Lecture Notes in Computer Science 4263

Commenced Publication in 1973
Founding and Former Series Editors:
Gerhard Goos, Juris Hartmanis, and Jan van Leeuwen

Albert Levi   Erkay Savaş
Hüsnü Yenigün   Selim Balcısoy
Yücel Saygın (Eds.)

Computer and Information Sciences – ISCIS 2006

21th International Symposium
Istanbul, Turkey, November 1-3, 2006
Proceedings

 Springer

Volume Editors

Albert Levi
Sabancı University, Istanbul, Turkey
E-mail: levi@sabanciuniv.edu

Erkay Savaş
Sabancı University, Istanbul, Turkey
E-mail: erkays@sabanciuniv.edu

Hüsnü Yenigün
Sabancı University, Istanbul, Turkey
E-mail: yenigun@sabanciuniv.edu

Selim Balcısoy
Sabancı University, Istanbul, Turkey
E-mail: balcisoy@sabanciuniv.edu

Yücel Saygın
Sabancı University, Istanbul, Turkey
E-mail: ysaygin@sabanciuniv.edu

Library of Congress Control Number: 2006934471

CR Subject Classification (1998): H, C, B, D, F, I

LNCS Sublibrary: SL 1 – Theoretical Computer Science and General Issues

ISSN   0302-9743
ISBN-10   3-540-47242-8 Springer Berlin Heidelberg New York
ISBN-13   978-3-540-47242-1 Springer Berlin Heidelberg New York

Springer is a part of Springer Science+Business Media

springer.com

© Springer-Verlag Berlin Heidelberg 2006
Printed in Germany

Typesetting: Camera-ready by author, data conversion by Scientific Publishing Services, Chennai, India
Printed on acid-free paper   SPIN: 11902140   06/3142   5 4 3 2 1 0

Preface

These are the proceedings of the 21st International Symposium on Computer and Information Sciences (ISCIS 2006) held in İstanbul, Turkey, November 1 – 3, 2006. ISCIS 2006 was organized by the Faculty of Engineering and Natural Sciences of Sabancı University.

These proceedings include updated versions of 106 papers selected by the program committee for presentation at the symposium. The increasing competition for presenting at the symposium, which relies on the success of previous ISCIS symposia, has led to many excellent papers and a higher standard overall. From a record-breaking 606 submissions, scheduling constraints dictated that only 106 papers could be accepted, resulting in a 17.5% acceptance rate. The program committee and external reviewers worked very hard and went through all submissions meticulously to select the best in a limited time frame. The selection process was especially hard when some of the good submissions could not be selected for publication due to space and time limitations.

Another interesting fact about the submissions is that they were by authors from 41 countries covering all habitable continents (excluding Antarctica). This is a clear indication of the ever-increasing popularity of ISCIS symposia among researchers all around the world as a medium to share and disseminate the results of their research activities.

In addition to the accepted papers, there were five invited presentations by leading researchers in their fields, three of which also appear as invited papers in this volume. The talk by Manfred Broy of the Technische Universität München, Germany, was titled "Requirements Engineering as a Key to Holistic Software Quality". The honorary chair of ISCIS 2006, Erol Gelenbe of Imperial College, London, gave a talk on "Analysis of Automated Auctions". Daniel Thalmann of the Ecole Polytechnique Fédérale de Lausanne, Switzerland delivered a talk titled "Advanced Mixed Reality Technologies for Surveillance and Risk Prevention Applications". These invited talks also appear as papers in this volume. Eric Badiqué of the European Commission, Belgium gave an informative speech on the European Union's Seventh Framework Programme. His speech was titled "Information and Communication Technologies in the EU's Seventh Framework Programme". Finally, Jacques G. Verly from the Université de Liège, Belgium, delivered a talk titled "Problems and Challenges of Image-Guided Neurosurgical Navigation and Intervention".

As always, ISCIS 2006 attracted submissions reporting on diverse aspects of computer and information sciences such as algorithms and theory, bioinformatics, computational intelligence, computer architecture, computer graphics, computer networks, computer vision, data mining, databases, embedded systems, information retrieval, mobile computing, parallel and distributed computing, performance evaluation, security and cryptography, and software engineering.

Many individuals and organizations contributed to making ISCIS 2006 a stimulating technical event. First and foremost, we would like to thank all authors who submitted papers, making the symposium possible, and the authors of accepted papers for their cooperation. The program committee and external reviewers deserve heartfelt thanks for their hard work and for sharing their expertise in the selection process. We are indebted to the invited speakers for their interesting and stimulating talks, which were the highlights of the symposium. Special compliments go to the faculty members and graduate students at the Faculty of Engineering and Natural Sciences, the staff at the Research and Graduate Policies of Sabancı University, and Dekon Congress & Tourism. We would like to thank the Scientific and Technological Research Council of Turkey (TÜBİTAK), the Turkey Section of the Institute of Electrical and Electronics Engineers (IEEE), and Sabancı University for their financial support. Last but not least, we would like to express our gratitude to Erol Gelenbe for his support, guidance and inspiration.

November 2006

Albert Levi
Erkay Savaş
Hüsnü Yenigün
Selim Balcısoy
Yücel Saygın

Organization

ISCIS 2006 was organized by the Faculty of Engineering and Natural Sciences, Sabancı University.

Honorary Chair

Erol Gelenbe   Imperial College, UK

Conference and Program Committee Chairs

Albert Levi   Sabancı University, Turkey
Erkay Savaş   Sabancı University, Turkey
Hüsnü Yenigün   Sabancı University, Turkey
Selim Balcısoy   Sabancı University, Turkey
Yücel Saygın   Sabancı University, Turkey

Program Committee

Abdullah Uz Tansel   City University of New York, USA
Adnan Yazıcı   Middle East Technical University, Turkey
Alain Jean-Marie   LIRMM/INRIA/CNRS, France
Alex Orailoğlu   University of California, USA
Ali Aydın Selçuk   Bilkent University, Turkey
Andrea D'Ambrogio   University of Rome "Tor Vergata", Italy
Athena Vakali   Aristotle University of Thessaloniki, Greece
Attila Gürsoy   Koç University, Turkey
Bakhadyr Khoussainov   University of Auckland, New Zealand
Berç Rustem   Imperial College, UK
Berk Sunar   Worcester Polytechnic Institute, USA
Berrin Yanıkoğlu   Sabancı University, Turkey
Bülent Örencik   İstanbul Technical University, Turkey
Carlos Juiz   University of the Balearic Islands, Spain
Cem Say   Boğaziçi University, Turkey
Cevdet Aykanat   Bilkent University, Turkey
Çağatay Tekmen   Qualcomm, USA
Damla Turgut   University of Central Florida, USA
Daniel Thalmann   EPFL, Switzerland
Danny Soroker   IBM T.J. Watson Research Center, USA

Doron Peled	University of Warwick, UK
Ethem Alpaydın	Boğaziçi University, Turkey
Eylem Ekici	Ohio State University, USA
Fatih Alagöz	Boğaziçi University, Turkey
Fatoş Yarman-Vural	Middle East Technical University, Turkey
Fevzi Belli	University of Paderborn, Germany
Francisco Rodriguez	CINVESTAV, Mexico
Gabriel Ciobanu	Romanian Academy, Romania
Giuseppe Iazeolla	University of Rome "Tor Vergata", Italy
Guy Vincent Jourdan	University of Ottawa, Canada
Gültekin Özsoyoğlu	Case Western Reserve University, USA
Hakan Erdoğan	Sabancı University, Turkey
Iain Duff	CCLRC Rutherford Appleton Laboratory, UK
Igor S. Pandzic	University of Zagreb, Croatia
İ. Budak Arpınar	University of Georgia, USA
İbrahim Körpeoğlu	Bilkent University, Turkey
Javier Barria	Imperial College, UK
Javier Garcia Villalba	Complutense University of Madrid, Spain
Jean-Michel Fourneau	Versailles Saint-Quentin-en-Yvelines University, France
Jeremy Pitt	Imperial College, UK
Johann Großschädl	IAIK TU Graz, Austria
Kainam Tom Wong	University of Waterloo, Canada
Kanchana Kanchanasut	Asian Institute of Technology, Thailand
Kemal Oflazer	Sabancı University, Turkey
Khaldoun El Agha	LRI, Paris-Sud University, France
Lale Akarun	Boğaziçi University, Turkey
Mariacarla Calzarossa	University of Pavia, Italy
Mehmet Keskinöz	Sabancı University, Turkey
Mehmet Orgun	Macquarie University, Australia
Mohamed Elfeky	Google, USA
Mohand Said Hacid	University of Lyon, France
Mustafa Ünel	Sabancı University, Turkey
Müjdat Çetin	Sabancı University, Turkey
Nahid Shahmehri	Linköping University, Sweden
Nassir Navab	Technical University of Munich, Germany
Onn Shehory	IBM Research Labs, Israel
Özgür B. Akan	Middle East Technical University, Turkey
Özgür Erçetin	Sabancı University, Turkey
Peter Harrison	Imperial College, UK
Philippe Jacquet	INRIA, France
Philippe Nain	INRIA, France
Pınar Yolum	Boğaziçi University, Turkey
Pierre Flener	Uppsala University, Sweden
Robert P. Kurshan	Cadence, USA

Robert Wrembel	Poznan University of Technology, Poland
Sibel Adalı	Rensselaer Polytechnic Institute, USA
Şahin Albayrak	Technical University of Berlin, Germany
Şule Gündüz Öğüdücü	İstanbul Technical University, Turkey
Tamer Özsu	University of Waterloo, Canada
Thomas Pedersen	Sabancı University, Turkey
Thomas Strang	DLR, Germany and University of Innsbruck, Austria
Tolga Çapın	Nokia, USA
Tonguç Ünlüyurt	Sabancı University, Turkey
Tuna Tuğcu	Boğaziçi University, Turkey
Ufuk Çağlayan	Boğaziçi University, Turkey
Uğur Çetintemel	Brown University, USA
Uğur Güdükbay	Bilkent University, Turkey
Uğur Sezerman	Sabancı University, Turkey
Ümit Uyar	City University of New York, USA
Vedat Coşkun	Işık University, Turkey
Yusuf Pisan	University of Technology Sydney, Australia

Local Organizing Committee

Alisher Kholmatov	Sabancı University, Turkey
Başak Alper	Sabancı University, Turkey
C. Emre Sayın	Sabancı University, Turkey
İlknur Durgar El-Kahlout	Sabancı University, Turkey
Özlem Çetinoğlu	Sabancı University, Turkey
Selim Volkan Kaya	Sabancı University, Turkey
Yılmaz Can Özmen	Sabancı University, Turkey

Congress Secretariat

Dekon Congress & Tourism	İstanbul, Turkey

Additional Referees

A. Esat Hızır	Afshin Akhsahni
Abdül Halim Zaim	Ahmet Koltuksuz
Abdülhakim Ünlü	Ahmet Murat Özdemiray
Achille Peternier	Ahmet Onat
Adnan Burak Gürdağ	Albert Özkohen
Adrian Tanasescu	Ahmet Şen

Haluk Bingöl
Haluk Gümüşkaya
Handan Gül Çalıklı
Harini Kulatunga
Hasan Ateş
Hasan Demirel
Hassan Abou Rajab
Hatice Tekiner
Hayretdin Bahşi
Hazem Elmeleegy
Hervé Rivano
Hidayet Aksu
Hitay Özbay
Hofhauser Andreas
Huaxin Zhang
Hüseyin Aygün
Hüseyin Özgür Tan
Hüsnü Türker Şahin
Ioan Toma
Işık Aybay
İbrahim Tekin
İlker Oyman
İmran Ergüler
Jacek Kopecky
Jean-Marc Desharnais
Jens-Peter Kaps
Jeong-Woo Lee
Jonathan Maïm
JongMin Jeong
Joonsang Baek
Jose-Luis Sanchez-Romero
Justin Pearson
Kaan Bür
Kamer Kaya
Kasım Sinan Yıldırım
Kayhan Erciyes
Kemal Bıçakçı
Kemal Kılıç
Kemalettin Erbatur
Kenneth Dockser
Kerem Bülbül
Kerim Yıldırım
Krzysztof Walkowiak
Kutluk Özgüven
Laurent Marsan

Levent Kandiller
Li Wei
Luisa Massari
M. Şükrü Kuran
Magnus Ågren
Marcin Paprzycki
Mahmut Şamil Sağıroğlu
Malik Magdon-Ismail
Manfred Aigner
Manuel González–Hidalgo
María José Abásolo
Marius Minea
Martin Feldhofer
Martin Groher
Martin Karresand
Melek Diker Yücel
Melike Erol
Meltem Turhan
Mert Akdere
Metin Koç
Metin Tekkalmaz
Michael Stollberg
Michel Dayde
Milagros Garcia
Mithat Dağlar
Mohamed Eltabakh
Mohamed Shehab
Mohammad Zubair Ahmad
Murat Ak
Murat Göksedef
Murat Şensoy
Mustafa Gök
Mustafa Kıraç
Mustafa Sert
Nesime Tatbul
Nusrettin Güleç
Oğuz Ergin
Oğuz Dönmez
Oliver Kutter
Orcun Mayuk
Osman Ünsal
Özgün Babür
Özgür Gürbüz
Özgür Kafalı
Özlem Keskin

Öznur Özkasap
Patrick Salamin
Peter McBrien
Pınar Şenkul
Poompat Saengudomlert
Prasun Choudhury
Renaud Ott
Reto Krummenacher
Reyhan Aydoğan
Ricardo Lent
Ronan Boulic
Rongquan You
Roy Küçükateş
Said Kalkan
Samir Tartir
Samira Hammiche
Samrat S. Batth
Sandrine Vial
Sayir Jossy
Sebastien Schertenleib
Selçuk Baktır
Selçuk Sümengen
Selim Çıracı
Selim Volkan Kaya
Sema Oktuğ
Semih Bilgen
Serdar Ayaz
Serdar Taşıran
Serhat Yeşilyurt
Shameem Shah Nawaz
Soraya Zertal
Stefan Tillich

Stephen Jarvis
Steven Martin
Süleyman Tosun
Suresh Chitturi
Syed Amjad Ali
Ş. İlker Birbil
Taneli Mielikäinen
Tayfun Küçükyılmaz
Theodosios Theodosiou
Tina Lindgren
Tolga Can
Tuğkan Tuğlular
Turgay Karlıdere
Türker Yılmaz
Uğur Ayan
Uli Harder
Veysi İşler
Viiveke Fåk
Vladimir Levin
Wei Jiang
William Knottenbelt
Xavier Carcelle
Y. İlker Topçu
Yagoubi Belabbas
Yakup Yıldırım
Yiğithan Dedeoğlu
Ying Xing
Young Ik Eom
Yusuf Sinan Akgül
Zehra Çataltepe

Sponsoring Institutions

- The Scientific and Technological Research Council of Turkey (TÜBİTAK)
- Sabancı University
- Institute of Electrical and Electronics Engineers (IEEE), Turkey Section
- International Federation for Information Processing (IFIP)

Table of Contents

Invited Papers and Talks

Invited Talks

Algorithms and Theory

Bioinformatics

Computational Intelligence

Computer Architecture

Computer Graphics

Computer Networks

Computer Vision

Data Mining

Databases

Embedded Systems

Information Retrieval

Performance Evaluation

Security and Cryptography

Software Engineering

Analysis of Automated Auctions*

Erol Gelenbe

Professor in the Dennis Gabor Chair
Intelligent Systems and Networks Group
Electrical and Electronic Engineering Department
Imperial College
London SW7 2BT, UK
e.gelenbe@imperial.ac.uk

Abstract. Web based computerised auctions are increasingly present in the Internet, and we can imagine that in the future automated buyer and seller agents will conduct automated transactions in this manner. The purpose of this paper is to model automated bidders and sellers which interact through a computerised auction. We model bidding process using random processes with discrete state-space. We obtain analytical solutions for a variety of single auction models, including English and Vickrey auctions, and relate the income per unit time to the other parameters including the rate of arrival of bids, the seller's decision time, the value of the good, and the "rest time" of the seller between successive auctions. We examine how the seller's "decision time" impacts the expected income per unit time received by the seller, and illustrate its effect via numerical examples.

1   Introduction

Auctions of different types are important n market based economies [3] and allow the bidding and selling process to be formalised and conducted in a timely fashion according to known rules. Their importance increases as much of the economy becomes network based, because through they are amenable to Internet based implementations [8,9,12]. Although we naturally think of auctions as being related to economic activity, it is also useful to think of them as a form of decision making that can also be used for resource allocation. More generally, auctions are a are an example of Computational Mechanisms [11] for the coordination of distributed and autonomous agents.

In this paper we will consider an auction for goods in which bidders' offers arrive sequentially at random time intervals. Successive bids are increasing in value, but the seller may not know the current market value of the good. The seller's problem is therefore to decide when it accepts a bid. Thus after each new bid, the seller may wait for a "decision delay or time" to determine whether to

---

* This research was undertaken as part of the ALADDIN (Autonomous Learning Agents for Decentralised Data and Information Systems) project and is jointly funded by a BAE Systems and EPSRC (Engineering and Physical Research Council) strategic partnership under Grant No. EP/C548051/1.

A. Levi et al. (Eds.): ISCIS 2006, LNCS 4263, pp. 1–12, 2006.

accept the offer. If a new bid arrives before that time expires, then the process is repeated for this new bid; at the end of the decision time, if a new bid has not arrived, the seller sells his good to the buyer who has so far made the most recent and therefore highest bid. After selling the good, the seller rests for a some time before initiating a new auction.

We will only consider single auction models in isolation and obtain analytical solutions for the price obtained and the income per unit time under certain assumptions, and relate the price obtained from an auction to the other parameters of the system, including the rate of arrival of bids, the seller's decision delay or wait time, the value of the good, and the rest time of the seller between successive auctions. Closed form expressions for all quantities of interest are provided in steady-state. We show how the average value of the seller's "decision time" impacts the expected income per unit time received by the seller, and illustrate its effect via numerical examples. Networked auctions will be studied in a subsequent paper.

2　An Auction with Unit Increments

We first analyse an auction in which bidders increase their offers in unit increments. We assume that bids arrive to the seller one at a time, according to a Poisson process of rate λ so that the average time that will elapse between successive bids is λ^{-1}. If a bid is not accepted by the seller, then the next bid will increment the value of the offer by 1 as long as the value V of the good for the buyers has not been reached. However the buyers will stop bidding and incrementing the offer when the most recent bid has reached the value V that the bidders associate with it.

The seller does not know the value V that buyers associate with the good. Thus after each new bid, the seller waits for some random "decision time" to determine whether to accept the offer. If a new bid arrives before that time expires, then the process is repeated for this new bid. However if a new bid does not arrive before this time expires, then the seller accepts the current bid. Of course, if the seller accepts the offer too quickly, then the price he will be getting may be low with respect to the price that he would have gotten had he been more patient. On the other hand, if the buyer waits a long time before accepting an offer he may ultimately get the highest possible price (which is V), but at the expense of wasting a lot of time. We may also have a situation where a bidder places a "time-out" on his offer so that the bid is withdrawn if the seller does not accept it before the time-out expires; however this case is not considered here.

2.1　The Mathematical Model

Assume that after each bid, the seller waits for an exponentially distributed time of parameter d to accept the bid. If a new bid arrives, then the process is repeated. Furthermore assume that after a bid is accepted, the auction has a random "rest time" of average value R, which is again modelled via an exponentially distributed time of rate $r = R^{-1}$. The auction repeats itself and infinite number of times, and all random variables and processes that we discuss are independent from each other in each of the success auctions, although they will always have the same distribution. In particular, the value V of the good beyond sold will be the random variable V_i for the $i - th$ successive auction, $i = 1, 2, \ldots$, with common distribution function $p(v)$. Thus for any of the auctions in the sequence, we model this system as a continuous time Markov chain $\{X_t : t \geq 0\}$ with state space $\{0, 1, \ldots , v, A_1, \ldots A_V\}$, where V is itself a random variable (so that we are dealing with a doubly stochastic process). Let $\{t_1, t_2, \ldots t_n, \ldots\}$ be the sequence of instants when the successive auctions begin. Then:

- $X_{t_n} = 0$ corresponds to the value of the state when the $n-th$ auction begins,
- The state $X_{t_n+t} = l$, for $t > 0$ and $1 \leq l \leq v$, corresponds to the case at time $t_n + t$ during the $n - th$ auction $(t_n + t < t_{n+1})$ where l bids have been received so that the offered price has reached the value l, while
- $X_t = A_l$, $t > 0$, is the state at time $t_n + t$ during the $n - th$ auction $(t_n + t < t_{n+1})$ where the bid has been accepted at the price l.

Clearly, the transition rate from state l to $l+1$, $1 \leq l \leq v-1$, is λ. The transition rate from state l for $1 \leq l \leq v$ to state A_l is d, and the transition rate from any state A_l to state 0 is r. In this model we are certain that the good will be sold in each successive auction, and the main question is then to evaluate the *income per unit time* that the auctions generate for the seller.

$P_v(.)$ denotes the stationary probability distribution of the Markov chain with state space $\{0, 1, \ldots , v, A_1, \ldots , A_v\}$, where we assume that V has a fixed value v. We will call this the *reduced* Markov chain, and denote by $\pi(l, v)$ the probability that the price that is obtained is l given that the value of the good is v. The average rest time after the bid is accepted is the time spent in any of the states A_l, $1 \leq l \leq v$; it is identical (and given by r^{-1}) for each auction. Thus $\pi(l, v)$ is the probability that the reduced Markov chain is in state A_l given that it is in one of the states $\{A_1, \ldots , A_v\}$, hence:

$$\pi(l, v) = \frac{P_v(A_l)}{\sum_{i=1}^{v} P_v(A_i)}, \ 1 \leq l \leq v. \tag{1}$$

2.2   Stationary Probability Distribution

Assuming that the value of the good is a constant v, we can write the equations satisfied by the stationary probabilities $P_v(.)$ as follows:

$$P_v(l)(\lambda + d) = \lambda P_v(l - 1), \ 1 \leq l \leq v - 1, \tag{2}$$

$$P_v(0)\lambda = r \sum_{l=1}^{v} P_v(A_l), \tag{3}$$

$$P_v(v)d = \lambda P_v(v - 1),$$

$$P_v(A_l)r = dP_v(l), \ for \ 1 \leq l \leq v,$$

$$1 = P_v(0) + \sum_{l=1}^{v} [P_v(l) + P_v(A_l)].$$

If we write $\rho = \frac{\lambda}{\lambda+d}$, after some calculations these equations yield:

$$P_v(l) = \rho^l P_v(0), \ 1 \le l \le v-1, \tag{4}$$

$$P_v(v) = \frac{\lambda}{d}\rho^{v-1} P_v(0),$$

$$P_v(A_l)r = dP_v(l), \ 1 \le l \le v,$$

$$P_v(0) = \frac{rd}{r\lambda + \lambda d + rd}.$$

As a consequence we can see that

$$\sum_{l=1}^{v} P_v(l) = \frac{\lambda}{d}P_v(0), \tag{5}$$

resulting in:

$$\pi(l,v) = \frac{d}{\lambda}\rho^l, \ 1 \le l \le v-1, \tag{6}$$

$$\pi(v,v) = \rho^{v-1}. \tag{7}$$

2.3 Expected Income

Using the probabilities $\pi(l,v)$ we can compute the expected income from a single auction for a good whose value is v directly as:

$$I_v = \sum_{l=1}^{v} l\pi(l,v), \tag{8}$$

$$= v\rho^{v-1} + \frac{1 - v\rho^{v-1} + (v-1)\rho^v}{1-\rho},$$

$$= \frac{1-\rho^v}{1-\rho}.$$

so that the expected price brought by the auction is

$$I = \frac{1 - E[\rho^V]}{1-\rho} \tag{9}$$

Note that the *total average time A that the auction lasts* is the average time it takes for a bid to be accepted, plus the reset time of average value r^{-1}, and is simply the total average time between two successive entries into state 0. Since the average time spent in state 0 in each auction is λ^{-1}, we use (5) to obtain:

$$P_v(0) = \frac{\lambda^{-1}}{A}, \tag{10}$$

$$A = \frac{1}{P_v(0)\lambda}, \tag{11}$$

$$= \frac{1}{\lambda} + \frac{r+d}{rd}, \tag{12}$$

which comes out to be independent of v the value of the good. The average income per unit time brought by this auction is then $\Phi_v = I_v/A$ or

$$\Phi_v = \frac{\lambda r(\lambda + d)}{\lambda r + \lambda d + rd}(1 - \rho^v). \tag{13}$$

We can also readily obtain the average income per unit time Φ for the auction as a whole, under the assumption that the value of the good being sold is a random variable V with probability distribution $\{p(v)\}$. We then have:

$$\Phi = \frac{\lambda r(\lambda + d)}{\lambda r + \lambda d + rd}[1 - E[\rho^V]], \tag{14}$$

where $E[x^V] = \sum_{v=0}^{\infty} p(v)x^v$ is the generating function associated with the probability distribution $\{p(v)\}$.

It is interesting to observe how Φ varies as a function of d, as shown in the numerical examples of Figure 1. We select the value V of the good to be uniformly distributed between 80 and 120 with an average value of 100, we set $r = 1$ to normalise the remaining parameters, and plot the income per unit time against the decision rate d for different values of the arrival rate of the bids λ. We see clearly that there is indeed an "optimum" value of d which differs for each set of parameters and which maximises the income from the auction. Thus the seller can adjust his/her "patience" so that the rate of income is maximised. We also see that faster decisions (greater d) need to be made when the rate at which bids are made is higher. The curves show that there is some optimum value of d that will maximise the seller's income. Furthermore, when λ is large we can afford to be less careful about waiting for some best value of the average decision time, and we can make decisions quite quickly (d large).

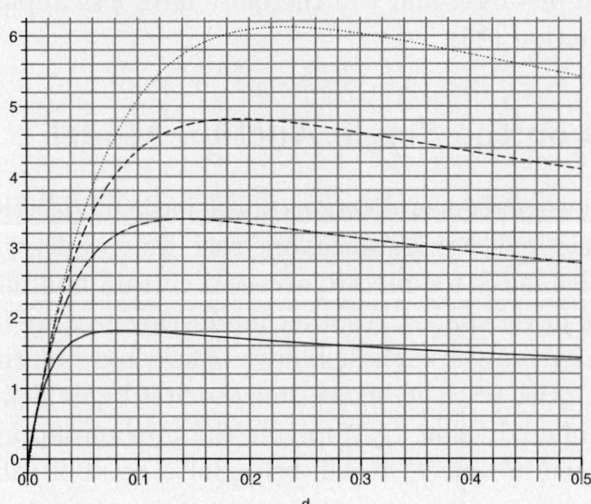

Fig. 1. Income per unit time versus the rate d at which decisions are made, for different values of the rate at which bids arrive ranging from 8 (top) to 2 (bottom). The value is uniformly distributed between 80 and 100. If the decision time is large (d less than 0.1), the income per unit time can drop significantly.

2.4 The Rate at Which Bids Arrive

For a given auction, requests to bid may arrive at some rate γ and this differs from the rate λ at which bids are made because a bidder may bid several times at an auction so that a bidder who is outbid by someone else will try again. In this section we discuss how γ and *lambda* are related. Let α be the stationary probability that a given auction is active, and $(1 - \alpha)$ be the probability that it is at rest before the next auction begins. During the rest period, we assume that bids are not made to this particular auction since bidders are aware that the auction is not open.

We know that out of Φ bids per unit time, only one will be successful and therefore the corresponding bidder will not return to the auction since he has been able to buy the good. Thus the probability that a bid is unsuccessful is $(\Phi - 1)/\Phi$. Thus when the auction is open the rate at which bids arrive is:

$$\lambda = \gamma + \lambda p \frac{\Phi - 1}{\Phi}, \tag{15}$$

$$= \gamma \frac{1}{(1 - p) + \frac{p}{\Phi}}.$$

where p is the probability that an unsuccessful bidder will try again with a new (and higher) bid. Thus the rate at which bids are made will in general be much large than the rate at which bidders arrive to the auction: $\lambda >> \gamma$. Furthermore, equations (15) tell us that the actual rate of bids depends on the number of bids that are made, and vice-versa. This analysis is illustrated in Figure 2 where we see that for low values of γ the income per unit time from the auction is just not "taking off", and when some threshold is exceeded it attains much higher values. Figure 3 confirms that when γ is large, λ will grow linearly as a function of γ because Φ will be larger and will therefore have less impact on the value of λ as shown by equation (15).

3 Variations on the Single Auction Model

Many other variations and generalisations of the basic models that were discussed earlier can be considered. For instance, one case that we have not considered is when each successive bid is required to exceed a certain minimum value. We will not detail this case in this paper. Another interesting case we now analyse is the "Vickrey" auction where the highest bidder is selected but the good is sold at the second highest price price [4], except for the first bid which (if accepted) will be accepted at its offered value. By applying the previous approach to a Vickrey auction, the expected income I_v^V it will bring for a good of value v becomes:

$$I_v^V = \sum_{l=2}^{v} (l - 1)\pi(l, v) + \pi(1, v), \tag{16}$$

$$= \frac{1 - \rho^v}{1 - \rho} - 1 + \frac{d}{\lambda}\rho, \tag{17}$$

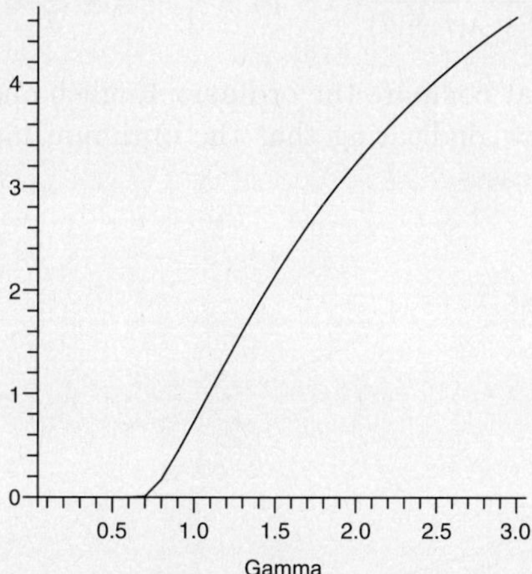

Fig. 2. Income per unit time (Phi) versus the rate Gamma at which bidders arrive. Here d=0.1, p=0.7 and r=1.

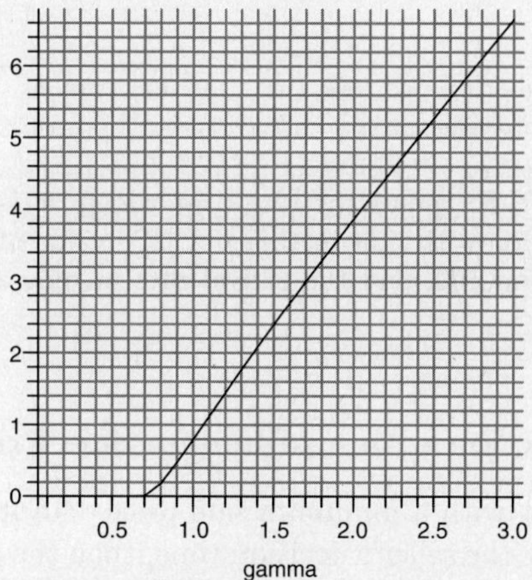

Fig. 3. Total bid arrival rate Lambda versus the rate Gamma at which bidders arrive. Here d=0.1, p=0.7 and r=1.

$$= \rho[\frac{1 - \rho^{v-1}}{1 - \rho} + \frac{d}{\lambda}], \tag{18}$$

The average income per unit time is then $\Phi_v^\nu = I_v^\nu/A$, leading to the average income per unit time Φ^ν for the Vickrey auction when the value of the good being sold is a random variable V with probability distribution $\{p(v)\}$, and using the fact that the average duration of each auction is the same as in the "English" case, we have::

$$\Phi^\nu = \frac{\lambda rd}{rd + \lambda(r+d)}[(1-\rho) + \frac{\lambda}{d} - (1 + \frac{\lambda}{d})E[\rho^V]].$$ (19)

Numerical examples that compare the ordinary English auction with a Vickrey auction are shown below, indicating that the optimum incomes per unit time are quite close in both cases.

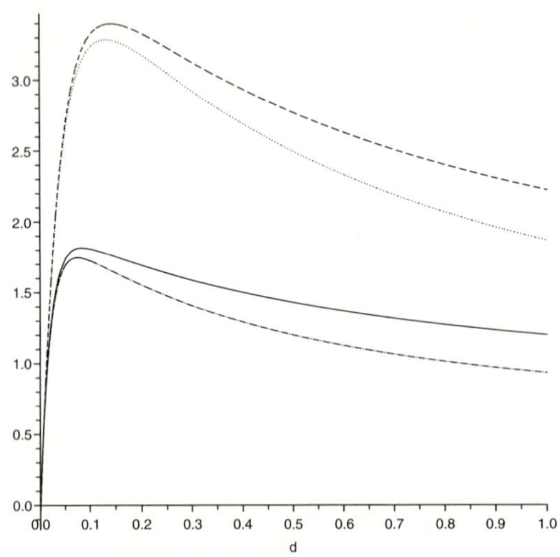

Fig. 4. Income per unit time versus the rate d at which decisions are made for the English and Vickrey auction with unit increments. The value of the good is uniformly distributed between 80 and 100, and the arrival rate of bids arrive is 4 (top) and 2 (bottom).

3.1   An English Auction with a Minimum Sale Price

Most auctions will start with a minimum sale price, call it s. If no bid is made for at least that price by the seller's decision time, then the auction ends without a sale. This case was not considered in the previous analysis in which the seller may wait indefinitely for the initial bid with $s = 1$.

Here we will denote by $P_v(A_0)$ the probability that the seller stops the auction because a bid with a price of at least s has not been received. When this happens, the auction "rests" for some time of average value r^{-1} and then restarts. In this case it is also normal to consider that the rate at which bids are made is a function of this threshold price, call it λ_s. Of course, unless the value v that buyers associate with the good is at least s, this auction will never result in a sale. Therefore we will take $v \geq s$.

The equations satisfied by the state probabilities now become:

$$P_v(l)(\lambda_s + d) = \lambda_s P_v(l-1), \; s < l \leq v - 1$$ (20)
$$P_v(s)(\lambda_s + d) = \lambda_s P_v(0),$$

$$P_v(0)(\lambda_s + d) = r \sum_{l=s}^{v} P_v(A_l) + r P_v(A_0),$$

$$P_v(v)d = \lambda_s P_v(v-1),$$

$$P_v(A_l) = \frac{d}{r} P_v(l), \ s \leq l \leq v, \ l = 0,$$

$$P_v(0) + P_v(A_0) + \sum_{l=s}^{v} [P_v(l) + P_v(A_l)] = 1. \tag{21}$$

If we set $\rho = \lambda_s/(\lambda_s + d)$ we obtain:

$$P_v(l) = \rho^{l-s+1} P_v(0), \ s \leq l \leq v-1, \tag{22}$$

$$P_v(v) = \frac{\lambda_s}{d} \rho^{v-s} P_v(0),$$

$$P_v(A_l) = \frac{d}{r} P_v(l), \ s \leq l \leq v, \ or \ l = 0,$$

$$P_v(0) = \frac{rd}{(\lambda_s + d)(r + d)}.$$

We are also interested in the probability that the price obtained is l given that the value of the good is v, with $v \geq s$. In that case we will have:

$$\pi(l, v) = \frac{P_v(A_l)}{P_v(A_0) + \sum_{i=s}^{v} P_v(A_l)}, \ s \leq l \leq v, \ l = 0, \tag{23}$$

$$\pi(l, v) = \frac{d}{d + \lambda_s} \rho^{l-s+1}, \ s \leq l \leq v-1, \tag{24}$$

$$= \rho^{v-s+1}, \ l = v,$$

$$= \frac{d}{d + \lambda_s}, \ l = 0,$$

so that the income from a single auction for a good whose value is $v \leq s$ is now:

$$I_v = \rho[s + \frac{\lambda_s}{d}(1 - \rho^{v-s})] \tag{25}$$

The numerical results in Figure 5 show that having a minimum price can yield much higher income per unit time, provided that decisions are taken much faster (larger d) than in an auction without a minimum price.

3.2   A Deterministic Model and Heuristic Rule

Consider an auction that begins at time $t = 0$ with successive bids arriving at $0 \leq a_1 \leq a_2 \leq \ldots$. Let $\alpha_{n+1} = a_{n+1} - a_n$. The $X_n > 0$, $n \geq 1$ are the increments that successive bids offer so that the value of the $n - th$ bid is $B_n = \sum_{i=1}^{n} X_i$. Suppose the seller decides to accept the $n - th$ bid at time $a_n + D_n$ provided no new bid arrives by that time. If W_n is the total wait time of the $n - th$ bidder, we see that:

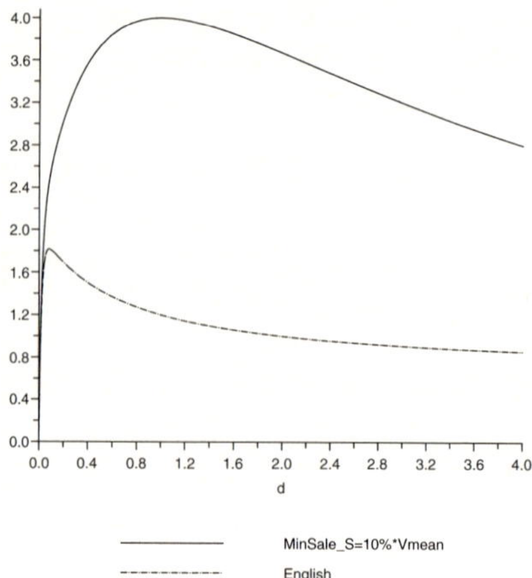

Fig. 5. Income per unit time versus the rate d at which decisions are made for an auction without a minimum sale price (lower curve), and for one where the minimum sale price of 10 (curve above). In both cases bids arrive at a rate of 2. The value V is uniformly distributed between 80 and 100. The minimum sale price has the effect of greatly improving the income per unit time, even though some of the auctions may end without a sale.

$$W_n = \alpha_{n+1}, \ if \ D_n > \alpha_{n+1}, \tag{26}$$
$$= D_n, \ otherwise.$$

since a bidder may leave the bidding process, if he so wishes, as soon as a higher bid is made.

We can also study how a decision may be made by the seller who is observing the successive bids. We may expect that the $n-th$ increment X_n will depend on the previous bid B_{n-1}, so that as time goes by at some point the bidding price has reached a high enough value, but the relative increase in the bid has somehow reached a point of diminishing returns. If the seller is interested in the income per unit time, he may well decide to accept the $k+1-th$ offer if:

$$\frac{B_k}{a_k} > \frac{B_{k-1}}{a_{k-1}}, \ and \tag{27}$$
$$\frac{B_{k+1}}{a_{k+1}} < \frac{B_k}{a_k}.$$

Equivalently, he accepts the $z-th$ bid where:

$$z = inf\{n : \frac{X_n}{B_{n-1}} < \frac{\alpha_n}{a_{n-1}}\}, \tag{28}$$

when the relative increase in the value of the bid is less than the relative increase in the time that the seller waits for the bid.

4 Conclusions

Auctions are common in the Internet as part of the web based economy. Thus in this paper we consider auctions for goods in which bidders' offers arrive sequentially at random time intervals. Successive bids are increasing in value, but the seller does not know what the market value of the good may be. The seller's problem is therefore to decide when to accept a bid. After each new bid, the seller may wait for some random "decision time" to determine whether to accept the offer. If a new bid arrives before that time expires, then the process is repeated for this new bid; at the end of the decision time, if a new bid has not arrived, the seller sells his good to the buyer who made the most recent bid. After selling the good, the seller rests for short time before initiating a new auction.

Here we have considered some basic auction models and studied them both in terms of the price a good will bring, and the income per unit time provided by the auction. This work introduces a methodology to evaluate the performance of an auction as a function of the rate at which bids arrive, and the speed with which the seller decides to close the auction. Our work shows that the decision time of the seller should be short enough to provide a high income per unit time, and that the seller should not just wait in order to obtain a price which is as high as possible.

Many interesting generalisations of these situations can be considered and will be the subject of future work. In particular we suggest that such models can be used to evaluate both the seller's satisfaction, in terms of income per unit time, and the buyers' needs. In particular our future work will investigate how buyers' interests can be best served by examining the opportunities offered by the large number of auctions which already populate the Internet, and how the buyers can perhaps automatically navigate through these auctions in order to maximise their benefit.

References

1. Y. S. Chow, S. Moriguti, H. Robbins and S. M. Samuels, Optimal selection based on relative rank (the "Secretary problem"), *Israel J. Math.* 2, 8190, 1964.
2. E. Gelenbe and I. Mitrani "Analysis and Synthesis of Computer Systems", Academic Press, New York and London, 1980.
3. P. R. Milgrom and R. Weber "A theory of auctions and competitive bidding", *Econometrica*, 50, 1089-1122, 1982.
4. R.P. McAfee and J. McMillan "Auctions and bidding", *J. Economic Literature*, vol. 25, 699–738, 1987.
5. E. Gelenbe. "Learning in the recurrent random neural network", *Neural Computation* 5(1), 154–164, 1993.
6. J. Medhi "Stochastic Processes" 2nd. Ed., Wiley Eastern Ltd., New Delhi, 1994.
7. E. Gelenbe and G. Pujolle "Introduction to Networks of Queues", 2nd Ed., J. Wiley & Sons, Chichester, 1998.
8. O. Shehory "Optimality and risk in purchase from multiple auctions", Lecture Notes in Artificial Intelligence, Vol. 2182, M. Klusch and F. Zambonelli (Eds.), 142-153. Springer, 2001.

9. O. Shehory "Optimal bidding in multiple concurrent auctions", *International Journal of Cooperative Information Systems*, Vol. 11(3-4), 315-327, 2002.

10. S. R. Finch "Optimal stopping constants", Mathematical Constants, Cambridge Univ. Press, 361363, 2003.

11. N.R. Dash, N.R. Jennings and D.C. Parkes "Computational mechanism design: a call to arms," *IEEE Intelligent Systems*, 40-47, Nov.-Dec. 2003.

12. E. David, A. Rogers, J. Schiff, S. Kraus, and N. R. Jennings "Optimal design of English auctions with discrete bid levels", *Proc. of 6th ACM Conference on Electronic Commerce (EC'05)* Vancouver, Canada, 98-107, 2005.

13. S. Fatima, M. Wooldridge and N. R. Jennings "Sequential auctions for objects with common and private values" *Proc. 4th Int Joint Conf on Autonomous Agents and Multi-Agent Systems*, Utrecht, Netherlands, 635-642, 2005.

Advanced Mixed Reality Technologies for Surveillance and Risk Prevention Applications

Daniel Thalmann[1], Patrick Salamin[1], Renaud Ott[1],
Mario Gutiérrez[2], and Frédéric Vexo[1]

[1] EPFL, Virtual Reality Laboratory,
Station 14, 1015 Lausanne, Switzerland
daniel.thalmann@epfl.ch
[2] ITESM Campus Toluca,
Edo. De México CP, 50110

Abstract. We present a system that exploits advanced Mixed and Virtual Reality technologies to create a surveillance and security system that could be also extended to define emergency prevention plans in crowdy environments. Surveillance cameras are carried by a mini Blimp which is tele-operated using an innovative Virtual Reality interface with haptic feedback. An interactive control room (CAVE) receives multiple video streams from airborne and fixed cameras. Eye tracking technology allows for turning the user's gaze into the main interaction mechanism; the user in charge can examine, zoom and select specific views by looking at them. Video streams selected at the control room can be redirected to agents equipped with a PDA. On-field agents can examine the video sent by the control center and locate the actual position of the airborne cameras in a GPS-driven map. The aerial video would be augmented with real-time 3D crowd to create more realist risk and emergency prevention plans. The prototype we present shows the added value of integrating AR/VR technologies into a complex application and opens up several research directions in the areas of tele-operation, Multimodal Interfaces, simulation, risk and emergency prevention plans, etc.

Keywords: Virtual Reality, Surveillance, Security, Teleoperation, Haptic Interfaces, Virtual Environments, Eye-tracking, Handheld Devices, Collaborative Environments.

1 Introduction

Information technology (IT) plays an important role in security and surveillance initiatives such as security. Security is a major concern for governments worldwide, which must protect their populations and the critical infrastructures that support them [1]. Together with IT, Virtual Reality offers a promising future as key component of surveillance, security systems and emergency plan preparation.

The approach to security that we follow in our work is based on video surveillance. Our system is based on mobile cameras that can be directed to a particular location while keeping an overview of the surveyed site. Airborne cameras are the most flexible solution for a mobile surveillance system.

A. Levi et al. (Eds.): ISCIS 2006, LNCS 4263, pp. 13–23, 2006.

The prototype we present in this paper shows that efficient cost-effective surveillance systems based on VR technologies can operate in complex environments with relatively low requirements in terms of equipment and personnel. Moreover, by using Augmented Reality techniques, we can extend this technology to training and emergency plan preparation.

2   Surveillance and Security Systems

A general surveillance and security system is composed of three main parts: *data acquisition, information analysis, on-field operation*. Any surveillance system requires means to monitor the environment and acquire data in the form of video, still images, audio, etc. The current state of our research focuses more on enhancing the interaction infrastructure of the three main parts composing a command and control surveillance system.

Following the *Command and Control* notion, we have designed an surveillance and security system composed of three main parts, covering the basic functions of a general surveillance system presented before: *data acquisition, information analysis, on-field operation*.

2.1   Data Acquisition

Data acquisition is performed by means of a set of video cameras. Several kind of cameras can be distinguished: fixed, orientable and mobile [2],[3]. Fixed cameras are an efficient alternative for outdoors use for surveying car traffic or crowds in public sites. They allow for focusing the attention on a particular point. However, there are circumstances under which there is no possibility to fix a camera in advance, due to cost restrictions or lack of appropriate locations for wide visibility. In this case it is necessary to use mobile cameras that are usually airborne.

Fig. 1. left : a UAV; Center: an orientable camera; right: A helicopter Wescam

In urban environments, blimps are the safest aerial devices for many reasons: they are light, easy to operate, and they fall slowly in case of problem, minimizing the risk of injuring people. We decided to base our system on a teleoperated mini-blimp and focused on implementing an intuitive and flexible interface that could take advantage of VR technologies.

2.2   Information Analysis

Information analysis is the central part of a surveillance system. In order to provide an appropriate response to a given incident within reasonable timing, all the information about the whole situation, needs to be gathered in one unique place. A control room for surveillance is composed, in most cases, by a large video wall and multiple screens displaying views from surveillance cameras, for a proper interpretation of the situation. A set of buttons and joysticks are used to select, move and setup appropriate views.

Fig. 2. Various control rooms

We decided to use VR devices for improving the ergonomics of existing systems. Visualization systems for video surveillance based on an Augmented Virtual Environment (AVE) are an important topic nowadays. AVE fuses dynamic imagery with 3D models in a real-time display to help observers comprehend multiple streams of temporal data and imagery from arbitrary views of the scene [4]. We provide a novel interface based on eye-tracking technologies which minimizes the use of keyboards and other interaction devices. The commander is immersed in a CAVE which displays live video enhanced with graphic overlays.

2.3   On-Field Operation

On-field operation is the result of decisions taken at the control center and require a team of surveillance agents to take action for controlling the situation on the ground. Common communication devices include: pagers, in-vehicle systems, radios and headsets; etc. Recent security studies and initiatives have pointed out the importance of permanent multimodal communication [5][6].

A common problem with handheld interfaces is that they usually present a scaled-down desktop-based interface composed of menus and buttons which are difficult to use on a small display. On-field agents require to concentrate their attention of the site, not on the interface. There is a need for a dynamic handheld interface that provides multimedia information and minimizes the use of menus and buttons.

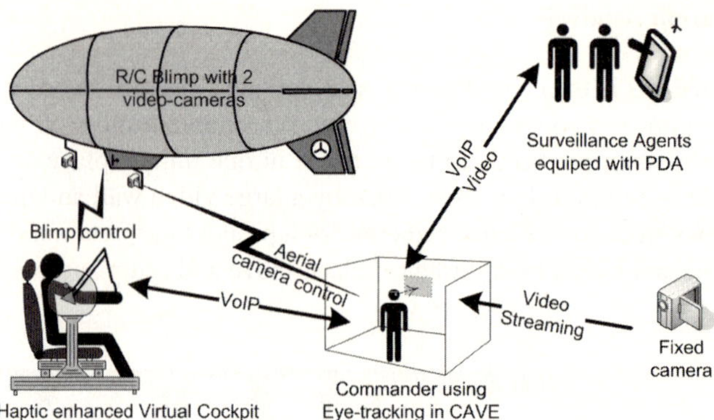

Fig. 3. The overall system architecture

3   System Architecture

This section describes the overall surveillance, security and training system that we have created. We can distinguish three main parts (figure 3) :

- Control of the aerial device (the Blimp) supporting the video cameras. This task is done by a single pilot seating on Haptic Workstation^{TM} inside a distant and closed environment. The pilot can control the blimp as if he were inside it.
- On-field agents : They are equipped with handheld devices in order to receive precise orders including multimedia content (text, selected images of a video stream, sound). They also may have a direct control on the cameras to better evaluate the situation.
- Coordinating on-field agents and blimp pilot. A commander communicates with the pilot and every agent and gives them spoken orders. He has also a real-time view of all the cameras (mobile and fixed), and can also send multimedia content to on-field agents.

3.1   R/C Blimp

Our blimp, as shown on figure 4, is a low-cost Unmanned Aerial Vehicle (UAV) that we use in our teleoperation research. The *R/C Blimp* is composed by a $6,75m$ long and $2,20m$ diameter. The blimp could fly up to $35km/h$. The range of the transmission of the radio controller is $1.5km$.

It is carrying two video-cameras and their transmission systems. The first camera can be controlled by the pilot using head movements. The other camera is used by the *Surveillance Control Room*. Thus it must have a good quality, allow for recording and zooming: we have chosen a Panasonic mini-DV TriCCD camera. We use the analogical output of these cameras with two systems of video transmission. The *R/C Blimp* is also equipped with a STXe GPS system, provided by GPS-Flight. It is used to give location, speed and altitude information. Finally, the actuators are controlled by a $40MHz$ 7-channels Futaba FX-18 and Graupner MC-10 radio controllers. We have used two USB SC-8000 Servo Controllers that allow a pc to control a radio controller.

Fig. 4. Photo of the R/C blimp

3.2   Virtual Cockpit

The *R/C blimp* is not so easy to pilot, even with the remote controller. Moreover, the *Virtual Cockpit* is in an isolated room without any direct-view of the *R/C Blimp*. Therefore the interface must be **precise** (for a fine control), **instructive** (to give location information) and **intuitive** (to avoid manipulation errors).

The visual part of the blimp is rendered to the pilot via an Head-Mounted Display (HMD). In order to have a virtual camera that moves according to the head movements, we have used an orientation tracker. The user is virtually seated inside a 3D gondola made of glasses. Finally, the GPS information transmitted to the pilot is overlayed on the window. Concerning haptics, we have used an Immersion Haptic Workstation^{TM}(see the photo on figure 5).

Fig. 5. The Blimp's Virtual Cockpit

3.3   Surveillance Control Room

In order to place the supervisor in the best disposition for taking decisions, our system displays several video streams in a CAVE. These allows the supervisor to select and send visual information to the *On-field Agents* intuitively and instantaneously.

The CAVE offers the possibility to display multiple video streams on four projection screens (see figure 7), providing full immersion of the user into the scene. The system is composed by four video projectors and four associated computers for recovering the video streams, displaying an eye picking area and sending the selected part of the

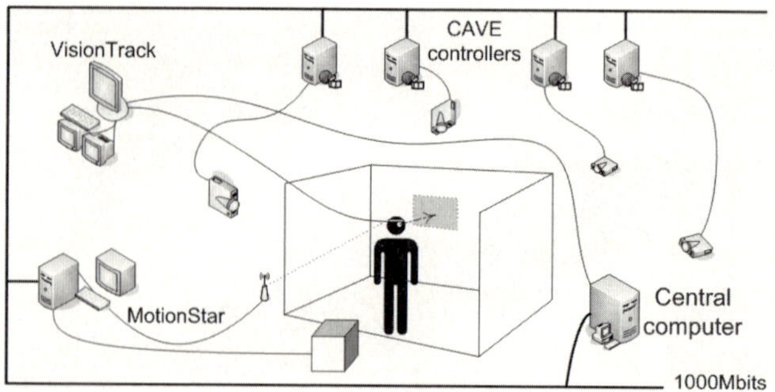

Fig. 6. The control room system

image to the *On-field Agents*. The video stream of the distant cameras is transmitted and rendered via the local area network using RTP.

A joystick allows the supervisor to move mobile cameras to get the most appropriate point of view (see figure7). By pressing a single button, the user validates his eye selection and sends it to the *On-field Agents*. The picture is sent via internet using virtual private network for security purposes. Passing the right information at the right moment is crucial. Since our camera is aerial, it gets a field of view covering a large area. In contrast, agents on the ground get a local view of the situation. It's important for them to be

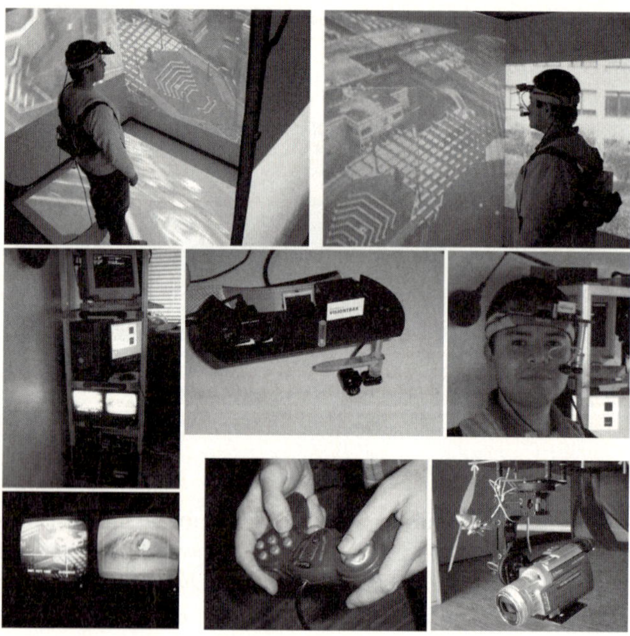

Fig. 7. The four sided CAVE: Advance Control Room

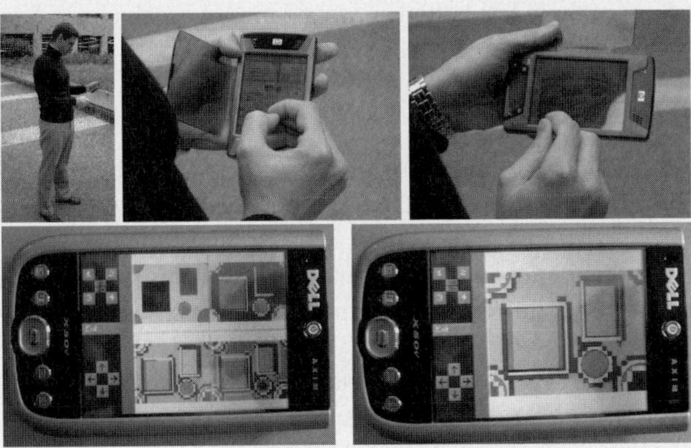

Fig. 8. On-field agent communication equipment

able to relate the received image to their field of action. For these reasons we needed, in addition to the zoom, to be able to send a cropped part of the full image. Notice that the on-field agents may sometimes require to move by themselves the cameras to better appreciate the situation. In these cases, the supervisor can gave them at any moment the possibility to control the cameras.

In order to select part of the image, the eye tracking system is used to compute the gaze direction and determine the gaze target on the cave. The vision system follows the eye movements and measures the position of the pupils. This system provides the supervisor with powerful tools to send visual and vocal information to *On-field Agents*.

3.4   On-Field Agent Equipment

Our handheld communication equipment (PDA) provided a dynamic interface that reacts to the way it was held by the agent. We then had to hold it vertically or horizontally depending on the information we wanted. But we finally decided to only use a simple and intuitive interface which the user gets quickly comfortable with.

At first, the user can see the images of every active cameras (four cameras at the maximum for the moment depending on our acquisition card) on his/her PDA screen, as shown hereinafter in figure 8. These pictures are selected at the control room as well as a map of the surveyed site and updated every time there are changes on the picture (i.e. something happened in the field of view of the camera). GPS information is used to point out on the map the current position of the blimp. When held horizontally (figure 8), the interface shows a higher resolution view of the live video stream. This way, *On-field Agents* can better appreciate specific details while maintaining communication with the control room.

On the left of the screen lies a panel with a few buttons the user can push to see one of the pictures on full screen or to see all of them together. Finally, some buttons can be used to control the current shown camera rotation and zoom. The on-field agent can the n apply the following basic operations: rotation to the left, right, up, down and zoom in and out. The use of these last buttons generate messages which are sent to the server what controls the camera servos embed on the blimp.

3.5   Modules Intercommunication

Video transport over internet in real-time is a complex problem that has often been addressed. Today, RTP [7], the Real-Time Transport Protocol, fulfilled most of the requirements necessary to this purpose, like asynchrony solving capacity, server/client traffic regulation or multiplexing of different kind of streams [8]. The streamed images are compressed using Motion JPEG [9], which provides a good compromise between image quality and size.

Our system uses a Voice Over IP communication between the *Virtual Cockpit* and the *Surveillance Control Room* and between the *Surveillance Control Room* and the *On-field Agents*. We use the freely available PC and PocketPC versions of Skype.

Moreover, as we presented it before, the PDAs of the on-field agents are also connected to the network and get jpeg pictures of the video streamings hown on the full screen or together. They also can control the camera direction and zoom when they are chosen by the supervisor.

4   Discussion and Results

After several trial sessions involving each of the components taken separately, we have put the whole system together and did some tests in the site of our university.

4.1   Virtual Cockpit

The use of a responsive head orientation tracker to drive the video camera of a tele-operated vehicle is an efficient method. It allows indeed to have mixed reality video stream coming from the *R/C Blimp* that is well positioned into the virtual 3D cockpit. This is also an intuitive way to move such a camera because it reproduces exactly what happens in the reality.

We have observed that the Haptic Workstation^{TM} is precise enough to offer a fine control on the blimp's actuators. As further work we plan to give extra force feedback to the pilot in order to improve the information that he gets, enhancing the multimodal aspect of the interface.

4.2   Surveillance Control Room

Standing into the CAVE gives you an amazing effect of immersion. You are literally feeling inside the scene. Using large display for aerial video surveillance, offers great benefits by balancing the effects of having a large field of view to detect small details. By surrounding the user with video information, We added orientation information by grouping the display of cameras according to their position. For example, we projected the aerial video from the blimp on the floor, producing the sensation of flying above the scene. The picking, done with the eye tracking system, offers an intuitive and efficient way to select and crop part of the selected image. The target follows smoothly the gaze and offers a visual feedback to the user on the selected zone.

4.3   On-Field Agent

We have tested our multimodal communication system with on-field agents. Interface proved to be easy to use and intuitive enough. We thought that minimizing the need for pressing buttons on the handheld device would make the use of this application easier but it almost does not change anything. Moreover, we always had to get the PDA inclination. Finally, we improved our interface Actions from the user are reduced to launching skype and loading the main web page on the PDA. Having a GPS driven map pointing out the position of the airborne camera (blimp) revealed to be very useful. Agents were able to have active interaction with the control room thanks to the visual feedback and the transparent VoIP communication.

Demand is growing among security professionals for systems that transmit video images to hand-held devices. If they have wireless access, security agents don't need to return to the control room to view an image before responding to an incident or rely on a dispatcher's description of a suspect, "A second-hand description of somebody is not necessarily the best" [10]. We believe our system responds well to current needs for mobility and intercommunication. We indeed made some experiments with on-field agents. This helped us to mainly improve the interface of the application on the PDA. We made it more intuitive and comfortable for the user. Moreover, we noticed during these experiments that the possibility for the agent to be able to control the camera is mandatory.

5   Potential Application Risk Prevention and Emergency Training

Based on aerial images, it could be nice to augment them with virtual elements such as crowds. This could be very helpful for the on-field agents training because we could simulate situations at risk which would lead to emergency ones. It would then be easier to manage the crowds for the agents if they know where the problem is and where they can redirect them.

Besides, it would be all the more interesting to be able to coach the agents to these situations. We think that if we could make these training directly on the manifestation terrain, this would improve the agents reactions and they could better evaluate and prevent unsecure and critical situations. As you can see in [11], our laboratory is currently working on a crowds engine. We model the crowd behavior, and how people interact each other while walking or running in several different directions. This could then be very interesting for the agents training to work with mixed reality, e.g. virtual crowds in the real environment to manage.

6   Conclusion

We have described a full surveillance, risk prevention and emergency system based on advanced Virtual Reality technologies. It also can help to prevent some risks by simulating with augmented reality some dangerous situations, e.g. crowds behavior in emergency. The system architecture is divided into three main components: data acquisition, analysis and operation. Our contribution focuses on the successful application of

Fig. 9. Example of mixed reality picture combining virtual crowds with a real aerial picture

state of the art Virtual Reality and multimedia technologies in a complex system with multiple participants. Our main goal was to maximize interaction and communication between the personnel implied in the tasks. A single user can teleoperate the airship used for data acquisition, while a second one can concentrate on analyzing the video streams. We put in practice the use of haptic interfaces for teleoperating a flying vehicle. Future work consist in taking full advantage of the new dimension provided by haptic feedback for conveying additional information to the pilot and ease the piloting task. In terms of information analysis which take place at the control room, we have obtained satisfactory results with the use of eye tracking technology within a CAVE system. We proposed an innovative interface for picking-up zones of interest from live video stream. The system is complemented with an efficient multimodal communication device based on a PDA. This solves a common demand of security agents who require more than just voice communication with the control room. This kind of VR and multimedia technology applications fit into the context of current initiatives for security and enhanced surveillance systems. Finally, it would be very interesting to use it, within the framework of augmented reality with our crowds engine, for the on-field agents training.

Acknowledgement

We wish to thank Sylvain Cardin and Achille Peternier for their useful hardware and software contribution to the system presented in this article.

References

1. Reiter, M., Rohatgi, P.: Homeland security. IEEE Internet Computing **8**(6) (2004) 16–17
2. Ellis, T.: Multi-camera video surveillance. In: Proceedings of the 36th Annual International Carnahan Conference on Security Technology. (2002) 228–233
3. Kumar, R., Sawhney, H., Samarasekera, S., Hsu, S., Hai, T., Yanlin, G., Hanna, K., Pope, A., Wildes, R., Hirvonen, D., Hansen, M., Burt, P.: Aerial video surveillance and exploitation. Proceedings of the IEEE (10) (2001) 1518–1539
4. Sebe, I.O., Hu, J., You, S., Neumann, U.: 3d video surveillance with augmented virtual environments. In: Proceedings of the First ACM SIGMM international workshop on Video surveillance, IWVS'03, New York, USA, ACM Press (2003) 107–112
5. Yuan, Y., Detlor, B.: Intelligent mobile crisis response systems. Commun. ACM (2) (2005) 95–98
6. Sawyer, S., Tapia, A., Pesheck, L., Davenport, J.: Mobility and the first responder. Communications of the ACM (3) (2004) 62–65
7. Schulzrinne, H., Casner, S., Frederick, R., Jacobson, V.: Rtp: A transport protocol for real-time applications. In: Request for Comment RFC-1889 of the Internet Engineering Task Force, IETF. (1996)
8. Benslimane, A.: Real-time multimedia services over internet. In: Proceedings of the 1st European Conference on Universal Multiservice Networks, ECUMN'00. (2000) 253–261
9. G.K. Wallace: The jpeg still picture compression standard. IEEE Transactions on Consumer Electronics (1992) xviii–xxxiv
10. Douglas, M.: Surveillance in the palm of your hand. Mobile Radio Technology Magazine (MRT). http://mrtmag.com/mag/radio_surveillance_palm_hand/ (2004)
11. Pettre, J., de Heras, P., Main, J., Yersin, B., Laumaond, J., Thalmann, D.: Real-time navigating crowds: Scalable simulation and rendering. In: Computer Animation and Virtual Worlds. Volume 16. (2006) 445–456

Requirements Engineering as a Key to Holistic Software Quality

Manfred Broy

Institut für Informatik, Technische Universität München
D-80290 München Germany
`broy@in.tum.de`
`http://wwwbroy.informatik.tu-muenchen.de`

Abstract. Adequate software functionality and quality is a crucial issue in a society that vitally depends on software systems. The rising expectations of software users, the distribution of software over networks, size and complexity of today's software systems bring our engineering abilities to limits. Functionality, the cost and the quality of software critically depend on an adequate requirements engineering. We argue in favor of systematic requirements engineering that is model-based, targeting comprehensive system architectures and deeply integrated into software life cycle models.

1 Introduction: Software-Intensive Systems

Software and systems engineering is the key discipline dealing with the construction of information-processing systems. In particular, software and systems engineering is devoted to issues such as requirements engineering, architectural design, implementation, reliability engineering and long-term maintenance. All these issues are of high importance not only from an economical point-of-view, but also with respect to safety and reliability in many areas of our everyday lives. Our critical infrastructures heavily depend on our ability to develop and operate safe and reliable software-intensive systems. Economically, our nations' abilities to be successful in a global market and worldwide competition depend critically on our ability to build software-intensive systems at reasonable cost and with high reliability.

In the following we address issues of requirements engineering by emphasizing its importance for engineering software-intensive systems, showing how requirements engineering can be improved by model-orientation, comprehensive notions of architecture and quality models. This relates four lines of research in our research group at the TU München: requirements engineering, model driven development, architecture centric processes, and holistic quality models.

2 The Engineering Challenge

Today, building complex software-intensive systems is still an unresolved challenge. In many application domains we observe a typical learning curve: at the start of the learning cycle, software is considered merely a minor issue among many others.

A. Levi et al. (Eds.): ISCIS 2006, LNCS 4263, pp. 24–34, 2006.

When the learning in the application domain has matured, software becomes more and more of a central engineering issue. Consequently, engineers in the domain start to develop their own individual processes and models to be able to manage their software issues. Apart from learning about software development itself, the move from an expertise to develop individual software intensive systems to a product line approach is a significant step, which has to be taken by software-intensive industries. In a product line approach, a rich family of related software-intensive systems is to be developed in a cost-effective manner with clearly tailored functionality as well as targeted quality including, in particular, safety and reliability.

For tackling the daunting challenges of complex software systems development, a number of new technical competencies will be mandatory. Among these competencies, we need a good understanding of system modeling (see [14]), and the effective use of models in a disciplined engineering process. Among other topics, this asks for a modeling theory of discrete event systems, which enriches and complements the classical mathematical approaches of system theory based on integral and differential equations.

2.1 Heterogeneity and Multi-functionality

One of the fascinating developments over the last ten to twenty years is the increasing multi-functionality of systems (for details about modeling such systems, see [8], [9], and [10]), accompanied by an increasing heterogeneity in the associated technical components. Traditionally, devices such as photo cameras, music players, and car phones were more-or-less devoted to only one particular function. Sometimes there were a number of possibilities for the devices to tailor those functions and to use the function in slightly different modes but, in the end, the devices served one functional purpose. With the arrival of software and devices, we witness more and more devices that are multifunctional. That means they combine a rich number of different, often quite unrelated functions.

The multi-functionality of our devices, which is in some sense patterned after the high programmability and extensibility of personal computers and laptops, brings of course many interesting questions, opportunities, and challenges. Typically, the elicitation and documentation of the required functionality for multi-functional systems is done during the requirements engineering phase. In this phase, one has to describe the detailed context in which the functionality is delivered, and most importantly, potentially harmful interactions between different features of the system (feature interactions) have to be identified. Different functionalities, even if they are conceptually independent, may be interdependent due to the fact that they use the same resources, such as access by the same keyboard, or presentation of results on the same screen. Therefore it is very important to establish very precisely how different functionalities are supposed to interact.

2.2 Reactivity and Timeliness

Another characterizing feature of embedded systems is their significant amount of interaction and reaction. The systems are connected to the environment by sensors and actuators. From sensors, they receive signals or most general events, and according to the system's state and its programmed reaction, the system responds to the input events by output actions, such as driving actuators, or communicating through the user interface.

Since an embedded software system often controls physical or technical processes, it has to perform in real-time. Thus the software system has to obey certain time properties. This means it has to react to events in a timely manner, but also not too early. Thus, physical and technical processes have to be coordinated in a uniform time frame.

The timely reaction is controlled by a software system. The execution of software also requires some time. Therefore a very critical issue is to make sure that the execution time of the algorithms producing the reaction to certain events is consistent with the time requirements for the output. Traditionally, classical real-time programming is often done in terms of low-level machine code using machine cycle times. Thus timely reaction is dependent heavily on machine cycles and scheduling. This machine-dependency, however, makes it very difficult to relate the application-specific timing requirements to the time properties of the software. Today the correct timing is done to a large extent in a trial and error mode, continually optimizing and fine-tuning the software until finally all the time requirements are implemented. Unfortunately, in most cases this means that the software is extremely machine-dependent and not portable. This makes it very difficult to change or port time-dependent software systems. As a result the same functionality has to be re-implemented on new hardware over and over again. What we need of course is a much more abstract, more stable way of realizing time properties.

2.3 Context-Specific Human Machine Interaction

Embedded systems in most cases have a specific context for human-machine interactions: both user environment, and machine context characterize interaction with the user. The user environment is the specific situation of the user of the system, such as a pilot, the driver of an automobile, or the person operating a phone. The machine context describes the particular properties of the embedded device, such as size, weight, and available energy. For instance, a mobile phone is rather small, and therefore it has a small screen and only a few keys. This means that in many cases we need tailored solutions for human machine interaction. This becomes particularly difficult, keeping in mind the multi-functionality of such systems.

2.4 Complex Hardware/Software Architectures

The hardware structures in embedded systems get more and more powerful and more complex. No longer does an embedded system consist of just one controller connected to sensors and actuators. An increasing number of embedded systems consist of several controllers. Premium cars have up to eighty controllers that are connected by up to five different bus systems. The bus systems in turn are connected by gateways or backbones. So surprisingly complex architectures are created consisting of dozens of controllers, several buses, actuators and sensors, including parts of the human machine interface. Multiplexing appears on all levels of such complex systems: communication devices, controllers, sensors and actuators, as well as the human-machine interface. This means the same devices are used in real-time for different functions while sharing limited resources.

This multiplexing often results in a very complex hardware structure, where the efficient deployment of the software onto the hardware is technically involved. In effect, choosing good hardware architecture along with a specific software deployment is a real challenge for engineering.

2.5 Heterogeneous Distribution

As shown by the hardware structures, a lot of the embedded systems are distributed today. In addition, connecting them through communication devices often combines a number of embedded software systems. The connection can be wireless or wire-bound. In any case, the connection results in an interdependency of several systems.

As a prominent example, we encounter frequently embedded software systems that are connected to the Internet in a way that on one hand, the embedded systems can download information from the Internet, and on the other hand, a remote user can control and operate certain embedded devices by the Internet. By this technique, for instance, heating systems in houses can be remotely controlled through the Internet.

2.6 Criticality

Many embedded devices are safety critical. This means if they fail or if they exhibit serious malfunctions, human lives can be in danger. In other cases, incorrect functioning of embedded systems could destroy high material values (see [12]).

In addition to safety criticality, reliability is a main issue. Reliability is measured in meantime-to-failure. Some of the systems of today are surprisingly reliable. Examples are software systems embedded in civil aircraft. They reach reliabilities of up to 10^9 hours of operation until meantime-to-failure. Such reliability results in the remarkable success that there has not yet been a single accident in civil air traffic as a mere consequence of a software bug. Admittedly, there were some problems with systems that did not react, as a pilot would have expected it in a certain situation such that finally an accident happened – which is in fact rather a systems problem, and, in particular, a requirements engineering issue. But it remains to conclude that safety problems are frequently rooted in requirements engineering and systems engineering, rather than in the detailed construction of the software [12].

Such reliability, on the other hand, is very expensive. It needs hardware redundancy and enormous quality assurance in the development processes.

2.7 Maintenance and Long Term Operation

The lifecycle time of software-intensive systems is beginning to vary considerably. Some systems live only a few weeks or months or years: For instance mobile telephones are often operated for a time-span of merely three to five years. Other systems, like automobiles, may be operated ten to fifteen years and more, with the additional possibility that they could even be operated much longer (for details, see [6]). Airplanes are often operated twenty to thirty years, but here sometimes the embedded devices are replaced earlier.

2.8 Domain Specificity

For most embedded software systems we see quite a number of domain-specific issues and aspects. The functions of the embedded devices are deeply integrated with domain-specific functionalities. Therefore the creation of embedded software devices is strongly connected and related to the specifics of the application domains.

3 Requirements Engineering

Solving the engineering challenges described above needs many research activities in software and systems engineering. We concentrate in the following on one particular topic and activity, namely requirements engineering, which we consider a key to master complexity and quality issues.

Requirements engineering is a critical activity in creation of novel "innovative" *system* concepts and *system* development when developing software-intensive systems. Requirements engineering involves:

- All life-cycle activities devoted to identifying business and user requirements.
- Identification of requirements and constraints derived from the target environment, implementation technologies.
- Analysis of those requirements to derive additional requirements.
- Documentation of the requirements (working out a specification).
- Validation and verification of the documented requirements against user needs.
- A clear, intuitive and unambiguous medium for communicating the product and feature ideas between the users and the developers.
- Development of innovative *product* concepts (e.g. the user experience), mainly driven by software.
- Maintenance of *product* requirements from deployment to sunset.

With clear and concise requirements, developers know what to build, clients know what to expect, and executives are able to make well-founded business decisions.

Fig. 1 shows the high level systematic of a "product model" for requirements engineering called REM as suggested by our research. It gives in all details the required "products" meaning results produced in the requirements engineering process. The arrows indicate the "work flow", however, they do not imply that the process is carried out in a "waterfall" manner. In REM both the product model and the related process model can be tailored. We, in particular recommend an iterative proceeding working out the products in a number of iterations.

Requirement engineering is a critical success factor since it determines the following most important aspects of systems:

- the *functionality* of a system and thus how useful a system is to its users and how difficult ("complex") the system is to develop,
- the *quality attributes* of a system, and thus to a large extend the costs and the value of a system.

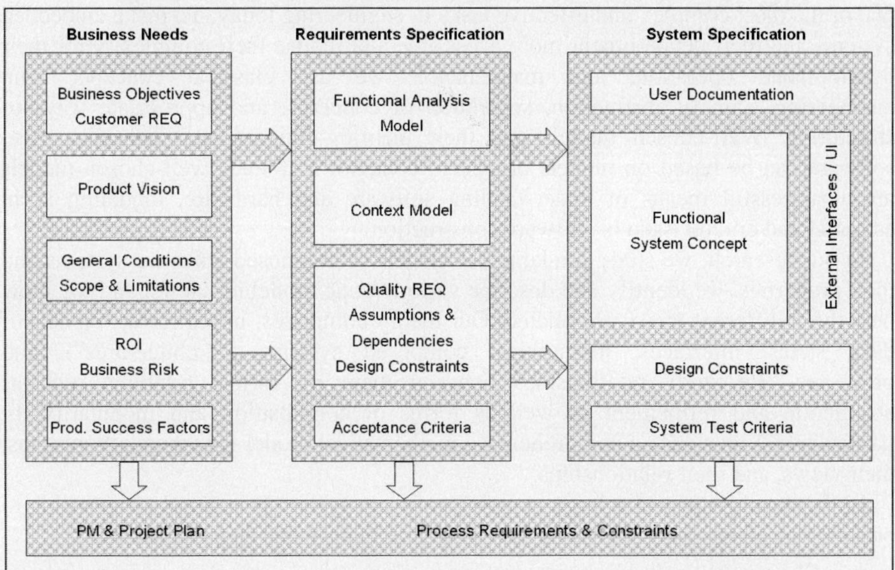

Fig. 1. A Requirements Engineering Reference Model (REM from [11])

This shows that requirements engineering is crucial. Actually, four out of ten critical success factors for the development of software address issues of requirements engineering.

Proper requirements engineering is one of the big challenges of software systems. One of the reasons is that today many software systems are innovative applications. We only have to learn how to design software intensive systems for certain purposes in a way that they really address the users' and market needs. In addition, often OEMs and their chain of suppliers produce the systems.

In such a situation, proper requirements engineering is a must in order to master the challenges of sub-processes carried out by suppliers.

4 Model-Based Development of Software-Intensive Systems

To overcome the complexity of software intensive-systems, we need appropriate ways to structure and model them.

Modeling is the heart of engineering. As yet, the theory of modeling for software-intensive systems is not complete (for work along these lines, see [2], [3], [4]). In the long run, we will need a comprehensive theory for modeling software-intensive systems. In these software-intensive systems, the software is distributed over networks of hardware devices and connected to sensors, actuators, human-machine interfaces and interconnected systems. Furthermore, the software is structured into logical components that interact over the network under hard or soft real-time conditions.

Development of software in general and, in particular, of embedded software is one of the most complex and effective tasks in engineering today. To make embedded systems and their development more accessible and reduce their complexity for their development, operation, and maintenance, we use classical concepts from engineering, namely abstraction, separation of concerns, and appropriate ways of structuring. Well-chosen models and their theories support such concepts. Also software can be based on models of system behavior and since well-chosen models are a successful means of understanding software and hardware, modeling is an essential and crucial issue in software construction.

In our research, we study fundamental models of composed software systems and their properties, we identify and describe various basic modeling views, and we show how these different views are related. Our theory comprises, in particular, models of data, states, interfaces, hierarchical composed systems ("architectures"), and processes. We study relationships between them by formal relations such as abstraction and refinement as well as forms of composition and modularity. In particular, we introduce a comprehensive mathematical model for composed systems, their views, and their relationships.

In the development of a large complex software system it is simply impossible to provide one comprehensive model for the system in only one step. Rather we

- specify a system or subsystem first in terms of its interface,
- add stepwise details by refinement,
- provide several views,
- decompose the hierarchical system into components, and
- construct a sequence of models at different levels of abstraction.

Each step in these activities introduces models, refines them, and verifies or integrates them. Based on a theory of modeling we may introduce description techniques (see, for instance, [5]) – and not the other way around – and based on appropriate methodology finally tool support (see, for instance, [1]).

5   A Reference Architecture Model for Software Intensive Systems

The modeling theory has, in particular, to target the architecture of software intensive systems.

As demonstrated architectures have shown many aspects, what we need in the end is an integrated understanding of architectures, which gives us a full picture of a system including the general system view, its embedded hardware part, although software is deployed on the hardware.

Due to the complexity of the software/hardware structures, the multi-functionality of systems, and the existence of distributed and concurrent engineering processes, the role of both hardware and software architecture of embedded software-intensive systems has become increasingly dominant. The connection from architecture to complexity, heterogeneity, and engineering practice is quite straightforward. First of all the architecture is most important for the quality attributes of systems, for instance to achieve reliability. In effect, it has to be designed in a way that it is redundant, allows us to spot errors, and supports error recovery or fail-safety. Second, the architecture is the

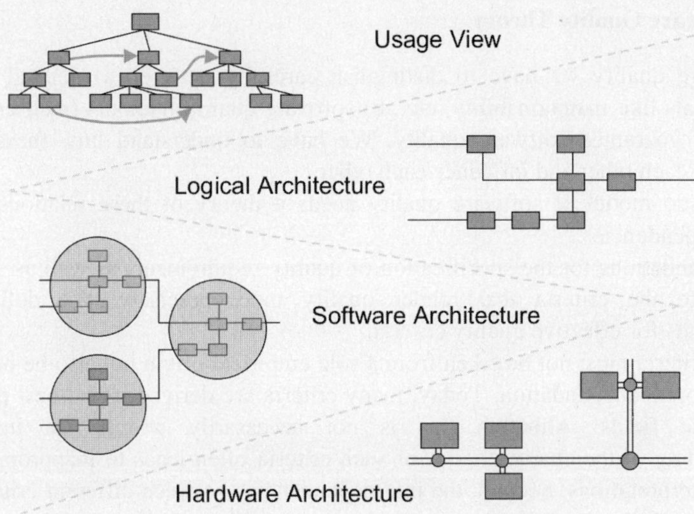

Fig. 2. Visualising the Architectural Levels

blueprint for the development process such as the distribution of work, and for the integration. Only if the different subsystems and the architectures and their interfaces are properly described, and only if the architecture is verified, can one be assured that the different subsystems that are developed and delivered by the suppliers fit together, and can be integrated into the overall systems in a cost-effective way.

Today our abilities to describe combined hardware and software architectures are too weak. A lot of the ideas for architecture that we find around are too specific either addressing only hardware issues or only software issues. What is really needed is a kind of a multilevel architectural view, where both views on an architecture and abstraction levels are considered, thus explaining all the different aspects of the system in an integrated architectural framework.

Fig 2. shows a set of architectural views as they typically are useful in a systematic approach.

6   Holistic Software Quality

If we understand how to support the whole development lifecycle by models, then we can develop a model-driven quality assurance. We can make sure of the quality of the system by analyzing, validating and verifying models. We can use the models to generate additional information that allows us to check certain properties of development artifacts. A very typical and extremely useful idea is the development of test cases from high-level models (see [13]).

We are aiming at a comprehensive, authentic, tractable, useful and realistic approach towards software quality keeping it simple but nevertheless taking care of all relevant factors. This is what we mean if we talk about a holistic approach (for details, see [7]).

6.1 Software Quality Theory

In software quality we have to distinguish carefully between a) general software quality goals like maintainability, etc., b) software quality numbers (metrics), and c) actions to guarantee software quality. We have to understand how these notions depend on each other and influence each other.

A holistic model of software quality needs a theory of these relationships and mutual dependencies.

The foundations for the specification of quality requirements as well as assurance actions are the criteria that render quality more precisely. We define three requirements for effective quality criteria.

First, criteria must not be taken from a sole empirical origin but also be based on a sound theoretical foundation. Today, many criteria are derived from "best practices" in specific fields. Although this is not necessarily wrong, the insufficient understanding of the characteristics of such criteria often leads to inappropriate uses and misinterpretations. Second, the interdependencies between different criteria must be understood. Our third requirement is that each quality criterion must be assessable, otherwise it cannot become effective. Note, that *assessable* does not necessarily mean automatically checkable with a tool. The inability to assess the satisfaction of criteria by automated static or dynamic source code analysis does not render it irrelevant. Generally, many useful criteria need to be assessed in semi-automated (e.g. tool supported analysis) or manual (e.g. reviews) ways.

We will only be able to evaluate and manage software quality if we can find quality criteria that are fine-grained enough to be actually assessed, and develop a clear understanding of their interdependencies. These criteria need to be integrated into a holistic quality model that describes all relevant quality criteria and how they depend on each other.

Of course, this model must be based on existing software engineering knowledge, but it is vital to design it in top-down manner without limiting oneself to "seen elsewhere" criteria. This is particularly important for criteria that are not assessable in an automated way.

6.2 Continuous Quality Controlling

Even a truly complete and correct quality model will not improve software quality if not enforced. We believe that such models need to be designed alongside a rigid, continuous, pro-active quality controlling process. Only if quality defects are detected in a timely manner they can be dealt with effectively.

Unfortunately there is widespread reluctance to install continuous quality controlling processes in software development as they are accepted in various other disciplines. This reluctance is usually justified by the costly nature of such processes. We believe that the inability of most project managers to foresee the long-term benefits of such measures is rooted in the remarkable insufficient understanding of software quality itself. If a holistic quality model could demonstrate the ROI for initially costly quality activities the mere change of mind of project manners would certainly improve overall software quality.

Key activity of the quality controlling process is the continuous assessment of the system. Where recent quality assurance activities are often carried out in an unstructured manner, a holistic quality model clearly defines which criteria need to be assessed in what way. Depending on the criteria and availability of tools this activity consists of automated data collection and manual reviews, whereas manual activities may be supported by tools (semi-automated assessment).

As the sole assessment of single criteria is not sufficient to evaluate system quality the assessment results need to be aggregated to be of real use. Since the quality model not only lists the criteria, but also describes their interdependencies, aggregation rules can be derived from the model itself.

All data and its aggregations must be made available in a central place so the ones in charge of quality controlling are enabled to quickly determine the systems quality or its deficiencies and react in an appropriate manner.

As continuous quality controlling is a highly complex and costly activity the availability of appropriate tools is compulsory. Controlling can only be successful if it applies scalable assessment tools and an adequate environment for collecting and aggregating assessment data that are centrally available.

Another important aspect of quality control concerns a meta quality level: The quality control process must define measures to assess itself and the underlying model such that deficiencies in either part can be as quickly determined and corrected as in the system they work on.

7 Conclusions: Requirements Engineering as a Model Driven Process

So far requirements engineering is done mainly be text in natural languages. Commercially available tools at its best support the structuring of text. Given a modeling approach to

- comprehensive functionality in terms of function hierarchies (along the lines of feature trees)
- comprehensive system architecture in terms of functionality, logical component architecture, hardware, software, and its deployment
- comprehensive quality model taking into account all kinds of quality aspects in terms of a quality profile

we can do requirements engineering in a much more systematic way in terms of formal or at least standardized models. This way the requirements engineering process and its products become measurable. Moreover, requirements tracing and verification can be done in a much more systematic way. Finally, tool support can be offered with a much higher level of automation.

As a step into the direction of a systematic requirements engineering we are currently developing a requirement engineering reference model (REM see Fig. 1) in close cooperation with Siemens Corporate Research Princeton (this is work based on [11]). The product model is essential for quality and progress control in projects.

Acknowledgement

It is a pleasure to thank Bernhard Schätz, Markus Pizka, Eva Geisberger, and Florian Deissenböck for discussions and feedback on topics of this paper.

References

[1] AutoFOCUS – Webseite, http://autofocus.in.tum.de, 2005

[2] D. Herzberg, M. Broy: Modeling layered distributed communication systems. Applicable Formal Methods. Springer Verlag, Volume 17, Number 1, May 2005

[3] M. Broy, K. Stølen: Specification and Development of Interactive Systems: FOCUS on Streams, Interfaces, and Refinement. Springer 2001

[4] M. Broy: Time, Abstraction, Causality, and Modularity in Interactive Systems. FESCA 2004. Workshop at ETAPS 2004, 1-8

[5] M. Broy: The Semantic and Methodological Essence of Message Sequence Charts. Science of Computer Programming, SCP 54:2-3, 2004, 213-256

[6] M. Broy: Challenges in Automotive Software Engineering. Key Note 28th International Conference on Software Engineering (ICSE 2006)

[7] M. Broy, F. Deißenböck, M. Pizka: A Holistic Approach to Software Quality at Work. 3rd World Congress for Software Quality (3WCSQ)

[8] M. Broy: Multi-view Modeling of Software Systems. Keynote. FM2003 Satellite Workshop on Formal Aspects of Component Software, 8-9 September 2003, Pisa, Italy

[9] M. Broy: Service-oriented Systems Engineering: Specification and Design of Services and Layered Architectures: *The JANUS Approach*. In: M. Broy, J. Grünbauer, D. Harel and T. Hoare: Engineering Theories of Software Intensive Systems, Marktoberdorf, 3–15 August 2004, Germany, NATO Science Series, II. Mathematics, Physics and Chemistry – Vol 195, Springer

[10] M. Broy, I. Krüger, M. Meisinger: A Formal Model of Services. TOSEM 2006, to appear

[11] E. Geisberger: Requirements Engineering eingebetteter Systeme – ein interdisziplinärer Modellierungsansatz. Dissertation, Technische Universität München, 2005. Shaker Verlag, ISBN: 3-8322-4619-3, www.shaker-online.com/

[12] G. Le Lann: An Analysis of the Ariane 5 Flight 501 Failure - A System Engineering Perspective. 10th IEEE Intl. ECBS Conference, March 1997, 339-346.

[13] A. Pretschner, W. Prenninger, S. Wagner, C. Kühnel, M. Baumgartner, B. Sostawa, R. Zölch, T. Stauner: One Evaluation of Model-Based Testing and its Automation. Proc. 27th Intl. Conf. on Software Engineering (ICSE), pp. 392{401, St. Louis, May 2005

[14] B. Selic, G. Gullekson. P.T. Ward: Real-time Object-oriented Modeling. Wiley, New York 1994

Problems and Challenges of Image-Guided Neurosurgical Navigation and Intervention

Jacques G. Verly[1],
Martin Kavec[2], Lara M. Vigneron[2], Christophe Phillips[2], Romain Boman[2],
Vincent Libertiaux[2], Jean-Philippe Ponthot[2], Serge Cescotto[2], Pierre Robe[2],
Didier Martin[2], David Wikler[3], Marc Levivier[3], and Jacques Brotchi[3]

[1] University of Liège, Liège, Belgium
Jacques.Verly@ulg.ac.be
[2] University of Liège, Liège, Belgium
[3] Free University of Brussels, Brussels, Belgium

Interventional MRI scanners now allow neurosurgeons to make images throughout the course of surgery. While these machines are still relatively rare today, they are bound to become a key instrument in the operating theatres of major medical centers. The successful use of such machines requires close collaboration between surgeons and engineers. This presentation describes the problem of neurosurgical navigation and discusses some of its algorithmic challenges, such as the joint use of multiple imaging modalities (CT, MRI, PET, etc), image registration, field-artifact removal, multi-modality image segmentation, biomechanical models of the brain, finite-element models (FEM) for tracking tissue deformation, and a generalization of FEM, known as XFEM, to handle the cuts, retractions, and resections occuring during surgery.

A. Levi et al. (Eds.): ISCIS 2006, LNCS 4263, p. 35, 2006.
© Springer-Verlag Berlin Heidelberg 2006

Information and Communication Technologies in the EU's Seventh Framework Programme

Eric Badiqué

European Commission, DG INFSO, Unit C2 - IST Strategy
BU31 1/58, B-1049 Brussels, Belgium
Eric.Badique@ec.europa.eu

After a broad overview of European support mechanisms to collaborative research, the presentation will give a summary of presently running EU projects within the IST Programme as part of the sixth Framework Programme (FP6). It will then focus on current activities that relate to Computer and Information Sciences including examples of key projects.

The core of the presentation will be an overview of the proposed orientations for the Seventh Framework Programme (FP7). The main strategic directions and the timetable for decision and implementation of the Programme will be given. This will be complemented by guidance and advice on future calls for proposals including practical information on calls timing and submission procedures.

A. Levi et al. (Eds.): ISCIS 2006, LNCS 4263, p. 36, 2006.
© Springer-Verlag Berlin Heidelberg 2006

The Greedy Prepend Algorithm
for Decision List Induction

Deniz Yuret[1] and Michael de la Maza[2]

[1] Koç University, Istanbul, Turkey
dyuret@ku.edu.tr
[2] Park Hudson Finance, Cambridge, MA 02139, USA

Abstract. We describe a new decision list induction algorithm called the Greedy Prepend Algorithm (GPA). GPA improves on other decision list algorithms by introducing a new objective function for rule selection and a set of novel search algorithms that allow application to large scale real world problems. GPA achieves state-of-the-art classification accuracy on the protein secondary structure prediction problem in bioinformatics and the English part of speech tagging problem in computational linguistics. For both domains GPA produces a rule set that human experts find easy to interpret, a marked advantage in decision support environments. In addition, we compare GPA to other decision list induction algorithms as well as support vector machines, C4.5, naive Bayes, and a nearest neighbor method on a number of standard data sets from the UCI machine learning repository.

1   Introduction

The Greedy Prepend Algorithm (GPA) is an induction system for decision lists. A decision list is an ordered list of rules where each rule consists of a pattern and a classification [1]. A new instance is classified by comparing it to the pattern of each rule, and the classification of the first matching rule is accepted. An example of a three rule decision list for the UCI house votes data set [2] is shown in Table 1.

To learn a decision list from a given set of training examples the general approach is to start with a default rule or an empty decision list and keep adding the best rule to cover the unclassified or misclassified examples. The new rules can be added to the end of the list [3], the front of the list [4], or other positions [5]. Other design decisions include the criteria used to select the "best rule" and how to search for it.

GPA works by prepending rules to the front of a growing decision list and distinguishes itself with its simple "best rule" definition. When a rule is added to a decision list, the increase in the number of correctly predicted training set instances is called the rule's *gain*. In GPA the best rule is defined to be the rule that has the maximum gain. Earlier decision list induction systems typically used variants of the Laplace preference function [6], which emphasizes the rule's individual accuracy rather than its contribution to the decision list as a whole.

A. Levi et al. (Eds.): ISCIS 2006, LNCS 4263, pp. 37–46, 2006.

Table 1. A three rule decision list for the UCI house votes data set

```
1. If adoption-of-the-budget-resolution = y
       and anti-satellite-test-ban = n
       and water-project-cost-sharing = y
   then democrat
2. If physician-fee-freeze = y
   then republican
3. If TRUE then democrat
```

We show that the simple maximum gain rule results in comparable or better overall accuracy on a number of standard data sets.

By default, GPA uses an efficient admissible search algorithm (OPUS [7]) which is guaranteed to find the maximum gain rule. However, in real world problems with a large number of training instances and distinct feature values such exhaustive search may become prohibitively expensive. To cope with large scale problems GPA introduces two novel heuristic search algorithms: one that restricts the rule set, and another that restricts the search algorithm.

To illustrate the performance of the algorithm on large scale problems we present two applications of GPA, one to the secondary structure prediction problem in bioinformatics (Section 3) and the second to English part of speech tagging (Section 4). Comparisons with other decision list inducers on these problems were not feasible due to the scale of the problems. Thus we compare the classification accuracy of GPA to other decision list inducers and well-known concept learning algorithms on a representative set of problems from the UCI Machine Learning Repository (Section 5). Section 2 describes the GPA algorithm.

2   The Greedy Prepend Algorithm

To construct the decision list in Table 1, GPA first generates the default rule (rule #3) which assigns every instance the majority class in the training set. Next, candidates for rule #2 are searched, and the one that results in the highest gain in accuracy for the training set is selected. The whole decision list is constructed from the bottom up until no further improvement can be made. Note that, when the completed decision list is applied to classify an instance, rules are applied from the top (rule #1) to the bottom (rule #3).

The high-level Greedy Prepend Algorithm is given in Table 2. MAX-GAIN-RULE finds the rule that results in the largest increase in the training set accuracy when added to the beginning of a decision list. By default, an admissible search algorithm (OPUS [7]) is used to search all possible rules. For large scale problems where this approach is not feasible, either the search algorithm (see Section 3) or the set of rules (see Section 4) can be restricted. The selection of rules based on gain, and the heuristic search methods distinguish GPA from other decision list algorithms such as Prepend [4].

Table 2. Greedy Prepend Algorithm

GPA(*data*)
1   *dlist* ← NIL
2   *default-class* ← MOST-COMMON-CLASS(*data*)
3   *rule* ← [if TRUE then *default-class*]
4   **while** GAIN(*rule*, *dlist*, *data*) > 0
5   **do** *dlist* ← PREPEND(*rule*, *dlist*)
6   *rule* ← MAX-GAIN-RULE(*dlist*, *data*)
7   **return** *dlist*

By default, GPA reserves 20% of its training set for validation. As more and more rules are added to the decision list, the performance on the validation set peaks, then starts dropping even though the training set performance is improved with every rule. GPA prevents overfitting by stopping the rule generation when the validation performance starts to drop.

The antecedents of the GPA rules can represent binary and nominal attributes naturally. Missing values do not pose a problem: an instance with a missing attribute will not match a rule that specifies a value for that attribute. For datasets with numeric attributes we use the MDL method of supervised discretization [8,9]. We force the resulting attributes to be binary (i.e. less than, greater than conditions) so that GPA can construct arbitrary ranges using only two terms of the form `attr >= x1 and attr <= x2` in the antecedent.

3   Secondary Structure Prediction

In this section, we present an application of GPA to a large scale problem and illustrate the use of its heuristic search algorithm. Specifying the tertiary structure of a protein, the location of all of its constituent amino acids in Euclidean space, is key to understanding its function and is one of the outstanding unsolved problems in biology. Ideally, the tertiary structure could be determined from the primary structure, the linear sequence of amino acids that compose the protein. A step towards the tertiary structure is the secondary structure which classifies each amino acids into one of three groups: alpha helix, beta strand, and loop.

Secondary structure prediction has been studied for several decades and dozens of standard machine learning techniques have been applied to the problem. Chou [10] described a simple rule based method for predicting secondary structure. Levin [11] introduced the notion of using multiple sequence alignment to improve prediction. Rost [12] combined neural networks and multiple sequence alignment. Huang [13] discusses the limitations of many secondary structure prediction techniques.

Data Set: Our GPA evaluation for the secondary structure prediction problem is based on the recommendations and the data set described in [14]. The data set, CB513, consists of 513 non-homologous proteins that have been used in a number of studies. These proteins, along with their homologues, were used with seven fold cross validation to obtain our accuracy figures. The data set includes 1.7 million instances, nine attributes with 180 distinct values, and three classes.

Methodology: Two decision lists were built to perform secondary structure prediction. The sequence-to-structure list takes a window of 9 adjacent residue names as input and outputs a prediction of one of three secondary structure assignments (helix, strand, or loop) for the center residue. The structure-to-structure list takes a window of 19 adjacent secondary structure *assignments* from the first decision list as input, and outputs a possible correction for the center residue. During testing both decision lists are applied to the test protein and its homologues, and final assignments are determined by majority vote. This type of organization is common in the literature [12], although implemented using different learners like neural networks.

Search Algorithm: Learning disjunctions is critical in the secondary structure prediction domain so that the decision lists can capture regularities across classes of residues. However, searching the space of all rules with disjunctions is computationally infeasible and current search techniques, such as OPUS [7], cannot be used in this problem domain.

We implemented a heuristic technique that finds good disjunctive rules. The search uses randomly selected instances to gradually construct a candidate rule. If the instance is misclassified by the current decision list and matches the class of the candidate rule, the rule is generalized to include the instance. If the instance is correctly classified by the current decision list but the candidate rule changes its classification, the rule is specialized to exclude the instance. After every modification, the change in the gain is computed and the modification is accepted if there is an overall increase in the rule's gain. The search terminates after a prespecified number of modifications fail to improve the candidate rule. A candidate rule is constructed for each class, and the one with the highest gain is accepted to the decision list.

Table 3. Performance results for the set of CB513 proteins

Algorithm:	PHD	DSC	Predator	NNSSP	GPA
Accuracy:	72.3	69.1	69.0	71.7	69.2

Results: GPA achieves a classification accuracy of 69.2% on CB513. To put this number in perspective, always predicting the most common class (loop) gives a prediction accuracy of 43%. Predicting the class based only on the identity of the center amino acid gives a prediction accuracy of 49%.

The secondary structure problem has been the subject of intense interest in computational biology and machine learning. Table 3 shows the classification accuracy of several of the leading algorithms on CB513. PHD is a neural network based system [12], DSC is a statistical technique [15], PREDATOR is a knowledge based system [16], and NNSSP is a nearest neighbor algorithm [17]. GPA gives a strong result and is the only one that produces human readable models.

4   Part of Speech Tagging

In this section, we present an application of GPA to a linguistic problem and illustrate the use of rule space restriction to cope with the large search space. Determining the part of speech of ambiguous words is a useful step in the analysis of natural language text. The sentence "Time flies like an arrow" can be interpreted in several different ways depending on the part of speech assignments. The word "time" can be a noun (time moves quickly just like an arrow does), a verb (measure the speed of flying insects like you would measure that of an arrow), or an adjective (a type of flying insect, "time-flies," enjoy arrows; compare "Fruit flies like a banana.") The problem of part of speech tagging is to decide what part of speech each word has depending on its context.

Data Set: We have used the Penn Treebank Wall Street Journal corpus [18] for evaluating the performance of GPA for part of speech tagging. The Penn Treebank uses a set of 45 distinct part of speech tags to annotate about a million words of newspaper text. The data set consists of one million instances with fifty attributes and half a million distinct attribute values. The data was split randomly intro training, validation, and test sets using a 4:1:1 ratio.

Methodology: To represent the context of a word to be tagged, we take a window of seven words centered around the target word and encode the following information about each one in the attributes:

1. The original word and its lowercase version.
2. The character types (upper case, numeric etc.) used in the word.
3. Prefixes and suffixes of the word up to four characters long.

Common domain specific optimizations were not performed on our GPA implementation: We did not use an explicit dictionary that lists the possible parts of speech for each word, or use previous part of speech predictions in the model, or train a separate model for the unknown words. Nevertheless GPA seems to extract the necessary information from the surface features of the surrounding words and achieve comparable accuracy to previously reported results.

The fact that these attributes are very redundant (e.g. the three character suffix of a word is correlated with its four character suffix) and mostly irrelevant (no attribute filtering was performed) does not seem to prevent GPA from getting a good result. More formal analysis of the robustness of GPA in the presence of redundant and irrelevant attributes needs to be performed.

Search Algorithm: The large size of the search space precludes an exhaustive search for the maximum gain rule. Representing the suffixes and strings of each word encountered during training creates a large number of distinct values for some attributes. To cope with the large search space, we limited the search to rules that add a single attribute to one of the already accepted rules in the decision list. As a result, after the default rule, only single attribute rules are searched. After the first single attribute rule, all the two attribute rules which share the same first attribute, and all the remaining single attribute rules are

Table 4. Performance results for part of speech tagging

Algorithm:	Post	Brill	Mxpost	GPA
Overall:	96.7	96.6	96.6	96.0
Unknown:	85.0	82.2	86.2	81.8

searched. This way each rule is forced to specify an exception to a previously accepted rule that can be expressed by a single attribute.

Results: Part of speech tagging is a much studied problem with a number of successful approaches. We present the results of three well known algorithms for comparison in Table 4. The "overall" column gives the overall accuracy, and the "unknown" column gives the accuracy on unknown words. Post is a Markov model based stochastic tagger [19], Brill's tagger uses transformation based learning [20], and Mxpost is based on a maximum entropy model [21].

5   UCI Machine Learning Repository

The UCI Machine Learning Repository [2] has a long and storied history in the machine learning community. Although its influence has waned in recent years, testing a new algorithm on a variety of UCI data sets serves as a sanity check on the algorithm's characteristics.

We present two sets of comparisons in this section. First, we compare the accuracy of GPA and the lengths of the decision lists it generates to other decision list induction algorithms analyzed in [4]. Then, we report results with a number of standard machine learning algorithms implemented in Weka [9].

Most UCI datasets are small enough to allow exhaustive search for the maximum gain rule. We therefore used the admissible OPUS algorithm [7] to find the best rule. On some problems a limit on the maximum number of terms in the antecedent of a rule was imposed for the sake of efficiency.

5.1   Comparison with Other Decision List Algorithms

Webb [4] compares the accuracy and average list length of a number of decision list induction algorithms. Prepend builds decision lists from the bottom towards the top like GPA, but uses the Laplace preference function which emphasizes the individual accuracy of a rule. GPA, in contrast, uses the maximum gain function which only measures the increase in the performance of the whole decision list caused by the new rule. Append is a variation of the CN2 algorithm [3] which builds decision lists from the top towards the bottom. Append-p2 implements rule pruning. C4.5rules is a standard algorithm which generates rules from a decision tree [22].

Table 5 presents accuracy and average list length for GPA and Prepend on the 11 problems used in [4]. The GPA results were obtained repeating 5 fold cross validation 100 times. The number of terms in the antecedents were limited to 3 for the sake of time.

Table 5. Comparison of GPA and Prepend on accuracy and list length on some UCI data sets (standard deviations are given in parentheses)

Data set	Accuracy		Length	
	GPA	Prepend	GPA	Prepend
audio	74.55 (5.78)	77.2 (5.4)	25.3 (2.15)	10.7 (0.9)
breast	71.96 (4.28)	61.2 (5.6)	4.5 (3.75)	9.6 (1.1)
votes	95.10 (2.41)	94.9 (2.5)	4.1 (1.76)	5.0 (0.5)
lymph	76.60 (7.27)	84.3 (7.4)	7.7 (2.19)	5.1 (0.6)
monks-1	100.0 (0.0)	100.0 (0.0)	5.9 (1.14)	4.7 (0.5)
monks-2	64.94 (2.07)	99.1 (1.5)	64.1 (4.8)	15.8 (0.4)
monks-3	98.92 (0.88)	97.9 (1.2)	4.0 (0.0)	4.9 (0.7)
mushroom	100.0 (0.0)	100.0 (0.0)	8.0 (0.0)	4.0 (0.0)
soybean	89.59 (2.69)	83.6 (5.3)	26.0 (8.6)	20.7 (0.8)
tic-tac-toe	98.41 (0.92)	96.9 (1.0)	9.0 (0.0)	12.0 (0.8)
tumor	40.8 (4.32)	39.1 (5.3)	11.1 (6.67)	16.8 (1.6)

A two tailed z test at 0.05 significance level was used to compare the GPA results to the ones reported in [4]. Compared to Prepend, GPA had significantly higher accuracy in 5 problems and worse in 3 problems. The list lengths were shorter than prepend 5 times and longer 6 times. GPA exceeds the performance of the original Prepend in accuracy and matches it in length. Comparison with the other algorithms is summarized in Table 6. The number triples indicate the number of problems in which GPA won, drew, and lost at the 0.05 significance level. GPA seems to achieve significantly higher accuracy than append and append-p2 and build shorter decision lists than append and c4.5rules.

Table 6. Win:draw:loss numbers comparing GPA to other rule based algorithms

Algorithm	Accuracy	Length
prepend-ip2	5:3:3	5:0:6
append	6:3:2	7:2:2
append-p2	5:4:2	5:1:5
c4.5rules	4:6:1	8:1:2

5.2   Comparison with Other Learning Algorithms

Table 7 summarizes GPA's performance versus naive Bayes, support vector machines (SMO), a nearest neighbor algorithm (IB5), C4.5 (J4.8), and a decision table learner (DTable) as implemented in the Weka tool [9]. All algorithms were run in their default settings. GPA was restricted to rules with at most three antecedent terms. Each of the 20 data sets were evaluated with five fold cross validation repeated 10 times. The results were compared with a two tailed paired t-test at 0.05 significance level.

The key result is that the performance accuracy of GPA is comparable to leading concept learning algorithms. For example, compared to support vector

Table 7. Comparison of GPA with other common learning algorithms. Standard deviations are given in parentheses. A (*) next to a result shows that it is statistically significantly worse than GPA and a (v) shows that it is significantly better than GPA. The last line gives the win:draw:loss numbers for each column.

Dataset	GPA	NBayes	SMO	IB5	J48	DTable
anneal	98.83(0.76)	86.80(2.41) *	97.37(1.10) *	96.97(1.30) *	98.62(0.76)	98.50(0.87)
audio	75.42(6.55)	71.37(4.44)	80.36(4.53)	60.67(5.22) *	77.57(4.77)	74.35(6.21)
balance	74.42(3.84)	89.97(1.31) v	87.82(1.96) v	87.60(1.70) v	78.11(2.49)	76.78(3.83)
breast	71.57(3.39)	73.21(5.00)	69.19(4.81)	74.02(3.52)	73.18(3.75)	71.47(4.80)
glass	69.27(6.59)	48.45(5.95) *	57.06(6.96) *	65.24(4.69)	67.45(7.13)	68.80(7.01)
heart-clev	79.24(5.81)	83.04(4.97)	83.40(4.37)	81.73(4.43)	76.24(4.80)	77.76(6.56)
heart-hung	78.47(4.24)	83.91(4.40) v	82.15(4.55)	81.84(4.68)	79.83(5.56)	79.77(4.68)
hepatitis	79.29(5.53)	83.42(5.09)	85.16(4.56)	84.32(4.88)	78.52(5.44)	78.77(6.22)
hypo	99.52(0.32)	95.33(0.48) *	93.58(0.29) *	93.26(0.40) *	99.50(0.26)	99.36(0.31)
iris	94.60(3.74)	95.47(3.55)	96.33(2.95)	96.13(3.04)	94.53(3.67)	93.73(3.27)
lymph	76.91(5.65)	82.71(7.02)	85.89(5.78) v	82.58(5.79)	76.11(6.53)	74.41(6.80)
monks-1	100.00(0.0)	74.62(2.75) *	74.64(2.77) *	98.44(1.37) *	97.73(3.80)	100.00(0.0)
monks-2	65.24(1.94)	62.33(2.54) *	65.72(0.22)	57.52(3.29) *	63.18(4.40)	65.72(0.22)
monks-3	98.92(0.80)	96.39(1.45) *	97.15(1.80)	97.71(1.29)	98.92(0.80)	98.92(0.80)
mushroom	100.00(0.0)	95.66(0.52) *	100.00(0.0)	99.98(0.05)	100.00(0.0)	100.00(0.0)
segment	94.44(1.15)	80.27(1.47) *	92.67(0.99) *	95.18(0.93)	96.47(1.14) v	91.60(1.71) *
sonar	70.76(6.68)	68.29(6.81)	76.39(5.86)	80.29(6.28) v	72.98(7.16)	70.74(7.15)
soybean	89.63(2.55)	92.65(1.92) v	93.03(1.61) v	89.66(2.18)	90.57(2.52)	85.78(2.76) *
tic-tac-toe	98.14(1.10)	70.26(2.91) *	98.33(0.84)	98.85(0.76)	83.98(2.26) *	77.40(2.89) *
tumor	40.62(4.49)	48.47(3.62) v	45.87(4.61)	46.96(4.36) v	40.64(4.35)	39.36(4.79)
		(9/7/4)	(5/12/3)	(5/12/3)	(1/18/1)	(3/17/0)

machines GPA is better ($p < 0.05$) on five data sets, worse ($p < 0.05$) on three data sets, and statistically indistinguishable on the rest.

6   Contributions

The Greedy Prepend Algorithm is a decision list induction system that achieves state-of-the art classification accuracy on secondary structure prediction and part of speech tagging and matches the performance of C4.5 and support vector machines on a representative set of data sets from the UCI Machine Learning Repository.

The main contributions of the GPA are its simple objective function for rule selection and its heuristic search extensions which allow decision lists to be applied to large scale problems with thousands of features and millions of instances. The results show that decision lists can be competitive with the best known algorithms in large scale real world problems. Unlike Bayesian methods, neural networks, nearest neighbor algorithms, and support vector machines, rule based learners like GPA produce output that is human readable. Hence GPA is a better fit in decision support environments where a decision maker benefits from an explanation for the recommendations made by automated concept learning systems. GPA demonstrates by example that high classification accuracy is possible while still preserving a representation that can be easily interpreted by humans.

A GPA implementation that runs within WEKA [9], an open source environment for running machine learning experiments, is available from the first author.

References

1. Rivest, R.L.: Learning decision lists. Machine Learning **2** (1987) 229–246
2. Newman, D.J., Hettich, S., Blake, C.L., Merz, C.J.: UCI repository of machine learning databases (1998) http://www.ics.uci.edu/~mlearn/MLRepository.html.
3. Clark, P., Niblett, T.: The CN2 induction algorithm. Machine Learning **3** (1989) 261–283
4. Webb, G.I.: Recent progress in learning decision lists by prepending inferred rules. In: Proceedings of the Second Singapore International Conference on Intelligent Systems (SPICIS '94), Singapore (1994) B280–B285
5. Newlands, D., Webb, G.I.: Alternative strategies for decision list construction. In: Proceedings of the Fourth Data Mining Conference (DM IV 03). (2004) 265–273
6. Clark, P., Boswell, R.: Rule induction with CN2: Some recent improvements. In Kodratoff, Y., ed.: Machine Learning – Proceedings of the Fifth European Conference (EWSL-91), Berlin, Springer-Verlag (1991) 151–163
7. Webb, G.I.: Opus: An efficient admissible algorithm for unordered search. JAIR **3** (1995) 431–465
8. Fayyad, U.M., Irani, K.B.: Multi-interval discretization of continuous-valued attributes for classification learning. In: Proceedings of the Workshop on Massive Datasets, Washington, DC, NRC, Committee on Applied and Theoretical Statistics (1993)
9. Witten, I.H., Frank, E.: Data Mining: Practical Machine Learning Tools and Techniques. 2 edn. Morgan Kaufmann (2005)
10. Chou, P.Y., Fasman, G.D.: Conformational parameters for amino acids in helical, beta sheet and random coil regions calculated from proteins. Biochemistry **13**(2) (1974) 211–222
11. Levin, J.M., Pascarella, S., Argos, P., Garnier, J.: Quantification of secondary structure prediction improvement using multiple alignment. Prot. Engin. **6** (1993) 849–854
12. Rost, B., Sander, C.: Prediction of protein secondary structure at better than 70% accuracy. Journal of Molecular Biology **232** (1993) 584–599
13. Huang, J.T., Wang, M.T.: Secondary structural wobble: The limits of protein prediction accuracy. Biochemical and Biophysical Research Communications **294**(3) (2002) 621–625
14. Cuff, J.A., Barton, G.J.: Evaluation and improvement of multiple sequence methods for protein secondary structure prediction. Proteins: Structure, Function, and Genetics **34** (1999) 508–519
15. King, R.D., Sternberg, M.J.E.: Identification and application of the concepts important for accurate and reliable protein secondary structure prediction. Protein Sci **5** (1996) 2298–2310
16. Frishman, D., Argos, P.: Seventy-five percent accuracy in protein secondary structure prediction. Proteins: Structure, Function, and Genetics **27** (1997) 329–335
17. Salamov, A.A., Solovyev, V.V.: Prediction of protein secondary structure by combining nearest-neighbor algorithms and multiple sequence alignments. Journal of Molecular Biology **247** (1995) 11–15
18. Marcus, M.P., Santorini, B., Marcinkiewicz, M.A.: Building a large annotated corpus of English: The Penn Treebank. Computational Linguistics **19**(2) (1993) 313–330
19. Weischedel, R., Meteer, M., Schwartz, R., Ramshaw, L.: Coping with ambiguity and unknown words through probabilistic models. Computational Linguistics **19**(2) (1993) 359–382

20. Brill, E.: Transformation-based error-driven learning and natural language processing: A case study in part-of-speech tagging. Computational Linguistics **21**(4) (1995) 543–565
21. Ratnaparkhi, A.: A maximum entropy model for part-of-speech tagging. In: Proceedings of the Conference on Empirical Methods in Natural Language Processing. (1996)
22. Quinlan, J.R.: C4.5: Programs for Machine Learning. Morgan Kaufmann (1993)

Heuristics for Minimum Brauer Chain Problem

Fatih Gelgi and Melih Onus

Department of Computer Science and Engineering
Arizona State University
{fagelgi, melih}@asu.edu

Abstract. The exponentiation problem is computing x^n for positive integer exponents n where the quality is measured by number of multiplications it requires. However, finding minimum number of multiplications is an NP-complete problem. This problem is very important for many applications such as RSA encryption and ElGamal decryption. Solving minimum Brauer chain problem is a way to solve the exponentiation problem. In this paper, five heuristics for approximating minimum length Brauer chain for a given number n is discussed. These heuristics are based on some greedy approaches and dynamic programming. As a result, we empirically get 1.1-approximation for the problem.

Keywords: Brauer chain, addition chain, exponentiation, greedy algorithms, dynamic programming.

1   Introduction

The exponentiation problem is computing x^n for positive integer exponents n. The quality of an exponentiation algorithm can be measured by number of multiplications it requires. A naive approach requires n multiplications which is very inefficient. The decrease-and-conquer technique requires at most $2 \lg n$ multiplications for any integer n. Since a trivial lower bound on number of multiplications for number n is $\lg n$, this algorithm is a 2-approximation algorithm.

The minimum exponentiation problem is finding minimum number of multiplications for computing x^n for positive integer exponents n. This problem is an NP-complete problem [1]. The exponentiation problem has many applications, several cryptosystems among them, e.g., RSA encryption and ElGamal decryption [2,3,4].

An addition chain [5,6] for a positive integer n is a sequence of integers $\langle a_1, a_2, ..., a_r \rangle$ such that $a_1 = 1$, $a_r = n$ and $a_i = a_j + a_k$ for some $1 \leq k, j < i$ and $2 \leq i \leq r$. For example, $\langle 1, 2, 3, 6, 9, 10, 15, 24 \rangle$ is an addition chain for 24 with length 8. The minimum exponentiation problem is equal to minimum addition chain problem.

A Brauer chain is an addition chain in which each member uses the previous member as an addend. Thus, a Brauer chain for a positive integer n is a sequence of integers $a_1, a_2, ..., a_r = n$ such that $a_1 = 1$, $a_r = n$ and $a_i = a_{i-1} + a_k$ for some $1 \leq k < i$ and $2 \leq i \leq r$.

A. Levi et al. (Eds.): ISCIS 2006, LNCS 4263, pp. 47–54, 2006.
© Springer-Verlag Berlin Heidelberg 2006

1.1 Our Contribution

In this work, we present five different heuristics for the minimum Brauer chain problem. The first three are greedy heuristics and the last two are based on dynamic programming. We run extensive experiments and compared our heuristics. The results are given in experiments section regarding to the optimum values. Simulation results show that all our heuristics have approximation ratio less than 1.5 and the heuristic based on dynamic programming have approximation ratio 1.1. To the best of our knowledge, this is the first work that presents empirical results on the topic.

1.2 Related Work

Most of the previous work is for addition chain problem [7,5]. Brauer's algorithm [8] and Yao's algorithm [9] requires $\lg n + (1 + o(1))(\lg n)/\lg\lg n$ multiplications for computing n^{th} power. Brauer's algorithm is based on the left-to-right 2^k-ary method. Knuth [7] has minor improvements on this algorithm. Pippenger's algorithm [10] uses the idea of computing products of specified subsequences of a sequence, and improves previous results for special cases.

1.3 Outline

In the following section, we present binary method and factor method as the background information. Our heuristics are given in Section 3. The experiments are presented in Section 4 and Section 5 concludes our work.

2   Background Information

This section provides two well-known methods to calculate Brauer chain and necessary background information for the heuristic methods we presented in this paper. The first of the two methods uses the binary representation of the given number n to find its Brauer chain whereas the latter uses factors of n.

2.1 Binary Method

This simple procedure starts with writing the number n in binary form. Then each 1 is replaced with DA and each 0 with D. After removing the leading DA, beginning from 1, the sequence is followed from left to right. For each D, the current number is doubled and for each A, the current number is added 1 [7]. For example, binary representation of 19 is 10011. Then the sequence is DADDDADA. When we remove the first DA, the sequence will be DDDADA. Then the sequence of numbers is 1, 2, 4, 8, 9, 18, 19. This method can be justified easily by binary number properties.

Let $l^*(n)$ is the minimum number of steps to reach n and $v(n)$ is the number of 1's in the binary representation of n.

Lemma 1. *For every positive integer n, $\lfloor \lg n \rfloor \leq l^*(n) \leq \lfloor \lg n \rfloor + v(n) - 1$.*

Proof. In the chain the current number at most doubles. So, $\lfloor \lg n \rfloor \leq \lg n \leq l^*(n)$. The binary method requires exactly $\lfloor \lg n \rfloor + v(n) - 1$ steps, so $l^*(n) \leq \lfloor \lg n \rfloor + v(n) - 1$. $\qquad\qquad\square$

Since lower bound is $\lfloor \lg n \rfloor$, binary heuristic is a trivially 2-approximation for the problem. The binary method finds optimal solution for $n = 2^m$ and finds long sequences for numbers $n = 2^m - 1$, m positive integer. For numbers $n = 2^m - 1$, an upper bound is proved by Brauer in 1939 [8]. This is the most famous theorem on Brauer chains.

Theorem 1 (Brauer Theorem). *For each positive integer m, $l^*(2^m - 1) \leq m + l^*(m) - 1$.*

2.2   Factorization Method

Let $n = p.q$ where n, p and q are positive integers. Factorization method first calculates Brauer chain for p and q, say $\langle a_1, a_2, ..., a_k \rangle$ and $\langle b_1, b_2, ..., b_m \rangle$ where $a_1 = 1$, $b_1 = 1$, $a_k = p$ and $b_m = q$ respectively. Then, $\langle a_1, a_2, \ldots, a_k, a_k.b_2, \ldots, a_k.b_m \rangle$ is a Brauer chain for $n = p.q$ (note that $a_k = p$ and $a_k.b_m = p.q$) [7].

Binary method will not always give minimum sequence. A counter example is 15. Binary method finds the sequence, 1, 2, 3, 6, 7, 14, 15. With factor method, 15=3.5, combining the sequence $\langle 1, 2, 3 \rangle$, $\langle 1, 2, 4, 5 \rangle$ will give the sequence, $\langle 1, 2, 4, 5, 10, 15 \rangle$.

Lemma 2. $l^*(p.q) \leq l^*(p) + l^*(q) - 1$ *for any positive integers p and q.*

Proof. It directly follows from factor method. Let $\langle a_1, a_2, ..., a_k \rangle$ and $\langle b_1, b_2, ..., b_m \rangle$ are sequences for p and q where $a_1 = 1$, $b_1 = 1$, $a_k = p$ and $b_m = q$. Then, $\langle a_1, a_2, ..., a_k, a_k.b_2, \ldots, a_k.b_m \rangle$ is a sequence for $n = p.q$ with $k + m - 1$ elements. $\qquad\qquad\square$

3   Proposed Heuristics

In this section, we present five different heuristics for the minimum Brauer chain problem. The first three are greedy heuristics and the last two are dynamic programming approaches.

3.1   2-*x*-*y* Heuristics

These heuristics contain three greedy approaches all of which are based on the same idea. The only difference is the starting pair (x, y). Here x and y refer to the numbers in the sequence following 2. (x, y) pair may be (3,5), (3,6) or (4,8). After that, the upcoming number is selected as the greatest possible number. Formally, the sequence $\langle a_1, a_2, ... \rangle$, starts with $a_1 = 1$, $a_2 = 2$, $a_3 = x$, $a_4 = y$ and continues with

$$a_{i+1} = a_i + max_j\{a_j\} \tag{1}$$

where $i \geq 4$ and $a_{i+1} \leq n$. For example, given $n = 25$, using the heuristic 2-3-5 will output the sequence $\langle 1, 2, 3, 5, 10, 20, 25 \rangle$ whereas 2-3-6 will give $\langle 1, 2, 3, 6, 12, 24, 25 \rangle$. On the other hand, 2-4-8 heuristic will lead the sequence $\langle 1, 2, 4, 8, 16, 24, 25 \rangle$. For this example lengths of resulting Brauer chains are the same for all of the greedy heuristics. However, 2-4-8 has the same affect as the binary method, and always produces the chain with the same length, hence similarly for numbers $n = 2^m$ it returns optimum solution, but does the same bad solution for the numbers $n = 2^m - 1$.

3.2   Factorization Heuristic

For the rest of the paper we will use the notation $l(n)$ to denote the length of the Brauer chain generated by the described heuristic in that subsection. The idea behind this heuristic is Lemma 2. It is a dynamic approach since for a given positive integer n, this algorithm searches for the minimum sum, $l(p) + l(q)$ such that $n = p.q$, and constructs the Brauer chain of n from the sequence of p and q as given in the factorization method. If n is prime, it simply uses the solution for $n - 1$ and only adds n at the end of the sequence.

Formally, let B_x denotes a Brauer chain for x and $f(B_p, B_q)$ be the function that generates the Brauer chain from B_p and B_q using the factorization method,

Definition 1 (Factorization function). *Let $B_p = \langle a_1, a_2, \ldots, a_k \rangle$ and $B_q = \langle b_1, b_2, \ldots, b_m \rangle$ be Brauer chains for p and q respectively. Factorization function f is*

$$f(B_p, B_q) = \langle a_1, a_2, \ldots, a_k, a_k.b_2, \ldots, a_k.b_m \rangle.$$

Proposition 1. *Given the factorization function f, $f(B_i, B_j)$ is a Brauer chain for $n = i.j$ with the length $l(i) + l(j) - 1$.*

Proof. Directly followed from the construction given in the factorization method, and from the Lemma 2. $\qquad\square$

The factorization heuristic, $H_f(n)$ that generates the Brauer chain for n is,

$$H_f(n) = \begin{cases} exhaustive(n) & \text{, if } n \leq \delta \\ H_f(n-1) \cdot \langle n \rangle & \text{, if } n > \delta \text{ and } n \text{ is prime} \\ f(H_f(p), H_f(q)) & \text{, otherwise} \end{cases} \tag{2}$$

and the length of the Brauer chain is,

$$l(n) = \begin{cases} l^*(n) & \text{, if } n \leq \delta \\ l(n-1) + 1 & \text{, if } n > \delta \text{ and } n \text{ is prime} \\ l(p) + l(q) - 1 & \text{, otherwise} \end{cases} \tag{3}$$

In these equation, δ is a small threshold for the base case of the function, and the heuristic function calculates the optimum Brauer chain exhaustively when

n is a small number. f is the factorization function, and '$\cdot$' is the operator to concatenate two sequences. The pair (p, q) is obtained by the formula,

$$\underset{\{(i,j)|n=i.j\}}{\arg\min} \ \{l(i) + l(j)\}.$$

3.3 Dynamic Heuristic

This heuristic is also based on dynamic programming; it uses the previous solutions to obtain the best solution for current n value. It is a heuristic since we store only one solution for each number.

Formally, the dynamic heuristic function, $H_d(n)$ is,

$$H_d(n) = \begin{cases} 1 & , \text{if } n = 1 \\ H_d(k) \cdot \langle n \rangle & , \text{otherwise} \end{cases} \tag{4}$$

and the length of the Brauer chain is,

$$l(n) = \begin{cases} 1 & , \text{if } n = 1 \\ l(k) + 1 & , \text{otherwise} \end{cases} \tag{5}$$

where

$$k = \underset{\{i|i<n,n-k\in H_d(k)\}}{\arg\min} \ \{l(i)\}.$$

The dynamic heuristic searches for the number k that its Brauer chain is minimum in length and contains $n - k$ in its Brauer chain – to guarantee the Brauer chain property.

4 Experimental Results

In this section, three experiments are presented. In the first one, Brauer chains for all numbers are calculated up to about 4,500. In the second one, within each interval of 200 up to 10,000, a number n is selected randomly and the Brauer chain for n is calculated. In the last experiment, we compared the factorization and the dynamic heuristics up to 20,000.

To calculate optimum lengths of the Brauer chains, we used exhaustive search with branch and bound technique. Although our pruning conditions make the search quite faster, we were able to calculate the optimum values up to 4,500 since the running time is $O(n!)$. Similar to the binary method, we can prove that all the heuristics we use are 2-approximation. The optimum function is logarithmic as expected, but not monotonic. Thus, it is quite hard to find better theoretical approximation ratios of the heuristics.

Figure 1 summarizes the performance of heuristics in the first experiment. The $l(n)/l^*(n)$ ratios are shown where $l^*(n)$ is the optimum length of the Brauer chain for n. All the heuristics clearly have 1.5 approximation ratios. Factorization has 1.25 approximation value. Dynamic heuristic performs much better than the

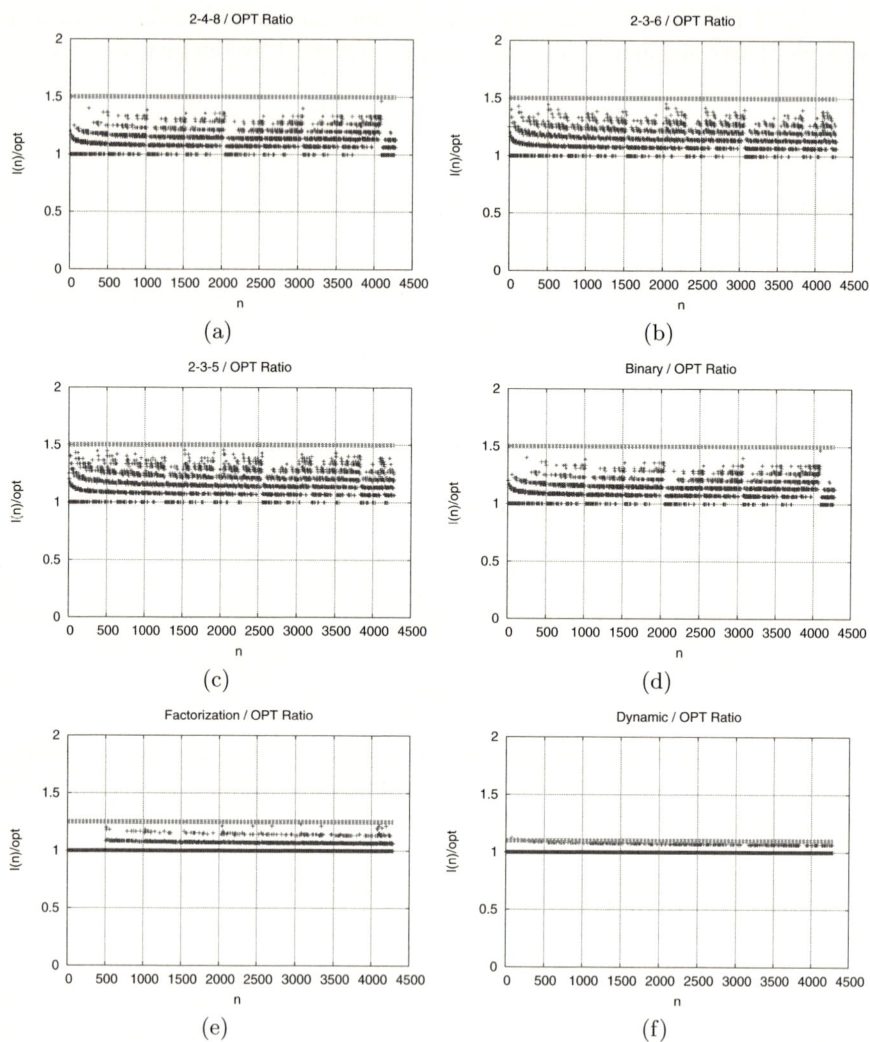

Fig. 1. The (heuristics / optimum) ratios are shown. Green line shows the empirical approximation ratios for heuristics. In (a), (b), (c), (d), approximation ratios are 1.5. In (e) and (f), the approximation ratios are 1.25 and 1.1 respectively.

others with approximation ratio with 1.1. Observe that the ratio in Figure 1(f) reduces monotonically. That promises a better approximation ratio in the long term.

The result of the second experiment makes easier to analyze the performances of heuristics in Figure 2. To obtain optimum values for larger n's and increase the quality of our experiments, for each interval with size 200, a random number

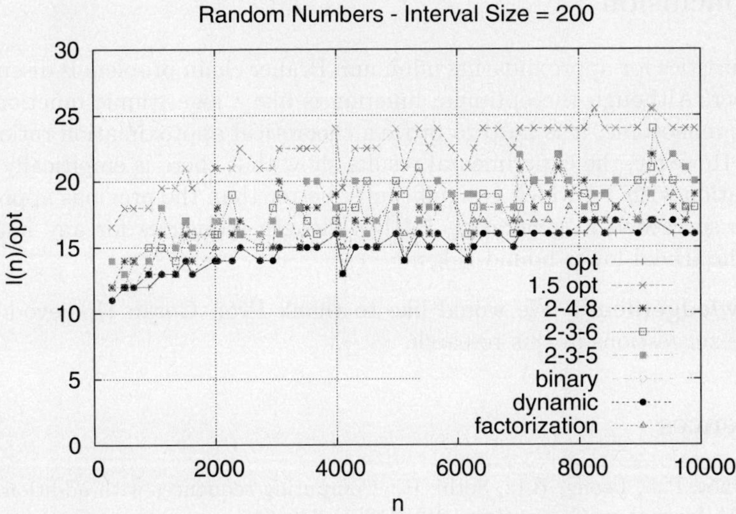

Fig. 2. The result for randomly chosen one n value per interval up to 10,000 where the interval size is 200

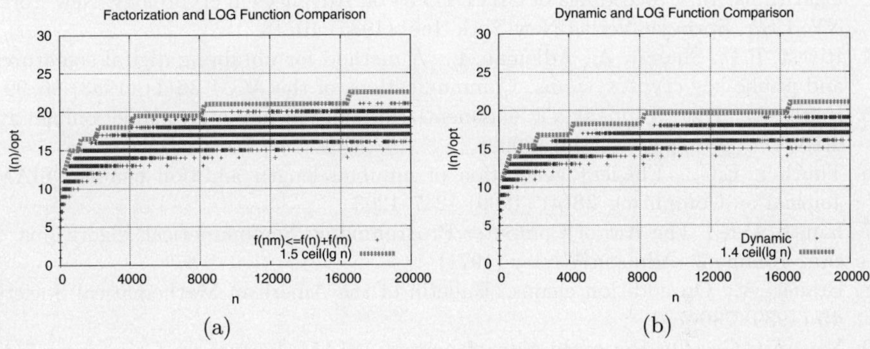

Fig. 3. Comparison of factorization (a) and dynamic (b) heuristics with logarithm function

n is selected and the calculated values are shown in the figure. All the solutions of heuristics are clearly smaller than 1.5 optimum. Especially dynamic heuristic performed amazingly well; it was able to find the optimum values except four misses which are only one step worse than the optimum.

The result of the third experiment is shown in Figure 3. It is surprising that empirically, factorization is even smaller than $1.5\lceil \lg n \rceil$ and dynamic is smaller than $1.4\lceil \lg n \rceil$. It means that for any n there is a solution with $1.4\lceil \lg n \rceil$. One can also observe that the gap between logarithm function and the dynamic heuristic increases monotonically.

5   Conclusion

Five heuristics for approximating minimum Brauer chain problem is discussed in the paper. Although the optimum function is like a logarithmic function, since it is not monotonic, it is hard to prove a theoretical approximation ratio better than 2. However, the experimental results show that there is empirically an approximation with 1.1 which is significantly better than the previous approaches. We also succeeded in generating $1.4\lceil \lg n \rceil$ length sequences for any number n where the trivial lower bound is $\lg n$.

Acknowledgements. We would like to thank Prof. Goran Konjevod for his valuable suggestions in this research.

References

1. Downey, P.J., Leong, B.L., Sethi, R.: Computing sequences with addition chains. SIAM Journal on Computing **10**(3) (1981) 638–646
2. Diffie, W., Hellman, M.E.: New directions in cryptography. IEEE Transactions on Information Theory **IT-22**(6) (1976) 644–654
3. Gamal, T.E.: A public key cryptosystem and a signature scheme based on discrete logarithms. In: Proceedings of CRYPTO 84 on Advances in cryptology, New York, NY, USA, Springer-Verlag New York, Inc. (1985) 10–18
4. Rivest, R.L., Shamir, A., Adleman, L.: A method for obtaining digital signatures and public-key cryptosystems. Communications of the ACM **26**(1) (1983) 96–99
5. Bernstein, D.: Pippenger's exponentiation algorithm. Available online at: http://cr.yp.to/papers.html (2002)
6. Thurber, E.G.: Efficient generation of minimal length addition chains. SIAM Journal on Computing **28**(4) (1999) 1247–1263
7. Knuth, D.E.: The Art of Computer Programming: Seminumerical Algorithms. 2 edn. Volume 2. Addison-Wesley (1971)
8. Brauer, A.: On addition chains. Bulletin of the American Mathematical Society **45** (1939) 736–739
9. Yao, A.C.C.: On the evaluation of powers. SIAM Journal on Computing **5**(1) (1976) 100–103
10. Pippenger, N.: On the evaluation of powers and monomials. SIAM Journal on Computing **9** (1980) 230–250

Dispatching Rules for Allocation of Component Types to Machines in the Automated Assembly of Printed Circuit Boards

Mehmet Bayram Yildirim[1], Ekrem Duman[2], and Dilek Duman[3]

[1] Wichita State University, Industrial and Manufacturing Engineering Department,
1845 Fairmount Wichita, KS 67260-0035, USA
Bayram.Yildirim@wichita.edu
[2] Dogus University, Industrial Engineering Department, Zeamet Sok. No.21,
Acibadem, Istanbul, Turkey
Eduman@dogus.edu.tr
[3] Intertech Information Technology and Marketing Inc., Kasap Sok. No.15,
Esentepe, Istanbul, Turkey
Dilek.Duman@denizbank.com

Abstract. In this paper, we propose a model and algorithms to solve a load balancing problem on a printed circuit board assembly line. On this line of two identical machines, the problem of allocation of component types to machines is analyzed in detail. Twenty eight dispatching rules are developed and extensive computational experimentation is performed. It has been observed that the imbalance per board increases as a function of the number of board types. Furthermore, the greedy dispatching rules perform better than the construction dispatching rules.

Keywords: Printed Circuit Board Assembly, Load Balancing, Heuristics.

1 Introduction

In this paper, we propose simple dispatching rules which can be implemented and used fairly easily in a production environment where there are two identical resources used in producing products which require processing by both of the resources. Each resource has access to separate storage areas (i.e., bins) with fixed capacity. Each bin stores certain components that must be placed on the product. Furthermore, it is assumed that the order which these components are placed on the product is not important. It is also assumed that there is no buffer where the semi-finished products can be stored. In our setting, we assume that a conveyor belt transfers the semi-finished product from resource 1 to resource 2. Thus, resource 1 can not start to work on a new part unless the second resource is idle.   Our goal is to assign components to bins in such a way that the total workload for each resource is balanced. This will ensure that both resources will be utilized efficiently and the total idle time for each resource will be minimized.

A. Levi et al. (Eds.): ISCIS 2006, LNCS 4263, pp. 55–64, 2006.

The use of numerically or computer controlled electronic component placement machines in assembling printed circuit boards (PCB) brings major gains in productivity and efficiency through their fast, error free and reliable component placement operations. To utilize these automatic machines efficiently, serious planning and scheduling decisions should be made on the production floor. Some of these decisions are allocation of component types to machines, determination of board production sequence, allocation of component types to feeder cells (feeder configuration) and determination of component placement sequence. All these problems are interdependent, i.e., the solution of one problem affects the solution of others. Such interdependency is more evident between the first two and last two problems. When an optimal solution is sought, all four problems should be solved simultaneously. However, since each of these problems is quite complex by itself, trying to build and to solve a monolithic model is quite difficult and intractable. Hence, usually, these problems are solved separately and iterative solution methods are deployed to cope for the interaction between them.

The literature on PCB assembly problems is quite extensive. However, most of the literature is related to the feeder configuration and placement sequencing problems. A general overview of PCB assembly problems is given by McGinnis et al. [2] and Ji and Wan [3]. Francis and Horak [4] consider the problem of choosing the numbers of reels of each type of components to be used in populating a printed circuit board by an SMT machine. The objective is to maximize the length of an uninterrupted machine production run, while using no more slots for reels than are available. Carmon et al. [5] minimize the total setup time to change the feeder configuration and propose the group set-up method (grouping similar boards), which can significantly reduce set-up times. Askin et al. [6] address the problem of minimizing the makespan for assembling a batch of boards with a secondary objective of reducing the mean flow time. Ben-Arieh and Dror [7] study the problem of assigning component types to insertion machines with the aim of balancing the workload assigned to machines. The study of Ho and Ji [8] is one of the few studies attempting to solve two PCB assembly problems (feeder configuration and placement sequencing) simultaneously.

Sadiq et al. [9] propose an iterative approach that minimizes the total production time for a group of PCB assembly jobs on a single machine when the sequencing and allocation of different component reels to feeder carriage are considered together. Ahmadi et al. [10] consider a placement machine, which features two fixtures for the delivery of components to the placement heads. They investigate the case where all components are accessible and the case of a static pick sequence. Crama et al. [11] propose a heuristic hierarchical approach to optimize the throughput rate of a line of several component placement machines with three placement heads, all devoted to the assembly of a single type of PCB. Given a line of placement machines and given a family of boards Klomp et al. [12] propose a heuristic for the feeder rack assignment problem. Hillier and Brandeu [13] develop the cost minimizing workload balancing heuristic to balance the workload among the semi-automatic placement machines and the manual assembly stations. Ben-Arieh and Dror [7] only consider the case where different board types require several different components and the demand for each board type is equal.

Although the use of electronic component placement machines has brought reliability and speed to the PCB assembly process, to get higher utilization, one needs to solve the resulting complex operations research problems efficiently. In this study, the problem of distributing the assembly workload to two machines deployed on an assembly line with two identical component placement machines to minimize the line idle time is considered. A mathematical model and several dispatching rules are proposed. We extend Ben-Arieh and Dror [7] model also to include demand information for all boards.

In the next section, the description setting considered in this study and the formulation of the problem is given. Some heuristics to solve this problem can be found in section three. In section four, the results and performances of these heuristics on randomly generated test problems are discussed. Finally, in section five, the concluding remarks are given.

2 Problem Description and Formulation

The form of the load balancing (component allocation) problems in automated PCB assembly shows a large variability. Some of the features that determine the underlying component allocation problem setting are differences in machine architecture (type), characteristics of the production processes and engineering preferences. In this study, the machine type considered is one with a component pickup device, a stationary placement head and a moving carrier board. In this machine, circular shaped turning component pickup device takes the role of the sequencer machine. The component tape is placed along the perimeter of the device and performs each placement just after the desired precise placement location is aligned beneath the head currently over the carrier board. The pickup device, which usually has 20 to 120 heads, picks up the components to its heads in the placement order from the component tapes. The placement sequencing problem turns out to be a Chebyshev Traveling Salesman Problem and the layout of the component tapes can be formulated as a simple allocation problem [1]. Two examples of this type of machines are the Universal 6287A and the Dynapert Intellisert V12000 axial component placement machines.

In our setting, the boards are populated by two machines sequentially. There is a conveyor belt between the machines, which carries the partially completed boards from machine 1 to machine 2 (see figure 1). It is assumed that the boards are produced in a high-mix, low-volume production environment, where the set of all

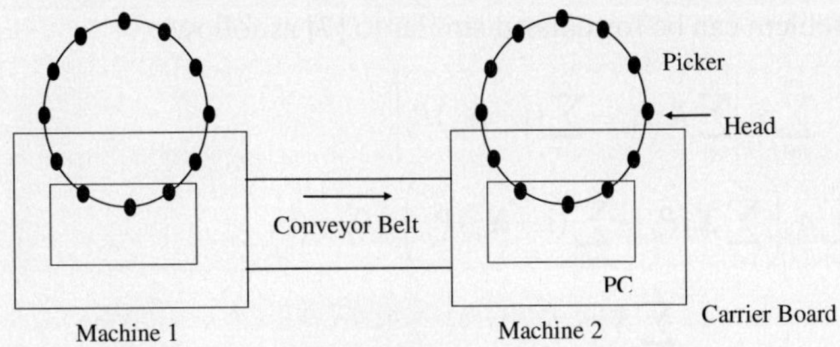

Fig. 1. Two Placement Machines on a Line

component types to be populated on all PCB types in the planning horizon, will be allocated to two identical placement machines with the same speed, the same nozzle sets and the same number of feeder locations. The demand for PCB types are known and fixed for the planning period under consideration. Furthermore, it is assumed that the insertion time is one unit for each of the components regardless of the PCB type and components' location on the boards. Component types are also identical in regard to their slot requirements in the feeder area and all use the same nozzle. Also the feeder capacity of each machine is strictly less than the minimum number of different components placed onto a single circuit board type, so that full assembly of each PCB type requires both machines. As a result, assembly of a new board cannot start unless both machines are cleared by the currently assembled one. The total number of component types is equal to the total number of feeder locations on two machines. It is assumed that there is no sequence dependent setup time when switching between different board types. However, the setup time to change a component type in a feeder is very high. Note that if this was not the case, then the load balancing problem would be considerably simplified: each time a board type is to be assembled, the feeders could be configured to balance that particular board type, by solving a single 2-partition problem (which is NP-Hard). Since the boards are reliably transferred by the conveyor belt, there is no engineering preference regarding population of the PCBs on a single machine. Buffer of partially completed boards is not desired due to the engineering preferences.

The objective is to partition the set of component types into two to maximize the average production rate. In other words, our objective is distribute the component types to the two machines so that, the workload among the machines has a good balance regarding each particular board type.

The problem stated above can be formulated as an integer program. Furst, we will introduce the notation. Let i be the component type index $(i=1,..,n)$, j be the board type index $(j=1,..,m)$, a_j be the number of boards of type j to be produced, P_{ij} be the number of components of type i to be placed on board type j and F be the feeder capacities of machine 1 and machine 2

In this problem, the decision is to assign the components to different machines in such a way that the total processing time required to process all of the demand on a machine is as close to the total amount of processing on the other machine. Note that we assume the total processing time is proportional to the total number of components placed. The decision variables are

$$X_i = \begin{cases} 1 & \text{if component type } i \text{ is assigned to machine 1} \\ 0 & \text{otherwise} \end{cases}$$

Now, the problem can be formulated similar to [7] as follows:

$$\text{Min} \quad \sum_{j=1}^{m} a_j \left| \sum_{i=1}^{n} X_i P_{ij} - \sum_{i=1}^{n} (1 - X_i) P_{ij} \right| \tag{1}$$

$$\text{s.t.} \quad \sum_{j=1}^{m} a_j \left(\sum_{i=1}^{n} X_i P_{ij} - \sum_{i=1}^{n} (1 - X_i) P_{ij} \right) \geq 0 \tag{2}$$

$$\sum_{i=1}^{n} X_i \leq F \tag{3}$$

$$X_i = 0 \text{ or } 1 \qquad\qquad I = 1,..,n$$

$\sum_{i=1}^{n} X_i P_{ij} - \sum_{i=1}^{n} (1 - X_i) P_{ij}$ reflects the total waiting (idle) time or imbalance of the machines for a particular board type j. As a result, in the above formulation, the objective function (1) shows the sum of the machine workload imbalances resulting from the assembly of each particular board type. Using constraint (2), it is ensured that the workload assigned to machine 1 is greater than or equal to the workload assigned to machine 2. This guarantees that a smaller amount of work-in-process inventory is accumulated between two machines. Constraint (3) is the feeder capacity constraint. Since

$$\sum_{j=1}^{m} a_j \left| \sum_{i=1}^{n} X_i P_{ij} - \sum_{i=1}^{n} (1 - X_i) P_{ij} \right| = \sum_{j=1}^{m} \left(2 a_j \sum_{i=1}^{n} X_i P_{ij} - N_j \right) \qquad (4)$$

where $N_j = \sum_{i=1}^{n} P_{ij}$ is the number of components required for board type j, the objective function and constraint (2) can further be simplified to the second term in equation (4).

When $a_j = 1$, $j = 1..n$, Ben-Arieh and Dror [7] prove that the resulting problem is NP-Complete. As a result, the problem formulated above is also NP-Complete. Below, we summarize the heuristic methods considered to solve the component allocation model presented above.

3 Solution Procedures Developed

A total of 28 dispatching rules are developed to find a good quality solution for the component allocation problem defined in the previous section in a reasonable amount of time. All of these algorithms have two mechanisms in their structure: component sorting and component assignment. Component sorting rules determine the order of the component assignment to the machines. On the other hand, component assignment rules decide which machine a given component type is to be assigned. Below, we present five component sorting and three component assignment rules:

3.1 Component Sorting Rules

i- Component Popularity (CP): The popularity of a component is measured by the number of board types on which it is used , i.e., $CP_i = \sum_{j=1}^{m} Y_{ij}$ where

$$Y_{ij} = \begin{cases} 1, & \text{if component type } i \text{ is placed on board type } j \\ 0, & \text{otherwise.} \end{cases}$$

In this sorting scheme, components are sorted in non-increasing CP values. If there are more than one component types with the same popularity, the one which is consumed more in the planning period gets higher priority.

ii- Component Usage (CU): The total number of placements of each component type over all boards is calculated (i.e., $CU_j = \sum_{j=1}^{m} a_j P_{ij}$) and the components are sorted in non-increasing order of CU values. This way, component types having higher usage are assigned to machines in a balanced manner in the earlier stages and it is hoped that the balance will not be much deteriorated by the least used component types.

iii- Standard Error (SE): The standard error for a component type i is given by the following equation:

$$ SE_i = \frac{\sum_{j=1}^{m} \left(\frac{P_{ij}}{m} - P_{ij} \right)^2}{\sum_{j=1}^{m} \frac{P_{ij}}{m}} \tag{5} $$

where m is the number of board types. Under this rule, the component types are ordered according to non-decreasing order of their *SE* values.

The logic for CP and CU rules is quite intuitive. SE sorting rule ensures that the component types which have a homogenous usage over all board types (which may imply component types used by most of the board types) are more important than the others and they should be handled first and distributed to machines as equally as possible. The numerator of the standard error expression (sum of squared errors) reflects this. On the other hand, among the component types, which have similar usage homogeneity, the ones with larger average usage are more important which is reflected by the expression in the denominator.

iv- Board-component Usage (BU): This is a two step component sorting rule; first, board types are ordered according to the number of components to be populated on them. Let N_j be the total number of components to be placed on board type j ($N_j = \sum_i a_j P_{ij}$). Board types requiring more components (i.e., the higher N_j) are prioritized in the BU order. Initially, the first board type in the order is selected. The components on that particular type of board are ordered in non-increasing order of their usage on that board. Then, the second board type is picked and the component types that exist on that board but not yet included in the ordered list before, are added at the end of the list using the same logic. This procedure continues until the BU list contains all component types.

v- RN (random): Component types are ordered in a random manner. This rule will be used as a benchmark for comparisons with other sorting rules.

3.2 Component Assignment Rules

i- Less Work Rule A (LWA): This rule selects a component type from a component order list described above and assigns the component to the machine with the least assigned workload. While processing the BU list, the assigned work of a machine is the total number of component placements for the board type being handled at that time.

ii- Less Work Rule B (LWB): This rule is same as LWA but differs only in heuristics containing the BU component sort rule. During the processing of the BU list, the assigned work of machines is considered as the total work related to all board types.

iii- Greedy Optimization (GR): This rule seeks a partial load balance at each step. Each time a new component type is picked up from a sorting list, the value of the objective function for the partial feeder configurations attained so far is calculated for both possible machine assignments, and the machine with the lower objective function value (imbalance) is chosen for assignment.

3.3 Proposed Dispatching Rules

In this research, 28 load balancing dispatching rules are experimented for the two identical machines case. A naming convention is used to identify the individual dispatching rules with respect to the sort and assignment rules deployed: A two letter code for component sort rule is first written in upper case and it is followed by the component assignment rule code in lower case (e.g. CUgr). The letters "a" and "b" are used to denote component assignment rules LWA and LWB, respectively. With RAN, component types in the RN sort list are assigned to machines in an alternating manner.

There are 4 sorting rules (excluding RAN) and 3 assignment rules, thus a total of 12 combinations. If the dispatching rule uses one component sort list partially and then another one, both sort rules are written one after the other and this is followed by a number (1, 2 or 3) which denotes the filling ratio of total feeder locations on both machines upon which the dispatching rule switches from the first sort list to the second: "1" denotes 25 percent filling ratio, whereas "2" and "3" denote 50 percent and 75 percent, respectively. If the filling ratio does not lead to an integer value for the number of feeder locations, it is rounded off to the nearest integer.

For example, if we have two identical machines, each having 15 feeder locations and if we are trying to assign 30 component types to these machines using CUBU1a dispatching rule, it will work as follows: A total of eight component types will be picked from the CU ordered list and will be assigned to either of the machines according to the LWA assignment rule. After this, the BU ordered list will be considered and starting from the first component type in the list that has not already been assigned to a machine, all component types of BU that are not yet assigned to a machine will be assigned to the machines according to the LWA rule.

Note that assignment for BU sort rule can be done according to both Less Work A and B rules. Considering all of these combinations, the total number of heuristics that can be considered is 28. Below is the list of the dispatching rules we experimented with for two identical machines case:

Cpa	CPgr	CPBU1a	CUBU1a	SEBU1a
CUa	CUgr	CPBU2a	CUBU2a	SEBU2a
SEa	SEgr	CPBU3a	CUBU3a	SEBU3a
BUa	BUgr	CPBU1b	CUBU1b	SEBU1b
BUb	RAN	CPBU2b	CUBU2b	SEBU2b
		CPBU3b	CUBU3b	SEBU3b

4 Computational Experimentation

In this section, we will first present the experimentation setup. Next, we will briefly compare the effectiveness of the proposed dispatching rules and discuss the results obtained to gain a better insight to the component allocation problem.

4.1 Experimental Setup

In generating the test problems the following design is considered: it is assumed that the production facility can produce 10 or 20 different types of boards. The demand for each board type is uniformly distributed between 1,000 and 10,000. The number of component types on a board varies between 20 and 120. The placement matrix (P), is generated as follows: with 0.40 probability, P_{ij} is zero (i.e., component i is not used on board type j). The P_{ij} value is 1, 2, 3, 4, 5, 6 and 7 with a probability of 0.15, 0.15, 0.08, 0.07, 0.06, 0.05 and 0.04, respectively.

The following naming convention has been utilized for the randomly generated test problems. PRnm is a problem with n components (the problem size), and m boards. In our experimental setting, test problems are generated for n=20, 30, 40, 60, 80, 100

Table 1. Deviation from the Best Solution, $m=10$

	CPa	CUa	SEa	BUa	CUBU1a	CUBU2a	CUBU3a	CPBU1a	CPBU2a	CPBU3a	SEBU1a	SEBU2a	SEBU3a	BUb	CUBU1b
PR2010A	1.06	1.43	1.82	0.85	1.31	1.20	1.04	1.16	0.86	1.00	1.24	1.57	1.63	1.35	1.22
PR3010A	2.10	1.81	2.55	2.79	2.42	2.02	1.61	2.14	2.27	1.96	2.35	1.28	1.69	1.48	1.48
PR4010A	1.60	2.07	2.40	3.00	2.77	2.33	2.24	3.11	1.65	1.34	3.10	2.67	1.85	1.58	2.32
PR6010A	2.62	2.93	4.68	4.71	4.89	3.78	2.93	4.08	4.09	2.54	4.93	4.17	4.31	3.96	3.02
PR8010A	5.89	4.79	6.84	7.88	5.84	4.67	3.93	6.00	6.08	5.07	6.96	5.36	3.93	3.14	5.22
PR10010A	5.58	3.82	4.59	6.17	5.82	4.57	5.36	5.54	4.98	4.46	5.59	5.15	3.88	3.03	3.87
PR12010A	6.80	6.15	6.45	9.13	6.97	6.11	4.38	7.86	6.77	6.89	6.71	6.66	5.68	5.44	5.32
Average	3.67	3.28	4.19	4.93	4.29	3.53	3.07	4.27	3.81	3.32	4.41	3.84	3.28	2.85	3.21

	CUBU2b	CUBU3b	CPBU1b	CPBU2a	CPBU3b	SEBU1b	SEBU2b	SEBU3b	CPgr	CUgr	SEgr	BUgr	RAN	MIN
PR2010A	1.28	1.33	1.03	1.16	1.20	0.98	1.34	1.44	0.16	0.35	0.43	0.40	1.10	0.16
PR3010A	2.13	1.83	1.51	1.53	1.96	1.49	2.29	1.75	0.54	0.34	1.23	0.09	3.47	0.09
PR4010A	1.85	2.25	2.28	1.38	1.50	1.93	2.40	1.97	0.55	0.44	1.16	0.16	2.86	0.16
PR6010A	2.62	2.84	3.51	3.06	2.46	3.50	3.26	4.62	0.85	0.09	2.27	0.48	4.93	0.09
PR8010A	4.15	4.56	4.18	4.65	4.96	4.24	4.32	4.58	0.65	0.19	1.28	0.37	5.33	0.19
PR10010A	4.21	4.23	4.23	3.83	5.17	4.66	4.46	4.87	0.30	0.11	1.40	0.40	3.97	0.11
PR12010A	5.54	5.54	4.63	5.76	6.85	4.86	4.91	5.84	0.34	0.21	3.14	0.50	5.62	0.21
Average	3.11	3.23	3.05	3.05	3.44	3.09	3.28	3.58	0.48	0.25	1.56	0.34	3.90	0.25

Table 2. Deviation from the Best Solution, $m=20$

	CPa	CUa	SEa	BUa	CUBU1a	CUBU2a	CUBU3a	CPBU1a	CPBU2a	CPBU3a	SEBU1a	SEBU2a	SEBU3a	Bub	CUBU1b
PR2010A	1.05	0.88	0.77	0.98	0.80	0.93	1.01	0.77	0.83	0.99	0.98	0.83	0.77	0.84	0.62
PR3010A	1.02	1.03	1.14	0.84	0.89	0.84	1.03	1.27	0.99	0.67	0.97	1.04	0.90	0.89	1.09
PR4010A	0.70	0.70	0.98	1.33	1.44	1.02	0.90	1.51	1.08	0.95	1.52	1.29	1.06	1.13	1.23
PR6010A	1.64	1.38	1.56	2.09	2.13	1.20	1.17	1.75	1.74	1.48	2.06	1.89	1.54	1.50	1.24
PR8010A	1.52	2.09	2.61	2.54	2.19	1.71	1.87	2.30	1.91	1.81	2.51	2.15	2.63	1.90	2.11
PR10010A	2.57	3.24	2.83	3.53	3.19	2.90	2.22	3.92	2.25	2.44	3.72	3.24	2.92	2.14	1.85
PR12010A	2.60	3.50	2.61	4.44	3.49	3.13	4.00	3.81	2.74	2.34	3.58	3.21	2.54	2.66	2.83
Average	1.59	1.83	1.79	2.25	2.02	1.68	1.74	2.19	1.65	1.53	2.19	1.95	1.76	1.58	1.57

	CUBU2b	CUBU3b	CPBU1b	CPBU2a	CPBU3b	SEBU1b	SEBU2b	SEBU3b	CPgr	CUgr	SEgr	BUgr	RAN	MIN
PR2010A	0.85	0.87	0.95	0.89	1.05	0.91	0.63	0.82	0.33	0.23	0.42	0.01	0.91	0.01
PR3010A	1.00	1.16	0.89	1.19	1.04	0.59	1.18	0.87	0.15	0.06	0.55	0.26	1.33	0.06
PR4010A	0.92	0.93	1.28	1.28	1.07	1.26	1.30	0.92	0.19	0.15	0.42	0.11	0.92	0.11
PR6010A	1.48	1.42	1.52	1.37	1.48	1.30	1.44	1.29	0.07	0.18	0.47	0.19	1.54	0.07
PR8010A	2.15	1.85	2.00	2.02	1.67	2.16	2.37	2.21	0.23	0.24	0.71	0.15	2.26	0.15
PR10010A	2.57	3.23	2.60	2.51	2.82	2.62	2.67	2.59	0.47	0.18	0.82	0.25	3.12	0.18
PR12010A	3.36	3.43	2.98	2.89	2.67	2.65	2.57	3.07	0.49	0.07	1.11	0.44	3.31	0.07
Average	1.76	1.84	1.75	1.73	1.69	1.64	1.74	1.68	0.28	0.16	0.64	0.20	1.91	0.16

and 120 and $m=10$ and 20. For each *(n,m)* combination, heuristics are tested on six randomly generated test problems. For all dispatching rules the percent deviations of the algorithms from the best solution are calculated and displayed on tables 1 and 2 (i.e., each entry in these tables shows the average imbalance percent deviation from the best solution of six problems having the same parameters). In these tables, the overall average for all problems (average) is also displayed.

4.2 Comparison of the Proposed Heuristics

When $m=10$, CUa, which is very similar to the algorithm proposed by Ben-Arieh and Dror [7], on average, behaves 328% worse than the best solution found by 28 dispatching rules as seen in table 1.   Among 28 dispatching rules, other than the greedy ones, when $m=10$, the best average solution obtained is worse than 285%. The greedy dispatching rules perform much better than the construction dispatching rules. On average SEgr finds solutions which are 156% worse then the best solution (SE's performance is 419%). The other greedy dispatching rules, on average find solution 35.6% worse than the best solution. Similar observations can be found when $m=20$ (see table 2). Among the greedy dispatching rules, BUgr provides better solutions when *n* is small. When *n* gets larger, CUgr is the most efficient dispatching rule. Another interesting point to note is that some dispatching rules perform worse than the random allocation.

To summarize, when average deviations are considered, it can be observed that the greedy dispatching rules certainly outperform the others: CUgr and BUgr are the first best and second best heuristics for both $m=10$ and $m=20$ problems. Also, note that the performance of CUgr dispatching rule gets better as the problem size increases.

5 Concluding Remarks

In this study, the problem of allocating component types to machines in PCB assembly is considered. The focus is on a two identical machines case. Twenty eight different dispatching rules are developed and their performances are tested. When the demand for each board type is different, the CUa dispatching rule proposed by Ben-Arieh and Dror [7] performs quite poor. Among the heuristics proposed in this study, the CUgr greedy dispatching rule performed the best.

For future research, one can extend the proposed dispatching rules to environments where there are restrictions on allocating certain components to specific machines, or when the slot requirements of component types are not the same, or when the machines have different nozzle sets that they can handle.

References

1. Duman E.: Optimization issues in automated assembly of printed circuit boards. Dissertation, Bogazici University, Turkey, 1998.
2. McGinnis, L.F., Ammons, J.C., Carlyle, M., Cranmer, L., Depuy, G.W, Ellis K.P., Tovey, C.A., Xu, H.: Automated process planning for printed circuit card assembly. IIE Transactions 1992; 24/4: 18-29.

3. Ji, P., Wan, Y.F.: Planning for printed circuit board assembly: The state-of-the-art review. Int. J. of Computer Applications in Technology 2001; 14 Nos.4/5/6: 136-144.
4. Francis, R.L., Horak, T.: A note on reel allocation problem. IIE Transactions 1994; 26/3: 111-114.
5. Carmon, T.F., Maimon, O.Z., Dar-El, E.Z.: Group set-up for printed circuit board assembly. International Journal of Production Research 1989; 27/10: 1795-1810.
6. Askin, R.G., Dror, M., Vakharia, A.J.: Printed circuit board family grouping and component allocation for a multimachine, Open-shop assembly cell. Naval Research Logistics 1994; 41: 587-608.
7. Ben-Arieh, D., Dror, M.: Part assignment to electronic insertion machines: Two machine case. International Journal of Production Research 1990; 28/7: 1317-1327.
8. Ho, W., Ji, P.: Component scheduling for chip shooter machines: a hybrid genetic algorithm approach. Computers and Operations Research 2003; 30/14: 2175-2189.
9. Sadiq, M., Landers, T.L., Taylor, G.D.: A heuristic algorithm for minimizing total production time for a sequence of jobs on a surface mount placement machine. International Journal of Production Research 1993; 11/6: 1327-1341.
10. Ahmadi, J., Grotzinger, S., Johnson, D.: Component allocation and partitioning for a dual delivery placement machine. Operations Research 1988; 36/2: 176-191.
11. Crama, Y., Kolen, A.W.J., Oerlemans, A.G., Spieksma, F.C.R.: Throughput rate optimization in the automated assembly of printed circuit boards. Annals of Operations Research 1990; 26: 455-480.
12. Klomp, C., Klundert, J., Spieksma, F.C.R., Voogt, S.: The feeder rack assignment problem in PCB assembly: A case study. International Journal of Production Economics 2000; 6: 399-407.
13. Hillier, M.S., Brandeu, N.L.: Cost minimization and workload balancing in printed circuit board assembly. IIE Transactions 2001; 33: 547-557.

Heuristic Approach to Schedule Crew for a Regional Airline

Byung Tech Kim and Young Hoon Lee

Department of Information and Industrial Engineering, Yonsei University,
134 Shinchon-Dong, Seodaemoon-Gu, Seoul 120-749, Korea
{kimbt, youngh}@yonsei.ac.kr

Abstract. Crew scheduling is a crux of running a regional airline. The regional airline is characterized as a crew dependant airline due to the fact that the flight operation of the airline is rather strictly constrained by crew availability and qualifications. Furthermore, the airline must accommodate frequent changes in flight crew requirements due to seasonal or monthly flight demand fluctuation. In this paper, a heuristic approach is proposed to schedule the airline's crew members. Additionally, an integer linear programming formulation is suggested to verify the feasibility of the heuristic approach. Evaluation purposes, the crew schedules of the operation of the regional airline were generated to check the computational advantages of the approach. The proposed heuristic approach finds a good crew schedule with computational efficiency for the airline.

1 Introduction

The air transportation market is becoming intensively competitive with increasing numbers of domestic regional airlines. The major air carriers handle most of air travelers, however, there are more domestic flights operated by rather small-sized air carriers, regional airlines. In this sense, the small-sized air carriers will be focused on relatively short routes with medium-sized airplanes to find a profitable and demanding air transportation market in domestic regional aviation.

To start and operate the regional airline, providing an affordable service to the customer remains a big task for the airline. The airline tends to operate domestic flights in the early stage of her operation, then crew scheduling is an area which they can seek to improve her flight operations. Additionally, the airline must establish the company as a flight safe air carrier in the early stage of the operation. Crew scheduling is the core element of a flight-safe operation since crew members especially, pilots, are responsible for running the flight operation. The flight safety is the paramount concern for the crew, therefore, the crew scheduling must accommodate the crew members' availability and qualification status. Furthermore, the airline needs a crew scheduling model to incorporate changes in the flight crew requirement due to seasonal or monthly flight demand fluctuation during the schedule planning process. Pursuing customer satisfaction and safety of the flight reputation, the company must focus on scheduling crew with the first priority in crew members' availability. The flight safety starts from a fine flight crew schedule with flight-ready crew members.

A. Levi et al. (Eds.): ISCIS 2006, LNCS 4263, pp. 65–74, 2006.

This eventually leads into customer satisfaction when the ready-flight-crew provides smooth and enjoyable flights.

In this paper, we develop a mathematical model with integer programming (IP) and a heuristic model to aid a Korean domestic regional airline's crew scheduling to enhance flight safety and improve flight operation. Therefore, we will produce an IP and a heuristic algorithm to generate a flight schedule from the data containing a flight-capable status of the regional airline's flight crews.

2 Literature Review

Airline crew scheduling problem is constantly searched by practitioners and scholars to obtain good crew schedules, which covers all the flights on the schedule and meets the rules and regulations concerning safety of flight. Marsten and Shepardson[6] reviewed crew scheduling applications. The crew scheduling problem is to pair aircrews to cover all required flight legs while minimizing costs. Formulated as an integer program over up to one month time period, this formula can be intractable for large domestic airlines. Ryan[8] and Gamache and Soumis[3] used the set partitioning problem (SPP) approach to model crew satisfaction and cost minimization. Teodorovic and Lucie[9] modeled with a "Day-by-day" allocation method which is to schedule flight crews at a starting day and move the remainder of the flight crews to the next day. Dawid et al.[2] introduced the bottleneck approach to SPP to allocate flight crew to solve the scheduling problem. Chang[1] applied the genetic algorithm to present efficient methods to solve various crew schedules of short routes. His work mainly focused on domestic or regional airline aircrew scheduling with some flexibility for the irregular flight operation. Guo et al.[4] generated flight pattern in a week, and was applied to the flight pattern for efficient allocation of an individual crew member. Using a Korean airline data, Kim and Lee[5] solved the cockpit crew scheduling problem with SPP. They developed a heuristic method to generate flight patterns and then those apply to cockpit crew scheduling. There are several case studies resulting from different researchers concerning cabin crew scheduling. Ozdemir and Mohan[7] introduce the genetic algorithm for flight graph presentation to solve flight schedule. The algorithm is to solve a single airline fleet which assigns any crew members to any flights. Yan and Lin[10] use Set Covering Problem to solve crew scheduling problem. They constructed a scheduling network, which formulated the dispatch regulations, to generate all feasible pairings of crew members. Yan and Tu[11] solve the Taiwan airline crew scheduling problem with the real constraint data using a pure network model. Yan et al.[12] extended the crew scheduling practice to solve using the column generation method. This approach discussed several case studies with multiple home bases, mixed aircraft type and multiple cabin classes into the crew scheduling.

In general, crew scheduling is divided into a flight pattern generation, and a crew allocation. However, this study mainly deals with effective crew allocation of flight schedule since the regional airline is in the beginning of the flight operation, so flight pattern part is rather easily solved using existing pattern generation methods. There has not been much effort for practical approach to solve regional airline's crew scheduling with prime focus on the constraints such as the status of an individual crew's availability and multi-qualifications. From the fluctuation of seasonal flight demand, crew scheduling with flexibility during the scheduling execution phase was not dealt in the previous studies. The objective of the crew scheduling in this study is allocate the crew member with equal amount of the flight among same qualified crew members. This factor is to address crew members' satisfaction of the aviation life with equity of the flight opportunities. Equalizing the number of the flight certainly brings a crew satisfaction of the flight operations as well as enhancing flight skills.

This paper is organized as follows. The third section focuses on modeling of the regional airline's crew scheduling. Section 4 presents case studies using both the IP and the heuristic model. Section 5 summarizes the results and the conclusions drawn as well as discusses recommendations for further studies.

3   Crew Scheduling Model

A regional airline furnishes a monthly crew schedule which contains all required route flights, maintenance flights, and other required flights. From the monthly crew schedule, given status of availabilities of all required crew members, the airline allocates required crew member to designated position in the airplane to fly the assigned flight. We used each member's qualification in designated position and monthly flight routes from the Korean regional airline[13]. The flights are divided into stand-by duty, maintenance, training and passenger flights, and the passenger flights further divided to the three main routes: Jeju-Seoul, Jeju-Busan, and Jeju-Daegu. The basic crew members are composed of a pilot (P), a co-pilot (CP), a chief flight attendant (CA), and a flight attendant (FA). Table 1 illustrates data for the regional airline crew scheduling.

Table 1. The data for the regional airline crew scheduing

Flight type	Required crew	Flight route	# of daily flight	Remarks
Passenger		Jeju-Seoul	12	
Passenger	P,CP,CA, FA	Jeju-Busan	4	※ Expected crew
Passenger		Jeju-Daegu	1	members with 80,
Stand-by		Hub airport	1	and project crew
Maintenance	P, CP, FA	Jeju-Jinju	As required	member with 160.
Training	P, CP	Hub airport		

3.1   Rules, Regulations and Limitations

The following rules and regulations are applied to the crew scheduling procedure by the airline's flight authority and the labor union.

(1) There will be no additional crew onboard in domestic flights.
(2) Crew must qualify in a designated flight position to fly a given flight.
(3) Any crew will not fly more than 120 flight hours a month.
(4) Crew qualification, proficiency test and physical examination will be conducted by the flight authority to determine the availability of the particular crew member.
(5) No one stands consecutive stand-by duties.
(6) Each individual crew member will fill in a monthly personal availability data.
(7) No one flies more than 4 consecutive days which means that there must be one day off after the 4th consecutive day of flights.

In order to allocate crew members effectively, the limitations of crew schedule such as personal availability, crew requirement changes, and equity of flight time are applied to the crew scheduling process for the designated flights. First, the status of an individual limits the availability of a crewmember to perform a designated task. These statuses include illness (or physical deficiency), leave, personal constraints, and so on. Secondly, it is important for the regional airline to accommodate frequent changes in crew requirement due to seasonal or monthly flight demand fluctuation. To accommodate the changes, the flight schedule model should have some flexibility to generate monthly flight schedule in the preparation phase of the flight scheduling. Lastly, equity of flight time among the same crew position is the most important concept when considering the flight operations. There are several reasons such as maintenance of basic airborne skill, fatigue, and so on. To model the above concept, a level of equity must be imposed to ensure that no one will fly too many or too few flights. The level of equity will be allowed deviation above and below the mean number of flights per crew member during the scheduling period. Additionally the consecutive flights will be another factor to consider during the crew scheduling process. These factors will be the main objective of the crew schedule model.

3.2 An Approach with Integer Programming Model

By approaching an IP model with an objective function which minimizes total flight differences between crew members among the same designated positions will be the most valuable solution to the crew scheduling problem. The mathematical formulation can be presented as follows:

<u>Notation</u>
i : the index for the crew member $(i = 1, 2, ..., I)$
j : the index for the flight type $(j = 1, 2, ..., J)$
m : the subset of the specific flight type index $(m = m1, m2, ..., mM)$
s : the index for the aircraft position $(s = 1, 2, ..., S)$
t : the index for the time period $(t = 1, 2, ..., T)$
T_0 : the maximum number of flights in a given time period
A_s : the set of crew members that are qualified to aircraft position s
$R_{j,s}$: the number of crew members of position s in flight type j
$Q_{i,s}$: 1 if crew member i is qualified to position s, 0 otherwise
$D_{i,t}$: 1 if crew member i is available on day t, 0 otherwise
Y_i : total number of flight types for crew member i during given time period

<u>Decision Variable</u>
$X_{i,j,s,t} = 1$, if crew member i is assigned to flight type j on position s for day t,
        0, otherwise

<IP Formulation>

$$Min \sum_{i \in A_s > i' \in A_s} Z_i - Z_{i'} \qquad (1)$$

subject to

$$Y_i = \sum_{j,s,t} X_{i,j,s,t} \quad \forall\, i \tag{2}$$

$$Y_i - \frac{\sum_{j,s} R_{j,s}}{I} = Z_i + Z_{i'} \quad \forall\, i, i \in A_s \,\rangle\, i' \in A_s \tag{3}$$

$$\sum_i X_{i,j,s,t} = R_{j,s} \quad \forall\, j, s, t \tag{4}$$

$$X_{i,j,s,t} \leq Q_{i,s} \quad \forall\, i,\, j,\, s,\, t \tag{5}$$

$$\sum_j \sum_s X_{i,j,s,t} \leq D_{i,t} \quad \forall\, i, t \tag{6}$$

$$\sum_t X_{i,j,s,t} \leq T_0 \tag{7}$$

$$X_{i,j,s,t} + X_{i,j,s,t+1} \leq 1 \quad for\ j \in m \tag{8}$$

$$\sum_j (X_{i,j,s,t} + X_{i,j,s,t+1} + X_{i,j,s,t+2} + X_{i,j,s,t+3}) \leq 4 \quad for\ \forall\, i, s, and\ j \notin m \tag{9}$$

$$X_{i,j,s,t} = \{0,\ 1\} \quad \forall\, i,\, j,\, s,\, t \tag{10}$$

The objective function is to minimize differences in the total number of flights among the same positions in a given time period. The constraints (2) and (3) are the formulas which convert the absolute value of the flights' differences among crew members. The constraint (4) which depicts a required station for the flight, combined with the constraint (5), the crew members' qualification status in a respective flight station, enforces proper designation of a crew with appropriate positional qualification onboard the airplane. The constraint (6) provides the availability status by each scheduled date for the crew members in a given scheduled time period. The constraint (7) shows limitation for number of flights in a given time period. The constraint (8) indicates flight restriction regarding a policy that no crew member is assigned to two consecutive flight types, the flight type profiles which are classified into a specified set, m, among the flight types. The constraint (9) requires that no one flies more than 4 consecutive days for flight types other than the specified sets including m.

3.3   An Approach with Heuristic Model

To accommodate all required qualifications sand personal availability for a given flight type profile for the flights, a heuristic approach can be utilized. The IP can be used to find an optimal solution, but it does not provide all optimal solutions regarding crew scheduling since it is known as NP-hard problem. Therefore, using the heuristic model provides a speedy and feasible solution to this type of crew scheduling. Fig. 1 depicts a general description of the heuristic algorithm, and the main body of the algorithm is in the red dotted box in the left side of the diagram.

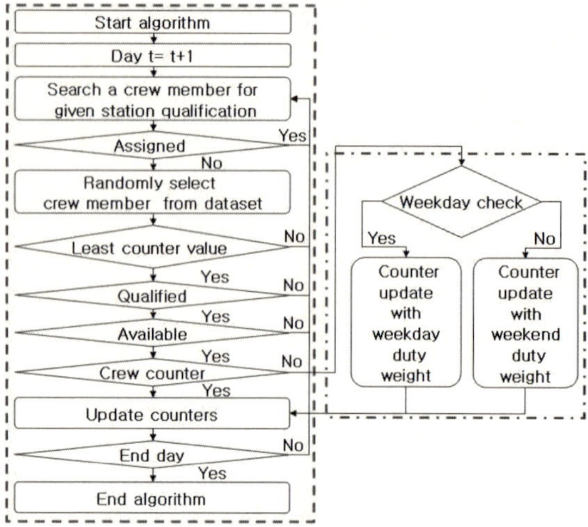

Fig. 1. Diagram for the heuristic model

With limited resources in the regional airline, the airline seldom underestimates the importance of reserve flight capable crew. A stand-by duty crew can play significant role in the airline, since the crew can serve extra flights such as unexpected maintenance flight, replacement flight due to assigned crews' unavailability, and so on. In this regard, we divide the heuristic model into two parts to generate the monthly schedule: a stand-by duty schedule, and a crew schedule. The IP model uses different set to separate the non consecutive schedule of the specified flight type such as m flight type. This approach can incorporate the same concept to schedule stand-by duty as a specified flight type for non consecutive schedule. The first part is to generate a monthly stand-by duty using positional qualifications and personal availability data. The second part generates crew schedule with produced the monthly stand-by duty and the existing positional qualification and personal availability data. Both parts use the algorithm to generate both monthly stand-by duty and monthly crew schedule.

The heuristic algorithm implements a greedy scheduling algorithm in Microsoft Visual Basic. A greedy algorithm is one that adds to a partial solution until it gets stuck at which point it stops or tries some more complicated procedure. In this paper, the algorithm first defines required crew positions for a designated profiled flight type on a given date. In the definition of the process, we can input the number of required crew dependant on the flight type. This process provides some flexibility to accommodate scheduling changes including change of certain composition of the crew in a specified flight type during the planning phase. With a defined crew flight requirement for the flight type, the algorithm accesses data from the data sets and searches non-assigned, smallest value of counter, qualified and available crew members. After the completion of the search, the process starts a random selection of a qualified and available crew member then it proceeds in a first-fit manner to fill in required crew station. The random selection of crew members improves both equity of the number of the flights among same positional groups. Once the algorithm finds qualified and available crew for the designated flights, then it stops the process. The selected crew member will have the assignment and his count will be updated. In this model, there is a separate counter for stand-by duty counter; the counter is blue dotted box shown in Fig. 1. The stand-by duty assignment for weekday and weekend has different values to enhance equal chance for crew members' assignment of week, and weekend duty. When a crew member is selected for a stand-by duty, then his stand-by duty counter will be updated with his assignment numbers for scheduling purposes. The crew schedule heuristic algorithm is similar to the following pseudo-code in Fig. 2.

```
For K = Start Day to End Day
    For J = First Crew Designation to Last Crew Designation
        Data Set = "Select data from database Where position =
            Aircraft Position (J) & category=Aircraft Category (J)"
        Assigned = False
        While Not (end of Data Set) And Not (assigned)
        Randomly select a crewmember from Data Set
        If crewmember is qualified and available Then
            If crewmember has no constraint* Then
                Mission (Day (K), Aircraft Position (J)) = crewmember
                Assigned = True
            End If
        End If
        Randomly select another crewmember
        from Data Set
        End While
    Next J
Next K.
```

Fig. 2. Pseudo-code for the heuristic algorithm

4 Computational Experiments

To evaluate the models, the monthly crew schedule was generated. The monthly planning horizon is divided into weekly intervals, and further divided into daily flight schedule. All the flights related to the schedules are to start and finish within a day. The flights leave an airport, and return to same airport within a day. The capabilities of each crewmember are the same in their designated crew position. For instance, a person qualified as an pilot with more experience in the position does not have any advantage over a person who have less experience but qualified in that same position.

For the purpose of two models' execution, we generated a case study with definition of flight requirements for monthly crew schedules. For the experimental purpose, computational environment of a Pentium 4, CPU 2.4Ghz, 512 RAM was used. OPL Studio 3.6.1 was also used for the IP model. The case study focuses on validity of the IP model and the quality of the heuristic model. The test sets use different combinations of crew, flight type, station, day, and crew's non-availability and crew requirements. To show the quality of two models, 8 different test sets representing 4 different seasons were used to generate monthly crew scheduling for 80 crew members, and 4 stations. These test sets also show the flexibility of the heuristic model to accommodate fluctuation of the flight demand by seasonal effect. The requirements for each test set is different since the sets represent peak travel seasons for spring and autumn, non-peak seasons such as winter and summer. Table 2 shows the results of crew schedules for the set problems using both the IP model and the heuristic algorithm. The IP model found optimal solutions from 108 to 522 seconds, and one test set with no solution within given time limit of 30 minutes. However, the heuristic model performed significantly well to solve these test sets with feasible solutions and short computation time. Another aspect of this case study is to show the flexibility of the heuristic model. Since the heuristic model has a feature to modify crew requirements, it is quite simple to change the requirement for the scheduling. For example, the heuristic model can view the change of the requirements, and input the data promptly while checking the requirement changes during the execution phase.

Table 2. The result of the seasonal crew schedule

Set	Season	# of Flight	Days of Non-availability	IP model using OPL		Heuristic	
				Obj. Value	Comp Time	Obj. Value	Comp Time
1	Winter	10	80	248	108.27	248	2.53
2		11	180	272	169.09	272	2.77
3	Summer	11	240	272	179.38	272	2.89
4		12	160	297	199.25	297	2.98
5	Autumn	15	140	372	338.67	372	3.12
6		16	120	396	395.20	396	3.32
7	Spring	17	80	421	522.08	421	3.35
8		18	60	-	-	462	3.57

For the realistic implementation of the schedule, we extend this 80-crew schedule into an extended 160-member-crew monthly schedule. The airline's projected number of the crew member is up to 160 individuals including 80 pilots and 80 flight attendants. The qualifications for the crew members were divided into 44 pilots, 36 co-pilots, 42 chief flight attendants, and 38 flight attendants. The total non-available days for the entire crew were counted as 640 days for using 30 flights per day. This monthly crew schedule can serve as a tool to forecast extended operations of the regional airline. To test this monthly crew schedule, we used similar regional crew members' data to generate the crew schedule. The IP model could not solve the monthly schedule; therefore, we divided the schedule into two different sets similar to second test case with 80 members each pilot and cabin crew. The combined solution using 2 sets solved the schedule in 866.6 seconds. One test set produced an optimal solution, but the other test set generated a feasible solution. For the heuristic model execution, we used applicable data for the crew schedule, and generated the duty schedule first. With a stand-by duty schedule, we solved the entire monthly crew schedule for 30 flight types including one stand-by duty crew ready. Total computation time for the heuristic model was 6.07 seconds. The heuristic provided a good solution in the range of lower and upper bound of the combined solution from the IP model. In reality, the comparison of computation time, the heuristic model was much faster than that of the IP model.

We compared the tightness of the crew schedule between the IP model and the heuristic model. The tightness of the crew schedule is as important as the equity of the crew schedule because it indicates the effectiveness of the allocation of the flight load among crew members. The tightness is measured in terms of consecutive assignments of each crew member in a given time period. The summation of the tightness of the IP model is 2168 days; however, the heuristic model shows a less tightened schedule with 2003 consecutive days. To measure the tightness in detail, we even look into the details of the total number of 2, 3, and 4 consecutive days to show the equity of the crew scheduling. Table 3 shows the details of the tightness of the both models.

Table 3. The comparison of the consecutive days of schedule from two models

Consecutive type	Model	Total # of Consecutive days	Mean	Variance
2 consecutive	IP	2168	23.83	10.70
days	Heuristic	2003	23.75	8.38
3 consecutive	IP	1235	15.01	7.83
days	Heuristic	1033	13.95	5.02
4 consecutive	IP	539	5.73	4.25
days	Heuristic	463	4.70	2.83

From the various comparisons of the schedule tightness, the heuristic performed better than the IP model. For instance, the differences of the variance of total consecutive days for three types were significant to mention that the heuristic model equitably allocated crew members for the monthly crew schedule. The means of the total number of consecutive days for three types also depicted that the heuristic model performed well. The case of three studies shows that the heuristic model does allocate crew members equitably. This heuristic model ultimately can provide a solution to the monthly crew schedule for the regional airline.

5 Conclusion and Discussion

Crew scheduling is the most important area for a regional airline to enhance safe-flight operation and to provide affordable service to the customers. For the crew scheduling, we propose a heuristic model which produces an output of a matrix of crew members and flight types indicating which crew to assign to what flight types during the crew scheduling period. The heuristic mode is to incorporate all flight requirements for the airline as well as crew members' availability and qualification status. Additionally, the model also accommodates frequent fluctuation of flights demands in the crew scheduling processes with a quick and reliable schedule generation. Therefore, this model ultimately provides a solution to the problem of the monthly crew schedule for the regional airline. In summary, this paper shows that the model not only produces flight schedules, but also serves as an effective tool to analyze the impact of changes on the flight operation of the airline since the model incorporates a fluctuation of the flight demand in the planning process. However, this paper can be future extended to study following additional area. Equality of flight hours is the key to operate a regional airline. This subject can be divided into further details in the model to accommodate any possible conflicts concerning the issue. Additionally, the maintain schedule can be incorporated to provide a specific airplane to fly a given flight type. Therefore, each airplane could be assigned to flight types as well as assigning the personnel.

References

1. Chang, S. C., "A new aircrew-scheduling model for short-haul routes," *Journal of Air Transportation Management,* Vol. 8, pp. 249-260, 2002.
2. Dawid, H., Konig, J., and Strauss, C., "An enhanced rostering model for airline crews," *Computers & Operations Research*, Vol. 28, pp. 671-688, 2001.

3. Gamache, M. and Soumis, F., "A method for optimally solving the rostering problem," Cahier GERAD, G-90-40, Ecole des Hautes Etutes Commerciales, Montreal, Canada, H3T 1V6, 1993.
4. Guo, Y., Mellouli, T., Suhl, L., and Thiel, M. P., "A partially integrated airline crew scheduling with time-dependant crew capacities and multiple home bases," *European Journal of Operational Research*, article in press, 2005.
5. Kim, G., and Lee, Y. H., "Cockpit Crew Scheduling using Set Partitioning Problem," *The Korean OR/MS,* Vol. 21, No. 1, pp. 39-55, Seoul, Korea, 2004.
6. Marsten, R. E., and Shepardson, F., "Exact Solution of Crew Scheduling Problems Using the Set Partitioning Model: Recent Successful Applications," *Networks*, Vol. 11, pp. 165-177, 1981.
7. Ozdemir, H. T., and Mohan, C. K., "Flight graph based genetic algorithm for crew scheduling in airlines," *Information Sciences*, Vol. 133, pp. 165-173, 2001.
8. Ryan, D.M., "The solution of massive generalized set partitioning problems in aircrew rostering," *Operations Research Society*, Vol. 43, pp. 459-467, 1992.
9. Teodorovic, D. and Lucic, P., "A fuzzy set theory approach to the aircrew rostering problem," *Fuzzy sets and system*, 95, pp. 261-271, 1998.
10. Yan, S., and Lin, C. I., "Optimization of airline crew pairing," *Journal of Chinese Institute of Civil and Hydraulic Engineering*, 9, pp. 303-313, Taiwan, 1997.
11. Yan, S., and Tu, Y. P., "A network model for airline cabin crew scheduling ," *European Journal of Operational Research*, Vol. 140, pp. 531-540, 2002.
12. Yan, S., Tung, T. T., and Tu, Y. P., "Optimal construction of airline individual crew scheduling," *Computers & Operations Research*, Vol.29, pp.341-363, 2002.
13. www.jejuair.net, "Regional Airlines," 2005.

Automatic Segmentation of the Liver in CT Images Using a Model of Approximate Contour

Marcin Ciecholewski[1] and Krzysztof Dębski[2]

[1] Institue of Automatics, AGH University of Science and Technology,
al. Mickiewicza 30, 30-059 Kraków, Poland
`ciechol@agh.edu.pl`
[2] Institue of Radiology and Nuclear Medicine, Medical University, Gdańsk, Poland

Abstract. The segmentation of the liver structure from a computed tomography (CT) image is an important function of the software designed to assist liver diagnostics, because it allows for the elimination of excess information from the diagnostic process. In this paper, the task of segmentation has been implemented through first finding the contour of the liver which is made up of a finite number of joint polylines approximating individual fragments of the liver boundary in the CT image. Next, the field outside the contour is divided into two polygons and eliminated from the image. The initial reference point for the calculations is the lumbar section of the spine which is a central point of any CT image of the liver. The automatic method of segmentation is to be used in a dedicated computer system designed to diagnose liver patients.

1 Introduction

Owing to the precision level it affords, Computed Tomography (CT) is now a commonly used method for imaging of the liver and the diagnostics of liver-related diseases. Nowadays, computer-assisted methods to facilitate the isolation of the boundaries of internal organs from medical images and thus improve the diagnostics of specific disorders are rapidly being developed.

The task of automatic extraction of liver boundary and segmentation of the liver structure is somewhat complex, because of the close proximity of other organs (Fig. 1). In the CT images there is also great diversity in the shapes of the liver, stemming from the individual features of the patients. The CT technology can be applied to the liver at three phases, such as parenchymatous, arterial and venal. The CT images may also present various disorders which also makes boundary extraction more difficult.

The task of liver segmentation in CT images has attracted fairly widespread interest among researchers. Bae et al. [1] used priori information about liver morphology and image processing techniques such as gray-level thresholding, Gaussian smoothing, mathematical morphology techniques and B-splines. Chen et al. [3] proposed a com-bination of the FBM (Fractional Brownian Motion) technique with a parametrically deformable active contour method, in order to determine an approximate liver con-tour. Ballerini [2] on the other hand

A. Levi et al. (Eds.): ISCIS 2006, LNCS 4263, pp. 75–84, 2006.
© Springer-Verlag Berlin Heidelberg 2006

presented the active contour method with the use of genetic algorithms. Seo et al. [9] had segmented the lumbar section of the spine and then determined the boundaries of the ROI (Region Of Interest), where the shape of liver is situated. The segmentation of the lumbar section of the spine is performed with the use of thresholding for fixed values of gray levels and histogram transformation. During the segmentation process, iterative filtration operations are performed such as dilatation and erosion. Husain et al. [5] used neural networks for feature-based recognition of the liver region.

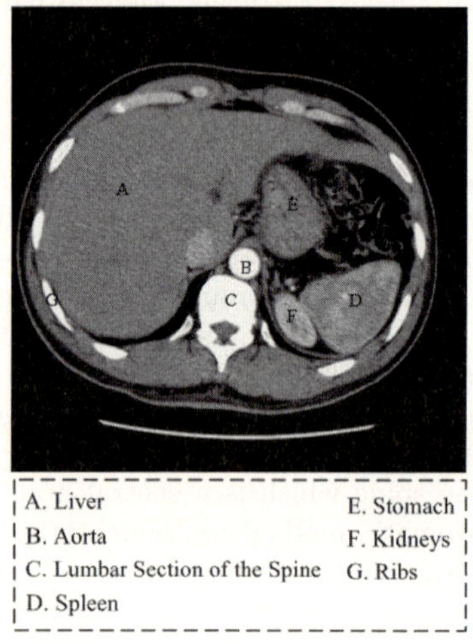

Fig. 1. CT image of the abdominal cavity. Description of the anatomical situation.

In this paper, the task of segmentation has been implemented through first finding the contour of the liver which is made up of a finite number of joint polylines approximating individual fragments of the liver boundary in the CT image. Next, the field outside the contour is divided into two polygons and eliminated from the image. The content of this paper is laid out as follows: section 2 presents the mathematical model used to describe the liver contour in the CT images; section 3 gives the algorithm of automatic detection of the liver contour; and section 4 describes the method for automatic segmentation of the liver structure in CT images. The penultimate section describes the experiments and presents their results, whereas the last section includes the conclusions and outlines the possible lines of our future research.

2 The Description of the Liver Contour: A Mathematical Model

In order to describe the boundary of the liver, a mathematical model has been defined, representing polygons, which may be formed by a finite number of joint polylines. Let $s = 1 \ldots 6$ and $j \in \{0, 1\}$. The polyline [10] means the set L_s^j of the form

$$L_s^j = \bigcup_{i=0}^{S} P_i P_{i+1} \tag{1}$$

$P_i P_{i+1}$ is a segment with the starting point P_i and the end-point P_{i+1}. The intersection $P_i P_{i+1} \cap P_{i+1} P_{i+2}$ is a single-element set containing the end-point of the segment $P_i P_{i+1}$ and the starting point of the segment $P_{i+1} P_{i+2}$. The intersection $P_i P_{i+1} \cap P_k P_{k+1}$ for $k > i + 1$ is empty. For $j = 0$ the set L_s^0 is empty, whereas for $j = 1$ the set L_s^1 is non-empty.

$$L_s^j = \begin{cases} L_s^1 & \text{for } s = 1 \ldots 5 \\ L_s^{j \in \{0,1\}} & \text{for } s = 6 \end{cases} \tag{2}$$

Let L be a polyline comprising at least five of the component polylines L_s^j, that is

$$L = \bigcup_{s=0}^{6} L_s^j \tag{3}$$

Each polyline approximates a corresponding fragment of a liver boundary in a CT image. The value of the variable j determines if the next component polyline can be formed. In Fig. 2 (b) for $s = 6$ we have $j = 1$, thus the component L_6^1 is the ending polyline approximating corresponding curvature, whereas in Fig. 2 (d) the last component polyline is L_5^1. In Fig. 2 (d) the polyline L is made up of five component polylines. Thus, for $s = 6$ we have $j = 0$, that is L_6^0. Let $t = 1 \ldots 6$ and $\in \{0, 1\}$. The given set of the form

$$R_t^j = \bigcup_{i=0}^{T} P_i P_{i+1} \tag{4}$$

also represents a polyline. For $j = 0$ the set R_t^0 is empty, whereas for $j = 1$ the set R_t^1 is non-empty.

$$L_s^j = \begin{cases} R_t^1 & \text{for } t = 1, 3 \\ R_t^{j \in \{0,1\}} & \text{for } t = 2, 4, 5, 6 \end{cases} \tag{5}$$

Let R be a polyline made of component polylines R_t^j, that is

$$R = \bigcup_{t=0}^{6} R_t^j \tag{6}$$

The set R is made up of at least two, and a maximum of three joint polylines. It is because it approximates shorter than the set L fragment of the liver boundary. The intersection $L \cap R$ is a two-element set containing a common starting point and end-point of the sub-sets L and R. In Fig. 2 (b) and 2 (d) the component R_3^1 is the ending polyline. In Fig. 2 (d) the polyline R is made up of two component polylines R_1^1 and R_3^1, thereofore for $t = 2, 4, 5, 6$ we have R_t^0. Figs. 2 (a) and 2 (c) present sample CT images of the abdominal cavity with the liver structure, whereas Figs. 2 (b) and 2 (d) present the corresponding models of liver contours formed by the polylines L and R. The point P_{ST} is a common starting point for the polylines L and R.

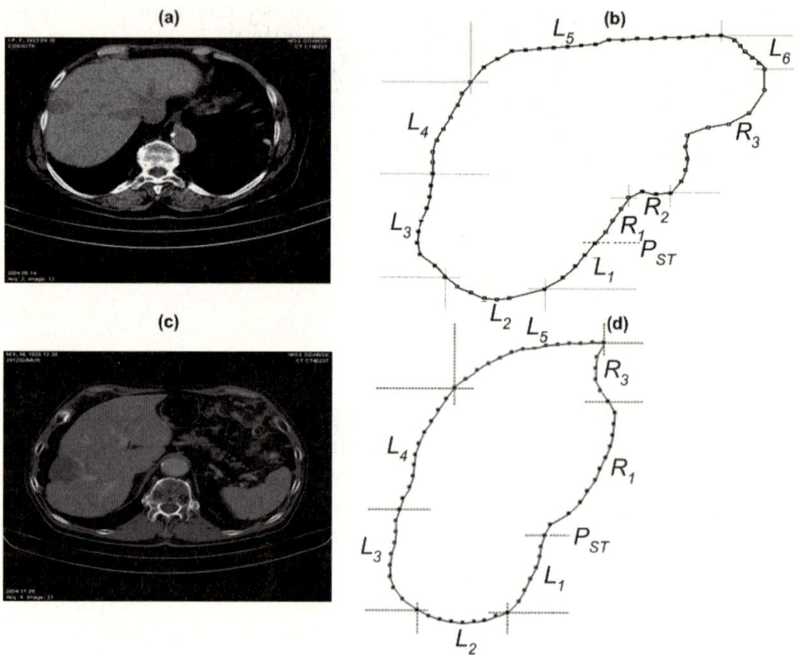

Fig. 2. CT images of the abdominal cavity and the liver. (a), (c) Sample CT images. (b), (d) Model of liver contours.

3   Proposed Algorithm for Detection of the Liver Contour

Let $g : M^2 \rightarrow Z$ be the gray-level image of the abdominal cavity with the liver structure and let $(x, y) \in [0, M] \times [0, M]$ determine the coordinates of the pixel. Then $(x, y) \in Z$. The set Z determines integral numbers from the range $[0, 2^B - 1]$, where B is an assumed number of bits for the representation of a single pixel. Assuming that a single pixel is represented by a one memory byte, we have $Z = \{g : g(x, y) \in [0, 255]\}$. The size of the image was 512×512 pixels. This is a standard resolution obtained in CT examinations, therefore it may be assumed that $M = 512$.

The first step in an algorithm operation is to find the starting point P_{ST}, which allows us to begin determination of the coordinates for polylines approximating the liver contour. The method of finding the point P_{ST}, together with the presentation of the algorithm for automatic detection of the liver contour by the use of component polylines determined by the relationships (3) and (6) were presented in the paper [4]. The determination of the point P_{ST} is performed in two stages (Fig. 3): The point P_{SP} situated at the boundary of the spine is found. Next, the point P_{SP} is projected along the X axis on to the boundary of the liver giving P_{ST}.

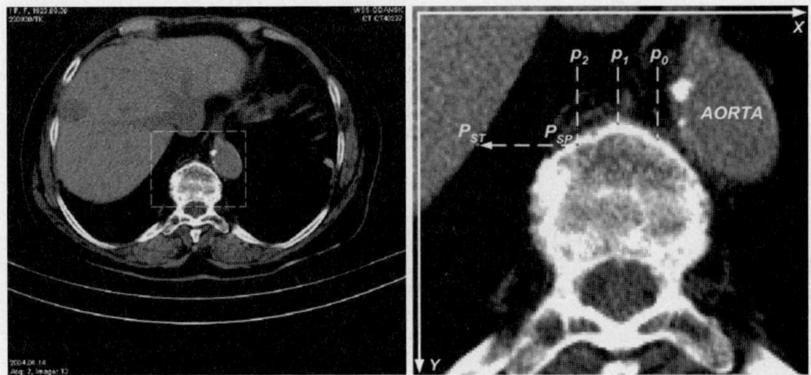

Fig. 3. CT of the liver. Locating the starting point P_{ST}.

The starting position which allows one to determine the point P_{SP} is the centre of the axis of symmetry of the CT image, that is $(xStart, yStart) = (M/2, M/2)$. As the aorta is located very close to the spine (Fig. 3) its presence may make the finding of the point P_{SP}. difficult. For this reason, it is assumed that three points p_i will be considered in calculations:

$$p_i = (x_i, y_i) = \begin{cases} x_i = xStart - D \cdot i \\ y_i = yStart \end{cases} \text{ for } i = 0, 1, 2 \qquad (7)$$

The value of y coordinate is incremented by one for each point p_i until one of the following conditions is satisfied: $\mid g(x_i, y_{i+1}) - g(x_i, y_i) \mid \in G_{SP}$ or $y_i - yStart > H$. Next, the coordinates of the $P_{SP} = (xP_{SP}, yP_{SP})$ are determined by comparing the distance between points p_i along the Y axis.

It was assumed that the distance between x_i coordinates along the X axis is defined as $D = \lfloor M/34 \rfloor = 15$ and the maximum distance along the Y axis from the starting point $(xStart, yStart)$ does not exceed $H = \lfloor M/D \rfloor = 70$. It was assumed that the interval of gray-levels of the spine is defined as $G_{SP} = \{g \in Z : g \in [190, 255]\}$.

The values of the constants which determine the ends of the interval G_{SP} and constant value of the variable H were assumed on the basis of tests and allow one finding the point P_{SP} and next P_{ST}.

From the starting point P_{ST} the defined conditions which determine the gray levels of the boundary coordinates are checked [4]. On this basis, the suitable arithmetic operations are performed either by increasing or decreasing the co-ordinates x or y in order find the next points of polylines approximating the contour of the liver. The boundary conditions which enable one to find the coordinates of the polyline L_1, are presented in Fig. 4 (c). In Fig. 4 (b) the pixels forming the sample polyline L_1 are marked, as well as the indexes of the boundary conditions met for them.

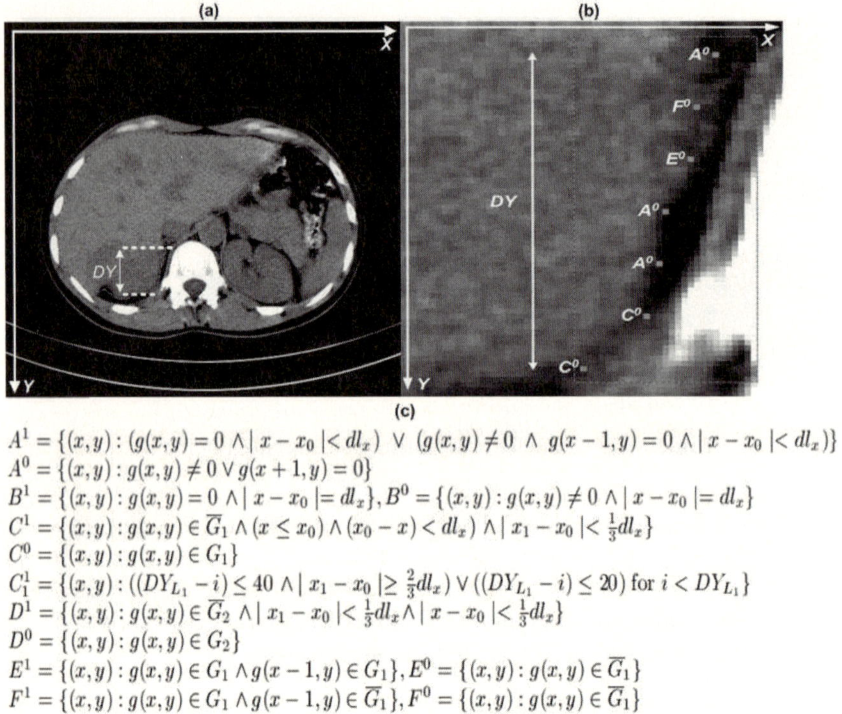

Fig. 4. CT of the liver. (a) Sample image with the marked distance DY of the polyline L_1. (b) Points of the polyline L_1 with symbols of boundary conditions. (c) Boundary conditions which enable determination of coordinates of the polyline L_1.

$$A^1 = \{(x,y) : (g(x,y) = 0 \wedge \mid x - x_0 \mid < dl_x) \vee (g(x,y) \neq 0 \wedge g(x-1,y) = 0 \wedge \mid x - x_0 \mid < dl_x)\}$$
$$A^0 = \{(x,y) : g(x,y) \neq 0 \vee g(x+1,y) = 0\}$$
$$B^1 = \{(x,y) : g(x,y) = 0 \wedge \mid x - x_0 \mid = dl_x\}, B^0 = \{(x,y) : g(x,y) \neq 0 \wedge \mid x - x_0 \mid = dl_x\}$$
$$C^1 = \{(x,y) : g(x,y) \in \overline{G}_1 \wedge (x \leq x_0) \wedge (x_0 - x) < dl_x) \wedge \mid x_1 - x_0 \mid < \tfrac{1}{3}dl_x\}$$
$$C^0 = \{(x,y) : g(x,y) \in G_1\}$$
$$C^1_1 = \{(x,y) : ((DY_{L_1} - i) \leq 40 \wedge \mid x_1 - x_0 \mid \geq \tfrac{2}{3}dl_x) \vee ((DY_{L_1} - i) \leq 20) \text{ for } i < DY_{L_1}\}$$
$$D^1 = \{(x,y) : g(x,y) \in \overline{G}_2 \wedge \mid x_1 - x_0 \mid < \tfrac{1}{3}dl_x \wedge \mid x - x_0 \mid < \tfrac{1}{3}dl_x\}$$
$$D^0 = \{(x,y) : g(x,y) \in G_2\}$$
$$E^1 = \{(x,y) : g(x,y) \in G_1 \wedge g(x-1,y) \in G_1\}, E^0 = \{(x,y) : g(x,y) \in \overline{G}_1\}$$
$$F^1 = \{(x,y) : g(x,y) \in G_1 \wedge g(x-1,y) \in \overline{G}_1\}, F^0 = \{(x,y) : g(x,y) \in \overline{G}_1\}$$

It was assumed that $DY_{L_1} = \lfloor M/6 \rfloor$. $DY \leq DY_{L_1}$. Intervals of gray-levels $G_1, \overline{G}_1, G_2, \overline{G}_2$ were determined as follows: $G_1 = \{g \in Z : g \in (0, 50)\}, \overline{G}_1 = \{g \in Z : g \in (50, 255]\}, G_2 = \{g \in Z : g \in (0, 100)\}, \overline{G}_2 = \{g \in Z : g \in (100, 255]\}$. It was assumed that the maximum distance along the X axis between the boundary pixels does not exceed $dl_x = 15$. The values of the constants which determine the ends of intervals $G_1, \overline{G}_1, G_2, \overline{G}_2$ were assumed on the basis of tests performed on a set of thirty CT images of the liver.

The actions associated with calculating coordinates belonging to the polylines L_i and R_i ($i = 1 \ldots 6$), on the basis of the defined boundary conditions were presented in the paper [4]. The computational complexity of the contour detection algorithm is a function of the class $O(N \cdot M)$, where N describes the number of points in a single polyline L_i and R_i $(i = 1 \ldots 6)$, while M is the maximum number of arithmetic operations required to find a single point of a polyline.

4 Liver Segmentation in the CT Image of the Abdominal Cavity

The proposed method for the liver structure segmentation in a CT image uses the calculated values of coordinates, which determine the liver contour with the use of component polylines (3) and (6).

Two polygons: W_1 and W_2 are given. It is assumed that the polygon W_1 is determined by the coordinates of the polyline L, which has $P_{ST} = (xP_{ST}, yP_{ST})$ as a starting point, and $P_E = (xP_E, yP_E)$ as an end-point. Next, the points for W_1 are: $P_1 = (xP_E, 0)$, $P_2 = (0, 0)$, $P_3 = (0, M)$, $P_4 = (xP_{ST}, M)$ and P_{ST}.

The polygon W_2 has points spaced along the coordinates of the polyline R, beginning at the point $P_{ST} = (xP_{ST}, yP_{ST})$ and ending at the point $P_E = (xP_E, yP_E)$. The remaining coordinates are: $P_1, Q_2 = (0, M), Q_3 = (M, M), P_4$ and P_{ST}. The

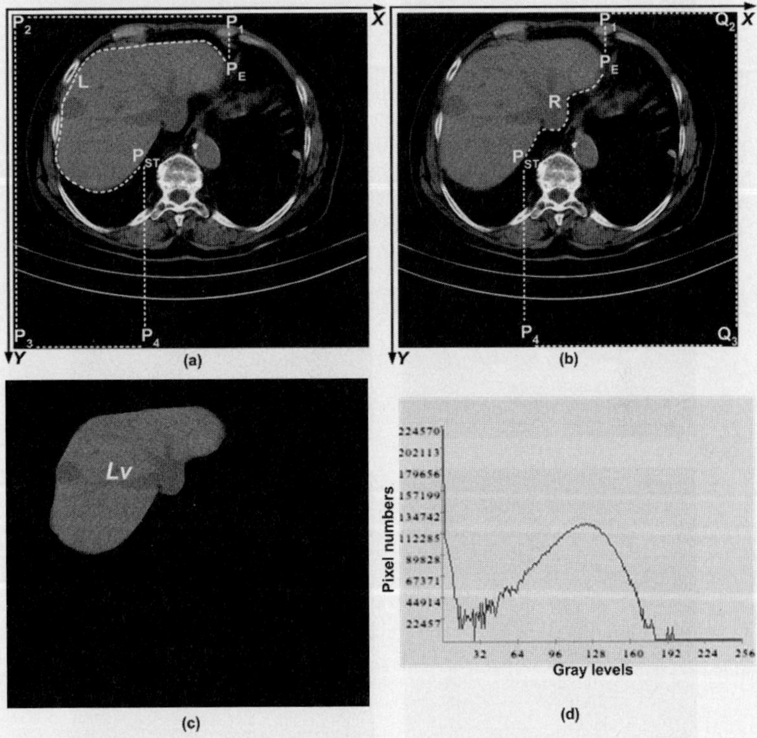

Fig. 5. Segmentation of the liver structure in CT images of the abdominal cavity. (a) The polygon W_1 containing the polyline L. (b) The polygon W_2 containing the polyline R. (c) Segmented structure of the liver. (d) Histogram of the image with the segmented structure of the liver.

polygons W_1 and W_2 are presented in Fig. 5 (a) and Fig. 5 (b) respectively. Thus, a CT image is divided into three component parts: the polygons W_1 and W_2 - representing background and Lv which is the liver structure (Fig. 5 (c)).

The segmentation is performed in such a way that in a CT image showing the liver and defined by the mapping $g : M^2 \rightarrow Z$, its fragment is replaced by the area made up by two polygons W_1 and W_2, in which pixels are set to black in colour. We obtain

$$g' = \begin{cases} g & \text{for } (x,y) \in W_1 \cup W_2 \\ 0 & \text{for } (x,y) \notin W_1 \cup W_2 \end{cases} \tag{8}$$

Fig. 5 (c) shows a sample CT image with the segmented liver structure.

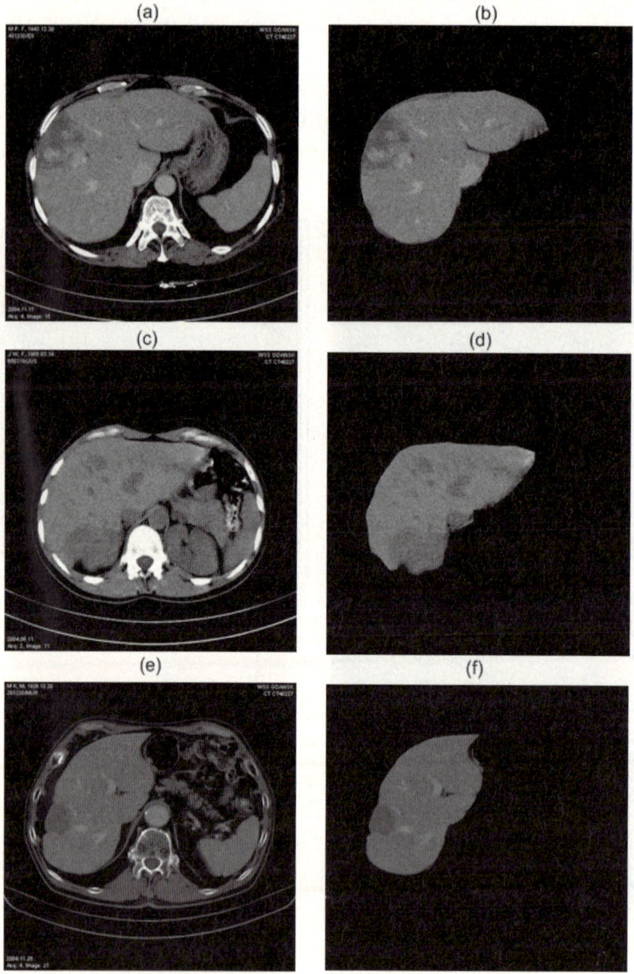

Fig. 6. Segmentation of the liver structure in CT images of the abdominal cavity. The left columns shows sample CT images, the right column shows the images with the segmented structure of the liver.

5   Experiments Conducted and Selected Research Results

During the studies on the analysis of CT images, the material from the Department of Image Diagnostics of the Provincial Specialist Hospital in Gdańsk, Poland, was used. The CT images were obtained with Somatom Emotion 6 (Siemens). CT images were performed with intravenous contrast enhancement. The parameters of exposure for the abdominal cavity were 130 kVp and 95 mAs for the venal phase, and 110 kVp and 90 mAs for the arterial phase, a 2 mm slice colimmation and a table speed of 15 mm/sec.

The experiments involved some 30 cases in various patients, either without any disease symptoms or with visible ailments such as hemangiomas and hepatomas. Figs.6 (a) and 6 (b) show images with hemangioma, whereas Figs. 6 (e) and 6 (f) show hepatomas. Fig. 6 (c) and Fig. 6 (d) show images with multi-focal hepatic lesions.

6   Conclusions and Further Directions of Research

This paper presents a new method for automatic segmentation of the liver structure in CT images of the abdominal cavity, using the lumbar section of the spine as a reference point. After the starting point is determined, an approximate contour of the liver is marked, consisting of joint polylines. The component polylines are the elements of two polygons which are then eliminated from the picture, leaving only the segmented shape of the liver. When applied in examination, this method yielded fairly accurate results for both healthy organs as well as those organs manifesting certain diseases or focal lesions within the liver. In order to fully verify the usefulness of the method it should be tested in a greater number of cases.

The presented method of the liver structure segmentation in CT images is a component part of a computer-assisted diagnostics software system. The system is developed in C++, with the use of an object-oriented programming technique. In other words, each component of the system may be replaced by a better one as soon as the latter is developed. The future direction of this research will be to develop effective methods for segmentation of the focal neoplastic lesions of the liver.

Acknowledgements

This work is supported from the Polish State Committee Research (KBN) Grant No. 3T11F03030.

References

1. Bae, K.T., Giger, M.L., Chen, C.T., Kahn, Jr. C.E.: Automatic segmentation of liver structure in CT images. Medical Physics, Vol. 20. (1993) 71–78.
2. Ballerini J.: Genetic Snakes for Medical Image Segmentation. LNCS, Vol. 1596. (1999) 59-73.

3. Chen, E.L., Chung, P.C., Chen, C.L.,Tsai, H.M.,Chang, C.I.: An automatic diagnostic system for CT liver image classification, IEEE Transactions on Biomedical Engineering, Vol. 45. No. 6. (1998) 783-794.
4. Ciecholewski M., Dębski K.: Automatic detection of liver contour in CT images. Automatics, semi-annual journal of the AGH University of Science and Technology, Vol. 10. No. 2. (2006).
5. Husain, S.A., Shigeru, E.: Use of neural networks for feature based recognition of liver region on CT images. Neural Networks for Sig. Proc.-Proceedings of the IEEE Work., Vol. 2. (2000) 831-840
6. Kass, M., Witkin, A., Terauzopoulos, D.: Snakes, Active Contour Models, Int. J. Computer Vision, Vol. 1. No. 4. (1987) 259-263.
7. Meyer- Bäse, A.: Pattern Recognition for medical imaging. Elsevier Academic Press (2004)
8. Ritter, G.X., Wilson, J.N.: Computer Vision Algorithms in Image Algebra, CRC Press, Boca Raton, Florida (2000)
9. Seo, K., Ludeman, L.C., Park S., Park, J.: Efficient liver segmentation based on the spine. LNCS, Vol. 3261. (2004) 400-409.
10. Schilling, R.J., Harris, S.L.: Applied numerical methods for engineers. Brooks/Cole Publishing Com., Pacific Grove CA (2000)

Unambiguous 3D Measurements by a Multi-period Phase Shift Method

E. Lilienblum and B. Michaelis

Institute for Electronics, Signal Processing and Communications
Otto-von-Guericke University Magdeburg
P.O. Box 4120, 39106 Magdeburg, Germany
{elilie, michaelis}@e-technik.uni-magdeburg.de
http://iesk.et.uni-magdeburg.de/TI/TI.html

Abstract. One problem of classical phase shift technique for 3D surface measurement is the occurrence of ambiguities due to the use of fringe projection. We propose a universal theory to calculate unambiguous values called projector coordinates. The projector coordinates can be used as a base for a reliable surface reconstruction without any ambiguity. The essence of our method is the application of pattern sequences with different periods. In contrast to combined techniques like hierarchical phase shift or phase shift with Gray code we use all pictures homogeneously which were taken for the measurement. This leads to a higher accuracy. Furthermore we are able to avoid some typical calculation errors that are produced in classical phase shifting.

1   Introduction

Methods with projection of structured light play an important role for optical 3D measurement of surfaces [1,2]. If non-moving objects are measured, the measuring accuracy can be substantially increased by the use of coded light sequences [3]. An important representative of methods based on coded light is phase shifting [4].

The basic idea of the phase shift method consists of capturing several images of phase shifted sinusoidal fringe patterns projected on the measuring object. The images are pixel separately processed, whereby for each pixel exactly one phase value is computed. That phase value is used as a measure for the calculation of the height information of the object. The surface reconstruction can take place via usual triangulation methods.

The periodicity of the fringe pattern leads directly to the periodicity of the computed phase value. That entails ambiguities with the reconstruction the object surface. To tackle that problem so far either approximate values of the object surface have been used [5] or additional methods like the Gray code technique have been applied [6,7]. One disadvantage of combined solutions based on an additional method is loss of information. Generally, additional pictures must be taken, which do not increase the measuring accuracy. Besides, a second method is always a source for additional errors.

A. Levi et al. (Eds.): ISCIS 2006, LNCS 4263, pp. 85–94, 2006.

An alternative is the projection of several phase-shift sequences, which differ in their local period. First ideas are proposed in [8]. In this paper we develop a universal mathematical approach to get a new basis for the phase shift method.

2   Phase Shifting

Basic principle for the classical phase shifting is the computation of a phase value $\varphi(u, v)$ on the pixel (u, v) from the grey tone images $G_1, G_2, \ldots, G_n$. For this different computation methods were suggested [9]. We use in our work

$$\varphi(u, v) = \frac{1}{2\pi} \, \arctan2 \left(\frac{\sum_{i=1}^{n} \cos\left(\frac{2\pi i}{n}\right) G_i(u, v)}{\sum_{i=1}^{n} \sin\left(\frac{2\pi i}{n}\right) G_i(u, v)} \right) + 0.5, \tag{1}$$

whereby arctan2 calculates the arctangent angle in the correct quadrant and without undefined (singular) values. In contrast to the actual classical phase value within the borders between $-\pi$ and π we have a range of values in the interval $[0, 1)$. Thereby, the use of the phase value is simplified significantly.

As an example of use figure 1 shows the measurements of some sphere objects. On the left side we see the original grey tone images. The phase values which we computed are shown as a so-called phase image on the right side.

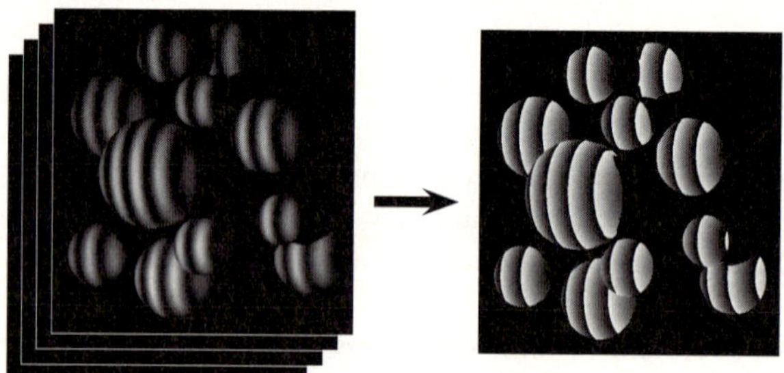

Fig. 1. Sequence of original gray tone images (left) and the computed phase image (right) of sphere objects

3   Projector Coordinates

For the reconstruction of a surface with stereo vision methods there is a basic premise. Along the epipolar lines we need measurements which are unambiguous, thus not periodic. However, the pattern we using are send from the projector. For this we consider the fringe patterns from projector view first.

A projected fringe pattern is characterized by a one-dimensional brightness function. We call the parameter of this function projector coordinate and we denote it with $\xi \in \mathbb{R}$. As a function of the projected pattern the brightness in a surface point of the measured object is always determined by exactly one projector coordinate. This of course also applies to the pixel of the camera, which "sees" this point of surface. Thus we can define a function $\xi(u, v)$, which gives the projector coordinate as a function of the pixel coordinate. Because this function is not periodic, the projector coordinate is the very value we are looking for.

3.1   Unambiguous Pattern Sequences

For the computation of the projector coordinate we need additional information, because the phase shifting supplies us with only one phase value. For this reason we use a set $S = \{M_1, M_2, \ldots, M_n\}$ of different pattern sequences. The M_i differ in their period, which we appoint with λ_i. According to our phase shift calculation and the definition of the projector coordinates we can also indicate a phase value function $\varphi_i(\xi) \in [0, 1)$ for each M_i. In addition, we assign a sequential natural number to each fringe of a pattern which we call fringe number and which we write as $\eta_i(\xi) \in \mathbb{N}$.

Figure 2 shows the interdependence between projector coordinate, phase value and fringe number. The phase value $\varphi_i(\xi)$ is shown for each pattern separately by a periodical graph. The fringe number $\eta_i(\xi)$ is shown as a numeral.

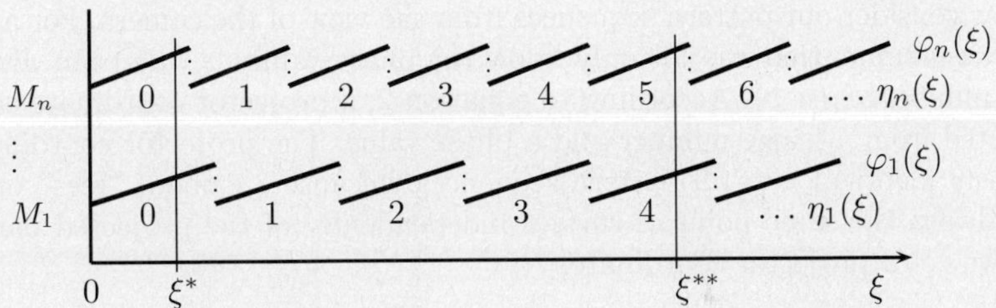

Fig. 2. Interdependence between coordinate, phase value and fringe number for fringe patterns with different periods

From figure 2 we can recognize a direct mathematical connection of the pattern sequences. To all $i = 1, 2, \ldots, n$ applies

$$\xi = \big(\eta_i(\xi) + \varphi_i(\xi)\big)\lambda_i \,. \tag{2}$$

This system of equations obviously becomes ambiguous, if the fringe numbers are unknown. We therefore need a side condition.

Concerning set S the ambiguity is generated exactly if two different projector coordinates $\xi^* \neq \xi^{**}$ yield the same phase values $\varphi_i(\xi^*) = \varphi_i(\xi^{**})$ for all pattern sequences $M_i \in S$. If we solve equation 2 for $\varphi_i(\xi^*)$ and $\varphi_i(\xi^{**})$ resp., we receive for all $i = 1, 2, \ldots, n$

$$\frac{\xi^*}{\lambda_i} - \eta_i(\xi^*) = \frac{\xi^{**}}{\lambda_i} - \eta_i(\xi^{**}) \tag{3}$$

and by further transforming we finally obtain

$$\xi^* - \xi^{**} = \big(\eta_i(\xi^*) - \eta_i(\xi^{**})\big)\lambda_i \,. \tag{4}$$

Since $\Delta\xi = \xi^* - \xi^{**} \neq 0$ is constant over all equations and the difference of two fringe numbers always results in an integer, there must be natural numbers $x_1, x_2, \ldots, x_n > 0$ with

$$x_i = |\eta_i(\xi^*) - \eta_i(\xi^{**})| \,, \tag{5}$$

which fulfill the equations

$$|\Delta\xi| = x_1\lambda_1 = x_2\lambda_2 = \cdots = x_n\lambda_n \,. \tag{6}$$

These equations form the basis of the computation of the least common multiples (LCM), which we can apply w.l.o.g. to the set of rational numbers $\mathbb{Q}$. If we postulate $\lambda_i \in \mathbb{Q}$ for all frequencies, then for the set S there is always a maximum projector coordinate

$$\xi_{\max}(S) = \mathrm{LCM}(\lambda_1, \lambda_2, \ldots, \lambda_n) \,, \tag{7}$$

up to which we can exclude ambiguity. Thus, with the condition $\xi < \xi_{\max}(S)$ the system of equation 2 becomes unambiguous.

3.2 Calculation of Fringe Numbers

We now consider our pattern sequences from the view of the camera. For a pixel (u, v) we assume, that we not only know the phase values $\varphi_i(u, v)$ but also the fringe numbers $\eta_i(u, v)$. According to equation 2, a projector coordinate can be computed from a fringe number and a phase value. The projector coordinate is obviously identical over all pattern sequences, because a camera "sees" on one pixel always the same point of surface independently of the projected pattern. Thus we get a projector coordinate

$$\xi(u, v) = \big(\eta_i(u, v) + \varphi_i(u, v)\big)\lambda_i \,, \tag{8}$$

which is independent of the pattern sequence M_i. If we equate the right sides from equation 8 for pairs of pattern sequences $(M_i, M_j) \in S \times S$, then we obtain after rearrangement

$$\lambda_i\,\eta_i(u, v) - \lambda_j\,\eta_j(u, v) = \lambda_j\,\varphi_j(u, v) - \lambda_i\,\varphi_i(u, v). \tag{9}$$

With reference to the right part of the equation 9 we introduce a phase difference vector $\Phi(u, v) = \boldsymbol{a}$ with the components

$$a_i = \lambda_1\,\varphi_1(u, v) - \lambda_i\,\varphi_i(u, v) \,. \tag{10}$$

If we again provide $\lambda_i \in \mathbb{Q}$, then we can define a map $H : P \to T$ for $P \subset \mathbb{R}^n$ and $T \subset \mathbb{N}^n$ with

$$H(\boldsymbol{a}) = \begin{cases} (h_1, h_2, \ldots, h_n) : & \begin{aligned} &\forall\, i\,\{\,\lambda_i h_i < \xi_{\max}(S), \\ &a_i = \lambda_i h_i - \lambda_1 h_1\,\} \end{aligned} \\ \text{undefined} : & \text{otherwise} \end{cases} \,. \tag{11}$$

The map H is well-defined, since ambiguities are excluded with $\lambda_i h_i < \xi_{\max}(S)$ as already shown for the derivation of the maximum projector coordinate. Let us provide $\xi(u, v) < \xi_{\max}(S)$ in equation 8 likewise, which can take place via the delimitation of the number of projected fringes. Then in connection with equation 9 and the correctness of H we get

$$H\big(\Phi(u, v)\big) = \big(\eta_1(u, v), \eta_2(u, v), \ldots, \eta_n(u, v)\big). \tag{12}$$

Thus at least theoretically we achieve the possibility to calculate our unknown fringe numbers.

3.3 Lookup Table

It is clear that on the basis of equation 1 we can compute $\Phi(u, v) = \boldsymbol{a}$ in a simple way. For the map $H : P \to T$ this is obviously not the case. However, from the definition of H in equation 11 it follows that both P and T must be a finite set. Thus we can already compute all possible function values of H before the actual measurement. That means we get in dependence on $\lambda_1, \lambda_2, \ldots, \lambda_n$ a lookup table by storing the function values $H(\boldsymbol{a})$ for all $\boldsymbol{a} \in P$. By structuring this lookup table efficiently we can thereby compute the fringe numbers very fast and direct.

However, our stated theory only works with accurate measurements. But in real world measurement we always get errors through noise. This means that equation 9 is only approximately correct. Thus it holds

$$\Phi(u, v) \approx \boldsymbol{a}. \tag{13}$$

Independently of measuring errors we can compute all $\boldsymbol{a} \in P$ accurately. In order to be able to use our lookup table, we need an additional rule of assignment for mapping the measured values $\Phi(u, v)$ to the theoretical values $\boldsymbol{a} \in P$. For this, we define $\lambda_i \in \mathbb{N}$ to all $i = 1, 2, \ldots, n$. With the left side of equation 9 it leads to $P \subset \mathbb{Z}^n$, where $\mathbb{Z}$ is the set of all integers. For the additional rule we choose rounding from real numbers to integers.

Practically seen we first compute the real vector $\Phi(u, v) = \boldsymbol{a} \in \mathbb{R}^n$ according to equation 1 and 10, and afterwards we round its components with the following definition

$$b_i = \max\{\, x \mid x \in \mathbb{Z}, \, x < a_i + 0.5 \,\}. \tag{14}$$

Note, that by rounding implicitly a certain signal-to-noise ratio between the measured values is given. Measurement errors lower than signal-to-noise ratio do not have any relevance for the computation of the fringe numbers, since incorrect phase vectors are corrected due to rounding. But the efficiency of the signal-to-noise ratio depends on the number of pattern sequences and their periods λ_i.

We are now able to compute the unknown fringe number for each pattern sequence from measured phase values only. With equation 2 we get the appropriate projector coordinate. We define an average projector coordinate as unique value over all pattern sequences by

$$\xi(u, v) = \frac{1}{n} \sum_{i=1}^{n} \big(\eta_i(u, v) + \varphi_i(u, v)\big)\lambda_i. \tag{15}$$

Since the set T is completely present in the entries of the lookup table, we execute part of the computations needed in equation 15 beforehand. For this we define the map

$$E(h_1, h_2, \ldots, h_n) = \sum_{i=1}^{n} \lambda_i h_i \tag{16}$$

and transform equation 15 to

$$\xi(u, v) = \frac{1}{n}\, E\Big(H\big(\Phi_{\mathbb{Z}}(u, v)\big)\Big) \sum_{i=1}^{n} \lambda_i \varphi_i(u, v)\,. \tag{17}$$

Thereby we have to dynamically compute only the rear part of the equation. The entire front part can be stored as a static constant in the lookup table. This results in a very fast computation of projector coordinates.

4   Implementation and Results

Basis of the implementation of the represented theory is the generation of the lookup table. We take a $(n-1)$-dimensional array which is indexed by the components $a_2, a_3, \ldots, a_n$ of the phase difference vector $\boldsymbol{a}$. The reason for skiping the first component follows from equation 10, because $a_1 = 0$ always holds true. With $\varphi_i(u, v) \in [0, 1)$ the expansion of our array is limited in each dimension by the inequations

$$-\lambda_i < a_i < \lambda_1\,. \tag{18}$$

The memory usage of the lookup table amounts to $\prod_{i=2}^{n}(\lambda_i + \lambda_1 - 1)$. This is hardly a problem for small n and λ_i. For example $n = 4$ and $\lambda_i < 50$, we need not more than 4MB of memory. Based on the condition of equation 18 we can build up a scheme, that allows us to compute the array elements by using the inverse of the lookup table.

Real test measurements show that false computations can occur caused by measuring noise at the jumps of the phase value function. But this happens rarely. For the solution of the problem we shift virtually the phase value of all pattern sequences by a constant offset value. Thus the jumps shift accordingly with the effect that at the problematic point an error free computation can take place. An example is shown in figure 3.

Altogether the proposed method yields very good results. We accomplished a comparison with a method based on the combination of Gray code and phase shifting. For this we used a measurement setup with a projector and two cameras. For statistical physicals we used a plane as a well-known test object and computed the standard derivation of the measuring error in a volume of 0.3×0.3 m^2. For example by using 10 images for Gray code and 6 images for phase shift we get a standard derivation of 10.2 μm. Using all 16 images for phase shifting with three different pattern sequences we get 8.6 μm. The increase of the accuracy is naturally due to the equivalent use of all images and the average operation

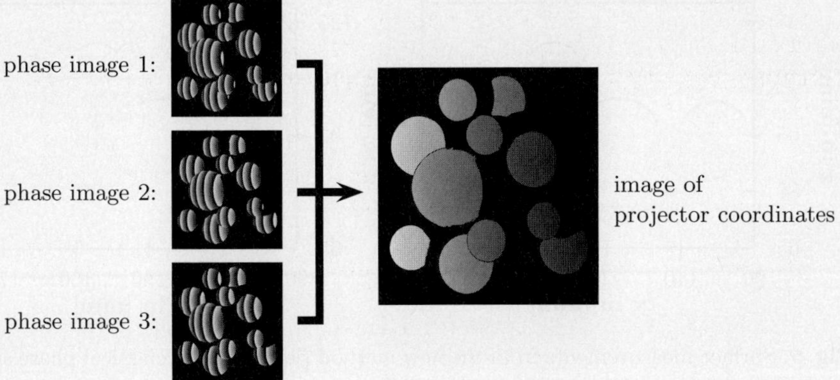

Fig. 3. Reconstruction of unambiguous measurements (projector coordinates) from three different pattern sequences

in equation 15. So, improvements in that range, we can confirm also for other objects and measurement setups.

The avoidance of typical phase shift errors is another advantage of the proposed technique. Discontinuities and reflections on the surface of the object normally lead to large deviations of the measured values and it is difficult to reduce errors like these automatically through mathematical methods. Using the lookup table in our method most of these bad phase values are not computed at all. This leads to a demarcation in the areas of discontinuity as shown in figure 3. The advantage of our method becomes obvious, if we compare our results of the 3d surface measurement with the results of the classical phases shifting without any error correction. As shown in figure 4 there are a lot of measurement errors in the surface computed by the classical method. Using a cut through the 3d sphere objects (outlined in left and right image) figure 5 represents the errors in more detail.

Even for tricky surfaces we get good results without any additional correction. Figure 6 shows on the right side the surface of a dolly and on the left side the three applied fringe patterns. Figure 7 represents the surface measurements of a

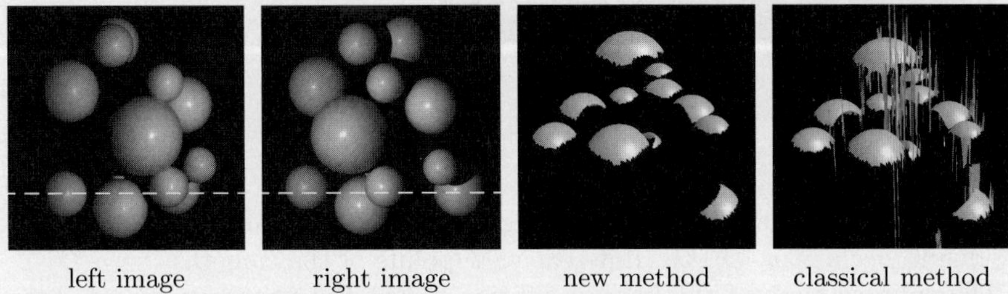

Fig. 4. 3d measuring results for the sphere objects

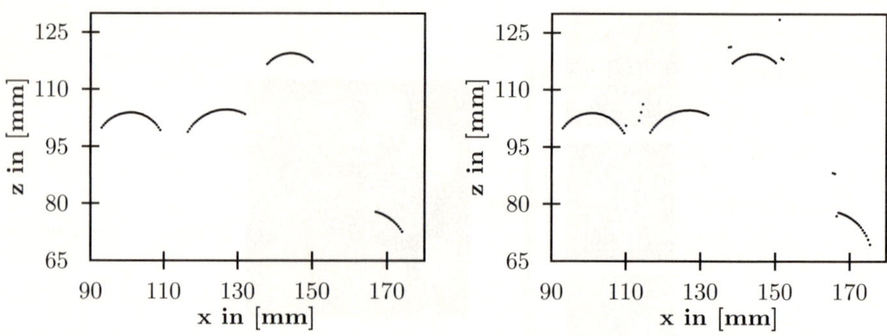

Fig. 5. Surface measurements from the new method (left) and the classical phase shifting (right) on a constant coordinate $y = 96.5$mm

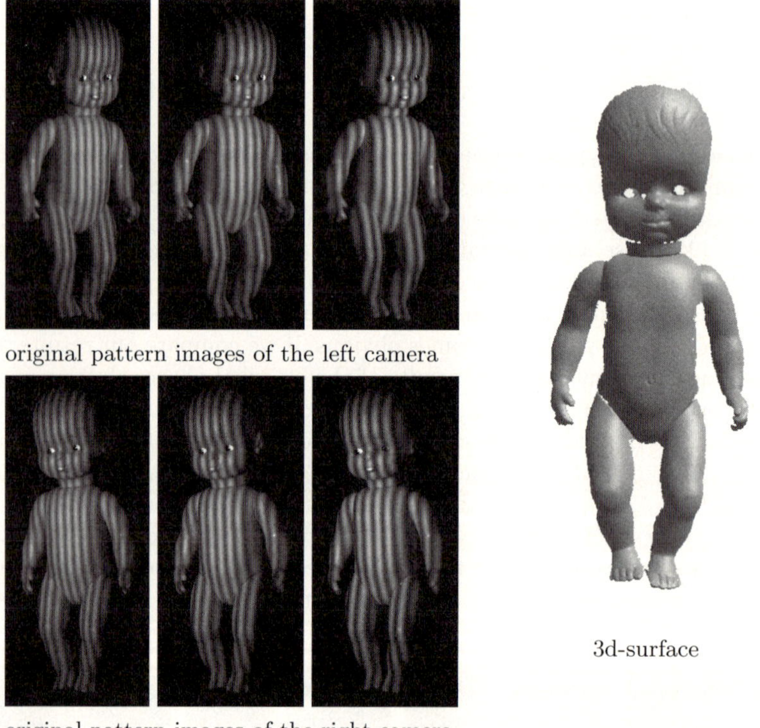

original pattern images of the left camera

3d-surface

original pattern images of the right camera

Fig. 6. Reconstruction of a dolly

regular monitor cable. The lack of surface points, both in figure 6 and in figure 7, are due to occlusions and the different view points of the cameras.

The running time of the implementation to get the unambiguous projector coordinates is very good. If n is the number of fringe patterns with different periods, than for each pixel one has to compute

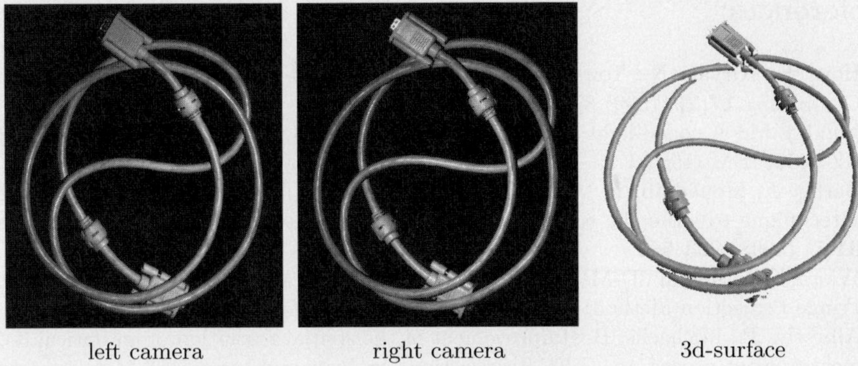

left camera   right camera   3d-surface

Fig. 7. Reconstruction of a regular monitor cable

- n phase values according to equation 1,
- $n - 1$ components of the phase difference vector according to equation 10,
- the summation of n addends according to equation 17
- and one access to the lookup table.

The operation to get the phase values (step 1) is the most expensive. It is the only one that depends on the number of images. However, all computations are linear. With a Pentium 4 standard PC the running time for computing projector coordinates using a one mega pixel camera and 24 images is less than one second. Thus, the time for compute the 3d surface is comparably to other implementations based on phase shifting.

5   Conclusion

The proposed method is an improvement over the classical phase shifting. By the use of several pattern sequences with different periods we get unambiguous measurements, which we call projector coordinates. Thereby, ambiguities in the solution of the correspondence problem are impossible. Thus no further information like approximate values or Gray code images are needed. The proposed method is very fast through the use of a lookup table and helps us to avoid systematic errors which are due to discontinuities and reflection points. By homogeneously using all images which were taken, the accuracy of a 3D measurement based on phase shifting can be increased.

Acknowledgements

This work was supported by LSA/Germany grants (FKZ: 3386A/0021B and XI3968A/0304D).

References

1. Horn, E., Kiryati, N.: Toward optimal structured light patterns. Image and Vision Computing **17**(2) (1999) 87–97
2. Wahl, F.M.: A coded light approach for 3dimensional (3d) vision. Technical Report RZ 1452, IBM (1984)
3. Batlle, J., Mouaddib, E., Salvi, J.: Recent progress in coded structured light as a technique to solve the correspondence problem: A survey. Pattern Recognition **31**(7) (1998) 963–982
4. Wiora, G.: Optical 3D-Metrology : Precise Shape Measurement with an extended Fringe Projection Method. PhD thesis, University Heidelberg (2001)
5. Albrecht, P., Michaelis, B.: Improvement of the spatial resolution of an optical 3-d measurement procedure. IEEE Transactions on Instrumentation and Measurement **47**(1) (1998) 158–162
6. Valkenburg, R.J., McIvor, A.M.: Accurate 3d measurement using a structured light system. Image and Vision Computing **16**(2) (1998) 99–110
7. Strutz, T.: Ein genaues aktives optisches Triangulationsverfahren zur Oberflächenvermessung. PhD thesis, University Magdeburg (1993)
8. Wolf, K.: Schnelle absolute 3D-Messung. 7. ABW-Workshop 3D-Bildverarbeitung, Technische Akademie Esslingen (2002)
9. Guan, C., Hassebrook, L., Lau, D.: Composite structured light pattern for three-dimensional video. Optics Express **11**(5) (2003) 406–417

Hybrid Techniques for Dynamic Optimization Problems

Demet Ayvaz[1], Haluk Topcuoglu[2], and Fikret Gurgen[1]

[1] Computer Engineering Department, Bogazici University,
Bebek, Istanbul, Turkey
{demet.ayvaz, gurgen}@boun.edu.tr
[2] Computer Engineering Department, Marmara University,
Goztepe, Istanbul, Turkey
haluk@eng.marmara.edu.tr

Abstract. In a stationary optimization problem, the fitness landscape does not change during the optimization process; and the goal of an optimization algorithm is to locate a stationary optimum. On the other hand, most of the real world problems are dynamic, and stochastically change over time. Genetic Algorithms have been applied to dynamic problems, recently. In this study, we present two hybrid techniques that are applied on moving peaks benchmark problem, where these techniques are the extensions of the leading methods in the literature. Based on the experimental study, it was observed that the hybrid methods outperform the related work with respect to quality of solutions for various parameters of the given benchmark problem.

1 Introduction

The fitness landscape change over time in dynamic environments, and the main goal in these environments is to track the global optimum. A set of evolutionary optimization techniques in dynamic environments have been proposed over the past few years, which have different design philosophies and characteristics. Researchers consider a set of syntactically-generated benchmarks [6] as well as benchmarks from real world problems [1,11] to measure the performance of their methods.

The problems in dynamic environments are not the same and the characteristics of the changes in an environment may generate different dynamic environments. Some of these characteristics are the frequency of change, the severity of change, the predictability of change, and the cycle length/cycle accuracy [4]. The frequency of change is a property defining how often an environment changes, which is the time for an algorithm to come up with a solution. The severity of change is the property defining the strength of changes in an environment. The predictability of change is a measure of correlation between successive changes. If there is a high correlation, it can be possible to predict next change when the past changes are given. Cycle accuracy/cycle length is the property defining the time for the optimum to return its previous location or a close location to old optimum.

A. Levi et al. (Eds.): ISCIS 2006, LNCS 4263, pp. 95–104, 2006.

The main motivation of this paper is to present hybrid techniques of leading algorithms in order to improve their performance. We propose two extensions of the leading methods. The first method hybridizes the self organizing scouts (SOS) [4,5] with local search technique by providing crossover hill-climbing [9] operator in place of simulated binary crossover operator. The second hybrid method combines multinational GA [10] with random immigrants method [7]. In our experimental study, a set of 13 leading evolutionary optimization techniques (including the two hybrid ones) from literature were implemented on a common platform and tested using the moving peaks benchmark.

The rest of this paper is organized as follows. In Section 2, we present the related work briefly, which is followed by details of hybrid methods given in Section 3. The experimental study is given in Section 4 which includes the performance metrics, the benchmark problem and results and discussions of the experiments. Finally, Section 5 concludes the paper.

2   Related Work

This section provides a classification of evolutionary optimization techniques that deal with dynamic environments. Additionally, algorithms that are part of the experimental study are briefly explained. Evolutionary optimization techniques can be broadly classified in three categories: (a) approaches for maintaining diversity throughout the run, (b) memory based approaches, and (c) multi-population approaches.

2.1   Approaches for Maintaining Diversity Throughout the Run

Random immigrants (RI) method [7] starts as a standard evolutionary algorithm. At each generation, random individuals are created and a fraction of the main population is replaced by these random individuals. Different replacement methodologies can be considered. The algorithm considered in [4] replaces the worst individuals in the population; and by this way, it maintains diversity throughout the execution.

Another evolutionary algorithm [4] (called P3 in the results) divides the population into three independent sub-populations of equal size. Each population explores the search space independently; and only the members of the same sub-population are allowed to recombine. Migration between sub-populations is not allowed in order to maintain high diversity.

The niching technique [12] uses the crowding selection and a replacement schema. The crowding selection chooses the second parent according to the similarity to the first parent. First, an individual from the population is selected; then a small group of individuals are selected from the population randomly. The individual which is the most similar to the first mate with respect to Euclidean distance is selected as the second mate. After recombination and mutation, the generated offspring replaces one of the old individuals according to the given replacement schema.

2.2   Memory-Based Approaches

The first algorithm in this group (called SEAm) [4] starts as a standard evolutionary algorithm; and at every xth generation, the best of population is written into the memory. Whenever memory becomes full, a memory replacement strategy is used. For this work, *mindist* strategy is applied as a replacement strategy. According to mindist strategy, the most similar two old solutions are selected from the memory, and the worst one is replaced by the entering solution only if the new solution is better than the old one. Whenever there is a change in environment, the main population and memory are merged; and the best n individuals are selected to form main population.

In RIm [4] algorithm, the random immigrants method is supported with an extra memory; and due to memory support, it is listed under the memory-based approaches. At every xth generation, the best individual is written into memory. In case of memory becoming full, mindist strategy is used for memory replacement.

This method (called P3m) [4] is the extended version of P3 with the addition of memory. At every xth generation, the best of all three populations is written into memory. As in the previous techniques, mindist strategy is considered for memory replacement. Whenever environment changes, one of the populations and the memory are merged and the best n individuals are selected to form new population.

Memory/Search algorithm [3,4] divides the population into two subpopulations, which are memory population and search population. At every xth generation, the best of two populations is written into memory; and whenever memory becomes full, mindist strategy is applied. In case of a change in the environment, the memory population and the memory are merged and the best n individuals are selected to form the memory population. The search population is reinitialized in order to increase diversity. A variant of this algorithm, Memory/2search algorithm uses two search populations instead of one. Its working procedure is the same as in the memory/search algorithm.

2.3   Multi-population Approaches

Self organizing scouts (SOS) [4,5] algorithm divides base population and the search space to find multiple optima in the search space. In each forking generation the base population is analyzed to check whether the forking conditions are satisfied. If that is the case, a small fraction of base population (scout population) is split from the base population and assigned to watch a small region which is thought to be a peak. Whenever a new scout is created, the base population is reinitialized. The scout populations may also move as new and better solutions are found by the scout. The sizes of the scout and base population are not fixed. At each forking generation the total number of individuals is divided between base and scout populations according to their quality. The quality of a scout is the linear sum of its relative fitness and relative dynamism.

The multinational GA (Multi-National) algorithm [10] considers the whole population as the world consisting of nations. Each nation is a subpopulation and it has a government, a policy and a population. The algorithm starts with a single nation and all members of the world are assumed to be from this single nation. The government of a nation are the best g members of the nation, where g is usually taken to be 8. At each generation each individual is first compared to its nations policy to detect if there is a valley between this member and its nation. If that is the case, this member migrates to another nation or it forms a totally new nation. Recombination is done on global and national level. For national recombination only the members of the same nation are recombined, while in global recombination any member in the population can be recombined. Distance to policy based mutation is applied after recombination. The idea of this operator is to mutate individuals according to their distance to policy.

3   Proposed Hybrid Techniques

In our first hybrid method (called SOS+LS algorithm), we propose a hybrid solution with the aim of improving the performance of SOS [4,5] method with local search based on crossover hill-climbing. Self organizing scouts algorithm splits the main population into base and scout populations which are responsible for exploration and exploitation, respectively. The scouts are isolated and recombination is only allowed for the members of the same scout. The low number of individuals in the scout population may degrade the exploitation capability of scout population. Moreover the number of individuals that a scout will own in the next generation is determined by the linear sum of the fitness and dynamism of the scout. If a scout population does not explore its search space effectively, this directly affects the division of population between scouts for the next generation. As a result of this degradation, a dynamic and promising area may seem less promising and lose its members in successive generations. To solve this problem, a way to increase the explorative power of a small population is needed. In this approach we support the scout population with a local search algorithm to increase its exploitation capability.

For each scout population the mates for recombination are selected with rank based selection. Instead of using simulated binary crossover as in SOS method, this algorithm uses crossover hill-climbing operator [9] to generate offsprings. The cross-over hill-climbing operator (given in Figure 1) is a genetic operator which uses hill-climbing as a move accepting criterion and uses crossover as a move operator. For each pair, crossover is applied for five times to create ten offsprings. The best of these offsprings replaces the worst parent. Then recombination is applied again to these new parents to create new offsprings. Again the worst parent is replaced and the resulting parents are returned as generated offsprings.

In our second hybrid method (called MN+RI algorithm), we consider the combination of multinational GA and the random immigrants method. This type of combination is considered in order to increase the area that multi-national GA algorithm searches. The hill-valley detection procedure used in this algorithm, takes two points and decides if the two points are on the same peak or there is a valley in between them so that they are on separate peaks. As a result, the performance of this algorithm strongly depends on the initial population.

Crossover Hill-Climbing(p_1, p_2, n_{off}, n_t)

1. $p_1' = p_1$ and $p_2' = p_2$

2. **Repeat** n_t times

3.   Generate n_{off} offspring $o_1, o_2, ...o_{n_{off}}$ by performing crossover on p_1' and p_2'

4.   Evaluate the fitness of $o_1, o_2, ...o_{n_{off}}$.

5.   Select the offspring o_{best} which has the best fitness value.

6.   Replace the worst of p_1' and p_2' with o_{best}, only if it is better.

7. **Return** p_1' and p_2'.

Fig. 1. Pseudocode for Crossover Hill-Climbing [9]

If the initial population only covers a small part of the whole search space, the algorithm only finds the peaks and valleys in this area. It can not direct the search to the other areas of the search space. Even if the initial population covers the whole search space, it can converge around a few promising peaks and can not find new peaks if they appear as a result of dynamism. By inserting random immigrants to the multinational GA algorithm, the diversity is kept high and search is directed to some unexplored areas in the search space. At each generation, if the total number of nations is lower than a predefined number, a fraction of the population is replaced by randomly generated individuals.

4   Experimental Study

4.1   Comparison Metrics

In order to compare the performance of algorithms we consider *offline error* metric, which is based on offline performance proposed by De Jong [8]. Since the optimum value of moving peaks benchmark is known at any point in time, offline error is used instead of offline performance in our experiments. Offline error is the running average of the difference between the best individual encountered so far and the optimum at any time. The formulation for offline error is as follows [4]:

$$E(T) = \frac{1}{T} \times \sum_{t=1}^{T} (opt_t - e_t') \tag{1}$$

$$e_t' = \max(e_\tau, e_{\tau+1}, ..., e_t) \tag{2}$$

In this formula τ is the time of last change. While calculating the offline error, only the evaluations made after the last change are considered. T is the total number of generations, opt_t is the optimal value at generation t, and e_t' is the best so far value obtained up to generation t.

4.2   Moving Peaks Benchmark

Moving peaks benchmark is considered for performance evaluation of the algorithms, which is a multimodal landscape consisting of peaks with changing heights, widths and locations in an n dimensional search space. In this work, we used the problem generator suggested by Branke [4] where the fitness landscape is formulated as follows :

$$F(\boldsymbol{x}, t) = \max(B(\boldsymbol{x}), \max_{i=1,\ldots,m} (P(\boldsymbol{x}, h_i(t), w_i(t), p_i(t)))) \tag{3}$$

In this formulation, $\boldsymbol{x}$ is a vector and $B(x)$ is the base function which is not dependent on time. The problem has m peaks and each of these peaks have its own time dependent height (h), width (w) and location (p) parameters.

There are several other parameters that define the characteristics of this dynamic problem. The height severity, the width severity and the shift length are the parameters defining the severity of changes in height, width and location of changes, respectively. The Δe is the parameter defining the number of generations before the environment changes, which is used for controlling frequency of changes. The λ is the parameter defining the correlation between successive moves of a peak. For $\lambda = 0$, peaks move in random ways without any correlation; for $\lambda = 1$, peaks move in linear directions. In this paper, our selected problem consists of 10 peaks in a 5 dimensional search space. The lower bound and the upper bound for each dimension is 0 and 100 respectively; and changes are applied at every 50 generations. The successive movements are not correlated. λ is taken to be zero and the peaks make random movement. The shift length is 1, height severity is 7 and width severity is 1. These values are considered in all experiments, unless otherwise stated.

4.3 Experimental Results

In our experiments, a population of 100 individuals is considered for each algorithm. The results presented in this section are the averages of 20 runs, where each run is performed with a different random seed to create different instances of the same problem. Real-valued representation and generational replacement with elitism of 1 is considered. Unless otherwise stated, two-point simulated binary cross-over and Gaussian random mutation is applied. The crossover probability is taken 0.6 and the mutation rate is set to 0.2. For memory supported algorithms, the memory size has been set to 10. The random immigrants (RI) and the random immigrants with memory (RIm) algorithms replace 25 percent of the individuals at each generation. The values of other algorithm-specific parameters are set with their original values presented in corresponding papers.

Selected parameters of the moving peaks benchmark are varied to provide different test cases or experiments. Specifically, influences of severity of change, frequency of change and correlation on performance of algorithms are presented in this section. It should be noted that results in the tables are grouped according to the classification of the algorithms. In addition to the algorithms mentioned in this paper, tables also include results of the SEA algorithm, which is the simple evolutionary algorithm.

Influence of Severity of Change. This experiment presents the effect of severity of change on the performance of different algorithms by changing the

shift length values. Shift length is the norm of the vectors that will be added to
the peak location; and a shift length of 1 means that each peak moves by one
unit at each change. Shift length values considered in our test cases are 1, 2 and
3. Table 1.(a) shows the offline errors of algorithms for different shift lengths.
As shift length increases, the performance of all algorithms degrades and offline
errors increase. As shift length increases, the degree of similarity between the
environments before and after a change decreases and the exploitable information
level decreases.

Table 1. Offline error values (a) for various shift lengths, and (b) for various change
frequencies

Algorithms	Shift Length		
	1.0	2.0	3.0
SEA	17,008	18,154	18,319
RI	11,07	11,89	12,058
P3	11,945	12,744	14,056
Niching	6,334	7,179	7,308
SEAm	17,236	18,2	18,714
RIm	13,193	13,626	14,008
P3m	12,398	13,196	14,911
Mem/Search	7,383	8,785	9,789
Mem/2Search	7,492	9,075	10,95
SOS	4,34	5,042	5,908
Multi-National	5,973	5,894	5,949
SOS+LS	**3,413**	**4,091**	**4,488**
MN+RI	4,337	5,052	5,242

Algorithms	Change Frequency		
	10	25	50
SEA	19,565	18,148	17,008
RI	15,568	13,027	11,07
P3	14,84	12,256	11,945
Niching	8,551	7,417	6,334
SEAm	18,646	18,175	17,236
RIm	15,043	13,716	13,193
P3m	14,43	12,838	12,398
Mem/Search	14,991	9,561	7,383
Mem/2Search	16,027	10,776	7,492
SOS	6,117	5,137	4,34
Multi-National	7,868	5,664	5,973
SOS+LS	**4,897**	**3,983**	**3,413**
MN+RI	5,329	4,628	4,337

All approaches which use a simple memory performs worse than their standard
approaches without memory and the difference increases as shift length increases.
That is because while peaks move, the memory becomes more useless. Since these
approaches reserve some part of the population to memory and can not use it effectively, they have worse performance than others. Mem/Search outperforms all
other algorithms except the multinational ones and the Niching algorithm. But as
the environment changes, memory/search is affected more than the others since
memory becomes less useful. When Memory/2Search is considered, the results
show that one search population is enough; therefore, the extra search population does not make any improvement. Niching algorithm performs better than all
memory based approaches since it uses crowding selection and a special replacement schema to maintain high diversity. It is better than Memory/Search while
exploring search space and not affected severely by the increase of shift length.

Multi-population approaches are much more efficient than others and they are
less affected from the change in severity since they are capable of detecting and
tracking multiple optima. The least affected algorithm is the multinational GA
because of using hill-valley detection. This clustering algorithm is able to predict
locations of peaks and valleys even if they move severely. The drawback of this
algorithm is that its performance strongly depends on the initial solutions. The

hybrid algorithm of multinational GA and random immigrants perform better than multinational GA since random immigrants makes this algorithm explore more unexplored regions and increase diversity. But it is more affected by the change in severity. SOS+LS gives the best results since it increases the search capacity of scout populations with a local search technique.

Influence of Frequency of Change. The second experiment aims to see the effect of frequency of change for different algorithms. For this purpose, algorithms are run in environments which change at every 10, 25 or 50 generations. As the frequency of changes increases, each algorithm has a shorter time to come up with a solution and the offline error increases for all algorithms (see Table 1.(b)).

The most heavily affected algorithms are the memory based ones, since the memorized individuals will not be good solutions after a short time and the memory becomes less useful as the environment changes more quickly. Diversity maintaining algorithms are less affected from the quick changes since they have high diversity and may explore for the new optimum more effectively. However, they also degrade in performance since they have less time to find an optimum solution before it changes. The least affected algorithms are the multi-population approaches. They are also degraded but not as much as other algorithms. Multi-population approaches divide the population to track the changes in all promising regions. Even if the environment changes more quickly, those algorithms still can detect and track changes in those promising areas. However they have also less time to climb the hills. As a result they can not find as good solutions as they find when changes are less frequent. As a consequence, their performance also degrades with the increase in frequency of change. The best performing algorithm is the SOS+LS algorithm because of employing a local search algorithm. The hybrid algorithm of multinational GA and random immigrants (MN+RI) performs better than the multinational GA; and the MN+RI algorithm is the least affected algorithm with respect to frequency of change, which can be due to insertion of immigrants. It takes an explicit action to increase diversity during optimization. These immigrants increase the adaptability of the algorithm as the environment changes.

Influence of Correlation. This experiment shows the effect of correlation between successive changes for different algorithms. In our previous experiments, we set λ to 0 and deal with peaks moving in random direction. In such a situation, peaks move around their initial locations. If λ is set to 1, each peak moves along a line. Different test cases are generated by changing the value of λ to see the effect of change predictability for different algorithms. In this experiment, λ values used are 0, 0.5 and 1.

Table 2 shows offline errors of different approaches for different λ values. The algorithms that maintain diversity throughout the run and multi-population approaches does not feel the effect of changes in correlation much. Only small changes occur when compared to memory based approaches, which is due to the memorization process. If peaks move around their initial conditions, the memorized solutions become more useful. Otherwise peaks move along and the old solutions in memory become useless and degrade the performance of algorithms.

Table 2. Offline error values of approaches for different correlation values

Algorithms	Correlation Value		
	0.0	0.5	1.0
SEA	17,008	17,24	17,412
RI	11,07	11,507	11,595
P3	11,945	12,825	13,291
Niching	6,334	6,662	6,812
SEAm	17,236	18,157	18,588
RIm	13,193	13,663	13,963
P3m	12,398	13,423	13,557
Mem/Search	7,383	8,59	9,888
Mem/2Search	7,492	8,97	10,137
SOS	4,34	4,54	4,563
Multi-National	5,973	5,772	5,661
SOS+LS	3,413	3,625	3,535
MN+RI	4,337	4,28	4,377

All multi-population approaches are nearly not affected and all diversity maintaining algorithms are slightly affected. The SOS+LS algorithm outperforms other methods considered in the experiments.

5   Conclusions

In this paper, we proposed two new techniques, which were constructed by hybridizing several leading approaches. The first one is the hybridization of self organizing scouts with local search provided by crossover hill climbing method, which is called SOS+LS algorithm in this paper. The second one is the combination of multinational GA method with random immigrants method, which is called MN+RI algorithm. The SOS+LS algorithm significantly outperforms the other 12 algorithms with respect to various problem parameters including severity of change, frequency of change, predictability of change and the problem complexity.

When the running time of the algorithms are considered, memory supported approaches work faster than the versions without memory, since memory is separated from the main population. All multi-population algorithms including the hybrid methods require more time than other methods except the niching algorithm. Even though niching algorithm makes less number of evaluations than SOS+LS and MN+RI, it has the highest time overhead since it uses the crowding selection and a special replacement schema.

References

1. C. Bierwirth and H. Copher, Dynamic task scheduling with genetic algorithms in manufacturing systems, Technical report, Department of Economics , University of Bremen, Germany, 1994.

2. J. Branke, Evolutionary Algorithms for dynamic optimization problems a survey, Technical Report 387, Institute AIFB, University of Kalsruhe, February 1999.
3. J. Branke, *Memory enhanced evolutionary algorithms for changing optimization problems*, In Congress on Evolutionary Computation, volume 3, pages 1875-1882, IEEE, 1999.
4. J. Branke, Evolutionary Optimization in Dynamic Environments, Kluwer, 2001.
5. J. Branke, T. Kauler, C. Schmidt, and H. Schmeck. *Multi-population approach to dynamic optimization problems*, In Adaptive Computing in Design and Manufacture - ACDM 2000, pages 299-308, Berlin, 2000, Springer Verlag.
6. J. Branke, E. Salihoglu, S. Uyar, *Towards an analysis of dynamic environments*, Proceedings of the Genetic and Evolutionary Computation Conference-GECCO-2005, pages 1433-1440, 2005.
7. J.J. Gerfenstette, *Genetic algorithms for changing environments*, Parallel Problem Solving From Nature 2, pages 137-144. North Holland, 1992.
8. K. De Jong, An analysis of the behavior of a class of genetic adaptive systems, PhD thesis, University of Michigan, Ann Arbor MI, 1975.
9. M. Lozano, F. Herrera, N. Krasnogor, and D. Molina, *Real-coded memetic algorithms with crossover hill-climbing*, Evolutionary Computation, vol. 12, no. 3, pp. 273302, 2004
10. Rasmus K. Ursem. Multinational GAs, *Multimodal optimization techniques in dynamic environments*, Proceedings of the Genetic and Evolutionary Computation Conference (GECCO-2000), Las Vegas, USA, 2000.
11. S. C. Lin, E. D. Goodman and W.F. Punch, *A genetic algorithm approach to dynamic job shop scheduling problems*, Seventh International Conference on Genetic Algorithms, pages 481-488, 1997.
12. W. Cedeno and V. R. Vemuri, *On the use of niching for dynamic landscapes*, In Intl. Conf. on Evolutionary Computation, IEEE, 1997.

Minimizing the Search Space for Shape Retrieval Algorithms

M. Abdullah-Al-Wadud and Oksam Chae[*]

Department of Computer Engineering, Graduate School of Kyung Hee University,
1 Seochun-ri, Kiheung-eup, Yongin-si, Kyunggi-do, Korea, 446-701
awsujon@yahoo.com, oschae@khu.ac.kr

Abstract. To provide satisfactory accuracy and flexibility, most of the existing shape retrieval methods make use of different alignments and translations of the objects that introduce much computational complexity. The most computationally expensive part of these algorithms is measuring the degree of match (or mismatch) of the query object with the objects stored in database. In this paper, we present an approach to cut down a large portion of this search space (number of objects in database) that retrieval algorithms need to take into account. This method is applicable in clustering based approaches also. Moreover, this minimization is done keeping the accuracy of the retrieval algorithms intact and its efficiency is not severely affected in high dimensionalities.

1 Introduction

To meet the need of the user or application, a shape retrieval method should have two properties: sufficiently high accuracy and speed. Some recent methods have employed complex shape matchers to gain high accuracy, making the system slower because of the relatively high pair-wise matching times. Some well-known methods include feature based methods (compare vectors of shape measurements such as circularity, eccentricity, and moments [3]), structural methods (represent shapes as parts and relationships using graphs, trees, or strings [4-7]), structural indexing methods (use shape parts to index objects [8, 9]), transform methods (match shapes represented in alternative domains; for example, by wavelet coefficients[10] or scale-space images [11]) and direct (often called correspondence or alignment) methods (represent shapes in their original form as spatial data, bring them into alignment, and then measure residual differences between them [16]).

Most of the earlier methods try to match the query shape with almost all the shapes in database. It is a straightforward approach with high accuracy, but the need of iterating the matching algorithm for each shape slows down the whole retrieval process. For this reason, many researchers have made approaches to reduce the number of shapes that have to be matched. [21] provides a free parameter that allows search accuracy to be reduced, thereby providing a substantially better speed-up versus accuracy tradeoff.

---

[*] Corresponding author.

A. Levi et al. (Eds.): ISCIS 2006, LNCS 4263, pp. 105 – 114, 2006.

Bottom-up methods, also called clustering methods, aim at identifying clusters embedded in data in order to reduce the search to clusters that potentially contain the nearest neighbor of the query [18-20]. Then the shape matcher is applied on the shapes of the identified cluster. Although these methods generally work well for low-dimensional spaces, their performance is known to degrade as the number of dimensions increases [17]. This phenomenon has been termed the *dimensional curse*. These methods are outperformed by a sequential scan whenever the dimensionality is above 10 [12].

A method is presented in [13] and [14] for block based motion estimation. The same method can be applied in shape matching by considering shapes instead of blocks. It applies matching algorithm only on those shapes/blocks that satisfy the triangular constraint. This gives a very good reduction in database shapes to be considered and as it uses the triangular constraint, it does not degrade the accuracy.

In this paper, we propose a method that relieves shape retrieval methods from matching the query shape with a huge number of database shapes. This paper has made use of a spherical constraint, triangular constraint and an ordering theorem to reduce the number of database shapes necessary to be taken into account. These constraints and theorem always assure the accuracy of the shape matcher. Our proposed algorithm also works on the clustering approach. It helps to exclude a number of shapes in the cluster from consideration of the shape matcher, hence speeds up the whole process. Moreover, the performance of the method does not degrade much in higher dimensional data sets.

The rest of the paper continues as follows: Section 2 covers some geometrical preliminaries, Section 3 presents the background of the paper, then our proposed method is described in detail in Section 4 and Section 5 reports the results to illustrate the performance. The paper concludes in Section 6 with a summary and some directions to make use of this method efficiently.

2 Geometrical Preliminaries

In this section, we present some preliminaries on Euclidian distances among points in Euclidian space. These include spherical constraint, triangle inequality, triangular constraint [1, 13, 14] and ordering theorem [2]. These constraints and the theorem can be extended to vector space, where the points may be regarded as position vectors and the distance may represent the magnitude of the vector connecting the heads of two position vectors. They can also be used in suitable shape spaces where the distances may represent the degree of dissimilarities among shapes.

2.1 Spherical Constraint

Suppose that P and Q are two points in the Euclidian space with Euclidian distance $PQ = r$. Let S_Q and S_P be the sets of all points contained in the sphere centered at Q and P with radii r and $2r$, respectively. Then from Fig. 1, it is clear that

$$\forall X \in S_Q \Rightarrow X \in S_P \text{ and } \exists X \notin S_P \Rightarrow X \notin S_Q . \tag{1}$$

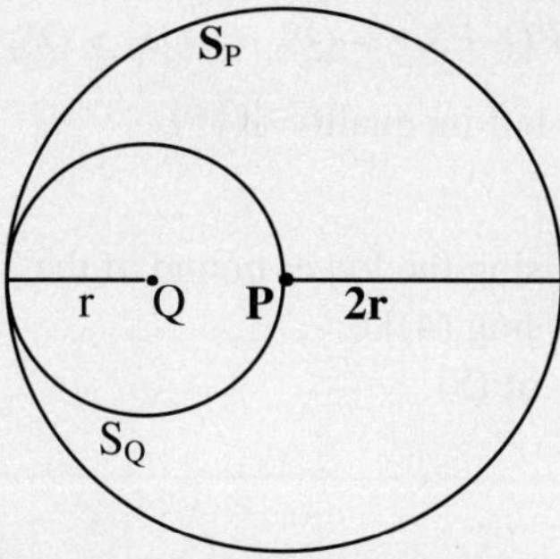

Fig. 1. Spherical Constraint. The center and radius of sphere S_Q are Q and r respectively while these are P and $2r$ for Sphere S_P

2.2 Triangle Inequality

If MN denotes the Euclidian distance between two points M and N, *then* a mathematical statement of triangle inequality applied to ΔPQY in Fig. 2 is

$$|PQ - PY| \leq QY \leq PQ + PY. \tag{2}$$

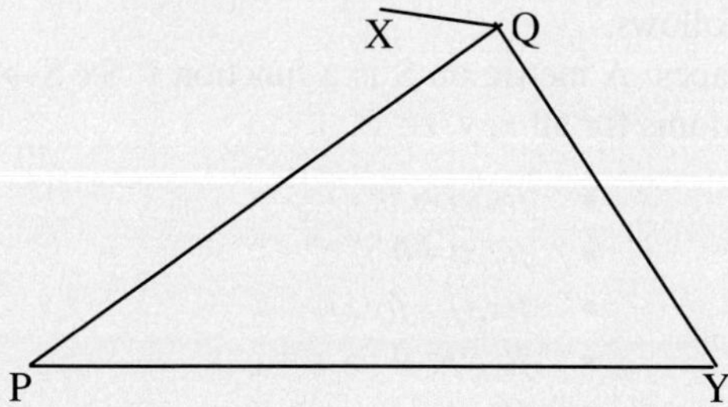

Fig. 2. Triangle Inequality and Triangular Constraint

2.3 Triangular Constraint

$$|PQ - PY| > QX \Rightarrow QY > QX. \tag{3}$$

Proof: Reversing the left inequality of (2), we get $QY \geq |PQ - PY|$. Substituting this in the left inequality of (3) gives its right inequality.

2.4 Ordering Theorem

For a point P, let S be a set of points such that,

$$S_0 = P \text{ and } S = \{S_i \mid i < j \Leftrightarrow PS_i \leq PS_j\}$$

where, S_i denotes the ith point in the set.   (4)

For any arbitrary point Q and $\forall \, k \geq j,$

$$|PQ\text{–}PS_j| > QS_i \Rightarrow QS_k > QS_i.$$ (5)

Proof: We proceed from the left inequality of (5).

$\quad |PQ\text{–}PS_j| > QS_i.$

$\Rightarrow \quad PS_j > QS_i.$ [Using the lower bound of the Triangle Inequality]

$\Rightarrow \quad PS_k > QS_i.$ [Using (4)]

$\Rightarrow \quad$ The right inequality of (5).

3 Background

Many shape retrieval algorithms calculate the similarity (or dissimilarity) between the features or contents of query shape and those of each shape in database. The most similar shape is retrieved finally. In a reverse procedure, we can think that the least dissimilar shape is retrieved. The straightforward retrieval method is that the query shape is matched or compared with each database shape and a degree of dissimilarity, dissimilarity index (DI), is calculated. Finally the shape with least DI is said to have the closest match with the query.

A number of similarity measures proposed in the literature explain similarity (or, more properly, dissimilarity) as a distance in some suitable feature space that is assumed to be a metric space [15]. It is preferable that dissimilarity measures satisfy the metric axioms [15] as follows.

Let S be a set of shapes. A metric on S is a function f: $S\times S \rightarrow \Re$, which satisfies the following metric axioms for all x, y, z$\in$ S.

- $f(x,y) \geq 0.$
- $f(x,x) = 0.$
- $f(x,y) = f(y,x).$
- $f(x,y) = 0 \Rightarrow x = y.$
- $f(x,y) + f(x,z) \geq f(y,z).$

Throughout this paper, we have used DI as a function for quantifying the dissimilarity between two shapes. It takes two shapes and outputs a real number that reflects the degree of dissimilarity between them. Hence DI is certainly a metric according to the abovementioned axioms.

In this paper we have extended the constraints and the theorem of previous section to shape space, where the points represent the shapes and DIs act as distances. Using these constraints we can throw out some of database shapes from further consideration in shape matcher. Thus it can help in speeding up shape retrieval applications.

The main problem in clustering based approaches in higher dimensionalities is that the number of partitions grows exponentially with dimension and the Nearst-Neighbor-Distances are expected to be large. Thus shapes are widely scattered and so the probability of being able to identify a good partitioning of the data space diminishes [12]. In our method, more shapes are included as the distances (DI) increases. So the efficiency become less. But for the same reason some shapes also fail to satisfy the constraints. This results in a reduction of number of shapes to be considered and the performance remains a good one as a whole.

The attractive feature here is that, to calculate the DIs, one can use any earlier shape matcher to measure shape similarities or dissimilarities and represent different DIs with different real values (that is the lower the DI, the higher is the similarity). If the algorithm measures the dissimilarity (Euclidean distance, for example, between points in a suitable feature space), then the proposed method can be applied directly. Otherwise if the shape matcher measures the similarity between two shapes, then the similarities, as real values, can be represented as similarity indices (SI). After that Sis can be subtracted from a sufficiently large value to get corresponding DIs and then the proposed method can be applied to get a minimized search space.

4   The Proposed Method

Our proposed algorithm works in two phases: preprocessing (offline) phase and retrieval (online) phase.

4.1   Preprocessing Phase

The preprocessing phase is done once as an initialization step and at the time of adding a new shape to the database. In this phase, a table or list is created for each shape, P, as follows

$$T_p = \{(d, j) \mid d = DI(j, p) \text{ and } j < k \Leftrightarrow DI(j, p) \leq DI(k, p)\}.$$

Thus in T_p all shapes are stored in non-decreasing order according to their DIs with shape p. In later sections, sometimes we have used $T_{i,j}(d)$ to denote $DI(i, j)$ that is stored in table Ti.

For n shapes in the database, here the space complexity $O(n^2)$ to store the tables, and the time complexity is $O(n^2 log n)$ for sorting the tables and $O(n^2 g(i,j))$ where $g(i,j)$ is the complexity of the shape matching algorithm for performing each matching.

It is, of course, very much time consuming and requires much memory to store the tables. But as it is done offline, it does not degrade the speed of retrieval process. Moreover, in retrieval phase only one table will be needed at a time. So, to get rid of using a huge memory for the tables, loading only the active table is sufficient for smooth running of applications. With the cost of memory and this preprocessing step, we can have a very fast retrieval phase.

4.2   Retrieval Phase

The algorithm for retrieval phase is given in Fig. 3. In statement 3 we have applied the spherical constraint on table T_S. Here it takes only the shapes that fall in the larger sphere of Fig.1 and excludes rest of the shapes. Thus it narrows down the scope. Here more shapes can be eliminated from consideration by applying the triangular constraint as it is done in [13] and [14]. Statement 4 is done implicitly by taking the elements sequentially from T_S as it was sorted in the preprocessing phase. It does not impose any extra cost here. After this, only the shapes in Y are taken into account further in procedure "Closest" given in Fig. 4.

Retrive(*q*)   /* *q is the query shape* */
1. Randomly choose a shape *s* from database.
2. *r = DI(q, s)*.
3. Make a list *Y(d, i)* from table T_S such that $T_{s,i}(d) < 2r$.
4. Sort *Y* in ascending order according to *d*.
5. Return *Closest(Y, s, r)*.

Fig. 3. The algorithm for the Retrieval phase

Closest (Y, s, r)
/* *This function returns the closest match* */
/* *So far s is having the minimum DI, r, with q* */

1. If $|V| = 1$ /* *There is only one item in V* */
          Then *return the only element in V*
2. Find an entry *(d, i)* in Y such that $x = DI(i, q) < r$
3. If *no such shape found* then *return s*

/* *Now make a new list V(d, j) = Y $\cap$ T$_i$ satisfying the constraints* */
4. For each shape, *j*, in T_i /* *Sequential scan* */
          a. If $j \notin Y$ or $j = s$ /* *No need to consider* */
                Then *Check the next shape*
          b. If $T_{i,j}(d) > 2x$ /* *Spherical constraint violated* */
                Then *go to step 5*   /* *No need to consider any other shape* */
          c. If $| Y_{s,j}(d) - r| \leq x$ and $|T_{i,j}(d) - x| \leq r$ /**Triangular constraint* */
                    Then *add (d, j) from T$_i$ to V*
          Else   /**Triangular constraint violated* */
                    If $|T_{i,j}(d) - x| > r$ /* *Ordering theorem satisfied* */
                          Then *go to step 5*
5. *Return* Closest *(V, i, x)*

Fig. 4. Function: *Closest (Y, s, r)*

In "Closest" at first a shape *i* is found from *Y* such that similarity between *i* and *q* is more than similarity between *s* and *q*. Then a list *V(d, j)* is created with the shapes from $T_i \cap Y$ that satisfy the spherical constraint. Fig. 5 shows a pictorial view of the creation of *V*. The scope is further narrowed down using the triangular constraint. At the time of forming *V*, if any shape *j* of T_i satisfies the ordering theorem then no further shape is needed to be considered from that table. Then in the following iterations of the recursive "Closest" procedure, only the shapes in *V* are considered. This helps the retrival to speed up confidently.

Here the worst case may occur when the initial shape, *s*, is very much dissimilar to the query shape. In this case the large value of *r*, in Fig. 3, forces the method to

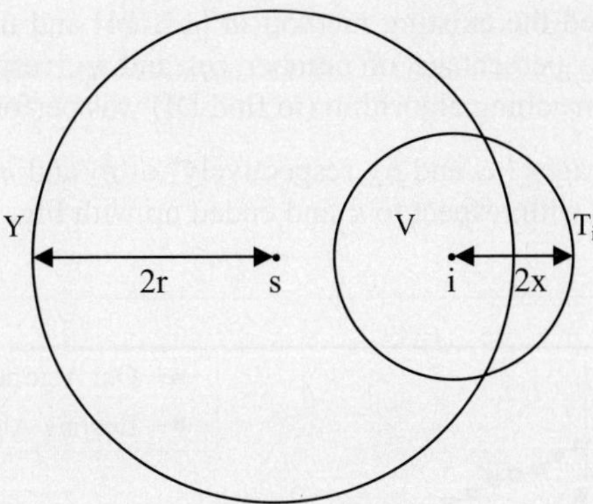

Fig. 5. Search space reduction using spherical constraint. Larger sphere (Y), centered at s, has radius $2r$ while the radius of the smaller one (T_i), centered at i, is $2x$. For next iteration (V), only the points in there intersection are needed to be checked.

consider more shapes. But even then, with the iterations of "Closest", the list Y gets shrinked quickly that improves the performance of the algorithm.

An improvement in "Closest". The proposed method is further improved by modifying the procedure "Closest". Here the key concepts are —

    (a) In Y the first shape is s where $DI(s, q)=r$, and $DI(s, s)= 0$.
    (b) For the last shape l in Y, we may expect $DI(s, l)$ to be almost $2r$.
    (c) Having (a) and (b), for shapes at the middle of Y, say m, we can expect —
        i. $DI\,(m, s)$ to be approximately r, and
        ii. $DI\,(m, q)$ to be less than $DI\,(s, q)$.

Bearing these in mind, step 2 of "Closest" can start from the middle shape of Y and continue to test the shapes in Y in both direction from the middle. This helps to find a shape with $x < r$ in less effort. Moreover here x is expected to be smaller than x that might be found in sequencial search. So the smaller value of x puts more constraint on the shapes to be selected for the next iteration of "Closest". And thus it helps V as well as Y to reduce in size rapidly and thereby speeds up the retrieval process.

5   Experimental Results

For simplicity of analysis, we represented the shapes as position vectors. Instead of using complex shape matching algorithms, we considered the distance between the heads of two position vectors as DI to denote the dissimilarity of two shapes. We generated the databases of shapes of various sizes (ranging from 10 to 1000). We did the following jobs iteratively 100 times for each size, κ, of database.

    a.   We randomly generated κ shapes (the vectors) for database, the query shape and the starting shape (initial s in Fig. 3)

b. We executed the existing method in [13, 14] and the proposed method and counted the percentage of number (η_1 and η_2, respectively) of shapes on which the matching algorithm (to find DI) was performed.

We took the averages (μ_1 and μ_2, respectively) of η_1 and η_2 in 100 iterations. Then we plotted μ_1 and μ_2 with respect to κ and ended up with Fig. 6.

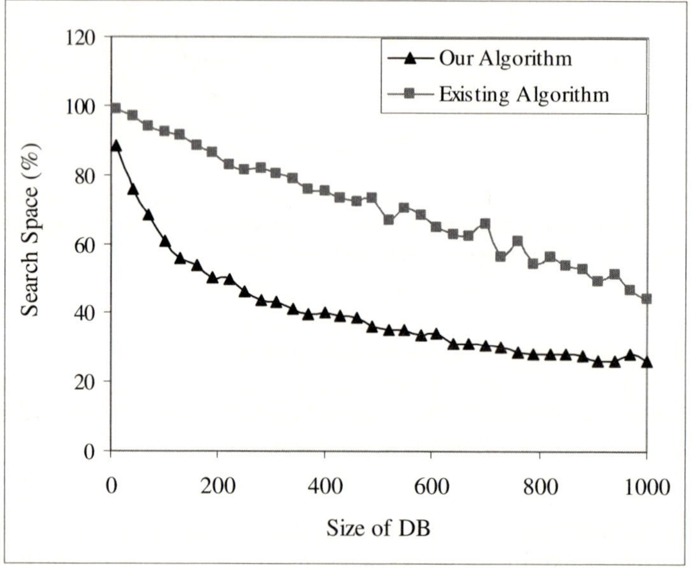

Fig. 6. Experimental results (Dim: 10) showing the percentage of necessary search spaces

In the graph presented in Fig. 6, the x-axis represents the total number of shapes in the database, κ, while the y-axis represents the percentage of the average number of shapes, μ_1 and μ_2 respectively, on which the shape matcher was applied. The upper curve represents the results of the retrieval method that makes use of the procedure in [13] and [14]. The lower curve shows the result of making use of the propesed method. Here we can easily find that the proposed method presents a noticeably good reduction in the search space. The more the number of shapes in the database, the less is the percentage which represents more reduction in the scope of the search space.

Fig. 6 presents results when the dimensionality was 10. We also applied our method in other dimensionalities. Fig. 7 shows some of these results. It shows that the performance degrades with the dimensionality. However, it still gives a very good minimization of the search space at higher dimensionalities while many other existing methods are outperformed by the simple sequential scan whenever the dimensionality is above 10. We can also notice that at 50, 75 and 100 dimensionalities, the perform-ance is almost same. This shows the stability of the performance of this approach when the dimensionality increases.

To test the stability of the proposed method on real data, we have also imple-mented the fixed-correspondence based technique presented in [16]. We have applied this method using both linear search and the proposed method on actual database of shapes. Here we have found that using the proposed method gives the same accuracy in shape retrieval as using linear scan, which proves the stability of the method on real world data. Again, we have found that the percentage of shapes, which the proposed method asks the fixed-correspondence based technique (using dimension 20) to consider, is similar to the graph presented in Fig. 7.

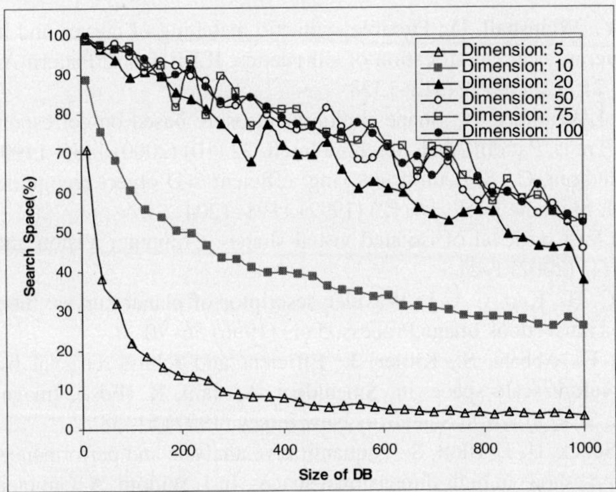

Fig. 7. Effect of increasing dimensions on the required search space of the proposed algorithm. It shows that the performance does not degrade severely in higher dimensionalities.

6 Conclusion

In this paper, we have proposed a method to minimize the search space for shape retrieval. The time-burden of the retrieval process is reduced at the expense of computing, sorting and storing the pair-wise distances of the shapes in the offline preprocessing phase.

Though this method needs a large memory to store the tables or lists, the application needs only one list to be loaded at a time in the memory. We have strictly followed some mathematically proven constraints of Euclidian geometry. As a result, the method shows a very good reduction in the search space while keeping the accuracy and flexibility of shape matcher unaffected. Moreover, it is stable even in high dimensionalities.

References

1. Greenspan, M., Godin, G., Talbot, J.: Acceleration of binning nearest neighbor methods. Vision Interface, Montreal, Canada (2000) 337–344
2. Greenspan, M., Godin., G.: A Nearest Neighbor Method for Efficient ICP. 3DIM01: Proceedings of the 3rd International Conference on 3-D Digital Imaging and Modeling, Quebec City, Quebec, Canada (2001)

3. Flickner, M., Sawhney, H., Niblack, W., Ashley, J., Huang, Q., Dom, B., Gorkani, M., Hafner, J., Lee, D., Petkovic, D., Steele, D., Yanker, P.: Query by image and video content: The QBIC system. IEEE Computer 28 (1995) 23–32

4. Zhu, S.C., Yuille, A.L.: FORMS: A flexible object recognition and modelling system. Internat. J. Computer Vision 20(3) (1996) 187–212

5. Chen, S.W., Tung, S.T., Fang, C.Y., Cherng, S., Jain, A.K.: Extended attributed string matching for shape recognition. Computer Vision and Image Understanding 70(1) (1998) 36–50

6. Gdalyahu, Y., Weinshall, D.: Flexible syntactic matching of curves and its application to automatic hierarchical classification of silhouettes. IEEE Trans. Pattern Analysis and Machine Intell. 21 (12) (1999) 1312–1328

7. Latecki, L., Lak€amper, R.: Shape similarity measure based on correspondence of visual parts. IEEE Trans. Pattern Anal. Machine Intell. 22 (10) (2000) 1185–1190

8. Stein, F., Medioni, G.: Structural indexing: efficient 2-D object recognition. IEEE Trans. Pattern Anal. Machine Intell. 14 (12) (1992) 1198–1204

9. Super, B.J.: Fast retrieval of isolated visual shapes. Computer Vision and Image Understanding 85 (1) (2002) 1–21

10. Chuang, G.C.-H., Kuo, C.-C.J.: Wavelet descriptor of planar curves: theory and applications. IEEE Transactions Image Process. 5 (1) (1996) 56–70

11. Mokhtarian, F., Abbasi, S., Kittler, J.: Efficient and robust retrieval by shape content through curvature scale space, in: Smeulders, A., Jain, R. (Eds.), Image Databases and Multi-Media Search. World Scientific, New Jersey (1997) 51–58

12. Weber, R., Schek, H.-J., Blott, S.: A quantitative analysis and performance study for similarity-search methods in high-dimensional spaces. In J. Widom, A. Gupta, and O. Shmueli, editors, VLDB'98, Proceedings of 24th International Conference on Very Large Data Bases (1998)24-27

13. Li, W., Salari, E.: Successive Elimination Algorithm for Motion Estimation. IEEE transactions on image processing. vol. 4, no. 1 (1995) 105-107

14. Salari, E., Li, W.: A Fast Quadtree Motion Segmentation for Image Sequence Coding. J. Signal Processing: Image Communication, Vol. 14 (1999) 811-816

15. Santini, S., Jain, R.: Similarity measures. IEEE Transactions on Pattern Analysis and Machine Intelligence, Volume 21, No. 9 (1999) 871 – 883

16. Super, B.J.: Fast Correspondence-based System for Shape Retrieval. Pattern Recognition Letters, Vol. 25, No. 2 (2004) 217-225.

17. Beyer, K.S., Goldstein, J., Ramakrishnan, R., Shaft, U.: When Is `Nearest Neighbor' Meaningful?. Proceedings 7th International Conference on Database Theory (ICDT'99), Jerusalem, Israel (1999) 217-235.

18. Berchtold, S., Böhm, C., Braunmüller, B., Keim, D.A., Kriegel, H.P.: Fast parallel similarity search in multimedia databases. In Proc. of the ACM SIGMOD Int. Conf. on Management of Data, Tucson, USA (1997) 1-12

19. Berchtold, S., Keim, D., Kriegel, H.P.: The X-tree: An index structure for high_dimensional data. In Proc. Of the Int. Conference on Very Large Databases (1996) 28-39

20. Katayama, N., Satoh, S.: The SR-tree: An index structure for high-dimensional nearest neighbor queries. In Proc. of the ACM SIGMOD Int. Conf. on Management of Data, Tucson, USA (1997) 369-380

21. Chen, J.-Y., Bouman, C.A., Allebach, J.P.: Fast image database search using tree-structured vq. In Proceedings of the International Conference on Image Processing, Santa Barbara, CA, October (1997) 26-29

Decision Support for Packing in Warehouses

Gürdal Ertek and Kemal Kilic

Sabanci University
Faculty of Engineering and Natural Sciences
Orhanli, Tuzla, 34956, Istanbul, Turkey

Abstract. Packing problems deal with loading of a set of items (objects) into a set of boxes (containers) in order to optimize a performance criterion under various constraints. With the advance of RFID technologies and investments in IT infrastructures companies now have access to the necessary data that can be utilized in cost reduction of packing processes. Therefore bin packing and container loading problems are becoming more popular in recent years. In this research we propose a *beam search* algorithm to solve a packing problem that we encountered in a real world project. The 3D-MBSBPP (Multiple Bin Sized Bin Packing Problem) that we present and solve has not been analyzed in literature before, to the best of our knowledge. We present the performance of our proposed beam search algorithm in terms of both cost and computational time in comparison to a greedy algorithm and a tree search enumeration algorithm.

1   Motivation

Managers of a major automobile manufacturer located in Bursa, Turkey, are undertaking an efficiency improvement program at their spare parts warehouse. Order packaging is one of the crucial processes that require further improvements, particularly for those items that are urgently demanded by their major service parts dealers. Everyday over 80 major service dealers, located at different cities in Turkey, submit their requests of urgent orders to the warehouse. These orders are pooled daily in an information system until 3:00 p.m. Then, the workers start picking the requested items and packing them into adequately sized boxes. By 5:00 p.m., trucks of a third-party logistics firm collect the boxes from the warehouse to deliver them to their destinations. The effectiveness of the order handling process during the two hours between 3:00-5:00 p.m. depends on the efforts of a workforce team of eight to ten workers and on the accuracy of the decisions regarding the selection of appropriate box types and quantities. Currently, at 3:00 p.m., two experienced foremen spend approximately 20 minutes on a PC to decide on and record the choice of boxes for each order. The foremen strive, solely based on their experience and wisdom, for determining a suitable set of boxes such that the posterior extra work of reallocating the items between boxes can be avoided. However in the current state of the operations, the warehouse workers still spend approximately 20 critical minutes each day for such

A. Levi et al. (Eds.): ISCIS 2006, LNCS 4263, pp. 115–124, 2006.

reallocations. The warehouse management decided to initiate the development and implementation of a decision support system that would help the foremen in their decision making and would eliminate the item reallocation process. Our motivation for this research is based on a project targeted at realizing this vision of the warehouse managers.

The heart of the decision support system to be developed is a metaheuristic algorithm which makes the decisions of how many boxes are used of each box type and how each item is placed in its box. The objective is the minimization of the total cost of the boxes used. The time limitations of the packing process (which has to be completed within two hours) oblige us to develop an algorithm that offers real-time solutions. In this paper we present three alternative algorithms that can serve as the solution engine of the decision support system, and compare them with respect to solution and running time performance.

2   Problem Definition

Everyday, major service parts dealers send urgent order requests that have to be handled separately from regular orders. The sizes and item characteristics of the urgent orders depend on the service dealers and exhibit seasonality. In general the contents of the orders range from a few items to nearly a hundred items. In this paper, we consider the packing problem for a single order, since the more general problem of meeting the orders of all the dealers with minimal box cost is decomposable to the independent problems of preparing each of the orders.

We have a set of n rectangular objects, i.e., items, ($O = \{o_i\}_{i=1,..,n}$), each with a height (h_i), a width (w_i) and a depth (d_i), that can be packed into a set of m larger rectangular objects, i.e., boxes, ($C = \{c_j\}_{j=1,..,m}$), each with a height (H_j), a width (W_j) a depth (D_j)and a cost (C_j). Our objective is to allocate the items into the boxes so that the total cost of boxes that are used is minimized. All the items within an order must be included and should not overlap with each other inside the boxes. We consider only the orthogonal arrangements of the items and allow them to be rotated around all three axis. The problem is a member of the cutting and packing problems family, namely a bin packing problem. Further refined typology of the problem is provided in the next section.

There are currently 22 different box types used for the urgent deliveries in the warehouse. However most of these are designed for special items and need not be considered in our study. Since only six of these box types are frequently used we have carried out our experiments for only six box types in our study, as well. In 2005, the cost of the boxes that are used for the shipment of the urgent orders alone was in the scale of tens of thousands of dollars. When the cost of labor is added to this figure, the total cost figure for handling urgent orders ramps even further. Thus, the decision support system we plan to develop and implement has the potential to bring significant savings since it will reduce both the cost of boxes and the cost of labor. Even though our research currently focuses only on the urgent orders, it is the forerunner of a more extensive research where the problem of efficiently packing regular orders (which have higher costs) will be handled.

In the warehouse the fragile items are packed separately. This constraint will be handled in the application with a simple if-then rule and is neglected in the scope of the paper. Therefore, we assume at this stage that all the items of an order can be packed together. Thousands of items with varying shapes and dimensions are present in the warehouse. However, a majority (%80-%85) of these items come in rectangular boxes. For the rest of our paper we assume that all the items have rectangular shape. This assumption was approved by the warehouse managers to be non-restrictive and is required for our computations.

3   Relevant Literature

The strong duality relation between the packing problems and the cutting problems makes it impossible to separate the research conducted on either of the two problems. While the packing problems deal with optimal arrangement of a set of smaller items (O) within larger items (C), the cutting problems aim to cut a larger item (stock) into smaller pieces.

The cutting and packing problems are some of the most extensively studied combinatorial optimization problem in the literature. In the editorial of the Special Issue of the European Journal of Operational Research on Cutting and Packing, Bisckhoff and Wäscher [2] present three reasons for the popularity of these problems. First of all, the cutting and packing problems have a wide range of applications in industry. This is quite true when one considers that the applications extend from production and distribution problems in supply chain logistics (e.g., cutting metal sheets into smaller pieces, order packaging in warehouses, loading the containers to trucks or ships, etc.), to applications as diverse as computer science and finance (e.g., memory allocation of processors [4], and capital budgeting problems [7]).

Second reason is the fact that the majority of such problems are strongly NP-Hard. Therefore, they receive a great deal of attention from researchers who focus on exact algorithms, as well as those who develop heuristic solutions for computationally complex problems.

The third reason is the diversity of the real world problems. Even small nuances in the objective function or the packing/cutting constraints result in new problem structures. In the knapsack packing problem, the space is limited and the goal is to choose the most valuable *(i.e., a set of)* small objects that would maximize the utility of the load packed into the larger object. On the other hand, the bin packing problems deal with the problem of packing *all* of the smaller objects so that the number of larger objects required is minimized. A special case is the pallet loading problem in which the smaller objects are usually *identical* or *weakly heterogenous* (relatively few small item types) and the objective is minimizing the number of *identical* (generally speaking) pallets required.

Since the seminal papers of Gilmore and Gomory in early 60's, over a thousand papers are published in problems related to cutting and packing problems. Such an extensive literature with many varieties of the problems necessitates a good typology. To our knowledge, two well-accepted typologies are present in the literature [5,15]. The most commonly accepted (and the earliest) is due to Dyckhoff [5] in which he proposes four criteria according to which the problems can be categorized; (1) Dimensionality (1D, 2D, 3D, ND) (2) Kind of assignment (all large objects and selected small objects - **B**, or all small objects and selected large objects -**V**) (3) Assortment of large objects (**O**ne, **I**dentical, **D**ifferent) and (4) Assortment of small objects (**F**ew items of few sizes, many items of **R**elatively few sizes, **M**any items of many sizes, **C**ongruent items).

In a recent paper, Wäscher et al. [15] argues that the classification scheme of Dyckhoff has major drawbacks in certain aspects such as inconsistency, lack of uniqueness and homogeneity. They improve the classification and propose a new typology similar to the Dyckhoff's in certain aspects but complements its deficiencies.

Given the overwhelming size of the literature, we refer the interested readers to one of the following extensive reviews: A historical development of the cutting and packing problems, with a brief discussion of the seminal and most important papers in major problem categories are presented by Dyckhoff et al.[7]. In an extensive review of the literature, Dyckhoff and Finke [6] investigate 308 papers that were published prior to 1992. They also provide a classification of the literature based on the typology proposed by Dyckhoff. In [15], 413 papers are reviewed and a classification based on the improved typology is provided.

Based on the typology of Dyckhoff [5], the problem studied in this paper is categorized as **3D/V/D/M**. None of the papers published prior to 1992 falls into this category. Actually, even three-dimensional packing problems were rarely studied prior to 1992. According to the typology of Washner[15], our problem is **3D-MBSBPP** (Multiple Bin Sized Bin Packing Problems). Again there are no papers published in this category between 1994-2004 [15]. Out of the 413 papers only four papers were published in the MBSBPP category and among these four papers, three of them were single-dimensional and the fourth one was two-dimensional. The closest category is 3D-MHLOPP (3D-Multiple Heterogenous Large Objects Placement Problems), which is basically a generalization of 3D-multiple container or pallet loading problems.

The object placement problems are categorized as the problems in which smaller objects have limited number of types (*weakly homogenous*) so that the proposed solutions exploit this constraint. The papers of Ivancic et al. [9] and Eley [8] fall into the 3D-MHLOPP category. Considering relatively few small number of items allows limited number of preassigned patterns of these small items and eases the computations. Being published in 2005, the work of Brunetta and Grégoire [3] was not included in the review, but also falls into 3D-MHLOPP category. Motivated from a real case in a biscuit factory with 15 different smaller objects size (in this case the smaller objects are boxes of sweeties), they propose a tree-search algorithm that implicitly explores the solution space in order to maximize volumetric utilization of multiple sized containers.

Another notable relevant paper is due to Martello et al. [11], in which the authors propose an exact solution for 3D-(Single Bin Sized) BPP.

To the best of our knowledge, our paper is the first work that proposes solution approaches to the 3D-MBSBPP.

4   Methodology

Let us assume that we have an order request $O = \{o_1, o_2, .., o_n\}$, a set of n items with dimensions (h_i, w_i, d_i) and that we have m boxes $(C = \{c_1, c_2, .., c_m\})$ with dimensions (H_j, W_j, D_j) and costs C_j. The problem is identifying the number of boxes of each type that will be used to fully ship a given order while minimizing the cost of boxes. We propose three solution algorithms, namely a greedy algorithm (G), a beam search algorithm (BS) and a tree search based implicit enumeration algorithm (TS).

The greedy algorithm (G) is based on a sequential assignment methodology. In this methodology, while there are objects that are not packed into a box, a single sized bin container loading problem (SSBCLP) is solved independently for each different box size, and the best box is selected according to a performance index $(I_{j,l})$. We used the tree search heuristic proposed by Pisinger [13], which loads the objects to the boxes layer by layer (guillotine cuttable) as the container loading algorithm (CLA). After the boxes are loaded independently, the best box is selected based on an index which is a function of the *filling ratio* and the *cost per volume* of the boxes. Next, those objects that are assigned to a box are deleted from the waiting list and the same procedure is applied sequentially. The filling ratio is defined as follows:

Let W_l denote a subset of item set (O) that contains the items that are not still packed in a box at level l. Let $A_{j,l}$ be a subset of W_l, which contains all of the items that are packed in the jth box by the container loading algorithm (CLA) at level l. The filling ratio, $q_{j,l}$, of the jth box type at level l is calculated as follows;

$$q_{j,l} = \frac{\sum\limits_{i=1}^{n} (V_i \times X_{i,j,l})}{V_j} \tag{1}$$

Where V_i is the volume of the ith object $(V_i = h_i \times d_i \times w_i)$, V_j is the volume of the jth box type $(V_j = H_j \times D_j \times W_j)$ and $X_{i,j,l}$ is the binary variable that equals to 1 if the CLA loads the ith object to the jth container at the lth level, and 0 otherwise. Considering the overall objective of minimizing the total cost of the boxes that are used for the shipment, we also included the cost per volume $(p_{j,l})$ in our performance index. Cost per volume for each container size is calculated as follows:

$$p_{j,l} = \frac{C_j}{\sum\limits_{i=1}^{n} (V_i \times X_{i,j,l})} \tag{2}$$

The proposed performance index is calculated as follows;

$$I_{j,l} = \frac{p_{j,l}}{q_{j,l}} \tag{3}$$

After the performance indices of each of the boxes are calculated, the box with the lowest index is selected (c_{j*}) as the next assignment. Later, the objects $A_{j*,l}$ that are loaded to the selected box are deleted from W_l and the remaining items are considered as W_{l+1} (i.e., $W_{l+1} = W_l \setminus A_{j*,l}$). This procedure is repeated until $W_{l+1} = \emptyset$.

The second algorithm we propose is a filtered beam search heuristic (BS). Beam search is a special type of tree search heuristic that mimics the infamous branch and bound algorithm. In the case of branch and bound one can prune the nodes after a guarantee of non-optimality, on the other hand in beam search the less promising nodes that do not seem to be leading to the optimal decisions are pruned. In this regard, beam search algorithm is faster but typically does not yield a solution as good as TS. Beam search was first used by Lowerre in a speech recognition program called HARPY [10]. Ow and Morton [12] present a thorough analysis of a filtered beam search methodology for different scheduling problems. Aktürk and Kilic [1] applied filtered beam search to a space mission scheduling problem and demonstrated that it outperforms other metaheuristics such as GRASP and Simulated Annealing for their problem.

A conventional filtered beam search has two decision parameters, the *beam width* (b) and the *filter width* (f). The most promising b nodes are determined based on a heuristic *global evaluation function,* which is typically the objective function value of a heuristic solution. Even though the heuristics utilized for this purpose are quite fast, they still might be undesirably time consuming and thus infeasible for real-time decision making, in particular for large scale problems. In order to overcome this problem, a second parameter f is introduced, which limits the number of the nodes where the *global evaluation function* is calculated. Under a *filtered* beam search scheme, at each level, firstly, the most promising f nodes are determined based on a *local evaluation function* and the rest of the nodes are pruned. Next among the filtered f nodes, the b most promising ones are selected based on a *global evaluation function.* In the proposed algorithm, the index introduced in Equation 3 is used as the local evaluation function, i.e. the filtering stage. On the other hand, the total cost of the boxes of the solution that is obtained by applying the greedy algorithm to the non-pruned nodes is utilized as the global evaluation function. Below we discuss the algorithm and the notation in detail.

Let $W_{t,b}$ be the set that contains the items that are still not packed in a box at level t for the bth beam of the tree. We intentionally denote the level by t, rather than l, so as to distinguish the description of the current algorithm (BS) from the previous (G). Let $S_{t,b}$ be the set of boxes that are already packed with objects prior to level t for beam b. The proposed algorithm is as follows;

Algorithm Beam Search.

Select f and b sizes
Initialize $t = 1$, $W_{1,b} = \{o_1, o_2, .., o_n\}$ $\forall\, b$,
While not *done do*

1. Procedure Filter_with_one_step
   (a) For all beams, $k = 1..b$ repeat the following
       i. For all $j = 1..m$ do the following
             Apply the container loading algorithm (CLA) with the set $W_{t,k}$
             Determine the local evaluation score, $I_{j,t,k}$
   (b) Select f boxes with the best (lowest) $I_{j,t,k}$

2. Let $F_{t,b}$ be the set of the indices of the boxes that are selected at step 1b on the bth beam.

3. $done = true$

4. Procedure Evaluate_the_global_evaluation_score_of the_nodes

    (a) For all beams, $k = 1..b$ repeat the following

        i. For each $j \in F_{t,k}$ repeat the following

            Develop an auxiliary problem with the remaining items that are not packed yet.

            Apply the greedy algorithm (G) and find a heuristic solution

            Evaluate the total cost of boxes (including the ones that assigned prior to that node)

    (b) Select b nodes yielding the lowest cost evaluated in step 4(a)i

    (c) Let $B_{t,b}$ be the set of the indices of the boxes on the bth beam that are selected at step 4b

    (d) For all beams, $k = 1..b$ repeat the following

        i. For each $j \in B_{t,k}$ do the following

            Augment the node (j^{th} box) to the kth beam.

            Let $P_{t,j,k}$ be the set of the *items* assigned to the fth box of the kth beam at step 1(a)i

            Let $W_{t,b} = W_{t,b} \setminus P_{t,j,k}$

            If $W_{t,b} \neq \{\}$ then $done = false$

5. Let $t = t + 1$

The third algorithm we propose is a depth-first tree search algorithm (TS) that implicitly enumerates the solution space. The nodes at each level of the tree hold information on which box types have been used until themselves, and a list of the remaining items to be allocated. The nodes are generated from their parents for each feasible box type. The best solution at any stage of the algorithm is used as an upper bound, and any children nodes that have a worse solution than the upper bound are pruned all-together with their subtrees. When a leaf node is reached the algorithm evaluates the cost of the complete allocation, compares it to the best solution until then, returns back to the leaf node's parent, and continues with generating the next node that allocates the remaining items in the parent to next box type.

5   Experimental Results and Discussion

The algorithms presented in the previous section were coded with C under the MS Visual Studio .NET environment and run on a PC with Intel Centrino 1700 Mhz processor and 512 MB of RAM. As a subroutine of our program we have used the C implementation of Pisinger's algorithm for container loading (CLA) [13], which we acquired from the Internet [14]. In this section we present the results of our experiments and compare the performances of the proposed algorithms with respect to costs of the boxes and computational times. The company currently doesn't store the dimensions of the items in its warehouse and is in the process of acquiring this data from its suppliers. Thus we generated the item sizes randomly within given bounds so as to represent various settings. We alos opted for using box types that we generated, whose volumes are roughly uniformly distributed. To determine the box costs, we initially plotted the costs of the 22 box types used in the warehouse against their volumes and found out that a power function in the form of $C(V) = aV^b$ fits the data extremely well. In this function $C(V)$ refers to the cost of the box, V refers to the volume of box, and a and b are constant real numbers. The costs of the generated box sizes were estimated according to this function.

The experiments were designed to cover the environment with regard to two aspects. Firstly, the order size, i.e., the number of items to be packed. For this purpose three different problem sizes were considered: Small order size ($n = 20$), medium order size ($n = 40$) and large order size ($n = 60$). The second aspect is the dimensions of the items compared to the dimensions of the boxes. Again three different problems are generated: Orders with smaller items (Case I), medium items (Case II) and larger items (Case III), in which the three dimensions of the items are randomly generated within the ranges [10-25], [15-30] and [20-35], respectively (in centimeters). For each experiment (altogether $3 \times 3 = 9$ cases), 10 instances were randomly generated. The execution of the TS was terminated after 5 minutes in solving more difficult problem instances. The results of the algorithms in terms of the average costs (approximately in \$) and the computational times (in seconds) are tabulated in Tables 1 and 2. For illustrative purposes, we depict the solution of the TS for a problem instance with 40 items in Figure 1. In this solution two large boxes of the same type, and two smaller boxes of different types are used to fully pack the sample order.

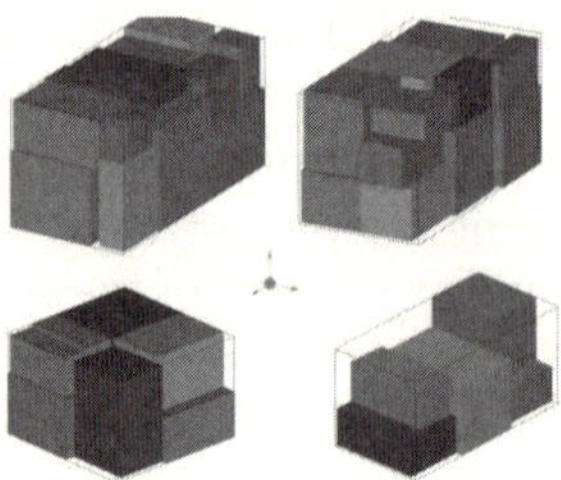

Fig. 1. The solution of the TS algorithm for a test instance with 40 items

As expected, GS has the worst performance in terms of the total costs, but is very fast. On the other hand, the implicit enumeration based TS requires extensive computational time and is not feasible to be used for orders with many items or with larger items. Both of these situations require usage of more boxes, which explodes the number of nodes in the search tree of TS. The greedy algorithm (G) and the beam search algorithm (BS) handle such situations efficiently, with G naturally running much faster.

Table 1. The performance of the algorithms in terms of the total costs (appr. in $)

	Case I			Case II			Case III		
	G	*BS*	*TS*	*G*	*BS*	*TS*	*G*	*BS*	*TS*
$n = 20$	2.20	1.78	1.78	3.83	3.54	3.54	7.04	6.62	6.56
$n = 40$	3.64	3.00	3.00	6.77	6.17	6.16	12.69	12.25	*
$n = 60$	5.04	4.25	*	9.32	8.76	*	19.23	12.11	*

Table 2. The performance of the algorithms in terms of the CPU time (seconds)

	Case I			Case II			Case III		
	G	*BS*	*TS*	*G*	*BS*	*TS*	*G*	*BS*	*TS*
$n = 20$	0.28	1.12	0.31	0.47	3.71	1.05	0.09	2.85	14.52
$n = 40$	2.85	19.07	3.88	0.65	13.77	30.35	0.19	8.60	*
$n = 60$	3.80	40.99	*	1.11	24.02	*	0.33	20.07	*

One may surprisingly observe that TS runs faster than BS on the average for some instance sets of Case I and Case II. We believe that this is due to the fact that we have listed the box types in descending order with respect to their volumes in the input file. TS starts by allocating the items to the largest boxes and quickly obtains a good upper bound, which enables it to prune most of the search tree.

It should be noted that BS performs significantly better than G for $n = 60$ in Case III, with only a slight increase compared to its running time for $n = 40$. BS yields results very close to TS and returns results fastly enough (¡25 seconds on the average) to be used in the company. In implementing the decision support system, one should specify the ranges of order sizes and items sizes in which each algorithm should be run.

6   Conclusion and Future Work

In this paper, being motivated by a real world case, we described the 3D-MBSBP problem and proposed three algorithms to solve it. Future stages of our research will involve implementing a functional and usable decision support system with a friendly GUI (Graphical User Interface), with the developed algorithms residing in it as the solution generating engine. Another future work is the improvement of our algorithms and software implementations to run more efficiently and produce better solutions. Finally, we are envisioning the extension of our work to scale up to the rest of the warehouse and yield significant monetary and ergonomic benefits.

Acknowledgement

The authors would like to thank Professor David Pisinger at University of Copenhagen for making the code of his container loading algorithm available on the

Internet. The authors would also like to thank Sabanci University undergraduate student Cem Sözeri for the 3D illustration of the sample solution, and Mr. Sinan Südütemiz and Mr. Rıza Altuğ from the company for their assistance during the project.

References

1. Akturk, M.S., Kilic, K.: Generating short-term observation schedules for space mission projects. Journal of Intelligent Manufacturing, **10**(5), (1999) 387–404
2. Bisckhof, E. E., Wäscher, G.: Cutting and packing. European Journal of Operational Research. **84**, (3) (1995) 503–505
3. Brunetta, L., Grégoire, P. A.: General purpose algorithm for three-dimensional packing. INFORMS Journal on Computing. **17**, (3) (2005) 328–338
4. Chung, F., Graham, R. and Varghese, G.: Parallelism versus memory allocation in pipelined router forwarding engines. ACM Symposium on Parallel Algorithms and Architectures, Proceedings of the sixteenth annual ACM symposium on Parallelism in algorithms and architectures, Barcelona, Spain (2004) 103–111
5. Dyckhoff, H.: A typology of cutting and packing problems. European Journal of Operational Research. **44**, (1990) 145–159
6. Dyckhoff, H., Finke, U.: Cutting and Packing in Production and Distribution. Springer Verlag, Berlin (1992)
7. Dyckhoff, H., Scheithauer, G., Terno, J.: Cutting and Packing. Annotated Bibliographies in Combinatorial Optimization. Dell'Amico, M., Maffioli F., and Martello, S. (eds) Wiley (1997) 393–412
8. Eley, M.: A bottleneck assignment approach to the multiple container loading problem. OR Spectrum **25** (2003) 45–60
9. Ivancic, N.J., Mathur, K., Mohanty, B.B.: An integer-programming based heuristic approach to the three-dimensional packing problem. Journal of Manufacturing and Operations Management **2**, (1989) 268–298
10. Lowerre, B.: The HARPY speech recognition system. Ph.D. Thesis, Carnegie Mellon University, PA (1976).
11. Martello, S., Pisinger, D., Vigo, D.: The three-dimensional bin packing problem. Operations Research, **48** (2), (2000) 256–267
12. Ow, P. S., Morton, T. E.: Filtered beam search in scheduling. International Journal of Production Research. **26**, (1988) 35–62
13. Pisinger, D.: A tree-search heuristic for the container loading problem. Ricerda Operativa. **28** (87), (1998) 31–48.
14. `http://www.diku.dk/~pisinger/`
15. Wäscher, G., Haußner, H., Schumann, H.: An improved typology of cutting and packing problems, Working Paper No. 24. Otto von Guericke University, Magdeburg (2006)

A Fast Partial Distortion Elimination Algorithm Using Selective Matching Scan

Jong-Nam Kim, Tae-Kyung Ryu, and Yongjae Jeong

Div. of Electronic Computer and Telecommunication Engineering, Pukyong University
jongnam@pknu.ac.kr

Abstract. Full search (FS) motion estimation has have been a big problem in real-time video coding because of enormous amount for calculation. Especially, the recent MPEG-4 AVC (advanced video coding) standard requires much more computations in motion estimation than the conventional MPEG-2 coding standard. In this paper, we propose a fast FS algorithm which can reduce only unnecessary computations significantly. Our algorithm is based on selective matching scan and elimination of unlike candidate blocks from initial matching error. According to the obtained matching order, we proceed to calculate matching errors and remove unlike candidate vectors based on PDE (Partial Distortion Elimination) method. Our algorithm takes about 4~10% of computations for block matching error compared with conventional FS algorithm without any degradation in prediction quality, thus our algorithm will be useful to real-time video coding applications using MPEG-4 AVC or MPEG-2 video coding standards.

1 Introduction

In MPEG-2 and MPEG-4 video compression, full search (FS) algorithm based on block matching algorithm (BMA) finds them optimal motion vectors which minimize the matching difference between reference block and candidate block. It has been widely used in video coding applications because of its simple and easy hardware implementation. However, heavy computational load of the full search with very large search range can be a significant problem in real-time video coding application. Many fast motion estimation algorithms to reduce the computational load of the full search have been studied in the last decades.

We classify these fast motion estimation methods into two main groups. One is lossy motion estimation algorithm with degradation of predicted images and the other is lossless one without any degradation of predicted images compared with the conventional FS algorithm. The former includes following subgroups : unimodal error surface assumption (UESA) techniques, multi-resolution techniques, variable search range techniques with spatial/temporal correlation of the motion vectors, half-stop techniques using threshold of matching distortion, integral projection technique of matching block, low bit resolution techniques, sub-sampling techniques of matching block, and so on [1]. The latter as fast full search technique contains following several algorithms: successive elimination algorithm (SEA) using sum of reference block and

A. Levi et al. (Eds.): ISCIS 2006, LNCS 4263, pp. 125 – 133, 2006.

candidate block and its modified algorithms [2]-[8], fast algorithm using fast 2-D FIR filtering method [9], vertical, horizontal and massive projection techniques for reference block and search range blocks [10], partial distortion elimination (PDE) method and its modified algorithms [11]-[13], and so on.

In lossless motion estimation algorithms, PDE is very efficient algorithm to reduce unnecessary computation for matching error calculation. To further reduce unnecessary computation in calculating matching error, J.N. Kim and et al. proposed fast PDE algorithms based on adaptive matching scan, which requires additional computation to get matching scan order [11]-[12]. But the additional computation for the matching scan order can be burden when cascading other fast motion estimation algorithm such as SEA.

In this paper, we propose a fast motion estimation algorithm to reduce computational load of the FS algorithm without any degradation of predicted images compared with the conventional FS algorithm. We reduced only unnecessary computations which doesn't affect predicted images from the motion vector. To do that, we use selective matching scan from initial matching and threshold based PDE algorithm. Instead of the conventional top-to-bottom matching order, we calculate the matching error adaptively according to the obtained computational order. Additionally, we remove unlike candidate vectors faster by using some threshold of initially estimated matching error. Our algorithm can control the trade-off between prediction quality and computational reduction for motion estimation. Our algorithm reduces about 90~94% of computations for block matching error compared with the conventional FS algorithm without any degradation of prediction quality.

This paper is organized as follows. In Section 2, conventional fast FS algorithms are described. Then, Section 3 explains the motivation of them proposed algorithm based on the previous works. In Section 4, experimental results for various test sequences and discussions of the results are presented. The conclusion is followed in Section 5.

2 Conventional Works

Most of the algorithms for fast motion estimation have degradation in predicted images because of coarse search or matching. In limited bit-rate applications, wrong motion vectors from these fast techniques can be serious problem because of increased error data from sub optimal prediction. For many hardware implementations of motion estimation, full search has been used due to its exactness of the prediction and simple search rule. Most of studies for motion estimation are about lossy motion estimation compared with full search algorithm. Famous lossless algorithms without any degradation of predicted images are SEA (successive elimination algorithm) and PDE (partial distortion elimination). We can organize like this. SEA algorithm removes impossible candidate motion vectors by using the sum of current block, the sum of candidate blocks and minimum SAD (Sum of Absolute Difference) at that time [2]. This algorithm called successive elimination algorithm (SEA). At first, one computes sum of the rows or the columns to reduce overlapped part of computing sum of reference block and sum of candidate blocks. After calculating initial matching error of determined search origin, one removes impossible candidate motion vectors.

A few algorithms of modified algorithms based on SEA have been reported. Speedup performance of the SEA depends on the initial matching error. Oliveira et al. [3] proposed the modified algorithm with less initial matching distortion from the adjacent motion vectors. Lu et al. [4] reduced more candidates by using hierarchical structure of Minkowski's inequality with pyramid of 5 levels. Coban et al. [5] used the concept of SEA to determine motion vectors with optimized rate-distortion. So, they extended SEA decision boundary by adding the weighted rate term to avoid enormous computation. Wang et al. [6] used SEA's concept adding PDE algorithm, square root and square term to reduce computations. Meanwhile, Gao et al. [7] reduced more impossible candidates vectors by using tighter boundary levels obtained by dividing each block into sub-blocks of normalized inequality Eq. (2) from SEA.

$$SSAD_L = \sum_{u=0}^{2^L-1} \sum_{v=0}^{2^L-1} |R_L^{(u,v)}(i,j) - C_L^{(u,v)}(i+x,j+y)| \tag{1}$$

$$SSAD_0 \le SSAD_1 \le \cdots \le SSAD_l \le \cdots \le SSAD_L \le SAD_{min} \tag{2}$$

Another algorithm to reduce them computational complexity efficiently is the PDE algorithm [11]-[13]. It used the partial sum of matching distortion to eliminate impossible candidates before complete calculation of matching distortion in a matching block. That is, if an intermediate sum of matching error is larger than the minimum value of matching error at that time, the remaining computation for matching error is abandoned. In Eq. (4). the *kth* partial SAD to check during the matching is as follows:

$$\sum_{i=1}^{k} \sum_{j=1}^{N} \left| f_t(i,j) - f_{t-1}(i+x,j+y) \right| \qquad k = 1,2,...N \tag{3}$$

where N represents matching block size. If there is $k<N$ making the partial SAD exceed current minimum matching error, then we can quit remaining calculation of matching error ($k+1$ to Nth rows). Kim et al. [11] calculated block matching error to reduce unnecessary calculations with four direction scan order, Top-to-bottom, Bottom-to-top, Left-to-right, Right-to-left sequentially based on gradient magnitude of image instead of matching scan using conventional Top-to-bottom scan order. Kim et al. [12] calculated block matching error to reduce unnecessary calculations with gradient magnitude of image instead of variable sequential matching scan. The above methods reduce only unnecessary computation for getting block matching error, but both of them require additional computation to determine matching scan order. Erol et al. [13] used the original PDE algorithm to real-time software codec.

3 Proposed Algorithm

Modified PDE algorithms have been published by using adjacent motion vectors in the spatial or temporal domain, spiral scan algorithm and cascaded algorithms to other fast ones [11]-[13]. Ability to reject impossible candidates in the PDE algorithm depends on the search strategy, which makes minimum matching error be detected faster. For the purpose, spiral search is very efficient. PDE algorithm with spiral search rejects impossible candidates faster than simple PDE [11]-[12]. Therefore, we employ the spiral search in the proposing matching scan algorithms. We summarize relationship between matching error and image gradient of matching block by using Taylor series expansion [11]-[12]. Let the image intensity at the position *(x,y)* of the *(t+1)*th frame be *{f_{t+1} (p), p=(x,y)}*, and the motion vector of position of p be *mv=(mvx, mvy)*. We can describe the relationship between reference frame and candidate frame in Eq. (4).

$$f_{t+1}(p)=f_t(p+mv) \tag{4}$$

$$
\begin{aligned}
d_{t+1}(p) &= \left| f_{t+1}(p) - f_t(p+cmv) \right| \\
&= \left| f_t(p+mv) - f_t(p+cmv) \right| \\
&\approx \left| \frac{\partial f_t(p+mv)}{\partial x}(cmvx - mvx) + \frac{\partial f_t(p+mv)}{\partial y}(cmvy - mvy) \right| \\
&\approx \left| \frac{\partial f_{t+1}(p)}{\partial x}(cmvx - mvx) \right| + \left| \frac{\partial f_{t+1}(p)}{\partial y}(cmvy - mvy) \right|
\end{aligned}
\tag{5}
$$

By using modified form of the Taylor series expansion, we can express relationship between the matching distortion and gradient magnitude of reference block in Eq. (5). Here, *cmv=(cmvx, cmvy)* means candidate motion vector corresponding to the matching distortion. From Eq. (5), we can find an important fact that the matching distortion at pixel p is proportional to the gradient magnitude of reference block in the current frame, which corresponds to the complexity of the image data. By localizing the image complexity well, we can get more reduction in unnecessary calculation. In general, image complexity is well localized in piece rather than the whole span of the image. In this paper, we calculate the matching error using 4x4 square sub-block instead of conventional 1x16 row vector to measure the complexity of matching block.

At this point, we try to seek complex square sub-block as soon as possible. In the previous algorithms, complex square sub-block was found by calculating gradient magnitude in the reference matching block, where the additional computation for calculating gradient magnitude can be neglected in some cases. The previous algorithms [11]-[12] can increase computational load more than the original PDE algorithm when both of them are cascaded to other fast algorithms such as TSS [1] or SEA [2]. Instead of calculating the gradient magnitude of the matching blocks, we find complex sub-blocks from initial SAD computation at center point of search range. At first, we calculate block matching error by the unit of square sub-block, and then accumulate the sum of sub-blocks. According to the accumulated sums of sub-blocks, we determine of the matching order for the following candidates. The idea further reduces only unnecessary computations without any sacrifice of additional ones. As described previously, our proposed algorithm use the matching order for sub-blocks in all candidates of the search range. Eq. (6) shows our modified PDE algorithm which employs sub-blocks and matching order of the sub-blocks from initial computation of SAD.

$$
\sum_{s}^{k} \sum_{i=1}^{N/s} \sum_{j=1}^{N/s} \left| f_t(i,j) - f_{t-1}(i+x, j+y) \right|
\tag{6}
$$

$$k = 1,2,...N/s*N/s,$$

$$s \in matching\_order[]$$

In Eq. (6), *matching_order[]* is from initial partial SADs value for each block. The pixel number of 4x4 square sub-block is 16. The matching order of 16 candidate sub-blocks is calculated for every reference block of the search range. Thus, we improve the probability of scan order that have larger matching first. The computational complexity sorting 4x4 sub-block is small and negligible in the total calculation of block matching algorithm.

Additionally, we further reduce unnecessary computation for motion estimation by using some threshold about initial matching error. After calculating initial matching error (SAD^1) of candidate vectors as shown in Eq. (7), we compare it with initial threshold (*Initial_Threshold*) in Eq. (7). The meaning of the symbols in Eq. (7) is the same as in Eq. (3). If the SAD^1 is larger than the *Initial_Threshold*, we don't have to calculate the remaining matching error for the candidate vector. The *Initial_Threshold* is determined by block size N, minimum SAD at that time SAD_{min}, and scaling factor *th*. We can control the trade-off between computational reduction and prediction quality by adjusting the scaling factor *th.*.

$$SAD^1 = \sum_{i=1}^{1} \sum_{j=1}^{N} \left| f_t(i, j) - f_{t-1}(i + x, j + y) \right|,$$

$$SAD^1 \geq Initial\_Threshold, \quad Initial\_Threshold = \frac{th}{N} SAD_{min}$$

(7)

If we cascade the SEA algorithm to our proposed algorithm, we can further remove only unnecessary computation. In the multilevel SEA algorithm, block size is 16x16 and sub-block size of adaptive matching scan is 4x4. If we employ the multilevel SEA instead of the original SEA, we can reduce more computations. At that time, the additional computation for matching scan order in the previous PDE algorithms can be considerable amount. Then, the proposed algorithm will be needed more.

4   Experimental Results and Discussions

To compare the performance of the proposed algorithm with the conventional algorithms, we use 100 frames of 'foreman', 'car phone', 'trevor', 'clair', 'akio' and 'grand mother' image sequences. In these sequences, 'foreman', and 'car phone' have big motions compared with other image sequences, while 'clair', 'akio' and 'grand mother' are almost inactive sequences compared with first two sequences. 'trevor' sequence has intermediate motions. Matching block size is 16x16 pixels and the search window is ± 7 pixels. Image format is QCIF(176×144) for each sequence and only forward prediction is used. The simulation results are shown in terms of average numbers of checking rows with reference of that of full search without any fast operation and peak-signal-to-noise ratio (PSNR). In the experiment, we put the scaling factor *th* as 1 and 4. All results in Table 1~ Table 2 was considered with overhead calculation for complexity measure. All the algorithms employed spiral search scheme to make use of the distribution of motion vectors.

Figure 1 ~ 2 show the reduced computation of average checking rows using 4x4 square sub-blocks based on partial SAD value comparison for the scaling factor *th=1*. The adaptive matching scan algorithm significantly reduces unnecessary calculations compared with conventional sequential scan algorithm. We apply our algorithm to MSEA [7] to prove usefulness of ours. As shown in Figure 1 ~2, our proposed algorithm shows the obvious difference in computational amount for PDE and MSEA algorithms.

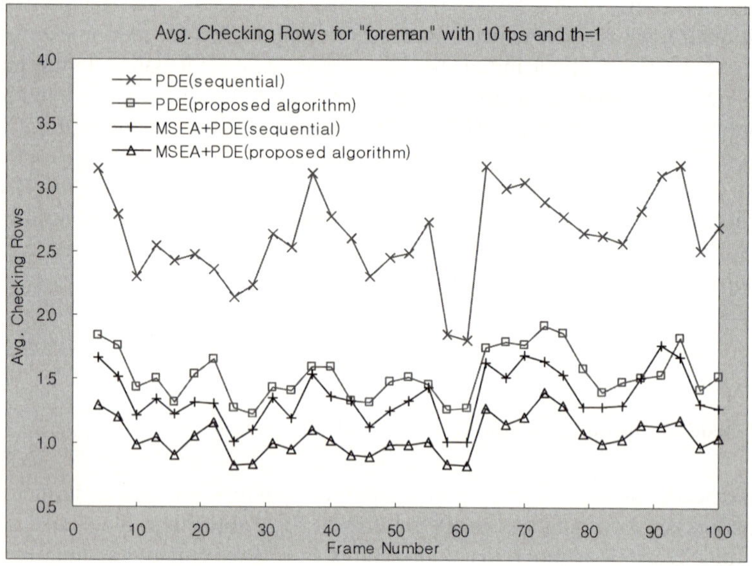

Fig. 1. Average computations for "foreman" sequence of the frame rate 10fps

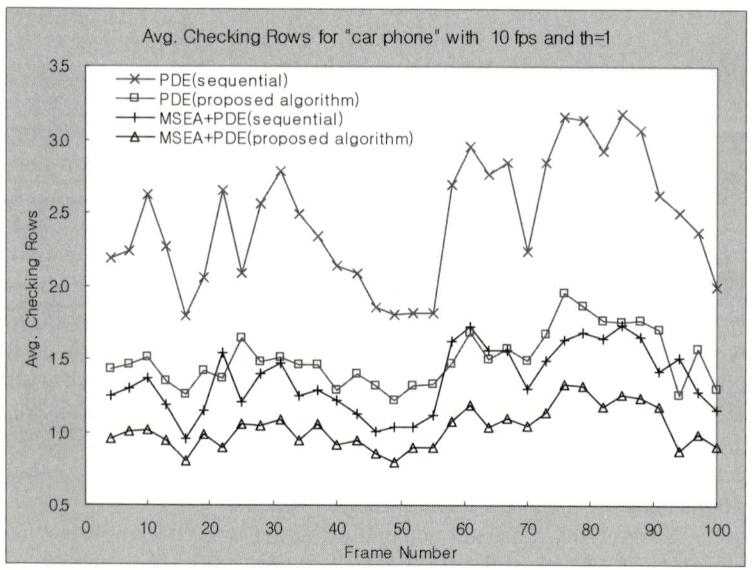

Fig. 2. Average computations for "carphone" sequence of the frame rate 10fps

Table 1 ~ Table 2 show computed average checking rows from various algorithms in all sequences for frame rate 10 fps and scaling factor $th=1, 4$. Average checking rows of conventional FS without any fast algorithm are matching block size, 16. As we described above, the references [11],[12] show importance and efficiency of spiral scan in PDE algorithm.

In "foreman" sequence of Table 1, we can see that the computational reduction ratio from the proposed algorithm for PDE are about 85~90 % and 90~96% for MSEA+PDE. Table 3~4 present PSNR for all sequences for 10 fps and $th=1, 4$. As described previously, PSNR is different for all sequences according to the scaling factors and algorithms. The main reason of different quality of predicted image is initial threshold and initial matching error from each algorithm. For $th=1$, there is no difference of prediction quality between the original FS and threshold based algorithms. With the experimental results, we can conclude that our adaptive matching scan algorithm can reduce computation efficiently without any degradation of prediction quality and additional computation for matching order by adjusting the scaling factor appropriately.

Table 1. Average computations for all sequences for 10 fps and th=1

Algorithms	Fore-man	Car phone	Trevor	Claire	Akio	Grand
Original FS	16.00	16.00	16.00	16.00	16.00	16.00
PDE (sequential)	2.63	2.45	2.40	1.68	1.40	2.18
PDE (proposed algorithm)	1.53	1.50	1.43	1.15	1.14	1.40
MSEA+PDE (sequential)	1.37	1.36	1.16	0.79	0.70	1.28
MSEA+PDE (proposed algorithm)	1.05	1.03	0.89	0.69	0.63	0.98

Table 2. Average computations for all sequences for 10 fps and th=4

Algorithms	Fore-man	Car phone	Trevor	Claire	Akio	Grand
Original FS	16.00	16.00	16.00	16.00	16.00	16.00
PDE (sequential)	4.20	4.32	3.85	3.83	1.78	4.11
PDE (proposed algorithm)	2.87	3.04	2.72	2.80	1.29	3.15
MSEA+PDE (sequential)	1.80	1.94	1.48	1.28	0.75	1.99
MSEA+PDE (proposed algorithm)	1.59	1.70	1.30	1.21	0.69	1.87

Table 3. Average PSNR of all sequences for 10 fps and th=1

Frame rate(10Hz, th=1)	Fore-man	Car phone	Trevor	Claire	Akio	Grand
Original FS	29.50	31.54	28.64	37.51	38.66	39.01
PDE (sequential)	29.24	31.18	28.25	37.23	38.55	38.84
PDE (proposed algo-rithm)	28.79	30.67	27.74	36.94	38.14	38.68
MSEA+PDE (sequen-tial)	29.24	31.18	28.25	37.23	38.55	38.84
MSEA+PDE (proposed algorithm)	28.79	30.67	27.74	36.94	38.14	38.68

Table 4. Average PSNR of all sequences for 10 fps and th=4

Frame rate(10Hz, th=4)	Fore-man	Car phone	Trevor	Claire	Akio	Grand
Original FS	29.50	31.54	28.64	37.51	38.66	39.01
PDE (sequential)	29.50	31.54	28.64	37.51	38.66	39.01
PDE (proposed algo-rithm)	29.51	31.56	28.64	37.50	38.66	39.01
MSEA+PDE (sequen-tial)	29.50	31.54	28.64	37.51	38.66	39.01
MSEA+PDE (proposed algorithm)	29.51	31.56	28.64	37.50	38.66	39.01

5 Conclusions

In this paper, we proposed a new block matching algorithm by sorting square sub-block and applying some scaling factor while keeping the same prediction quality compared with the original FS algorithm. Unlike the conventional fast PDE algo-rithms, Our algorithm doesn't need additional computation for matching order. Be-cause of that, our algorithm can be cascaded to other fast algorithms such TSS or SEA. Additionally, we can control easily trade-off between prediction quality and computational reduction for motion estimation. Experimentally, our algorithm re-duces up to 90% of computations compared with conventional FS algorithm without any degradation of prediction quality. Thus our algorithm will be useful in real-time video coding applications using MPEG-4 AVC or MPEG-2 standards.

Acknowledgement. This work was supported by The Regional Research Centers Program (Research Center for Logistics Information Technology), granted by the Korean Ministry of Education & Human Resources Development.

References

1. F. Dufaus and F. Moscheni, "Motion estimation techniques for digital TV: A review and a new contribution," *IEEE Proceeding*, vol. 83, pp. 858-876, Jun. 1995.
2. W. Li and E. Salari, "Successive elimination algorithm for motion estimation," *IEEE Trans. Image Processing*, vol. 4, pp. 105-107, Jan. 1995.
3. G.C. de Oliveira and A. Alcaim, "On fast motion compensation algorithms for video coding," *Proc. PCS*, pp. 467-472. 1997.
4. J.Y. Lu, K.S. Wu, and J.C. Lin, "Fast full search in motion estimation by hierarchical use of Minkowski's inequality (HUMI)," *Pattern Recog.*, vol. 31, pp. 945-952, 1998.
5. M.Z. Coban and R.M. Mersereau, "A fast exhaustive search algorithm for rate-constrained motion estimation," *IEEE Trans. Image Processing*, vol. 7, pp. 769-773, May 1998.
6. H.S. Wang and R.M. Mersereau, "Fast algorithms for the estimation of motion vectors," *IEEE Trans. Image Processing*, vol. 8, pp. 435–438, Mar. 1999.
7. X.Q. Gao, C.J. Duanmu, and C.R. Zou, "A multilevel successive elimination algorithm for block matching motion estimation," *IEEE Trans. Image Processing*, vol. 9, pp. 501-504, Mar. 2000.
8. T.G. Ahn, Y. H. Moon and J.H Kim, "Fast full-search motion estimation based on Multilevel Successive Elimination Algorithm," *IEEE Trans. Circuits System for Video Technology*, vol. 14, pp. 1265-1269, Nov. 2004.
9. Y. Naito, T. Miyazaki, and I. Kuroda, "A fast full-search motion estimation method for programmable processors with a multiply-accumulator," *Proc. ICASSP*, pp. 3221-3224, 1996.
10. V.L. Do and K.Y. Yun, "A low-power VLSI Architecture for full-search block-matching motion estimation," *IEEE Trans. Circuits System for Video Technology*, vol. 8, pp. 393-398, Aug. 1998.
11. J.N. Kim, "Adaptive matching scan algorithm based on gradient magnitude for fast full search in motion estimation," *IEEE Trans. Consumer Electronics*, vol. 45, pp. 762-772, Aug. 1999.
12. J.N. Kim, S.C. Byun, Y.H. Kim and B.H. Ahn, "Fast Full Search Motion Estimation Algorithm Using Early Detection of Impossible Candidate Vectors", *IEEE Trans. Signal Processing*, vol. 50, pp. 2355-2365, Sept. 2002.
13. B. Erol, F. Kossentini, and H. Alnuweiri, "Efficient Coding and mapping algorithms for software-only real-time video coding at low bit rates," *IEEE Trans. Circuits Syst. for Video Technol.*, vol. 10, pp. 843-856, Sept. 2000.

Variable Neighborhood Search for the Orienteering Problem

Zülal Sevkli[1] and F. Erdoğan Sevilgen[2]

[1] Fatih University, Department of Computer Engineering, Büyükçekmece, Istanbul, Turkey
zsevkli@fatih.edu.tr
[2] Gebze Institute of Technology, Department of Computer Engineering, Gebze,
Kocaeli, Turkey
sevilgen@gyte.edu.tr

Abstract. The Orienteering Problem (OP) is a version of TSP with profits in which instead of a cycle, a path is sought. In this paper, we consider three variations of Variable Neighborhood Search (VNS) and present the first algorithm solely based on VNS to solve the OP. The experimental results for the benchmark problems indicate that the algorithm, designed by using Reduced VNS instead of the local search phase of the traditional VNS, is the best amongst other variations of VNS we tried; it is the most robust and produces the best results, in terms of solution quality, within a reasonable amount of time. Moreover, it improves the best known results for several benchmark problems and reproduces the best results for others.

1 Introduction

The Orienteering Problem (OP) is a subset selection version of well-known Traveling Salesman Problem with profits. The objective of the Orienteering Problem is to construct a path starting at an origin and ending at a destination that maximizes the total profit without violating prescribed limits. The problem is inspired from and named after an outdoor sport usually played on mountains or forest areas.

The Orienteering Problem can be described in detail as follows: Let $G = (V, E)$ be a graph where V denotes the set of nodes (control points) and E denotes the set of edges between nodes in V. Each node v_i in V ($1 \leq i \leq n$) has a score $S_i \geq 0$ and the scores of v_1 (the origin node) and v_n (the destination node) are set to 0; i.e. $S_1 = S_n = 0$. Each edge between v_i and v_j has a cost $c_{i,j}$ associated with it. The objective of the OP is to find an acyclic path from v_1 to v_n that maximizes the total score of the nodes on the path without violating a cost constraint (e.g., the total cost of the edges on the path is not more than a specified limit, $T_{\max}$). Because of this limitation, the path needs not to visit all control points and each node on path is visited at most once. Golden et al. [7] prove that the OP is NP-hard. The mathematical model of the OP can be found in [17].

A. Levi et al. (Eds.): ISCIS 2006, LNCS 4263, pp. 134 – 143, 2006.

The OP is used to model many practical problems such as inventory/routing, customer/vehicle assignment [6] and production scheduling [1]. Additionally, a variation of the OP with time windows has applications to problems including postal delivery or school bus routing [13].

Table 1. Exact solution methods for the OP

Reference	Solution Strategy	Year
Hayes and Norman [12]	Dynamic Programming	1984
Kataoka and Morito [14]	Branch and Bound	1988
Laporte and Martello [16]	Branch and Bound	1990
Ramesh et al.[20]	Branch and Bound	1992
Leifer and Rosenwein [17]	0-1 Integer Programming	1993
Fishetti et al.[5]	Branch and cut	1998

There exist a number of exact methods for the OP as summarized in Table 1. By using these exact methods, small sized instances of the OP problem can be solved in a reasonable amount of time. However, when the problem size increases, the computational time grows exponentially and these methods become impractical. Therefore, many researchers focus on heuristic algorithms.

Table 2. Heuristic methods used for the OP

Reference	Solution Strategy	Year
Tsiligirides [23]	greedy insertion	1984
Tsiligirides [23]	sweep-based insertion	1984
Golden et al. [7,8]	greedy insertion, path improvement	1987
Keller [15]	random insertion, path improvement	1989
Keller [15]	greedy insertion, path improvement	1989
Ramesh and Brown [19]	random insertion, path improvement	1991
Chao et al. [3]	random insertion, path improvement	1996

Heuristic methods generally solve the OP in two stages; **path construction** and **path improvement**, respectively. Several **path construction** approaches are proposed in the literature. One way is that; each point is given a weight calculated by various formulations using point scores and/or edge costs [7, 8, 15, 23]. A point selected by using a greedy strategy (based on the weights) is inserted to an initially empty path, until no more insertion is possible. Random point selection is alternatively used [15, 19]. Tsiligrides [23] presents another path construction approach based on the sweep algorithm [25]. In this approach, search space is divided into sectors, dynamically and paths are constructed based on the sectors. An alternative construction approach which is driven by a partition of the points into a set of feasible paths is also proposed [3]. Feasible paths are built up with a greedy insertion strategy. After path construction stage, path improvement stage starts. In **path improvement** stage, generally 2-opt, 3-opt are used for decreasing the total cost and point insertion, deletion, and exchange are used for increasing the total score. Table 2 summarizes heuristic approaches for solving the OP.

In addition to heuristic methods, several meta-heuristics are applied to the OP. Wang et al. [24] use artificial neural network. Tasgetiren and Smith [22] use genetic algorithm to solve the OP. Recently, ant colony algorithm and tabu search are used by Liang et al. [18]. The heuristics proposed by Ramesh and Brown [19], and Chao et al. [3] can also be considered as the meta-heuristic approaches (tabu search and deterministic annealing, respectively [4]). Tasgetiren's and Liang's results are competitive to the best known results; though Tasgetiren's computational time is relatively high. Meta-heuristic approaches for solving the OP are provided in Table 3.

Table 3. Meta-heuristic methods used for the OP

Reference	Solution Strategy	Year
Wang et al [9,12]	Neural Network	1995
Tasgetiren and Smith [16]	Genetic algorithm	2000
Liang et al.[18]	Ant Colony	2001
Liang et al.[18]	Tabu search	2001

In this paper, we present an algorithm based on the philosophy of Variable Neighborhood Search (VNS) to solve the OP. VNS [10] is a meta-heuristic proposed in 1997 for solving combinatorial and global optimization problems. VNS is applied to many problems such as the p-Median [11], the k-Cardinality tree [2], the degree constraint MST [21], successfully and competitive results are obtained. Further applications of VNS can be found in [9].

We consider the Euclidean OP where the nodes are in the Euclidean plane. In such a problem, the graph is a full graph and the score of an edge in the graph is the distance between nodes and determined by the geographical measure. The following three versions of VNS are applied to the Euclidean OP:

- VNSwithVND: VND is a variation of VNS in which the shaking step is omitted. In this version, VND is used in local search step of VNS.
- VNSwithRVNS: Reduced VNS (RVNS) is a variation of VNS in which the local search step is omitted. In this version, RVNS is used in local search step of VNS.
- Pure RVNS.

All three variations of VNS are implemented and tested using 107 benchmark problems. All three methods provided good results but VNSwithRVNS is the best amongst them. It improves the best known results for 11 benchmark problems and produces the solution in a comparable amount of time. The performance of VNSwithRVNS can be attributed to the elimination of exhaustive local search since it is expensive for large problems.

2 Variable Neighborhood Search

The basic idea of VNS algorithm is to search solution space with a systematic change of neighborhood. The pseudo-code of VNS algorithm is given in Figure 1, where N_k, represents k^{th} neighborhood structure (k=1,...,k_{max}), S represents the set of all feasible solutions and N_k(s) represent the set of solutions in the kth neighborhood of the solution s. Both the choice and the order of neighborhood structures are critical for the performance of the algorithm. The algorithm starts with selection of an initial solution from S. In the course of following two nested loops, the algorithm explores the solutions in S and tries to find the best solution. **LocalSearch** and **Shake** functions perform this exploration, systematically. The function **Shake** diversifies the solution; it selects an alternative solution s' randomly from N_k(s). Neighborhood structures are usually ranked in such a way that VNS algorithm explores increasingly further away from s. The result of **Shake**, s', is used as the starting point for the **LocalSearch**. After exploring local area thoroughly, the best solution of the local search, s" is compared with s. If s" is better than s, it replaces s and the algorithm starts all over again with k=1. Otherwise, k is incremented and algorithm continues from shaking phase with next neighborhood structure. This inner loop is terminated after all neighborhood structures are exhausted. The outer loop iterates until a stopping condition is met. Possible stopping conditions include maximum CPU time allowed, maximum number of iterations or maximum number of iterations between two improvements.

```
Procedure VNS
   Define neighborhood structures N_k (k=1,...,k_max)
   Generate initial solution s ∈ S
   while stopping condition is not met do
      k ← 1
      while k ≤ k_max do
         s' ← Shake(s), s' ∈ N_k(s)
         s" ← LocalSearch(s'), s" ∈ S
         if (Fitness(s") < Fitness(s))
            s ← s"
            k ← 1
         else
            k ← k+1
      end-while
   end-while
End-Procedure
```

Fig. 1. The pseudo-code of VNS algorithm

There are several variations of the VNS including Variable Neighborhood Descent (VND), RVNS, and etc. In VND, shaking phase is removed from VNS so that the algorithm explores local optima by using neighborhood structures only. VND can be used as a part of VNS in the local search phase. As opposite of VND, RVNS use only shaking phase while exploring the solutions. RVNS is useful for problems where local search is expensive. The details of the version and extension of VNS can be found in [9].

3 Variable Neighborhood Search for the Orienteering Problem

In this section, we describe our application of VNS to solve the OP; firstly, we present the representation of OP solution and neighborhood structures used. Secondly, we explain the details of VNS application i.e., the methods used in shaking and local search phases.

3.1 Problem Representation

Candidate solutions of the OP are formed by using permutations of control points not including the origin and the destination. In order to obtain the feasible OP solution from a permutation, the points are inserted between the origin and destination one by one starting from the first point in the permutation until a prescribed cost limit is exceeded. In other words, let $\left(v_{i_1}, v_{i_2}, \ldots, v_{i_{n-2}}\right)$ be a permutation of control points, the solution obtained from the permutation is $\left(v_0, v_{i_1}, v_{i_2}, \ldots, v_{i_k}, v_n\right)$ where feasibility criterion $c_{0i_1} + c_{i_1 i_2} + c_{i_2 i_3}, \ldots + c_{i_{k-1} i_k} + c_{i_k n} \leq T_{\max}$ is satisfied.

3.2 Neighborhood Structures

The neighborhood structures are the key elements of VNS and the performance depends on both the choice and the order of the neighborhood structures. In this study, the following four neighborhood structures are employed:

Insert: It defines the closest neighborhood considered. This structure performs an insertion of a control point chosen randomly from the permutation, in front of another randomly chosen control point. Using this structure, following effects can be observed:

- A control point inside the solution can be deleted from the solution.
- A control point outside the solution can be inserted into the solution.
- The position of a control point inside the solution can be changed to another location inside the solution.
- The position of a control point outside of the solution can be changed. This operation does not change the current solution but may affect the results of subsequent operations.

Exchange: It is the other neighborhood structure used to explore new solutions in a little further vicinity of a solution. In this structure, two randomly selected control points are simply swapped. Again, depending on whether the control points are in the solution or not, the meaning of the operation varies:

- A control point in the solution can be swapped with a control point outside of the solution. This operation is like performing a deletion followed by an insertion at the same position.
- Two control points in the solution can be swapped.
- Two control points outside of the solution are swapped.

Path insert: It is similar to insert structure apart from a randomly selected sub-path instead of only one control point is inserted. Three control points are chosen randomly in permutation: Two of them signify the beginning and the end of the sub-path, the other one shows the position where the insertion to be done. Note that using this structure, it is possible to search solutions in more distant neighborhoods than ones achievable by insert and exchange structures.

Path exchange: It exchanges two randomly selected sub-paths of equal length. This structure facilitates exploration of further away neighborhoods than all other structures.

3.3 Variations of VNS for the OP

In this study, we consider application of three variations of VNS for the OP as summarized in **Table 4:**

- **VNSwithVND:** VND is used as local search method in VNS. VND searches all the neighbors of the incumbent solution defined by a neighborhood structure and selects the best one that becomes the new incumbent solution for subsequent searches. Two neighborhood structures, namely the insert and exchange which explore solutions in close proximity to the incumbent solution, are employed in VND. Path insert and path exchange, other two neighborhood structures, are utilized in shaking phase of VNS.
- **RVNS:** It is a variation of VNS where random solutions are selected from a neighborhood without having local search phase. RVNS provides better performance results for problems where local search is expensive and size of instances are very huge. In our application of RVNS, all of the aforementioned neighborhood structures are used.
- **VNSwithRVNS:** This variation of VNS uses RVNS instead of the local search phase of basic VNS. So, the solutions are explored in two nested shaking phases; namely the distant and nearby shaking. Path insert and path exchange are used in distant shaking phase while insert and exchange are used in nearby shaking phase. Nearby shaking terminates when the number of iterations exceeds the square of the problem size (i.e., the number of control points).

Table 4. The neighborhood structures used in the VNS variations

		RVNS	VNSwithVND	VNSwithRVNS
Shaking		1.insert 2.exchange 3.path insert 4.path exchange	1. path insert 2. path exchange	1. path insert 2. path exchange
LocalSearch		-	1. insert 2. exchange	1. insert 2. exchange

4 Experimental Results

All three variations of VNS algorithm are implemented in Borland C and tested for several benchmark problems. Experimentation is performed on an Intel P4 2.6 GHz PC with 512 MB memory. There are 107 benchmark problems in the literature: Problems with 32 (dataset 1 includes 18 problems), 21 (dataset 2 includes 11 problems), 33 (dataset 3 includes 20 problems) control points are provided by Tsiligirides [23], 32 (dataset 1 includes 18 problems), 66 (dataset 5 includes 26 problems) and 64 (dataset 6 includes 14 problems) control points are provided by Chao [3].

Table 5. Comparison of VNS variations: results for datasets 1,2,3 and 4 based on CPU time (seconds) , RPE , ARPE

	CPU			RPE			ARPE		
	RVNS	**VNS with VND**	**VNS with RVNS**	**RVNS**	**VNS with VND**	**VNS with RVNS**	**RVNS**	**VNS with VND**	**VNS with RVNS**
Dataset 1	0.91	6.86	2.79	1.16	0.00	0.00	9.06	0.50	0.12
Dataset 2	0.43	0.69	0.15	1.02	0.00	0.00	4.65	0.52	0.00
Dataset 3	1.05	9.99	0.89	0.86	0.00	0.00	6.50	0.22	0.04
Dataset 4	0.85	6.58	0.62	1.05	0.00	0.00	9.39	0.52	0.05
	0.81	**6.03**	**1.11**	**1.02**	**0.00**	**0.00**	**7.40**	**0.44**	**0.05**

Each problem is run 10 times and results are compared based on computational time (CPU), average relative percentage error (ARPE) and relative percentage error (RPE). RPE is the error in the best solution in all repetitions with respect to the best known solution. It indicates whether an algorithm finds the best known solution throughout the repetitions. ARPE is the average error of all the solutions in the repetitions. ARPE specifying the robustness of an algorithm, will be smaller if more repetitions find good solutions.

The results of three variations of VNS for the first four datasets with respect to above mentioned performance measures are given in Table 5. In order to make better judgment for different variations, the results are given for different number of iterations. While RVNS is executed 10000 iterations, VNSwithVND and VNSwithRVNS are executed for 1000 iterations. Results indicate that, RVNS is the fastest method in the expense of larger error values. Although, RVNS could not find the best known solution for several problems, both VNSwithVND and VNSwithRVNS produce the best known solution for all problems. Moreover, robustness of RVNS is poorer than robustness of the competitors. On the other hand, VNSwithVND has a good error characteristic in the expense of larger execution time. The computational time of VNSwithVND is much larger than the others. VNSwithRVNS achieves the best RPE and APRE values and comparably good computational time. Therefore, it can be claimed that it is the best method among the others.

Table 6. Comparison of results on test problems dataset 5 and 6

Dataset 5

Tmax	TA	CGW	VNS	TA	CGW
5	10	10	10		
10	40	40	40		
15	100	120	120	+	
20	190	195	**205**	+	+
25	290	290	290		
30	400	400	400		
35	460	460	**465**	+	+
40	575	575	575		
45	645	650	650	+	
50	730	730	730		
55	820	825	825	+	
60	915	915	915		
65	980	980	980		
70	1070	1070	1070		
75	1140	1140	1140		
80	1215	1215	1215		
85	1265	1270	1270	+	
90	1340	1340	1340		
95	1390	1380	**1395**	+	+
100	1455	1435	**1465**	+	+
105	1515	1510	**1520**	+	+
110	1550	1550	**1560**	+	+
115	1590	1595	1595	+	
120	1635	1635	1635		
125	1655	1655	**1670**	+	+
130	1670	1680	1680	+	
Summary of VNS vs. Previous Heuristic Methods				13+ 0-	7+ 0-

Dataset 6

Tmax	TA	CGW	VNS	TA	CGW
15	90	96	96	+	
20	258	294	294	+	
25	354	390	390	+	
30	432	474	474	+	
35	516	570	**576**	+	+
40	642	714	714	+	
45	732	816	816	+	
50	828	900	900	+	
55	906	984	984	+	
60	978	1044	**1062**	+	+
65	1020	1116	1116	+	
70	1110	1176	**1188**	+	+
75	1152	1224	**1236**	+	+
80	1200	1272	1272	+	
Summary of VNS vs. Previous Heuristic Methods				14+ 0-	4+ 0-

The results obtained from VNSwithRVNS are also compared with the results in literature for datasets 5 and 6. The comparison with

- CGW: heuristic by Chao, Golden and Wasil and
- TA: heuristic by Tsiligirides

are given in Table 6. Better results have been observed for 11 problems in total.

5 Conclusions

In this paper, we propose VNS for solving the OP problem and examine the performance of our approach based on solution quality and execution time. Two well-known variations of VNS; VNSwithVND and RVNS and one which is the combination of VNS and RVNS are implemented and tested on 107 benchmark problems. VNS with RVNS outperforms other two methods. It finds the best known solution for all the problems and improves the best solution for 11 benchmark problems. As future research, we would like to apply same techniques to the team based TSP, especially team orienteering problem.

Acknowledgements

We would like to thank Fatih Taşgetiren for his helpful comments on the problem and Mehmet Şevkli for helping in development of preliminary versions of the algorithm.

References

1. Balas, E.:The prize collecting traveling salesman problem. Networks, 19 (1989) 621-636.
2. Brimberg, J., Urosevic, D., Mladenovic, N.: Variable neighborhood search for the vertex weighted k-cardinality tree problem. Eur. J. Oper. Res., 2004.
3. Chao, I.-M., B. L. Golden, E. A. Wasil: A fast and effective heuristic for the orienteering problem. Eur. J. Oper. Res., 88(3) (1996) 475-489.
4. Feillet, D., Dejax, P., Gendreau, M.: Traveling Salesman Problems with Profits. Transportation Science, 39 (2005) 188-205.
5. Fischetti, M., Gonzalez, J. S., Toth, P.: Solving the orienteering problem through branch-and-cut. INFORMS J. Comput., 10(2) (1998)133-148.
6. Golden, B.L., Assad A., Dahl, R.: Analysis of a large-scale vehicle routing problem with inventory component. Large Scale Systems, 7 (1984) 181-190.
7. Golden, B.L., Levy, Vohra, R.: The Orienteering Problem. Naval Res. Logist, 34(3) (1987) 307-318.
8. Golden, B.L., Wang, Q. , Liu, L.: A Multifaced heuristic for the orienteering problem. Naval Res. Logist, 35 (1988) 359-366.
9. Hansen, P., Mladenovic N.: An introduction to variable neighborhood search, in Metaheuristics, advances and in local search paradigms for optimization, i.S.V.e. al, Kluwer Academic Publishers: Dordrecht. (1999) 433-458.
10. Hansen, P., Mladenovic, N.:Variable neighborhood search: principles and applicatons. Eur. J. Oper. Res., 130 (2001) 449-467.
11. Hansen, P., Mladenovic, N.: Variable neighborhood search for the p-Median. Location Sci., 5 (1997) 207-226.
12. Hayes, M., .Norman., J., M.:Dynamic Programming in Orienteering:Route Choice and the Siting of Controls. J. Oper. Res. Soc., 35(9) (1984) 791-796.
13. Kantor, M.G., Rosenwein, M., B.: The orienteering problem with time windows. J. Oper. Res. Soc., 43(6) (1992) 629-635.
14. Kataoka, S., Morito, S.: An algorithm for the single constraint maximum collection problem. J. Oper. Res. Soc., 31(4) (1988) 515-530.

15. Keller, C.P.: Algorithms to solve orienteering problem: A Comparision. Eur. J. Oper. Res., 41 (1989) 224-231.
16. Laporte, G., Martello, S.: The selective traveling salesman problem. Discrete Applied M, 26 (1990)193-207.
17. Leifer, A.C., Rosenwein, M., B.: Strong Lineer Programming relaxations for orienteering problem. Eur. J. Oper. Res., 73 (1994) 517-523.
18. Liang, Y.-C., Kulturel-Konak., S., Smith, A.E.: Meta Heuristic For the Orienteering Problem. in Proceeding of the 2002 Congress on Evolutionary Computation (CEC'02). (2002), Hawaii.
19. Ramesh, R., Brown, K. M.: An efficient four-phase heuristic for the generalized orienteering problem. Comput. Oper. Res., 18(2) (1991)151-165.
20. Ramesh, R., Yoon, Y.-S. , Karwan, M. H.: An optimal algorithm for the orienteering problem. ORSA J. Comput., 4(42) (1992) 155-165.
21. Ribeiro, C., C., Souza, M.,C.: Variable Neighborhood Search for the degree-constrained minumum spaning tree problem. Discrete Applied M, 118 (2002) 43-54.
22. Tasgetiren, F.M., Smith, A. E.: A genetic algorithm for the orienteering problem. in Congress Evolutionary Comput. (2000) San Diego, CA.
23. Tsiligirides, T.: Heuristic methods applied to orienteering. J. Oper. Res. Soc., 35(9) (1984) 797-809.
24. Wang, Q., Sun, X. , Golden, B. L. , Jia, J .: Using artificial neural network to solve orienteering problem. Ann. Oper. Res., 61 (1995)111-120.
25. Wren, A., Holliday, A.: Computer scheduling of vehicles from one or more depots to a number of delivery points. Oper. Res. Quart., 23 (1972) 333-344.

Extracting Gene Regulation Information from Microarray Time-Series Data Using Hidden Markov Models

Osman N. Yoğurtçu, Engin Erzin, and Attila Gürsoy

Computer Engineering, Koç University, Istanbul, Turkey
{oyogurtcu, eerzin, agursoy}@ku.edu.tr

Abstract. Finding gene regulation information from microarray time-series data is important to uncover transcriptional regulatory networks. Pearson correlation is the widely used method to find similarity between time-series data. However, correlation approach fails to identify gene regulations if time-series expressions do not have global similarity, which is mostly the case. Assuming that gene regulation time-series data exhibits temporal patterns other than global similarities, one can model these temporal patterns. Hidden Markov models (HMMs) are well established structures to learn and model temporal patterns. In this study, we propose a new method to identify regulation relationships from microarray time-series data using HMMs.

We showed that the proposed HMM based approach detects gene regulations, which are not captured by correlation methods. We also compared our method with recently proposed gene regulation detection approaches including edge detection, event method and dominant spectral component analysis. Results on Spellman's α-synchronized yeast cell-cycle data clearly present that HMM approach is superior to previous methods.

1   Introduction

Gene regulatory networks are control mechanisms of the gene expression level of a cell. They regulate and decide which genes in the cell will be transcribed into RNA (and then possibly translated to protein) and which others will remain silent along the cell cycle. With microarray technology, expression levels of thousands of genes can be measured simultaneously. Particularly, time series expression data from microarray measurements can be used to extract regulatory relationships among gene pairs.

There are a number of approaches to extract such information from time-series data. Simple correlation analysis [1], edge detection method [2], event method [3], Bayesian networks modeling [4], differential equations [5] and dominant spectral component decomposition [6] are the methods published in the recent literature.

Methods based on correlation coefficient of two time-series fail to locate many regulatory gene pairs, since these methods emphasize signal similarity. In [2], it is reported that only about 20% of known regulatory gene pairs can be identified

A. Levi et al. (Eds.): ISCIS 2006, LNCS 4263, pp. 144–153, 2006.
© Springer-Verlag Berlin Heidelberg 2006

using Pearson correlation on Spellman's yeast cell-cycle data. To overcome the limitations of correlation approach, they proposed the edge detection method, which focuses on the local features of data, the temporal behavior variations at the edges and the turning points of gene expression levels. Although edge-detection improves upon correlation, it still fails to to identify many known activations and can not be used for inhibitions. The event method proposed by [3] converts gene expression time-series data to an event string and calculates a score based on the sequence alignment of gene pair event strings. Event method, in addition to activations, is capable of detecting inhibitions. Another approach reported by [6] is based on finding dominant spectral components of time-series data using auto-regressive modeling. A component-wise correlation algorithm is then used to detect regulations.

In this study, we propose an alternative method based on hidden Markov models (HMMs). HMM approach is a well-known and widely used statistical method of characterizing temporal or sequential behaviors of a pattern. HMMs have been employed extensively in computational biology for protein sequence alignment problems [7,8,9]. In this study we used HMM to model time-series expression data of regulated gene pairs. Regulated gene pairs, either activations or inhibitions, are expected to carry temporal correlations or patterns in their experimental time-series microarray data. Figure 1 presents example expression patterns for activation and inhibition regulations and for an arbitrary gene pair (unknown regulation) from Spellman's α-synchronized cell-cycle experimental data. Hypothetically, as one of the gene pairs activate/inhibit the other gene, the expression of inhibitee/activatee does not necessarily exhibit strong signal correlation. However, HMM structure is capable of learning significant temporal patterns. In our case HMM learns the temporal behavior of the different classes of gene pairs like gene activation, inhibition or neither. Then the trained HMM can be used to classify a given time-series data of a gene pair.

The paper is organized as follows. Section 2 introduces our HMM based approach. The performance of the proposed method and comparison with the prior work including correlation, edge detection, event method and component-wise correlation, are given in Section 3.

2   Methods

In this study the temporal patterns of regulated gene pairs are modeled through HMM structure. Temporal expression data of gene pairs are treated as two dimensional observations from certain stochastic processes. This two dimensional observation stream is used to model known and unknown regulations with different HMM structures after a learning phase, in which some partial time-series data from known and unknown regulations are utilized to train HMMs.

An HMM structure includes states, state transitions and input observation probabilities. A sample HMM structure is given in Figure 2. Let us represent HMM as $\lambda = (\boldsymbol{A}, \boldsymbol{B}, \boldsymbol{\Pi})$ with the following parameter set:

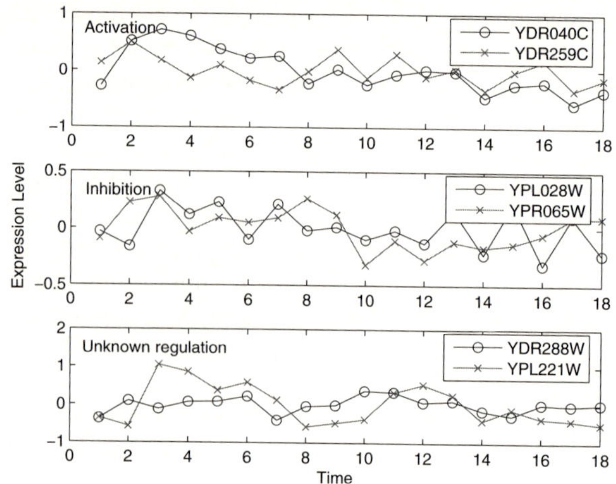

Fig. 1. Temporal behavior of three gene pairs (in activation, inhibition, and unknown regulation) from Spellman's α-synchronized cell-cycle experimental data

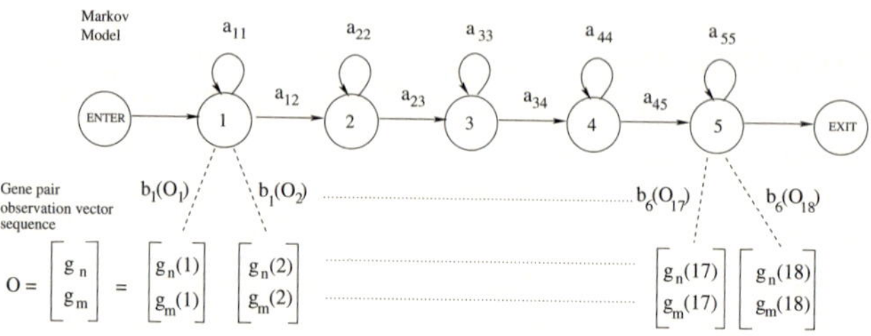

Fig. 2. A 5-state left-to-right HMM model. Observation vector includes expression levels of the gene pair (g_n, g_m).

- N is the number of states, where states are denoted by $S = \{s_1, s_2, \cdots, s_N\}$.
- $A = \{a_{ij}\}$ is the matrix of state transition probabilities where a_{ij} is the probability of making a transition from state i to j, such that $a_{ij} = P(q_{\tau+1} = s_j | q_\tau = s_i)$, where q_τ is the state at time τ. The state transition probabilities are assumed to be time independent.
- $B = \{b_j(o)\}$ is the vector of observation probabilities associated with each emitting state j, where
  $b_j(o) = P(o | q_\tau = s_j)$.
- $\Pi = \{\pi_i\}$ is the vector with the initial state probabilities of entering the model at state i such that $\pi_i = P(q_1 = s_i)$.

Since gene pair expression levels evolve forward in time, the transition probability matrix A is normally constrained to only allow self-loops or transitions from left to right, as plotted in Figure 2.

In the proposed HMM structure, states correspond to statistically correlated time-series segments, and state transitions correspond to segment-to-segment transitions. The probability density functions of expression levels in each segment are the corresponding observation probabilities, which are modeled using Gaussian density functions. Let, g_n represents the n-th gene in time-series microarray data, and the expression level of g_n at time instant t is denoted by $g_n(t)$. Then, the observation vector at time instant t is defined by $\boldsymbol{o}_t = [g_n(t), g_m(t)]'$ for genes g_n and g_m. The relation between observation vector and a left-to-right HMM structure is plotted in Figure 2. The probability of observing gene-pair time-series expressions, $\boldsymbol{O} = (\boldsymbol{o}_1, \boldsymbol{o}_2, ..., \boldsymbol{o}_T)$, given HMM model λ is defined as,

$$P(\boldsymbol{O}|\lambda) = \sum_{all\ \boldsymbol{q}} P(\boldsymbol{O}, \boldsymbol{q}|\lambda), \tag{1}$$

where $\boldsymbol{q} = (q_1, q_2, ..., q_T)$ is a possible state transition sequence. Further we can write the joint probability of the observation sequence and the state transition sequence given the model as,

$$P(\boldsymbol{O}, \boldsymbol{q}|\lambda) = P(\boldsymbol{O}|\boldsymbol{q}, \lambda)P(\boldsymbol{q}|\lambda), \tag{2}$$

where

$$P(\boldsymbol{O}|\boldsymbol{q}, \lambda) = b_{q_1}(\boldsymbol{o}_1)b_{q_2}(\boldsymbol{o}_2) \cdots b_{q_T}(\boldsymbol{o}_T), \quad and$$
$$P(\boldsymbol{q}|\lambda) = \pi_{q_1} a_{q_1 q_2} a_{q_2 q_3} \cdots a_{q_{T-1} q_T}.$$

The resulting class conditional probability from Equation (1) will be in the form of,

$$P(\boldsymbol{O}|\lambda) = \sum_{all\ \boldsymbol{q}} \pi_{q_1} b_{q_1}(\boldsymbol{o}_1) a_{q_1 q_2} b_{q_2}(\boldsymbol{o}_2) a_{q_2 q_3} \cdots$$
$$\cdots b_{q_{T-1}}(\boldsymbol{o}_{T-1}) a_{q_{T-1} q_T} b_{q_T}(\boldsymbol{o}_T), \tag{3}$$

in which observation symbol probabilities, $b_j(\boldsymbol{o})$, are modelled using Gaussian mixture densities as,

$$b_j(\boldsymbol{o}_t) = \sum_{l=1}^{L} \omega_{jl} \mathcal{N}(\boldsymbol{o}_t, \boldsymbol{\mu}_{jl} \boldsymbol{\Sigma}_{jl}). \tag{4}$$

For each state j, observation vector probabilities are represented as the weighted sum of L Gaussian mixture densities with means μ_{jl}, covariance matrices Σ_{jl} and weights ω_{jl}, such that $\sum_l \omega_{jl} = 1$ and $0 < \omega_{jl} \leq 1$.

2.1   Gene Regulation Detection

The detection of regulated gene pairs from time-series microarray data is modeled as a two-class classification problem. All possible gene pairs are split into two classes, where the first class λ_k includes all known regulations, and the second class λ_u includes the remaining gene pairs with unknown regulation information. (A pair of genes, which is not in the known regulations, is referred as unknown regulation throughout the paper.) The class conditional probability models, $P(\boldsymbol{O}|\lambda_k)$ and $P(\boldsymbol{O}|\lambda_u)$, respectively for known and unknown regulations, are extracted using HMM structures. The detection of known and unknown regulations is then formulated with the following maximization,

$$\lambda_* = \arg\max_{\lambda_k,\lambda_u} P(\boldsymbol{O}|\lambda), \tag{5}$$

where λ_* is the detected class for the observation vector $\boldsymbol{O}$, which is the time-series expression levels of a gene pair. Hence, given any pair of gene, one can detect whether the gene pair belongs to known or unknown regulation classes using Equation (5).

The detection mechanism in Equation (5) does not convey a measure of confidence for the decision. However, a confidence measure for known-regulation class, ρ, can be defined based on the following log-likelihood ratio,

$$\rho(\boldsymbol{O}) = \log P(\boldsymbol{O}|\lambda_k) - \log P(\boldsymbol{O}|\lambda_u). \tag{6}$$

Note that, the regulation confidence measure ρ is expected to be positive for regulated gene pairs, and expected to increase with increasing contribution of known regulation class and with decreasing contribution of unknown regulation class.

In this study, the known regulation class λ_k can be any of the following: (i) only known activations (λ_a), (ii) only known inhibitions (λ_i), or (iii) all known regulations, activations and inhibitions, (λ_r).

3   Experimental Results

Experiments have been conducted using Spellman's α-synchronized yeast cell-cycle data [10] (publicly available at http://genome-www. stanford.edu/cellcycle), which contains 6178 yeast genes. Each gene expression consists of 18-point temporal mRNA level measurements at a sampling rate of 7 min/sample. [2] identified a subset of genes (288 out of 6178 yeast genes), which are involved in 439 pairs of known regulations of which 343 are activations and 96 are inhibitions. Let us denote this subset of 288 genes, which are involved in these regulations, with $\mathcal{G}$, and the set of all possible gene pairs with $\mathcal{P}$. Note that, the set $\mathcal{P}$ includes 41328 possible gene pairs of which 439 gene pairs ($\mathcal{P}_r$) are known to be regulated and the regulation informations of the remaining gene pairs ($\mathcal{P}_u$) are unknown. Note that, the set of known regulations, $\mathcal{P}_r$, includes ordered gene pairs (g_1, g_2), where gene g_1 regulates gene g_2. Furthermore, the set of known gene regulations, $\mathcal{P}_r$, can be split into two sets, which are known activations ($\mathcal{P}_a$) and known inhibitions ($\mathcal{P}_i$).

The detection of regulated gene pairs using HMM approach requires to have two individual HMM models λ_k and λ_u, respectively for known and unknown regulations. The known regulation class λ_k can be further modeled as λ_r using all known gene regulations, or as λ_a using only known activations, or as λ_i using only known inhibitions. These HMM models can be extracted by the well-known

Baum-Welch algorithm [11], which employs expectation-maximization training procedure using a set of training data from known and unknown regulations. In this study, the HMM modeling is carried out using the HTK HMM tool kit [12]. The training and testing of the HMM models should be performed on independent data for fair evaluation of the gene regulation detection system. In order to get independent training and testing data, the sets of known and unknown regulations, $\mathcal{P}_k$ and $\mathcal{P}_u$, are partitioned into ten disjoint subsets of equal size, such that,

$$\mathcal{P}_k = \bigcup_{n=1}^{10} \mathcal{P}_k^n \text{ and } \mathcal{P}_u = \bigcup_{n=1}^{10} \mathcal{P}_u^n. \tag{7}$$

Note that, P_k can be any of the known regulation classes among P_r, P_a and P_i. In the extraction of experimental results, ten independent training and testing phases are performed using the leave-one-out scheme. That is, in the n-th training and testing phase, the subsets $\mathcal{P}_k^n$ and $\mathcal{P}_u^n$ are used for testing, and the training of the HMM models for known and unknown regulations, λ_k and λ_u, are performed using the remaining known regulations, $\bigcup_{j \neq n} \mathcal{P}_k^j$, and unknown regulations, $\bigcup_{j \neq n} \mathcal{P}_u^j$, respectively. The ten independent test results are combined together for the performance analysis of the detection of gene pair regulations.

3.1 Classification Rate Analysis

The impact of the number of HMM states to the classification performance is investigated. The classification rates of Equation (5) using λ_r and λ_u are calculated for varying number of states, (N_r, N_u). The best classification rate is achieved at number of states (5,5) with 64.92%. Note that, the classification rate of known regulations using Pearson correlation is reported as 20% in [2]. Later, we fixed N_r to 5, since it yields the best known regulation detection, and we investigate the effect of changing the number of states for unknown regulation class λ_u. When N_u changes from 4 to 6 states, we observed that while the classification rate for known regulations are increasing the classification rate of unknown regulations are decreasing. This observation is found to be useful for top-k analysis that we discuss in the following section.

3.2 Comparative Performance Analysis

Figure 3 plots the number of known regulations (activations or inhibitions) in top-k candidates for HMM(5,4), HMM(5,6) and Pearson correlation. Here HMM(5,4) refers to the HMM classifier with number of states $N_r = 5$ and $N_u = 4$. Top-k lists for HMM approach are prepared by sorting 41328 possible gene pairs using the regulation confidence measure ρ, which is defined in Equation 6. It is clear that HMM based approach significantly outperforms Pearson correlation. Further, HMM(5,6) performs better than HMM(5,4) for the first

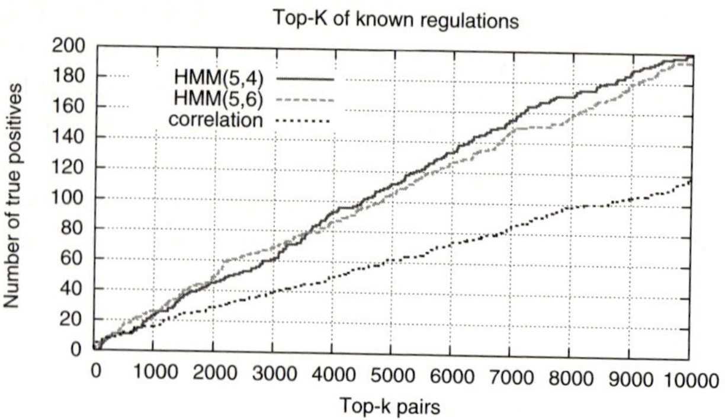

Fig. 3. Number of known regulations (activations or inhibitions) contained in the top-k pairs for correlation and our HMM based methods

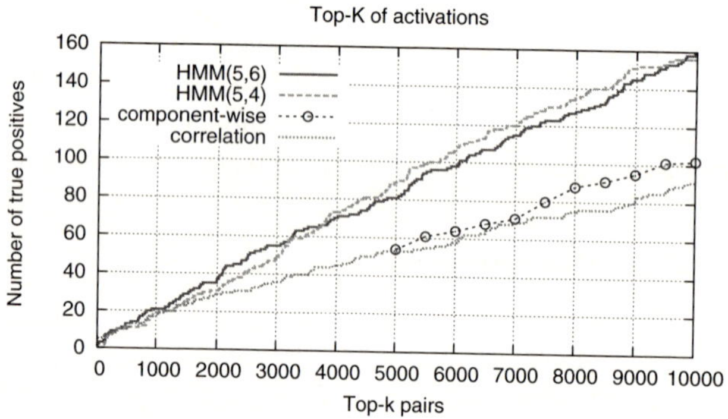

Fig. 4. Number of known activations contained in the top-k pairs for component-wise [6] and our HMM based methods

3500 top-k, after that HMM(5,4) performs better. Since the number of unknown regulations is significantly more than that of known regulations, for large k it is beneficial to have higher classification rate for unknown regulations. Note that, HMM(5,4) has better top-k performance for large k, since its classification rate for unknown regulations is higher. This can be used selecting proper HMM model for the region of interest in the top-k.

Figure 4 compares the top-k performances of the proposed HMM method and the correlation of dominant spectral components [6]. Since the results of component-wise method were reported for activations only, the top-k performances are evaluated using only activations λ_a. The HMM method is observed to be superior than the component-wise method and the event method [3], which is reported to be comparable to Pearson correlation. A similar comparison between edge function [2] and the proposed HMM approach for activations is presented in Table 1. The HMM approach is observed to detect more number of true activations as the total number of gene pairs increases. Figure 5 presents top-k

Table 1. Comparing classification performances of edge detection and our HMM based methods for activations

| Edge detection | | HMM method | |
Top-K	Activations	Top-K	Activations
96	5	79	3
223	5	223	9
557	13	568	14
1581	26	1564	31

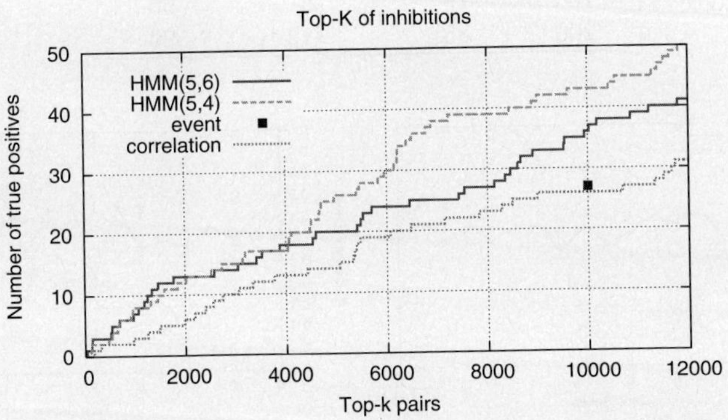

Fig. 5. Number of known inhibitions contained in the top-k pairs for correlation and our HMM based methods

performances for classification of inhibition pairs. The proposed HMM outperforms Pearson correlation and event method, which reports 27 inhibitions in top 10000.

Table 2 shows the number of common regulated gene pairs for the top-k regulations after they are ordered according to Pearson correlation and regulation confidence measure ρ. Note that, for the top 20 activations there are no common pairs between correlation and HMM methods. In the top 60 pairs, there are 4 activations out of 343 and 38 inhibitions out of 96. This observation indicates that correlation and HMM methods model different patterns of the regulated gene pairs and carry complementary regulation informations. This behavior is expected, since it is known that only about 20% of the known regulations can be detected using correlation method on Spellman's yeast cell-cycle data. It is expected to observe that HMM learns regulation patterns other than signal correlation, since we model regulation information with the stochastic HMM model after a learning phase using a subset of the known regulations, which are known to include about 80% weak signal correlation [2]. For example, Figures 6 (a) and (b) are respectively activation and inhibition cases with low Pearson correlation and low edge detection scores. However, the activation pair YLR182W and YLR286C is scored as 14th in activation top-k list of HMM among 41232 pairs. Similarly the inhibition pair YNL229C and YLR256C is scored as 25th in inhibition top-k list of HMM among 40985 pairs.

Table 2. Number of common regulations for Pearson correlation and our HMM based method in the top-k ranking among 439 known regulations of which 343 are activations and 96 are inhibitions

| | Number of common regulations | | |
Top-K	Regulations	Activations	Inhibitions
20	-	-	4
40	2	1	17
60	4	4	38
80	8	10	66
100	19	20	96
200	85	112	96

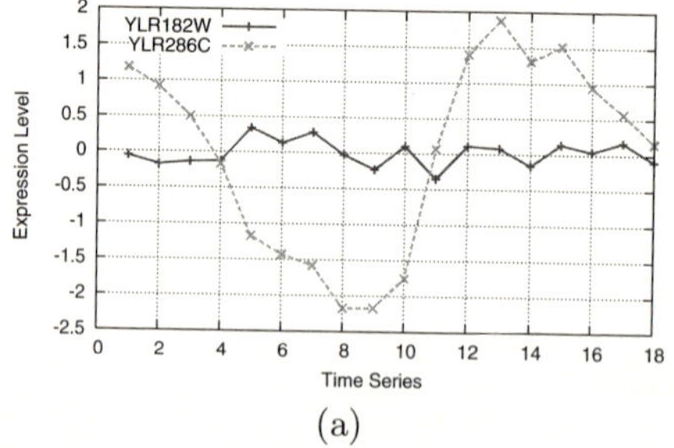

(a)

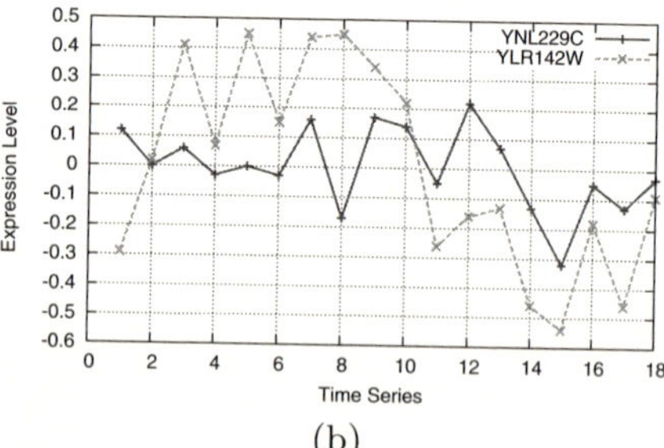

(b)

Fig. 6. (a)Temporal behavior of a known activation between genes YLR182W and YLR286C from Spellman's alpha-synchronized cell cycle experimental data. It has a high regulation confidence measure ρ and low Pearson and edge detection correlations. (b) Temporal behavior of a known inhibition between genes YNL229C and YLR256C from Spellman's alpha-synchronized cell cycle experimental data. It has a high regulation confidence measure ρ and low Pearson and edge detection correlations.

4   Conclusion

We present an HMM based method to infer potential gene regulations from microarray time-series data. The proposed HMM method learns temporal patterns from a set of known activations and inhibitions, as well as unknown regulations. Using two separately trained HMM models, one for known and one for unknown regulations, a two class classifier is used to detect potential gene regulations.

In the experimental studies using Spellman's α-synchronized yeast cell-cycle data, we show that HMM method clearly outperforms edge detection, event, component-wise and Pearson correlation methods, which are recently reported for gene regulation detection, in top-k analysis. We also demonstrate that HMM approach detects gene regulations, which are not captured using Pearson correlation method. Furthermore, HMM approach can be extended to model not only gene pairs but also a set genes that are co-regulated. This can be used to infer potential gene regulatory networks.

References

1. Eisen, M., Spellman, P., Brown, P., Bolstein, D.: Cluster analysis and display of genome-wide expression patterns. Proc. Natl. Acad. Sci. USA **95** (1998) 14863–14868
2. Filkov, V., Skiena, S., Zhi, J.: Analysis techniques for microarray time-series data. J. Comput. Biol. **9** (2002) 317–330
3. Kwon, A., Hoos, H., Ng, R.: Inference of transcriptional regulation relationships from gene expression data. Bioinformatics **19** (2003) 905–912
4. Friedman, N., Linial, M., Nachman, I., Pr, D.: Using bayesian networks to analyze expression data. J. Comput. Biol. **7** (2000) 601–620
5. De Hoon, M., Imoto, S., Miyano, S.: Inferring gene regulatory networks from time-ordered gene expression data using differential equations. In: Fifth International Conference on Discovery Science. Volume 2534 of Lecture Notes in Computer Science., Lbeck, Germany, Springer-Verlag (2002) 267–274
6. Yeung, L.K.e.: Measuring correlation between microarray time-series data using dominant spectral component. Bioinformatics **20(5)** (2004) 742–749
7. Churchill, G.: Stochastic models for heterogeneous DNA sequences. B. Math. Biol. **51** (1989) 79–94
8. Cardon, L., Stormo, G.: Expectation maximization algorithm for identifying protein-binding sites with variable lengths from unaligned dna fragments. Journal of Molecular Biology **223** (1992) 159–170
9. Krogh, A., Brown, M., Mian, S., Sjolander, K., Haussler, D.: Hidden markov models in computational biology: Applications to protein modeling. Journal of Molecular Biology **235** (1994) 1501–31
10. Spellman, P., Sherlock, G., Zhang, M., Iyer, V., Anders, K., Eisen, M., Brown, P., Botstein, D., Futcher, B.: Comprehensive identification of cell cycle-regulated genes of the yeast saccharomyces cerevisiae by microarray hybridization. Mol. Biol. Cell **9** (1998) 3273–3297
11. Baum, L.: An inequality and associated maximization technique in statistical estimation of probabilistic functions of a Markov process. Inequalities **3** (1972) 1–8
12. Young, S., Evermann, G., Hain, T., Kershaw, D., Moore, G., Odell, J., Ollason, D., Povey, D., Valtchev, V., Woodland, P.: The HTK Book (for HTK version 3.2.1). Cambridge University Engineering Department (2002)

Asymptotical Lower Limits on Required Number of Examples for Learning Boolean Networks*

Osman Abul[1], Reda Alhajj[2,3], and Faruk Polat[4]

[1] Dept of Cancer Research and Molecular Medicine, Norwegian University of Science and Technology, Trondheim, Norway
osmanabul@hotmail.com
[2] Dept of Computer Science, University of Calgary, Calgary, Alberta, Canada
alhajj@cpsc.ucalgary.ca
[3] Dept of Computer Science, Global University, Beirut, Lebanon
rhajj@gu.edu.lb
[4] Dept of Computer Engineering, Middle East Technical University, Ankara, Turkey
polat@ceng.metu.edu.tr

Abstract. This paper studies the asymptotical lower limits on the required number of samples for identifying Boolean Networks, which is given as $\Omega(logn)$ in the literature for fully random samples. It has also been found that $O(logn)$ samples are sufficient with high probability. Our main motivation is to provide tight lower asymptotical limits for samples obtained from time series experiments. Using the results from the literature on random boolean networks, lower limits on the required number of samples from time series experiments for various cases are analytically derived using information theoretic approach.

1   Introduction

Cells in living organisms contain thousands of genes together with their associated products, *i.e.*, proteins. The machinery in the genetic material determines which/when genes are going to be expressed and their abundance. Genetic regulatory network modeling studies uncovering code of this machinery. So, the uncovered models are abstractions of this machinery. Since gene expression data is a snapshot of what this machinery does, it helps to uncover its code. Note that this is a kind of reverse engineering. Lots of snapshots (samples) are usually required to reach meaningful models. The models for various cases are possible, *e.g.*, model under normal conditions, model under a specific stress, dynamic model from temporal data, model for genetic mutations, among others [1]. The objective in the modeling is to get insights in the cell machinery. If almost correct model is induced, then computational methods can be applied for a number of goals, including simulating, predicting, controlling, and treatment.

The advance in microarray technology has influenced the ongoing research on computational biology, and hence attracted the attention of several research

---

* Osman Abul carried out part of this work during his tenure as ERCIM fellowship.

A. Levi et al. (Eds.): ISCIS 2006, LNCS 4263, pp. 154–164, 2006.

groups who have mainly concentrated on analyzing microarray datasets for identifying models for gene regulation network. Given the time series gene expression data, the dynamic model that generated the data can be reverse engineered. Numerous approaches are proposed to construct the model. The approaches include, boolean networks [3,4,12,13,17], probabilistic boolean networks [15,16], bayesian networks [8,9,21], differential equations [6], petri nets [14], linear/quasi linear regression [7,19], markov chains [11], and others.

Boolean networks and probabilistic boolean networks are discrete; Bayesian networks can be either discrete or continuous. Modeling continuous gene expression levels with discrete models makes sense because it has been observed that qualitative approximation works well and human reasoning is qualitative most of the time. However, inference of discrete models from gene expression data is not trivial. Reasons for such difficulty include high dimension, continuous valued expression data, limited number of samples, and coarse and uneven sampling.

Dynamics of discrete networks can be explored within the discrete Markov Chains framework, *i.e.*, their dynamics can be collapsed into Markov chains to ease the analysis. The number of input/output pairs (samples) is very important for correctly inducing the underlying mechanism regardless of the modeling approach. This problem is studied in the literature in the context of boolean Networks [2,3,4,10]. Particularly, Akutsu *et al.* [2] present the analytical results on the lower limits for fully random samples. They also addressed the non-random (sequential) sampling case, as it is the typical one for genetic networks and presented the asymptotical lower limits from simulation studies. The current work is mainly motivated from the authors work to provide the analytical results instead of simulation results.

It has been observed that dynamics of genetic boolean networks resemble random boolean networks with small and constant in-degree. So, this suggests the use of results from dynamics of random boolean networks to study the behavior of genetic boolean networks. We make use of the results from random boolean network dynamics to analytically find lower limits on the required number of samples when the sampling is from a time-series experiment. Our results show that this quantity depends on network properties (chaotic vs. ordered, small vs. large in-degree, etc.) of the underlying random boolean network.

The rest of this paper is organized as follows. Section 2 covers boolean networks as an approach for modeling genetic regulatory networks. Section 3 provides some relevant results from random boolean networks literature. Section 4 gives our main result of the lower limits on the required number of samples problem for induction of boolean networks. Section 5 is conclusions.

2 Boolean Networks

Boolean (Genetic) Networks (BNs) were originally introduced by Kauffman [10], and extensively studied later [2,3,4,13]. In this approach, expression levels of genes are represented as boolean variables. So, binary discretization of continuous expression values are pre-requisite to model gene networks using boolean values. For any gene, the expression level is 1 when the gene is expressed (activated), and 0 when the gene is repressed (not-activated)[2]. Each gene is assigned a boolean variable, which is a boolean function of values of some other variables (genes). A particular state of the network is an instantiation of all of its variables. So, given N genes, the state space contains 2^N states. Since state transitions happen at discrete times and the state space is finite, BNs are sometimes called *discrete BNs*.

Definition 1 (Boolean Network). A boolean network (BN) with in-degree K is a tuple $G =< V, F >$, with a set of nodes V and a set of boolean functions $F = \{f_v | v \in V\}$; where f_v specifies gene regulation rule for node v. Gene v is expressed (repressed, resp.) if f_v computes to 1 (0, resp.). f_v is a deterministic boolean function of a subset of V with K elements, *i.e.*, $f_v(v_{i_1}, \ldots, v_{i_K})$; so the value of the K-subset completely determines the state of gene v; the genes not in the K-subset are either irrelevant or indirectly relevant to v. □

To define the dynamics of BNs, let the state of nodes at time step t be ψ_t; if gene v is expressed at time t, then $\psi_t(v) = 1$, otherwise $\psi_t(v) = 0$. The state of the nodes at time $t+1$ is defined by ψ_{t+1}, and this value is determined based solely on ψ_t of the K-subset: $\psi_{t+1}(v) = f_v(\psi_t(v_1), \ldots, \psi_t(v_K))$. The state of the network is defined as a vector S, and its value at time t is given by $S(t) =< \psi_t(v_1), \psi_t(v_2), \ldots \psi_t(v_N) >$, where $N = |V|$.

It is trivial to simulate any BN given an initial state $S(0)$; just apply $f_v, \forall v \in V$. For any initial state, since the state space is finite and the transitions are deterministic, after some time T', the simulation starts looping with period T, namely $S(T') = S(T' + T), S(T' + 1) = S(T' + T + 1)$, and so on. It is clear that both $T', T \leq 2^N$. The cycle $S(T'), S(T' + 1), \ldots, S(T' + T)$ is called *attractor* of the respective BN. If the length of this cycle is 1 (self-loop), it is called *point attractor*, otherwise it is called *cycle attractor*. A BN may have one or more attractors. States not in any attractor cycles are called *transient*. Biologically, attractors correspond to stable states of the cell, while transient states are unstable. It is evident that without any external perturbation, there is no exit from any of the attractors. So, it is clear that states of BN can be partitioned into equivalence classes based on their attractors, so called *basins*.

Time series gene expression data is needed to infer dynamic BNs. After the proper pre-processing (feature selection, discretization, etc), the input dataset to the inference procedure is obtained in the following way. Let the dataset be D and its length be $M + 1$; D is indexed from $D(0), D(1), \ldots, D(M)$. The input to the inference procedure is input/output pairs[3] of the form $< D(t), D(t + 1) >$, $\forall t \in \{0, 1, \ldots, M - 1\}$. This way, one-step back dependency is assumed. Although this is the canonical way of casting experiments to input/output pairs for dynamic BNs, there are approaches that assume multi-step back dependency.

---

[2] In practice, gene expression levels are quantized into ternary values (-1, 0 and 1), where 0 is used for baseline level, -1 for repression and 1 for over expression. Results for BNs apply for ternary networks and in general for *n*-ary networks.

[3] The terms *example*, *input/output pair*, and *sample* are used interchangeably.

The *consistency* problem is defined as finding functions for every node of the network with a complete agreement to data. Closely related to the consistency problem is the *best-fit extension* problem. In the best-fit extension approach, the function with the smallest disagreement to the input/output pair is searched. In this sense, the consistency problem (in which the disagreement is 0) is a special case of the best-fit extension [12,17]. So, inference can be done under this approach as well.

The authors of [3] present an exhaustive algorithm for finding consistent boolean functions (functions not violating input/output patterns) with the given input/output pairs under the constraint of bounded in-degree K. The algorithm considers all boolean functions for all K-subsets of V for any node v. For the maximum in-degree K, the number of boolean functions become at most 2^{2^K}, for any node v and for a specific K-subset of V. For N genes and $\binom{N}{K}$ combinations, the run time complexity of the exhaustive algorithm is clearly $O(2^{2^K} N^{K+1} M)$. The authors of [4] present an improved randomized algorithm, but the complexity is still high, between $O(N^{K-1})$ and $O(N^K)$.

An information theoretic algorithm named REVEAL is provided by Liang *et al.* [13] for the inference of BNs from experimental data. The maximum in-degree is assumed to be bounded by a constant K; otherwise the problem is NP-Hard. The algorithm is iterative: first consider 1-subsets, then 2-subsets and finally K-subsets. If any combination of subsets explains the whole variability consistently, the respective subset is selected with corresponding function as determiner for any node v. The measure for variability is mutual information. They have observed that the probability of identifying incorrect solutions reduces exponentially with the number of input/output pairs. The authors report that relatively less number of samples are enough for correct identification of BNs, though the complexity of the inference algorithm is relatively high.

3   Random Boolean Networks

Random Boolean Networks (RBN) are boolean networks where state-transitions happen according to randomly assigned (but fixed through time) boolean functions. In this work, we only consider the synchronous RBNs. They are sometimes referred to as random NK networks, where N is the number of nodes in the network and K is the maximum in-degree.

Although RBNs are conceptually simple, their dynamics exhibit interesting properties [20]. Their asymptotical (for large Ns) nature of dynamics strongly depends on K, as well as homogeneity value p, which is simply the ratio of ones or zeroes in the state vector. Note that p depends on the random functions assigned to nodes. Here, we present some of the proven or conjectured results related to their dynamics.

Result 1 (Kauffman [10]). If $\lambda = 2 K p (1-p)$, then the behavior is **chaotic** when $\lambda > 1$, otherwise it is **ordered**. $\square$

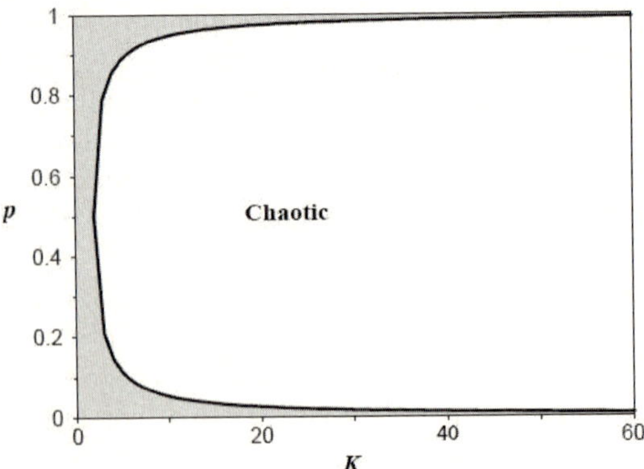

Fig. 1. Regions of chaotic and ordered behaviors for RBNs. Adapted from [5].

The *chaotic* behavior is a divergent behavior (similar states diverge to states far away), while *ordered* behavior is convergent (similar states converge to same state). *Chaotic* and *ordered* regions are depicted in Figure 1. The white region corresponds to *chaotic* behavior and the gray region represents *ordered* behavior.

Lemma 1. The critical value for K is 2 to guarantee an ordered behavior.

Proof : Letting $p = .5$ gives maximum value for $p(1-p)$; at this level it is clear that it is sufficient to have $K \leq 2$ in order to make $\lambda \leq 1$.   □

An important interest related to RBNs is how the number of attractors, number of states in attractor cycles and steps spent in transient states before reaching an attractor state, change as functions of K, N and p. Let na, nas, and nts denote these values of interest, respectively.   □

Result 2 (Somogyvari *et al.*[18]). nas and nts have same asymptotical growth (complexity) regardless of K and p.   □

The importance of Result 2 is that even though the complexity of nas and nts may change depending on K and p, their complexity ratio is constant. We would like to indicate that Result 2 is also valid for small N. In the following, the growth of these parameters is characterized.

Result 3 (Aldana [5]). When the network behavior is chaotic, nas grows exponentially, while when it is ordered, it grows algebraically.   □

It is clear from Results 3 and 1 that when K is in the order of N, there are exponential states in attractor cycles. The particular interest is when K is small and constant (not depending on N). This is because in genetic networks, the average K is constant and small (usually $K \leq 5$).

Result 4 (Aldana [5]). When $K = 1$, the values na, nas and nts grow unpredictably. But it has been shown that on the average nas and nts growth is constant; this is because cycle length drops exponentially with N and, therefore na grows exponentially.   □

Result 5 (Kauffman [10]). *na*, *nas* and *nts* grow with $\sqrt{N}$ when $K = 2$. □

Result 6 (Aldana [5]). When $K > 2$ and RBN is not chaotic, *na*, *nas* and *nts* grow algebraically (mostly polynomial). □

4   Required Number of Examples for Boolean Network Induction

The induction of BNs from given input/output pairs (samples) can be considered as a model fitting problem. There are several approaches developed for this problem within the context of inferring genetic BNs. The question is data complexity, *i.e.*, how much data we need to infer such a consistent network. For consistent datasets, the problem can be articulated as: how many samples do we need to uniquely identify the model that generated data?

The authors of [2] analyze the number of controlled experiments (instead of random) to be done for guaranteed identification of BNs. Their main result can be stated as follows: if the number of manipulated (intensionally set to either 0 or 1) genes are in the order of N, the problem can be solved with $O(logN)$ number of experiments. However, if the manipulated genes are restricted to at most a constant d, the problem can be solved with $O(N^{2d})$ number of experiments; for details see [2]. As it is clear, the complexity changes depending on the experimental protocol followed. If we follow the former protocol, we need considerably less number of experiments, but for true biological networks following such a protocol is almost impossible because of the need for controlling large number of genes in parallel.

The easiest protocol, of course, is getting random snapshots (input/output pairs) from the network. Akutsu *et al.* [3,4,2] studied the required number of observed input/output pairs (*i.e.*, not controlled) needed for identifying and inferencing BNs. It has been shown that the number of experiments required from uniformly random input/output pairs is $\Omega(logN)$; but with a considerable constant factor. Indeed, $\Omega(logN)$ complexity has been first observed by Liang *et al* [13] in their simulations. Finally, the main result of Akutsu *et al.* is articulated next in Theorem 1.

Theorem 1 (Akutsu *et al.* [3]). Given $O(2^{2K} \cdot (2K + \alpha) \cdot log(N))$ random samples, the following holds with probability of at least $1 - \frac{1}{N^\alpha}$: there exists at most one BN of N nodes with maximum in-degree $\leq K$, which is consistent with the given input/ouput pairs.

Proof: Refer to [3] for the complete proof. □

The information theoretic lower bound can also be developed as shown next.

Lemma 2. The number of bits obtained from a fully random sample of NK BN is N bits.

Proof: Since there are 2^N possible states for NK network, the information obtained from a random sample is $log(2^N) = N$ bits. □

Lemma 3. $\Omega(2^K N + NKlogN)$ bits of information are necessary to identify a NK BN.

Proof: For each node, there are $\Omega(N^K)$ possible combinations of input nodes, and 2^{2^K} possible boolean functions per node. There are $\Omega((2^{2^K}N^K)^N)$ BNs whose maximum in-degree is at most K. It suffices to take the logarithm of this quantity. Therefore, $\Omega(2^K N + NKlogN)$ bits are required to identify a BN. $\square$

Algorithm 1. Uniquely identifying a BN from time series samples

---

Require: number of genes N, in-degree K given

   $Network \leftarrow$ Randomly construct a random NK BN

  repeat

    select an initial state $s(0)$ randomly

    $s \leftarrow s(0)$

    repeat

      if Is the $Network$ is uniquely identified **then**

        Return

      end if

      $s \leftarrow$ state of $Network$ following s

    until a cycle is detected

  until Forever

Theorem 2 (Akutsu *et al.* [3]). $\Omega(2^K + KlogN)$ input/output pairs are necessary in the worst case to identify BN of maximum in-degree $\leq K$.

Proof: Since the total information required to identify a BN is $\Omega(2^K N + NKlogN)$ bits (From Lemma 3) and the information obtained from a single experiment is N bits (From Lemma 2), therefore $\Omega(2^K + KlogN)$ experiments are necessary in the worst case. $\square$

The corollary to Theorems 1 and 2 is that $\Theta(logN)$ experiments are necessary and sufficient, with high probability, to induce a NK BN from random samples when K is constant.

Both Theorems 1 and 2 apply for BNs with random sampling with in-degree of at most K. On the other hand, time series experiments are not random, but the next sample (at time $t + 1$) is completely dependent on the current sample (at time t). The authors address this case as well and show that the number of required samples is still $\Omega(logN)$ based on their simulations, *i.e.*, this is not an analytic result. They obtained $\Omega(logN)$ complexity (but with a much larger constant factor, $\approx$ 20 times larger compared to random sampling) with the experimental protocol given in Algorithm 1.

The experimental protocol given in Algorithm 1. is a typical time series protocol. The outer loop starts with a random initial state $s(0)$ and the inner loop generates next states along the trajectory until a cycle is detected. Since there is no point to follow the trajectory afterwards, the outer loop starts from another random start state. Note that given the initial state, the trajectory is uniquely determined as state transitions are always deterministic. The outer and inner loops are executed until the underlying network is uniquely identified. We would like to emphasize here that only the initial state $s(0)$ is random, but other states along the trajectory are not random or only random within the states of respective basin as there is no way of moving to states of other basins.

Motivated by the authors simulation results from time series experiments, we attempt to analytically, instead of by simulations, derive lower bounds on the required number of examples for the experimental protocol given in Algorithm 1.. We use information theoretic lower bounds and exploit the results for RBNs from Section 3.

Theorem 3. The average number of information units obtained from time series experiments for a network with N nodes and $(nas + nts)$-long trajectory is $\left(\frac{N+C(nas+nts-1)log(nas+nts-1)}{(nas+nts)}\right)$ bits.

Proof: The total information can be calculated as the total information obtained from the first random experiment and the information obtained from $nas + nts - 1$ dependent experiments. By Lemma 2, the first term is N. Since each of the dependent experiments can be in one of $nas + nts - 1$ states following the initial state, and then $nas + nts - 2$, and so on until 1, thereby the total information content of all dependent experiments amounts to $log(nas + nts - 1) + log(nas + nts - 2) + \cdots + log(1) = log((nas + nts - 1)!) = \Theta((nas + nts - 1)log(nas + nts - 1))$. This is because we exploit the information from the previous experiments to restrict the outcome for the given the input. We can replace $\Theta((nas+nts-1)log(nas+nts-1))$ by $C(nas+nts-1)log(nas+nts-1)$, where C is the constant involved in the growth. Since the total information obtained is $N + C(nas + nts - 1)log(nas + nts - 1)$, dividing this by the total number of experiments gives the average number of information units. $\square$

Theorem 4. The required number of samples required for identifying NK BN is $\Omega\left(\frac{2^K N+N \cdot K \cdot log(N)}{N+C(nas+nts-1)log(nas+nts-1)}(nas + nts)\right)$.

Proof: From Theorem 2, the required total number of bits that should be obtained is $\Omega(2^K N + NKlogN)$; and from Lemma 3, the total number of bits obtained from a trajectory is $C(nas + nts - 1)log(nas + nts - 1)$. By taking their ratio, we find the number of trajectories, and multiplying this ratio with the number of samples $(nas + nts)$ in each trajectory gives the result. $\square$

Our interest is on the lower bound on the required number of examples for constant K values as it is the case for true genetic networks. Note that it is enough to characterize this by finding the value of $(nas + nts)$. The corollaries below make use of Theorem 4.

Corollary 1. For a NK BN, where $K = 1$, the required number of examples is $\Omega(logN)$.

Proof: From Theorem 4, this is evident by plugging constant $K = 1$ and assuming $(nas + nts) = constant$ (recall Result 4). $\square$

Corollary 2. For a NK BN, where $K = 2$, the required number of examples is $\Omega(\sqrt{N}logN)$.

Proof: From Theorem 4, this is evident by plugging constant $K = 2$ and assuming $(nas + nts) = \sqrt{N}$ (recall Result 5).   □

Corollary 3. For a NK BN with constant $K > 2$ and when network behavior is chaotic, the required number of examples is $\Omega(logN)$.

Proof: From Theorem 4, this is evident by plugging constant K and assuming $(nas + nts)$ exponential, *e.g.*, $(nas + nts) = 2^N$ (recall Result 3).   □

Corollary 4. For a NK BN with constant $K > 2$ and when network behavior is ordered, the required number of examples is $\Omega(N)$.

Proof: From Theorem 4, this is evident by plugging constant K and assuming $(nas + nts)$ polynomial, *e.g.*, $(nas + nts) = N^2$ (recall Result 6).   □

Note that if we do not exploit the information from the previous experiments along the trajectory, then in any experiment the information obtained is N. In that case, we need to replace the term $log(nas + nts - 1)$ with N in Theorem 4. As a result, for a fixed K, all the lower bounds in Corollaries 1, 2, 3 and 4 will give the same bound of $\Omega(logN)$. Though this bound is correct, it is not tight for certain cases, *e.g.*, Corollary 2 and 4. In this respect, our analysis gives tight bounds for certain cases.

5   Conclusions

Motivated from the work of Akutsu *et al.* [2], we tackled the problem of analytically proving the required number of samples from time series experiments for induction of BNs. Their main result is that $\Theta(logN)$ experiments are required and sufficient with high probability when inducing BNs from fully random samples. For the samples generated from time series experiments, however, the lower limit was not so clear. Their conjecture of lower limit, from simulations, is $\Omega(logN)$.

We have shown that the required number of examples change compared to random sampling case. We have also shown that, depending on the network parameters and chaoticity, the lower limits change as well. Although the lowest lower limit $\Omega(logN)$ is valid for all cases we identified; for some cases we have found better lower limits using information theoretic approach and exploiting results from random BN research.

RBFs show fascinating properties, quoting Kauffman "It has been more than 20 years since I discovered those features of random networks, and they still surprise me"; our results also show some interesting properties on the required number of examples. For example, the lower limit for $K = 1$ is same as when K is constant and RBF is chaotic. On the other hand, the results show that larger number of samples are required when K is constant and RBF is ordered.

References

1. Osman Abul. Controlling discrete genetic regulatory networks. *PhD Thesis, Middle East Technical University*, January 2005.
2. Tatsuya Akutsu, Satoru Kuhara, Osamu Maruyama, and Satoru Miyano. Identification of genetic networks by strategic gene disruptions and gene overexpressions under a boolean model. *Theoretical Computer Science*, 298:235–251, 2003.
3. Tatsuya Akutsu, Satoru Kuhara, and Satoru Miyano. Identification of genetic networks from a small number of gene expression patterns under the boolean network model. In *Proc. of Pacific Symposium on Biocomputing*, pages 17–28, 1999.
4. Tatsuya Akutsu, Satoru Miyano, and Satoru Kuhara. Algorithms for 'identifying boolean networks and related biological networks based on matrix multiplication and fingerprint function. In *Proc. of Research in Computational Molecular Biology*, pages 8–14, 2000.
5. Maximino Aldana. Boolean dynamics of networks with scale-free topology. *Physica D*, 2003.
6. Ting Chen, Hongyu L. He, and George M. Church. Modelling gene expression with differential equations. In *Proc. of Pacific Symposium on Biocomputing*, pages 29–40, 1999.
7. Patrik D'haesseleer, Shoudan Liang, and Roland Somogyi. Genetic network inference: from co-expression clustering to reverse engineering. *Bioinformatics*, 16(8):707–726, 2000.
8. Nir Friedman, Michal Linial, Iftach Nachman, and Dana Peer. Using bayesian networks to analyze expression data. *Computational Biology*, 7:601–620, 2000.
9. Seiya Imoto, Takao Goto, and Satoru Miyano. Estimation of genetic networks and functional structures between genes by using bayesian networks and nonparametric regression. In *Proc. of Pacific Symposium on Biocomputing*, pages 175–186, 2002.
10. S.A. Kauffman. The origins of order: Self organization and selection in evolution. *Oxford University Press, New York*, 1993.
11. Seungchan Kim, Huai Li, Edward R. Dougherty, Nanwei Cao, Yidong Chen, Michael Bittner, and Edward B. Suh. Can markov chain models mimic biological regulation. *Biological Systems*, 10(4):337–357, 2002.
12. Harri Lahdesmaki, Ilya Shmulevich, and Olli Yli-Harja. On learning gene regulatory networks under the boolean network model. *Machine Learning*, 52:147–167, 2003.
13. Shoudan Liang, Stefanie Fuhrman, and Roland Somogyi. REVEAL: A general reverse engineering algorithm for inference of genetic network architectures. In *Proc. of Pacific Symposium on Biocomputing*, pages 18–29, 1998.
14. Hiroshi Matsuno, Atsushi Doi, Masao Nagasaki, and Satoru Miyano. Hybrid petri net representation of gene regulatory network. In *Proc. of Pacific Symposium on Biocomputing*, pages 341–352, 2000.
15. Ilya Shmulevich, Edward R. Dougherty, Seungchan Kim, and Wei Zhang. Probabilistic boolean networks: a rule-based uncertainty model for gene regulatory networks. *Bioinformatics*, 18(2):261–274, 2002.
16. Ilya Shmulevich, Edward R. Dougherty, and Wei Zhang. Control of stationary behavior in probabilistic boolean networks by means of structural intervention. *Biological Systems*, 10:431–446, 2002.
17. Ilya Shmulevich, Olli Yli-Harja, and Jaakko Astola. Inference of genetic regulatory networks under the best-fit extension paradigm. *Computational and Statistical Approaches to Genomics*, 2002.

18. Z. Somogyvari and Sz. Payrits. Length of state cycles of random boolean networks: ananalytic study. *J. Phys. A:*, 33:6699–6706, 2000.
19. D.C. Weaver, C.T. Workman, and G.D. Stormo. Modeling regulatory networks with weight matrices. In *Proc. of Pacific Symposium on Biocomputing*, 1999.
20. A. Wuensche. Genomic regulation modeled as a network with basins of attaction. In *Proc. of Pacific Symposium on Biocomputing*, pages 89–102, 1998.
21. C. Yoo, V. Thorsson, and G.F. Cooper. Discovery of cuasal relationships in a gene regulation pathway from a mixture of experimental and observational DNA microarray data. In *Proc. of Pacific Symposium on Biocomputing*, pages 498–509, 2002.

Modified Association Rule Mining Approach for the MHC-Peptide Binding Problem

Galip Gürkan Yardımcı, Alper Küçükural, Yücel Saygın, and Uğur Sezerman

Faculty of Engineering and Natural Sciences,
Sabanci University, Turkey
{yardimci, kucukural}@su.sabanciuniv.edu,
{ysaygin, ugur}@sabanciuniv.edu

Abstract. Computational approach to predict peptide binding to major histocompatibility complex (MHC) is crucial for vaccine design since these peptides can act as a T-Cell epitope to trigger immune response. There are two main branches for peptide prediction methods; structural and data mining approaches. These methods can be successfully used for prediction of T-Cell epitopes in cancer, allergy and infectious diseases. In this paper, association rule mining methods are implemented to generate rules of peptide selection by MHCs. To capture the binding characteristics, modified rule mining and data transformation methods are implemented in this paper. Peptides are known to bind to the same MHC show sequence variability, to capture this characteristic, we used a reduced amino acid alphabet by clustering amino acids according to their physico-chemical properties. Using the classification of amino acids and the OR-operator to combine the rules to reflect that different amino acid types and positions along the peptide may be responsible for binding are the innovations of the method presented. We can predict MHC Class-I binding with 75-97% coverage and 76-100% accuracy.

Keywords: Peptides, MHC Class-I, Association rule mining, reduced amino acid alphabet, data mining.

1 Introduction

Peptide binding prediction is a crucial step for vaccine design since it enables the understanding of the mechanism of the immune response to foreign bodies and how vaccines work. There are numerous experimental research results regarding this subject. These experiments take too much time and are costly since there are a vast number of peptides to be tried as a vaccine candidate even for a single MHC. Therefore, there is an urgent need for developing effective computational methods to solve the peptide binding problem to the MHC. The methods developed in finding peptide sequences specific for the target MHCs can be also used for developing therapeutical proteins as well for other types of receptors.

MHCs recognize antigens which are foreign macromolecules that cause an immune response in the body. There are two types of immune responses to the antigens: humoral and cellular immune response. Class II MHC molecules are involved in humoral immune response whereas Class I MHC molecules are involved in the

A. Levi et al. (Eds.): ISCIS 2006, LNCS 4263, pp. 165–173, 2006.

cellular immune response which is the response after the antigen enters the cell [9]. In this paper we will focus on cellular response which involves recognition of antigenic fragments by Class I MHCs. After foreign bodies enter the cell they are cleaved into smaller pieces that are called peptides.   These peptides are picked up by Class I MHCs and brought to the cell surface. There are on average three to four different type of Class I MHCs in the human cell, which all bind to different types of peptides including self and antigenic peptides. The T-Cells recognize the infected cell upon binding to the antigenic peptide-MHC complex, which triggers a cascade of events leading to the cellular immune response to foreign bodies. In both Class I and Class II pathways the most important molecule initiation of the recognition of infected cells is major histocompatibility complex (MHC). Knowing which peptides that are yielding from the cleavage of antigens will be picked up by the MHC molecule and understanding the mechanism of the binding of the peptides (sequence motifs) will be of great use in vaccine design. A peptide presented to a T-Cell together with a MHC molecule is called T-Cell epitope.   If the cell is infected, it can be induced to apoptosis by T-Cell. In this paper, we investigate the Class I pathway for prediction of T-Cell epitopes.

Laboratory experiments can be used to determine which peptides bind to which kind of MHC molecules. The peptides that are known to bind to Class I MHCs have variable length but the majority of them have between 8 to 10 residues. Conducting laboratory experiments for all types of peptide binding combinations is not feasible since there are 20^8 to 20^{10} possible peptides using 20 amino acid alphabet, but only a few are selected by the MHC[12]. We combine structural and data mining based methods for prediction of T-Cell epitopes. Association rule mining techniques are used for finding correlations between positions of the bound peptides and determining the binding motifs for each type of MHC.   These rules will be useful for understanding the mechanism of peptide binding.

2   Background and Related Work

There are two main approaches to the peptide prediction problem: profile based approaches and machine learning. Profile based approaches build profile scoring matrices from the alignment of the binding peptides. These methods control the peptide sequence for the availability of the preferred sequences at certain positions of the peptide as predicted by the scoring matrix. Up to now most successful methods are machine learning methods, like SVMHC[7].

Profile based methods, SYFPEITHI[11], Rankpep[13], and ProPred1 [15], only take into account the positive cases to derive the information therefore they do not have high specifity as compared to machine learning approaches where the non binder class information is also taken into account to distinguish the properties of binders. [4]

The second group of researchers used machine learning approaches such as Support Vector Machines and Artificial Neural Networks to find the correlations between the positions of the peptide to build a valid probabilistic model using both the binding and non binding peptides' data [5],[6],[7]. Another method done by Milledge et. al. that was used for predicting peptides for HLA 0201 type of MHC has created sequence structural patterns by using association rules to reflect the MHC binding characteristics of peptides [10].

2.1 Association Rule Mining

The problem of finding association rules among items is formally defined by Agrawal et al. in [1], [2] as follows:

Let $I = \{i_1, i_2, ..., i_m\}$ be a set of all items. Let T be a transaction consisting of a set of items such that $T \subseteq I$. We call D a database of transactions. We say that a transaction T contains X, a set of some items in I, if $X \subseteq T$. An association rule is an implication of the form $X \Rightarrow Y$, where $X \subset I$, $Y \subset I$ and $X \cap Y = \varnothing$. An item set X has support s if s% of the transactions contain X. We say that the rule $X \Rightarrow Y$ holds with confidence c if c% of the transactions in D that contain X also contain Y. The rule $X \Rightarrow Y$ has support s if s% of transactions in D contain $X \cup Y$.

Association rule mining algorithms scan the database of transactions and calculate the support and confidence of the candidate rules to determine if they are significant or not. For that purpose, threshold values are used by the algorithms to prune the insignificant rules. A rule is significant if its support and confidence is higher than the user specified minimum support and minimum confidence threshold. In this way, algorithms do not retrieve all the association rules that could possibly be generated from a database, instead only a very small subset of rules which satisfies the threshold values are retrieved.

Support of an association rule mimics the coverage of that rule, and confidence of the rule specifies the accuracy. Both of these measures are important for determining the significance of a rule. Therefore we used a combined support confidence measure (CSC-Measure)[1]. The formula for the CSC-measure is obtained by taking the harmonic mean of the support and confidence measure, which is formulated below:

$$CSC(s,c) = \frac{2 \cdot s \cdot c}{s + c}$$

where s is the support and c is the confidence of the rule. CSC-Measure takes both the confidence and support of the rule into account, so rules which have high confidence values and which cover more transactions over the data set will be more valuable.

3 Association Rule Mining Methods for (Peptide-Binding) Prediction

Our data set D contain amino acid sequences of peptides which are known to bind to Class I MHC molecules [3]. In D, there are 198 transactions (peptides) known to bind to 4 different MHCs. We have worked with nine amino acid long sequences only since the majority of the known peptides were nine-mers. Each peptide is represented by an item-set of nine elements, based on it sequence. So in our case there are 180 different items since there are nine different positions and twenty different amino acids. Set I has 20^9 different item-sets, each set has nine elements for nine positions and each element can be one of the 20 different items. The position of each amino acid in the sequence is important so we have turned the sequences into item sets X of

---

[1] In information retrieval context, precision and recall measures are combined in the same way to calculate the F-measure.

the form A_p where A is the one letter code of each amino acid and p is the position of the amino acid in the sequence. The rules mined will be as follows $\{V_1\} \Rightarrow \{G_2\}$, meaning that the presence of a Valine in first position of the peptide sequence implies that there will be Glycine in the second position in the peptide sequence. For simplicity, we'll omit the curly brackets in the following sections.

But MHC molecules are not very decisive when binding the peptides, it can accommodate different types of amino acids at the same position of the peptide. There are pockets at the binding site of MHC, some of these pockets have to be filled with certain types of amino acids for the binding requirements to be fulfilled [19]. Sometimes the second position of the peptide fills the appropriate pocket and sometimes the third position of the peptide occupies the same pocket. Therefore different amino acids and different positions of the peptide may have the same role in defining the peptides' binding characteristics; association rules cannot catch this property well. So we have decided to change the rule structure to deal with this problem.

Our association rules have the form $\{V_2\} \vee \{A_2\} \vee \{L_3\} \Rightarrow \{I_9\}$ meaning that the presence of a Valine or an Alanine in the second position or a Leucine in the third position of the peptide implies that the ninth position of the peptide sequence will be an Isoleucine. Such rules can capture the binding characteristics better. This rule structure with ORs ($\vee$) will also increase the CSC-Measure of the rules, resulting with more globally correct binding characteristic rules. The support and the confidence measures' definitions remain unchanged, the only difference is that the calculations are done taking the OR into account.

3.1 Candidate Generation and Rule Mining

The candidate generation step is generally done by the apriori algorithm and its variations [2]. Since using OR as a rule increases the number of candidates so much that the apriori algorithm will not have a reasonable runtime. We first extracted rules with one amino acid on each side by the conventional rule mining algorithm. Then we have combined these rules with the OR operator, to yield rules which reflect the binding characteristic better. The confidence of a new combined rule will be between the values of the minimum and the maximum of confidences of the rules which were combined to yield the new rule. The support will obviously increase as the number of sequences which contain the amino acids on the left side are increasing because of the OR operator between them.

First we have mined the database for association rules of the form $X_i \Rightarrow Y_j$ where X and Y are amino acids and i and j are their positions. Small confidence (50%) and support (20%) thresholds are used for two reasons. The first is that we expect these values to go up as we combine the rules with the OR operator so we want as many rules as possible. The second is that low support values imply that the number of sequences or the transactions which contain both of the combined amino acids will be small.

The combining process will be as follows, over the set of all one amino acid rules of the form $X_i \Rightarrow Y_j$, we will combine the rules which have the same implication, then generate all the possible two amino acid combinations of these rules.

After we have the two amino acid rules, again we combine these rules to yield three amino acid rules. This time the process will be similar to the apriori algorithm.

We combine k amino acid rules which share k-1 amino acids and which have the same implication. Combining these rules yield k+1 amino acid rules. The fact that we are using the OR operator guarantees that new rules' support values will never decrease so we don't have to check support values. The pruning criterion is CSC-Measure of the new rules. If CSC measure does not improve by at least 2% by addition of the new OR rule, the new rule is pruned.

3.2 Amino Acid Classification

Evolution allows for sequence variability; to capture this information, we have also classified the amino acids according to their physico-chemical properties as given in Table 1. Different classes of amino acids are obtained from a previous study by Sezerman et. al. which used an encoding decoding algorithm that classified amino acids based on similarity scoring matrices [14]. The classification scheme given in Table 1 yielded the best results for us. Using the classification table enabled us to distinguish the binding rules according to their physico-chemical properties e.g. HLA-A2 molecule prefers a peptide with a bulky hydrophobic residue at position two (Class F) and a small hydrophobic residue at position nine (Class A) for binding.

The classification step reduces the number of items and item-sets, reducing the number of rules but making the rules more compact. The number of possible item-sets reduces to 129 from 209 and number of items reduces to 108 from 180.

Table 1. Classification of amino acids

Class	Amino Acid(s)		Class	Amino Acid(s)
A	I,V,L,M,A		G	W
B	R,K		H	H
C	D,E		J	G
D	S,T		K	Q,N
E	Y		L	C
F	F		M	P

4 Implementation and Experimental Results

First datasets are downloaded from SYFPEITHI[11]. The peptide sequences are re-written using the classes in Table 1 as a preprocessing operation.

Nine amino acid long binding sequences of different kinds of MHC molecules are used for rule extraction explicitly. The amount of binding peptides for different kinds of MHC molecules varied from 24 to 107. The nature of our data set required data cleaning. Peptide sequences are obtained experimentally. In some cases they obtain MHC bound peptides and these are sequenced and stored in the databases. In other cases they artificially create polyalanine peptide sequences of length nine, check the binding affinity of this peptide to the specific MHC of interest. They mutate each position to different amino acid types separately and look at the binding affinity of the mutated peptide and compare it with the original one. Therefore many binding peptides coming from these studies had alanine (which is a neutral small amino acid that would not have any impact on the binding) in many positions. Since we are looking for the support and confidence of the binders, this would cause a bias for that amino acid type in our association rules therefore we cleaned our data of such sequences. A peptide sequence was removed from our data set if it had the same amino acid in four consecutive positions.

Table 2. Some of the best rules for four types of MHC molecule using four fold cross validation

Molecule	Rule	Avg. Support %	Avg. Confidence %	Avg. CSC-Measure %	Avg Accuracy %
HLA-A020110	A1VA5VA6VA7⇒A2	69,3	83,22	75,59	76,38
	A1VA6VA7VA8⇒A2	69,3	86,89	77,01	76,38
	A1VA5VA6VA7VA8⇒A2	71,92	83,71	77,32	78,88
HLA-A02019	A1VA3VA5VA6⇒A2	77,25	93,25	84,48	82,19
	A1VA3VA5VA6VA7⇒A2	83,48	93,71	88,29	85,93
	A1VA3VA4VA6VA7VA8⇒A9	85,66	93,85	89,56	87,82
HLA-B089	A1VA4VA2⇒B3	68,05	74,17	70,96	83,33
	A1VC1VM2VA6VA8⇒A9	72,22	75,63	73,84	87,5
	C4VB5VA6VA7VA8⇒A9	75	77,28	76,11	87,5
HLA-B27059	B1VA3VA6⇒B2	79,27	100	88,41	92,85
	B1VA3VA6VA9⇒B2	90,80	100	95,17	100
	B1VA3VA5VA6VA7VB9 ⇒B2	95,4	100	97,64	100

4.1 Testing Method

The data set we have used for the association rule mining is non-redundant and the number of sequences in the data set is not large enough especially for certain MHC data to split the database to yield a test and training set. We have used only binding peptides (positives) for the rule mining and testing processes. Since we haven't worked with nonbinding (negatives) peptides, we can only calculate sensitivity of our rules. Therefore we refer to sensitivity as the accuracy of our method. For the testing process, rules whose accuracy values are among the top 80% of all accuracy values are used. Some of the best rules are presented in Table 2. The values in Table 2 are obtained by using a training set of 198 peptides total on 4 different MHC types. We can predict the binding up to 100% accuracy and 97% coverage for some cases. (Table 2).

We have used four fold cross-validation to test the accuracy and validity of the rules we have mined. The data set was split in to four sub-data sets randomly. We obtained the association rules using three data sets and tested it on the fourth set. Then we switched the test set and the training sets until we run all possible combinations of training and test sets. The testing procedure involved using the association rules generated by the training set to identify binders. The values in Table 2 are average values of the four tests. The cross validation showed that association rules can predict between 76% and 100% accuracy.

Accuracy of the resulting rules are dependent on the confidence and support thresholds. For some MHC classes, dataset size is not sufficiently large, thus small confidence and support thresholds must be used. For sufficiently large datasets, large support and confidence thresholds can be set, yielding 90% percent accuracy.

CSC measure gives a better picture of success of our method. CSC values varied between 71% and 92%. Our methods yield approximately 81% percent accuracy. Brusic et.al. report a predictive value of 78% for binding to human MHC HLA-A2 and 88% for mouse MHC H-2K^B using ANNs[6]. Udaka et.al report approximately 80% accuracy using a scoring program for prediction on three mouse MHC binding sequences [17]. Dönnes et. al. report 90% of all the peptides that are known to bind to MHC can be predicted with 90% specificity using support vector machines on 21 MHC data[7]. In another article, Udaka et al reports that HMMs achieve %84 precision, assessing their method by using a so called precision recall curve analysis in [16]. SYFPEITHI uses a profile based method, evaluating the contribution of each amino acid in a peptide to binding process and assigns an overall score to a given peptide. The scoring process is based on the knowledge of anchor and auxiliary anchor positions. For a given protein, all possible octamers, nonamers and decamers are evaluated and SYFPEITHI reports that the naturally presented epitope is among the top scoring 2% of all peptides in 80% of all predictions.[11] The methods reported here use different data-sets with varying data preprocessing steps so our results are not directly comparable to theirs, except for SYFPEITHI with which we share our dataset.

5   Discussion and Perspectives

The novelties of our approach are the use of the OR operator and reduced amino acid alphabet classification. We have used a new association rule mining operator (OR) to combine the rules to describe binding preference of MHC molecules. This combination gives better explanation to the importance of specific sites at the binding peptide. Second and ninth positions appear most frequently in the motifs. These positions have highly correlated hydrophobicity values which is also supported by Zhang et al.[19] Zhang et al. also report that HLA-A02 classes require isoleucine, valine, leucine, methionine (class A according to our amino acid classification) as consensus anchors for binding, and HLA-B classes need charged residues (class B and C according to our classification) as consensus anchors. These finding also correlate with our rules. We also used a reduced amino acid alphabet which helped us to determine important physical and chemical properties of amino acids required at significant positions for a successful binding to MHC. Deriving general rules for binding is a crucial contribution of our method. Profile based methods assume contribution of each position on the peptide even though some would contribute more than the others depending on the frequency of occurrence at the given position. Even though a peptide has the binding motif at the key positions, the scores coming from the other sites can cause it to be classified as non binder. According to Gulukota et. al. [8] profile based methods have 30% accuracy in prediction of binders. Our method points out key positions and significant features for binding. Machine learning based methods can predict the binders with high accuracy and specificity but cannot give out features that are important for binding, which is crucial information for vaccine design. Therefore, they are not well suited for this type of application.

Up to now we did not consider the information coming from non binders in this work. So, for future work, we are developing a new approach which takes non binders' information into account as well. We are also trying to scan for explicit pairs or triplets in peptide sequences using a Bayesian approach and compare its efficiency with our method.

References

[1] R.Agrawal, T. Imielinski, and A. Swami. Mining association rules between sets of items in large databases. In *Proc 1993 ACM-SIGMOD Int. Conf: Management of Data (SIGMOD'93)*, Washington, DC, pp. 207-216 , May 1993.

[2] R.Agrawal and R. Srikant. Fast algorithms for mining association rules. In Proc. *1994 Int. Conf. Very Large Data Bases (VLDB'94)*, Santiago, Chile, Sept, pp. 487-499, 1994.

[3] M. Bhasin, H. Singh, G. P. S. Raghava. MHCBN: A Comprehensive Database of MHC Binding and Non-Binding Peptides. *Nucleic Acids Research*, Vol. 19 no.5 pp. 665-666, 2002.

[4] V. Brusic, V.B. Bajica, N. Petrovsky. Computational methods for prediction of T-cell epitopes—a framework for modelling, testing, and applications. *Methods,* 34(4):436-43, 2004.

[5] V. Brusic and D.R. Flower. Bioinformatics tools for identifying T-cell epitopes. *DDT: BIOSILICO Vol. 2, No. 1,* pp. 18-23, January 2004.

[6] V. Brusic, G. Rudy, L. C. Harrison. Prediction of MHC Binding Peptides Using Artificial Neural Networks. *Complexity International*, Volume 2, 1995

[7] P. Dönnes, A. Elofsson. "Prediction of MHC class I binding peptides, using SVMHC". *Bioinformatics*, 3:25, 2002.

[8] K. Gulukota, J. Sidney, A. Sette, C. DeLisi. Two complementary methods for predicting peptides binding major histocompatibility complex molecules. *J Mol Biol*, 267:1258-1267, 1997

[9] P. M. Kloetzel. The proteasome and MHC class I antigen processing. *Biochimica et Biophysica Acta 1695*, pp. 217-225, 2004.

[10] T. Milledge, G. Zheng, G. Narasimhan. An Application Of Association Rule Mining to Hla-A*0201 Epitope Prediction. *ICBA, 2004.*

[11] H. G. Rammensee, J. Bachmann, N.P.N. Emmerich, O.A. Bachor, and S. Stevanovic. SYFPEITHI: database for MHC ligands and peptide motifs. *Immunogenetics*, 50(3-4):213-219, 1999.

[12] H.G. Rammensee, T. Friede, S. Stevanovic. MHC ligands and peptide motifs: 1st listing. *Immunogenetics* 41, pp. 178-228, 1995.

[13] P.A. Reche, J. P. Glutting, and E.L. Reinherz. Prediction of MHC Class I Binding Peptides Using Profile Motifs. *Hum. Immunol.*, 63:701-709, 2002.

[14] O.U. Sezerman, R. Islamaj and E. Alpaydin. Three dimensional representation of amino acid characteristics. *IEEE EMBC*, Vol. 3 2903-2906, 2001

[15] H. Singh and G.P.S. Raghava. ProPred1: prediction of promiscuous MHC Class-I binding sites. *Bioinformatics*, Vol. 19 no. 8 pp. 1009-1014, 2003.

[16] K. Udaka, H. Mamitsuka, Y. Nakaseko and N. Abe. Empirical Evaluation of a Dynamic Experiment Design Method for Prediction of MHC Class I-Binding Peptides. *The Journal of Immunology,* 169:5744 – 5753, 2002

[17] K. Udaka, K.H. Wiesmuller, S. Kienle, G. Jung, H. Tamamura, H. Yamagishi, K. Okumura, P. Walden, T. Suto, T. Kawasaki. An automated prediction of MHC class I-binding peptides based on positional scanning with peptide libraries. *Immunogenetics*, pp. 816-828, 2000.

[18] J. Zeng, H. R. Treutlein & G. B. Rudy. Predicting sequences and structures of MHC-binding peptides: a computational combinatorial approach. *Journal of Computer-Aided Molecular Design*, pp. 573-576, 2001.

[19] C. Zhang, A. Anderson , C. DeLisi . Structural principles that govern the peptide-binding motifs of class I MHC molecules. *J. Mol Biol*, 929 – 947, 1998.ï

Prediction and Classification for GPCR Sequences Based on Ligand Specific Features

Bekir Ergüner, Özgün Erdoğan, and Uğur Sezerman

Biological Sciences and Bioengineering, Sabanci University, Orhanli – Tuzla
34956 Istanbul, Turkey
{bekir, ozgune}@su.sabanciuniv.edu,
ugur@sabanciuniv.edu

Abstract. Functional identification of G-Protein Coupled Receptors (GPCRs) is one of the current focus areas of pharmaceutical research. Although thousands of GPCR sequences are known, many of them are orphan sequences (the activating ligand is unknown). Therefore, classification methods for automated characterization of orphan GPCRs are imperative. In this study, for predicting Level 1 subfamilies of GPCRs, a novel method for obtaining class specific features, based on the existence of activating ligand specific patterns, has been developed and utilized for a majority voting classification. Exploiting the fact that there is a non-promiscuous relationship between the specific binding of GPCRs into their ligands and their functional classification, our method classifies Level 1 subfamilies of GPCRs with a high predictive accuracy between 99% and 87% in a three-fold cross validation test. The method also tells us which motifs are significant for class determination which has important design implications. The presented machine learning approach, bridges the gulf between the excess amount of GPCR sequence data and their poor functional characterization.

Keywords: G-Protein Coupled Receptors (GPCRs), ligand specificity, GPCR sequence.

1   Introduction

GPCR (G-Protein Coupled Receptors) are a large family of trans-membrane proteins responsible for signal transduction. The GPCRs receive various external stimuli ranging from chemical to physical and in turn activate intracellular G-proteins. Cells can accept and respond different extracellular and physical signals. Acceptance of a signal occurs principally in two different transduction pathways. One is mediated by tyrosine kinase receptors and the other by G protein-coupled receptors (GPCR)[4].

GPCR is an essential subject of many recent biomolecular projects. They are responsible for diverse physiological processes such as neurotransmission, secretion, cellular metabolism rowth and cellular differentiation as well as inflammatory and immune responses. Therefore, they are vital for the research and development for new drugs [3].

A. Levi et al. (Eds.): ISCIS 2006, LNCS 4263, pp. 174–181, 2006.

Various databases have been created in order to observe and categorize different characteristics of GPCRs. These databases hold sequences, mutation data and ligand binding data. Moreover, these databases are further improved by multiple sequence alignments, two dimensional visualization tools, three dimensional models and phylogenetic trees [5].

Even though thousands of GPCR sequences are known as a result of ongoing genomics projects , the crystal structure has been solved only for one GPCR sequence using electron diffraction at medium resolution (2.8 A) to date and for many of the GPCRs the activating ligand is unknown, which are called orphan GPCRs [11]. Hence, based on sequence information, a functional classification method of those orphan GPCRs and new upcoming GPCR sequences is crucial to identify and characterize novel GPCRs.

In the current literature, to classify GPCRs in different levels of families, there exist different attempts, such as using prim database search tools, e.g., BLAST [1], FASTA [8]. However, these methods only work if the query protein sequence is highly similar to the existing database sequences in order to work properly. In addition to these database search tools, the same problem is addressed by using Hidden Markov Models [10], bagging classification trees [6] and SVMs [7]. One other method studies the tertiary structure of GPCRs by using only the amino acid sequence (MembStruck) and the binding site and binding energy of various ligands to GPCRs (HierDock) [9]. Out of all these methods Karchin et al. (2001) showed that SVMs gave the highest accuracy in recognizing GPCR families [7]. In SVMs, an initial step to transform each protein sequence into a fixed-length vector is required and the predictive accuracy of SVMs significantly depends on this particular fixed-length vector. Karchin et al., pointed out that the SVM performance could be increased by using most relevant feature vectors, since SVMs do not identify the features most responsible for class discrimination. Therefore, for an accurate SVM classification, feature vectors should reflect the unique biological information contained in sequences, which is specific to the type of classification problem. In a recent work Bakir et al. used a fixed length feature vector of 40 most distinguishing patterns to classify amine sub-family GPCRs with 97% accuracy using SVMs[2].

2   System and Methods

In this paper we used several machine learning approaches to classify GPCRs according to their ligand specificities rather than their subfamilies. The GPCR groups we chose to work on were selected according to the ligands they bind to: amines, peptides, olfactory and rhodopsin. The binding of ligand to GPCR occurs outside of the cell therefore to understand interaction of GPCR and ligands; we decided to examine the primary sequence information of extracellular regions of GPCRs. Since The GPCR is a 7TM protein, meaning that it has 7 trans-membrane regions, the regions we observed were an N-terminus and three extracellular loops. We acquired the GPCR amino acid sequences from GPCRDB database which also groups GPCR proteins into subfamilies (http://www.gpcr.org/7tm/multali/multali.html) [12]. Total of 352, 1998, 595, 355 and 56 proteins from *amine, olfactory, peptide, rhodopsin* and *prostanoid* subfamilies derived from GPCRDB respectively. After derivation of proteins from database their secondary structure is determined by using TMHMM (trans-membrane hidden Markov model) server. The dataset is available upon request. Thus we could isolate the n-terminus and extracellular loop sequences. Using different alphabetic coding systems for amino acids, we created a database consisting of amino acid triplet frequencies of each extracellular sequences for each ligand class studied.

Our database was created using MYSQL due to its user friendly nature. Another important factor in choosing MYSQL as our database system was being able to control the MYSQL database through Microsoft Visual C++ by MYSQL++ implementation (http://tangentsoft.net/mysql++).

We randomly separated each existing GPCR group into 2 subgroups as 'train' and 'test' in a 2:1 ratio for amine, rhodopsin, prostanoid subfamilies, 5:1 ratio for peptide subfamily and 9:1 ratio for olfactory subfamily. For both subgroups, the amino acid sequence of n-terminus, loop1, loop2 and loop3 regions were grouped into triplets. For 'n' amino acid long sequences, this would provide us with 'n-2' possible triplets. Using triplets seemed to be the optimal choice since using single amino acids would not help to determine neighborhood information in the sequence. The reasoning behind this was to focus on more specific patterns in the amino acid sequence while not losing vital patterns. Since it is too specific, using 5-amino-acid bundles would greatly diminish the number of matches, possibly ignoring positive matches that would have been spotted using triplets.

The 'train' subgroups were loaded into the database to create the basis for prediction patterns which would later be applied to the 'test' subgroup. These final results would show us how efficient the prediction patterns were.

The results of these pattern searches provided us with certain information such as the number of triplet occurrences and in how many proteins a certain pattern was spotted. In order to find specific patterns for different ligand groups we compared the results of each group with one another. The over-expression of a specific pattern in one of the two GPCR groups compared showed us that this pattern was characteristic of that certain GPCR group. However, this method was not precise enough since a pattern that separates amines-peptides might not do so for amines-olfactory. Therefore, to further enhance our statistical precision, we compared the results of each group to that of all the remaining GPCR groups combined.

We also applied an index search on amino acid sequences to check whether the positions of dominant triplets carried an importance in the separation of GPCR groups. We were hoping to spot a parallelism between triplet densities and their positions in the extra cellular portions of the protein.

All of these comparison methods were first used on a 11-letter amino acid alphabet (Table 1), then repeated on 6-letter and 20-letter alphabets. The usage of different alphabet systems allowed us to examine the effect of a single amino acid compared to the general biochemical properties of the group it belongs to. The classifications of amino acids were done according to their physical and chemical properties. Evolution allows for conserved mutations that do not change the physical and chemical nature of mutation site since these mutations do not disrupt the function of the molecule. By

Table 1. Classification of amino acids

Class	Amino Acid(s)	Class	Amino Acid(s)
a	I,V,L,M	g	G
b	R,K,H	h	W
c	D,E	i	C
d	Q,N	j	Y,F
e	S,T	k	X,P
f	A		

using classification of amino acids we can capture this nature of evolution. Since the patterns we expect to observe can vary allowing acceptable mutations.

For each comparison of classes we found the ratio of existence of a triplet at a certain location (e.g loop 1) in one class against the other class. We ranked the triplets with these ratios. The words with highest ratios would make up the important features. This is done for six times comparing each class to another class. These important features are selected from training set only. Then starting from the highest ratio we search how many sequences in the training set can be selected with this motif only. Going down the ratio ranking we add a new motif to important motif list if it helps to identify new sequences other than the previous motifs. We carry on until no new sequence can be identified with the rest of the motifs. This is done for each classification problem and we get a list of important motifs for each class. Then given the test sequence we look at existence of these motifs in the query sequence. We assign the query sequence to the class that has the highest hits on the query sequence. Unlike the patterns obtained in Bakir's work, the selected patterns are observed only in the specific group and not the other groups [2]. In the previous work, selected patterns had to be present in at least 50% of the sequences in the selected group, presence of the same pattern in other classes were not checked.

3   Results

The motifs obtained from amine peptide comparison are listed in Table 2. Showing how many sequences in the training set they occur and how many new sequences they help to identify. We keep the motifs that cause no misclassification between these classes. In determining the most important motifs the patterns that occur in most of the given class that do not occur in the other classes are ranked according to number of occurrences in the given class. The most important motif distinguishing amine from the peptide is existence of word bhe in loop1. Since it helps to classify 33 amine GPCRs without any misclassification.

By running all possible comparisons of classes we obtain the list of important features that helps us to identify a given class. The list is derived from ranked

    B. Ergüner, Ö. Erdoğan, and U. Sezerman

Table 2. Occurences of motifs for amine versus peptide classification

n-terminal			loop2			loop1			loop3		
motif	occur	new	motif	occur	New	motif	occur	new	motif	Occur	new
Ddh	13	13	dkf	26	26	bhe	33	33	ibc	27	27
Ief	11	11	cij	22	21	egb	27	12	bak	20	19
Dif	10	3	ckg	19	14	aic	26	23	fai	19	12
Fkh	8	8	kbi	15	12	hka	25	9	kia	13	13
Hfa	7	3	dic	14	14	ihj	16	16	abk	12	8
Chc	6	6	ggi	12	12	afi	15	14	kkc	12	6
Hff	6	5	kdi	12	8	ejg	14	4	cid	10	9
Ffh	5	5	iic	11	3	abi	13	13	jbk	9	4
Hck	5	3	bij	10	5	aha	12	7	kcj	9	3
Hdg	5	5	cci	10	9	bah	12	8	gke	8	8
Fbh	4	3	jfa	10	4	jhf	12	11	jid	7	6
Dhk	3	3	eki	5	4	ehi	11	9	jef	5	4
			gdi	5	5	fgj	10	10	dai	4	4
			hdd	4	3	jic	8	3	ibf	4	3
			jbi	4	4	bfh	6	6	aie	3	3
			cig	3	3	bhc	4	4	bfh	3	3
						fjh	3	3	icc	3	3
									jig	3	3

important features table. We start from the most distinguishing feature and add on a new feature if it helps us to classify a new GPCR sequence correctly. The motif list ends when the remaining motifs s can only classify already distinguished sequences thus yielding to no new classifications. Using these motif lists, we try to determine the class of the sequences in the test set. The results can be seen in Table 3. Success rate of classification varies between 87% and 99% and we can also determine the important motifs for each class.

We had problem with prostanoids therefore we eliminated them from our search. There were only few prostanoids to be able determine any kind of significant patterns. The search yielded very few patterns with such stringent determination of patterns. Therefore any class compared with the prostanoid binding group gave more hits. Therefore only 28% of the prostanoids could be identified and all the others were classified to other classes. Currently we are allowing for more errors in pattern identification to overcome this problem.

In order to check how accurate the results were, we used a program called CART, a software program or building regression trees. For testing the accuracy of patterns that recognize amines, 40 patterns were given as predictors and 18 test proteins were used. The result of patterns comparing amine versus all ligand classes are shown in Figure 1. The importance of the patterns in classification of amines are summarized in Table 4. Unlike the patterns used in the previous method, the patterns used in CART distinguish one ligand class from all the other 4 ligand classes. For example distinguishing patterns for amines used in CART are the best patterns in the combination of amines vs. peptides, amines vs. olfactory, amines vs. rhodopsin and amines vs. prostanoid pattern sets in the first method. Thus patterns in Table 4 can differ from the ones in Table 2. For example pattern 'caa' is the most important pattern in Table 4 but it is not seen in Table 2. This is because 'caa' is important for amines vs. rhodopsin and amines vs. prostanoid classification but not as important for amines vs. peptides and amines vs. olfactory classification. Since Table 2 shows the patterns for amines vs. peptides, 'caa' pattern is not seen.

The main novelty of this method is to determine motifs using reduced alphabet representation and using information theory for determining significance of the motifs. This increased the prediction accuracy drastically while enabling the end users (pharmaceutical companies) to determine significant motifs for ligand determination that can be used for drug design purposes.

Table 3. Total success rates of classifications

	Correct	**total**	**success**
amines	104	120	0.87
peptides	98	102	0.96
olfactory	195	195	1
rhodopsin	87	111	0.87
prostanoid	5	18	0.28

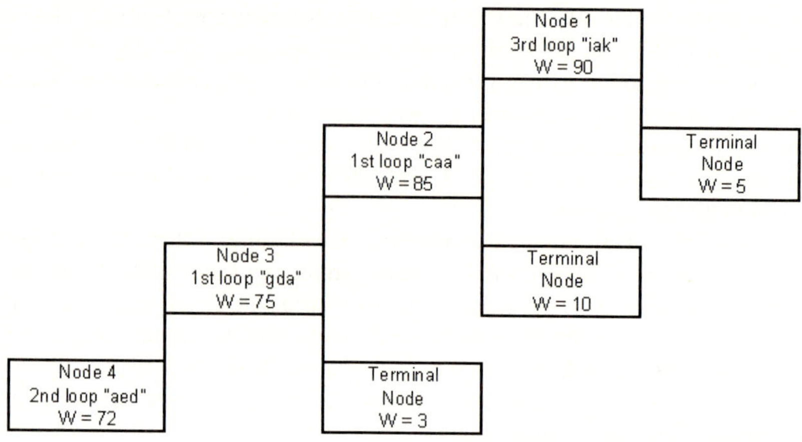

Fig. 1. The classification table showing the only patterns determining amines from all others. The figure shows that pattern "iak" occurring in 3rd loop of extracellular region is the most crucial pattern determining amines of all ligand groups with weight 90. The increasing number of the nodes are in the decreasing order of importance of determining amines. W is the number of sequences populating a given node.

Table 4. Variable importance of the amine determining patterns

Patterns	Relative Importance
Loop 1 'caa'	100
Loop 1 'gbh'	97.46
Loop 3 'iak'	83.767
Loop 1 'gjh'	64.62
Loop 1 'gda'	51.101
Loop 2 'aed'	44.942
Loop 1 'agj'	43.636
Loop 1 'aag'	31.099
Loop 1 'dca'	22.736
Loop 3 'akc'	17.737
Loop 1 'hjj'	16.511
N-term 'afa'	12.811
N-term 'eea'	0

Acknowledgements

The authors wish to thank to Alper Kucukural, Gurkan Yardimci, Berkay Kaya, Hanife Kebapci, Emir Tinaztepe, Nalan Liv and Yekta Yamaner for their help in different parts of the project.

References

1. Altshul,S. et al. Basic local alignment search tool. *J. Mol. Biol.*, 215, (1990) 403-410
2. Bakir ,B. Sezerman, U.Functional Classification of G proteins based on their specific ligand coupling patterns, LNCS, 2006
3. Bouvier, M. Structural and functional aspecs of g protein-coupled receptor oligomerization. *Biochem. Cell Bio.* 76, (1998) 1-11
4. Thomas Gudermann, Torsten Schöneberg, and Günter Schultz. Functional And Structural Complexity of Signal Transduction via G-protein Coupled Receptors. *Annu. Rev. Neurosci.* 20, (1997) 339-427
5. F. Horn, J. Weare, M. W. Beukers, S. Hörsch, A. Bairoch, W. Chen, Ø. Edvardsen, F. Campagne and G. Vriend, GPCRDB: an Information System for G Protein-Coupled Receptors. *Nucleic Acids Res.* 1, (2003) 294-7
6. Huang,Y. et al. Classifying G-protein Coupled receptors with bagging classification tree. *Computational Biology and Chemistry,* 28, (2004) 275-280
7. R. Karchin, K. Karplus, D. Haussler. Classifying G-protein Coupled Receptors with Support Vector Machines. *Bioinformatics.* 18, (2002) 147-59
8. Pearson,W. and Lipman,D. Improved tools for biological sequence analysis. *Proceedings of National Academic Science*, 85, (1988) 2444–2448. Database search tool is available at: http://www.ebi.ac.uk/fasta33
9. N. Vaidehi, W. B. Floriano, R. Trabanino, S. E. Hall, P. Freddolino, E. J. Choi, G. Zamanakos, W. A. Goddard III. (2002) *PNAS.* 99,20,12622-7
10. Sreekumar,K.R. et al. Predicting GPCR-G-Protein coupling using hidden Markov models, *Bioinformatics,* 20, (2004) 3490-3499
11. Tusnády,G.E. and Simon,I. The HMMTOP transmembrane topology prediction server. *Bioinformatics*, 17 (2001) 849-850. Available at: http://www.enzim.hu/hmmtop
12. G Protein-Coupled Receptor Data Base, http://www.gpcr.org/7tm/multali/multali.html

An Efficient Algorithm for the Identification of Repetitive Variable Motifs in the Regulatory Sequences of Co-expressed Genes

Abanish Singh and Nikola Stojanovic

Department of Computer Science and Engineering, The University of Texas at Arlington, Arlington, TX 76019, USA

Abstract. Over the last several years there has been an explosion in the number of computational methods for the detection of transcription factor binding sites in DNA sequences. Although there has been some success in this field, the existing tools are still neither sensitive nor specific enough, usually suffering from the detection of a large number of false positive signals. Given the properties of genomic sequences this is not unexpected, but one can still find interesting features worthy of further computational and laboratory bench study. We present an efficient algorithm developed to find all significant variable motifs in given sequences. In our view, it is important that we generate complete data, upon which separate selection criteria can be applied depending on the nature of the sites one wants to locate, and their biological properties. We discuss our algorithm and our supplementary software, and conclude with an illustration of their application on two eukaryotic data sets.

1   Introduction

Gene expression is regulated by a network of protein–DNA and protein–protein interactions. Most of them occur within a few hundred bases upstream of the transcription start sites, although many can be quite distant. It is also generally accepted that the binding of transcriptional enzymes is directed by specific motifs in DNA sequence. However, while there are proteins which bind specifically to exact sequences of bases, most transcription factors are rather promiscuous in their choice of a preferred binding consensus. This indicates that sequence motifs may only be a part of the regulatory signal.

The search for transcription factor binding sites is one of the most popular subfields of bioinformatics, and many algorithms have been developed over more than a decade of intensive research. The early approaches relied on a rather naive assumption that the target sites of proteins must feature information content sufficient for them to be recognized. Disillusionment soon followed, as any attempt to isolate functional elements in DNA resulted in an enormous number of false positives. Recent methods have thus concentrated on the incorporation of additional information to the raw sequence data. They often relied on phylogenetic conservation [17,11,15,8] or search for clusters whose elements matched experimentally confirmed consensus motifs [11,15], retrieved from databases such

A. Levi et al. (Eds.): ISCIS 2006, LNCS 4263, pp. 182–191, 2006.
© Springer-Verlag Berlin Heidelberg 2006

as TRANSFAC [13] or Jaspar [14]. The latter methods exploited the fact that proteins involved in the initiation of transcription rarely, if ever, act in isolation.

With the advances in microarray technology large sets of putatively co-expressed genes became available, stimulating the development of new methods to detect conserved motifs in their upstream sequences [10,11]. It is intuitive that if a group of genes is coordinately regulated, it should be controlled by the same transcription factors. From the hypothesis that protein binding is directed by DNA sequence motifs it follows that same motifs should be present in all regulatory sequences, moreover as a cluster, or clusters. This led to the exploitation of motif over-representation in the target sequences. In addition, it has been observed in yeast that the promoter regions are often characterized by multiple occurrences of the same binding motif [20], and it has been postulated that it may be the case in higher eukaryotes, too. These assumptions stimulated the search for over-represented, or "surprise", motifs in related sequences [2,21].

Along with the sequencing of a large number of eukaryotic genomes which have taken place over the last several years, the efforts to characterize non-coding functional DNA elements have intensified [18]. A comprehensive study of the effectiveness of many motif–finding tools [19] has shown that, while there has been some success in the binding site recognition, the existing methods are not nearly satisfactory. There are several reasons for that. Spatial configuration of DNA, along with other epigenetic phenomena, may be a major factor in transcription factor binding, and no software tool incorporates this information. Transcription factors generally feature very non-specific binding preferences [3], and that permits for wide variations in the motif consensus. To make things worse, transcription factor binding sites are short, and their detection may be hampered by pieces of randomly conserved short sequences. Our own previous study has shown that it is indeed the case [17]. This, in turn, may force us to comparatively look at homologous or paralogous sequences that have diverged so much that the proteins that bind there are only similar, but no longer same. The solution to this problem may lie in the simultaneous study of a large number of related sequences, a method of choice for the recent initiatives such as ENCODE [18].

Genomic sequence is not a random assembly of 4 letters. We have done extensive simulations [16] in which the number of repeated elements in randomly generated synthetic sequences was almost perfectly conforming to the Poisson expectation, but the number of repeated motifs in repeat–masked random intergenic DNA was far greater than expected. In consequence, any search for over-represented sequences is bound to return many results. Depending on what we search for, most would likely be false positives.

Even assuming a pure Poisson model, the number of short repeats expected by chance can be large in any significant sequence interval. Ideally, when examining m upstream sequences of related genes we would like to set the length such that m or more occurrences of even a short motif would be significant. Unfortunately, as shown in Table 1, the sequence lengths needed to assure 0.01 significance of a motif of length k in m different segments, if it occurs m or more times, would be unacceptably short. If we would want to include all bases upstream of the

Table 1. Maximal size L_i of individual upstream regions necessary to guarantee 0.01 level significance for a motif of length k repeated m or more times in m sequences

	$k = 3$	$k = 4$	$k = 5$	$k = 6$	$k = 7$	$k = 8$
$m = 2$	4	19	76	304	1216	> 2000
$m = 3$	9	37	148	595	> 2000	> 2000
$m = 4$	13	52	210	843	> 2000	> 2000
$m = 5$	16	65	261	1047	> 2000	> 2000
$m = 6$	19	76	304	1218	> 2000	> 2000
$m = 7$	21	85	340	1363	> 2000	> 2000
$m = 8$	23	92	371	1487	> 2000	> 2000

genes likely to contain regulatory signals the observed sequences would become so long that a short motif would need to be excessively redundant in order to be recognized as significant. With these sequence lengths many more motifs would start showing up by chance. If we consider a 5' regulatory region of a gene to consist of about 500 bases, then the minimal length of a detectable motif is about 6. These are the numbers for exact repeats — if we permit some variability then we would be forced to either look at much shorter regions, include more co-regulated genes (if any), or seek long motifs only.

Positional conservation can be sometimes used to filter the motifs, using sequence alignments. However, this approach is vulnerable to the quality of the alignment, and may miss quite a few positionally conserved elements simply by not aligning them precisely on the top of one another.

In our approach we aim to detect everything that appears significant and then filter the results according to the number of regions sharing the motif, motif composition (simple sequence, tandem repeat structure or perfectly conserved bases at loci suggesting a helix-loop-helix, zinc fingers or leucine zipper structure, for instance), database hits, clustering patterns or positional conservation. We have thus written a program which searches through gene regulatory sequences and lists all significant variable motifs shared within subsets of these sequences. Our algorithm favorably compares to other methods for detecting weak similarities in many sequences, such as Gibbs sampling [12] (as it can rapidly detect all significant motifs) or the BEST [7] suite of tools (featuring better sensitivity in our tests on known regulatory motifs described in TRANSFAC [13]).

2   Algorithm

The algorithm receives a set of sequences in which significant motifs should be located, and outputs the list filtered by specific (user–definable) criteria: minimal motif length, minimal number of input sequences in which it should be found, likelihood of its occurrence by chance and the permitted degeneracy (minimal percentage of conserved bases in all occurrences of the motif). This output can be further processed by a set of tools we have developed (such as cross–matching, filtering and graphical representation of motif positions).

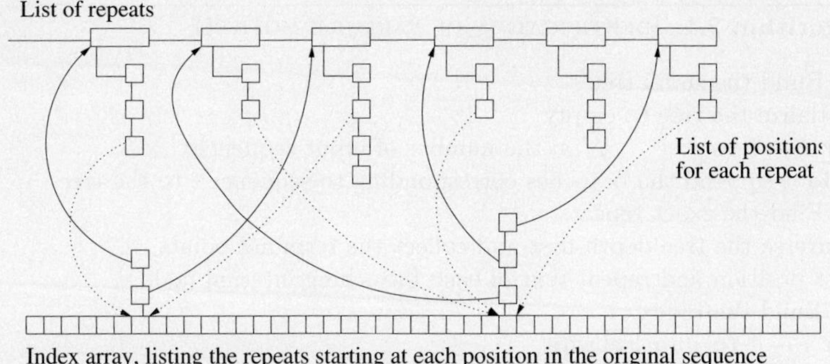

Fig. 1. A schematic representation of the indexing for finding neighboring repeats

We start by identifying all exact repeated strings of length 2 or more in the input sequences, both strands, using the suffix tree data structure [22]. This method is well known, and widely used in similar applications [2,1,4], so we shall omit the details of its construction and use. After the original list has been built, we identify the repeats which co-occur at least twice, at a constant distance, and name them potential mates. We use all sites of co-occurrence to build the putative consensus sequence of the variable motif according to the following rules: (1) if the bases at the m-th positions of all loci where the mates have been found are identical (uppercase letter in the consensus), we record the number of loci as the number of conserved characters; (2) if there is a majority base at the m-th positions of all loci of co-occurrence (lowercase consensus letter), we record the number of occurrences of the majority base as the number of conserved characters; (3) if the m-th position of all putative consensus locations does not feature a majority base, we assign 'N' to that position and record the number of occurrences of the most common base as the number of conserved characters[1]. We then determine whether the percentage of conserved characters exceeds a given threshold (95% in our tests). If that holds we accept the consensus and attempt further refinement, by recursively searching for additional elements co-occurring with the newly built consensus. The identification of pairs can be efficiently done due to an indexing scheme shown in Figure 1.

Finally, we combine the consensus motifs with the remaining exact repeats, reindex the list and attempt to collapse substantially overlapping elements. This is necessary because components of the motifs may have separate occurrences elsewhere, and thus could have been identified as separate, distinct repeats. If their separate occurrences permit the inclusion in the broader consensus, that is done now. A high–level pseudo–code of our algorithm is shown in Figure 2.

Our algorithm finds all repeated motifs (with user–definable significance) where a certain (a parameter) percentage of bases are conserved, and in which at least two dinucleotides are conserved in at least two copies, at a fixed distance.

---

[1] Alternatively, we could have used the information content, but it would not be of much help unless we could confirm a bias in the overall distribution of bases.

Algorithm 2.1: IDENTIFICATION OF VARIABLE MOTIFS()

// Build the suffix tree
Initialize the tree to empty
for $i \leftarrow 1$ **to** s // s: the number of input sequences
  do {Append the branches corresponding to sequence i to the tree
// Find the exact repeats
Traverse the tree depth-first and collect the terminal points
List position and repeat text of each branching internal node
// Build the Index
for $i \leftarrow 1$ **to** $num\_repeats$
  do $\begin{cases} \textbf{for } j \leftarrow 1 \textbf{ to } num\_positions[i] \\ \quad \textbf{do } \{\text{Create an index array entry at } position[j] \end{cases}$
// Identify variable motifs by their consensus sequences
for $i \leftarrow 1$ **to** $num\_repeats$
  do $\begin{cases} // \text{ Create a list of motifs} \\ \text{CREATE\_CONSENSUS}(i) \qquad // \text{ Function call listed below} \end{cases}$
Merge the list of consensus motifs with simple repeats
Rebuild the index of repeat (motif) position
// Refine the list of identified motifs
for $i \leftarrow 1$ **to** num_motifs
  do $\begin{cases} \textbf{repeat} \\ \quad \text{Attempt to merge neighbors of } i \text{ in a single consensus} \\ \textbf{until } \text{no further refinement possible} \end{cases}$
// Report the significant motifs
Filter the motifs according to significance and other criteria

---

Algorithm 2.2: CREATE_CONSENSUS($seed$)

for $i \leftarrow 1$ **to** max_gap_size
  do $\begin{cases} // \text{ Find repeated neighbors for } i \qquad \text{(fixed gap size)} \\ \textbf{for } j \leftarrow 1 \textbf{ to } num\_positions[seed] \\ \quad \textbf{do } \begin{cases} \text{List the neighbors of } seed \text{ at } j \text{ using the index} \\ \textbf{for each } \text{neighbor } N \text{ occurring more than once} \\ \quad \textbf{do } \begin{cases} \text{Build consensus } C \text{ of } seed \text{ and } N \\ \text{CREATE\_CONSENSUS}(C) \qquad // \text{ Recursive call} \end{cases} \end{cases} \end{cases}$

Fig. 2. Psudo–code of the variable motif finding algorithm

The maximal allowable distance between the anchoring exact repeats is a parameter to the program, and by default set to 5. No motif copy is lost until the final filtering of the list, however these that partially overlap and fail to create a consensus scoring above the threshold will be considered separate motifs, and may not be sufficiently significant to be reported.

2.1   Algorithm Performance

The running time of our algorithm is the sum of the processing of the suffix tree and the building of the consensus sequences of variable motifs. If we denote the number of sequences in the input by s, and their maximal length by L, then we need $O(sL)$ time to identify the original (anchoring) exact repeats. However, we also need to maintain records of all their positions. This adds another complexity factor of q, the total expected number of positions featuring an occurrence of a repeat. Under the Poisson model

$$q = \sum_{i=2}^{L} 4^i \left(\sum_{j=2}^{sL} j \frac{\left(\frac{L}{4^i}\right)^j e^{-\frac{L}{4^i}}}{j!} \right) = \sum_{i=2}^{L} 4^i \left(\sum_{j=2}^{sL} \frac{\left(\frac{L}{4^i}\right)^j e^{-\frac{L}{4^i}}}{(j-1)!} \right) \tag{1}$$

The expected number of repeats (each counted only once) is estimated as

$$r = \sum_{i=2}^{L} 4^i \left(\sum_{j=2}^{sL} \frac{\left(\frac{L}{4^i}\right)^j e^{-\frac{L}{4^i}}}{j!} \right) \tag{2}$$

While it is difficult to express these estimates in a closed form, our simulations over relevant ranges have shown that r was bounded by sL, and q was slightly super-linear to sL (the function we compared it with was logarithmic).

Locating the mates and extending the repeat consensus is primarily dependent on r, since we need to make an attempt for each repeat in our list. The time necessary to handle the neighborhood of one repeat $\mathcal{R}$ is bounded by $gh\mathcal{T}_0 \sum_{j=1}^{r_i} hs$, where g is the number of positions we allow to separate exact repeats (while still considering them mate candidates), h is the number of repeats examined (and thus the upper bound to the number of mates themselves) and r_i is the number of occurrences of $\mathcal{R}$ (so $\sum_{j=1}^{r_i} hs$ is the time necessary to examine the neighborhood at every occurrence of $\mathcal{R}$). Although r_i can theoretically be as large as sL, in practice it would be around q/r on average. $\mathcal{T}_0$ is the time necessary to recursively refine and extend the initial consensus, whenever a co-occurring pair is found. As we look for variable motifs with only a very limited number of spaces between their conserved parts, we can consider g as a constant. Due to our indexing scheme (Figure 1), the same applies to h. However, for each repeat we still need to look at all of its occurrences. The estimate for $\mathcal{T}_0$ is similar to the time needed to build the original consensus, i.e. proportional to $gh\mathcal{T}_1 \sum_{j=1}^{r_i} hs$, where $\mathcal{T}_1$ is the complexity of further extensions. Since a large number of extensions would imply very large motifs, which are rare under the conditions in which this program has been designed to run, we can consider it as a very small constant (2 to 3), on average. We shall denote this value by t. The total execution time for the location of mates and building consensuses for one repeat is thus $O((q/r)^t)$, on average. This cost would apply to all r repeats, so the total cost of forming initial motifs would be $O(r(q/r)^t)$.

The final refinement step will on average take time proportional to the final number of motifs. The creation of each consensus can potentially add another repeat to our list, if these identified as mates also have separate occurrences that cannot be merged. Consequently, the number of motifs can grow as large as $O(r(q/r)^t)$. However, due to the re-indexing step before the refinement this last step can be done in time proportional to the number of motifs. Since any motif that has been merged ceased to exist independently, multiple iterative refinements in this step cannot add to the complexity. The total time needed for the execution of our algorithm, on average, is thus $O(r(q/r)^t)$.

The space needed is dominated by that necessary to store all original repeats and the discovered consensus motifs, since the suffix tree uses space proportional to the number of its leaves, sL. As the number of motifs cannot exceed the time needed for their discovery, the space requirement is also $O(r(q/r)^t)$.

Usually t, the exponential factor in our estimates, will be very small (2 or 3), and q/r (the number of occurrences of an average repeat) is a small number, too, so the algorithm would be efficient. However, there are some real–world scenarios under which our program would not perform well. If the sequences examined consist of, for instance, ALU repeats or nearly identical genomic regions, this would result in many extensions, and consequently very large values of t. This would lead to poor performance, in terms of both time and space. Fortunately, such sequences are simple to detect and filter before the program is applied, and we have not encountered this problem in practical runs.

3 Applications

In order to study the performance of our software, we looked at several eukaryotic datasets, including the CAVEOLIN cluster and MLL target genes.

Our first data set was taken from the caveolin gene regions of 8 vertebrates. Caveolins encode integral membrane proteins that act as scaffolds to sequester and organize lipids and proteins in signaling complexes [6]. Their expression is highly regulated, and CAV1 and CAV2 are target genes for PPARγ. However, previous studies were unable to identify sequences matching the DR-1 consensus binding element (AGGTCAnnnAGGTCA) of the PPARγ/RXR heterodimer. Indeed, we have found only a fraction of this element, as motif AGGTCACNNAGC, repeated twice in the upstream sequences of CAV2 and CAV3 genes.

Table 2. The number of significant short variable motifs discovered in the (left) promoter sequences of 8 vertebrate CAV1 genes, and (right) 8 random synthetic 4-letter sequences, under various stringency levels: the columns represent the minimal number of motif occurrences and the rows show the minimal motif length

	4/8	5/8	6/8	7/8	8/8	4/8	5/8	6/8	7/8	8/8
5	231	127	92	44	23	100	73	45	21	19
6	224	111	71	35	18	99	72	42	19	18
7	194	93	57	29	13	92	66	39	16	17
8	159	59	29	11	1	74	41	26	4	1

Table 3. Highest scoring repeated motifs found in the upstream sequences of caveolin genes. SH — significance in homology; SP — significance in paralogy; OC — occurrences, homology; OP — occurrences, paralogy.

Consensus	SH	SP	OH	OP	TRANSFAC hits	Hit strength
CCccCC	0	4×10^{-5}	59	4	human SP1–4	100%
GGctcCC	2×10^{-16}	10^{-4}	39	3	human NF-Atp	100%
					rat MAPF2, YY1	100%
CAtccCT	3×10^{-15}	4×10^{-5}	28	5	human NIP, PEA3	100%
CCACAC	7×10^{-10}	6×10^{-4}	12	4	multiple	80%
CAGgGA	2×10^{-5}	10^{-4}	15	3	multiple	80%
GGgNGA	2×10^{-4}	10^{-7}	16	7	multiple	91.7%
ACttTT	8×10^{-4}	4×10^{-3}	12	6	multiple	80%

We first concentrated on the upstream regions of CAV1, CAV2 and CAV3 genes in the human sequence. With shortest reportable motif length set to 5, consensus strength at 0.95 and the likelihood of occurring by chance at less than 0.01, there were 416 significant motifs occurring in at least 2 out of 3 sequences, and 126 occurring in all 3. With these numbers in mind, we were interested to determine if any of these motifs were phylogenetically conserved.

Using the Ensembl browser [5], we have extracted 8 sequences of length 500 located upstream of the Caveolin-1 gene in fugu, zebrafish, chicken, mouse, rat, dog, chimpanzee and human. The number of short motifs discovered under varying stringency levels (all highly significant) is depicted in Table 2, along with the number of significant motifs discovered in completely random synthetic sequences of 4 DNA letters, which served as a control.

Looking at the intersection of the sets of motifs discovered in the promoter regions of CAV1, CAV2 and CAV3 in the human sequence, on one side, and the motifs discovered in the promoter regions of CAV1 in 8 vertebrates, we again identified large sets under various stringency levels. When we imposed a requirement that a motif must be present in all 3 human genes, and in all 8 vertebrate CAV1, with minimal reportable length of 6, we identified 7 motifs shown in Table 3. Top two of these motifs had a perfect hit with the TRANS-FAC [13] database, and the remaining could be found as weaker matches. Although our goal was solely to identify the short repeated variable elements in promoter regions of related genes, such TRANSFAC hits may help elucidate their role. The spatial distribution of these motifs in the upstream regions of human caveolins is shown in Figure 3. In general, very few significant repeated motifs exhibit positional conservation, when they can be detected by multiple alignments, and they may thus serve for further refinement of the repeats from our lists.

In another test, we have applied our software to 7 putative target genes of the MLL transcriptional complex (Mixed Lineage Leukemia genes [9]). After filtering for poly-A and other simple sequence, including tandem repeats, our program has identified 27 significant motifs, including several that warrant further experimental study, currently being pursued (manuscript in preparation).

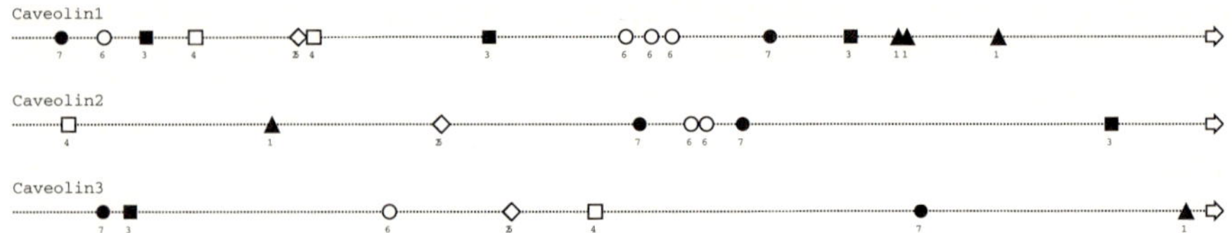

Fig. 3. The layout of the motifs in the upstream sequences of caveolin genes

4   Discussion

Our software has so far performed well. It was finding the motifs efficiently, and it has shown good sensitivity. In recent tests it was able to identify several motifs described in the TRANSFAC database which were missed by all but one of the programs included in the BEST suite [7]. The number of motifs reported by our tool tends to be large, however this is a common problem shared by all motif finders, and stems from the structure of genomes, or at least the eukaryotic genomes. In another study [16] we have described and quantified the remarkable micro-repetitive structure of the human genome, and shown that it is impossible to reliably identify functional motifs solely based on the occurrence counts, even after all known repeats have been excluded.

Our current approach cannot identify motifs featuring insertions and deletions. While more than one or two such modifications of a consensus would probably result in a loss of binding affinity, permitting some would further improve the sensitivity of our software. In one of our experiments done on yeast genes we have failed to recognize a well described common promoter, as almost all of its variants featured an indel. However, even our present algorithm detects an overabundance of significant motifs, and one can easily imagine that with permitted insertions and deletions this number would substantially increase.

Acknowledgments

The authors would like to thank Dr. Cedric Feschotte of UTA Biology for comments on repetitive elements in DNA, and Dr. Subhrangsu Mandal of UTA Biochemistry for help in the application of our software to putative MLL targets. This work has been partially supported by UTA REP grant 14 7487 62 to NS.

References

1. E.F. Adebiyi, T. Jiang, M. Kaufmann. An efficient algorithm for finding short approximate non–tandem repeats. *Bioinformatics*, 17:S5–S12, 2001.
2. A. Apostolico, M.E. Bock, S. Lonardi and X. Xu. Efficient detection of unusual words. *J. Comput. Biol.*, 7:71–94, 2000.
3. J.P. Balhoff and G.A. Wray. Evolutionary analysis of the well characterized *endo16* promoter reveals substantial variation within functional sites. *PNAS*, 102:8591–8596, 2005.

4. H. Bannai, S. Inenaga, A. Shinohara, M. Takeda, S. Miyano. Efficiently finding regulatory elements using correlation with gene expression. *J. Bioinform. Comput. Biol.*, 2:273–288, 2004.

5. E. Birney, D. Andrews, M. Caccamo *et al.*. Ensembl 2006. *Nucleic Acids Res.*, 34:D561–D453, 2006.

6. E. Burgermeister, L. Tencer and M. Liscovitch. Peroxisome proliferator–activated receptor-γ upregulates Caveolin-1 and Caveolin-2 in human carcinoma cells. *Oncogene*, 22:3888–3900, 2003.

7. D. Che, S. Jensen, L. Cai and J.S. Liu. BEST: Binding–site Estimation Suite of Tools. *Bioinformatics*, 21:2909–2911, 2005.

8. D.L. Corcoran, E. Feingold, J. Dominick, M. Wright, J. Harnaha, M. Trucco, N. Giannoukakis and P.V. Benos. Footer: A quantitative comparative genomics method for efficient recognition of *cis*–regulatory elements. *Genome Res.*, 15:840–847, 2005.

9. J.L. Hess. MLL: a histone methyltransferase disrupted in leukemia. *Trends Mol. Med.* 10:500–507, 2004.

10. J.D. Hughes, P.W. Estep, S. Tavazoie and G.M. Church. Computational identification of *cis*–regulatory elements associated with groups of functionally related genes in *Saccharomyces cerevisiae*. *J. Mol. Biol.*, 296:1205–1214, 2000.

11. A.G. Jegga, S.P. Sherwood, J.W. Carman, A.T. Pinski, J.L. Phillips, J.P. Pestian and B.J. Aronow. Detection and visualization of compositionally similar *cis*–regulatory element clusters in orthologous and coordinately controlled genes. *Genome Res.*, 12:1408–1417, 2002.

12. C.E. Lawrence, S.F. Altschul, M.S. Boguski, J.S. Liu, A.F. Neuwald and J.C. Wootton. Detecting subtle sequence signals: a Gibbs Sampling strategy for multiple alignment. *Science*, 262:208–214, 1993.

13. V. Matys, O.V. Kel–Margoulis, E. Fricke *et al.* TRANSFAC®and its module TRANSCompel®: transcriptional gene regulation in eukaryotes. *Nucleic Acids Res.*, 34:D108–D110, 2006.

14. A. Sandelin, W. Alkema, P. Engstrom, W. Wasserman and B. Lenhard. JASPAR: an open-access database for eukaryotic transcription factor binding profiles. *Nucleic Acids Res.*, 32:D91–D94, 2004.

15. R. Sharan, I. Ovcharenko, A. Ben–Hur and R.M. Karp. CREME: a framework for identifying *cis*–regulatory modules in human–mouse conserved segments. In *Proc. of the 11th International Conf. on Intelligent Systems in Mol. Biol.*, 283–291, 2003.

16. A. Singh and N. Stojanovic. Computational Analysis of the Distribution of Short Repeated Motifs in Human Genomic Sequences. To appear in *Proc. BIOT-2006*.

17. N. Stojanovic, L. Florea, C. Riemer, D. Gumucio, J. Slightom, M. Goodman, W. Miller and R. Hardison. Comparison of five methods for finding conserved sequences in multiple alignments of gene regulatory regions. *Nucleic Acids Res.*, 27:3899–3910, 1999.

18. The ENCODE Project Consortium. The ENCODE (ENCyclopedia Of DNA Elements) Project. *Science*, 306:636–640, 2004.

19. M. Tompa, N. Li, T.L. Bailey *et al.* Assessing computational tools for the discovery of transcription factor binding sites. *Nature Biotechnology*, 23:137–144, 2005.

20. J. van Helden, B. Andre and J. Collado–Vides. Extracting regulatory sites from the upstream region of yeast genes by computational analysis of oligonucleotide frequencies. *J. Mol. Biol.*, 281:827–842, 1998.

21. J. van Helden. Metrics for comparing regulatory sequences on the basis of pattern counts. *Bioinformatics*, 20:399-406, 2004.

22. P. Weiner. Linear pattern matching algorithms. *Proceedings of the 14th IEEE Symposium on Switching and Automata Theory*, 1–11, 1973.

An Intelligent Shopping Agent for Optimal Purchasing Decision on the Semantic Web

Hak-Jin Kim[1], Wooju Kim[2,*], and Jungmyong Kim[2]

[1] School of Business
[2] Department of Information and Industrial Engineering,
Yonsei University,134 Shinchon-dong, Seoul, 120-749, Korea
`hakjin@yonsei.ac.kr, wkim@yonsei.ac.kr, zzang94@daum.net`

Abstract. Shopping in the Internet does not proceed smoothly as customers expect currently. In particular customers have many obstacles in finding an optimal combination of products and shopping malls to minimize the total purchasing cost. To solve such problems, this paper proposes a new framework of an intelligent shopping agent based on the Semantic Web and the Integer Programming technologies. Starting from the search of products, it will show how to build an intelligent agent by using concepts of the Semantic Web and how to connect information to formulating and solving an optimization problem to achieve a customer's goal.

Keywords: Semantic Web, Integer Programming, OWL, SWRL, Internet Shopping Agent.

1 Introduction

When customers purchase products in Internet shopping malls, they experience difficulties in many ways. One comes from the conventional search systems. Current search systems are keyword-based such as in Amazon.com and Buy.com – they use combinations of words, phrases and sentences in query and search for items that contain the specified combinations. This kind of search method does not, however, satisfy customers with vague ideas about what they want. Also, even with clear ideas on products, they have to visit lots of shopping malls to find their best deals. While some websites such as MySimon.com and Dealtime.com try to give customers services of comparing products, it is still far behind what they want. When customers purchase multiple products from Internet shopping malls, they may still visit many websites to compare products from various shopping malls and struggle to handle complicating business rules such as price policy, sales taxes and delivery costs. After collecting all necessary information, finding an optimal combination of products and shopping malls with the lowest cost is not easy to customers.

W3C proposed the Semantic Web with implementation languages such as RDF, OWL and SWRL as a step to make more intelligent Web. The Semantic Web makes an agent understand meanings on the Web and process the data to provide what customers want while the conventional approach can't. RDF is a language for

---

[*] Corresponding author.

A. Levi et al. (Eds.): ISCIS 2006, LNCS 4263, pp. 192–201, 2006.

representing information about resources in the Internet. OWL, an extension of the concepts in RDF, describes Web ontologies of information for objects that can be identified on the Web and make them processed by applications; so, it is quite useful when information of products needs to be represented on the Web. SWRL, a semantic web rule language combining OWL and RuleML, helps to describe relations between Web ontologies.

Benefits of the Semantic Web technology have enticed many researchers to apply the technology to various applications: medical and biological information search [6] and product information representation in e-commerce. [5] and [3] applied the technology to product information search while [4] and [2] addressed product information integration and tracking. All the preceding works, however, address only a part of the whole process of shopper's decision making. This paper will address how to support the whole process of shopper's decision making with the Semantic Web and the Integer Programming technologies. It will propose how to make an agent more intelligent by using the Integer Programming (IP) as a reasoning method. With this reasoning method, the agent can deduce what customers really want such as an optimal combination of products and shopping malls. More details will be showed in the following: customer-product information description using the Web Ontology; description of business rules using SWRL; query generation method based on the Web Ontology; the price minimization of multiple products based on the Integer Programming. The agent will be explained with the case of purchasing CDs.

This paper is organized in four sections. The first is this section. The second shows how the proposed agent works to solve the problems mentioned above. The third section will show details of implementation, and finally a conclusion follows.

2 How Ontology Rule and IP-Based Intelligent Agent Works

The agent collects information about CDs from Internet shopping malls and finds an optimal selection to achieve the goal a customer sets. The agent starts with receiving an ID and a password from a customer and showing the registered shopping malls the customer can access to. Also, it displays the status of the customer's membership for each shopping mall, stored in each shopping mall's ontology.

Next, the agent displays a dialogue box with three fields to get data keywords necessary to search for a CD. The keywords include the name of an album, the list of songs and the artist's name. A query to search for the CD is generated in RDQL and is conducted in an ontology, Whole CD Ontology, containing information of all CDs. After the search, the agent displays the result in a table. The customer may put the found CDs into the shopping cart, and either continue shopping or go to the table showing all information about the chosen CDs. Then, the customer puts the number of each CD to purchase in the shopping cart.

In the next step, the agent retrieves all information about shopping malls stocking the chosen CDs and business rules from Shopping Mall Ontologies. A table called Price Table appears and shows the prices for CDs, delivery rates and discounts shopping malls are proposing. In other words, the agent queries information about

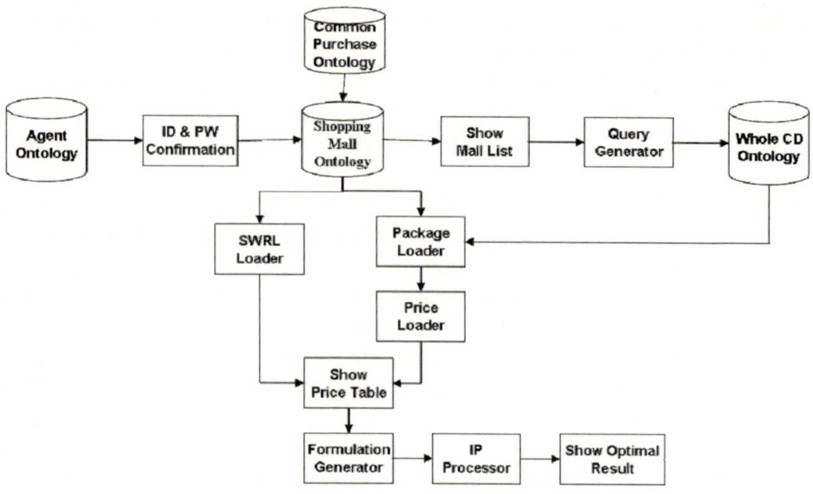

Fig. 1. The Agent Architecture

products from Shopping Mall Ontologies and extracts price information by Price Loader. If a package product is found by Package Loader, the module makes separate rows in the table and provides the information for the customer. SWRL Loader reads and shows in the table the information about delivery rates and discount policies, stored in Shopping Mall Ontologies. In this step the agent may give the customer several choices of goals such as "minimize the total expense", "minimize the use of saving points", "minimize delivery charge," and so on; this choice provides a criterion to find an optimal choices of products and shopping malls.

An IP model is formulated from the information of Price Table to find out an optimal combination of products and shopping malls and then the IP Processor solves the model. A result window finally shows an optimal combination about products and shopping malls. The architecture of the intelligent shopping agent is described in Fig. 1.

3   An Implementation of the Intelligent Shopping Agent

3.1   An Ontology Representation of Product-Customer Information

Whole CD Ontology is the one that combines information about CDs from all Shopping Mall Ontologies to search CDs only. It stores the names of albums, the lists of songs and artists' names as attributes. Fig. 2 shows a part of Whole CD Ontology, and Fig. 3 a part of XML code to represent the ontology.

To build an implementation of the agent, ontologies for 6 shopping malls are constructed in this research. While Whole CD Ontology contains all CDs on sale, each Shopping Mall Ontology has only a subset of CDs according to the state of the shopping mall's inventory. Each ontology keeps information about customers' memberships, product information and business rules. The membership information includes IDs and passwords for customer confirmation. The product information

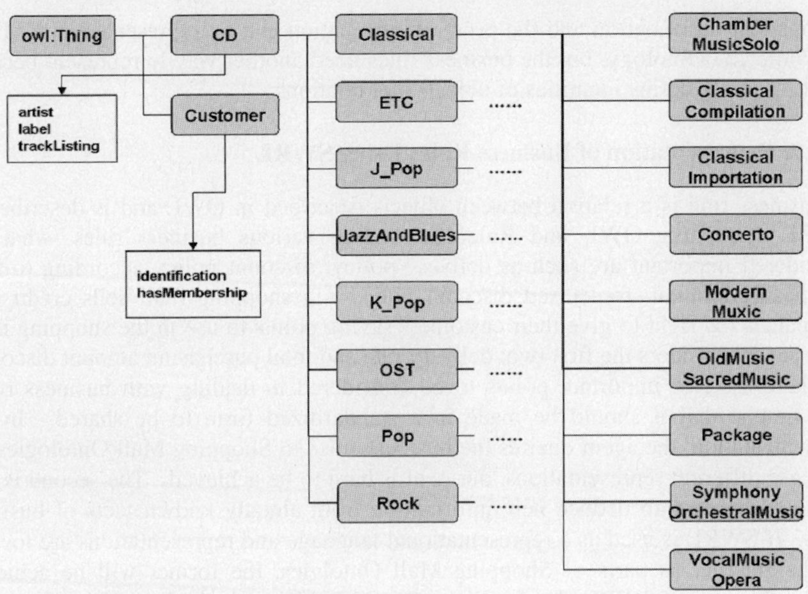

Fig. 2. Class Hierarchy and Properties of Whole CD Ontology

```
<owl:Ontology rdf:about=""/>
<owl:Class rdf:ID="ForeignFilm">
  <rdfs:subClassOf><owl:Class rdf:ID="OST"/></rdfs:subClassOf>
</owl:Class>
<owl:Class rdf:ID="KoreanFilm">
  <rdfs:subClassOf><owl:Class rdf:about="#OST"/></rdfs:subClassOf>
</owl:Class>
<owl:Class rdf:ID="JNBCompilation"/>
  <rdfs:subClassOf><owl:Class rdf:ID="JazzBlues"/></rdfs:subClassOf>
</owl:Class>
<owl:Class rdf:ID="HardROckHeavyMetal">
  <rdfs:subClassOf><owl:Class rdf:ID="Rock"/></rdfs:subClassOf>
</owl:Class>
<owl:Class rdf="Group">
  <rdfs:subClassOf><owl:Class rdf:ID="KPOP"/></rdfs:subClassOf>
</owl:Class>
<owl:Class rdf="WorldMusic">
  <rdfs:subClassOf><owl:Class rdf:ID="POP"/></rdfs:subClassOf>
</owl:Class>
<owl:Class rdf="Trot">
  <rdfs:subClassOf><owl:Class rdf:about="#KPOP"/></rdfs:subClassOf>
</owl:Class>
```

Fig. 3. A Part of XML code for Whole CD Ontology

consists of the names of albums, the lists of songs in each album, the names of artists, and sale prices. The business rules are policies of a shopping mall for delivery rate and discount from the total amount of sales. In Shopping Mall Ontologies, the membership information and the product information can be represented in XML as in Whole CD Ontology, but the business rules need another way to represent because OWL can only define identities of objects, not relations.

3.2   A Representation of Business Rules Using SWRL

A business rule is a relation between objects described in OWL and is described in SWRL combining OWL and RuleML. Among various business rules, what are considered important are such as delivery policy, discount policy according to total purchasing amount, franchised discount policy – a shopping mall sells credit card companies the right to give their customers saving points to use in the shopping mall. This paper considers the first two: delivery rate and total purchasing amount discount.

There are two important points to be considered in dealing with business rules. The first is that it should be made in a standardized form to be shared. In our implementation, the agent queires the business rules to Shopping Mall Ontologies. If they use different representations, our goal is hard to be achieved. The second is that it should be easy to deduce new information from already known facts of business rules. If SWRL is used as a representational language and representations are located on the Internet as parts of Shopping Mall Ontolgies, the former will be achieved easily. The use of SWRL also facilitates the second because the language is based on rule-based reasoning.

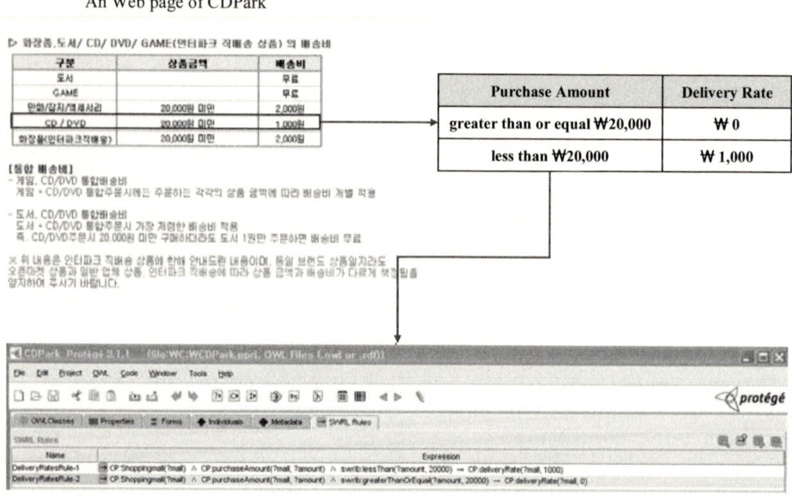

Fig. 4. The Delivery Policy of CD Park and its SWRL Representation

```
DeliveryRatesRule-1:
  CP:Shoppingmall(?mall)∧CP:MallName(?mall, "CDParks") ∧
  CP:purchaseAmount(?mall, ?amount) ∧
  swrlb:lessThan(?amount, 20000)
   →CP:deliveryRate(?mall, 1000)
```

Fig. 5. An Example of A Delivery Rate Rule

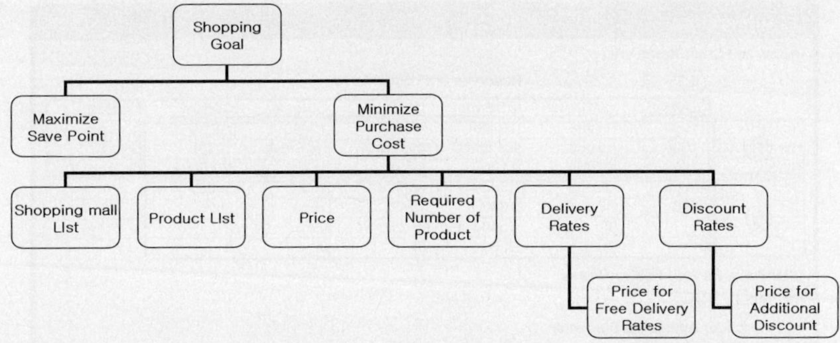

Fig. 6. The Class Hierarchy of Shopping Goal Ontology

The shopping malls we studied on delivery policy have simple types of policies: each either may charge delivery cost or exempt it. This may be extended to be piecewise linear delivery rate. Fig 4 shows how a delivery policy is transformed in SWRL with Protégé tool. Fig. 5 is a SWRL representation of the first delivery rate in Fig. 4. The first predicate of the antecedent identifies a variable "?mall" belonging to a class "shoppingmall" of an ontology "CP". Here CP means a Common Purchase Ontology in Fig. 1 that defines general purchasing activities. This is imported to a Shopping Mall Ontology to define SWRL atoms. The predicate atom "shoppingmall" says that a variable "?mall" is a shopping mall. In the second, predicate "pusrchaseAmount" says that the amount purchased in a shopping mall "?mall" is "?amount". The third predicate means that the purchased amount is less than 20000. If all of those predicate are satisfied, the delivery rate for the shopping mall is charged by 1000.

Discount from the total purchasing amount is also handled in the same way. It is defined in a Common Purchase Ontology and imported to a Shopping Mall Ontology. When the agent queries the rule about discount, it is scanned and necessary information is extracted. As in the delivery policy, a simple case of discount is considered: a discount rate is applied only for the total amount exceeding a given threshold.

3.3   Extracting Data from Ontologies and SWRL

Customers may intend to take advantages other than saving time in Internet shopping: they may amass saving points provided by Internet shopping malls to use for future shopping, and they may search the variety of delivery and discount policies to find an optimal combination of products and shopping malls so that they can minimize the total cost of purchase. This paper focuses on the latter for exemplification.

The agent refers to an ontology of Fig. 6 located in a Common Purchase Ontolgy and generate a Price Table in Fig. 7. Necessary data is a list of shopping malls, a list of products the customer chose, sale prices, purchasing quantities, delivery rates and reference amounts for delivery charge, discount rates and reference amounts for discount.

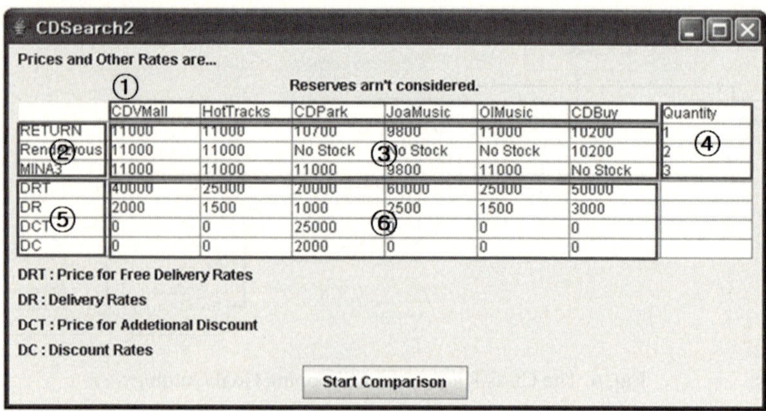

Fig. 7. The Screenshot of a Price Table

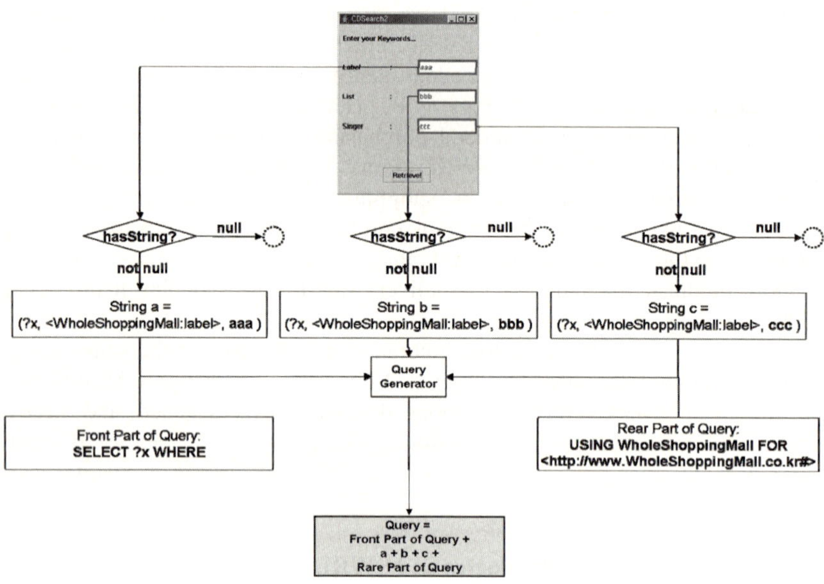

Fig. 8. The Procedure of Query Generation for Finding a Product

To find data on the product stored in RDF format, the agent generates queries in a query language RDQL. Fig. 8 shows how each component of a query to search for a CD is generated in RDQL. From the response of a customer about "label", "list" and "singer", the agent makes the corresponding strings, "a", "b", "c", and combines them as the body part of a query. A query is built out by adding the front and the rear parts to the body part. The resulted query shown in Fig. 9 commands to search for the product whose values of attributes, label, track listing and artist attributes, are "RETURN", "temptation" and "Mina". The last line indicates the namespace WholeShoppingMall used in this query.

After finding products, the extraction of price information from each shopping mall is needed. The required queries to shopping malls are the same but should have different namespaces because each shopping mall has its own namespace. CDV Mall with its URL http://www.CDVMall.co.kr# has its namespace CDVMall for example.

The agent has a profile for each customer where a shopping mall may be added or deleted easily. Fig. 10 is an RDQL code to extract shopping malls from the profile.

When the agent queries each Sopping Mall Ontologies about delivery rates, discount rates and their reference amounts in vain, it searches Common Purchase Ontologies for business rules represented in SWRL. As for rules of delivery, it looks for all rules whose consequents have a predicate atom "deliveryRate", and then finds one whose consequent has the non-zero second argument. It also identifies a predicate atom "pruchaseAmount" and a builtin atom "swrlb:lessThan". A delivery rate is set to the second argument of "deliveryRate" predicate and a reference amount for deliver charge to the second argument of "swrlb:lessThan" predicate (See Fig. 5.). A discount rate and a reference amount for discount are extracted in the same way.

```
SELECT    ?x
WHERE     (?x,<WholeShoppingMall:label>,"RETURN")
          (?x,<WholeShoppingMall:trackListing>,"temptation")
          (?x,<WholeShoppingMall:artist>,"Mina")
USING     WholeShoppingMall FOR
           <http://www.WholeShoppingMall.co.kr#>
```

Fig. 9. An Example of RDQL to Find a Product

```
SELECT    ?x
WHERE     (?z,<http://www.CDSearch.co.kr#password>,"PW")
          (?z,<http://www.CDSearch.co.kr#identification>,"ID")
          (?z,<http://www.CDSearch.co.kr#regShoppingmall>,?x)"
USING     CDSearch FOR <http://www. CDSearch.co.kr#>
```

Fig. 10. RDQL to Extract Information of Shopping Malls

3.4 Total Cost Minimization by the Integer Programming

The agent suggests an optimal choice of combination of products and shopping malls by solving an integer programming problem. Let us i denote a shopping mall and j a product. Let n be the number of shopping malls, m the number of unpackaged products, and k the number of package products. Also, let N_j be the quantity of product j the customer is about to purchase. P_{ij} denotes the price of product j in shopping mall i and X_{ij} the purchase quantity of product j from shopping mall i. If a shopping mall i has no stock for a product j, an arbitrary big number M is assigned to its price. Since the customer minimizes the total purchasing cost, the objective is

$$Minimize \qquad \sum_{i=1}^{n} \sum_{j=1}^{m+k} P_{ij} X_{ij} \qquad\qquad (1)$$

Since the total quantity of purchases from all shopping malls for each product equals the quantity the customer wants to purchase, a simple constraint $\sum_{i=1}^{n} X_{ij} = N_i$ is added in the case of no package products. However, when package products are considered, it is a little complicating. If product p and product q form a package r, then the constraints for product p and product q have additional terms as follows:

$$\sum_{i=1}^{n} X_{ip} + \sum_{i=1}^{n} X_{ir} = N_p, \quad \sum_{i=1}^{n} X_{iq} + \sum_{i=1}^{n} X_{ir} = N_q \tag{2}$$

The delivery rate depends on the total purchasing amount from a shopping mall. Let DR_i be a delivery rate shopping mall i charges, DRT_i a reference amount for delivery charge; if the purchasing amount exceeds this amount, the shopping mall does not charge any delivery cost. Also let Y_{i1}, Y_{i2}, Y_{i3} be binary variables that has value 1 if the total amount of purchase is 0, less than DRT_i and greater than or equal to DRT_i, respectively. Then the following constraints are imposed.

$$\sum_{j=1}^{m} P_{ij} X_{ij} = DRT_i \cdot \lambda_{i3} + M \cdot \lambda_{i4}$$
$$\lambda_{i1} \leq Y_{i1}, \quad \lambda_{i2} \leq Y_{i1} + Y_{i2}, \quad \lambda_{i3} \leq Y_{i2} + Y_{i3}, \quad \lambda_{i4} \leq Y_{i3} \tag{3}$$
$$\lambda_{i1} + \lambda_{i2} + \lambda_{i3} + \lambda_{i4} = 1, \quad Y_{i1} + Y_{i2} + Y_{i3} = 1$$

The customer may have discount if the total amount to purchase products from a shopping mall exceeds a certain amount according to the shopping mall's discount policy. Let DC_i be the discount amount from shopping mall i and DCT_i a reference amount for discount. So, if the total amount from Shopping Mall i does not exceed DCT_i, DC_i will be zero. Also, define another kind of binary variables Z_i that has value 1 if the total amount of purchase is greater than or equal to DCT_i ; otherwise 0. Then the following constraints are added:

$$\sum_{j=1}^{m} P_{ij} X_{ij} - DCT_i \leq M \cdot Z_i$$
$$DCT_i - \sum_{j=1}^{m} P_{ij} X_{ij} \leq M \cdot (1 - Z_i) \tag{4}$$

Now if we consider the delivery policy and the discount, the objective function becomes as follows

$$Minimize \quad \sum_{i=1}^{n}\sum_{j=1}^{m+k} P_{ij} X_{ij} + \sum_{i=1}^{n} DR_i \cdot Y_{i2} - \sum_{i=1}^{n} DC_i \cdot Z_i \tag{5}$$

Since all data required to formulate this integer programming model may be obtained as mentioned in the last section, the model can be solved by an integer programming solver. For example, the solution to Fig. 7 suggests that the customer purchases 2 "Rendezvous" and 1 "MINA3" in "HotTracks", 1 "RETURN", 2 "MINA3" in "CDPark with total cost 63,700.

4   Conclusion

In this paper, we proposed an implementation of an intelligent shopping agent, based on the Semantic Web and the Integer Programming technologies, which finds an optimal combination of products and shopping malls for purchasing. This idea still is seminary and needs to be made concrete further. Especially, it requires implementing a modeling language to formulate Integer Programming models automatically for further study.

Acknowledgement. This work was supported by Korea Research Foundation Grant.

References

1. Antoniou, G., van Harmelen, F.: Semantic Web Primer Chapter 1. The Semantic Web Vision. available from <http://www.ics.forth.gr/isl/swprimer/ presentations/Chapter1.ppt>
2. Guo, M., Li, S., Dong, J., Fu, X.., Hu, Y., Yin, Q.: Ontology-Based Product Data Integration. 17th International Conference on Advanced Information Networking and Applications (AINA'03) (2003) 530
3. Heinecke, J., Toumani, F.: A Natural Language Mediation System for E-Commerce applications: an ontology-based approach. Proceedings of ISWC 2003, October (2003)20-23
4. Ketkar, V.N., Whitman, L., Malzahn, D.: Ontology-based Product Tracking System. Proceedings of 11th Annual Industrial Engineering Research Conference IERC-2002: May (2002) 19-21 2002.
5. Kim, W., Choi, D.W., Park, S.-U.: Intelligent Product Information Search Framework Based on the Semantic Web. Proceedings of ISWC 2004, November (2004) 7-11
6. Marquet, G., Golbreich, C., Burgun, A.: From an ontology-based search engine towards a mediator for medical and biological information integration. Proceedings of the Semantic Integration Workshop Collocated with the ISWC-03, October 20 (2003)
7. Nemhauser, G.L., Wolsey, L.A.: Integer and Combinatorial Optimization. John Wiley & Sons (1988)
8. Silverman, B., Bachann, M., Al-Akharas, K.: A Markov Decision Processing Solution to Natural Language Querying of Online e-Commerce Catalogs: The EQUIsearch Agent. Available at < http://www.seas.upenn.edu/~barryg/mdp.pdf>
9. Sproule, S., Archer, N.: A Knowledgeable Agents for Search and Choice Support in E-commerce: A Decision Support Systems Approach. Journal of Electronic Commerce Research, 1(4). (2000) 152-165
10. Wooldridge, M.: An Introduction to MultiAgent Systems. John Wiley & Sons Publishers, available from <http://www.csc.liv.ac.uk/~mjw/pubs/imas/>

Adapting the Pyramid Technique for Indexing Ontological Data

Övünç Öztürk, Tuğba Özacar, Murat Osman Ünalır, and Ata Önal

Department of Computer Engineering,
Ege University
Bornova, 35100, Izmir, Turkey
{ovunc.ozturk, tugba.ozacar, murat.osman.unalir, ata.onal}@ege.edu.tr

Abstract. This paper describes the implementation of an indexing mechanism on a Rete-based reasoner working with ontological data in order to optimize memory consumption of the reasoner. This newly introduced indexing mechanism is known as the Pyramid Technique [1]. Our work organizes three dimensional ontological data in a way that works efficiently with this indexing mechanism and it constructs a subset of the querying scheme of the Pyramid Technique that supports querying ontological data. This work also implements an optimization on the Pyramid Technique. Finally, it discusses the performance analysis of the reasoner in terms of time and memory consumptions.

1   Introduction

Handling large and combined ontologies is essential for many semantic web tools including reasoners. Although there are a number of rule based reasoners, that can manage medium sized ontologies with fairly good performances, it is hard to say the same for large ontologies [2]. Since reasoning is a time and memory consuming process, many of the reasoners can not manage with large ontologies. A solution approach is serializing the inference results to speeding up the querying process. This approach can be very useful unless you change the data dynamically.

In the case of dynamically updated data it is reasonable to use algorithms such as Rete that only tests the newly added or deleted ontology triples against rules without starting the algorithm again. Although Rete is an optimized forward chaining algorithm, it lacks memory while dealing with large ontologies.

This work introduces a solution for reducing memory consumption of a Rete reasoner by adapting an indexing method to ontological data. This method is known as the Pyramid Technique.

Next section represents the problem statement in detail. Section three describes mapping Semantic Web resources to numerical values in order to support the input format required by the Pyramid Technique. Section four represents how three dimensional ontological data is indexed using the Pyramid Technique. This section also has a subsection that represents a subset of the querying scheme of

A. Levi et al. (Eds.): ISCIS 2006, LNCS 4263, pp. 202–211, 2006.

the Pyramid Technique that supports querying ontological data. The second subsection describes an optimization method on the Pyramid Technique in order to get better query response times. Section five compares the memory consumptions and performances of our reasoner with and without implementation of the Pyramid Technique. Finally section six concludes this paper with an outline of some potential future research.

2   Problem Statement

Rete[3][4] is an optimized forward chaining algorithm. An inefficient forward chaining algorithm applies rules for finding new facts and whenever a new fact is added to or removed from ontology, algorithm starts again to produce facts that are mostly same as the facts produced in the previous cycle. Rete is an optimized algorithm that remembers the previously found results and does not compute them again. Rete only tests the newly added or deleted facts against rules and increases the performance dramatically.

Rete algorithm is based on the reasoning process of Rete network. Following definitions give a formal representation of the concepts in a Rete network.

Let $\mathcal{O} = (\mathcal{W}, \mathcal{R})$ be an ontology where $\mathcal{W} = \{w \mid w = (s, p, o) \wedge s, p, o \in \mathcal{U}\}$ is the set of all facts in the ontology and $\mathcal{R}$ is the set of all rules related with the ontology, then every fact $w \in \mathcal{W}$ consists of a subject s, a predicate p and an object o and $\mathcal{U}$ denotes the set of constants. Given a $r \in \mathcal{R}$, $r = (lhs, rhs)$ where both lhs and rhs are lists of atoms. An atom $at = (a, i, v)$ consists of an attribute a, an identifier i and a variable v where $a, i, v \in \mathcal{T}$ and $\mathcal{T} = \mathcal{U} \cup \mathcal{V}$ where $\mathcal{V}$ denotes the set of variables. A lhs atom is called a condition. $\mathcal{C}$ is the set of all conditions of all rules $r \in \mathcal{R}$. Given a Rete network of the ontology $\Omega(\mathcal{O}) = (\alpha, \beta)$, we denote by α the alpha network and by β the beta network. $\alpha = \{\delta(c) \mid c \in \mathcal{C}\}$ and $\delta : \mathcal{C} \to \mathcal{D}$ is a function where $\mathcal{D} = \{x \mid x \subseteq \mathcal{W}\}$. $\delta(c)$ returns the set $\{w \mid w = (s, p, o) \wedge c = (a, i, v) \wedge ((s = a) \vee (a \in \mathcal{V})) \wedge ((p = i) \vee (i \in \mathcal{V})) \wedge ((o = v) \vee (v \in \mathcal{V}))\}$ denoting all matching facts with condition c. β network consists of beta memories and join nodes where beta memories store partial instantiations of rules, which are called tokens, and join nodes perform tests for consistency of variable bindings between conditions of rules. Figure 1 explains the relationships among the formal definitions with the help of an illustration existing in [4]. In this figure rectangles show beta memory nodes, ovals show alpha memories and circles show join nodes.

The set of all beta memories is $\mathcal{PI} = \{\phi(s) \mid s \in \mathcal{S}\}$ where $\mathcal{S} = \{x \mid x = (c_1 \wedge ... \wedge c_n) \wedge r = (lhs, rhs) \wedge lhs = (c_1, ..., c_t) \wedge (1 \leq n \leq t) \wedge r \in \mathcal{R}\}$ and $\phi : \mathcal{S} \to \mathcal{I}$ is a function where $\mathcal{I} = \{x \mid x \text{ is a conjunctive set of } w \in \mathcal{W}\}$. $\phi(s)$ returns the conjunctive sets of facts that are matching with s. The instantiations at the end of the Rete network are handled as production nodes, abbreviated as p-nodes. $\mathcal{P} = \{\phi(s) \mid s = (c_1 \wedge ... \wedge c_t) \wedge r = (lhs, rhs) \wedge lhs = (c_1, ..., c_t) \wedge r \in \mathcal{R}\}$. Whenever a propagation reaches the end of the Rete network in other words a p-node gets activated, it indicates that a rule's conditions are completely matched and the right handside atoms of the rule produces a new fact that will be added

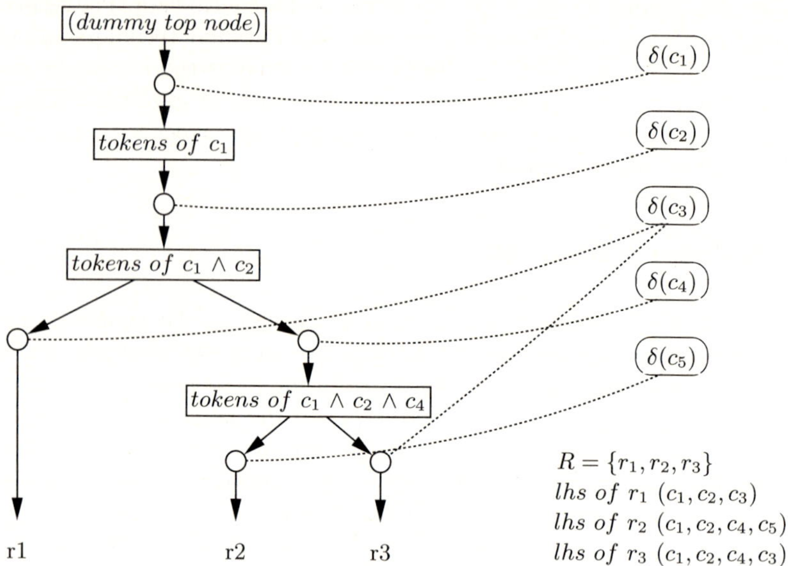

Fig. 1. An example RETE Network

to the ontology. Adding a new fact to the ontology triggers Rete network and new facts are inferred by these newly added facts without recomputing the previously found facts.

Our Rete based reasoner uses the syntax and semantics described in OWL Rules Language for rules, which is a special case of axiom-based approach[5]. The reasoner modifies some well known optimization heuristics[6],related with ordering conditions in the rules and queries, in needs of the semantic web and uses these independent heuristics together[7]. However, there is still a need to improve the memory performance in order to manage large ontologies.

Ontological data consists of facts where each fact is a triple containing a subject, a predicate and an object. Queries on ontological data are based on these three parts of the triple, in other words ontological data has three dimensions. Our analysis proved that the indexes, that we created on these dimensions, in order to reduce time consumption, make up a big percentage of the memory consumption. In order to reduce the memory consumption by sacrificing a reasonable amount of performance, we decided to implement a new indexing mechanism that is known as the Pyramid Technique.

3   Mapping Semantic Web Resources to Numerical Values

The Pyramid Technique indexes d-dimensional data using d-dimensional points as input. Ontological data has three dimensions (these dimensions are *subject*, *predicate* and *object*) where every dimension is a Semantic Web resource represented by an URI[1]. Thus, it is required to map the three dimensional ontological data to a three dimensional point in order to support the input format required by the Pyramid Technique. Originally the Pyramid Technique has numerical dimension values between 0-1 but we mapped every URI to a 16-digit long number because of the inadequacy when dealing with rational numbers. The cause of this inadequacy is that in computational environment rational numbers are represented using a floating point encoding with limited precision smaller than 16.

We slightly modified the mapping scheme in [8], in needs of semantic web resources. The mapping mechanism will assign a unique 16-digit long number for every semantic web resource residing in the ontology. The first six digits of this number represent the namespace and the remaining ten digits represent the reference name. In other words, mapping scheme supports an ontology having namespaces up to 10^6, and reference names up to 10^{10}.

In this mapping algorithm, every namespace is numbered sequentially from 0 to 10^6 and every reference name is numbered sequentially from 0 to 10^{10}. Given an URI to be mapped u, let n be the number assigned to the namespace of u, r be the number assigned to the reference name of u and x be the 16-digit long number that is the result of the mapping procedure, then $x = (n \times 10^{10}) + r$.

Mapping semantic web resources to long values comes with an additional benefit beyond supporting the input format required by the Pyramid Technique. During the reasoning process we deal with long values instead of strings. Comparison and evaluation of long values are not as time and memory consuming as strings. Since there are huge numbers of comparison and evaluation of semantic web resources, representing these resources as long values makes a significant impact on time and memory performance of the reasoner.

4   Adapting the Pyramid Technique for Indexing Ontological Data

The basic idea of the Pyramid Technique is to transform the d-dimensional data points into one dimensional values and then store and access the values using an efficient index structure such as the $B^+ - tree$. In our case, this technique transforms a three dimensional point into a one dimensional value. The Pyramid Technique partitions the data space into 2d (in our case 6) pyramids having the center point of the data space as their top. Then each of six pyramids is divided into several partitions each corresponding to one data page of the $B^+ - tree$. The Pyramid Technique transforms a three dimensional ontological data into a one dimensional value $(i + h_v)$ where i is the index of the according pyramid p_i and h_v is the height of v within p_i. Whenever we need to access ontological data, we first compute the pyramid value and query the $B^+ - tree$ using this value as a key. The resulting data pages of the $B^+ - tree$ contain points which constitute the answer of the query. Thus it is necessary to sequentially search these data pages in order to find the exact points corresponding to the query answer.

---

[1] Anonymous nodes and literals in ontologies are handled by assigning unique numbers to each of them programmatically.

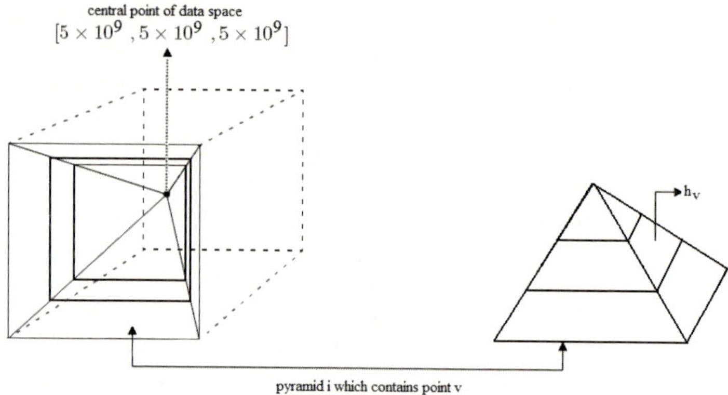

Fig. 2. Indexing 3-dimensional ontological data using the Pyramid Technique

The Pyramid Technique is an index structure for managing high-dimensional data. Our motivation to choose this index mechanism for indexing relatively low dimensional data (three dimensions) is to support potential index requirements. The Pyramid Technique allows to increment the dimension size in a flexible way and without sacrificing the performance.

4.1   Querying Indexed Ontological Data

Transformed ontological queries construct a subset of the queries described in the Pyramid Technique. The queries of the Pyramid Technique consist of point queries and range queries that are a set of d-dimensional intervals represented by r where $r = [q0_{min}, q0_{max}], \ldots, [q_{d-1_{min}}, q_{d-1_{max}}]$. Ontological queries consists of point queries and a subset of the range queries which is also a set of d-dimensional intervals represented by r' where $r' = [q0_{min}, q0_{max}], \ldots, [q_{d-1_{min}}, q_{d-1_{max}}]$ and $((q_{x_{min}} = q_{x_{max}})$ or $(q_{x_{min}} = 0$ and $q_{x_{max}} = 10^{10}))$ and $0 \leq x \leq d - 1$.

The two types of the ontological queries are defined below and all possible cases of range queries on ontological data with their transformations are presented in Table 1 :

- *Point Queries:* The query answer is a simple yes/no. This type of queries is used in searching or editing ontological data. In this case, a point is given and the answer specifies whether the given point is in the data space. Every dimension of the point is specified in the query. This problem is solved by first computing the pyramid value of the point, then querying the $B^+ - tree$ using this value as a key.
- *Range Queries:* This kind of queries returns a group of ontological data. The answer set is a range in the data space rather than a point. In this case, a three dimensional interval is given and the result is a data region that includes the answer set. This data region is searched sequentially for obtaining the exact answer set.

Table 1. All possible forms of range queries

Ontological Query	Transformed Range Query
$*, *, *$	$[0, 10^{10}][0, 10^{10}][0, 10^{10}]$
$pv_s, *, *$	$[pv_s, pv_s][0, 10^{10}][0, 10^{10}]$
$*, pv_p, *$	$[0, 10^{10}][pv_p, pv_p][0, 10^{10}]$
$*, *, pv_o$	$[0, 10^{10}][0, 10^{10}][pv_o, pv_o]$
$pv_s, pv_p, *$	$[pv_s, pv_s][pv_p, pv_p][0, 10^{10}]$
$pv_s, *, pv_o$	$[pv_s, pv_s][0, 10^{10}][pv_o, pv_o]$
$*, pv_p, pv_o$	$[0, 10^{10}][pv_p, pv_p][pv_o, pv_o]$

4.2 Optimizing the Pyramid Technique

In [9], it is proven that the Pyramid Technique may be worse than sequential
scan in some cases. Figure 3 shows the difference between querying a data range
near the center of the pyramid and near the corner of the pyramid. When queries
return a data range near the corner, the answer set make up a big percentage of
this range. Consequently data accessed is much more than the answer set and
sequential search for the answer set in this data makes the Pyramid Technique
quite inefficient.

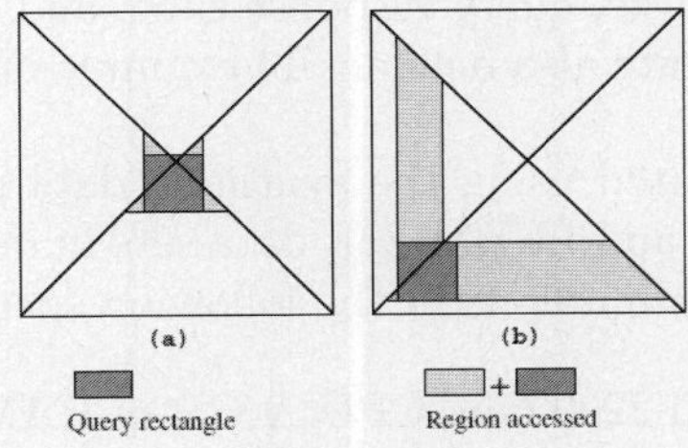

Fig. 3. The difference between querying a data range near the center of the pyramid
and near the corner of the pyramid

Thus it makes sense to shift our data near the center point of the data space.
This shifting can be done modifying the mapping scheme slightly. In the modified
mapping algorithm,every reference name is numbered sequentially from 0 to 10^{10}
and every namespace numbered proceeding through the following way :

Let s_i be the number assigned to the i_{th} namespace, $s_0 = 5 \times 10^5$ and $s_{x+1} = \delta(s_x)$ then;

$$\delta(s_x) = \begin{cases} (5 \times 10^5 - \mid 5 \times 10^5 - s_i \mid) & \text{if } s_i < 5 \times 10^5 \\ (5 \times 10^5 + \mid 5 \times 10^5 - s_i \mid + 1) & \text{otherwise} \end{cases}$$

Given a URI to be mapped u, let n be the number assigned to the namespace
of u, r be the number assigned to the reference name of u and x be the 16-digit
long number that is the result of mapping procedure, then $x = (n \times 10^{10}) + r$.
Figure 4 depicts the effect of this new scheme on data distribution.

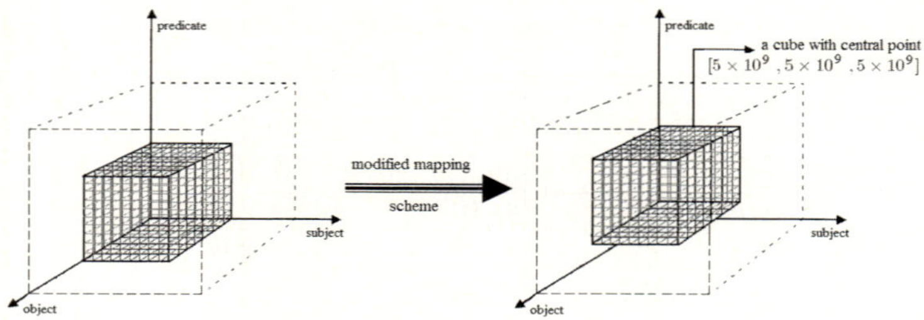

Fig. 4. Data distribution using the modified namespace numbering scheme

5   Performance Analysis

We use Lehigh University Benchmark [2] in order to evaluate the performance of the inference engine and to see the effects of the Pyramid Technique on performance and scalability. Lehigh University Benchmark is developed to evaluate the querying performance of Semantic Web repositories over a large data set. The data set is generated according to one ontology, named univ-bench, using the synthetic data generation tool provided with the benchmark. The performance of the repositories is evaluated through a set of metrics including data loading time, repository size, query response time, and query completeness and soundness. Benchmark suite also includes 14 example queries that cover a range of types.

Our data set is generated using the synthetic data generation tool. We use LUBM(1,0), LUBM(2,0) and LUBM(3,0) data sets in our benchmark. The tests are done on a desktop computer with the following specifications:

- AMD Athlon 64 3500 2200 Ghz CPU; 2 GB of RAM;320 GB of hard disk
- Windows XP Professional OS, .NET Framework 1.1

The evaluated inference engine, Aegont Inference Engine, is a part of the Aegean Ontology Environment Project. The inference engine is developed to work in correspondence with the Aegont Ontology Editor. Ontology Editor is used to load and query ontologies, in other words, ontology editor can be seen as a graphical user interface to the ontology repository residing in memory. Aegont inference engine is a forward chaining reasoner like OWLJessKB [10], this means once it loads the ontology, the ontology is complete and sound according to the rules defined in the system and there is no need to make inference while answering the queries.

In order to get more accurate query execution times, they are measured ten times and then their average is calculated. In our system all queries are answered with full completeness and soundness, this results in a high F-measure value, calculated according to the formula in [2]. The system's inference level is between OWL Lite and OWL DL. This inference level is satisfied by approximately 30 rules, which are written according to the OWL entailment tests [11]. Query execution times of all queries can be seen on Table 2.

Table 2. Query Execution Time

Query	Metrics	LUBM(1,0)	LUBM(2,0)	LUBM(3,0)
1	Time(ms)	762.0	540.0	440.2
	Answers	4	4	4
	Completeness	100	100	100
2	Time(ms)	705.8	434.0	433.8
	Answers	0	0	2
	Completeness	100	100	100
3	Time(ms)	868.6	340.2	421.6
	Answers	6	6	6
	Completeness	100	100	100
4	Time(ms)	40.0	646.4	105.6
	Answers	34	34	34
	Completeness	100	100	100
5	Time(ms)	121.8	502.6	665.2
	Answers	719	719	719
	Completeness	100	100	100
6	Time(ms)	315.0	499.6	596.6
	Answers	7790	17878	26258
	Completeness	100	100	100
7	Time(ms)	874.8	577.6	577.6
	Answers	67	67	67
	Completeness	100	100	100
8	Time(ms)	90.2	718.0	674.4
	Answers	7790	7790	7790
	Completeness	100	100	100
9	Time(ms)	705.8	693.4	634.0
	Answers	208	449	692
	Completeness	100	100	100
10	Time(ms)	462.0	634.0	374.6
	Answers	4	4	4
	Completeness	100	100	100
11	Time(ms)	899.6	765.0	655.4
	Answers	224	224	224
	Completeness	100	100	100
12	Time(ms)	727.6	868.4	340.0
	Answers	15	15	15
	Completeness	100	100	100
13	Time(ms)	687.2	530.8	777.6
	Answers	1	4	8
	Completeness	100	100	100
14	Time(ms)	537.0	280.6	633.6
	Answers	5916	13559	19868
	Completeness	100	100	100

The memory consumption of the reasoner is reduced by seventy percent by implementing the Pyramid Technique (Figure 5). The first row in the figure shows the memory consumption of the reasoner without the Pyramid Technique.

The second, third and fourth rows show the memory consumption of the reasoner with the Pyramid Technique. By using the Pyramid technique the reasoner can open a three times larger data set, LUBM(3,0), with the same amount of memory.

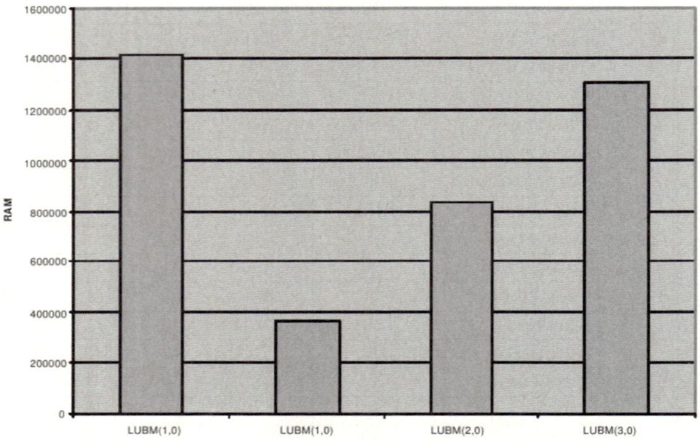

Fig. 5. Memory consumption of the reasoner with the Pyramid Technique

6   Conclusion and Future Work

This paper describes a Rete based inference engine with a special indexing mechanism based on the Pyramid Technique and evaluates the improvement in the memory consumption of the inference engine. The Pyramid Technique makes the inference engine to be able to find the closure of the 2-university data set with one gigabyte of memory, where OWLJessKB [8] can open 1-university data set with same amount of memory [1]. Although some repositories in the literature can open larger data sets, these repositories are not immune to changes in the ontology. Since they do not use algorithms like Rete, when the ontology is changed, they start inference procedure from scratch.

References

1. Berchtold, S., Böhm, C., Kriegel, H.P.: The pyramid-technique: Towards breaking the curse of dimensionality. In Haas, L.M., Tiwary, A., eds.: SIGMOD 1998, Proceedings ACM SIGMOD International Conference on Management of Data, June 2-4, 1998, Seattle, Washington, USA, ACM Press (1998) 142–153
2. Guo, Y., Pan, Z., Heflin, J.: An evaluation of knowledge base systems for large owl datasets. In: International Semantic Web Conference. (2004) 274–288
3. Forgy, C.: Rete: A fast algorithm for the many patterns/many objects match problem. Artif. Intell. **19** (1982) 17–37
4. Doorenbos, R.B.: Production matching for large learning systems. Technical report, Pittsburgh, PA, USA (2001)

5. Franconi, E., Tessaris, S.: Rules and queries with ontologies: A unified logical framework. In: PPSWR. (2004) 50–60
6. Ishida, T.: Optimizing rules in production system programs. In: National Conference on Artificial Intelligence. (1988) 699–704
7. Ünalir, M., Özacar, T., Öztürk, Ö.: Reordering query and rule patterns for query answering in a rete-based inference engine. In: WISE Workshops. (2005) 255–265
8. Jagadish, H.V., Koudas, N., Srivastava, D.: On effective multi-dimensional indexing for strings. In: SIGMOD '00: Proceedings of the 2000 ACM SIGMOD international conference on Management of data, New York, NY, USA, ACM Press (2000) 403–414
9. Zhang, R., Ooi, B.C., Tan, K.L.: Making the pyramid technique robust to query types and workloads. In: ICDE. (2004) 313–324
10. Kopena, J., Regli, W.C.: Damljesskb: A tool for reasoning with the semantic web. In: International Semantic Web Conference. (2003) 628–643
11. Carroll, J.J., Roo, J.D.: Owl web ontology language test cases (2004)

Comparison of Different Neural Networks Performances on Motorboat Datasets

M. Fatih Amasyalı[1], Mert Bal[2], Uğur B. Çelebi,
Serkan Ekinci[3], and U. Kaşif Boyacı[4]

[1] Yıldız Technical University, Computer Engineering Department
İstanbul, Turkey
mfatih@ce.yildiz.edu.tr
[2] Yıldız Technical University, Mathematical Engineering Department
İstanbul, Turkey
mertbal@yildiz.edu.tr
[3] Yıldız Technical University, Naval Architecture Department
İstanbul, Turkey
ucelebi@yildiz.edu.tr, ekinci@yildiz.edu.tr
[4] National Research Institute of Electronics and Cryptology ,TÜBİTAK, UEKAE
Gebze, Kocaeli, Turkey
ukasif@uekae.tubitak.gov.tr

Abstract. Calculation of the required engine power and displacement takes an important place in the initial design of motorboats. Recently, several calculation methods with fewer parameters and with a possible gain of time compared to classical methods have been proposed. This study introduces a novel calculation method based on neural networks. The method requires less data input and hence is more easily applicable than classical methods. In this study several different neural network methods have been conducted on data sets which have principal parameters of motorboats and the respective performances have been presented. From the results obtained, displacement and engine power prediction for motor boats can be used at a suitable level for ship building industry.

1 Introduction

At the predesign stage, the necessary information to calculate ship displacement and engine power is usually obtained by testing similar ship models in the towing tank. These data are converted into characteristic curves, tables and empiric equations via principal dimensions of ship. Moreover, with the developing computer technology, today it is also possible to calculate engine power and displacement using specific computer programs for the dimensions of the ship as inputs.

Recently, calculating design parameters with neural network is found to be much better than the traditional calculation methods in terms of time and costs. In the literature there are some applications of neural networks into naval architecture: neural network applications in naval architecture and marine engineering

[1], design of a robust neural network structure for determining initial stability particulars of fishing vessels [2], modeling and simulation of ship main engine based on neural network [3], determination of approximate main engine power for chemical cargo ships using radial basis function neural network [4] can be given as examples.

In this study, different neural network models are applied for determining the engine power and displacement based on principal parameters of current motorboats which have a length of 8 to 25 meters. Input data for the model are used ship length, breadth, draught and speed as principal parameters. System output is the engine power and displacement to be predicted and then the results of these methods are compared to examine which method give better results.

A motorboat's profile and upper view are given below in Figure 1. Main dimensions and related parameters in the illustrations are defined below.

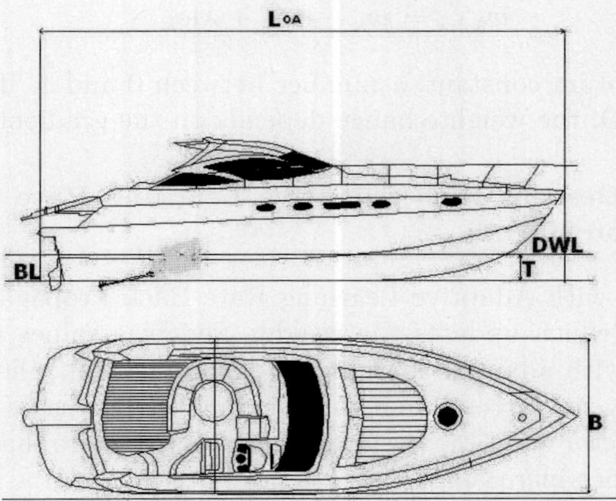

Fig. 1. A motorboat's profile and upper view

(BL) Baseline: The horizontal line parallel to the design waterline (DWL), which cuts the midship section at the lowest point of ship. The vertical heights are usually measured from the baseline.

(LOA) Length Overall: The total length of the ship from one end to the other, including bow and stern overhangs.

(T) Draught: The vertical distance from the waterline at any point on the hull to the bottom of the ship.

(B) Breadth: The distance from the inside of plating on one side to a similar point on the other side measured at the broadest part of the ship.

(V) Ship speed (Knot): The distance in miles taken in an hour.

(∇) Water Displacement ($\mathbf{m}^3$): The water displacement equals the volume of the part of the ship below the waterline including the shell plating, propeller and rudder.

(Δ) Displacement (ton): The displacement is weight of the volume of water displaced by the ship.

$$\Delta(\text{ton}) = \nabla(\text{m}^3)\gamma(\text{ton}/\text{m}^3) \tag{1}$$

2 Neural Network Models

In this study different Neural Network architecture and learning algorithms were used. Their basic explanations are given in this section.

2.1 Gradient Descent Back Propagation with Momentum (GDM)

Gradient Descent Back Propagation with Momentum is a generalization of GD introducing the concept of "momentum" in order to avoid trapped in a local minimum. The new weight formula is as follows:

$$w_{k+1} = w_k - \alpha g_k + \lambda w_{k-1} \tag{2}$$

where λ is momentum constant, a number between 0 and 1. If the momentum is 0, then as in GD, the weight change depends on the gradient.

2.2 Gradient Descent with Adaptive Learning Rate Back Propagation (GDA)

Gradient Descent with Adaptive Learning Rate Back Propagation (GDA) is a learning function which updates the weights and bias values according to the gradient descent with adaptive learning rate. At each step, the learning rate is either increased by the factor 1.05 if the performance decreases toward the goal, or decreased by factor 0.7 if the performance grows by more than the factor 1.05 and the performance increasing change is not applied.

2.3 Levenberg Marquardt Method

Levenberg-Marquardt method is one of the best known curve-fitting algorithms. The method works better than the Gauss-Newton method even if the starting point is very far off the desired minimum. To better illustrate the advantage of LM method over Newton method, consider a multilayer feedforward neural network.

The Newton method calculates the weight function recurrently as:

$$w_{n+1} = w_n - [H\psi(w_n)]^{-1}\nabla\psi(w_n) \tag{3}$$

where $\psi : \mathbb{R}^K \to \mathbb{R}$ is the corresponding error function

$$\psi(w) = \frac{1}{2}e(w)^T e(w) \tag{4}$$

The exact Hessian matrix calculation is too expensive and the condition that Hessian matrix should be positive definitive is too restrictive.

To overcome these difficulties, LM method proposes a positive-definite approximation $H\psi(\boldsymbol{w}) \approx \boldsymbol{J}(\boldsymbol{w})^T \boldsymbol{J}(\boldsymbol{w}) + \mu \boldsymbol{I}$ where

$$\boldsymbol{J}(\boldsymbol{w}) = \begin{bmatrix} \dfrac{\partial e_{11}(\boldsymbol{w})}{\partial w_1} & \dfrac{\partial e_{11}(\boldsymbol{w})}{\partial w_2} & \cdots & \dfrac{\partial e_{11}(\boldsymbol{w})}{\partial w_K} \\ \vdots & \vdots & \ddots & \vdots \\ \dfrac{\partial e_{L1}(\boldsymbol{w})}{\partial w_1} & \dfrac{\partial e_{L1}(\boldsymbol{w})}{\partial w_2} & \cdots & \dfrac{\partial e_{L1}(\boldsymbol{w})}{\partial w_K} \\ \vdots & \vdots & \ddots & \vdots \\ \dfrac{\partial e_{1Q}(\boldsymbol{w})}{\partial w_1} & \dfrac{\partial e_{1Q}(\boldsymbol{w})}{\partial w_2} & \cdots & \dfrac{\partial e_{1Q}(\boldsymbol{w})}{\partial w_K} \\ \vdots & \vdots & \ddots & \vdots \\ \dfrac{\partial e_{LQ}(\boldsymbol{w})}{\partial w_1} & \dfrac{\partial e_{LQ}(\boldsymbol{w})}{\partial w_2} & \cdots & \dfrac{\partial e_{LQ}(\boldsymbol{w})}{\partial w_K} \end{bmatrix} \tag{5}$$

is the Jacobian matrix, $\mu > 0, \boldsymbol{I}$ is an identity matrix of size $K \times K$.

The LM method weight recurrence is then [8]

$$\boldsymbol{w_{n+1}} = \boldsymbol{w_n} - [\boldsymbol{J}(\boldsymbol{w_n})^T \boldsymbol{J}(\boldsymbol{w_n}) + \mu_n \boldsymbol{I}]^{-1} \nabla \psi(\boldsymbol{w_n}) \tag{6}$$

So, each iteration requires the calculation of the inverse of $\boldsymbol{J}(\boldsymbol{w_n})^T \boldsymbol{J}(\boldsymbol{w_n}) + \mu_n \boldsymbol{I}$ which explains the only drawback of the LM method compared to the Newton method, namely the relative sloth if the starting parameters and the functions are "nice".

2.4   Radial Basis Function (RBF) Neural Network

The Radial Basis Function networks have a simple architecture comprising an input layer, a single (usually Gaussian) hidden layer and an output layer, the nodes of which are expressed as a linear combination of the outputs of the hidden layer nodes. For a one-node output layer, the global input-output relationship of an RBF Neural Network can be expressed as a linear combination of K basis function as follows:

$$f(\boldsymbol{x}) = \sum_{k=1}^{K} w_k \phi_k(\boldsymbol{x}) \tag{7}$$

where $\boldsymbol{x} = [x_1, x_2, \ldots, x_M]^T$ is the M-dimensional input vector, w_k are the weighting coefficients of the linear combination, and $\phi_k(\boldsymbol{x})$ represents the response of the kth neuron of the hidden layer. Typically, the basis function $\phi_k(\boldsymbol{x})$ are assumed to be Gaussian shaped with scale factor σ_k; their values decrease monotonically with the distance between the input vector $\boldsymbol{x}$ and the center of each function $\boldsymbol{c_k} = [c_{k1}, c_{k2}, \ldots, c_{km}]^T$ [7].

$$\phi_k(\boldsymbol{x}) = exp(-\frac{\| \boldsymbol{x} - \boldsymbol{c_k} \|^2}{\sigma^2}) \tag{8}$$

2.5   General Regression Neural Network (GRNN)

Suggested by Specht D.F., the General Regression Neural Network given enough data can solve any smooth approximation. The method is simple but suffers from high estimation cost. GRNN can be considered as a normalized RBF network. The GRNN consists of an input layer (where the inputs are applied), a hidden layer and a linear output layer. The hidden layer is usually expressed by a multivariate Gaussian function ϕ with an appropriate mean and an auto variance matrix as follows:

$$\phi_k[\boldsymbol{x}] = exp[-(\boldsymbol{x} - \boldsymbol{v}_k^x)^T(\boldsymbol{x} - \boldsymbol{v}_k^x)/(2\sigma^2)] \tag{9}$$

When $\boldsymbol{v}_k^x$ are the corresponding clusters for the inputs, $\boldsymbol{v}_k^y$ are the corresponding clusters for the outputs obtained by applying clustering technique of the input/output data that produces K cluster centers. $\boldsymbol{v}_k^y$ is defined as

$$\boldsymbol{v}_k^y = \sum_{y(p)\in \text{ cluster k}} y(p) \tag{10}$$

N_k is the number of input data in the cluster center k , and

$$d(\boldsymbol{x}, \boldsymbol{v}_k^x) = (\boldsymbol{x} - \boldsymbol{v}_k^x)^T(\boldsymbol{x} - \boldsymbol{v}_k^x) \tag{11}$$

with

$$\boldsymbol{v}_k^x = \sum_{\boldsymbol{x(p)}\in \text{ cluster k}} \boldsymbol{x(p)} \tag{12}$$

The outputs of the hidden layer nodes are multiplied with appropriate interconnection weights to produce the output of the GRNN [6]. The weight for the hidden node k (i.e.,w_k) is equal to

$$w_k = \frac{\boldsymbol{v}_k^y}{\sum_{k=1}^K N_k exp[-\frac{d(\boldsymbol{x},\boldsymbol{v}_k^x)^2}{2\sigma^2}]} \tag{13}$$

3 Experimental Results

In this study, engine power and displacement are modeled by using different neural network architectures and training algorithms. Both of problems are function approximation. Many different parameters are used for each architecture and training algorithms. Function approximators's abbreviations and explanations are given at Table 1.

Training and test sets are composed of 92 and 22 samples respectively. The problems share same 4 inputs but differ from the outputs. The inputs are B, L, V and T for each problem. In the first problem the output is displacement while the engine power is the output of second problem. Samples have 4 inputs and 1 input. For each problem, all possible combinations of inputs are given to neural network models to be able to see the prediction abilities of inputs. Training data sets of four single inputs, two and three inputs each with six, and single four input pairs are obtained.

Each train/test set pairs (datasets) are used in 17 different networks varies architecture, algorithms and parameters. In other words 255 (15*17) training and testing process is done for each function approximation problem.

Table 1. Function approximators

Abbreviation	Architecture parameters	Architecture and Learning algorithms
LM-1	No hidden layer (Linear Model)	Multi Layer Perceptron
LM-10-1	Hidden layer with 10 neuron	trained by
LM-20-1	Hidden layer with 20 neuron	Levenberg-Marquardt
LM-100-1	Hidden layer with 100 neuron	optimization
GDA-1	No hidden layer (Linear Model)	Multi Layer Perceptron
GDA-10-1	Hidden layer with 10 neuron	trained by
GDA-20-1	Hidden layer with 20 neuron	gradient descent with
GDA-100-1	Hidden layer with 100 neuron	adaptive learning rate
GDM-1	No hidden layer (Linear Model)	Multi Layer Perceptron
GDM-10-1	Hidden layer with 10 neuron	trained by
GDM-20-1	Hidden layer with 20 neuron	gradient descent
GDM-100-1	Hidden layer with 100 neuron	with momentum
GRNN	Spread = 1.0	Generalized Regression Neural Network
RBF-10	Spread =10	
RBF-20	Spread =20	Radial Basis Function
RBF-50	Spread =50	Neural Network
RBF-100	Spread =100	

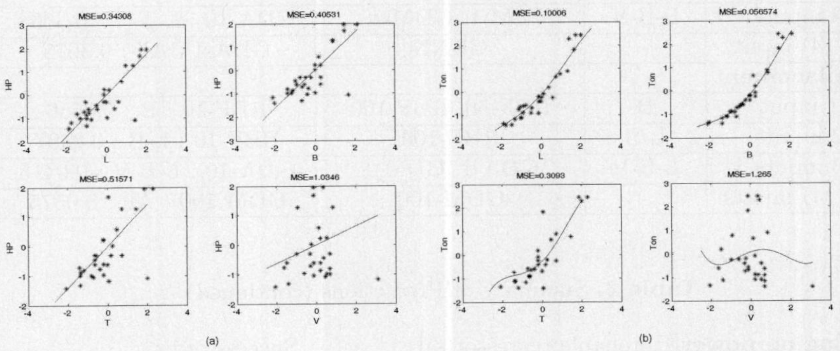

Fig. 2. The stars are test samples while the line is approximated function (a) engine power with GDA linear model (b) displacement with RBF network spread=50

In Figures, Mean Square Error's are given at the top of each experiment. In Figure 2.a, GDA linear models and their engine power approximations are given for each single input. The predicted function of displacement with RBF network in Figure 2.b. X and Y axis show the single input and the output of the functions respectively.

In Figure 3, GDM and RBF models and their engine power function approximations are given for the same dataset with two inputs.

In Table 2, 3, and 4, engine power and displacement prediction experiments are summarized. For each number of inputs, the best feature, the best regressor, the best experiment, the unreliable regressor(s), mean success order and obser-

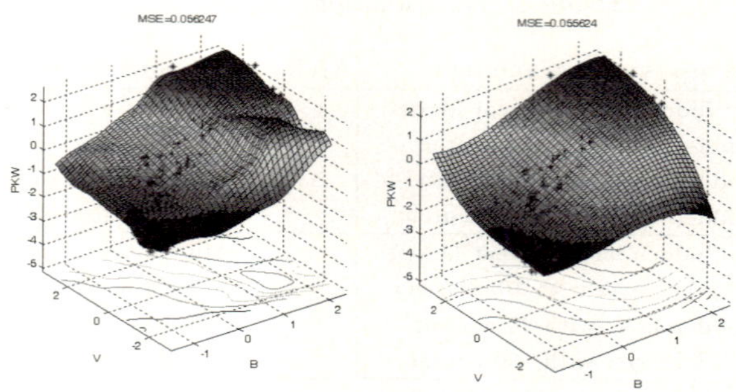

Fig. 3. GDM 20 neuron at the hidden layer, RBF 50. Blue and red stars are train and test sets respectively. The surface is approximated engine power function.

Table 2. Summary of Predictions

Engine power	The Best feature(s)	The average best regressor	The best experiment (Model : Feature(s) : MSE)
1 input	B	LM-1,GDA-1, GDM-1	GDM-10-1 : L : 0.2981
2 inputs	L-B	LM-1, GDM-1	GDM-20 : L-V : 0.255
3 inputs	L-B-V	LM-1, GDM-1	GDA-10 : L-T-V : 0.3068
All (4) inputs	-	GRNN	GDA-1 : All : 0.3075
Displacement			
1 input	B	RBF-50, RBF-100	RBF-10 : B : 0.0556
2 inputs	L-B	RBF-100	RBF-10 : L-B : 0.0497
3 inputs	L-B-V	GDA-1, GDM-1	GDA-10 : L-B-V : 0.0418
All (4) inputs	-	GDM-100	GDM-100 : All : 0.0575

Table 3. Summary of Predictions (continued)

Engine power	Unreliable regressor(s)	Success order
1 input	LM	GRNN>RBF>GDA>GDM>>LM
2 inputs	LM, RBF	GRNN>GDM>GDA>RBF>>LM
3 inputs	LM, GDA, RBF	GRNN>GDM>>LM>GDA>RBF
All (4) inputs	LM, RBF	GRNN>GDM>GDA>>RBF>LM
Displacement		
1 input	LM	RBF>GDM>GRNN>GDA>>LM
2 inputs	LM, RBF	GDM>GRNN>GDA>RBF>>LM
3 inputs	LM, GDA, RBF	GDM>GRNN>LM>GDA>RBF
All (4) inputs	GDA, RBF	GDM>GRNN>LM>>RBF>GDA

vations are given. The best features, the best regressors and success orders are obtained from average values of experiments having different number of inputs. For the explanations of regressor abbreviations see Table 1.

Table 4. Prediction Observations

Number of Inputs	Engine Power Observations
1 input	LM, GDA and GDM have similar characteristics. MSE increases with the number of neurons in the hidden layer. LM gives unreliable results when the number of neurons in the hidden layer is above 20. LM, GDA and GDM have very similar performance when linear model is used (no hidden layer). The effect of RBF's spread value over the performance is very few.
2 inputs	LM is very sensitive to the number of hidden neurons. LM and GDM have similar MSEs with linear model. The spread value of radial basis functions in RBF is effective in the performance.
3 inputs	LM and GDM's linear models have similar performances and they are the best regressors for 3 inputs. In RBF, the MSEs decrease while spread value increases.
All (4) inputs	GDA and GDM have similar characteristics. MSE increases with the number of neurons in the hidden layer. LM, GDA and GDM have very similar performance when linear model is used. In RBF, the MSEs decrease while spread value increases. RBF has not robust results when the spread value is 10 or 20.
Number of Inputs	Displacement Observations
1 input	The effect of RBF's spread value over the performance is very few. LM, GDA and GDM give similar MSEs when linear model is used.
2 inputs	LM and GDM give similar MSEs when linear model is used. The spread value of radial basis functions in RBF is effective in the performance.
3 inputs	LM and GDM give similar MSEs when linear model is used. In RBF, the MSEs decrease while spread value increases.
All (4) inputs	In GDM, MSEs decreases while the number of neurons in hidden layer increase. LM and GDM give similar MSEs when linear model is used. In RBF, the MSEs decrease while spread value increases. RBF has not robust results when the spread value is 10 or 20.

4   Conclusion

In naval engineering, in order to calculate the engine power and the water displacement, classical methods use several parameters [5] , some of which require tedious work and long experiments. This study aims to estimate the engine power and displacement by the help of only easily accessible parameters. As estimation models, several ANN techniques are used where the samples have 4 inputs and only one output. In this study, two analysis have been conducted to find:

1. The most effective input(s)to determine the output
2. The most successful ANN architecture and/or training algorithm

For the first one, using each possible input combinations 15 different training and test sets have been created. For the second analysis, 17 regressors comprising different architecture, algorithm and parameters in modeling have been used. Some important results have been summarized as follows:

- GDA and RBF give most accurate estimations in some situations but, they have also some unreliable results.
- GDM is the best choice for these two datasets because of high performance and always reliable results.
- When the number of hidden neurons increase LM's results get unreliable.
- GRNN is the best choice for engine power prediction.
- RBF and GRNN's approximated functions are smoother than GDA, GDM and LM's ones.
- When the number of features increased, unreliable results appears more.
- For both of datasets, prediction abilities of inputs are ordered as "B>L>V>T" when they are used alone.
- Engine power is better modeled with linear functions than the non-linear ones.
- Displacement is better modeled than engine power with neural networks. The minimum MSEs of displacement and engine power are 0.042 and 0.255 respectively.

References

1. Raya, T., Gokarna, R.P., Shaa, O.P. :Neural network applications in naval architecture and marine engineering. Artificial Intelligence in Engineering, 10(3), pp.213-226 (1996)
2. Alkan A.D., Gulez K., Yilmaz H. :Design of a robust neural network structure for determining initial stability particulars of fishing vessels, Ocean Engineering (31), pp.761-777 (2004)
3. Xiao J., Wong X., Boa M. :The modeling and simulation of ship main engine based on Neural Network, Shanghai Maritime Universty, Proceedings of the 4th World Congress on Intelligent Control and Automation, (2002)
4. Kapanoglu B., Çelebi U.B., Ekinci S., Yıldırım T. :Determination Of Approximate Main Engine Power For Chemical Cargo Ships Using Radial Basis Function Neural Network, Turksh Naval Academy, Journal of Naval Science and Engineering 2(2), pp:115-115 (2004)
5. Baykal R., Dikili A.C. :Ship Resistance and Engine Power, I.T.U, ISBN 975-561-196-7, Istanbul (in Turkish) (2002)
6. Popescu I., Kanatas A., Constantinou P., Nafornita I. :Applications of General Regression Neural Networks for Path Loss Prediction, Proc. of International Workshop "Trends and Recent Achievements in Information Technology", Cluj Napoca (2002)
7. Corsini G., Diani M., Grasso R., De Martino M., Mantero P., Serpico S.B. :Radial Basis Function and Multilayer Perceptron Neural Networks for Sea Water Optically Active Parameter Estimation in Case 2 Waters: A Comparison, International Journal Remote Sensing 24(20) (2003)
8. Chen Y., Wilamowski B.M. :TREAT: A Trust-Region-based Error-Aggregated Training Algorithm for Neural Network, Proc. IEEE International Joint Conference on Neural Networks-IJCNN 2002, Honolulu Hawaii (2002)

Dynamic Role Assignment for Multi-agent Cooperation

In-Cheol Kim

Department of Computer Science, Kyonggi University
San94-6, Yiui-dong, Youngtong-gu, Suwon-si, 442-760, South Korea
kic@kyonggi.ac.kr

Abstract. In this paper, we introduce a dynamic role assignment mechanism for a team of cooperative virtual agents working in interactive computer games. This role assignment mechanism is a new one different from both existing static and dynamic mechanisms, in which decisions regarding role assignment are made all at once either in the design phase or in the execution phase. According to our mechanism, all situation-dependent role sets are predefined in the design phase. Detail decisions regarding which member agent has to take what specific role, however, are made in the execution phase. This mechanism can minimize the negotiation effort for role assignment in the execution phase. Therefore, this mechanism is quite effective in real-time multi-agent environments like interactive computer games. Through experiments, we show the superiority of our dynamic role assignment mechanism.

1 Introduction

A multiagent system which involves several agents that collaborate towards the achievement of joint objectives can be viewed as a team of agents. In order to effectively coordinate a team of agents in the execution of cooperative tasks, each member agent has to perform a unique role that determines its actions during the cooperation [1]. Generally, the role assignment can be viewed as a task allocation problem. The allocation of tasks to a group of agents is necessary when tasks cannot be performed by single agents or when single agents perform them inefficiently [8]. Agents may have different degrees of efficiency in task performance due to their differing capabilities or positions. Task allocation should be done with respect to these differences. Several researches have studied this task allocation problem or role assignment problem, both for multi-agent systems (MAS) and distributed robots [4, 5]. However, most of them suggested pure static or pure dynamic mechanisms, in which decisions regarding role assignment are made all at once either in the design phase or in the execution phase. In this paper, we introduce a new dynamic role assignment mechanism for a team of cooperative virtual agents working in interactive computer games. According to our mechanism, all situation-dependent role sets are predefined in the design phase. Detail decisions regarding which member agent has to take what specific role, however, are made in the execution phase. This mechanism

A. Levi et al. (Eds.): ISCIS 2006, LNCS 4263, pp. 221 – 229, 2006.

can minimize the negotiation effort for role assignment in the execution phase. Therefore, this mechanism is quite effective in real-time dynamic multi-agent environments. Through experiments, we show the superiority of our dynamic role assignment mechanism.

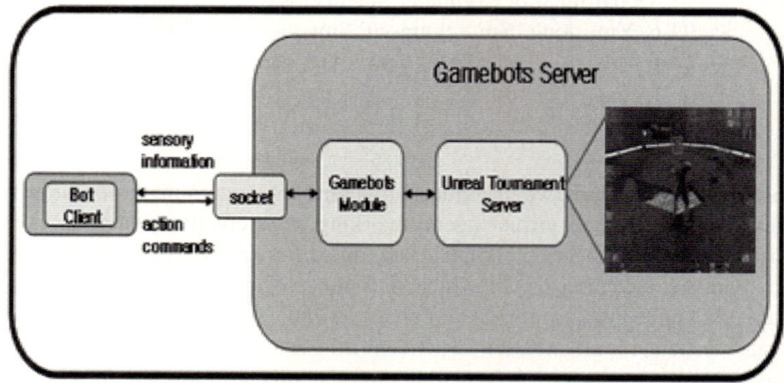

Fig. 1. Architecture of the Gamebots System

2   UT Domination Games

Unreal Tournament (UT) is a category of video games known as first-person shooters, where all real time players exist in a 3D virtual world with simulated physics. Every player's senses are limited by their location, bearings, and occlusion within the virtual world. The Gamebots [2] is a multi-agent system infrastructure derived from Unreal Tournament. Fig. 1 shows the architecture of the Gamebots system. The Gamebots allows UT characters to be controlled over client-server network connections by feeding sensory information to client agents and delivering action commands issued from client agents back to the game server. In a dynamic virtual environment built on the Gamebots system and the UT game engine, agents must display human-level capabilities to play successfully, such as planning paths, learning a map of their 3D environment, using resources available to them, coordinating their activities with considering adversaries.

Fig. 2 (a) shows a screenshot of the UT Domination game, which is a popular one of game types provided by Unreal Tournament. As shown in Fig. 2 (b), there are several control points on the map (indicated by colored rectangles), and each team needs to have possession of them for a while in order to score a point. One team wins by scoring the required amount of points first. This game requires a lot of team work. As the match progresses, for example, each team has to be organized so that while at least one or two players are defending a control point, other players should try to roam the map covering the other control points.

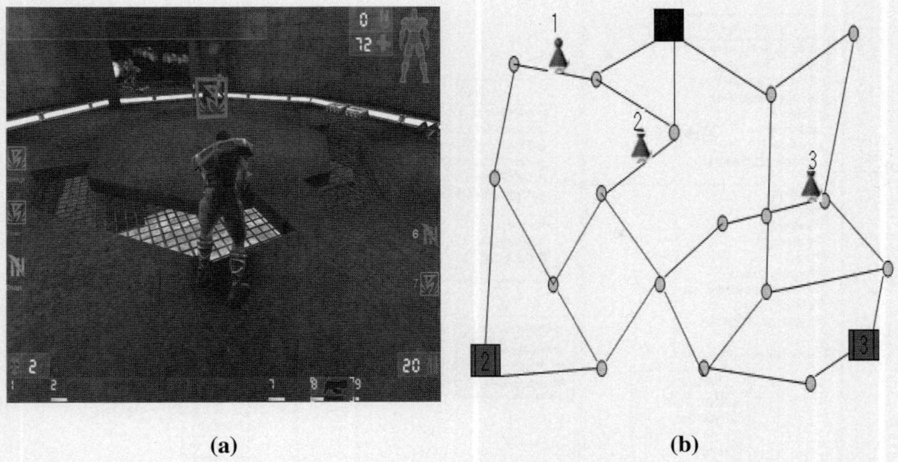

(a)   (b)

Fig. 2. UT domination game: (a) a screenshot, (b) a team of agents on the map

3   CAA UTBot

The CAA UTBots are intelligent virtual agents working in UT Domination game environments. They are all implemented as bot clients of the Gamebots system. The CAA UTBot adopts the CAA(Context-Sensitive Agent Architecture) as its brain to decide proper behaviors to execute in response to the dynamically changing environment. Our CAA consists of (1) a world model; (2) an internal model; (3) a behavior library; (4) an interpreter; and (5) a set of sensors and effectors. The UML class diagram of Fig. 3 shows the major components of the CAA. The world model of the CAA UTBot contains various domain-specific objects. This world model contains both static and dynamic information. Static information does not change during the course of a game. Static information includes, for example, the agent's name and ID, the team number, the number of team members, the maximum team score, and the address of the game server. In contrast, dynamic information continually changes during the game. Dynamic information includes, for example, the agent's position and direction, the health and skill information, the current weapons and armors, a partial world map, and the discovered domination points. The UT internal model contains an internal mode and the related parameters. There are five distinct internal modes: Explore, Dominate, Collect, Died, and Healed. The internal parameters such as the starting position and the target object may accompany one of the Explore, Dominate, and Collect modes.

The behavior library contains a set of pre-defined behavior objects. The behavior class has three sub-classes: external behavior, internal behavior and conversational behavior. While external behaviors change the state of the environment through effectors, internal behaviors change the internal state – namely, the internal mode and

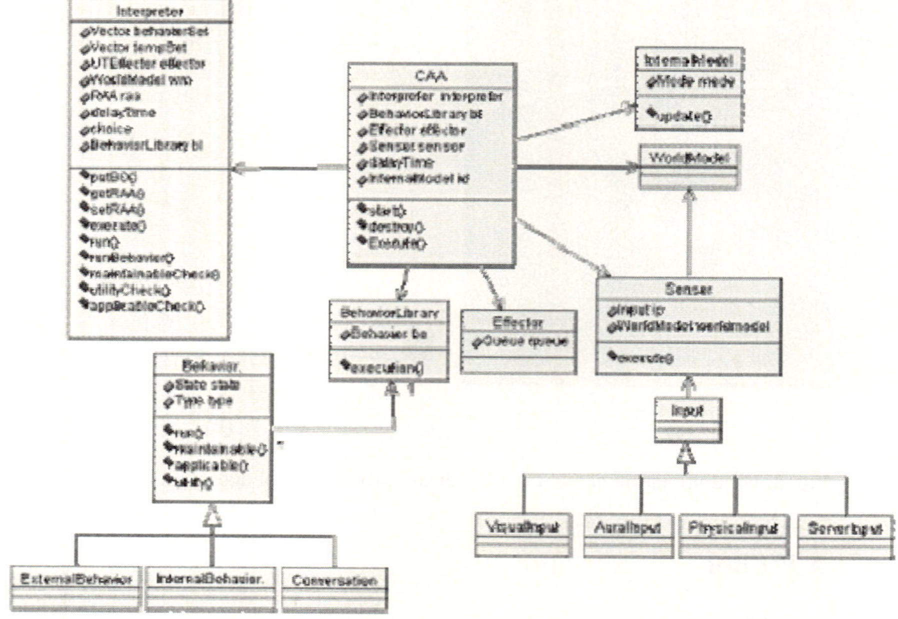

Fig. 3. UML class diagram of the CAA

parameters- without any change of the environment. Conversational behaviors can be used to communicate with other agents in a certain agent communication language or protocol. Conversational behaviors can be also viewed as a special kind of external behaviors. The behavior class has five main member methods: applicable(), utility(), maintainable(), run(), and failure(). The applicable() method checks if the preconditions of a behavior can be satisfied against the world model and the internal model. The utility() method computes the relative utility of an applicable behavior by considering the current world model and internal model. Whenever multiple behaviors are applicable for a given situation, the highest-utility behavior is automatically selected and executed from them. The maintainable() method continually checks the context of a behavior throughout the execution of the behavior once it starts execution, to make sure that the behavior is still applicable to the intended situation. The run() method is the main body of a behavior. It is called when the selected behavior starts execution. This method usually generates one or more atomic actions, sets some member variables, and returns. Finally, the failure() method is a procedural specification of what the agent should do when a plan fails. In the CAA, the life cycle of a behavior object consists of seven distinct states: create, waiting, executing, interrupt, fail, resume, and finish.

The CAA UTBot has a variety of external behaviors such as Explore, Attack_Point, Defend_Point, Collect_Powerup, Collect_Weapon, Collect_Armor,

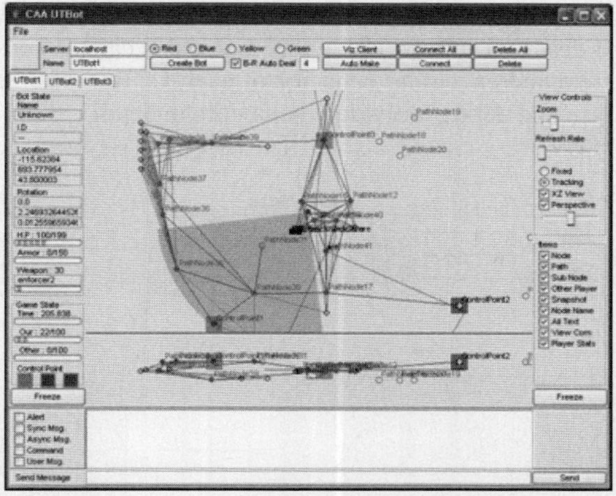

Fig. 4. Visualization tool of the CAA UTBot

Chase, Attack, Retreat, and MoveTo. Table 1 lists available internal modes and the associated external behaviors. Although more than one external behavior is applicable at a certain internal mode, the utility values may be different among them. To transit from one internal mode to another, the CAA UTBot has a set of internal behaviors such as ExploreToDominate, DominateToCollect, and CollectToDominate.

Table 1. The internal modes and the associated external behaviors

Internal Modes	External Behaviors
Explore	MoveTo, Explore, Attack, Chase, Retreat
Dominate	MoveTo, Attack_Point, Defend_Point
Collect	MoveTo, Collect_Powerup, Collect_Weapon, Collect_Armor, Retreat, Attack
Died	No Behaviors
Healed	No Behaviors

The interpreter controls the execution of the entire CAA UTBot. Whenever there is new or changed information in the world model or internal model, the interpreter determines a set of applicable behaviors by calling the applicable() method of each behavior. From this set of applicable behaviors, it selects the highest-utility behavior by using the utility() methods. By invoking the run() method of the selected behavior, the interpreter starts the execution of the behavior. Once the selected behavior starts execution, the interpreter continually checks the behavior's context by calling the maintainable() method periodically. If the context of the behavior gets unsatisfied with either the current state of the world model or of the internal model, the interpreter immediately stops the execution of the behavior, and then replaces it with a new behavior appropriate to the changed situation.

Fig. 4 shows the unique visualization tool of the CAA UTBot. With this tool, users can launch and destroy UTBots. Using this tool, users can also easily keep track of both the current state and executing behavior of each UTBot. Therefore this tool can help users to analyze and debug individual behaviors in detail.

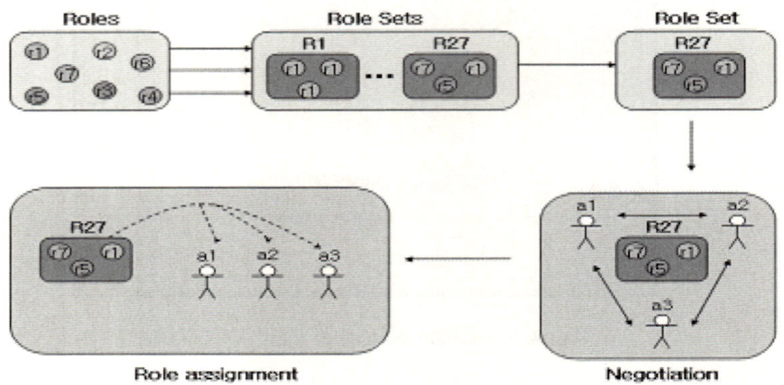

Fig. 5. Role assignment process

4   Dynamic Role Assignment

Many existing mechanisms for role assignment are either pure static or pure dynamic ones. According to a pure static mechanism, all decisions regarding role assignment should be made at once before the execution phase and never be changed after that. These approaches may be effective only when the multiagent system (MAS) designer should be able to completely predict and deal with possible situations occurring in the execution phase. On the other hand, pure dynamic approaches postpone all decisions until the execution phase. In real-time multiagent environments like interactive computer games, however, these pure dynamic approaches are also not much desirable considering the required amount of runtime communication and computation. We suggest a new dynamic role assignment mechanism for a team of cooperative virtual agents deploying in interactive computer games. According to our mechanism, all situation-dependent role sets are predefined in the design phase. Detail decisions regarding which member agent takes what specific role, however, are made in the execution phase. This mechanism for role assignment can minimize the negotiation effort in execution phase. Fig. 5 shows the whole process of role assignment for co-operative virtual agents.

Our mechanism for role assignment can be formulated as a tuple M={A, R, S, t_i, m_i, F_i}, where

A= {a_1, a_2, .., a_n}: a team of n member agents,
R= {r_1, r_2, ..., r_k}: a set of k possible roles,
S = {s_1, s_2, ..., s_m}: a set of m possible states,
t_i : (R_{i-1}, s_i) $\rightarrow$ R_i: a role-set transition function,

$(R_{i-1}, R_i \subset R,$

  R_{i-1}: the previous role set,

  s_i: the current state,

  R_i: the new role set)

m_i: $R_i \rightarrow A$: a role assignment function,

$F_i = <A, R_i, m_i>$: a team formation.

We assume that the role-set transition function t_i is given in the design phase as well as the set A, R, and S. However, the role assignment function m_i can be actually determined through negotiation among member agents during the execution phase. Fig. 6 shows an example of role-set transition diagram. All member agents in a team share the same role-set transition function. Through the shared role-set transition function, each agent can decide what role set their team has to perform whenever the situation changes.

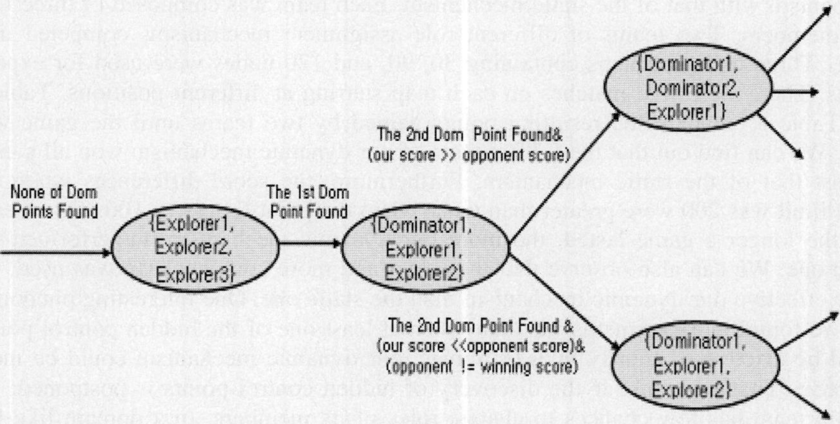

Fig. 6. Role-set transition diagram

Role determination step in the execution phase implements dynamic role assignment through explicit communication. Since a known, small number of member agents are collaborating, we chose to use a system of broadcast messages to share information. This message contains each agent's current position as well as its local map. In order to shorten the negotiation process for role assignment, we chose to use an auction mechanism. Whenever a new role set R_i is determined, each member agent calculates its own cost and revenue with respect to a specific one r_k in the role set. The cost function c and the revenue function v of each member agent depend on the shared information such as its current position. For example, the cost function of a "Dominator" role may be the distance to the given control point, while the cost function of a "Explorer" role may be the distance to the frontier of the current partial map. In similar way, the revenue function of a "Dominator" role may use the estimated score points obtained by possessing the control point, while the revenue function of a

"Explorer" role may use the number of newly discovered nodes and edges. Based on the values of these cost and revenue functions, each agent can estimate its own profit gained by taking a specific role, and then decides the bid as much as its profit. In similar way, it can determine the other members' bids based upon the shared information. Comparing bids with respect to a specific role r_i, each member agent decides whether it has to take the role over or not. If its own bid is the highest of them, the corresponding agent takes the role over. Otherwise, it gives up the role and then continues to bid on another role.

5 Experiments

In order to investigate the effectiveness of our dynamic mechanism for role assignment, we conducted some experiments using UTBots and UT Domination games. Through experiments, we tried to compare the performance of a team of our dynamic mechanism with that of the static mechanism. Each team was composed of three UTBot members. Two teams of different role assignment mechanisms competed in a game. Three different maps containing 30, 90, and 120 nodes were used for experiments. There were five matches on each map starting at different positions. Table 2 and Table 3 compare the resulting points gained by two teams until the game was over. We can find out that the UTBot team of our dynamic mechanism won all games against that of the static mechanism. Furthermore, the score differences when the point limit was 200 were greater than those when the point limit was 100. This means that the longer a game lasted, the more our dynamic mechanism outperformed the static one. We can also observe that the larger and more complex map was used, the more effective our dynamic mechanism than the static one. One interesting phenomenon we found in experiments was that when at least one of the hidden control points could be discovered shortly by a teammate, our dynamic mechanism could be more effective. That's because if the discovery of hidden control points is postponed, the UTBot team has few chances to change roles of its members. In a domain like UT Domination game, thus, the exploring capability of each member agent or a group of agents is as important as the role assignment mechanism for the overall performance of the team.

Table 2. Dynamic vs. static role assignment team (when the point limit = 100)

	Map 1 (# of Nodes=30)	Map 2 (# of Nodes= 90)	Map 3 (# of Nodes= 120)
1	100 : 58	100 : 24	100 : 18
2	100 : 46	100 : 34	100 : 22
3	100 : 48	100 : 30	100 : 12
4	100 : 65	100 : 38	100 : 30
5	100 : 57	100 : 35	100 : 28

Table 3. Dynamic vs. static role assignment team (when the point limit = 200)

	Map 1 (# of Nodes=30)	Map 2 (# of Nodes= 90)	Map 3 (# of Nodes= 120)
1	200 : 109	200 : 55	200 : 23
2	200 : 113	200 : 47	200 : 29
3	200 : 99	200 : 51	200 : 41
4	200 : 130	200 : 62	200 : 46
5	200 : 101	200 : 58	200 : 62

6 Conclusions

We introduced a dynamic role assignment mechanism for a team of cooperative virtual agents working in interactive computer games. This mechanism for role assignment can minimize the negotiation effort in execution phase. Through experiments, we showed that our dynamic role assignment mechanism is superior to the static one. We are now planning on conducting some experiments to compare ours with other dynamic mechanisms in terms of time efficiency and resulting performance.

References

1. Chaimowicz, L., Campos, M. F. M., Kumar, V.: Dynamic Role Assignment for Cooperative Robots. (2002).
2. Kaminka, G.A., et al.: GameBots : A Flexible Test Bed for MultiAgent Team Research. Communications of ACM, 45(1) (2002) 43-45.
3. J. E. Laird, J.E.: Research in Human-Level AI Using Computer Games. Communications of the ACM, 42 (2002) 32-35.
4. Nair, R., Tambe, M., Marsella, S.: Role Allocation and Reallocation in Multiagent Teams: Towards A Practical Analysis. (2003).
5. Scerri, P., Farineli A., Okamoto S., Tambe M.: Allocating Roles in Extreme Teams. Proceedings of the 3rd International Joint Conference on Autonomous Agents and Multiagent Systems (2004)
6. Sterren, W.: Squad Tactics: Team AI and Emergent Maneuvers. AI Game Programming Wisdom, Charles River Media Inc (2002).
7. Stone, P., Veloso, M.: Task Decomposition and Dynamic Role Assignment for Real-Time Strategic Teamwork. Proceedings of the International Conference on Multiagent Systems (1998).
8. Weiss, G.: Multiagent Systems. MIT Press, (1999).

Lexical Ambiguity Resolution for Turkish in Direct Transfer Machine Translation Models

A. Cüneyd Tantuğ[1], Eşref Adalı[1], and Kemal Oflazer[2]

[1] Istanbul Technical University Faculty of Eletrical-Electronic Engineering
Computer Engineering Department
34469, Maslak, Istanbul, Türkiye
`{cuneyd, adali}@cs.itu.edu.tr`
[2] Sabancı University
Faculty Of Engineering and Natural Sciences
34956, Orhanlı, Tuzla, Türkiye
`oflazer@sabanciuniv.edu`

Abstract. This paper presents a statistical lexical ambiguity resolution method in direct transfer machine translation models in which the target language is Turkish. Since direct transfer MT models do not have full syntactic information, most of the lexical ambiguity resolution methods are not very helpful. Our disambiguation model is based on statistical language models. We have investigated the performances of some statistical language model types and parameters in lexical ambiguity resolution for our direct transfer MT system.

1 Introduction

This paper presents a statistical lexical ambiguity resolution method in direct transfer machine translation models in which the target language is Turkish. This resolution method is based on statistical language models (LM) which exploit collocational occurrence probabilities. Although, lexical ambiguity resolution methods are generally required for some NLP purposes like accent restoration, word sense disambiguation, homograph and homophone disambiguation, we focus only on lexical ambiguity of word choice selection in machine translation (MT).

The direct transfer model in MT is the transfer of the sentence in the source language to the sentence in the target language on word-by-word basis. While this model is the simplest technique for MT, it nevertheless works fine with some close language pairs like Czech-Slovak [1], Spanish-Catalan [2]. We have been implementing an MT system between Turkic Languages, the first stage of the project includes the Turkmen-Turkish language pair.

The lexical ambiguity problem arises when the bilingual transfer dictionary produces more than one corresponding target language root words for a source language root word. Hence, the MT system has to choose the right target word root by means of some evaluation criteria. This process is called *word choice selection* in MT related tasks. Most of the methods developed to overcome this problem are based on

A. Levi et al. (Eds.): ISCIS 2006, LNCS 4263, pp. 230–238, 2006.

some syntactic analysis or domain knowledge. However, there is no such syntactical analysis or any other deeper knowledge in MT systems that utilize direct transfer models.

2 Previous Work

The general task of "word sense disambiguation" (WSD) studies the assignment of correct sense labels to the ambiguous words in naturally occurring free text. WSD has many application areas like MT, information retrieval, content and thematic analysis, grammatical analysis, spelling correction, case changes and etc. In general terms, *word sense disambiguation* (WSD) involves the association of a given word in a text or discourse with a definition or meaning (*sense*) which is distinguishable from other meanings potentially attributable to that word. In the history of the WSD area, supervised and unsupervised statistical machine learning techniques are used as well as other AI methods. A Bayesian classifier was used in work done by Gale et al [5]. Leacock et al [6] compared the performances of Bayesian, content vector and neural network classifiers in WSD tasks. Shütze's experiments showed that unsupervised clustering techniques can get results approaching the supervised techniques by using a large scale context (1000 neighbouring words) [7]. However, all these statistical WSD suffer from two major problems: need for manually sense-tagged corpus (certainly for supervised techniques) and data sparseness.

The lexical ambiguity resolution in MT is a related task of WSD which focuses on deciding the most appropriate word in the target language among a group of possible translations of a word in the source language. There are some general lexical ambiguity resolution techniques; unfortunately, most of the successful techniques require complex information sources like lemmas, inflected forms, parts of speech, local and distant collocations and trigrams [8].

Most of the disambiguation work use syntactic information with other information like taxonomies, selectional restrictions and semantic networks. In recent work, complex processing is avoided by using partial (shallow) parsing instead of full parsing. For example, Hearst [9] segments text into noun and prepositional phrases and verb groups and discards all other syntactic information. Mostly, the syntactic information is generally simply part of speech used conjunction with other information sources [10]. In our work, there is no syntactic transfer so there is not any syntactic level knowledge but the part of speech. So we have developed a selection model based on the statistical language models.

Our disambiguation module performs not only the lexical ambiguity resolution but also the disambiguation of source language morphological ambiguities. Our translation system is designed mainly for translation from Turkic languages to Turkish. One serious problem is the almost total lack of computational resources and tools for these languages to help with some of the problems on the source language side. So all the morphological ambiguities are transferred to the target language side. Apart from the lexical disambiguation problem, our disambiguation module should decide the right root word by considering the morphological ambiguity. For example the Turkmen word "akmak" (`foolish`) has two ambiguous morphological analyses:

```
akmak+Adj                                              (fool)
ak+Verb+Pos^DB+Noun+Infl+A3sg+Pnon+Nom                 (to flow)
```

These analyses can not be disambiguated until the transfer phase because there is no POS tagger for the source language. The transfer module converts all the root words to the target language as stated below.

```
ahmak+Adj                                              (fool)
budala+Adj                                             (stupid)
ak+Verb+Pos^DB+Noun+Infl+A3sg+Pnon+Nom                 (to flow)
```

Note that there are two possible translations of the source word regarding its "fool" sense. The disambiguation module that will be designed has to handle both the lexical ambiguity and the morphological ambiguity.

3   Language Models

Statistical language models define probability distributions on word sequences. By using a language model, one can compute the probability of a sentence S $(w_1 w_2 w_3 \ldots w_n)$ by the following formula:

$$P(S) = P(w_1)P(w_2|w_1)P(w_3|w_1 w_2)\ldots P(w_n|w_1\ldots w_{n-1})$$

This means that the probability of any word sequence can be calculated by decomposition using the chain rule but usually due to sparseness, most terms above would be 0, so n-gram approximations are used.

3.1   Training Corpus

Since Turkish has an agglutinative and highly inflectional morphology, the training corpus cannot be just texts collected from various sources. In order to calculate frequencies of the root words, these texts should be processed by a lemmatizer. However, some of our models require not only the root words but also some other morphological structures so the words in the training corpus should be processed with a morphological analyzer and the morphological ambiguity should be resolved manually or by using a POS-Tagger.

We have used such a corpus which is composed of texts from a daily Turkish newspaper. Some statistics about the corpus is depicted in Table 1.

Table 1. Training Corpus Statistics

# of tokens	948,000
root word vocabulary size	25,787
root words occurring 1 or 2 times	14,830
root words occurring more than 2 times	10,957

3.2 Baseline Model

At first glance, the simplest way of word choice selection can be implemented by incorporating word occurrence frequencies collected from a corpus. We took this model as our baseline model. Note that this is same as the unigram (1-gram) language model.

3.3 Language Model Types

We have used two different types of language models for lexical ambiguity resolution. The first LM Type 1 is built by using only root words and dismissing all other morphological information. LM Type 2 uses the probability distributions of root words and their part of speech information.

All types of these language models are back-off language models combined with Good-Turing discounting for smoothing. Additionally, we have used a cutoff 2 which means n-grams occurring fewer than two times are discarded. We have computed our language models by using CMU-Cambridge Statistical Language Modeling Toolkit [11].

3.4 LM Parameters

Apart from the type of the LM, there are two major parameters to construct a LM. The first one is the order the model; the number of successive words to consider. The second parameter is the vocabulary size. It might be better to have all the words in a LM. However this is not practically possible because a large LM is hard to handle and manage in real world applications, and is prone to sparseness problems. Therefore, a reduction in vocabulary size is a common process. So, deciding how many of the most frequent words will be used to build a LM becomes the second parameter to be determined.

4 Implementation

We have employed our tests on a direct MT system which translates text in Turkmen Language to Turkish. The main motivation of this MT system is the design of a generic MT system that performs automatic text translations between all Turkic languages. Although the system is currently under development and it has some weaknesses (like the small coverage of the source language morphological analyzer, insufficient multi-word transfer block), the preliminary results are at an acceptable level. The system has following processing blocks:

1. Tokenization
2. Source Language (SL) Morphological Analysis
3. Multi-Word Detection
4. Root Word Tansfer
5. Morphological Structure Transfer
6. Lexical & Morphological Ambiguity Resolution
7. Target Language (TL) Morphological Synthesis

Our word-to-word direct MT system generates all possible Turkish counterparts of each input source root word by using a bilingual transfer dictionary (while the morphological features are directly transferred). As the next step, all candidate Turkish words are used to generate a directed acyclic graph of possible word sequence, as shown in Figure 1.

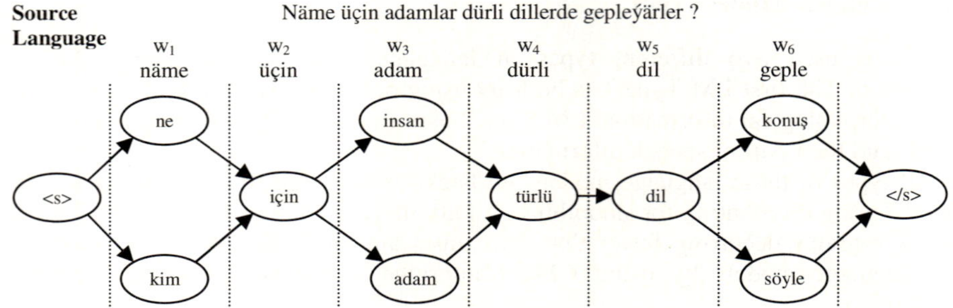

Fig. 1. The process of decoding the most probable target language sentence

As seen in the figure, each root word of the sentence in the source language can have one or more Turkish translations which produce lexically ambiguous output. The transition probabilities are determined by the language model.

As an example, the probability of the transition between "dil" and "konuş" is determined by the probability P("konuş"|"dil") which is calculated from the corpus in the training stage of the bigram language model. Then, the ambiguity is disambiguated by trying to find the path with the maximum probability by using the Viterbi algorithm [13].

5   Evaluation

In the evaluation phase of our work, the aim is to find the LM type, order and vocabulary size which performs best with our direct MT model. We have conducted our tests for n=1,2,3,4 and root word vocabulary size =3K, 4K, 5K, 7K and 10K. Note that 10K is nearly the vocabulary size of the training corpus which means that all the root words are used to construct the LM.

The performance evaluation of the proposed resolution method is investigated by means of NIST scores achieved by each LM type for different parameters. NIST is a widely used, well-known method for evaluating the performance of the MT systems [14]. We have used the BLEU-NIST evaluation tool *mteval* that can be accessed from NIST. These evaluations are calculated on 255 sentences. In order to find out which LM type and parameters are better, we have run our direct transfer system with different LMs. For a fair evaluation, we have measured the performances of these LMs against the performance of our baseline model. The results are given in figure 2 and figure 3.

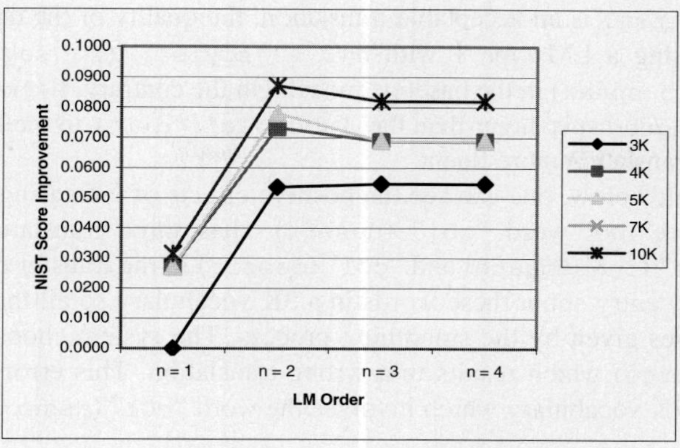

Fig. 2. LM Type 1 (Root Word) Results

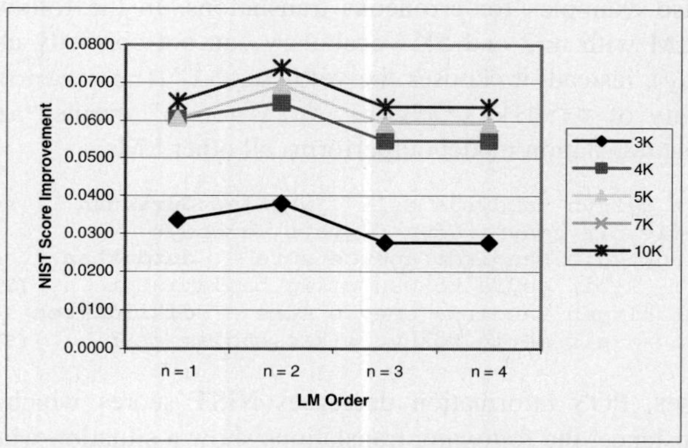

Fig. 3. LM Type 2 (Root Word + POS Tag) Results

In our tests, the root word language model (type 1, n=2 and vocabulary size = 7K) performs best. We examined that there is absolutely no difference between 7K and 10K vocabulary selection. This is why the 7K and 10K lines in the graphs are superposed. An interesting and important result is the decrease of the score with n higher than 2 for all LM types and parameters (except type 1 with 3K vocabulary). This can be explained with the fact that most of the dependencies are between two consecutive words. Also, as expected, the NIST score improvement increases for larger vocabulary sizes, but it is clear that using a LM which has a 5K vocabulary is meaningful.

As an example, the translation of the Turkmen sentence in the figure 1 by using our baseline model is below:

```
Input   : Näme üçin adamlar   dürli dillerde gepleýärler  ?
Output1: ne    için insanlar türlü dillerde söylüyorlar  ? (Type1,n=1,3K)
Output2: ne    için insanlar türlü dillerde konuşuyorlar ? (Type2,n=2,3K)
```

Although `Output1` is an acceptable translation, the quality of the translation can be improved by using a LM type 1 with n=2. `P("söyle")` `(to say)` is larger than `P("konuş")` `(to speak)` in the baseline model. On the contrary, `P("konuş"|"dil")` (`dil` means `language`) is larger than the `P("söyle"|"dil")` in the LM with n=2 so this makes the translation more fluent.

In the example below, one can see the positive effects of increasing the vocabulary size. The source root word "çöl" (desert) has three translations; "seyrek" (scarce), "kıt" (inadequate) and "çöl" (desert) in the transfer dictionary, there is no probability entry about these words in a 3K vocabulary so all three target words have probabilities given by the smoothing process. The system chooses the first one "seyrek" (scarce) which results in a wrong translation. This error is corrected by the LM with a 7K vocabulary which involves the word "çöl" (desert).

```
Input   : Bir adam  çölüň     içinde kompas tapypdyr   .
Output1: bir insan  seyreğin  içinde pusula bulmuştur . (Type1,n=1,3K)
Output2: bir insan  çölün     içinde pusula bulmuştur . (Type1,n=1,7k)
```

There are also examples for erroneous translations. In the following translation instances, the LM with n=2 and 5K vocabulary can not correctly choose the word "dur" (to stay), instead, it chooses the verb "dikil" (to stand) because of the higher probability of `P("dikil"|"sonra")` ("sonra" means "after"). In this case, the baseline translation model outperforms all other LMs.

```
Input   : Hamyr gyzgyn tamdyrda esli   wagtlap durandan    soň  , ondan
          tagamly bir zadyň  ysy      çykyp ugrapdyr      .
Output1: hamur kızgın tandırda epeyce süre    durduktan   sonra , ondan
          tatlı    bir şeyin kokusu çıkıp başlamıştır .  (Type1,n=1,3K)
Output2: hamur kızgın tandırda epeyce süre    dikildikten sonra , ondan
          tatlı    bir şeyin kokuyu çıkıp başlamıştır .  (Type1,n=2,5K)
```

In some cases, POS information decreases NIST scores which is opposed as expected. For instance, the following translations show a situation where the baseline system produces the right result by choosing the verb "var" (to exist) whereas the more complex (type 2 with n=2 and 5K vocabulary) LM generated a false word choice by selecting the verb "git" (to go).

```
Input   : Sebäbi meniň içimde goşa ýumruk ýaly gyzyl bardy
Output1: nedeni benim içimde çift yumruk gibi altın vardı. (Type1,n=1,3K)
Output2: nedeni benim içimde çift yumruk gibi altın gitti. (Type2,n=2,5K)
```

6 Conclusions

Our major goal in this work is proposing a lexical ambiguity resolution method for Turkish to be used in our direct transfer MT model. The lexical ambiguity occur mainly because of the transfer of the source language root words. We have built language models for statistical resolution of this lexical ambiguity and then these LMs are used to generate Hidden Markov Models. Finding the path with the highest probability in HMMs has done by using the Viterbi method. By this way, we can disambiguate the lexical ambiguity and choose the most probable word sequences in the target language.

Two types of language models (root words and root word+POS tag) are used and we have investigated the effects of the other parameters like LM order or vocabulary size. The LM built by using root words performs best with the parameters n=2 and 7K vocabulary.

Since Turkish is an agglutinative language, taking NIST as the evaluation method may not be very meaningful because NIST considers only surface form matching of the words, not the root word matching. Even though the model chooses the right root word, the other morphological structures can make the surface form of the translated word different from surface forms of the words in the reference sentences. This means that the real performance scores are equal or probably higher than the actual performance scores.

We are expecting higher NIST score improvements with the development and extending of our translation model. There are some problems like SL morphological analyzer mistakes and transfer rule insufficiencies to handle some cases.

Acknowledgments

This project is partly supported by TÜBİTAK (The Scientific and Technical Research Council of Turkey) under the contract no 106E048.

References

1. Hajič, J., Hric J., Kubon, V. : Machine Translation of Very Close Languages. Applied NLP Processing, NAACL, Washington (2000)
2. Canals, R., et.al. : interNOSTRUM: A Spanish-Catalan Machine Translation System. EAMT Machine Translation Summit VIII, Spain (2001)
3. Hirst, G. Charniak, E. : Word Sense and Case Slot Disambiguation, In AIII-82, pp. 95-98 (1982)
4. Black, E. : An Experiment in Computational Discrimination of English Word Senses, IBM Journal of Research and Development 32(2), pp. 185-194 (1988)
5. Gale, W., Church, K. W., and Yarowsky, D. : A Method for Disambiguating Word Senses in a Large Corpus, Statistical Research Report 104, Bell Laboratories (1992)
6. Leacock, C.; Towell, G., Voorhees, E. : Corpus-based statistical sense resolution, Proceedings of the ARPA Human Language Technology Worskshop, San Francisco, Morgan Kaufman(1993)
7. Schütze, H. : Automatic word sense discrimination, Computational Linguistics, 24(1), (1998)
8. Yarowsky, D. : Unsupervised word sense disambiguation rivaling supervised methods. In Proceedings of the 33rd Annual Meeting of the Association for Computational Linguistics (ACL'95), Cambridge, MA. (1995)
9. Hearst, M. A. : Noun homograph disambiguation using local context in large corpora. Proceedings of the 7th Annual Conf. of the University of Waterloo Centre for the New OED and Text Research, Oxford, United Kingdom, 1-19 (1991)

10. McRoy, S. W. : Using multiple knowledge sources for word sense discrimination. Computational Linguistics, 18(1) 1-30 (1992)
11. Clarkson, P.R., Rosenfeld R. : Statistical Language Modeling Using the CMU-Cambridge Toolkit. Proceedings ESCA Eurospeech (1997)
12. Fomey, G.D., Jr. : The Viterbi Algorithm, IEEE Proc. Vol. 61, pp. 268-278 (1973)
13. NIST Report (2002) Automatic Evaluation of Machine Translation Quality Using N-gram Co-Occurrence Statistics.
http://www.nist.gov/speech/tests/mt/doc/ngramstudy.pdf

Design of a Feature Set for Face Recognition Problem

Emre Akbaş and Fatoş T. Yarman-Vural

Department of Computer Engineering,
Middle East Technical University, Ankara, Turkey
{eakbas, vural}@ceng.metu.edu.tr

Abstract. An important problem in face recognition is the design of the feature space which represents the human face. Various feature sets have been and are continually being proposed for this purpose. However, there exists no feature set which gives a *superior* and *consistent* recognition performance on various face databases. Concatenating the popular features together and forming a high dimensional feature space introduces the curse of dimensionality problem. For this reason, dimensionality reduction techniques such as Principal Component Analysis is utilized on the feature space. In this study, first, some of the popular feature sets used in face recognition literature are evaluated over three popular face databases, namely ORL [1], UMIST [2], and Yale [3]. Then, high dimensional feature space obtained by concatenating all the features is reduced to a lower dimensional space by using the Minimal Redundancy Maximal Relevance [4] feature selection method in order to design a *generic* and *successful* feature set. The results indicate that mRMR selects a small number of features which are satisfactory and consistent in terms of recognition performance, provided that the face database is statistically stable with sufficient amount of data.

1 Motivation and Introduction

The problem of *representation*, namely the design of the feature spaces, is one of the open issues and a hot research topic in the field of pattern recognition. There is no formal method of designing "the best" feature space for a broad variety of problem domains. In most of the pattern recognition systems, the feature space is designed heuristically. Naturally, face recognition is no exception. Various feature spaces have been proposed and are being continually developed for face recognition problem.

The motivation behind this study is to develop a rather generic feature space for face recognition problem. As a first step, one should investigate the existence of such a generic feature set. In this study, we assume that there exists at least one representation, which provides "reasonably" satisfactory results for a wide range of face images, provided that the images come from a statistically stable source with sufficient amount of data. The next question is how to design a generic feature space which is superior compared to the available features in the literature.

A. Levi et al. (Eds.): ISCIS 2006, LNCS 4263, pp. 239–247, 2006.

The word *generic* is used in the context of consistency of recognition performance over various face recognition databases, and 'being *superior* to the available feature sets' refers to the desirable situation that the feature set which is sought for exhibits a better, at least comparable, recognition performance than those of the available feature sets.

Feature extraction in face recognition can be divided into 3 categories [5]:

1. Holistic (appearance-based) methods: These methods use the face image (or region) as a whole to compute the features. Eigenfaces [6] is one of the most widely used holistic approaches.
2. Feature-based (structural) methods: These methods attempt to extract local features such as the eyes, nose and mouth, then their locations and local statistics (geometric and/or appearance) are used as features. Some examples for this representation type are: pure geometric methods, dynamic link architecture and transformation-based features.
3. Hybrid methods: These methods uses both holistic features and feature-based features. Modular eigenfaces and component-based features can be given as examples.

In this study, we first evaluated the performances of five feature sets, namely Eigenfaces [6], Laplacianfaces [7], Haar features, Gabor features and C2 features [8], over three face recognition databases. Then, we attempted to find an answer to the motivation presented at the beginning of this section by using a feature selection method.

We have chosen the feature sets mentioned above due to their popularity and success stories in the literature. Eigenfaces and Laplacianfaces are holistic approaches. Eigenfaces method is based on Principal Component Analysis (PCA). Laplacianfaces method also utilizes PCA (generalized version), however, different from the eigenfaces approach, it tries to find a "locality-preserving" subspace. Haar, Gabor and C2 features are wavelet transformation-based approaches. It is worth to mention that the C2 feature set, proposed recently in [8], is inspired by visual cortex and is based on Gabor wavelet-transform.

The organization of the paper is as follows: in section 2, mRMR feature selection method is explained. Experimental results can be found in section 3 and we conclude with a discussion of the experimental results in section 4.

2   mRMR: Minimal Redundancy Maximal Relevance Feature Selection Method

The mRMR method selects *good* features according to the maximal statistical dependency criterion based on mutual information. In pattern recognition problems, the optimal characterization condition of a set of features can be defined by the minimal classification error, and this minimal error usually requires the *maximal statistical dependency* of the class labels on the data distribution in the subspace of the selected features [4].

In mRMR, maximal statistical dependency is based on mutual information. Given two random variables x and y, mutual information of these variables is defined by:

$$I(x;y) = \int\int p(x,y) log \frac{p(x,y)}{p(x)p(y)} dx dy \tag{1}$$

where $p(\cdot)$ denotes probabilistic density function.

Since it is difficult to directly implement the maximal dependency condition, an equivalent form called minimal-redundancy-maximal-relevance is proposed and proved to be equivalent to maximal dependency. See [4] for the proof.

The method works as follows: let S denote the set of m features which we are trying to find. Let Ω denote the set of all features. The maximal-relevance criterion is defined as:

$$\max_{S \subset \Omega} \frac{1}{|S|} \sum I(f_i; c) \tag{2}$$

where f_i is the ith feature and c is the class label. By this criterion, features which are maximally relevant to the class label c are selected. However, these features could have high redundancy. To eliminate redundancy, minimal-redundancy criterion is utilized:

$$\min_{S \subset \Omega} \frac{1}{|S|^2} \sum_{i,j \in S} I(f_i; f_j) \tag{3}$$

By optimizing (2) and (3) simultaneously, we obtain a *good* set of features which satisfy the maximal dependency condition. The complexity of this method is $O(|S| \cdot |\Omega|)$.

A critical issue in feature selection by mRMR is the determination of the number of features to select. In the following subsection, this problem is addressed.

2.1   Finding the Optimal Number of Features

We propose the following algorithm to find the optimal number of features to be selected by mRMR:

1. For a given dataset (a pair of training and testing sets)
2. Set $max = 0$.
3. For i from 1 to D_{max}:
   (a) Select i features from the training set by mRMR.
   (b) Apply leave-N-out cross-validation M times on the training set using only the i selected features.
   (c) Set *current* as the median of the results of these 100 runs.
   (d) If *current* $\geq$ *max* then, set *max* = *current*. Set *best_i* = i.
4. Return *best_i*.

3   Experiments

Three well-known face databases are used in the experiments: ORL [1], UMIST [2] and Yale Face Database [3]. ORL database consists of 400 face images of 40 subjects. For each subject, there are only 10 images with varying facial expressions, details and lighting conditions. UMIST face database contains 564 images of 20 subjects. In our experiments the pre-cropped version of the database, which consists of 575 images of 20 subjects, is used. On the average there are 28 images for each subject covering a range of poses from frontal to profile view. Yale database consists of 165 face images of 15 subjects. There are 11 images per subject having different facial expressions (i.e. normal, happy, sad, sleepy, surprised, wink) and configurations (i.e. center-light, left-light, right-light, glasses, no-glasses). Examples from these databases can be seen in figure 1.

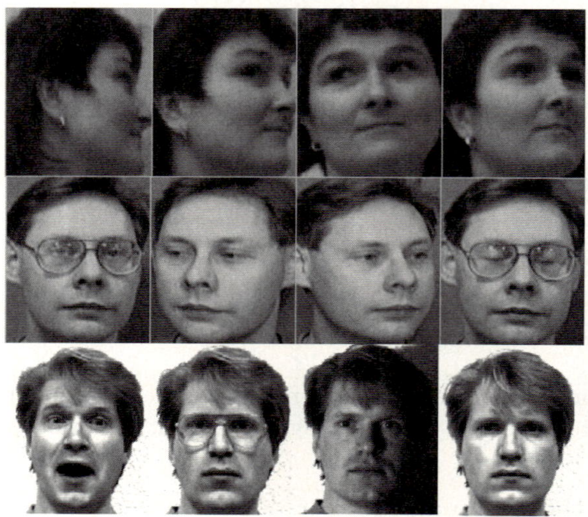

Fig. 1. Example face images. First row: UMIST database, second row: ORL database, third row: Yale database (images are cropped for demonstration)

As a pre-processing step, all images are histogram-equalized.

3.1   Feature Extraction

Five feature sets are utilized on the databases mentioned above.

For extracting eigenfaces and Laplacianfaces, the images are scaled to 46x56 pixels for the purpose of reducing the computation time. Originally, the images in ORL and UMIST databases are 92x112 pixels, whereas the images in Yale database have dimensions of 320x243. In both eigenfaces and Laplacianfaces, all non-zero principal components of the covariance matrix are used in projection.

Haar features are extracted similarly as in [9]. First, the image is scaled to 128x128 pixels and a 4-level 2D Haar wavelet transformation is applied on the image. The values in the 16x16 matrix from the upper-left corner of this transformation is concatenated row by row and are used as the feature vector. The standard deviation of the values in this 16x16 upper-left corner matrix is also added to the feature vector. Then, a 5-level 2D Haar wavelet transformation is applied on the same 128x128 image and the values in the 8x8 upper-left corner matrix are added to the feature vector.

Gabor features are extracted by applying a family of Gabor filters to the face images. Gabor filters are obtained by modulating a 2D sine wave with a Gaussian envelope. To obtain the Gabor filters, we use 5 different frequencies at 4 different orientations. The images are convolved by a 15x15 Gaussian kernel and the output is downsampled by a factor of 64.

C2 features are extracted as described in [8]. For each dataset, the training images are taken as the set of *positive* images. The number of random patches is taken as 50. Features are extracted by using the software [11] available from MIT-CBCL.

3.2   Recognition Results

Fuzzy k-NN [10] is used as the recognition method, simply because it is a robust technique and easy to implement. The experiments were conducted on the GNU/Linux platform using MATLAB.

Average recognition results on each dataset using all features concatenated, each feature set individually and the features selected by mRMR are listed in Table 1. These results were obtained by repeating the following experiment 10 times on each database and averaging the results: in each experiment, the set of all images are randomly split into two equal-size sets: one being the training, other being the testing set. While splitting, the ratio of training images to testing images, which is 1, is preserved over each class.

Table 1. Recognition results averaged on 10 experiments on each face dataset. In each experiment, all samples are randomly divided into two equal-sized groups: training and testing.

Dataset	All features	Eigenfaces	Laplacian-faces	Haar	Gabor	C2	Features selected by mRMR
ORL	82.05%	78.90%	68.30%	94.00%	76.35%	80.90%	81.95%
UMIST	94.91%	95.61%	91.82%	95.58%	91.30%	87.93%	95.79%
Yale	69.33%	18.67%	64.40%	64.67%	62.67%	62.80%	69.87%

A close look at Table 1 shows that Haar features are quite successful on ORL and UMIST databases. On the other hand, eigenfaces is only successful on UMIST database which has a comparable performance to Haar. Concatenating all features improves the performance only on the Yale database. Therefore, one can judge that concatenation is not always a good approach to improve the performance. Finally, reducing the dimension by mRMR gives satisfactory results for UMIST and Yale databases, however it gives poor performance on the ORL database. This is basically because of the insufficient amount of data of the ORL database for 40 subjects which is a quite high number compared to the class numbers of other databases. The standard deviation of the results in Table 1 can be found in Table 2.

In each experiment, the optimal k-value is found by repeating 100 times leave-N-out cross-validation method on the training set, where N corresponds to 20% of the number training samples. The k-value which gets the highest vote is selected as the k-value to be used in testing. The average of the k-values found by cross-validation can be seen in Table 3.

Table 2. Standard deviation of the results listed in Table 1

Dataset	All features	Eigenfaces	Laplacian-faces	Haar	Gabor	C2	Features selected by mRMR
ORL	2.32%	2.75%	8.94%	1.87%	3.00%	2.71%	3.33%
UMIST	0.63%	1.11%	1.86%	0.74%	1.45%	1.55%	1.28%
Yale	3.68%	3.16%	4.34%	5.27%	4.22%	5.25%	4.73%

Table 3. Average of the optimal k-values found by leave-N-out cross-validation method in 10 experiments on each database

Dataset	All features	Eigenfaces	Laplacian-faces	Haar	Gabor	C2	Features selected by mRMR
ORL	2.00	2.00	4.40	2.10	2.20	2.80	2.20
UMIST	2.00	2.00	2.00	2.00	2.00	2.00	2.00
Yale	3.40	2.70	2.50	3.60	4.60	4.20	2.50

3.3 Feature Selection by mRMR

In order to find the optimal number of features to be selected by the mRMR method, the algorithm described in section 2.1 is used. In this algorithm, the following parameters are used: $D_{max} = 1000$, $M = 100$, and $N = 20\%$. Since mRMR is designed to work with discrete features, we discretized our continuous features with a discretization threshold of 0.01.

The algorithm in section 2.1 selected on average 116 features with a standard deviation of 133.62 on the ORL database, 467 features with a standard deviation of 192.80 on the UMIST database and, 217 features with a standard deviation of 195.66 on the Yale database.

After finding the optimal number of features (only using the training sets), we use the selected features on the testing sets. The recognition rates obtained by the selected features is given at the last column of Table 1.

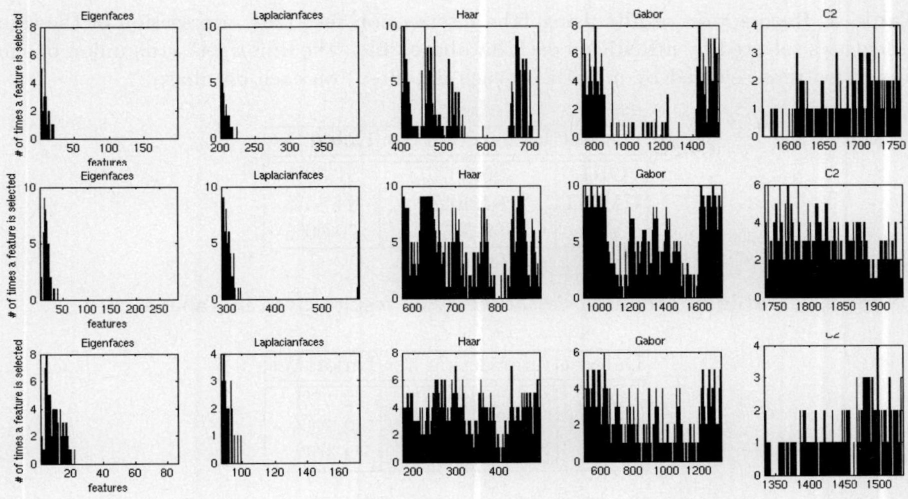

Fig. 2. Histogram of features selected by mRMR. First row: ORL database, second row: UMIST database, third row: Yale database.

In order to see which features are selected by mRMR, we plotted the histograms of the selected features on each database. These histograms are given in figure 2. Notice that mRMR has failed to select Haar features on the ORL database. This explains the relatively low performance of mRMR compared to Haar in ORL.

To test the *genericness* of the features selected by mRMR, we formed two feature sets as follows: "the intersection set": the set of common features selected on all of the 3 databases, and "the union set": the union of all selected features on all datasets. The intersection set has 331 features, whereas the union set has 1135 features. The visualization of these feature sets is given in figure 3.

The recognition results using "the intersection set" and "the union set" on each database are given in Table 4. The standard deviation of these results are in Table 5. Compared to the results in Table 1, "the union set", which has 1135 features, performs better on the Yale database. The performances on other

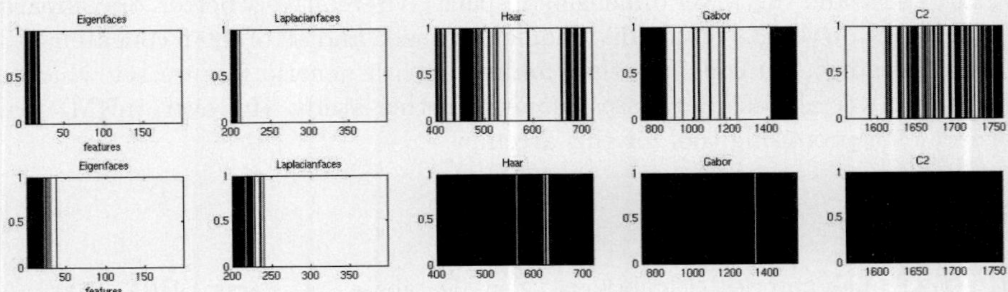

Fig. 3. First row: Intersection of sets of features selected by mRMR on each database. Second row: Union of sets of features selected by mRMR on each database.

Table 4. Recognition results using "the intersection set" (the intersection of the sets of features selected by mRMR on each database) and "the union set" (the union of the sets of features selected by mRMR on each database) on each database

Dataset	Intersection Set	Union Set
ORL	80.60%	81.50%
UMIST	94.49%	94.84%
Yale	69.33%	70.00%

Table 5. Standard deviation of the results given in Table 4

Dataset	Intersection Set	Union Set
ORL	2.92%	2.17%
UMIST	1.03%	0.70%
Yale	3.93%	3.40%

databases are nearly the same with the rates listed in Table 1 for concatenated features. Considering that a feature set gives different recognition results on different databases (See eigenfaces and Haar in Table 1), both "the intersection set" and "the union set" can be utilized on a face database of which characteristics are not known in advance.

4   Results and Discussion

In this study, we try to design a generic feature space which yields consistent and satisfactory results over a wide range of face databases. Experiments indicate that the performance of the same feature set varies significantly over different databases. Using a filter method such as mRMR gives successful results, when there is sufficient amount of data for each subject. Therefore, it can be concluded that the success of mRMR depends on the statistical sufficiency of the database used. Haar features seem to be the best feature set for the ORL database. This may be attributed to the nature of the data and robustness of the Haar features to the low number of samples. It is noted that mRMR, at least, reduces the dimension of the feature space and this lower dimensional space gives relatively better, or comparable, recognition results than individual feature sets, and all of them concatenated.

At this point, we conclude that finding such a generic feature set which is successful over all face databases requires further study. However, mRMR can be seen as a promising tool for this attempt.

References

1. AT&T Laboratories Cambridge: The Database of Faces. URL: `http://www.cl.cam.ac.uk/Research/DTG/attarchive/facedatabase.html`, (1994)
2. Graham, D. B., Allinson, N. M.: Face Recognition: From Theory to Applications. NATO ASI Series F, Computer and Systems Sciences, Vol. 163, pp 446-456 (1998)

3. Belhumeur, P. N., Kriegman,D. J.: The Yale face database. URL: `http://cvc.yale.edu/projects/yalefaces/yalefaces.html`, (1997)
4. Peng, H., Long, F., Ding, C.: Feature selection based on mutual information: criteria of max-dependency, max-relevance, and min-redundancy. IEEE Transactions on Pattern Analysis and Machine Intelligence, Vol. 27, No. 8, pp.1226-1238, (2005)
5. Zhao, W., Chellappa, R., Rosenfeld, A., Phillips, P.: Face recognition: A literature survey. UMD CfAR Technical Report CAR-TR-948 (2000)
6. Turk, M., Pentland, A.: Eigenfaces for Recognition. Journal of Cognitive Neuroscience, Vol. 3, No. 1, pp. 71-86, (1991)
7. He, X., Yan, S., Hu, Y., Niyogi, P., Zhang, H.-J.: Face Recognition Using Laplacianfaces. IEEE Transactions on Pattern Analysis and Machine Intelligence, Vol. 27, No. 3, Mar. (2005)
8. Serre, T., Wolf, L., Poggio., T.: Object Recognition with Features Inspired by Visual Cortex. Proceedings of 2005 IEEE Computer Society Conference on Computer Vision and Pattern Recognition (CVPR), IEEE Computer Society Press, San Diego, June. (2005)
9. Wang, J. Z., Wiederhold, G., Firschein, O., Wei, S. X.: Content-Based Image Indexing and Searching Using Daubechies' Wavelets. International Journal on Digital Libraries, vol. 1, no. 4, pp. 311-328, Springer-Verlag, (1998)
10. Keller, J. M., Gray, M. R., Givens, J. A.: A Fuzzy K-Nearest Neighbour Algorithm. IEEE Trans. Syst., Man, Cybern., vol. SMC-15, 4, pp580-585, (1985)
11. The Center for Biological & Computational Learning (CBCL), MIT: A new biologically motivated object recognition system (Source Code). URL: `http://cbcl.mit.edu/software-datasets/standardmodel/index.html`, (2005)

Low-Cost Microarchitectural Techniques for Enhancing the Prediction of Return Addresses on High-Performance Trace Cache Processors

Yunhe Shi[1], Emre Özer[2], and David Gregg[1]

[1] Department of Computer Science, Trinity College Dublin
[2] ARM Ltd., Cambridge, UK
yshi@cs.tcd.ie, emre.ozer@arm.com, david.gregg@cs.tcd.ie

Abstract. This paper discusses the effects of the prediction of return addresses in high-performance processors designed with trace caches. We show that a traditional return address stack used in such a processor predicts return addresses poorly if a trace cache line contains a function call and a return. This situation can often be observed for processors demanding aggressive instruction fetch bandwidth. Thus, we propose two potential schemes to improve the prediction accuracy of return addresses. We demonstrate that the proposed schemes increase the return address prediction rates reasonably using minimal hardware support. We also analyze the effects of various trace cache configurations on the return address prediction accuracy such as trace cache set associativity, cache size and line size. Our experimental results show that the average return address prediction accuracy across several benchmarks can be up to 11% better than a traditional return address stack in a high-performance processor with a trace cache.

1   Introduction

The trace cache is an approach to fetching multiple basic blocks in a single cycle in the Instruction-Level Parallelism (ILP) processors that have a large number of functional units. These functional units need to be supplied with multiple instructions in each cycle. Supplying several instructions involves in fetching instructions from instruction cache that are not contiguous in program order. Thus, the trace cache can largely increase the fetch bandwidth of the processor by collecting the snapshots of executed instruction stream and by storing them as trace cache lines. This provides a mechanism to place instructions from non-contiguous execution path into contiguous locations in the trace cache. When a trace cache line is predicted correctly, the entire trace cache line can be fetched in a single cache access.

A return from a function can be accurately predicted with a return address stack (RAS). Once a function is invoked, the next-PC address after the function call is pushed onto the RAS. After returning from the function call, the PC address from the RAS is popped off to continue fetching after the call instruction. When constructing trace cache lines, a trace cache line may contain a function call and end with a return instruction. In this case, the RAS cannot be used to predict the next fetch address because the next-PC address of the function call has not been pushed onto the RAS yet. This situation does not usually appear in the processors with a low instruction bandwidth. However, the higher instruction fetch bandwidth demand results in long traces of instructions that may contain one or even more function calls ending with a return in the same fetch cache line. When such a case occurs, the traditional RAS mispredicts the return address by popping off a wrong address because the last call in the same trace cache line has not been pushed onto the RAS yet.

Thus, we propose two low-cost microarchitectural techniques that potentially alleviate this problem and improve the return address prediction accuracy rate. The first technique is a *forwarding logic* that detects a call or multiple calls along with a return in the same trace cache line, and then forwards the next-PC address of the last call without using the RAS. Alternatively, the second technique *embeds the next-PC address* at the end of the trace cache line if the cache line contains a call or multiple calls and ends with a return. The return address stored at the end of the line is used to predict the next fetch address instead of popping off the RAS. The common feature of both techniques is that the next-PC address of the last function call in the trace cache line is *not* pushed onto the RAS.

The organization of the paper is as follows: *Section 2* describes the related work about the return address prediction. Then, *Section 3* discusses the return address prediction on trace caches and introduces our proposed schemes for improving the return address prediction accuracy. Next, *Section 4* presents the experimental framework and the initial return address prediction results by comparing the traditional return address stack with our proposed schemes, and then shows the incremental improvement in the return address prediction accuracy results by varying several trace cache configurations. Finally, *Section 5* concludes the paper.

2   Related Work

Predicting return addresses in trace caches have been discussed in [1] [2] [3] [4]. *Patel* [1] uses a RAS to predict return addresses but no special focus is made for improving the prediction of return addresses. Also, *Jacobson et al.* [2] predict next trace addresses instead of predicting individual instructions. Hence, their predictor does not use a RAS but they propose a return history stack structure that keeps the branch history before each function call. The return history stack only provides the past history before the call to the next-trace predictor. *Santana et al.* [4] uses a RAS as part of the next-stream predictor, which is similar to the next-trace predictor. A stream consists of basic blocks between two taken branches, and therefore contains only one call or a return in a single stream.

3   Return Address Prediction on Trace Cache

3.1   Trace Cache Model

Our trace cache model is based on the trace cache model as described in [1]. A trace cache system consists of an instruction cache, the trace cache, a multiple-branch predictor, a branch target buffer (BTB), a fill unit and a RAS. Each trace cache line stores multiple basic blocks for an execution path and may contain up to n instructions with no more than m conditional branches. Each trace cache line is accessed by the address of the first instruction in the first basic block, and contains the number and directions of branches.

The multiple-branch predictor predicts m conditional branches and the BTB provides branch target addresses. In addition to the multiple-branch predictor and BTB, the RAS predicts return addresses for return instructions. Instruction cache supplies instructions to the functional units when there is a trace cache miss. The fill unit constructs trace cache lines and places them into the trace cache as instructions retire from the functional units. So, the instructions are stored in decoded form in the trace cache lines. A trace cache line is terminated when it contains n instructions or m conditional branches, or if it ends with an *indirect branch*, *return* or a *trap* instruction. If there is a trace cache line starting as the same address, the new trace cache line replaces the existing trace cache line only when it is longer or follows a different execution path (i.e. *keep-longest* write policy).

3.2   Prediction of Return Addresses

Return addresses can be predicted accurately using the RAS [5] [6]. The RAS can be updated using two different mechanisms: 1) Update on fetch and 2) Update on commit. In the former, the function call address is pushed onto the stack as soon as the trace cache line containing the call is fetched. In the latter, the call address is pushed onto the stack when the call instruction is executed and committed. The advantage of the latter case is that the RAS is not corrupted by the misspeculated calls or returns but its drawback is that the call address cannot be pushed onto the stack by several pipeline cycles, which can cause return address mispredictions by successive return instructions.

In processors with speculative execution, mispeculation of branches causes corruption of the RAS. Speculatively executing call and return instructions push and pop the RAS speculatively and this causes misalignment of non-speculative call-return pairs if there is a branch misprediction. *Skadron et. al.* in [7] provides a simple mechanism to save the top of the stack along with the top of the stack entry after each branch prediction. Similarly, *Jourdan et. al.* in [8] checkpoints the whole RAS at each branch prediction. A separate RAS per thread is shown to be effective for simultaneous multithreading [9] and distributed RAS structures are proposed for speculative multithreaded processors [10].

In this paper, we use the *update-on-fetch* mechanism and the corruptions due to misspeculated calls/returns are fixed using the techniques mentioned above such as *saving the top-of-the stack* or *full stack checkpointing*.

In theory, there is no limitation on the number of unconditional branches or calls that are packed in a trace cache line. So, the entire trace cache line may consist of function calls, in which case the next-PC addresses of all calls must be pushed onto the RAS in the same cycle before the next fetch. **Figure 1a** shows a situation where three function calls exist in a trace cache line. Here, the trace

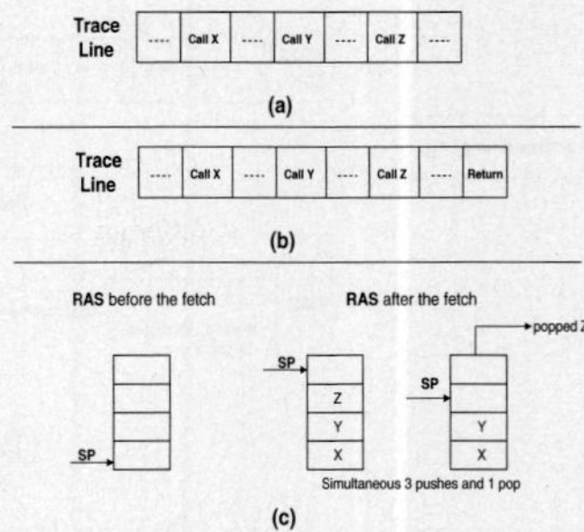

Fig. 1. (a) A trace cache line with multiple function calls, **(b)** a trace cache line with multiple function calls and a return, **(c)** the status of the RAS before and after the fetch

cache line consists of three function calls. After fetching this trace cache line, the next-PC addresses of function calls X, Y and Z must be pushed onto the RAS simultaneously in the order they appear in the trace cache line. If there is a return instruction in the next trace cache line, the RAS is popped off to predict the return address and the popped value from the RAS must be the next-PC address of the function call Z.

3.3   Simultaneous Updating of Multiple Calls and a Return

A trace cache line may contain one or more function calls and also may end with a return instruction. If this is the case, the return instruction must pop off the RAS after all call addresses must be pushed onto the stack.

Figure 1b and **Figure 1c** show a situation where three function calls and a return in a trace cache line. After fetching the trace cache line, the next-PC addresses of function calls X, Y and Z need to be pushed onto the RAS, and at the same time the return instruction pops off the RAS to get the predicted return address, which, in this particular case, is the next-PC address of the function call Z.

Pushing all the addresses onto the RAS and popping them off in the same cycle is not possible with the current RAS model. If this model is used, the return instruction pops off the RAS before the calls push their addresses. Hence, the value popped off the RAS is not the correct return address, and this results in a return address misprediction. In order to alleviate this problem, we propose two alternative schemes: 1) Return address forwarding logic, 2) embedding return addresses at the end of the trace cache line. Both will be discussed in the following sections.

Return Address Forwarding Logic: This is a mechanism that forwards the return address as the next fetch address by detecting call and return instructions in the same trace cache line. If there are more than one call instruction in the

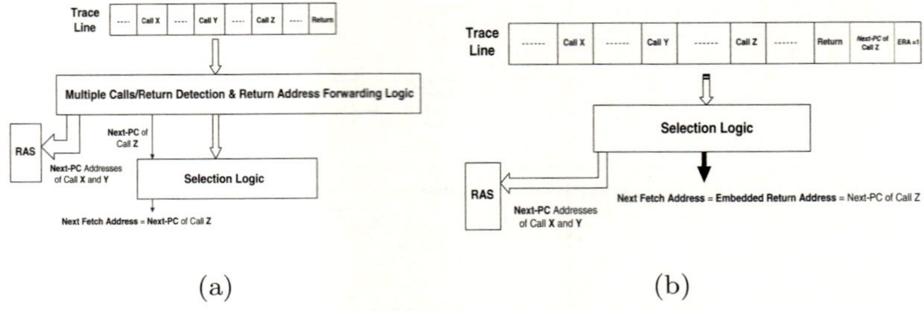

Fig. 2. **(a)** Return address forwarding logic, **(b)** embedded return address

line and the line ends with a return instruction, the next-PC address of the last call is forwarded. When such a trace cache line is detected, the last call is not pushed onto the RAS and also the return instruction is prevented to pop off the RAS. The detection and forwarding logic is inserted before the *Selection Logic* in the trace cache microarchitecture that generates the next fetch address.

Figure 2a shows the multiple calls and a return detection and the return address forwarding logic stage before the *Selection Logic*. It reads the opcodes of all instructions in the cache line and detects calls and/or a return. In the figure, calls X, Y and Z and a return are detected. So, the condition of having a call and a return in the same cache line is met. First, the next-PC addresses of X and Y are sent to the RAS in that order. The return instruction is not allowed to pop off the RAS and the next-PC address of Z is not sent to the RAS but forwarded as the next fetch address for the fetch engine.

Embedding Return Addresses: Despite its simplicity, the return address forwarding logic before the *Selection Logic* is on the critical path of the processor and therefore it may put pressure on the processor clock cycle time. An alternative solution is to add extra intuitive information to trace cache lines at trace cache fill time by the fill unit. This is a much simpler solution than the forwarding scheme and does not effect the processor cycle time since the fill unit is not on the critical path of the processor.

The fill unit detects the condition of having a call and a return in the same trace cache line. As soon as this is detected, the next-PC address of the last function call is saved at the end of the trace cache line after the return instruction. This does not demand extra space because trace cache lines already store the next fetch address at the end of the trace cache line. However, this space is currently *not used* for trace cache lines ending with a *return* instruction in the trace cache [1] because return instructions are predicted using the RAS. An extra bit called the *Embedded Return Address(ERA)* is also appended to the cache line to notify the *Selection Logic* that the return address is embedded into the trace line. When the ERA bit is set, the *Selection Logic* does not allow the next-PC address of the last call to be pushed onto the RAS and disables the popping off the RAS by the return instruction. The next fetch address is taken directly from the embedded return address at the end of the line. **Figure 2b** shows the embedded return address scheme.

Table 1. Trace cache parameters

1024-entry directed-mapped Trace cache
Trace Cache Write Policy: *keep-longest*
Trace lines of **16 instructions** with **at most 3 branches**
2-level conditional branch predictor Global History Size = 8 - Pattern History Table Size = 1024-entry
BTB size = 512 × 4
Return Address Stack (RAS) Size = 8-entry

4   Experimental Results

4.1   Experimental Framework

The SPECint2000 benchmark suite is used to evaluate different trace cache configurations/strategies and their influences on the return address prediction. Reduced data sets [11] are used as inputs for SPECint2000 benchmarks that run to completion. We integrate our trace cache model into *sim-bpred* in the *SimpleScalar* 3.0 [12] simulator. The trace cache parameters used in the simulator are shown in **Table 1**.

4.2   Trace Cache Line Statistics

Table 2 presents the percentage of trace cache lines with single call, multiple calls, and multiple calls-and-a return. The first part of the table with three columns shows the statistics about trace cache lines with 1, 2 and 3 calls. The second part consisting of a single column provides the percentage of cache lines with at least 1 call ending with a return.

The first part implies that the RAS hardware structure needs to have at most *three ports* to maintain simultaneous updating of it in the same cycle although the percentage of having 3 calls in the same trace cache line is very small. No cache lines with 4 calls is observed in any of the benchmarks.

The second part of the table shows that the percentages of having at least 1 call ending with a return in the same trace cache line is relatively higher in *twolf, parser, crafty, mcf* and *gcc*. This is particularly significant in *mcf* by 26%, and therefore the improvement in the return address prediction rate in *mcf* is also expected to be quite significant. In general, the benchmarks that contain relatively short functions (i.e. the ones that return immediately after performing a simple operation) benefit more from these two proposed techniques because such a function may easily fit into a single trace cache line.

Table 2. Statistics of the percentage of trace cache lines with multiple calls, and multiple calls with a return: Column **A** is "1 Call", Column **B** is "2 Calls", Column **C** "3 Calls" and Column **D** is "At Least 1 Call and a Ret"

Benchmarks	A	B	C	D
twolf	12.2%	0.05%	0%	0.6%
bzip2	9.2%	1.3%	0%	0.007%
vortex	24.6%	0.7%	0%	0.05%
gap	8.5%	0.7%	0%	0.09%
perlbmk	8.2%	0.001%	0%	0.07%
eon	16.5%	0.009%	0%	0.009%
parser	21%	1.4%	0%	2.6%
crafty	10.8%	0.7%	0%	0.8%
mcf	29.3%	0%	0%	26.2%
gcc	8.6%	0.2%	0%	0.5%
vpr	13.4%	0.005%	0%	0%
gzip	8.3%	0%	0%	0%
MEAN	**14.2%**	**0.4%**	**0%**	**2.6%**

4.3   Initial Results

The return address prediction accuracy of the base RAS is compared with the enhanced RAS model with one of our proposed schemes (i.e. *return address forwarding logic* or *embedded return addresses*) since both techniques perform equally well due to their same functionality.

Figure 3a shows return address prediction rates, and the last column denotes the arithmetic mean of prediction rates across all benchmarks. The highest improvement occurs in *mcf* by about 75% due to a high number of trace cache lines with at least one call and a return. Overall, the average return address prediction accuracies across all benchmarks are 90.92% for *Base RAS* and 98.97% for *Enhanced RAS*, which provides an average improvement of 8.05%.

4.4   Effects of Various Trace Cache Configurations

Here, we measure the effects of varying several trace cache parameters on the prediction of return addresses such as the trace cache size, set associativity and line size.

Figure 3b shows the percentage improvement of return address prediction rates for three trace line sizes of 128, 256, 512, 1024, 2048 and 4096 entries. The slight improvement in the prediction rates can be observed as the number of entries is increased. After 2048 entries, the improvement in the prediction rates becomes minor. When the cache size get larger, the number of conflict misses diminishes, and thereby the instruction fetch engine uses the trace cache more often than the instruction cache. Resorting to the trace cache more often increases the frequency of fetching trace cache lines with a call and a return in the same cache line. Hence,

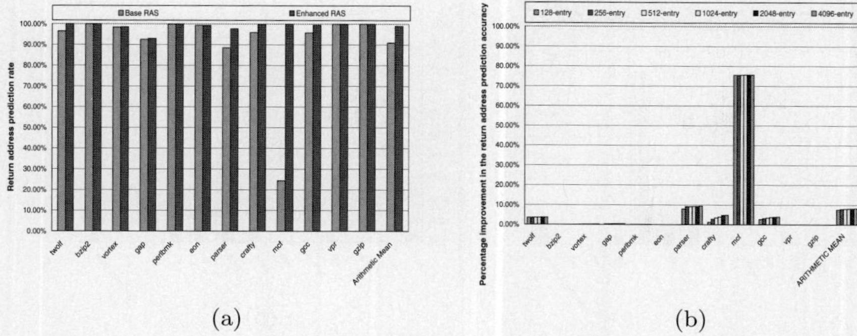

(a)   (b)

Fig. 3. (a) Initial return address prediction rates, **(b)** Percentage improvement of return address prediction rates for direct-mapped trace cache sizes of 128, 256, 512, 1024, 2048 and 4096 entries

the traditional RAS performs poorly as the size of the trace cache increases. The average percentage improvement in the prediction rates for 2048 entries rises to 8.14% from 8.05% for 1024 entries and from 7.6% for 128 entries.

We also vary the set associativity of the trace cache with 2, 4 and 8-way sets for 2048-entry trace cache. **Figure 4a** shows the percentage improvement of return address prediction rates of each cache configuration including 1-way or direct-mapped cache. Increasing the set associativity also increases the percentage improvement of return address rate due to the reduction in conflict misses, similar to the observations made in the cache size analysis. After 4-way set associativity, no obvious improvement is observed, though. An average of 8.64% and 8.72% improvements in the return address prediction rates is possible with 2 and 4-way 2048-entry trace caches.

So far, we have assumed a fixed number of branches (i.e. 3 branches with up to 16 instructions) in a trace cache line. However, future processors demand more instruction fetch rate, so we increase the trace cache line size to 4 and 5 branches and measure the improvement in the return address prediction rates. **Figure 4b** shows the percentage improvement of return address prediction rates for three trace line sizes of 3-branch-16-instruction (i.e. the base model), 4-branch-20-instruction and 5-branch-24-instruction using 4-way 2048-entry trace cache. As the trace cache line becomes longer, the chance of having a call and a return in the same trace cache line increases. Therefore, the base RAS in 4 and 5-branch models encounters many more mispredictions than the base RAS of the 3-branch model while the enhanced RAS prediction rates for all three models do not change. **Table3** shows the statistics of trace cache lines with multiple calls with a return for 5-branch line size. The average percentage of trace cache lines with at least one call and a return has increased to 4.7% in 5-branch line size from 2.6% in 3-branch line size in **Table 2**.

Overall, the average percentage improvement of the RAS prediction rate rises from 8.72% in 3-branch model to 9.71% in 4-branch model and to 10.98% in 5-branch model.

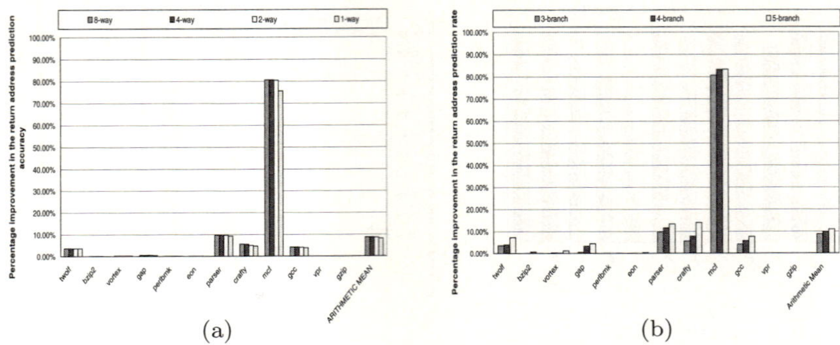

(a)   (b)

Fig. 4. Percentage improvement of return address prediction rates **(a)** for 1, 2, 4 and 8-way set associative trace cache of 2048 entries, **(b)** for trace line sizes of 3-branch-16-instruction, 4-branch-20-instruction and 5-branch-24-instruction

Table 3. Statistics of trace cache lines with at least 1 call and a return for trace cache line size of 5 branch-24-instruction

twolf	*bzip2*	*vortex*	*gap*	*perlbmk*	*eon*
1.8%	0.04%	0.5%	1.4%	0.1%	0.2%

parser	*crafty*	*mcf*	*gcc*	*vpr*	*gzip*	***MEAN***
5.7%	4%	41.5%	1.4%	0.003%	0.005%	**4.7%**

5   Conclusion

In this paper, we have discussed the effects of using the trace cache on the prediction of return addresses. We propose two schemes to improve the prediction accuracy of return addresses for processors with trace caches. We have demonstrated that the proposed schemes improves the return address prediction rates using only minimal hardware support.

We have analyzed various trace cache configurations such as varying trace cache size and set associativity and cache line size to measure their effects on return address prediction accuracy. Our experimental results have shown that the average return address prediction accuracy across several benchmarks using one of the two proposed techniques is about 11% better than a traditional trace cache model.

References

1. Patel, S.J.: Trace Cache Design for Wide-Issue Superscalar Processor. PhD thesis, Computer Science and Engineering in The University of Michigan (1999)
2. Jacobson, Q., Rotenberg, E., Smith, J.: Path-based next trace prediction. In: Proceedings of the 30th Annual ACM/IEEE International Symposium on Microarchitecture. (1997)

3. Rotenberg, E., Bennett, S., Smith, J.E.: A trace cache microarchitecture and evaluation. IEEE Transactions on Computers (1999)
4. Santana, O.J., Falcon, A., Ramirez, A., Larriba-Pey, J.L., Valero, M.: Next stream prediction. Technical Report UPC-DAC-2002-15, Technical Report (2002)
5. Webb, C.F.: Subroutine call/return stack. IBM Tech. Disc. Bulletin **30**(11) (1988)
6. Kaeli, D.R., Emma, P.G.: Branch history table prediction of moving target branches due to subroutine returns. In: Proceedings of the 18th Annual International Symposium on Computer Architecture (ISCA-18). (1991)
7. Skadron, K., Ahuja, P.S., Martonosi, M., Clark, D.W.: Improving prediction for procedure returns with return-address-stack repair mechanisms. In: Proceedings of the 31st Annual ACM/IEEE International Symposium on Microarchitecture. (1998)
8. Jourdan, S., Stark, J., Hsing, T.H., Patt, Y.N.: Recovery requirements of branch prediction storage structures in the presence of mispredicted-path execution. International Journal of Parallel Programming **25**(5) (1997)
9. Hily, S., Seznec, A.: Branch prediction and simultaneous multithreading. In: Proceedings of the 1996 Conference on Parallel Architectures and Compilation Techniques (PACT '96). (1996)
10. Zahran, M.M., Franklin, M.: Return-address prediction in speculative multithreaded environments. In: Proceedings of the 9th International Conference on High Performance Computing. (2002)
11. KleinOsowski, A., Lilja, D.J.: Minnespec: A new spec benchmark workload for simulation-based computer architecture research. Computer Architecture Letters **Vol.1** (2002)
12. Austin, T., Larson, E., Ernst, D.: Simplescalar: An infrastructure for computer system modeling. Computer, IEEE Computer Society (2002) 59–67

Recovery Logics for Speculative Update Global and Local Branch History

Jong Wook Kwak[1] and Chu Shik Jhon[2]

[1] SoC R&D Center, System LSI Division, Samsung Electronics Co.
Giheung-eup, Yongin-City, Gyeonggi-do, Korea
jongwook.kwak@samsung.com
[2] Department of Electrical Engineering and Computer Science,
Seoul National University, Shilim-dong, Kwanak-gu, Seoul, Korea
csjhon@riact.snu.ac.kr

Abstract. Correct branch prediction is an essential task in modern microarchitectures. In this paper, to additionally increase the prediction accuracy, recovery logics for speculative update branch history are presented. In local or global branch predictors, maintaining speculative update history provides substantial prediction accuracy. However, speculative update history requires a suitable recovery mechanism. This paper proposes recovery logics for speculative update branch history, for both global- and local-history. The proposed solutions provide higher prediction accuracy and guarantee the correctness of program, and they can be efficiently implemented with low hardware costs.

Keywords: Branch Prediction, Branch History, Speculative Update Branch History, Recovery Logic, *gshare* Predictor.

1 Introduction

To realize the performance potential of today's widely-issued, deeply pipelined superscalar processors, the accurate branch predictor is an essential part of modern microprocessor architectures and embedded systems [1][2][3]. Since the introduction of two-level branch predictor, the dynamic branch history has been a major input vector to index the Pattern History Table (PHT). The two-level branch predictors or their variations maintain the history of the last k "committed-branches" encountered and the branch behavior for the last s occurrences of the specific pattern of these k branches [4]. However, the history of committed-branches may not efficiently reflect the correlations among branch instructions, because there are possibly many in-flight branches between the last committed-branch and the currently predicted branch.

Fig. 1 shows the motivation of this paper. In Fig. 1 (a), Br3 has a strong correlation with Br1 and Br2. That is, if we know the results of Br1 and Br2, we can easily predict the direction of Br3. However, as mentioned above, there are many in-flight branches and the results of Br1 and Br2 may not be reflected in history register yet, which makes the prediction of Br3 difficult. As shown in Fig. 1 (b), when we predict the direction of Br3, the history used to index the

A. Levi et al. (Eds.): ISCIS 2006, LNCS 4263, pp. 258–266, 2006.

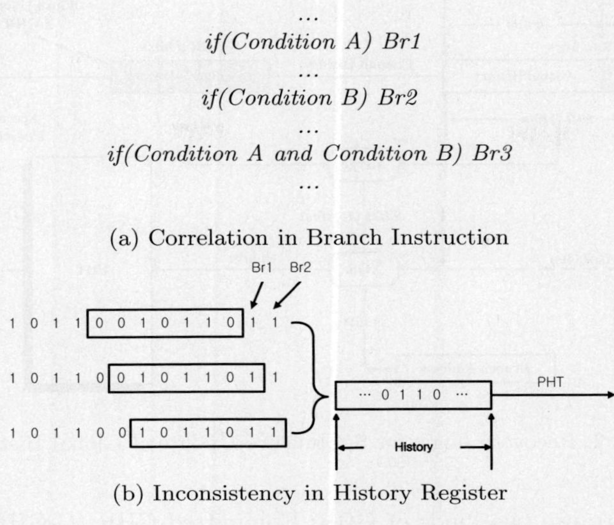

Fig. 1. The Need for Speculative History Utilization

PHT may be different for each time. This is due to the dynamic events like cache misses, other miss-predictions and resource shortages, and these events cause the instruction-window contents to vary.

However, speculative history resolves these problems, and it guarantees that each prediction uses the most recent branch history consistently. Previous research shows the benefits for maintaining speculative update branch history [5]. The branch predictor of the modern state-of-the-art microprocessors, such as *Alpha EV8*, maintains the speculative histories as well [6]. However, although the branch predictors with speculative update branch history increase the prediction accuracy substantially, they require suitable recovery mechanisms, after detecting the miss-speculative update branch history. Despite the definite necessity of speculative update branch history, few previous studies provide the implementation details about recovery logics for utilizing speculative history, within the knowledge of our survey. This paper proposes hardware-efficient recovery logic for speculative update branch history, for both global- and local-history.

2 Recovery Logics for Speculative History

2.1 Recovery Logic for Global History

Fig. 2 shows the recovery logic for speculative update of global history. Global history predictors, such as *GAg* [4] or *gshare* [7], maintain a Global History Register (GHR). Among them, *gshare* predictor is generally considered as a default global history predictor in many researches [8][9]. Further, although we describe the recovery logic with *gshare* predictor, the proposed logic can be implemented in any global branch predictors which use the GHR.

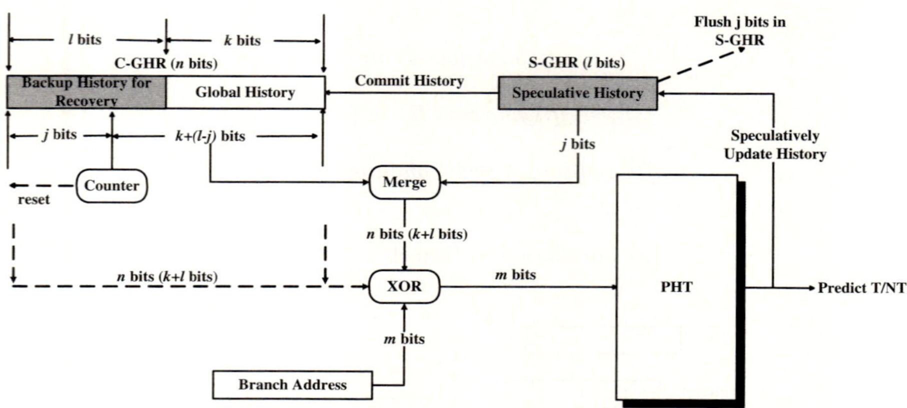

Fig. 2. Recovery Logic for Speculative Update of Global History

In Fig. 2, we use two kinds of GHR: Committed GHR (C-GHR) and Speculative GHR (S-GHR). S-GHR contains the speculative update global history. After correctly committing the speculative update branch instruction, the oldest bit in S-GHR is moved into C-GHR. C-GHR is further divided into (1) Global History and (2) Backup History for Recovery (BHR). Whenever one entry in S-GHR is moved into C-GHR, C-GHR is shifted left and the entry of BHR is incremented. The counter in Fig. 2 indicates the number of currently occupied entries in BHR which is equal to the number of currently utilized S-GHR bits $(j \leq l)$. Consequently, when predicting the branch with speculative history, n bit speculative history, which is obtained by merging (1) $k + (l - j)$ bits in C-GHR and (2) j bits in S-GHR, is *exclusive-or*ed with m bit branch address. Then, the PHT is indexed by m bit input vector $(m \leq n)$.

However, the utilization of speculative history in branch prediction requires a suitable recovery mechanism, after detecting miss-speculative update history. In case of recovery in our mechanism, it is sufficient to restore the branch history to committed history, by flushing j bits in S-GHR and resetting the counter, as shown in Fig. 2 (the dotted line). Then, n (i.e., $k + l$) bit C-GHR is used, without any S-GHR bits.

Although the necessity of speculative update history is definite, only [10] provides the implementation details about recovery logics for utilizing speculative global history, within the knowledge of our survey. Compared to the prior work, the additional hardware costs of our logic are trivial. The additional hardware overheads in [10] is (the number of global history bits)×(the queue entries for the number of in-flight branches), whereas our logic requires l bit S-GHR and $\log_2 l$ bit counter. For example, if we use 4K entry PHT with 2 bit counter and allow 20 maximal speculative histories, then [10] requires additional 240 bits (12 bits × 20) in 8000 bit (4K × 2 bits) table, whereas our logic requires about 25 bits (20 bits $+\log_2 20$), i.e., 90% reduction in additional hardware costs, which is almost trivial without violating program correctness.

2.2   Recovery Logic for Local History

In case of the recovery logic for speculative update local history, we present two mechanisms: Committed History based (CH-based) and Speculative History based (SH-based).

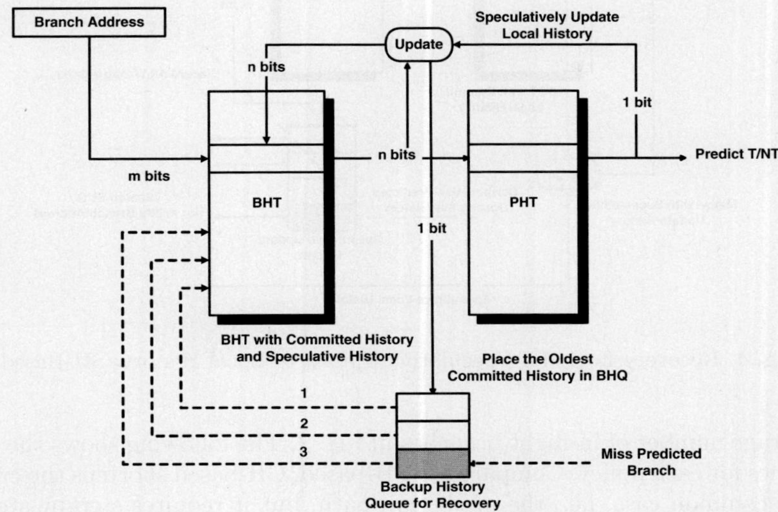

Fig. 3. Recovery Logic for Speculative Update of Local History: CH-Based

At first, Fig. 3 shows CH-based recovery logic. In Fig. 3, Backup History Queue (BHQ) stores the oldest committed history which is truncated by newly updated speculative history. The Branch History Table (BHT) in CH-based mechanism contains n bit local history, which is composed of committed history and speculative history. Then, the PHT is indexed by n bit speculative update local history. In case of detecting the miss-speculative history, each entry in BHT is recovered from BHQ in reverse order, as shown in the dotted line. When the branch instruction is correctly committed, the BHQ entry is deleted.

SH-based recovery logic, on the other hand, is shown in Fig. 4. Compared to CH-based, the queue, which is called Speculative Update Queue (SUQ), stores speculative history. At this time, the BHT contains only committed histories, without any speculative history. When predicting a new branch with m bit address, the PHT is indexed by merged n bit local history from proper entries in BHT and SUQ. In case of recovery for miss-speculative history, the SUQ entries are flushed, from SUQ tail to miss-speculative SUQ entry, as shown in the dotted line. When the branch instruction is correctly committed, the SUQ entry is deleted and the BHT is updated with correct history.

The main additional hardware costs for both mechanisms are BHQ and SUQ, with the size of (1 bit history $\times$ the number of in-flight branches). We will discuss

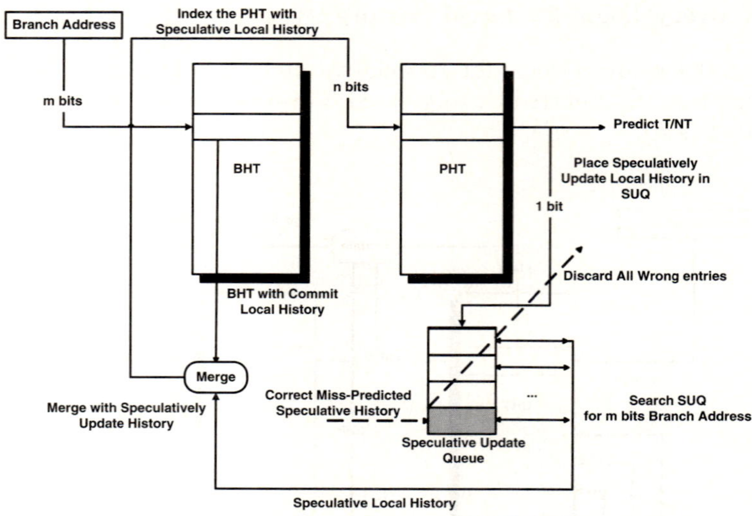

Fig. 4. Recovery Logic for Speculative Update of Local History: SH-Based

the average number of in-flight branches in Fig. 7. The following shows the characteristics for each policy. Compared to SH-based, CH-based shortens the critical path in common case, i.e., the prediction path, but it requires step-by-step recovery processes. However, the recovery time of CH-based can be overlapped by miss-prediction penalty if branch prediction system requires high miss penalty. On the contrary, SH-based has a simple recovery. Flushing the SUQ entries is enough, because the BHT already contains the correct committed history. However, it may lengthen the prediction path, resulting in the slight increase of prediction time. Therefore, CH-based is more suitable for high prediction accuracy applications and SH-based is more suitable for low miss penalty systems.

3 Performance Evaluation

In this section, we evaluate the performance of our proposal. We use an event-driven simulator, *SimpleScalar* [11], for our simulation. As benchmark programs, we use the *SPEC 2000* application suits [12]. Table 1 shows the detailed simulation environment and system parameter.

Fig. 5 shows the performance of the Recovery Logic for Global History; the prediction accuracy for *SPEC 2000*. As shown in Fig. 5, speculative update with recovery (SU w/ Rec, the proposed solution) provides prediction accuracy of up to 5.6%, compared to previous commit-time update (CT_Update). Meanwhile, as shown in the results of SU w/o Rec, speculative update history without utilizing recovery mechanism is clearly not sensible. Rather, even CT_Update vastly outperforms the SU w/o Rec.

Table 1. Simulation Parameters

System Parameter	Value
Fetch Queue	4 entries
Fetch and Decode Width	4 insructions
ROB entries	16 entries
LSQ entries	8 entires
Functional Units(Int and FP)	4 ALUs, 1Mult/Div
I-TLB	$64(16 \times 4ways)$ entries, 4K pages, 30 cycle miss
D-TLB	$128(32 \times 4ways)$ entries, 4K pages, 30 cycle miss
Predictor Style	*gshare*
BTB entries	$2048(512 \times 4ways)$ entries
RAS entries	8 entries
Extra Miss Penalty	3 cycles
L1 I-Cache	16KB, direct-map, 32B line, 1 cycle
L1 D-Cache	16KB, 4-ways, 32B line, 1 cycle
L2 Cache(Unified)	256KB, 4-ways, 64B line, 6 cycles
Memory Latency	first chunk=18 cycles, inter chunk=2 cycles

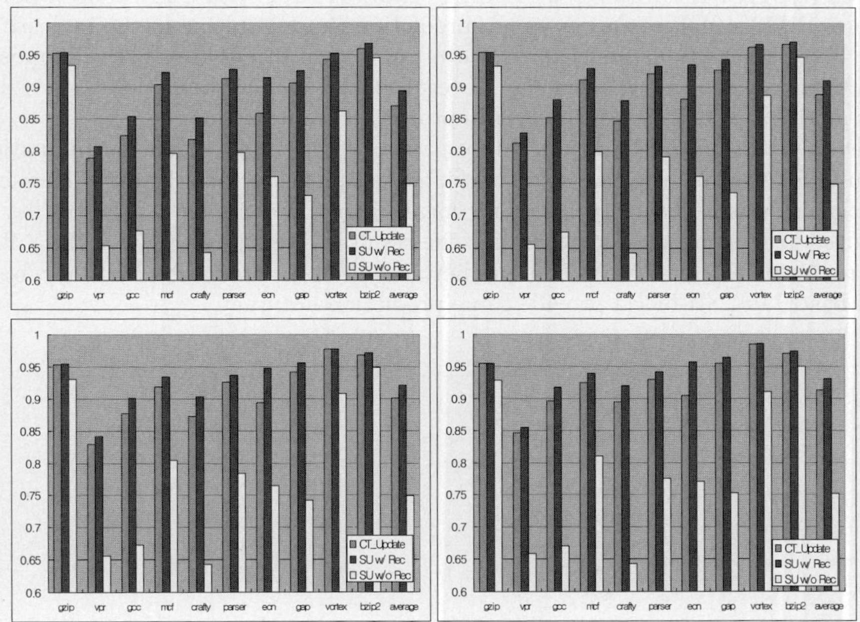

Fig. 5. Branch Prediction Accuracy

In addition, Fig. 6 shows the average prediction accuracy for all applications in each PHT size. As shown in Fig. 6, the prediction accuracies of PHT with i-K entry in SU w/ Rec generally outperform those of PHT with 2i-K entry in CT_Update.

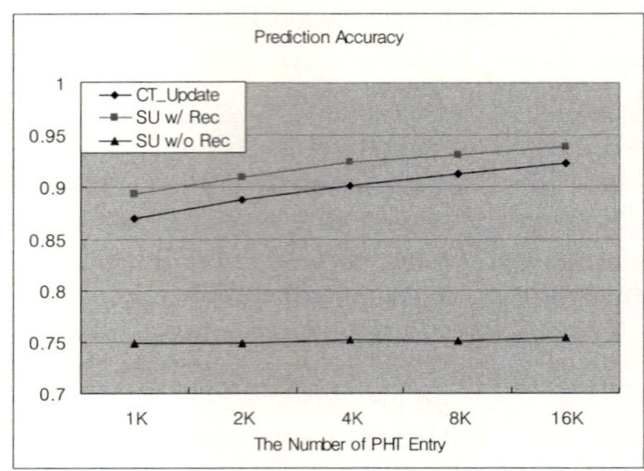

Fig. 6. The Average Branch Prediction Accuracy

Further, the prediction accuracies of PHT with i-K entry is almost similar or slightly inferior to those of PHT with 4i-K entry in CT_Update, which shows the usefulness of the proposed logic in the strict hardware resource constraint environments (eg. 2K PHT with SU w/ Rec vs. 4K or 8K PHT with CT_Update). Large size of PHTs usually requires longer prediction time, resulting in the increase of the overall execution time [13]. However, as shown in our result, the proposed mechanism is also more beneficial, in terms of the branch prediction time which has a critical relation with the overall program execution time.

Due to the space limitation of this paper, we briefly describe the simulation results for the recovery logics for speculative update of local history. The simulation results of recovery logics for local history are similar to the results of recovery logic for global history. Like the result of Fig. 5 and Fig. 6, SU w/ Rec outperforms CT_Update in local predictors as well. In prediction accuracy, both CH-based and SH-based provide same prediction accuracy.

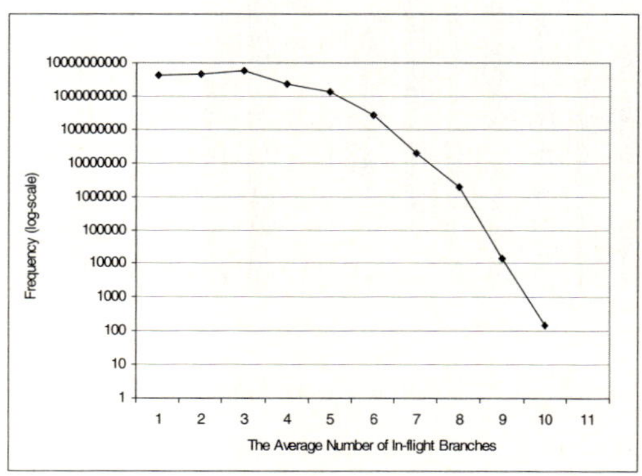

Fig. 7. The Average Number of In-Flight Branches

Fig. 7 shows the average number of in-flight branches for *SPEC 2000* benchmark programs, which indirectly indicates the additional hardware costs for managing the speculative history. The result in Fig. 7 is shown in *log-scale*. Based on this result, we can infer the proper number of S-GHR entries (l bits) in our branch predictor. From this result, we can conclude that the average number of in-flight branches is mostly less than 5 in common case and 8 in-flight branches are enough to make speculative update history more beneficial (i.e., cost-effective), for all applications.

4   Conclusion

In this paper, new recovery logics for speculative update branch history are proposed. The proposed logics provide higher prediction accuracy and do not violate the program correctness. In case of recovery logic for speculative update of global history, its simple structure results in almost 90% reduction in additional hardware costs, compared to the prior works, and it provides improvement of up to 5.6% in prediction accuracy. In case of recovery logic for speculative update of local history, we present two versions of recovery logics: Committed History based and Speculative History based, and their hardware requirements are modest as well. The two distinct recovery mechanisms in local predictors can be applied differently, according to application characteristics and system environments.

References

1. J. L. Hennessy and D.A Patterson, "Computer Architecture : A Quantitative Approach", Third Edition, Morgan Kaufmann Publishers, Inc, 2001.
2. Intel XScale Core Developer's Manual, January, 2004
3. Steve Furber, "ARM System-on-Chip Architecture", 2nd edition, Addison-Wesley, 2000
4. Yeh, T. Y. and Patt, Y. N., "Two-level adaptive branch prediction", In Proceedings of the 24th ACM/IEEE International Symposium on Microarchitecture, 51-61, 1991
5. E. Hao, P.-Y. Chang, and Y. Patt, "The effect of speculatively updating branch history on branch prediction accuracy, revisited," In Proc. of the 27th MICRO, pp. 228-232, Nov. 1994
6. A. Seznec, S. Felix, V. Krishnan, and Y. Sazeid'es. "Design tradeoffs for the ev8 branch predictor", In Proc. of the 29th ISCA, pp. 295-306, May 2002.
7. McFarling, S., "Combining branch predictors. Tech. Rep. TN-36m", Digital Western Research Lab., June, 1993
8. J. W. Kwak, J.-H. Kim, and C. S. Jhon, "The Impact of Branch Direction History combined with Global Branch History in Branch Prediction", IEICE Transactions on Information and System, Vol. E88-D, No. 7, pp. 1754-1758, July 2005
9. David Tarjan, Kevin Skadron, "Merging path and gshare indexing in perceptron branch prediction", ACM Transactions on Architecture and Code Optimization (TACO), Volume 2 Issue 3, September 2005

10. K. Skadron, M. Martonosi, and D. Clark. "Speculative updates of local and global branch history: A quantitative analysis", JILP, vol. 2, Jan. 2000
11. D. Burger, T. M. Austin, and S. Bennett, "Evaluating future micro-processors: the SimpleScalar tool set", Tech. Report TR-1308, Univ. of Wisconsin-Madison Computer Sciences Dept., 1997
12. SPEC CPU2000 Benchmarks, http://www.specbench.org
13. D. A. Jimenez, S. W. Keckler, and C. Lin, "The impact of delay on the design of branch predictors", In Proc. 33rd Int'l Symp. on Microarchitecture, pp. 67-76, 2000.

An ILP Formulation for Task Scheduling on Heterogeneous Chip Multiprocessors

Suleyman Tosun[1], Nazanin Mansouri[2], Mahmut Kandemir[3],
and Ozcan Ozturk[3]

[1] Computer Engineering Department, Selcuk University, Konya, Turkey
stosun@selcuk.edu.tr
[2] EECS Department, Syracuse University, Syracuse, NY, USA
namansou@ecs.syr.edu
[3] Computer Science and Engineering Department, The Pennsylvania State University,
University Park, PA, USA
{kandemir, ozturk}@cse.psu.edu

Abstract. One of the main difficuties to map an embedded application onto a multiprocessor architecture is that there are multiple ways of this mapping due to several constraints. In this paper, we present an Integer Linear Programming based framework that maps a given application (represented as a task graph) onto a Heterogeneous Chip Multiprocessor architecture. Our framework can be used with several objective functions such as energy, performance, and fallibility (opposite of reliability). We use Dynamic Voltage Scaling (DVS) for reducing energy consumption while we employ task duplication to minimize fallibility. Our experimental results show that over 50% improvements on energy consumption are possible by using DVS, and the fully task duplicated schedules can be achieved under tight performance and energy bounds.

Keywords: Reliability, duplication, energy minimization, DVS, heterogeneous chip multiprocessors.

1 Introduction

Increasing complexity of embedded applications and their large dataset sizes make it imperative to consider novel embedded architectures that are efficient from both performance and power angles. Heterogeneous Chip Multiprocessors (HCM) are one such example where multiple processor cores are placed into the same die. While it is possible to put together multiple processor cores, interconnect and necessary memory components and build an HCM architecture, programming it in an effective manner is an entirely different matter.

The main difficulty comes from the fact that there are typically multiple ways of mapping a given embedded application to HCM. Favoring one way over the other is not easy, as it depends strongly on the constraints to be met and the objective function to be optimized. In particular, a typical real-time execution environment may demand proper balancing among different metrics such performance, power/energy,

A. Levi et al. (Eds.): ISCIS 2006, LNCS 4263, pp. 267–276, 2006.

code/ memory size, and reliability/fault tolerance. Therefore, software optimizers and other automated tools can be of great help in such situations since they can optimize the input code automatically under multiple criteria and a given objective function. Unfortunately, with a couple of exceptions, most of the previously proposed optimization frameworks in the literature exclusively target at minimizing the execution cycles of the application code. The power, code/data size, and reliability aspects of doing so have received relatively less attention.

In this paper, our goal is to map a given real-time embedded application (represented as a task graph) onto an HCM architecture. This mapping is implemented within a publicly available ILP (integer linear programming) tool [1] and operates under an objective function and multiple criteria (constraints). The objective function to be optimized and constraints to be satisfied can be functions of energy, performance or fallibility (opposite of reliability). Therefore, our framework can be used for three different purposes: (1) maximizing performance under energy and fallibility constraints; (2) minimizing energy under performance and fallibility constraints; and (3) minimizing fallibility under performance and energy constraints.

What makes this problem even more interesting is the fact that each processor in the HCM architecture can have different characteristics from the others in terms of maximum clock speed, available voltage/frequency levels (that could be used for reducing energy consumption), attached memory capacity, etc.. We use Dynamic Voltage Scaling (DVS) for reducing energy consumption while we employ task duplication to minimize fallibility. Our experimental evaluation shows that, with a small increase in energy consumption or a small decrease in performance, we can have designs with zero fallibility (i.e., all tasks are duplicated). In addition, by employing voltage scaling, we reduce the energy consumption over 50% as compared to the case where no voltage scaling is used.

The remaining of this paper is organized as follows. In the next section, we review related work. In Section 3, we explain performance, energy, and fallibility metrics and describe our task graph model and our target architecture. In Section 3, we give our ILP formulation and objective functions. We discuss the experimental results in Section 4. Finally, we conclude the paper in Section 5.

2 Related Work

Dynamic Voltage Scaling (DVS) has been a promising energy reduction technique since Weiser et al. [2] introduced the idea to the community. Exploiting the availability of the processors that run on multiple voltages, most of the prior work focused on using voltage scaling as the primary energy reduction technique. While some researchers used ILP for voltage selection [3], others employed heuristic approaches to find the solutions faster [4]. However, such studies do not take reliability related issues into account. There are also several research efforts at the system level focusing on reliability-aware high-level synthesis [5] and hardware/ software co-design [6], [7]. In [7], for example, Xie et al. employs duplication to improve the reliability of the design. However, they do not consider the energy consumption introduced by adding new tasks to the system. We reported the preliminary version of this work in [8]. Our work differs from the prior studies in at least two aspects. First, we embed the energy consumption and the fallibility (reliability) metrics at the same time into the scheduling problem unlike above mentioned efforts. Second, our approach is flexible in that it can optimize any of several objective metrics, such as the fallibility, energy consumption, and/or performance, based on a set of constraints. To the best of our knowledge, this is the first study that integrates all these three important parameters in a framework that targets heterogeneous chip multiprocessors.

3 Preliminaries

Dynamic voltage scaling (DVS) is one of the most commonly used techniques to reduce the energy consumption of the tasks in the design. Its attraction comes from the fact that tasks consume less energy (proportional to the square of the supply voltage) when they run under low supply voltages. However, the drawback is that they also take more time (proportional to the supply voltage) to execute. When a task executes on a lower voltage, its WCET increases at a rate which is proportional to the following expression:

$$t = \frac{C_L.v}{k.(v-v_t)^\alpha},\tag{1}$$

where C_L is the output load capacitance of the circuit, k is a constant that depends on the process technology employed and gate size, v_t is the threshold voltage, and α is a variable that ranges between 1.2 and 2. In this paper, we assume α is 2 and v_t is 0.6V for our numerical evaluations. Consequently, if the WCET and energy consumption of a task when using a high voltage v_h is known, its corresponding WCET and energy consumption on a lower voltage v_j can be determined by the following expressions:

$$t_{v_l} = t_{v_h} \cdot \frac{v_l}{v_h} \cdot \left(\frac{v_h - v_t}{v_l - v_t} \right)^2 \quad \text{and} \quad E_{v_l} = E_{v_h} \cdot \left(\frac{v_l}{v_h} \right)^2 \tag{2}$$

In this work, we assume that we know the worst case execution times and energy consumptions of the tasks when using the highest voltage/frequency level available for each processor in our HCM.

Our next concern in this paper is to minimize the fallibility (maximize the reliability) of the design. To do this, we introduce duplication to the task graph. The duplicated tasks in our designs can be the exact copy of the primary tasks or the scaled down versions of them (as a result of voltage scaling). When a task is duplicated, we also add a checker circuitry to check the correctness of the computation. As our reliability metric, we use the percentage of duplicated tasks in the design. The fallibility of the design is the opposite of the reliability value, which is the number of tasks that are not duplicated.

We use a *task graph* to represent the given embedded application. Task graph is a directed-acyclic graph where vertices (nodes) represent the tasks and edges represent the dependencies among these tasks. An example task graph is given in Figure 1(a). For a given task graph, we add source (t_0) and sink (t_{n-1}) tasks to make our scheduling formulations simpler. In Figure 1(a), tasks 0 and 4 are the source and sink tasks, respectively. The deadline is the maximum allowed time that a task should finish its execution. While each task in the graph may have its own deadline, in this work, we use a single deadline for the entire task graph, though our approach can be extended to handle the case where multiple nodes have their own deadlines. A fully duplicated task graph example is shown in Figure 1(b).

The target architecture has an important role in our framework. Its configuration affects the resulting design in many aspects such as performance, cost, and energy consumption. In our target architecture, each processor has its own memory and the communication between processors (tasks) is conducted via shared bus. In fact, the mapping of each task onto a processor may result in different memory area consumption and communication overhead. These problems (minimizing the memory cost and communication overhead) have been studied extensively in the literature, and they are beyond the scope of this work. In Figure 1(c), we illustrate a possible mapping of fully duplicated task graph (shown in Figure 1(b)) onto our target architecture. In this figure, we assume that we have only two processors, each differing in clock speed/frequency, energy/power consumption, and memory consumption (cost). As can be seen from this figure, we may map the primary task and its duplicate onto the same processor or onto the different processors to minimize our objective function. However, mapping the primary task and its duplicate onto the same processor may cause a problem if that processor (specifically, its data path) is faulty. This is because; the results of a task and its duplicate on a faulty processor will be the same and faulty. However, these faulty results will be passed as correct results, since both the faulty results will be the same as far as the checker circuitry is concerned. This can be avoided by forcing the duplicate of a task to be executed on a different processor, which brings extra energy consumption since the duplicate of the task will not be mapped to its best alternative.

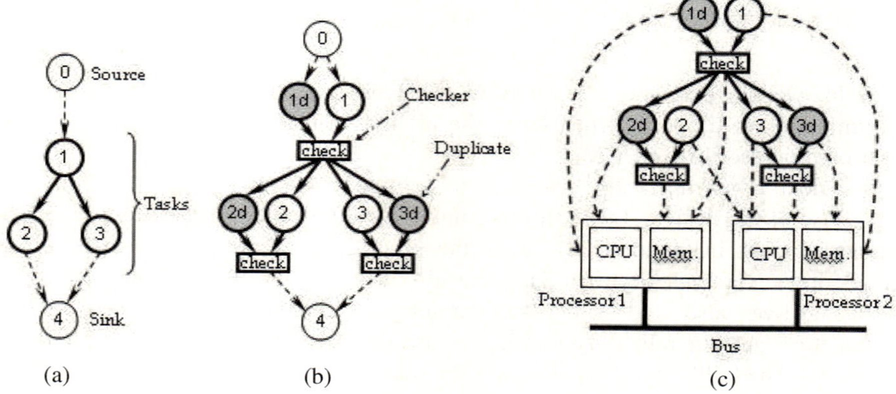

Fig. 1. (a) An example task graph, (b) its fully duplicated version, (c) a possible mapping of fully duplicated task graph onto the target architecture with two processors

4 Task Scheduling

In this section, we give our ILP formulation for the task scheduling problem. First, we define a binary variable $b_{i,j,v}$, which indicates whether task i is assigned to processor j that runs under voltage level v. The duplicates may not necessarily be assigned to a processor since we may not know if a node is duplicated or not. The duplication criterion depends on the energy, fallibility, and/or performance constraints. Expressions (3) and (4) capture this constraint. In these expressions, n, m, and o represent the number of tasks, processors, and voltage levels, respectively.

$$\sum_{j=1}^{m}\sum_{v=1}^{o} b_{i,j,v} = 1 \, , \forall i : 0 \le i < n \tag{3}$$

$$\sum_{j=1}^{m}\sum_{v=1}^{o} b_{i,j,v} \le 1 \, , \, \forall i : n \le i < 2n - 2 \tag{4}$$

Next, we need to assign the most appropriate execution time d_i and energy consumption E_i values to the tasks and their duplicates. For each task, we have several alternatives for both the execution time and energy consumption values since these values can vary depending on the processor used. Additionally, these values will be different for each voltage level on a processor. We then assign these time and energy values to each task using the expressions below. In these expressions, $t_{i,j,v}$ and $E_{i,j,v}$ are the WCET and energy consumption, respectively, of task i on processor j that runs under voltage level v.

$$\forall i : \quad d_i = \sum_{j=1}^{m}\sum_{v=1}^{o} t_{i,j,v} \cdot b_{i,j,v} \quad \text{and} \quad E_i = \sum_{j=1}^{m}\sum_{v=1}^{o} E_{i,j,v} \cdot b_{i,j,v} \tag{5}$$

Each task i and its duplicate must be assigned a start time s_i, an integer variable that we define as:

$$\forall i : 0 \le s_i \le l - d_i \, , \tag{6}$$

where l is the deadline and d_i is the WCET of task i.

In order to ensure the correct execution order for the tasks, the sequencing constraints must be satisfied. This means that a task can start its execution only after its predecessors have finished their executions (i.e., no task can start its execution unless all its input data are available). To express the sequencing constraints, we need to know when a task finishes its execution. As we mentioned earlier, some of the tasks may be duplicated. After each task and its duplicate, we need to insert a checker circuitry (an additional node in the task graph), which introduces some extra delay to the design. As a result, we should add the delay of the checker after the task and its duplicate complete their executions. To do this, we need to know which one finishes its execution later so that we add the delay of the checker circuitry to this task. Consequently, we define a binary variable $c_{i,k}$, which is set 1 when task i finishes its execution later than its duplicate k ($k=i+n$-1). Expressions (7), (8), and (9) below are used to capture this constraint, where et_i is the finish time of a task, disregarding the checker circuitry:

$$\forall i: et_i = s_i + d_i , \tag{7}$$

$$et_i - et_k \leq (l+1).c_{i,k} - 1, \quad \forall i : 0 \leq i < n \tag{8}$$

$$et_k - et_i \leq l - (l+1).c_{i,k}, \quad \forall i : 0 \leq i < n \tag{9}$$

We then define a binary variable r_i, which is set to one if task i is duplicated:

$$r_i = \sum_{j=1}^{m}\sum_{v=1}^{o} b_{i,j,v} , \forall i : n \leq i < 2n - 2 \tag{10}$$

We combine binary variables $c_{i,k}$ and r_i from Expressions (8), (9), and (10) to obtain binary variable ch_i, given in Expression (11), which is set to 1 if task i is duplicated and it finishes its execution later than its duplicate. We then add the checker delay t_{ch} to the end time et_i of the task i to find the exact end time e_i of the task after checker insertion, if the task is duplicated.

$$ch_i \geq c_{i,k} + r_i - 1 , \forall i : 0 \leq i < n \tag{11}$$

$$e_i = et_i + t_{ch}.ch_i , \forall i : 0 \leq i < n \tag{12}$$

$$e_i = et_i + t_{ch}.(1 - c_{i-n+1,i}) , \forall i : n \leq i < 2n - 2 \tag{13}$$

Expressions (14) and (15) below ensure that the tasks and their duplicates start execution after their predecessor and predecessors' duplicates complete. In these expressions, *Edge* represents the edge set, where the existence of an edge (i, k) in this set means task k is a direct successor of task i.

$$s_k \geq e_i \wedge s_k \geq e_{i+n-1} , \tag{14}$$

$$s_{k+n-1} + l - l.r_k \geq e_i \wedge s_{k+n-1} + l - l.r_k \geq e_{i+n-1} , \tag{15}$$
$$\forall i,k : 0 < i,k < n; (i,k) \in Edge$$

An additional timing constraint states that there cannot be two tasks on the same processor with overlapping time frames. We formulate this constraint by adopting an approach similar to that used in [9]. Specifically, we define a binary variable $a_{i,k}$, which is set to one if tasks i and k are scheduled on the same processor. We use the following expression:

$$\forall i,k,j \text{ such that } i > j ; \quad a_{i,k} \geq \sum_{v=1}^{o} b_{i,j,v} + \sum_{v=1}^{o} b_{k,j,v} - 1 . \tag{16}$$

If task i starts its execution earlier than task k, then binary variable $f_{i,k}$ is set to 1:

$$\forall i,k,j \text{ such that } i > j ; \quad s_k - s_i \leq (l+1).f_{i,k} - 1, \tag{17}$$

$$\forall i,k,j \text{ such that } i > j ; \quad s_i - s_k \leq l - (l+1).f_{i,k} , \tag{18}$$

Finally, we adopt the following expressions from [9], which ensure that there will be no two tasks that are mapped onto the same processor and their execution times overlap with each other.

$$\forall i, k, j \text{ such that } i > j \qquad s_k \geq et_i - (3 - f_{i,k} - 2a_{i,k}).l \,, \tag{19}$$

$$\forall i, k, j \text{ such that } i > j \qquad s_i \geq et_k - (2 - f_{i,k} + 2a_{i,k}).l \,, \tag{20}$$

As we explained in Section 2, the duplicate of a task may be forced to be mapped onto a different processor. The following expression captures this constraint.

$$\forall i, j: \qquad \sum_{v=1}^{o} (b_{i,j,v} + b_{n-1+i,j,v}) \leq 1 \tag{21}$$

Expressions (22), (23), and (24) below give the fallibility, performance, and energy consumption constraints of the design respectively.

$$F_s \geq n - 2 - \sum_{i=n}^{2n-2} \sum_{j=1}^{m} \sum_{v=1}^{o} b_{i,j,v} \tag{22}$$

$$s_{n-1} \leq l \tag{23}$$

$$TE = \sum_{i=1}^{2n} E_i \leq E\max \tag{24}$$

In this paper, we focus on three different objective functions:
Minimize energy under fallibility (F_s) and performance (l) constraints.

$$MIN: \; TE = \sum_{i=1}^{2n} E_i \text{ under Expressions (22) and (23).}$$

Minimize fallibility (i.e., maximize the number of duplicated tasks) under performance (l) and energy ($Emax$) constraints.

$$MIN: \; n - 2 - \sum_{i=n}^{2n-2} \sum_{j=1}^{m} \sum_{v=1}^{o} b_{i,j,v} \text{ under Expressions (23) and (24).}$$

Minimize execution time of the task graph (i.e., maximize performance) under energy and fallibility constraints.

$$MIN: \; s_{n-1} \text{ under Expressions (22) and (23).}$$

5 Experimental Results

In this section, we test the impact of our approach through two sets of experiments, each having a different objective function and a different set of constraints to be satisfied. In our experiments, we use task graphs extracted from embedded appli cations; namely, G721decode and G721encode from Mediabench, Mismatch_test from Trimaran GUI, and a custom task graph tg01. Since a uniprocessor system is a special case of an HCM, we consider HCMs from two to five heterogeneous processors in our experiments. For each processor, we employ five different levels of supply voltages. These voltage levels range from 2.0V to 3.3V (specifically, 2.0V, 2.4V, 2.7V, 3.0V, and 3.3V). We tested our approach on randomly generated task graphs as well. However, due to lack of space, we report only one of the experiments (Experiment 2) here.

Experiment 1: In our first set of experiments, we study the impact of voltage scaling on energy reduction. We also show how fallibility affects the energy improvement brought by voltage scaling. To do this, we scheduled three benchmarks (G721encode, G721decode, and Mismatch_test) under a fixed performance constraint. We assume that we have three processors and three voltage levels (2.0V, 2.7V, and 3.3V) in our target architecture. Then, we change the percentage of duplicated tasks from 0% to 100%. Note that under given performance constraints, we may not be able to fully duplicate the given task graph.

In Figures 2(a), 2(b), and 2(c), we give the comparisons of energy consumptions with and without dynamic voltage scaling (DVS) under a fixed performance cons traint for G721encode, G721decode, and Mismatch_test benchmarks, respectively. In Figure 2(d), we summarize the percentage energy improvements brought by our approach over a scheme that does not use DVS. As can be seen from this bar-chart, when we increase the number of duplicated tasks in the design the energy improvement reduces. This is because when we add more duplicated task to the design, we may not scale down all the tasks to meet the performance bound, resulting in less energy improvement (i.e., our energy consumption will be closer to the energy consumption of the scheme without DVS when we decrease fallibility).

Experiment 2: In this set of experiments, we schedule the task graph tg01 under different performance and energy bounds, with the objective of minimizing fallibility. For the target architecture, we assume that we have three processors that can use three different supply voltages. In Figure 3, we show how the percentage of duplicated tasks changes as a function of the different energy and performance bounds. As can be seen from this bar-chart, a very small energy and/or performance bound relaxation allows us to duplicate more tasks. Beyond certain performance and energy bounds, however, increasing the bounds further does not bring any additional improvements on fallibility since the application reaches its maximum energy savings under the given deadline, and the fallibility is minimized to zero (i.e., the task graph is 100% duplicated).

Our experiments show how the proposed ILP-based approach can be used effectively for scheduling a real-time embedded application on an HCM under several constraints, and for optimizing the desired cost function. It can be observed that our approach is flexible in the sense that it can be employed for several scheduling problems from simple schedules that do not consider fault-tolerance and/or power to very complex schedules that involve all three metrics in some fashion.

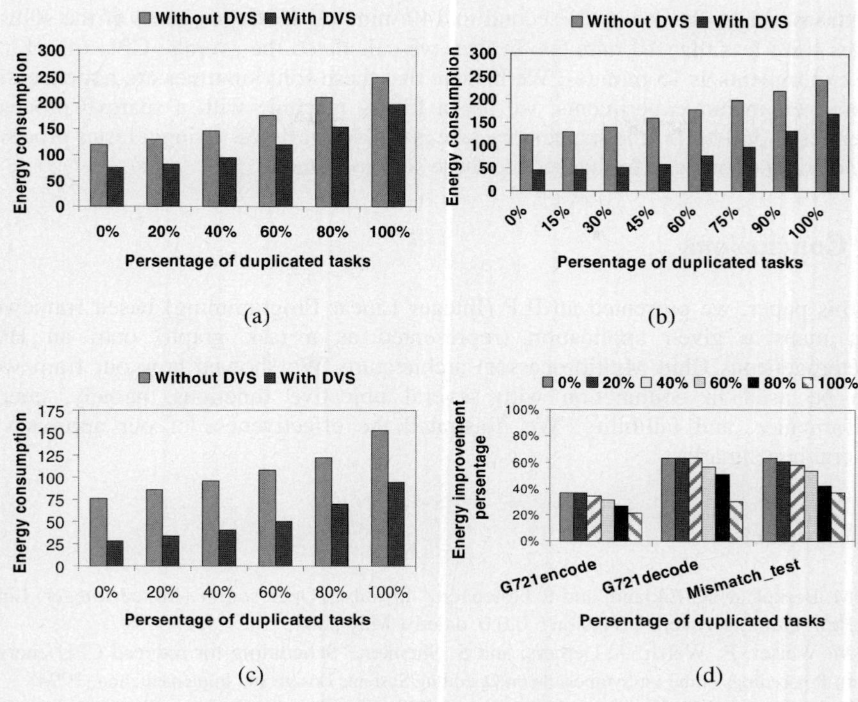

Fig. 2. Energy consumptions under different percentage of duplicated tasks with and without DVS for (a) G721encode, (b) G721decode, and (c) Mismatch_test benchmarks, and (d) the percentage energy improvements brought by our approach

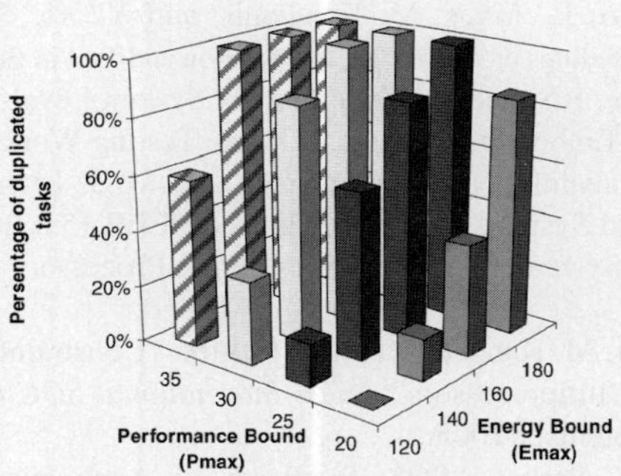

Fig. 3. Maximum percentage values of duplicated tasks with respect to energy and performance bounds for tg01

One of the concerns for ILP based approaches is the solution time required for the given problem, depending highly on its complexity. When the complexity increases, producing an output using an ILP can become too time-consuming, sometimes even impossible in a reasonable amount of time. In our experiments, the CPU time of the solutions ranges from one (1) second to 140 minutes. However, most of the solution times were less than 10 minutes. In fact, we calculated the average CPU time for all the experiments as 15 minutes. We believe that these solution times are not excessive. Moreover, in our experiments, we use a UNIX machine with a sparcv9 processor operates at 360 MHz, and its memory size is 128 MegaBytes. Using a faster processor and a better solver can further reduce these solution times.

6 Conclusions

In this paper, we presented an ILP (Integer Linear Programming) based framework that maps a given application (represented as a task graph) onto an HCM (Heterogeneous Chip Multiprocessor) architecture. We showed how our framework can be used in conjunction with several objective functions, namely, energy, performance, and fallibility. We illustrated the effectiveness of our approach on several benchmarks.

References

1. M. Berkelaar, K. Eikland, and P. Notebaert, "lp_solve: Open source (Mixed-Integer) Linear Programming system", Version 5.0.0.0. dated 1 May 2004.
2. M. Weiser, B. Welch, A. Demers, and S. Shenker, "Scheduling for reduced CPU energy", In Proceedings of the 1st Symposium on Operating Systems Design and Implementation, 1994.
3. T. Ishihara and H. Yasuura, "Voltage scheduling problem for dynamically variable voltage processors", Proc. of the 1998 International Symposium on Low Power Electronics and Design, 1998.
4. J. Luo and N. K. Jha, "Power-Conscious Joint Scheduling of Periodic Task Graphs and Aperiodic Tasks in Distributed Real-Time Embedded Systems", ICCAD, 2000.
5. S. Tosun, N. Mansouri, E. Arvas, M. Kandemir, and Y. Xie, "Reliability-Centric High-Level Synthesis", Proceedings of the Design, Automation and Test in Europe (DATE'05), 2005.
6. C. Bolchini, L.Pomante, F.Salice and D.Sciuto, "A System Level Approach in Design Dual-Duplex Fault Tolerant Embedded Systems," Online Testing Workshop, 2002.
7. Y. Xie, L. Li, M. Kandemir, N. Vijaykrishnan, and M. J. Irwin, "Reliability-Aware Co-synthesis for Embedded Systems", in Proceedings of IEEE 15th International Conference on Application-specific Systems, Architectures and Processors (ASAP'04), pp. 41-50, September 2004.
8. S. Tosun, N. Mansouri, M. Kandemir, and O. Ozturk, "Constraint-Based Code Mapping for Heterogeneous Chip Multiprocessors", *IEEE International SOC Conference (SOCC 2005)*, Washington, D.C., September 2005.
9. S. Prakash and A. C. Parker, "SOS: Synthesis of Application-Specific Heterogeneous Multiprocessor Systems", Journal of Parallel and Distributed Computing, December 1992, Vol. 16, pp. 338-351.

Hardware Designs for Local Alignment of Protein Sequences

Mustafa Gök and Çağlar Yılmaz

Cukurova University, Dept. of Comp Eng. Balcali, 01330 Turkey

Abstract. Local alignment of two protein sequences shows the similar regions between these proteins. Usually, a query protein sequence is aligned with several hundred thousands of protein sequences stored in databases. Since this procedure is computationally demanding, various hardware units are designed to get high quality results in a practically useful time. This paper presents efficient hardware designs that compute the local alignment scores of protein sequences. The presented designs are compared with the reference designs. All designs are implemented using ASIC and FPGA technologies. Syntheses results show that compared to the reference designs the proposed ASIC implementations achieve frequency improvements up to 250 % and hardware gains up to 40 %, and the proposed FPGA implementations achieve frequency improvements up to 29 % and hardware gains up to 48 %.

1 Introduction

In bioinformatics, the similar regions between two sequences usually indicate functional relationship [1]. Sequence alignment procedure is used to point-out the global similarity of two sequences or local similar regions between two sequences. The local alignment of sequences usually gives more useful results than the global alignment of sequences. To find the best aligning database sequences with a query sequence, several hundred thousands of sequences in bioinformatics databases are scanned, and sequences with highest similarity scores are chosen for each alignment. In order to get high quality results in a practically useful time, various high-performance algorithms are developed. One of the well-known local alignment algorithm is Smith-Waterman (SW) algorithm [2], [3]. This algorithm gives optimal results, but it is computationally more demanding compared to other faster but non-optimal sequence alignment algorithms.

Special hardware units can execute SW algorithm several hundreds times faster than the software applications [4], [5]. In most designs, SW algorithm is mapped on a systolic linear array. The advantages of using the linear array structure for SW implementations are throughly explained in [6]. Recent SW implementations are mapped on FPGAs due to the cost and design advantages of these platforms [5], [7], [8], [9]. On the other hand, mapping SW on ASIC provide the best area/performance ratio [6], [10], [11], [12]. In general, the previous SW implementations mainly differ by their cell designs. These implementations either over simplify the cells [4], [7], [8] or directly map the iterative equations of

A. Levi et al. (Eds.): ISCIS 2006, LNCS 4263, pp. 277–285, 2006.

algorithm [5], [6]. The first approach gives practically non-useful hardware that computes only the edit distance between two sequences. The second method increases the area of the design. Inefficient cell design also decreases the clock frequency of the design. This paper presents SW hardware units for protein sequence alignments. The presented designs use a novel cell design method, which has the following advantages:

- *Efficient use of the hardware resources in the cell.* This decreases the area and increases the clock frequency of the overall implementation without sacrificing the practical functionality of the design.
- *Better scaling with the precision of the score.* Increasing the score precision does not change the delay, and slightly increases the area for the proposed designs.

In order to use an SW hardware on a computer system, an interface logic is required. The interface passes the database sequences to SW hardware and sends the score results generated by the SW unit to the computer. These score results are used to identify best aligned sequences. The computer reconstructs the local alignments that fits the score criteria. This paper focuses only on the design of SW unit.

The rest of the paper is organized as follows. Section 2 explains the Smith-Waterman algorithm for performing local alignment. Section 3 presents the proposed design. Section 4 compares the presented design with the reference design presented in [6]. Section 5 presents the conclusions.

2   Local Alignment of Protein Sequences

SW algorithm is used to identify the best-aligned subsequences between a query sequence $Q = q_1 q_2 \ldots q_m$ and a database sequence $P = p_1 p_2 \ldots p_n$. The degree of the similarity is determined by a score. Let $H(i, j)$ be the similarity score for two subsequences of Q and P ending in q_i and p_j, respectively. $H(i, j)$ is computed for local alignments using the following iterative equations

$$F(i, j) = max(H(i - 1, j) - g_o, F(i - 1, j) - g_e) \qquad (1)$$
$$E(i, j) = max(H(i, j - 1) - g_o, E(i, j - 1) - g_e) \qquad (2)$$
$$H(i, j) = max(0, H(i - 1, j - 1) + S(i, j), E(i, j), F(i, j)) \qquad (3)$$

Initial values of the iterations are set as $H(i, 0) = E(i, 0) = F(i, 0) = 0$, for $i \geq 0$ and $H(0, j) = E(0, j) = F(0, j) = 0$, for $j \geq 0$. $S(i, j)$ is a match, or a mismatch cost. g_o is the gap opening cost and g_e is the gap extension cost. Setting the gap extension cost less than the gap opening cost usually gives more useful results. This model is called affine-gap penalty model and favors gap extension. The regular-gap penalty model assigns the same cost for a gap opening and a gap extension.

SW can be used for aligning nucleic acid sequences or proteins. When it is used for aligning nucleic acid sequences, substitution costs can be set to simple

(a) The Dayhoff PAM250 Matrix

	A	R	N	D	C	Q	E	G	H	I	L	K	M	F	P	S	T	W	Y	V
A	2																			
R	-2	6																		
N	0	0	2																	
D	0	-1	2	4																
C	-2	-4	-4	-5	12															
Q	0	1	1	2	-5	4														
E	0	-1	1	3	-5	2	4													
G	1	-3	0	1	-3	-1	0	5												
H	-1	2	2	1	-3	3	1	-2	6											
I	-1	-2	-2	-2	-2	-2	-2	-3	-2	5										
L	-2	-3	-3	-4	-6	-2	-3	-4	-2	2	6									
K	-1	3	1	0	-5	1	0	-2	0	-2	-3	5								
M	-1	0	-2	-3	-5	-1	-2	-3	-2	2	4	0	6							
F	-3	-4	-3	-6	-4	-5	-5	-5	-2	1	2	-5	0	9						
P	1	0	0	-1	3	0	1	0	0	2	3	1	2	5	6					
S	1	0	1	0	0	-1	0	1	-1	-1	-3	0	-2	-3	1	2				
T	1	2	0	0	-2	-1	0	0	-1	0	-2	0	-1	-3	0	1	3			
W	-6	2	-4	-7	-8	-5	-7	-7	-3	-5	-2	-3	-4	0	-6	-2	-5	17		
Y	-3	-4	-2	-4	0	-4	-4	-5	0	-1	-1	-4	-2	7	-5	-3	-3	0	10	
V	0	-2	-2	-2	-2	-2	-2	-1	-2	4	2	-2	2	-1	-1	-1	0	6	2	4

(b) The BLOSUM62 Matrix

	A	R	N	D	C	Q	E	G	H	I	L	K	M	F	P	S	T	W	Y	V
A	4																			
R	-1	5																		
N	-2	0	6																	
D	-2	-2	1	6																
C	0	-3	-3	-3	9															
Q	-1	1	0	0	-3	5														
E	-1	0	0	2	-4	2	5													
G	0	-2	0	-1	-3	-2	-2	6												
H	-2	0	1	-1	-3	0	0	-2	8											
I	-1	-3	-3	-3	-1	-3	-3	-4	-3	4										
L	-1	-2	-3	-4	-1	-2	-3	-4	-3	2	4									
K	-1	2	0	-1	-3	1	1	-2	-1	-3	-2	5								
M	-1	-1	-2	-3	-1	0	-2	-3	-2	1	2	-1	5							
F	-2	-3	-3	-3	-2	-3	-3	-3	-1	0	0	-3	0	6						
P	-1	-2	-2	-1	-3	-1	-1	-2	-2	-3	-3	-1	-2	-4	7					
S	1	-1	1	0	-1	0	0	0	-1	-2	-2	0	-1	-2	-1	4				
T	0	-1	0	-1	-1	-1	-1	-2	-2	-1	-1	-1	-1	-2	-1	1	5			
W	-3	-3	-4	-4	-2	-2	-3	-2	-2	-3	-2	-3	-1	1	-4	-3	-2	11		
Y	-2	-2	-2	-3	-2	-1	-2	-3	2	-1	-1	-2	-1	3	-3	-2	-2	2	7	
V	0	-3	-3	-3	-1	-2	-2	-3	-3	3	1	-2	1	-1	-2	-2	0	-3	-1	4

Fig. 1. Two Commonly Used Scoring Matrices

values. For example using a match score of 1 and a mismatch score of -1 are very common. When SW is used for comparing proteins more complex scoring schemes are used. Various scoring matrices are developed to determine the costs for the substitution of amino acids [13]. Figure 1 shows two commonly used amino acid substitution matrices, the BLOSUM62 and the PAM250. In general, the BLOSUM matrices seems to capture more distance type of variations found in protein families while the PAM matrices can be more useful in capturing the relations between protein families that have short evolutionary distances [1]. We preferred to use BLOSUM62 matrix in the proposed designs. In BLOSUM62 the minimum and the maximum cost values are -8 and 11, respectively. Thus, all the cost values can be represented using five bits. The proposed design can be easily modified to use PAM250 matrix.

3   The Proposed SW Hardware Unit

Figure 2 shows the general block diagram for the proposed SW design method. In this design, all the SW cells are identical, and placed in a linear array. When the load1 signal is high, letters that represent amino acids of the query sequence, q_i, are stored in the unit, and when load2 signal is high the gap penalty values are stored. The presented design can be adapted for ASIC or FPGA implementations. Based on the implementation platform different methods used for storing the substitution matrix. For ASIC implementations all columns of the BLO-SUM62 matrix are stored in the LUT of each SW cell, and for FPGA implementations only a column of the BLOSUM62 is stored. For FPGA implementations the columns of the substitution matrix are stored at the initialization step. The gap opening and gap extension penalties are set to any values in the range of -1 to -15. After these initializations, the load1 and load2 signals are set to low,

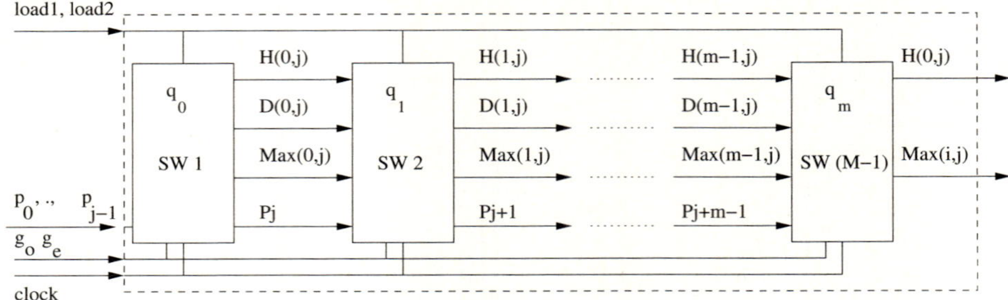

Fig. 2. The Linear Array Structure

and the database sequences are fed into the array. In each iteration, a SW cell computes a score, $H(i,j)$, a maximum value, $Max(i,j)$, and a 2-bit difference value, $D(i,j)$. The maximum score computed in each alignment is output by the last cell. The maximum scores are used to identify the best aligned sequences.

3.1   The Design of The SW Cell

The design of the SW cell is the most important part of the systolic implementation, since the performance and the size of the SW cell mainly determines the clock frequency and the area of the overall architecture. The SW cell consists of adders, registers, and maximum generation units that implement Equations (1)-(3). Direct implementation of these equations causes inefficient use of hardware resources, due to the following reasons:

1. The precision of the score, $H(i,j)$, determines the size of adders and maximum generation units in the cell. This precision is always larger than the precisions of the cost values. In most applications, the precisions of $S(i,j)$, g_e, and g_o are 4 bits or less, whereas the precision of $H(i,j)$ is at least 16 bits.
2. To map Equations (1) and (2) on hardware, significant resources are required.

To decrease the hardware used to implement a SW cell, the following property is used: *The intermediate values used to compute $H(i,j)$ differ from $H(i-1,j-1)$ by a small amount.* In relation to that property, $H(i,j)$ differs from $H(i,j-1)$ by a small amount as well. The maximum difference is determined by the maximums of the cost and gap penalty values. Assume that the precision of $H(i,j)$ is 16, and the precision of the cost and gap penalty values is 5 (for BLOSUM62), then the difference vectors are defined as follows

$$D(i,j-1) = H(i,j-1)_{15:4} - H(i-1,j-1)_{15:4}$$
$$D(i-1,j) = H(i-1,j)_{15:4} - H(i-1,j-1)_{15:4}$$
$$D(i,j) = H(i,j)_{15:4} - H(i-1,j)_{15:4}$$

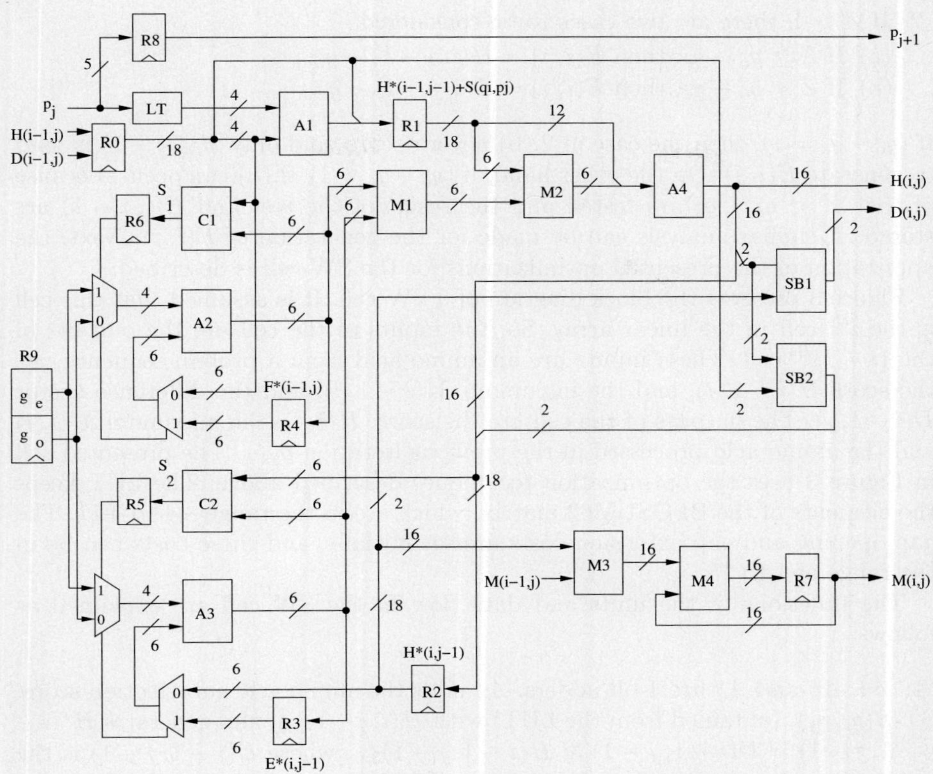

Fig. 3. The SW Cell

Also, $D(i-1, j-1)$ is defined as the value of carry or borrow out of the addition $H(i-1, j-1)_{3:0} + S(q_i, p_j)$. All the other difference values are generated by 2-bit subtracters, since they can be only -1, 0, or $+1$. By concatenating $H(x, y)_{3:0}$ to $D(x, y)$ the intermediate values are represented. These new representations for the intermediate values are 6 bits. Therefore, the size of the adders and maximum generators that use these values in the generation of $H(i, j)$ are reduced to process 6-bit vectors. Moreover, the sizes of those units do not change even if the score precision is increased.

The hardware that generates $E(i, j)$ and $F(i, j)$ vectors is also reduced. The details for the reduction are explained by analyzing generation of $E(i, j)$. According to the Equations (1)-(3) $H(i, j-1)$ is greater than or equal to $E(i, j-1)$, therefore, $Z = H(i, j-1) - E(i, j-1) \geq 0$ is always true. This inequality is used in the analysis as follows:

1. If $Z = 0$, then $H(i, j-1) - g_o < E(i, j-1) - g_e$, and,
   $E(i, j) = H(i, j-1) - g_e = E(i, j-1) - g_e$ $(g_o > g_e)$.

2. If $Z > 0$, there are two cases to be considered
   (a) If $Z \geq g_o - g_e$, then $E(i,j) = H(i,j-1) - g_o$.
   (b) If $Z < g_o - g_e$, then $E(i,j) = E(i,j-1) - g_e$.

If $(g_o - g_e = 1)$, then the case in 2.(b) never occurs, and only $H(i,j-1)$ is used to generate $E(i,j)$. On the other hand, if $(g_o - g_e > 1)$, 2.(b) can occur, because of that $Z < g_o - g_e$ are tested and the result of the test and $E(i,j-1)$ are stored. A similar analysis can be made for the generation of $F(i,j)$. Next, the application of the presented optimizations for the SW cell is described.

Figure 3 presents the block diagram of a SW cell. It is assumed that this cell is the ith cell in the linear array. So, the inputs of the cell are the outputs of the $(i-1)^{th}$ cell. These inputs are an amino acid from a protein sequence, p_j, the score $H(i-1,j)$, and the maximum $M(i-1,j)$, and the difference vector $D(i-1,j)$. The outputs of the cell are the score, $H(i,j)$, the maximum $M(i,j)$ and the amino acid processed in the previous iteration p_{j+1}. The presented cell in Figure 3 uses the optimization techniques described above. The LUT keeps the elements of the BLOSUM62 matrix, which are in the range -4 to $+11$. The gap opening and gap extension costs are set initially, and these costs can be in the range of 1 to 15.

The functions of the units and data flow in the SW cell are explained as follows:

1. *A1*, *A2* and *A3* are 4-bit adders. *A1* adds the amino acid substitution score, $S(q_i, p_j)$, (obtained from the LUT) with $H(i,j-1)_{3:0}$, and generates $H^*(i-1,j-1) = D(i-1,j-1)$ & $H(i-1,j-1)_{3:0}$, where $D(i-1,j-1)$ is the carry or borrow out from the adder, and $H(i-1,j-1)_{3:0}$ is the four sum bits generated by the adder. *A2* adds g_o or g_e with $H^*(i-1,j)$ or $F^*(i-1,j)$ based on the value of control signal $S1$, and generates $F^*(i,j)$. *A3* adds the g_o or g_e to $H^*(i,j-1)$ or $E^*(i,j-1)$ based on the value of control signal $S2$, and generates $E^*(i,j)$.

2. *M1*, *M2* and *M3* are 6-bit maximum generation units. *M1* outputs the maximum of $F^*(i-1,j)$ and $E^*(i,j-1)$. *M2* compares the output of *M1* with $H^*(i-1,j-1)$ and outputs the maximum of the two.

3. *C1* and *C2* units generate control signals, $S1$ and $S2$, respectively. Each of these units consists of a 6-bit subtracter and a 4-bit comparator. In *C1* the inequality, $(H^*(i-1,j) - F^*(i-1,j)) < (g_o - g_e)$, is tested, and if it is true, $S1$ is set. In *C2*, the inequality, $(H^*(i,j-1) - E^*(i,j-1)) < (g_o - g_e)$, is tested, and if it is true, $S2$ is set.

4. *SB1* and *SB2* are 2-bit subtracters which compute $D(i,j)$ and $D(i,j-1)$, respectively. $D(i,j)$ is sent to the next cell. $D(i,j-1)$ is used in the generation of $H(i,j-1)$.

5. *M3* and *M4* are 16-bit maximum generation units, these units compare the maximum value from the previous cell, $M(i-1,j)$ the maximum value generated in this cell, and the score generated in the previous iteration, $M(i,j-1)$ and generate the maximum of three as $M(i,j)$. By this way maximum value generated in each alignment is passed up to the last cell.

Table 1. The Units In The Proposed and Reference [6] SW Cells

		16-Bit Score			24-Bit Score			32-Bit Score		
		16-bit	12-bit	6-bit	24-bit	18-bit	6-bit	32-bit	28-bit	6-bit
Adders	Ref.	5	-	-	5	-	-	5	-	-
	Prop.	-	1	6	-	1	6	-	1	6
Max. Gen	Ref.	5	-	-	5	-	-	5	-	-
	Prop.	2	-	4	2	-	4	2	-	4
FFs	Ref.	109			157			205		
	Prop.	79			105			121		

6. Registers $R0$ to $R9$ stores the values, $H(i, j-1)$, $D(i, j-1)$, $H(i-1, j-1)_{15:4} + S(q_i, p_j)$, $H^*(i, j-1)$, $E^*(i, j-1)$, $F^*(i-1, j)$, $S1$, $S2$, $Max(i, j)$, p_{j+1}, g_o, and g_e, respectively.

4   Results

The SW implementations designed by using the presented methods in this paper are compared with the SW implementations designed by the methods presented in [6]. Chow *et. al*'s work is chosen as reference, since most of the previous studies use similar design strategies and/or use their work as reference. The maximum generation function in the reference and presented designs are implemented using the method presented in [5]. Table 1 presents the main units in the proposed and the reference SW cells, except the LUTs. These main units are the adders, the maximum generation units, and the registers. Instead of giving the numbers of various sizes of the registers the total number of FFs are given. The scaling advantage of the proposed designs over the reference designs can be observed in Table 1. As the score precision increases, the sizes of one adder, two maximum generation units, and three registers in the proposed SW cell increase, while the sizes of all units increase in the reference SW cell.

To compare the proposed and the reference designs by syntheses, VHDL codes for 16, 24 and 32-bit implementations are written. Each of these implementations consists of 100 cells. The ASIC syntheses are performed using Leonardo Synthesis Tool and TSMC 0.18 micron technology cells. The FPGA syntheses are performed using Xilinx's ISE 8.1 and Virtex II XC2V6000 platform. The individual SW cells are optimized for speed, and the systolic array structures are optimized for area with high effort. Table 2 presents the ASIC and FPGA syntheses results. This table shows the number of gates and clock frequencies for ASIC implementations, and the slice counts and the clock frequencies for FPGA implementations. In general, the presented designs are smaller and faster than the reference designs, and the percentage gains increase as the precisions of the designs increase. The frequency gains for the proposed ASIC implementations are especially significant. The frequencies of the proposed FPGA implementations do not change as the precision increases, but the frequencies of the reference FPGA

Table 2. The Syntheses Results For The Proposed and The Reference [6] SW Designs

		ASIC		FPGA	
		Gates	Freq(MHz.)	Slices	Freq(MHz.)
16-Bit	Ref	274,788	233.6	13,512	74.49
	Prop	197,605	102.3	9,170	80.97
	Gain	28 %	128 %	32 %	9 %
24-Bit	Prop	374,211	79.4	20,152	67.45
	Ref	233,812	195.8	11,257	80.97
	Gain	37 %	146 %	44 %	20 %
32-Bit	Ref	532,714	62.4	26,796	62.84
	Prop	296,215	157.6	13,899	80.97
	Gain	44 %	152 %	48 %	29 %

implementations decrease as the precision increases. The percentage hardware gains for the proposed FPGA implementations are significant as well. Since the hardware resources are fixed on FPGA platforms, the slice counts can be used to estimate the number of SW cells that can fit on a single device. For instance, the presented 24-bit SW designs can contain approximately 1.8 times more SW cells than the reference 24-bit implementation when both are mapped on an XC2V6000 FPGA platform.

5   Conclusion

This paper presented novel hardware designs for the local alignment of protein sequences. The main contribution of the presented work is the development of design techniques that improves the scaling of the implementations. The presented designs are compared with the reference implementations that are designed by the methods described in [6]. The comparisons of all designs are conducted by using ASIC and FPGA syntheses tools. In general, the syntheses results for the presented designs are better than the ones for the reference designs. The percentage frequency gains for the proposed ASIC implementations are especially outstanding. For example, the percentage frequency gain for the proposed 24-bit ASIC implementations is 146 %. On the other hand, for the proposed FPGA implementations the percentage hardware savings are up to 48 %. The frequency for FPGA implementations also do not decrease as the size of the design increases. FPGA implementations are ideal for sequence alignment applications that use variable cost values and the ASIC implementations are ideal for the sequence alignment applications that use fixed cost values. To improve the gains obtained by the presented techniques, mixed platforms that contain both ASIC and FPGA technology can be used to implement the proposed designs. Our future work will look for mapping the proposed designs on such platforms. Also, the application of the presented optimization techniques on other alignment algorithms will be studied.

References

1. Mount, D.W.: Bioinformatics and Genome Analysis. CSHL Press (2004)
2. T.F. Smith, M.W.: Identification of common molecular subsequences. Journal of Molecular Biology **147**(1) (1981) 195–197
3. Waterman, M., Eggert, M.: A new algorithm for best subsequence alignments with application to trna-rrna comparisons. Journal of Molecular Biology. **197** (1987) 723–728
4. Lopresti, D.: P-nac: systolic array for comparing nucleic acid sequences. Computer **20**(7) (1987) 98–99
5. Oliver, T.F., Schmidt, B., Maskell, D.L.: Hyper customized processors for bio-sequence database scanning on fpgas. In: FPGA. (2005) 229–237
6. Chow, E.T., Peterson, J.C., Waterman, M.S., Hunkapiller, T., Zimmermann, B.A.: A systolic array processor for biological information signal processing. In: ICS '91: Proceedings of the 5th international conference on Supercomputing, New York, NY, USA, ACM Press (1991) 216–223
7. Hoang, D.T., Lopresti, D.P.: FPGA implementation of systolic sequence alignment. In: Field-Programmable Gate Arrays: Architectures and Tools for Rapid Prototyping. (1992) 183–191
8. Guccione, S.A., Keller, E.: Gene matching using jbits. In: Field-Programmable Logic and Applications. (2002) 1168–1171
9. Yamaguchi, Y., Maruyama, T., Konagaya, A.: High speed homology search with fpgas. In: Pacific Symposium on Biocomputing. (2002) 271–282
10. Yu, C.W., Kwong, K.H., Lee, K.H., Leong, P.H.W.: A smith-waterman systolic cell. In: FPL. (2003) 375–384
11. Han, T., Parameswaran, S.: Swasad: An asic design for high speed dna sequence matching. In: ASP-DAC '02: Proceedings of the 2002 conference on Asia South Pacific design automation/VLSI Design, Washington, DC, USA, IEEE Computer Society (2002) 541
12. Smith, S.F.: A scalable coprocessor for bioinformatic sequence alignments. In: ESA/VLSI. (2004) 303–308
13. Lesk, A.M.: Introduction to Bioinformatics. Oxford University Press (2002)

A New Model of BAM: Alpha-Beta Bidirectional Associative Memories

María Elena Acevedo-Mosqueda[1], Cornelio Yáñez-Márquez[2],
and Itzamá López-Yáñez[3]

Centro de Investigación en Computación, Instituto Politécnico Nacional,
Laboratorio de Inteligencia Artificial,
Av. Juan de Dios Bátiz s/n, México, D. F., 07738, México
[1] eacevedo@ipn.mx
[2] cyanez@cic.ipn.mx
[3] ilopezb05@sagitario.cic.ipn.mx

Abstract. Most models of Bidirectional associative memories intend to achieve that all trained pattern correspond to stable states; however, this has not been possible. Also, none of the former models has been able to recall all the trained patterns. In this work we introduce a new model of bidirectional associative memory which is not iterative and has no stability problems. It is based on the Alpha-Beta associative memories. This model allows, besides correct recall of noisy patterns, perfect recall of all trained patterns, with no ambiguity and no conditions. An example of fingerprint recognition is presented.

Keywords: Bidirectional associative memories, Alpha-Beta associative memories, perfect recall.

1   Introduction

The first bidirectional associative memory (BAM), introduced by Kosko [1], was the base of many models presented later. Some of this models substituted the learning rule for an exponential rule [2-4]; others used the method of multiple training and dummy addition in order to reach a greater number of stable states [5], trying to eliminate spurious states. With the same purpose, linear programming techniques [6], and the descending gradient method [7-8] have been used, besides genetic algorithms [9] and BAM with delays [10-11]. Other models of non-iterative bidirectional associative memories exist, such as morphological BAM [12] and Feedforward BAM [13]. All these models have arisen to solve the problem of low pattern recall capacity shown by the BAM of Kosko. However, none has been able to recall all the trained patterns. Also, these models demand the fulfillment of some specific conditions, such as a certain Hamming distance between patterns, solvability by linear programming, orthogonality between patterns, among others.

  The model of bidirectional associative memory presented in this paper is based on the Alpha-Beta associative memories [14], is not an iterative process, and does not present stability problems. Pattern recall capacity of the Alpha-Beta BAM is maximal,

A. Levi et al. (Eds.): ISCIS 2006, LNCS 4263, pp. 286 – 295, 2006.

being $2^{\min(n,m)}$, where m and n are the input and output patterns dimension, respectively. Also, it always shows perfect pattern recall without imposing any condition.

In section 2 we present the Alpha-Beta autoassociative memories, base of our new model of BAM, and the theoretical sustentation of Alpha-Beta BAM. In section 3 the model is applied to fingerprint recognition. Conclusions follow in section 4.

2   Alpha-Beta Bidirectional Associative Memory

In this section the proposed model of bidirectional associative memory is presented. However, since it is based on the Alpha-Beta autoassociative memories, a summary of this model will be given before presenting our proposal, the new model of bidirectional associative memory.

2.1   Alpha-Beta Associative Memories

Basic concepts about associative memories were established three decades ago in [15-17], nonetheless here we use the concepts, results and notation introduced in the Yáñez-Márquez's PhD Thesis [14]. An associative memory $\mathbf{M}$ is a system that relates input patterns, and outputs patterns, as follows: $\mathbf{x} \rightarrow \mathbf{M} \rightarrow \mathbf{y}$ with $\mathbf{x}$ and $\mathbf{y}$ the input and output pattern vectors, respectively. Each input vector forms an association with a corresponding output vector. For k integer and positive, the corresponding association will be denoted as $\left(x^k, y^k\right)$. Associative memory $\mathbf{M}$ is represented by a matrix whose ij-th component is m_{ij}. Memory $\mathbf{M}$ is generated from an *a priori* finite set of known associations, known as the fundamental set of associations.

If μ is an index, the fundamental set is represented as: $\left\{ \left(x^\mu, y^\mu\right) \middle| \mu = 1,2,...,p \right\}$ with p the cardinality of the set. The patterns that form the fundamental set are called fundamental patterns. If it holds that $x^\mu = y^\mu, \forall \mu \in \left\{1,2,...,p\right\}$, $\mathbf{M}$ is *autoassociative*, otherwise it is *heteroassociative*; in this case it is possible to establish that $\exists \mu \in \left\{1,2,...,p\right\}$ for which $x^\mu \neq y^\mu$. A distorted version of a pattern x^k to be recalled will be denoted as $\tilde{x}^k$. If when feeding a distorted version of x^ϖ with $\varpi = \left\{1,2,...,p\right\}$ to an associative memory $\mathbf{M}$, it happens that the output corresponds exactly to the associated pattern y^ϖ, we say that recall is perfect.

Among the variety of associative memory models described in the scientific literature, there are two models that, because of their relevance, it is important to emphasize: morphological associative memories which were introduced by Ritter *et al.* [18], and Alpha-Beta associative memories, which were introduced in [14, 19-20]. Because of their excellent characteristics, which allow them to be superior in many aspects to other models for associative memories [18], morphological associative memories served as starter point for the creation and development of the Alpha-Beta associative memories.

The Alpha-Beta associative memories are of two kinds and are able to operate in two different modes. The operator α is useful at the learning phase, and the operator β is the basis for the pattern recall phase. The properties within the algebraic operators

α and β, allow the Alpha-Beta memories to exhibit similar characteristics to the ones inherent to the binary version of the morphological associative memories, in the sense of: learning capacity, type and amount of noise against which the memory is robust, and the sufficient conditions for perfect recall.

The heart of the mathematical tools used in the Alpha-Beta model, are two binary operators designed specifically for these memories. These operators are defined as follows: First, we define the sets A={0,1} and B={00,01,10}, then the operators α and β are defined in tabular form:

$$\alpha \; : \; A \times A \rightarrow B$$

x	y	$\alpha(x,y)$
0	0	01
0	1	00
1	0	10
1	1	01

$$\beta \; : \; B \times A \rightarrow A$$

x	y	$\beta(x,y)$
00	0	0
00	1	0
01	0	0
01	1	1
10	0	1
10	1	1

The sets A and B, the α and β operators, along with the usual $\wedge$ (minimum) y $\vee$ (maximum) operators, form the algebraic system $(A,B,\alpha,\beta,\wedge,\vee)$ which is the mathematical basis for the Alpha-Beta associative memories.

The ij-th entry of the matrix $y \oplus x^t$ is: $\left[y \oplus x^t \right]_{ij} = \alpha(y_i, x_j)$.

If we consider the fundamental set of patterns: $\left\{ (x^\mu, y^\mu) \middle| \mu = 1,2,\ldots,p \right\}$ where

$$x^\mu = \begin{pmatrix} x_1^\mu \\ x_2^\mu \\ \vdots \\ x_n^\mu \end{pmatrix} \in A^n \qquad\qquad y^\mu = \begin{pmatrix} y_1^\mu \\ y_2^\mu \\ \vdots \\ y_m^\mu \end{pmatrix} \in A^m$$

then, the ij-th entry of the matrix $y^\mu \oplus \left(x^\mu\right)^t$ is: $\left[y^\mu \oplus \left(x^\mu\right)^t \right]_{ij} = \alpha\left(y_i^\mu, x_j^\mu\right)$

The following two important results, which were obtained in [14], are presented:

Let $x \in A^n$ and let **P** be a matrix of dimensions $m \times n$. The operation $\mathbf{P}_{m \times n} \bigcup_\beta x$ gives as a result a column vector of dimension m, with i-th component:

$$\left(\mathbf{P}_{m \times n} \bigcup_\beta x \right)_i = \bigvee_{j=1}^n \beta(p_{ij}, x_j).$$

Let $x \in A^n$ and let **P** be a matrix of dimensions $m \times n$. The operation $\mathbf{P}_{m \times n} \bigcap_\beta x$ gives as a result a column vector of dimension m, with i-th component:

$$\left(\mathbf{P}_{m \times n} \bigcap_\beta x \right)_i = \bigwedge_{j=1}^n \beta(p_{ij}, x_j).$$

Below are shown some characteristics of Alpha-Beta autoassociative memories:

1. The fundamental set takes the form $\{(\mathbf{x}^\mu, \mathbf{x}^\mu) \mid \mu = 1, 2, ..., p\}$.
2. Both input and output fundamental patterns are of the same dimension, denoted by n.
3. The memory is a square matrix, for both kinds, $\mathbf{V}$ and Λ. If $\mathbf{x}^\mu \in A^n$ then

$$v_{ij} = \bigvee_{\mu=1}^{p} \alpha\left(x_i^\mu, x_j^\mu\right) \quad \text{and} \quad \lambda_{ij} = \bigwedge_{\mu=1}^{p} \alpha\left(x_i^\mu, x_j^\mu\right)$$

and since $\alpha\colon A \times A \to B$, v_{ij} and $\lambda_{ij} \in B$, $\forall i \in \{1, 2, ..., n\}$, $\forall j \in \{1, 2, ..., n\}$.

In the recall phase, when a pattern $\mathbf{x}^\mu$ is presented to memories $\mathbf{V}$ and Λ, the i-th components of recalled patterns are:

$$\left(\mathbf{V}\Delta_\beta \mathbf{x}^\omega\right)_i = \bigwedge_{j=1}^{n} \beta(v_{ij}, x_j^\omega) \quad \text{and} \quad \left(\Lambda\nabla_\beta \mathbf{x}^\omega\right)_i = \bigvee_{j=1}^{n} \beta(\lambda_{ij}, x_j^\omega)$$

2.2   Alpha-Beta Bidirectional Associative Memories

The model proposed in this paper has been named Alpha-Beta BAM since Alpha-Beta associative memories, both *max* and *min*, play a central role in the model design. However, before going into detail over the processing of an Alpha-Beta BAM, we will define the following.

In this work we will assume that Alpha-Beta associative memories have a fundamental set denoted by $\{(\mathbf{x}^\mu, \mathbf{y}^\mu) \mid \mu = 1, 2, ..., p\}$ $\mathbf{x}^\mu \in A^n$ and $\mathbf{y}^\mu \in A^m$, with $A = \{0, 1\}$, $n \in \mathbf{Z}^+$, $p \in \mathbf{Z}^+$, $m \in \mathbf{Z}^+$ and $1 < p \leq \min(2^n, 2^m)$. Also, it holds that all input patterns are different; M that is $\mathbf{x}^\mu = \mathbf{x}^\xi$ if and only if $\mu = \xi$. If $\forall \mu \in \{1, 2, ... p\}$ it holds that $\mathbf{x}^\mu = \mathbf{y}^\mu$, the Alpha-Beta memory will be *autoassociative*; if on the contrary, the former affirmation is negative, that is $\exists \mu \in \{1, 2, ..., p\}$ for which it holds that $\mathbf{x}^\mu \neq \mathbf{y}^\mu$, then the Alpha-Beta memory will be *heteroassociative*.

Definition 1 (One-Hot). *Let the set A be $A = \{0, 1\}$ and $p \in \mathbf{Z}^+$, $p > 1$, $k \in \mathbf{Z}^+$, such that $1 \leq k \leq p$. The k-th one-hot vector of p bits is defined as vector $h^k \in A^P$ for which it holds that the k-th component is $h_k^k = 1$ and the rest of the components are $h_j^k = 0$, $\forall j \neq k$, $1 \leq j \leq p$.*

Remark 1. In this definition, the value $p = 1$ is excluded since a one-hot vector of dimension 1, given its essence, has no reason to be.

Definition 2 (Zero-Hot). *Let the set A be $A = \{0, 1\}$ and $p \in \mathbf{Z}^+$, $p > 1$, $k \in \mathbf{Z}^+$, such that $1 \leq k \leq p$. The k-th zero-hot vector of p bits is defined as vector $\overline{\mathbf{h}}^k \in A^P$ for which it holds that the k-th component is $h_k^k = 0$ and the rest of the components are $h_j^k = 1$, $\forall j \neq k$, $1 \leq j \leq p$.*

Remark 2. In this definition, the value $p = 1$ is excluded since a zero-hot vector of dimension 1, given its essence, has no reason to be.

Definition 3 (Expansion vectorial transform). *Let the set A be A = {0, 1} and n∈ $\mathbf{Z}^+$, y m∈ $\mathbf{Z}^+$. Given two arbitrary vectors* $\mathbf{x} \in A^n$ *and* $\mathbf{e} \in A^m$, *the expansion vectorial transform of order m,* $t : A^n \to A^{n+m}$, *is defined as* $t(\mathbf{x}, \mathbf{e}) = \mathbf{X} \in A^{n+m}$, *a vector whose components are:* $X_i = x_i$ *for* $1 \le i \le n$ *and* $X_i = e_i$ *for* $n + 1 \le i \le n + m$.

Definition 4 (Contraction vectorial transform). *Let the set A be A = {0, 1} and n∈ $\mathbf{Z}^+$, y m∈ $\mathbf{Z}^+$ such that* $1 \le m < n$. *Given one arbitrary vector* $\mathbf{X} \in A^{n+m}$, *the contraction vectorial transform of order m,* $t : A^{n+m} \to A^m$, *is defined as* $t(X, m) = \mathbf{c} \in A^m$, *a vector whose components are:* $c_i = X_{i+n}$ *for* $1 \le i < m$.

In both directions, the model is made up by two stages, as shown in figure 1.

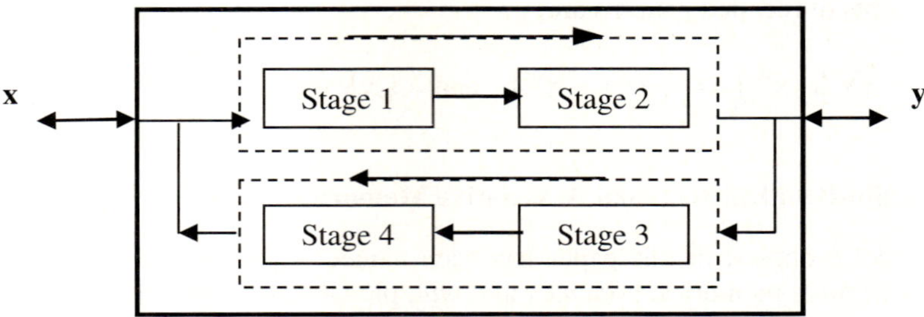

Fig. 1. Graphical schematics of the Alpha-Beta bidirectional associative memory

For simplicity, first will be described the process necessary in one direction, in order to later present the complementary direction which will give bidirectionality to the model (see figure 2).

The function of Stage 2 is to offer a $\mathbf{y}^k$ as output ($k = 1, ..., p$) given a $\mathbf{x}^k$ as input.

Now we assume that as input to Stage 2 we have one element of a set of p orthonormal vectors. Recall that the *Linear Associator* has perfect recall when it works with orthonormal vectors. In this work we use a variation of the *Linear Associator* in order to obtain $\mathbf{y}^k$, parting from a *one-hot* vector $\mathbf{v}^k$ in its k-th coordinate.

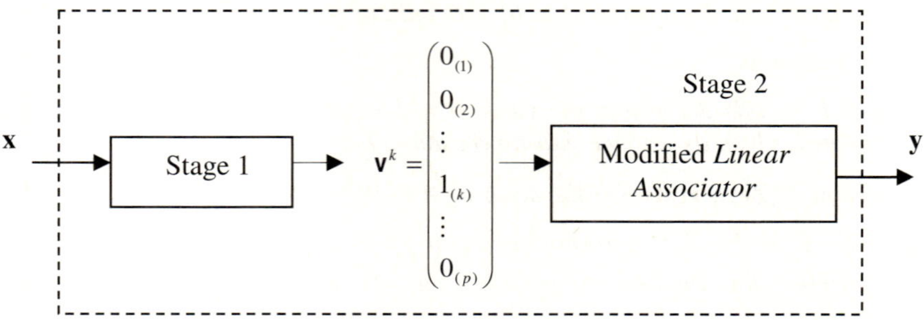

Fig. 2. Schematics of the process done in the direction from $\mathbf{x}$ to $\mathbf{y}$. Here are shown only Stage 1 and Stage 2. $v_k{}^k = 1$, $v_i{}^k = 0$ $\forall i \neq k$, $1 \le i \le p$, $1 \le k \le p$.

For the construction of the modified Linear Associator, its learning phase is skipped and a matrix $\mathbf{M}$ representing the memory is built. Each column in this matrix corresponds to each output pattern $\mathbf{y}^{\mu}$. In this way, when matrix $\mathbf{M}$ is operated with a one-hot vector $\mathbf{v}^{k}$, the corresponding $\mathbf{y}^{k}$ will always be recalled.

The task of Stage 1 is: given a $\mathbf{x}^{k}$ or a noisy version of it ($\tilde{\mathbf{x}}^{k}$), the *one-hot* vector $\mathbf{v}^{k}$ must be obtained without ambiguity and with no condition. In its learning phase, stage 1 has the following algorithm:

1. For each index $k \in \{1, ..., p\}$ do expansion $\mathbf{X}^{k} = \tau^{e}(\mathbf{x}^{k}, \mathbf{h}^{k})$
2. Build an Alpha-Beta autoassociative memory max $\mathbf{V}$ with fundamental set

$$\left\{ \left(\mathbf{X}^{k}, \mathbf{X}^{k} \right) \mid k = 1,..., p \right\}$$

3. For each index $k \in \{1, ..., p\}$ do expansion $\overline{\mathbf{X}}^{k} = \tau^{e}(\mathbf{x}^{k}, \overline{\mathbf{h}}^{k})$
4. Build an Alpha-Beta autoassociative memory min Λ with fundamental set

$$\left\{ \left(\overline{\mathbf{X}}^{k}, \overline{\mathbf{X}}^{k} \right) \mid k = 1,..., p \right\}$$

Recall phase is described through the following algorithm:

1. Present, at the input to stage 1, a vector from the fundamental set $\mathbf{x}^{\mu} \in A^{n}$, for some index $\mu \in \{1, ..., p\}$.

2. Build vector $\mathbf{u} \in A^{p}$ in the following manner: $\mathbf{u} = \sum_{i=1}^{p} \mathbf{h}^{i}$

3. Do expansion $\mathbf{F} = \tau^{e}(\mathbf{x}^{\mu}, \mathbf{u}) \in A^{n+p}$

4. Operate Alpha-Beta autoassociative memory max $\mathbf{V}$ with $\mathbf{F}$, in order to obtain a vector $\mathbf{R}$ of dimension $n + p$: $\mathbf{R} = \mathbf{V}\Delta_{\beta}\mathbf{F} \in A^{n+p}$

5. Do contraction $\mathbf{r} = \tau^{c}(\mathbf{R}, n) \in A^{p}$

6. If ($\exists\, k \in \{1, ..., p\}$ such that $\mathbf{h} = \mathbf{r}^{k}$) it is assured that $k = \mu$, and the result is $\mathbf{h}^{\mu}$. STOP.
   Else:

7. Build vector $\mathbf{w} \in A^{p}$ so that $w_{i} = u_{i} - 1, \forall i \in \left\{ 1,..., p \right\}$

8. Do expansion $\mathbf{G} = \tau^{e}(\mathbf{x}^{\mu}, \mathbf{w}) \in A^{n+p}$

9. Operate Alpha-Beta autoassociative memory min Λ with $\mathbf{G}$, in order to obtain a vector $\mathbf{S}$ of dimension $n + p$: $\mathbf{S} = \Lambda\nabla_{\beta}\mathbf{G} \in A^{n+p}$

10. Do contraction $\mathbf{s} = \tau^{c}(\mathbf{S}^{\mu}, n) \in A^{p}$

11. If ($\exists\, k \in \{1, ..., p\}$ such that $\overline{\mathbf{h}}^{k} = \mathbf{s}$) then it is assured that $k = \mu$, and the result is $\mathbf{h}^{\mu}$. STOP.
    Else:

12. Do operation $\mathbf{r} \wedge \overline{\mathbf{s}}$, where $\wedge$ is the symbol of the logical AND operator, and $\overline{\mathbf{s}}$ is the negated vector of $\mathbf{s}$. The result of this operation is $\mathbf{h}^{\mu}$.
STOP.

The process in the contrary direction, which is presenting pattern $\mathbf{y}^k$ ($k = 1, ..., p$) as input to the Alpha/Beta BAM and obtaining its corresponding $\mathbf{x}^k$, is very similar to the one described above. The task of Stage 3 is to obtain a one-hot vector $\mathbf{v}^k$ given a $\mathbf{y}^k$. Stage 4 is a modified Linear Associator built in similar fashion to the one in Stage 2.

Now, lets analyze the time complexity of this algorithm; in particular that of the recalling phase, since this is the portion of the whole algorithm that requires a greater number of elemental operations. If we define EO as elemental operation, *n_pares* as the number of associated pairs of patterns, and n as the dimension of the patterns plus the addition of the *one-hot* or *zero-hot* vectors, the algorithm of the recalling phase can be summarized as:

```
u = 0; (1)
   while(u<n_pares) (2)
          i = 0;  (3)
            while(i<n)  (4)
                  j = 0;  (5)
                    while(j<n)  (6)
                            if(y[u][i]==0 && y[u][j]==0) (7)
                                        t=1;  (8)
                            else if(y[u][i]==0 && y[u][j]==1) (9a)
                                        t=0;
                            else if(y[u][i]==1 && y[u][j]==0) (9b)
                                        t=2;
                            else               t=1;
                            if(u==0) (10)
                                        Vy[i][j]=t; (11)
                            else
                                    if(Vy[i][j]<t)  (12)
                                            Vy[i][j]=t;  (13)
                            j++;  (14)
                  i++;  (15)
          u++;  (16)
```

(1)   1 EO, assignation

(2)   *n_pares* EO, comparison

(3)   *n_pares* EO, assignation

(4)   *n_pares*n EO, comparison

(5)   *n_pares*n EO, assignation

(6)   *n_pares*n*n EO, comparison

(7a) *n_pares*n*n EO, comparison: y[u][i]==0

(7b) *n_pares*n*n EO, relational operation AND: &&

(7c) *n_pares*n*n EO, comparison: y[u][j]==0

(8) There is always an allocation to variable t, *n_pares*n*n EO

(9) Both a and b have the same probability of being executed, *n_pares*n*(n/2)

(10) *n_pares*n*n EO, comparison

(11) This allocation is done only once, 1 EO

(12) (*n_pares*n*n)-1 EO, comparison

(13) Allocation has half probability of being run, *n_pares*n*(n/2)

(14) $n\_pares*n*n$ EO increment
(15) $n\_pares*n$ EO, increment
(16) n_pares EO, increment

The total number of EO's is: Total = $1+n\_pares(3+3n+9\ n^2)$

From the total of EO's obtained, n_pares is fixed with value 50, resulting in a function only dependant on the size of the patterns: $f(n) = 1+50(3+3n+9n^2)$.

Let f and g be functions from a set of integer or real numbers to a set of real numbers. Now, using the Big-O notation, it is said that $f(x)$ is $O(g(x))$ if there exist two constants C and k such that: $|f(x)| \le C\ |g(x)|$ when $x > k$

The number of elemental operations obtained from our algorithm was:

$$f(n) = 1+50(3+3n+9\ n^2)$$

A function $g(x)$ and constants C and k must be found, such that the inequality holds. We propose: $50(3n^2+3n^2+9n^2) = 150n^2+150n^2+450n^2 =750n^2$

Then if $g(n) = n^2$, $C = 750$ and $k = 1$, we have that

$$|f(n)| \le 750\ |g(n)| \text{when } n > 1, \text{therefore } O(n^2).$$

3   Simulations

The Alpha-Beta BAM model was applied as a Fingerprint Identifier. The fingerprints used were obtained from the Fingerprint Verification Competition (FPV2000) located at the web page `http://bias.csr.unibo.it/fvc2000/download.asp`. Originally the images have dimensions of 240 x 320 pixels. The image editing software *Advanced Batch Converter* was used to crop the size of the images in order to fit 40 fingerprints in one screen, thus ending with dimensions of 80 x 170 pixels. Each fingerprint was associated to a number, from 1 to 40 inclusive. These numbers are images of 10 x 10 pixels. Both sets of images, fingerprints and numbers, are binary.

The process of creation of the Alpha-Beta BAM amounts to 1 minute and 34 seconds, approximately. For this purpose a Sony® VAIO® laptop, equipped with an Intel® Pentium® 4 processor at 2.8 GHz was used.

The program allows choosing an input pattern among both sets of images. If the chosen input pattern is a number then, automatically, the chosen number and its corresponding output pattern, which will be a fingerprint, are shown (see figure 3a). If the chosen image is a fingerprint, then the fingerprint and its corresponding recalled pattern are shown (see figure 3b).

First, we choose as input patterns each one of the 40 fingerprints, and all corresponding output patterns were perfectly recalled. Then, every number image was chosen as input pattern, and again the corresponding fingerprints were perfectly recalled.

For recall in both directions, no condition whatsoever was imposed; this means that the patterns did not need to be orthonormals, nor have a certain Hamming distance between them. Our model does not need convergence of a solution and has no stability problems.

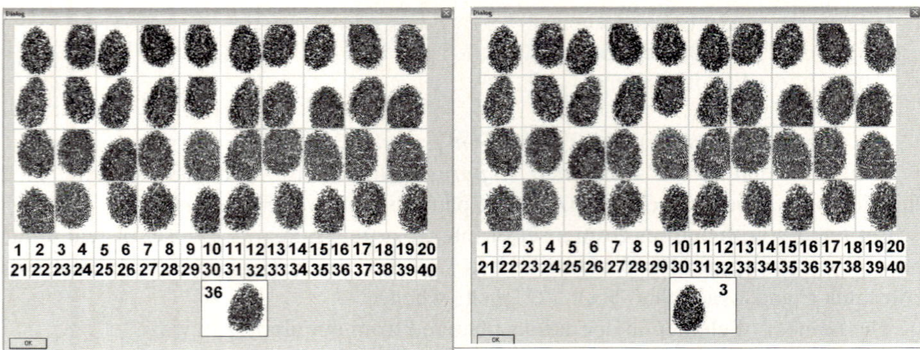

Fig. 3. The bidirectional process of the model is shown in both screens. (a) A number is chosen as input pattern and its corresponding fingerprint is perfectly recalled. (b) The input pattern is now a fingerprint, its corresponding output pattern a number.

4   Conclusions

Presented results show that the Alpha-Beta BAM model, introduced in this paper, has perfect recall of all patterns in the fundamental set. This perfect recall requires no condition. The trained patterns do not need to fulfill certain properties for the Alpha-Beta BAM to be able to recall them in a perfect manner. The algorithm of this BAM is not an iterative process and does not require convergence for its solution; also, it does not present any stability problem.

Acknowledgements. The authors would like to thank the Instituto Politécnico Nacional (Secretaría Académica, COFAA, SIP, and CIC), the CONACyT, and SNI for their economical support to develop this work.

References

1. Kosko, B.: Bidirectional associative memories, IEEE Transactions on Systems, Man, and Cybernetics, Vol. 18, No. 1 (1988) 49-60.
2. Jeng, Y.-J., Yeh, C.-C., Chiveh, T.D.: Exponential bidirectional associative memories, Electronics Letters, Vol. 26, Issue 11 (1990) 717-718
3. Wang, W.-J., Lee, D.-L.: Modified exponential bidirectional associative memories, Electronics Letters, Vol. 28, Issue 9 (1992) 888-890Chen, S., Gao, H., Yan, W.: Improved exponential bidirectional associative memory, Electronics Letters, Vol. 33, Issue 3 (1997) 223-224
5. Wang, Y.-F., Cruz J. B., Jr., Mulligan, Jr.: Two coding strategies for bidirectional associative memory, IEEE Transactions on Neural Networks, Vol. 1, Issue 1 (1990) 81-92
6. Wang, Y.-F., Cruz J. B., Jr., Mulligan, Jr.: Guaranteed recall of all training pairs for bidirectional associative memory, IEEE Transactions on Neural Networks, Vol. 1, Issue 6 (1991) 559-56
7. Perfetti, R.: Optimal gradient descent learning for bidirectional associative memories, Electronics Letters, Vol. 29, Issue 17 (1993) 1556-1557

8. Zheng, G., Givigi, S. N., Zheng, W.: A New Strategy for Designing Bidirectional Associative Memories, Lecture Notes in Computer Science, Springer-Verlag, Vol. 3496 (2005) 398-403

9. Shen, D., Cruz, J. B., Jr.: Encoding strategy for maximum noise tolerance bidirectional associative memory, IEEE Transactions on Neural Networks, Vol. 16, Issue 2 (2005) 293-300

10. Arik, S.: Global asymptotic stability analysis of bidirectional associative memory neural networks with time delays, IEEE Transactions on Neural Networks, Vol. 16, No. 3 (2005) 580-585

11. Park, J.: Robust stability of bidirectional associative memory neural networks with time delays, Physics Letters A, Vol. 349 (2006) 494-499

12. Ritter, G. X., Diaz-de-Leon, J. L., Sussner, P.: Morphological bidirectional associative memories, Neural Networks, Vol. 12 (1999) 851-867

13. Wu,Y., Pados, D. A.: A feedforward bidirectional associative memory, IEEE Transactions on Neural Networks, Vol. 11, Issue 4 (2000) 859-866

14. Yáñez-Márquez, C.: Associative Memories Based on Order Relations and Binary Operators (In Spanish). PhD Thesis. Center for Computing Research, México (2002)Kohonen, T.: Self-Organization and Associative Memory. Springer-Verlag, Berlin Heidelberg New York (1989)Hassoun, M. H.: Associative Neural Memories. Oxford University Press, New York (1993)

17. Kohonen, T.: Correlation Matrix Memories. IEEE Transactions on Computers. 21(4) (1972) 353-359

18. Ritter, G. X., Sussner, P., Diaz-de-Leon, J. L.: Morphological Associative Memories. IEEE Transactions on Neural Networks. 9 (1998) 281-293

19. Yáñez-Márquez, C., Díaz de León-Santiago, J. L.: Memorias Asociativas Basadas en Relaciones de Orden y Operaciones Binarias. Computación y Sistemas. México, 6(4) (2003) 300-311

20. Yáñez-Márquez, C., Díaz de León-Santiago, J. L.: Memorias Asociativas con Respuesta Perfecta y Capacidad Infinita. In: Albornoz, A., Alvarado, M. (eds.): Taller de Inteligencia Artificial TAINA'99. México (1999) 245-257

PARM: Data Structure for Efficient Volume Ray Casting

Sukhyun Lim and Byeong-Seok Shin

Inha University, Dept. Computer Science and Information Engineering,
253 Yonghyun-dong, Nam-gu, Inchon, 402-751, Rep. of Korea
slim@inhaian.net, bsshin@inha.ac.kr

Abstract. We propose a new data structure to accelerate the color computation step of CPU-based volume ray casting. To ensure interactive frame rates on a PC platform, we store interpolated scalar value and gradient vector required for color computation step in volume ray casting. However, it is difficult to store those two values in preprocessing step because sample points can lie in arbitrary position in a cell. Therefore, after determining candidate cells that contribute to the final images, we partition each candidate cell into several sub-cells. Then, we store trilinearly interpolated scalar value and an index of encoded gradient vector for each sub-cell. Because the information that requires time-consuming computations is already stored in our data structure, color values are determined without further computations.

1 Introduction

Volume visualization is a research area that deals with various techniques to extract meaningful and visual information from volume data [1], [2]. Volume datasets can be represented by *voxels*, and adjacent eight voxels form a cube called a *cell*. One of the most frequently applied techniques is direct volume rendering, producing high-quality 3D rendered images directly from volume data without intermediate representation. Volume ray casting is a well-known direct volume rendering method [1]. In general, it is composed of two steps [3]: after a ray advances through transparent region (*leaping step*), the ray integrates colors and opacities as it penetrates an object boundary (*color computation step*). Although volume ray casting produces high-quality images, the rendering speed is too slow. To solve the problem, a number of researchers have concentrated on skipping over transparent region because the region does not contribute to the final images [3]. However, computing color values from an object boundary also requires several time-consuming calculations such as trilinear interpolation and gradient vector estimation. To avoid these calculations, we propose a data structure that stores the information required to compute color values of the volume ray casting. At preprocessing time, after determining candidate cells that contribute to the final images, we divide each candidate cell into several sub-cells. Then, we store trilinearly interpolated scalar value and an index of encoded gradient vector for each sub-cell. During the rendering stage, when a ray lies on an arbitrary sample point in a candidate cell after skipping over transparent region, a color value can be determined

A. Levi et al. (Eds.): ISCIS 2006, LNCS 4263, pp. 296–305, 2006.

without time-consuming computations because most values to compute a color value are already stored in our data structure. As a result, our method is at least 53% faster than conventional methods.

The next section gives a brief description of previous work, and we explain our data structure in detail. In Section 4, we present a method for reducing the storage. Experimental results are presented in Section 5. Finally, we conclude our work.

2 Related Work

Several software-based acceleration techniques for direct volume rendering have been proposed to reduce rendering time. Yagel and Kaufman exploited the use of a ray template to accelerate ray traversal, using spatial coherence of the ray trajectory [4]. However, it is difficult to apply their method to applications involving perspective projection. The shear-warp method introduced by Lacroute and Levoy rearranges the voxels in memory to allow optimized ray traversal (shearing the volume dataset) [5]. Although this method can produce images from reasonable volumes at quasi-interactive frame rate, image quality is sacrificed because bilinear interpolation is used as a convolution kernel. Parker et al. demonstrated a full-featured ray tracer on a workstation with large shared memory [6]. Unfortunately, this method requires 128 CPUs for interactive rendering and is specialized for isosurface rendering. Although Knittel presented the interleaving of voxel addresses and deep optimizations (by using the MMX^{TM} instruction) to improve the cache hit ratio [7], it generates only 256×256 pixel images. If we want a high-resolution image, the 256×256 image can be magnified by using graphics hardware. Mora et al. proposed a high performance projection method that exploits a spread-memory layout called object-order ray casting [8]. However, this also does not support perspective projection. Grimm et al. introduced acceleration structures [9]. They used a gradient cache, and a memory-efficient hybrid removal and skipping technique for transparent regions. This method achieves fast rendering on a commodity notebook PC, but it is not applicable to perspective projection.

3 PARM(Precomputed scAlar and gRadient Map)

Our method focuses on accelerating color computation step of volume ray casting. Through the next section, we can recognize the method to accelerate the step.

3.1 Review of Color Computation Step in Volume Ray Casting

The color computations step in volume ray casting is composed of three steps. First, when a ray lies on arbitrary sample point in a cell, it computes a scalar value by using a resampling operation for transparency evaluation. In general, a trilinear interpolation is exploited as the resampling filter in volume ray casting. Since the trilinear interpolation is composed of seven linear interpolations, the computation speed is slow.

Second, the ray evaluates the eight gradient vectors in eight voxels of the cell. Although there are several methods to estimate the gradient vector in a voxel [10], [11], most of them randomly access the memory and take a long time to compute it. In addition, to compute the gradient vector for the sample point in the cell, we have to estimate eight gradient vectors in the enclosing eight voxels of the cell. This causes increasing the rendering time.

Third, the ray interpolates the estimated eight gradient vectors by using trilinear interpolation to calculate the gradient vector for the sample point. To compute it, we have to perform three trilinear interpolations because a gradient vector has three components (x-, y-, and z-element).

These three steps are repeated for all rays. From the first to third step, we can recognize that the color computation step can be accelerated when trilinearly interpolated scalar value and gradient vector for a sample point in a cell are already computed. Our method is motivated the fact that we precompute the values at preprocessing time, and refer to them in the rendering stage. For this reason, we propose a new data structure to store the values.

3.2 Generation of PARM

We call a cell of which the enclosing eight voxels are all transparent as a *transparent cell*, and a cell with eight opaque voxels is an *opaque cell*. The *candidate cell* means a cell that contributes to the final images. After dividing each candidate cell into N_{sc}^{3} cells, where N_{sc} is a representative on one axis to divide one candidate cell into several cells, we call the resulting cell as a *sub-cell*. That is, a single candidate cell contains N_{sc}^{3} sub-cells. Fig. 1 shows the structure of a candidate cell.

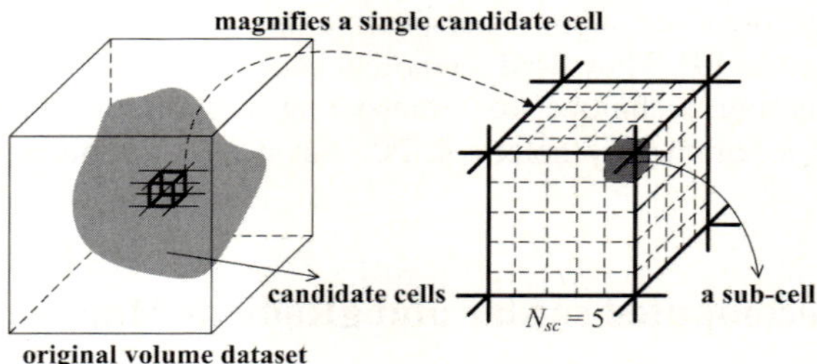

Fig. 1. Structure of a single candidate cell. A candidate cell is composed of several sub-cells. In this example, one candidate cell is composed of 125 sub-cells (that is, N_{sc}=5).

To generate our data structure, we determine candidate cells from the entire volume because we require large-sized memory if we generate it for entire cells. A simple way is to exploit an Opacity Transfer Function (OTF) proposed by Levoy [12]. Let the position where the transparency is changed from a transparent to a nontransparent region be τ. Based on τ, we determine the candidate cells. However, computing the positions of sample points is not feasible because the points can lie in an arbitrary position in a candidate cell. Therefore, after dividing each candidate cell into N_{sc}^{3} sub-cells, we compute the required values per sub-cell. From Section 3.1, we can recognize that the color computation step can be accelerated when trilinearly interpolated scalar value and gradient vector for a sample point are already computed. So, we store two items in the *DATA BUFFER*. Since the volume dataset and the user-defined N_{sc} value are determined and they are independent of viewing conditions, we can compute them at preprocessing time.

However, if we store trilinearly interpolated gradient vector, we require three bytes per a sub-cell because a vector is composed of three components (x-, y- and z-element). If the number of candidate cells is large, this is a burden. So, we apply the *gradient encoding method* proposed by Rusinkiewicz and Levoy [13]. This method maps the gradient vectors on a grid in each of the six faces of a cube. In conventional method [13], they exploited 52x52x6=16,224 different gradient vectors. However, we increase the grid size as 104x104x6 (approximately 2 bytes) to reduce visual artifacts. It leads to a mean error of below 0.01 radian. As a result, after computing trilinear interpolated gradient vector, we store an index.

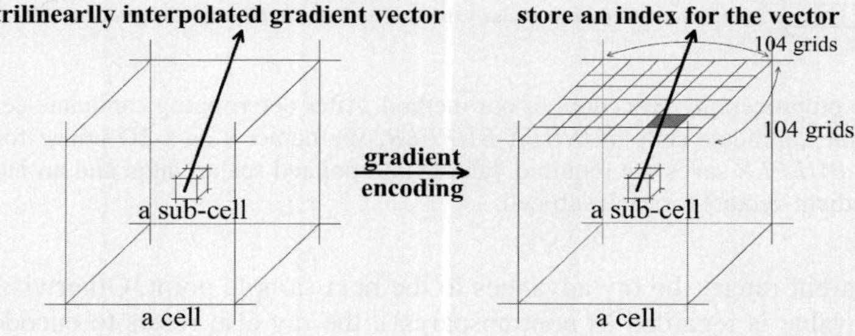

Fig. 2. By the gradient encoding method, we store an index of the gradient vector instead of three components of interpolated vector

To refer the computed values from the *DATA BUFFER*, we require a data structure stored on the indices of the candidate cells (we call it *INDEX BUFFER*). It has a null value when the scalar value of a voxel is less than τ, otherwise we store the accumulated indices of the candidate cells. As a result, our data structure is composed of two structures: *DATA BUFFER* and *INDEX BUFFER*. Fig. 3 illustrates the preprocessing procedure of our method. Even if one of the enclosing eight voxels of a cell is non-transparent, we regard it as a candidate cell. If not, visible artifacts can occur because the cell can contribute to the final images.

3.3 Ray Traversal Scheme

The ray-traversal procedure of our method is as follows: first, a ray is fired from each pixel on an image plane. After traversing the transparent cells using the conventional space-leaping methods, it reaches a candidate cell. Second, our method refers to an index of the candidate cell from the *INDEX BUFFER*, and selects the nearest sub-cell. Third, it refers to the precomputed scalar value from the *DATA BUFFER* by the index. Because the scalar value on a sample point is already interpolated in our data structure, it does not require time-consuming trilinear interpolation. If the value is within

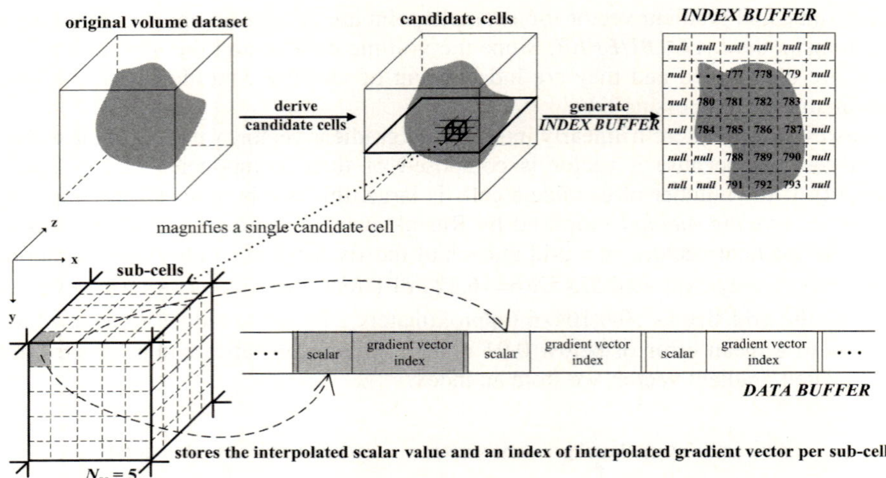

Fig. 3. The preprocessing procedure of our method. After determining candidate cells, we store indices of the candidate cells in *INDEX BUFFER*. We depict it as a 2D image for simplicity. The *DATA BUFFER* saves the required values (interpolated scalar value and an index of interpolated gradient vector) for each sub-cell.

the transparent range, the ray advances to the next sample point. Otherwise (that is, if the scalar value is regarded as nontransparent), the ray also refers to encoded gradient vector index from the *DATA BUFFER*. To decode representable vector from the index quickly, we use a lookup table [13]. Lastly, a color value is determined from the referred gradient vector. These steps continue for all rays of the image plane.

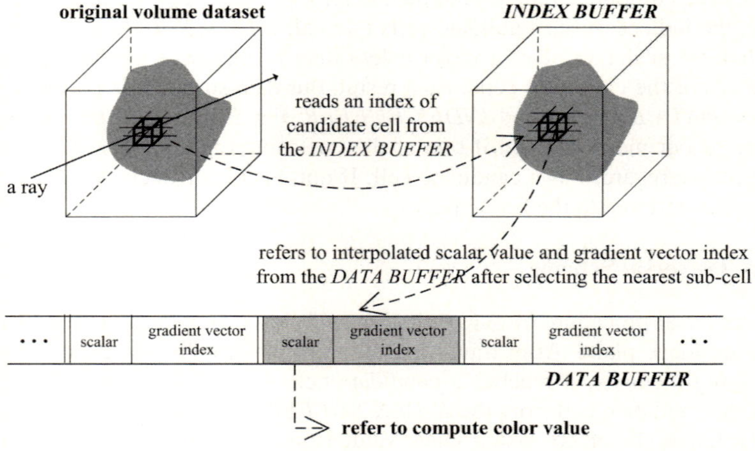

Fig. 4. An example of a ray traversal. If the ray reaches an arbitrary candidate cell, it refers to the trilinearly interpolated scalar value and an index of encoded interpolated gradient vector from the *DATA BUFFER* by referring an index through the *INDEX BUFFER*.

4 Techniques to Reduce Storage

Although the method using the transparency threshold value (τ) mentioned in Section 3.2 reduces the number of candidate cells, a lot of storage is required when the number of voxels with scalar values greater than τ is numerous. Therefore, we propose a view-independent method to reduce the number of candidate cells without affecting image quality. At preprocessing time, we define an outermost or innermost boundary based on τ. Then, we perform 3D morphological dilation or erosion to determine translucent region from the boundary. At the same time, we exploit the property that when a ray reaches a fully opaque cell during ray traversal in the rendering stage, the color computation for the ray is ended by the *Early Ray Termination* (ERT) scheme [12]. We use this property in the preprocessing stage without firing rays. On performing the 3D morphological operation, if the examining cell is enclosed by previously generated opaque cells, we disregard the cell, and mark it as opaque. In this case, rays are not entirely entered into the examining cell in rendering stage even it is transparent because the opacity values of them is already reached 1.0 in previously generated opaque cells. Therefore, the cell is skipped while the procedure to determine candidate cells in preprocessing step is completed. Fig. 5 illustrates our scheme.

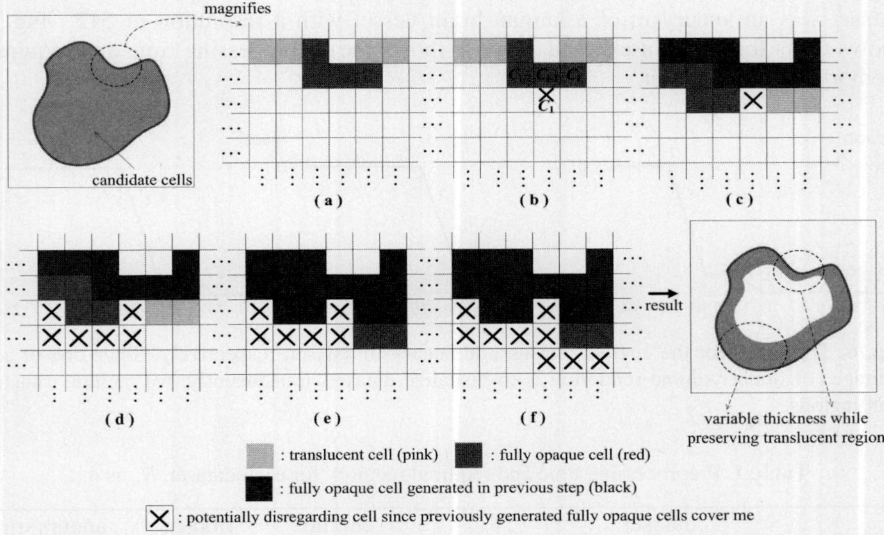

Fig. 5. A procedure to determine candidate cells possessing variable thickness. (a) Step 1: Outermost isosurface. (b) Step 2: The examining cell C_1 is enclosed by previously generated opaque cells ($C_{i-2} \sim C_i$) , so we disregard that cell C_1 (marked as **X**) since rays are entered into C_1 cell. (c) Step 3: 3D morphological erosion is performed from the previously generated cells without considering the C_1 cell. (d) Step 4: In the same way, we determine a potentially disregarding cell enclosing previously generated opaque cells, and mark it as **X**. (e) Step 5: Performing the morphological erosion operation once again without considering potentially disregarding cells marked **X**. (f) Step 6: We define potentially disregarding cells such as Step 2 and Step 4, and mark it as **X**. Then, the procedure is stopped because the boundary is fully enclosed with potentially disregarding cells.

If we stop the extraction procedure in the boundary, our method only renders an isosurface (that is, first-hit volume ray casting). However, by performing the 3D morphological operation, we determine the candidate cells including the translucent region. As a result, our method reduce a set of candidate cells in preprocessing time without firing rays while preserving translucent region.

When we deal with numerous candidate cells, the voxel size to store *INDEX BUFFER* is increased. To solve the problem, we exploit a summed-area table [14]. It contains the accumulated number of candidate cells along the z-axis, and the *INDEX BUFFER* stores only the indices of the candidate cells per xy-plane. By this approach, we reduce the size of it below half. To determine an index of a candidate cell in rendering stage, this method performs one addition between the result of the *INDEX BUFFER* and that of the summed-area table.

5   Experimental Results

All the methods were implemented on a PC equipped with an AMD Athlon64x2™ 4200+ CPU, 2 GB main memory, and GeForce™ 6600 graphics card. The graphics card capabilities are only used to display the final images. The first and second dataset were an engine block and a bonsai with a resolution of 256^3, respectively. The third dataset was an aneurysm of a human brain vessel with a resolution of 512^3. Fig. 6 shows OTfs for the datasets, and Table 1 shows the preprocessing time and required memory for each dataset.

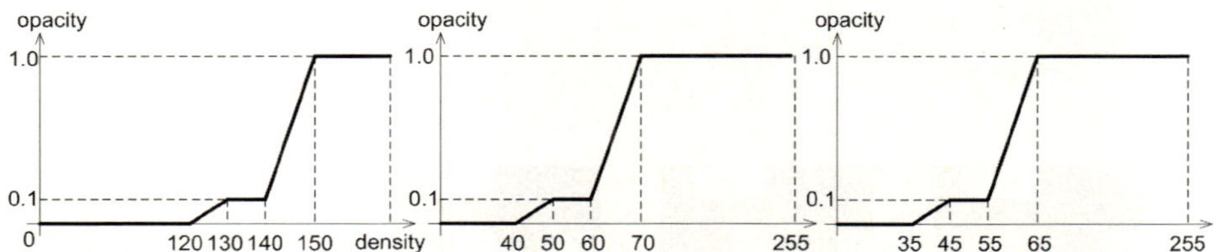

Fig. 6. The OTFs for the engine, bonsai, and aneurysm dataset, respectively. Since one of advantages of direct volume rendering is to visualize datasets translucently, we include translucent regions.

Table 1. Preprocessing time and required memory for each dataset. N_{sc} is 4.

dataset	engine	bonsai	aneurysm
the number of candidate cells (voxels)	1,031,929	829,726	1,015,800
candidate cell determination time (A) (secs)	0.93	0.76	0.95
generation time (B) (secs)	30.21	23.88	29.60
total preprocessing time (A+B) (secs)	31.14	24.64	30.55
required memory (MB)	232	193	463

The rendering times to produce the perspective view are shown in Table 2. Since our method is focused on speedup of color computation step of the volume ray casting, adequate space-leaping method to skip over transparent cells is required. Therefore,

Table 2. Rendering improvements for each dataset before/after our method (unit: %). The time for space leaping is included in our method. All results are rendered to a perspective projection.

dataset	engine	bonsai	aneurysm	**average**
improvements	57	54	49	**53**

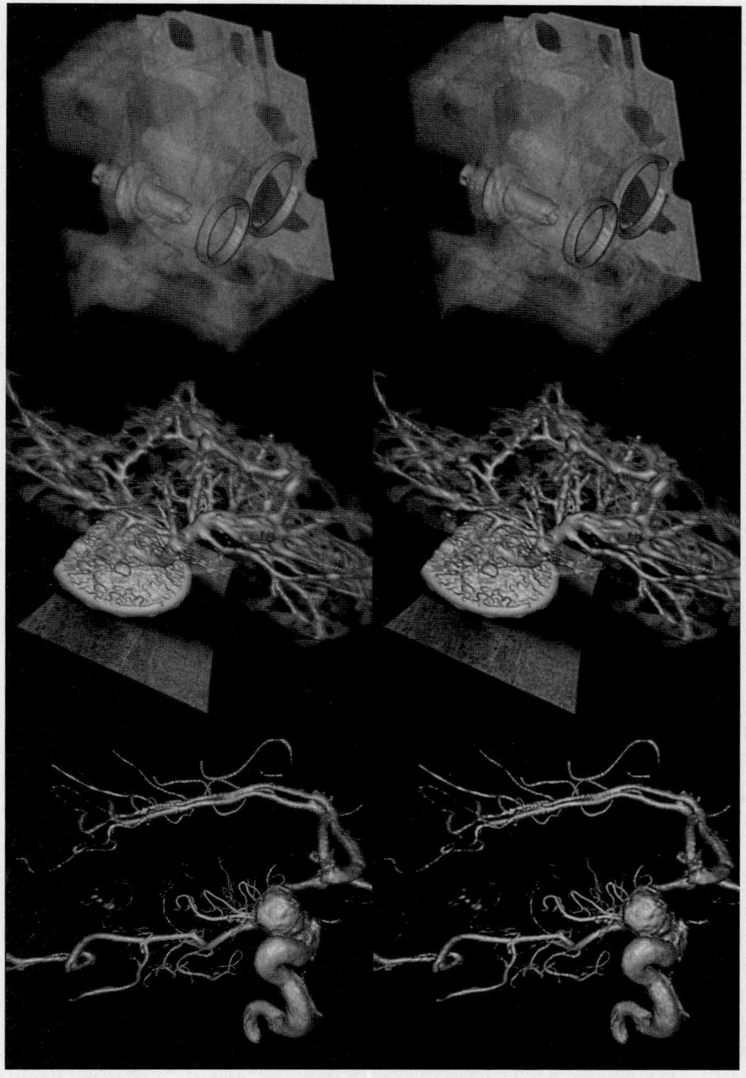

Fig. 7. Comparisons of image quality: conventional volume ray casting (left) and N_{sc}=4 (right). The RMSE results are 2.42, 5.20, and 4.02 for each dataset. The engine is rendered to parallel projection, and the bonsai and aneurysm are projected to perspective viewing.

we exploit the hierarchical min-max octree [6], [7], [8], [9], [15], [16], [17], [18], which is widely used for efficient space-leaping. All the results of our method show average computation time and include the space-leaping time. Our method is at least 53% faster than the method using the previous hierarchical min-max octree.

Fig. 7 shows the image quality when we apply the number of N_{sc} as four. We compute the *Root Mean Square Error* (RMSE) [19] for accurate comparisons. It is the square root of the average of the squared error, and one of the most commonly used generalized standard deviations. Compared with the conventional volume ray casting, the mean value of RMSE results is about 3.88. This is marginal against increasing the rendering speed.

6   Conclusion

The most important issue in volume visualization is to produce high-quality images in real time. Although most of researchers have concentrated on skipping over transparent region, we focused on the accelerating color computation step for the CPU-based volume ray casting. To achieve interactive frame rates on a PC platform, we precompute interpolated scalar value and an index of encoded gradient vector for each sub-cell in the preprocessing stage. Although most accelerated methods depend on projection methods, the rendering performance of our method reaches interactive rates even for perspective projection without additional calculations or degrading the image quality. In addition, our approach can be combined with any kind of space-leaping methods for CPU-based volume ray casting because it is not dependent on them. However, when the OTF is changed, we must regenerate our data structure because the isosurface value is changed. Of course, it is not necessary to compute all values since we can only update the changed cells. After comparing eight voxels in a candidate cell, we determine the update procedure easily. The experimental results show that our method reduces rendering time and produces high-quality images.

Acknowledgment

This work was supported by IITA through IT Leading R&D Support Project.

References

1. Levoy, M.: Display of Surface from Volume Data. IEEE Computer Graphics and Applications, Vol. 8, No. 3 (1988) 29-37
2. Kaufman, A.: Volume Visualization. 1st ed., Ed. IEEE Computer Society Press (1991)
3. Krishnamurthy, B., Bajaj, C.: Data Visualization Techniques. 1st ed., Ed. John Wiley & Sons (1999)
4. Yagel, R., Kaufmann, A.: Template-based Volume Viewing. Computer Graphics Forum, Vol. 11 (1992) 153-167
5. Lacroute, P., Levoy, M.: Fast Volume Rendering Using a Shear-Warp Factorization of the Viewing Transformation. Proc. SIGGRAPH 1994 (1994) 451-457

6. Parker, S., Shirley, P., Livnat, Y., Hansen, C., Sloan, P.: Interactive Ray Tracing for Iso-surface Rendering. Proc. IEEE Visualization 1998 (1998) 233-238
7. Knittel, G.: The UltraVis System. Proc. IEEE Volume Visualization 2000 (2000) 71-79
8. Mora, B. Jessel, J.P., Caubet, R.: A New Object Order Ray-Casting Algorithm. Proc. IEEE Volume Visualization 2002 (2002) 203-210
9. Grimm, S., Bruckner, S., Kanitsar, A., Gröller, E.: Memory Efficient Acceleration Structures and Techniques for CPU-based Volume Raycasting of Large Data. Proc. IEEE Volume Visualization 2004 (2004) 1-8
10. Yagel, R., Cohen, D., Kaufmann, A.: Normal Estimation in 3D Discrete Space. The Visual Computer, Vol. 6 (1992) 278-291
11. Möller, T., Machiraju, R., Muller, K., Yagel, R.: A Comparison of Normal Estimation Schemes. Proc. IEEE Visualization 1997 (1997) 19-26
12. Levoy, M.: Efficient Ray Tracing of Volume Data. ACM Transactions on Graphics, Vol. 9 (1990) 245-261
13. Rusinkiewicz, S., Levoy, M.: QSplat: A Multiresolution Point Rendering System for Large Meshes. Proc. SIGGRAPH 2000 (2000) 343-352
14. Crow, F.C.: Summed-Area Tables for Texture Mapping. Proc. SIGGRAPH 1984 (1984) 207-212
15. Lim, S., Shin, B.S.: Reliable Space Leaping Using Distance Template. Lecture Notes in Computer Science, Vol. 3337 (2004) 60-66
16. Hadwiger, M. Sigg, C., Scharsach, H., Bühler, K., Gross, M.: Real-time Ray-casting and Advanced Shading of Discrete Isosurfaces. Graphics Forum, Vol. 24 (2005) 303-312
17. Lim, S., Shin, B.S.: RPO: A Reverse-Phased Hierarchical Min-Max Octree for Efficient Space-Leaping. Proc. Pacific Graphics 2005 (2005) 145-147
18. Lim, S., Shin, B.S.: Efficient Space-Leaping Using Optimal Block Sets. IEICE Trans. on Information and Systems, Vol. E88-D (2005) 2864-2870
19. Kim, K., Wittenbrink, C.M., Pang, A.: Extended Specifications and Test Data Sets for Data Level Comparisons of Direct Volume Rendering Algorithms. IEEE Trans. on Visualization and Computer Graphics, Vol. 7 (2001) 299-317

Triangle Propagation for Mass-Spring Chain Algorithm

Alpaslan Duysak

Computer Engineering Department, Dumlupinar University,
Main Campus 43100 Kutahya, Turkey
aduysak@dumlupinar.edu.tr

Abstract. The paper proposes some major modifications on the mass-spring chain algorithm. The original algorithm takes into account individual springs of the 3 D lattice representing a deformable object and deforms springs. In this proposed version, deformation algorithm loops through triangles of the 3 D mesh and performs deformation. Two additional improvements are also provided: A new formula, which produces smooth deformations, is used for deformation calculation. A simple and fast algorithm for crossing test in order to avoid vertex penetration is also employed. Modified mass-spring chain algorithm is used in several applications and is compared against the original algorithm. The proposed method is faster than the original algorithm and suitable for deformation simulations in virtual realty applications where real time performance is required.

Keywords: Modeling, mass-spring chain, animation, deformation simulation.

1 Introduction

Accuracy and computing speed are two main concerns in simulation of deformable objects. Depending on the requirements of the applications, researchers may use different simulation techniques for such simulations [1]. The finite element method (FEM) is a common choice if accuracy is the main concern while the mass spring systems (MSS) may be preferred if speed is essential. It is important to note that, even with the MSS, real-time performance, which is essential in many simulation applications, is difficult to achieve, since most real applications involve a large number of modeling (e.g. vertices and springs) elements and the calculation is iterative over a large number time steps. Therefore, whilst much research effort has been spent on improving such techniques in the area of physical accuracy and performance (introducing nonlinear finite elements and adaptive sampling for FEM [2] and optimization [3] and approximated implicit methods [4] for MSS), other methods, such as the ChainMail algorithm [5] and mass-spring chain [6], have been proposed aiming at interactive frame rates.

The ChainMail algorithm was designed to produce very high frame rates because only simplistic deformation rules are defined between the individual elements of the chain (vertices connected with links) [5]. It aimed at interactive applications for large networks at the price of accuracy. This algorithm was later improved [7], where the modeling capabilities of the original ChainMail algorithm were expanded to handle

A. Levi et al. (Eds.): ISCIS 2006, LNCS 4263, pp. 306–315, 2006.

inhomogeneous materials. A detailed analysis of the ChainMail algorithm and its applications are given in [8].

Inspired by MSS and ChainMail methods, mass-spring chain algorithm (MSC), which introduces an element of physical modeling into a procedural approach, was developed [6]. MSC method combines the strengths of both mass-spring systems and ChainMail algorithms. It is therefore able to achieve good accuracy with interactive frame rates. MSC algorithm was successfully applied to simulation of facial tissue deformations for craniofacial surgery, [9]. In this paper, modifications on the MSC algorithm and its applications are presented. In the following sections, the original MSC algorithm is described (see [6, 9] for more details), first. Next, contributions of the paper over the original algorithm are provided in detail.

2 Mass-Spring Chain Algorithm

The basic idea of mass-spring chain algorithm is to treat the deformable objects in a similar way to that of the mass spring systems, but replace their computation procedure by a set of new rules. Deformation starts from the displaced mass-points and propagates over the entire 3D lattice of springs. Spring movement is limited between two extremes: rigid movement and elastic movement. The spring length is also constrained between the allowed maximum compression and elongation.

2.1 Deformation Propagation

When a point in 3D mesh is subject to an external force (by grabbing it and moving it) this particular point becomes an *active point* or, in other words, a *source point* for the deformation. An active point (**A**) is shown as green in Fig. 1a. Driven by the active point, the deformation, starting from the active point, travels through the rest of the lattice in every direction following the springs. Deformation algorithm first determines the springs, called *active springs,* connected to the active point. These springs are represented with green lines. Arrows on these lines show the direction of propagation of the deformation (Fig. 1). Deformation algorithm then, determines the other end points of the active springs, called the *semi-active points* (**B** and **C** in Fig. 1a). Semi-active points will be repositioned (causing deformation), and will become active points themselves in the next step. Springs connecting the semi-active points are called *semi-active spring* and they have arrows at both ends representing deformation at both ends. Semi-active springs are shown in blue in Fig. 1a. This is regarded as the first step of propagation and it involves one active and two semi-active points in this example.

Fig. 1b shows the second step of the deformation propagation. The previous semi-active points (**B** and **C**) have now become active points, shown as green in Fig. 1b. The previous active points, active and semi-active springs are now shown in red implying that these elements from the previous step are turned off to prevent backwards propagation. Semi-active points (**D**, **E** and **F**) and semi-active springs are found by deformation algorithm and deformation is performed. Another step is given in Fig. 1c, where points **D**, **E** and **F** are now active points acting as source for deformation. Semi-active points and springs are determined and after deformation is performed, MSC algorithm moves to next phase. Deformation propagation terminates when all active and semi-active points as well as springs are processed (deformed).

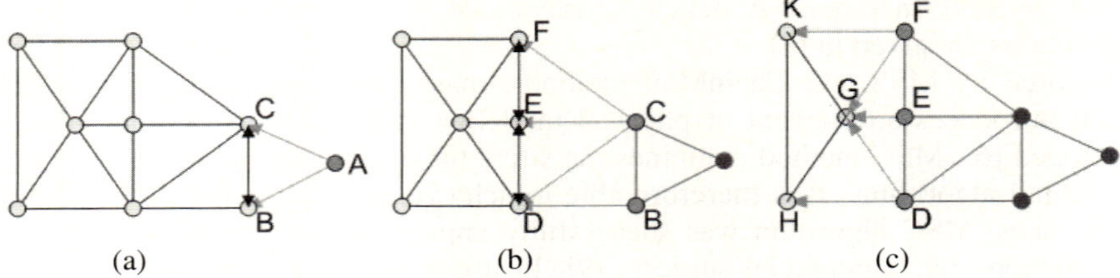

Fig. 1. Deformation propagation of the original algorithm: (a) first wave; an active point **A** is moved (b) second wave; **B** and **C** are now active points (c) third step; and deformation propagation moves forward

2.2 Movement Limits

Deformation algorithm considers two possible extreme cases of spring movements in order to deform springs; *rigid* and *elastic* movements. When a point is moved, any connected spring will move accordingly. If there was no elasticity in the spring and no rotation, rigid movement occurs and the spring concerned would move like a rigid bar. The moved spring would be in a parallel position with the initial spring. This extreme movement is illustrated in Fig. 2a, where the initial triangle is represented by **ABC** and vertex **A** is moved to a new location **a**. In the case of rigid movement, spring **AB** will rigidly move to the new position **ab**. The following vector is called the *rigid movement limit vector*:

$$\vec{u} = b - a \tag{1}$$

which sets the rigid limit or, in other words, the upper limit beyond which there will not be any movement. The opposite situation is known as the *elastic movement*. If the spring offered no resistance to its movement, when one end of the spring moves, the other end would stay still. The vector linking the moving end to the stationary end of the spring is given below:

$$\vec{v} = B - a \tag{2}$$

This vector sets the elastic limit and is called the *elastic movement limit vector*. It is assumed that the moved and deformed spring will be placed somewhere between the rigid and elastic movement limit vectors. Deformation algorithm employs a vector called the *orientation vector* whose purpose is to specify where the spring lies between movement limit vectors,

$$\vec{w} = \alpha \vec{u} + (1-\alpha)\vec{v} \tag{3}$$

where α represents the deformation characteristic of the object under consideration. As shown in Fig. 2b, the orientation vector is located between limit vectors and points to the new location of the semi-active point. Notice **B** is relocated to $\underline{b}$.

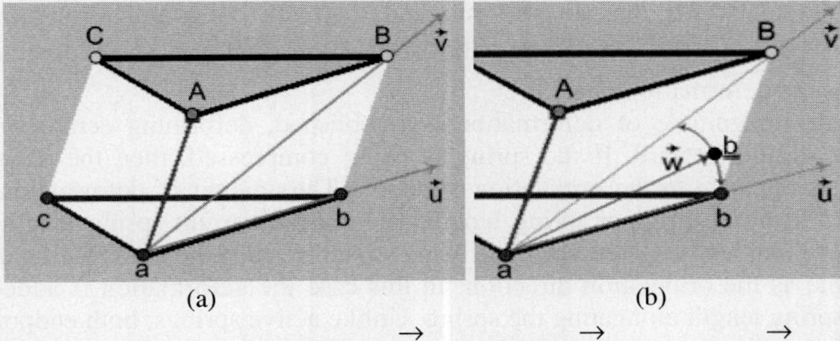

Fig. 2. Vectors used by the algorithm (a) $\vec{u}$ (rigid) and $\vec{v}$ (elastic), (b) $\vec{w}$ (orientation) vector pointing the new location of semi-active point

The parameter α, whose value is in the range of [0, 1], can also be considered as a control factor for the spring movement. Fig. 3 shows (after C is deformed) the new locations (green lines) of triangle **ABC** for different values of α (0.0, 0.4, 0.8, and 1.0). These new locations are called as new orientations for the original triangle. These new locations do not include the deformations of the related springs.

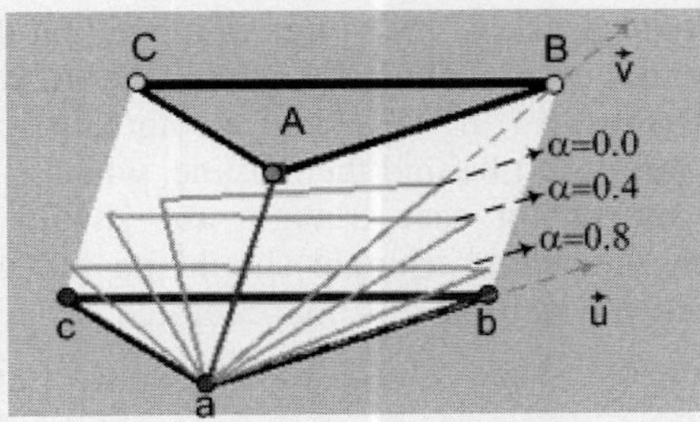

Fig. 3. Initial triangle is given by **ABC** while rigid movement is given by **abc**. The other triangles between them (green) are obtained using different values of α.

2.3 Deformation Magnitude and Direction

Once the new locations (orientations) of the springs are found, deformation algorithm calculates the amount of the deformation for each spring. Springs are allowed to stretch or compress for a certain percentage of their original lengths r_0. The current spring length r varies between the maximum compression length and the maximum stretch length. Similar to the MSS algorithm, the current spring lengths are found and compared with their initial (pre-set) lengths. There are three possible outcomes from this comparison: no spring deformation; spring stretched; spring compressed. The magnitude of deformation is calculated using equation 4,

$$def = d_{max} (1 - e^{-\beta \frac{|dr|}{r_0}}) \qquad (4)$$

where d_{max} stands for the allowed maximum stretch or compression, dr is the difference between the current and the rest length, and the slope parameter β represents the deformation rate.

Once the magnitude of deformation is established, deforming active springs is relatively straightforward. If the spring is being compressed, then the deformation direction is opposite to the orientation direction. The amount of deformation is then subtracted from the original spring length, leaving the current spring length shorter than the original length. If the spring is being stretched, then the deformation direction is the same as the orientation direction. In this case the deformation is added to the original spring length elongating the spring. Unlike active springs, both endpoints of a semi-active spring are moving at the same time. Spring deformation is computed separately from both ends, and the results obtained are combined to give the final deformation of the spring [6].

2.4 Shape Alteration (Vertex Penetration)

In this case the building blocks, triangles, are forced to change their original shapes. The MSS does not consider any shape violation because it is not able to detect shape alterations. Shape alteration is also known as *vertex penetration*, because it happens when one of the vertices of the triangle penetrates one of the edges of the same triangle. This situation only occurs if the vertex is moved on the same surface where the triangle lies. If **A** is moved to **a** (Fig. 4a) while line **BC** remains unchanged and forms the triangle **aCB** (Fig. 4b), it will yield an unrealistic solution. In practice, vertices **B** and **C** should not be left behind the red line, which is parallel to the original edge **BC**. In the rigid movement case triangle **abc** should be formed. Although compression may occur, the whole triangle should be moved below the red line. Vertex penetration distorts the result and is not permitted.

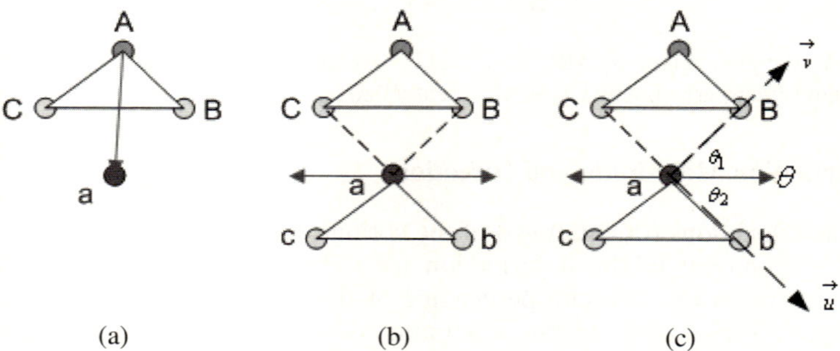

Fig. 4. Vertex **A** penetrates the edge (**BC**) of the same triangle (a), for the rigid movement triangle **abc** is formed (b) and detection the crossing (c)

The original MSC algorithm uses a correction algorithm to prevent vertex penetration. The idea is very simple; correction algorithm measures the angles between red line (described above) and elastic limit as well as between the red line and rigid limit, Fig. 4c. If the sum of these angles is equal to the angle measured between elastic and rigid limit, vertex crossing occurs.

3   Improvements

The mass-spring chain algorithm is modified in terms of deformation propagation, vertex crossing test and deformation formula.

3.1   Triangle Propagation

The original algorithm, when a point is picked, determines active springs connected to the active points. The algorithm then loops all found active springs and determines semi-active points which are the other end points of the active springs. Another loop is also necessary in the original algorithm to determine semi-active springs which are connecting semi-active points. MSC algorithm then moves and deforms these springs according to the defined rules [6, 9]. Instead of using individual springs, individual triangles can be used for deformation propagation.

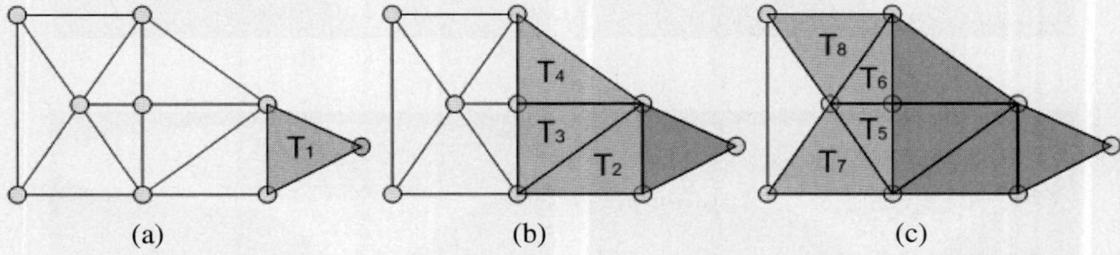

Fig. 5. Deformation process based on triangular propagation; (a) start of the deformation process, (b) second wave of deformation, (c) third wave and deformation propagation goes on

The same image of the Fig. 1 is given in the Fig. 5, where a vertex is moved externally and connected triangle becomes active triangle. Springs of the active triangle (**T1** is an active triangle shown in green) are deformed during this first wave of the deformation. When the first wave completed connected triangles are found (from a pre-set list) and added to the deformation list to be performed in the next wave. Before the next wave starts deformed triangle of the first phase is turned off (red in the Fig. 5b) similar to the original algorithm that turns off the individual springs. Second wave is shown in Fig. 5b, where there are now three active triangles named as **T2**, **T3** and **T4**. These triangles are processed and connected triangles are found and added to the deformation list before triangles of this wave of deformation are turned off. The next wave is shown in Fig 5c where triangles **T1**, **T2**, **T3** and **T4** are turned off, shown in red. New active triangles are shown as green. After the third wave, there is only one triangle left to be processed as can be seen from the Fig. 5c, shown as white.

For each active triangle, elastic and rigid movement limits for the springs are found. This process is the same as in the original algorithm. Different than original algorithm, two active and one semi-active springs forming the triangle are already known. Therefore, looping active springs to determine semi-active points and looping semi-active points to determine semi-active springs are eliminated. In fact, there is no looping in this process now, once triangles are picked from the list, picked vertex or vertices are the active points and springs connected to active points are active springs.

Remaining springs and vertices of the picked triangles are classified as semi-active springs and points.

Propagating the deformation using triangles is shown in Fig. 6. First image of the Fig. 6 is the result of the first wave, which only moves and deforms few triangles. As can be seen from the figure that the process is not complete and connections between deformed triangles (very few during the first wave) and the deformable object should not be considered as local deformation. The image in the Fig. 6b shows the second wave and more of the deformed triangles. The fifth and tenth steps are shown in Fig. 6c and 6d respectively. The final image, Fig. 6d, shows that almost all triangles in the mesh are processed (deformed).

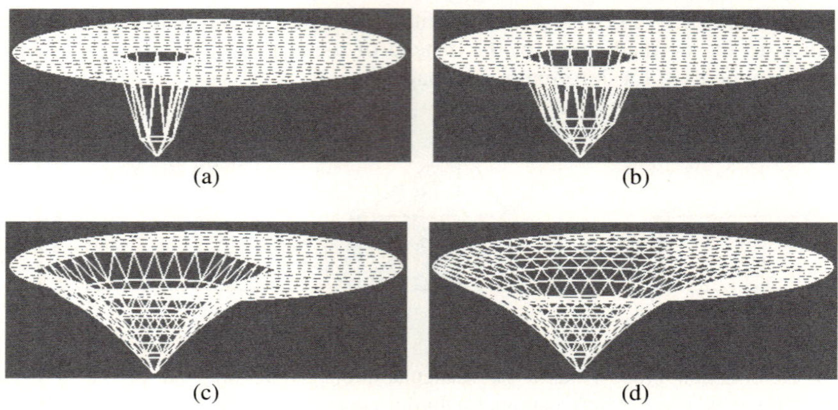

(a)   (b)

(c)   (d)

Fig. 6. A flat net is deformed by moving one of its vertices. The resultant deformation is propagated using triangles: (a) first, (b) second, (c) fifth and (d) tenth wave of triangle propagation.

3.2   Crossing Test

Performing a crossing test is essential in the mass-spring chain algorithm. In this process, it is important to prevent vertices crossing edges of the triangle causing inversion of the same triangle. Preventing vertex penetration in the original algorithm is computationally expensive. Calculations involve determining the red line (Fig. 4), computing three angles and comparing them [6, 10]. Since vertex penetration only occurs when one (or two) vertex of a triangle moves on the same surface where triangle lies and crosses one of the edges of the triangle, crossing test is actually finding ray segment intersection.

Vertex **A** in Fig. 7a moves to a new location given as **a** and crosses the segment defined by two end point **BC** (one of the edges of the triangle **ABC**). If a ray is defined by **Aa**, ray (**Aa**) segment (**BC**) crossing test can be performed. If ray-segment algorithm finds intersection deformation algorithm replaces elastic limit vector to prevent crossing as in the original algorithm. A simple and fast test given in [10] is used to determine crossing in this work. Fig. 7a shows a crossing example and deformation of the triangle **ABC** without crossing test (blue triangle) and with a crossing and correction (green triangle). Rigid movement case is represented by triangle **abc**. In order to demonstrate more fully the correction algorithm for vertex penetration, a simple 2D figure whose one vertex is moved externally to instigate vertex penetration, as shown in Fig. 7b, is simulated. Several vertex penetrations occur in this example and they are handled successfully as can be seen from the Figure.

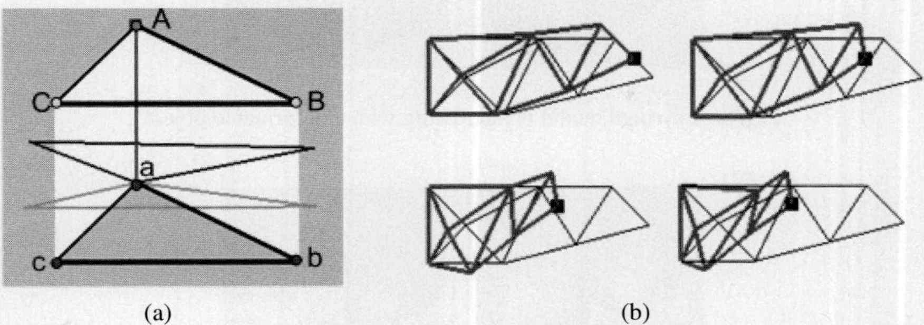

(a)   (b)

Fig. 7. Deformation of a triangle with (green) and without (blue) crossing test, (a) and a simple deformation example shows vertex penetrations (b)

3.3 Deformation Calculation

Original algorithm uses a deformation calculation formula given by Equation 4. This formula requires negative values of the length change (current length is less than original length) converted to positive values. The function given by Equation 5, on the other hand, works for both compression and elongation cases. The term in parenthesis is the famous tangent hyperbolic function which   produces smooth deformations for changes in the spring length (dr).

$$def = d_{\max} \left(\frac{e^{\beta dr} - e^{-\beta dr}}{e^{\beta dr} + e^{-\beta dr}} \right) \tag{5}$$

4 Applications and Results

The modified mass-spring chain algorithm is used in several deformation simulation cases. It is important to note that both algorithms produce very similar deformations since improvements focus on speeding up the original algorithm. Examples are given in Fig. 8 and Fig. 9, where syringe is deforming an object and a stomach model is interacting with a knife respectively.

The third example is an animation of a moon character. The character is manipulated by moving one of its vertices as given in Fig. 10. Mass-spring chain algorithm (MSC) and its modified version are used in these examples. Although visually very similar results are obtained, a performance gain is achieved as shown in Table 1. Results are obtained on 2.40 GHz. Pentium 4 computer. The proposed algorithm therefore provides even faster simulation times required for many computer graphics applications such as virtual realty simulations.

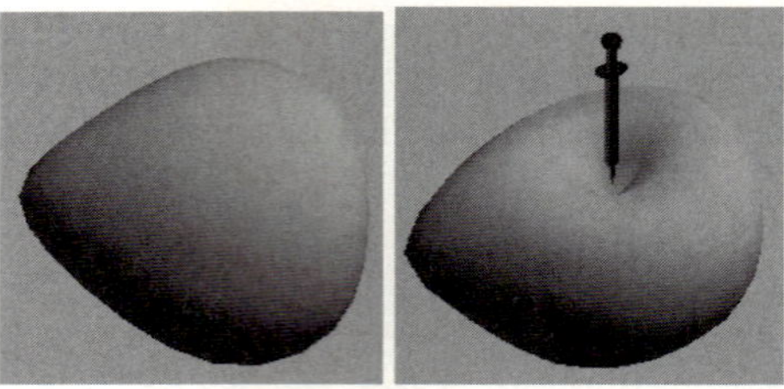

Fig. 8. A syringe model is interacting with a deformable object

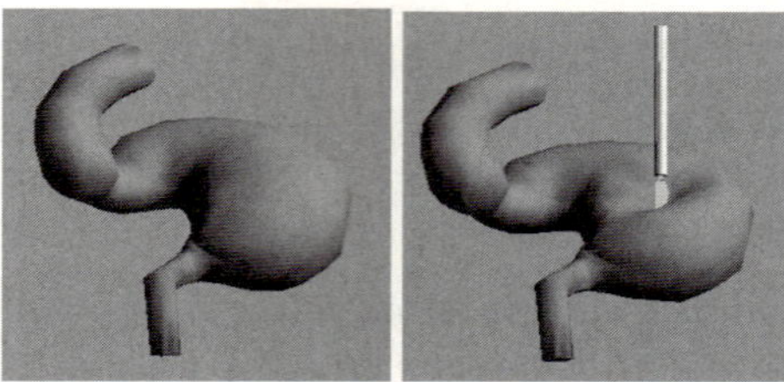

Fig. 9. A knife is deforming the stomach model

Table 1. Performance comparison of the original and modified mass-spring chain algorithms

Model	Spring Number	Vertex number	MSC seconds	Modified MSC seconds
Moon	9504	3198	0.016	0.011
Stomach	3206	1071	0.013	0.009

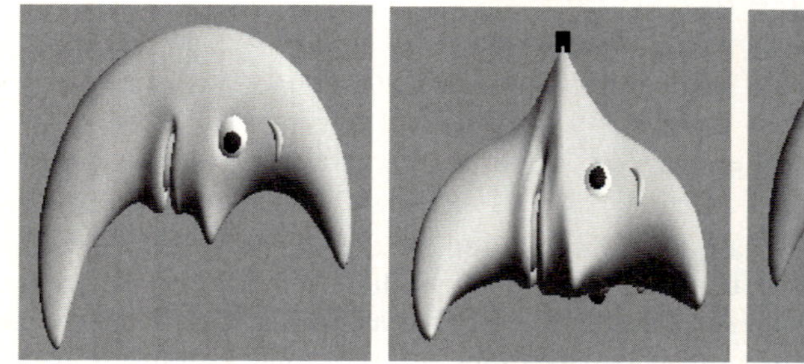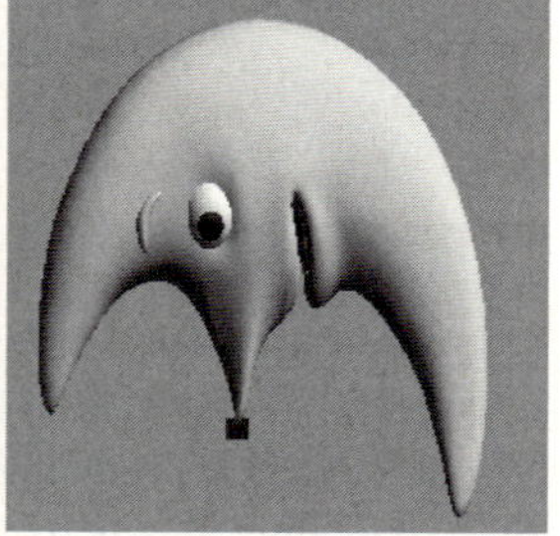

Fig. 10. A moon character is deformed by moving vertices

Future work will include exploring new ways of determining triangle movements (movement limits) and parameter settings for accuracy improvements. Application of the proposed algorithm to more complex deformable objects is already undertaken.

References

1. Nealen, A., Müller, M., Keiser, R., Boxermann, E., Carlson, M.: Physically Based Deformable Models in Computer Graphics. Proceedings of Eurographics, 71-94, (2005)
2. Wu, X., Downes, M.S., Goktekin, T., Tendick, F.: Adaptive nonlinear finite elements for deformable body simulation using dynamic progressive meshes. EUROGRAPHICS, Vol. 20, 349-358, (2001)
3. Teschner, M., Girod, S., Girod, B.: Optimization approaches for soft-tissue prediction in craniofacial surgery simulation. Second Int. Conf. On Medical Image Computing and Computer-Assisted Intervention MICCAI, 1183-1190, (1999)
4. Kang, Y. M., Choi, J. H., Cho, H. G.: Fast and stable animation of cloth with an approximated implicit method. Proceedings of the Computer Graphics International (CGI'00), 247-255, (2000)
5. Gibson, S. F. F.: 3D Chainmail: A Fast Algorithm for Deforming Volumetric Objects. Proc. Symp. Interactive 3D Graphics, 149-154, (1997)
6. Duysak, A., Zhang, J. J.: Fast Simulation of Deformable Objects. International symposium on Computer Animation, The 8th International Conference on Information Visualization, IEEE Computer Society, 422-427, (2004)
7. Schill, M. A., Gibson, S. F. F., Bender, H. J., Manner, R.: Biomedical Simulation of the Vitreous Humor in the Eye using an Enhanced ChainMail Algorithm. MICCAI, 679-687, (1998)
8. Gibson, S. F. F.: Using Linked Volumes to Model Object Collisions, Deformation, Cutting, Carving, and Joining. IEEE Transactions on Visualization and Computer Graphics, Vol. 5, No 4, 333-348, (1999)
9. Duysak, A., Zhang, J. J.: Fast Simulation of Facial Tissue Deformations Using Mass-Spring Chain Algorithm. Theory and Practice of Computer Graphics, the 23rd Conference organized by the UK chapter of the Eurographics Association, 139-145, (2005)
10. Sunday, D.: Intersections of Rays and Segments with Triangles in 3D, May 2001 algorithms:http://softsurfer.com/Archive/algorithm_0104/algorithm_0104B.htm#Line%20 Intersections, (09/01/2006)

Hardware Acceleration of Terrain Visualization
Using *ef*-Buffers

Hyun-Duk Chang and Byeong-Seok Shin

Department of Computer Science and Information Engineering, Inha University
253 Yonghyeon-Dong, Nam-Gu, Inchon, 402-751, Korea
`biggreat@inhaian.net, bsshin@inha.ac.kr`

Abstract. Quadtree-based terrain visualization methods have been used in a lot of applications. However, because most procedures are performed on the CPU, the rendering speed is slow. In this paper, we present a quadtree-based terrain visualization method working on the GPU with specially designed data structure, the error-buffer and flag-buffer named *ef*-buffers. In pre-processing step, error metrics are computed in world space and the error metrics are transferred to the error-buffer. In rendering time, LOD selection and view-frustum culling are processed by evaluating the error metrics. The result is stored into the flag-buffer. To remove cracks or T-junction, the flag-buffer is refined. Then triangulation is performed using the flag-buffer. This method reduces CPU load and performs time consuming jobs such as LOD selection and view-frustum culling on the GPU. We can conclude that our method much faster than CPU-based rendering method without loss of image quality.

1   Introduction

Terrain visualization methods have been used in many applications such as GIS (Geographic Information System), computer games and flight simulations. A quadtree-based CLOD method is one of the ways to visualize terrain datasets [1], [2], [3]. A quadtree provides a fast CLOD (Continuous Level-Of-Detail) computation and a view-frustum culling. So, it can generate a moderate quality image in real-time. However, since a quadtree-based terrain visualization method processes most operations on a CPU, rendering performance is fully dependent on the performance of the CPU.

Generally, the GPU is much faster than the CPU for graphics operations. Also a vertex processor and a fragment processor have parallel architecture adequate to massively parallel graphics processing. In this paper, to achieve high-speed terrain visualization, we take advantages of the GPU as mentioned above. Our terrain visualization method is based on a quadtree structure. Unfortunately, since a traditional quadtree method exploits a hierarchical data structure, the GPU cannot handle those hierarchical data structure. We propose the error-buffer (*e*-buffer) and flag-buffer (*f*-buffer) to implement quadtree-based terrain visualization on the GPU. In pre-processing step, error metrics are computed in world-space for all nodes and edges, and stored in our *e*-buffer. In rendering time, LOD selection and view-frustum culling is performed on the GPU. We determine the visibility of each node and edge, and store the conditions into the *f*-buffer. That is, values of *f*-buffer are exploited as an

A. Levi et al. (Eds.): ISCIS 2006, LNCS 4263, pp. 316–324, 2006.

enabling flag to determine inclusion of a node or an edge in a final mesh. To prevent cracks or T-junctions, the f-buffer should be refined. Finally, a terrain mesh is generated using the refined f-buffer and sent to GPU for rendering.

In Sect. 2, we introduce a brief description of previous works. In the Sect. 3, we explain the e-buffer and f-buffer in detail and how to use them for a quadtree-based terrain visualization. Experimental results are presents in Sect. 4. Finally we conclude our method.

2   Related Works

Lindstrom introduced a terrain visualization method based on a quadtree [1]. It splits a terrain dataset into four quadrant recursively and performs efficient a CLOD (Continuous Level-Of-Detail) and a view-frustum culling. Röttger et. al [2] provide a quadtree-based method to make a simple crack elimination and geomorphing by using top-down strategy. Shin and Choi proposed a method to maintain constant frame rate without flickering by controlling the number of triangles in view frustum [3]. Duchaineau proposed ROAM (Real-time Optimally Adaptive Meshes) [4]. ROAM uses triangle bintrees to visualize terrain dataset efficiently. Both methods are helpful for adaptive terrain rendering because it has a hierarchical mesh model that can be selected optimally according to viewing conditions. However these hierarchical structures should be performed on the CPU due to hierarchical structure that cannot be handled on GPU. As a result, it is entirely dependent on CPU performance and its rendering speed is relatively slow due to lack of parallel processing scheme.

In recently year, the GPU has been widely used and its performance is increasing continuously. So, a lot of terrain visualization methods using the GPU were proposed [5], [6], [7]. The geometry clipmap [5] technique applies the clipmap [8] to terrain visualization. In the geometry clipmap, however, a LOD is selected in world space based on several rectangular regions. Therefore it can not achieve an accurate CLOD computation. The geometry clipmap uses degenerated triangles and texture transitions to remove visual continuity of the mesh. However, the method is not a radical solution because it does not connect physical geometry.

3   Quadtree-Based Triangulation Using *ef*-Buffers

In conventional quadtree-based terrain rendering method, most process is performed on the CPU such as computation of view-dependent error metric, edge splitting and view-frustum culling. We propose a method working these operations on GPU. With this approach, we can reduce the rendering time without loss of image quality. Our method uses the e-buffer and f-buffer for efficient transferring of error metrics and node/edge information between GPU and CPU. We call those two buffers as *ef*-Buffers. Fig. 1 presents a diagram of our terrain visualization method.

The input data is a height field of which the size is $n \times n$ ($n = 2^k + 1$, where k is quadtree height). Our method stores geometric errors into the e-buffer. In most cases,

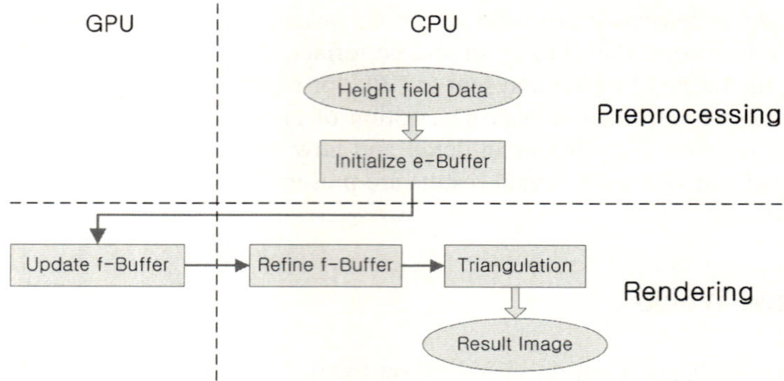

Fig. 1. A procedure of our terrain visualization method using the *ef*-buffer

because height values for specific terrain are not changed, this step can be performed in a preprocessing time only once. However, for a varying height field such as water surface in ocean simulations, the *e*-buffer should be initialized in each frame.

During rendering, a triangle mesh is created using the value of *f*-buffer. Enabling (visibility) flags of nodes and edges are determined by computing error metrics in *e*-buffer and stored in *f*-buffer. In order to avoid T-junctions, refinement step is required. Lastly, a terrain mesh is generated using our *f*-buffer.

3.1 Initialization of the *e*-Buffer

In this step, the geometric error values are computed in world space for all nodes and edges in a quadtree, and stored into a 2D texture (*e*-buffer) to exploit CLOD technique. Since initialization of the *e*-buffer requires hierarchical traversal of quadtree, this step is done on the CPU. An error metric for an edge e_i ($i = 0...3$) of a specific node in m-th level is denoted as δ_{ei}^m and it is distance between a vertex in the finer

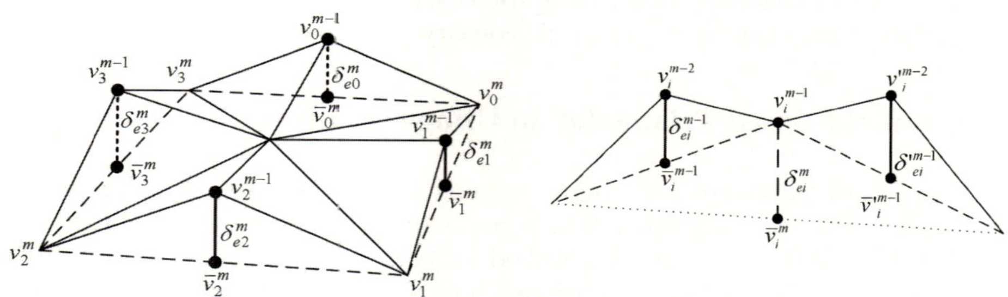

Fig. 2. Error metric δ_{ei}^m ($i = 0...3$) of an edge at the finest level ($m=1$, left image) and the other levels ($1<m<k$, right image). A solid line denotes an edge of mesh in m-2-th level. A dashed line represents an edge of mesh in m-1-th level and a dotted line means the lowest (m-th) level. v_i^m is a vertex in m-th level. And $\bar{v}_i^m$ is an intermediate vertex between v_i^m and v_{i+1}^m. δ_{ei}^{m-1} and δ'_{ei}^{m-1} are edge errors in the m-1-th level.

level (v_i^{m-1}) and mid point of the edge in current level (v_i^m). To compute δ_{ei}^m, we have to consider v_i^{m-1}, v_i^m, v_{i+1}^m, δ_{ei}^{m-1}, δ'^{m-1}_{ei} as described in Eq. (1) and (2).

$$\delta_{ei}^m = \left| v_i^{m-1} - \bar{v}_i^m \right| = \left| v_i^{m-1} - \left(v_i^m + v_{i+1}^m \right)/2 \right|. \qquad (i = 1,\ldots,3 \text{ and } m=1) \tag{1}$$

$$\delta_{ei}^m = \max\left(\left| v_i^{m-1} - \left(v_i^m + v_{i+1}^m \right)/2 \right|, \ \delta_{ei}^{m-1}, \ \delta'^{m-1}_{ei} \right). \qquad (i = 1,\ldots,3 \text{ and } 1<m<k) \tag{2}$$

Fig. 3 shows how to compute edge errors from the height map and store them into *e*-buffer in case of using a height field of which the resolution is 5×5 .

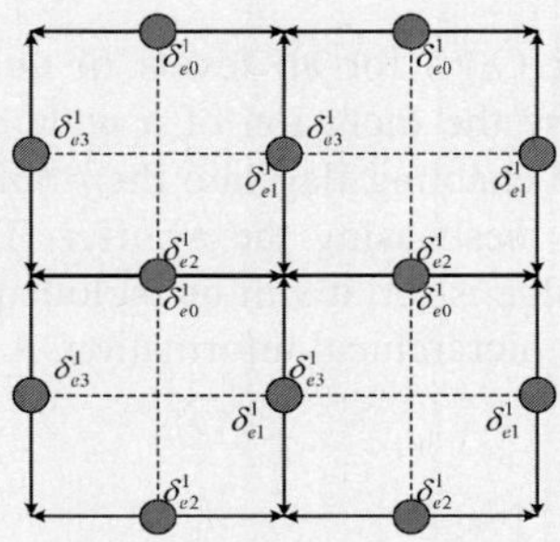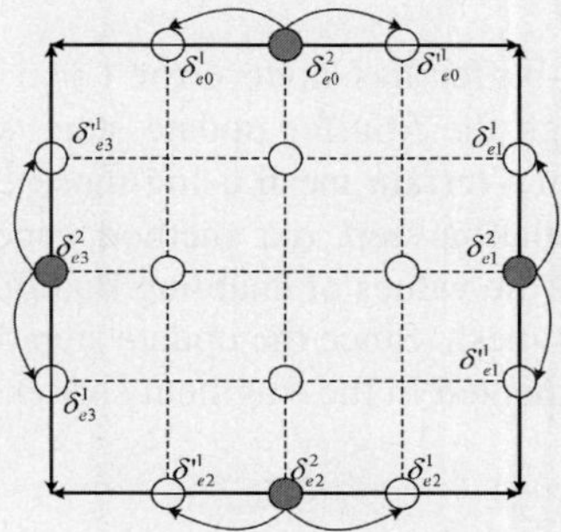

Fig. 3. Indexing of a height value for computing edge errors in level 0 (left) and level 1(right). The gray circle denotes an edge's error metric in a current level; the blank circle represents an edge's error metric in upper level.

Error metric of a node p_i (δ_{pi}^m) can be obtained from δ_{ei}^m as shown in Eq. (3) and (4). To compute node error, we need an error metric of the neighboring edges and its child nodes. At the finest level, the node error is the maximum value of its four edge's

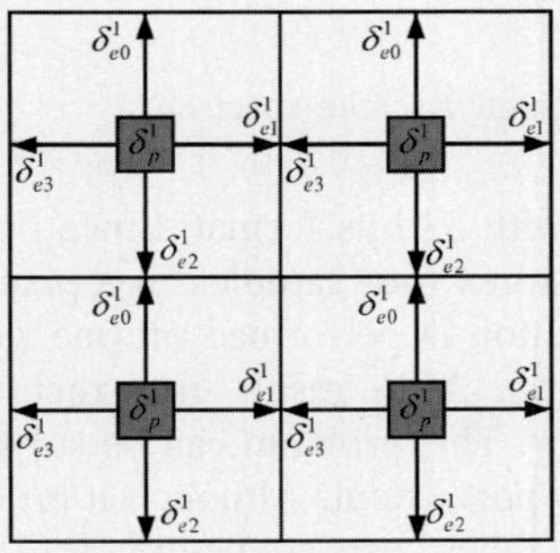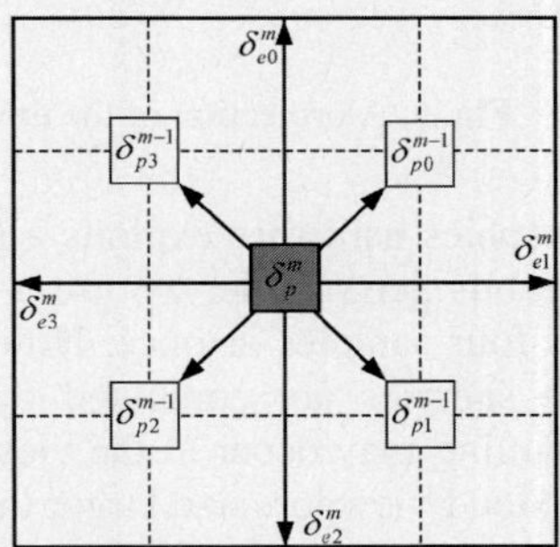

Fig. 4. An example of computing a node error (δ_{pi}^m) in level 0 (left) and level m (right). The gray rectangle denotes a node error in current level, and the blank rectangle represents errors of child node's in finer level.

error metrics. In the other levels, the node error is the maximum value of four edge's error metrics as well as errors of four child nodes as described in (4). Fig. 4 shows how to store and index the node error in an e-buffer.

$$\delta_p^m = \max_{i=0}^{3}\left(\delta_{ei}^m\right). \quad (m=1) \tag{3}$$

$$\delta_p^m = \max\left[\max_{i=0}^{3}\left(\delta_{ei}^m\right), \max_{i=0}^{3}\left(\delta_{pi}^{m-1}\right)\right]. \quad (1<m<k) \tag{4}$$

3.2 Triangulation Using the f-Buffer

The e-buffer has node error (δ_{pi}^m) and edge error (δ_{ei}^m) for all levels of quadtree. Through the f-buffer update step, we can determine the inclusion of a node and an edge in a terrain mesh using those errors, and store enabling flag into the f-buffer. In triangulation step, our method generates a terrain mesh using the f-buffer. That is, only if the values of enabling flag of a node or an edge is set, it will be included in the terrain mesh. Since the update step does not require hierarchical information, it can be implemented in the fragment shader of GPU.

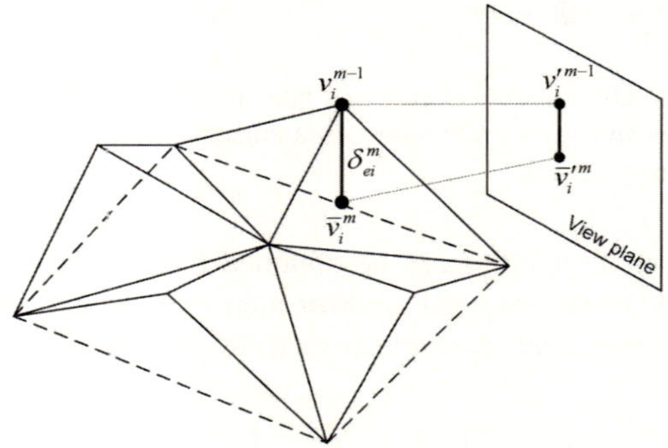

Fig. 5. A projection of the error metric to compute a screen-space error

The graphics hardware exploits a render target with 32-bits format. Since f-buffer requires 8-bits per sample, we use a method that stores four samples in a pixel and processes four samples at once. However, a projection is performed on one sample and three samples are computed by approximation. As a result, incorrect view-frustum culling may occur at the viewport boundary. This problem can be solved by slightly extend viewport size larger than actual viewport extent. Although it produces little additional polygons and takes some more time, thoes costs are negligible.

3.2.1 The f-Buffer Update
The f-buffer is updated using error metrics in the e-buffer. In update step, LOD selection and view-frustum culling is performed to determine visibility of each edges and nodes. In our method, LOD selection and view-frustum culling are performed on the

screen space. So all vertices are must projected on the view plane. A vertex in the world space (v_i^m) can be calculated using a height map. A projected vertex ($v_i^{\prime m}$) can be computed by transforming v_i^m using World-View-Projection matrix (see Fig. 5).

For LOD selection, we compute a projected error metric by measuring the distance between two projected vertices ($v_i^{\prime m-1}$ and $\bar{v}_i^{\prime m}$) in successive levels of detail. The projected error metric means the number of influenced pixels when switching two levels. Therefore, if the projected error metric is greater than a user-defined threshold (τ), lower level can be selected. Otherwise upper level should be selected to prevent popping.

View-frustum culling is performed by testing whether $v_i^{\prime m-1}$ is in the viewport or not. If so, the node or the edge is included in the terrain mesh because it means the correspond vertex in world space (v_i^m) is in the view-frustum.

By the results of LOD selection and view-frustum culling, visibilities of all vertices are determined. The visibilities are stored into the *f*-buffer as boolean values. By using values in the *f*-buffer, a terrain mesh is generated.

3.2.2 The *f*-Buffer Refinement

Because the updated *f*-buffer was generated without relationship of neighbor nodes, T-junction or cracks might be occurred in a result of triangulation. So it is not suitable for a fine terrain mesh. To remove the problems, we refine the *f*-buffer to make a restricted quadtree by following criteria [9].

- An enabling flag of the node is true when at least one edge is enabled among the four adjacent edges to the node.
- An enabling flag of the edge is true when at least one node is enabled among the two adjacent nodes to edge of upper level.

3.2.3 A Terrain Mesh Generation

To generate the terrain mesh, we traverse the refined *f*-buffer hierarchically using the block-based method [2]. And we generate a triangle-fan for each node according to visibilities of vertices in the *f*-buffer.

4 Experimental Results

Our method has been implemented on dual Intel Pentium Xeon™ 3.0GHz and 2GB main memory. Graphics accelerator was NVIDIA GeForce™ 6600GT with 128MB video memory and it installed on PCI Express×4 BUS. We set τ for projected error as one pixel. The viewport size is 512×512. We use Puget and Grand-Canyon dataset. Because a rendering performance is dependent upon the viewing condition, we measure the rendering time under two viewing conditions.

Fig. 6 describes elapsed times of the update, refinement and triangulation stage for two datasets in two cases of viewing conditions. Among the three stages, the update stage takes the most time during render a scene. GPU-based implementation significantly accelerates its update time. So overall performance increased up in comparison to the CPU-based method.

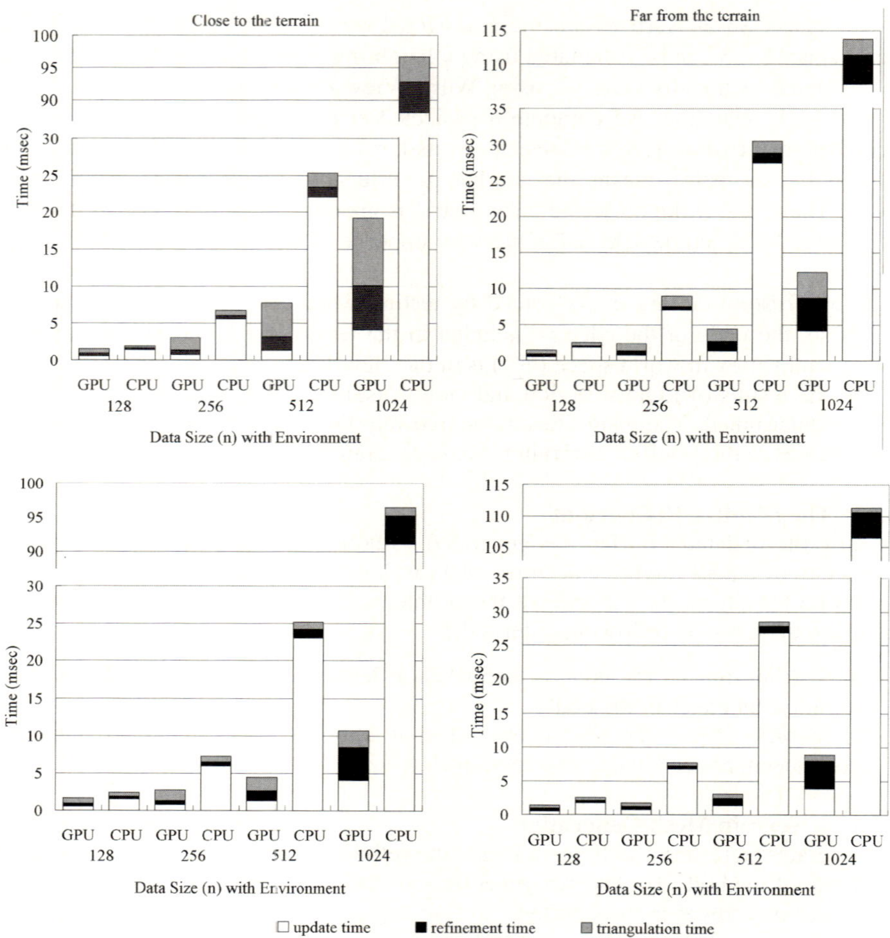

Fig. 6. Performance comparison of each stage for two datasets and two viewing conditions. Grand-Canyon dataset is on the upper row and Puget dataset is on the lower row. A left column is results when viewer is close to the terrain. A right column is results when viewer is far from the terrain.

We use the GPU only for the update step of the f-buffer. Therefore, the refinement step of the f-buffer in two approaches is identical. In a triangulation step, however, a GPU-based approach requires more time compared with the CPU-based approach because more polygons is rendered by limitation of graphics accelerator capabilities as mentioned in Sect 3.1. However the update step of the f-buffer is accelerated by GPU. So it makes up for wasted polygon and time for transferring the f-buffer contents via system bus.

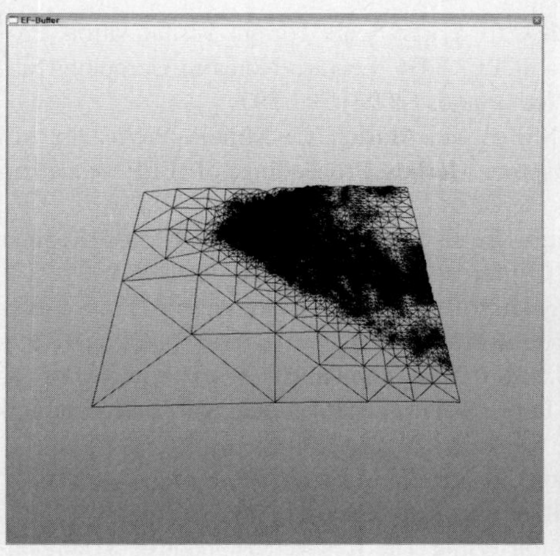

Fig. 7. Resulting images rendered with our method. The left image shows a triangulated mesh of our method using Grand-Canyon dataset (513×513). The right image is a rendered image using a lightmap to prevent shading artifacts.

5   Conclusion

We propose the *e*-buffer and the *f*-buffer for performing quadtree-based terrain visualization on the GPU. By using the *e*-buffer and the *f*-buffer, fast LOD selection and view-frustum culling in the fragment shader is possible. As a result, we achieved seamless terrain visualization in real-time. Also we confirm a GPU-based method is at least five times faster than CPU-based approach in the largest dataset (1025×1025). In our method, it takes a long time for read back the *f*-buffer from the GPU. However, since system bus is enhancing continuously, we expect that performance of our method will be improved in the future architectures.

Acknowledgements

This research was supported by the MIC (Ministry of Information and Communication), Korea, under the ITRC (Information Technology Research Center) support program supervised by the IITA (Institute of Information Technology Assessment).

References

1. Lindstrom, P., Koller, D., Ribarsky, W., Hodges, L., Faust, N., Turner, G.: Real-time, Continuous Level of Detail Rendering of Height Fields. Proceedings of ACM SIGGRAPH 96, Addison Wesley (1996) 109-118
2. Röttger, S., Heidrich, W., Slusallek, P., Seidel, H.: Real-Time Generation of Continuous Levels of Detail for Height Fields. Proceedings of 6th International Conference in Central Europe on Computer Graphics and Visualization (1998) 315-322

3. Shin, B., Choi, E.: An Efficient CLOD Method for Large-Scale Terrain Visualization. Proceedings of The Entertainment Computing – ICEC 2004. Lecture Notes in Computer Science, Vol. 3166. Springer, Eindhoven, The Netherlands (2004) 592-597
4. Duchaineau, M., Wolinsky, M., Sigeti, D., Miller, M., Aldrich, C., Mineev-Weinstein, M.: ROAMing Terrain: Real-time Optimally Adapting Meshes. Proceedings of IEEE Visualization 97 (1997) 81-88
5. Losasso, F., Hoppe, H.: Geometry Clipmaps: Terrain Rendering Using Nested Regular Grids. Proceedings of the 2004 SIGGRAPH Conference, Vol. 23 (2004) 769-776
6. Schneider, J., Westermann, R.: GPU-Friendly High-Quality Terrain Rendering. Proceedings of Journal of WSCG, Plzen-Bory Czech Republic (2006) 49-56
7. Agrawal, A., Radhakrishna, M., Joshi, R.C.: Using Programmable GPU Hardware for Increased Visual Effects and Photorealism in Large-Scale Terrain Visualization. Proceedings of Map India (2006)
8. Tanner, C., Migdal, C., Jones, M.: The clipmap: A Virtual Mipmap. Proceedings of the 25th annual conference on Computer graphics and interactive techniques (1998) 151-158
9. Pajarola, R.: Large Scale Terrain Visualization Using The Restricted Quadtree Triangulation. Proceedings of IEEE Visualization 98 (1998) 19-26

Computer Simulation of Woven Fabric Defects Based on Faulty Yarn Photographs

Hakan Özdemir and Güngör Başer

Dokuz Eylül University, Department of Textile Engineering, 35100 İzmir, Turkey
hakanoz.demir@deu.edu.tr, gungor.baser@deu.edu.tr

Abstract. In this work, the appearance of woven fabric defects due to yarn faults has been simulated by a method developed which is based on photographs taken from yarns along their lengths. Simulation of woven fabric is based on yarn and fabric cross sectional geometry as well as on yarn measurements and images. The transformation of yarn from a straight circular cylinder to a flattened and crimped form in fabric structure is modelled mathematically and this is applied to obtain its projected image on the fabric surface by resizing the yarn image on the photographic plane. The resized yarn images thus obtained are, then, rearranged to simulate pixel based fabric surface appearance onto which images of faulty yarn sections are superposed. This is achieved by a suitable software developed, based on raster graphics. The faulty fabric simulations are confined to single fabrics of plain, matt and twill weaves with neps, slubs, thick and thin places.

Keywords: Fabric simulation, fabric appearance, woven fabric faults, elastica curve, yarn flattening.

1   Introduction

Because staple fibres are not regularly included and twisted in yarn structure, spun yarns contain both random and periodic irregularities. These irregularities include defects such as thick and thin places, neps (small fibre entanglements), hairiness, random or planned futures such as slubs (irregularity created during spinning). Irregularities in yarn may be small (in the range of a millimetre or two) or long (in the range of tens of millimetres or longer). Yarn imperfections often have great effects, which may be desirable or undesirable, on the visual appearance of a finished fabric.

Many computer software exist in the market to design woven fabrics of simple and complex structures which enable the designer to create a fabric, guiding the designer in the selection of numerous design parameters, and also showing the fabric appearance simulated on the computer screen. To mention a few, there are software of Fashion Studio, Nedgraphics, Pointcarré and Wonder Weaves Systems which provide fabric simulations from simulated yarn images. Uster Zellweger, Zweigle and Loepfe, on the other hand, provide fabric simulation software to examine probable fabric defects due to faulty yarns to evaluate fabric quality. Adabala, Thalmann and Fei developed a technique for visualizing woven textiles in real time, while optimising a realistic fabric appearance. The proposed approach supports rendering of

A. Levi et al. (Eds.): ISCIS 2006, LNCS 4263, pp. 325–333, 2006.
© Springer-Verlag Berlin Heidelberg 2006

complex weave patterns by adopting Weaving Information File (WIF), a standard used in Computer Aided Design (CAD) of textile for representing the grammar of weaving [1]. Křemenáková, Sirková and Garg developed a textile design system which focused on the prediction of the structure as well as properties of the fibres, yarns and of the fabrics. The principal aim of the system is to obtain fabric design optimisation on the basis of virtually created fabrics [9]. Keefe proposed a methodology to take into account potential effects of compressibility on a twisted assembly. His approach assumes that an individual yarn in compression could be approximated by a single element with an elliptical cross-section [7]. In another work, Keefe used elliptical cross sectional yarns in the basic plain weave pattern [8].

Fabric simulations mentioned above are generally based on artificially constructed yarn images from given or measured yarn parameters by some mathematical algorithm developed. However, work was reported previously by the authors on the simulation of plain woven fabric based on yarn photographs taken by still camera [11]. This would provide a more realistic real time simulation of fabric appearance. It is the aim of the work reported here to develop a method to simulate the defective woven fabric appearance based on actual yarn photographs taken by a stationary camera.

2 Theoretical

2.1 Mathematical Model

The mathematical model developed for the resizing of yarn image on the photographic plane to its appearance as its top view on the fabric surface may briefly be explained as follows:

Fig.1 shows how the cylindrical surface of yarn is generated from yarn image and transformed into an elliptic cylinder surface and re-projected on the fabric plane. It

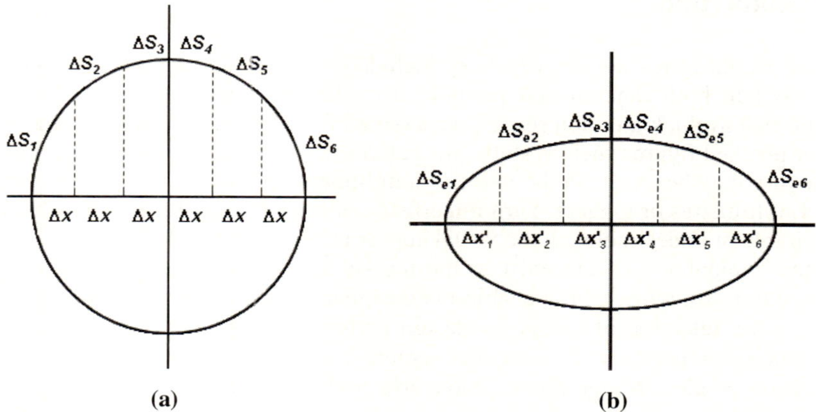

Fig. 1. (a) Constituting surface development of yarn cylinder from the planar projection of yarn cylinder, **(b)** Transforming the surface development of yarn cylinder to elliptical surface

was assumed that circular yarn cross section was deformed to an elliptical cross section of the same circumference [3] and that yarns were flattened along the major diameter in medium sett fabrics [5].

The crimped shape of the yarn central axis in plain weave structure, whose cross section is shown in Fig. 2, was modelled by elastica curve [12] lying in a plane perpendicular to fabric surface as shown in Fig. 3a. To simulate the top view of the yarn in fabric structure, it is necessary to define the projection of elastica curve onto x axis as shown in Fig. 3b. The processes for both the transformation of circular yarn cross section to a flattened elliptic section and the projection of elastica curve onto x axis were performed by equations given in earlier work [11].

Fig. 2. Cross sectional view of plain weave

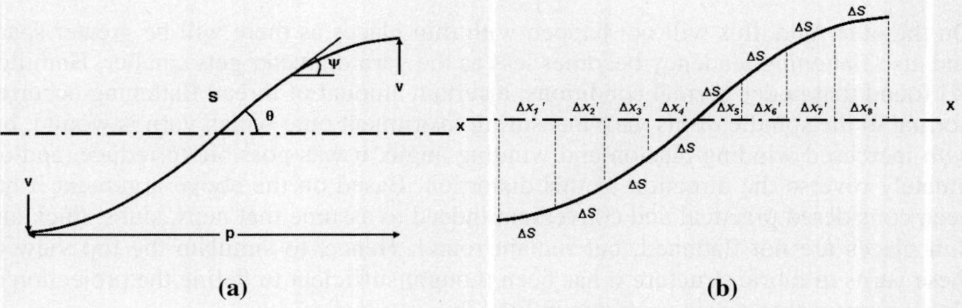

(a)   (b)

Fig. 3. (a) Modelling of yarn axis by elastica curve, **(b)** Projection of elastica curve onto x axis

2.2 Modelling Structures Other Than Plain Weave

Method of simulating plain weave fabric appearance was reported earlier [11]. For simulating various woven structures other than plain weave such as 2/2 twill, 1/3 twill and 2/2 matt, the assumption was made that the yarn path followed the elastica curve in intersecting parts whereas it remained straight in flat portions, namely floats. Cross sections of these weaves based on Hamilton's models of fabric cross sections [5] are displayed in Fig. 4. In all three weaves the reverse version of a cross section can be obtained from the original one using symmetry properties. Ashenhurst's 1st Setting Theory [2] was used in fabric simulations to calculate appropriate yarn spaces for fabric simulations.

2.3 Modelling Faulty Yarns

Thick places, slubs and neps are flattened along the major yarn diameter first, and are pressed in the course of weaving along fabric plane by the pressure of adjacent yarns.

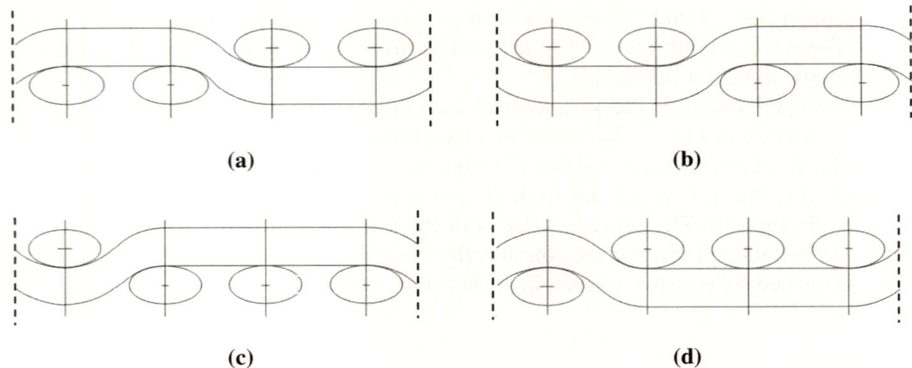

(a)   **(b)**

(c)   **(d)**

Fig. 4. Cross sectional views: **(a)** Cross sectional view of 2/2 matt in first two cross sections both in weft and warp direction, the same as the first cross section both in weft and warp direction in 2/2 twill, **(b)** Cross sectional view in the reverse manner to that above, **(c)** Cross sectional view of the forth weft in 1/3 twill, **(d)** Cross sectional view of the first warp in 1/3 twill

On the other end, this will not happen with thin places as there will be greater space and also flattening tendency becomes less as the yarn diameter gets smaller. Hamilton [4] found that under normal conditions, a certain amount of thread flattening occurred normal to the spindle of his yarn measuring instrument onto which yarn is wound, but with increased winding tension and winding angle, it was possible to reduce, and ultimately reverse the direction of this distortion. Based on the above argument it has been considered practical and convenient indeed to assume that neps, slubs, thick and thin places are not flattened, but remain round. Hence, to simulate the top view of these yarns in fabric structure it has been thought sufficient to define the projection of elastica curve onto x axis as shown in Fig. 3b.

3 Experimental

3.1 Materials

Photographs of 50 tex carded cotton yarn bobbins were used to generate fabric simulations. Photographs of faulty yarn portions (slubs, neps, thick and thin places) removed by the yarn clearing device of the winding machine were employed in defective fabric simulations.

3.2 Taking Yarn Photographs

As a preliminary experiment, photographs of yarns both in horizontal direction and in stationary state were taken by a Sony TRV 40E model digital video camera assembled on a photograph taking platform. The camera is moveable in vertical direction. Digital video camera was arranged to manual focus mode and therefore a fixed focus length was used during recordings. Both digital video cassette and memory stick were used to store the images obtained.

4 Image Processing Methods

Yarn photographs taken by digital video camera were transferred to the computer directly by means of a connection cable as JPEG. The computer used in processes had Pentium(R) IV CPU and 1 GB RAM.

4.1 Processing Yarn Images for Simulations

Each picture file was converted to Photoshop PSD and PPM file with Photoshop 6.0 to enable it being processed with both Photoshop 6.0 and C programming codes. The ground colour was erased and the images were cropped in pixel values related to the thread spacing by both Photoshop 6.0 and Matlab 5.3. In Photoshop, these processes can be done by Mask Pro 3 Tool or by Magic Wand Tool or by Colour Range Command. Cropped yarn images whose ground colours were erased were copied to new layers whose grounds were transparent. The new layers were then saved as picture file in TIFF format. In Photoshop, these processes are saved as action and applied to the directory selected. In Matlab, these processes are performed by converting RGB image to binary image by im2bw function, whose one of its parameters is threshold value. While RGB values of colour image are stored in 3D arrays, values of binary image are stored in 2D arrays in Matlab. In addition to this, images are processed with program codes in C by dynamic memory management functions which allocate a memory (RAM) for arrays. RGB and binary image values are transferred to arrays by C codes. While elements of arrays of RGB image are strucks with 3 elements, elements of binary image are unsigned char. Programs both in Matlab and in C perform processes by applying matrix operations on the yarn images on pixel level. Coordinates of elements of array are determined by controlling yarn colour in binary image. If yarn colour is light, binary value of yarn image value will be 1, but if yarn colour is dark, binary value of yarn image value will be 0. So, processes required are performed at elements of RGB image arrays in parallel to elements of binary image arrays.

Binary and RGB values of frames are transferred to a different array consecutively in rows. As in previous work [11], the problems of defining yarn outlines, of orienting yarns parallel to x axis and of aligning yarn segments appearing in separate frames which have to be joined later on are to be solved by programs written in Matlab and C.

With programs written in Matlab and C, bottom and top boundary of yarns in images are found by controlling yarn colour, areas of yarn images, centres of gravities of yarn images, average vertical lengths (average yarn diameters) and orientations of yarn images are calculated by image processing methods developed using available algorithms [6],[13].

Small faulty areas resulting from rotating in the first and last rows in binary image are controlled. Then value of 0 or 1 is appointed in binary image and value of white colour (255) is appointed in colour image. Arrays whose numbers of rows are changed because of rotating will be transferred to an array whose number of rows is equal to the crop width, side by side and by centring them in array.

Attributes of image mentioned above are calculated again. If y values of centre of gravity of images are different from y values of centre of crop, images will be transferred so that y values of centre of gravity of images will be equal to y values of centre of crop. Rotated and non rotated images are joined end to end to become one of the horizontal yarn images. Ground colour value is appointed for horizontal yarn image either by C codes directly or via keyboard.

The alternative methods mentioned above give similar results, so any one of them may be employed.

4.2 Resizing Yarn Images

While the projections of intersecting segments were images resized in directions both perpendicular to yarn axis and along the yarn axis, the projections of the floating segments were resized only in direction perpendicular to yarn axis. While the increments of Δx along the yarn diameter in the projected image were resized to the increments of x_i', the increments of ΔS along the straight yarn length were resized to the increments of $\Delta x_i''$ in order to create the yarn image in fabric structure from the processed and joined frames. For faulty yarn portions, resizing process was applied only in one direction along the yarn axis.

Weaves have different cross sections in weft and warp directions, so unit lengths of segments to resize are different from each other. While in 2/2 twill and 2/2 matt weaves, resizing procedure is applied for repeats comprising of half the total arc length of elastica for cross over section plus a length equal to (or a certain amount shorter in 2/2 matt than) its projection for the flat section, in 1/3 twill weave resizing is applied along the whole weave unit comprising of a length equal to two total arc lengths of elastica curve plus a length equal to their projections. On the other hand, lengths of repeat to resize in plain weave will be equal to the arc length of the elastica curve. Yarn images resized for plain weave are shown in Fig. 5.

Fig. 5. Yarn images resized: (**a**) Yarn image resized for plain weave, (**b**) Image of thick place resized for plain weave, (**c**) Image of thin place resized for plain weave, (**d**) Image of nep resized for plain weave, (**e**) Image of slub resized for plain weave

In the application of the theory developed to calculate resizing factors, the eccentricity of elliptic yarn cross section, $e = b / a$, was assumed to be 0.6. As for the calculation of resizing factors to be applied to the yarn photographs in the direction of yarn axis, a weave angle of $\theta = 40°$ was assumed, which gave a crimp factor, S/p, equal to 1.27. This represents a medium to high sett fabric.

A computer program in C was written to calculate the resizing values, to resize these cropped yarn images in vertical and horizontal directions and to lay these resized yarn images side by side in vertical and horizontal directions to align the intersecting yarn sections.

4.3 Weave Simulation by Faulty Yarns

Space is allocated for an array of fabric simulation whose number of rows and columns are equal to the number of columns of resized horizontal image in pixel. Horizontal yarn images are rotated 90° clockwise to obtain vertical yarn images. Procedures were built in the program to simulate weave structures by transferring pixel values of horizontal or vertical image arrays of fabric simulation according to the particular weave structure required, by controlling ground colour and by transferring pixel values of crossing yarn image. Faulty yarn portions resized for the crimped shape according to fabric cross sections of the particular weave structure are superposed on the fabric simulation from normal yarns, by using these portions in place of the normal yarn portions, the starting points being selected by random numbers defined by random function. This is achieved by transforming this random number to row and column numbers first and then multiplying it with crop width in pixels. If faulty yarn portions are placed in horizontal (weft) direction, transformed column numbers are modified so as to be one more than a whole multiple of the repeat size of the weave unit. If faulty yarn portions are placed in vertical (warp) direction, the modification procedure will be applied to row numbers in similar way. The array of fabric simulation is recorded as PPM file. Space assigned in memory for all images are set free.

Example of faulty plain fabric simulation achieved is shown in Fig. 6 in versions as in actual fabric dimensions. A thick place is seen on top left of the picture and following this a nep in middle extreme right, a slub on bottom left and two thin places on bottom right can be observed.

5 Discussion and Conclusions

For the application of resizing algorithms realistic and consistent geometrical models for both yarn flattening and yarn curve are necessary. It was thought that a constant perimeter deformation of the cross sectional yarn shape in flattening is more realistic than constant area deformation especially in cotton yarns which are more compressible [3]. Elliptic cross sectional shape seems to be more realistic when actual photographs of fabric sections are examined [10], [14]. As for the degree of flattening, a value of 0.6 may be considered a reasonable value for medium sett fabrics and it is a convenient value to display an appreciable resizing. It may however be changed as desired.

The application of the elastica curve in plain weave geometry presents no difficulty and should be preferred being closer to reality than a sinus curve. A weave angle of 40° represents medium to high sett fabrics, but because of inadequate number of pixels obtained in yarn image due to camera resolution, a smaller weave angle could not be employed. The weave angle calculated, using Peirce's simplified formulas, for a fabric sett according to Ashenhurst's 1st Theory [2] is 30° and this represents a medium or normal sett fabric giving a crimp factor of 1,14.

Fig. 6. Simulation of plain weave with nep, slub, thick and thin places in weft direction

Obtaining fabric simulation with yarn faults by the method developed is not difficult, because applying mathematical transformations and procedures, and reaching elements of image arrays presenting pixels are easy.

Although the crimped shape of the faulty yarn portions is not expected to be too different from that of a normal yarn portion, it is obvious that the distortion of the faulty yarn cross section will be very different from that of a normal yarn during weaving.

Except in high sett and jammed fabrics and in high sett fabrics of weaves with long floats, yarn flattening occurs in vertical direction to fabric plane [5]. In faulty yarn portions, however, there will be compression in horizontal direction (along major diameter) due to adjacent yarns if faulty portion is a nep or a slub or a thick place. In such a case flattening may occur along two perpendicular directions and the final shape cannot, at all, be assumed. Moreover, there will be jamming of the normal yarns in the neighbourhood of a thick place and a few of next or prior weft yarns may also be curved. It will, however, be very difficult to work out a more realistic simulation model as such and develop mathematics to reflect the actual distortion on the fabric structure due to a thick place. It may, though, not be so necessary, from a practical point of view.

It may be stated that with the proposed method many fabric defects due to yarn faults can be simulated, but for a more realistic simulation structural models of yarn and fabric distortions should to be developed for each type of yarn fault.

Acknowledgements. The authors wish to acknowledge the technical support of TARİŞ Spinning Plant, İzmir. Thanks are also due to Dr. S. GUMUSTEKIN, Dr. M. CINSDIKICI, L. CETIN, MSc. and O. SAHİN, BSc. for their help and valuable discussions.

References

1. Adabala, N., Thalmann, N. M., Fei, G.: Real-time Visualization of Woven Textiles. Journal of Textile Institute, Vol. 86, No. 4 (1995) 635-648
2. Ashenhurst, T. R.: A Treatise on Textile Calculations and the Structure of Fabrics. J. Broadbent and Co., London (1884)
3. Baser, G.: The Transverse Compression of Helices with Special Reference to the Compression of Yarns. PhD thesis. The University of Leeds, Leeds (1965)
4. Hamilton, J. B.: A Direct Method for Measuring Yarn Diameters and Bulk Densities under Conditions of Thread Flattening. Journal of Textile Institute, Vol. 50, T 655 (1959)
5. Hamilton, J. B.: A General System of Woven Fabric Geometry. Journal of Textile Institute, Vol. 55, No.1, T 66 (1964)
6. Jain, R., Kasturi, R., Schunck, B. G.: Machine Vision. McGraw-Hill, New York (1995)
7. Keefe, M.: Solid Modeling Applied to Fibrous Assemblies Part I: Twisted Yarns. Journal of Textile Institute, Vol. 85, No. 3 (1994) 338-349
8. Keefe, M.: Solid Modeling Applied to Fibrous Assemblies Part II: Woven Structure. Journal of Textile Institute, Vol. 85, No. 3 (1994) 350-358
9. Křemenáková, D., Sirková, B. K., Garg A.: Computer Aided Textile Design. 3rd Indo-Czech Textile Research Conference, Liberec (2004)
10. Meriç, B.: Dokumada Kıvrım Oluşumunun ve Değişiminin % 100 Pamuklu ve % 100 Polyester Kumaşlar Üzerinde Mekanik ve Yapısal Etkilerinin Araştırılması. PhD Thesis. Uludağ University, Bursa (1995)
11. Özdemir, H., Başer, G.: Computer Simulation of Woven Structures Based on Actual Yarn Photographs. 17th IMACS World Congress Scientific Computation, Applied Mathematics and Simulation, Paris (2005)
12. Peirce, F. T.: The Geometry of Cloth Structure. Journal of Textile Institute, Vol. 28, T 45 (1937)
13. Pitas, I.: Digital Image Processing Algorithms. Prentice Hall, New Jersey (1993)
14. Snowden, D. C.: Thread Spacings in Woven Fabrics. Institut Textile de France, No. 4 (1965) 331-341

Bidirectional Distancemap
for Efficient Volume Ray Casting

Sukhyun Lim and Byeong-Seok Shin

Inha University, Dept. Computer Science and Information Engineering,
253 Yonghyun-dong, Nam-gu, Inchon, 402-751, Rep. of Korea
`slim@inhaian.net, bsshin@inha.ac.kr`

Abstract. A method using a ray-coherence in volume ray casting skips over transparent region efficiently because a current ray advances as the amount of the leaping distance between an image plane and the object boundary of a representative ray. If the ray jumps over the object boundary, a user-selected constant distance of which the size is larger than the unit distance is commonly used to reach the boundary quickly. However, since we cannot determine an accurate distance, the traversal speed depends on the constant distance. In this paper, to support efficient space-leaping in transparent region and to determine the distance from inside of an object to its boundary, we generate a distancemap for transparent region as well as for nontransparent region, named bidirectional distancemap. In rendering step, a current ray advances as the amount of the leaping distance of a representative ray. If it lies on transparent region, we use our distancemap for transparent region such as the previous approaches. Otherwise, when it already jumps over an object boundary, the distancemap for nontransparent region is exploited.

1   Introduction

Volume visualization is a research area that deals with various techniques to extract meaningful and visual information from volume data [1], [2]. One of the most frequently applied techniques is direct volume rendering, producing high-quality 3D rendered images directly from volume data without intermediate representation. Volume ray casting is a well-known direct volume rendering method [1]. In general, it requires two steps [3]. First, a ray advances through transparent region. Second, the ray integrates colors and opacities as it penetrates an object boundary. Since the transparent region does not contribute to the final image [3], [4], [5], skipping the region increases rendering performance without affecting image quality.

A number of researchers have proposed space-leaping methods to skip over transparent region. A distance-transform-based (distancemap-based) approach proposed by Zuiderveld *et al.* [6] is one of the space-leaping methods. It computes the distance from each voxel to the nearest nontransparent voxel, and saves it in a distancemap structure. Since the distance values are the minimum distance to reach the object boundary, a ray leaps over transparent region without entering the inside of a structure. Later, it was surveyed as a proximity-clouds method by Cohen and Sheffer [7]. Yagel and Shi introduced a C-buffer (Coordinates-buffer) based method to accelerate

A. Levi et al. (Eds.): ISCIS 2006, LNCS 4263, pp. 334–342, 2006.

the process of volume rendering in a sequence of images [8]. It is based on exploiting temporal coherence by using consecutive images. Another technique by Wan *et al.* [9] has used temporal and spatial coherence, simultaneously. For exploiting temporal coherence, they project visible cells from the previous frame onto the image plane of the current frame, and update the depth buffer to be used for the current frame. Sramek and Kaufman proposed a view-sensitive extension of the distancemap-based approach [10]. Recently, Lakare and Kaufman exploited a ray-coherence [11]. After firing some rays to detect how far an object is from the image plane (*representative rays*), other adjacent rays use the result to leap over transparent region.

In this paper, we call a distance between an image plane and an object boundary (surface) as a *leaping distance*, and assume that the image size is N^2, the i-th ray is r_i $(0 \leq i < N^2)$, and the leaping distance of a r_i is d_i. The procedure of the previous method using a ray-coherence [11] is as follows: firstly, the r_i advances as the amount of the leaping distance d_{i-1} of a representative ray. Then, if the r_i lies on transparent region, it also refers a distancemap to reach the boundary (see Fig. 1 (a)). Otherwise (that is, when it locates at the inside of an interesting object), it performs backtracking until it arrives at the boundary (see Fig. 1 (b)).

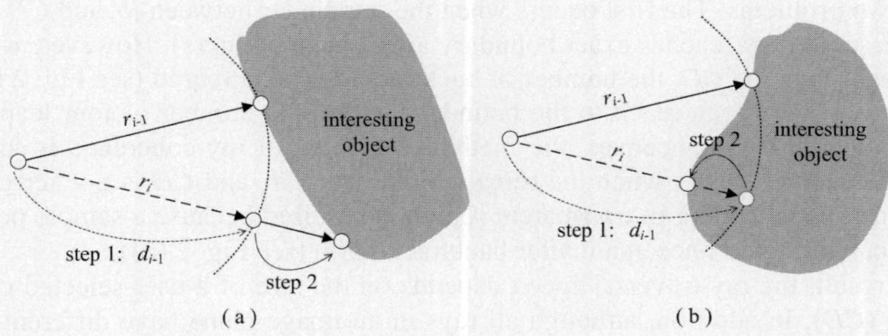

Fig. 1. The previous space-leaping method using a ray-coherence. There are two cases: (a) After a r_i advances as the amount of the d_{i-1} (step 1), our method refers a distancemap to reach the boundary of an interesting object because a sample point lies on transparent region (step 2). (b) When the r_i already jumps over the boundary after leaping (step 1), it backtracks to the boundary (step 2).

Since distance values in a distancemap are the minimum distances to reach non-transparent voxels, a ray refers to the distancemap several times to reach exact boundary. Therefore, the method using a ray-coherence property can reduce traversal time. However, if the ray jumps over the boundary, we cannot determine an optimal distance to reach the boundary. The simple way is that it backtracks to the object boundary by advancing as the amount of the unit distance 1.0. In this case, however, because the time for backtracking is slow, a user-defined constant distance whose size is larger than 1.0 is commonly used. We call this previous approach as a *Constant Backtracking Method (CBM)*. However, because the constant distance is only estimated by experiment (that is, it depends on the volume datasets and viewing conditions), the ray-traversal time is affected to the distance. To solve the problem, we propose a *bidirectional distancemap*. In preprocessing step, we generate a distancemap for transparent region as in the conventional distancemap approaches [6], [7], [10]. Then, we update it for nontransparent region. In rendering step, after exploiting a ray-coherence property, if a ray lies on transparent region, we use a bidirectional distancemap to skip over transparent region. When the ray already jumps over the object boundary, our distancemap generated for nontransparent region is also used. Therefore, our approach supports efficient space-leaping since distance values exist in our distancemap structure for transparent and nontransparent region simultaneously.

In section 2, we review the problems of the CBM. Then, we explain our structure in detail in section 3. Experimental results are shown in section 4. Finally, we conclude our work.

2   The Problems of the Constant Backtracking Method

We assume that a distance between an arbitrary sample point inside the interesting object and its boundary of the r_i is ib_i, and the size of a user-selected constant distance is CD. The simple way is that we set the CD as the unit distance 1.0. However, because it increases the traversal time, the CD of which the size is larger than 1.0 is commonly used. In this case, although a ray reaches an object boundary quickly, it causes two problems. The first occurs when the remainder between ib_i and CD is zero. In this case, the ray reaches exact boundary after backtracking(s). However, when the ib_i is longer than the CD, the number of backtrackings is increased (see Fig. 2 (a)). In this figure, if the r_i can reach to the boundary within the number of four leaps using only conventional distancemap, the method exploiting a ray-coherence is less efficient. The second occurs when the remainder between ib_i and CD is not zero. In this case, extra space-leaping in transparent region is required because a sample point lies on transparent region once again after backtracking(s) (see Fig. 2 (b)).

As a result, the ray-traversal speed depends on the size of a user-selected constant distance (CD). In addition, although all rays in an image plane have differently optimal distance to reach their boundaries, the CBM exploits only identical CD for all rays.

3   Bidirectional Distancemap

If we can determine an accurate distance to reach an object boundary quickly even if a ray lies on the inside of an object, we solve the two problems as denoted in Sect. 2. Therefore, we propose a bidirectional distancemap.

3.1   Preprocessing

The preprocessing stage is composed of three steps. Firstly, we generate a distancemap for transparent region. This is identical to the conventional distancemap approaches [6], [7], [10]. Secondly, we invert an OTF (Opacity Transfer Function). That is, we regard transparent region as nontransparent one, and vice versa. Then, we perform distance-transform operation once again. In this case, a distancemap is generated for nontransparent region (interesting object).

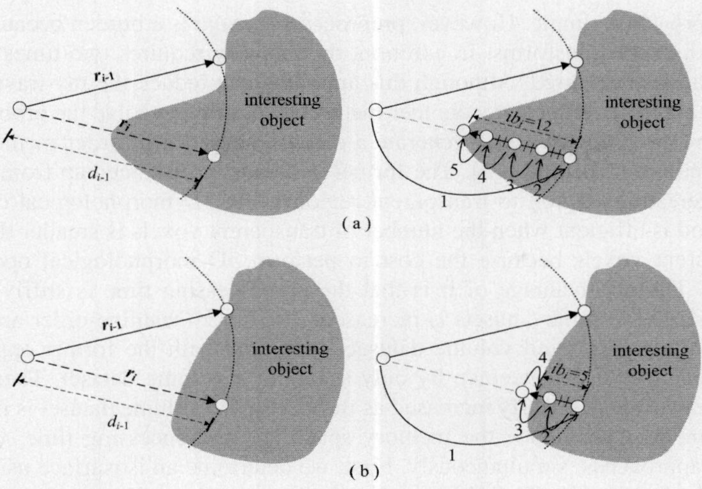

Fig. 2. Two possible cases when we use the CBM. Assume that a user-selected constant distance (CD) is 3. (a) After advancing as the amount of d_{i-1} (left), the r_i reaches to the object boundary by performing four times backtrackings (right, from step 2 to step 5). (b) The r_i advances as the amount of d_{i-1} (left). After two times backtrackings (step 2 and step 3), it has to refer a distancemap once again (step 4) because a sample point locates at transparent region again (right).

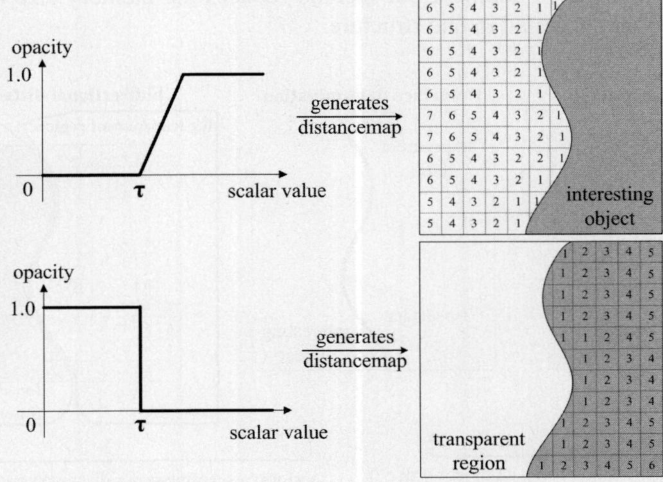

Fig. 3. The preprocessing stage to generate a bidirectional distancemap. Since there are no translucent voxels in nontransparent region, we regard the shape of an OTF as the binary type. τ means the changing position of an opacity value.

This approach is simple. However, preprocessing stage is a burden because we perform two distance-transforms. In addition, the memory requires two times since two distancemaps are required. Although this approach can reduce the ray-traversal time, we cannot exploit it. Therefore, another method is required to solve the problems.

There are two approaches to generate a distancemap: object-order method [6], [7] and scanline-order method [12]. The former generates a distancemap from nontransparent (interesting) region to transparent region using 3D morphological operations. This method is efficient when the number of transparent voxels is smaller than that of nontransparent voxels because the cost to perform 3D morphological operations is expensive. The disadvantage of it is that the preprocessing time is stiffly increased when the size of volume datasets is increased. The latter (scanline-order approach) is appropriate for large-sized volume datasets compared with the former approach because it generates a distancemap by only scanning a volume dataset. Therefore, the preprocessing time is linearly increased as the size of the volume dataset is increased.

In our method, to reduce the memory space and preprocessing time, we exploit those two approaches, simultaneously. First, we determine an isosurface using object-order methods [6], [7]. The object-order methods make a distancemap by adding distance values from nontransparent voxels to transparent voxels by 3D morphological operations. Therefore, if we stop the procedure after the first iteration, we easily determine an isosurface. Then, we generate a distancemap using scanline-order method [12] from the isosurface. In this case, the distancemap is generated from the isosurface to transparent and to nontransparent region, simultaneously. As a result, by this approach, we can reduce the preprocessing time because additional isosurface determination step is only required compared with the conventional scanline-order distancemap method. In addition, our method reduces the memory size because two distancemaps are generated in one structure.

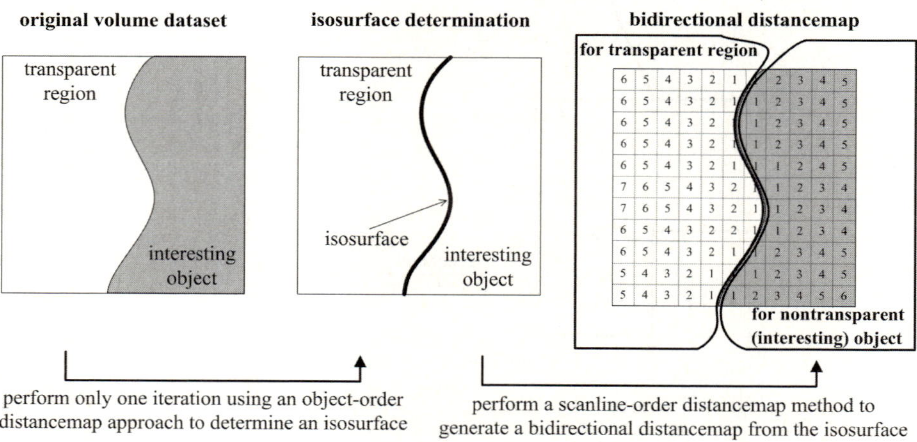

Fig. 4. The structure of a bidirectional distancemap. After determining an isosurface using object-order distancemap approaches, we generate a bidirectional distancemap by exploiting scanline-order methods. As a result, we reduce the memory space and preprocessing time simultaneously.

3.2 Ray Traversal

The ray-traversal scheme is as follows: after firing a ray r_i from a pixel, it advances as the leaping distance d_{i-1} of a representative ray. Then, we refer to a scalar value of the original dataset related to a sample point for the ray. If the scalar value is regarded as transparent by an OTF, the r_i forwards to an object boundary as the amount of stored distance value in a bidirectional distancemap since it means that the r_i still lies on transparent region. Otherwise (that is, the current scalar value is estimated as non-transparent), it backtracks to an object boundary as the amount of stored distance value because the r_i already jumps over the boundary. Then, it performs the conventional volume ray casting to compute a color value. These procedures are repeated for all rays.

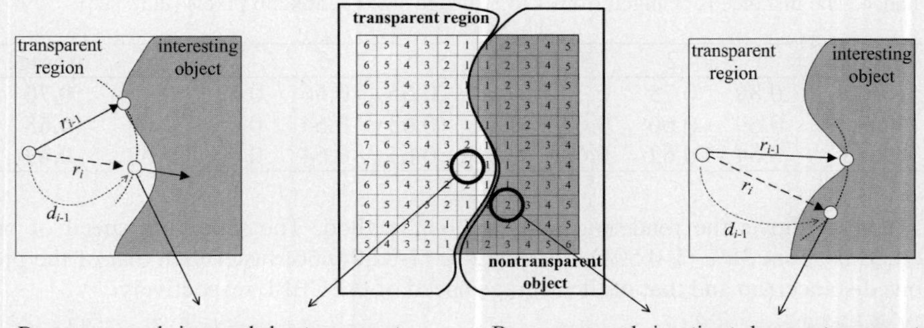

Because a sample is regarded as transparent, the r_i forwards to the boundary as the amount of two

(a)

Because a sample is estimated as nontransparent, the r_i backwards to the boundary as the amount of two

(b)

Fig. 5. The ray-traversal scheme. We cannot determine distance values that are for transparent and nontransparent region by only referring to a bidirectional distancemap. Therefore, we regard it by an OTF. (a) After leaping as the amount of d_{i-1}, the r_i forwards to the boundary because the scalar value for a sample point is transparent. (b) When the sample point locates inside an object (that is, the scalar value for a sample point is nontransparent), the r_i backwards to the boundary.

4 Experimental Results

Our method was implemented on a PC equipped with an AMD Athlon64x2^{TM} 4200+ CPU, 2 GB main memory, and GeForce^{TM} 6600 graphics card. The graphics card capabilities are only used to display the final image. We used three datasets. The first dataset was a teapot scanned at a resolution of 512^3, and the second was a bunny that had a resolution of $512 \times 512 \times 360$. The last dataset was a human head with a resolution of 256^3.

Table 1 shows the preprocessing time. We used the Euclidian distance transform approximated integers as 10, 14 and 17 according to directions [10]. In our method, the time for determination of isosurfaces is included.

Table 1. Comparison of the preprocessing time (unit: sec)

dataset	previous distancemap	our method	**additional time**
teapot	43.03	44.94	**4.4 %**
bunny	33.06	34.08	**3.1 %**
head	5.57	5.80	**4.1 %**

Table 2 shows the rendering time of the CBM [11] under fixed viewing conditions. We experiment on the CBM by changing the distance value from 1 to 8 because we cannot estimate an optimal constant distance to reach an object boundary.

Table 2. Comparison of the rendering time in the CBM according to the size of a constant distance. The distance is changed from 1 to 8. Image size is 256x256 pixels (unit: sec).

dataset	1	2	3	4	5	6	7	8	**average**
teapot	0.80	0.75	0.72	0.68	0.65	0.66	0.67	0.70	**0.70**
bunny	0.69	0.66	0.63	0.62	0.63	0.64	0.65	0.68	**0.65**
head	0.64	0.62	0.60	0.61	0.63	0.64	0.66	0.68	**0.63**

Table 3 shows the rendering time for our method. The rendering speed of our method is about 38% (1-0.50/0.80) and 24% (1-0.50/0.66) faster than that of the previous distancemap and that of the average speed of the CBM, respectively.

Table 3. Comparison of the rendering time. Viewing conditions are identical with the Table 2 (unit: sec).

dataset	previous distancemap	CBM (average)	our method
teapot	0.82	0.70	0.51
bunny	0.80	0.65	0.50
head	0.79	0.63	0.49
average	**0.80**	**0.66**	**0.50**

Fig. 6 shows the image quality without changing the viewpoint or viewing directions. The images in the left column are the results generated using the previous distancemap method [12], and those of the right column are generated by our method. To verify the differences between the images, we compute the RMSE (Root Mean Square Error) value [13]. It is the square root of the average of the squared error, and one of the most often used generalized standard deviations. After comparing the RMSE value of each dataset, we confirm that there are little differences between them (see Fig. 6). Therefore, we confirm that our method normally renders volumetric scenes.

5 Conclusion

We propose a bidirectional distancemap to support efficient space-leaping when we exploit a ray-coherence property. In preprocessing step, we generate our distancemap

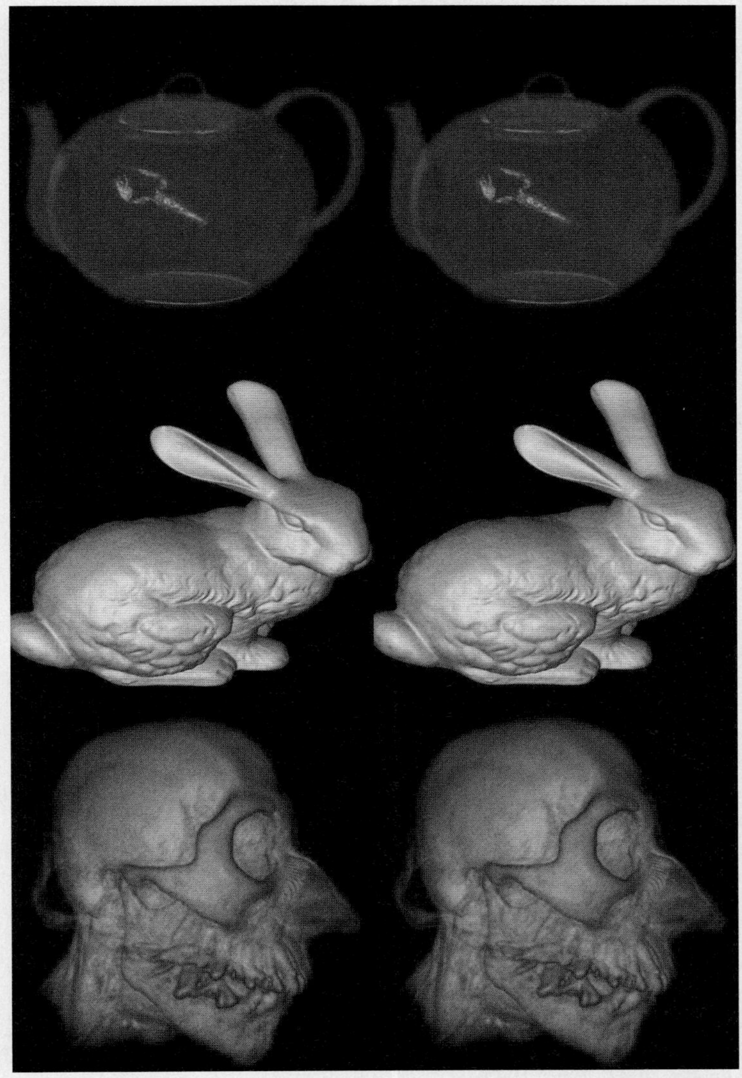

Fig. 6. Comparison of image quality: the teapot and bunny are projected to parallel view, and the head is rendered to perspective projection. The RMSE result of each dataset is 0.188, 0.191 and 0.152, respectively.

for transparent and nontransparent region using conventional object-order and scanline-order distance transform approaches, simultaneously. In rendering step, after exploiting a ray-coherence property, when a ray lies on transparent region, our method refers to a bidirectional distancemap generated for transparent region. If the ray already jumps over an object boundary, it also quickly reaches the boundary by referring our distancemap generated for nontransparent region. Although the performance of the previous approaches depends on the size of a user-selected constant distance, our method supports optimal distances to reach an object boundary for all rays of an image plane. The memory requirement is reduced as the size of one distancemap structure, and additional preprocessing is below 5% compared with conventional distancemap method. Experimental results show that our method normally produces high-quality images and requires less rendering time compared with the previous method.

Acknowledgment

This work was supported by grant No. RTI05-03-01 from the Regional Technology Innovation Program of the Ministry of Commerce, Industry and Energy(MOCIE).

References

1. Levoy, M.: Display of Surface from Volume Data. IEEE Computer Graphics and Applications, Vol. 8, No. 3 (1988) 29-37
2. Kaufman, A.: Volume Visualization. 1st ed., Ed. IEEE Computer Society Press (1991)
3. Krishnamurthy, B., Bajaj, C.: Data Visualization Techniques. 1st ed., Ed. John Wiley & Sons (1999)
4. Levoy, M.: Efficient Ray Tracing of Volume Data. ACM Transactions on Graphics, Vol. 9 (1990) 245-261
5. Yagel, R. Cohen, D., Kaufman, A.: Discrete Ray Tracing. IEEE Computer Graphics and Applications, Vol. 12, No. 5 (1992) 19-28
6. Zuiderveld, K., Koning, A., Viergever, M.: Acceleration of Ray-Casting Using 3D Distance Transforms. Visualization in Biomedical Computing 1992 (1992) 324-335
7. Cohen, D., Sheffer, Z.: Proximity Clouds: An Acceleration Technique for 3D Grid Traversal. The Visual Computer, Vol. 11, No. 1 (1994) 27-28
8. Yagel, R., Shi, Z.: Accelerating Volume Animation by Space-leaping. Proc. IEEE Visualization 1993 (1993) 62-69
9. Wan, M., Sadiq, A., Kaufman, A.: Fast and Reliable Space Leaping for Interactive Volume Rendering. Proc. IEEE Visualization 2002 (2002) 195-202
10. Sramek, M., Kaufman, A.: Fast Ray-Tracing of Rectilinear Volume Data Using Distance Transforms. IEEE Trans. on Visualization and Computer graphics, Vol. 6, No. 3 (2000) 236-252
11. Lakare, S., Kaufman, A.: Light Weight Space Leaping Using Ray Coherence. Proc. IEEE Visualization 2004 (2004) 19-26
12. Saito, T., Toriwaki, J.: New Algorithms for Euclidean Distance Transformations of an n-Dimensional Digitized Picture with Applications. Pattern Recognition, Vol. 27, No. 11 (1994) 1551-1565
13. Kim, K., Wittenbrink, C., Pang, A.: Extended Specifications and Test Data Sets for Data Level Comparisons of Direct Volume Rendering Algorithms. IEEE Trans. on Visualization and Computer Graphics, Vol. 7, No. 4 (2001) 299-317

Segmenting Free-Form 3D Objects by a Function Representation in Spherical Coordinates

Olcay Sertel and Cem Ünsalan

Computer Vision Research Laboratory
Yeditepe University, İstanbul 34755, Turkey

Abstract. Segmenting 3D object surfaces is required for various high
level computer vision and computer graphics applications. In computer
vision, recognizing and estimating poses of 3D objects heavily depend on
segmentation results. Similarly, physically meaningful segments of a 3D
object may be useful in various computer graphics applications. Therefore, there are many segmentation algorithms proposed in the literature.
Unfortunately, most of these algorithms can not perform reliably on free-
form objects. In order to segment free-form objects, we introduce a novel
method in this study. Different from previous segmentation methods, we
first obtain a function representation of the object surface in spherical
coordinates. This representation allows detecting smooth edges on the
object surface easily by a zero crossing edge detector. Edge detection
results lead to segments of the object. We test our method on diverse
free-form 3D objects and provide the segmentation results.

1 Introduction

Advances in modern range scanning technologies and integration methods allow
us to obtain high precision representations of complex, detailed 3D models of
real world objects. These 3D models are widely used for recognition and representation purposes both in computer vision and computer graphics. Computer
vision practitioners are shifting their interests to 3D models instead of 2D images
or video sequences, due to powerful representation capabilities of these 3D models. Campbell and Flynn [1] provide a through survey on 3D representation and
recognition algorithms in computer vision and computer graphics applications.

In order to represent 3D objects for recognition purposes, researchers have
introduced many segmentation and edge detection methods on range images.
The aim is to partition the 3D surface to meaningful subparts. We can divide
the range image segmentation methods to three main categories as: region based
[2,3,4], edge based [5,6], and hybrid (region and edge based) [7,8,9]. This list is
far from being complete, more through review on the subject can be found in
[3]. Hoover *et. al.* [10] offer a comparison tool for the state of the art range image
segmentation methods. They conclude that, segmenting range images is still a
major problem in computer vision due to problems in the correct identification
of small surfaces and the preservation of the edge location. Unfortunately, these
issues are extremely important for 3D object modeling and recognition.

A. Levi et al. (Eds.): ISCIS 2006, LNCS 4263, pp. 343–352, 2006.

To overcome these problems, we introduce a novel free-form 3D object segmentation method in this study. Campbell and Flynn [1] define *free-form* object as: "a free-form object is often assumed to be composed of one or more nonplanar, nonquadric surfaces". Most previous work deals with surfaces composed of planar or quadratic surfaces. Although they have fairly good segmentation results, their applicability to free-form objects is relatively poor.

Our method is distinct from the previous segmentation methods in the way we represent the object surface by a function form in spherical coordinates. This function representation allows us to detect smooth edges on the object surface reliably. As we obtain the function representation, we apply a Laplacian of Gaussian (LoG) filter with an adjustable smoothing parameter to detect edge locations. LoG filter also takes into account noise on the object boundary. Finally, we detect zero crossings on the filter response and segment the object surface. Although the function representation is applicable to star shaped objects only, we decompose free-form objects to star shaped subparts and apply our method to each separately. Hence, we can obtain segments of free-form objects without any difficulty.

We start with explaining the effect of changing the coordinate system from cartesian to spherical. Then, we define how to obtain the function representation of star shaped and free-form objects in spherical coordinates. We next define edge detection on the function representation and obtain segments on the object. We test our segmentation method on various free-form 3D objects in the experiments section. Finally, we discuss the results and provide a road map for future studies.

2   The Effect of Changing the Coordinate System

Most of the commercial range scanners provide the point set of the 3D object in cartesian coordinates. Besides the point set, they also provide the spatial neighborhood of these points encoded by triangulations. There are also many commercial software, providing triangulation if we only have the point set of the 3D surface. For segmentation, we need these triangulation and coordinate information.

Researchers have focused on cartesian coordinate representations to introduce segmentation and edge detection for 3D surfaces. Unfortunately, applying edge detection in cartesian coordinates do not provide acceptable results. The main reason for this poor performance is that, most edge detectors are designed for step edges in grayscale images (it is assumed that, these step edges correspond to boundaries of objects in the image) [11]. In range images (3D surfaces), we do not have clear step like changes corresponding to the actual edges of the object. On the contrary, for most objects we have smooth transitions not resembling a step edge. Therefore, applying edge detection on these surfaces do not provide good results.

To overcome this problem, we hypothesize that if we represent the same object surface in spherical coordinates, we can detect most smooth edges easily. Therefore applying edge detection on this new representation provides improved results. As we detect edges on the spherical representation, we can obtain the cartesian coordinates of the edges and project them back to actual 3D surface to obtain edge points on the actual surface.

Let's start with a simple example to test our hypothesis. We assume a slice of a generic 3D object (at $z = 0$) for demonstration purposes. We can represent the point set at this slice by a parametric space curve $c(t) = (x(t), y(t), 0)$ as:

$$c(t) = \begin{cases} (\cos(t), \sin(t), 0) & t \in [0, \pi/3) \bigcup [2\pi/3, \pi) \\ (\cos(t), \sin(t) + 0.3 sin(3t - \pi), 0) & t \in [\pi/3, 2\pi/3) \end{cases} \tag{1}$$

This space curve is plotted in Fig. 1 (a). As can be seen, the curve is composed of two parts. However, applying edge detection directly on this representation will not give good results, since we do not have step edge like transition between those two curves.

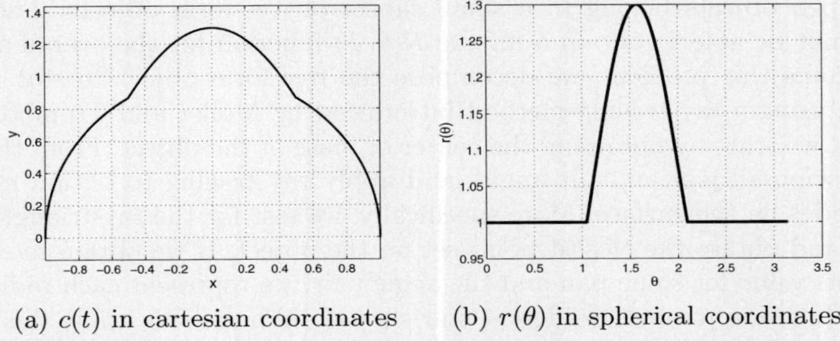

(a) $c(t)$ in cartesian coordinates (b) $r(\theta)$ in spherical coordinates

Fig. 1. A simple example emphasizing the effect of changing the coordinate system on detecting edges

We can obtain the spherical coordinate representation of $c(t)$ by defining $\theta = t$ and $r(\theta) = \sqrt{x^2(\theta) + y^2(\theta)}$. Now, our curve becomes:

$$r(\theta) = \begin{cases} 1 & \theta \in [0, \pi/3) \bigcup [2\pi/3, \pi) \\ 1 + 0.6 sin(\theta) sin(3\theta - \pi) + 0.09 sin^2(3\theta - \pi) & \theta \in [\pi/3, 2\pi/3) \end{cases} \tag{2}$$

As we plot $r(\theta)$ in Fig. 1 (b), we observe that the change in the curve characteristics is more emphasized similar to a step edge. This change can easily be detected by an edge detector. Now, we can explore our hypothesis further for 3D objects.

2.1 A Function Representation for Star Shaped Object Surfaces

For an object to be star shaped, the requirement is that there exists at least one center point such that, every surface point (x, y, z) can be seen from it without intersecting other surface points. Therefore, if we apply change of coordinates from cartesian to spherical (taking the center point as the center of our coordinate system) we obtain a function representation, $R(\theta, \phi)$, in terms of pan (θ) and tilt (ϕ) angles as:

$$R(\theta, \phi) = \sqrt{x^2 + y^2 + z^2} \tag{3}$$

where

$$\theta = \arctan\left(\frac{y}{x}\right) \tag{4}$$

$$\phi = \arctan\left(\frac{\sqrt{x^2 + y^2}}{z}\right) \tag{5}$$

We will apply edge detection on $R(\theta, \phi)$. If our object violates star shaped condition, we can not obtain $R(\theta, \phi)$. We will consider this issue next.

2.2 Multiple Functions for Free-Form Object Surfaces

Star shaped objects belong to a small subset of free-form objects. Therefore, we may not be able to obtain a unique $R(\theta, \phi)$ function for the overall surface. To overcome this problem, we decompose the free-form object to star shaped subparts using a ray tracing method introduced by Moller and Trumbore [12]. To do so, we start by obtaining the center of mass of the object. From this center, we swipe all pan and tilt angles and apply ray tracing to obtain multiple intersections on the surface. More specifically, we test for the ray-triangle intersections and obtain the closest point set on the object. If we obtain more than one radius value for some pan and tilt angle pair, we represent each radius in a different function to obtain different star shaped subparts. We apply this procedure iteratively, until we obtain a full decomposition such that each one is star shaped. Therefore, we obtain multiple non-overlapping $R(\theta, \phi)$ representations for the same object.

We test this decomposition operation on the crocodile object given in Fig. 2. For most of the surface points we do not have multiple radius values except the tail part. As we apply our decomposition method, we obtain two star shaped subparts one representing the body of the crocodile, and the other representing part of the tail (top of the second figure). We provide the $R(\theta, \phi)$ functions for the crocodile in Fig. 3 (a) and (b).

3   Edge Detection on the $R(\theta, \phi)$ Function

As we obtain $R(\theta, \phi)$ functions representing the object, segmentation problem simplifies to detecting edges on these functions separately and combining the final segmentation on the object. In grayscale intensity images, object boundaries can be modeled by step changes. Therefore, most edge detectors are justified for detecting step edges in intensity images to extract object boundaries.

As we apply cartesian to spherical coordinate transformation and obtain $R(\theta, \phi)$ functions, we have similar step like changes corresponding to physically meaningful segments on the actual 3D object. In order to detect these step like

Fig. 2. The crocodile object

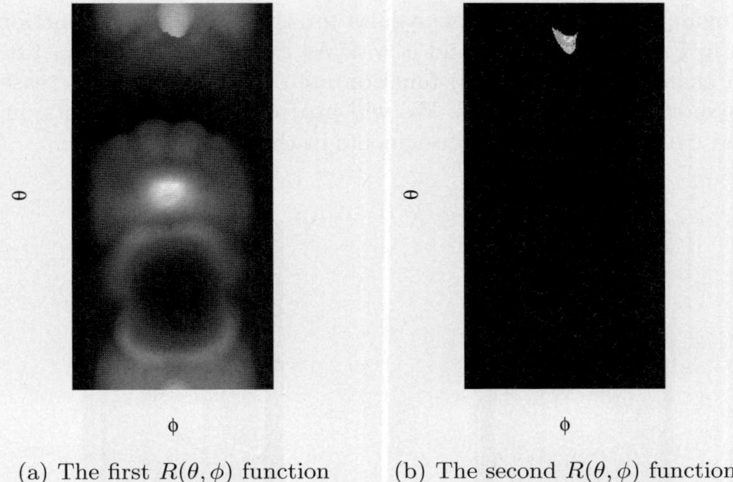

(a) The first $R(\theta, \phi)$ function   (b) The second $R(\theta, \phi)$ function

Fig. 3. Decomposing the crocodile object to two $R(\theta, \phi)$ functions

changes, we tested different edge detectors on $R(\theta, \phi)$ functions. Based on the quality of the final segmentations obtained on the 3D object, we picked Marr and Hildreth's [13] zero crossing edge detector. Zero crossing edge detector is based on filtering each $R(\theta, \phi)$ by the LoG filter:

$$F(\theta, \phi) = \frac{1}{\pi \sigma^4} \left(\frac{\theta^2 + \phi^2}{2\sigma^2} - 1 \right) \exp \left(-\frac{\theta^2 + \phi^2}{2\sigma^2} \right) \tag{6}$$

where σ is the scale (smoothing) parameter of the filter. This scale parameter can be adjusted to detect edges in different resolutions, such that a high σ value will lead to coarse edges. Similarly, a low σ value will lead to fine edges.

To label the edge locations from the LoG filter response, we extract zero crossings with high gradient magnitude. Zero crossing based edge detection has many desirable properties. First of all, obtained edge points will form closed boundaries.

The zero crossing operation is more robust to noise. Smooth transitions (as in our case) are handled well on zero crossing edge detectors.

Besides the desirable properties of zero crossing edge detector, our edge detection method has also some desirable characteristics. If the object is rotated around its center of mass, the corresponding $R(\theta, \phi)$ function will only translate. Therefore, the new edges obtained will be definitely same as in the original representation.

As we the label edge points on each $R(\theta, \phi)$, we project them back to the original 3D object and obtain the final segmentation for the object. In practical applications, one should remember that $R(\theta, \phi)$ function should be wrapped around since an edge at one corner may correspond to the continuum of another edge at the opposite corner. We handle this wrapping around problem by taking $R(\theta, \phi)$ function as periodic wrt. (θ, ϕ) and applying edge detection on more than one period of this function.

We provide the edge detection results for the first $R(\theta, \phi)$ function of the crocodile in Fig. 4 for $\sigma = 1.8$ and $\sigma = 4$. As can be seen, for $\sigma = 1.8$ most of the small changes on the $R(\theta, \phi)$ function are detected. As we increase $\sigma = 4$, more coarse changes are labeled. We will project these edge points on the 3D object and extract corresponding segments in the following section.

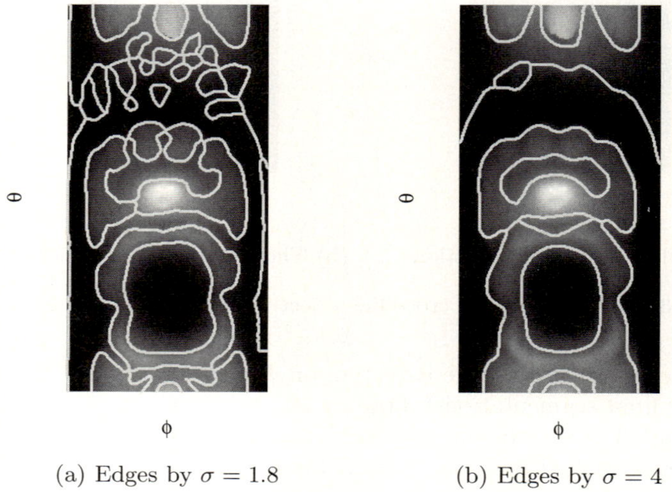

(a) Edges by $\sigma = 1.8$ (b) Edges by $\sigma = 4$

Fig. 4. Edge detection results for the first $R(\theta, \phi)$ function of the crocodile with two different scales

4   Segmentation Experiments

We test our segmentation method on seven different free-form objects with two different filter scale parameters, $\sigma = 1.8$ (to obtain a fine or detailed segmentation) and $\sigma = 4$ (to obtain a coarse segmentation). We provide the coarse and

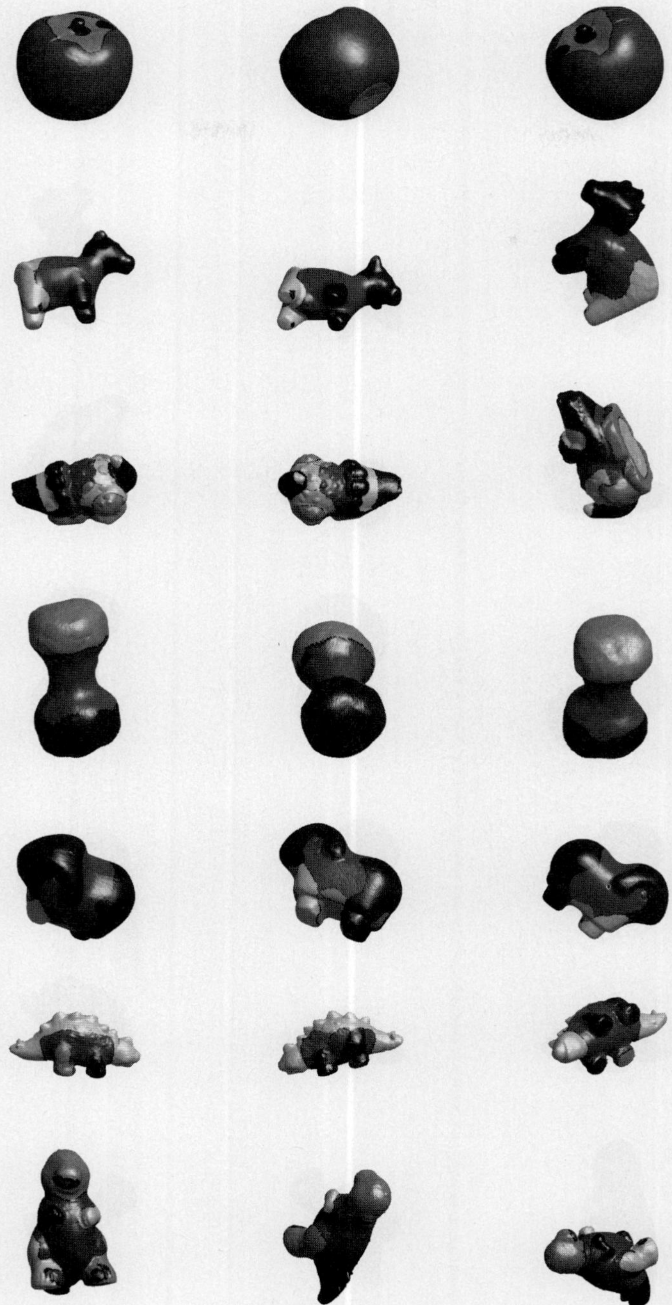

Fig. 5. Coarse segments (with $\sigma = 4.0$) obtained from the apple, cow, crocodile, dumb-bell, lamb, orange dino, and red dino (for each row)

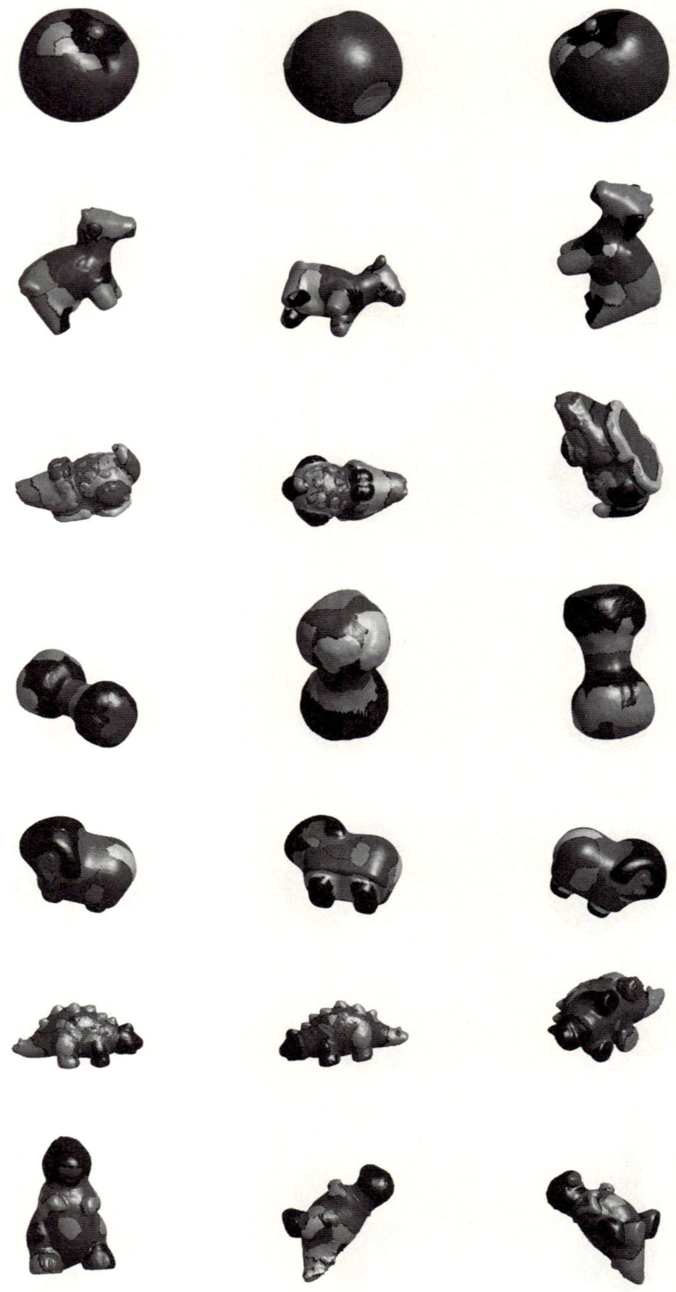

Fig. 6. Fine segments (with $\sigma = 1.8$) obtained from the apple, cow, crocodile, dumbbell, lamb, orange dino, and red dino (for each row)

fine segmentation results in Figs. 5 and 6 respectively. We provide three different views of segmentation results for each object in these figures.

As can be seen from Figs. 5 and 6, our segmentation method works fairly well on seven different free-form 3D objects having fairly diverse characteristics. Almost all the segments labeled on the actual objects correspond to different object parts. In general, there are minor edge detection problems due to the scale of the filter for $\sigma = 1.8$. At this scale, obtained edges become weaker, hence there may be missing links on some objects. However, this problem can be fixed by a post processing step.

5 Future Work

We introduced a free-form 3D object segmentation method by changing the coordinate system and representing the object surface as functions in the spherical coordinates. Based on experimental results on diverse objects, we can claim that our method works fairly well in segmenting free-form objects. We plan to use these segments for 3D object recognition in our future studies. Since most of the segments obtained in this study correspond to some physical parts of the actual object, this decomposition may be used for animation purposes in computer graphics applications.

Acknowledgments

We would like to thank Prof. Dr. Patrick J. Flynn for providing the *apple, cow, crocodile, dumbbell, lamb, orange dino, red dino* objects.

References

1. Campbell, J.R., Flynn, P.J.: A survey of free-form object representation and recognition techniques. Computer Vision and Image Understanding **81** (2001) 166–210
2. Besl, P.J., Jain, R.J.: Segmentation through variable-order surface fitting. IEEE Trans. on PAMI **10** (1988) 167–192
3. Srikantiah, P., Boyer, K.L., Flynn, P.J.: Saliency sequential surface organization for free-form object recognition. Computer Vision and Image Understanding **88** (2002) 152–188
4. Gotardo, P.F.U., Bellon, R.P.O., Boyer, K.L., Silva, L.: Range image segmentation into planar and quadric surfaces using an improved robust estimator and genetic algorithm. IEEE Trans. on SMC **34** (2004) 2303–2316
5. Wani, M.A., Batchelor, B.G.: Edge region based segmentation of range images. IEEE Trans. on PAMI **16** (1994) 314–319
6. Jiang, X., Bunke, H.: Edge detection in range images based on scan line approximation. Computer Vision and Image Understanding **73** (1999) 183–199
7. Yokoya, N., Levine, M.D.: Range image segmentation based on differential geometry: A hybrid approach. IEEE Trans. on PAMI **11** (1989) 643–649
8. Al-Hujazi, E., Sood, A.: Range image segmentation with applications to robot bin-picking using vacuum gripper. IEEE Trans. on SMC **20** (1990) 1313–1325

9. Ghosal, S., Mehrotra, R.: An orthogonal moment-based integrated approach. IEEE Trans. on Robotics and Automation **9** (1993) 385–399
10. Hoover, A., Jean-Baptiste, G., Jiang, X., Flynn, P.J., Bunke, H., Goldgof, D.B., Bowyer, K., Eggert, D.W., Fitzgibbon, A., Fisher, R.B.: An experimental comparison of range image segmentation algorithms. IEEE Trans. on PAMI **18** (1996) 673–689
11. Sonka, M., H.V., Boyle, R.: Image Processing, Analysis and Machine Vision. 2. edn. PWS Publications (1999)
12. Moller, T., Trumbore, B.: Fast, minimum storage ray-triangle intersection. Journal of Graphics Tools **2** (1997) 21–28
13. Marr, D., Hildreth, E.C.: Theory of edge detection. Proceedings of the Royal Society of London. Series B, Biological Sciences **B-207** (1980) 187–217

Applying Natural Neighbor Coordinates for Electromagnetic Tracker Calibration*

Yi Li, Weidong Chen, Dongming Lu, and Lei Zhao

College of Computer Science and Technology, Zhejiang University,
310027, Hangzhou, Zhejiang, P.R. China
liyi9810857@gmail.com, {chenwd, ldm, cszhl}@zju.edu.cn

Abstract. In this paper, we use the natural neighbor coordinates and its properties as a tool for electromagnetic tracker calibration. We have established a framework for computing the three-dimensional natural neighbor coordinates and used it for the calibration process for which we wish to eliminate the distortion error presented in the electromagnetic field. Our work comprises of two main parts. The first is about the computational model of the natural neighbor coordinates while the second is a discussion on the result we get after calibrating the electromagnetic tracker distortion. Our result has shown that the natural neighbor coordinates can be a promising method for approximating the distortion in the electromagnetic field and for calibrating the distorted field data.

Keywords: Natural Neighbor Coordinate, Laplace interpolant, electromagnetic tracker calibration, virtual reality.

1 Introduction

Natural neighbor coordinates are used in natural neighbor interpolation which is a multivariate data interpolation scheme, first proposed by Sibson [16]. Works described in [12,15,17] are some of the works to extend the methods to three or even higher dimensional spaces. Recent advances in the field of natural neighbor interpolation have revealed that, natural neighbor interpolation can be widely used in the field related to multivariate interpolation such as surface smoothing [3], image reconstruction [13], solution of PDEs [17] and so on. Early implementations of natural neighbor interpolation in three or higher dimensions can be found in Owen [12] and Boissonnat [3]. Watson [18] used the so called 'Compound signed decomposition' to compute the polyhedron volume.

The 6DOF electromagnetic tracker systems have been widely used in various virtual reality environments as position and orientation reporter relying on three orthogonal electromagnetic fields to generate 3D position and orientation values. However, the electromagnetic fields are very sensitive to internal fields and metals present in the operating environment, which will cause field distortion and decrease in the accuracy of the system and further influences the quality of

---

* This work was fully supported by National Basic Research Program of China (NO.2002CB312106).

A. Levi et al. (Eds.): ISCIS 2006, LNCS 4263, pp. 353–362, 2006.

users' experience and perception as well as the performance of the virtual reality system. This problem can be corrected via the procedure referred to as tracker calibration. Raab et al. [14] foresaw the need for calibration and suggested that the correction of the distorted measurements can take the form of additive vectors for location error correction and a sequence of rotations for orientation error correction and can be stored either in a look-up table or as polynomials in the position space. Bryson [6] and Kindratenko [10] both used a weighted look-up table to correct the errors. Briggs [5] used the look-up table scheme similar to the one described in [11]. The difference between them is in the way that the look-up tables are re-sampled from the measurements taken on an irregular grid. In Briggs's work [5] , he also applied a $4th$ order polynomials. Ghazisaedy [9], Czernusenko [7] and Livingston [11] implemented a tri-linear interpolation to compensate for the errors in reported location. Besides, Zachmann [19] proposed an interpolation scheme using Hardy's Multi-Quadric method. Borst [4] developed a new method by using interpolating cubic spline with C^2-continuity to model tracked space distortion as a piecewise tricubic deformation of the true space.

The goal of our work is to use the natural neighbor coordinates to calibrate the electromagnetic tracker in a CAVE in order to provide users with a better sense of immersion and better interaction. First, the raw data reflecting distortion of the field was collected. Second, adjustment to the natural neighbor interpolation framework was made. The following paper contains three parts. The first part introduces our implementation framework and computing procedure. The second part shows our experiment results and gives a discussion. Finally we conclude and give a future way.

2   Computing Natural Neighbor Coordinates

2.1   Natural Neighbor Coordinates

Generally speaking, the natural neighbor interpolation scheme has the following form:

$$f(x) = \sum_{k=1}^{n} f_k(x)f(x_k) \tag{1}$$

The unknown functional values at point x is $f(x)$, $x_1, x_2, \ldots, x_n$ are the k natural neighbors of point x, $f(x_k)$ is the corresponding functional value at each natural neighbor point. It is a key component in the procedure of natural neighbor interpolation. Up to now, there are two main methods for computing natural neighbor coordinates. The first one is Sibson's shape function [16], while the other one can be found in both Belikov [2] and SuKumar's [17] work.

Sibson's shape function is depicted in Equation 2 :

$$\phi_k(x) = L(T_k)/ \sum_{i=1}^{n} L(T_i) \tag{2}$$

Here, the natural neighbor coordinate is defined as the ratio between the Lebesgue measure (length, area, volume,... in one, two, three dimensions,...) of T_k and T, where T is the Voronoi cell of point x and T_k is the intersection of the first order Voronoi cell of x_k and T. The Sibson's shape function can provide a C^∞-continuity within the interpolated vicinity, and is C^0 continued at the boundaries. It is obvious that the derivatives are also C^∞ except at the boundaries.

Another form presented in Belikov [2] and Sukumar's [17] work is called Laplace interpolant. It has the form as:

$$\phi_k(x) = \alpha_k / \sum_{i=1}^{n} \alpha_k, \quad \text{where } \alpha_k = l_k/d_k \tag{3}$$

Here, l_k is the Lebesgue measure of the $(d-1)$-d facet shared by the Voronoi cells of point x and its kth natural neighbor, d_k is the Euclidean distance between the two points.

To extend the natural neighbor interpolation to three or higher dimensions, the Sibson's shape function requires more computational work, the Laplace interpolant, however, only requires a Lebesgue measure on a lower dimension. The advantage on the computational cost is more significant especially in higher dimensions. So we are in favor of Laplace interpolant for its computational efficiency.

2.2   Computing the Natural Neighbor Coordinates

There are two issues concerned in the computational process. One is to locate all natural neighbors for a specific point and the other is to compute the natural neighbor coordinates for all neighbors.

To locate all natural neighbors is equivalent to find out all the tetrahedra whose circumscribing balls contain the point. The union of vertices of these tetrahedrons is the set of natural neighbors. If the size of data set is only in a few thousands, searching through all the triangles is a feasible choice, though with a complexity of $O(n^2)$. If the number of data set is of $O(10^5)$ or higher, as Sukumar [17] said, the walking-triangle algorithm [8] which is of $O(n)$ complexity may be a suitable choice. Since the walking-triangle algorithm is a stochastic process, sometimes it would eventually reach the destination after several trials. Our goal is to report a result just for one trial, so this algorithm may not be suitable. But scanning the whole triangle list linearly is a much slower process. So we make a compromise between the two schemes.

As the union of all tetrahedrons containing natural neighbors of point x form a star-shaped region, we can first locate a tetrahedron whose circumscribing ball including the point, then by looking through the first level, second level and higher levels of natural neighbors in these tetrahedrons until no more neighbors could be found, the full list of natural neighbors can then be obtained. All vertices of these tetrahedrons form the set of natural neighbors. To know which tetrahedron to start with, we can simply do it by searching out the whole tetrahedral list one by one until the first match is found, then we can start neighbor searching from this tetrahedron. The pseudo code for our search process is shown as follows.

let *NList* be the list of tetrahedra whose circumscribing ball contains *x* and
PList be the list of all natural neighbor vertices.*I* is a list of all tetrahedrons
for each tetrahedron *t* in the list *T* do
    let *ct* be the center of the circumscribing ball of *t* and *rt* be its radius
    if distance between *ct* and *x* are smaller than *rt*
       set *NList*[0]=*t*, break
    set *end*=false
    current=0
    while(*end* is not true)
       let *tlist* be the neighbor tetrahedra of *Nlist*[current], add tetrahedra in
tlist whose circumsphere also contains *x*, and increases the size of *Nlist*.
     if *current* is less than the size of *Nlist*
       current=*current*+*1*
    else *end* = true;break

Add all vertices of tetrahedras in *NList* to *PList* .*PList* is a list of natural
neighbor points needed.

Fig. 1. Pseudo code for finding all natural neighbors

After seeking out all natural neighbors, the next step is to compute the natural
neighbor coordinates. There are two steps involved in this procedure. First, we
need to compute the Voronoi diagrams and Delaunay tessellation for the data
set. Many existing algorithms and tools are available to do so. In our work, we
select the *qhull* package, which is based on the *quickhull* algorithm [1] and uses
less space and executes faster for inputs with no extreme points and easy to
use. Here we maintain lists recording the information of the Voronoi diagrams
and Delaunay tessellation. Then we need to find out the common facets between
the two Voronoi cells in our three-dimensional interpolation. The set of natural
neighbors of a point x is denoted as $NA = \{n_k, k = 1, 2, \ldots, n\}$, where n is the
size of the set. A list of Voronoi vertices, named $V = \{v_1, v_2, \ldots, v_m\}$, determines
the Voronoi diagrams for the data set and the point x. By the property of Voronoi
diagrams, we see that if two Voronoi cells have the common facets, the vertices
of the shared facet are located on the perpendicular biplane between the two
points. This can be proved from the definition of Voronoi cells. Suppose P is
the Voronoi cell of point x, Q is the Voronoi cell of point x_k, if a point $p \in Q$,
then $distance(p, x_k) \leq distance(p, x)$, respectively. Now that the point $p \in (P \cap
Q)$, then $distance(p, x) = distance(p, x_k)$. So p is located on the perpendicular
biplane of the two points. Another obvious fact is that the number of common
vertices shared by the two cells in three-dimensional space is greater than or
equal to three at least. Thus the common facet between the Voronoi cell of
point x and its kth natural neighbor can be determined, which is marked as
a polygon composed of a set of vertices $V_k = \{V_{k1}, V_{k2}, \ldots, V_{kn}\}$. Then the
Lebesgue measure of this facet that is the area of this two-dimensional polygon
can be determined using the following formula:

$$Area(V_k) = \frac{1}{2} \left| N \cdot \left\{ \sum_{i=1}^{k_n} V_{ki} \times V_{k(i+1)} \right\} \right| \tag{4}$$

Here, N is the unit vector perpendicular to the plane where the polygon lies and
V_{ki} are the vertices of the polygon in counterclockwise order. When $i = n$, the

next vertex is the first one V_1. With the area of each common facet between the Voronoi cells of point x and each of its natural neighbors known, the third step involved is to compute the natural neighbor coordinates. This can be simply done by involving the previously computed area and the distance between the point x and its natural neighbors.

3   Experiment Result and Discussions

The goal of our experiment is to establish a correspondence between the true space in a CAVE environment and the position reported by the tracker.When we move the tracker sensor in the volume, the tracker reported position values are collected. Then the corresponding value at the true space is computed and reported. By measuring the actual physical position of the tracker in our working volume defined in a CAVE as well as those value reported by the tracker relative to the tracker transmitter, then applying natural neighbor interpolation on these data, we can build such a map between these two data sets.

3.1   Apparatus and Data Collection

To do the calibration work, a raw data set reported by the receiver in the tracking system reflecting the relative position to the origin of the tracker transmitter must be first collected. A total number of about 67000 scattered data at intervals of 10cm in our $2.4 \times 2.4 \times 2.4m^3$ workspace was collected. To avoid the influence of metal objects or other interference, a wooden frame is used which has three long bars of $2.4m$ in length. The two vertical bars can be moved in Z direction in our CAVE volume, the horizontal bar in Y direction, then the receiver is moved in X direction. Each bar is marked with a graduation of $5cm$. the receiver is then placed on the horizontal bar by aligning with each scale on a fixed orientation. So the influence of the orientation on the reported location data can be eliminated. At each location, 100 successive readings were taken and averaged to determine the tracker reported position. The wooden frame we use is depicted in Fig.

The whole space is divided into 48 vertical surfaces with an interval of 5cm, while each surface is further divided into 48 horizontal lines. The data gathered

Fig. 2. Wooden frame we use for original data collection. Wooden frame we use for original data collection. Left is the three bars, the left most is the horizontal bar and the other two are the vertical ones, right is the wooden frame in CAVE.

were equally distributed on these lines at 5cm interval. After almost two weeks'
work, a total number of 67045 valid data points with known true space location
are gathered with the precision of double 18-bits and the corresponding x, y,
z, values reported by the receiver in the tracking system. By collecting such a
large data set, we can test the effectiveness and accuracy of the natural neighbor
interpolation with different nodal intensities of 5cm, 10cm, 15cm and 20cm. Then
we could reach a balance between the speed and the accuracy.

The electromagnetic tracker system we use is Ascension's Flocks of Birds,
installed in a CAVE of the size $2.4 \times 2.4 \times 2.4m^3$. The machine running our
framework is a PC with a 2.4GHz Pentium 4, equipped with 1GB RAM under Windows 2000 professional. We only tested the location data but not the
orientation data. Since previous on the tracker calibration work revealed [10],
the error on the orientation data is related to position only, the principle of the
location and orientation error calibration is the same.

3.2   Experiment Results

The first part of our experiment is to build the map from the true space in
CAVE to that distorted field in the tracker system. We do this by comparing the
data result reported by the tracker at a few fixed true space positions with the
data interpolated from its neighboring data. The natural neighbor interpolation
used here is to describe the filed distortion at these fixed points. We tested a
total number of 540 data points distributed on three vertical planes from near
to far away from the transmitter with averagely 180 data points on each plane.
With the values reported by the receiver already known, we want to see the
error between the reported value and the interpolated value to determine the
efficiency of the natural neighbor interpolation in describing the electromagnetic
field distortion. The following table shows the result when comparing these two
data sets.

Table 1. The result of comparing tracker reported value with that interpolated by
natural neighbor interpolation. Here, values along the three axis are shown as well as
a statistical result of the data set.

Names	Mean	Max Deviation	Min Deviation
X	0.0031	0.01799	-0.00038
Y	-0.0006	0.02142	0.00038
Z	-0.0031	-0.02046	-0.00088
distance	0.0044	0.034	0.0010
Std	(-0.0070, 0.0051, 0.0061)		

These data values are measure in the true space which are in the range of
$[-1, 1]$ covering a length of 2.4m. So by converting the reported values into
distance, the average distance between the tracker reported location and the
true location in our CAVE environment is about 0.37cm in X direction, 0.07cm

in Y direction and 0.37cm in Z direction. Though we can not say that this is of high accuracy approximating the distortion of the electromagnetic field compared with other existing but more accurate methods, it is acceptable for our application, since the absolute error in the 2.4m frame is less than 1cm, which is about 0.1% respectively. This result shows that natural neighbor interpolation can be used as a tool for describing the distortion of the electromagnetic field with high accuracy in our working frame. From another aspect, if the original data acquisition equipment is other than our wooden frame but with much higher precision, the result would be much better.

A second part of our experiment is to do just the inverse of the first part, that is, to build a map from the distorted field to the true space in the CAVE. To do this, we selected a whole vertical plane as test plane with a total number of 1596 data points uniformly distributed on the plane as our test data. The purpose is that, from the data value reported by the tracker, we can compute out the corresponding value at the CAVE space. This is done by applying the natural neighbor interpolation framework using tracker reported data as input, preprocessing the original data set with known tracker reported data value and treating the corresponding true space location in the CAVE as the function value, to find out all natural neighbors within the data set and then compute the corresponding position in our CAVE environment. The result of this part of work is shown in Fig. 3.

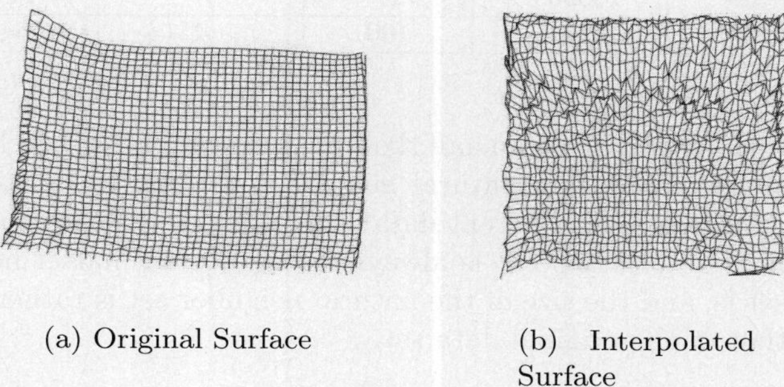

(a) Original Surface   (b)   Interpolated Surface

Fig. 3. Experiment result after testing on the surface

From the figures we can see that the shape of the whole plane is successfully confined to a square, which is in our desire. The table below shows some statistical results.

The third part of our experiment is to test the time efficiency of our interpolation framework. For experimental purpose, we tested the searching efficiency at different size of data points. The number of data points for each set is 100, 500, 1000, 5000, 10000 and 50000, which are randomly generated normal distributed data in our CAVE space. The corresponding number of tetrahedrons after applying delaunay tessellation are 544, 3162, 6463, 33364, 66959 and 337403. The result is shown as follows.

Table 2. Statistical results obtained by applying natural neighbor interpolation to a whole surface in the space. The definitions are the same with the table above.

Names	Mean	Max Deviation	Min Deviation
X	-0.0023	-0.054809	-0.0011674
Y	-0.0101	0.15159	0.0031361
Z	-0.0393	-0.10309	0.0000308
distance	0.0407	0.19134	0.0033464
Std	(0.0287, 0.0146, 0.0227)		

Table 3. Time efficiency of natural neighbor interpolation on the test data set. The first colume is the total point number, the second is the number of tetrahedrons after applying delaunay tessellation, the third colume shows the time needed to determine the natural neighbors, while the fourth is the time required to compute the natural neighbor interpolation resulat and the last is the total time required to finish computing on one point.

Point number	Tetra number	Search (ms)	Compute (ms)	Total (ms)
100	544	3	4	7
500	3162	3	4	7
1000	6463	3	4	7
5000	33364	10	4	14
10000	66959	17	4	21
50000	337403	100	4	104

The table shows that more than half the time is spent on the searching process. The time spent on computing natural neighbor coordinates by using Laplace interpolant is constant over different data sizes. This shows that the number of natural neighbors of a data point is always a constant no matter how large the original data set is, and the size of the natural neighbor set is rather small when compared to that of the original data set.

3.3   Discussion

From the above three experiments, we can see that the natural neighbor interpolation could be an efficient tool for doing the electromagnetic tracker calibration. The first part of the experiment shows that it can properly describe the distortion of the electromagnetic field with high accuracy. The second part shows that it is also capable of building an inverse map from the distorted electromagnetic field to that of the true space in our CAVE environment. By looking at tables and figures, we notice that there is still some disturbance in the calibrated data. The average error is relatively larger than that reported in the first step. The reason for this may be in that, in the first test, our task is to build a map from a vertical or horizontal plane to a curved plane, while in this test, the purpose is to build a map from a curved plane to a vertical or horizontal plane, when using the same method in both situations, the result would be better in the first, for the original data set values, that is the function parameters, are more accurate than that in the second one. While in the second test, the more accurate value is the function results not the input data values used for the preprocessing. Another fact that influences the accuracy of the interpolation framework may be due to the method and equipment used for original data acquisition. The wooden frame we used can greatly reduce the original error in the data acquisition period, but it is far away from the accuracy can be reached by using equipment such as ultrasonic sound or others. Finally, as the data acquisition process is done manually by humans, some human-related factors such as aligning by sight or moving by hand would also introduce errors in the whole process. Though our framework is not perfect, it can also reduce the distortion greatly, which can be tens of centimeters originally. The remaining errors are still tolerable in our application. In the third part of our experiment, that is concerning the time efficiency, we see that as the data set number increases from 1000 to 5000 then to 10000, the searching time increased greatly at the same time. 10000 points with 66959 tetrahedrons may be an upper limit for our application. If data number increases over the number, this scheme can never be suitable for use in our CAVE environment, since most of the time will be spent on the search, there is no more time left doing other computation work, such as collision detection or rendering. A suitable balance between the data size and time efficiency and the accuracy may be of several thousands in our current framework. But if other more accurate data acquisition methods and devices could be available or the search algorithm could be improved to achieve an complexity of $O(n)$ or better, the data size may be increased then.

4   Conclusion and Future Work

In this paper, we present a framework for electromagnetic tracker calibration problem by using natural neighbor interpolation to eliminate distortion in the electromagnetic field. Our experiment shows that the natural neighbor interpolation could be used as a good interpolation scheme to describe the distortion of the electromagnetic field and could also be used to build a map between the true space such as CAVE environment to the field distortion reported by the electromagnetic tracker. Since our framework is limited by both the data acquisition equipment and the search algorithm in the calibration framework, the efficiency of our framework could be improved if both conditions can be improved. This shows the future direction of our current work.

References

1. Barber, C.B., Dobkin, D.P., Huhdanpaa, H.T., The Quickhull algorithm for convex hulls. ACM Transactions on Mathematical Software. **22** (1996) 469–483
2. Belikov, V.V. and Andrie, Yu. S., Non-Sibsonian interpolation on arbitrary system of points in Euclidean space and adaptive isoline generation. Applied Numerical Mathematics. **32** (2000) 371–380

3. Boissonnat, J.D. and Cazals, F., Smooth surface reconstruction via natural neighbor interpolation of distance functinos. Computational Geometry. **22** (2002) 185–203

4. Borst, C.W., Tracker calibration using tetrahedral mesh and tricubic spline models of warp. Proceedings of IEEE Virtual Reality 2004, (2004) 19–26

5. Briggs, W., Magnetic calibration by tetrahedral interpolation. Proceedings of NIST-ASME Industrial Virtual Reality Symposium, Chicago, IL. **9** (1999) 27–32

6. Bryson, S., Measurement and calibration of static distortion of position data from 3D trackers. Proceedings of SPIE Conference on Stereoscopic displays and applications III, San Jose, CA. Feb 12–13 (1992) 244–255

7. Czernuszenko, M., Sandin, D. and DeFanti, T., Line of sight method for tracker calibration in projection-based VR systems. Proceedings of the 2nd International Immersive Projection Technology Workshop, Ames, Iowa, May 11–12 (1998)

8. Devillers, O., Pion, S. and Tellaud, M., Walking in a triangulation. Proceedings of the 7th Annual Symposium on Computational Geometry(SCG'01), Medford, Massachusetts, USA. (2001) 106–114

9. Ghazisaedy, M., Adamczyk, D., Sandin, J., Kenyon, R.V. and DeFanti,T., Ultrasonic calibration of a magnetic tracker in a virtual reality space. Proceedings of the Virtual Reality Annual International Symposium, Research Triangle Park, NV, March (1995) 179–188

10. Kindratenko, V. and Bennett, A., Evaluation of rotation correction techniques for electromagnetic position tracking systems. Proceedings of the Virtual Environments 2000 Eurographics Workshop, Amesterdam, the Netherland, June (2000) 13–22

11. Livingston, M.A. and State, A., Magnetic tracker calibration for improved augmented reality registration. Teleoperator and Virtual Environment, **16** (1997) 532–546

12. Owen, S.J., An implementation of natural neighbor interpolation in three dimensions. Master's thesis, Brighham Young University (1992)

13. Prak, S., Linsen, L., Kreylos,O., Owens, J.D. and Hamann, B., Discrete sibson interpolation. IEEE Transactions on Visualization and Computer Graphics. **12** (2006) 243–253

14. Raab, F., Blood, E., Steiner, T. and Jones, R., Magnetic position and orientation tracking system. IEEE Transactions on Aerospace and Electronic Systems. **15** (1979) 709–718

15. Sambridge, M., Braun, J. and McQueen, H., Computational methods for performing natural neighbor interpolation in two and three dimensions. Proceedings of the 7th Biennial Conference on Computational Techniques and Applications (CTAC'95). (1995) 685–692

16. Sibson, R., A brief description of natural neighbor interpolation. Interpreting Multivariate Data. (1981) 21–36

17. Sukumar, N., The natural element method in solid mechanics. Ph. D. Thesis, Northwestern University, Evanston, IL, USA, June (1998)

18. Waston, D.F., Compound signed decomposition, the core of natural neighbor interpolation in n-Dimensional space. See ftp://ftp.iamg.org/Waston/core.ps.gz(2001)

19. Zachmann, G., Distortion correction of magnetic fields for position tracking. Proceedings of Computer Graphics International (CGI'97), Hasselt, Belgium, June 23–27, (1997), 213–220

Minkowski Sum Based Octree Generation for Triangular Meshes

Engin Deniz Diktaş and Ali Vahit Şahiner

Computer Engineering Department, Boğaziçi University, Istanbul/Turkey

Abstract. This paper presents an easy-to-implement and efficient method to calculate the Minkowski Sums of simple convex objects. The method is based on direct manipulation of planes in 3D space. The paper then explains how this method is used for generating octrees for scenes consisting of triangular meshes.

1   Introduction

In graphic and haptic applications, Minkowski sums are mainly used in the context of collision detection. When checking collision for two objects, one of the objects (the pivot object) is shrunk to a point while the other is grown (dilated) by the amount equal to that of the pivot (the grown object actually is the Minkowski sum of the two objects). This process allows the detection of collisions between these objects simply by checking if the shrunk point is inside the grown object. If the objects subject to collision tests undergo only translations with respect to each other, the growth operation needs to be performed only once. The single copy of the grown object can be tested against any reference point to answer all the collision queries, instead of costly object-object intersection tests. Minkowski sums can also be used to find the penetration depth of one object intersecting the other along a certain direction, to evaluate minimum/maximum distance queries between two convex objects, and in topology simplification and correction.

In the literature, various methods have been proposed to compute the Minkowski sum of two convex polyhedra in R^3. Flato and Halperin [1] present algorithms for robust construction of planar Minkowski sums. Their methods are based on an arrangement-package of a software library called Computational Geometry Algorithms Library (CGAL). Guibas et al. [2] introduced the definition of the convolution operation based on the kinetic framework in two dimensions, which is a superset of the Minkowski sum operation, and its use in a various algorithmic problems. An output-sensitive algorithm for computing Minkowski sums of polytopes was introduced in [3]. Gritzmann and Sturmfels [4] obtained a polynomial time algorithm in the input and output sizes for computing Minkowski sums of k polytopes in R^d for a fixed dimension d, while Fukuda [5] provided an output sensitive polynomial algorithm based on linear programming concepts. Ghosh [6] presented a unified algorithm for computing 2D and 3D Minkowski sums of both convex and non-convex polyhedra based on a slope diagram representation. Computing the Minkowski sum amounts to

A. Levi et al. (Eds.): ISCIS 2006, LNCS 4263, pp. 363–373, 2006.

computing the slope diagrams of the two objects, merging them, and extracting the boundary of the Minkowski sum based on the merged diagram. Bekker and Roerdink [7] apply a few variations on this idea, where the slope diagram of a 3D convex polyhedron is represented as a 2D object, thus reducing the problem to a lower dimension. Fogel and Halperin [8] follow the same approach, where they first construct the dual representations of both 3D convex polyhedra under a special type of Gaussian Map called Cubical Gaussian Map (CGM), overlay the two planar arrangements of these dual representations, from which they pass back to the primal representation of the desired Minkowski sum. Their method results in significant performance improvements compared to the other methods they list. All of these methods involve utilization of complex data structures requiring costly initializations and updates and usually have high time-complexities. In this paper, we propose a geometric method for calculating the Minkowski sums for simple convex objects and evaluate it within the context of octree generation.

The paper is divided into 4 sections. Section 1 introduces the Minkowski Sum and provides a literature survey. Section 2 presents our method for Minkowski Sum computation and briefly discusses two alternative methods. Section 3 explains the key issues in octree generation using Minkowski sums. Section 4 presents some performance evaluation results, our conclusions and planned future work.

2   Minkowski Sums

If A and B are two convex polyhedra in R^3, then the Minkowski sum of A and B is defined as the convex polyhedron

$$M = A \oplus B = \{a + b \mid a \in A, b \in B\} \tag{1}$$

meaning that M is the union of all translated polyhedra B^a, such that $M = \bigcup_{a \in A} B^a$, where B^a is the polyhedron translated by a single point a, $a \in A$. In other words, the Minkowski sum of two polyhedra geometrically, is nothing but the convex hull of a set of vertices obtained by placing copies of one polyhedron at all vertices of the other. This is shown in Fig. 1 for a triangle and a rectangle. The set of vertices $\mathcal{V} = \{v_i\}$, whose convex hull is to be computed, can be given by

$$\mathcal{V} = (\mathcal{V}_T \times \mathcal{V}_R) \cup \mathcal{V}_T \tag{2}$$

where $\mathcal{V}_T$ is the set of all vertices of the triangle, $\mathcal{V}_R$ is the set of all vertices of the rectangle and $\times$ denotes the Cartesian product operation.

2.1   Proposed Method

The geometric method we describe in this paper generates the convex hull directly by translating lines in 2D space (planes in 3D space), instead of generating the convex hull using conventional convex hull algorithms, like with Graham's method in 2D or Incremental Method in 3D [9], which have large computational overheads when applied to simple convex objects.

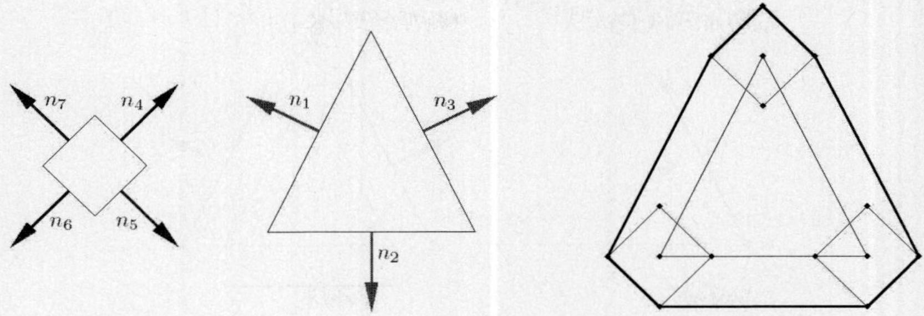

Fig. 1. The 2D Minkowski Sum of a triangle and a rectangle

Our method is based on the fact that every edge normal in the 2D Minkowski sum comes from the set of edge normals of both polygons, i.e. every edge in the Minkowski sum is parallel either to an edge of the triangle or to an edge of the rectangle. The vertices in the Minkowski sum are those that are extremal along these normals. For the example given in Fig. 1, the set of normals $\mathcal{N}$ is given by

$$\mathcal{N} = \mathcal{N}_T \cup \mathcal{N}_R \tag{3}$$

where $\mathcal{N}_T$ is the set of normals of the triangle and $\mathcal{N}_R$ is the set of normals of the rectangle. That is, $\mathcal{N}$ consists of the set $\{n_1, \cdots, n_7\}$, where the first 3 normals come from the triangle and, the remaining ones come from the rectangle. Minkowski sum calculation for this example can be analyzed as the two following cases:

(a) Calculating edges parallel to those of the triangle: This is simply achieved by shifting a line passing through the origin with normal $n_i \in \mathcal{N}_T$, in the direction of its normal until the most distant vertex is found. Figure 2 shows this process for the stippled line with normal n_1. Here v_1 and v_2 are the extreme vertices, also the end-points of the edge e_1. The set of extreme vertices for a given normal n_i is thus given by

$$\{\, v_k \mid v_k \cdot n_i = \max_j v_j \cdot n_i, \quad v_j \in \mathcal{V}, \, n_i \in \mathcal{N} \,\} \tag{4}$$

where $\mathcal{V}$ is the set of all vertices given by (2). Repeating this procedure for all normals $n_1 \ldots n_3$ coming from the triangle: we get the edges shown in Fig. 2 (right).

(b) Calculating the edges parallel to the edges of the rectangle: Here the same procedure is repeated for the lines with normals coming from the rectangle. Shifting the stippled line in Fig. 3, which is parallel to one of the edges of the rectangle along the normal n_4 we get extreme vertices v_3 and v_4, and therefore the edge e_4 of the Minkowski sum. Repeating this procedure for all normals $n_4 \ldots n_7$ coming from the triangle, we get the edges shown Fig. 3(right).

2.2   Minkowski Sum Generation in 3D

The Minkowski sum of two polyhedrons A and B, where B is the pivot polyhedron can be computed by

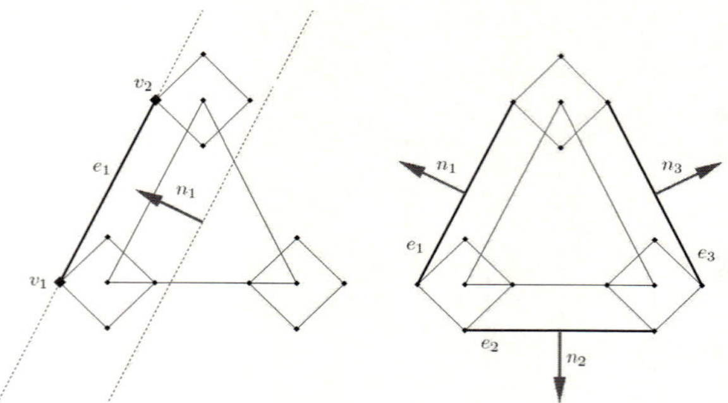

Fig. 2. Edges obtained by shifting lines parallel to triangle-edges

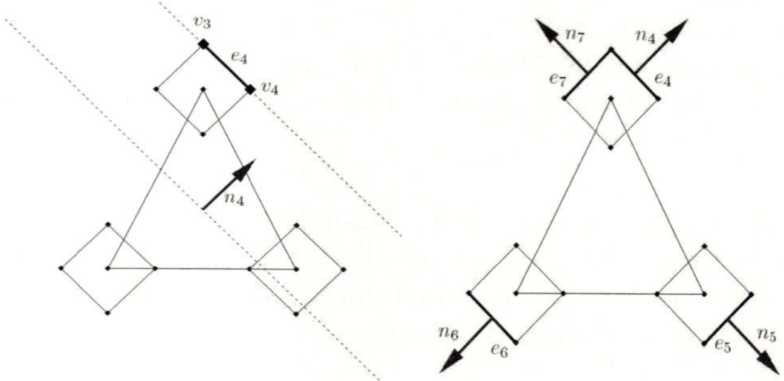

Fig. 3. Edges obtained by shifting lines parallel to rectangle-edges

1. Generating the vertex set $\mathcal{V}$ from which the extreme vertices will be chosen
2. Generating the normal set for all possible facets of the resultant polyhedron
3. Generating the facets by pushing the planes along their normals starting from the origin

These steps will be explained on an example, where the polyhedron A is a cube and B is an octahedron. We can generate the vertex set $\mathcal{V}$ simply by placing one copy of B at each vertex of A, as shown in Fig. 4. The set of vertices of the resultant object is the set $\mathcal{V}$ given by

$$\mathcal{V} = (\mathcal{V}_A \times \mathcal{V}_B) \cup \mathcal{V}_A \tag{5}$$

where

$$\mathcal{V}_A \times \mathcal{V}_B = \{v_{ij}\} = \{v_i^A + v_j^B\} \qquad i = 1 \ldots |\mathcal{V}_A|, \; j = 1 \ldots |\mathcal{V}_B| \tag{6}$$

v_i^A and v_j^B being the ith and j^{th} vertices of A and B, respectively. In the second step, we have to bear in mind that the facets in the Minkowski sum have normals coming from three possible sources (as opposed to the two sources in 2D case):

- normals coming from the facets of A (Fig. 5 left)
- normals coming from the facets of B (Fig. 5 middle)
- 'new' normals coming from facets generated by sweeping the edges of B along the edges of A (Fig. 5 right)

The normal set $\mathcal{N}_M$ of the Minkowski sum M is a subset of the normal set $\mathcal{N}$, or $\mathcal{N}_M \subseteq \mathcal{N}$, where $\mathcal{N}$ is given by

$$\mathcal{N} = \mathcal{N}_A \cup \mathcal{N}_B \cup \mathcal{N}_{AB} \tag{7}$$

where $\mathcal{N}_{AB}$ consists of normals $\{n_{ij}\}$ with

$$n_{ij} = e_i^A \times e_j^B \qquad i = 1 \ldots |\mathcal{N}_A|,\ j = 1 \ldots |\mathcal{N}_B| \tag{8}$$

Here e_i^A is the direction vector of the ith edge of the polyhedron A and e_j^B is the direction vector of the jth edge of the polyhedron B. In step 3, we generate a set

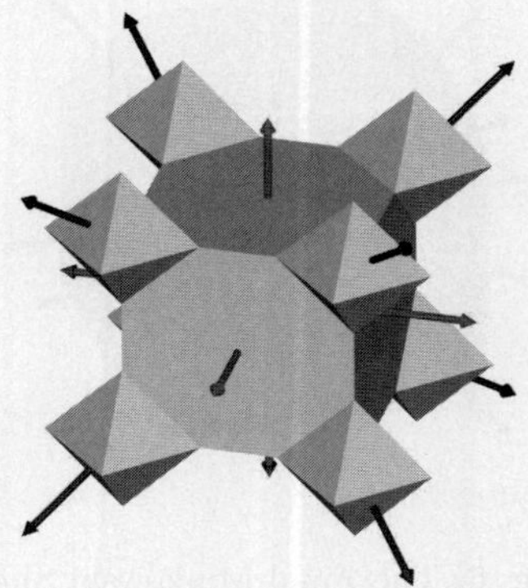

Fig. 4. Multiple Copies of B placed at all vertices of A

of planes each with a normal drawn from the set $\mathcal{N}$ and re-position these planes by *pushing* them until extreme vertices from the set $\mathcal{V}$ are encountered. This is done by projecting each vertex onto the normal vector of the corresponding plane and keeping track of all vertices forming the same *maximum* dot-product with the corresponding plane-normal. During this stage of the algorithm the candidate plane is assigned the number of extreme vertices it contains, i.e. all vertices forming the same extremal dot-product with the candidate plane-normal are assigned to that candidate plane. Once this set contains at least 3 non-collinear vertices, the plane is guaranteed form a facet of the Minkowski sum. Another way of stating this is as follows:

$$\mathcal{F}_i = \{\, v_k \mid v_k \cdot n_i = \max_j v_j \cdot n_i,\quad v_j \in \mathcal{V},\ n_i \in \mathcal{N}_M \,\} \tag{9}$$

where $\mathcal{F}_i$ is the set of vertices belonging to the ith facet of the final Minkowski sum. Since the set N_M contains normals from A and B, the planes having normals drawn from $\mathcal{N}_A$ or $\mathcal{N}_B$ are guaranteed to form facets in the Minkowski sum

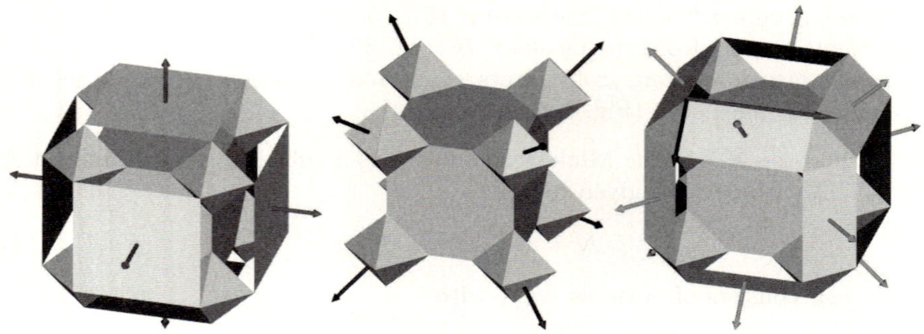

Fig. 5. Three types of faces encountered during Minkowski sum construction

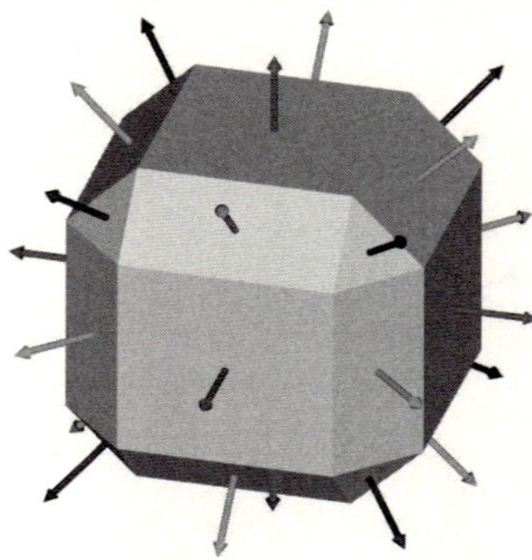

Fig. 6. The Final Minkowski Sum

after being translated to their respective extreme vertices. This can be observed Fig. 5 (left, middle), where the normals of all facets of A and B appear as facet-normals of the Minkowski sum. Figure 5 (right) also shows that additional facets are formed by pushing planes having normals drawn from the set $\mathcal{N}_{AB}$.

However, it is important to realize that not all of the normals in the set $\mathcal{N}_{AB}$ have to form facets in the final Minkowski sum. In fact, a plane having a normal from the set $\mathcal{N}_{AB}$, cannot form a facet if

- A candidate plane is assigned less than 3 non-identical vertices
- If (at least 3) vertices assigned to the candidate plane are collinear

In fact, this is why the normal set of the Minkowski sum is a subset of set of all normals $\mathcal{N}$. The rules above are implemented in [7, 8] using a Gaussian Map. A plane having the normal obtained by taking the cross-product of the direction vectors of two edges will contribute to the final Minkowski sum if their dual images under the Gaussian Map intersect. But in our application, since the number of normals, thus the number of the tests to be performed are very small, constructing the dual representations is a relatively time consuming process compared to our method. If visualization of the Minkowski sum is needed, some vertices need to be eliminated and only those vertices that are assigned to at least 3 distinct incident facets need to be retained. The final Minkowski sum is shown in Fig. 6. Here, red arrows represent the normals coming from the static polyhedron A, blue arrows represent those from the pivot polyhedron B and green arrows represent the normals of facets obtained by sweeping.

2.3 Incremental Convex Hull Construction

Since the Minkowski sum geometry is a convex hull, it can be computed using Convex Hull construction methods. One widely used technique is the incremental convex hull construction method, which is $O(n^2)$ [9]. This method starts by constructing a tetrahedron from an initial set of 4 non-coplanar points. The algorithm takes all remaining points one by one and at each step, it identifies which triangles of the current polyhedron are visible and which are not, which results in a shadow boundary between the visible and non-visible triangles. It then eliminates all faces visible from the current point and constructs new triangles by connecting each edge on the identified shadow boundary with the current point. It continues with the next point in the list and repeats the same set of operations until no points are left in the point-list.

When computing the Minkowski sum of two convex objects A and B, consisting of n and m vertices respectively, this method will have $O(n^2m^2)$ computational complexity. In addition to that, the complex update mechanisms involved will add algorithmic overhead to the method.

2.4 Dual Graph Method

It has been published that, Minkowski sum construction using dual representations can achieve asymptotically faster rates compared to convex hull construction methods. In [8], the Cubical Gaussian Map (CGM) is used to represent the dual graphs of two convex objects. CGM-based Minkowski sum calculation is done in 3 steps as follows:

- Construct the CGM-representation of both convex objects
- Calculate the overlay of both dual graphs
- Calculate the Minkowski sum by passing from the overlayed dual representation to the primal representation

Note that since a sphere can be covered by at least 6 planar patches, the CGM-method must generate and hold 6 planar arrangements to store the dual graph of each convex object. In addition to that since duals of some edges or vertices may fall in more than one planar patch, the algorithm should handle such situations. In the second step, again 6 planar arrangements need to be overlayed, i.e. the intersections of edges must be calculated, the intersected edges should be splitted and newly generated enclosed regions should be identified.

In the last step, the algorithm finds out which points in the dual representation (faces in the primal representation) are enclosed in which polygons in the dual representation (vertices in the primal representation) to be able to find out which faces of one object need to be translated by what amount. Since there will be faces obtained by sweeping the edges of one object with the corresponding edges of the other object, the algorithm also needs to keep track of the information regarding which edges intersect which edges in the dual graph. In essence, the intersection point of the dual representation of the edges corresponds to the normal of the face obtained by sweeping the corresponding primal edges, which can also be obtained by taking the cross-product of the direction vectors of the primal edges.

Although the CGM method is known to produce superior performance compared to other methods when generating Minkowski sums for arbitrarily complex convex objects, it is computationally more costly than our geometric method when only simple convex objects are considered.

3   Octree Generation Using Minkowski Sums

A commonly used hierarchical space partitioning technique involves the utilization of Octrees. Octree construction is based on recursive subdivision of cubes into eight subcubes, starting with the scene bounding cube, such that each leaf node of the octree contains a small number of geometric primitives. When generating an octree for triangular meshes, every triangle in the scene is assigned to a node of the octree by checking if the respective cube is intersected by that triangle. Our method for constructing an octree, is based on the use of Minkowski sums for intersection calculations. An important structural property of the octree is the fact that cubes of an octree at a fixed depth are nothing but dimensionally equal copies displaced relative to each other with the same orientation. In this respect we can think of the cubes of an octree as multiple copies of a single prototype cube. Therefore it would be sufficient to construct the Minkowski Sum only once, and use it multiple times to evaluate all the intersection queries for other cubes placed at different locations in the tree.

In a Minkowski sum based method, we only need to evaluate a simple point-in-polyhedron test, i.e. we need to check if the center of the cube falls inside the Minkowski-Sum, which is bounded by planes found with our method. This requires simple signed distance computations that can be performed with a single dot-product operation per bounding plane. The number of the required dot-products can be roughly calculated as follows:

- $6 + 2 = 8$ planes coming from the facets of the cube and the triangle
- $2 \times (3 \times 3) = 18$ upper bound for those coming from sweept edges

totaling to a maximum of $8 + 18 = 26$ planes. In practice this upper bound is rarely reached. In addition to that, being as simple as calculating dot-products, the method is very easy to implement and it takes care of all possible degenerate cases.

3.1   Index Tracking

The additional advantage of using Minkowski sums is based on the fact that all cubes of an octree have the same orientation, i.e. their face-normals or principal directions are all the same. This means that for cubes having different depth values, the only thing that changes is the size of the cubes. As shown in Fig. 7, the Minkowski sums of cubes having the same orientation but different sizes have the same topology, i.e. their facets have the same set of normals and they are essentially the same geometric entity except their facets-sizes, edge-lengths and vertex locations. Taking into account these observations, it is easy to see

Fig. 7. Minkowski sums of the triangle and cubes at different depths

that once we calculate the Minkowski Sum of a triangle and a cube *at any depth*, then all Minkowski sums of the cubes at other depths with the same triangle can quickly be calculated by keeping track of the index of the vertex (being the extreme vertex found by shifting the corresponding plane along its normal) selected as the origin of the bounding plane in the final Minkowski Sum. We refer to this method as *index tracking*.

The Minkowski sum output of our method is a set of bounding planes, each represented by a normal and a support-point that originates from the set of vertices $\mathcal{V}$. Since at each depth of the octree the vertex set $\mathcal{V}$ is obtained in the same manner, we label each vertex in V with a global vertex index that would indirectly encode the way the vertex is calculated. That is, the vertex set $\mathcal{V} = \{v_k\}$ consists of vertices given by

$$v_k = v_i^c + v_j^t \qquad i = 1\ldots8, \, j = 1\ldots3 \tag{10}$$

where $k = i + 8 \cdot j$, v_i^c and v_j^t are the ith and j^{th} vertices of the cube and the triangle, respectively. Therefore k encodes the information which vertex of the cube should be added to which vertex of the triangle. This information can be recovered using $i = k \bmod 8$ and $j = \lfloor k/8 \rfloor$.

4   Evaluation and Conclusions

Table 1 presents the processing times for the octree generation for a mesh with 33K triangles. In this table, *Old Method* refers to our previous implementation

Table 1. Elapsed time for generating the octree (all results are given in *seconds*)

Depth	Index Tracking	Minkowski Sum	Old Method
1	27.422	27.329	200.687
2	38.328	51.672	408.204
3	49.578	77.000	642.140
4	60.953	103.266	922.171
5	74.500	129.235	1296.297

which employs classic intersection tests, *Minkowski Sum* refers to our geometric method, while *Index Tracking* refers to our improved method with index-tracking.

The results given in Table 1, show that Minkowski sums based octree generation,is significantly faster than using brute force intersection tests. The octree generation application has been particulary interesting for the fact that two important features of Minkowski sums, namely the translational invariance and the topological invariance were observed to be valid within this context. Index tracking has also proved to be very efficient especially for octrees with high depth values. We must note that using Minkowski sums purely for binary (yes/no) intersection decisions is more expensive than separating axis based techniques [10] which are optimized for the underlying geometry. An analysis in this respect can be found in [11]. However, our intention in using Minkowski sums for Octree generation was to address the distance/proximity queries as well as handling the intersection tests using the same computational framework.

Since our geometric method can efficiently calculate the Minkowski sum of any simple geometric entity with the cubes of an octree. This makes it easier to use, for example, in intersection detection of cubes and Voronoi regions, for generating a Proximity Octree [12]. On the other hand, if method of separating axes is to be used then all intersection conditions should be formulated and optimized individually for each and every type of Voronoi region.

We should also point out that since the Minkowski sum is actually a polyhedron, when a proper set of partitioning planes are selected, the intersection tests can potentially be performed much faster. Currently we are looking into the problem of partitioning the Minkowski sum with an optimal set of partitioning planes such that the number of dot-product operations is minimized.

Due to its simplicity and the absence of complicated data structures, the proposed method could be implemented entirely on a Graphical Processing Unit to achieve interactive rates. This is another research area that is part of our future work plan.

References

[1] P. K. Agarwal, E. Flato, D. Halperin. Polygon decomposition for efficient construction of Minkowski sums. *Comput. Geom. Theory Appl.*, vol. 21, 2002, pp. 39-61.

[2] L. J. Guibas, L. Ramshaw, J. Stolfi. A kinetic framework for computational geometry. *Proc. 24th Annu. IEEE Sympos. Found. Comput. Sci.*, 1983, pp. 100-111.

[3] L. J. Guibas and R. Seidel. Computing convolutions by reciprocal search. *Disc. Comp. Geom.*, vol. 2, 1987, pp. 175-193.

[4] P. Gritzmann and B. Sturmfels. Minkowski addition of polytopes: Computational complexity and applications to Grobner bases. *SIAM J. Disc. Math*, vol. 6, no. 2, 1993, pp. 246-269.

[5] K. Fukuda. From the zonotope construction to the Minkowski addition of convex polytopes. *Journal of Symbolic Computation*, vol. 38, no. 4, 2004, pp. 1261-1272.

[6] P. K. Ghosh. A unified computational framework for Minkowski operations. *Comp. Graph.*, vol. 17, no. 4, 1993, pp. 357-378.

[7] H. Bekker and J. B. T. M. Roerdink. An efficient algorithm to calculate the Minkowski sum of convex 3d polyhedra. *Proc. of the Int. Conf. on Comput. Sci.-Part I*, Springer-Verlag, 2001, pp. 619-628.

[8] E. Fogel and D. Halperin. Exact and Efficient Construction of Minkowski Sums of Convex Polyhedra with Applications. *To appear in ALENEX 2006, Miami, Florida*, 2006.

[9] J. O'Rourke. Computational Geometry In C. *Cambridge University Press*, 1994.

[10] D. Eberly, Dynamic Collision Detection using Oriented Bounding Boxes, http://www.geometrictools.com/

[11] E.D. Diktas, *A Space Subdivision Framework for Virtual Reality and Haptic Applications*, MSc Thesis, Department of Systems & Control Engineering, Bogazici University, June 2006.

[12] E.D. Diktas, A.V. Sahiner, *Closest Feature Tracking Using Proximity Octrees*, MediaLab Technical Report, Department of Computer Engineering, Bogazici University, 2006.

Hardware-Oriented Visualisation of Trees

C. Rebollo, I. Remolar, M. Chover, and J. Gumbau

Departamento Lenguajes y Sistemas Informáticos
Universitat Jaume I, 12071 Castellón, Spain
{rebollo, remolar, chover, gumbau}@uji.es

Abstract. Real-time rendering of vegetation is currently a problem in need of a solution. The large number of polygons that form this kind of objects means that current hardware cannot achieve interactive rendering of outdoor scenes. This paper deals with the problem and it presents a multiresolution scheme that allows us to represent the whole geometry of the trees using both uniform and variable levels of detail. The method presented here models the trees using two multiresolution models. This is due to the different characteristics of the geometry that forms them. The trunk is modelled by *LodStrips*, a model oriented towards representing continuous meshes, and the foliage is modelled by the multiresolution model *Level of Detail Foliage*, presented in a previous work. In this paper, it has been efficiently implemented and extended to allow us to change the level of detail in a variable way, by adapting the resolution of this part of the tree to certain criteria determined by the application. Both of them have been designed to be hardware-oriented. They take advantage of the graphics hardware by adapting the data structures and the rendering algorithms to make the visualisation time efficient. Finally, the multiresolution scheme presented in this paper is compared with the only work that has appeared up to now that uses the same technique.

1 Introduction

Most interactive applications currently available are set in outdoor scenes. In these environments, trees and plants make the scenes more similar to the real world. A vast number of works on modelling vegetal species have appeared up to now, nowadays it is therefore possible to obtain very realistic tree models. However, the problem arises when real-time rendering is required by the application. The more realistic the vegetation objects are, the greater the number of polygons they contain.

Depending on the technique used to solve this problem, methods can be divided into two important groups: image-based and geometry-based rendering. Geometric representation has many advantages, the most important of which is that trees do not lose realism even when the camera is extremely near the object. Another important advantage is that geometry can be stored either in the main memory or directly in the graphics card, thus taking advantage of current graphics-hardware. Moreover, using geometry to represent objects makes it

A. Levi et al. (Eds.): ISCIS 2006, LNCS 4263, pp. 374–383, 2006.

possible to obtain shadows and different lighting effects, as well as greater acceleration in rendering. Geometry-based approaches have used several techniques to achieve interactivity, such as replacing the basic display primitive triangle by points and lines, or using multiresolution modelling techniques.

Multiresolution geometric models have proved to be a good solution for visualising objects made up of a vast number of polygons in interactive applications. These models adapt the geometric detail of the objects to the capacity of present-day graphics systems. Using this technique, objects are represented by means of multiple resolutions, with varying complexities, called levels-of-detail (LoDs). The application can visualise the object using the most suitable LoD and thus avoid, for instance, wasting time on visualising imperceptible details. These models provide two possible solutions: levels of detail of uniform resolution and levels of detail of variable resolution. Multiresolution models do not work properly with the representation of trees because of the characteristics of their geometry [1]: the trunks are modelled by continuous meshes and a set of isolated polygons is used for the foliage.

This paper presents a new hardware-oriented multiresolution approach to represent the geometry of these vegetal species. Two different multiresolution models are used to represent the tree objects: *LodStrips* [2] for the trunk and branches, and *Level of Detail Foliage* LoDF [3] for the foliage. Both of them have been designed within a hardware-oriented approach, thus considerably reducing the visualisation time of the LoDs that are required. In order to adapt the resolution of the different parts of the foliage depending on certain criteria, the data structures and retrieval algorithms of LoDF has been both extended. Finally, these models are compared with the ones used in [4] to represent trees, the results showing how this approach reduces the extraction and visualisation time even if hardware storage is not applied.

After reviewing previous work in section 2, the multiresolution model used to represent the trunk and branches is set out in section 3. Next, section 4 includes an analysis of the one used to represent the foliage. The data structure designed for this model and the retrieval algorithms for a uniform and a variable level of detail of the foliage are presented. Section 5 analyses the results of comparing this new method against the one used in [4] and, finally, in section 6 some ideas for future research are discussed.

2   Related Work

Research into real-time visualisation of detailed vegetal species is aimed at adapting the number of polygons used to represent those plants to the requirements of graphics hardware. As it was said in the previous section, research into interactive visualisation of vegetal species can be grouped into two broad directions: work that uses images or work that uses only geometry to represent the plants.

Image-based rendering. This is one of the commonest methods to represent trees because of its simplicity. Impostors are the most popular example of image-based rendering. This method replaces the geometry of the object with an image of it textured on a polygon immersed in the scene. Nevertheless, it presents some disadvantages, such as, for example, the loss of realism when the object is close to the viewer. Max [5] adds depth information to the precalculated images. This information allows them to recalculate different views from the stored images of the scene. Other authors obtain 2D images from volumetric textures and combine them depending on the position of the camera, [6]. Some authors, such as Remolar et al. [7], divide the scene into zones depending on the distance from the object to the viewer. Objects farther away from the camera are represented by an image and objects near the viewer are depicted by geometry. García et al. [8] solve the parallax problem by using textures that group sets of leaves.

Geometry-based rendering. This approach does not lose realism when the viewer moves towards the model, but the number of polygons that form the tree objects makes it necessary to use certain techniques to obtain interactive visualisation. Most of the works published to date change the display primitive for points or lines [9]. Works such as the ones presented by [1] [10] allow us to interactively adapt the number of points depending on the importance of the object in the final rendered image.

In recent years, several works based on multiresolution models have appeared. Meyer et al. [11] and Lluch et al. [12] use a representation based on multiresolution models of images. The only method so far that works with multiresolution representation of the tree based exclusively on polygons is [7], which the authors have called *VDF*. This work is focused on tree foliage. It adapts the number of leaves that form the foliage in real time.

3   Trunk Representation

The trunk is represented by a continuous general mesh, where the polygons are connected to each other. In our scheme, it is modelling using *LodStrips*. This continuous multiresolution method noticeably improves on previous models, in terms of storage and visualisation cost. The model is entirely based on optimised hardware primitives, triangle strips, and manages the level of detail by performing fast strip updating operations. In addition, it uses stripification techniques oriented towards exploiting vertex buffering.

4   Foliage Representation

Foliage is formed by isolated polygons that represent the leaves. In the presented scheme, it is represented using the multiresolution model LoDF.

In general, a multiresolution representation is constructed from two main elements: the original geometry of the object and the different approximations given by a simplification method. LoDF is based on the *Foliage Simplification Algorithm* (FSA) [13], which provides the coarsest approximation F_{n-1} from the original foliage F_0. The basic simplification operation of this algorithm is *leaf collapse*: two leaves are collapsed into a new one. This operation conditions a hierarchical structure based on trees. The sequence of leaf-collapse operations is processed to build the new multiresolution representation F^r (Figure 1 left). The LoDF data organisation is a forest of binary trees, where the root-nodes are the leaves that form F_{n-1}, the coarsest approximation, and the leaf-nodes are the leaves of the original tree model, F_0. In the example shown in Figure 1, F_0 is formed by 9 leaves, and F_{n-1} is made up of 3 leaves.

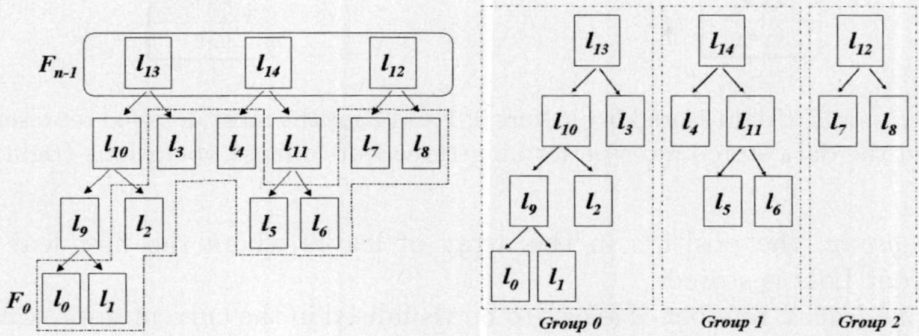

Fig. 1. Example of an F^r structure and the data stored for clusters 0, 1 and 2

In the multiresolution model the inverse operation has been performed in order to increase the level of detail, the refinement operation has been called *leaf split*: one leaf is divided into the two leaves that formed it.

The main characteristic of F^r is that the foliage is divided into independent clusters. As each simplification operation creates a new leaf, each leaf can only belong to one binary tree. Thus, every set of leaves in a binary tree of the data organisation forms one cluster. Following with the previous example, Figure 1 (right) shows the three clusters representing it. These groups determine the data structure used in our model.

4.1   Data Structure of the Foliage

The basic data structure of the LoDF model is an array of clusters (Figure 2). Each cluster stores all the leaves that form a binary tree of the data organisation F^r and some additional information.

In order to make it possible to perform the leaf collapse or split operations quickly, leaves l_i are stored in the clusters following the order of simplification established by the FSA, i.e. by levels of proof in the binary tree. Furthermore, leaves in each cluster are linked following the visualisation order: first of all the leaves that form the original representation are linked and then the ones obtained in the simplification process. These links also follow the order of creation determined by the FSA. This step makes it possible to extract the leaves that form the current LoD quickly. In Figure 2 the link of each leaf in the cluster is represented by n_j, j being the position of the leaf in the array.

In addition, some necessary data for leaves visualisation are also stored in each cluster. These data are:

Left group (clusters 0, 1 and 2 — most detailed representation):

	leaf	next	leaf	next	leaf	next
Init_group	0		0		0	
Active_leaves	4		3		2	
leaf_number next	l_0	n_1	l_5	n_1	l_7	n_1
	l_1	n_2	l_6	n_2	l_8	n_2
	l_2	n_4	l_4	n_3	l_{12}	n_{-1}
	l_9	n_5	l_{11}	n_4		
	l_3	n_3	l_{14}	n_{-1}		
	l_{10}	n_6				
	l_{13}	n_{-1}				

Right group (after performing three leaf collapse operations):

	leaf	next	leaf	next	leaf	next
Init_group	4		2		0	
Active_leaves	2		2		2	
leaf_number next	l_0	n_1	l_5	n_1	l_7	n_1
	l_1	n_2	l_6	n_2	l_8	n_2
	l_2	n_4	l_4	n_3	l_{12}	n_{-1}
	l_9	n_5	l_{11}	n_4		
	l_3	n_3	l_{14}	n_{-1}		
	l_{10}	n_6				
	l_{13}	n_{-1}				

Fig. 2. Example of data stored in clusters 0, 1 and 2 for the most detailed representation (left) and the data stored after performing three leaf collapse operations (right)

- *Init_group*: the position in the array of leaves where the first leaf of the current LoD is stored.
- *Active_leaves*: number of leaves to be visualised in the current approximation.

In order to extract the sequence of leaves that form the required LoD, we must start traversing the group from the position indicated in the *Init_group*. The number of links that the algorithm must consider is the value stored in *Active_leaves*.

In addition to this structure, the multiresolution model also needs to store the numbers of the clusters where every simplification operation that is processed to obtain F_{n-1} from F_0 is performed. This data structure is called *Changed_groups*. Following the example of the data shown in Figure 2, the data stored in this structure are represented in Figure 3.

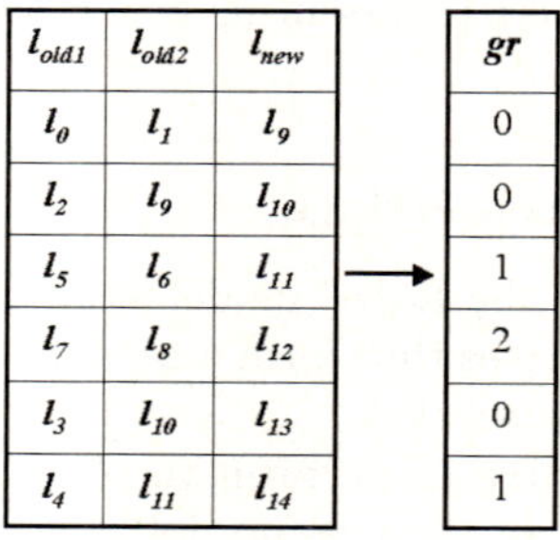

l_{old1}	l_{old2}	l_{new}		gr
l_0	l_1	l_9		0
l_2	l_9	l_{10}		0
l_5	l_6	l_{11}		1
l_7	l_8	l_{12}		2
l_3	l_{10}	l_{13}		0
l_4	l_{11}	l_{14}		1

Fig. 3. Left: Data obtained from the FSA. Right: Data stored in *Changed_groups*.

The LoDF data organisation is well adapted to graphics hardware. The geometric data of the model is initially stored in the graphics card. When a change in the LoD is required by the application, the affected clusters are updated. The only information that will be sent to the hardware are the leaves of these updated clusters. The rest of the groups will remain in the graphics card without undergoing any kind of modification, that is to say, just as they were before the change of LoD. Visualisation time is considerably reduced due to the fact that only the information about the updated clusters is sent to the graphics card instead of sending all the geometry of the foliage.

4.2   Rendering Algorithms for a Uniform LoD

In order to obtain a uniform resolution in the foliage, the leaf collapse operations have to be performed in the order established by the FSA. This sequence has been stored in the array *Changed_groups*. Once the application where the foliage is included establishes the number of leaves for the appropriate LoD, the extraction algorithm determines the number of leaf split or collapse operations that have to be performed in the foliage. Then, a pointer crosses the *Changed_groups* array and updates the *Init_group* and the *Active_leaves* fields in each cluster where an operation has to be performed.

Due to the storing order of the leaves in the clusters, a leaf-collapse is simply performed by increasing the *Init_group* by two units, and a leaf-split by decreasing this field by two units. These operations allow us to automatically update the position where the extraction algorithm starts traversing the leaves of the group. Figure 2 right shows how three leaf collapses affect the initial data, situated on the left of the figure. According to the information stored in *Changed_groups*, two of them are performed in the 0 and one in the 1 clusters. The leaves to be visualised are shaded.

Once the necessary operations have been processed, the visualisation process begins. This algorithm starts traversing the group from the position indicated in the *Init_group*. It follows the links stored in the leaves to achieve the leaf visualisation sequence. The number of links that the algorithm has to consider is stored in *Active_leaves*.

4.3   Rendering Algorithms for a Variable LoD

The main advantage of data organisation is that different clusters can be visualised at different resolutions. This fact makes it possible to represent the foliage with different detailed zones coexisting in the same representation. The application assigns a certain number of leaves to represent the foliage of a tree and the leaves that are visualised can be distributed following some specific criteria.

To retrieve a variable resolution LoD, a criterion or a set of criteria is needed. These criteria decide which part of the object is to be simplified and which part is to be refined. They depend on the final application where the multiresolution object is to be included. In the case of LoDF, a criterion has been implemented in order to determine the most detailed zone. This criterion is the *distance to the viewer*. Clusters situated near the camera require more detail than those farther away from it. The function *MostDetailedZone* calculates the appropriate number of leaves in the cluster depending on this criterion. This function evaluates each cluster and returns the appropriate number of leaves in each one following a linear function. Figure 4 shows two trees where part of their foliage is less detailed than the rest.

The number of leaves to visualise allows us to know the number of leaf collapse or split operations that have to be performed in the clusters: if the number of leaves to be visualised in the required LoD is higher than the number of leaves currently being visualised, then some leaf split operations have to be performed. In the other case, if the new LoD requires less leaves than the one currently being visualised, the algorithm has to perform the appropriate number of leaf collapses. This information is used to obtain the *Init_position* in the leaf array of the cluster. The number of links to be traversed is the number of leaves that we want to visualise, which is returned by the function *MostDetailedZone* and stored in the *Active_leaves* field of the cluster.

Nevertheless, more criteria can easily be added to LoDF if the application makes it necessary to do so.

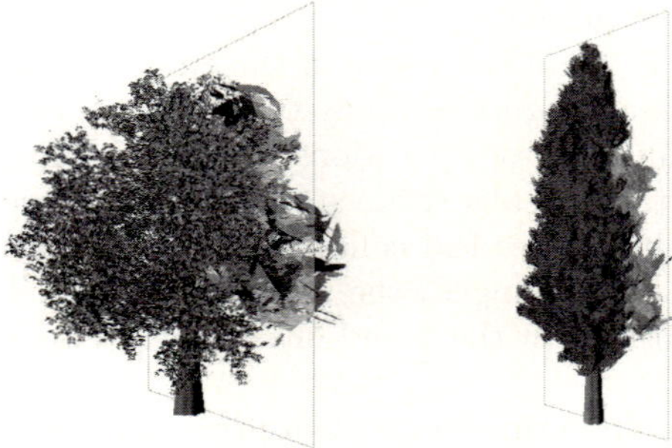

Fig. 4. Example of variable resolution according to the implemented criterion. A part of the tree is more detailed than other.

5   Results

All the tests used here were implemented in C++ with OpenGL as the graphics library. The trees used in our study was modelled with the Xfrog application [14]. The trunks are made up of 34.202 and the foliages consist of another 95.679.

The method is compared with the one presented by Remolar et al. [7], that is, *VDF+MOM*. In order to achieve a better comparison, the tests designed for use here were performed on a computer with the same characteristics as the one used in that work.

The multiresolution methods *VDF+MOM* are not hardware-oriented, so first of all they were compared with the methods presented in this paper, *LoDF+LodStrip* but without taking advantage of the graphics hardware. In other words, all the geometric data about the *LoDF+LodStrip* models are stored in the main memory in the same conditions as the data in *VDF+MOM*. Two tests were designed in this case: one for uniform changes in the LoD and other one for variable changes. Results are shown in Figure 5.

The tests we carried out consist in traversing different LoDs. In all of them, the LoD varies between 0 and 1, 0 being the most detailed approximation and

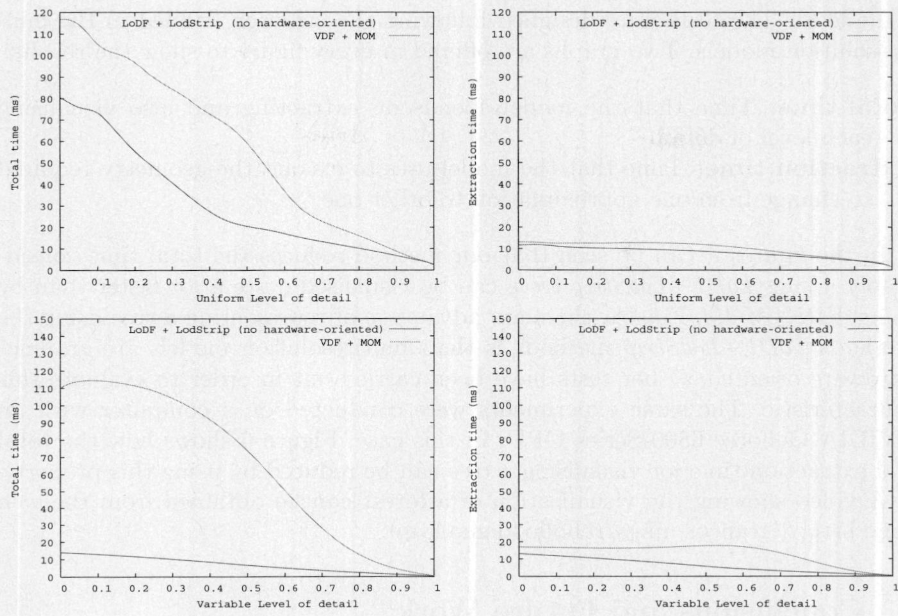

Fig. 5. Results obtained on comparing *VDF+MOM* with *LoDF+Lodstrip*

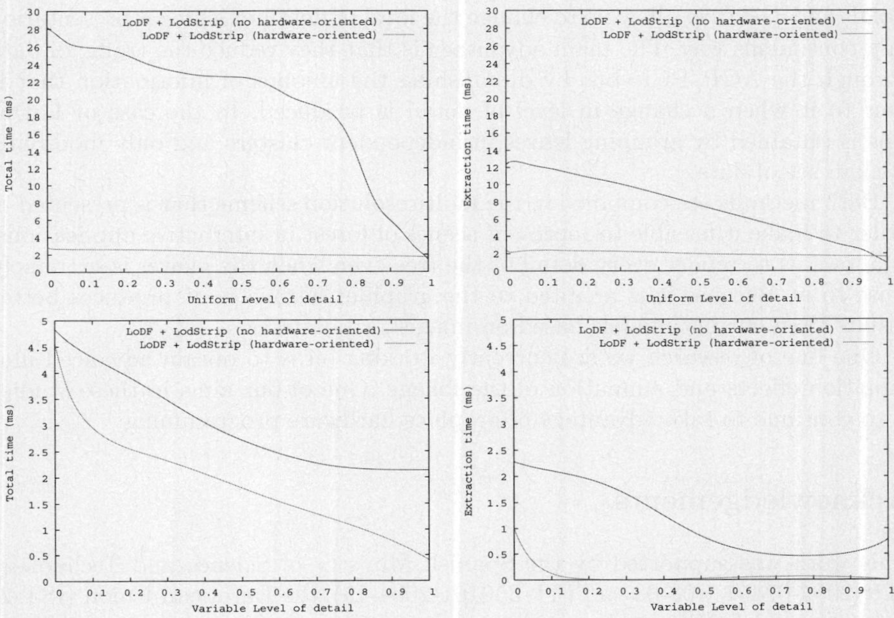

Fig. 6. Results obtained on comparing *LoDF+LodStrip* with and without taking advantage of the graphics hardware

1 the least. The tests were designed following the criterion defined in the multiresolution models. Two graphs are offered in every figure to show the results:

Total time. Time that the model spends on extracting and also visualising each level of detail.
Extraction time. Time that the model uses to extract the geometry required to change from one approximation to other one.

In the figures it can be seen that our method reduces the total time considerably. Using *LoDF+LodStrip* trees can be visualised quite a lot faster than by using *VDF+MOM*. Finally, the main advantage of representing a tree using the methods *LoDF+LodStrip* methods is that multiresolution models are graphics hardware oriented. Other tests have been carried out in order to evaluate this characteristic. The same experiments were conducted on a computer with an NVIDIA GeForce 6800 Series GPU. In this case, Figure 6 shows how the total and extraction time for visualising a tree can be reduced by using this property.

A video showing the visualisation of a forest can be obtained from the web page http://graficos.uji.es/rebollo/demo.html.

6 Conclusions and Future Work

In this article we have presented a new multiresolution approach that exploits the characteristics of current graphics hardware. The models *Level of Detail Foliage* LoDF and *LodStrip* allow us to change the level of detail of a tree representation in a continuous way. The main advantage is that they reduce the traffic of data through the AGP/PCIe bus by diminishing the amount of information that is sent to it when a change in level of detail is produced. In the case of LoDF, this is obtained by grouping leaves in independent clusters and only modifying a small set of data.

Both methods are combined in the multiresolution scheme that is presented in order to make it feasible to represent scenes of forest in interactive applications. It allows us to render every detail of the tree even when the viewer is extremely close to it. Because it is adapted to the graphics hardware, it produces better results than current models based on images or points.

One line of research we are currently working on is to obtain advanced illumination effects and animation of the foliage. One of our aims in these studies is to continue to take advantage of graphics hardware programming.

Acknowledgements

This work was supported by the Spanish Ministry of Science and Technology (TIN2004-07451-C03-03 and FIT-350101-2004-15), the European Union (IST-2-004363) and FEDER funds.

References

1. Deussen, O., Colditz, C., Stamminger, M., Drettakis, G.: Interactive visualization of complex plant ecosystems. In: VIS '02: Proceedings of the conference on Visualization '02, IEEE Computer Society (2002) 219–226
2. Ramos, J.F., Chover, M.: Lodstrips: Level of detail strips. In: International Conference on Computational Science. (2004) 107–114
3. Rebollo, C., Remolar, I., Chover, M., Ripollés, O.: An efficient continuous level of detail model for foliage. In: Proc. of 14-th International Conference in Central Europe on Computer Graphics, Visualization and Computer Vision (WSCG 2006), UNION agency (2006) 335–342
4. Remolar, I., Rebollo, C., Chover, M., Ribelles, J.: Real time tree rendering. In: Lecture Notes in Computational Science 3039. (2004) 173–180
5. Max, N.: Hierarchical rendering of trees from precomputed multi-layer z-buffers. In Pueyo, X., Schrder, P., eds.: Rendering Techniques '96, Proceedings of the Eurographics Workshop, Eurographics, Springer-Verlag (1996) 165–174
6. Reche, A., Martin, I., Drettakis, G.: Volumetric reconstruction and interactive rendering of trees from photographs. ACM Transactions on Graphics (SIGGRAPH Conference Proceedings) **23**(3) (2004) 720–727
7. Remolar, I., Chover, M., Ribelles, J., Belmonte, O.: View-dependent multiresolution model for foliage. Journal of WSCG'03 **11**(2) (2003) 370–378
8. García, I., Sbert, M., Szirmay-Kalos, L.: Leaf cluster impostors for tree rendering with parallax. In: Proc. Eurographics 2005 (Short Presentations), Eurographics (2005)
9. Stamminger, M., Drettakis, G.: Interactive sampling and rendering for complex and procedural geometry. In S.Gortler, C.Myszkowski, eds.: Proceedings of the 12th Eurographics Workshop on Rendering Techniques, Springer-Verlag (2001) 151–162
10. Gilet, G., Meyer, A., Neyret, F.: Point-based rendering of trees. In E. Galin, P.P., ed.: Eurographics Workshop on Natural Phenomena. (2005)
11. Meyer, A., Neyret, F., Poulin, P.: Interactive rendering of trees with shading and shadows. In: Eurographics Workshop on Rendering, Springer-Verlag (2001)
12. Lluch, J., Camahort, E., Vivo, R.: An image based multiresolution model for interactive foliage rendering. Journal of WSCG'04 **12**(3) (2004) 507–514
13. Remolar, I., Chover, M., Belmonte, O., Ribelles, J., Rebollo, C.: Geometric simplification of foliage. In Navazo, I., Slusallek, P., eds.: Proc. Eurographics 2002 (Short Presentations), Eurographics (2002)
14. Xfrog: Greenworks: Organic software. `http://www.greenworks.de/` (2005)

A Multi-resolution Technique for Real-time Animation of Large Crowds

Ingu Kang[1,2], Young Ik Eom[3], and JungHyun Han[1,*]

[1] Game Research Center, College of Information and Communications
Korea University, Seoul, Korea
[2] Nexon Co., Ltd
[3] School of Information and Communications Engineering
Sungkyunkwan University, Suwon, Korea

Abstract. This paper proposes a multi-resolution technique for real-time animation of large crowds, which is useful for massively multi-player online games. Skinning is used to animate non-player characters (NPCs) at close proximity as well as player characters, vertex keyframe animation is used for middle-distance NPCs, and impostors are used for rendering long-distance NPCs. Both of skinning and vertex keyframe animation are accelerated by GPU, and each character is animated independently of the others. The experiments show that hundreds of thousands of characters can be animated at real-time.

Keywords: character animation, skinning, vertex keyframe animation, impostor, large crowds rendering, GPU.

1   Introduction

Recently, *multi-player online games* (MOGs) have experienced an amazing success. A large number of MOGs are currently in service that can accommodate thousands of simultaneous players, which are called *massively multi-player online games* (MMOGs). Animation of large crowds is essential in MMOGs.

The dominant approach to character animation in games has been the *linear blend skinning*[1], which is simply called *skinning*. The skinning algorithm is based on a hierarchy of bones, and each vertex in the mesh is assigned a set of influencing bones and a blending weight for each influence. During animation, the current position of a vertex is computed through the weighted sum of vertices rigidly moved by its influencing bones.

The most popular online game genre is *role playing game* (RPG), which typically requires rendering of *non-player characters* (NPCs). For rendering an NPC in close proximity, skinning is needed because the NPC can interact with the player character and the interaction may cause various actions of the NPC. However, an NPC at a distance does not interact with the player character, performs a limited set of actions, and therefore can be efficiently rendered by *vertex*

---

* Corresponding author.

A. Levi et al. (Eds.): ISCIS 2006, LNCS 4263, pp. 384–393, 2006.

keyframe animation[1]. Finally, consider a long-distance NPC. It also shows a limited set of actions. Further, it usually takes a small number of pixels in screen. Then, the best choice for rendering such an NPC would be the *animated sprites* or *impostors*[2,3].

This paper proposes a multi-resolution technique for real-time animation of large crowds, where skinning is used to animate NPCs at close proximity as well as player characters, vertex keyframe animation is used for middle-distance NPCs, and finally impostors are used for rendering long-distance NPCs.

The experiment results show that the proposed approach is appropriate for rendering extremely large crowds. Even with hundreds of thousands of characters, the proposed algorithm works in real-time.

2   Related Work

Animation of large crowds is an area of research that has been receiving an increased amount of interest. Most of the works in this area have adopted the image-based rendering technique based on impostors. Tecchia *et al.*[4] proposed to use pre-generated impostors in place of geometric models. Aubel *et al.*[5] proposed dynamically-generated impostors, which use less memory than pre-generated ones. A new impostor is generated, for example, when the camera pose has significantly changed. Heigeas *et al.*[6] proposed a similar approach for simulating a larger non-photorealistic impostor crowd in an ancient Greek agora of Argos.

Pre-generated impostors are not appropriate for characters in close proximity. On the other hand, dynamically-generated impostors are not good for a rapidly-changing scene. Dobbyn *et al.*[7] proposed a hybrid technique for large crowds rendering, where polygon meshes are used for characters in close proximity and pre-generated impostors are used for distant characters. However, the number of polygonal characters is strictly limited (100 in their article) to achieve the interactive frame rate.

In OpenGL and DirectX, rendering an object requires invoking a *drawcall*. Suppose an object is repeatedly rendered with a distinct color and world matrix. Then, repeated drawcalls are needed. There is a non-zero overhead associated with each state-changing drawcall. In order to resolve the drawcall overhead, *hardware instancing*[8] has been proposed in DirectX, where multiple instances of an object are rendered through a single drawcall. In OpenGL, a large number of constant register settings prior to drawcalls results in a large amount of driver's work. In order to resolve the overhead, *pseudo instancing*[9] has been proposed, where the constant register setting overhead can be minimized by providing the rendering data in terms of texture coordinates through APIs such

---

[1] It was popular in the old-time games such as Quake, and was often called *deformable mesh animation*. Its obvious disadvantage is that the animation data size is huge because the complete mesh has to be stored for every keyframe. As a result, the number of animations is strictly limited.

as `glTexCoord()`. However, both of the techniques are good only for rendering static meshes. They are inappropriate for rendering skinning meshes.

Skinning algorithm can be implemented using either CPU or GPU, and works efficiently for a small number of characters. A vertex shader implementation has been reported by ATI[10], where the bone matrices are recorded in the constant registers. The number of bones for a character is limited to 20, the 3×4 bone matrix is stored in three constant registers, and a single drawcall renders four characters. In total, 240 $(20 \times 3 \times 4)$ constant registers are needed. Due to the limited number of constant registers, the vertex shader-based skinning is not good for rendering large crowds.

Recently, GPU-based algorithms for real-time skinning animation of large crowds have been proposed by [11] and [12], where each character is animated independently of the others. The performance of the algorithms is excellent enough to render thousands of characters at real-time. However, the algorithms cannot handle extremely large crowds, e.g. hundreds of thousands of characters.

3   Crowd Rendering System

This paper proposes to use three levels of detail for real-time animation of large crowds: skinning, vertex keyframe animation, and impostors.

3.1   Skinning

This subsection summarizes the GPU-based two-pass algorithm proposed by [11], and discusses the optimization issues. In skinning, each vertex is assigned a set of influencing bones, and a blending *weight* is determined for each influence. The skinning data for a vertex consist of position, normal, bone indices and weights, and bone matrices. They are passed to GPU through 1D textures. Shown in the left-hand side of Fig. 1 are the skinning data. A vertex is influenced by up to 4 bones. The bone matrices are computed every frame, and each row of the 3×4 matrix is recorded in a separate texture, as shown in the right-hand side of Fig. 1.

In the first pass of the algorithm, skinning is computed using a pixel shader and the transformed vertex data are written into the *render target texture*. It is done through a single drawcall. Shown in the middle of Fig. 1 is the render target

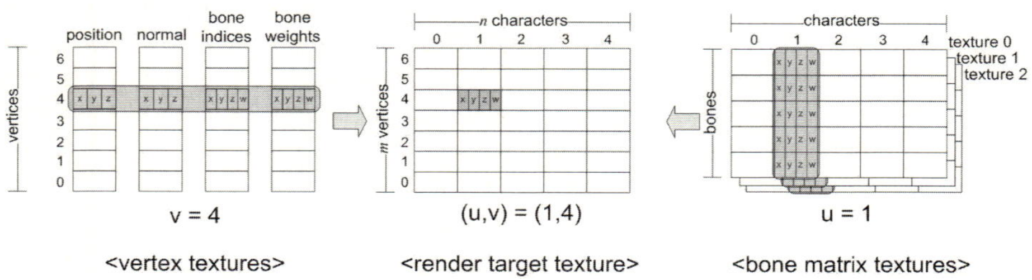

Fig. 1. Skinning and render target texture

texture for n characters each with m vertices[2]. For implementing the skinning algorithm in the pixel shader, the vertex shader renders a quad covering the render target. Then, the pixel shader fills each texel of the render target texture, which corresponds to a vertex of a character. Unlike the vertex shader-based skinning discussed in Section 2, the data needed for skinning are obtained from the textures, not constant registers. Therefore, the proposed approach is free from the constant register size limitation.

With the transformed vertices, the second pass renders the large crowds. The render target texture is copied to a vertex buffer object (VBO)[13], and then each character is rendered by the vertex shader using a given index buffer. For all of the render target texture, VBO and pixel buffer object (PBO)[14], 32-bit float format is used for each channel of RGBA/xyzw for the sake of accuracy.

In the current implementation, the render target texture contains vertex data for 64 characters, i.e. n is set to 64. Suppose that view frustum culling decides to render 240 characters. Then, three invocations of drawcall will render 64×3=192 characters. The remaining 48 characters are then rendered by the 4th invocation of drawcall, where the render target texture is not completely filled. Even though not completely filled, the entire render target texture is copied to VBO. Our experiments show that such unnecessary copy incurs negligible overhead. When the render target texture was made larger, however, noticeable inefficiency was found for rendering a small number of characters.

Consider a horse character with 1,084 polygons and 555 vertices. In rendering such a low-polygon character, the render target texture of 64 characters shows the best performance because 16-bit vertex indices are enough. Suppose that 1,024 characters are rendered where the character is composed of 1,024 vertices. Then, the 16-bit vertex index requires 16 drawcalls. In contrast, a single drawcall is enough if we adopt 32-bit vertex index. However, 16 drawcalls using the 16-bit index shows better performance than a single drawcall using the 32-bit index due to the limited bandwidth for index data.

It is worth mentioning that the vertex textures lead to efficient per-vertex lighting for white-colored light. Skinning and per-vertex lighting can be done at the same time by the pixel shader, and then the lighting intensity value can be stored in the w-component of the render target texture.

In the current implementation, the bone matrices are computed by CPU, and such load balancing between CPU and GPU leads to the best performance. In CPU-intensive applications such as AI-based games, however, the bone matrices may need to be computed by GPU. The choice between CPU and GPU depends on applications.

3.2   Vertex Keyframe Animation

In the traditional vertex keyframe animation, the keyframe vertices are interpolated by CPU. On the other hand, the GPU-based implementation stores a

---

[2] The number of characters n is recommended to be a power of 2 because the GPU automatically makes the texture size 2^k through padding.

keyframe mesh into a vertex buffer, and invokes a drawcall by providing the vertex shader with two keyframes as streams. Then, interpolation is done by the vertex shader. A large number of keyframes leads to the drawcall overhead. This subsection proposes a pixel shader-based 2-pass algorithm, which requires a single drawcall.

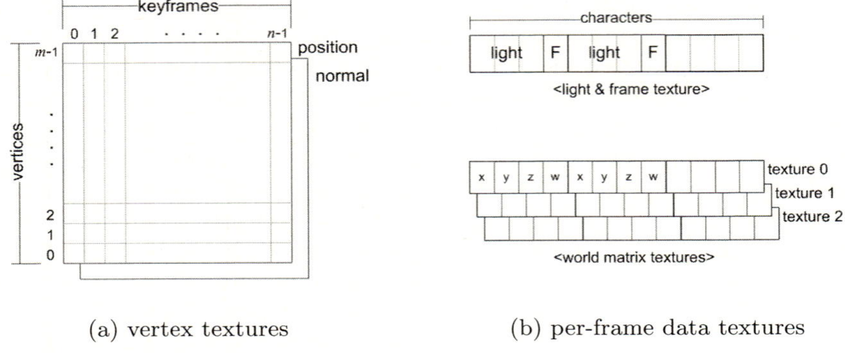

(a) vertex textures   (b) per-frame data textures

Fig. 2. Vertex textures and per-frame data textures

The data required for vertex keyframe animation are stored as textures. Fig. 2-(a) shows the vertex information (position and normal) stored in 2D textures. Fig. 2-(b) shows {light, frame-number} information stored in a 1D texture, and the world matrix stored in three 1D textures. A character instance is assigned {light, frame-number}, where (x,y,z) information can be either position or direction depending on the light source type. Each row of the 3×4 world matrix is recorded in a separate 1D texture.

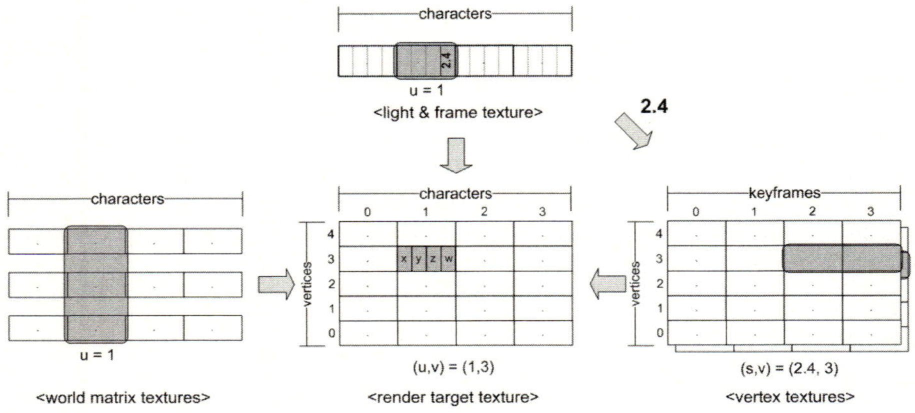

Fig. 3. Vertex keyframe animation and render target texture

The shader implementation of the vertex keyframe animation works in two passes. The vertex shader renders a quad covering the render target. Then, the pixel shader fills each texel of the render target texture. For example, given the render target texture coordinates $(u,v)=(1,3)$ in the middle of Fig. 3, u-coordinate of the render target texture is used to retrieve the world matrix, light, and frame number. Then, the retrieved frame number s and the render target texture's v-coordinate constitute the texture coordinates $(s,v)=(2.4,3)$, which is used to retrieve the interpolated vertex from the vertex textures. *Linear filtering* is set for texturing, and therefore interpolation is done by hardware, leading to superior performance. The interpolated vertex is transformed by the world matrix, and the lighting intensity is computed. A texel of the render target texture contains the final vertex position and the lighting intensity. Finally, the second pass renders all characters using the render target texture.

3.3   Impostors

For each keyframe, sprites are captured from 256 viewpoints, as shown in Fig. 4. For experiments, two characters are used: bird and horse. For bird rendering, 16×16 viewpoints are sampled in the spherical coordinates (ρ,ϕ), i.e. 16 along the longitude ρ in the range $[0,\pi]$, and 16 along the latitude ϕ in the range $[0,2\pi]$. For horse rendering, the viewpoint cannot fall below the ground, and therefore 8×32 viewpoints are sampled, i.e. 8 in the range of $\rho=[0,\pi/2]$, and 32 in the range of $\phi=[0,2\pi]$. For a character, 11 keyframes are used to generate the sprite textures, i.e. a character has 11 sprite textures.

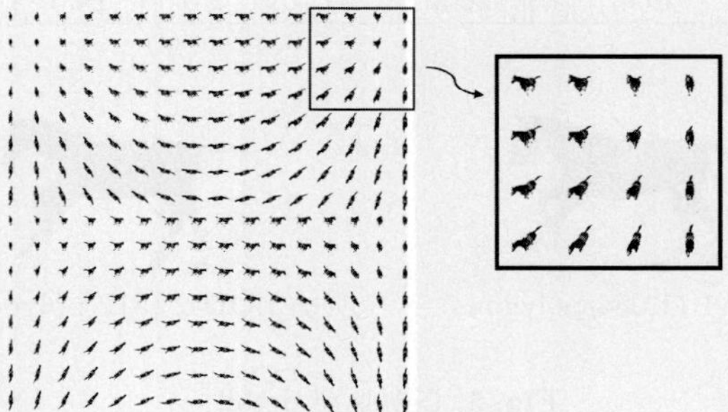

Fig. 4. Sprite texture

A keyframe's 256 sprites are stored in a 512×512 texture. See Fig. 4. Then, the impostors (animated sprites) are rendered through hardware-accelerated *point sprites*, for rendering of which both OpenGL and DirectX have standard interfaces. For a world space position p where an impostor is to be rendered, the API is supplied with the impostor's texture coordinates (u,v). Then, a square centered at the screen space position p' is automatically created, and each of the square's corner vertices is assigned a texture coordinate, which the pixel shader computes using (u,v).

4   Implementation and Result

The proposed algorithm has been implemented in C++, OpenGL and Cg on a PC with 3.2 GHz Intel Pentium4 CPU, 2GB memory, and NVIDIA Geforce 7800GTX 256MB. For experiments, two characters are animated: a bird character with 24 bones, 360 vertices and 473 polygons, and a horse character with 38 bones, 555 vertices and 1,084 polygons. Table 1 compares the frame rates of the vertex shader skinning and the proposed 2-pass skinning. (For performance evaluation, view frustum culling is disabled and 'all' characters are processed by GPU.) When rendering 1024 horses, for example, the proposed approach is almost six times faster than the vertex shader skinning. In contrast, the performance gain is not so great in the bird case because the bird character has smaller vertices than the horse.

Table 1. FPS comparison of vertex shader (VS) skinning and proposed 2-pass skinning

# characters	bird		horse	
	VS	2-pass	VS	2-pass
1	1800	1830	2680	1723
4	1721	1759	1555	1590
16	1476	1545	577	1235
64	924	1032	164	649
256	320	411	43	209
1024	83.3	121	10	57.2
2048	41.5	62.4	5	28.7
4096	20.3	31	2.5	14.3

(a) LOD-1 (1,084 polygons)   (b) LOD-2 (312 polygons)

Fig. 5. Levels of detail

In the current implementation, discrete LOD (levels of detail) techniques are used. Fig. 5 show 2 levels of detail for the horse character. Table 2 shows that the skinning algorithm's performance with LOD-1 is comparable to that with LOD-2. For the proposed 2-pass skinning, the bottleneck lies in CPU, which computes bone matrices. As LOD-1 and LOD-2 have the same number of bones, CPU does the same amount of work for both meshes. In contrast, the vertex keyframe animation's performance with LOD-2 is superior to that with LOD-1 because CPU actually does nothing.

Table 3 shows how the performance changes in FPS on the ratio of skinning and impostor rendering when 1,000 horses are rendered. Obviously, the rendering

Table 2. FPS comparison of 2-pass skinning and 2-pass vertex keyframe animation

	skinning		keyframe	
# characters	LOD-1	LOD-2	LOD-1	LOD-2
1	1725	1723	1757	1740
4	1594	1590	1641	1705
16	1236	1240	1318	1598
64	649	651	752	1250
256	209	212	255	679
1024	56.2	56.9	70	225
2048	28	27.8	35.3	119
4096	13.3	13.5	17.3	61

Table 3. FPS change on the ratio of skinning and impostor rendering

		FPS	
# skinning	# impostor	bird	horse
1000	0	83.8	57
800	200	101	70
600	400	130	91
400	600	180	124
200	800	279	207

Fig. 6. Rendering 102,400 horses with LOD and frustum culling

Fig. 7. Rendering 102,400 birds with LOD and frustum culling

performance is improved as as the ratio of impostor rendering to skinning is increased.

Fig. 6 shows snapshots of rendering 102,400 horses. Depending on the distance from the viewpoint, a character is rendered through skinning, vertex keyframe animation or impostor rendering. In Fig. 6, hundreds of horses are skin animated, thousands are animated through vertex keyframe animation, and the others are rendered using impostors. The average FPS is 25 with view frustum culling enabled. Fig. 7 shows snapshots of rendering 102,400 birds. The average FPS is 30.

5   Conclusion

This paper presented a multi-resolution technique for real-time animation of large crowds in games, where skinning is used to animate non-player characters (NPCs) at close proximity as well as player characters, vertex keyframe animation is used for middle-distance NPCs, and impostors are used for rendering long-distance NPCs. The experiment results show that the proposed approach is attractive for massively multi-player online games, especially where huge NPCs such as soldiers or animals should be rendered. Real-time performance has been achieved even with hundreds of thousands of characters.

Acknowledgements

This work was supported by grant No. R01-2006-000-11297-0 from the Basic Research Program of the Korea Science & Engineering Foundation.

References

1. Lewis, J.P., Cordner, M., Fong, N.: Pose space deformations: A unified approach to shape interpoalation and skeleton-driven deformation. SIGGRAPH2000 165–172
2. Guymon, M.: Pyro-techniques: Playing with fire. Game Developer **7** (2000) 23-27.
3. Maciel, P., Shirley, P.: Visual navigation of large environments using textured clusters. Proc. Symposium of Interactive 3D Graphics(1995).
4. Tecchia, F., Loscos, C., Chrysanthou, Y.: Image based crowd rendering. IEEE Computer Graphics and Applications 22 (2002)
5. Aubel, A., Boulic, R., Thalmann, D.: Real-time display of virtual humans: levels of details and impostors. IEEE Transactions on Circuits and Systems for Video Technology **10** (2000) 207-217.
6. Heigeas L., Luciani A., Thollot J., Castagne N.: A physically-based particle model of emergent crowd behaviors. In Proc. Graphikon '03 (2003).
7. Dobbyn, S., Hamill, J., O'Conor, K., O'Sullivan, C.: Geopostors : A real-time geometry / impostor crowd rendering system. ACM Transactions on Graphics(2005) 933
8. Microsoft: Instancing sample. DirectX SDK. February 2006
9. Zelsnack, J.: GLSL pseudo-instancing. NVIDIA Technical Report. November 2004
10. Gosselin, D. R., Sander, P. V., Mitchell, J. L.: Drawing a crowd. ShaderX3. CHARLES RIVER MEDIA. (2004) 505–517

11. Kang, I., Han, J.: Real-time Animation of Large Crowds (Poster). International Conference on Entertainment Computing. (2006).
12. Wu, O.: Animation with R2VB. ATI SDK. (2006).
13. NVIDIA: Using vertex buffer objects. NVIDIA White Paper. October 2003
14. NVIDIA: Fast texture downloads and readbacks using pixel buffer objects in OpenGL. NVIDIA User Guide. August 2005

A Framework for Working with Digitized Cultural Heritage Artifacts

Can Ozmen and Selim Balcisoy

Sabanci University, Turkey
canozmen@su.sabanciuniv.edu, balcisoy@sabanciuniv.edu
http://graphics.sabanciuniv.edu

Abstract. In this paper, we present our work in designing, implementing, and evaluating a set of 3D interactive spatial measurement tools in the context of Cultural Heritage Toolbox (CH Toolbox), a framework for computer-aided cultural heritage research. Our application utilizes a bi-manual, spaceball and mouse driven user interface to help the user manage visualized 3D models digitized from real artifacts. We have developed a virtual radius estimator, useful for analyzing incomplete pieces of radial artifacts, and a virtual tape measure, useful in measurement of geodesic distances between two points on the surface of an artifact. We tested the tools on the special case of pottery analysis.

1 Introduction

Using digital models of cultural heritage artifacts, obtained through 3D scanner and modeling technology, has the following advantages. It is faster, cheaper, and safer to store, transport, search, sort, and re-arrange digitized models instead of the real pieces. Digitization is also beneficial for the computational analysis of these artifacts as it makes it easier to compute and verify the results.

Although the use of digitized models in cultural heritage research is beneficial, the adoption of such techniques is problematic because nearly all experts are trained for using the traditional methods. Thus, practitioners of the field cannot easily transfer their expertise with traditional tools to new software based tools without further education [1]. Similar problems arise in the medical field as well, where the disparency between computer tools and formal education methods is acknowledged. The generally preferred solution to this problem is to present a familiar interface to the underlying software system.

In the following subsections we will present two traditional tools, the tape measure and the bordimeter, and discuss their usage in the special case of archaeological pottery classification.

1.1 Tape Measure

The tape measure is used for determining the dimensions of a sherd and the surface distance between any two points on the sherd. These measurements are used for classifying a piece, along with its weight and thickness. It is also used

A. Levi et al. (Eds.): ISCIS 2006, LNCS 4263, pp. 394–400, 2006.
© Springer-Verlag Berlin Heidelberg 2006

for measuring fracture lengths to aid in reconstruction. The main purpose of the tape measure is to find geodesic distances either on the surface, along the rim, if the sherd is part of the rim, or along the fractured edges.

The tool is used with two hands. The protrusion on the edge of the tape is fastened to one of the end-points of the distance to be measured, then it is held in place using one hand while the other hand pulls the measure and extends the tape to the other end-point. The measurement can be more easily read by locking the tape at the desired length. The tape measure is, in essence, an easier to use metered rope.

1.2 Bordimeter

A bordimeter, also called a rim chart, is a set of concentric circles drawn on a piece of paper or cardboard. It is used for estimating the rim radius of a vessel given a sherd belonging to the vessel's rim. The rim radius is used in calculating the rim size, which in turn helps archaeologists to assess a pot's usage. Radius estimation is also used in volume, and consequently capacity estimation. Both assessments help in the classification of the vessel.

The tool is placed on a flat surface, then a rim sherd is put rim-side down to find the best fitting circle, which is then used to estimate the radius. Because the bordimeter is a solid piece of paper, radius estimation cannot be done with pieces other then rim sherds.

2 Related Work

The most common approach in working with digitized cultural heritage artifacts is to use existing 3D modeling software. The problem is that effectively using these programs needs expertise with the software and user interface which the researcher may lack. They are also general purpose programs, mostly geared toward digital content creation, architecture, or technical drawing and thus may not mimic the traditional way cultural heritage researchers work with artifacts. Applications targetting specific archaeological tasks exist, but they are limited by their tight focus and cannot be easily extended to other domains in analytical cultural heritage research.

2.1 Geodesics

A geodesic curve is the shortest path between two points on a surface. Common areas of use include navigation, path-finding, motion planning and network optimization. It is also an important step in many computer graphics algorithms such as mesh parametrization, mesh segmentation and mesh editing [4,5,6]. Current graphics hardware all use a triangular mesh format to process and visualize 3D geometries, thus most geodesics research is done for the discrete case [7].

The Djikstra shortest-path algorithm is not sufficient to solve the discrete geodesic problem because the shortest path on a surface does not always follow along the edges of the mesh. The simplest solution is to augment the original mesh with extra points before running Djikstra. Lanthier et. al. [9] compare different ways of populating a mesh with additional vertices on existing edges, called Steiner points, and show that a bounded approximation to the geodesic can be obtained with this method. The error bound and complexity of the algorithm depends on the number and distribution of these Steiner points. An description of the algorithm using a fixed-point distribution scheme, which we used, will be presented in the next section. A survey of approximate algorithms can be found in [8].

Several algorithms giving an exact solution to the discrete geodesic problem have been proposed. The "single source - all destinations" algorithm described by Mitchell, Mount and Papadimitriou (MMP) uses the continuous Djikstra method and it has a worst case running time of $O(n^2 \log n)$, where n is the number of vertices. The MMP algorithm was recently implemented by Surazhky et. al. [11], who conclude that it performs much better than the worst case analysis suggests. An exact algorithm with $O(n^2)$ running time based on surface unfoldings was proposed by Chen and Han [12].

2.2   Circle Fitting

The problem of fitting a circle to a given set of co-planar points is called 2D circle fitting. It is a nonlinear least squares problem, which can be solved iteratively by reducing it to a set of linear least squares problems [3]. The numerical solution we used will be presented in the next section.

3   CH Toolbox

CH Toolbox is a 3D application framework for analytical cultural heritage research. It visualizes digitized models of artifacts in 3D and allows the user to analyze the pieces using a spaceball and mouse driven interface. It has a bi-manual user interaction scheme, where the mouse is used to switch between tools, toggle visualization modes and select the artifacts to be manipulated and the spaceball is used to translate and rotate the selected artifacts. Bi-manual interaction is a familiar human trait, and increases productivity in 3D manipulation tasks [13].

CH Toolbox is developed in C++, using the open-source scenegraph library OpenSceneGraph [14] that helps visualizations in OpenGL by providing an organizational hierarchy. The CH Toolkit and the interactive spatial measurement tools developed for it are available for all the operating systems that OpenSceneGraph supports. Our application runs in real-time on desktop PCs.

We developed a radius estimation and a surface distance measurement tool for the CH Toolbox. They are used interactively inside the framework and allow quick and precise measurements. The next subsections detail their implementation and usage.

3.1   Virtual Tape Measure

The virtual tape measure is used for measuring the surface distance between two points on a model. The user fixes a point then moves the mouse to interactively visualize and measure geodesics originating from the start point as seen in Figure 1.

We solve the geodesic problem in the pre-processing stage before the artifact model is visualized inside the CH Toolbox environment. The approximate geodesic solution proposed by Lanthier et. al. [9] is used. The algorithm is as follows:

1. The original mesh is loaded and converted to a triangle mesh.
2. Original edges are sub-divided to create extra vertices, called Steiner points.
3. New edges are created between two Steiner points if they are adjacent on the same triangle edge or they lie on different edges of the same triangle.
4. The single-source all-destinations Djikstra is run for each vertex.

We used a fixed scheme to evenly add two Steiner points per edge, therefore 6 vertices and 27 edges are added to a triangle in the pre-processing stage. Lanthier et. al. [9] proved that the algorithm runs in $O(n^5)$ for the single-source all-destinations problem, where n is the number of triangles in the original mesh.

The geodesic is visualized by traversing vertices on the shortest path between the two end points of the tape measure. We choose to visualize the extra edges only if they lie on the shortest path solution, thus the tool has negligible impact on the interactivity of CH Toolbox. The bi-manual interaction scheme of the framework is also conserved while using the virtual tape measure.

Fig. 1. Screenshot of the tape measure in action

3.2   Virtual Bordimeter

Virtual Bordimeter is a radius estimation tool for digitized artifacts. A best fit circle is computed and displayed interactively as the user moves the mouse over visualization of the artifact model as seen in Figure 2.

The tool works as follows:

1. The plane defined by moving the mouse is intersected with the model to obtain a set of points on the plane.
2. The average of the points is taken as the initial estimate for the circle.
3. The circle is fit iteratively using least squares fitting to these selected points (see Figure 3).
4. The center and the radius of the circle is computed.

Even if the least squares solution does not converge, the iteration for fitting the circle is stopped after a certain number of steps to maintain interactivity. We found that the solution converges in sufficient time if the points are not nearly linear. Otherwise, a warning message is displayed. This is not a problem with our test case since archaeological pottery has a curved surface.

The circle and its center is visualized in addition to the text display of the location of the center and its radius because it helps the expert to visually verify the suitability of the numeric solution as the rotational axis of the artifact. During the measurement process the expert can use the spaceball to move and orient the model. She can also change the transparency of the circle visualization to prevent it from obscuring the artifact.

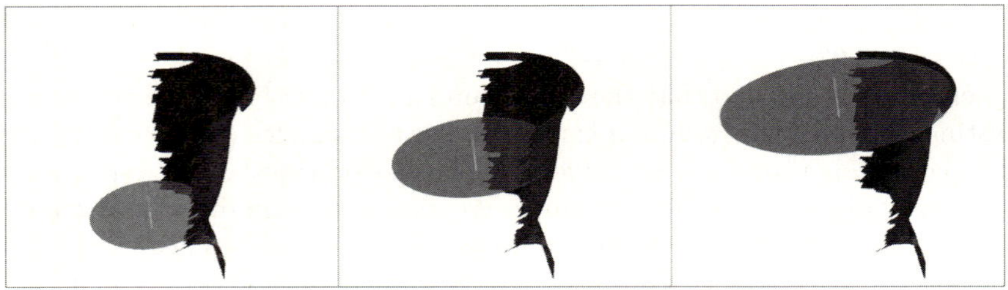

Fig. 2. Screenshot of the virtual bordimeter in action

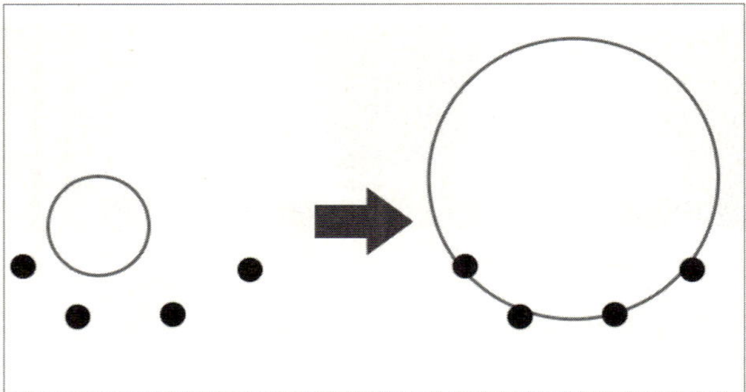

Fig. 3. Circle fitting

4   Results

We tested the surface distance algorithm on a Pentium IV 2.6GHz PC with 1GB RAM and a dual Xeon 3.4GHz workstation with 4GB RAM. For a sherd mesh with 17K triangles, our algorithm takes 16 seconds on the Pentium IV and 14 seconds on the Xeon as seen in Table 1. The number of extra vertices and edges, and its impact on performance is also reported. Although the perfomance is not adequate for real-time interaction, our interviews with cultural heritage experts show that the it is acceptable for real world use cases [1].

Table 1. Performance of approximate geodesic algorithm

Model	Vertices	Faces	Stn. points	Stn. edges	time 1 (s)	time 2 (s)
Sherd	9183	17696	62967	427304	16.2003	14.0507
Sphere	25502	50986	178502	1230534	47.5673	41.2052
Sphere	102302	204552	716102	4938138	202.2870	175.5850

We also compared rim estimations and surface distances measured on a real pot with the approximate results we got using our virtual tools on a sherd mesh (Table 2). The error rate of the geodesic is very small, and it is consistent with the bound proven by Lanthier et. al. [9]. Again, the error was found to be acceptable by experts [1] although it includes the error from the 3D scanning process as well.

Table 2. Error rate of virtual tools

Tool	Real (cm)	Virtual (cm)	Rel. error
Tape	15.35	15.44	0.6%
Bordimeter	12.74	12.17	4.5%

5 Conclusion and Future Work

Our contribution is the development of a platform for interactive computer-aided cultural heritage tasks. We implemented measurement tools that archaeologists daily use in real life by adapting algorithms developed for other computational geometry tasks. The algorithms we chose are suitable for use in a real-time interactive environment.

Accuracy problems of the radius estimation tool must be further researched. We suspect the relatively high error rate is due to errors in the 3D scanning technology we used. Our tools should be tested with models obtained from other scanning technologies.

CH Toolbox was approved by the cultural heritage experts who have seen it. We plan to release CH Toolbox as an open-source application to aid researchers in the cultural heritage domain.

Acknowledgements

This research was supported by TUBITAK EEAG 104E155.

References

1. Personal communication with Prof. Bernard Frischer, Univ. of Virgina. (2006)
2. Preim, B., Spindler, W., Oldhafer, K. J., Peitgen, H.-O.: 3d distance measurements in medical visualizations. Interactive Medical Image Vis. and Analysis (2001), 31-36

3. Gander, W., Golub, G. H., Strebel, R.: Least squares fitting of circles and ellipses. BIT 34 (1994), 556-577
4. Krishnamurthy, V., Levoy, M.: Fitting smooth surfaces to dense polygon meshes. Proc. of SIGGRAPH 96 (1996) 313–324
5. Funkhouser, T., Kazhdan, M., Shilane, P., Min, P., Kiefer, W., Tal, A., Rusinkiewicz, S., Dobkin, D.: Modeling by example. Proc. of SIGGRAPH 2004 (2004) 652-663
6. Floater, M. S., Hormann, K.: Parameterization of triangulations and unorganized points. Tutorials in Multiresolution in Geometric Modeling (2002) 287-315
7. Mitchell, J. S. B., Mount, D. M., Papadimitriou, C. H.: The discrete geodesic problem. SIAM J. of Computing 16(4), 647-668
8. Mitchell, J. S. B.: Geometric shortest paths and network optimization. Handbook of Computational Geometry (2000) 633-702
9. Lanthier, M., Maheshwari, A., Sack, J.-R.: Approximating weighted shortest paths on polyhedral surfaces. Proc. 13th Annu. ACM Symp. Computational Geometry (1997) 274-283
10. Martinez, D., Velho, L., Carvalho, P. C.: Geodesic paths on triangular meshes. Proc. of SIBGRAPI/SIACG. (2004) 210-217
11. Surazhsky, V., Surazhsky, T., Kirsanov, D., Gortler, S. J., Hoppe, H.: Fast exact and approximate geodesics on meshes. ACM Trans. on Graphics 24(3) (2005), 553-560
12. Chen, J., Han, Y.: Shortest paths on a polyhedron: part I: computing shortest paths. Int. J. of Computational Geometry and Applications 6(2) (1996) 127-144
13. Hinckley, K., Pausch, R., Profitt, D., Kassel N. F.: Two handed virtual manipulation ACM Trans. on Human Computer Interaction, Vol 5(3) (1998) 260-302
14. OpenSceneGraph: www.openscenegraph.org

On the Stability of Application-Layer Multicast Tree

Ke Xu[1], Jiangchuan Liu[2], Lizheng Fu[3], and Chunyu Liu[4]

[1] Department of Computer Science and Technology, Tsinghua University
`xuke@tsinghua.edu.cn`
[2] School of Computing Science, Simon Fraser University
`jcliu@cs.sfu.ca`
[3] Research Institute, Bitway Network Technology Ltd. Co.
`fulz@bit-way.com`
[4] Department of Computer Science and Technology, Tsinghua University
`liuchunyu@csnet1.cs.tsinghua.edu.cn`

Abstract. A tree structure has been widely used in constructing application-layer overlays. It is known that the instability of a tree will significantly reduce the performance of the overlay. In this paper, we propose a novel stochastic model that captures the (in)stability characteristics of an application-layer multicast tree. Our model has considered various important factors related to the tree stability, and we have derived closed-form solutions to a class of typical multicast trees. Our results offer a better understanding on the (in)stability of application-layer multicast trees, and also suggest three effective enhancements to improve their stability.

Keywords: Application-Layer Multicast, Stability, Stochastic model.

1 Introduction

Multicast has a broad spectrum of applications, ranging from Internet-based TV broadcasting to large-scale multi-peer games. While IP multicast provides an efficient vehicle for multicast application, its deployment remains quite limited due to many practical and political issues. Recently, application-layer multicast (ALM) is advocated by many researchers as a flexible and readily deployable alternative.

In application-layer multicast, an end user can serve as a relay. As does in IP multicast, a tree structure is widely adopted in ALM systems. Many of them have focused on forming a high quality tree structure out of the application-layer overlay, with high throughput or short delay. However, unlike IP multicast, where the internal tree nodes are dedicated routers, an overlay node is autonomous, which can join or leave the overlay at will, or even crash without notification. The (in)stability thus becomes a key problem in an ALM tree, which can significantly impact the user experience.

In this paper we present an initiative discuss on the impact of dynamic user behaviors to the stability of ALM trees. We assume that, when a parent node departs from the multicast tree, fails, or suffers from congestion, and then all its descendents will be affected. This assumption generally holds for existing tree-based ALM protocols if repairing algorithms are ignored. We then propose a novel stochastic

A. Levi et al. (Eds.): ISCIS 2006, LNCS 4263, pp. 401–412, 2006.

model that captures the (in)stability characteristics of an ALM tree. Our model has considered various important factors related to the tree stability, and we have derived closed-form solutions to a class of typical multicast trees. Our results offer a better understanding on the (in)stability of ALM trees, and also suggest three effective enhancements to improve their the stability.

The rest of this paper is organized as follows. Section 2 presents the related work. The models and definition of stability are discussed in Section 3. In Section 4, we analyze the stability for different multicast trees, and we further analyze the impact of stable nodes in Section 5. Finally, Section 6 concludes the paper.

2   Related Work

Application layer research has been a hotspot in today's network research. Due to the limit of network layer multicast, shift this function to application layer is a kind of solving method. Up to date, there has been considerable research in this field. In this section, we will introduce some related work of application layer multicast.

2.1   Application Layer Multicast

ALM up shifts the network layer functions that used to be realized by routers in IP multicast to application layer nodes. As such, there is no fundamental change needed in the network infrastructure. The main target of an application layer multicast protocol is to efficiently deliver data to all the end users, and we can classify them into two: unstructured ALM and structured ALM.

An unstructured application layer multicast scheme does not maintain an explicitly structure. A node can obtain data from one or more neighboring nodes through flooding, random searching, etc. In Peercast [1], there is only one neighboring node, where as in Coolstreaming [2], there are 4 neighboring nodes, which potentially enhances robustness.

The unstructured ALM is relatively simple to implement. However, they often suffer from the low efficiency without an explicit structure. On the contrary, structured application layer multicast scheme preserves an explicit structure among the overlay nodes. They maintain a control topology and a data topology. The group members in the control topology periodically exchange update messages to identify each other and recover from node failures. The data topology is a subset of control topology, and is for identifying the data routes used in multicast forwarding. In existing protocols, a tree topology is widely used; examples include Yoid [5] and Overcast [6].

2.2   Stability of Multicast Tree

Since an overlay node can join or leave at will, or even crash without notification, (in)stability becomes a great challenging in application-layer multicast. We are aware that there are several previous studies on the stability of a tree topology or multicast. The stability of a shortest path tree is defined in [8]. Zhang et al. [9] proposed a link-dependent model and the dependent-degree model for modeling congestion bottlenecks in a tree. They also defined a real-valued dependency-degree factor to quantify all possible degrees of dependency between the random variables in the Markov chain's one-step transition probabilities. In [7, 10], we have applied stochastic model analysis to the stability of layered multicast congestion control. Our work is motivated by these studies, yet we focus on the stability issues specifically in application-layer multicast.

3   Model and Definitions

In order to evaluate and quantify application layer multicast tree stability, we first give a definition of stability:

Definition 1: Assume that the total node number of multicast tree T is $N(T)$, $\Delta(T)$ represents the number of nodes affected by a malfunctioned (leave, fail, or congested) node, and $E(\Delta(T))$ represents the expected value of $\Delta(T)$. We define the stability factor of multicast tree as $S(T) = 1 - E(\Delta(T))/N(T)$. Intuitively, the higher the stability factor of the multicast tree T, the more stable it is.

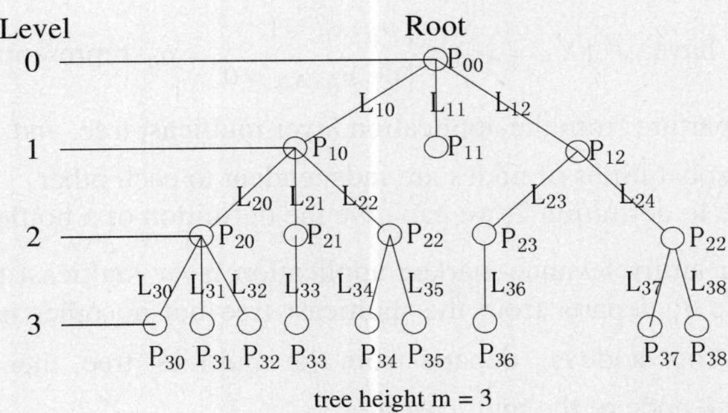

Fig. 1. An application layer multicast tree model

There are many factors that have impact on the stability of an application layer multicast tree: the probability of nodal departure, the nodal service capacity, the topological structure of the multicast tree, the height of the multicast tree, etc. In order to investigate the impact these factors, we now give a multicast tree analytical model which labels stochastically the irrelevances.

Definition 2: A random irrelevance-marked application layer multicast tree is an application layer multicast tree with labels being independent stochastic variables. The height of the tree is m and the node set which composes the tree is P. It meets these four conditions:

1: All the nodes of set P are marked in the multicast tree T, and $P = \{P_{00}, P_{10}, \cdots, P_{1j_1}, P_{20}, \cdots, P_{2,j_2}, \cdots, P_{m,0}, \cdots, P_{m,j_m}\}$, as is shown in Fig.1. Here,

P_{ij} represents node j (from the left) on layer i, link L_{ij} links the adjoining upstream nodes of nodes P_{ij} and P_{ij} in multicast tree T.

2: In order to identify the relation between two nodes in a multicast tree, we define some simple operations:

1) Adjoining links: we use $NU(T, P_{ij}, P_{i+1,l})$ to represent adjoining links, where $P_{i,j}$ and $P_{i+1,l}$ represent respectively a node on layer i and layer $i+1$ in the multicast tree. $NU(T, P_{ij}, P_{i+1,l})$ meets following expression:

$$NU(T, P_{ij}, P_{i+1,l}) = \begin{cases} 1, if\ P_{i+1,l}\ is\ the\ neighbor\ upstream\ node\ of\ P_{ij} \\ 0, else \end{cases}$$

2) upstream link set: We express the upstream link set as $NUL(T, P_{ij})$, which denotes a set L' for all the links in the route from root node P_{00} to node P_{ij}.

3) upstream path node set: We express the upstream path node set as $NUP(T, P_{ij})$, which denotes a set P' for all the nodes in the route from root node P_{00} to node P_{ij} .It is worth noting that root node P_{00} always belongs to set P', and $NUP(T, P_{00}) = \{P_{00}\}$.

3: Assume that the stochastic variable X_{ij} represents the mark state of node P_{ij}, and

$X_{ij} \in \{0,1\}$. We have: $P_r\{X_{ij} = x_{ij}\} = \begin{cases} p_{ij}, x_{ij} = 1; \\ 1 - p_{ij}, x_{ij} = 0; \end{cases}$ $\cdot p_{ij}$ represents the probability

of node P_{ij}'s departure from the application layer multicast tree, and $0 < p_{ij} < 1$.

4: The mark probabilities of nodes are independent to each other.

With reference to definition 2, we can give the definition of a bottleneck node.

Definition 3: For an irrelevance-marked application layer multicast tree (height $=m$), if a nonleaf node P_{ij} departs from the multicast tree but no other node in the route from node P_{ij} to root node P_{00} departs from the multicast tree, then this node P_{ij} is called a bottleneck node of the multicast tree.

The following theorem gives the stability factor of an ALM tree.

Theorem 1: For a relevance-marked application layer multicast tree T (height $= m(m \geq 2)$) as given by definition 2, $SubT(T, P_{ij})$ defines a subtree in tree T, whose root node is node P_{ij}. When $P_{ij} = P_{00}$, $SubT(T, P_{00}) = T$. If we use $\Delta(T)$ to represent the number of nodes departed from the tree T due to the existence of the bottleneck node, then the expected values of $\Delta(T)$, $E(\Delta(T))$ and stability factors $S(T)$ are:

$$E(\Delta(T)) = \sum_{i=1}^{m} \sum_{all\ j} \Psi_d(T, P_{ij}) \cdot N(SubT(T, P_{ij})) \tag{1}$$

$$S(T) = 1 - E(\Delta(T))/N(T) . \tag{2}$$

P_{ij} is any node but P_{00} in multicast tree T, $1 \leq i \leq m$.

4   Stability Analysis of ALM Tree

After giving the definition of stability of application layer multicast tree, we now analysis the typical topology model of ALM tree and its stability model.

4.1   Multicast Tree Topology Model

Before analyzing the stability of an ALM tree, we first introduce a tree topology model. Without loss of generality, we consider a multicast tree as composed of three parts of links, as shown in Fig.2.

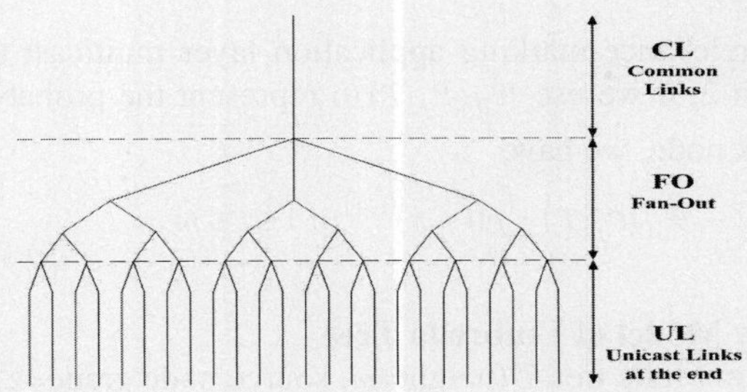

Fig. 2. A model for application layer multicast tree

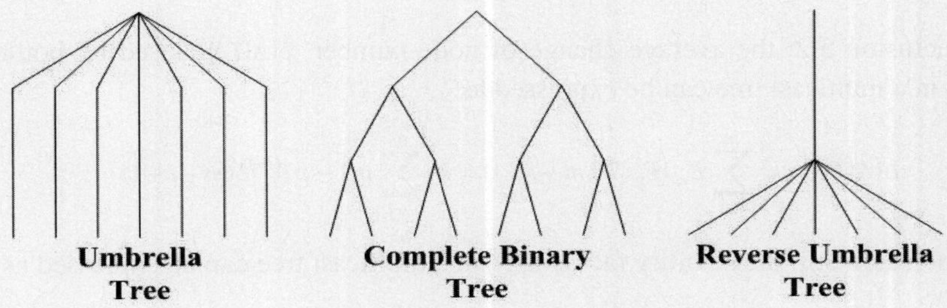

Fig. 3. Three basic tree types

(1) Common links: height is CL. That is for all receiving hosts.

(2) Fan shape links: height is FO. The degree of the uppermost nodes in this fan shape link is k, while the degree of other nodes is 2.

(3) Line shape links: height is UL. In these links, the degree of every node is 1, and there is no common links between nodes.

Given different combination of three types of links, we will have different types of multicast trees. We will focus on three representative basic types, as shown in Fig. 3.

(1) Umbrella tree: The leftmost tree type in Fig.3, which begins with a short sector link (FO = 1), followed by a long line style link (very large UL value). The unique feature of the umbellate form multicast tree is that few links are shared among receiving hosts. Such tree types are similar to the Mbone.

(2) Complete binary tree: The tree type in the middle of Fig.3, where every node has two child nodes (very large FO value).

(3) Reverse umbrella tree: The rightmost tree type in Fig.3, where the subgroup first transmits along a long general purpose link, then ends in a short sector link (fairly large CL, FO=1).

4.2 The Stability Models of the Basic Tree Types

We now give the stability factors of the three basic tree types. For simplicity, we consider only homogeneous trees, i.e., for $\forall i, j$, we have $0 < p_{ij} = p < 1$. Then the following theorem holds.

Theorem 2: For a relevance-marking application layer multicast tree T (height $=m$) defined in definition 2, if we use $\Psi_d(P_{ij}, T)$ to represent the probability for node P_{ij} to become a bottleneck node, we have

$$\Psi_d\left(P_{ij}, T\right) = p(1-p)^{(i-1)}, \text{if } 1 \le i \le m \ . \tag{3}$$

4.2.1 The Stability Model of Umbrella Tree
Theorem 3: For an umbrella tree T (height$=m$, source node grade$=k$), we have
  Conclusion 3.1: the number of nodes $N(T)$ in a multicast tree can be expressed as:

$$N(T) = m \cdot k + 1 \ . \tag{4}$$

Conclusion 3.2: the average change of node number $E(\Delta(T))$ caused by bottleneck nodes in a multicast tree can be expressed as:

$$E(\Delta(T)) = k \cdot \sum_{i=1}^{m} \Psi_d\left(P_{ij}, T\right)(m-i+1) = k \cdot \sum_{i=1}^{m} p(1-p)^{(i-1)}(m-i+1) \ . \tag{5}$$

Conclusion 3.3: the stability factor $S(T)$ in a multicast tree can be expressed as :

$$S(T) = 1 - E(\Delta(T))/N(T) = 1 - \frac{k}{m \cdot k + 1} \cdot \sum_{i=1}^{m} p(1-p)^{(i-1)}(m-i+1) \ . \tag{6}$$

4.2.2 The Stability Model of 2-Ary Balanced Tree
Theorem 4: For a 2-ary balanced tree defined in *definition 2* (height $= m$), we have:

$$N(T) = 2^{m+1} - 1 \ . \tag{7}$$

$$E(\Delta(T)) = \sum_{i=1}^{m} 2^i \cdot \Psi_d\left(P_{ij}, T\right)(2^{m-i+1} - 1) = \sum_{i=1}^{m} p(1-p)^{(i-1)}(2^{(m+1)} - 2^i) \ . \tag{8}$$

$$S(T) = 1 - E(\Delta(T))/N(T) = 1 - \frac{1}{2^{m+1} - 1} \cdot \sum_{i=1}^{m} p(1-p)^{(i-1)}(2^{(m+1)} - 2^i) \ . \tag{9}$$

4.2.3   The Stability Model of Reverse Umbrella Tree

Theorem 5: For a reverse umbrella tree T (height $= m$, source node grade= k) defined in definition 2, if $CL = m - 1$, $FO = 1$, the dimension number of chain circuit FO is k , then we have:

$$N(T) = m + k \ . \tag{10}$$

$$E\big(\Delta(T)\big) = k \cdot p(1-p)^{(m-1)} + \sum_{i=1}^{m-1} p(1-p)^{(i-1)}(m-i+k) \ . \tag{11}$$

$$S(T) = 1 - \frac{k}{m+k} \cdot p(1-p)^{(m-1)} - \frac{1}{m+k} \cdot \sum_{i=1}^{m} p(1-p)^{(i-1)}(m-i+k) \ . \tag{12}$$

Proof can be found in [11].

4.3   Numerical Results

We now use Matlab to observe the stability of these three basic types of multicast tree. We use the following default settings: the height of the multicast tree is 7, i.e., $CL + FO + UL \le 7$; the maximum node number of the multicast tree is 128. We focus on the results describing the variation of multicast tree factors compared to node numbers, the conclusion is shown as in Fig.4.

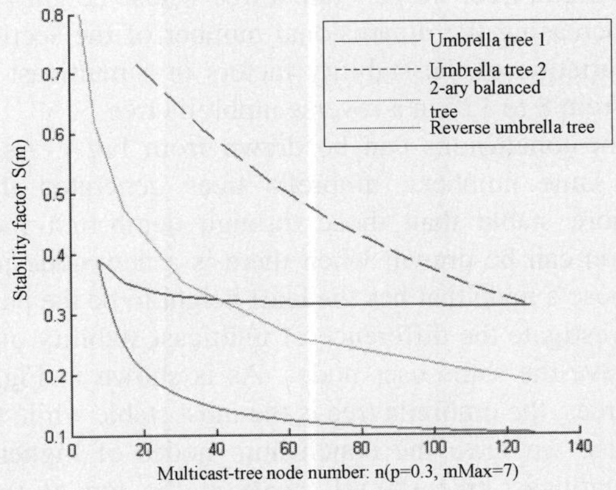

Fig. 4. The variation of stability factors

For an umbrella tree, we investigate the impact of an increase of nodes on the stability of the tree is in two aspects: (1) depth-first: first, we generate an umbrella tree whose height is 7 and dimensional number 1, node number 8; then we increase the dimensional number; the node number increases by 7 when the dimensional number is increased by 1; stop increasing the dimensional number when it reaches 18,so the node number is 7*18+1=127. (2) breadth-first: first generate an umbrella tree whose height is 1 and dimensional number 18; gradually increase the height of the tree, the node number increasing by 18 each time; stop increasing the height of the tree when it reaches 7. The node number at this time is still 7*18+1□127.

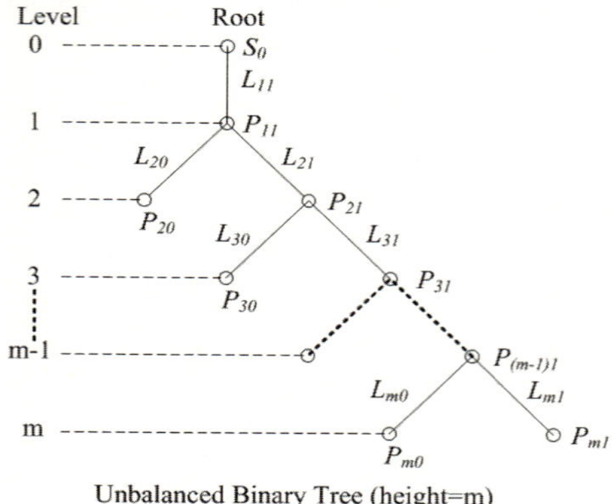

Fig. 5. Unbalanced binary tree (height=m)

For a 2-ary balanced tree, first, we observe a 2-ary balanced tree whose height is 1 and node number 3; then we increase the height of the complete binary tree, 1 by each time; when the height of the tree reaches 6, the node number of the tree is 127.

For a reverse umbrella tree, we generate a tree whose height is 7, and increase the node number by increasing the dimensional number of the sectional nodes. We can see the curve of variation of the stability factors in a multicast tree when the node number increased from 8 to 127 in a reverse umbrella tree.

Several important conclusions can be drawn from Fig.4. As is shown in Fig.4, when having the same numbers, umbrella trees generated through breadth-first method are far more stable than those through depth-first methods. Hence, one important conclusion can be drawn: when there is a new node joining the multicast tree, we should choose a node that has the least height to be the parent node.

Next we will investigate the difference of multicast stability of the three basic tree types when they have the same user nodes. As is shown in Fig.4, among the three types of multicast trees, the umbrella tree is the most stable while the reverse umbrella tree the least. Hence we have the conclusion: nodes of higher competence in an application layer multicast tree should locate at the top of the multicast tree to minimize the value of CL so that the multicast tree could be even more stable.

5   Impact of Stable Nodes

In this section we will discuss the impact of stable nodes (which have zero probability of departure) on the stability of ALM trees. We have researched on two types: unbalanced binary tree and k-ary balanced tree. Due to space limit, we only presented results of unbalanced binary tree here. Interested readers can find more results in [11].

5.1 Unbalanced Binary Tree

Theorem 6: For an unbalanced binary tree (height $= m$) defined in definition 2, as is shown in Fig.5, we have the following conclusions.

Conclusion 6.1: if $m < \infty$, and for arbitrary i and j, $0 < p_{ij} = p < 1$, then the probability for node P_{k1} to become a bottleneck node can be expressed as:

$$\Psi_d(P_{k1}, p, m) = p(1-p)^{(k-1)}, \text{if } 1 \le k \le m-1 . \tag{13}$$

The impact of intermediate node P_{k1}'s becoming a bottleneck node on the number of nodes $\Delta(P_{k1}, p, m)$ can be expressed as:

$$\Delta(P_{k1}, p, m) = 2(m-k) + 1 + (k-1)p, \text{if } 1 \le k \le m-1 . \tag{14}$$

The probability that there is no bottleneck node can be expressed as:

$$\Psi(m) = (1-p)^{(m-1)} . \tag{15}$$

When there is no bottleneck node in a multicast tree, the change in node number $\Delta(p, m)$ can be expressed as:

$$\Delta(p, m) = m \cdot p . \tag{16}$$

The average change of node number $E(p, m)$ in a multicast tree can be expressed as:

$$E(p, m) = p \cdot (2m-1) + (1-p)(E(p, m-1) + p) . \tag{17}$$

The stability factor of a multicast tree $S(p, m)$ can be expressed as:

$$S(p, m) = \frac{(2 - 3p + p^2)}{p(2m-1)} + \frac{2(m-1)}{p(2m-1)} \cdot (1-p)^{m-1} + \frac{2}{2m-1} \cdot (1-p)^m . \tag{18}$$

Conclusion 6.2: if $m < \infty$ and for arbitrary i, $p_{i1} = \begin{cases} p, 0 < p < 1, \text{if } i \ne j \\ 0, \text{if } i = j \end{cases}$,

The probability for intermediate node P_{k1} to become a bottleneck node $\Psi_d(P_{k1}, p, m, j)$ can be expressed as:

$$\Psi_d(P_{k1}, p, m, j) = \begin{cases} p(1-p)^{(k-1)}, \text{if } 1 \le k < j; \\ 0, \text{if } k = j \\ p(1-p)^{(k-2)}, \text{if } j < k \le m-1 \end{cases} . \tag{19}$$

The impact of intermediate node P_{k1}'s becoming a bottleneck node on the number of nodes can be expressed as:

$$\Delta(P_{k1}, p, m, j) = 2(m-k) + 1 + (k-1)p, \text{if } 1 \le k \le m-1; . \tag{20}$$

The probability that there is no bottleneck node $\Psi(m, j)$ can be expressed as:

$$\Psi(m, j) = (1 - p)^{(m-2)} \, .$$ (21)

When there is no bottleneck node in the multicast tree, the change of node number in the tree $\Delta(p, m, j)$ can be expressed as:

$$\Delta(p, m, j) = m \cdot p \, .$$ (22)

The stability factor $S(p, m, j)$ in the multicast tree can be expressed as:

$$S(p, m, j) = 1 - \frac{1}{2m-1} \cdot \left\{ \Psi(m, j) \cdot \Delta(p, m, j) + \sum_{k=1}^{m-1} \Psi_d \left(P_{k1}, p, m, j \right) \cdot \Delta(P_{k1}, p, m, j) \right\} \cdot$$ (23)

Proof can be found in [11].

5.2 Numerical Results

We use Matlab to investigate the impact of different factors on multicast stability. First, we consider the impact of different parameters on the bottleneck nodes, and then we study the impact of these parameters on the stability of the multicast tree.

5.2.1 Impact of User Departure

We will focus on an unbalanced binary tree. Fig.6 (a) presents the results of the variation of stability factors against the node departure probability p in 10 unbalanced binary trees whose height varies from 1 to 10. We can see in the figure that as p increases the stability of the multicast tree decreases rapidly; the decreasing rate of S is in proportion to the height m of the multicast tree. For an unbalanced binary tree whose height is 10, even if the node departure probability p is only 0.1, there will be 40% nodes departing from the multicast tree (multicast tree stability factor is 0.6).

5.2.2 Impact of the Height of a Stable Node on the Stability Factor

From conclusion 6.2, we can see the change of the stability factors in an unbalanced binary tree when stable nodes appear. In Fig.6 (b), suppose the height of an unbalanced binary tree $m=6$, the height j of stable nodes varies from 0 to 5, i.e., the departing probability of user node P_{j1} is $P_{j1=0}$. Specifically, $j=0$ means that there is no stable node in the multicast tree. Just as we expect, the existence of stable nodes will improve the stability factors in a multicast tree. Especially, with the increase of the departing probability p of unstable nodes, the promotion of stability is more apparent. It is worth noting is that when $j=1$, i.e., when the user node on the uppermost level is stable, the stability of the multicast tree increase considerably.

5.2.3 Impact of the Height of a Multicast Tree on the Stability Factor

Fig.6 (c) presents the curve of the change of stability factor S against the height m in an unbalanced binary tree. The curves in the figure represent respectively the locations of stable nodes in the multicast tree. We can see very clearly that as the height of the tree increases, the stability of the tree drop rapidly. But the existence of stable nodes promotes the stability of the multicast tree. Especially, when the height

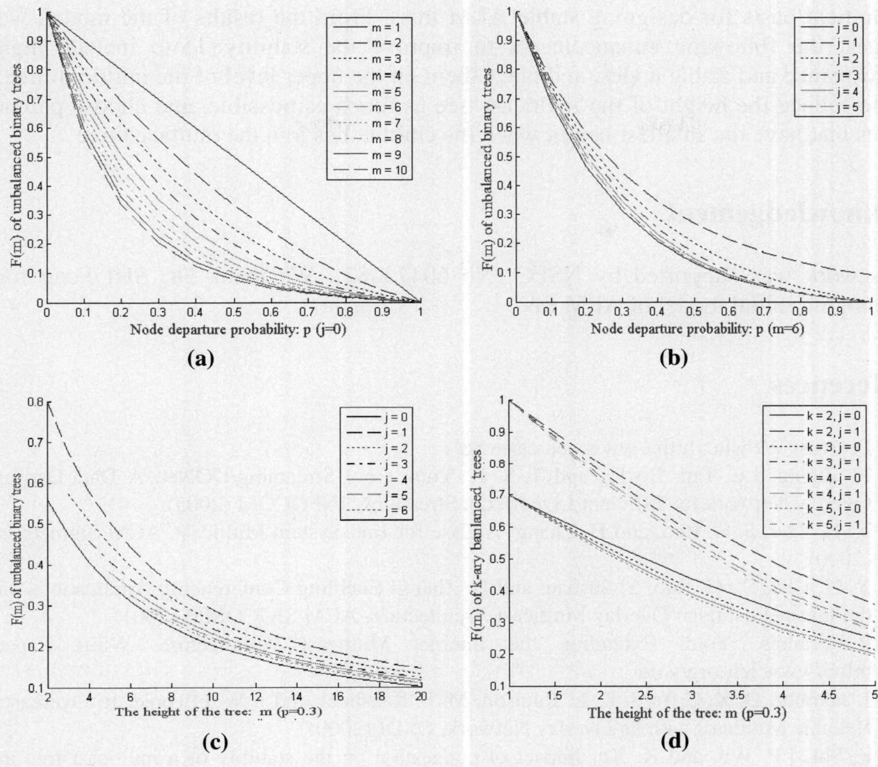

Fig. 6. Numerical Results

of the tree is not large (e.g. $m = 4$), the stable nodes can even improve the stability factor from 0.4 to 0.6.

We continue to observe the impact of the height of the tree on the stability factor. In Fig.6 (d) we make a comparison of multicast trees of different dimensions and different stable nodes to see their impact on the stability factor. We can see in the figure, for multicast trees with the same height, the larger the dimensional number k, the less stable the tree is. However, this impact is not as apparent as is shown in the figure. But when a stable node appears at the nearest node to the source ($j = 1$), the stability of the multicast tree is greatly promoted.

6   Conclusion

In this paper, we presented an initiative discuss on the impact of dynamic user behaviors to the stability of ALM trees. We proposed a novel stochastic model that captures the (in)stability characteristics of an ALM tree. Our model has considered various important factors related to the tree stability, and we have derived closed-form solutions to a class of typical multicast trees. These solutions have established a theoretical basis for designing stable ALM tress. From the results of the model, we suggest the following enhancements to improve the stability:(1) to include high performance and stable nodes, and place them on the upper level of the multicast tree; (2) to reduce the height of the multicast tree as much as possible, and choose parent nodes that have the smallest height when the child nodes join the multicast tree.

Acknowledgement

This work was supported by NSFC (No 60473082). We thank Dr. SHI Feng for developing initial model of ALM tree.

References

1. Peercast Website: http://www.peercast.org/
2. X. Zhang, J.C. Liu, Bo Li, and T.-S. P. Yum: Cool Streaming/DONet: A Data-Driven Overlay Network for Efficient Live Media Streaming. INFOCOM (2005)
3. Y.-H. Chu, S. G. Rao, and H. Zhang: A Case for End System Multicast. ACM Sigmetrics (2000)
4. Y.-H, Chu, S.. G. Rao, S. Seshan, and H. Zhang: Enabling Conferencing Applications on the Internet using an Overlay Multicast Architecture. ACM SIGCOMM (2001)
5. P. Francis. Yoid: Extending the Internet Multicast Architecture. White Paper http://www.icir.org/yoid
6. J. Jannotti, D. K. Gifford, K. L. Johnson, M. F. Kaashoek and J. W. O'Toole, Jr: Overcast: Reliable Multicast with an Overlay Network. OSDI (2000)
7. F. Shi, J.P. Wu, and K. Xu. Impact of congestion on the stability of a multicast tree in cumulative layered multicast. IEE Proceeding Communication, (2003) 150(5):371-376
8. P.V. Mieghem, M. Janic, Stability of a Multicast Tree. INFOCOM(2002)
9. X. Zhang, K.G. Shin, Statistical Analysis of Feedback-Synchronization Signaling Delay for Multicast Flow Control. INFOCOM(2001)
10. F. Shi, J. Wu, K. Xu, Stability of a Multicast Tree in Cumulative Layered Multicast Congestion Control. IPCCC(2003)
11. K XU, JC Liu, F. Shi. On the Stability of Application-Layer Multicast Tree (extended version). http://netlab.cs.tsinghua.edu.cn/~xuke/ALMStability 20051127.pdf

Extended Authentication Integrating Scheme for Beyond 3G Wireless Networks[*]

JongMin Jeong[1], GooYeon Lee[2,**], and SangJae Moon[3]

[1] School of Electrical and Computer Engineering,
Cornell University, Ithaca, NY 14853, USA
jj248@cornell.edu
[2] School of Information Technology, Kangwon National University,
192-1, Hyoja-dong, Chunchen, Kangwon 200-701, Korea
leegyeon@kangwon.ac.kr
[3] School of Electronic and Electrical Engineering, Kyungpook National University,
1370, Sankyuk-dong, Taegu 702-701, Korea
sjmoon@ee.knu.ac.kr

Abstract. This paper considers the global communication environment of B3G wireless networks when integrating security mechanism of two wireless networks, WLAN and 3G cellular networks. As a result, the existing integration paradigms are extended to a more realistic network model for B3G based on dividing the cellular network into the visited network and the home network. Also, we presents a security analysis based on a formal model of the cryptographic mechanisms.

1   Introduction

Over the last few years, the integration of various diverse wireless technologies has been a topic of intense research and standardization the most notable of which is the integration of WLAN into wide area 3G cellular networks. The complementary characteristics of 3G cellular networks and WLAN make them attractive for integration to offer the best of both technologies.

Another exciting aspect of integrating various 3G wireless networks is that it represents the beginning stage of the future convergence of networks beyond 3G (B3G). Therefore, these integrating researches should eventually fulfill requirements of B3G wireless networks. One of the most significant requirement is a global roaming environment (GRE).

Motivation. Despite various studies on the integration of 3G cellular and WLAN [1]-[7], none has considered the GRE feature that the two core networks of the cellular system should be independent. Therefore, existing integrating results do not provide the ideal architectural model from the B3G network-architectural standpoint, even though they offer procedural approaches for integration.

---

[*] This research has been supported by University IT Research Center Project.

[**] Corresponding Author. The work of GooYeon Lee has been supported by grant No. B1220-0501-0289 from the University Fundamental Research Program of the Ministry of Information Communication in Republic of Korea.

A. Levi et al. (Eds.): ISCIS 2006, LNCS 4263, pp. 413–423, 2006.

Contributions. Therefore, the main goal is to extend the existing authentication integration schemes between WLAN and 3G networks to a more realistic network architecture as considering the GRE, which explicitly divides the core network of the cellular system into the visited network (VN) and the home network (HN). Then, the protocols are analyzed from the standpoint of security.

Related Work. There have already been a number of studies on the integration of WLAN and 3G wireless networks from various perspectives, such as network architectural models [1]-[3], QoS management [4], mobility management [5], and security [6]-[7]. However, none of the existing integration schemes for WLAN and 3G cellular network authentication has considered any of the distinguishable features of B3G networks, and just focus on the integration of authentication.

Section 2 outlines the basic system model of the schemes proposed by this study, then section 3 describes two extensions. Section 4 analyzes the proposed protocols, and some final conclusions are given in section 5.

2   System Model

2.1   Basic Approaches

The following is a summary of the basic approaches for the extended integration of authentication schemes.

- **Separation of roles for cellular core networks:** The role of the core network of the cellular system is divided into two distinguishable networks: the visited network and the home network.
- **Compatibility:** The proposed extensions preserve the existing basic security mechanism for backward compatibility. Therefore, the EAP (extended authentication protocol) of WLAN and UMTS-AKA (authentication key agreement) of cellular networks are considered as the basic frameworks.
- **Cellular-centric architecture:** The authentication centers used for WLAN authentication are replaced with the authentication entities of cellular networks, meaning that the basic framework of authentication follows cellular-centric authentication schemes.

2.2   Network Integrating Model

There are three possible network layer level architectures for interworking between WLAN and 3G cellular networks. [6][8][11];

- **Loosely-coupled:** This calls for the introduction of a new element in WLAN, a WLAN gateway. The gateway connects to the Internet and does not have any direct link to a 3G network element.
- **Tightly-coupled:** Here, the WLAN system is connected to a 3G cellular network as an alternative radio access network. This is based on the idea of making use of the WLAN radio interface as a bearer for 3G cellular networks with all the network control entities in the core network integrated.

- **No-coupling:** No-coupling is based on the Mobile IP protocol and both networks are peers. This involves two independent networks that may belong to different operators.

The loosely-coupled method can be easily implemented, as the two wireless networks are considered as independent networks. There is no need for a major conversion to recognize messages from or to the corresponding networks. Conversely, in a tightly-coupled, the WLAN and cellular systems have to recognize messages from the corresponding part. However, tightly-coupled is a more suitable model for real convergence concepts. We adopt a tightly-coupled model as the network architecture.

3   Protocols

Two extension protocols are proposed for the existing integration of the authentication mechanism between WLAN and a 3G cellular network.

3.1   Protocol 1: Visited Network-Centric Authentication

The VN-centric protocol uses the visited network for user authentication and is divided into the following three stages: authentication request (Stage 1), mutual authentication between the VN and the HN (Stage 2), and mutual authentication between the user and the cellular network (Stage 3). Stage 1 and Stage 3 are processes between the WLAN interfaces, while Stage 2 is a cellular network relating process.

There is little difference between Stages 1 and 3 and existing integration studies. Thus, Stage 1 and Stage 3 are only addressed for the overall procedure, while Stage 2 is described in detail.

Stage 1: Authentication Request. The user and WLAN access network begin the authentication request by providing identities. After establishing the WLAN connection, the EAP is initiated using a WLAN technology-specific procedure.

Stage 2: Mutual Authentication between Core Networks. This stage is the essential part of the VN-centric protocol and involves two processes: mutual authentication between the VN and the HN and the secure transmission of the authentication vectors from the HN to the VN.

`M1. Mutual Authentication Request(MAReq)`

$$VN \rightarrow HN : \langle T_{MAReq}, ID_{VN}, ID_{HN}, RAND_{VN}, AUTN_{VN}, MAC_{VN}, N1 \rangle$$

The VN starts the mutual authentication with MAReq. $T_{MAReq} \in \mathbb{N}$ indicates the message type. $ID_x \leftarrow \{0,1\}^m$ for $x \in \{VN, HN, MU\}$ is the unique ID of principle x where m is size of identification. $RAND_{VN} \leftarrow \{0,1\}^r$ is the random number generated by the VN, where r is a size of $RAND_{VN}$.

$AUTN_{VN} = \{SQN_{VN}, AMF_{VN}, MAC^A_{VN}\}$ is its authenticator which is generated with the shared security key, where SQN is the the sequence number, AMF is the authentication management field. MAC_{VN} is the integrity code for the whole message. $N1$ is nonce to prevent a replay attack.

M2. Mutual Authentication Response (MARes)

$HN \rightarrow VN : \langle T_{MARes}, ID_{VN}, ID_{HN}, RES_{HN}, MAC_{HN}, N2 \rangle$

Upon receiving the MAReq message, the HN verifies the identity of the VN. The HN checks whether the $AUTN_{VN}$ has been generated with the correct shared secret key. If and only if it is true, the HN calculates the authentication response, $RES_{HN} \leftarrow (RAND_{VN} \parallel K)$, based on the shared secret key, then sends it to the VN. MAC_{HN} is the message authentication code. $N2$ is nonce which is generated by $N1$.

M3. Authentication Data Request (ADReq)

$VN \rightarrow HN : \langle T_{ADReq}, ID_{VN}, ID_{HN}, ID_{MU}, N3 \rangle$

After receiving the MARes, the VN examines the RES_{HN} using the same algorithm used to generate the RES_{HN} in the HN. If the RES_{HN} is correct, the mutual authentication between the VN and the HN is normally finished. The VN then requests authentication vectors AVs to authenticate the WLAN user.

M4. AuthDataResponse (ADRes)

$HN \rightarrow VN : \langle T_{ADRes}, ID_{VN}, ID_{HN}, ID_{MS}, \{AVs\}_{SK}, MAC_{HN}, N4 \rangle$

The HN transfers the user authentication vectors $AVs=\{RAND, XRES, CK, IK, AUTN\}$ which are encrypted using the new session secret key SK between the VN and the HN. This session key is generated using an existing UMTS confidential key generation algorithm. The AVs are the authentication vectors for the mutual authentication between the VN and the user.

Stage 3: MA between End User and Network. After receiving the AVs in Stage 2, the VN begins the mutual authentication with the end user via an EAP request/AKA challenge. Upon receiving the challenge request, the WLAN user calculates the RES_{MU} with their secret key and sends an EAP response/AKA challenge. This phase is almost identical to that described in EAP-AKA scheme [10].

3.2   Protocol 2: Home Network-Centric Through Tunneling

The HN-centric protocol uses the HN for user authentication, and is also divided into two stages: authentication request (Stage 1) and mutual authentication through tunneling (Stage 2). Only the tunneling stage is detailed below, as Stage 1 is similar to that in the VH-centric protocol and other existing integration schemes.

Stage 1: Authentication Request. The WLAN connection is first established according to WLAN specifications, then an authentication request message is received by the 3G cellular network. Thus, the main difference from the authentication request stage of the VH-centric protocol is that the authentication request message is received by the HN, rather than the VN.

Stage 2: Mutual Authentication between End User and Home Network through Tunneling. This procedure guarantees confidentiality from the VN through tunneling. Thus, although the VN relays messages, it is unable to read the encrypted authenticating data.

M1. Authentication Request through Tunneling (AReqTunneling)

$$HN \rightarrow MU/WLAN : \langle T_{AReqTunneling}, ID_{MU}, ID_{HN}, MAC_{HN}, \{RAND_{HN}, ATUN_{HN}\}_K \rangle$$

Upon receiving the authentication request, the HN generates a $RAND_{HN} \leftarrow \{0,1\}^r$ and calculates the $AUTN_{HN}$ using the shared secrete key, K. The HN then sends AReqTunneling including the $RAND_{HN}$ to the user via the VN.

M2. Authentication Response through Tunneling (AResTunneling)

$$MU/WLAN \rightarrow HN : \langle T_{AResTunneling}, ID_{MU}, ID_{HN}, MAC_{MU}, \{RES_{MU}\}_K \rangle$$

After receiving AReqTunneling, the WLAN user checks the $AUTN_{HN}$ as to whether it has been generated using the shared key, K. If it is correct, the user then calculates the RES_{MU} using the shared secret key K, and sends it to the HN via the VN. The HN finally checks whether or not the RES_{MS} is equal to its results, $XRES_{HN} \leftarrow (RAND_{HN} \| K)$

4   Security Analysis

There are several formal cryptographic models for MAC function security. Bellare et al. stated that the chaining block cipher (CBC)-MAC, an international standard [13], is secure if the underlying block cipher is secure [12]. Plus, Ludy and Rackoff suggested that a good block cipher can be assumed to behave as a good pseudorandom function (PRF) [14]. Bellare et al. showed that the CBC-MAC of a pseudorandom function is itself a pseudorandom function [12]. The security of the CBC-MAC as a MAC then follows, as it is well known that any PRF is a secure message authentication code. As such, proof of a PRF is utilized as the formal proof for a MAC, which is a reduction approach. Meanwhile, Goldwasser et al. designed the formal proof model for symmetric key encryption based on applying the reduction concept to PRF [15]. Thus, to prove the security of a MAC or symmetric-key encryption, an alternative way is to show that it preserves pseudo-randomness. The current analysis was also based on these two reduction models, as the key components of the proposed schemes are a MAC and symmetric-key encryption.

First, the security model of a PRF is defined, as reported by Bellare et al [12]. The security of F as a PRF is measured by an adversary's inability to distinguish between the pseudo-randomness and truly real randomness.

Definition 1. *Suppose $F_{prf} : \{0,1\}^l \to \{0,1\}^L$ is a PRF function family, where l is the message space of F_{prf} and L is the output space of F_{prf}. Then for any PRF adversary A let*

$$Adf_{F_{prf}}(A) \overset{def}{=} |\, Pr[f \overset{R}{\leftarrow} F_{prf} : A = 1] - Pr[f \overset{R}{\leftarrow} Rand^{l \to L} : A = 1]\,|$$

Second, the security definition of the message authentication function (MAF) is defined according to [12]. A secure MAC must resist an existential adversary (forgery) under adaptive chosen message attacks. It is assumed that an adversary is allowed to mount a chosen message attack through which they can obtain the MACs for messages of their choice aided by a random oracle. After several training sessions, the adversary outputs a pair message M and its MAC, δ. If M is not a pair obtained from the oracle during the chosen message attack training course and the pair is correct, the pair is considered a valid forgery. The experiment of adversary A who tries to forge the MAC is depicted as follows:

Experiment $Forge(F_{mac}, A)$
    $K \overset{R}{\leftarrow} \{0,1\}^k$
    $(M, \delta) \leftarrow A^{Fmac(K, \cdot)}$
    If $F_{mac}(K, M) = \delta$ and M was not a query of A to its oracle,
    then return 1, else return 0

Definition 2. *Suppose $F_{mac} : \{0,1\}^k \times \{0,1\}^m \to \{0,1\}^s$ is a MAC function family, where k is the key space for F_{mac}, m is the message space for F_{mac} and s is the MAC space for F_{mac}. The success probability of adversary A is then defined as*

$$Adf_{F_{mac}}(A) \overset{def}{=} Pr[Forge(F_{mac}, A) = 1]$$
$$= |\, Pr[f \overset{R}{\leftarrow} F_{mac} : A = 1] - Pr[f \overset{R}{\leftarrow} Rand^{m \to s} : A = 1]\,|$$

Associated with F_{mac} is an insecurity function $Adv_{F_{mac}}(\cdot, \cdot)$ defined for any integers $q, t \geq 0$ via

$$Adv_{F_{mac}}(q, t) \overset{def}{=} \max_{A}\{Adv_{F_{mac}}(A)\}$$

The maximum is over all forgers A at most q times, and the running time of A is at most t.

Finally, a specific symmetric encryption scheme $SE = (K, E, D)$, key generation algorithm K, encryption algorithm E, and decryption algorithm D are included. An adversary is a program that has access to the oracle to which it can input any pair (M_0, M_1) of equal length messages. The oracle then returns a cipher text of either $C = E(K, M_0)$ or $C = E(K, M_1)$, the choice of which is made according to the random bit $b \in \{0, 1\}$. If an adversary can not obtain a significant advantage in distinguishing the cases $b = 0$ and $b = 1$ given access to the oracle, the SE is considered secure against the chosen plain text attack (cpa).

Experiment $cpa(SE, A, b)$

$\qquad b \overset{R}{\leftarrow} \{0, 1\}$

$\qquad K \overset{R}{\leftarrow} \{0, 1\}^k$

$\qquad d \leftarrow A^{E_K(\{M_0, M_1\}, b)}$

$\qquad$ if $d = b$ then return 1 else return 0

Definition 3. *Suppose $SE = (K, E, D)$ is a symmetric encryption scheme with the key generation function K, encryption algorithm E, and decryption algorithm D. The success probability of adversary (distinguisher) A is defined as*

$$Adv_{SE}^{cpa}(A) \overset{def}{=} Pr[(cpa(SE, A, b) = 1]$$
$$= |\, Pr[C \leftarrow E(M_1, K) : A = 1] - Pr[C \leftarrow E(M_0, K) : A = 1]\, |$$

Associated with SE is an insecurity function $Adv_{SE}^{cpa}(\cdot, \cdot)$ defined for any integers $q, t \geq 0$ via

$$Adv_{SE}^{cpa}(q, t) \overset{def}{=} \max_A \{Adv_{SE}^{cpa}(A)\}$$

The maximum is over all distinguishers A making it to the oracle at most q times, and the running time is at most t.

Definition 4. *Suppose $F_{mac} : \{0, 1\}^k \times \{0, 1\}^m \rightarrow \{0, 1\}^s$ is an MAF family and $SE(K, E, D)$ is a symmetric-key block encryption algorithm. The proposed scheme $Ex \in \{$ VN-centric, HN-centric $\}$ is secure if the advantage of both the forger $Forge(F_{mac}, A)$ and the distinguisher $cpa(SE, A, b)$ are negligible and the advantage of the underlying PRF is also negligible within the security parameter k.*

Using the above four definitions, the security proof for the proposed schemes is as follows:

Lemma 1. *Let $F_{mac}^{Ex} : \{0, 1\}^k \times \{0, 1\}^m \rightarrow \{0, 1\}^s$ be a MAC function family, and $q, t,$ and $t' > 1$ be integers. The advantage of an adversary who simulates Experiment $Forge(F_{mac}^{Ex}, A)$ to try to forge the MAC function used in the proposed scheme, Ex, is*

$$Adv_{mac}^{Ex\text{-}forge}(q, t) \leq Adv_{prf}^{Ex}(q, t') + \tfrac{1}{2^s}$$

where $t' = t + O(s + m)$.

Proof. Let A by any forger attacking the message authentication code F_{mac}^{Ex}. Assume the oracle in Experiment $Forge(F_{mac}^{Ex}, A)$ is invoked at most q times and the running time of A is at most t.

Let B_A be given an oracle for function $f : \{0,1\}^l \rightarrow \{0,1\}^L$. This will run A as a subroutine, providing an environment in which A's oracle queries are answered by B_A. When A finally outputs a forgery, B_A checks whether it is correct, and if so bets that f must have been an instance of the family MAC rather than a $Rand^{m \rightarrow s}$.

In the case f is an instance of a MAC, then B_A is the same as in experiment $Forge(F_{mac}^{Ex}, A)$. Therefore, when A makes a successful forgery, B_A returns 1.

And if f is a real random function, the success probability is 2^{-s}.

$$Pr[f \overset{R}{\leftarrow} Rand^{l \rightarrow L} : B_A = 1] \le \tfrac{1}{2^s}$$

A distinguisher B_A can also be designed for a MAC versus $Rand^{m \rightarrow s}$ according to definition 2, such that

$$Adv_{prf}^{Ex}(B_A) \ge Adv_{mac}^{Ex\text{-}forge}(A) - \tfrac{1}{2^s}$$

B_A will run in time t' and make at most q queries to its oracle. This implies equation (1), because

$$\begin{aligned}
Adv_{mac}^{Ex\text{-}forge}(q,t) &= \max_A\{Adv_{mac}^{Ex\text{-}forge}(A)\} \\
&\le \max_A\{Adv_{prf}^{Ex}(B_A) + \frac{1}{2^s}\} \\
&= \max_A\{Adv_{prf}^{Ex}(B_A)\} + \frac{1}{2^s} \\
&\le \max_B\{Adv_{prf}^{Ex}(B_A)\} + \frac{1}{2^s} \\
&= Adv_{prf}^{Ex}(q,t') + \tfrac{1}{2^s}
\end{aligned}$$

$\blacksquare$

3GPP defines f_8 as a confidential algorithm, which is the basis for the proposed tunneling method. Therefore, the f_8 algorithm is adopted for the formal proof of confidentiality. The encryption mode f_8 is based on the block cipher KASUMI and this is a pseudorandom permutation ensemble [16]. Plus, the operation mode of KASUMI is a variant of the output feedback (OFB) mode. Yet, the difference is that an initial nonce is not sent to the receiver. Thus, f_8 works as follows:

Algorithm f_8

$\quad\quad IV \leftarrow g'(ctr)$

$\quad\quad Reg_1 = IV$

$\quad\quad$ **For** $i = 1$ **to** n

$\quad\quad\quad\quad o_i = g(Reg_i)$

$\quad\quad\quad\quad y_i = o_i \oplus x_i$

$\quad\quad\quad\quad Reg_{i+1} = IV \oplus i \oplus o_i$

$\quad\quad$ **End for**

$\quad\quad$ **Return** $(y_i, \ldots, y_n)$

Lemma 2. *Let $F_{prf} : \{0,1\}^l \to \{0,1\}^L$ be a family of functions and $F_{SE}^{Ex} : \{0,1\}^k \times \{0,1\}^m \to \{0,1\}^e$ be a symmetric encryption algorithm. The advantage of distinguisher A who simulates the experiment $cpa(F_{SE}^{Ex}, A, b)$ is as follows:*

$$Adv_{cpa}^{Ex}(q, t) \leq Adv_{prf}^{Ex}(q, t') + \frac{q(q-1)}{2^{l+1}}$$

where $t' = t + O(l + m + e)$.

Proof. In the case of f_8 function, the probability of success of distinguisher is according to the collision event, i.e. $Reg_i = Reg_j$ for $i \neq j$ in Algorithm f_8. If $Reg_i = Reg_j$ for $i \neq j$, then also $o_i = o_j$. Therefore, $y_i \oplus y_j = x_i^b \oplus x_j^b (b = 1, 2)$. This means that b is revealed if $x_i^1 \oplus x_j^1 = x_i^2 \oplus x_j^2$ [16].

Let D_A be given an oracle for function $g : \{0,1\}^l \to \{0,1\}^L$. This then runs A as a subroutine and replies to A's oracle queries.

Distinguisher D_A picks the challenge bit b representing the choice for A, then waits to see if A will succeed in guessing the value of this bit. If it does, it bets that f is an instance of F, otherwise it bets that f is an instance of $Rand^{l \to L}$.

Then, D_A returns 1 when A makes a successful forgery.

$$Pr[g \xleftarrow{R} F : D_A = 1] = Adv_{cpa}^{Ex}(A)$$

However, in other cases, because g is a real random function, D_A has no information to guess correctly. The success probability is as follows:

$$Pr[g \xleftarrow{R} Rand^{l \to L} : D_A = 1] \leq \frac{q(q-1)}{2^{l+1}}$$

The proof of this inequality is related to a birthday attack. That is, it is the probability that the q-th ball collides with one of the previous ones in 2^{l+1} number bins. More details about the formal proof can be found in Lemma 7 in [16].

A distinguisher D_A can also be designed for $Ex\_Rand^{l \to L}$ versus $Rand^{l \to L}$ according to definition 3, such that

$$Adv_{cpa}^{Ex}(D_A) \geq Adv_{cpa}^{Ex}(A) - \frac{q(q-1)}{2^{l+1}}$$

D_A will run in time t' and make at most q queries to its oracle. This implies equation (2), because

$$\begin{aligned}
Adv_{cpa}^{Ex}(q, t) &= \max_A \{Adv_{cpa}^{Ex}(A)\} \\
&\leq \max_A \{Adv_{prf}^{Ex}(D_A) + \frac{q(q-1)}{2^{l+1}}\} \\
&= \max_A \{Adv_{cpa}^{Ex}(D_A)\} + \frac{q(q-1)}{2^{l+1}} \\
&\leq \max_B \{Adv_{prf}^{Ex}(D_A)\} + \frac{q(q-1)}{2^{l+1}} \\
&= Adv_{prf}^{Ex}(q, t') + \frac{q(q-1)}{2^{l+1}}
\end{aligned}$$

∎

Theorem 1. Let $F_{prf} : \{0,1\}^l \to \{0,1\}^L$ be the PRF function family that is underlying the MAC and symmetric encryption algorithm. Also, let $F_{mac}^{Ex} : \{0,1\}^k \times \{0,1\}^m \to \{0,1\}^s$ be the MAC function family and be $F_{SE}^{Ex} : \{0,1\}^k \times \{0,1\}^m \to \{0,1\}^e$ the symmetric encryption algorithm used for the proposed schemes. Then, according to the reduction of the PRF, the advantage of an attacker breaking the proposed schemes is negligible.

Proof. The underlying cryptographic mechanisms are identical in both the VN-centric and HN-centric schemes, therefore Lemma 1 and Lemma 2 are applicable to both schemes. The main difference is the association of the two cryptographic mechanisms. The VN-centric scheme can be broken if an adversary is successful in forging or distinguishes at least one message, while the HN-centric scheme can not be broken until an adversary succeeds in forging the MAC and then distinguishes the plain-text from the known cipher-text without the shared secret key.

In the VN-centric scheme, there are two authentication messages and one confidential message. Therefore, the advantage of an attacker is

$$Adf_{Ex}^{VN-centric} = 3Adf_{Ex}^{prf} + \frac{1}{2^{s-1}} + \frac{q(q-1)}{2^{l+1}}$$

In the HN-centric scheme, there are two messages and both consist of an authentication and confidential process. Therefore, the advantage of an attacker is

$$Adf_{Ex}^{HN-centric} \simeq 2\{Adf_{Ex}^{prf}\}^2 + \frac{q(q-1)}{2^{s+l+1}}$$

$\blacksquare$

5   Conclusion

This paper focused on extending the integration of authentication procedures for 3G cellular networks and WLAN. The main motivation is that integration research should also consider the requirement of B3G wireless networks. However, existing integration schemes between 3G cellular networks and WLAN have only dealt with the interaction of these two networks. The significant nature of a B3G wireless network is its global communication features,which require enhancement of the role of the visited network. Consequently, an extension of authentication integration between two wireless networks was proposed based on dividing the core networks of the cellular networks into two independent networks. Furthermore, the security of the proposed schemes was confirmed based on proof models of the cryptographic mechanism.

References

1. Salkintzis, A.K.: Interworking Technique and Architectures for WLAN/3G Integration toward 4G Mobile Data Networks. IEEE Wireless Comm., Vol.11, Issue 3 (2004) 50-61
2. 3rd Generation Partnership Project: 3GPP System to Wireless Local Area Network Inter-working; System Description (Release 6). 3GPP TS 23.234 V1.6.0, Feb 2004

3. Karlich, S., Zahariadis, T., Jennings, B., Korrias, V., and Magedanz, T.: A Self-Adaptive Service Provisioning Framework for 3G+/4G Mobile Applications. IEEE Wireless Comm., Vol.11, Issue 5 (2004) 48-56

4. Zhuang, W., Gan, Y.-S., and Chua, K-C.: Policy-Based QoS Management Architecture in an Integrated UMTS and WLAN Environment. IEEE Communication Magazine, Vol. 41, Issue 11 (2003) 118-125

5. Varma, V.K., Ramesh, S., Wong, K. D., and Friedhoffer, J.A.: Mobility Management in Integrated UMTS/WLAN Networks. IEEE International conference on Vol.2 (2003) 1048-1053

6. Koien, G. M. and Haslestad, T.: Security Aspects of 3G-WLAN Interworking. IEEE Communication Magazine, Vol. 41., Issue 11 (2003) 82-88

7. 3rd Generation Partnership Project: Wireless Local Area Network Inter-working Security (Release 6). 3GPP TS 33.234 V0.40 (2003)

8. Buddhikot, M., Chandranmenon, G., Han, S., Lee, Y. W., Miller, S., and Salgarelli, L.: Integration of 802.11 and Third Generation Wireless Data Network. INFOCOM 2003 (2003)

9. Aboba, B. and Beadles, M.: The Network Access Identifier. RFC2486 (1999)

10. Arkko, J. and Haverinen, H.: EAP AKA Authentication. IETF Internet Draft, draft-arkko-pppext-eap-aka-10.txt (2003)

11. Fitzek, F., Munari, N., Pastesini, V., Rossi, S., and Badia, L.: Security and Authentication Concepts for UMTS/WLAN Convergence. VTC 2003-Fall (2003) 2343-2347

12. Bellare, M., Kilian, J., and Rogaway, P.: The Security of the Cipher Block Chaining Messages Authentication code. Crypto 94, LNCS 839, Springer-Verlag (1994)

13. ISO/IEC 9797, Data cryptographic techniques - Data integrity mechanism using a cryptographic check function employing a block cipher algorithm (1989)

14. Luby, M. and Rackoff, C. : How to construct Pseudorandom Permutations from Pseudorandom function, SIAM J. Computation, Vol. 17 (1988)

15. GoldWasser, S. and Bellare, M.: Lecture Notes on Cryptography. MIT Lab of Computer Science (2001)

16. Kang, J. S., Shin, S.U., Hong, D. and Yi, O.: Provable Security of KASUMI and 3GPP Encryption Mode f8. ASIACRYT 2001, LNCS 2248, Springer-Verlag (2001) 255-271

A New Function for Optimization of Working Paths in Survivable MPLS Networks

Krzysztof Walkowiak

Chair of Systems and Computer Networks, Faculty of Electronics, Wroclaw University of
Technology, Wybrzeze Wyspianskiego 27, 50-370 Wroclaw, Poland
Krzysztof.Walkowiak@pwr.wroc.pl

Abstract. We consider the problem of working paths optimization in survivable
MPLS network. Both restoration methods: global and local repair are addressed. We focus on an existing facility network, in which only network flows
can be optimized to provide network survivability. The lost flow due to a single
failure of a network link is applied as the performance metric. Since joint optimization of working and recovery paths is very complex, we suggest to partition the problem into two simpler subproblems and first optimize working
routes. We introduce a new objective function for optimization of working
routes and propose a heuristic algorithm to solve the considered problem. Next,
simulation performance of various methods for working paths assignment is
examined.

1 Introduction

Recent development of IP-based broadband networks makes the availability of communication service to failures to become a crucial issue. The network survivability
implies the capability to detect failures and recover from these failures. Connection-
oriented network technologies like MultiProtocol Label Switching (MPLS) use quite
simple and effective method to enable network survivability. The main idea of this
approach is as follows. Each connection, i.e. label switched path (LSP), has a working
path (route) and a recovery (backup) path (route). The working route is used for
transmitting of data in normal, failure-free state of the network. After a failure of the
working path, the failed connection is switched to the backup route. There are two
main configurations of working and recovery paths in MPLS networks [12]: local
repair (LR) and global repair (GR). In the former method the backup path is established around the failed element (link or node) and the node immediately upstream of
the fault is the one to start recovery. In the latter method the reaction to a failure takes
place from an end-to-end viewpoint for each connection. For more details on survivable MPLS networks refer to [6], [12].

In this work we focus on an existing facility network, i.e. we do not consider facility capacity planning and topological design. We propose a new function for optimization of working routes. Next, we present results of extensive simulations for various
network topologies and demand patters of this new method and other approaches
developed previously. Comparing to our earlier work on this subject [13-14], in which
we focused on local recovery, in this work we also address global recovery method.

A. Levi et al. (Eds.): ISCIS 2006, LNCS 4263, pp. 424–433, 2006.

2   Related Work and Discussion

Most of previous works on optimization of survivable networks focus on the problem of spare capacity planning to enable full restoration after a network failure. The objective is to minimize the cost of extra capacity [6], [10]. In our approach we assume that the network is in an operational phase and augmenting of its resources (links, capacity) is not possible in a short time perspective. The goal of optimization is to minimize consequences of network failure. Since the resources of spare capacity are limited, it can happen that some connections cannot be restored after the failure. The objective function is lost flow [9], [13-14], i.e. we want to restore as much as possible of traffic carried on failed elements. Mutual assignment of working and recovery paths is a very complex problem. Therefore, we first optimize working routes in order to prepare the network for future failures and restoration. Backup paths are calculated for already established working routes. Such an approach simplifies the optimization process. However, the key question is: what should be the objective function for working paths optimization? The overall goal is to minimize the lost flow after a network failure and restoration process. However, calculation of lost flow requires much complexity. Most of optimization techniques need many repetitive calculations of the objective function in order to evaluate the temporary solutions and find the final solution. Therefore, the preferred objective function should be relatively simple for calculation and should show how the network is prepared for the failure.

The first work using this approach was [9], in which only the local recovery method was addressed and the k-shortest path (KSP) function was used as the objective. In [13-14] we proposed a new function called LFL (Lost Flow in Link) function, which offers comparable performance to KSP, however has much lower complexity, what yields lower calculation time. Both functions – KSP and LFL – show the local situation in the network in terms of network survivability. Since the local repair acts locally around the failed link, it is possible to develop analytically a function for each network link or node that indicates how much traffic can be restored. For global repair the situation is not so simple. In this method the restoration is spread more widely over the network as a whole. Thus, it is very difficult to identify and develop analytically objective function that tries to estimate the capability of the network to run global repair after a network failure. Therefore, we have decided to develop a new function that seems to be effective for optimization of working paths in a network using path restoration. Some inspiration was taken from papers on online routing of MPLS networks. In online problems, in which new incoming calls arrive one-by-one and are not known a priori, the most common approach is the shortest path first (SPF) algorithm. The main issue is the selection of link metric applied for the path calculation. One of the first works on dynamic MPLS routing was [7]. However, the proposed algorithm MIRA has much higher time complexity than other algorithms. According to results presented in [1] and our own experience [14] good results in dynamic routing of MPLS can be obtained for much simpler link metrics that makes use of local information on link flow and capacity. According to these results, we have decided to use as objective function for offline optimization of working paths the function based on the reciprocal of residual capacity. This metric is used in Constraint Shortest Path First (CSPF) algorithm [4]. Also LIOA (Least Interference Optimization Algorithm)

[1] applies similar metric. Furthermore, we propose to add to the objective function the LFL scaling factor as proposed in [14].

The definition of LFL and results presented in [13-14] confirm that application of LFL scaling factor in optimization should improve the network survivability for link repair. The main idea of LFL function is to compute residual flow of each node that represents the potential capability to perform local repair. LFL is a relatively tight lower bound of the lost flow because the restoration is performed locally. Now we consider briefly the LFL function in the context of global repair method. In GR origin nodes of connections perform the rerouting of failed LSPs. The source of physical failure is not on average adjacent to the end nodes of failed paths. However, every node still has to provide some residual capacity required under this scenario. A major difference from LR is that many end-node pairs are affected and each node-pair is concerned only with restoration of a portion of flow that the failed link carries [6]. Consequently, LFL scaling factor could also improve the performance of optimization algorithms for global repair method, but probably, according to theoretical considerations, the performance improvement will not be as substantial as for local repair. In Section 5 we use the simulations to verify our hypothesis.

Another function that seems to be attractive for our goal is the network congestion [2]. The objective of congestion problem is to maximize the minimum residual capacity of network links. This lead to quite proportional allocation of residual capacity resources in the network what should improve network survivability, especially for global repair. In [15] we present a heuristic algorithm CA (Congestion Avoidance) for non-bifurcated version of congestion problem.

Network delay function applied in [3] and many other works on network optimization [3], [8], [11] should also provide proportional allocation of flows. The delay function includes the capacity constraint as a penalty function. Therefore, optimizing routes according to this function leaves more open capacity on each link that can be used for restoration after a failure.

3 Problem Formulation

To mathematically represent the problem we introduce the following notations.

Sets:

V set of n vertices representing the network nodes.

A set of m arcs representing network directed links.

P set of q connections in the network.

Π_p the index set of candidate working paths (routes) for connection p.

X_r set (selection) of variables x_p^k, which are equal to one. X_r determines the unique set of currently selected working paths

Indices:

p connections (demands) in the network, used as subscript

k candidate routes, used as superscript

a arcs (directed links), used as subscript

r selections, used as subscript

Constants:

δ_{pa}^k equal to 1, if arc a belongs to path k realizing connection p; 0 otherwise

Q_p volume (estimated bandwidth requirement) of connection p

c_a capacity of arc a

Variables:

x_p^k decision variable, which is 1 if working route $k \in \Pi_p$ is selected for connection p and 0 otherwise

f_a flow of arc a

According to considerations presented in previous section we formulate a new objective function called RCL (Residual Capacity with LFL) for assignment of working routes in survivable MPLS networks in the following way

$$RCL(X_r) = \sum_{a \in A} \frac{(1 + \alpha \cdot l_{ar}^{LFL})}{(c_a - f_{ar})} \tag{1}$$

l_{ar}^{LFL} is an arc weight (metric) calculated according to LFL function for flows given by paths defined in X_r. α is a calibration parameter used to tune the objective function. Formulation of l_{ar}^{LFL} and exhaustive discussion on LFL function can be found in [13-14]. Applying function RCL we formulate the optimization problem WP_RCL of working paths assignment as follows

$$\min_{X_r} \quad RCL(X_r) \tag{2}$$

subject to

$$\sum_{k \in \Pi_p} x_p^k = 1 \qquad \forall p \in P \tag{3}$$

$$x_p^k \in \{0,1\} \quad \forall p \in P, \forall k \in \Pi_p \tag{4}$$

$$f_{ar} = \sum_{p \in P} \sum_{k \in \Pi_p} \delta_{pa}^k x_p^k Q_p \quad \forall a \in A \tag{5}$$

$$f_{ar} \le c_a \quad \forall a \in A \tag{6}$$

Condition (3) states that the each connection can use only one working route. Constraint (4) ensures that decision variables are binary ones. (5) is a definition of a link flow. (6) denotes the capacity constraint.

4   Algorithm FD_RCL

In order to solve the WP_RCL problem (2-6) we have developed a heuristic algorithm called FD_RCL. The main idea of FD_RCL is based on Flow Deviation (FD) algorithm for non-bifurcated flows proposed in [5] and used for many optimization problems [2-3], [10], [13-14]. Similar algorithm was applied to related problem in [14]. The only difference is using various objective function and link metric.

We use the following metric for arc a to calculate the shortest route

$$l_{ar}^{RCL} = \frac{(1 + \alpha \cdot l_{ar}^{LFL})}{(c_a - f_{ar})^2} \tag{7}$$

Let X_1 denote a feasible initial solution. In order to find X_1 we apply an algorithm based on the initial phase of the FD algorithm [5]. Let $RCL(H)$ denote a value of the RCL function (1) for a selection H. We start with $r := 1$.

Algorithm FD_RCL

<u>Step 1.</u> Find a selection $SR(X_r)$ of variables x_p^k associated with the shortest routes π_p^k under the metric l_{ar}^{RCL} (7). Set $p:=1$ and go to step 2.

<u>Step 2.</u> Let $H := X_r$.

a) Calculate a selection F from the selection H in the following way $F := \left(H - \{x_p^i\}\right) \cup \{x_p^k\}$ where $x_p^i \in H$, $x_p^k \in SR(X_r)$. Routes for other connections except connection p remain unchanged.

b) If F is a feasible selection and $RCL(F) < RCL(H)$ then set $H:=F$.

c) If $p=q$ the go to step 3. Otherwise set $p:=p+1$ and go to step 2a.

<u>Step 3.</u> If $H=X_r$ stop the algorithm, since the solution cannot be improved. Otherwise set $r:=r+1$, $X_r:=H$ and go to step 1.

For detailed analysis of algorithm FD for non-bifurcated flows refer to [13].

5   Results

The major goal of numerical experiments is comprehensive evaluation of the new objective function proposed in previous section against other methods used for working paths assignment. As the performance metric we apply the lost flow (LF) after a single failure of any network link. To find the lost flow the following procedure is applied. After setup of all LSPs according to selected algorithm, each network link is cut sequentially, one at a time, and next the process of recovery is performed, in which we try to find new paths for broken LSPs according to selected restoration strategy. In global repair recovery paths are found between end nodes of failed LSP. In local repair, the backup path is calculated between end nodes of failed link. A simple greedy algorithm is applied for this task. If the network is congested, some LSPs are not recovered due to limited resources of residual capacity. The lost flow function is a sum of bandwidth of such LSPs that are not restored. Consequently, LF shows the network performance after a failure of a single link failure. Obviously, also other failure scenarios (node failures, multiple failures) could be considered, however we focus on the most common case.

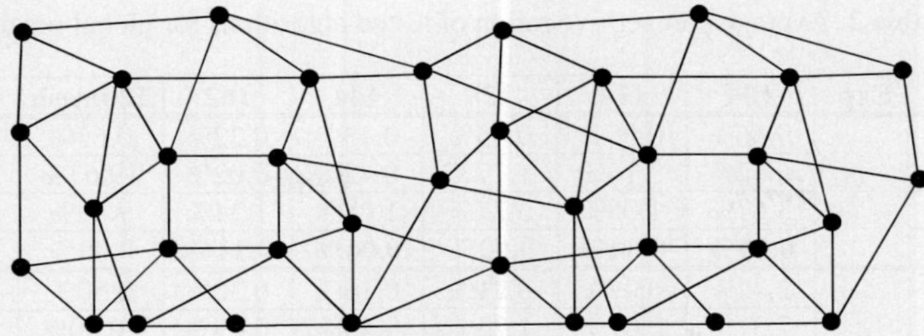

Fig. 1. Topology of network 162

We test the following algorithms: FD_RCL presented above and using the RCL function, FD_DEL [5] applying the delay function, FD_LFL using LFL function [13], CA optimizing the network congestion [15] and CARel minimizing the relative congestion. CARel is based on CA. Relative congestion is defined as the maximum ratio over all arcs of flow f_a divided by the capacity c_a. All methods were coded in C.

Algorithms are studied in detail on a family of networks having irregular mesh topology consisting of a master network and a series of progressively sparser networks derived from the master network. Moreover, two regular topology networks are analyzed. Table 1 summarizes the parameters of all sample networks. The first column specifies the name of the parameter, next columns includes values of these parameters for each network. Let bandwidth unit (BU) denote an arbitrary unit of bandwidth, for instance 1 Mb/s. In Fig. 1 we show the master network, which is referred to as 162.

Table 1. Parameters of tested networks

Name of network	104	114	128	144	162	108ring	120mesh
Number of nodes	36	36	36	36	36	36	36
Number of links	104	114	128	144	162	108	120
Node degree (average)	2.89	3.17	3.56	4.00	4.50	3.00	3.33
Node degree (minimum)	2	2	3	3	3	3	2
Node degree (maximum)	5	5	6	6	6	3	4
Topology	irregular mesh					ring	regular mesh

We run three sets of experiments. In experiments A and B, all arcs have the capacity 4800 BU to model the capacity ratio of OC-48. In experiment C, arcs have the capacity kx1200 BU, where k=1,2,…,8 . In experiment A, it is assumed that there is a requirement to set up a connection for each direction of every node pair. Thus, the total number of demands (commodities) is 1260. All connections have the same bandwidth requirement in a given demand pattern. In experiments B and C, 2500 random demands are generated, i.e. origin node, destination node and bandwidth requirement are chosen for each demand at random. For each experiment we test 10 demand patterns for each network, what gives in total 210 various demand patterns.

To compare results we apply *competitive ration* performance indicator. The competitive ration, which indicates how well the particular algorithm performs comparing to performance of other algorithms. The competitive ration is defined as the difference

Table 2. Average competitive ration of tested algorithms for global repair

Algorithm	Exp.	104	114	128	144	162	120mesh	108ring
FD_DEL	A	0.66%	0.05%	0.45%	0.13%	0.22%	0.65%	0.13%
FD_LFL		6.67%	3.16%	1.77%	0.42%	0.02%	19.67%	0.13%
CA		3.67%	1.06%	3.27%	1.68%	1.34%	9.48%	**0.02%**
FD_RCL		**0.00%**	**0.00%**	**0.00%**	**0.06%**	**0.11%**	**0.00%**	0.12%
FD_DEL	B	2.42%	0.07%	0.21%	0.16%	0.30%	0.50%	10.03%
FD_LFL		7.31%	2.01%	1.23%	0.45%	0.49%	20.50%	10.03%
CA		9.05%	1.42%	3.52%	1.50%	1.01%	26.67%	**3.90%**
FD_RCL		**0.27%**	**0.02%**	**0.01%**	**0.03%**	**0.01%**	**0.00%**	10.00%
FD_DEL	C	1.66%	1.36%	0.88%	2.24%	1.03%	0.91%	0.93%
FD_LFL		6.23%	4.83%	7.67%	1.94%	3.06%	17.93%	6.96%
CA		8.63%	6.82%	13.40%	8.64%	5.71%	18.89%	6.65%
CARel		4.23%	2.17%	4.51%	3.55%	2.88%	13.26%	4.62%
FD_RCL		**0.23%**	**0.03%**	**0.69%**	**1.04%**	**0.35%**	**0.53%**	**0.30%**

Table 3. Average competitive ration of tested algorithms for local repair

Algorithm	Exp.	104	114	128	144	162	120mesh	108ring
FD_DEL	A	0.59%	**0.00%**	0.41%	0.17%	0.28%	0.43%	0.13%
FD_LFL		7.76%	5.20%	1.82%	0.80%	0.60%	19.49%	0.13%
CA		8.67%	7.31%	3.75%	4.69%	5.89%	11.85%	**0.02%**
FD_RCL		**0.00%**	0.04%	**0.00%**	**0.00%**	**0.13%**	**0.01%**	0.19%
FD_DEL	B	2.23%	0.04%	0.23%	0.07%	0.54%	**0.09%**	10.01%
FD_LFL		8.88%	3.28%	1.25%	0.75%	0.57%	19.23%	10.01%
CA		10.97%	6.98%	4.40%	4.90%	6.62%	27.11%	**3.89%**
FD_RCL		**0.31%**	**0.01%**	**0.00%**	**0.03%**	**0.08%**	**0.09%**	10.02%
FD_DEL	C	2.02%	3.32%	**3.12%**	4.29%	3.95%	**0.52%**	**0.54%**
FD_LFL		5.36%	6.82%	10.18%	**2.17%**	5.51%	18.24%	9.17%
CA		9.27%	6.12%	14.93%	9.68%	4.27%	19.03%	9.01%
CARel		3.98%	**2.01%**	5.23%	5.82%	**1.86%**	13.15%	3.97%
FD_RCL		**1.58%**	3.28%	3.32%	4.63%	4.55%	0.93%	1.88%

between result obtained for a particular algorithm and the minimum value of objective function yielded by the best algorithm. For instance, if for the test consisting of simulations of various algorithms the minimum value of lost flow is 2000 and the considered algorithm yields 2500; the competitive ration is calculated as follows: (2500-2000)/2500=20%.

The first step of simulations was tuning of the calibration parameter of the RCL function in algorithm FD_RCL. We run experiments for the following values of parameter $\alpha = \{0.0; 0.2; 0.4; 0.6; 0.8; 1.0; 1.2; 1.4; 1.6; 1.8; 2.0\}$. Results of FD_RCL presented below are the best among all tested values of parameter α.

In Tables 2 and 3 we report values of aggregate competitive ration of tested algorithms for global and local repair, respectively. The best results are typed bold. For experiments A and B we don't show results for CARel, because in these cases all network links have the same capacity, consequently CA and CARel yield the same

Table 4. Average ranking of tested algorithms

Algorithm	Global repair			Local repair		
	A	B	C	A	B	C
FD_DEL	4.26	3.84	3.77	4.27	4.21	3.76
FD_LFL	2.91	2.83	2.30	3.00	3.19	2.46
CA	2.97	2.43	1.64	2.59	2.19	2.21
CARel	2.97	2.43	2.86	2.59	2.19	3.33
FD_RCL	4.80	4.74	4.49	4.60	4.54	3.30

results. Comparing Table 2 against Table 3 indicates that for both restoration methods performance of particular algorithms is comparable. In both cases, the largest differences in results can be observed for regular topologies: 108ring and 120mesh.

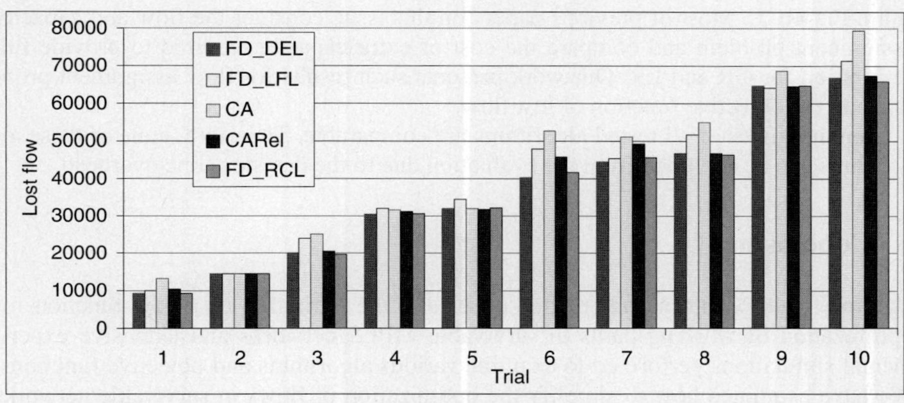

Fig. 2. Lost flow for various demand patterns for network 128, global repair and experiment C

Table 4 shows the ranking of all tested algorithms for global and local repair. We apply the following ratings. For each of 210 cases (various in terms of network topology, traffic pattern, and experiment) we give 5 points for the best algorithm, which yields the lowest value of lost flow, 4 points for the second algorithm, 3 points for the third place, etc. Next, we take the average value of these scores over 70 trials for each experiment. Fig. 3 depicts detailed results of 10 demands patterns obtained for network 128, experiment C and global repair.

Results presented in Tables 2-4 and Fig. 3, show that FD_RCL outperforms other methods. The delay function (FD_DEL) provides results close to RCL. It is evident since both functions have similar construction – the capacity constraint placed in the denominator is a kind of penalty function. However, adding the LFL factor to the numerator improves the performance in terms of network survivability expressed by the lost flow function. It should be noted that according to our results, there are some specific demand patterns and topologies for which each of FD_LFL, CA or CARel can also find a configuration of working routes with the lowest value of lost flow.

Table 5. Aggregate average lost flow for global repair and local repair

	Exp.	104	114	128	144	162	120mesh	108ring
Global repair	A	44482	44339	131324	78727	76608	67026	99132
Local repair		54331	67898	137159	120078	117274	69098	99155
Global repair	B	19518	32001	66104	57626	57659	63394	76571
Local repair		21344	41756	69939	76664	97136	74886	76602
Global repair	C	27584	27290	37024	36803	36533	44314	23415
Local repair		33970	40866	64023	73747	76443	63048	31571

Another, quite evident observation derived from detailed analysis of results is that global repair provides lower values of lost flow than local repair. This intuitive conclusion confirms theoretical considerations on both methods presented in [6]. In Table 5 we report the comparison of GR and LR in terms of lost flow obtained for algorithm FD_RCL. Most of previous papers on this issue consider the flow and capacity assignment problem and compare the cost of extra capacity required to provide full restoration for GR and LR. Our work presents such results for flow assignment problem and the objective function of lost flow.

Running times of all tested algorithms are comparable. Therefore, none of these algorithms can be excluded from the evaluation due to the decision time overhead.

6 Conclusion

The two major contributions of this paper are: the definition of a new function for optimization of working paths in survivable MPLS networks and extensive experimental simulations performed to examine various algorithms and objective functions. We have examined how to simplify the optimization of flows in survivable networks by decoupling the problem of joint working and paths assignment into two subproblems. First, we optimize working routes according to a selected objective function, which should indicate the capability of the network to restoration. Second, we find backup routes for established working paths according to selected restoration method and failure scenario. We have proposed several objective function for working paths assignment. Since analytical evaluation of these functions is difficult, we have run extensive simulations to verify effectiveness of particular approaches. Based on these experimental results, our conclusion is that the new function RCL proposed in this paper provides the best results. Comparable results to FD_RCL have been obtained for FD_DEL that facilitates the network delay function. The relative performance of tested functions and algorithms depends on the network topology and the traffic demand pattern. In other words, each of proposed heuristic can provide the best result for some specific simulation scenario. In this work we have focused on MPLS, however, it should be mentioned that approaches and conclusions reported in this paper can be also used to other connection-oriented techniques.

Acknowledgements. This work was supported by a research project of the Polish State Committee for Scientific Research carried out in years 2005-2007.

References

1. Bagula, B., Botha, M., Krzesinski, A.: Online Traffic Engineering: The Least Interference Optimization Algorithm. In proccedigs of IEEE ICC 2004, Paris, France, (2004)
2. Bienstock, D.: Potential function methods for approximately solving linear programming problems. Theory and Practice. Kluwer Academic Publishers, Boston (2002)
3. Burns, J., Ott, T., Krzesinski, A., Muller, K.: Path selection and bandwidth allocation in MPLS networks. Performance Evaluation, 52 (2003) 133-152
4. Crawley, E., Nair, R., Jajagopalan, B., Sandick, H.: A framework for QoS-based routing in the Internet. RFC2386 (1998)
5. Fratta, L., Gerla, M., Kleinrock, L.: The Flow Deviation Method: An Approach to Store-and-Forward Communication Network Design. Networks (1973) 97–133
6. Grover, W.: Mesh-based Survivable Networks: Options and Strategies for Optical, MPLS, SONET and ATM Networking. Prentice Hall PTR, Upper Saddle River, New Jersey (2004)
7. Kar, K., Kodialam, M., Lakshman, T.: Minimum interference routing of bandwidth guaranteed tunnels with MPLS traffic engineering applications. IEEE JSAC, 12 (2000), 2566-2579
8. Markowski, M., Kasprzak, A.: The web replica allocation and topology assignment problem in wide area networks: algorithms and computational results. Lecture Notes in Computer Science, LNCS 3483 (2005) 772-781
9. Murakami, K., Kim, H.: Virtual Path Routing for Survivable ATM Networks. IEEE/ACM Transactions on Networking, 2 (1996) 22-39
10. Pióro, M., Medhi, D.: Routing, Flow, and Capacity Design in Communication and Computer Networks. Morgan Kaufman Publishers (2004)
11. Ryba, P., Kasprzak, A.: The gateways location and topology assignment problem in hierarchical wide area networks: algorithms and computational results. Lecture Notes in Computer Science, Vol. 3982 (2006) 1100-1109
12. Sharma, V., Hellstrand, F. (ed.): Framework for MPLS-based Recovery. RFC 3469 (2003)
13. Walkowiak, K.: A New Method of Primary Routes Selection for Local Restoration. Lecture Notes in Computer Science, Vol. 3042 (2004) 1024-1035
14. Walkowiak, K.: Survivable Online Routing for MPLS Traffic Engineering. Lecture Notes in Computer Science, Vol. 3266 (2004) 288-297
15. Walkowiak, K.: An Heuristic Algorithm for Non-bifurcated Congestion Problem. In proceedings of 17th IMACS World Congress, Paris, France, (2005)

HIMUTSIS: Hierarchical Multi-tier Adaptive Ad-Hoc Network Security Protocol Based on Signcryption Type Key Exchange Schemes

Attila Altay Yavuz[1], Fatih Alagoz[1], and Emin Anarim[2]

[1] Bogazici University, Department of Computer Engineering,
Bebek, Istanbul 34342, Turkey
[2] Bogazici University, Department of Electrical and Electronic Engineering,
Bebek, Istanbul 80815, Turkey
{attila.yavuz, fatih.alagoz}@boun.edu.tr,
anarim@boun.edu.tr

Abstract. Mobile Ad-hoc networks (MANETs), providing infrastructure-free wireless instant communication, play important role in tactical military networks. However, providing security in tactical military MANETs, having very large and dynamic structure without infrastructure support in hostile environments, is a very difficult task. In order to address security problems in tactical military MANETs, we propose a new HIerarchical MUlti-Tier adaptive ad-hoc network security protocol based on SIgncryption type key exchange Schemes: HIMUTSIS. Our protocol makes contribution to the military MANETs in three major points: Architectural design, cryptographic methods used in military MANETs and key management techniques. Novel architectural design of HIMUTSIS facilitates certification and key management procedures, provides flexibility and reduces cryptographic workload of the military MANETs. In HIMUTSIS, as a novelty, we offer to use DKEUTS (Direct Key Exchange Using TimeStamp) protocol providing security and performance advantages when compared to some traditional cryptographic methods. Also, multi-security level approach provides adaptive solutions for each layer of the HIMUTSIS. As a key management technique, HIMUTSIS uses hybrid key management approach which reduces rekeying workload of the networks significantly while minimizing single point of failure risk of the military MANET.

1 Introduction

Mobile Ad-hoc networks (MANETs) are infrastructure-free wireless communication networks. MANETs are considered as ideal technology for instant communication networks in both military and civilian applications. Nowadays, tactical military networks are the main application area of MANETs. Tactical military networks, having critical operation environments, require very high security and performance together. Hostile environment of tactical military networks and infrastructureless-wireless characteristic of MANETs make these networks vulnerable to various attacks and compromises.

A. Levi et al. (Eds.): ISCIS 2006, LNCS 4263, pp. 434–444, 2006.

In this paper, in order to answer these challenges, we propose a new HIerarchical MUlti-Tier adaptive ad-hoc network security protocol based on SIgncryption type key exchange Schemes: HIMUTSIS. In HIMUTSIS, we make contributions to the military MANETs for three major points. These are design and security architecture, cryptographic methods used in MANETs and key management techniques.

In HIMUTSIS, we use hierarchical multi-tier architecture including novel approaches for design aspects. Two tiered UAV-MBN (Unmanned Aerial Vehicle-Mobile Backbone Networks) networks have been recently proposed for digital battlefields utilizing heterogeneous structure of military MANETs [1], [2]. In HIMUTSIS, as a novel approach, using same heterogeneity principle, we divide MBN layer into MBN1 and MNB2 layers. This approach significantly facilitates key management and certification procedures of military MANETs and reduces the threshold cryptography requirements. Particularly, when UAVs are not available in military MANETs, this architecture provides flexibilities to the traditional approaches.

Many cryptographic methods have been proposed to secure MANETs [3]. In a secure MANET, availability, confidentiality, integrity, authentication, unforgeability and non-repudiation goals must be achieved [4]. In HIMUTSIS, as a novel approach, we use signcryption type key exhange scheme DKEUTS (Direct Key Exchange Using Time Stamp) [5] as a major cryptographic method. This method achieves all aforementioned cryptographic goals together while preventing network from some of the active attacks. Also, this method provides advantages for bandwidth and computational resource usage when compared to the classical methods. Apart from these, we propose a new multi-level security approach which provides high security for each layer while preventing system overloaded due to unnecessary cryptographic workloads.

In HIMUTSIS, we use hybrid key management techniques in order to scale very large and dynamic structure of military MANETs. We adapt independency of layers principles of [6], [7] and [17] to the MANETs. This approach significantly reduces workload of the rekeying which is required to provide forward and backward security. Also, single point of failure problem is minimized using hybrid key management architecture.

2   Related Works and Background

In order to provide major cryptographic goals in Ad-hoc networks, many cryptographic methods utilizing public key and hybrid cryptography have been proposed. In Ad-hoc network, due to the lack of infrastructure, a static Trusted Third Party (TTP) may not be avaliable. Thus, key exchange and key establishment schemes based on Diffie-Hellman (DH) variants are frequently used for collaborative key exchange. Especially, for hierarchical key agreement in Ad-hoc networks, extending DH to the groups, Group Diffie-Hellmann GDH-1-2 [8] protocols are used. Moreover, Hybercube , Octopus and the Burmester-Desmedt protocols are used for hierarchical group key exchange [9]. In addition to these, key agreement protocols using generic password-based authenticated key exchange schemes and DH variants with extensions to the multi-party versions have been proposed in [3]. There are many other protocols using variants of these approaches [10]. Another important technique, which is frequently used in Ad-hoc network security, is the threshold cryptography. Threshold cryptography can be used to construct distributed public key management service to solve trusted certification problem. Using this approach, if some components of the system are compromised, single point of failure problem will not occur especially for certification issues. In [4], a distributed public-key management service for Ad-hoc networks has been proposed using these approaches.

Many different key management protocols have been proposed to solve various problems of key management in large and dynamic groups. Mainly, we can classify group key management protocols into three main categories: Centralized, decentralized and hybrid key management protocols [11], [12]. In centralized group key management protocols, there is only one central entity that controls whole group. No auxiliary entity (TTP) is required to perform key distribution. However, Single Point of Failure (SPoF) problems may arise. In these protocols, hierarchical approaches, which scale group size logarithmically, are generally used. LKH (Logical Key Hierarchy) [13], OFT (One-Way Function Three) [14], and ELK (Efficient Large Group Key) [15] are well-known protocols using these approaches. In decentralized group key management protocols, the large group is split into small sub-groups. Different controllers are used for each sub-group. Iolus [16] is based on this approach. Hybrid protocols integrating these two approaches can be found in [6], [7], [17]. Note that, even if [6], [7] and [17] focus on satellite multicast systems, hybrid key management techniques of these studies can be applied to any very large and dynamic network system.

3   Architectural Design of HIMUTSIS

HIMUTSIS uses hierarchical multi-tier architecture to secure and scale large and dynamic MANETs. Notice that, this architecture is especially compatible with naturally existing hierarchical structure of the military networks. HIMUTSIS utilizes generic architecture of hierarchical military MANETs such as [18] , [1], [2]. This architecture consists of UAVs (Unmanned Aerial Vehicles), MBN (Mobile Backbone Networks) and RGN (Regular Ground Nodes). Each UAV sets up and controls a MBN group having terrestrial mobile units in hierarchical manner. Also, each MBN sets up and controls RGN groups in hierarchical manner. In HIMUTSIS, we use a novel design approach and divide MBN into MBN1 and MBN2 layers having different properties and duties. HIMUTSIS utilizes existing heterogonous structure and additional possibilities of MBN nodes in modern armies. This approach provides advantages for both security and performance aspects.

UAV-MBN1 layer consist of UAVs and MBN nodes having extensive communication capabilities such as long range missile batteries and mobile tactical centers. Notice that, as a reasonable assumption, both UAVs and MBN1 type nodes have advanced tamper resistant mechanism (for UAVs, an appropriate self-destruction mechanism can be applied) [2]. Thus, even if they are destroyed or captured by enemy, they will not comprise their cryptographic keys or certificates. Dividing MBN into MBN1 and MBN2 layers, we extend advantages of tamper resistant mechanism into MBN layer and obtain some advantages for key management architecture. In our protocol, UAVs are mainly responsible for key distribution and certification processes as well as being bridge between MBN clusters for communication. Since number of MBN1 type nodes is limited, both storage and computational workload of UAVs are neglible.

MBN1-MBN2 is the second layer of our protocol. MBN2 nodes are generally mobile units used in classical UAV-MBN structure having high communication abilities. Special fighting units like trucks, tanks having beam-forming antennas can offer high-speed point-to-point direct wireless links in this layer [19]. MBN1-MBN2 layer utilizes possibilities of existing heterogeneous formation in MBN layer especially for armies having specialized ground units. This approach uses same heterogeneity principle which leads the creation of UAV-MBN networks. Notice that, our protocol can still function if MBN1 type nodes are not available. In this case, MBN2 type nodes will carry out duties of MBN1 type nodes using specific cryptographic techniques such as threshold cryptography in order to solve trust issues of certification [4].

MBN2-RGN is the third layer of our protocol. Each MBN2 controls RGNs including light weight equipped soldiers. In this layer, cryptographic algorithms are different from other layers. Details are given in section 4 and 6.

4   Cryptographic Techniques and Security Level Architecture of HIMUTSIS

In HIMUTSIS, we use a new multi-level security architecture including cryptographic methods which have not been used in MANETs as far as our concern.

In HIMUTSIS, as a novel approach, we use signcryption based key exchange schemes as a major cryptographic method. Signcryption is a relatively new concept in cryptography. Signcryption scheme is a cryptographic method that fulfills both the functions of secure encryption and digital signature, but with a cost smaller than that required by sign-then-encrypt approach [20]. Many efficient signcryption schemes and their applications for various security problems have been proposed [21]. For instance, in [17], multi-recipient signcryption scheme has been used. In HIMUTSIS, we use DKEUTS (Direct Key Exchange Protocol Using a Timestamp) based on SDSS1 type signcryption scheme [5].

In HIMUTSIS, we suggest using a secure block cipher with appropriate modes such as AES in first and second layers as symmetric encryption part of the signcryption process. Notice that, first layer of the architecture particularly requires very high security. Thus, we suggest using at least 256 bit block cipher in this layer. Each signcryption scheme uses cryptographic hash functions to provide integrity and authentication. We suggest using at least 512 bit hash function such as SHA-512 [22]. Notice that, SHA-1 has been broken and threats for hash functions are in increase. Also, bit length of public key parameters should be hold as large as possible. We call security criteria determined for first layer as "Security level 1" (SL1). Same security approach, sligthly reducing bit length of block ciphers, hash functions and public key parameters can be applied to the second layer. Notice that, security requirements are still high in second layer. We call this slightly reduced security level as "Security Level 2" (SL2).

In third layer, taking into consideration computational capabilities and communication scope of its nodes, we suggest using T-function combined stream ciphers such as ABC [23] as an alternative symmetric key cryptography method. Stream ciphers are especially preferred for their high speed encryption properties. Also, we use key transport protocol in this layer instead of key exchange protocol like DKEUTS or [7]. Bit length requirements are reduced and cryptographic methods are changed in this layer. We call this setting as "Security Level 3" (SL3).

5   Detailed Description of HIMUTSIS

Major principle behind key management techniques of HIMUTSIS is providing independency of layers while preventing MANETs from performance deterioration and security problems. In order to provide forward and backward security (rekeying problem), we utilize independency of layers and local rekeying principles for each layer of the HIMUTSIS. We use ELK protocol as a major key management protocol in each layer. ELK protocol has advantages for rekeying cost and size of the packets when compared to some well-known protocols such as LKH and OFT [15]. Whenever a node join-leave event occurs in the theaters (active regions in military operations), ELK protocol is applied only related parts of the layer and other parts of the network are not affected from modifications. This provides significant performance gain and drastically reduces rekeying workload of the overall network. Notice that, some of these approaches have been effectively used in [7] and [17]. However, in HIMUTSIS, key management techniques are modified because architectural design of [7] and [17] are completely different from HIMUTSIS and can not be applied directly. Apart from these, we also utilize batch keying mechanism of [6], [7] adapting them to the architecture and requirements of HIMUTSIS.

We use certification procedures to provide authentication for public key's of the nodes in each layer. In [2], authors proposed an certification services for UAV-MBN networks. Our approach utilizes some principles of [2] but differs for cryptographic methods and key management techniques. We adapt DKEUTS scheme to the our multi-tier hierarchical military MANET architecture. Following notations are used:

$K_{i,j}^{s,d}$:Directed secret key in key exchange procedure. It is transmitted from $i'th$ source s_i to $j'th$ destination d_j. Source or destination can be following node types, $u : UAV$, $m_1 : MBN1$ $node$, $m_2 : MBN2$ $node$. All other internal keys adapted from DKEUTS obey same notation rules. $KT_i^{\gamma_l}$: This is intra-theater group communication key generated by theater manager. γ_l represents theater level and index i denotes index of the group manager in level l. $su_{i,j}$: Seed value transmitted from $i'th$ theater manager to $j'th$ node in that theater. These seed values are used for moderate-time batch keying purposes. SKG (Symmetric Key Generator): Generate keys obeying security level which is send as a parameter to the function. Also, it may take a seed value to generate keys with related security level. $SGNKG$ (signcryption Key Generator): Similar to SKG but generates signcryption related paramteres such as, p :Large prime number, q :A large prime factor for $(p-1)$, g :Generator of the group with order q modulo p and other signcryption parameters: $xa_{i,j}^{s,d}$, $xb_{i,j}^{s,d}$ are private parameters and $ya_{i,j}^{s,d}$, $yb_{i,h}^{s,d}$ are public parameters of signcryption based schemes. H :Unkeyed cryptographic hash function, $H_{K_{i,j}^{s,d}}$:Keyed cryptographic hash function, $(E-D)_{K_{i,j}^{s,d}}$:Symmetric encryption-decryption function. n, n_{type}, n_{type_i} : Number of total nodes, number of $type$ nodes and number of $type$ nodes in the $i'th$ theater in MANET, respectively. M : Messages. Other notations are given when they are needed. We represent certificates as $CERT_j^{l,i}$. Now, we give details of the first layer operations:

UAV-MBN1 Layer
5.2.1 Key Generation

$UAVs$: $(su_{i,j}, KT_i^{\gamma_1}, K_{i,j}^{u,m_1}, x_{i,j}^{u,m_1}) = SKG(SL1)$, obtain $y_j^{m_1,u}$ from MBN1 nodes and $(p_i, q_i, g_i, xa_{i,j}^{u,m_1}) = SGNKG(SL1)$.

$MBN1\ Nodes$: $(K_{j,i}^{m_1,u}, x_{j,i}^{m_1,u}) = SKG(SL1)$, obtain y_i^{u,m_1} from UAVs and $xb_{j,i}^{m_1,u} = SGNKG(SL1)$ where $1 \leq i \leq n_u$, $1 \leq j \leq n_{m_{1_i}}$ for each i and $l = 1, 2$.

5.2.2 DKEUTS Steps

$UAVs\ Key\ Transport$: $(k_{1,i,j}^{u,m_1}, k_{2,i,j}^{u,m_1}) = H((y_i^{m_1,u})^{x_{i,j}^{u,m_1}} \bmod p_i)$ and each UAV gets their current time-stamps $TS_{i,j}^{u,m_1}$.

$c_{i,j}^{u,m_1} = E_{k_{1,i,j}^{u,m_1}}(K_{i,j}^{u,m_1}, TS_{i,j}^{u,m_1})$, $r_{i,j}^{u,m_1} = H_{k_{2,i,j}^{u,m_1}}(K_{i,j}^{u,m_1}, TS_{i,j}^{u,m_1}, CERT_j^{\gamma_l,i})$, $s_{i,j}^{u,m_1} = x_{i,j}^{u,m_1}(r_{i,j}^{u,m_1} + xa_{i,j}^{u,m_1})^{-1} \bmod q_i$ and UAVs transmit $(c_{i,j}^{u,m_1}, r_{i,j}^{u,m_1}, s_{i,j}^{u,m_1})$ tuples to the MBN1 nodes.

$MBN1\ Nodes\ Verification$: $(k_{1,i,j}^{u,m_1}, k_{2,i,j}^{u,m_1}) = H((y_{i,j}^{u,m_1} \cdot g_i^{r_{i,j}^{u,m_1}})^{s_{i,j}^{u,m_1} \cdot xb_{j,i}^{m_1,u}} \bmod p_i)$, $(K_{i,j}^{u,m_1}, TS_{i,j}^{u,m_1}) = D_{k_{1,i,j}^{u,m_1}}(c_{i,j}^{u,m_1})$ then perform following control:

$If(Freshness(TS_{i,j}^{u,m_1} == true) \wedge (H_{k_{2,i,j}^{u,m_1}}(K_{i,j}^{u,m_1}, TS_{i,j}^{u,m_1}) == r_{i,j}^{u,m_1}))$ then accept else reject.

$MBN1\ Nodes\ Key\ Transport$: $(k_{1,j,i}^{m_1,u}, k_{2,j,i}^{m_1,u}) = H((y_i^{u,m_1})^{x_{j,i}^{m_1,u}} \bmod p_i)$ and each MBN1 node gets their current time-stamps $TS_{j,i}^{m_1,u}$.

$c_{j,i}^{m_1,u} = E_{k_{1,j,i}^{m_1,u}}(K_{j,i}^{m_1,u}, TS_{j,i}^{m_1,u})$, $r_{j,i}^{m_1,u} = H_{k_{2,j,s}^{m_1,u}}(K_{j,i}^{m_1,u}, TS_{j,i}^{m_1,u}, CERT_j^{\gamma_l,i})$, $s_{j,i}^{m_1,u} = x_{j,i}^{m_1,u}(r_{j,i}^{m_1,u} + xa_{j,i}^{m_1,u})^{-1} \bmod q_i$ and UAVs transmit $(c_{j,i}^{m_1,u}, r_{j,i}^{m_1,u}, s_{j,i}^{m_1,u})$ tuples to the MBN1 nodes.

$UAVs\ Key\ Verification$: $(k_{1,j,i}^{m_1,u}, k_{2,j,i}^{m_1,u}) = H((y_{j,i}^{m_1,u} \cdot g_i^{r_{j,i}^{m_1,u}})^{s_{j,i}^{m_1,u} \cdot xa_{i,j}^{u,m_1}} \bmod p_i)$, $(K_{j,i}^{m_1,u}, TS_{j,i}^{m_1,u}) = D_{k_{1,j,i}^{m_1,u}}(c_{j,i}^{m_1,u})$ then perform following control:

$If(Freshness(TS_{j,i}^{m_1,u} == true) \wedge (H_{k_{2,j,i}^{m_1,u}}(K_{i,j}^{u,m_1}, K_{j,i}^{m_1,u} TS_{j,i}^{m_1,u}) == r_{j,i}^{m_1,u}))$ then accept else reject.

5.2.3 Complete Key Exchange

Both UAVs and MBN1 nodes: $K_{i,j}^* = K_{i,j}^{u,m_1} \oplus K_{j,i}^{m_1,u}$ then unique shared key pairs $K_{i,j}^*$ have been created among UAVs and MBN1 nodes. As an optional step: UAV: $tag_{i,j}^{u,m_1} = MAC_{K_{i,j}^*}(TS_{i,j}^{u,m_1})$ and send tags to the MBN1 nodes. MBN1 nodes verify tags $if(MAC_{K_{i,j}^*}(TS_{i,j}^{u,m_1}) == true)$.

5.2.4 Secure Communication and Key Transmission

$UAVs$: $M_{i,j}^{u,m_1} = (KT_i^\gamma, su_{i,j})$, $M_{i,j}^* = E_{K_{i,j}^*}(M_{i,j}^{u,m_1})$, $M_i' = E_{KT_i^\gamma}(m_i^\gamma)$ where $M_{i,j}^{u,m_1}$ message includes intra-theater communication keys and batch keying seeds for each nodes. For each nodes, $M_{i,j}^{u,m_1}$ are encrypted with shared keys $K_{i,j}^*$.

$MBN1$: $M_{i,j}^{u,m_1} = D_{K_{i,j}^*}(M_{i,j}^*)$ and recover $KT_i^\gamma, su_{i,j}$ keys from $M_{i,j}^*$. Now, each MBN1 nodes in related theaters have intra-theater communication keys KT_i^γ . Using these, , $m_i^\gamma = D_{KT_i^\gamma}(M_i')$ and each MBN1 nodes obtain intra-theater message m_i^γ. MBN1 nodes can communicate with their UAV using $K_{i,j}^*$.

5.2.5 Member-Join Leave

Whenever a MBN1 node join-leave event occurs in a UAV theater, UAV applies ELK key update rules using $K_{i,j}^*$ unique keys of each MBN1 nodes.

MBN1-MBN2 and MBN2-RGN Layers. In MBN1-MBN2 layer, similar to upper layer, DKEUTS key exchange is realized among MBN1 and MNB2 nodes. MBN1 may use same batch keying mechanisms. Key generation and parameter bit lengths obey SL2 criteria. As an optional step, MBN1 nodes can generate their directed unique keys $K_{i,j}^{m_1,m_2}$ using $su_{i,j}$ seeds. Then, each key update in MBN1-MBN2 layer can be tracked by UAVs. If this is not desired, key generation rules for these keys can be done similar to the upper layer. Due to space limitation, we can not give detailed steps of this layer. Details of mathematical transformations can be found in [24]. Important difference of this layer from classical architectures is minimizing threshold cryptograpy requirement. In MBN2-RGN layer, we suggest using SL3 criteria. As discussed in section 4, instead of joint key exchange, a key transport mechanism like [6] or multi-recipient signcryption scheme like [17] can be used. Benefits of this approach are given in section 6 and details can be found in [24].

6 Performance Analysis of HIMUTSIS

Properties of Cryptographic Methods Used in HIMUTSIS. Major cryptographic method used in our protocol is DKEUTS key exchange protocol. DKEUTS protocol is based on signcryption and it inherently utilizes all security properties of signcryption schemes. We summarize benefits of DKEUTS protocol to the some traditional cryptographic methods below:

- DKEUTS protocol provides confidentiality, authentication, integrity, unforgeability and non-repudiation. Notice that, many traditional cryptographic methods can not provide these five major cryptographic goals together. Freshness of the messages is provided by either time-stamps or nonces.

– Signcryption, when compared to the classical sign-then-encrypt approach, has both computational and bandwidth advantages. When compared to the sign-then encrypt approach using Shcnorr and and El-Gamal signature, in average, signcryption provides 58% computational and 78 % communication overhead advantages for RSA based signatures [5]. We denote cryptographic advantages of the DKEUTS protocol for both bandwitdh and computational effort as c_{sgn} and cryptographic cost of traditional methods as c_{trd} .

Apart from benefits coming from DKEUTS, HIMUTSIS has a multi-security level architecture which provides many advantages when compared to the traditional approaches. In traditional approaches, generally, all components of the network are enforced to use same cryptographic methods without regarding their heterogeneous computational and storage possibilities. In HIMUTSIS, we use three different security levels having two different cryptographic approaches. In first and second layers, joint key exchange method DKEUTS has been preferred instead of key transport protocol used in [17] or [6] . The reason is that, in the first layer , trust level (military ranks and rights, possibilities and hardness of the capturing of the nodes can be criteria) and computational availability of UAV and MBN1 nodes are close to each other both of them having tamper resistant possibilities. Thus, both parties of the communication should have right to determine their unique key pairs $K_{i,j}^*$ in equal manner. Similarly, it is also reasonable for MBN1-MBN2 nodes to realize joint key exchange having equal rights. Security level of each layer depends on three major criteria: Communication scope, importance of the information and computational-storage possibilities of the nodes in that layer. In first layer and second layers, which have large communication scope, high information context importance and computational possibilities, nodes use very high and high security parameters in first and second layers, respectively. In third layer, RGNs, which have low communication possibilities and communication scope, nodes use stream ciphers focusing on high speed and low storage requirements. Also, since there is important possibilities and trust difference among MBN2 and RGNs, we use key transport protocol similar to [17] or [6]. Apart from these, in third layer, using a different approach, we suggest using T-function supported stream ciphers [23].

Architectural Design and Key Management Properties of HIMUTSIS.
Architectural desing of HIMUTSIS provides advantages for security, scabilitiy and performance aspects.HIMUTSIS utilizes heterogenic structure of MBN layer and divides MBN layer into MBN1 and MBN2 layers. MBN1, having tamper resistant properties, facilitates certification procedures when central manager of the theater is destroyed. Duplication of the certificates of the UAVs is now possible for MBN1 layer and this approach reduces threshold cryptography requirement. Main principles behind of the hybrid key management techniques of the HIMUTSIS can be given as follows. Pure decentralized architectures are not suitable for naturally hierarchical and central entity based military applications. Pure centralized architectures cause SPoF problems. This problem becomes much severe for highly dynamic military MANETs where survability

of nodes can not be guaranteed. HIMUTSIS divides very large and dynamic MANET into subgroups like decentralized approaches in order to prevent SPoF. At the same time, HIMUTSIS uses centralized key management technique in each theater in order to provide scalability and forward-backward security. Similar approach is also used in [18].

In HIMUTSIS, significant performance gain is obtained from independent multi-ELK-theater approach. In each theater, whenever a node join-leave event occurs, in order to provide forward and backward security, key update (rekeying) is realized on only related part of the theater using ELK and other parts of the system are not affected from these processes. This approach minimizes rekeying workload of MANET and provides significant performance gain. We define ORW (Overall Rekeying Workload) measurement for cost of the rekeying operation. Measurement is defined according to the three major criteria: Number of join-leave event for certain time period in certain scope of the network, r_{scope}, cost of the rekeying protocol used in network, $c_{protocol}$ (also related with number of members affected from rekeying), and cost of the cryptographic methods used in key management, c_c. ORW can be determined approximately as $r_{scope} \cdot c_{protocol} \cdot c_c$.

We compare HIMUTSIS to some Pure Centralized Key Management Protocols (PCKMP) such as LKH, OFT and ELK protocols in the context of their ORW measurements. In pure centralized approach, rekeying of all network components is done by only central entity. Thus, for aforementioned protocols, number of affected nodes is represented by n, which is all nodes in the network. In HIMUTSIS, for each node join-leave, only related theater is affected. Thus, number of affected nodes is represented with thr where $thr << n$. Also, number of rekeying in a single theater, r_{thr}, is much smaller than rekeying of all network, r, for certain time period and $r_{thr} << r$. m denotes benefits coming from batch keying and this factor additionally reduces ORW of the HIMUTSIS. k denotes branching factor of the logical key tree. Detailed cost analysis of LKH, OFT and ELK protocols can be found in [11], [14]. Comparison results are given at Table 1 below.

Table 1. Comparison of HIMUTSIS with some PCKMP for ORW

	ORW	Storage Cost	SPoF Problem
LKH	$c_{trd}O(k \log_k n - 1)r$	$O(\log_k n |K|)$	Yes
OFT	$c_{trd}O(\log_k n)r$	$O(\log_k n |K|)$	Yes
ELK	$c_{trd}O(\log_k n) \Pr(leave)r$	$O(\log_k n |K|)$	Yes
HIMUTSIS	$c_{sgn}O(\log_k thr) \Pr(leave)r_{thr}m^{-1}$	$O(\log_k (thr) |K|)$	No
PDC	Trust problems, not suitable for military applications		No

As we have seen, HIMUTSIS has significant advantages over the pure implementation of the centralized approaches. These advantages stem from the decentralized properties of HIMUTSIS and both $r_{thr} << r$ (most important gain) and $thr << n$. Thus, performance of HIMUTSIS is better than pure implementation of these protocols. Also, in pure centralized approach, SPoF problem occurs while this problem is minimized in HIMUTSIS. When compared to Pure Decentralized Approach (PDA), HIMUTSIS is more appropriate for military MANETs as discussed above.

7 Conclusion

In this paper, we have proposed a new hierarchical multi-tiered adaptive Ad-hoc network security protocol based on signcryption type key establishment schemes: HIMUTSIS. HIMUTSIS brings novelties for architectural design of military MANETs, cryptographic methods used in MANETs and usage of hybrid key management approaches. Architectural design of HIMUTSIS consists of UAV, MBN1-MBN2 and RGN layers in hierarchical manner. Architectural design of HIMUTSIS differs from traditional UAV-MBN networks with MBN1-MBN2 layers utilizing heterogeneity of MBN layer and tamper resistant possibilities of MBN1 nodes. This approach makes possible to give centralized certification rights of the UAVs' to the MBN1 (tamper resistant) which reduces threshold cryptography requirement and facilitates certification procedures. HIMUTSIS uses multi-security level approach for its layers applying high security parameters with DKEUTS signcryption type key exchange in its two layers and stream ciphers based key transport schemes in the third layer. Adapted DKEUTS provides all security and computational-bandwidth advantages of signcryption schemes to the HIMUTSIS when compared to the traditional cryptography approaches. Also adapted DKEUTS prevents MANETs from some active attacks. HIMUTSIS utilizes hybrid key management techniques to the military MANETs. HIMUTSIS divides military MANETs into hierarchical layers and theaters using decentralized approach preventing system SPoF problem. In each theater, HIMUTSIS uses ELK centralized protocol to scale large and dynamic military MANETs. As a result, HIMUTSIS is especially suitable for very large and dynamic military MANETs requiring very high security and performance.

Acknowledgements

This work is supported by the State Planning Organization of Turkey under "Next Generation Satellite Networks Project", and Bogaziçi University Research Affairs.

References

1. D. L. Gu, G. Pei, H. Ly, M. Gerla, and X. Hong. Hierarchical Routing for Multi-layer Ad-hoc Wireless Networks with UAVs. In IEEE MILCOM, 2000.
2. J. Kong, H. Luo, K. Xu, D. Lihui Gu, M. Gerla, and S. Lu, "Adaptive Security for Multi-layer Ad Hoc Networks," Wireless Communications and Mobile Computing, Special Issue on Mobile Ad Hoc Networking, vol. 2, pp. 533– 547, 2002.
3. N. Asokan and P. Ginzboorg. Key Agreement in Ad-hoc Networks. In Computer Communications, 23(18), pp. 1627-1637, 2000.
4. L. Zhou and Z. Hass. Securing ad hoc networks. IEEE Network, 13(6), pages 24-30, November/December 1999.

5. Y. Zheng. Shortened digital signature, signcryption, and compact and unforgeable key agreement schemes (A contribution to IEEE P1363 Standard for Public Key Cryptography), July 1998.
6. A. Altay Yavuz, F. Alagoz , E. Anarim. A new satellite multicast security protocol based on elliptic curve signatures. IEEE International Conference on Information Communication Technologies (ICTTA) , April 2006.
7. A. Altay Yavuz, F. Alagoz, E. Anarim. Three-Tiers satellite multicast security protocol based on ECMQV and IMC methods. Computer-Aided Modeling, Analysis and Design of Communication Links and Networks (CAMAD'06).
8. M.Steiner, G. Tsudik, M. Waidner, "Diffie-Hellman Key Distribution Extended to Groups", Proc. 3rd ACM Symp. on Computer and Communications Security, Vol. 1, pp31-37, March 1996.
9. G. Yao, K. Ren, F. Bao, R. Deng and D. Feng, "Making the Key Agreement Protocol in Mobile Ad Hoc Network More Efficient" In Proc. of ACNS 2003, LNCS, Vol. 2846, p343-356, 2003.
10. D. Augot and R. Bhaskar and V. Issarny and D. Sacchetti. An Efficient Group Key Agreement Protocol for Ad hoc Networks, IEEE Workshop on Trust, Security and Privacy in Ubiquitous Computing, Taormina, Italy, 2005.
11. D. H. S. Rafaeli. A survey of key management for secure group communications. ACM Comp. Surveys, vol. 35, no. 3, Sept 2003, pp. 309–29.
12. A. Menezes, P. Van Oorschot, and S. Vanstone. Handbook of applied cryptography. CRC press, 1996.
13. D. Wallner, E. Harder, and R. Agee. Key management for multicast: Issues and architectures. IETF, RFC2627, June 1999.
14. D. Balenson et al. Key management for large dynamic groups: One way function trees and amortized initialization. IETF Draft, work-in progress, draft-balenson-groupkeymgmt-oft-00.txt, February 1999.
15. A.Perrig, D.Song, and J.D. Tygar. ELK, a new protocol for efficient large-group key distribution. IEEE Security and Privacy Symposium May 2001.
16. S. Mittra. Iolus: A framework for scalable secure multicasting.In Proceedings of the ACM SIGCOMM'97, September 1997.
17. A. Altay Yavuz, F. Alagoz, E. Anarim. NAMEPS: N -Tier Satellite Multicast Security Protocol Based on Signcryption Schemes. To appear on IEEE Globecom Conference, San Francisco, 2006.
18. Rhee, Y. Park and G. Tsudik. A group key management architecture in mobile ad-hoc wireless networks. Journal Of Communication and Networks, Vol. 6, No. 2, pp. 156-162, June 2004.
19. D. L. Gu, G. Pei, H. Ly, M. Gerla, B. Zhang, and X. Hong. UAV-aided Intelligent Routing for Ad-hoc Wireless Network in Single-area Theater. In IEEE WCNC, pages 1220–1225, 2000.
20. Y. Zheng. Digital signcryption or how to achieve Cost(Signature Encryption) $<<$ Cost(Signature) + Cost(Encryption). Advances in Cryptology – Crypto'97, Lecture Notes in Computer Science, Vol. 1294, pp. 165-179, Springer-Verlag, 1997.
21. Y. Zheng and H. Imai. Compact and unforgeable key establishment over an ATM network. Proceedings of IEEE INFOCOM'98 , pp.411-418, 29/3-3/4, 1998.
22. D. Stinson. Cryptography Theory and Practice. CRC Press, Third Edition, 2005.
23. V. Anashin , A. Bogdanov, I. Kizhvatov. ABC : A New Flexible Stream Cipher.
24. A. Altay Yavuz. Novel Methods for Security Mechanisms and Key Management Techniques in Wireless Networks Based on Signcryption and Hybrid Cryptography. MS Thesis, Boğaziçi University, 2006.

Dual-Level Traffic Smoothing Technique over Switched Ethernet for Hard Real-Time Communication*

Hai Jin, Minghu Zhang, and Pengliu Tan

Cluster and Grid Computing Lab
School of Computer Science and Technology
Huazhong University of Science and Technology, Wuhan, 430074, China
hjin@hust.edu.cn

Abstract. This paper introduces a novel dual-level traffic smoothing technique for hard real-time communication over Fast/Gigabit switched Ethernet without any modification to existing Ethernet hardware. First, the necessary restricted conditions for hard real-time communication over switched Ethernet are analyzed using the network calculus theory. Then the dual-level traffic smoothing scheme, which combines the node-level traffic smoothing with the global-level traffic smoothing, is introduced. Finally, we make thorough measurements and the results show that the dual-level traffic smoothing mechanism can provide very good hard real-time communication performance with low system overheads and has more potential for most hard real-time and embedded control systems than other existing approaches.

1   Introduction

With the emerging distributed hard real-time applications such as command and control systems, industrial process control and distributed medical imaging, the ability of handling hard real-time traffic is becoming more and more important. In order for these applications to be usable, they require the network to guarantee bounded end-to-end delays between hundreds of microseconds to tens of milliseconds.

Ethernet has been used for hard real-time communication for its advantages of popularity, high-speed, simplicity, and low-cost. In recent years, the switched Ethernet has more and more been the network topology for industry control systems. Hard real-time communication without hardware support over switched Ethernet is still an open problem for researchers.

This paper introduces the dual-level traffic smoothing technique to realize hard real-time communication over Fast/Gigabit switched Ethernet. To achieve true hard real-time communication, the scheme is built under the real-time micro-kernel.

The organization of this paper is as follows. The related works are summarized in Section 2. Section 3 analyzes the constraining conditions for hard real-time communication over switched Ethernet using the network calculus theory. The dual-level

---

* This paper is supported by the National Natural Science Foundation of China under grant No.90412010.

A. Levi et al. (Eds.): ISCIS 2006, LNCS 4263, pp. 445–454, 2006.

traffic smoothing technique is addressed in Section 4 in detail. The detail measurements are discussed in Section 5. Finally, Section 6 concludes this paper.

2 Related Work

Many proposed real-time communication solutions are based on shared-medium Ethernet. RETHER [1] adopts a circulating token representing the permission to transmit data through the shared channel. MARS [2] uses TDMA to provide real time guarantee on Ethernet in process control environments.

Most real-time communications over switched Ethernet either provide additional QoS mechanisms inside the switches or use intelligent switches. EtheReal [3] includes a bandwidth reservation scheme inside the switches. Many efforts associated with the delay bound are presented in [4, 10], where deterministic end-to-end delay over switched Ethernet are analyzed using the network calculus theory. The traffic smoothing technique [6, 8] is firstly proposed to realize soft real-time communication over shared medium Ethernet. Loeser et al. [5] use traffic shaping technique to implement hard real-time communication on commodity networks. Like other traffic smoothing approaches, Loeser's approach considers only at local level without a global opinion, where some periodic real-time messages may loss their deadlines due to the failure of the extra admission request. Hard real-time communication without hardware support over switched Ethernet is still an open problem.

3 Background and System Model

Three types of components are defined in switched Ethernet, shown in Fig. 1: the service node (*SN*), the control node (*CN*), and the Ethernet switch (*ES*). The *SN* sends (receives) traffics to (from) other nodes. The *CN* collects the information of all traffics at the global level and distributes reserved bandwidths to all *SNs*. The *ES* can be considered as a multiplexer which stores and forwards incoming frames.

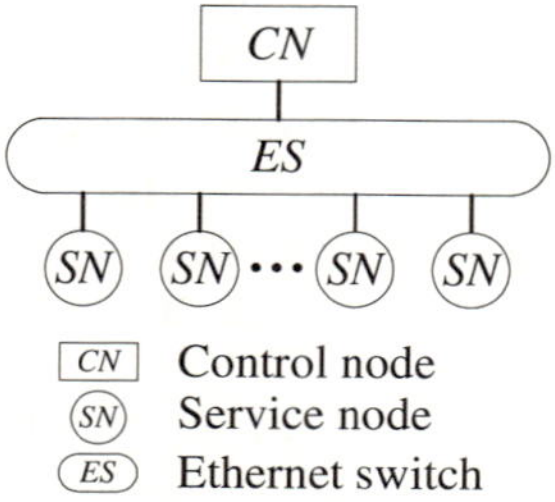

Fig. 1. Single-hop switched Ethernet

We denote all the traffics from node i to node j as a "*stream*" and only one stream exists from one node to another, where nodes i and j are either *SNs* or *CNs*.

Table 1 shows the parameter definitions which are related to traffic transmission.

Table 1. Parameter definitions

Notation	Definition
t_{es}	The delay of a Ethernet frame through the Ethernet switch
t_{nic}	Message processing delay at the Ethernet adapter
r, ρ	The long term transmission rate and the burst length
α, β	The arrival curve and the service curve
C_{switch}	The physical transmission rate of the Ethernet switch
C_{host}	The physical transmission rate of the Ethernet adapter
C_{stack}	The processing rate of the communication protocol stack

3.1 Service Node (*SN*)

Based on the network calculus theory [11], the NIC (*Network Interface Card*) can be considered as a multiplexer. Multiple streams may arrive to the NIC at maximal rate of C_{stack} and NIC processes these streams at the rate of C_{host}. To sender *SN i*, the arrival curve α_i and the service curve β_i are given as fellows, where K streams are established from sender *SN i* to other nodes $j_1, j_2, ..., j_K$, $MAAS_i$ presents the *maximal accumulative arrival size* of all streams from node i during one *refresh period (RP)*.

$$\alpha_{i,j}(t) = \rho_{i,j} + r_{i,j} \cdot t, \sum_{j=j_1}^{j_K} \rho_{i,j} \leq K \cdot MTU \leq MAAS_i, \sum_{j=j_1}^{j_K} r_{i,j} \leq C_{stack}$$

$$\alpha_i(t) = \sum_{j=j_1}^{j_K} \alpha_{i,j}(t) = \sum_{j=j_1}^{j_K} (\rho_{i,j} + r_{i,j} \cdot t) = \sum_{j=j_1}^{j_K} \rho_{i,j} + \sum_{j=j_1}^{j_K} r_{i,j} \cdot t \tag{1}$$

$$\beta_i(t) = max(0, C_{host} \cdot (t - t_{nic}))$$

Fig. 2 illustrates the arrival and the service curves of *SN i* at the case of C_{stack} is faster than C_{host} (C_{stack} is faster than C_{host} in normal Fast/Gigabit Ethernet).

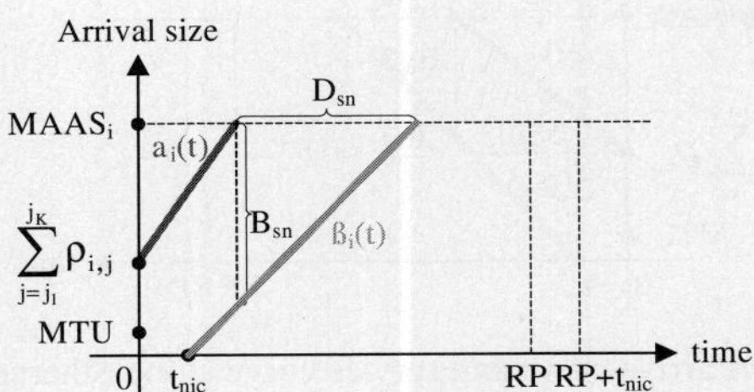

Fig. 2. Arrival curve and service curve at the sender *SN*

The maximal backlog B_{sn} and the maximal delay D_{sn} can be obtained as the maximal vertical and horizontal differences between α_i and β_i, respectively.

$$B_{sn} = min(MAAS_i, MAAS_i + t_{sn} \cdot C_{host} - (MAAS_i - \sum_{j=j_1}^{j_K} \rho_{i,j}) \cdot C_{host} / C_{stack})$$

$$D_{sn} = MAAS_i / C_{host} + t_{sn} - (MAAS_i - \sum_{j=j_1}^{j_K} \rho_{i,j}) / C_{stack} \tag{2}$$

3.2 Ethernet Switch (*ES*)

Fig. 3 shows a typical full duplex Ethernet switch with *N* input/output ports.

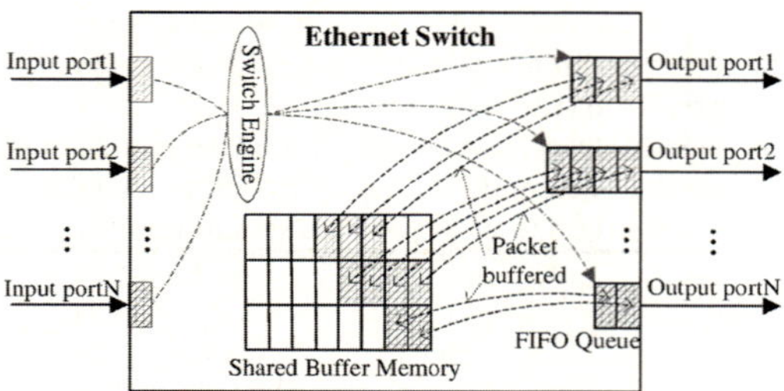

Fig. 3. FIFO Ethernet switch with *N* input/output ports

To a given output port *j*, its arrival curve α_j and the service curve β_j are given as follows, where i_1, i_2,..., i_{N-1} are input ports of the switch excluding input port *j*.

$$\alpha_{i,j}(t) = \rho_{i,j} + r_{i,j} \cdot t, \ \rho_{i,j} \le MTU, \ r_{i,j} \le C_{host}$$

$$\alpha_j(t) = \sum_{i=i_1}^{i_{N-1}} \alpha_{i,j} = \sum_{i=i_1}^{i_{N-1}} (\rho_{i,j} + r_{i,j} \cdot t) = \sum_{i=i_1}^{i_{N-1}} (\rho_{i,j}) + \sum_{i=i_1}^{i_{N-1}} (r_{i,j}) \cdot t \tag{3}$$

$$\beta_j(t) = \max(0, C_{switch} \cdot (t - t_{es}))$$

Fig. 4 shows the arrival and service curves of output port *j*, where $MAAS_j$ is limited to the shared buffer memory allocated to output *j*.

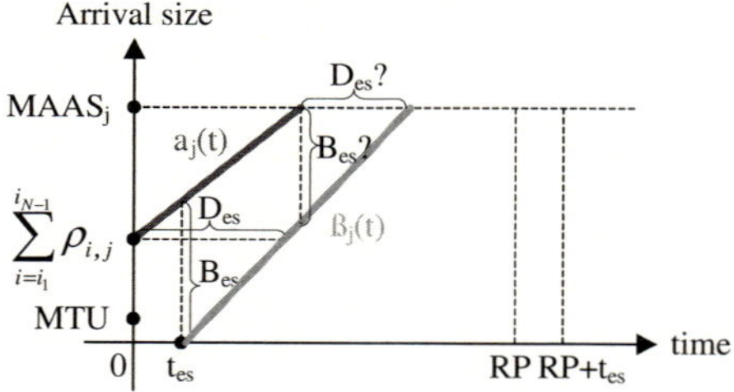

Fig. 4. The arrive curve and service curve at the Ethernet switch

The accumulative rate to output port *j* may be either larger or smaller than C_{switch} and the maximal backlog B_{es} and the maximal delay D_{es} can be obtained as:

$$B_{es} = \max((N-1) \cdot MTU + \sum_{i=i_1}^{i_{N-1}} (r_{i,j}) \cdot t_{es}, \min(MAAS_j,$$

$$MAAS_j + t_{es} - C_{switch} \cdot (MAAS_j - \sum_{i=i_1}^{i_{N-1}} \rho_{i,j}) / \sum_{i=i_1}^{i_{N-1}} (r_{i,j}))) \tag{4}$$

$$D_{es} = \max(MAAS_j / C_{switch} + t_{es} - (MAAS_j - \sum_{i=i_1}^{i_{N-1}} \rho_{i,j}) / C_{host}, (N-1) \cdot MTU / C_{switch} + t_{es})$$

4 Dual-Level Traffic Smoothing Mechanism

4.1 Node-Level Traffic Smoothing

Each node may send multiple streams to other nodes and each stream is smoothed by one traffic smoother. The traffic smoother is leaky bucket based with two parameters, *RP* and *MAAS*. *RP* is fixed and the transmission rates of the stream from node i to nodes j is set as:

$$r_{i,j} = MAAS_{i,j} / RP, \quad j = j_1, j_2, \ldots, j_K \tag{5}$$

Let C_{ave} be the average arrival rate of all streams from sender *SN* i to nodes j_1, j_2, ..., j_K. Thus, the smoothed arrival curve α'_i and service curve β'_i are as follows:

$$C_{ave} = \sum_{j=j_1}^{j_K} r_{i,j} = \sum_{j=j_1}^{j_K} (MAAS_{i,j}) / RP$$

$$\alpha'_i(t) \approx C_{ave} \cdot t, \; \beta'_i(t) \approx \max(0, C_{ave} \cdot (t - t_{nic})) \tag{6}$$

Fig. 5 shows both the original curves (α_i and β_i) and the smoothed curves (α'_i and β'_i), where $[C_{stack}]$, $[C_{host}]$ and $[C_{ave}]$ present the slopes of the curves.

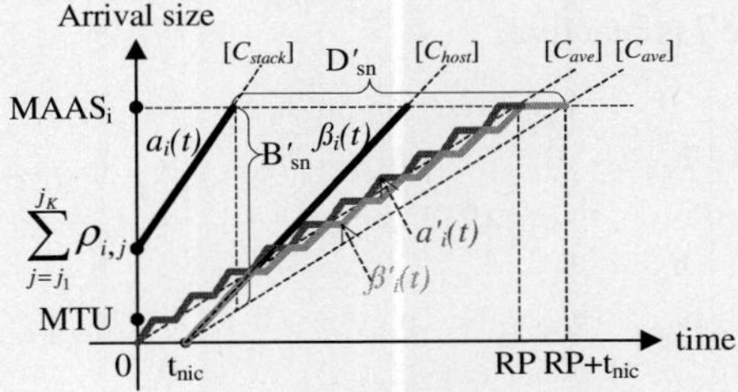

Fig. 5. The smoothed arrival curve and service curve at the sender node

We can achieve the smoothed maximal delay and backlog as follows:

$$B'_{sn} = \boldsymbol{min}(MAAS_i, MAAS_i + t_{nic} - C_{ave} / C_{stack} \cdot (MAAS_i - \sum_{j=j_1}^{j_K} \rho_{i,j}))$$

$$D'_{sn} = RP + t_{nic} - (MAAS_i - \sum_{j=j_1}^{j_K} \rho_{i,j}) / C_{stack} \tag{7}$$

Conditions in (7) show that the smoothed maximal delay and backlog is related to the value of *RP*. Thus constrained conditions of the node-level traffic smoothing are:

$$C_{ave} \le C_{host}, \quad \sum_{j=j_1}^{j_L} \rho_{i,j} \le MAAS_i \tag{8}$$

4.2 Global-Level Traffic Smoothing

The main function of the global traffic smoothing is to avoid multiple incoming streams flooding to individual nodes. Thus, the conditions in (9) must be constrained:

$$\sum_{i=i_1}^{i_N}(r_{i,j})\le C_{switch} \tag{9}$$

The maximal delay and backlog in the switch are readjusted as fellows:

$$B'_{es}=(N-1)\cdot MTU+\sum_{i=i_1}^{i_N}(r_{i,j})\cdot t_{es}\le(N-1)\cdot MTU+C_{switch}\cdot t_{es}$$
$$D'_{es}=(N-1)\cdot MTU/C_{switch}+t_{es} \tag{10}$$

The conditions show that the smoothed maximal delay and backlog in the Ethernet switch have nothing to do with the value of *RP*.

4.3 Parameter Control for Traffic Smoothing

A traffic stream may consist of three types of messages, including the periodic real-time (*PRT*) messages, aperiodic real-time (*ART*) messages and non real-time (*NRT*) messages. During current *RP*, each service node sends the parameter requirements of its streams in the next *RP* to the control node through a vector $\boldsymbol{B_i}$ $(b_{i,1}, b_{i,2},..., b_{i,i-1}, 0, b_{i,i+1},..., b_{i,N})$, where $b_{i,j}$ represents the long term transmission rate for the *PRT* messages. The control node collects all parameter requirements from the service nodes and composes a global bandwidth matrix $\boldsymbol{M_{periodic}}$, where $b_{i,j}$ is set to 0 if i equals to j, or either node i or node j is inactive:

$$\boldsymbol{M}_{periodic}=\begin{vmatrix}\boldsymbol{B_1}\\\boldsymbol{B_2}\\\vdots\\\boldsymbol{B_i}\\\boldsymbol{B_{i+1}}\\\vdots\\\boldsymbol{B_{N-1}}\\\boldsymbol{B_N}\end{vmatrix}=\begin{vmatrix}0 & b_{1,2} & \cdots & b_{1,i} & b_{1,i+1} & \cdots & b_{1,N-1} & b_{1,N}\\b_{2,1} & 0 & \cdots & b_{2,i} & b_{2,i+1} & \cdots & b_{2,N-1} & b_{2,N}\\\cdots & \cdots & 0 & \cdots & \cdots & \cdots & \cdots & \cdots\\b_{i,1} & b_{i,2} & \cdots & 0 & b_{i,i+1} & \cdots & b_{i,N-1} & b_{i,N}\\b_{i+1,1} & b_{i+1,2} & \cdots & b_{i+1,i} & 0 & \cdots & b_{i+1,N-1} & b_{i+1,N}\\\cdots & \cdots & \cdots & \cdots & \cdots & 0 & \cdots & \cdots\\b_{N-1,1} & b_{N-1,2} & \cdots & b_{N-1,i} & b_{N-1,i+1} & \cdots & 0 & b_{N-1,N}\\b_{N,1} & b_{N,2} & \cdots & b_{N,i} & b_{N,i+1} & \cdots & b_{N,N-1} & 0\end{vmatrix} \tag{11}$$

At the same time, the control node calculates an additional bandwidth matrix $\boldsymbol{M_{other}}$ which includes each active stream's reserved bandwidth, $v_{i,j}$, for the *ART* and *NRT* messages of each service node in the next *RP*:

$$\boldsymbol{M}_{other}=\begin{vmatrix}0 & v_{1,2} & \cdots & v_{1,i} & v_{1,i+1} & \cdots & v_{1,N-1} & v_{1,N}\\v_{2,1} & 0 & \cdots & v_{2,i} & v_{2,i+1} & \cdots & v_{2,N-1} & v_{2,N}\\\cdots & \cdots & 0 & \cdots & \cdots & \cdots & \cdots & \cdots\\v_{i,1} & v_{i,2} & \cdots & 0 & v_{i,i+1} & \cdots & v_{i,N-1} & v_{i,N}\\v_{i+1,1} & v_{i+1,2} & \cdots & v_{i+1,i} & 0 & \cdots & v_{i+1,N-1} & v_{i+1,N}\\\cdots & \cdots & \cdots & \cdots & \cdots & 0 & \cdots & \cdots\\v_{N-1,1} & v_{N-1,2} & \cdots & v_{N-1,i} & v_{N-1,i+1} & \cdots & 0 & v_{N-1,N}\\v_{N,1} & v_{N,2} & \cdots & v_{N,i} & v_{N,i+1} & \cdots & v_{N,N-1} & 0\end{vmatrix} \tag{12}$$

$$v_{i,i}=0, v_{i,j}=0 \;(if\; node\; i\; or\; node\; j\; is\; inactive)$$
$$v_{i,j}=\boldsymbol{min}((C'_{host}-\sum_{k=1}^{N}b_{i,k})/(M-1),(C'_{switch}-\sum_{k=1}^{N}b_{k,j})/(M-1)) \tag{13}$$

where M ($\leq N$) is the number of active node in the system, C'_{host} ($\leq C_{host}$) the available transmission rate of the NIC, and C'_{switch} ($\leq C_{switch}$) the available rate of the switch.

5 Performance Measurements

The dual-level traffic smoothing technique is implemented in the 16-node cluster system. Fig. 6 shows the communication architecture of each cluster node.

The OS structure combines the real-time micro-kernel RTAI [12] with the Linux kernel. The SS-RTUDP lightweight real-time network communication protocol stack, which is modified from RTNET [13], is built under RTAI. The traffic smoothers locate within the RTMAC (*Real-Time Medium Access Control*) layer. More about the SS-RTUDP protocol stack can be found in our previous works [7, 9].

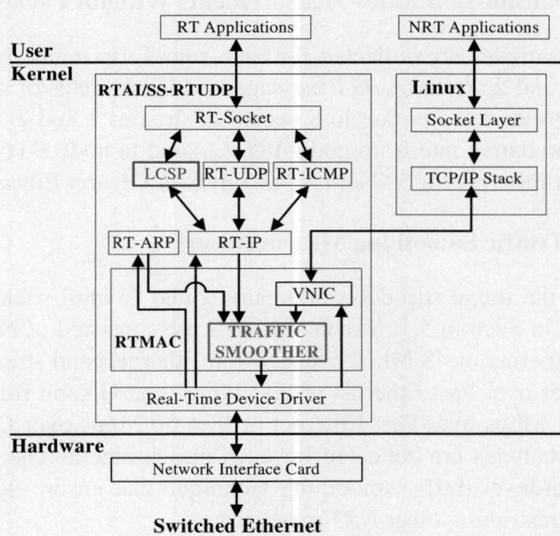

Fig. 6. Network communication architecture

The detail testing configurations are shown in Table 2. All the sender and receiver applications are processed through inserting the kernel modules.

Table 2. Testing configurations

Hardware	Intel Celeron 2.0 GHz; 256MB DDRAM; 32 bits 33 MHz PCI buses
Software	RedHat 9.0; Linux kernel 2.4.20;RTAI 3.0 r4; RTNET 0.8.0
Adapters	3COM 905B Fast Ethernet adapter Intel PRO/1000MT Gigabit adapter
Switches	TP-Link TL-SF1024 Fast switch; TP-Link TL-SG1024 Gigabit switch

Six streams are produced for each measurement, shown in Fig. 7. The round trip delay measurements between node A and node B are based on the "ping-pong" method (streams 1 and 2) with different local traffic loads (streams 3 and 4) and global traffic loads (streams 5 and 6).

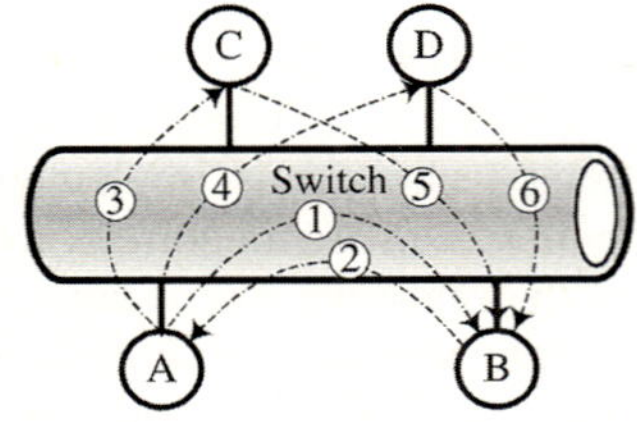

Fig. 7. Traffic streams for round trip delay measurements

5.1   Available Transmission Rates Measurements Without Packet Loss

Total of 100,000 samples are collected for each round trip delay measurement. The rates of streams 1 and 2 are fixed *PRT* messages, while the rates of streams 3 to 6 are increased from 0 to the rates packet loss occurs in streams 1 and 2. We can find that the maximal accumulative rate from node A (C'_{host}) and to node B (C'_{switch}) are 84 and 88 *Mbps* over Fast Ethernet, or 508 and 528 *Mbps* over Gigabit Ethernet, respectively.

5.2   Dual-Level Traffic Smoothing Measurements

We first measure the round trip delays (streams 1 and 2) until packet loss occurs of the measurements in Section 5.1. Streams 1 and 2 are consisted of *PRT* messages (12 Mbps over Fast Ethernet or 48 Mbps over Gigabit Ethernet) and streams 3~6 are *PRT* messages (24 Mbps over Fast Ethernet or 200 Mbps over Gigabit Ethernet) with *NRT* messages (0 to 14 Mbps over Fast Ethernet or 0 to 50 Mbps over Gigabit Ethernet). Total of 100,000 samples are collected for each measurement. The results (Table 3) show that the dual-level traffic smoothing technique can ensure no packet loss for *PRT* messages by restricting other *NRT* messages.

Table 3. The delay bounds using dual-level traffic smoothing mechanism

Environment	Streams	Rates of streams (Mbps)						Round trip delays (µs)				Packet loss (stream 1)
		1	2	3	4	5	6	Max.	Min.	*Average*	*Standard deviation*	
Fast Ethernet	Original	12	12	36	38	38	40	1106	586.3	912.1	142.3	126
	Smoothed	12	12	32	32	33.3	33.3	865.4	586.4	680.6	54.2	0
Gigabit Ethernet	Original	48	48	230	240	240	250	394.6	146.5	181.6	68.5	158
	Smoothed	48	48	220	220	226.7	226.7	321.9	146.1	171.6	21.7	0

Next, we measure the bounded delay for the *PRT* message with MTU size. The rates of streams 1~4 are set to 28 Mbps (1 Mbps *PRT* and 27 Mbps *ART*), and the rates of streams 5 and 6 are set to 30 Mbps (3 Mbps *PRT* and 27 Mbps *ART*). Total of 100,000 are collected for each measurement and no packet loss occurs to stream 1.

The final measuring results (Table 4) show that the dual-level traffic smoothing approach can provide less than 1 millisecond bounded end-to-end delay for a MTU frame with low system overheads, which can satisfy most of current hard real-time applications which require bounded delay at the order of 10 milliseconds.

Table 4. End-to-end delay bounds measurements

Environment	Refresh period	CPU load	End-to-end delay bounds	
			Calculated	Observed
Fast Ethernet	1 ms	21.3%	1309.1 µs	993.5 µs
	10 ms	10.2%	9787.6 µs	6895.4 µs
Gigabit	1 ms	25.2%	750.6 µs	447.5 µs
Ethernet	10 ms	11.2%	6458.6 µs	4825.3 µs

5.3 Performance Comparison

Since most current real-time communication approaches on switched Ethernet are soft real-time based and we only compare our approach with Loeser's approach [5]. The rates of streams 1 and 2 are set to 0.5 Mbps (*PRT* type, 64 bytes frame every one millisecond), while the rates of streams 3~6 are set to 50 Mbps (40 Mbps *PRT* and 10 Mbps *NRT*) over Fast Ethernet, or 260 Mbps (240 Mbps *PRT* and 20 Mbps *NRT*) over Gigabit Ethernet. Total of 500,000 samples are collected for each measurement. The results (Table 5) indicate that our approach can provide lower maximal delay than Loeser's approach. On the other hand, Loeser's approach does not consider the delay introduced by the local streams (streams 3 and 4), while these cases exist in most distributed hard real-time systems. Therefore our approach has more potential for distributed hard real-time and embedded control systems.

Table 5. End-to-end delay comparison

Approaches	Environment	Accumulative rates of streams		Max. delay
		From source node	To destination node	(64 bytes)
Ours	Fast Ethernet	82.9 Mbps	85.5 Mbps	486 µs
	Gigabit Ethernet	498.9 Mbps	512.1 Mbps	450µs
Loeser's	Fast Ethernet	0.512 Mbps	92.5 Mbps	1300 µs
	Gigabit Ethernet	0.512 Mbps	480.5 Mbps	906 µs

6 Conclusion and Future Works

In this paper, a novel dual-level traffic smoothing technique, which combines the node-level traffic smoothing with the global-level traffic smoothing, is introduced to realize hard real-time communication over Fast/Gigabit switched Ethernet under the real-time micro-kernel. This mechanism ensures all period real-time messages are satisfied within their deadlines. The testing results demonstrate that the dual-level traffic smoothing mechanism can provide reliable packet transmission with bounded transmission delays with low system overhead and can satisfy most current hard real-time communication requirements.

In our future work, we will consider fault-tolerant to the dual-level traffic smoothing mechanism and extend it to realize hard real-time communication over multihop switched Ethernet.

References

[1] C. Venkatramani, *The Design, Implementation and Evaluation of RETHER: a Real-Time Ethernet Protocol.* PhD thesis, State University of New York at Stony Brook, Jan. 1997.

[2] H. Kopetz, A. Damm, C. Koza, "Distributed fault-tolerant real-time systems: the Mars approach", *IEEE Micro*, Vol.9, No.1, Feb. 1989, pp.25-40.

[3] S. Varadarajan and T. Chiueh, "EtheReal: A host-transparent real-time Fast Ethernet switch", *Proceedings of ICNP*, Oct. 1998.

[4] J-P Georges, E. Rondeau, and T. Divoux, "Evaluation of switched Ethernet in an industrial context by using the Network Calculus", *Proceedings of the 4th IEEE International Workshop on Factory Communication Systems*, Vasteras, Sweden, Aug. 28-30, 2002, pp. 19-26.

[5] J. Loeser and H. Haertig, "Low-latency hard real-time communication over switched Ethernet", *Proceedings of 16th Euro-micro Conference on Real-Time Systems (ECRTS'04)*, 30 June-2 July 2004, pp.13-22.

[6] L. LoBello, G. A. Kaczynski, and O. Mirabella, "Improving the Real-Time Behavior of Ethernet Networks Using Traffic Smoothing", *IEEE Transactions on Industrial Informatics,* Vol.1, No.3, Aug. 2005, pp.151-161.

[7] H. Jin, M. Zhang, P. Tan, and L. Xu, "Lightweight Hard Real-time Network Communication for Commodity Cluster Systems", *Proceedings of the International Conference on Sensing, Computing and Automation*, May 5~8, 2006, pp.3562-3567.

[8] S. K. Kweon, M. G. Cho, and K. G. Shin, "Soft real-time communication over Ethernet with adaptive traffic smoothing", *IEEE Transactions on Parallel and Distributed Systems*, Vol.15, No.10, Oct. 2004, pp.946-959.

[9] H. Jin, M. Zhang, P. Tan, H. Chen, and L. Xu, "Lightweight Real-time Network Communication Protocol for Commodity Cluster Systems", *Proceedings of the 2005 IFIP International Conference on Embedded And Ubiquitous Computing (EUC'05)*, Nagasaki, Japan, Dec. 2005, pp.1075-1084.

[10] J. Jasperneite, P. Neumann, M. Theis, and K. Watson, "Deterministic Real-Time Communication with Switched Ethernet", *Proceedings of the 4th IEEE International Workshop on Factory Communication System*, Vasteras, Sweden, Aug. 28-30, 2002, pp.11-18.

[11] J. L. Boudec and P. Thiran, *Network Calculus: A Theory of Deterministic Queuing Systems for the Internet,* Springer Verlag, LNCS 2050, May 2004.

[12] Available: http://www.rtai.org/index.php.

[13] Available: http://www.rts.uni-hannover.de/rtnet/.

A Model of a Packet Aggregation System

Jung Ha Hong[1], Oleg Gusak[1], Neal Oliver[2], and Khosrow Sohraby[1]

[1] Dept. of Computer Science and Electrical Engineering
University of Missouri - Kansas City
5100 Rockhill Road, Kansas City, MO 64110, USA
{jhhk86, gusako, sohrabyk}@umkc.edu
[2] Intel Europe, 1515 Route 10 Parsippany, NJ 07054, USA
neal.oliver@intel.com

Abstract. The decision and ability to aggregate packets can have significant impact on the performance of a communication system. The impact can be even more substantial when the system operates under a heavy load. In this paper, we present a queuing model which describes a packet encapsulation and aggregation process. Using this model, we provide analysis of the end-to-end delay of a packet transmitted by the system. The analytical model is verified by a simulation model of the system. We calculate the maximum number of packets in a single frame for which packet aggregation minimizes the average total delay of a packet. It is numerically shown that when the load is high, the higher the variability of the packet service time, the higher the maximum allowed number of packets in the frame should be to achieve the minimum average total packet delay. However, the impact of the variability of the packet service time is insignificant when the system load is moderate or low.

1 Introduction

In attempt to increase data throughput, many modern data transmission protocols provide capabilities for aggregating of transmitted data fragments into larger packets at the time of encapsulation at a particular OSI layer. Thus, in Frame Relay systems [7] every packet transmitted over the system is encapsulated into a frame. Frame Relay technology also allows packing of small packets into a single frame as in the case of voice packets transmission defined in FRF.11 (see [7] for details). The decision and ability to aggregate packets into a larger packet, which we will call a frame, can have significant impact on the performance of a communication system especially when the load is high.

The packet encapsulation and aggregation process can be described by a well-known concatenation queuing model in which packets are served in batches. The number of packets inserted into a frame and transmitted as a batch is limited by K, the maximum number of packets that the frame can accommodate. In the existing models, the overhead due to the transmitted frame header usually is not considered. The literature on queueing models with batch service is rather rich and goes back to Bailey [4]. In that model, if the server, after finishing service of the batch, finds less than K packets in the queue, it takes all the packets for

A. Levi et al. (Eds.): ISCIS 2006, LNCS 4263, pp. 455–463, 2006.

service. If the server finds more than K packets waiting, then it takes for service only K packets, while other in excess of K wait in the queue for a next round of service. Variation and generalization of this model where both a minimum and a maximum batch size is considered are given in [8] and [11]. For other works in this area see, for instance, [5,6,13] and the recent edition of Medhi's book [10].

This paper analyzes a packet encapsulation and aggregation process for Poisson arrivals and a phase-type packet service time distribution using a Markov chain model. Frame header of constant size is assumed. Using the proposed model, we provide analysis of the end-to-end delay of a packet transmitted by the system. We verify analytical results with a simulation model of the system. Based on results of experiments with the model, we provide the maximum number of packets in a frame for which packet aggregation minimizes the average total delay of a packet. It is numerically shown that when the load is high, the higher the variability of the packet service time, the higher the maximum allowed number of packets in the frame should be to achieve the minimum average total packet delay. However, the impact of the variability of the packet service time is insignificant when the system load is moderate or low.

In the next section, we present the queuing model and give its analysis for a frame consisting of K packets. In section 3, we provide analysis of the total delay of a packet transmitted by the system, and in section 4, we present numerical results of experiments with the model of the system.

2   Model of the System and Its Analysis

We assume that interarrival time of packets follows an exponential distribution with mean $1/\lambda$. Arriving packets are stored in an infinite buffer until they are transmitted to the destination peer. The transmission is done frame by frame. Each frame is comprised of a header of constant size and a number of data packets. The maximum number of data packets which can be aggregated in a single frame is K. Whenever the system is ready for transmission and the buffer is not empty, a frame is created of packets currently residing in the buffer starting from the head of line packet. If the number of packets in the queue is larger than K, then only K packets are inserted into the frame. The transmission time of the frame consists of transmitting the constant size header and k packets, $k = 1, 2, \ldots K$. We assume that the frame is transmitted as a single entity and hence, the transmission time of an individual packet is the transmission time of the frame the packet belongs to. Upon arrival at a non-empty buffer having i packets waiting for transmission, the arriving packet waits in the queue until the current frame and $\lfloor i/K \rfloor$ frames are transmitted, where $\lfloor \cdot \rfloor$ denotes the largest integer not exceeding the argument. Upon arrival at an empty buffer, a frame consisting of the single arrived packet is formed and its transmission starts immediately.

We assume that the packet size and hence its transmission time has a phase-type distribution [12] of order m with irreducible representation (α, T). Phase-type distributions measure the time until the transition into the absorbing state

$m+1$ in a Markov chain with $m+1$ states. The entries of square matrix $T = (q_{i,j})$, $1 \leq i,j \leq m$ represent the transition rates from state i to j $(i \neq j)$. The parameters $q_{i,m+1}$, $1 \leq i \leq m$ denote the transition rate from state i to the absorbing state $m+1$, which are given as the entries of the vector T^o. Vector T^o satisfies equation $Te + T^o = 0$, where e is a column vector of ones. The entries of the $1 \times m$ vector $\alpha = (\alpha_1, \alpha_2, \cdots, \alpha_m)$ represent the probability distribution of the Markov chain being in any non-absorbing state at the initial time. The nth moment of the phase-type distribution is given by $\mathrm{m}_n = (-1)^n n! \alpha T^{-n} e$, where $n \geq 1$. Note that m_1 is the average size of the transmitted packets.

To model this system as a Markov chain, we approximate transmission of the constant size header of a frame by an Erlang-M distribution having mean of $1/h$. Later, we obtain results for the constant transmission time of the frame header by taking M, the number of stages of the Erlang distribution, to infinity.

Let $\rho = \lambda \mathrm{m}_1$, $H = 1/h$, and $\gamma = Mh$ be the parameter for Erlang-M distribution. We assume that $\rho + \lambda H/K$ is strictly less than one for the stability of the system. The described system is a Markov chain with the states $\xi = \{(0), (i, j, k), (i, 0, l)\}$, where state (0) represents the empty system, $i = 0, 1, \ldots$ denotes the number of packets in the queue, $j = 1, 2, \ldots K$ is the number of packets in the current frame which are not transmitted including the currently transmitted packet, $k = 1, 2, \ldots m$ is the phase of the transmission time of the currently transmitted packet, and $l = 1, 2, \ldots M$ is the phase of the Erlang-M distribution corresponding to transmission of the header. The Markov chain is given by the following balance equations:

$$\lambda p_{(0)} = \gamma p_{(0,0,M)}, \tag{1}$$

$$(\lambda + \gamma) p_{(0,0,1)} = \sum_{k=1}^{m} q_{k,m+1} p_{(0,1,k)},$$

$$(\lambda + \gamma) p_{(0,0,l)} = \gamma p_{(0,0,l-1)}, \quad 2 \leq l \leq M,$$

$$(\lambda - q_{k,k}) p_{(0,1,k)} = \lambda \alpha_k p_{(0)} + \alpha_k \sum_{k'=1}^{m} q_{k',m+1} p_{(0,2,k')} + \gamma \alpha_k p_{(1,0,M)} + \sum_{s=1,s \neq k} q_{s,k} p_{(0,1,s)}, 1 \leq k \leq m,$$

$$(\lambda - q_{k,k}) p_{(0,j,k)} = \gamma \alpha_k p_{(j,0,M)} + \sum_{s=1,s \neq k}^{m} q_{s,k} p_{(0,j,s)} + \alpha_k \sum_{k'=1}^{m} q_{k',m+1} p_{(0,j+1,k')},$$
$$2 \leq j \leq K - 1, 1 \leq k \leq m,$$

$$(\lambda - q_{k,k}) p_{(0,K,k)} = \gamma \alpha_k p_{(K,0,M)} + \sum_{s=1,s \neq k}^{m} q_{s,k} p_{(0,K,s)}, 1 \leq k \leq m,$$

$$(\lambda + \gamma) p_{(i,0,1)} = \lambda p_{(i-1,0,1)} + \sum_{k=1}^{m} q_{k,m+1} p_{(i,1,k)}, \quad i \geq 1,$$

$$(\lambda + \gamma) p_{(i,0,l)} = \lambda p_{(i-1,0,l)} + \gamma p_{(i,0,l-1)}, \quad i \geq 1, 2 \leq l \leq M,$$

$$(\lambda - q_{k,k}) p_{(i,j,k)} = \lambda p_{(i-1,j,k)} + \alpha_k \sum_{k'=1}^{m} q_{k',m+1} p_{(i,j+1,k')} + \sum_{s=1,s \neq k}^{m} q_{s,k} p_{(i,j,s)},$$
$$i \geq 1, 1 \leq j \leq K - 1, 1 \leq k \leq m,$$

$$(\lambda - q_{k,k}) p_{(i,K,k)} = \lambda p_{(i-1,K,k)} + \gamma \alpha_k p_{(K+i,0,M)} + \sum_{s=1,s \neq k}^{m} q_{s,k} p_{(i,K,s)}, i \geq 1, 1 \leq k \leq m,$$

where $p_{(\xi)}$ is the stationary probability of state ξ. For a finite M, the Markov chain is quasi birth-death (QBD) with complex boundaries [1,2,3]. The complexity of the solution increases as M increases. Here, we use the probability generating function approach in which the complexity of the solution is independent of M.

Let $H_l(z) \triangleq \sum_{i=0}^{\infty} p_{(i,0,l)} z^i$, $1 \le l \le M$, and $F_{j,k}(z) \triangleq \sum_{i=0}^{\infty} p_{(i,j,k)} z^i$, $1 \le j \le K$, $1 \le k \le m$ be generating functions on $|z| \le 1$. Then, from the balance equations (1) and for $1 \le k \le m$ we get the following:

$$H_l(z) = \left(\frac{\lambda + \gamma - \lambda z}{\gamma}\right)^{M-l} H_M(z), \ 1 \le l \le M, \tag{2}$$

$$H_1(z) = \frac{1}{\lambda + \gamma - \lambda z} F_1(z) T^o, \tag{3}$$

$$F_1(z) = [F_2(z) T^o + \gamma p_{(1,0,M)} + \lambda p_{(0)}] X(z), \tag{4}$$

$$F_j(z) = [F_{j+1}(z) T^o + \gamma p_{(j,0,M)}] X(z), 2 \le j \le K - 1, \tag{5}$$

$$F_K(z) = g(z) X(z), \tag{6}$$

where

$$g(z) = \frac{\gamma}{z^K} \left[H_M(z) - \sum_{i=0}^{K-1} p_{(i,0,M)} z^i \right], \tag{7}$$

$F_j(z) = [F_{j,1}(z), F_{j,2}(z), \cdots, F_{j,m}(z)]$, $1 \le j \le K$, $X(z) = \alpha[(\lambda - \lambda z)I - T]^{-1}$, and I is a square identity matrix of the size equal to that of T. From (2),

$$\sum_{l=1}^{M} H_l(z) = \frac{\left(1 + \frac{\lambda(1-z)}{\gamma}\right)^M - 1}{\lambda(1-z)} \gamma H_M(z), \tag{8}$$

and from (5) and (6), we get

$$F_{K-j}(z) = \left[g(z)\{X(z)T^o\}^j + a_j(z) \right] X(z), \ \ 0 \le j \le K - 2, \tag{9}$$

where $a_j(z) = \sum_{i=1}^{j} \gamma p_{(K-i,0,M)} \{X(z)T^o\}^{j-i}$. Substituting $F_2(z)$ from (9) into (4), we get

$$F_1(z) = \left[g(z)\{X(z)T^o\}^{K-1} + a_{K-1}(z) + \lambda p_{(0)} \right] X(z). \tag{10}$$

Substituting (10) and $H_1(z)$ from (2) into (3), we obtain

$$H_M(z) = \frac{f_1(z) - z^K \left[f_2(z) + p_{(0,0,M)}\{\beta(z)\}^{K-1} \right]}{1 - [z\beta(z)]^K \left(\frac{\lambda - \lambda z + \gamma}{\gamma}\right)^M}, \tag{11}$$

where $f_1(z) = \sum_{i=0}^{K-1} p_{(i,0,M)} z^i$, $f_2(z) = \sum_{i=1}^{K-1} p_{(i,0,M)} [\beta(z)]^{K-i}$, and $\beta(z) = \{X(z)T^o\}^{-1}$.

Now, we consider a constant header size by taking M to infinity. Let $x_i \triangleq \lim_{M \to \infty} Mh p_{(i,0,M)}$, where $i \ge 0$. Also, let $\Phi(z) \triangleq \lim_{M \to \infty} Mh H_M(z)$ on $|z| \le 1$. From (11), $\Phi(z)$ can be obtained in terms of x_i, $i = 0, 1, \ldots, K-1$, as

$$\Phi(z) = \sum_{i=0}^{\infty} x_i z^i = \frac{\sum_{i=0}^{K-1} x_i z^i - z^K f_3(z)}{1 - e^{\lambda(1-z)H} [z\beta(z)]^K}, \tag{12}$$

where $f_3(z) = \sum_{i=1}^{K-1} x_i[\beta(z)]^{K-i} + x_0[\beta(z)]^{K-1}$. Assuming the same notations $p_{(0)}, H_l(z)$, and $F_j(z)$ for the constant header size as for the case of finite M, from (1), (9), and (10), $p_{(0)} = \frac{x_0}{\lambda}$,

$$F_1(z) = \left[G(z)[b(z)]^{K-1} + \sum_{i=1}^{K-1} x_{K-i}[b(z)]^{K-1-i} + x_0 \right] X(z),$$

$F_{K-j}(z) = \left[G(z)[b(z)]^j + \sum_{i=1}^{j} x_{K-i}[b(z)]^{j-i} \right] X(z), \ 0 \le j \le K - 2$, where $b(z) = X(z)T^o$, and $G(z) \triangleq \lim_{M\to\infty} g(z) = \frac{1}{z^K} \left[\Phi(z) - \sum_{i=0}^{K-1} x_i z^i \right]$, which is obtained from (7). Now let $\mathcal{F}(z) \triangleq \sum_{j=1}^{K} F_j(z)\mathrm{e}, \mathcal{H}(z) \triangleq \sum_{l=1}^{\infty} H_l(z)$. Then,

$$\mathcal{F}(z) = \left[G(z)\frac{1 - [\beta(z)]^K}{1 - \beta(z)} + \sum_{i=1}^{K-1} x_i \frac{1 - [\beta(z)]^i}{1 - \beta(z)} + x_0 \right] X(z)\mathrm{e}$$

and (8) becomes $\mathcal{H}(z) = \frac{e^{\lambda(1-z)H}-1}{\lambda(1-z)}\Phi(z)$. Using L'Hôpital's rule, we obtain

$$\mathcal{F}(1) = \mathrm{m}_1 \left[K\Phi(1) + x_0 + \sum_{i=1}^{K-1} ix_i - K \sum_{i=0}^{K-1} x_i \right]. \tag{13}$$

$\mathcal{H}(1) = \Phi(1)H$, where $\Phi(1)$ is given by

$$\Phi(1) = \frac{(1 - \rho)\{K \sum_{i=0}^{K-1} x_i - \sum_{i=1}^{K-1} ix_i\} + \rho x_0}{(1 - \rho)K - \lambda H}, \tag{14}$$

Expression (14) is obtained from (12) using L'Hôpital's rule as well. Finally, the normalization condition is given by $\frac{x_0}{\lambda} + \mathcal{H}(1) + \mathcal{F}(1) = 1$.

It can be shown that $\mathcal{F}(1) = \rho$ by solving the normalization condition with respect to x_0 and substituting x_0 into the right side of (13). We remark that this result is obtained before the system is solved completely.

Let $\Xi(z)$ and $\Delta(z)$ be the numerator and denominator of $\Phi(z)$ in (12), respectively. Then, we have

$$\Delta(z) = 0 \implies z = e^{-\lambda H(1-z)/K} X(z)T^o. \tag{15}$$

Note that $X(z)T^o$ is equal to $B^*(\lambda - \lambda z)$, where $B^*(\cdot)$ denotes the Laplace Stieltjes Transform (LST) of the packet service time distribution.

The sequence $x_i, i = 0, 1, \cdots, K-1$, is obtained using the analyticity of $\Phi(z)$ inside and on the unit circle. At each root of (15) inside and on the unit circle, $\Xi(z)$ should vanish. Now, for $k = 0, 1, \cdots, K-1$, we consider the following iteration with $z_0 = 0$:

$$z_{n+1} = e^{-\lambda H(1-z_n)/K} e^{i2\pi k/K} X(z_n)T^o, \quad n \ge 0. \tag{16}$$

For each k, if $|z_n| \le 1$, then $|z_{n+1}| = |e^{-\lambda H(1-z_n)/K}||B^*(\lambda - \lambda z)|$, which is ≤ 1.

Thus, iteration (16) provides K roots of (15) on $|z| \leq 1$, which includes the root $z = 1$ for $k = 0$. Substituting $K - 1$ roots for $k = 1, 2, \cdots, K - 1$ (i.e., root $z = 1$ is excluded) into $\Xi(z)$, we obtain $K - 1$ linear equations in terms of x_i for $i = 0, 1, \cdots, K - 1$. Solving these equations with the normalization condition, we obtain all K unknowns resulting in the complete set of x_i's and hence stationary probabilities of all states of the system.

Let $Q(z)$ be the probability generating function of the number of packets in the queue. Then, $Q(z) \triangleq \sum_{n=0}^{\infty} P[L_q = n]z^n = \frac{x_0}{\lambda} + \mathcal{F}(z) + \mathcal{H}(z)$ and the average queue length $E[L_q] = \left. \frac{dQ(z)}{dz} \right|_{z=1}$. Using Little's law, we obtain the average waiting time of a packet in the queue, $E[W_q]$, which is equal to $E[L_q]/\lambda$.

Now, we consider the distribution of the number of packets in the frame in terms of the sequence x_i found earlier. Recall that a frame is completely transmitted when the transmission of the last phase of its header is performed. Hence, the stationary frame size is identical to the number of packets in the queue at the departure epoch of the frame. Therefore, if there are i, $1 \leq i \leq K - 1$, packets in the queue at the departure epoch of a frame, then the next frame has i packets aggregated in it. If $i = 0$, then the frame consists of a single packet. If $i \geq K$, then the number of packets in the frame is equal to K.

Denote $\tilde{\pi}_n^K$ as the stationary probability that a frame consists of n packets, then $\tilde{\pi}_1^K = \frac{x_0 + x_1}{\Phi(1)}$, $\tilde{\pi}_n^K = \frac{x_n}{\Phi(1)}$, $2 \leq n \leq K - 1$, $\tilde{\pi}_K^K = \frac{\sum_{n=K}^{\infty} x_n}{\Phi(1)} = 1 - \frac{\sum_{n=0}^{K-1} x_n}{\Phi(1)}$, where $\Phi(1)$ is given by expression (14). Thus, the average number of packets, $\bar{k}$, in a frame is $\bar{k} \triangleq \sum_{n=1}^{K} n \tilde{\pi}_n^K = \frac{\mathcal{F}(1)}{m_1 \Phi(1)}$. Noting that $\mathcal{F}(1) = \rho$, the expression for $\bar{k}$ can be written as $\bar{k} = \frac{\lambda}{\Phi(1)}$.

In the next section, we present analysis of the total delay of a packet transmitted by the system.

3   Analysis of the Total Packet Delay

We obtain the LST of the packet waiting time in the queue, $W^*(s)$, and the LST of the total time spent by a packet in the system, $S^*(s)$, by conditioning on the state of the Markov chain which the packet sees at its arrival epoch. Assuming that there are i packets in the queue at the arrival epoch of a packet, the waiting time of the packet in the queue is the sum of the remaining service time of a frame in transmission and the service time of $\lfloor \frac{i}{K} \rfloor$ frames.

Let $B^*(s)$ be the LST of the service time of a packet, $B_H^*(s) = e^{-sH}$ the LST of the service time of a constant header, $R^*(s) = \frac{1 - B^*(s)}{sm_1}$ the LST of the remaining service time of a packet when sampled at a random point, and $R_H^*(s) = \frac{1 - e^{-sH}}{sH}$ be the LST of the remaining service time of a constant header. By the PASTA (Poisson arrivals see time averages) property, the stationary distribution at the arrival epoch of a packet is the same as the one at an arbitrary time. Hence, $W^*(s)$ is obtained as $W^*(s) \triangleq E[e^{-sW_q}] = P_{(0)} + \sum_{i=0}^{\infty} \left[\{B^*(s)\}^K B_H^*(s) \right]^{\lfloor \frac{i}{K} \rfloor} \{ \sum_{j=1}^{K} \sum_{k=1}^{m} P_{(i,j,k)} R^*(s) [B^*(s)]^{j-1} B_H^*(s) + R_H^*(s) \sum_{l=1}^{\infty} P_{(i,0,l)} \}$.

The analysis of the total packet delay is complicated because it depends on the state of the system at the arrival epoch of a packet and the packet arrival process while the packet is waiting in the queue. The total time spent by a packet in the system is the sum of the packet's waiting time in the queue and the service time of the frame the packet belongs to. Thus, we focus on the frame which contains the packet of interest. The size of this frame is determined by the number of packets arriving to the queue during the time interval corresponding to the waiting time of the packet.

Assume now that there are i packets in the queue and j remaining packets in transmission at the arrival epoch of the packet. Also, let $i = nK + r$, for $n \geq 0$ and $r = 0, 1, \cdots, K - 1$. Then, $A_{i,j}$, the number of packets arriving during the packet queuing time has the probability generating function

$$\sum_{k=0}^{\infty} P[A_{i,j} = k]z^k = R^*(\lambda - \lambda z)[B^*(\lambda - \lambda z)]^{j-1+nK}[B_H^*(\lambda - \lambda z)]^{n+1}. \quad (17)$$

Given i and j, let u_x be the probability that the frame size is equal to x. Then, it is clear that u_x is equal to the coefficient of z^{x-r-1} in (17) for $r + 1 \leq x \leq K - 1$ and $u_K = 1 - \sum_{x=r+1}^{K-1} u_x$. Let v_y be the probability that the number of packets in the frame is equal to y given that there are i packets in the queue and the header is in transmission at the arrival epoch of the packet of interest. Similarly, v_y is obtained as the coefficient of z^{y-r-1} in $R_H^*(\lambda - \lambda z)[B^*(\lambda - \lambda z)]^{nK}[B_H^*(\lambda - \lambda z)]^n$ for $r + 1 \leq y \leq K - 1$ and $v_K = 1 - \sum_{x=r+1}^{K-1} v_x$. Therefore, the LST of the total delay of the packet, $S^*(s) \triangleq E[e^{-sT}] = p_{(0)}B^*(s)B_H^*(s) + \sum_{n=0}^{\infty} \sum_{r=0}^{K-1} \sum_{j=1}^{K} \sum_{k=1}^{m} \sum_{x=r+1}^{K} P_{(nK+r,j,k)}u_x R^*(s)[B^*(s)]^{j-1+nK+x}[B_H^*(s)]^{n+2} + \sum_{n=0}^{\infty} \sum_{r=0}^{K-1} \sum_{l=1}^{\infty} \sum_{y=r+1}^{K} P_{(nK+r,0,l)}v_y R_H^*(s)[B^*(s)]^{nK+y}[B_H^*(s)]^{n+1}$. Finally, the average waiting time of a packet, $E[W_q] = -\frac{d}{ds}W^*(s)|_{s=0}$ and the average total delay of a packet transmitted by the system, $E[S] = -\frac{d}{ds}S^*(s)|_{s=0}$.

4 Numerical Results and Future Work

In all experiments of this section, the average size of transmitted packets, m_1, is set to 1. First, we verify results of our analysis with numerical results of a simulation model of the system. We compare analytical and simulation results for $\bar{k}$, the average number of packets aggregated in a frame, as a function of K for different values of ρ.

The results which we do not tabulate here show that for $\rho = 0.5$, the difference between analytical and simulation results is less than 2.3%. For $\rho = 0.7$, the difference does not exceed 4.9%, and for $\rho = 0.9$, the difference is less than 12%. The larger difference between simulation and analytical results for larger values of ρ is due to a higher variance of the number of packets in a frame for larger values of ρ.

95% confidence intervals for the simulation results does not exceed 0.7% for experiments in which $\rho = 0.5$ and $\rho = 0.7$. The confidence intervals does not exceed 2.5% for experiments in which $\rho = 0.9$.

Table 1. $\tilde{K}$ for different ρ, c^2, and $H_1 = 0.05$, $H_2 = 0.1$, $H_3 = 0.15$

c^2	$\rho=0.3$			$\rho=0.5$			$\rho=0.7$			$\rho=0.8$			$\rho=0.9$		
	H_1	H_2	H_3	H_1	H_2	H_3	H_1	H_2	H_3	H_1	H_2	H_3	H_1	H_2	H_3
0.5	1	1	1	1	1	1	2	2	2	2	3	4	4	6	6
1	1	1	1	1	1	1	2	2	3	2	3	4	4	6	8
4	1	1	1	1	1	2	2	3	3	3	4	5	6	9	11
10	1	1	1	1	2	2	2	3	4	4	6	7	8	12	16

The results also show that for $\rho = 0.5$ and $\rho = 0.7$, the average number of packets transmitted in a frame essentially does not depend on K, for $K \geq 5$. Note also that the difference in $\bar{k}$ for the case of $\rho = 0.5$ and $\rho = 0.7$ is small. On the other hand, when $\rho = 0.9$, $\bar{k}$ is roughly twice larger than in the case of the moderate load.

In Table 1, we provide values of $\tilde{K}$, the maximum number of packets in the frame which provides the minimum average total packet delay, for different values of ρ, H, and c^2 of the packet size distribution. Results of Table 1 show that when system load is low or moderate ($\rho < 0.8$), $\tilde{K}$ is almost independent of c^2. There is also little dependency of $\tilde{K}$ on H in this case. As the system load gets higher ($\rho \geq 0.8$), $\tilde{K}$ increases with increasing c^2 and H. For instance, when $\rho = 0.9$, $c^2 = 10$, and $H = 0.15$, $\tilde{K}$ is two times larger than in the case when $H = 0.05$ and the other parameters are the same. Note also that for each of the chosen values of H, when $\rho = 0.9$ and $c^2 = 10$, $\tilde{K}$ is two times larger comparing to the case when $c^2 \leq 1$. The same conclusion also holds for $\rho = 0.8$ and each value of $H = 0.05$ and $H = 0.1$.

As a continuation to this work, we are planing to consider analysis of the system for infinite K. Also, it is interesting to investigate the system with a general packet arrival process modeled by a Markov modulated Poisson process. We also plan on investigating distribution of the total packet delay and its tail behavior for infinite K.

References

1. Akar, N., Oguz, N.C., Sohraby, K.: A Novel Computational Method for Solving Finite QBD Processes, Communications in Statistics, Stochastic Models 16.2 (2000).
2. Akar, N., Oguz, N.C., Sohraby, K.: Matrix-Geometric Solution in Finite and Infinite $M/G/1$ Type Markov Chains: A Unifying Generalized State-Space Approach, IEEE J. on Selected Areas in Communications 16 (5) (1998).
3. Akar, N., Sohraby, K.: An Invariant Subspace Approach in $M/G/1$ and $G/M/1$ Type Markov Chains, Communications in Statistics, Stochastic Models 13 (3) (1997).
4. Bailey, N.T.J.: On queuing process with bulk service, J. of Royal Statistical Association 16 Series B (1954) 80-87.
5. Chaudhry, M.L., Templeton, J.G.C.: A First Course in Bulk Queues, Wiley New York (1983).

6. Chaudhry, M.L., Medhi, J., Sim, S.H., Templeton, J.G.C.: On a two hetrogeneous-server Markovian queue with general bulk service rule, Sankhyā 49 Series B (1987) 35-50.
7. Flanagan, W. A.: Voice over Frame Relay, Telecom Books New York (1997).
8. Medhi, J.: Waiting time distribution in a Poisson queue with general bulk service rule, Management Sci. 21 (1975) 777-782.
9. Medhi, J.: Recent Developments in Bulk Queueing Models, Wiley Eastern New Delhi (1984).
10. Medhi, J.: Stochastic Models in Queueuing Theory, 2nd ed., Academic Press (2003).
11. Neuts, M.F.: A general class of bulk queues with Poisson input, Ann. Math. Stat. 38 (1967) 759-770.
12. Neuts, M.F.: Matrix-Geometric Solutions to Stochastic Models-An Algorithmic Approach, The Johns Hopkins University Press Baltimore (1981).
13. Sim, S.H., Templeton, J.G.C.: Steady state results for the $M/M(a,b)/c$ batch service system, Euro. J. Operations Research 21 (1985) 260-267.

On the Use of Principle Component Analysis for the Hurst Parameter Estimation of Long-Range Dependent Network Traffic

Melike Erol[1], Tayfun Akgul[2], Sema Oktug[3], and Suleyman Baykut[4]

[1,3]Department of Computer Engineering
[2,4]Department of Electronics and Communications Engineering
Istanbul Technical University
Maslak, 34469, Istanbul, Turkey
[1]`erol@ce.itu.edu.tr`, [2]`tayfun@ehb.itu.edu.tr`, [3]`oktug@ce.itu.edu.tr`,
[4]`baykut@ehb.itu.edu.tr`

Abstract. Long-range dependency and self-similarity are the major characteristics of the Internet traffic. The degree of self-similarity is measured by the Hurst parameter (H). Various methods have been proposed to estimate H. One of the recent methods is an eigen domain estimator which is based on Principle Component Analysis (PCA); a popular signal processing tool. The PCA-based Method (PCAbM) uses the progression of the eigenvalues which are extracted from the autocorrelation matrix. For a self-similar process, this progression obeys a power-law relationship from which H can be estimated. In this paper, we compare PCAbM with some of the well-known estimation methods, namely; periodogram-based, wavelet-based estimation methods and show that PCAbM is reliable only when the process is long-range dependent (LRD), i.e., H is greater than 0.5. We also apply PCAbM and the other estimators to real network traces.

1 Introduction

The Internet traffic is known to be self-similar since 1990s [1]. The recognition of self-similarity in Internet traffic has led to a large number of studies. Some of these works focus on accurately modeling the traffic [1,2] where some focus on the causes and effects of self-similarity [3,4,5]. Besides these, there are various works on robust estimation of the degree of self-similarity.

The degree of self-similarity is measured by the Hurst parameter and there are a handful of methods to estimate H. These methods usually exploit time, spectral or wavelet domain properties of a self-similar process [6,7,8]. A newly proposed method uses Principle Component Analysis; a technique that is widely employed in signal processing applications for reducing the dimension of a data set. The PCA-based Method (PCAbM) utilizes the eigen domain properties of a self-similar process [9,10].

In this paper, we compare the performance of PCAbM with periodogram and wavelet based methods. We test and compare these methods on artificial data and real network traffic. For artificial data, we produce self-similar traces

A. Levi et al. (Eds.): ISCIS 2006, LNCS 4263, pp. 464–473, 2006.

via several methods; random midpoint displacement [11], Fourier-based spectral generation [12], wavelet-based generation [8], circulant embedding method [13,14] and show that PCAbM produces similar results to the other estimation methods for all of the artificial traces when $H > 0.5$. Next, we apply PCAbM, periodogram and wavelet-based estimation methods to two real traffic traces collected at UNC (University of North Carolina) DIRT (Distributed and Real-Time Systems) laboratory in 2002. We show that PCAbM is a reliable estimator for LRD network traffic.

This paper is organized as follows. In Section 2, we give a brief introduction to self-similarity and long-range dependency. We introduce PCAbM in Section 3. In Section 4, we demonstrate our simulations and in Section 5, we apply the estimation methods to real Internet traces. We conclude our paper in Section 6.

2   Self-similarity and Long-Range Dependency

A self-similar process can be defined in time domain using its invariance along scales. Formally, a Statistically Self-similar (SSS) process, $x(t)$ has the scaling form [15]:

$$x(t) =^d a^{-H} x(at) \tag{1}$$

where $=^d$ denotes the equality of distributions and a is a positive real constant. H, defined between 0 and 1, is the Hurst parameter that is used to characterize the correlation structure of the SSS process. When $0.5 < H < 1$ the SSS process is long-range dependent which is usually the case for the network traffic. The samples of long-range dependent time series are correlated even for large lags, in other words the correlation function decays slowly. On the other hand, if there is correlation only between closely spaced samples then $0 < H < 0.5$ and the time series is short-range dependent. If the samples are uncorrelated then $H = 1/2$ and the process is white noise [15].

The spectral behavior of an SSS process obeys a power-law relation:

$$S_x(\omega) \sim \sigma_x^2 |\omega|^{-\gamma} \tag{2}$$

where $S_x(\omega)$ is the empirical power spectrum and σ_x^2 is the variance of $x(t)$, ω is the angular frequency and γ is the spectral exponent [8]. Here, γ is related to H as $\gamma = 2H + 1$ for fBm (fractional Brownian motion), and $\gamma = 2H - 1$ for fGn (fractional Gaussian noise) [16]. fBm and its incremental stationary version fGn are widely used to model self-similar (or $1/f$) processes. Network traffic is assumed to be stationary within a few hours and it is widely modeled by fGn.

3   Hurst Parameter Estimation with PCA

There are various Hurst parameter estimation methods defined in different domains where time, frequency and wavelet domain properties of an SSS process have been used [6,7,8]. Recently, eigen domain interpretation is shown to be applicable to fBm traces [9]. In [10], it is analytically proven that the Principle Component Analysis-based Method (PCAbM) can only be used for fBm series when $0 < H < 0.5$. In this paper, by simulations, we show that it can be employed to LRD fGn traces, i.e., fGn traces with $0.5 < H < 1$. As network traffic typically shows LRD, we suggest that PCAbM can be used for network traffic.

PCA is a linear transformation which formes a new coordinate system for the data set such that the most representative features lie on the first axis (the first principal component) and the second most representative features lie on the second axis and so on. This enables the lower-order principle components (eigenvalues) contain sufficient information about the data set, hence PCA reduces the dimension of a data set while keeping its most important characteristics.

PCAbM uses the eigenvalues obtained from the autocorrelation matrix, $\mathbf{R}$, of a self-similar process. The progression of these eigenvalues is then used to estimate H. The eigenvalues can be determined via:

$$\mathbf{R}\varphi_n = \lambda_n \varphi_n \tag{3}$$

where λ_n and φ_n, $n = 1, ..., N$ are the eigenvalues and the eigenvectors, respectively, for $N \times N$ dimensional $\mathbf{R}$. Here, N is the data length. The progression of the eigenvalues (sorted in decreasing order) and the indices are proportional [9,10];

$$\lambda_n \sim n^{-\gamma} \tag{4}$$

The spectral exponent γ is calculated by taking the logarithm of both sides of (4) and as we already know $\gamma = 2H - 1$ for fGn.

In Figure 1, we provide a sample regression plot for PCAbM. We present an artificial trace with $H = 0.8$ that is generated by the wavelet based generation method (as described in Section 4). PCAbM estimates $\hat{H} = 0.8246$ which is close to the original H value.

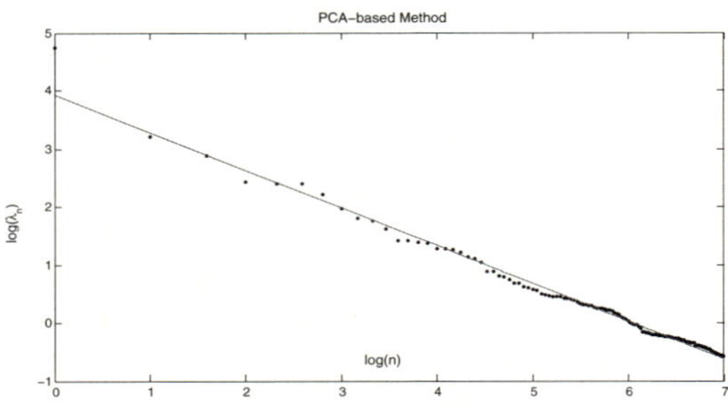

Fig. 1. PCAbM example for artificial data with H=0.8 generated via wavelet based method where N=8192 ($\hat{H}$=0.8246)

4   Simulations

In this section, the performance of PCAbM is analyzed in detail. We also provide the overall results of the simulations including periodogram and wavelet based methods. Before the simulation results, we briefly introduce artificial fGn generation methods and the other two estimation methods; periodogram and wavelet-based estimation methods.

4.1   Self-similar Process Generation

We compare the performance of the estimation methods using artificial fGn data sets that are generated with random midpoint displacement [11], fourier-based spectral generation [12], wavelet-based generation [8] and circulant embedding methods [13,14]. We use different generation methods to make our comparisons fair and independent of generation methods.

Random Midpoint Displacement

Random Midpoint Displacement Method (RMDM) [11] starts with two initial points at 0 and N where N is the desired data length. Initially, these points are interpolated by placing a point at $N/2$. This method is based on recursively placing midpoints until the process with N points is achieved. These midpoints are calculated by using the variance relation of an fBm process.

Fourier-based Spectral Generation

Fourier-based Spectral Generation Method (FbSGM) [12] uses the spectral property of a self-similar process given in (2). First the spectrum is constructed according to H and then by an inverse Fourier transform the corresponding fGn process is formed.

Wavelet-based Generation

Wavelet-based method can be used in estimating the H parameter as well as self-similar trace generation. The wavelet transform of a self-similar process, $x(n)$, gives the wavelet coefficients, x_k^m, which are mutually uncorrelated, zero-mean, Gaussian random variables with variances obeying the power-law relationship [8]:

$$var \left\{ x_k^m \right\} = \sigma^2 2^{-\gamma m} \tag{5}$$

Wavelet-based Generation Method (WbGM) first calculates the variances of the wavelet coefficients according to H parameter (or γ), then produces zero-mean, Gaussian random noise with the specified variances. These are used as the wavelet coefficients in the inverse wavelet transform to generate the self-similar trace.

Circulant Embedding Method

Circulant Embedding Method (CEM) [13,14] decomposes the circulant matrix $\mathbf{S}$ that is formed by embedding the covariance matrix $\mathbf{R}$ of a self-similar process. The entries of $\mathbf{R}$ are computed according to the given H parameter and NxN $\mathbf{R}$ is embedded into $2M$x$2M$ $\mathbf{S}$ such that $M \geq N - 1$. Later, $\mathbf{S}$ is decomposed as $\mathbf{S}{=}\mathbf{FDF}^H$. Here, $\mathbf{F}$ is a $2M$x$2M$ matrix with entries $f_{ij} = 1/2M$ x $\exp(-2\pi ij/2M)$ and $\mathbf{F}^H$ is the conjugate transpose of $\mathbf{F}$. The sample path of the SSS process is attained by using D in $y = FD^{1/2}v$ where v is a complex vector with i.i.d entries. Here, imaginary or real part of $\mathbf{y}$ can be used as the self-similar trace.

4.2   Hurst Parameter Estimation

At this point, we describe the H parameter estimation methods which are used to compare the performance of PCAbM. We do not discuss some well-known

time domain methods such as, R/S, aggregated variances or Higuchi methods
due to their computational inefficiency for long data sets; e.g. network traces
considered in Section 5.

Periodogram-based Method

Periodogram is commonly used in power spectral density (PSD) estimation. The
PSD of a self-similar process is given in (2). Periodogram-based Method (PbM)
estimates γ from the logarithmic plot of $S_x(\omega)$ versus ω of (2) [6].

Wavelet-based Estimation Method

Wavelet-based Estimation Method (WbEM) is widely used in networking community. There is a readily available wavelet-based analysis tool on the web [7],
however, we use an implementation based on [8] which gives similar results.
WbEM first calculates the wavelet coefficients by taking the wavelet transform
of the self-similar process. It estimates γ from the progression of the variances
of the wavelet coefficients by taking the logarithm of both sides of (5).

4.3   Simulation Results

We generate processes with varying H values between 0.1 and 0.9 with 0.1 increments. For each of the four generation methods (RMDM, FbSGM, WbGM and
CEM) and nine different H values, we generate $K = 50$ traces of length N=8192
and compute mean, variance, mean-square error (MSE) where MSE is defined as:

$$MSE = \frac{1}{K} \sum_{i=1}^{K} (H_i - \hat{H}_i)^2 \tag{6}$$

Here, $\hat{H}_i$ denotes the estimated Hurst parameter. The estimation results for
PbM, WbEM, PCAbM are given in Table 1. Our simulation results show that
PCAbM can not be used for fGn when $H \leq 0.5$. For $H > 0.5$, i.e. when the
process is LRD, PCAbM can be used. In this range, it produces estimates with
small $\sqrt{\varepsilon}$ (square root of MSE) values. Our results suggest that, PCAbM is
suitable for the Internet traffic which is a typical example of LRD process. Here,
we only focus on the performance of PCAbM because PbM and WbEM are
well-known estimators and their comparisons can be found in [15]. In the next
section, we give the estimation results for real Internet traces.

5   Application of the PCA-Based Method to Network Traffic

We use two byte count processes formed from the Internet traffic traces that are
collected from a link between UNC (University of North Carolina) and its service provider at 2002. The traces are available from the web site of UNC DIRT
laboratory [17]. The byte count processes are formed by binning the traces over
1 ms and 10ms periods. We choose the byte count processes binned at 10ms on

Table 1. $\mu_{\hat{H}}$, $\sigma_{\hat{H}}^2$ and $\sqrt{\varepsilon}$ values for 50 realizations for $N = 8192$. (Generation methods are given in rows and estimation methods are given in columns.)

		Estimation Methods								
	Generation	PbM			WbEM			PCAbM		
H	**Methods**	$\mu_{\hat{H}}$	$\sigma_{\hat{H}}^2(\times 10^{-3})$	$\sqrt{\varepsilon}$	$\mu_{\hat{H}}$	$\sigma_{\hat{H}}^2(\times 10^{-3})$	$\sqrt{\varepsilon}$	$\mu_{\hat{H}}$	$\sigma_{\hat{H}}^2(\times 10^{-3})$	$\sqrt{\varepsilon}$
0.1	RMDM	0.1134	0.5125	0.0263	0.2154	3.7822	0.1308	0.5742	0.0468	0.4742
	FbSGM	0.0308	0.0206	0.0693	0.1419	10.7084	0.1117	0.5576	0.0759	0.4576
	WbGM	0.0950	0.4625	0.0221	0.1982	7.0818	0.1294	0.5766	0.3601	0.4767
	CEM	0.0289	0.5948	0.0752	0.1572	11.9817	0.1235	0.5943	0.0505	0.4944
0.2	RMDM	0.2134	0.7160	0.0299	0.2754	2.8396	0.0924	0.5692	0.0417	0.3693
	FbSGM	0.1745	0.0222	0.0259	0.2343	4.9542	0.0783	0.5463	0.0468	0.3463
	WbGM	0.1975	0.3200	0.0181	0.2697	5.5752	0.1022	0.5705	0.3015	0.3706
	CEM	0.1750	0.6277	0.0354	0.2255	4.8276	0.0740	0.5870	0.0270	0.3870
0.3	RMDM	0.3001	0.4965	0.0223	0.3445	1.7879	0.0614	0.5637	0.0340	0.2638
	FbSGM	0.2897	0.0204	0.0112	0.3169	2.0073	0.0479	0.5372	0.0648	0.2372
	WbGM	0.2988	0.2613	0.0162	0.3415	2.5739	0.0655	0.5666	0.3119	0.2667
	CEM	0.2900	0.5670	0.0258	0.3209	2.5860	0.0550	0.5755	0.0344	0.2756
0.4	RMDM	0.4006	0.4487	0.0212	0.4162	0.6779	0.0307	0.5588	0.0436	0.1589
	FbSGM	0.3967	0.0385	0.0070	0.3995	0.6479	0.0255	0.5274	0.0289	0.1274
	WbGM	0.3996	0.3013	0.0168	0.4133	0.8787	0.0325	0.5585	0.2648	0.1586
	CEM	0.3938	0.4474	0.0220	0.4054	1.3621	0.0373	0.5637	0.0307	0.1638
0.5	RMDM	0.4941	0.4860	0.0228	0.5047	0.5651	0.0242	0.5512	0.0168	0.0514
	FbSGM	0.4999	0.0308	0.0056	0.5009	0.4942	0.0223	0.5156	0.0240	0.0156
	WbGM	0.5009	0.2818	0.0174	0.5069	0.7321	0.0279	0.5513	0.2572	0.0516
	CEM	0.5008	0.7769	0.0279	0.5011	0.9022	0.0301	0.5515	0.0231	0.0518
0.6	RMDM	0.5970	0.6101	0.0249	0.5846	0.3989	0.0252	0.5988	0.1113	0.0106
	FbSGM	0.6038	0.0328	0.0069	0.6018	0.2876	0.0171	0.6122	0.1361	0.0128
	WbGM	0.5999	0.2321	0.0152	0.5972	0.3407	0.0187	0.6030	0.2899	0.0062
	CEM	0.5973	0.5824	0.0243	0.6035	0.5095	0.0228	0.6131	0.1005	0.0165
0.7	RMDM	0.7011	0.3593	0.0190	0.6761	0.2128	0.0280	0.6993	0.1121	0.0106
	FbSGM	0.7031	0.0178	0.0052	0.6987	0.1534	0.0125	0.7217	0.0989	0.0220
	WbGM	0.6976	0.3023	0.0175	0.6892	0.1730	0.0170	0.7055	0.2775	0.0076
	CEM	0.7039	0.6568	0.0259	0.7054	0.3865	0.0204	0.7259	0.1295	0.0283
0.8	RMDM	0.7996	0.5848	0.0242	0.7660	0.3639	0.0390	0.8008	0.1380	0.0118
	FbSGM	0.8012	0.0286	0.0055	0.8007	0.1110	0.0106	0.8321	0.1741	0.0323
	WbGM	0.8015	0.3416	0.0185	0.7892	0.0647	0.0135	0.8169	0.5674	0.0185
	CEM	0.7974	0.6234	0.0251	0.7991	0.3372	0.0184	0.8305	0.1625	0.0331
0.9	RMDM	0.8916	0.5367	0.0246	0.8611	0.2451	0.0419	0.9076	0.2067	0.0163
	FbSGM	0.9035	0.0238	0.0060	0.8990	0.0984	0.0100	0.9441	0.1504	0.0442
	WbGM	0.8980	0.3642	0.0192	0.8869	0.1067	0.0167	0.9243	0.4264	0.0251
	CEM	0.9024	0.4388	0.0211	0.9009	0.3152	0.0178	0.9446	0.2122	0.0469

April 11 and 12 between 3-5 AM. We pick these traces after analyzing all of the provided traces. The traces that contain trend and periodicity are excluded because they are known to be misleading the estimation methods [18].

In Figure 2, we give the first trace[1]. In Figure 3, we give the regression plots of the estimation methods for this trace. The Hurst parameters estimated by PbM, WbEM and PCAbM are 0.7629, 0.7997, 0.7890, respectively.

---

[1] File name: 2002_Apr_11_Thu_0300.7260.sk1.10ms.B_P.ts.

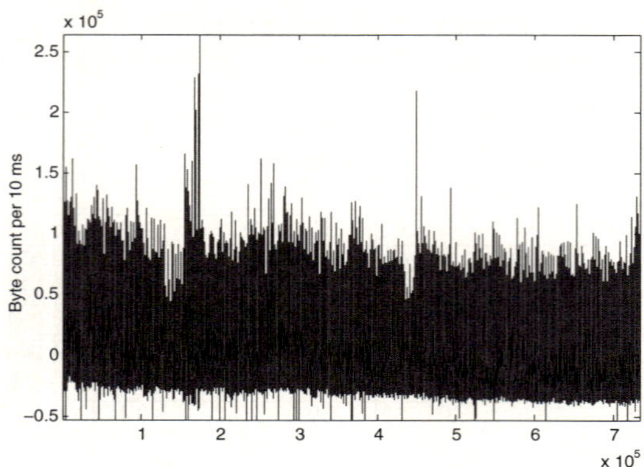

Fig. 2. Two hour-long trace on April 11, 2002 between 03:00-05:00 AM

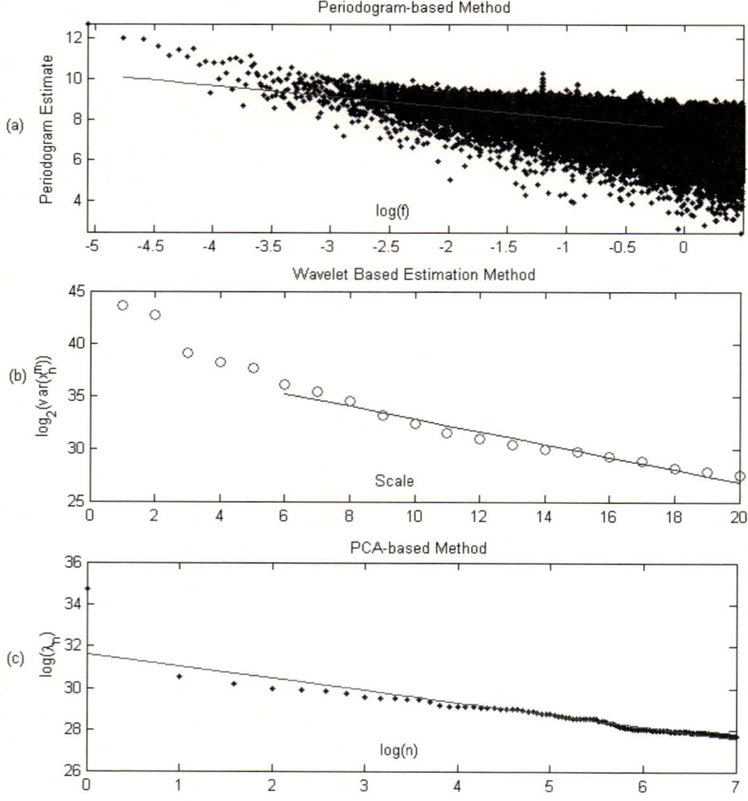

Fig. 3. The regression plots for (a) PbM $\hat{H}$=0.7629, (b) WbEM $\hat{H}$=0.7997, (c) PCAbM $\hat{H}$=0.7890 for the trace collected at UNC on 11 April 2002

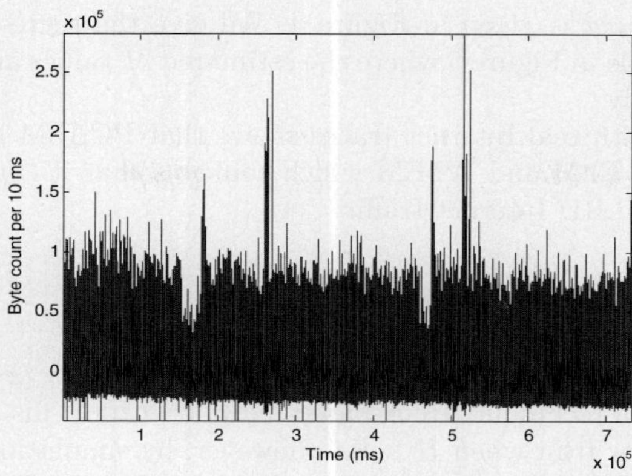

Fig. 4. Two hour-long trace on April 12, 2002 between 03:00-05:00 AM

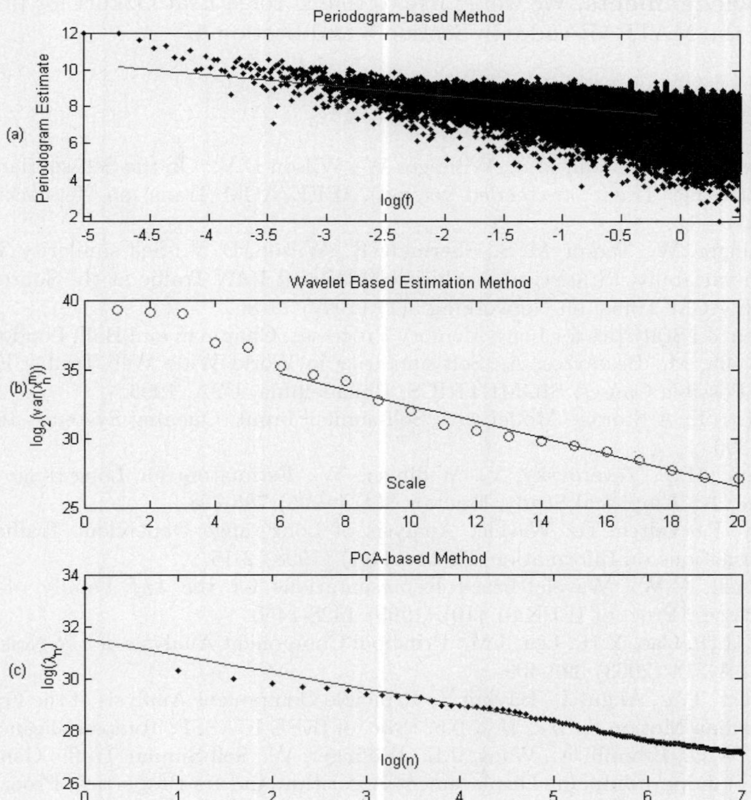

Fig. 5. The regression plots for (a) PbM $\hat{H}$=0.7794, (b) WbEM $\hat{H}$=0.7927, (c) PCAbM $\hat{H}$=0.8182 for the trace collected at UNC on 12 April 2002

The second trace[2] is given in Figure 4. We give the regression plots of the estimation methods in Figure 5 where the estimated H values are 0.7794, 0.7927, 0.8182, respectively.

Our analysis with real Internet traces shows that PCAbM method produces close estimates to PbM and WbEM which confirms that it can be used in estimating H for the LRD Internet traffic.

6   Conclusion

In this paper, we discuss the estimation results of a recently proposed Hurst parameter estimation technique, PCA-based method [9,10]. This method is known to be unreliable for fBm when $H > 0.5$, however, by simulations, we show that it can be used for fGn when $H > 0.5$. We also show that the PCA-based method produces reliable estimates for LRD network traffic.

Acknowledgements. We would like to thank Tolga Esat Ozkurt for providing some of the MATLAB codes in Section 3 and Section 4.

References

1. Leland, W.E., Taqqu, M.S., Willinger W., Wilson D.V.: On the Self-similar Nature of Ethernet Traffic, (extended version). IEEE/ACM Trans. on Networking 2(1) (1993) 1-15.
2. Willinger, W., Taqqu, M. S., Sherman, R., Wilson, D. V.: Self-similarity Through High-variability: Statistical Analysis of Ethernet LAN Traffic at the Source Level. IEEE ACM Trans. on Networking 5(1) (1997) 71-86.
3. Beran, J.: Statistics for Long-Memory Processes. Chapman and Hall, London, 1994.
4. Crovella, M., Bestavros, A.: Self-similarity in World Wide Web Traffic: Evidence and Possible Causes. SIGMETRICS, Philadelphia, USA, 1996.
5. Norros, I.: A Storage Model with Self-similar Input. Queuing Systems, 16 (1994) 387-396.
6. Taqqu, M.S., Teverovsky, V., Willinger, W.: Estimators for Long-range Dependence: An Empirical Study. Fractals 3(4) (1995) 785-798.
7. Abry, P., Veitch, D.: Wavelet Analysis of Long-range Dependent Traffic. IEEE Transactions on Information Theory 44(1) (1998) 2-15.
8. Wornell, G.W.: Wavelet-based Representations for the $1/f$ Family of Fractal Processes. Proc. of IEEE 81 (10) (1993) 1428-1450.
9. Gao, J.B., Cao, Y.H., Lee, J.M.: Principal Component Analysis of $1/f$ Noise. Phys. Lett. A 314 (2003) 392-400.
10. Ozkurt, T.E., Akgul T., Baykut S.: Principle Component Analysis of the Fractional Brownian Motion for $0 < H < 0.5$. Proc. of IEEE ICASSP, Toulosse, France, 2006.
11. Lau, W.C., Eramilli A., Wang, J.L., Willinger, W.: Self-Similar Traffic Generation: The Random Midpoint Displacement Algorithm and Its Properties. Proc. of ICC, Seattle, USA, 1995.
12. Paxon, V.: Fast, Approximate Synthesis of Fractional Gaussian Noise for Generating Self-Similar Network Traffic, Comp. Comm. Rew. 27 (1997) 5-18.

---

[2] File name: $2002\_Apr\_12\_Fri\_0300.7260.sk1.10ms.B\_P.ts$.

13. Dietrich, C.R., Newsam, G.N.: Fast and Exact Simulation of Stationary Gaussian Processes Through Circulant Embedding of the Covariance Matrix. Siam J. Sci. Comput. 18(4) (1997) 1088-1107.
14. Perrin, E., Harba, R., Jennane, R., Iribarren, I.: Fast and Exact Synthesis for 1-D Fractional Brownian Motion and Fractional Gaussian Noises. IEEE Signal Processing Letters 9(11) (2002) 382-384.
15. Doukhan, P., Oppenheim G., Taqqu M.S.: Theory and Applications of Long-Range Dependence. Birkäuser, Basel, 2003.
16. Mandelbrot, B.B., Van Ness, J.W.: Fractional Brownian Motions, Fractional Noise and Applications, SIAM Review 10(4) (1968) 422-437.
17. UNC DIRT Laboratory Internet traces, http://www-dirt.cs.unc.edu/ts/
18. Erol, M., Akgul, T., Baykut, S., Oktug, S.: Analysis of the Hurst Parameter Estimation Methods for Network Traffic Containing Periodicity. *submitted to* Elsevier Computer Networks 2006.

Throughput Analysis of UDP and VPN Traffic in 802.11g Networks

Süheyla Ikiz[1] and Y.M. Erten[2]

[1] Informatics Institute, Middle East Technical University, Ankara - Turkey
suheylaikiz@gmail.com
[2] Computer Engineering Department, TOBB Economics and Technology University,
Ankara - Turkey
erten@etu.edu.tr

Abstract. In this study the effects of using VPNs on the throughput of wireless LANs are investigated. To this end we have set up a test bed and based our observations on the actual measurements obtained from the experiments performed using this test bed. The wireless LAN we have used is an IEEE 802.11g network and we compared the throughput values obtained by employing IPSec in this network with the calculated ones. We performed the tests using periodically generated traffic with 1ms and 5 ms intervals between successive packets. We have also considered the case for random traffic generated according to exponential distribution. We present the variations of the throughput with respect to packet size for different input traffic patterns.

1 Introduction

Wireless networks are being deployed at offices, homes and public places at an increasing rate. They are easier to setup, more flexible and offer cost savings over their wired counterparts. There are, however, many parameters which make the use of these networks different. Due to the characteristic of the medium and protocols used, the error rates are higher and maximum achievable throughput is lower than the expected maximum as shown in [6].

Security is another issue where wired networks are superior. Considerable research is carried out in wireless network security where there are many challenging areas open to further study. Wireless networks use Wired Equivalent Privacy (WEP) for secure communications but the authentication and integrity offered by this scheme does not completely protect a network against Man-in-the-Middle, Peer-to-Peer and Denial Service attacks [9]. Wi-Fi Protected Access which is introduced by Wi-Fi Alliance as part of the emerging 802.11i standard improves wireless LAN security considerably by enhanced encryption, authentication and key management methods. 802.11i, however, is not immune against threats such as RF jamming and Denial of Service (DoS) attacks. Furthermore, security methods of 802.11i have not been tested long enough to be proven to be as strong as claimed [9].

A. Levi et al. (Eds.): ISCIS 2006, LNCS 4263, pp. 474–482, 2006.

It may be possible to create a secure environment in wireless networks based on Virtual Private Network technology which is well understood and widely used in wired networks. The main purpose of using VPN is to provide a secure connection between remote users over the Internet or public telecommunications infrastructures. In this approach secure tunnels are established between the distant locations and the data inside the tunnels is encrypted after both sites agree on the cryptographic entities. One of the most widely used VPN protocol is IPSec which provides security at the network layer and achieves message integrity using encryption.

Current recommendations for wireless deployments suggest the use of VPN for wireless clients to provide both authentication and privacy [8], [9]. This combination is usually referred to as Wireless Virtual Private Networks (WVPNs) [7]. Some universities already started to implement VPN to secure their wireless data networks [8]. In this study we have attempted to investigate how the performance of WLANs are affected when VPNs are used to provide end-to-end security for wireless LAN users.

As the wireless links have limited bandwidth and higher error rates, introducing VPN into the connections may influence the QoS parameters such as error rate and packet loss as well as the throughput. Munasinghe et al evaluated the use of wireless VPN in IEEE 802.11b networks in [7]. We have, on the other hand, measured the effects of using IPSec connections on the throughput of IEEE 802.11g networks using the testbed that we have set up as described in section 3. We tested the network under uniform traffic with different size packets generated at fixed intervals. We have also measured the performance of the network with packets generated according to exponential distribution. We compared the measured throughput with the calculated one for UDP and IPSec traffic. Our contribution has been the use of an IEEE 802.11g network, comparison of the measured throughput with the calculated one and introduction of random traffic into the studies. Although IEEE 802.11g network performance has been investigated in [3], the authors did not consider VPN connections in that study.

The rest of the paper is organized as follows. In section 2 we have introduced the calculations of the throughput in the wireless LANs. The methodology used for the experiments is explained in Section 3 in detail. The results are presented and discussed in section 4 and conclusions are included in section 5 together with proposed further research areas.

2 Throughput Analysis in Wireless LANs

In general, the packets transmitted in a network contains both the payload and protocol overheads. Throughput, which is defined as the amount of payload transmitted in unit time, can be calculated for wireless networks taking these overheads into consideration [1],[3]-[6].

IEEE 802.11 networks use CSMA/CA for transmission of packets. The details of this protocol is presented in different sources [2], [5]. We shall just present the related time parameters for the calculation of throughput in the following paragraphs. As we have not used RTS/CTS in this study we ignored their effects. Since there is a single source there are no collisions, hence they were also omitted.

In CSMA/CA protocol the source waits for a distributed coordination function inter frame spacing (DIFS) period before transmission. This period, T_{DIFS}, is given as

$$T_{DIFS} = 2 \times T_{SLOT} + T_{SIFS} \tag{1}$$

where T_{SLOT} is the slot time which is 9 μs for IEEE 802.11g neworks and T_{SIFS} is the short interframe space time as explained below.

Following this period there is the time for the contention window, CW, and the delay associated with this, T_{BOFF}, is given in equation 2.

$$T_{BOFF} = \frac{CW_{MIN} \times T_{SLOT}}{2} \tag{2}$$

The transmission time of the data frame, T_D, depends on the payload size and can be calculated as shown in equation 3 for IEEE 802.11g networks transmitting at the defined 54 Mbps rate.

$$T_D = \frac{Payload\,Si\,ze \times 8}{54 \times 10^6} \tag{3}$$

The transmitted packet is acknowledged by the receiver after a short inter frame spacing (SIFS), T_{SIFS}, which is equal to 10 μs for the standard under study. Time to transmit 14 bytes of acknowledgement data, T_{ACK}, is calculated from the given 802.11g bit rates as 2.07 μs.

Layers 3 and 4 as well as the MAC layer adds some protocol overheads to the frame which are also transmitted. The overheads are 8 bytes for UDP, 20 bytes for IP and 34 bytes for the MAC protocols respectively. These account for protocol overhead time, T_{POH}, and based on the data rates can be shown to be 9.19 μs. The physical layer introduces physical layer convergence procedure (PCLP) header and a preamble, the transmission time of which, T_{PHY}, is given in Table 1. There is also a signal extension period which we call T_{SX}. This parameter is given as 6 μsec in IEEE 802.11g specifications [3]. Table 1 gives the values of these parameters calculated or defined for 802.11g networks.

Based on these parameters and Figure 1 which illustrates the above defined IEEE 802.11 MAC layer components, data transmission time, T_P, can be calculated as:

$$T_P = T_{SIFS} + T_{ACK} + T_{DIFS} + T_{BOFF} + T_{POH} + 2 \times T_{PHY} + T_D \tag{4}$$

The reason we have used T_{PHY} twice in this expression is because it is transmitted both for the payload and the acknowledgement, and T_{SX} is included in T_{PHY} for the calculations.

In our experiments we used 1 msec and 5 msec interframe gap between successive frames, therefore, as long as the time required for the transmission of packets is less than this period the throughput is equal to:

$$Throughput = (Frames\ size\ in\ bytes \times 8)/Payload Generation Rate \tag{5}$$

Table 1. IEEE 802.11g parameters

Parameter	802.11g (sec)
T_{ACK}	2.07407E-06
T_{SIFS}	1.0E-05
T_{SLOT}	9.00E-06
T_{DIFS}	2.80E-05
T_{PHY}	2.21E-05
T_{BOFF}	1.4E-04
T_{POH}	9.19E-06
T_{SX}	6.0E-6

If on the other hand actual packet generation time (T_G) exceeds the data transmission period then calculations should be revised accordingly. In this case throughput would be:

$$Throughput = (Frames\ size\ in\ bytes \times 8)/T_G \qquad (6)$$

It should be noted that normally $T_G = T_P$, but T_G may be higher than T_P since there are overheads such as processing delay, retransmission due to packet loss etc..

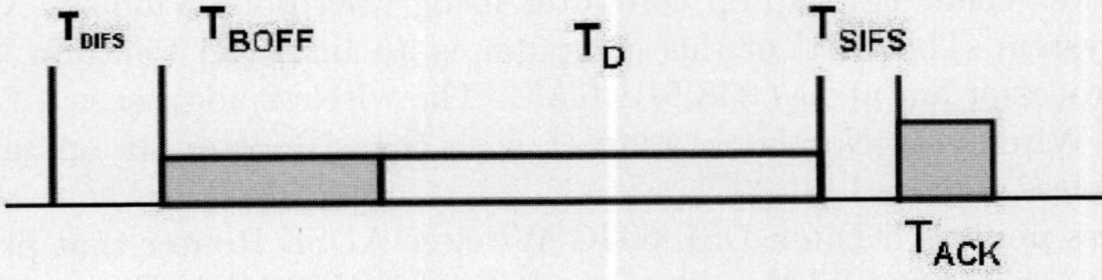

Fig. 1. IEEE 802.11 MAC Layer Mechanism. The protocol overheads are assumed to be included in the data transmission time and propagation delays are ignored.

We have also considered the case where the data packets are produced based on exponential distribution in which case the packet arrival would be a Poisson process. For this case the probability that number of packets, N, arriving during a time period t being equal to n is given as

$$P(N = n) = e^{-\lambda t}(\lambda t)^n / n! \qquad (7)$$

Assuming transmission of the first packet is realized, we calculated the probability of having at least one packet arrive during the transmission of the previous frame. This is given in expression 8

$$P(N \geq 1) = 1 - P(N = 0) \qquad (8)$$

where N is the number of packets generated during period t and $P(N = 0)$ is the probability of having 0 packets generated. Substituting $n = 0$ in equation 7 this expression becomes:

$$P(N \geq 1) = 1 - e^{-\lambda t} \tag{9}$$

and substituting previously calculated T_P for t, equation 9 becomes

$$P(N \geq 1) = 1 - e^{-\lambda T_P} \tag{10}$$

Plots of calculated throughput for different values of packet size are shown in the following sections together with the measured values.

3   Experimental Setup

An experimental network is set up to measure the effects of using VPN in wireless Local Area Networks. The setup includes two computers one of which is a wireless client and the second one is a server. The wireless network connection between them is established through an access point.

Microsoft Windows 2000 Server is used as the server with minimal features installed. This hardware has Intel(R) Pentium (R) 4 Central Processor Unit (CPU) operating at 3.00 GHz and has 1 GB Random Access Memory (RAM). To connect the server to the network a Realtek RTL8139 (A)-Fast Ethernet Adapter is used. This network card supports 100 Mbps connection speeds and it is connected to the access points using 4 meters of 100BaseT cable.

The wireless client is a laptop computer using Microsoft Windows XP Pro operating system. The CPU of this computer is an Intel (R) Pentium (R) III 995 MHz processor and it has 248 MB RAM. The wireless adapter is a Linksys WPC54GS Wireless-G Notebook adapter with SpeedBooster. It operates on 802.11g wireless standard.

The access point is a Dlink DSL-604G Wireless ADSL Router that provides 802.11g/802.11b wireless LAN connection. It has four 100 Mbps Ethernet ports. The antenna transmit power is set to be maximum and only 802.11g protocol is used on the wireless connections. The DSL port is unplugged and it has not been activated. The access point service is enabled and the channel number is set to be 6. No security mechanism such as WEP or WPA is activated. The access point's DHCP service is enabled and only one IP address is assigned to the IP pool. The access point is placed 3-3.5 meters away from wireless client.

This setup is shown in Figure 2. To verify that the connections are active the ping utility is used.

The trial version of Check Point VPN-1 Pro NGX software is used to establish VPN connections. The components of this software suite is used to configure VPN parameters, VPN connections and users. The software suite has firewall utility, but to obtain pure VPN connection performance, this utility is disabled. Only one policy is defined on the server and the encryption algorithm chosen is 3DES with MD5 algorithm for authentication.

The Check Point Secure Remote is used on the client side. This enables us to create a VPN tunnel between a remote user and the server.

The server verifies the client with username and password. This username and password is set on the policy. After the IKE negotiation ends successfully, a

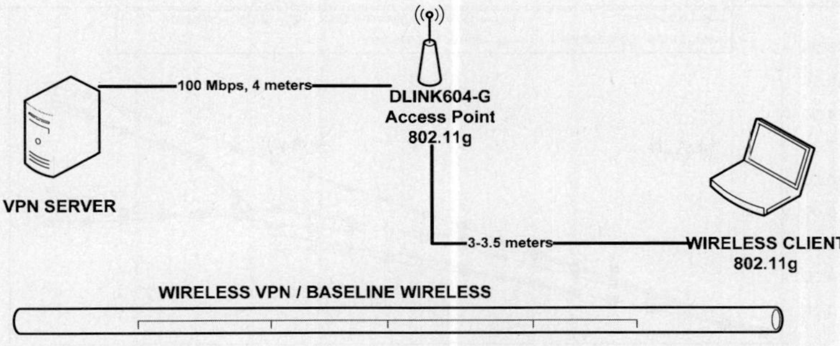

Fig. 2. Experimental Setup

secure connection (a VPN connection) is established between the client and the server.

For the purpose of traffic generation trial version of LAN Traffic v2 software is installed on both the client and the server. The software allows users to change the inter frame time between the packets and in the experiments we used two inter frame times, 1 msec and 5 msec. We also used traffic generated randomly during the experiments and we adopted exponential distribution with $\lambda = 7$ to generate packets. The traffic generator program also allows users to establish multiple simultaneous connections between the peers. Up to three simultaneous connections are used during the experiments.

Throughput of the network is measured using the logging capability of the software as the average amount of data payload transferred from the wireless client.

During the tests the transmitted payload size is modified between 25-1600 bytes for each configuration, and 10000 packets are sent for each trial. Tests are repeated 5 times and the average value is taken.

The throughput sampling is done every 2 msec and UDP timeout value is set to 700 msec. The receiver and sender buffer sizes are set to 25000 bytes separately. To reduce the chance of fragmentation the related parameter was set to 2048 in the wireless network. The test results are discussed in the following sections.

4   Results

Figure 3 shows the results of calculated and measured throughput for 1 ms interframe time. The plots show the throughput for 1 baseline UDP connection, and for one, two and three IPSec connections. The same calculations were repeated for 5 msec inter frame spacing and the results are presented in Figure 4.

As can be observed from the graphs, if the inter frame time is assigned 1 msec then maximum throughput achieved is around 7.7 Mbps for baseline connections. The observed throughput agrees with the calculated one upto packet sizes of 800 bytes. After this it settles to approximately 7.7 Mbps. The explanation for this

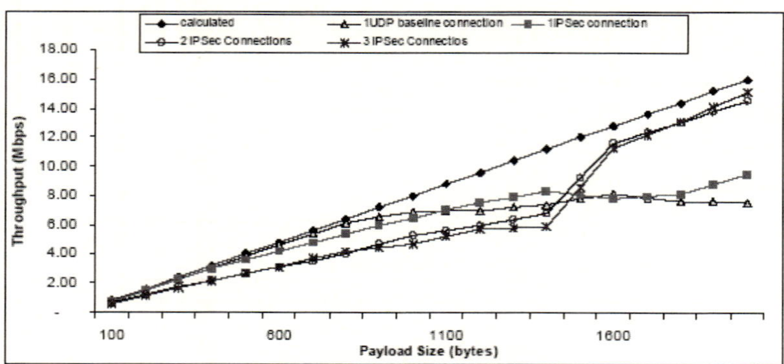

Fig. 3. Calculated and measured Throughput versus frame size for 1 msec inter frame time. The measured values are for 1 baseline and 1,2 and 3 IPSec connections.

is thought to be that it takes longer than 1 ms to generate the larger packets hence the imposed interframe spacing loses its meaning. For one or more IPSec connections with 1 ms interframe time, the achieved throughput is lower than the baseline UDP for packet sizes upto 1500 bytes, after which an improvement is observed for two and three VPN connections. This could be due to fragmentation as the total traffic from two and three IPSec connections form a burst and this burst size exceeds the threshold for fragmentation. The smaller packets thus formed are handled by the system more efficiently as the overheads are lower. In

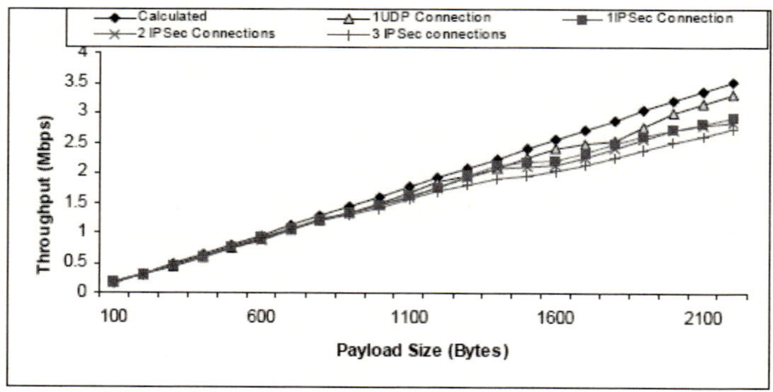

Fig. 4. Calculated and measured Throughput versus frame size for 5 msec inter frame time. The measured values are for 1 baseline and 1,2, and 3 IPSec connections.

the case of 5 ms interframe time, the observed throughput is very similar to the calculated one for packet sizes of upto about 1000 bytes after which a degradation in the throughput starts. UDP baseline connection gives the best throughput of 3.3 Mbps for packet sizes of 2200 bytes and it exhibits an increasing trend. As this interframe time is large enough for packet generation we do not observe the decrease in the throughput as we did for the 1 ms case.

Using IPSec connections with 5 ms interframe time causes a decrease in the throughput. At 2200 byte packet sizes 2.9, 2.85, and 2.74 Mbps throughput is observed for one, two and three simultaneous VPN connections respectively. This is due to the processing overhead and extra data introduced by the IPSec protocol.

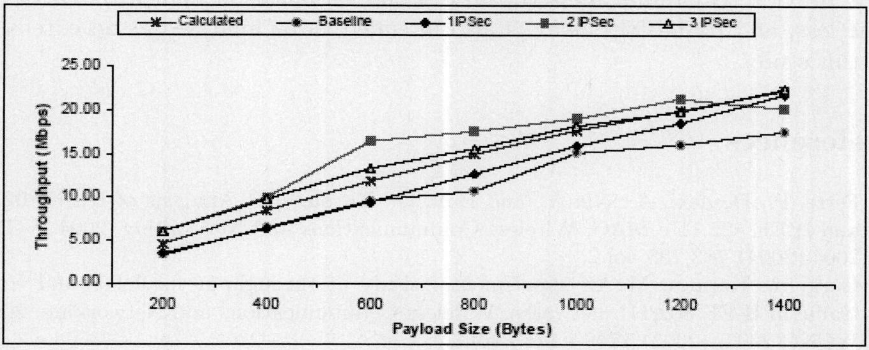

Fig. 5. Calculated and measured Throughput versus frame size for random packets. The payload packets are generated according to exponential distribution as explained in the text.

For random traffic a throughput of upto 22 Mbps is obtained for packet sizes of 1400 bytes. IPSec traffic behaves better than expected for most of the payload sizes and performs fairly closely to the calculated results especially for high packet sizes as shown in Figure 5. In this case we have only included packets upto 1400 bytes because accurate measurements could not be obtained for larger values. The observed throughput is higher because we are not forcing the source to generate packets periodically as in the previous cases. The maximum throughput is still lower than the theoretical maximum of 54 Mbps.

We have compared our results with those found in [7] for IEEE 802.11b network. The results show an improvement in the IEEE 802.11g network as expected due to the higher bit rates offered. The observed throughput for single baseline UDP connection in an IEEE 802.11b network was reported to be 5.97 Mbps there, where as the same throughput is measured to be 7.79 Mbps in our case. IPSec connections in [7] also show worse performance compared to the baseline one, but accurate readings are not possible from the graphs.

5   Conclusions

In this study, an experimental setup is used to evaluate the throughput of IEEE 802.11g networks when IPSec VPNs are used. The analysis point out that the inter frame time between the packets, number of simultaneous VPN connection and packet sizes are important parameters affecting throughput in these networks. As the frames are generated more frequently an improvement in the throughput is observed as expected. For high payload sizes the difference between the actual and calculated results increase as packet generation takes longer. Random traffic generates best throughput and using VPN connections reduce the throughput for most of the cases.

Computer simulation of the infrastructure using ns2 or a similar simulator may provide a more flexible setup to test the various aspects of wireless VPNs. The loss, and round trip delay is also intended to be analysed as an extension to this study.

References

1. Ferre, P., Doufexi, A., Nix,A., and Bull, D.: Throughput Analysis of IEEE 802.11 and IEEE 802.11 e MAC, Wireless Communications and Networking, 2004 WCNC 2004,(2004) 783-788 vol.2.
2. Garg, S.; Kappes, M.;An experimental study of throughput for UDP and VoIP traffic in IEEE 802.11b networks, Wireless Communications and Networking, 2003. WCNC 2003. (2003) 1748 - 1753 vol.3.
3. Wijesinha, A.L., Yeong-tae Song Krishnan, M., Mathur, V., Ahn, J., and Shyama-sundar, V.,Throughput measurement for UDP traffic in an IEEE 802.11g WLAN, Sixth International Conference onSoftware Engineering, Artificial Intelligence, Networking and Parallel/Distributed Computing, 2005 and First ACIS International Workshop on Self-Assembling Wireless Networks. SNPD/SAWN 2005. (2005),220 - 225 .
4. Jun, J., Peddabachagari, P., and Sichitiu, M.,Theoretical maximum throughput of IEEE 802.11 and its applications, Second IEEE International Symposium onNetwork Computing and Applications, 2003. NCA 2003, (2003) 249-256.
5. Wang, S.-C., Chen, Y.-M., Lee, T-H., and Helmy, A.,Performance evaluations for hybrid IEEE 802.11b and 802.11g wireless networks, 24th IEEE InternationalPerformance, Computing, and Communications Conference, 2005. IPCCC 2005. (2005), 111 - 118
6. Xiao, Y., and Rosdahl, J.,Throughput and delay limits of IEEE 802.11, IEEE Communications Letters, Volume 6, Issue 8, Aug. 2002, 355 - 357.
7. Munasinghe, K.S., and Shahrestani, S.A., Wireless VPNs: an evaluation of QoS metrics and measures, International Conference on Mobile Business, (2005), 616 - 622. ICMB 2005.
8. Allen, J. and Wilson, J., Securing a wireless network. In Proceedings of the 30th Annual ACM SIGUCCS Conference on User Services November 2002, 213-215.
9. Fazal, L., Ganu, S., Kappes, M., Krishnakumar, A.S., Krishnan, P., Tackling security vulnerabilities in VPN-based wireless deployments, IEEE International Conference on Communications, 2004 Volume 1, June 2004,100 - 104.

Path Loss Rate Driven Burst Assembly in OBS Networks*

Burak Kantarci and Sema Oktug

Istanbul Technical University, Department of Computer Engineering,
Computer Networks Research Lab.
34469 Maslak, Istanbul, Turkey
{burak, oktug}@ce.itu.edu.tr
http://www.ce.itu.edu.tr

Abstract. In this paper a novel optical burst assembly technique, namely path loss rate driven burst assembly which is an enhancement on an adaptive threshold based burst assembly is proposed. Path loss rate driven burst assembly adjusts the threshold values based on the feedback obtained from the network. Each egress node sends feedback packets periodically to each ingress node informing them on the contention level along the path. As the traffic along the corresponding path becomes lighter, an ingress node allows the corresponding burst generator to use greater time and size threshold values. Conversely, under heavy traffic along the path, the corresponding burst generators are forced to decrease the time and size threshold parameters. The results are obtained in terms of byte loss rate and delay, and compared with those obtained under nonadaptive (static) burst assembly and previously proposed link loss rate based adaptive threshold burst assembly. It is observed that the proposed technique significantly decreases the byte loss rate as the traffic gets heavier by keeping the end to end delay in a feasible range.

1   Introduction

Optical Burst Switching *(OBS)* uses the advantages of wavelength routing and optical packet switching and attempts to eliminate the disadvantages of these paradigms in *Wavelength Division Multiplexing (WDM)* networks [1]. At the ingress nodes, incoming IP packets are collected in virtual queues for each destination to form optical bursts. A *Burst Header Cell (BHC)* is formed upon forming an optical burst. BHC is transmitted a pre-determined offset time prior to the corresponding payload to reserve available resources on the path.

The performance metrics of the OBS network are affected by the arrival pattern of the bursts and the burst size[2]. Therefore the process of assembling incoming IP packets into optical bursts is a challenging issue. Basically, burst assembly schemes can be classified as *time threshold based* techniques [3], *size threshold based techniques* [4], and *hybrid* techniques [5].

* This work is supported by the Turkish State Planning Organization under Grant no 2001K120750.

A. Levi et al. (Eds.): ISCIS 2006, LNCS 4263, pp. 483–492, 2006.

We previously proposed an adaptive threshold (time and size) technique to enhance the performance of OBS networks [6]. That technique monitors the loss rate on the corresponding outgoing fiber, and based on this value, it determines the maximum size of the virtual queue and the upper bound of the burstification time threshold value. However, in that model, ingress nodes do not have sufficient information on the characteristics of the traffic along the path to destination nodes. The horizon technique [1] is used in order to schedule the optical bursts on the wavelengths.

In this paper, as an enhancement on the performance of the adaptive threshold based burst assembly, a novel burst assembly scheme is proposed in which the burst generators are guided by the loss rates along the paths. Upon the arrival of the first BHC from an ingress node, each egress node starts sending feedback packets periodically to the source node by using the same path in reverse direction. The feedback packet is supposed to carry the maximum byte loss rate along the path from source to destination. Each intermediate node compares the loss rate on the corresponding link and updates the control information field of the feedback packet if necessary. Upon receiving the feedback packet, the ingress node adjusts its time and size threshold values based on the most congested link where the byte loss rate is maximum along the path.

Variable size IP packet traffic that is coherent with the properties given in [8] is generated. The results obtained are compared with those obtained by using the *hybrid burst assembly* and the *link loss rate based adaptive threshold burst assembly* [6] under Poisson and self-similar traffic. It is shown that as the network traffic gets heavier, the proposed technique significantly outperforms these techniques.

The rest of the paper is organized as follows. In Section 2, we present the previously proposed burst assembly algorithms, especially the link loss rate based adaptive threshold burst assembly is explained. The path loss rate driven burst assembly is explained in Section 3. The simulation results showing the performance of the proposed technique are given in Section 4. We conclude the paper in Section 5 by giving some future directions.

2 Burst Assembly in OBS Networks

In an OBS network, at each ingress node incoming IP packets are buffered electronically in the appropriate virtual queues for each destination and assembled into optical bursts. The burst assembly process is expected to be based on an carefully selected policy since the performance of the OBS network is closely related to the *burstification* technique [2].

2.1 Static Threshold Based Schemes

The well-known and practical burst assembly techniques are *time threshold based*, *size threshold based*, and *hybrid* burst assemblies. In [3] the time threshold based approach is proposed where IP packets are collected unless the timer reaches a time threshold (TTh). However, it is shown that, when the incoming IP traffic is bursty [5], burst sizes vary significantly under light loads [9].

In the size threshold based burst assembly [5], only the virtual queue size is used as the threshold to form the optical bursts. In hybrid burst assembly [5], the burst generator forms an optical burst if either the size of the virtual queue exceeds STh or the corresponding timer exceeds TTh. The hybrid burst assembly brings advantages on the performance of OBS networks in comparison to the other static techniques[9].

2.2   Link Loss Rate Based Adaptive Burst Assembly

In [6], we propose an adaptive burst assembly technique in which the threshold values are arranged dynamically based on the byte loss rate on the outgoing fiber leading the corresponding destination. If the loss rate on the outgoing link is 'too high' (greater than upper loss threshold, LTh_{upper}) , it triggers the burst generator to decrease the size and time threshold values for the corresponding virtual queue in order to generate shorter bursts that are less likely to contend. Conversely, when the outgoing link has 'low enough' (smaller than lower loss threshold, LTh_{lower}) byte loss rate, the burst generator is allowed to increase the threshold values for that queue in order to form longer bursts. Whenever the measured loss rate is neither 'too high' nor 'low enough', than the burst generator selects the threshold values to form bursts of medium size. Based on the loss rate values obtained, the time threshold values are selected among three values determined in advance which are TTh_{low}, TTh_{medium}, and TTh_{high}. Similarly, the size threshold values are also selected among three pre-determined values of STh_{short}, STh_{medium}, and STh_{long}.

In [6], it is shown that, under various traffic types, such a burst assembly technique outperforms the hybrid burst assembly in terms of byte loss rate, and keeps the end-to-end delay in a feasible range which is less than the maximum burstification delay (TTh_{high}).

3   Path Loss Rate Driven Burst Assembly

In the link loss rate based adaptive burst assembly, as the time goes on, the nodes become unaware of the traffic along the path to destinations since each ingress node adjusts its threshold parameters based on the loss rate on the outgoing links to the corresponding destinations.

In path loss rate driven burst assembly, when an egress node (destination node) initially receives a BHC that informing the arrival of a data burst from an ingress node (source node), it starts sending feedback packets periodically by using the same path in the reverse direction to the ingress node. The feedback packet contains a 4 byte field ($MaxLoss$) that points out the maximum byte loss rate along the path from source node to the destination node. The feedback packet is forwarded to the related source by the intermediate nodes. Each intermediate node (and the source node) along the path compares the $MaxLoss$ field in the feedback packet with the loss rate on the reverse link where it has received the feedback packet. If the loss rate on the reverse direction of the link is greater than the *MaxLoss* parameter, the node updates the *MaxLoss* field with the measured loss value. The source node configures the time and size threshold values based on the *MaxLoss* value.

In Figure 1, a simple scenario is illustrated on informing the source node about the congestion level along the path to a specific destination. Here, node S attempts to send a data burst to node D (assume that such a transmission is not occurred earlier). At t_0 the BHC is transmitted by S. D receives the BHC informing that a data burst is about to arrive at t_2. Receiving the BHC at t_3, D generates a feedback packet at t_4 and sets the initial value of the *MaxLoss* field to zero, and forwards it to B (on the reverse path from S to D). The intermediate nodes along the reverse path compare the loss rates on the corresponding reverse links with the *MaxLoss* value received and update the field if necessary. At t_7, S has the feedback packet and performs the necessary action to calculate the *MaxLoss* rate on the *S-D* path. Based on the *MaxLoss* value, S configures the time and size threshold values to generate bursts for D.

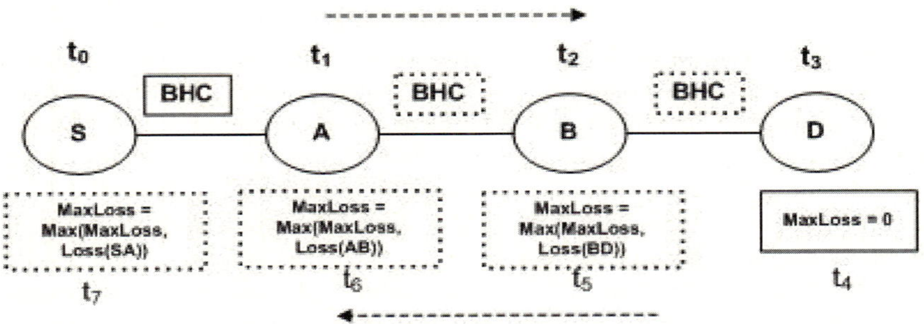

Fig. 1. A simple scenario for the feedback mechanism in path loss rate driven burst assembly

The maximum loss rate along the path (*MaxLoss*) is compared with two loss thresholds, namely the lower loss threshold (LTh_{lower}) and the upper loss threshold (LTh_{higher}). If (*MaxLoss*) exceeds the upper loss threshold, the burst generator is expected to form shorter bursts. To form short bursts, the burst generator requires shorter *STh* and lower *TTh* values (STh_{short} and TTh_{low}). Conversely, if *MaxLoss* is between the lower and the upper loss threshold, the burst generator is expected to form medium size bursts. When *MaxLoss* is lower than the lower loss threshold, the burst generator is expected to form longer bursts. To form medium and long size bursts, the burst generator has to select $STh_{medium}, TTh_{medium}$ and STh_{long}, TTh_{high}, respectively.

Due to the transmission and propagation delay of the feedback packet, instantaneous changes may occur with a low probability along the path on some links that are more than one hop away from the source node. This may affect the current loss rate on the path. Therefore, in order to filter the effect of such anomalies that occur with a low probability, we define a filtering interval of 2ϵ around the upper and the lower threshold values. Instead of immediately comparing

MaxLoss with the loss threshold values, the burst generator first checks whether *MaxLoss* is in $[LTh_{upper} - \epsilon,\ LTh_{upper} + \epsilon]$. If it is, then the burst generator configures the threshold values to be medium or short with equal probability. If it is not, then the burst generator checks if *MaxLoss* is in $[LTh_{lower} - \epsilon,\ LTh_{lower} + \epsilon]$. If it is, then the threshold values are configured to be high(long) or medium with equal probability.

The configuration process of the threshold values is given as follows:

```
Configure Thresholds ()
begin
if (MaxLossRate is in [LTh_upper − ε, LTh_upper + ε])
      TTh := TTh_low, STh := STh_short with a probability of 1/2
      TTh := TTh_medium, STh := STh_medium with a probability of 1/2
else if (MaxLossRate is in [LTh_lower − ε, LTh_lower + ε])
      TTh := TTh_medium, STh := STh_medium with a probability of 1/2
      TTh := TTh_high, STh := STh_long with a probability of 1/2
else if (MaxLossRate >= LTh_upper)
      TTh := TTh_low, STh := STh_short
else if (MaxLossRate <= LTh_lower)
      TTh := TTh_high, STh := STh_long
else
      TTh := TTh_medium, STh := STh_medium
end.
```

Optical burst generators use the algorithm described above to configure the time and size threshold values of the virtual queues. The algorithm which is run by a burst generator for each virtual queue is very similar to the Link Loss Rate Based Adaptive Threshold algorithm [6]. However, this scheme takes the loss threshold parameter as the maximum link loss rate along the path, and employs an anomaly filter to the maximum loss rate obtained as a feedback from the egress nodes. As it can be seen, only the bursts of three pre-determined sizes are allowed to be formed. If the virtual queue size is between the two size threshold values, the shorter one is selected to be the size of the burst to be formed. The reason of this behavior is that, it is known that the longer bursts are more likely to contend [7]. Therefore instead of padding to an upper threshold value, the burst generator takes the bytes of the smaller size threshold, and re-buffers the remaining bytes. The burst generator only use padding when the virtual queue size is less than low size threshold value (STh_{low}) in order to prevent the wavelength channels to be under utilized by too short bursts.

4 Simulation Results

The simulation software is developed using Visual C++ and run on a Pentium 4 3.00GHz with 3.50GB memory space. The NSFNET topology given in [11] is used in our simulation scenarios. Each link consists of two unidirectional fibers for each direction. It is assumed that each fiber has 32 wavelengths each having a bandwidth of 10Gbps. Each node in the topology can act both as an ingress node and an egress node. Each node performs source routing based on Dijkstra's shortest path algorithm. An average switching time of $1\mu s$ is assumed while the average packet processing time is taken as $10\mu s$.

Poisson traffic and the self-similar traffic with H = 0.8 are generated as explained in [12] to be used in our simulations. The traffic sources generate an aggregated traffic at line rate 80 Gbps. The simulations run for a virtual duration of ten minutes. The results obtained provide minimum confidence interval of 90%.

The *horizon* scheduling algorithm is used to schedule the bursts on wavelength channels. The loss threshold values LTh_{low} and LTh_{high} are determined emprically in advance and set to 0.15 and 0.25 respectively. The three size threshold values STh_{long}, STh_{medium}, and STh_{short} are selected as 80 μs (100 KB on 10Gbps), 60 μs (75 KB on 10Gbps), and 40 μs (50 KB on 10Gbps) respectively. The three time threshold values TTh_{high}, TTh_{medium}, and TTh_{low} are selected as 100, 60, and $20\mu s$, respectively. The threshold parameters used in the hybrid burst assembly are static STh of 60 μs (75 KB on 10Gbps) and TTh of 100 μs.

In the path loss rate driven burst assembly, we select the ϵ value based on the instantaneous incoming load at each node. By using the time between two consecutive burstification processes and the number of bytes buffered during this time, an ingress node calculates its instantaneous load. The instantaneous load lower than 0.7 Erlang is marked as light, the instantaneous load greater than and equal to 0.7 Erlang is marked as heavy. When running the path loss rate driven burst assembly algorithm, if the instantaneous load is heavy, ϵ is selected as 0.03. Similarly, if the instantaneous load is light, ϵ is selected as 0.01.

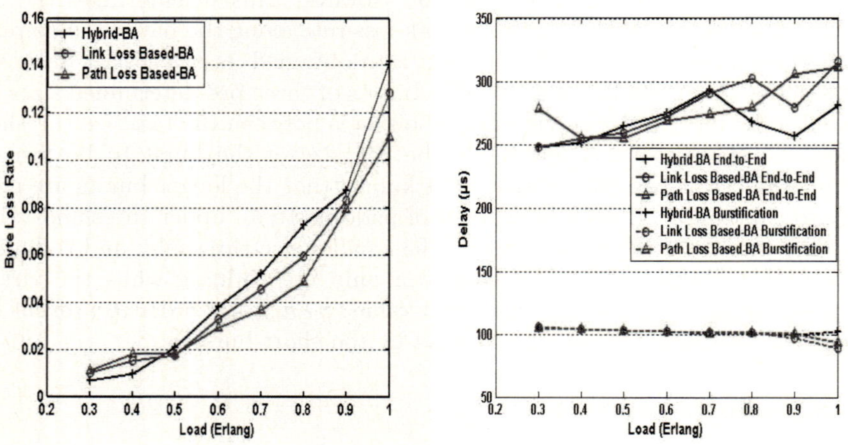

Fig. 2. Byte loss rate comparison under Poisson traffic

Fig. 3. Burstification and end-to-end delay comparison under Poisson traffic

In Figure 2, the results taken under Poisson traffic are shown in which the hybrid burst assembly, the link loss rate based, and path loss rate based adaptive burst assembly are compared in terms of byte loss rate. As it is seen from the figure, since the adaptive techniques are reactive to the increase in byte loss rates on the links, they outperform the hybrid burst assembly as the traffic gets heavier. In addition, starting from the moderate link loads, path loss rate based adaptive burst assembly leads to better byte loss values in comparison to the other two techniques. The reason of this behavior is that the path loss rate driven burst assembly uses global information on the link losses along the path from source to destination. Although the link loss rate based technique adapts the burst sizes by monitoring the congestion level on its outgoing link it is not aware of the traffic characteristics on the other links along the path. The congestion level on the links along the path increases as the traffic gets heavier. Therefore, informing the source node on the congestion level along the path is emergent important.

Figure 3 compares the three techniques in terms of burstification and end-to-end delays per burst. The hybrid burst assembly uses a $100\mu s$ of static time threshold. However, the adaptive techniques use three different TTh values two of those are less than 100μ. However, as we explain in the previous section, at the time of burstification if the virtual queue size is greater than the STh of that time instant, a burst of size STh is formed and the remaining bytes are re-buffered. At high loads, the loss rate on links tend to increase more oftenly than the lighter loads, and the adaptive techniques react such changes by decreasing TTh. Therefore, at high loads, the burstification delay slightly decreases.

As a result of the re-buffering of the remaining bytes, the adaptive techniques are expected to have greater average burst size which causes a significant latency in end-to-end transmission of the bursts. As it is seen in Figure 3, the average end-to-end delay per burst increases as the load gets heavier. As the traffic gets heavier, the virtual buffer size increases faster which causes to re-buffer more number of bytes in burstification stage. Between the loads of 0.6 and 0.9 Erlang, the path loss rate driven burst assembly performs better than the link loss rate based technique. As the traffic gets heavier than 0.8 Erlang, the path loss rate driven burst assembly start to react the congestion along the path more than link loss rate based technique since it has the loss rate information on the links that are more than one hop. Therefore it re-buffers more bytes by decreasing the threshold values, and this behavior causes a significant increase in the end-to-end delay per burst. However, the increase caused by path the loss rate driven burst assembly (and also the link loss rate based burst assembly) is not as much as the burstification period of the hybrid burst assembly. Therefore it can be stated that the proposed technique keeps the increase in the end-to-end transmission delay in a feasible range.

In Figure 4, the performance comparison of the three techniques in terms of byte loss rate under self-similar traffic with $H = 0.8$ is shown. The results obtained are similar to those obtained under Poisson traffic. Path loss rate driven

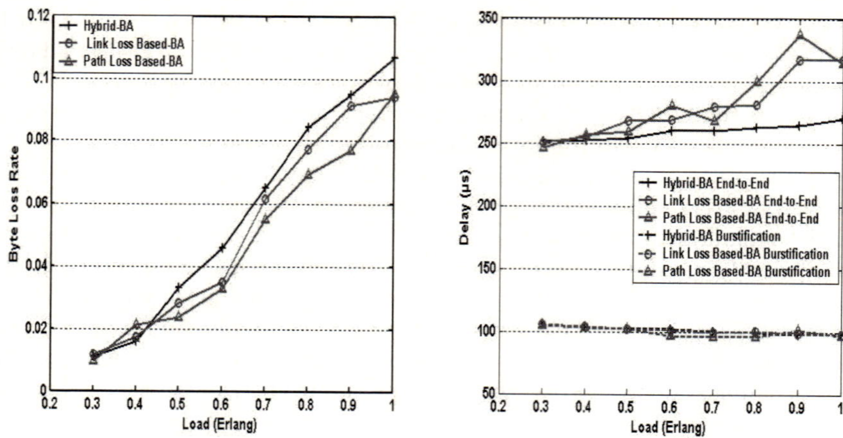

Fig. 4. Byte loss rate comparison under self-similar traffic with H = 0.8

Fig. 5. Burstification and end-to-end delay comparison under self-similar traffic with H = 0.8

burst assembly gives lower byte loss in comparison to the other techniques. The only difference is that at the load of 1.0 Erlang, the performance of path loss rate based and link loss rate based burst assemblies coincide. As the traffic gets heavier, the loss characteristics of the links along the path also tend to coincide.

In Figure 5, the burstification and end-to-end delay comparison of the three techniques are illustrated under the self-similar traffic with H = 0.8. The proposed technique does not cause an increase in burstification delay and keeps the average value of burstification delay close to that of the hybrid burst assembly. The hybrid burst assembly leads to lower end-to-end transmission delay as a result of using static time and size thresholds. Using static size and time thresholds shapes the incoming traffic by reducing the long range dependence degree [9]. Therefore the hybrid burst assembly leads to lower end-to-end transmission delay. The re-buffering scheme and the self-similar nature of the incoming traffic affect the burst sizes of the adaptive techniques. This causes an increase in the end-to-end transmission delay. However, the increase in end-to-end delay is in a feasible range here.

5   Conclusion and Future Work

In this paper we propose a novel burst assembly scheme, namely the path loss rate driven burst assembly to improve the performance of OBS networks. We use the maximum byte loss rate on the links along the path from source to destination to decide the threshold values (TTh, STh) of the related virtual queue. The maximum loss rate on each path to an egress node is sent periodically to the related ingress node using the feedback packets generated by the egress node.Each intermediate node along the path updates the maximum loss rate field in the feedback packet according to the loss rate on its outgoing link to the egress node. Bursts are forced to have one of four sizes in order to let the physical implementation practical. We evaluate the performance of the proposed technique in terms of byte loss rate, end-to-en delay, and burstification delay $(\mu_{min}, STh_{short}, STh_{medium}, STh_{long})$.

The results obtained are compared with those of the hybrid burst assembly and another adaptive threshold burst assembly, namely the link loss rate based burst assembly. It is shown that the proposed technique outperforms the hybrid burst assembly, and the link loss rate based burst assembly with respect to byte loss rate under the traffic employed. It is also shown that the proposed technique does not lead to an increase in burstification delay. However, at some load values the path loss rate driven technique experiences larger end-to-end delays since it allows larger bursts when the feedback corresponds to a low amount of maximum delay along the path, and as a result of re-buffering of the remaining bytes of the virtual queue to form the burst only of those four sizes.

As a future work we are focusing on the performance evaluation of the proposed technique by using the burst scheduling algorithms other than the *horizon*. Besides, we are planning to include quality of service into the burst scheduling phase.

References

1. Xu J., Qiao C., Li J., Xu G.: Efficient Channel Scheduling Algorithms in Optical Burst Switched Networks. Proc. IEEE International Conference on Computer Communications (INFOCOM), Vol.3, (March 2003) 2268–2278.
2. Chen Y., Qiao C., Li J., Xu G.: Optical Burst Switching: A New Area in Optical Networking Research. IEEE Network, Vol 18, (May-June 2004) 16–23
3. Ge A., Callegati F., Tamil L. : On Optical Burst Switching and Self-similar Traffic. IEEE Communication Letters, Vol 4, Issue 3, (March 2000) 98–100
4. Oh S., Kang M. : A Burst Assembly Algorithm in Optical Burst Switching Networks. Proc. Optical Fiber Communications Conference and Exhibit (OFC). (May 2003) 771–773
5. Luo J., Zen Q., Chi H., Zhang Z., Zhao H. : The impacts of burst assembly on the traffic properties in optical burst switching networks. Proc. IEEE International Conference on Communication Technology. Vol 1, (April 2003) 521–524
6. Kantarci B., Oktug S. : Adaptive Threshold Based Burst Assembly in OBS Networks. To appear in Proc. Canadian Conference on Electrical and Computer Engineering (CCECE),(May 2006)
7. Battestilli T., Perros H. : A Performance Study of an Optical Burst Switched Network with Simultaneous Dynamic Link Possession. Computer Networks, Vol 50, Issue 2, (Feb 2006) 219–236
8. Cano M. D., Malgosa-Sanahuja J., Cerdan F., Garcia-Haro J. : Internet Measurements and Data Study Over the Regional. Proc IEEE Pacific RIM Conference on Communications, Computers and Signal Processing, Vol 2, (August 2001) 393–396.
9. Kantarci B., Oktug S., Atmaca T. : Performance of Optical Burst Switching Techniques under Self-similar and Poisson Traffic Based on Various Burst Assembly Techniques, under review in Elsevier Computer Communications, 2006.

10. Hu G., Dolzer K., Gauger C. : Does Burst Assembly Really Reduce Self-similarity?
    Optical Fiber Communications Conference (OFC), Vol 86, OSA Trends in Optics
    and Photonics Series (2003), 124–126
11. Vokkarane V. M., Qiong Z., Jue J. P., Biao C. : Generalized Burst Assembly and
    Scheduling Techniques for QoS Support in Optical Burst-Switched Networks. Proc.
    IEEE Global Telecommunications Conference, Vol 3, (Nov 2002) 2747–2751
12. Taqqu M. S., Willinger W., Sherman R. : Proof of a Fundamental Result in Self-
    similar Traffic Modeling. ACM/SIGCOMM Computer Communications Review,
    Vol 27, (1997), 5–23

Pixel Domain Spatio-temporal Denoising for Archive Videos

M. Kemal Güllü, Oğuzhan Urhan, and Sarp Ertürk

Kocaeli University Laboratory of Image and Signal processing (KULIS),
Electronics and Telecom. Eng. Dept., University of Kocaeli, 41040, Kocaeli, Turkey
{kemalg, urhano, sertur}@kou.edu.tr

Abstract. A new pixel domain spatio-temporal video noise filter for archive film restoration has been proposed in this paper. The proposed filtering method takes motion changes and spatial information into account. Firstly, temporal filtering is carried out considering temporal changes adaptively. Afterwards, interpolation between degraded and temporally filtered images is carried out to preserve edge information using local standard deviation values. With respect to pixel domain techniques proposed in the literature, the proposed method gives better results for various test videos and particularly provides superior results for archive film.

1 Introduction

Restoration and storage of archive film materials are important for the transfer of cultural heritage to next generations. Archive films include many types of defects like flicker, blotch, scratch, and noise that are caused by storage medium conditions, playing and copying of films etc. Noise is a typically encountered degradation in archive films. After removing strong blotches that cause enormous temporal discontinuity in archive video, transparent dust effects and film-grain noise remain. These remained defects should be suppressed from archive film for improved visual quality.

Spatial (2-D) and spatio-temporal (3-D) filters [1-6] have been proposed in the literature to remove video noise. Spatial filters take only spatial information into account and as an effect can cause spatial blurring at high noise levels. This blurring effect can be reduced using both temporal and spatial information and the filtering performance can be improved at low noise levels also in this way.

A wavelet domain spatial filter whose coefficients are manipulated using a Markov Random Field (MRF) image model has been proposed in [1]. In [2], a Wiener filter is utilized in the wavelet domain in order to remove image noise. A fuzzy logic based image noise filter that takes directional deviations into account has been proposed in [3]. In [4], a recursive estimator structure has been proposed to estimate the clean image from the film-grain noisy image. Noise is considered to be related to exposure time in the form of non-Gaussian and multiplicative structure in [4].

A pixel based spatio-temporal adaptive filter that calculates new pixel values adaptively using the weighted mean of pixels over motion compensated frames has been proposed in [5]. In [6], an edge preserving spatio-temporal video noise filter that

A. Levi et al. (Eds.): ISCIS 2006, LNCS 4263, pp. 493 – 502, 2006.

combines 2D Wiener and Kalman filters has been presented. A non-linear video noise filter which calculates new pixel values using a 3D window has been proposed in [7]. This method arranges pixels in the form of a 3D window according to their difference with respect to related pixel values and averages the pixels in the window after weighting them according to their sorting order. This method gives good results in case of no- or slow local motion, but deforms image regions in cases of abrupt local motion. Video denoising using 2D and 3D dual-tree complex wavelet transforms has been proposed in [8]. In the case of local motion, the 3D filtering performance of the method is highly reduced. In order to increase the 3D filtering performance of the method proposed in [8], 2D wavelet based filtering and temporal mean filtering that uses pixel based motion detection has been proposed in [9]. A wavelet transform based video filtering technique that uses spatial and temporal redundancy has been proposed in [10]. In [11], a content adaptive video denoising filter has been proposed recently. This method filters both impulsive and non-impulsive noise but the filtering performance is highly reduced in case of Gaussian noise with high variance.

In this work, a new pixel based spatio-temporal video noise filter that takes motion changes and spatial standard deviations into account is proposed. The main objective is to suppress noise in archive video, and it is shown that the proposed method provides a successful visual quality for archive videos.

2   The Proposed Filtering Method

2.1   Noise Model

Noise can be defined as an unwanted component of the video and generally occurs as Gaussian noise, film-grain noise and quantization noise in archive video. In general, noise can be grouped as: additive (impulse, Gaussian noise) and multiplicative (film grain noise) noise. Image independent noise is described by an additive noise model as in (1).

$$I_n(x, y) = I_o(x, y) + \eta(x, y) \tag{1}$$

where I_o denotes the original image, I_n is the noisy image. The noise η is often considered as zero-mean Gaussian distribution and described by its variance σ_n^2 $(\eta(0, \sigma_n^2))$. In this work the noise for each pixel is handled as zero-mean Gaussian, independent and identically distributed (i.i.d.) (Additive White Gaussian Noise-AWGN).

2.2   Temporal Filtering Considering Local Motion

Only spatial noise reduction techniques give limited filtering performance and can produce frustrating artifacts [14]. Taking the advantage of the i.i.d. property of the noise, lost or degraded image information can typically be attained from previous and/or subsequent image frames for the current pixel $I_n(x, y, t)$ more accurately. Therefore filtering performance is increased for video sequences.

Similar to video de-noising methods in the literature, a 3D window (of size $ws \times ws \times ws$) around the (x, y, t) position has been constructed for each pixel (See Fig. 1) to obtain temporal information to the noise suppression process in our method.

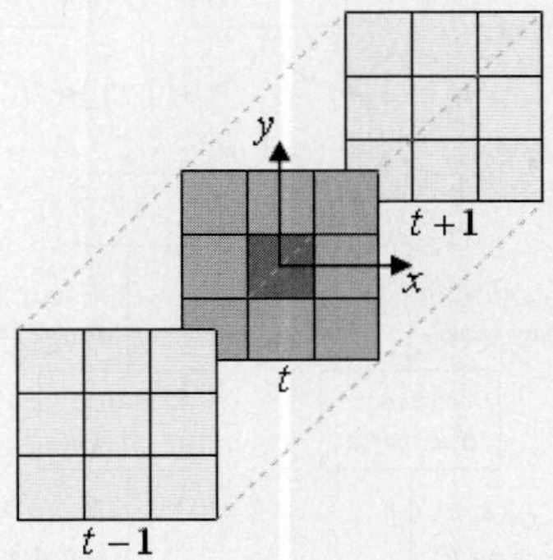

Fig. 1. The 3D window used for temporal video denoising

Suppose that preceding and subsequent frames are the same as the current frame and AWGN (Additive White Gaussian Noise) is added to each frame independently. Basically, linear average of the pixels in this 3-D window can give good results for less detailed regions in this assumption. While filtering real sequences, global and local motion effects should be taken into account to reduce temporal filtering artifacts such as blurring. Global motion effect can be recompensed using global motion compensation. However, image regions that include local motion in the preceding and/or succeeding frames that are non-matching parts of the 3-D window should not taken into account or local motion compensation should be done while filtering.

In the proposed method, two temporal contribution thresholds are calculated for each pixel in the current frame to determine which pixels from preceding and succeeding frames are to be used in the 3-D window while filtering. For this purpose, initially absolute image frame differences are thresholded using T_i and the Euclidean distance is measured over the binary difference image. Then, obtained distance images are smoothened using SOR (Successive Over-Relaxion) to avoid crisp changes [13]. Smoothened distance images are subsequently converted to temporal threshold images using a linear function $f_t(.)$ as given in (2). The proposed adaptive temporal threshold selection process is shown in Fig. 2.

$$T(x, y) = f_t(E(x, y)) = \begin{cases} \left[\dfrac{0.5 - E(x, y)}{0.5}\right] \times T_s, & E(x, y) \leq 0.5 \\ 0, & otherwise \end{cases} \tag{2}$$

here $E(x, y)$ is Euclidean distance value for a given (x, y) pixel and T_s is the temporal deviation threshold.

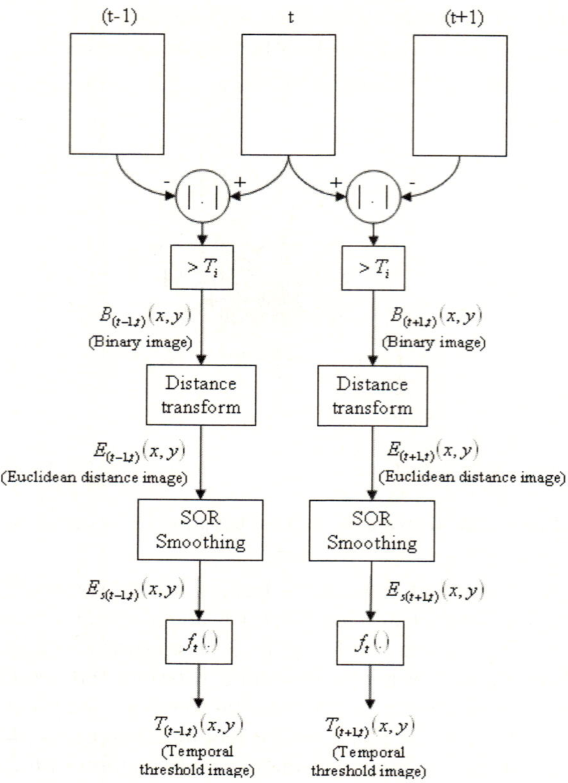

Fig. 2. Proposed adaptive temporal threshold selection stage

A simple SOR smoothing approach is utilized, which can be formulated as

$$E^{i+1}(x, y) = E^i(x, y) -$$
$$\lambda\left(4E^i(x, y) - E^i(x-1, y) - E^i(x+1, y) - E^i(x, y-1) - E^i(x, y+1)\right)/4 \tag{3}$$

where i is the iteration order, and λ determines the smoothness of the operation. In this work, the maximum smoothness value is selected ($\lambda = 1$). Temporal threshold images for frame #1160 of Mount archive video are given in Fig. 3.

After temporal threshold selection, local mean calculation of the $ws \times ws$ square window of t'th frame is carried out as given (4).

$$\mu(x, y, t) = \frac{1}{ws \times ws} \sum_{m=1}^{ws} \sum_{n=1}^{ws} I_n\left(x + m - \frac{ws+1}{2}, y + n - \frac{ws+1}{2}, t\right) \tag{4}$$

$\mu(x, y, t)$ is used to decide pixels which can be used for temporal filtering from the previous and subsequent frames in the 3D window in case of local motion (denoted as P_b and P_f). This operation is carried out as given in (5).

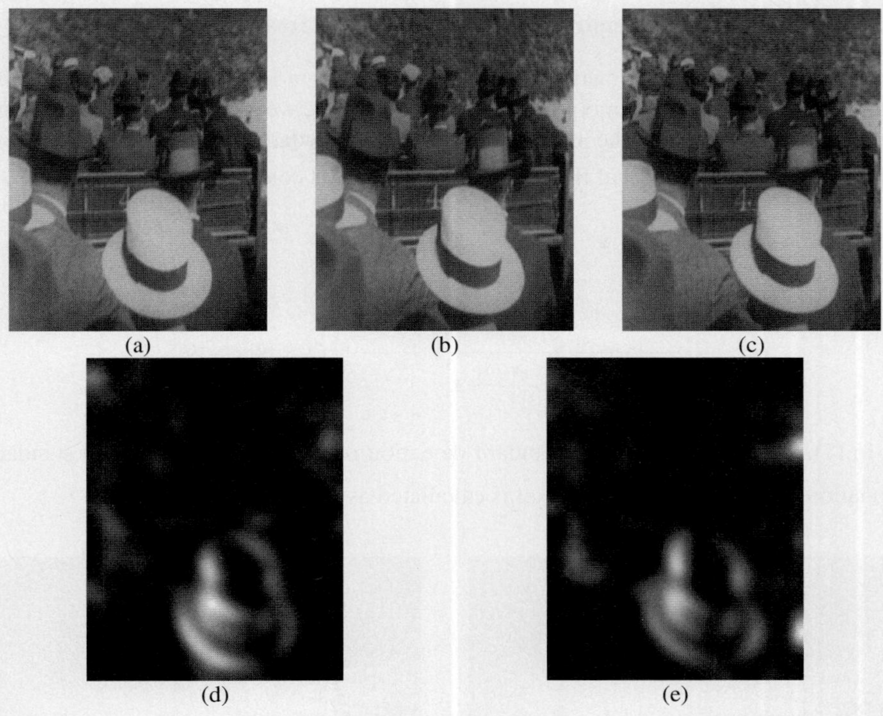

Fig. 3. Original frames a) #1159, b) #1160, c) #1161 of Mount archive video, d) $T_{(t-1,t)}$ and, e) $T_{(t+1,t)}$ threshold images

$$P_b = \left\{ \forall I_n(x, y) \middle| I_n(x+m, y+n, t-1) - \mu(x,y,t) \middle| < T_{(t-1,t)}(x, y) \right\}$$
$$P_f = \left\{ \forall I_n(x, y) \middle| I_n(x+m, y+n, t+1) - \mu(x,y,t) \middle| < T_{(t+1,t)}(x, y) \right\},$$

$$m, n = -1, 0, 1 \tag{5}$$

$$P_u = P_b \cup P_f$$

The temporal filtering result $\mu_u(x, y, t)$, which will replace each pixel value in the following stage is obtained as the average value of all pixels in P_u as shown in (6).

$$\mu_u(x, y, t) = \frac{1}{NUP} \sum_{m=1}^{NUP} P_u(m) \tag{6}$$

Here, NUP is the total number of used pixel in the temporal filtering process for a given (x, y, t) pixel.

2.3 Interpolation of Temporally Filtered and Noisy Image Data

Preservation of edge information is the main problem in image and video denoising techniques. In this work, interpolation is carried out between temporally filtered and degraded images taking the block based standard deviation into account to retain edges successfully. The final filtered image frame I_o' is constructed as given in (7).

$$I_o'(x,y,t) = \begin{cases} \mu_u(x,y,t) & , \quad \sigma_u(x,y,t) < T_a(t) \\[2em] \dfrac{I_n(x,y,t) \times \dfrac{\sigma_u(x,y,t)}{T_a(t)} + \mu_u(x,y,t)}{\dfrac{\sigma_u(x,y,t)}{T_a(t)} + 1} & , \quad \text{otherwise} \end{cases} \tag{7}$$

In (7), $\sigma_u(x,y,t)$ shows the standard deviation of P_u for each pixel. The standard deviation value of P_u for each pixel is calculated as given in (8).

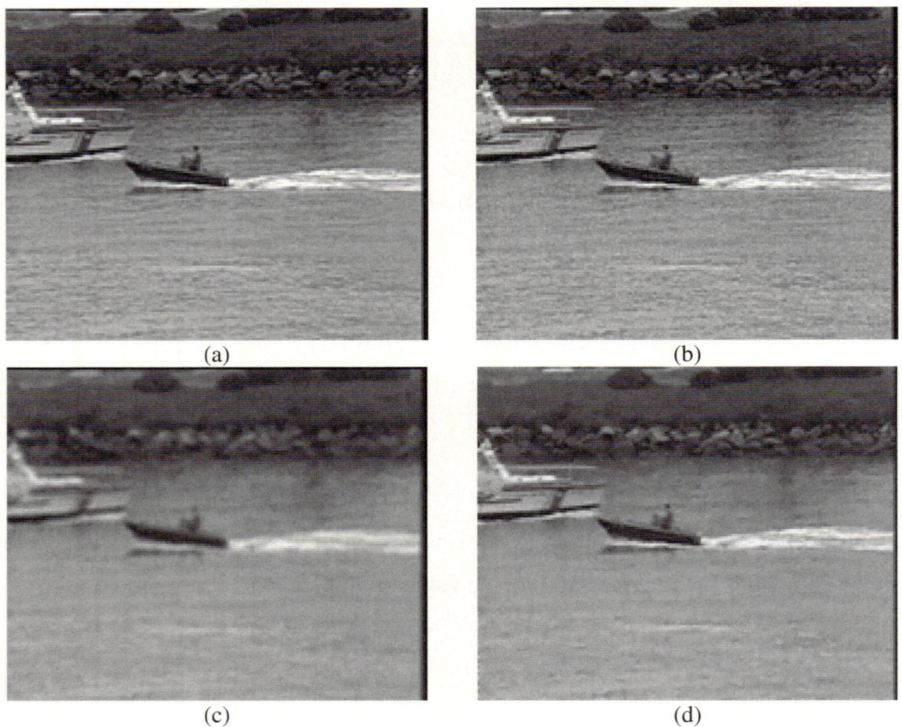

(a)   (b)

(c)   (d)

Fig. 4. Coastguard sequence a) original frame #25, b) $\sigma = 5$ AWGN added frame #25, c) temporal filtering result, and d) output of the proposed filter

$$\sigma_u(x, y, t) = \sqrt{\frac{1}{NUP} \sum_{m=1}^{NUP} [P_u(m) - \mu_u(x, y, t)]^2} \tag{8}$$

T_a is an adaptive threshold that is determined for the entire image using (9).

$$T_a(t) = \frac{1}{w \times h} \sum_{m=1}^{w} \sum_{n=1}^{h} \sigma_u(m, n, t) \tag{9}$$

If $\sigma_P(x, y, t) < T_\alpha(t)$ less detail around the pixel region is detected and $I'_o(x, y, t)$ is kept as $\mu_u(x, y, t)$. Interpolation is carried out if $\sigma_P(x, y, t) \geq T_\alpha(t)$ to preserve the spatial details in the image frame. In Fig. 4, the temporally filtered image frame and result of spatial interpolation are given for frame #25 of the Coastguard sequence with $\sigma = 5$ AWGN added.

In this figure smoothed details are successfully retained overall but on the sea area some details can not preserved effectively.

3   Experimental Results

The standard deviation value of noise in archive videos is generally low. Therefore, the proposed method is examined for $\sigma = 2$, $\sigma = 5$ and $\sigma = 10$ values of AWGN, artificially introduced into the first 100 frames of commonly used test sequences. To compare the objective performance of the proposed method against several pixel domain methods, Zlokolica's [7] and Chan's [11] pixel domain methods as well as the Wiener filter [12], and the Peak Signal to Noise Ratio (PSNR) measure is used. The PSNR is calculated as given in (10).

$$MSE = \frac{1}{w \times h} \sum_{x=1}^{w} \sum_{y=1}^{h} [I'_o(x, y) - I_o(x, y)]^2$$

$$PSNR = 20 \log_{10} \frac{255}{\sqrt{MSE}} \tag{10}$$

Table 1. Average PSNR (dB) values of compared methods for various test sequences (AWGN with $\sigma = 2$)

Sequence	Wiener [12]	Chan [11]	Zlokolica [7]	**Proposed**
Akiyo	39.01	39.69	38.20	42.97
Coastguard	30.01	35.76	30.23	32.32
Foreman	34.30	37.66	35.18	38.78
Hall Monitor	35.07	38.89	33.86	39.48
Mother	37.00	38.77	37.79	41.49
Salesman	33.21	36.94	35.49	36.22
Silent	33.65	36.77	33.87	38.00
Average	34.60	37.78	34.95	**38.47**

T_i and T_s thresholds are experimentally set to 20 in the proposed method. It is seen from Table 1, Table 2 and Table 3 that the proposed method gives the highest average PSNR values for all standard deviation values of the noise. PSNR graphics are given for AWGN added Foreman sequence ($\sigma = 2$, $\sigma = 5$) in Fig. 5 to evaluate

Table 2. Average PSNR (dB) values of compared methods for various test sequences (AWGN with $\sigma = 5$)

Sequence	Wiener [12]	Chan [11]	Zlokolica [7]	**Proposed**
Akiyo	37.38	36.31	36.83	39.57
Coastguard	29.74	33.74	29.97	31.67
Foreman	33.67	35.08	34.45	36.78
Hall Monitor	34.26	35.86	33.39	37.36
Mother	35.97	35.90	36.57	38.53
Salesman	32.60	34.72	34.63	34.80
Silent	33.18	34.53	33.38	36.22
Average	33.83	35.16	34.17	**36.42**

Table 3. Average PSNR (dB) values of compared methods for various test sequences (AWGN with $\sigma = 10$)

Sequence	Wiener [12]	Chan [11]	Zlokolica [7]	**Proposed**
Akiyo	34.23	29.77	33.92	35.07
Coastguard	28.91	29.00	29.11	30.25
Foreman	32.01	29.43	32.46	33.53
Hall Monitor	32.27	29.75	31.91	34.09
Mother	33.60	29.71	33.73	34.36
Salesman	31.02	29.38	32.48	32.20
Silent	31.86	29.28	31.71	33.17
Average	31.99	29.47	32.19	**33.24**

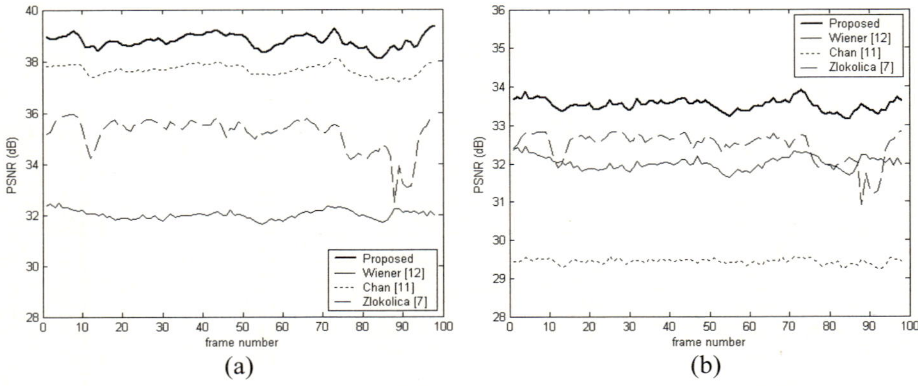

Fig. 5. PSNR graphics for Foreman sequence AWGN added with a) $\sigma = 2$, b) $\sigma = 10$

the characteristics of the methods in case of different standard deviation values of the AWGN and local motion.

It is clearly seen from Fig. 5-a that the proposed method gives better results than the compared methods for the case of AWGN with $\sigma = 2$. The Wiener filter gives poor results compared to the others. PSNR results of Zlokolica's method are on the average lower by 3.5dB mainly because this method distorts the shape of image regions in case of local motion. Fig. 5-b presents the performance results of the compared techniques for the case of AWGN with $\sigma = 10$. It is obviously seen from this figure that the proposed method outperforms compared methods. Performances of the Wiener filter and Zlokalica's method increase with higher standard deviation values of the AWGN but Zlocalica's method is still influenced by local motion. Chan's method gives poor results for higher standard deviation values of AWGN compared to the other methods.

4 Conclusion

A new pixel domain spatio-temporal video noise filter for archive video restoration has been proposed in this paper. The proposed filtering method takes motion changes and spatial information into account. Initially, temporal filtering is carried out considering temporal changes for this purpose. Then, interpolation is utilized between degraded and temporally filtered images to preserve edge information taking standard deviation values into account. Filtering results are compared with several pixel domain filtering methods and the results show that the proposed method outperforms compared pixel domain filtering techniques in terms of PSNR and provides successful visual results for archive film.

Acknowledgement

This work was supported by the Turkish Scientific and Technical Research Council (Tübitak), under grant EEEAG/103E007.

References

1. Malfait M., and Roose D.: Wavelet-Based Image Denoising Using a Markov Random Field a Priori Model. IEEE Trans. on Image Processing, Vol. 6, No. 4, (1997) 549-565
2. Kazubek M.: Wavelet Domain Image Denoising by Thresholding and Wiener Filtering. IEEE Signal Processing Letters, Vol. 10, No. 11, (2003) 324-326
3. Van De Ville D., Nachtegael M., Van der Weken D., Kerre E. E., Philips W., and Lemahieu I.: Noise Reduction by Fuzzy Image Filtering. IEEE Trans. on Fuzzy Systems, Vol. 11, No. 4, (2003) 429-436
4. Sadhar S. I., and Rajagopalan A. N.: Image Estimation in Film-Grain Noise. IEEE Signal Processing Letters, Vol. 12, No. 3, (2005) 238-241
5. Ozkan M. K., Sezan I., and Tekalp A. M.: Adaptive Motion Compensated Filtering of Noisy Image Sequences. IEEE Trans. on Circuits and Systems for Video Technology, Vol. 3, No. 4, (1993) 277-290

6. Dugad R., and Ajuha N.:Video Denoising by Combining Kalman and Wiener Estimates. IEEE Int. Conf. on Image Processing, Kobe, Japan, 4, (1999) 152-161
7. Zlokolica V., Philips W., and Van De Ville D.: A New Non-Linear Filter for Video Processing. 3rd IEEE Benelux Signal Processing Symposium (SPS-2002), Leuven, Belgium, (2002) 13-16
8. Selesnick I. W., and Li K. Y.: Video Denoising Using 2d and 3d Dual-Tree Complex Wavelet Transforms. In Wavelet Applications in Signal and Image Processing (SPIE 5207), San Diego, 5207, (2003) 607-618
9. Pizurica A., Zlokolica V., and Philips W.: Combined Wavelet Domain and Temporal Video Denoising. IEEE Conf. on Advanced Video and Signal Based Surveillance (AVSS'03), (2003) 334-341
10. Gupta N., Swamy M. N. S., and Plotkin E. I.: Low-Complexity Video Noise Reduction in Wavelet Domain, IEEE 6th Workshop on Multimedia Signal Processing, (2004) 239-242
11. Chan T.-W., Au O. C., Chong T. S., and Chau W.-S.: A Novel Content-Adaptive Video Denoising Filter. IEEE Int. Conf. on Acoustics, Speech, and Signal Processing (ICASSP), Philadelphia, PA, USA, Vol. 2, (2005) 649-652
12. Lim J. S.: Two-Dimensional Signal and Image Processing. Englewood Cliffs, NJ: Prentice Hall, (1990) 536-540
13. Press W. H., Teukolsky S. A., Vetterling W. T., and Flannery B. P.: Numerical Recipes in C, 2nd edition New York: Cambridge Univ. Press, (1992)
14. Brailean J., Kleihorst R., Efstratiadis S., Katsaggalegos A., and Lagendijk A.: Noise Reduction Filters for Dynamic Image Sequences: A Review, Pcoc. Of IEEE 83 (9), (1995) 1272-1292

Fast Sub-pixel Motion Estimation by Means of One-Bit Transform

Orhan Akbulut, Oğuzhan Urhan, and Sarp Ertürk

Kocaeli University Laboratory of Image and Signal processing (KULIS),
Electronics and Telecom. Eng. Dept., University of Kocaeli, 41040, Turkey
orhanakbulut@gmail.com, {urhano, sertur}@kou.edu.tr

Abstract. In this study sub-pixel motion estimation using one-bit transform is presented. The utilization of low bit depth representations for full-pixel motion estimation exist in the literature [1,7]. However sub-pixel motion estimation employing these kinds of transforms has not been tried until now. In this paper, it is shown that one-bit transform can also be utilized for sub-pixel motion estimation, significantly improving motion estimation accuracy. Hence a fast sub-pixel motion estimation approach is facilitated using one-bit transform.

1 Introduction

Video compression enables effective utilization of both memory and bandwidth. Motion estimation and compensation are employed for exploiting temporal redundancy between consecutive image frames to obtain better compression performance. Efficient motion estimation and compensation enable effective compression of video data. However motion estimation comprises most of the coding time and computational complexity.

Block based motion estimation methods are generally used in video coding standards. In block based motion estimation, image frames are initially divided into blocks. Then, each block of the current frame is searched for in the previous frame within a pre-defined search window. The best matched block is regarded to be the motion compensated prediction and is subtracted from the current block to form the residual, and both the difference (residual) and motion vectors are encoded [2].

The full search strategy uses exhaustive search of all possible candidate locations within the search window, hence the best match is ensured. However, the computational load is extremely high. Many fast search methods have been proposed to reduce the computational burden of the full search approach, at the cost of lower accuracy. These methods commonly decrease the number of search points to reduce computational load. Some of the fast search approaches are three step search (3SS) [3], 2D logarithmic search (2DLOG) [4] and new three step search (N3SS) [5].

Several matching criteria have been proposed for block based motion estimation. Minimum absolute difference (MAD) is one of the error criteria commonly used for the matching process. Another matching criterion is the mean square error (MSE) which gives better Peak Signal to Noise Ratio (PSNR) according to other matching

A. Levi et al. (Eds.): ISCIS 2006, LNCS 4263, pp. 503–510, 2006.
© Springer-Verlag Berlin Heidelberg 2006

criteria, but on the other hand, it is more difficult to implement the MSE criterion in hardware. Alternative matching error criteria for easier hardware calculation have been proposed in the literature.

Reduced bit resolution motion estimation methods have been proposed to obtain low-complexity matching criteria in [1,2,7]. In these cases, the matching criterion can be calculated faster using these low bit representation image frames using Boolean only operations. The exclusive-or (XOR) function is very efficient and can be easily implemented in hardware to perform matching criteria computation.

The one-bit (1BT) transform proposed in [1] is one of the first methods which uses low bit resolution representations. The main purpose of the 1BT transform is to represent image frames as binary images reducing the bit resolution. In this method, the 8-bit gray scale image frames are initially filtered using a multi band-pass filter kernel as given in (1).

$$K_{i,j} = \begin{cases} \frac{1}{25}, & i,j \in [0,4,8,12,16] \\ 0, & \text{otherwise} \end{cases} \tag{1}$$

After the filtering operation binary image frames ($G_{i,j}$) are obtained using (2) where $F_{i,j}$ denotes the original frame and $F'_{i,j}$ denotes the filtered frame obtained by filtering the original frame with the kernel K.

$$G_{i,j} = \begin{cases} 1, & F_{i,j} \geq F'_{i,j} \\ 0, & \text{otherwise} \end{cases} \tag{2}$$

The one-bit transform based motion estimation approach uses XOR (exclusive or) operation to compute block matching criteria. The calculation of the matching criteria for a given block is expressed as

$$\|G(t), G(t-1)\| = \sum_{i=1}^{N} \sum_{j=1}^{N} G_{i,j}(t) \otimes G_{i,j}(t-1) \tag{3}$$

where $\otimes$ and N show the XOR process and block size respectively. Hence, the 1BT transform uses the XOR process to perform block comparison. Therefore, a significant performance increment can be achieved in terms of speed in the case of hardware implementation of 1BT motion estimation approach. It is noted in [1] that the 1BT allows for a roughly 15:1 speed improvement with respect to the traditional architecture.

In this work 1BT based motion estimation method is modified for sub-pixel accuracy to improve the motion estimation performance. Firstly image frames are up-sampled by a factor of 2 and 4 for 0.5 and 0.25 pixel accuracy respectively. Appropriate kernels are utilized according to the image frame up-sampling factor to obtain 1-bit binary images. Then standard full search is employed using EXOR based matching criteria to obtain the motion vectors. Experimental results show that the proposed sub-pixel motion estimation approach via one-bit transform significantly outperforms the standard full-pixel 1BT based motion estimation approach, and can be used to facilitate fast sub-pixel motion estimation accuracy.

2   Sub-pixel Accuracy 1BT Matching

In block motion estimation, improved block matching results can be achieved if the motion vector is calculated with sub-pixel accuracy. MPEG2 and H.263 video coding standards support half (0.5) pel accuracy motion vectors. On the other hand, MPEG4 and H.264 standards support one-quarter (0.25) and one-eighth (0.125) pel accuracy motion vectors. Obviously better motion compensation accuracy can be obtained with higher resolution motion vectors. In other words, sub-pixel motion estimation can provide better compression than integer pixel motion estimation, at the expense of increased complexity.

In this work, the 6-tap FIR filter approach with tap values (1,-5, 20, 20,-5, 1) is used to up-sample image frames by 2 and 4 times, and the interpolation process is performed using this filter.

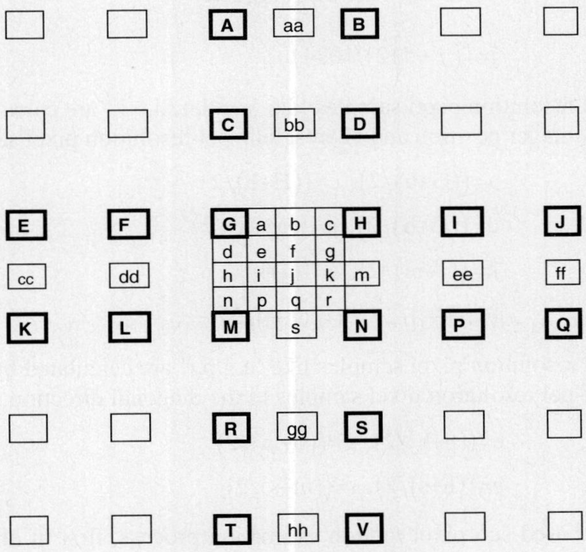

Fig. 1. Telenor up-sampling filter

Actually, several different interpolation filters exist in the literature such as the Bi-linear filter, Wiener filter and Telenor filter [8]. The tap values of the filter and the filter length changes according to the desired filter structure. In this study the Telenor filter is used. The interpolation process with quarter-pel resolution consists of two stages. The first stage is interpolation to half-pel resolution. In other words, the image frame is up-sampled 2 times. In the second stage, the up-sampled image frame is again up-sampled by a factor of 2. As a result of this process, an interpolation with quarter-pel resolution is obtained. The Telenor filter is used to calculate new pixel values as shown in Figure1. Each pixel value is calculated as follows,

- Half-pel resolution pixel samples like 'b' are calculated by applying the 6-tap filter to the nearest integer position samples in the horizontal direction. Half-pel resolution pixel samples like 'h' are calculated by applying the 6-tap filter to the nearest integer position samples in the vertical direction.

$$b = (E-5F+20G+20H-5I+J)$$
$$b = ((b+16)/32) \tag{4}$$

$$h = (A-5C+20G+20M-5R+T)$$
$$h = ((h+16)/32) \tag{5}$$

- Half-pel resolution pixel samples like 'j' are calculated by applying the 6-tap filter to the nearest half-pel resolution samples in the horizontal direction or vertical direction.

$$j = cc-5dd+20h+20m-5ee+ff$$
$$j = aa-5bb+20b+20s-5gg+hh \tag{6}$$

$$j = ((j+512)/1024) \tag{7}$$

- Quarter-pel resolution pixel samples like 'a,c,d,n,f,i,q,k' are calculated by averaging nearest integer position and nearest half-pel resolution pixel samples.

$$a = ((G+b)/2), \quad c = ((H+b)/2)$$
$$d = ((G+h)/2), \quad n = ((M+h)/2)$$
$$k = ((j+m)/2), \quad q = ((j+s)/2) \tag{8}$$
$$f = ((b+j)/2), \quad i = ((h+j)/2)$$

- Quarter-pel resolution pixel samples like 'e,g,p,r' are calculated by averaging two nearest half-pel resolution pixel samples in the diagonal direction.

$$e = ((b+h)/2), \quad g = ((b+m)/2)$$
$$p = ((h+s)/2), \quad r = ((m+s)/2) \tag{9}$$

For the 1BT based sub-pixel motion estimation process, first of all, the interpolation process is applied and frames are converted into binary bit plane representations similar to [1]. However different kernel sizes are used for half-pel and quarter-pel interpolated versions. Then, the block in the reference frame, is searched for in the 1BT of the previous frame using XOR matching.

An important point is that, if we use half-pixel resolution, the size of the maximum vector displacement that is used to determine the search window size, is increased by a factor of 2 (2:1 resolution). Similarly, if we use quarter-pixel resolution, the size of the maximum vector displacement is increased by a factor of 4 (4:1 resolution). Another important point is the size of the multi band-pass filter. The standard kernel filter given in (1) should not be applied on the interpolated image frames, and it is required to modify the filter kernel appropriately. Hence, new kernel filters (modified kernel matrices) are used in this application for the 1BTs of the up-sampled image frames. Mathematical expressions of the kernel filters are given in equations (10) and (11) respectively for 0.5 pixel and 0.25 pixel accuracy. The frequency response of the modified kernel matrix for half-pel accuracy motion estimation is shown in Figure 2.

$$K_{i,j} = \begin{cases} \dfrac{1}{25}, & i,j \in [0,8,16,24,32] \\ 0, & \text{otherwise} \end{cases} \tag{10}$$

$$K_{i,j} = \begin{cases} \dfrac{1}{25}, & i,j \in [0,16,32,48,64] \\ 0, & \text{otherwise} \end{cases} \tag{11}$$

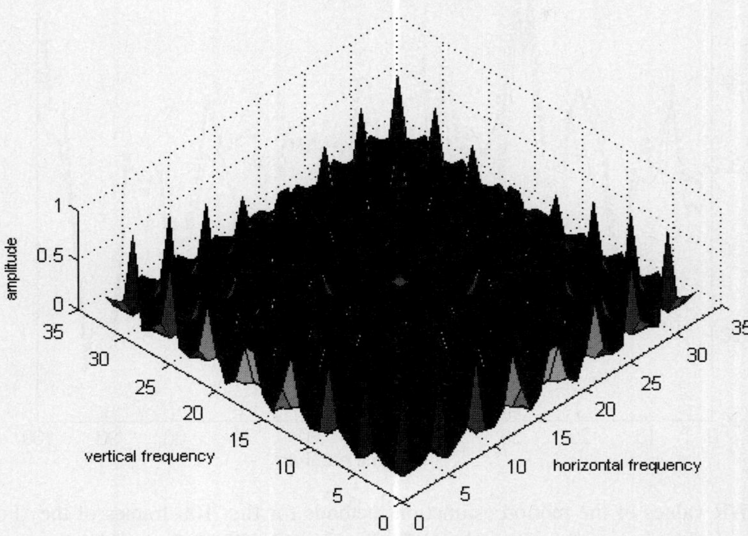

Fig. 2. Frequency response of modified filter kernel for half-pel accuracy motion estimation

3   Experimental Results

Several experiments are performed to evaluate the performance of the proposed sub-pixel motion estimation approach for various video sequences. Performance evaluation is made in terms of peak signal to noise ratio (PSNR) that is computed between the original frame and the reconstructed frame obtained from the previous frame using motion vectors computed by the proposed sub-pixel accuracy 1BT motion estimation scheme. PSNR values of the proposed approach with respect to frame numbers are given in Fig 3 for the first 100 frames of the "Foreman" sequence. It is clearly seen from this figure that the proposed sub-pixel based 1BT approaches generally outperform the standard full-pixel 1BT method proposed in [1], as expected.

Performance of the various motion estimation approaches for different sequences for block sizes of 16×16 and 8×8 are given in Table 1 and 2 respectively. MAD block matching criteria approach using sub-pel accuracy with full search (FS) is also performed and results are provided in these tables. As clearly shown from these tables sub-pixel accuracy motion estimation approach gives better performance than full-pixel MAD and full-pixel 1BT. Moreover, quarter-pixel accuracy 1BT approach provides up to 1.5 dB than the full-pixel 1BT for some test sequences. Quarter-pixel accuracy 1BT generally shows even better performance than the full-pixel 2BT method proposed in [7].

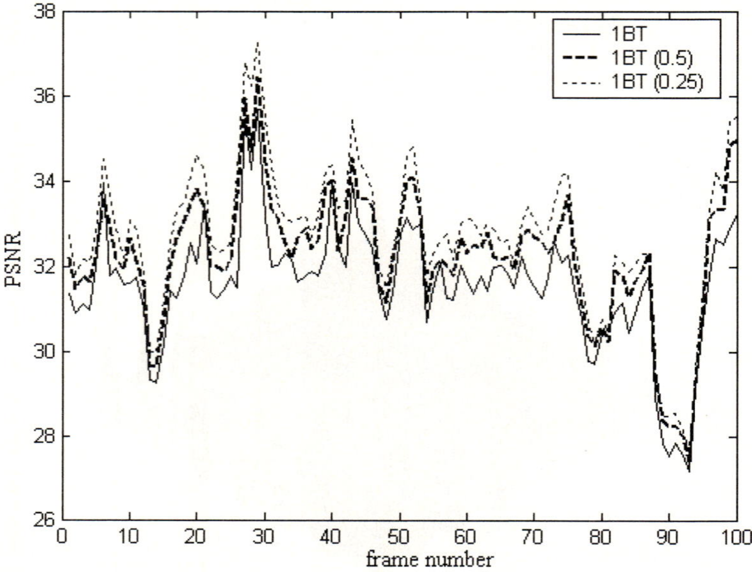

Fig. 3. PSNR values of the motion estimation methods for first 100 frames of the "Foreman" sequence at the block size of 8×8 pixels (1BT= One-bit [1], 1BT (0.5) = half-pel accuracy one-bit), 1BT (0.25) = Quarter-pel accuracy one-bit)

Table 1. Average PSNR values (dB) of several sequences for various motion estimation methods with block size of 16×16 pixels

METHOD	VIDEO SEQUENCES					
	Football (352x240) (125 frames)	Flower garden (352x240) (115 frames)	Mobile (352x240) (140 frames)	Tennis (352x240) (112 frames)	Coastguard (352x288) (299 frames)	Foreman (352x288) (299 frames)
MAD	22.88	23.79	22.99	29.87	30.48	32.11
MAD (0.5 pel)	23.50	24.86	24.87	30.60	31.21	33.56
MAD (0.25 pel)	23.82	25.52	25.80	30.98	31.82	34.19
2BT	22.08	23.43	22.72	28.89	29.93	30.71
1BT	21.83	23.32	22.71	28.77	29.84	30.44
1BT (0.5 pel)	22.31	24.15	24.49	29.27	30.36	31.13
1BT (0.25 pel)	22.53	24.61	25.27	29.49	30.79	31.54

Table 2. Average PSNR values (dB) of several sequences for various motion estimation methods with block size of 8×8 pixels

METHOD	VIDEO SEQUENCES					
	Football (352x240) (125 frames)	Flowergarden (352x240) (115 frames)	Mobile (352x240) (140 frames)	Tennis (352x240) (112 frames)	Coastguard (352x288) (299 frames)	Foreman (352x288) (299 frames)
MAD	24.73	25.22	23.88	31.25	31.59	32.90
MAD (0.5 pel)	25.78	26.88	26.30	32.23	32.61	34.72
MAD (0.25 pel)	26.24	27.85	27.57	32.68	33.42	35.53
2BT	23.36	24.55	22.99	29.91	30.50	30.64
1BT	22.70	24.11	22.73	29.22	29.20	29.84
1BT (0.5 pel)	23.38	25.09	24.73	29.71	29.64	30.87
1BT (0.25 pel)	23.68	25.57	25.42	29.80	30.19	31.41

Comparing the performance of 1BT based sub-pixel motion estimation with conventional MAD sub-pixel motion estimation, it is seen that there is a performance drop of about 1 dB for a block size of 16×16 pixels, and a drop of about 2.5 dB for a block size of 8×8 pixels. As the interpolation scheme of both approaches is the same, and the gain in 1BT is low-complexity matching of single bit-planes, the speed improvement can be regarded as 15:1 in accordance with [1].

4   Conclusion

Low bit resolution representations have been presented in the literature for motion estimation [1,7]. However sub-pixel motion estimation employing these kinds of transforms has not been tried until now. In this work, sub-pixel motion estimation via one-bit transform using interpolation of image frames followed by 1BT is proposed. Experimental results show that the proposed approach outperforms standard full-pixel 1BT method in terms of PSNR. Furthermore, better PSNR results are obtained than full-pixel 2BT for quarter-pel accuracy of 1BT. Fast search approaches can be used with 1BT to further decrease the computational load at sub-pixel level.

References

[1] B. Natarajan, V. Bhaskaran, and K. Konstantinides, "Low-Complexity Block-Based Motion Estimation via One-Bit Transforms," IEEE Trans. on Circuits and Systems for Video Technology, Vol. 7, No. 4, pp. 702-706, Aug. 1997.

[2] P. H. W. Wong and O. C. Au, "Modified One-Bit Transform for Motion Estimation," IEEE   Trans. Circuits Syst. Video Technol., Vol. 9, No. 7, pp. 1020-1024, Oct. 1999.

[3] T. Koga, K. Iinuma, A. Hirano, Y. Iijima, and T. Ishiguro, "Motion-Compensated Interframe Coding for Video Conferencing," Proc. of Nat. Telecommun.Conf., pp. G5.3.1-5.3.5, Nov./Dec. 1981.

[4] J. R. Jain and A. K. Jain, "Displacement Measurement and Its Application in Interframe Image Coding," IEEE Trans. Communication., Vol. COM-29, pp. 1799-1808, Dec. 1981.

[5] R. Li, B. Zeng, and M. L. Liou, "A New Three-Step Search Algorithm for Block Motion Estimation," IEEE Trans. on Circuits and Systems for Video Technology, Vol. 4, No. 4, pp. 438-442, Aug. 1994.

[6] A. M. Tekalp, Digital Video Processing. Englewood Cliffs, NJ: Prentice-Hall, 1995, pp. 432-455.

[7] A. Ertürk and S. Ertürk, "Two Bit Transform for Binary Block Motion Estimation " IEEE Trans. On Circuits and Systems for Video Technology, Vol. 15, No. 7, pp. 938-946, July 2005.

[8] G. Bjontegaard, "Motion Compensation with 1/4 pixel accuracy", ITU-T SG16/Q15, Geneva, Feb. 2000.

Neighborhood Decomposition of Convex Structuring Elements for Mathematical Morphology on Hexagonal Grid

Syng-Yup Ohn

Hankuk Aviation University,
Department of Computer and Information Engineering,
Seoul, Korea
syohn@hau.ac.kr

Abstract. In this paper, we present a new technique to find the optimal neighborhood decomposition for convex structuring elements used in morphological image processing on hexagonal grid. In neighborhood decomposition, a structuring element is decomposed into a set of neighborhood structuring elements, each of which consists of the combination of the origin pixel and its six neighbor pixels. Generally, neighborhood decomposition reduces the amount of computation required to perform morphological operations such as dilation and erosion. Firstly, we define a convex structuring element on a hexagonal grid and formulate the necessary and sufficient condition to decompose a convex structuring element into the set of basis convex structuring elements. Secondly, decomposability of a convex structuring element into the set of primal bases is also proved. Furthermore, cost function is used to represent the amount of computation or execution time required for performing dilations on different computing environments and by different implementation methods. The decomposition condition and the cost function are applied to find the optimal neighborhood decomposition of a convex structuring element, which guarantees the minimal amount of computation for morphological operations. Example decompositions show that the decomposition results in great reduction in the amount of computation for morphological operations.

1 Introduction

Mathematical morphology provides powerful tools in the fields of image processing and computer vision. The basic operations of mathematical morphology are dilation and erosion shown in the below, which stem from Minkowski addition and subtraction[1],[2],[3]. In the below, A and B are subsets of E^N or Z^N, where E^N or Z^N are the N-dimensional Euclidean or the digital image space. For example, a 2-dimensional binary image can be represented by a subset of Z^2, which is the set of the coordinates of foreground pixels with value 1 in the image.

Dilation:

$$A \oplus B \in \{\, a + b \mid a \in A, b \in B \}$$

(1)

A. Levi et al. (Eds.): ISCIS 2006, LNCS 4263, pp. 511–521, 2006.

Erosion:

$$A\ominus B = \{c \mid c+b\in A \ \text{ for every } \ b\in B\} \tag{2}$$

In the above, A generally represents an image and B is called a structuring element. Different image processing tasks could be achieved by choosing structuring elements of appropriate sizes and shapes, and putting the dilation and erosion operations as well as set operations in chained sequences. The structuring elements used in morphological operation play the important role of the probe to detect and extract the geometrical characteristics of an input image, and one should choose the structuring element with the size and the shape suitable for the purpose of the operation [4],[5],[6].

Dilation and erosion operation can be implemented by simple algorithms. But, it's often inefficient to use a large structuring element when an input image has a large amount of data. Also, some parallel architectures can only compute with structuring elements that fit inside a 3×3 window centered on the origin. Therefore, it is desirable to decompose a large structuring element into a sequence of dilation of smaller structuring elements. By the chain rule for dilations[3],[7], if structuring element B is decomposed into $B_1, B_2, \ldots B_n$, i.e.

$$B = B_1 \oplus B_2 \oplus \ldots \oplus B_n, \tag{3}$$

then the dilation of A by B can be computed by the sequence of dilations as

$$A\oplus B =((A\oplus B_1)\oplus B_2)\oplus\ldots\oplus B_n. \tag{4}$$

instead of a single dilation by the original structuring element. Generally, the amount of computation for the sequence of dilations as in (4) is less than that for a single dilation operation as $A \oplus B$. Also, the erosion of A by B can be computed by

$$A\ominus B = (((A\ominus B_1)\ominus B_2)\ominus\ldots)\ominus B_n. \tag{5}$$

Erosion can be benefited by decomposition similarly. In the rest of this paper, we discuss the decompositions for dilation only since an analogous discussion can be made for erosion.

Due to their regularity and simplicity, morphological operations are often implemented on parallel processing architectures or VLSI for fast processing of images [8], [9],[10]. Most parallel image processing hardwares are designed to efficiently perform local window operations within a window with size of 3×3, and for pipelined architectures such as Cytocomputer, the size of the local window is restricted to 3×3[11]. Thus, the neighborhood decomposition of a structuring element, in which every component structuring element is a neighborhood structuring element consisting of a subset of the origin and its neighborhood pixels, is an important issue.

The decomposition of structuring elements was first investigated by Zhuang and Haralick[11]. Xu[12] and Park[13] developed the methods to decompose a convex structuring element into a set of neighborhood structuring elements. The convex-shaped structuring elements are frequently used for morphological operations in image processing and computer vision tasks because of its good mathematical characteristics. Even though much research efforts are made to develop the theory and techniques for the decomposition for morphological operations on a rectangular grid, the decomposition on a hexagonal grid is yet to be explored. The theories and the techniques for decomposition on a rectangular grid are not easily extended to a hexagonal grid because the two grid systems have different geometric properties.

Due to its symmetry and uniformity in connectivity and distance between pixels, hexagonal grids are preferred than rectangular grids and shown to be optimal in some applications[14], [15]. For example, many types of display devices have hexagonal grid frames. Furthermore, Serra presented most of his theories and practices of morphology on hexagonal grids. Despite the advantage of the hexagonal grid, it is not widely used in practice because of a lack of efforts to develop mathematical foundations and applications on hexagonal grids[16].

In this paper, we present the conditions for decomposition of a convex structuring element used by morphological operations on the hexagonal grid into a set of basis convex structuring elements and propose a new technique for neighborhood decomposition. The structuring elements in a neighborhood decomposition are neighborhood structuring elements, each of which is a subset of a set consisting of the origin pixel and its 6 neighborhood pixels. Furthermore, we prove decomposability of a convex structuring element by showing it always can be decomposed into the set of primal bases.

In the previous works in[12], [13], their algorithms result in the optimal decomposition for single case or single type of hardware. However, in our approach, different optimal decompositions for different implementations of morphological operations can be easily obtained thanks to the cost functions representing the optimal criteria for the implementations of morphological operations.

The optimal decompositions of a structuring element are different for different computer architectures and implementation methods. Since different parallel processing machines exploit different modes of parallelism, one should choose the decomposition which provides a feasible implementation also requiring the minimum amount of computation on a particular parallel processing architecture. In this paper, cost function is used to represent the total amount of computation or time required to perform a sequence of dilations by the structuring elements in a decomposition[17]. By obtaining the solutions satisfying the decomposition condition and minimizing the cost functions representing the optimal criteria for different cases at the same time, the optimal decompositions for different cases can be obtained.

This paper is organized as follows. In Section 2, a convex structuring element on a hexagonal grid is defined. In Section 3, we present the conditions for the decomposition of a convex structuring element into the set of bases. In Section 4, decomposability of a convex structuring element into the minimal set of primal bases is shown. A new method for the optimal neighborhood decomposition of convex structuring element is proposed in Section 5, and example decompositions are shown in Section 6. Finally, Section 7 is our conclusion. We avoid the unnecessary mathematical elaborations and rely on figures to give intuitive explanation for the proofs of propositions in this paper.

2 Convex Structuring Element on Hexagonal Grid

2.1 Hexagonal Grid

In this paper, an oblique coordinate frame is used to index all hexagonal grid points by integers as in Fig. 1. Each point on hexagonal grid has six neighbor points. The hexagonal grid has the advantage that all neighbor points of a point have the same form of contact with the point, and the distances from a point to its all neighbors are same. In a square grid, we must distinguish between strong neighbors (horizontal or vertical neighbors) and weak neighbors (diagonal neighbors), and the distances to the two types of neighbors are different. The discussions on hexagonal grids can be found in [14],[15],[16].

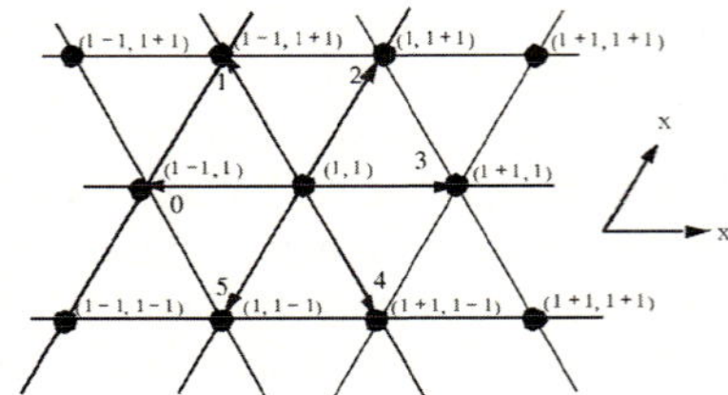

Fig. 1. Hexagonal grid and chain code directions to six neighbor points

2.2 Convex Structuring Elements on Hexagonal Grid

In our method, a convex structuring element on hexagonal grid is represented using its boundary chain codes as follows. See Fig. 1 for the different chain code directions.

Definition 1. The set of hexagonal grid points A is a called a hexagonal convex structuring element, HCSE in short, if the boundary of the image can be represented as a chain code in the form of $0^{c0}1^{c1}2^{c2}3^{c3}4^{c4}5^{c5}$ and it has no holes inside.

In Definition 1, each chain code direction corresponds a side of a polygon shape. If a c_i=0 for the ith chain code direction, then the side corresponding to the chain code direction degenerates to a vertex.

Definition 2. Suppose the boundary of HCSE P is represented as chain code sequence $0^{c0}1^{c1}2^{c2}3^{c3}4^{c4}5^{c5}$. The length of the ith edge of HCSE P, denoted as e(P, i), is defined as the chain code length c_i in the chain code sequence.

See Fig. 2 for an example HCSE . The chain code representation of the boundary of P is $0^5 1^3 2^4 3^3 4^5 5^2$, starting with point S and the lengths of edges of P are e(P, 0) = 5, e(P, 1) = 3, e(P, 2) = 4, e(P, 3) = 3, e(P, 4) = 5, e(P, 5) = 2.

In [12], [13], convex structuring elements on rectangular grid were defined using chain codes similarly to the above.

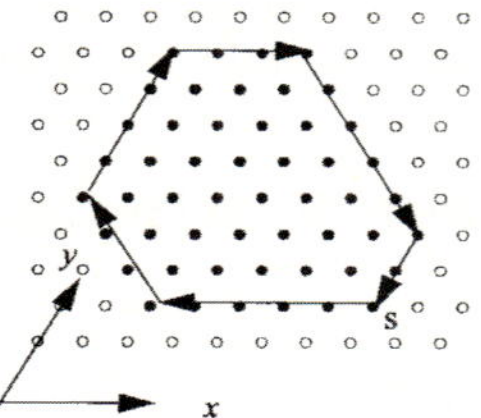

Fig. 2. Example HCSE P

3 Decomposition of HCSE

In this section, the decomposition condition of a HCSE is presented. First, the condition for a HCSE to be decomposed into two basis HCSEs is derived and it is extended into linear combination form. We consider only the shapes and ignore the positions of HCSEs for decomposition at this time, and the considerations on the positions will be added later.

Proposition 1 shows the relationship of the lengths of the edges of original HCSE and bases in a decomposition.

Proposition 1. Suppose P, Q, and R are HCSEs.

$$P = Q \oplus R, \tag{6}$$

if and only if

$$e(P, i) = e(Q, i) + e(R, i) \tag{7}$$

for $i = 0, 1, \ldots, 5$.

The necessary and sufficient condition for a HCSE to be decomposed into two HCSEs is that the length of each edge of the original HCSE should be equal to the sum of the lengths of the corresponding edges of the HCSEs in the decomposition. Fig. 3 shows an illustrative example of Proposition 1. In the figure, $P = Q \oplus R$, and $e(P, i) = e(Q, i) + e(R, i)$ for $i = 0, 1, \ldots, 5$.

Proposition 1 can be extended to a linear combination form as in Proposition 2. In the below, nQ represents the n-fold dilation of image Q.

Proposition 2. Suppose that P and Q_ks, where $k = 1, 2, \ldots, n$, are HCSEs.

$$P = a_1Q_1 \oplus a_2Q_2 \oplus \ldots \oplus a_nQ_n, \tag{8}$$

if and only if

$$e(P,i) = \sum_{k=1}^{n} a_k e(Q_k, i) \tag{9}$$

for $i = 0, 1, \ldots, 5$, where a_k is a non-negative integer.

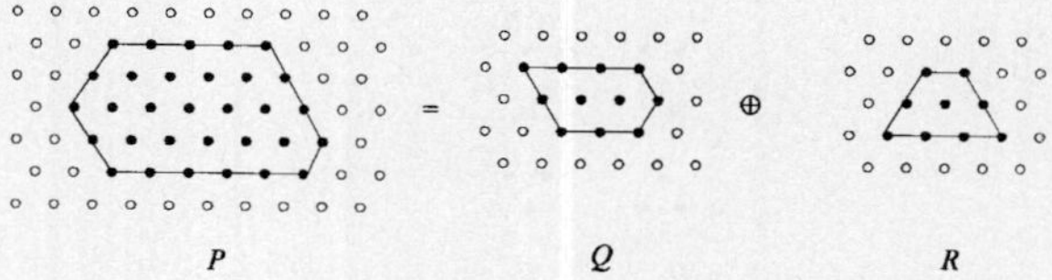

Fig. 3. Illustration of Proposition 1

Finally, the positions of HCSEs in decomposition are considered. Suppose A, B, and C to be the sets of points such that $C = A \oplus B$. Then $\min_x(C) = \min_x(A) + \min_x(B)$, where $\min_x(C)$ denotes the minimum x-coordinate of the region occupied by C, and similarly for y-coordinates. Thus, if $P = a_1Q_1 \oplus a_2Q_2 \oplus \ldots \oplus a_nQ_n$, then $\min_x(P) =$

$a_1\min_x(Q_1) + a_2\min_x(Q_2) + \ldots + a_n\min_x(Q_n)$, and similarly for y-coordinates. Taking the relationships of positions into consideration, we show the decomposition condition for HCSE P to be decomposed into the combination of $a_1\,Q_1$s, $a_2\,Q_2$s, $\ldots$, $a_n\,Q_n$s. in Proposition 3.

Proposition 3. Suppose that P and Q_k, where $k = 1,\ldots, n$ are HCSEs.

$$P = a_1Q_1 \oplus a_2Q_2 \oplus \ldots \oplus a_nQ_n, \tag{10}$$

if and only if

$$e(P,i) = \sum_{k=1}^{n} a_k e(Q_k,i) \tag{11}$$

for $i = 0, 1,\ldots, 5$, and

$$\min_x(P) = a_1\min_x(Q_1) + a_2\min_x(Q_2) + \ldots + a_n\min_x(Q_n)$$
$$\min_y(P) = a_1\min_y(Q_1) + a_2\min_y(Q_2) + \ldots + a_n\min_y(Q_n) \tag{12}$$

where a_ks are a non-negative integers.

In Proposition 3, the solution n-tuple, $(a_1, a_2, \ldots, a_n)$, satisfying (11) and (12) determines a decomposition of P into a set of bases, $\{Q_1, Q_2, \ldots, Q_n,\}$ since (11) and (12) is the necessary and sufficient condition for (10). Furthermore, all the possible decomposition of P into the basis set are determined by the set of all the solution n-tuples satisfying (11) and (12).

4 Primal Bases and Decomposability of HCSE

In this section, we present the minimal set of primal basis HCSEs and prove decomposability of a HCSE. The minimal set of primal bases is the set of HCSEs with the minimum number of elements with which any non-singleton HCSE can be composed by dilation. In turn, any non-singleton HCSE has at least one decomposition consisting of primal bases. We consider only the shapes of HCSEs in the discussion of primal basis and decomposability of HCSEs in this section. Fig. 4 shows the minimal set of primal bases. There are 41 neighborhood HCSEs, and they are denoted as H_0, H_1, $\ldots H_{40}$, of which we have 5 primal bases, H_0, H_1, H_2, H_6, H_7.

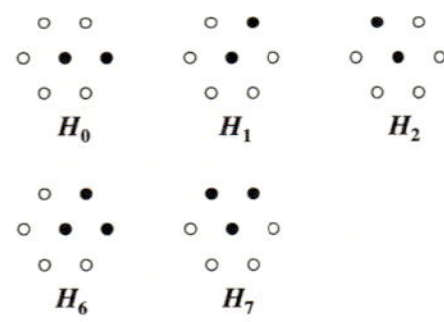

Fig. 4. Primal basis HCSEs

In the following, it is shown that there always exists a solution n-tuple determining a decomposition for any HCSE that satisfies (9) involving the set of primal bases. For any HCSE P, one of the solution 6-tuples $(a_0, a_1, a_2, a_6, a_7)$ satisfying (9) and determining the decomposition such that $P = a_0H_0 \oplus a_1H_1 \oplus a_2H_2 \oplus a_6H_6 \oplus a_7H_7$ is as follows.

Case i. In case that $e(P, 0) \le e(P, 3)$,

$$
\begin{aligned}
a_0 &= e(P, 0), \\
a_1 &= e(P, 2), \\
a_2 &= e(P, 4), \\
a_6 &= 0, \\
a_7 &= e(P, 3) - e(P, 0).
\end{aligned}
\tag{13}
$$

Case ii. In case that $e(P, 0) > e(P, 3)$,

$$
\begin{aligned}
a_0 &= e(P, 3), \\
a_1 &= e(P, 5), \\
a_2 &= e(P, 1), \\
a_6 &= e(P, 0) - e(P, 3), \\
a_7 &= 0.
\end{aligned}
\tag{14}
$$

It is easy to show that 6-tuples $(a_0, a_1, a_2, a_6, a_7)$ in each case satisfy condition (9) in terms of P and primal bases, H_0, H_1, H_2, H_6, and H_7, using the fact that a HCSE has the property on the lengths of edges as follows.

$$
\begin{aligned}
e(P, 0) + e(P, 1) &= e(P, 3) + e(P, 4) \\
e(P, 1) + e(P, 2) &= e(P, 4) + e(P, 5) \\
e(P, 2) + e(P, 3) &= e(P, 5) + e(P, 0)
\end{aligned}
\tag{15}
$$

5   Neighborhood Decomposition of HCSE

5.1   Neighborhood Decomposition

In Proposition 3, an n-tuple $(a_1, a_2, ..., a_n)$ which satisfies conditions (11) and (12) determines a decomposition of HCSE P into the set of bases $\{Q_1, Q_2, ..., Q_n\}$, and the solution space of n-tuples contains all the possible decompositions of P into the set of bases. The decomposition conditions for HCSE can be immediately applied to the decomposition of a HCSE into the set of neighborhood HCSEs. A neighborhood HCSE is a HCSE which consists of a subset of the set of origin pixel and its six neighbors. In case of neighborhood decomposition, the set of 41 neighborhood HCSEs is used as the bases for decomposition.

5.2   Cost Function

We use cost function to represent optimal criteria for decomposition[17]. The total processing cost or time required to perform the sequence of dilation operations with structuring elements of $a_1 Q_1$s, $a_2 Q_2$s, ..., $a_n Q_n$s can be formulated as

$$
\sum_{k=1}^{n} a_k c_k ,
\tag{16}
$$

where c_k is the processing cost to perform a dilation operation with structuring element Q_k with an input image. Generally, it is reasonable to assign a constant cost to each structuring element since the processing time for a dilation operation does not depend on the contents of an input image but on the size. A cost function can be used to represent the optimal criterion of decomposition for different implementation methods of dilation operation. The optimal decomposition for a particular implementation of dilation is the one that minimizes the computation time or cost to perform dilation by the implementation and different optimal decompositions can be obtained for different implementation methods.

On a general-purpose computer with single CPU, dilation can be performed by ORing the set of translated input images. The cost to perform a dilation operation with a structuring element is proportional to the number of the OR operations required to perform the dilation operation, which is equal to the number pixels having value 1 contained in the structuring element. In case of parallel processing architectures, different optimal decomposition criteria can be obtained according to the modes of parallelism that the architectures exploit.

5.3   Optimization Problem

The problem of finding the optimal decomposition of a HCSE can be converted into a linear optimization problem. In the optimization problem, the constraints are the set of linear integer equations on the conditions for the decomposition and the location involving the original HCSE and the set of the decomposition bases as in (11) and (12). The objective function to be minimized is the cost function representing the optimization criterion of the algorithm or the computer architecture for a dilation operation as in (16).

5.4   Finding Solution for Neighborhood Decomposition

The solution n-tuple that minimizes a cost function and satisfies the decomposition condition at the same time can be found by linear integer programming technique[18]. The objective function to be minimized is the cost function representing the optimal criterion for an implementation method of dilation operation. The constraints of the linear integer programming are the set of linear integer equations generated by the decomposition conditions, (11) and (12), involving the original structuring element and the set of 41 the neighborhood bases.

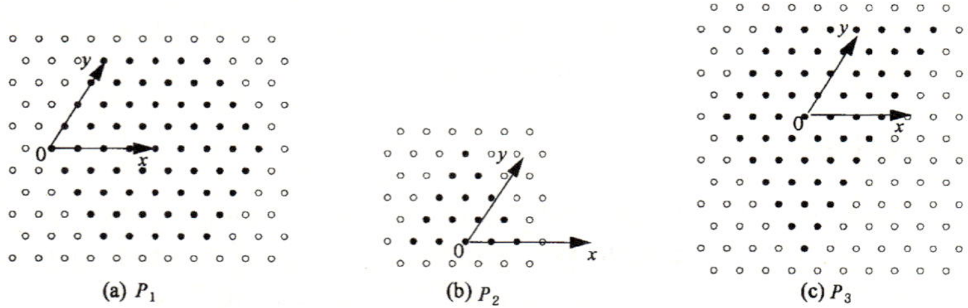

Fig. 5. Example HCSEs

6   Decomposition Examples

The optimal neighborhood decompositions of example convex structuring elements in Fig. 5 for general-purpose computers are shown in Table 1. The neighborhood HCSEs in the decompositions are listed in Fig. 6. Also, in Table 2, the costs for performing dilations with the sequence of the structuring elements in the optimal neighborhood decompositions are compared to the costs with the original structuring elements. In this case, the cost is the number of OR operations with translated input images required for dilation operation. For each example HCSE, the decomposition reduces the amount of computation or the execution time required for dilation.

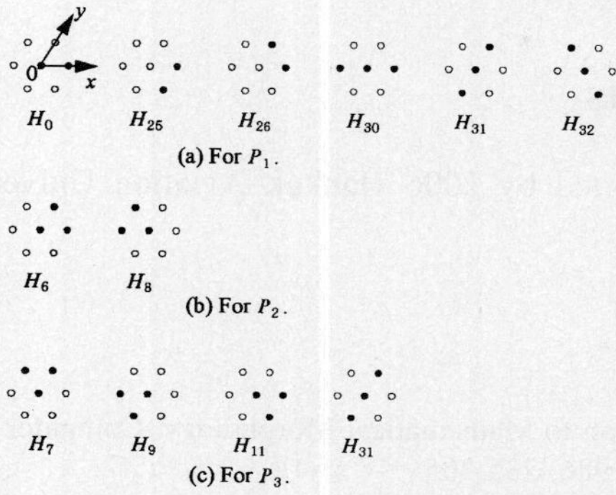

$$H_0 \qquad H_{25} \qquad H_{26} \qquad H_{30} \qquad H_{31} \qquad H_{32}$$

(a) For P_1.

$$H_6 \qquad H_8$$

(b) For P_2.

$$H_7 \qquad H_9 \qquad H_{11} \qquad H_{31}$$

(c) For P_3.

Fig. 6. Neighborhood bases in the decompositions of example HCSEs

Table 1. Decomposition results for example HCSEs in Fig. 5

Example HCSE	Example
P_1	$2H_0 \oplus 2H_{25} \oplus 2H_{26} \oplus H_{30} \oplus H_{31} \oplus H_{32}$
P_2	$2H_6 \oplus 2H_8$
P_3	$3H_7 \oplus H_9 \oplus 2H_{11} \oplus 2H_{31}$

Table 2. Comparison of the numbers of OR operations of images required for dilation by original structuring elements and by decomposed sequences of optimal local decomposition

Example HCSE	Original Structuring Element	Decomposed Sequence by Optimal Neighborhood Decomposition
P_1	61	21
P_2	15	12
P_3	66	24

7 Conclusion

In this paper, we presented the decomposition condition for convex structuring elements on hexagonal grid and proved the existence of decomposition into the primal basis convex structuring elements. Furthermore, the condition is applied to the neighborhood decomposition, in which each basis is a small structuring element consisting of a subset of the set of origin pixels and its six neighbors. Cost function represents the different optimal criteria on the decomposition for different implementations of morphological operations. The optimal decompositions which satisfy the decomposition condition and minimize the cost function at the same time can be found by linear integer programming. Thanks to the cost function, our method can be used to obtain different optimal neighborhood decompositions for different cases. We also showed that the optimal neighborhood decomposition greatly reduces the amount of computation for dilation operation by example decompositions.

Acknowledgements

This work was supported by 2006 Hankuk Aviation University Faculty Research Grant.

References

1. Serra, J.: Introduction to Mathematical Morphology. Computer Vision, Graphics and Image Processing 35 (1986) 285-305
2. Serra, J.: Image Analysis and Mathematical Morphology. Academic Press London(1982)
3. Haralick, R. M., Sternberg, S.R., Zhuang, X.: Image Analysis Using Mathematical Morphology. IEEE Trans. on PAMI 9 (1987) 532-550
4. Aykac, D., Hoffman, E.A., McLennan, G., Reinhardt, J.M.: Segmentation and analysis of the human airway tree from three-dimensional X-ray CT images. IEEE Transactions on Medical Imaging **22** (2003) 940 – 950
5. Zana, F., Klein, J.-C.: Segmentation of vessel-like patterns using mathematical morphology and curvature evaluation. IEEE Trans. on Image Processing on Vol. 10. (2001) 1010 – 1019
6. Soille, P., Pesaresi, M.: Advances in mathematical morphology applied to geoscience and remote sensing. IEEE Trans.on Geoscience and Remote Sensing, Vol. 40. (2002) 2042–2055
7. Zhuang, X., Haralick, R. M.: Morphological Structuring Element Decomposition. Computer Vision, Graphics and Image Processing 35 (1986) 370-382
8. Dadda, L.; Parallel algorithms and architectures for CPUs and dedicated processors: development and trends Algorithms and Architectures for Parallel Processing ICAPP 95 vol. 2 (1995) 939 - 948
9. Svolos, A.I.; Konstantopoulos, C.G.; Kaklamanis, C.: Efficient Binary Morphological Algorithms on a Massively Parallel Processor. International Parallel and Distributed Processing Symposium 2000 Proceedings (2000) 281 - 286
10. York, G., Managuli, R., Kim, Y.: Fast Binary and Grayscale Mathematical Morphology on VLIW. Proc. Of SPIE: Real-Time Imaging IV (1999) 45–55
11. Levialdi, S.: Computer Architectures for Image Analysis. 9th International Conference on Pattern Recognition vol.2 (1988) 1148 - 1158
12. Xu, J.: Decomposition of Convex Polygonal Morphological Structuring Elements into Neighborhood Subsets. IEEE Trans. on PAMI 13 (1991) 153-162
13. Park, H., Chin, R.T,: Optimal Decomposition of Convex Morphological Structuring Elements for 4-connected Parallel Array Processors. IEEE Trans. on PAMI, Vol. 16 (1994) 304-313

14. C.A. Wuthrich, P. Stucki, An algorithmic comparison between square- and hexagonal grids. CVGIP:Graphical Models Image Processing, Vol. 53. (1991) 324-339
15. I. Her, C.-T. Yuan: Resampling on a pseudo-hexagonal grid. CVGIP: Graphical Models Image Processing, Vol. 56. (1994) 336-347
16. Innchyn Her: Geometric transformations on the hexagonal grid. IEEE Trans. on Image Processing, Vol. 4. (1995) 1213-1222
17. Syng-Yup Ohn: Decomposition of 3D Convex Structuring Element in Morphological Operation for Parallel Processing Architectures. Lecture Notes in Computer Science, Vol. 3656. (2005) 644-651
18. Syslo, M. M., Deo, N., Kowalik, J. S.: Discrete Optimization Algorithms. Prentice Hall Englewood Cliff (1983)

Block Motion Estimation Using Modified Two-Bit Transform

Begüm Demir and Sarp Ertürk

Kocaeli University Laboratory of Image and Signal Processing (KULIS),
Electronic and Telecomm. Eng. Dept., Veziroglu Campus, 41040 Kocaeli, Turkey
{begum.demir, sertur}@kou.edu.tr

Abstract. Modified two-bit transform based block motion estimation is presented in this paper. Initially video frames are converted into two-bit representations using the two-bit transform (2BT) and binary block based motion estimation is performed using these two bit-planes. Modification to the original 2BT based motion estimation scheme is introduced by conditional local or full searches using the MAD criterion to improve the initial motion estimation accuracy. Experimental results show that the proposed modified 2BT-based motion estimation technique can significantly improve peak signal-to-noise radio performance compared to 2BT without modification, and also outperforms the modified one-bit transform (1BT) based motion estimation approach.

1   Introduction

Video compression is necessary in a wide range of application to reduce the total data amount required for the transmission or storage of video data. Motion estimation/compensation plays a significant role in removing temporal redundancies between image frames in video coding systems. Motion estimation performs up to 50% of the computations encountered in the entire coding system, and is commonly remarked as the computationally most intensive part of the video coding system [1].

Block matching, that divides the frame into rectangular blocks and searches for the best matching block inside a certain search window in the previous frame, is the most popular technique used for motion estimation in video coding systems [2]. The optimal matching search strategy is full search (FS) that exhaustively checks all candidate locations within the search window for the best matching block. However the computational complexity of full search is extremely high as all candidate locations are investigated, making it particularly unsuitable for real-time video coding. The mean absolute difference (MAD) or mean square error (MSE) matching criteria are considered to be statistically optimal solutions to the matching process.

Various methods have been proposed to reduce the high computational load of the FS-MAD based block motion estimation technique. Approaches proposed for this purpose can be divided into three main categories [3]. The first category of techniques use fast search algorithms to evaluate only part of the candidate search locations. These methods reduce computation complexity by selecting a subset of the possible

A. Levi et al. (Eds.): ISCIS 2006, LNCS 4263, pp. 522–531, 2006.

search candidate locations. Three-step search (3SS) [4], 2-D logarithmic search (LOGS) [5],cross search [6], conjugate direction search (CDS) [7], new three step search [8], four step search (4SS) [9], block based gradient descent search (BBGDS) [10], diamond search (DS) [11], polynomial search (PS) [12], zonal search [13] and adaptive irregular pattern search [14] are examples for methods falling into this category.

The second category of techniques comprises methods that use pattern or motion vector sub-sampling approaches to reduce computational complexity [15-18]. In [15], a fraction of the pixels within the block is used in the matching and the motion field is computed for a fraction of the blocks only, while the motion vectors of the remainder blocks are interpolated from the computed motion vectors. Hexagonal sub-sampling is proposed in [16]. Adaptive pixel decimation using selective pixels whose features are important to determine a match has been proposed in [17]. Adaptive block matching scan and the utilization of representative pixels obtained by Taylor series expansion has been proposed in [18].

The approaches falling into the third category concentrate on using different matching criteria instead of MAD to achieve reduction in computational complexity. In [19], the block mean is used as threshold to represent pixels using a single bit-plane through a one-bit transform (1BT). The bit-plane of an image frame is constructed as

$$B(i, j) = \begin{cases} 1, & \text{if } I(i, j) \ge t_{bm} \\ 0, & \text{otherwise} \end{cases} \tag{1}$$

where t_{bm} is the threshold value (i.e. block mean). In [20], the original image frame has been compared with a multi band-pass filtered version to create one-bit /pixel representations. A 17×17 sized multi band-pass filter kernel which is used to filter the image frame, is defined in the form of

$$K(i, j) = \begin{cases} 1/25, & \text{if } i,j \in [0,4,8,12,16] \\ 0, & \text{otherwise} \end{cases} \tag{2}$$

Then, one-bit representations of image frames are calculated as

$$B(i, j) = \begin{cases} 1, & \text{if } I(i, j) \ge I_F(i, j) \\ 0, & \text{otherwise} \end{cases} \tag{3}$$

where $I_f(i, j)$ is the filtered form of the image frame $I(i, j)$. When a single bit is used in the representation of image frames, bad motion vectors can be obtained, particularly for small block sizes. In [21], a conditional local search algorithm has been added to the 1BT based motion estimation approach to improve the estimation accuracy at the cost of higher computational complexity. Block based motion estimation using a two-bit/pixel representation has been proposed in [22], to improve the motion estimation accuracy and reduce bad motion vectors compared to 1BT.

In this paper, modified two-bit transform based motion estimation is presented. A modification similar to the one proposed for 1BT based motion estimation in [21] is utilized in this paper for modified 2BT based motion estimation. Conditional searches are added to 2BT in order to improve motion estimation accuracy. Experimental results are obtained for different video sequences using various conditional search constraints, and compared with standard 1BT and 2BT as well as modified 1BT based motion estimation. It is shown that modified 2BT based motion estimation can be used to improve motion estimation accuracy compared to 2BT at the cost of increased computational complexity. Note that the total computational will still be substantially lower than standard FS-MAD motion estimation.

This paper is organized as follows. In the following section, initially the two-bit transform is reviewed and the two step search modification is described. In the third section experimental result are presented. Conclusions are given in the final section.

2 Modified 2BT Based Block Motion Estimation

Two-bit transform based motion estimation has been proposed in [22]. The proposed 2BT, obtains a two-bit representation using block based transformations. Local mean and standard deviation values are computed to convert image frames into two-bit representations. In 2BT based motion estimation, low motion estimation complexity is achieved though binary matching criteria and low bit depth representations. It is shown in [22] that 2BT improves motion estimation accuracy compared to 1BT.In 2BT, local mean (μ) and variance (σ^2) values are computed as,

$$\mu = E[I_{tw}]$$
$$\sigma^2 = E[I_{tw}] - E^2[I_{tw}]$$
(4)

where I_{tw} shows pixel values in the local threshold window constructed around the transforming block. Standard deviation values can be obtained from the variance using a square root operation or a linear approximation to this operation as presented in [22].The 2BT can then be obtained in the form of

$$B_1(i,j) = \begin{cases} 1, & \text{if } I(i,j) \ge \mu \\ 0, & \text{otherwise} \end{cases}$$

$$B_2(i,j) = \begin{cases} 1, & \text{if } I(i,j) \ge \mu+\sigma \text{ or } I(i,j) \le \mu-\sigma \\ 0, & \text{otherwise} \end{cases}$$
(5)

where $B_1(i,j)$ and $B_2(i,j)$ represent the resulting two bit-planes, hence a total of four separate classes are derived.

The number of non-matching defined as

$$NNMP(m,n) = \sum_{i=0}^{N-1}\sum_{j=0}^{N-1} \{B_1^t(i,j) \oplus B_1^{t-1}(i+m,j+n)\} \|$$
$$\{B_2^t(i,j) \oplus B_2^{t-1}(i+m,j+n)\},$$
$$-s \le m, \text{n} \le \text{s-1}$$
(6)

is used as matching criterion to find the best matching block. Here, $NNMP(m,n)$ is the number of non-matching points for a displacement (i.e. motion vector) of (m,n) pixels,

$B_{1,2}^{t}(i,j)$ shows the current image frame, $B_{1,2}^{t-1}(i,j)$ shows the previous image frame, s determines the search range, N determines the block size, $\oplus$ represents the Boolean Exclusive-OR operation, and $\|$ represents the Boolean OR operation.

The modification approach presented in this paper is based on multiple candidate two-step search, and is inspired by [21]. The main reason why the strategy of [21] was adopted is that 2BT normally outperforms 1BT based motion estimation, and as the modification in [21] significantly improves the accuracy of 1BT, the same modification can be considered to be appropriate for 2BT as well.

In the modified two-bit transform (M2BT) motion estimation approach presented in this paper, initially, the first and second best motion vectors are obtained using conventional 2BT based motion estimation as presented in [22] for each block. Then, distortion measures corresponding to first and second best motion vectors are calculated. The sub-sampled sum of differences (SSAD) is used as the block distortion measure. Note that although two different sub-sampling patterns have been presented in [21] for the SSAD computation, only the one shown in equation 1 is used in this paper, as this one results in higher motion estimation accuracy. The utilized distortion measure can be expressed in the form of

$$D = \sum_{(i \bmod 2 = j \bmod 2)} \left| I(i,j) - I_{t-1}(i - mv_x, j - mv_y) \right| \tag{7}$$

where (i,j) is used as pixel index, $I(i,j)$ shows the pixels within the current block, and $I_{t-1}(i - mv_x, j - mv_y)$ shows the pixels within the corresponding block of the previous frame having a motion vector displacement of (mv_x, mv_y).

Once this distortion measure is computed for the first and second best motion vectors obtained using 2BT motion estimation, the resulting distortions are compared against a threshold value (T). If the distortion corresponding to the first best motion vector (mv_1) is below T , the final block motion vector is assigned as mv_1 . Otherwise, the second best motion vector (mv_2) distortion is evaluated and if this value is below T , the final block motion vector is assigned as mv_2 . If both distortion values are above the threshold, multiple-candidate two step search (M2SS) is performed around mv_1 and mv_2 to find the final motion vector. Figure 1 shows the two-step search path utilized. First, SSAD is computed for five locations centered at mv_1 and mv_2 (marked as diamonds in Fig. 1, and the point with the lowest distortion measure is identified. Then, a second search is carried out for eight locations (marked as circles in Fig. 1) around the point with the lowest distortion measure to determine the point with the lowest distortion measure at this stage. This process is carried out around mv_1 and mv_2 , and the location with the lowest distortion measure is identified. If this distortion is below the threshold value (T), the corresponding displacement is assigned as the motion vector of the block. Otherwise, full-search with the distortion computed as given in (7) is utilized as final prospect to find an acceptable match and the motion vector computed through FS is assigned as the final motion vector of the block.

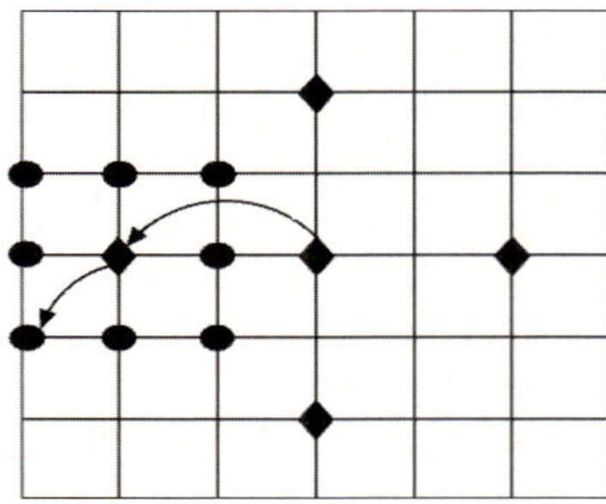

Fig. 1. The utilized two step search path

3   Experimental Results

In order to evaluate the performance of the proposed modified two-bit transform (referred to as M2BT), motion estimation has additionally been performed using standard full-search with MAD matching (referred to as MAD), standard one-bit transform (referred to as 1BT), standard two-bit transform (referred to as 2BT) and modified one-bit transform (referred to as M1BT) for various video sequences for block sizes of $16{\times}16$ pixels with a search range of 16 pixels as well as block sizes of $8{\times}8$ pixels with a search range of 8 pixels. In order to assess the motion estimation accuracy, each frame is reconstructed from the previous frame using motion vectors computed with the mentioned approaches and peak signal-to-noise ratio (PSNR) values between reconstructed and original frames are computed.

Tables 1-3 show results for the "football", "tennis" and "foreman" test sequences for block sizes of $16{\times}16$ pixels with a search range of 16 pixels. For the M1BT and M2BT, various threshold values are investigated to observe the influence of the threshold value which is used to decide if any additional search is required, and results for several threshold values are shown in the tables. In addition to PSNR values, the percentage of motion vectors computed without additional local search, i.e. directly from 1BT or 2BT only (denoted as %mv-stage1); the percentage of motion vectors computed with additional multiple-candidate two-step search (M2SS) after 1BT or 2BT (denoted as %mv-stage2); and the percentage of motion vectors calculated after the final full-search stage with MAD (denoted as %mv-stage3) are also provided for M1BT and M2BT. It is seen in these tables, that M2BT provides about the same or a slightly better motion estimation accuracy compared with M1BT for block sizes of $16{\times}16$ pixels with a search range of 16 pixels, however a higher percentage of motion vectors is decided in earlier stages of the motion estimation process, resulting in faster computation and lower computational load in M2BT.

Tables 4-6 show results for the "football", "tennis" and "foreman" test sequences for block sizes of $8{\times}8$ pixels with a search range of 8 pixels. In this case M2BT not only provides improved motion estimation accuracy, but also results in a lower computational load compared with M1BT. It is seen in particular that the PSNR gap increases if the number of motion vectors computed using FS-MAD is reduced through the utilization of a higher threshold value.

Table 1. Results for the "football" sequence (block size: 16×16 , search range of 16 pixels)

Method		Football (352×240) (125 frames)			
		PSNR	%mv-stage1	%mv-stage2	%mv-stage3
MAD		22.88	NA	NA	NA
1BT [20]		21.83	NA	NA	NA
2BT [22]		22.08	NA	NA	NA
M1BT [21]	T=1500	22.72	68.45	23.83	7.72
	T=3000	22.24	91.28	8.33	0.39
	T=3500	22.13	94.27	5.59	0.14
M2BT	T=1500	22.73	69.02	24.41	6.57
	T=3000	22.36	92.79	7.07	0.14
	T=3500	22.29	95.65	4.32	0.03

Table 2. Results for the "tennis" sequence (block size: 16×16 , search range of 16 pixels)

Method		Tennis (352×240) (112 frames)			
		PSNR	%mv-stage1	%mv-stage2	%mv-stage3
MAD		29.87	NA	NA	NA
1BT [20]		28.77	NA	NA	NA
2BT [22]		28.89	NA	NA	NA
M1BT [21]	T=1500	29.53	94.00	4.28	1.72
	T=3000	29.07	98.07	1.30	0.63
	T=3500	28.99	98.43	1.12	0.45
M2BT	T=1500	29.50	94.04	4.47	1.49
	T=3000	29.03	97.17	2.63	0.20
	T=3500	28.98	98.00	1.88	0.12

Table 3. Results for the "foreman" sequence (block size: 16×16 , search range of 16 pixels)

Method		Foreman (352×288) (299 frames)			
		PSNR	%mv-stage1	%mv-stage2	%mv-stage3
MAD		32.10	NA	NA	NA
1BT [20]		30.36	NA	NA	NA
2BT [22]		30.71	NA	NA	NA
M1BT [21]	T=1500	31.13	96.48	2.86	0.66
	T=3000	30.71	99.14	0.80	0.06
	T=3500	30.65	99.38	0.58	0.04
M2BT	T=1500	31.14	96.83	2.69	0.48
	T=3000	30.81	99.40	0.58	0.02
	T=3500	30.75	99.621	0.37	0.009

Table 4. Results for the "football" sequence (block size: 8×8, search range of 8 pixels)

Method		Football (352×240) (125 frames)			
		PSNR	%mv-stage1	%mv-stage2	%mv-stage3
MAD		24.73	NA	NA	NA
1BT [20]		22.72	NA	NA	NA
2BT [22]		23.36	NA	NA	NA
M1BT [21]	T=300	24.42	64.46	26.07	9.47
	T=500	24.03	82.64	15.15	2.21
	T=700	23.63	90.93	8.52	0.55
M2BT	T=300	24.49	66.79	25.06	8.15
	T=500	24.23	85.30	13.22	1.48
	T=700	23.96	93.16	6.60	0.24

Table 5. Results for the "tennis" sequence (block size: 8×8, search range of 8 pixels)

Method		Tennis (352×240) (112 frames)			
		PSNR	%mv-stage1	%mv-stage2	%mv-stage3
MAD		31.25	NA	NA	NA
1BT [20]		29.23	NA	NA	NA
2BT [22]		29.91	NA	NA	NA
M1BT [21]	T=300	30.63	91.20	6.75	2.05
	T=500	30.25	96.55	2.31	1.14
	T=700	29.95	97.88	1.45	0.67
M2BT	T=300	30.70	92.05	6.17	1.78
	T=500	30.44	97.10	1.91	0.99
	T=700	30.26	98.30	1.10	0.60

Table 6. Results for the "foreman" sequence (block size: 8×8, search range of 8 pixels)

Method		Foreman (352×288) (299 frames)			
		PSNR	%mv-stage1	%mv-stage2	%mv-stage3
MAD		32.89	NA	NA	NA
1BT [20]		29.82	NA	NA	NA
2BT [22]		30.64	NA	NA	NA
M1BT [21]	T=300	31.38	89.97	8.57	1.46
	T=500	30.72	96.27	3.33	0.40
	T=700	30.37	98.15	1.70	0.15
M2BT	T=300	31.61	91.48	7.59	0.93
	T=500	31.14	97.42	2.36	0.22
	T=700	30.91	98.84	1.09	0.07

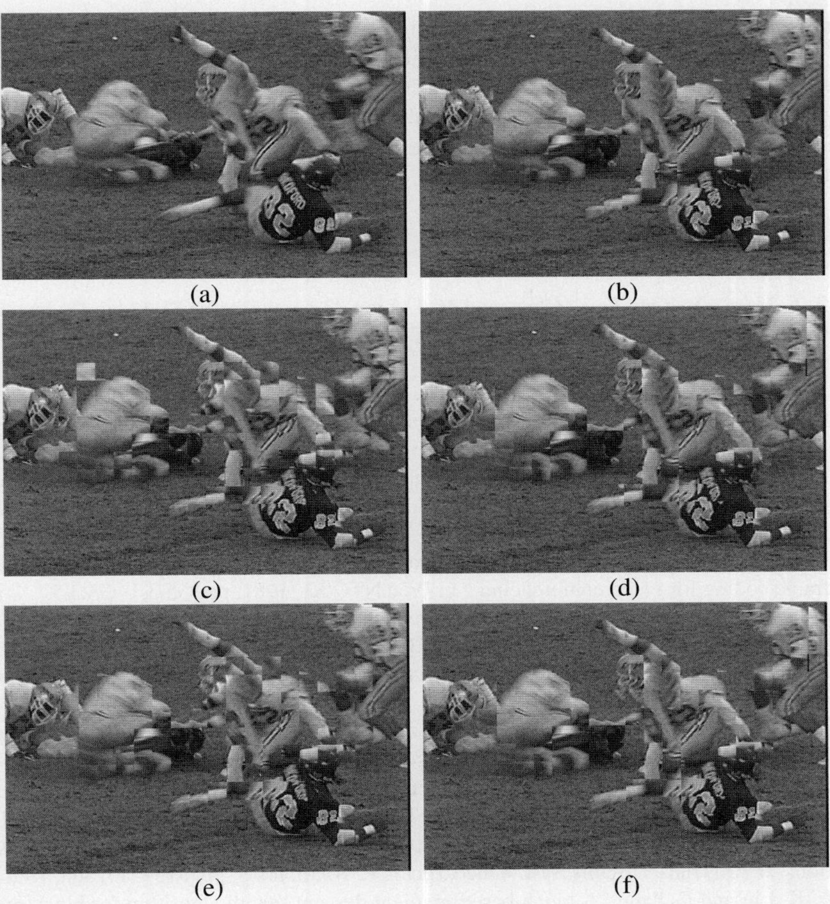

Fig. 2. Sample results for the "football" test sequence, with a block size of 16x16 and search range of 16 pixels. (a) Original frame #15. Frame #15 reconstructed from the previous frame with motion vectors of (b) MAD (PSNR=22.97dB). (c) 1BT (PSNR=21.25dB). (d) 2BT (PSNR=22.08). (e) M1BT (PSNR=22.17dB) using T=3000. (f) M2BT using (PSNR=22.41dB) using T=3000.

Fig. 2 shows an example frame of the "football" sequence together with images reconstructed from the previous frames using motion vectors computed with the aforementioned methods. It is seen that M2BT not only provides improved PSNR results compared to M1BT, but the visual appearance is much more acceptable in M2BT as the number of bad motion vectors is lower than M1BT.

4   Conclusions

Modified two-bit transform (M2BT) based block motion estimation has been presented in this paper. Conditional searches with MAD criterion are added to two-bit transform based motion estimation to improve the motion estimation accuracy at the cost of computational complexity. If 2BT estimation accuracy is below a certain threshold, additional MAD based searches are executed. It is shown that M2BT improves the motion estimation accuracy compared to standard 2BT based motion estimation. It is also shown that M2BT outperforms M1BT based motion estimation in terms of accuracy and computational load.

References

1. Z.-L. He, C.-Y. Tsui, K.-K. Chan, and M. L. Liou, "Low-power VLSI design for motion estimation using adaptive pixel truncation," IEEE Trans.Circuits Syst. Video Technol., vol. 10, no. 8, pp. 669–678, Aug. 2000

2. J. M. Jou, P.-Y. Chen, and J.-M. Sun, "The gray prediction search algorithm for block motion estimation," IEEE Trans. Circuits Syst. Video Technol., vol. 9, no. 6, pp. 843–848, Sep. 1999.

3. M. Mattavelli and G. Zoia, "Vector-tracing algorithm for motion estimation in large search windows," IEEE Trans. Circuits Syst. Video Technol., vol. 10, no. 12, pp. 1426–1437, Dec. 2000.

4. T. Koga, K. Linuma, A. Hirano, Y. Lijima, and T. Ishiguro, "Motion-compensated inter-frame coding for video conferencing," in Proc.NTC'81, 1981, pp. G5.3.1–G5.3.5.

5. J. Jain and A. Jain, "Displacement measurement and its application in internal image coding," IEEE Trans. Commun., vol. 29, no. COM–12, pp. 1799–1808, Dec. 1981.

6. M. Ghanbari, "The cross-search algorithm for motion estimation," IEEE Trans. Commun., vol. 38, no. 7, pp. 950–953, Jul. 1990.

7. R. Srinivasan and K. Rao, " Predictive coding based on efficient motion estimation," IEEE Trans. Commun., vol. 33, no. 8, pp. 888–896, Aug. 1985.

8. R. Li, B. Zeng, and M. L. Liou, "A new three-step search algorithm for block motion estimation," IEEE Trans. Circuits Syst. Video Technol., vol. 4, no. 4, pp. 438–442, Aug. 1994

9. L. M. Po and W. C. Ma, "A novel four-step search algorithm for fast block motion estimation," IEEE Trans. Circuits Syst. Video Technol., vol. 6, no. 3, pp. 313–317, Jun. 1996.

10. L. K. Liu and E. Faig, "A block-based gradient descent search algorithm for block motion estimation in video coding," IEEE Trans. Circuits Syst. Video Technol., vol. 6, no. 4, pp. 419–422, Aug. 1996.

11. S. Zhu and K.-K. Ma, "A new diamond search algorithm for fast blockmatching motion estimation," IEEE Trans. Image Process., vol. 9, no. 2, pp. 287–290, Feb. 2000.

12. C. J. Kuo, C. H. Yeh, and S. F. Odeh, "Polynomial search algorithm for motion estimation," IEEE Trans. Circuits Syst. Video Technol., vol. 10, no. 5, pp. 813–818, Aug. 2000.

13. A.M. Tourapis, O.C. Au, and M.L. Liou, "Fast Motion Estimation using Circular Zonal Search", Proc. of SPIE Sym. of Visual Comm. & Image Processing, VCIP'99, Vol. 2, pp. 1496-1504, Jan. 25-27, 1999.

14. Y. Nie, K.K. Ma, "Adaptive Irregular Pattern Search With Matching Prejudgment for Fast Block-Matching Motion Estimation", IEEE Trans. Circuits Syst. Video Technol., vol.15, no. 6, pp. 789-794, June 2005.

15. B. Liu and A. Zaccarin, "New fast algorithm for motion estimation of block motion vectors," IEEE Trans. Circuits Syst. Video Technol., vol. 3, no. 2, pp. 148–157, Apr. 1993.

16. K. T. Choi, S. C. Chan, and T. S. Ng, "A new fast motion estimation algorithm using hexagonal subsampling pattern and multiple candidates search," in Proc. ICIP, vol. 2, 1996, pp. 497–500.

17. Y. Wang, Y. Wang, and H. Kuroda, "A globally adaptive pixel-decimation algorithm for block-motion estimation," IEEE Trans. Circuits Syst. Video Technol., vol. 10, no. 6, pp. 1006–1011, Sep. 2000.

18. Kim and T. Choi, "A fast full-search motion-estimation algorithm using representative pixels and adaptive matching scan," IEEE Trans. Circuits Syst. Video Technol., vol. 10, no. 7, pp.1040–1048, Oct. 2000.

19. J. Feng, K.-T. Lo, H. Mehrpour, and A. E. Karbowiak, "Adaptive block matching motion estimation algorithm using bit plane matching," in Proc. ICIP', 1995, pp. 496–499.

20. B. Natarajan, V. Bhaskaran, and K. Konstantinides, "Low-complexity block-based motion estimation via one-bit transforms," IEEE Trans. Circuits Syst. Video Technol., vol. 7, no. 4, pp. 702–706, Aug. 1997.

21. P. H. W. Wong and O. C. Au, "Modified one-bit transform for motion estimation," IEEE Trans. Circuits Syst. Video Technol., vol. 9, no. 7, pp.1020–1024, Oct. 1999.

22. A.Ertürk, S. Ertürk, "Two-Bit Transform for Binary Block Motion Estimation", IEEE Trans. Circuit and Syst. Video Technol, vol. 15, no. 7, pp. 938-946, Jul. 2005

3D Face Tracking Using Appearance Registration and Robust Iterative Closest Point Algorithm[*]

Fadi Dornaika and Angel D. Sappa

Computer Vision Center
Edifici O, Campus UAB
08193 Bellaterra, Barcelona, Spain
{dornaika, sappa}@cvc.uab.es

Abstract. Recently, researchers proposed deterministic and statistical appearance-based 3D face tracking methods that can successfully tackle the image variability and drift problems. However, appearance-based methods dedicated to 3D face tracking may suffer from inaccuracies since they are not very sensitive to out-of-plane motion variations. On the other hand, the use of dense 3D facial data provided by a stereo rig or a range sensor can provide very accurate 3D face motions/poses. However, this paradigm requires either an accurate facial feature extraction or a computationally expensive registration technique (e.g., the Iterative Closest Point algorithm). In this paper, we propose a 3D face tracker that is based on appearance registration and on a fast variant of a robust Iterative Closest Point algorithm. The resulting 3D face tracker combines the advantages of both appearance-based trackers and 3D data-based trackers. Experiments on real video data show the feasibility and usefulness of the proposed approach.

1 Introduction

The ability to detect and track human heads and faces in video sequences is useful in a great number of applications, such as human-computer interaction and gesture recognition. There are several commercial products capable of accurate and reliable 3D head position and orientation estimation (e.g., the acoustic tracker system Mouse[1]). These are either based on magnetic sensors or on special markers placed on the face; both practices are encumbering, causing discomfort and limiting natural motion. Vision-based 3D face tracking provides an attractive alternative since vision sensors are not invasive and hence natural motions can be achieved [1]. However, detecting and tracking faces in video sequences is a challenging task.

Recently, deterministic and statistical appearance-based 3D face tracking methods have been proposed and used by some researchers [2,3,4]. These methods can successfully tackle the image variability and drift problems by using

---

[*] This work was supported by the MEC project TIN2005-09026 and The Ramón y Cajal Program.

[1] www.vrdepot.com/vrteclg.htm

A. Levi et al. (Eds.): ISCIS 2006, LNCS 4263, pp. 532–541, 2006.

deterministic or statistical models for the global appearance of a special object class: the face. However, appearance-based methods dedicated to full 3D face tracking may suffer from some inaccuracies since these methods are not very sensitive to out-of-plane motion variations. On the other hand, the use of dense 3D facial data provided by a stereo rig or a range sensor can provide very accurate 3D face motions. Unfortunately, computing the 3D face motions from the stream of dense 3D facial data is not straightforward. Indeed, inferring the 3D face motion from the dense 3D data needs an additional process. This process can be the detection of some particular facial features in the range data/images from which the 3D face pose can be inferred. For example, in [5], the 3D nose ridge is detected and then used for computing the 3D face pose. Alternatively, one can perform a registration between 3D data obtained at different time instants in order to infer the relative 3D motions. The most common registration technique is the Iterative Closest Point (ICP) [6]. The ICP algorithm and its variants can provide accurate 3D motions but they are computationally very expensive.

The main contribution of this paper is a robust 3D face tracker that combines the advantages of both appearance-based trackers and 3D data-based trackers. First, the 3D face pose is recovered using an appearance registration technique. Second, possible errors associated with the obtained 3D face pose are reduced using a robust Iterative Closest Point algorithm, which registers a 3D mesh to a 3D facial surface provided by a stereo system. We show that this scheme is extremely faster than a raw implementation of the ICP algorithm.

The remainder of this paper proceeds as follows. Section 2 introduces our deformable 3D facial model. Section 3 summarizes the adaptive appearance-based tracker that tracks in real-time the 3D face pose and some facial actions. It gives some evaluation results. Section 4 describes an improvement step based on a robust ICP algorithm. Section 5 gives some experimental results.

2   Modeling Faces

A deformable 3D model. In our study, we use the 3D face model *Candide* [7]. This 3D deformable wireframe model was first developed for the purpose of model-based image coding and computer animation. The 3D shape of this wireframe model is directly recorded in coordinate form. It is given by the coordinates of the 3D vertices $\mathbf{P}_i, i = 1, \ldots, n$ where n is the number of vertices. Thus, the shape up to a global scale can be fully described by the $3n$-vector $\mathbf{g}$; the concatenation of the 3D coordinates of all vertices $\mathbf{P}_i$. The vector $\mathbf{g}$ is written as:

$$\mathbf{g} = \mathbf{g}_s + \mathbf{A}\,\tau_a \tag{1}$$

where $\mathbf{g}_s$ is the static shape of the model, τ_a the animation control vector, and the columns of $\mathbf{A}$ are the Animation Units. In this study, we use six modes for the facial Animation Units (AUs) matrix $\mathbf{A}$. We have chosen the six following AUs: lower lip depressor, lip stretcher, lip corner depressor, upper lip raiser, eyebrow lowerer, outer eyebrow raiser. These AUs are enough to cover most common facial animations. Moreover, they are essential for conveying emotions.

In equation (1), the 3D shape is expressed in a local coordinate system. However, one should relate the 3D coordinates to the image coordinate system. To this end, we adopt the weak perspective projection model. We neglect the perspective effects since the depth variation of the face can be considered as small compared to its absolute depth. Thus, the state of the 3D wireframe model is given by the 3D face pose parameters (three rotations and three translations) and the internal face animation control vector $\boldsymbol{\tau_a}$. This is given by the 12-dimensional vector $\mathbf{b}$:

$$\mathbf{b} = [\theta_x,\, \theta_y,\, \theta_z,\, t_x,\, t_y,\, t_z,\, \boldsymbol{\tau_a}^T]^T \tag{2}$$

Shape-free facial textures. A face texture is represented as a shape-free texture (geometrically normalized image). The geometry of this image is obtained by projecting the static shape $\mathbf{g}_s$ (neutral shape) using a centered frontal 3D pose onto an image with a given resolution. The texture of this geometrically normalized image is obtained by texture mapping from the triangular 2D mesh in the input image (see figure 1) using a piece-wise affine transform (see [7] for more details).

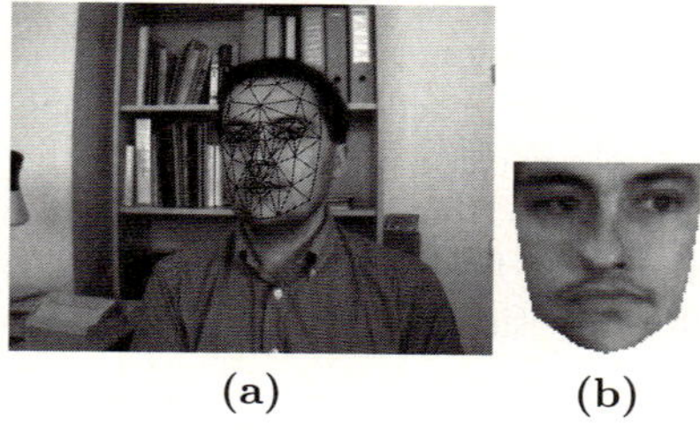

(a)   (b)

Fig. 1. **(a)** an input image with correct adaptation. **(b)** the corresponding shape-free facial image.

3   Tracking Using Adaptive Appearance Registration

Tracking the face and facial actions in a video is carried out by estimating the vector $\mathbf{b}_t$ for every frame. In [8], we have developed an efficient technique for the estimation of the vector $\mathbf{b}$ from the stream of images, by minimizing a distance between the incoming warped frame and the current *shape-free* appearance of the face. This minimization is carried out using a Gauss-Newton method. The statistics of the *shape-free* appearance as well as the gradient matrix are updated every frame. This scheme leads to a fast and robust tracking algorithm. On a 3.2 GHz PC, a non-optimized C code of the approach computes the 3D face pose and the six facial actions in 50 ms. About half that time is required if one is only interested in computing the 3D face pose parameters.

3.1   Accuracy Evaluation

Figure 2 depicts the proposed monocular tracker errors associated with a 300-frame long sequence which contains rotational and translational out-of-plane face motions. This evaluation has been obtained by the joint use of facial surfaces and of the ICP algorithm [9]. The nominal absolute depth of the head was about 65 cm, and the focal length of the camera was 824 pixels. As can be seen, the out-of-plane motion errors can be large for some frames for which there is a room for improvement. Moreover, this evaluation has confirmed the general trend of appearance-based trackers, that is, the out-of-plane motion parameters are more affected by errors than the other parameters.

One expects that the monocular tracker accuracy can be improved if an additional cue is used. In our case, the additional cue will be the 3D data associated to the mesh vertices provided by stereo reconstruction. Although the use of stereo data may seem as an excess requirement, recall that cheap and compact stereo systems are now widely available (e.g., [www.ptgrey.com]).

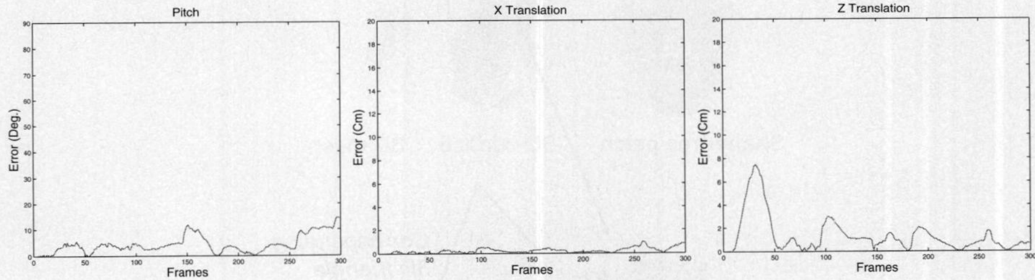

Fig. 2. 3D face pose errors computed by the ICP algorithm

4   Improving the 3D Face Pose Using a Robust ICP Algorithm

In this section, we describe the proposed improvement which is based on a fast and robust Iterative Closest Point algorithm. The ICP algorithm is widely used for geometric alignment of 3D models of rigid objects when an initial estimate of the relative transform is known, or equivalently the two surfaces are roughly aligned. This is consistent with our case since the 3D mesh is roughly aligned with the current 3D facial surface using the estimated appearance-based 3D face

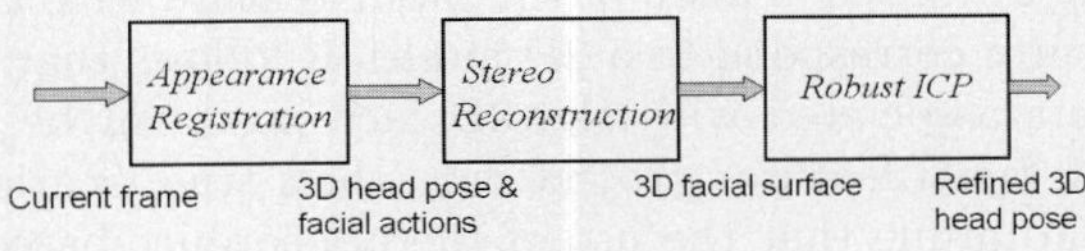

Fig. 3. The main steps of the developed 3D face tracker

(a)   (b)

Fig. 4. (a) An ideal case where the appearance-based 3D face pose corresponds to the true 3D face pose. **(b)** A real case where the appearance-based 3D face pose does not exactly correspond to the true 3D face pose. It follows that the improvement is simply the rigid 3D displacement $[\mathbf{R}|\mathbf{T}]$ that aligns the two surfaces. This rigid 3D transform can be recovered using a robust Iterative Closest Point algorithm.

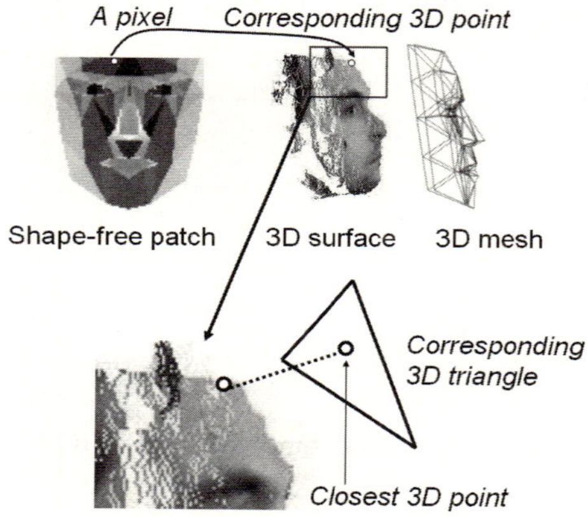

Fig. 5. At any iteration of the ICP algorithm, the computation of the closest points is carried out by exploiting the labelled 3D points and projecting them onto their triangles. This scheme can be very fast compared to the classical closest point computation.

pose. Many variants of the ICP algorithm have been proposed. A comparative study can be found in [10]. Figure 3 illustrates the main steps of the proposed approach. Notice that the stereo reconstruction only concern a subset of pixels that belong to the face region in the current image.

Since the monocular tracker provides the 3D face pose and the facial deformations by matching a warped version of the input texture with the facial texture model (both textures correspond to a 2D mesh), it follows that the out-of-plane motion parameters associated with the 3D face pose can be inaccurate even when most of the facial features project onto their true location in the image. We use this fact to argue that the use of the appearance-based tracker results and the 3D mesh model will greatly help the refinement step in the sense that i) it will provide the initial 3D pose required by the ICP algorithm, ii) it will adapt the deformable model (mesh) to the current facial expression, and iii) it will make the search for the closest points simple and fast. Indeed, the most expensive step in any ICP algorithm is the computation of the closest points. In our case, we use a robust version of the ICP algorithm that registers the 3D mesh to the current facial surface. The provided registration will be considered as the 3D face pose improvement.

Figure 4 illustrates the basic idea that is behind the improvement step, namely the robust 3D registration. Figure 4.**a** illustrates an ideal case where the estimated appearance-based 3D face pose corresponds to the true 3D pose. In this case, the mapped 3D mesh is perfectly registered with the 3D facial surface provided by the stereo system. Here the mapping is provided by the appearance-based 3D face pose. Figure 4.**b** illustrates a real case where the estimated appearance-based 3D face pose does not correspond exactly to the true one. In this case, the improvement can be estimated by recovering the 3D rigid displacement $[\mathbf{R}|\mathbf{T}]$ between the 3D mesh and the current facial surface. To this end, we will use a robust ICP algorithm where the surfaces to be aligned are the current 3D facial surface and the 3D mesh - a piecewise planar surface. Note that both surfaces are expressed in the same coordinate system.

4.1 Computing the Closest Points

Any ICP algorithm should include the selection and matching of 3D points on the surfaces to be registered. In our case, the rough registration provided by the appearance-based registration will be used to get these correspondences rapidly. The process is illustrated in Figure 5. At any iteration of the ICP algorithm, the computation of the closest points is carried out using the following. A pixel in the shape-free patch is mapped onto the input range image in order to get the corresponding 3D coordinates on the 3D facial surface. Then, the obtained 3D point is orthogonally projected onto its corresponding 3D triangle in the 3D mesh (recall that the shape-free patch is a 2D representation of the 3D mesh). This scheme is very fast compared to the classical closest point computation. Once the set of 3D-to-3D points is computed we invoke a robust technique for estimating the 3D rigid transform between the 3D mesh and the facial surface. We point out that the use of robust techniques is required since some pairs will have large points-to-points distance due to possible self-occlusions associated with the 3D mesh. Robust ICP variants have been proposed in recent literature (e.g., see [13,14]). In our work, we use a RANSAC-like technique that computes an adaptive threshold for outlier detection. The tracking algorithm associated with one frame in the video is given in Figure 6. Notice that the number of points used by the robust ICP algorithm may vary from one iteration to another.

Computational cost. On a 3.2 GHz PC, a non-optimized C code of the whole approach takes about 1 second working on 1300 facial points with four iterations. This time can be considered as few hundred times faster than a classical ICP algorithm which usually takes between 5 and 10 minutes to register two facial surfaces.

1. Compute the 3D face pose and the facial actions using the appearance registration technique (see Section 4).
2. Iterate until the maximum number of iterations is reached or the registration error in two consecutive iterations is below a certain threshold: Compute a set of putative 3D-to-3D points between the 3D surface and the 3D mesh $\{\mathbf{S}_i \leftrightarrow \mathbf{M}_i\}$, $i = 1, \ldots, N$ using the technique illustrated in Figure 5.
   Random sampling: Repeat the following three steps K times
   (a) Draw a random subsample of 3 different pairs of points. We have three pairs of 3D points $\{\mathbf{S}_i \leftrightarrow \mathbf{M}_i\}$, $i = 1, 2, 3$.
   (b) For this subsample, indexed by k ($k = 1, \ldots, K$), compute the 3D rigid displacement $\mathbf{D}_k = [\mathbf{R}_k | \mathbf{T}_k]$, where $\mathbf{R}_k$ is a 3D rotation and $\mathbf{T}_k$ a 3D translation, that brings these three pairs into alignment. $\mathbf{R}_k$ and $\mathbf{T}_k$ are computed by minimizing the residual error $\sum_{i=1}^{3} |\mathbf{S}_i - \mathbf{R}_k \mathbf{M}_i - \mathbf{T}_k|^2$. This is carried out using the quaternion method [11].
   (c) For this solution $\mathbf{D}_k$, compute the median M_k of the squared residual errors with respect to the whole set of N points. Note that we have N residuals corresponding to all points $\{\mathbf{M}_j \leftrightarrow \mathbf{S}_j\}$, $j = 1, \ldots, N$. The squared residual associated with an arbitrary point $\mathbf{M}_j$ is $|\mathbf{S}_j - \mathbf{R}_k \mathbf{M}_j - \mathbf{T}_k|^2$.
   Solution:
   (a) For each solution $\mathbf{D}_k = [\mathbf{R}_k | \mathbf{T}_k], k = 1, \ldots, K$, compute the number of inliers among the entire set of vertices (see [12]). Let n_k be this number.
   (b) Choose the solution that has the highest number of inliers. Let $\mathbf{D}_i$ be this solution where $i = \arg\max_k(n_k), k = 1, \ldots, K$.
   (c) Refine $\mathbf{D}_i$ using all its inlier pairs.
3. Based on the above 3D motion update the 3D face pose and go to 2.

Fig. 6. Tracking the 3D face pose and the facial actions in each video frame using appearance registration and a robust ICP algorithm

5   Experimental Results

Figure 7 displays the face and facial action tracking results associated with a 300-frame-long sequence (only four frames are shown). The tracking results were obtained using the adaptive appearance and the robust ICP algorithm described in Sections 3 and 4, respectively. The upper left corner of each image shows the current appearance model and the current shape-free texture. In this sequence, the nominal absolute depth of the head was about 80 cm. As can be seen, the tracking results indicate good alignment between the mesh model and the images.

Figure 8 displays the face and facial action tracking results associated with a 300-frame-long sequence (only four frames are shown). In this sequence, the nominal absolute depth of the head was about 65 cm. Figure 9 displays the 3D rigid motion computed by the robust ICP algorithm, that is, the expected improvement to the appearance-based 3D face pose (shown by a solid horizontal line). The improvements associated with the vertical translation and the pitch angle are quite small.

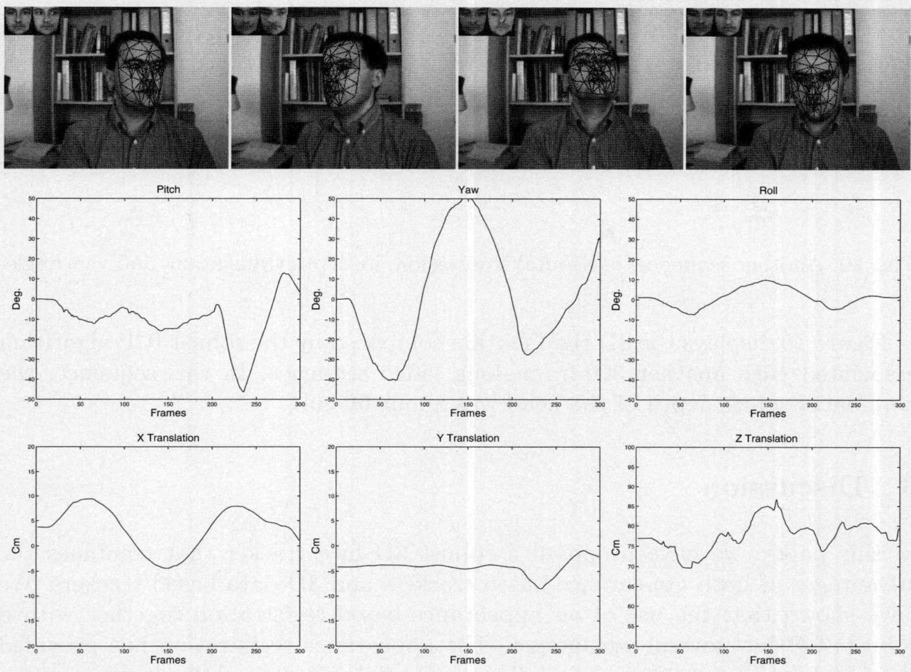

Fig. 7. Tracking the 3D face pose using the proposed technique. The sequence length is 300 frames. Only frames 38, 167, 247, and 283 are shown.

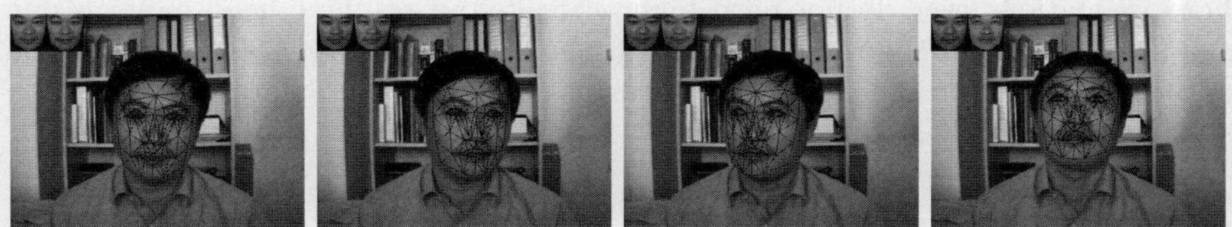

Fig. 8. Applying the developed tracker to a 300-frame long video sequence

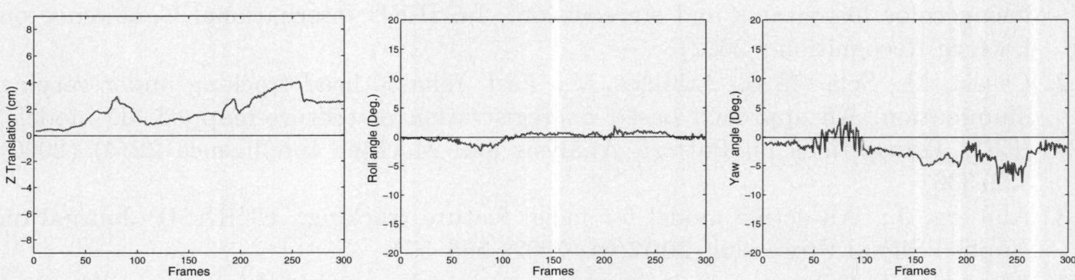

Fig. 9. The 3D rigid motions computed by the robust ICP algorithm associated with the sequence depicted in Figure 8: in-depth translation, roll angle, and yaw angle.

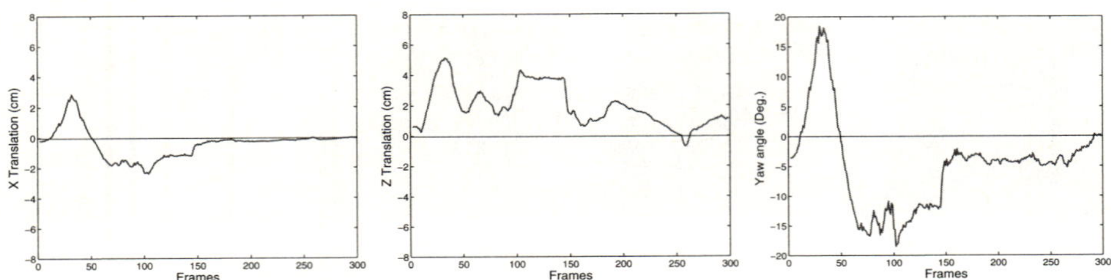

Fig. 10. Another sequence: horizontal translation, in-depth translation, and yaw angle.

Figure 10 displays the 3D rigid motion computed by the robust ICP algorithm associated with another 300-frame-long video sequence. In this sequence, the nominal absolute depth of the head was about 60 cm.

6   Discussion

In this paper, we have proposed a robust 3D face tracker that combines the advantages of both appearance-based trackers and 3D data-based trackers. We have shown that the use of an appearance-based registration together with a robust ICP has several advantages. The appearance registration has provided the facial action parameters as well as the initial estimate of the parameters for the robust ICP algorithm. On the other hand, the ICP algorithm has provided an accurate out-of-plane face motion. Due to the fact that the two surfaces are different not all degrees of freedom associated to the head pose can be improved. For applications that do not need high accurate out-of-plane head motions one can skip the use of the robust ICP algorithm. The proposed framework can be applied to tracking deformable surfaces as long as their deformations can be statistically modelled.

References

1. Moreno, F., Tarrida, A., Andrade-Cetto, J., Sanfeliu, A.: 3D real-time tracking fusing color histograms and stereovision. In: IEEE International Conference on Pattern Recognition. (2002)
2. Cascia, M., Sclaroff, S., Athitsos, V.: Fast, reliable head tracking under varying illumination: An approach based on registration of texture-mapped 3D models. IEEE Transactions on Pattern Analysis and Machine Intelligence **22**(4) (2000) 322–336
3. Ahlberg, J.: An active model for facial feature tracking. EURASIP Journal on Applied Signal Processing **2002**(6) (2002) 566–571
4. Matthews, I., Baker, S.: Active appearance models revisited. International Journal of Computer Vision **60**(2) (2004) 135–164
5. Malassiotis, S., Strintzis, M.G.: Robust real-time 3D head pose estimation from range data. Pattern Recognition **38**(8) (2005) 1153–1165

6. Besl, P., McKay, N.: A method for registration of 3-D shapes. IEEE Transactions on Pattern Analysis and Machine Intelligence **14**(2) (1992) 239–256
7. Ahlberg, J.: Model-based coding: Extraction, coding, and evaluation of face model parameters. PhD thesis, No. 761, Linköping University, Sweden (2002)
8. Dornaika, F., Davoine, F.: On appearance based face and facial action tracking. IEEE Transactions on Circuits and Systems for Video Technology (To appear)
9. Dornaika, F., Sappa, A.: Appearance-based tracker: An evaluation study. In: IEEE International Workshop on Visual Surveillance and Performance Evaluation of Tracking and Surveillance. (2005)
10. Rusinkiewicz, S., Levoy, M.: Efficient variants of the ICP algorithm. In: IEEE International Conference on Pattern Recognition. (2001)
11. Horn, B.: Closed-form solution of absolute orientation using unit quaternions. J. Opt. Soc. Amer. A. **4**(4) (1987) 629–642
12. Rousseeuw, P., Leroy, A.: Robust Regression and Outlier Detection. John Wiley & Sons, New York (1987)
13. Chetverikov, D., Stepanov, D., Kresk, P.: Robust Euclidean alignment of 3D point sets: the trimmed iterative closet point algorithm. Image and Vision Computing **23** (2005) 299–309
14. Fitzgibbon, A.: Robust registration of 2D and 3D point sets. Image and Vision Computing **21** (2003) 1145–1153

Video as Input: Spiral Search with the Sparse Angular Sampling

Tatiana V. Evreinova, Grigori Evreinov, and Roope Raisamo

TAUCHI Computer-Human Interaction Unit
Department of Computer Sciences
FIN-33014 University of Tampere, Finland
+358 3 215 8549
{etv, grse, rr}@cs.uta.fi

Abstract. This paper presents an improved cross-correlation algorithm for template-based object tracking: the reduced spiral search with a sparse angular sampling. The basic parameters of the algorithm for the real-time face tracking were evaluated regarding their impact on the algorithm performance. They are the minimum number of pixels and the size of the template, the correlation threshold and drifting, and the parameters of the search - radius, shift, direction, and rotation of the template. We demonstrated that the information provided by the grid-like template might be reduced to 16 pixels with a grid step of 15 pixels. A spiral search in 8 directions with a minimum shift of 1 pixel decreases the number of computations by 20 times. Being activated sequentially the template rotation does not increase the performance, but doing the tracking adaptive and robust.

1 Introduction

There is a challenge to employ head-, face-, and eye-tracking in mobile applications for access control, games and entertainment. In the last decade, new algorithms for real-time object recognition and tracking have been developed being appropriate for a large variety of objects with different colors and textures [2], [5], [7], [8], [9], [11], [12]. Still, to ascertain and recognize the tracked features, the algorithms are executed by employing a lot of system resources being allocated for processing video stream.

Cross-correlation (CC) has been a conventional approach to feature detection by template matching in computer vision since the 1960's. Several schemes to accelerate computation of the CC for image processing have been proposed [4], [10], [12]. Nowadays, the method has been widely used in machine vision for industrial applications and for real-time tracking of body features [1], [2], [6].

The dots (pixels) which are composing the template that has to be tracked, have two basic parameters: the coordinates and brightness. These dots can be selected as a rectangular grid with a fixed step along X and Y axes. Alternatively, the template grid might have a variable step which depends on a particular brightness gradient of the dots captured. When a template of the pixels presents a grid with a fixed step it seems an easy way for processing. The research presented in this paper was carried out with

A. Levi et al. (Eds.): ISCIS 2006, LNCS 4263, pp. 542–552, 2006.

the use of a rectangular grid-like template, by assuming that the template movements occurred in a two-dimensional plane. It can be shown that there is a potential to optimize a real-time face tracking performed with reasonable efficiency for a variety of interaction tasks. Below we will present the results of the systematic assessment of the improved version of the CC-algorithm: the spiral search with the sparse angular sampling.

2 The Template Matching Techniques

Since 1996 the methods of motion detection and tracking have been described in a number of patents related to computer vision and input techniques. It is noteworthy that the area of an early mouse image sensor was 16 by 16 pixels. In contrast to a camera-mouse, for instance presented in [2], [7], [9], tracking of the optical mouse does not require any adjusting and additional system resources. An optical mouse motion produces successive frames of pixel values, which are compared by autocorrelation using the nearest-neighbor approach to ascertain the direction and amount of movement [3]. Herewith, a physical aperture of the optical subsystem limits the size of the template. The compact CC-algorithm was integrated in a DSP optical sensor making the optical mouse the most popular and reliable input device that does not require any adjusting or additional system resources for video processing.

In two-dimensional camera tracking of facial landmarks, detection of the particular image region within a search area is commonly structured as follows. The first procedure is the initialization to store the template to be tracked. The initialization may include zooming and positioning the entire image to efficiently fit it within a search area. The next procedure is an inspection of the search area to detect the sample candidate which resembles the template with the maximum correlation. This stage is the subject of the current investigation.

The search area might be processed with the predefined shift of the sample array in all locations, for instance starting from the left top pixel, as it is implemented in the raster search. The raster search is a CPU-time consuming procedure. The restricted head movements normally occur near the neutral head position. Therefore, in the case of tracking facial landmarks the detection probability of the template is highest along eight basic directions near the previous location of the landmark. Proceeding from the assumption of the formal congruence between the grid-like template and head movements, to detect a sample resembling the template within a search area, we have proposed to employ a spiral search. In particular, when correlation of the sample-candidate is less than the predefined threshold (0.8) the next locations to be inspected would be the points sequentially shifted in eight directions with the angular step of 45 degrees starting from the left top pixel in clockwise direction with the predefined radial shift of 1 pixel. Thus, the initial search looks like a *circle* having a radius of R pixels (R capture) for each dot of the template. When the correlation coefficient between the sample candidate and the template is more or equal to the threshold the search procedure will stop and coordinates of the reference point (e.g., the center or the left top pixel of the sample) will be selected as a start point for the next search in the new capture window. The matching is always performed regarding the same template throughout the tracking. When the correlation coefficient is less than the threshold in eight directions the search radius will increase with a predefined shift and the search procedure will be repeated. Finally, when all of the sample candidates within maximum capture radius were failed the search will start again from the reference point where the template was initially stored. To facilitate a spatial synchronization of the tracking the person might follow to the initial (neutral) head position. The failed records may occur when a correlation is too low, for instance a sample is beyond of the working area or dynamic range of the parameters predefined.

3   The Features That Affect the Template Matching Performance

The faster matching procedure is the more features can be processed in real-time to increase resolution and reliability of the tracking techniques. Employing Microsoft Video for Windows (VfW) and API functions that enable an application to process video data takes different time. We used the fastest method of the image copying through display device context (Windows GDI), which takes less than 0.7ms (Intel Pentium 4, 3201.0 MHz Cache 2MB) to grab an image (320×240 pixels) from the capture window. However, when we did an evaluation of the algorithm performance, the time of copying a part of the image from the capture window during the template detection was excluded from consideration.

3.1   The Number of Pixels in the Template

How many pixels should be processed to conclude that the sample candidate resembles the template with a high degree of similarity? Francois Bérard used the template the size of which was 32 by 32 pixels and the (raster) search area was restricted to a square of 60 by 60 pixels. In a case of the spiral search, the search area can be translated to the capture radius of 14 pixels (R capture). The author noted that image processing to ascertain a new location of the template (in the orig. "the target") took of about 16 ms with correlation matching and the equipment he used: processor running at 350MHz and a built-in frame grabber [1]. A study performed by Margrit Betke [2] to determine parameters of the template and a search region showed that the template of 15 by 15 pixels and a search region of 40 by 40 pixels around each previous location (R capture = 13 pixels) seemed as the optimal tradeoff between algorithm performance and a camera frame rate of 30 Hz. However, to process video information the researchers used a separate PC mentioned as a *vision computer* running at 550MHz.

Facial landmarks can be considered as relatively rigid surface having almost the same brightness within a small region as 0.2-0.5% of the entire face image. That is, a region of 12×12 pixels may have not a significant brightness gradient within a frame of 320×280 pixels. While the template having a size of 1.5-2.5% of the entire face image, composed of about 1600-2300 pixels, might have many dissimilar features.

Guided by these reasoning, we have considered optimizing the size of the skin region and the number of dots (pixels) which compose the template. As can be seen in

Fig. 1, the 16-pixel template has a relatively unique signature of the brightness gradient. But, it seems that this template was received as the template with higher resolution averaged over some number of pixels. For visual matching the pattern with higher resolution is shown again near the pattern having a low resolution and covered with a grid the cell of which conforms to the 16-pixel template.

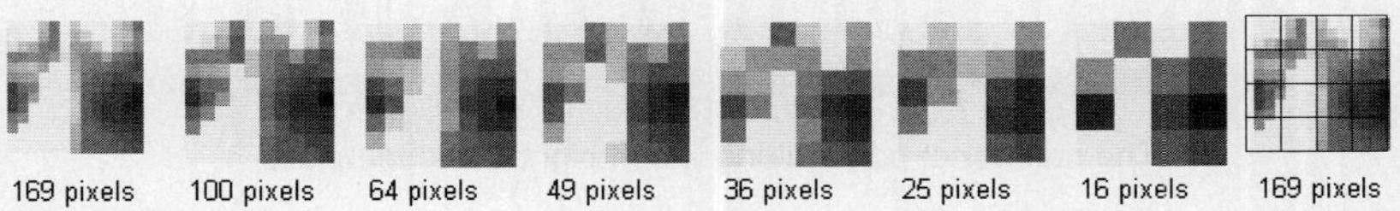

Fig. 1. The region between two eyes captured as a pattern of 40×40 pixels at the different number of the dots in the template. The right picture covered with a grid the cell of which conforms to the 16-pixel template. All these templates can be tracked with correlation 0.95.

Brightness is a more general parameter than color that may vary significantly depending on a type of the lighting and reflection conditions. As a signature of the image region, the dots should compose an array having unique features, if it is possible. They can be selected, for instance, as a rectangular grid with a fixed step along X-axis and Y-axis presenting the unique gradient of brightness, or vice versa, the template can present a particular layout of dots with near-equal brightness. The connected dots having a similar brightness and being localized in some distances can present the unique pattern as well. However, the higher are requirements to the template detection and matching, the greater are demands to the lighting conditions.

The absolute brightness of each dot (pixel) for 8-bit gray level images can vary in a range of 0-255. While a phase of varying the brightness of the connected dots in rows and columns of the grid-like template remains almost the same at the head movements within a small region, for example, yaw at less than ±20 degrees and pitch at about ±15 degrees. It can be shown that correlation between two samples calculated on the relative brightness of their dots is the same as that which is being calculated on the absolute brightness. By the relative brightness, we assign a difference between brightness of any pixel minus the mean brightness over all pixels in the template (B_i − $\bar{B}$). Still, the correlation calculated on the relative brightness is less sensitive to changes in image intensity with different lighting conditions [10].

According to the equation, a correlation depends less on the number of pixels in the template and a sample candidate. In practice, Fig. 2 illustrates how the number of pixels in the template affects the radius within of which a sample candidate was detected with correlation more than a predefined value 0.8. To easily arrange the dots within the rectangular grid layout, both wide and height of the template had a small variation in size (1600-1764 pixels). The search procedure was implemented in 8 directions with a maximum capture radius of 40 pixels near the previous location of the template and with a shift of 1 pixel. The data were averaged over 500 records.

The samples composed of 36-16 pixels, matched to the template with correlation of 0.8, had the mean variation of R capture of about 1.32 pixels (STD = 0.033 pixels). The maximum capture radius recorded was 6 pixels. Herewith, the sample composed of 16

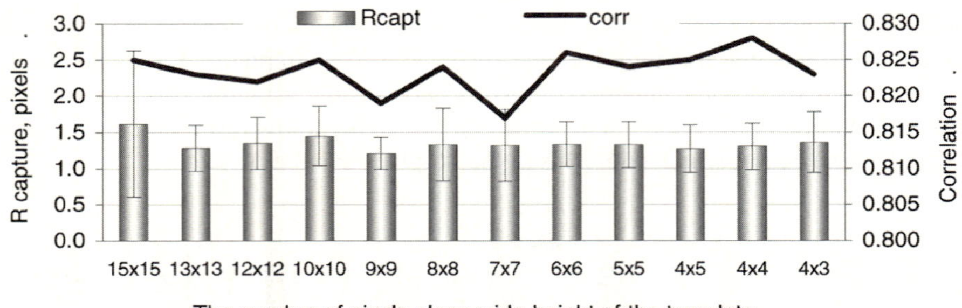

Fig. 2. R capture (the search area) and correlation recorded when the template was composed of the different number of pixels. Template size: width = 40-42 pixels, height = 40-42 pixels. Search parameters: 8 directions, shift 1 pixel, R_{capt} = 40 pixels, correlation threshold 0.8.

pixels (layout 4×4) had the higher correlation coefficient. The template composed of 225 pixels (layout 15×15) had the maximum variation of the search region, from 1 to 30 pixels, and the mean of R capture was of about 1.62 pixels (STD = 2.03 pixels).

With the raster search, a sample candidate has to be checked through correlation over all search area with a minimum consequent displacement. That is, when the template size of 40×40 pixels composed of 16 dots and it has to be detected in a search area of 120 by 120 pixels ($R_{capt.}$ = 40 pixels), the correlation computation in 6400 possible locations might be performed. The great number of computations in real-time still is a problem at designing the applications for devices with a low-performance processor. The spiral search in 8 directions with the sparse angular sampling and a minimum shift of 1 pixel decreases a number of computations by 20 times. And such an improvement has a good performance (Fig. 2 and Fig. 3).

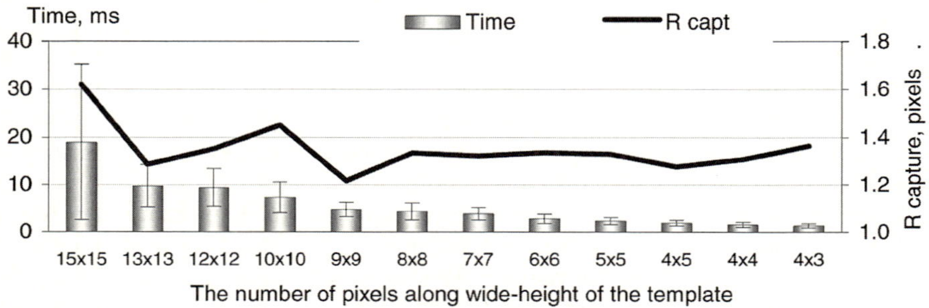

Fig. 3. The algorithm performance when the template was composed of the different number of pixels. The conditions are the same as in Fig. 2.

The number of locations to be inspected, to ascertain the sample that resembles the template, is proportional to the number of sample displacements, that is, R_{capt} divided by shift. Further decreasing of the directions (to 6, 4, 3) insignificantly reduces the number of computations, but the number of failed records increases. Thus, eight directions can be considered as the efficient optimizing to increase the performance of the template matching through cross-correlation.

Fig. 3 shows the evaluation of the algorithm performance implemented with the use of the QueryPerformanceCounter function. Apparently, the lesser number of pixels is the faster those locations of the template candidates can be processed. In particular, 2.3 ms (STD = 0.57 ms) was required for the templates composed of 36-16 pixels. Search and matching of the template composed of 225 pixels happened within an interval of about 19 ms (STD = 32.63 ms). Moreover, the lesser number of pixels was used the higher correlation was recorded within the search area.

3.2   The Correlation Threshold and Drifting

The problem of a sample drifting originates from the tracking algorithm. In particular, correlation coefficient may change due to the error of calculation (rounding), a minimal shift of the sample, lighting and other non-controlling factors.

The correlation threshold 0.8 was chosen as sufficient to suppose that the sample-candidate resembles the template and to support a variety of conditions with a minimum of failed records. We have stored all the correlations (of about 500-700 records) throughout the tests that normally took about 25-30 seconds. Fig. 4 shows a distribution of the correlation occurrences throughout the test when samples were recorded for 64-pixel template. 90.2% of the records had correlation within a range of 0.8-0.855 with the mean of 0.813 (STD = 0.011). Employing higher threshold is possible and might decrease drifting of the sample location. However, the probability of failed records might be increased when the algorithm is being evaluated with a variation of lighting or shift of the sample displacement within a search area, the number of directions is less than 8.

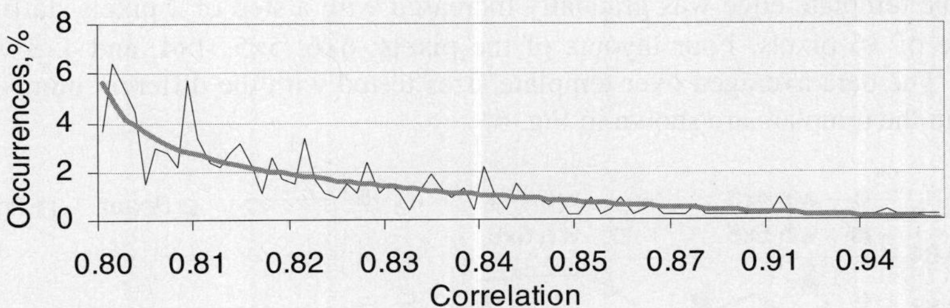

Fig. 4. The correlation occurrences through 470 records when correlation threshold was set at 0.8, the template composed of 64 pixels (8×8). Logarithmic trendline shows the data tendency.

The drifting of the template location in the neutral head position, which was recorded on 500 counts, was limited to 1.08 pixels with a minimum of 1 pixel, a maximum of 7 pixels, STD=0.48 (Fig. 5, black line). It can be considered as a *physiological noise* (tremor-like micromovements) as displacement of the reference point may occur with equal probability in any of 8 directions when no significant involuntary movements were produced.

The correlation drifting is differed of the system instability. Fig. 5 (gray line) illustrates a measurement of the correlation drifting at recording the static object. As can be seen the *system noise* has a random variation with the mean of 0.852 (with a minimum of 0.834, a maximum of 0.869, STD = 0.006) within a narrow search area $R_{capt.}$ = 1 pixel (STD=0.0). At correlation threshold 0.95 *system noise* had a random variation within a search area of about 1 pixel (STD=0.0) with a minimum of 0.951, a maximum of 0.997, STD = 0.009 and the mean of 0.98. To stabilize displacements of the reference point that can be converted into the location of cursor in the application program, the moving average might decrease drifting of the output coordinates.

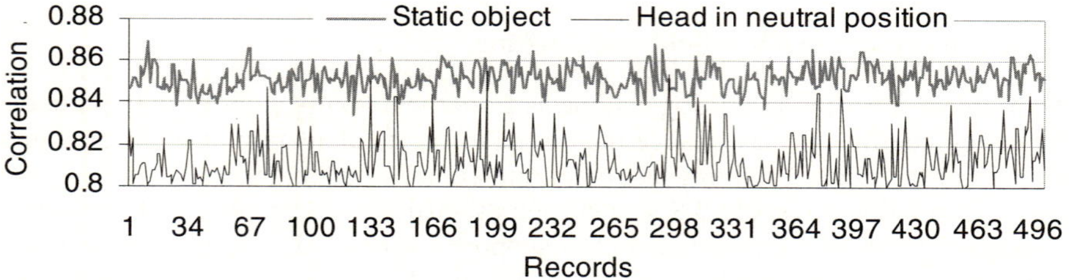

Fig. 5. Measurements of the correlation drifting. Template size: 64 pixels, layout 8×8. Search parameters: 8 directions, shift 1pixel, R_{capt} = 20 pixels, correlation threshold 0.8.

3.3 Frame Size and the Number of Pixels in the Template

A template size should be commensurable with the working area of the video frame. Initially, the size of the template was chosen as a square with the edge of 40-42 pixels to easily arrange the dots within the rectangular grid layout. The template size might be evaluated and optimized. The algorithm performance was tested in more detail when the template edge was gradually increased with a step of 2 pixels starting from the size of 36 pixels. Four layouts of the pixels: 6×6, 5×5, 4×4, and 4×3 were explored. The data averaged over template sizes tested with the different number of the pixels in the template are shown in Fig. 6.

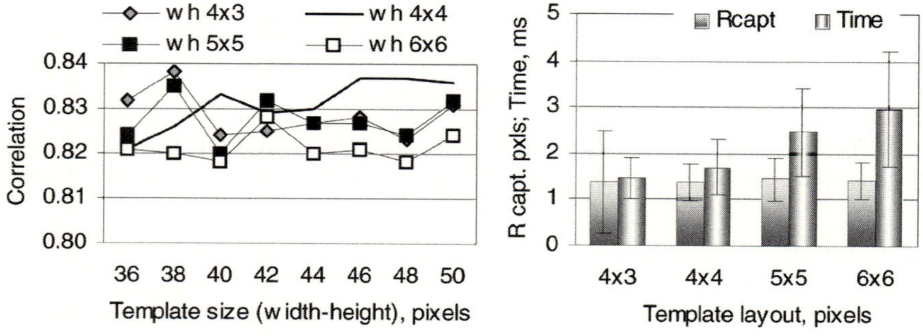

Fig. 6. The algorithm performance tested with the different size and the number of pixels in the template. 8 directions, shift 1 pixel, R_{capt} = 40 pixels, correlation threshold 0.8.

The search area was small and almost the same when the size of the template was changed from 36×36 to 50×50 pixels and the number of pixels composing the template was 12, 16, 25 or 36 (Fig. 6). R capture varied from 1 to 2 pixels nearly independently of other parameters. The tendency in correlation changing is shown in Fig. 6 (left chart). When size of the template was 46×46 or 48×48 pixels and the template composed of 16 pixels (layout 4×4) the correlation value was higher than 0.83 and the object tracking was performed smoothly as $R_{capt.}$ was held at a minimum.

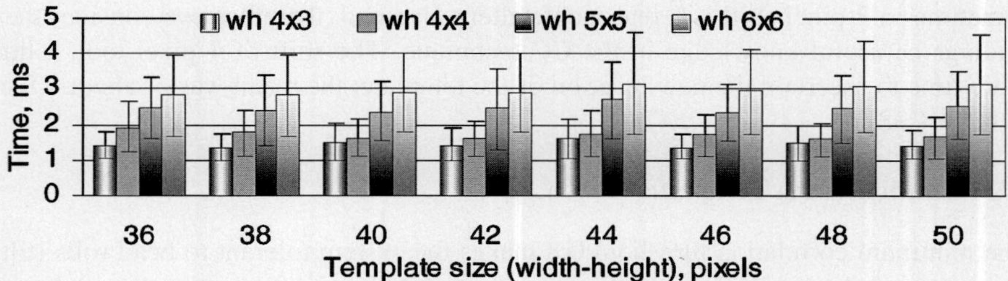

Fig. 7. The algorithm performance tested with the different size and the number of pixels in the template. The conditions are the same as in Fig. 6.

As shown in Fig. 7, the search time and its variation were proportional to the number of pixels in the template. Both 12- and 16-pixel templates demanded shorter time with the mean of about 1.45 ms (STD=0.89) and 1.7 ms (STD=1.18) correspondingly. The 25- and 36-pixel templates demanded twice more time, of about 1.9 – 3 ms. Herewith, the search area of the 12-pixel template (the mean 1.37 pixels, STD=2.2 pixels) varied by three times higher than in the case of 16-pixel template (the mean 1.37 pixels, STD=0.79 pixels).

3.4   Shift of the Template During the Search Procedure

As it can be seen from Fig. 8 the shift of 3 pixels provided the higher performance. It took in average the shorter time, of about 1.2 ms (STD = 0.46) and relatively small R

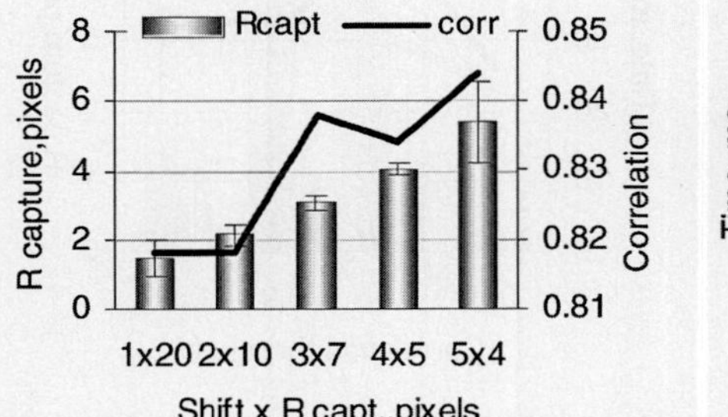

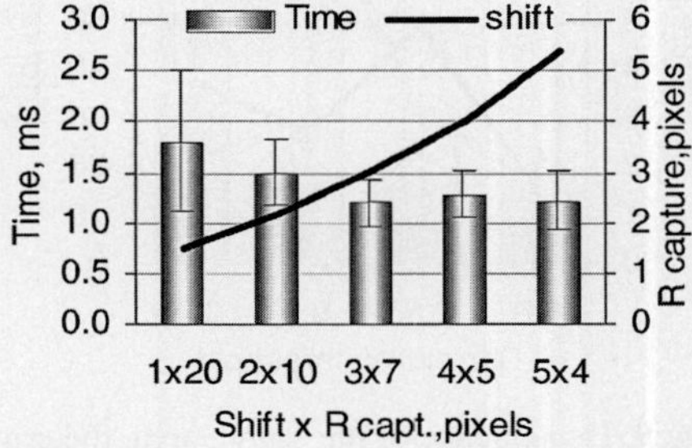

Fig. 8. R capture, correlation and the search time recorded with the different shift of the sample in 8 directions. Template size: wide = 48 pixels, height = 48 pixels, layout 4×4. Search parameters: shift 1…5 pixels, R_{capt} = 20 pixels, correlation threshold 0.8.

capture, of about 3.06 pixels (with a minimum of 3 pixels, a maximum of 9 pixels, STD = 0.48).

However, this parameter is crucial when the template shifts have to be translated into a displacement of the cursor position at a screen resolution of 1024×768 pixels. The direct calculation shows that the shift of the template with 3 pixels in consequent frames can occur in opposite directions, that is, 6 pixels displacement in the working area of 160×120 pixels would be translated to 38.4 pixels or about 1.3 cm. Thus, drifting will increase proportionally to the minimum shift of the template. Nevertheless, sometimes a 3-pixel shift is a reasonable alternative and, therefore, we consider these findings as useful knowledge in the CC technique. The shift of 1 pixel took a little more time to ascertain the new location of the template; the mean was of about 1.8 ms (STD = 1.38).

3.5 Rotation of the Template

The minimum correlation threshold 0.8 makes the system tolerant to head rolls (tilts) in a range of about ±18 degrees. To increase a probability of detection a sample candidate which could resemble the template being rotated ±28 degrees within a search area, this feature was added to augment the correlation matching (Fig. 9). Still, it is difficult to predict which rotation direction would be preferable at any moment. Therefore, the matching was implemented as follows. When search in 8 directions with a maximum search area of 20 pixels and a shift of 1 pixel was failed, the template is rotated 10 degrees counter-clockwise and the procedure is repeated. When the first rotation brings no positive result, the template is rotated 10 degrees clockwise and the search will continue. Just after 3 rounds the search of the sample candidate will be stopped.

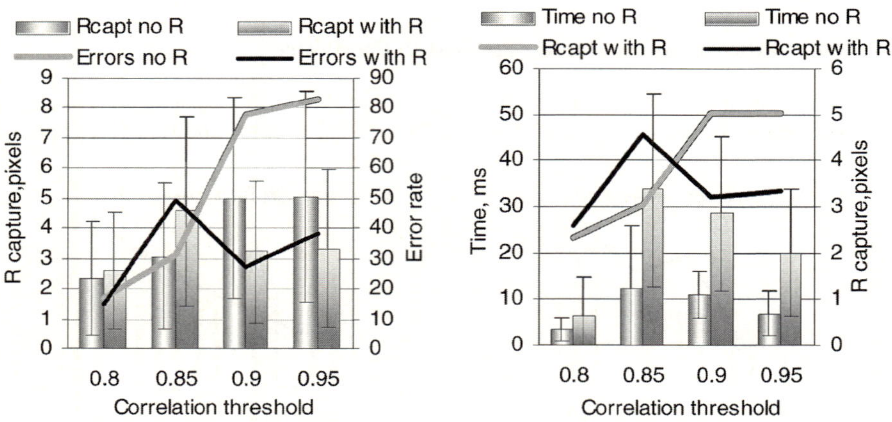

Fig. 9. Dependence of the search area, the error rate and the search time required to ascertain a sample candidate that resembles the template being rotated. Template size: 48×48 pixels, layout 4×4. Index R shows the data collected when the rotation procedure was activated.

It was recorded that the sample varied in a high degree due to a coercive head rotation. However, just only 1.6-2% cases of overall 500-700 records in any trial indicated that the rotation procedure was activated. In such a case, when matching was failed for a normal position of the template, the search time was drastically increased and the mean was of about 36.63 ms (STD = 25.79). Both R capture and correlation indicated no difference with head movements produced within a restricted region as a matching procedure with rotated template was performed in the same search area with the same criterion. Being activated *sequentially* the template rotation did not increase the performance, but extended the algorithm flexibility, doing the tracking more adaptive and robust.

4   Conclusion

We demonstrated that the information provided by the grid-like template reduced to 16 pixels (layout 4×4, step 15 pixels) is sufficient for tracking a facial landmark in various positions and orientations at the correlation threshold of 0.8. The matching procedure based on the spiral search had a good performance employing the minimum PC resources for computation. The matching procedure in eight directions with a minimum shift of 1 pixel and capture radius of 20 pixels decreases a number of computations by 20 times in a comparison to the techniques when the sample candidate has to be checked through correlation over all search area with a minimum consequent displacement. Being activated sequentially the template rotation does not increase the performance, but extends the algorithm flexibility, doing the tracking more adaptive and robust. Still, there is a potential to make the correlation higher when the spiral search could spatially be synchronized with object axes.

Acknowledgements. This work was financially supported by the Academy of Finland (grant 200761), and the project "MICOLE" funded by the EU Commission, eInclusion, IST-2003-511592 STP.

References

1. Bérard, F.: The perceptual window: Head motion as a new input stream. IFIP Conference on Human-Computer Interaction. (1999) 238–244.
2. Betke, M., Gips, J. and Fleming, P.: The Camera Mouse: Visual Tracking of Body Features to Provide Computer Access For People with Severe Disabilities. IEEE Transactions on Neural Systems and Rehabilitation Engineering, Vol. 10, No. 1, (2002) 1-10.
3. Blalock, T.N. et al.: Method and Device for Tracking Relative Movement by Correlating Signals From an Array of Photoelements, US Patent 5729008, 1998.
4. Brunelli, R., Poggio, T.: Face recognition: features versus templates. IEEE Trans. Pattern Analysis and Machine Intelligence, Vol. 15, No. 10, (1993) 1042-1052.
5. Comaniciu, D., Ramesh, V., Meer P.: Real-Time Tracking of Non-Rigid Objects using Mean Shift, IEEE Conf. Computer Vision and Pattern Recognition (CVPR'00). Vol. 2, (2002) 142-149.
6. Crowley, J.L., Berard, F. and Coutaz J.: Finger Tracking as an Input Device for Augmented Reality, Int. Workshop on Face and Gesture Recognition. (1995) 195-200.

7. FaceMOUSE. Product information. Web site (2005), http://www.aidalabs.com/
8. Intel Image Processing library "Open CV". http://www.intel.com/technology/~/opencv/
9. Jilin Tu, T. Huang, T, Hai Tao: Face As Mouse Through Visual Face Tracking. Proc. of the 2nd Canadian Conf Computer and Robot Vision. (2005) 339-346.
10. Lewis, J. P.: Fast Template Matching. Vision Interface (1995) 120-123.
11. Product information on EyeTwig.com. Website 2005. http://www.eyetwig.com
12. Si-Cheng Zhang, Zhi-Qiang Liu. A robust, real-time ellipse detector. J. Pattern Recognition 38 (2005) 273 – 287.

An Adept Segmentation Algorithm and Its Application to the Extraction of Local Regions Containing Fiducial Points

Erhan AliRiza İnce and Syed Amjad Ali

Eastern Mediterranean University, Electrical and Electronic Engineering
Famagusta, North Cyprus
`erhan.ince@emu.edu.tr, syed.ali@emu.edu.tr`

Abstract. Locating human fiducial points like eyes and mouth in a frontal head and shoulder image is an active research area for applications such as model based teleconferencing systems, model based low bit rate video transmission, computer based identification and recognition systems. This paper proposes an adept and efficient rule based skin color region extraction algorithm using normalized r-g color space. The given scheme extracts the skin pixels employing a simple quadratic polynomial model and some additional color based rules to extract possible eye and lip regions. The algorithm refines the search for fiducial points by eliminating falsely extracted feature components using spatial and geometrical representations of facial components. The algorithm described herein has been implemented and tested with 311 images from FERET database with varying light conditions, skin colors, orientation and tilts. Experimental results indicate that the proposed algorithm is quite robust and leads to good facial feature extraction.

1   Introduction

Extracting face regions containing fiducial points and recovering pose which are two challenging problems in computer vision have been widely explored by researchers. Many vision applications such as video telephony, face recognition, hybrid access control, feature tracking, model based low bit rate video transmission and MPEG-4 coding require feature extraction and pose recovery. There exist various methods for the detection of facial features and a detailed literature survey about these techniques is available in [1-6]. One of the very first operation that is needed for facial feature detection is the face localization. To achieve face localization many approaches such as segmentation based on skin color [2,3], clustering [7], Principal Component Analysis [8], and neural nets [9] have been proposed. Once the face region is located it can be made more evident by applying a region growing technique [10]. Facial features can then be extracted from the segmented face region by making use of image intensity, chromaticity values and geometrical shape properties of the face.

It has been clearly demonstrated in [11] that local facial components based recognition will outperform the global face based approaches since the global

A. Levi et al. (Eds.): ISCIS 2006, LNCS 4263, pp. 553–562, 2006.
© Springer-Verlag Berlin Heidelberg 2006

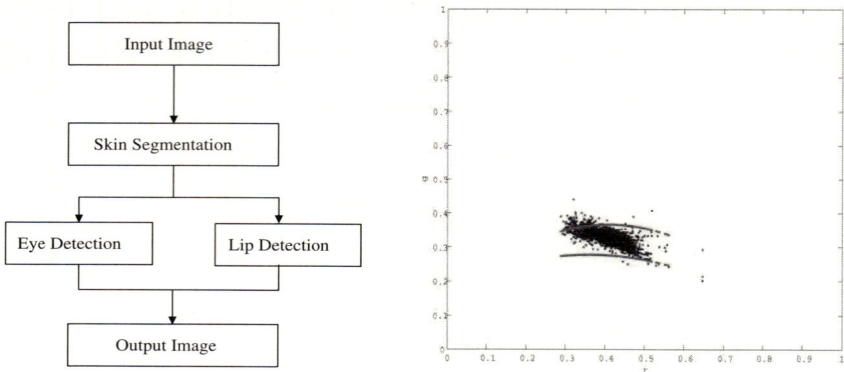

Fig. 1. (a) Feature detection archetype (b) Skin color cluster in $(r - g)$ space

approaches are more sensitive to image variations caused by translations and facial rotations. Hence this paper suggests an efficient segmentation algorithm for locating and cropping local regions containing fiducial points. In order to reduce the search area in the input images skin-pixels are extracted using a quadratic polynomial model. Also to alleviate the influence of light brightness in extracting skin pixels, the proposed algorithm adopts the r-g chromatic color coordinates for color representation. Over the r-g plane the skin pixels will form a compact region and the algorithm's computational cost is lower in comparison to probabilistic and neural network based models. Since the objective is to design a real-time system it is essential that the complexity of the algorithm chosen is not high.

Unlike many published works in the literature this paper adopts an approach in which the eyes and the mouth features are extracted independently of each other. As depicted in Fig. 1(a) this will provide the extra advantage of being able to run the two extraction routines in parallel for better time management.

The paper is organized as follows: section 2 provides details about the standard color FERET database and explains how the collection of 311 images belonging to 30 subjects was chosen. Section 3 introduces the rule-based skin segmentation and sections 4 and 6 detail how to generate the feature and lip maps respectively. Sections 5 and 7 are about rules for facial component verifications and simulation results. Details about the efficiency in extracting each individual feature are given in section 8. Finally conclusions are made in section 9.

2   The Standard Color FERET Database

The database used in the simulations is a subset of the color FERET database [12,13] which has been specifically created in order to develop, test and evaluate face recognition algorithms. We have selected 30 subjects randomly from the pool and accumulated 311 pictures in total using only the FA, FB, QL, QR, RB and RC poses for each subject. FA and FB are frontal images, QR and QL are poses with the head turned about 22.5 degrees left and right respectively, and RB and RC are random images with the head turned about 15 degrees in either direction. The standard color FERET database contains images with multiple faces under various illumination conditions. The images come in two different sizes. The large ones are (512×768) and the small ones are (256×384). Profile left/right (PL,PR) and half left/right (HL,HR) poses have been intentionally left out because no authorized user of a hybrid access system making use of facial feature based identification is expected to pose in front of the camera at an angle more than 22.5 degrees.

3   Skin Segmentation

For humans, skin-tone information is a useful mean for segmenting skin region. The RGB, normalized r-g, YC_bC_r and HSV color spaces or their variations are used frequently in literature [1,14] for skin segmentation. In this work, we have used both the RGB and normalized r-g color spaces. The normalized red-green components are computed by using the following relations

$$r = \frac{R}{R + G + B} \tag{1}$$

$$g = \frac{G}{R + G + B} \tag{2}$$

Once the r-g components are obtained a simple quadratic polynomial model [15] is used to determine the upper and lower thresholds for the skin region as shown in Fig. 1(b).

$$f_{upper}(r) = -1.3067r^2 + 1.0743r + 0.1452 \tag{3}$$

$$f_{lower}(r) = -0.7760r^2 + 0.5601r + 0.1766 \tag{4}$$

Finally, skin segmentation is done by applying together the following three rules

S1. $f_{lower}(r) < g < f_{upper}(r)$
S2. $R > G > B$
S3. $R - B > 10$

to obtain a raw binary mask (BM) as follows:

$$BM = \begin{cases} 1 & \text{if all segmentation rules S1, S2 and S3 are true,} \\ 0 & \text{otherwise.} \end{cases}$$

The binary mask is refined by first selecting the largest connected binary region in the image and then filling the holes inside the region. Lastly, closing the gaps (holes) connected to the background in the upper part of the binary image (mostly eye and eyebrow in a left or right rotated head create such regions). The outcome of each phase of the skin segmentation algorithm in shown in Fig. 2.

In order to close the holes connected to the background in the upper part of the image we first define *toprow, bottomrow, leftcolumn* and *rightcolumn* as

Fig. 2. Left to right: (a) Original image (b) Binary mask (BM) (c) Largest connected binary mask with holes filled (d) Binary mask after closing the gaps

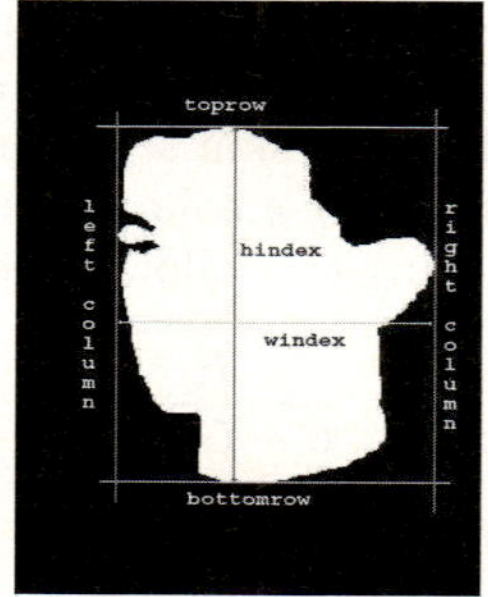

Fig. 3. Binary face mask with marked boundaries

shown in Fig. 3. For each column of the binary map we apply the processing from *toprow* down to 45% elements of the height (*hindex*). The mechanism for closing the gaps can be explained using a simple example.

Suppose $x = \begin{pmatrix} 1\,1\,1\,1\,0\,0\,1\,1\,1\,0\,0\,0\,1\,1\,0 \end{pmatrix}$ contains the binary pixels of any selected column. Finding the starting and ending index of contiguous 1's we get $y = \begin{pmatrix} 1 & 7 & 13 \\ 4 & 9 & 14 \end{pmatrix}$. Now filling indices (5 6) and (10 11 12) with 1's, the modified column values become $x = \begin{pmatrix} 1\,1\,1\,1\,1\,1\,1\,1\,1\,1\,1\,1\,1\,1\,0 \end{pmatrix}$. The number of columns from both left and right side of the image are chosen to be 30% of the width (*windex*).

Skin segmentation for binary face map has the advantage that the processing required to extract fiducial points needs to be carried out only inside this map. Secondly, it is possible to locate eyes and lip region independent of each other so that their performance will not depend on each other. Independent search to locate eyes and the lip region also has the benefit that they can be carried out in parallel to speed up the processing.

4   Feature Map Generation

Most approaches for eye and mouth detection are template based. However, in this paper we directly locate eyes and mouth based on measurements derived from the r-g, RGB and YC_bC_r color space components of the images. In order to locate the possible eye region we first create a feature map (FM) using the equations and conditions below.

$$f_{upper}(r) = -1.3067r^2 + 1.0743r + 0.1452 \tag{5}$$

$$f_{lower}(r) = -0.7760r^2 + 0.5601r + 0.1766 \tag{6}$$

S1. $f_{lower}(r) < g < f_{upper}(r)$
S2. $R > G > B$
S3. $R - G > 10$
S4. $65 < C_b < 125$ and $135 < C_r < 165$

$$FM = \begin{cases} 1 & \text{if all segmentation rules S1, S2, S3 and S4 are true,} \\ 0 & \text{otherwise.} \end{cases}$$

Once FM is obtained it is complemented and the components touching the borders are cleared to obtain the composite feature map (CFM). Afterwards the CFM is masked by the binary face mask (BM) obtained in previous section and finally the eye region is extracted using:

$$eyereg = CFM(toprow + 0.19 * hindex : toprow + (0.52 * hindex)) \tag{7}$$

where $hindex$ represents the height of the binary skin segmented image (see Fig. 3). The steps, as described above for the extraction of the region containing the eyes can be seen in Fig. 4.

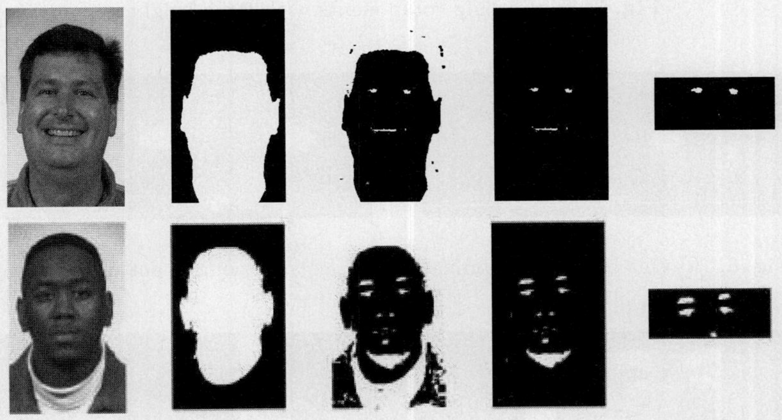

Fig. 4. Obtaining the region containing the eyes

5   Rules for Eye Component Verifications

Among all the extracted possible eye candidates only the largest 5 components are kept. If fewer than 5 components remain then all components are kept. From the selected possible eye components there exist some false candidates that needs to be eliminated. In order to remove these falsely extracted components, the proposed algorithm performs component verifications based on a set of rules which are discussed below.

A. If the height for any candidate is larger than a threshold value then those components should be eliminated (refer to Fig. 5).
B. If the right vertical border of any component is to the left of a vertical line at a distance equal to one-eight of the image width or the left vertical border is to the right of a vertical line at seven-eight of the image width then they should be eliminated (refer to Fig. 6a).
C. Knowing that in an image the eyes are always horizontally aligned (symmetric), we first detect the top, bottom, left and right boundaries for each possible eye component and scan the left and right side within the vertical boundaries to see if other components exist. If we find any component/s in the searched bands the component under test is kept but if no other component is found the candidate should be eliminated (refer to Fig. 6b).

Fig. 5. Eliminating components with large height

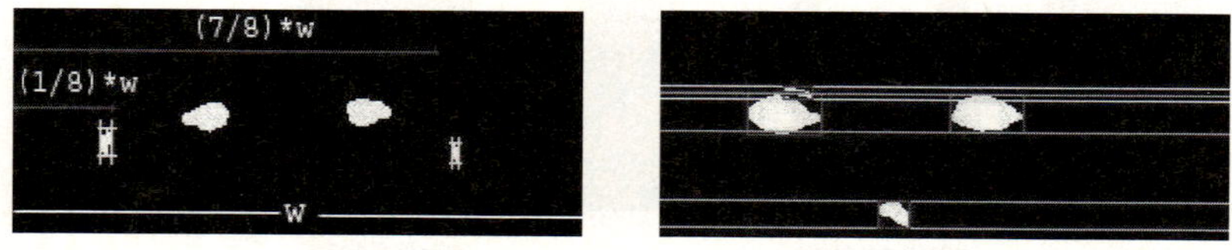

Fig. 6. (a) Out of bounds elimination (b) Isolated component elimination

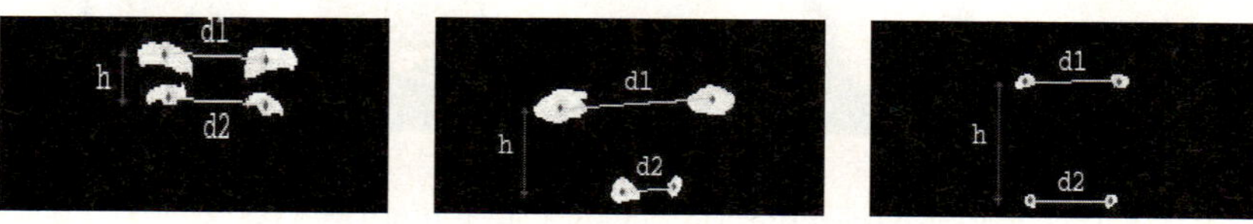

Fig. 7. Possible four component cases

D. In the case of having 4 remaining components which also satisfy the symmetry
   property the decision is based on two criterions. At first we find the horizontal
   distance between the two symmetric components namely $d1$ and $d2$ and secondly the vertical distance h between them. If the horizontal distances $d1$ and
   $d2$ are comparable but the vertical distance between them is small we choose
   the lower two components as eyes, since the upper components are eyebrows.
   If the horizontal distances $d1$ is fairly greater than $d2$ and h is also relatively
   large we choose the upper two components as eyes, as the lower components
   are due to nostrils. If the horizontal distances $d1$ and $d2$ are comparable but h
   is quite large we again choose the upper two components as eyes, as the lower
   components are due to the lip corners (refer to Fig. 7).
E. If there exist more than two components that are aligned in a horizontal
   band, find the center (half of $windex$) and choose the two components that
   are at a minimum horizontal distance from the center.

6   Lip Map Generation

Lip detection as discussed in [15] states that the lip color distribute at the lower
areas of the crescent area defined by the skin colors on the r-g plane. Hence, as
before we can define another quadratic polynomial discriminant, $l_r(r)$, for the
extraction of the lip pixels. How to combine the three polynomial discriminants
and the RGB color space information in order to obtain a lip map (LM) is
shown below.

$$f_{upper}(r) = -1.3067r^2 + 1.0743r + 0.1452 \tag{8}$$

$$f_{lower}(r) = -0.7760r^2 + 0.5601r + 0.1966 \tag{9}$$

$$l_r(r) = -0.7760r^2 + 0.5601r + 0.2563 \tag{10}$$

$$LM = \begin{cases} 1 & \text{if } g > f_{lower}, g < l_r, R > 60, G > 30, B > 30 \\ 0 & \text{otherwise.} \end{cases}$$

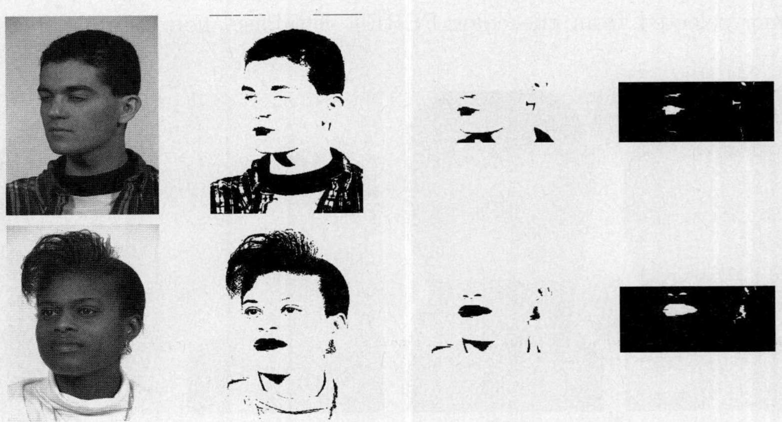

Fig. 8. Extracting the mouth regions

where R, G and B are the intensity values in the red, green and blue channels of the RGB color space. Final step in the processing is to crop the lip map using equation (11) to get the mouth region.

$$MouthRegion = LM(bottomrow - ceil(0.60 * hindex) : bottomrow - 25)$$
(11)

The above described processing steps are depicted in Fig. 8.

7   Rules for Mouth Component Verifications

To remove falsely extracted mouth candidates the following set of rules are applied.

A. If the right vertical border of any component is to the left of a vertical line at a distance equal to 16 % of the image width or the left vertical border is to the right of a vertical line at 80 % of the image width then they should be eliminated.
B. Remove all components whose width to height ratio is below 1.8.
C. If the area (number of connected 1's) for a candidate is less than a fixed threshold value then remove this component.
D. If the area (number of connected 1's) for a candidate is greater than a fixed threshold value then also remove this component.
E. If more than 2 components remain select the largest two.
F. Compute the ratio $A \cdot \left(\frac{w^2}{h}\right)$ for each of the two components where, A is the area, w is the width and h is the height of the component considered. Finally, select the one with the larger ratio.

8   Simulation Results

We tested the proposed algorithm on 311 test images (30 subjects) that we have randomly selected from the color FERET database. Four sample faces with

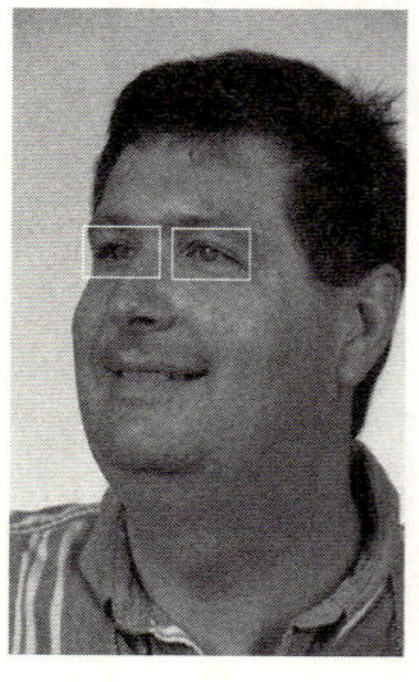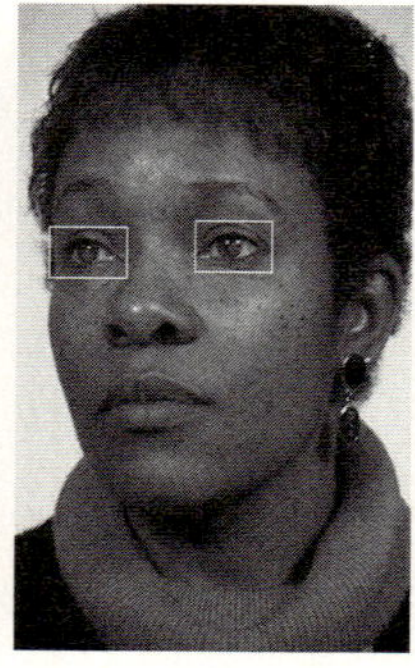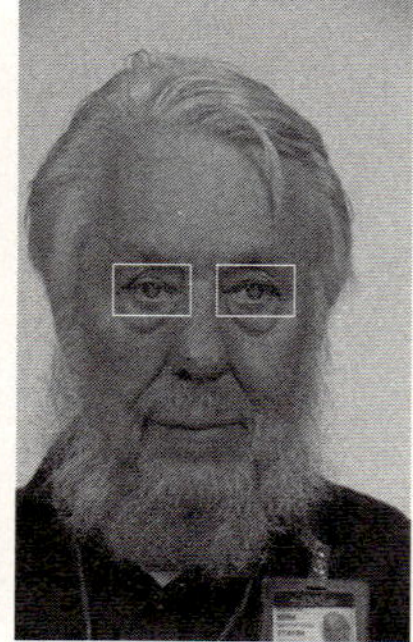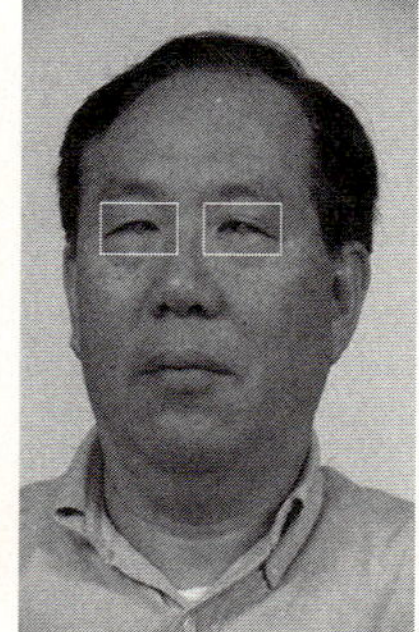

Fig. 9. Marked eye features

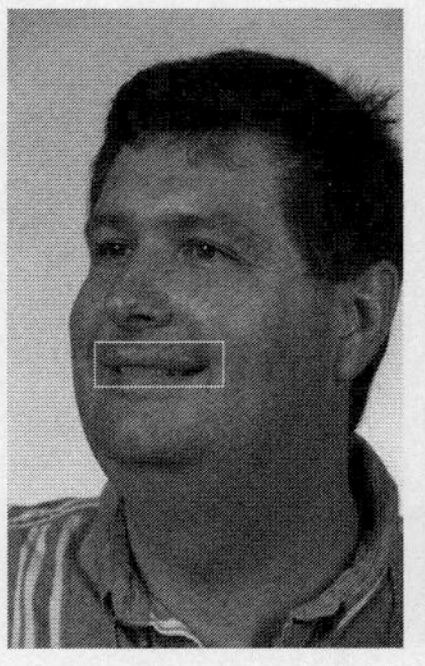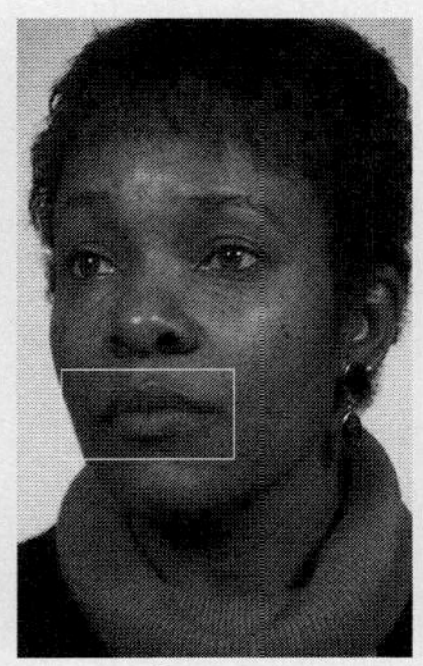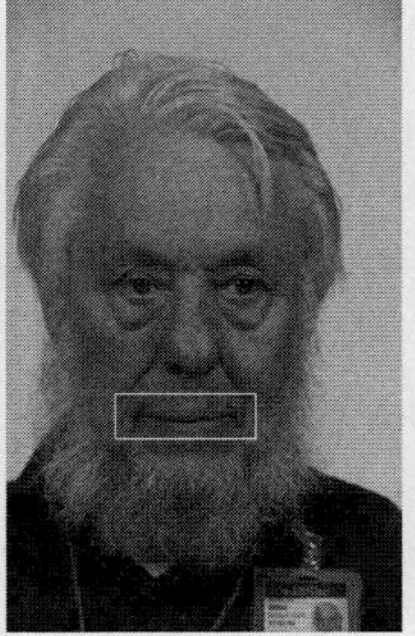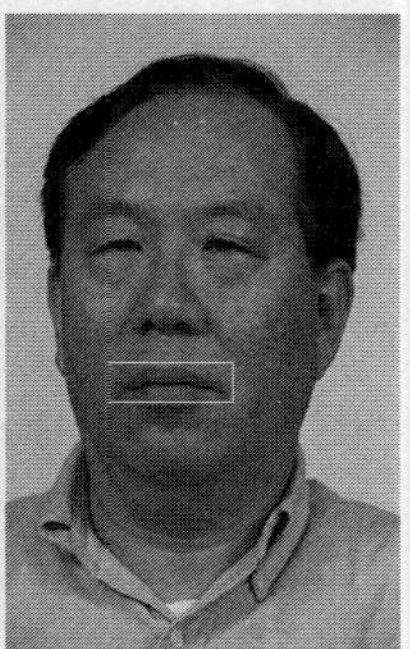

Fig. 10. Marked mouth features

detected features using the proposed algorithm are shown in Fig. 9 and Fig. 10. The experimental results show that the algorithm can robustly detect the local regions for people with varying skin-tones.

Table 1 provides a summary for the correct detection rates for the left eye, right eye and the mouth regions. As can be seen from the results all three rates are very promising.

Also since this method does not extract the mouth corners based on the lip-cut, it is not required that the subject's mouth is closed.

Table 1. Performance in extracting component regions from FERET database

region containing left eye	92.53
region containing right eye	94.02
region containing mouth	91.00

9   Conclusion

A efficient rule based local region extraction algorithm making use of quadratic polynomial discriminants derived from the r-g chromatic coordinates and the RGB color space information is proposed. The algorithm will eliminate the false feature candidates using spatial and geometrical representations of facial components. The paper adopts an approach in which the feature and lip maps are generated independently and hence provides the flexibility of being able to run the two extraction routines in parallel for better time management. Preliminary simulation results indicated in Table 1 implies that the proposed algorithm is quite effective. Authors believe that if the affine transform parameters are estimated and the transformations are reversed then the correct extraction rates can be even higher. Finally, since the mouth region extraction is not based on determining the lip-cut there is no restriction on the mouth mimics.

Acknowledgment

The work presented herein is an outcome of research carried out under Seed Money Project *EN-05-02-01* granted by the Research Advisory Board of Eastern Mediterranean University.

References

1. Rein-Lien, H., Abdel-Mottaleb, M.: Face detection in colour images, *IEEE Trans. on Pattern Analysis and Machine Intelligence*, Vol. 24, No:5, pp. 696-706, May 2002.
2. Ming-Hsuan, Y., Kriegnam, D. J., Ahuja, N.: Detecting faces in images: a survey, *IEEE Trans. on Pattern Analysis and Machine Intelligence*, Vol. 24, No:1, pp. 34-58, January 2002.
3. Alattar, A. M., Rajala, S. A.:Facial Features Localization In Front View Head And Shoulders Images, *IEEE International Conference on Acoustics, Speech, and Signal Processing*, Vol. 6, pp. 3557-3560, March 1999.
4. Rein-Lien, H., Abdel-Mottaleb, M., Jain, A. K.:Face detection in color images, *Tech. Report MSU-CSE-01-7*, Michigan State University, March 2001.
5. İnce., E. A., Kaymak., S., Çelik., T.: Yüzsel Öznitelik Sezimi İçin Karma Bir Teknik, *13. IEEE Sinyal İsleme ve İletisim Uygulamaları Kurultayı*, pp. 396-399, May 2005.
6. Hu, M., Worrall, S., Sadka A. H., Kondoz, A. M.: Face Feature Detection And Model Design For 2D Scalable Model-Based Video Coding, *International Conference on Visual Information Engineering*, pp. 125-128, July 2003.
7. Sung, K., Poggio, T.: Example based Learning for View-based Human Face Detection, *C.B.C.L.* , Paper No: 112, MIT, 1994.
8. Moghaddam, B., Pentland, A.: Face Recognition using View-Based and Modular Eigenspaces, *IEEE Transactions on Pattern Analysis and Machine Intelligence*,Vol. 20, No:1, pp. 23-38, January 1998.
9. Rowley, H., Baluja, S., Kanade, T.: Neural Network Based Face Detection, *IEEE Trans. on Pattern Analysis and Machine Intelligence*, Vol. 24, No:1, pp. 34-58, January 2002.
10. Adams, R., Bischof, L.: Seeded Region Growing, *IEEE Trans. on Pattern Analysis and Machine Intelligence*, Vol. 16, No:6, pp. 641-647, June 1994.
11. Heisele, B., Ho, P., Wu, J., Poggio, T.: Face Recognition: Component-based versus Global Approaches, *Computer Vision and Image Understanding 91*, 6-21, February 2003.
12. Phillips P. J., Wechsler H., Huang J., Rauss P.: The FERET database and evaluation procedure for face recognition algorithms, *Image and Vision Computing J.*, Vol.16, No.5, pp. 295-306, 1998.
13. Phillips P. J., Moon H., Rizvi S. A.,Rauss P. J.: The FERET Evaluation Methodology for Face Recognition Algorithms, *IEEE Trans. Pattern Analysis and Machine Intelligence*, Vol. 22, pp. 1090-1104, 2000.
14. Terrillon, J. C., Shirazi, M. N., Akamatsu, S.: Comperative performance of different skin chrominance models and chrominance spaces for the automatic detection of human faces in color images, *Proc. IEEE Int. Conf. Automatic Face and Gesture Recognition*, pp. 54-61, 2000.
15. Chiang, C-C., Tai, W-K., Yang, M-T., Huang, Y-T., Huang, C-J.: A novel method for detecting lips, eyes and faces in real time, *Real-Time Imaging 9* , Vol. 9, pp. 277-287, 2003.

Lossless Compression of Volumetric Medical Data

Samy Ait-Aoudia, Fatma-Zohra Benhamida, and Mohamed-Azzeddine Yousfi

INI – Institut National d'Informatique, BP 69M, Oued-Smar 16270, Algiers, Algeria
s_ait_aoudia@ini.dz

Abstract. Medical imaging applications produce large sets of similar images. Thus a compression technique is useful to reduce space storage. Lossless compression methods are necessary in such critical applications. Volumetric medical data presents strong similarity between successive frames. In this paper we investigate predictive techniques for lossless compression of video sequences applied to volumetric data. We also make a comparative study with other existing compression techniques dedicated to volumetric data.

1 Introduction

Medical imaging applications produce a huge amount of 3D data. Among these medical data we can mention CT (Computed Tomography), MR (Magnetic Resonance), PET (Position Emission Tomography) Ultrasound, X-Ray and Angiography images. Storing such amount of data need a lot of disk space. That is why compression is required in that field. In addition, medical images must be stored without any loss of information since the fidelity of images is critical in diagnosis. This requires lossless compression techniques. Lossless compression is an error free compression. The decompressed image is the same as the original image.

Classical image compression techniques (see [1,3,4,6,7,8,10]) concentrate on how to reduce the redundancies presented in an individual image. This model ignores an additional type of redundancy that exists in sets of similar images, the temporal redundancy. Volumetric 3D data compression techniques exploit the correlation that exists among successive image slices to achieve better compression rates.

Due to the fact that volumetric medical data presents strong similarity between successive frames, we investigate, in this paper, predictive techniques for lossless compression of video data. We also make a comparative study with other existing compression techniques dedicated to volumetric data..

This paper is organized as follows. We define in section 2, the correlation coefficient that quantify similarity between images. The predictions schemes for 3D data compression are explained in section 3. We briefly present in section 4, the coding methods used for the compression. Experimental results on medical samples datasets are given in section 5. Section 6 gives conclusions.

2 Images Similarity

There is a strong similarity between every two successive frames in a volumetric dataset. This similarity must somehow be mathematically quantified to show the degree of

A. Levi et al. (Eds.): ISCIS 2006, LNCS 4263, pp. 563–571, 2006.

resemblance. Two images are said to be similar or statistically correlated if they have similar pixel intensities in the same areas.

The correlation coefficient is used to quantify similarity. For two datasets $X=(x_1,x_2,\ldots x_N)$ and $Y=(y_1,y_2,\ldots y_N)$ with mean values x_m and y_m, Neter et al. [11] defined this coefficient as :

$$r=\frac{\sum_{i=1}^{N}(x_i-x_m)(y_i-y_m)}{\sqrt{\sum_{i=1}^{N}(x_i-x_m)^2}\sqrt{\sum_{i=1}^{N}(y_i-y_m)^2}} \tag{1}$$

The correlation coefficient is also called Person's r. To avoid the manipulation of negative values, r^2 is often used instead of r. For to datasets X and Y, a value of r^2 close to 0, means that no correlation exits between them. A value of r^2 close to 1, means that strong correlation exits between the two datasets. X and Y are perfectly correlated if $r^2=1$. In context of images, a value r^2 close to 0 means that the two images are totally dissimilar, a value r^2 close to 1 indicates "strong" similarity and a value $r^2=1$ means that the images are identical.

We give two examples to quantify the similarity between images. Figure 1 shows two successive MR chest scans of a same patient. The value $r^2=0.997$ indicates strong similarity between these two images. Figure 2 depicts two non similar images. The correlation parameter $r^2=0.005$ indicates that the two images are non correlated.

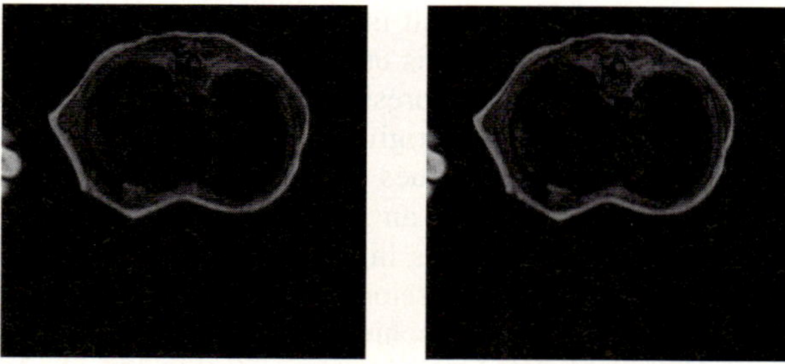

Fig. 1. Two successive MR chest scans

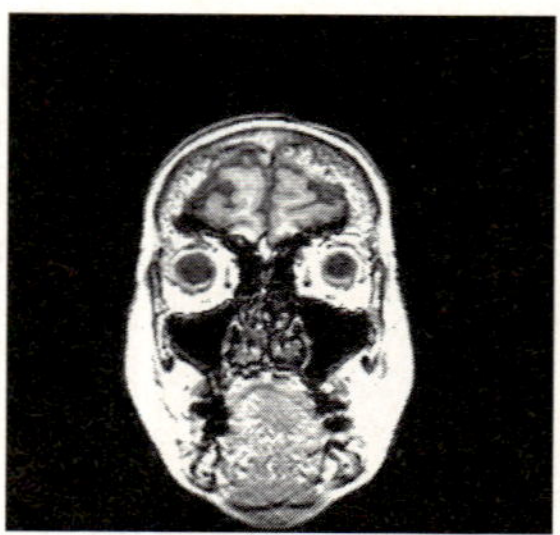

Fig. 2. Two dissimilar images

3 Prediction Schemes

A prediction model is used to predict pixel values and replace them by the error in prediction. The resulting image is called the residual image or error image. The remaining structure is then captured by a statistical or universal model prior to encoding. The first step is called decorrelation and the second step is called error modeling. The images are processed in a in raster scan order and a pixel is predicted on the basis of pixels which have already treated in the current and previous frames. In the frame k, we denote the current pixel $P_k[i,j]$ and its predicted value by $\underline{P}_k[i,j]$. The prediction error is then given by : $\underline{P}_k[i,j] - P_k[i,j]$.

3.1 DPCM

The simplest way to extract the temporal redundancy is to subtract adjacent pixels values in two successive frames. This principle is called DPCM (Differential Pulse Code Modulation). The predicted pixel value is given by :

$$\underline{P}_k[i,j] = P_{k-1}[i,j] \tag{2}$$

3.2 3D JPEG-4

The lossless JPEG predictors are effective in removing spatial correlations present in individual frames. The JPEG standard provides eight different predictors from which the user can select. Table 1 lists the eight predictors used. Figure 3 shows the notation used for specifying neighboring pixels of the pixel being predicted.

Fig. 3. Notation used for specifying neighboring pixels of current pixel P[i,j]

Table 1. JPEG predictors for lossless coding

Mode	Prediction
0	0 (no prediction)
1	N
2	W
3	NW
4	N+W-NW
5	W+(N-NW)2
6	N+(W-NW)/2
7	(N+W)/2

For a video sequence or a volumetric data, using these predictors in each frame does not take into account temporal correlation. Memon et al.[9] used 3-dimensional versions of the JPEG predictors. The 3D predictors were obtained by simply taking the average of the 2D predictors in each of the three planes that can pass through a given pixel in three dimensions. According to Memon et al. [9] The 3D version of the predictor specified by mode 4 of lossless JPEG gave the best performance among all the 3D predictors. This predictor, that will be used in our experiments, is given by :

$$\underline{P}_k[i,j] = \frac{2*(P_k[i,j-1]+P_k[i-1,j]+P_{k-1}[i,j])}{3} - \frac{P_{k-1}[i-1,j]+P_{k-1}[i,j-1]+P_k[i-1,j-1]}{3} \quad (3)$$

3.3 3D JPEG-LS

LOCO-I (LOw COmplexity LOssless COmpression for Images) [13] uses a non-linear predictor with edge detecting capability. The approach in LOCO-I consists on performing a test to detect edges. Specifically, the LOCO-I predictor guesses:

$$\text{Predicted\_pixel} \begin{cases} \min(N,W) & \text{if } NW \geq \max(N,W) \\ \max(N,W) & \text{if } NW \leq \min(N,W) \\ N + W - NW & \text{otherwise} \end{cases}$$

LOCO-I is the algorithm at the core of the standard compression of continuous-tone images, JPEG-LS ([13]). The predictor used in LOCO-I was renamed during the standardization process "median edge detector" (MED).

From the MED predictor, we have derived and used in our experiments a 3D predictor called 3D JPEG-LS. We define it as follows:

- if $(\min(P_k[i-1,j-1], P_{k-1}[i-1,j], P_{k-1}[i,j-1]) >= \max(P_k[i-1,j], P_k[i,j-1], P_{k-1}[i,j]))$
  $\underline{P}_k[i,j] = \min(P_k[i-1,j], P_k[i,j-1], P_{k-1}[i,j])$
- if$(\max(P_k[i-1,j-1], P_{k-1}[i-1,j], P_{k-1}[i,j-1]) <= \min(P_k[i-1,j], P_k[i,j-1], P_{k-1}[i,j]))$
  $\underline{P}_k[i,j] = \max(P_k[i-1,j], P_k[i,j-1], P_{k-1}[i,j])$
- otherwise

$$\underline{P}_k[i,j] = \frac{2*(P_k[i,j-1]+P_k[i-1,j]+P_{k-1}[i,j])}{3} - \frac{P_{k-1}[i-1,j]+P_{k-1}[i,j-1]+P_k[i-1,j-1]}{3}$$

4   Encoding the Residual Images

In a predictive lossless image compression technique, there are two distinct steps, decorrelation and coding. In the decorrelation step, spatial and temporal redundancies among pixels are reduced, resulting in a image called the residual image.

If the decorrelation step is effective, than the every residual image has significantly lower zero-order entropy compared to the original image slice in the 3D dataset. Several coding schemes were tested in the residual image encoding phase.

In our studies, we will restrict ourselves to the three techniques that gave good results. We will use arithmetic coding, PPMd and LZMA algorithms. PPMd is a PPM (Prediction by Partial Matching) based algorithm. It is a finite-context statistical modeling technique. This algorithm is mostly based on Dmitry Shkarin's work [12] The LZMA algorithm is a derivative of the Lempel-Ziv algorithm. It is an improved and optimized version of LZ77 algorithm [17].

5   Experimental Results

5.1   Test Images

The evaluation compressions methods is made on sample medical images. We present experimental results on the same CT and MR volumetric datasets used in [2,15,16] for easy comparisons. All images were gray-level, and were scaled to 8 bits/pixel. The volumetric medical data are described in table 2. The first slice of each dataset is given in figure 4.

Tabel 2. Description of the datasets used in the experiments

Type	History	Age	Sex	File name	Size
CT	Apert's syndrom	2	M	Aperts	256x256x96
	Internal carotid dissection	41	F	Carotid	256x256x64
	Tripod fracture	16	M	Skull	256x256x192
	Healing scaphoid fracture	20	M	Wrist	256x256x176
MR	Normal	38	F	Liver_t1	256x256x48
	Normal	38	F	Liver_t2e1	256x256x48
	Congenital heart disease	1	M	Ped_chest	256x256x64
	Left exophthalmoses	42	M	Sag_head	256x256x48

5.2   Compression Results

All lossless coding results are based on real compressed file sizes. In the first experiment, we have compressed the volumetric data by general purpose lossless compressors:

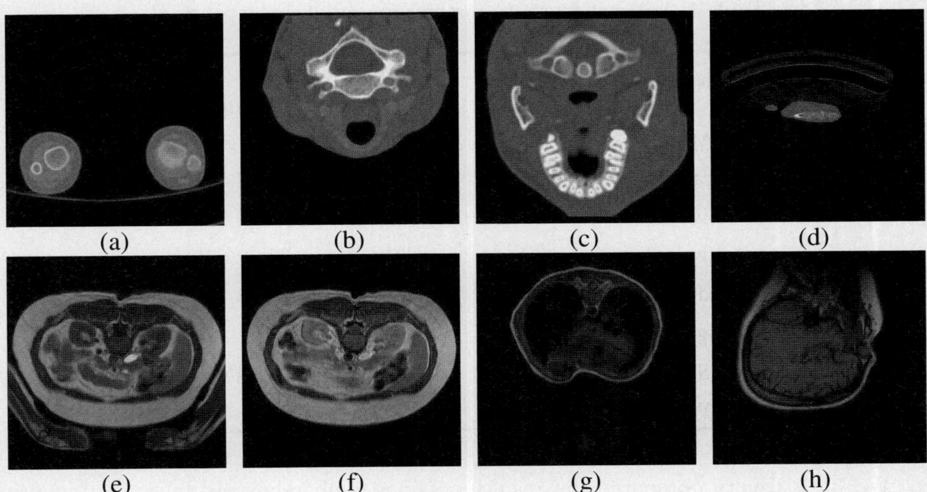

Fig. 4. Volumetric medical images : First slice of each data set. (a) Aperts (b) Carotid (c) Skull (d) Wrist (e) Liver_t1 (f) Liver_t2e1 (g) Ped_chest (h) Sag_head.

Table 3. Lossless compression results in bit per pixel using standard lossless compressors

Name	UNIX Compress	WIN ZIP	WIN RAR	JPEG LS	CALIC
Aperts	1.739	1.789	1.494	1.063	1.047
Carotid	2.782	2.825	2.288	1.738	1.654
Liver-t1	5.304	5.294	3.882	3.158	3.047
Liver-t2	3.938	3.738	3.033	2.369	2.243
Ped-Chest	4.333	4.509	3.796	2.928	2.810
Sag-Head	3.595	3.569	3.323	2.556	2.585
Skull	4.135	3.944	3.741	2.846	2.725
Wrist	2.720	2.801	1.901	1.653	1.691

Unix-compress, Win-Zip and Win-Rar. We also compressed the 3D data by JPEG-LS [13] the ISO/ITU standard for lossless compression of continuous tone-images and CALIC (Context-based Adaptive Lossless Image Coding) [14]. Lossless compression results in bit per pixel (bpp) using these compressors are given in table 3.

In the second experiment, we have compressed the volumetric data by first decorrelating these data and then coding them. The decorrelation phase was made by using the three predictors DPCM, 3D JPEG-3 and 3D JPEG-LS. In the coding phase we have used several techniques. In our experiments three methods gave good results. These methods are : arithmetic coding, LZMA algorithm and PPMd algorithm.

Table 4, table 5 and table 6 give lossless compression results in bit per pixel (bpp) when using for the coding step arithmetic coding, LZMA algorithm and PPMd algorithm respectively.

Table 4. Arithmetic lossless compression results in bit per pixel

Name	DPCM Arithmetic	3D JPEG-4 Arithmetic	LS-3D Arithmetic
Aperts	1.192	1.238	1.330
Carotid	1.940	1.965	2.083
Liver-t1	2.941	3.125	3.330
Liver-t2	2.555	2.622	2.675
Ped-Chest	1.839	2.768	3.112
Sag-Head	2.453	2.758	2.898
Skull	2.631	3.112	3.174
Wrist	1.384	1.652	1.818

We have finally compared the results obtained with relatively recent volumetric data compression that uses wavelets. In table 7, the columns '3D SPIHT' and '3D

Table 5. LZMA lossless compression results in bit per pixel

Name	DPCM LZMA	3D JPEG-4 LZMA	LS-3D LZMA
Aperts	1.062	1.199	1.236
Carotid	1.733	1.859	1.995
Liver-t1	2.722	3.290	3.483
Liver-t2	1.905	2.478	2.500
Ped-Chest	1.757	2.853	3.053
Sag-Head	2.232	2.752	2.809
Skull	2.182	2.972	3.102
Wrist	1.151	1.555	1.713

Table 6. PPMd lossless compression results in bit per pixel

Name	DPCM PPMD	3D JPEG-4 PPMD	LS-3D PPMD
Aperts	0.867	1.004	1.119
Carotid	1.471	1.625	1.817
Liver-t1	2.390	3.039	3.320
Liver-t2	2.025	2.406	2.509
Ped-Chest	1.689	2.687	3.112
Sag-Head	2.127	2.619	2.747
Skull	2.119	2.716	2.928
Wrist	1.029	1.372	1.569

Table 7. Bits rates for lossless compression, average bitrate in bits per pixel (bpp)

Name	3D SPIHT	3D AT-SPIHT	3D ES-COT	3D CB-EZW	3-D NL ($\delta=0$)	DPCM PPMD
Aperts	1.054	1.039	0.9	1.013	0.933	**0.867**
Carotid	1.497	1.497	**1.4**	1.455	1.650	1.471
Liver-t1	2.399	2.369	**2.2**	2.415	2.376	2.390
Liver-t2	1.748	1.744	**1.6**	1.753	1.856	2.025
Ped-Chest	2.104	2.054	1.9	2.117	1.770	**1.689**
Sag-Head	2.240	2.202	**2.0**	2.356	2.136	2.127
Skull	2.113	2.166	**2.0**	2.204	2.405	2.119
Wrist	1.368	1.355	1.2	1.327	1.144	**1.029**

AT-SPIHT' refer to the results with lossless variations of 3D SPIHT [5].The columns
'3D ESCOT' and '3D CB-EZW' refer to the lossless results with 3D ESCOT [15] and

3D CB-EZW [2]. The column '3-D NL (δ=0)' refers to the 3D wavelet based two-stage lossless coder described in [16]. All these results can be found in [16]. The last column refers to DPCM-PPMd the best predictive technique in the tests conducted. Boldface entry in each column indicates the best result for the corresponding dataset.

5.3 Discussion

From the results shown in previous tables, we see that most of the 3D compressions methods carry out an improvement compared to individual image standard compression. From table 7, we see that the DPCM-PPMd method performed the best for three of eight test sequences. This can be explained by the fact that high similarity is present in the three sequences (CT_Aperts, MR_Ped-Chest and CT_Wrist). The correlation coefficient for every two successive slices in each of these datasets is always superior to 0.99. When the correlation coefficient decreases (as this is the case for MR_Liver-t2 sequence) the DPCM-PPMD will not be effective.

6 Conclusion

One of the best application areas for volumetric compression methods is medical imaging. Medical image databases usually store huge amount of similar images. This paper attempts to evaluate the performance of lossless volumetric compression on sample datasets of grayscale similar images. In this study, only the effect of compressing sets of grayscale images was evaluated. Further works must consider compressing sets true color images. Spectral decorrelation must then be taken into account. 3D compression methods can also be tested on many other application areas. Satellite image databases, for example, often contain sets of images taken over the same geographical areas, and under similar weather or lighting conditions. They necessarily contain inter-image redundancy.

References

[1] Bekkouche H. and Barret M., Adaptive multiresolution decomposition: application to lossless image compression, ICASSP 2002, Orlando Florida, USA, May 2002.

[2] Bilgin A., Zweig G., and Marcellin M.W., Three-Dimensional Image Compression with Integer Wavelet Applied Optics, vol.39, n°11, pp. 1799-1814, April 2000.

[3] Celik M.U., Sharma G., and Tekalp A.M., Gray-level embedded lossless image compression, ICASSP 2003, 6-10 April 2003, Honk-Kong, pp. III_245-248.

[4] Chang C.C. and Chen G.I, Enhancement algorithm for nonlinear context-based predictors, IEE Proc.–Vis Image Signal Processing, vol. 150, n° 1, February 2003.

[5] Cho S., Kim D. and Pearlman W.A, Lossless Compression of Volumetric Medical Images with Improved Three-Dimensional SPIHT Algorithm, Journal of Digital Imaging, vol.17, n°1, pp. 57-63, March 2004.

[6] Clunie D., Lossless compression of grayscale medical images and Effectiveness of traditional and state of the art approaches, in Proc. SPIE-Medical Imaging, Vol. 3980, 2000

[7] Falkowski B.J., Compact representations of logic functions forlossless compression of grey-scale images, IEE Proc.-Comput. Digit. Tech., Vol. 151, No. 3, May 2004, pp 221-230.

[8]   Jiang J., Guo B. and Yang S.Y., Revisiting the JPEG-LS prediction scheme, IEE Proc.–Vis Image Signal Processing, vol. 147, n° 6, Decembre 2000.

[9]   Memon N.D., and Sayood K., Lossless Compression of Video Sequences, IEEE trans. On Communications, 44(10), pp.1340-1345, Oct.1996.

[10] Memon N.D., and Wu X., Recent Developments in Context-Based Predictive Techniques for Lossless Image Compression, The Computer Journal, Vol.40(2/3), pp.127-136, 1997.

[11] Neter, J., Wasserman W., and Kutner M.H., Applied Linear Regression Models, IRWIN Burr Rigde, IL, 1989.

[12] Shkarin, D., Improving the efficiency of PPM algorithm, Problems of Information Transmission, Volume 37, Number 3, July 2001, pp. 226-235(10).

[13] Weinberger M. J., Seroussi G., and Sapiro G., The LOCO-I Lossless Image Compression Algorithm: Principles and Standardization into JPEG-LS, IEEE Transactions on Image Processing, Vol. 9, N°. 8, August 2000, pp. 1309-1324.

[14] Wu X. and Memon N., Context-based, adaptive, lossless image codec" IEEE Trans. Commun., vol. 45 (4), Apr. 1997, pp. 437-444.

[15] Xiong Z., Wu X., Cheng S. and Hua J., Lossy to Lossless Compression of Medical Volumetric Data Using Three-Dimensional Integer Wavelet Transforms, IEEE trans. On Medical Imaging, vol. 22, n°3, pp. 459-470, March 2003.

[16] Yea S., Cho S. and Pearlman W.A., Integrated Lossy, Near-lossless, and Lossless Compression of Medical Volumetric Data, ,"*Image and Video Communications and Processing 2005*, IS&T/SPIE Symposium on Electronic Imaging, 2005, Proc. SPIE 5685, Vol. 2, pp. 151-159, Jan. 2005.

[17] Ziv J., and A. Lempel, A universal algorithm for sequential data compression, IEEE Trans. Inf. Theory, vol. IT-23, no. 3, pp. 337-343, May 1977.

Identification of Luminal and Medial Adventitial Borders in Intravascular Ultrasound Images Using Level Sets

Ali Iskurt, Sema Candemir, and Yusuf Sinan Akgul

GIT Vision Lab
Gebze Institute of Technology
Department of Computer Engineering,
Gebze, Kocaeli, Turkey
{iskurtali, scandemir, akgul}@bilmuh.gyte.edu.tr
http://www.bilmuh.gyte.edu.tr

Abstract. Extraction of the media and plaque boundaries from the intravascular Ultrasound (IVUS) images is gaining popularity as a biomedical application. This paper presents a novel system for the fully automatic extraction of the boundaries of the media and the plaque visible in the IVUS images. The system utilizes an enhanced level set technique to derive the evolution of two coupled contours as the zero level sets of a single higher dimensional surface. Moreover, the system utilizes the surface features to impose the expected media thickness. By using the single surface as a communication path between the contours, the system carries all the advantages of using two evolving surfaces and it becomes more efficient, less complex, easily extensible, and faster. Additionally, the capability of using different dynamic behaviors for the segmentation of the inner and outer walls makes our system even more flexible. The derived surface evolution equations capture the domain dependent information in an elegant and effective manner and address many practical issues, such as the missing wall sections or very weak boundary contrast. We have verified the accuracy and effectiveness of our system on synthetic and real data.

1   Introduction

Intravascular ultrasound (IVUS) is a relatively new medical imaging technique which can provide information complementary to angiography. An ultrasound transducer on the tip of a catheter provides cross-sectional images of the coronary arteries, which produces the morphological views of both the plaque and the arterial wall as shown in Fig.1. It has been shown that IVUS can demonstrate[10] diseases in cases where angiography is misleading proper coronary therapy[9]. Geometric information about the lumen, plaque, and vessel wall can be easily obtained by IVUS. In addition, IVUS can supply crucial data about the plaque type which is really important for the identification of sections of vessels likely to rupture. As a result, IVUS is becoming a popular technique for direct visualization of the coronary arteries.

A. Levi et al. (Eds.): ISCIS 2006, LNCS 4263, pp. 572–582, 2006.
© Springer-Verlag Berlin Heidelberg 2006

Traditionally, the manual analysis of IVUS images is laborious, time consuming, and subject to large interobserver and intraobserver variability which prevents us from taking the full advantages of IVUS technology. Computerized segmentation of IVUS images will address these problems since the results will be objective. It will not require intense manual intervention and the overall cost will be less.

There are a number of techniques for the semi-automatic segmentation of IVUS images. An overview of the common 2-D and 3-D segmentation and reconstruction systems was presented in [4]. One classical approach is the 3D segmentation of Li *et al.*[11], which performs both longitudinal and cross-sectional semiautomatic contour detection based on a minimum cost algorithm. This algorithm was performed in clinical applications by von Birgelen *et al.*[2]. Knowledge-based solutions was proposed by Sonka *et al.*[6] and this research soon led to 3D modeling using this [1]. This segmentation is based on a graph-search approach within a manually determined elliptical region of interest(ROI). Despite the popularity of IVUS, there are no fully automatic systems available.

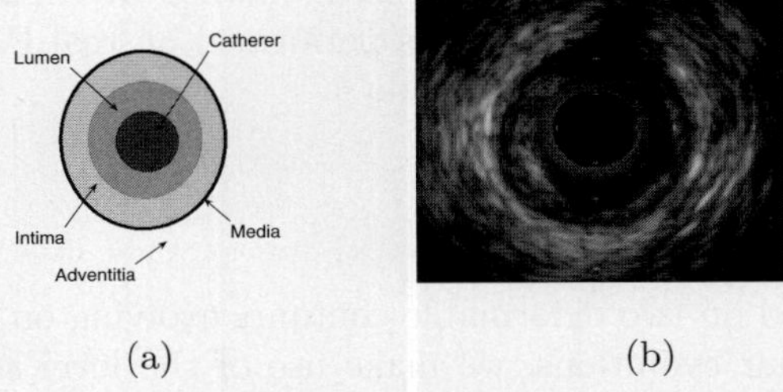

(a)   (b)

Fig. 1. (a) The layers of a coronary artery wall. (b) An intravascular ultrasound image.

This paper presents a novel technique for the segmentation of the IVUS images. The technique is based on evolving two contours with different dynamics and stopping them with the constraint of media thickness and uniquely address many IVUS specific problems. If one of the image boundaries is missing or has weak image contrast, the information obtained from other contour can be employed to find the expected position. Similarly, if both contours have missing image data, the system can impose a media thickness constraint on the boundary position to come up with an estimate. This property is especially useful for obtaining media segment in IVUS images.

Among all other techniques for the segmentation of images in Computer Vision, level sets method is utilized in our research because of the advantages they offer. First, it is very easy in the level set theory to go to an upper dimension. Thus, once the 2D image segmentation is formulated, it will be straightforward to use it in the 3D reconstruction of a vessel. Second, it is possible to impose constraints in level sets for special case studies like IVUS. For instance, one constraint will be the media thickness. Levels set methods have already been applied to 3D medical image segmentation[3], detection of vessel borders in magnetic resonance angiography (MRA) images[5], segmentation of white and gray matters in MRI images[13] and many other areas.

The straightforward usage of level sets was not applicable for IVUS image segmentation. Therefore, level set theory had to be refined to capture the IVUS related constraints and to address the emerging problems. Thus, we extend the classical level set framework in several novel ways. The zero set contours of a single three dimensional surface would correspond to the inner and outer wall boundaries. The surface movement along the normal direction moves the boundaries towards each other and the inherent geometric constraints on the surface makes the contours keep a distance that enforces a thickness constraint of the media. The local surface properties, such as the directional surface derivatives, make it possible to elegantly define different evolution behaviors for the two contours.

Rest of this paper is organized as follows. Section 2 provides information about how we refine classical level set methods and the novel extensions that we introduce with this paper. The experiments on system validation on synthetic images under varying controlled noise and anomalies are explained in Section 3. Section 3 also includes the experiments performed on real IVUS data. Finally, we provide concluding remarks in Section 4.

2   Segmentation

Our system is based on two deformable contours evolving on the IVUS images. To drive the contour evolutions, we make use of the level set methods which were introduced[7] to Computer Vision for recovering shapes of objects in two or three dimensions. The basic idea of level set methods is to embed the shape of the objects as the zero level set of a higher dimensional surface. While the surface evolves, the zero level set contours might develop singularities and sharp corners or they might change topology. Finally, contour evolution stops at desired boundaries.

The contours are evolved in a way that they try to move smoothly towards each other while seeing some resistance from the image features at likely boundary positions. The two contours are not allowed to come too close or stay too far from each other. At the end of the deformations, the inner and outer media boundaries are localized.

Consider two time-dependent, i.e. moving, closed contours $c_1(t)$ and $c_2(t)$ on R^2. The contours c_1 and c_2 never intersect and c_1 is always inside c_2 for $t \geq 0$. Our motivation is to use the contours c_1 and c_2 to extract the inner and outer walls of media. We will write the motion equations for these contours that will move them towards the wall boundaries and stop them when the destination is reached.

Let C be the set of points on $c_1(0)$ and $c_2(0)$. Consider a function s,

$$s(\mathbf{x}) = \begin{cases} 0, & \text{if } \mathbf{x} \in C; \\ -d(x), & \text{if } \mathbf{x} \text{ is outside } c_1(0) \text{ but inside } c_2(0); \\ d(x), & \text{otherwise,} \end{cases} \tag{1}$$

where d is the shortest distance to C from point $\mathbf{x} \in R^2$. We define the time dependent surface $\varphi(\mathbf{x}, t = 0)$ by

$$\varphi(\mathbf{x}, t = 0) = G(\alpha|s(\mathbf{x})|) * s(\mathbf{x}), \tag{2}$$

where $G(\sigma)$ is the two dimensional Gaussian with variance σ^2, $\alpha > 0$ is a weighting constant, and $*$ is the standard convolution operation. Note that when $\mathbf{x} \in C$, the surface φ is the same as the function s because the σ of the Gaussian function becomes zero at those points. Note also that Equation (2) implies that

$$C = (\mathbf{x}|\varphi(\mathbf{x}, t = 0) = 0). \tag{3}$$

The original idea of level sets is to define a smooth higher dimensional function that represents the lower dimensional contours (the interface or the front) to be extracted/tracked as the zero level set of the higher dimensional function. If we take the intersection of the X-Y plane with the function $\varphi(\mathbf{x}, t = 0)$, the two closed contours $c_1(0)$ and $c_2(0)$ are obtained (See Fig. 2). We would like to expose the surface φ to a velocity field that depends on geometry, position, and image data. While φ moves under the influence of the velocity field, the contours c_1 and c_2 also move to find the desired wall boundaries.

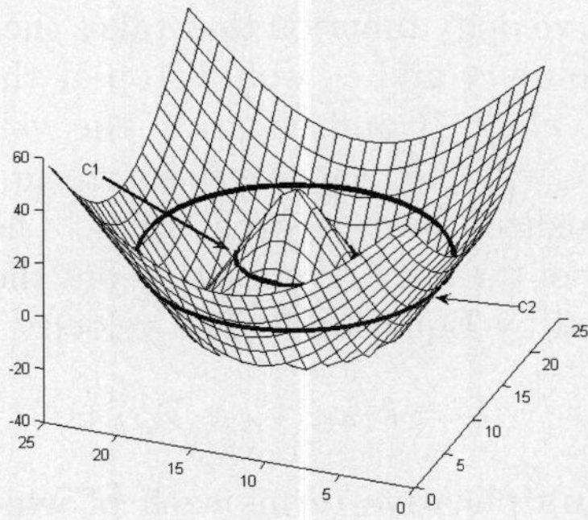

Fig. 2. The surface φ at $t = 0$. The zero level set of φ produces the contours c_1 and c_2.

The elementary equation of motion under the velocity field can be written[8] as

$$\frac{\partial \varphi}{\partial t} + V|\nabla \varphi| = 0, \tag{4}$$

where V is the normal component of the desired velocity of the front and $|\nabla \varphi| = \sqrt{\frac{\partial \varphi}{\partial x}^2 + \frac{\partial \varphi}{\partial y}^2}$.

Furthermore, the geometric properties of the contours c_1 and c_2 (the front), such as the normal or the mean curvature, can easily be calculated from the surface. The normal to the front is simply the gradient of the surface, $\nabla\varphi$. The mean curvature of the front can be conveniently obtained by

$$\kappa = -\nabla\frac{\nabla\varphi}{|\nabla\varphi|}. \tag{5}$$

We recognize that the normal vectors of the points on $c_1(t)$ and $c_2(t)$ have opposite directions. If the velocity field contains constant velocity values for all points, then we expect the contour c_1 to expand and c_2 to shrink according to the Equation 4. This is a desirable feature of our design of the level set function because our motivation of using coupled dual contours is to obtain a contour movement that pushes the contours together until they find the correct boundaries. This natural movement of the surface φ governed by the Equation 4 greatly simplifies our system both in terms of mathematical complexity and computational efficiency. Other systems that use levels sets to perform multiple contour extraction, such as Yezzi *et al.*[12], use more than one evolving surface.

We need a mechanism for stopping the contours when they are close to the desired borders. We also need to establish a communication path between these contours so that they would stop moving if they come too close when there is no image feature to stop them. The next section describes how we use the image data and surface geometry information to achieve this goal.

2.1   Recovering the Boundaries

We would like to define a velocity function that takes the image data into account so that the moving contours c_1 and c_2 would stop at the boundaries. We follow the notation of Malladi *et al.*[7] and separate the velocity function into two additive components. We will keep the advection term component, V_A, so that the two contours are pushed towards each other. The other component, V_G depends on the geometry of the front. It smoothes out the high curvature sections of the front and is defined by Equation 5. The velocity function we have is

$$V = k_I k_G(V_A + V_G), \tag{6}$$

where k_I and k_G are multiplicative terms each of which can stop the surface evolution if they become zero. In our implementation, each of the four terms have weighting constants to adjust the influence of the term on the overall velocity. The weighting constants were removed from the formula for the presentation clarity.

If portions of the image data is missing or very weak as in IVUS, boundaries will be localized incorrectly. For correct localization the thickness constraint is utilized by looking at the ridges between the contours in spatial gradient. For obtaining spatial gradient, we look at φ which is differentiable even around the minima points between the contours c_1 and c_2, so the partial derivatives of φ with respect to x and y should vanish around the minima points, which should make the spatial gradient $|\nabla\varphi|$ values close to zero around the vicinity of the extrema region. This idea is incorporated into the multiplicative velocity term k_G at $\mathbf{x}$ as

$$k_G(\mathbf{x}) = \begin{cases} 0, & \text{if } |\nabla\varphi(\mathbf{x})| < \gamma \text{ and } \varphi(\mathbf{x}) < 0; \\ |\nabla\varphi(\mathbf{x})| - \gamma, & \text{otherwise,} \end{cases} \tag{7}$$

where $\gamma > 0$ is a constant. k_G will slow down the contour movement when the contours get close and depending on the γ value, it will stop the contour evolution completely. Note that $|\nabla\varphi|$ also vanishes for the center region of the inner contour, which can be dealt with by checking the sign of the surface height.

Note that if we let the surface φ evolve on a flat image with no features, the contours c_1 and c_2 will be attracted towards each other but they will never collide due to the multiplicative velocity term k_G. There will be a distance between the contours at the end of the evolution process and this distance depends on the α value of Equation 2 and γ value of Equation 7. In other words, the α and γ values are parameters that directly affect the extracted media thickness. The ability of accepting expected media thickness is a flexible feature for a practical system because it allows one to input beneficial data to the system for extra robustness.

Even though the evolutions of both media contours are strongly tied to the same 3D surface evolution, our formulations allow different evolution characteristics for each contour in an elegant way. Formally, checking the signs of the directional derivatives of the surface towards the highest surface position inside the inner contour will give us the information about which boundary that point belongs. The sign to check for this information can be calculated using

$$sign(\nabla\varphi(\mathbf{x}).\mathbf{x}). \tag{8}$$

The information produced by equation 8 is valuable for a number of applications that can define different properties for the inner and outer boundaries. In IVUS data, inner walls has better contrast and can easily be identified. It is preferable to give more weight to easily identified sections and let this information affect the other boundary extraction, which can be achieved in our system by simply choosing different weights for the inner and outer contours image velocity components.

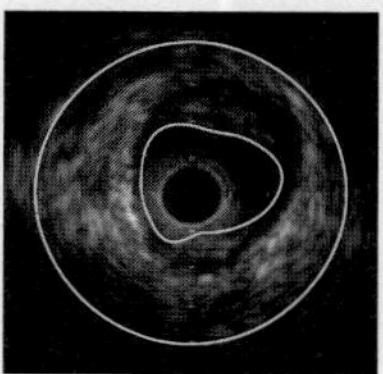

Fig. 3. Lumen-intima interface captured

Using the above mechanism, we first evolve the inner contour and capture the lumen-intima interface as shown in Fig.3. During this evolution, outer contour stands still which is seen as the blue contour. Then, we evolve the inner contour to outer side for a few pixels with normal velocity without the influence of the image. The inner contour now left the lumen-intima wall behind and can go on evolving for finding the media segment together with outer contour. At this time, image gradient features are not permitted to be dominant over the geometry term that imposes thickness constraints. We also increase the influence of the curvature term. This is because we expect a ring-like structure in the end and do not want the contours to be influenced by non-circular gradients. At the end of the surface evolutions, the two level set contours will find the high gradient contour regions that are separated by a distance of certain thickness.

3   Experiments and Validation

We validated the system using both synthetic data and real IVUS images. Synthetic images are used for the quantitative evaluation of the system. The real IVUS images validated the system in the real world.

3.1   Localization of Circular Structure

In order to test the ability for correctly extracting a ring structure with a certain width in a noisy environment, synthetic test images are used. Like the IVUS images, test images are not of very high quality and they contain artifacts. Moreover, the images have missing ring sections. The types of noise added were chosen to reflect the problems seen in IVUS images. Zero mean Gaussian, speckle, and salt & pepper noise types are added to the images with varying amounts.

Fig. 4 shows a few examples of the images used in the experiments. The images are about 100 by 100 pixels in size and the object has a contrasts of

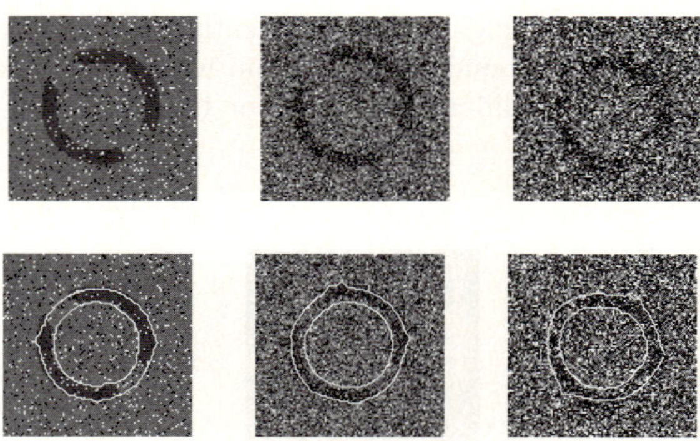

Fig. 4. Example synthetic images used for testing are shown at the top row. The bottom row shows the automatically extracted contours by our system for the same images.

50 gray levels. The wall extraction system produced two ring boundaries, which were compared to the ground truth contours that were used to produce the synthetic images. Table. 1 and Fig. 5 show the error values measured under changing noise and artifact conditions. We observe from the error data that our system performs very well even under high amounts of noise and artifacts. We are especially encouraged by the handling of missing wall sections.

Table 1. Noise Levels and Average Pixel Errors

	1	2	3	4	5	6	7	8	9	10	11	12
Gaussian (σ^2)	0	0	0.01	0	0.02	0.02	0.05	0.08	0.15	0.2	0.3	0.3
Salt and Pepper (%)	0	0	0	0	2	2	5	5	8	10	10	20
Speckle (σ_λ^2)	0	0	0	0	0	0	0.05	0.1	0.1	0.1	0.1	0.2
Missing Walls (%)	0	5	0	15	0	5	15	15	15	20	20	20
Average Pixel Error	0.95	1.03	1.37	1.42	1.82	2.15	2.22	2.58	3.00	3.16	3.67	4.09

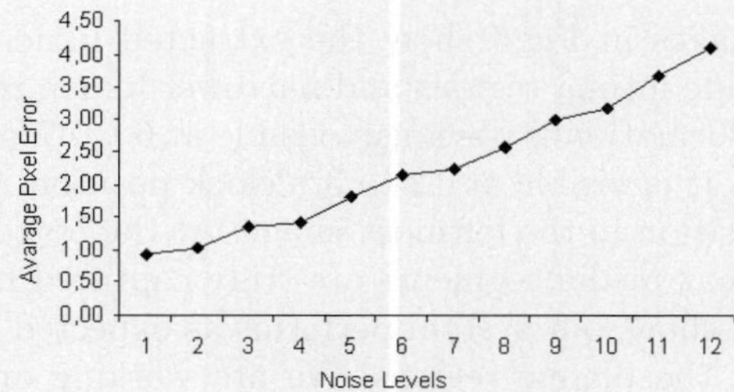

Fig. 5. The graph of the error values for Fig. 1

3.2 Application to Intravascular Coronary Ultrasound

The boundaries of the artery walls, which yields crucial information about the artery blockages, are obtained from the fully automatic segmentation of the IVUS images. The artery wall consists of three layers: intima, media, and adventitia (see Fig. 1-a). The interface between lumen and intima is referred as inner wall and the interface between media and adventitia is defined as the outer vessel wall. IVUS images are ring-shaped, not very contrasty and not clean around the artery wall sections(see Fig. 1-b).

We have applied our segmentation mechanism on various IVUS images of different patients and obtained very satisfying results. Since it is not possible to produce ground truth for the real IVUS images, we validated our results visually. Figure 6 shows only the results for two of them. We automatically removed the catheter boundaries from the image during the experiments. As can be seen in the IVUS images, the inner vessel wall has a better contrast and it should lead the extraction of the outer boundary.

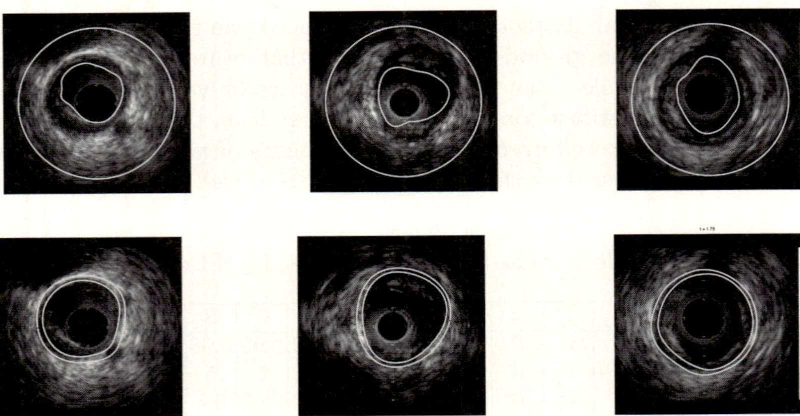

Fig. 6. Lumen-intima interfaces at images on top . Media segments of the same images at bottom.

The top three images in Fig.6 show the extracted lumen-intima interfaces. Both images have wide intima regions and narrower lumen regions. On the leftmost image, plaque formation is obviously visible at 6 to 12 o'clock position and on the middle image it is visible at 12 to 3 o'clock position. Intima is thin only at 12 to 2 o'clock position in the leftmost image. At the bottom images in Fig.6, it can be observed that media segments are truly captured by double contours. As the visual results show, our system performs as expected and correctly finds the vessel walls and the plaque regions. We are working on obtaining several contours produced manually by experts to compare our results numerically.

4   Conclusions

We presented a Computer Vision system that extracts the inner and outer boundaries of vessels simultaneously in IVUS images. The system captures many domain dependent constraints without using any complicated rule sets or hard constraints. We introduced several novel ideas that make our system computationally efficient, robust against the imaging problems, and flexible to use in practice. At the center of our system, there is a single evolving surface whose zero level set contours represent the wall boundaries. The natural dynamics of our system push the contours together until they find the destination, which makes our system simple but powerful. The contours can evolve under different criteria without complicating the surface evolution mechanism. Another novel feature of our system models the expected thickness of the media by using the evolving surface geometry to decide if the approximate media thickness is reached. This feature is very effective for the missing sections of the media.

We have validated our system by applying it to synthetic and real images. Synthetic localization experiments showed our system's accuracy under controlled varying conditions with the thickness constraint. Application to IVUS images proved that our method can be used in segmenting images of vessels with a considerable success.

As for the future research, we are actively working on the extensions of this work towards 3D boundary recovery and 2D + time analysis of video sequences. Specifically, we employ IVUS image sequences while the catheter is being pulled inside the vessel. This 3D analysis of IVUS images produce a better and more reliable information about the possible plaque.

Acknowledgements

The authors thank Dr.Bekir Sitki Cebeci and Dr.Lutfi Hocaoglu for providing the IVUS images.

References

1. S. A.Wahle, G.P.M.Prause and M.Sonka. Geometrically correct 3-d reconstruction of intravascular ultrasound images by fusion with biplane angiographymethods and validation. *IEEE Transactions on Medical Imaging*, 18(8), 1999.
2. W. L. J. C. H. S. C. J. S. P. J. d. F. J. R. T. C. R. C. von Birgelen, C. Di Mario and P. W. Serruys. Morphometric analysis in three-dimensional intracoronary ultrasound: An in-vitro and in-vivo study performed with a novel system for the contour detection of lumen and plaque. *American Heart Journal*, 132:516–527.
3. T. Deschamps, R. Malladi, and I. Ravve. Fast evolution of image manifolds and application to filtering and segmentation in 3d medical images. *IEEE Transactions on Visualization and Computer Graphics*, 10(5):525–535, 2004.
4. G. K. J. H. C. R. J. Dijkstra, A. Wahle and M. Sonka. Quantitative coronary ultrasound: State of the art. *Whats New in Cardiovascular Imaging? (Developments in Cardiovascular Medicine) J. H. C. Reiber and E. E. van der Wall Eds. Dordrecht, The Netherlands: Kluwer*, 204:79, 1998.
5. C. Jian and A. Amini. Quantifying 3-d vascular structures in mra images using hybrid pde and geometric deformable models. *IEEE Transactions of Medical Imaging*, 23(10):1251–1262, 2004.
6. M. S. M. S. B. S. C. D. S. M. M. Sonka, X. Zhang and C. R. McKay. Segmentation of intravascular ultrasound images: A knowledge-based approach. *IEEE Transactions on Medical Imaging*, 14:719–732.
7. R. Malladi, J. Sethian, and B. Vemuri. Shape modeling with front propagation: A level set approach. *IEEE Transactions on Pattern Analysis and Machine Intelligence*, 17(2), February 1995.
8. S. Osher and N. Paragios. *Geometric Level Set Methods in Imaging, Vision, and Graphics*. Springer, 2003.
9. C. S. J. B. R. Blasini, F. J. Neumann and A. Schomig. Comparison of angiography and intravascular ultrasound for the assessment of lumen size after coronary stent placement: Impact of dilation pressures. *Cathet. Cardiovasc. Diagn.*, 42:113, 1997.
10. E. J. Topol and S. E. Nissen. Our preoccupation with coronary luminology. the dissociation between clinical and angiographic findings in ischemic heart disease. *Circulation*, 92:2333, 1995.

11. C. D. M. E. E. N. d. P. W. Li, C.vonBirgelen and N.Bom. Semi-automatic contour detection for volumetric quantification of intravascular ultrasound. In *Proc. Computers in Cardiology 1994: IEEE-CS Press*, pages 277–280, Los Alamitos, CA, 1994/95.
12. A. Yezzi, Jr., A. Tsai, and A. Willsky. A fully global approach to image segmentation via coupled curve evolution equations. *Journal of Visual Communication and Image Representation*, 13(1/2):195–216, March 2002.
13. X. S. Zhou, A. Gupta, and D. Comaniciu. An information fusion framework for robust shape tracking. *IEEE Transactions on Pattern Analysis and Machine Intelligence*, 27(1):115–129, January 2005.

Prediction of Moving Object Location Based on Frequent Trajectories

Mikołaj Morzy

Institute of Computing Science
Poznań University of Technology
Piotrowo 2, 60-965 Poznań, Poland
Mikolaj.Morzy@put.poznan.pl

Abstract. Recent advances in wireless sensors and position technology provide us with unprecedent amount of moving object data. The volume of geospatial data gathered from moving objects defies human ability to analyze the stream of input data. Therefore, new methods for mining and digesting of moving object data are urgently needed. One of the popular services available for moving objects is the prediction of the unknown location of an object. In this paper we present a new method for predicting the location of a moving object. Our method uses the past trajectory of the object and combines it with movement rules discovered in the moving objects database. Our original contribution includes the formulation of the location prediction model, the design of an efficient algorithm for mining movement rules, the proposition of four strategies for movement rule matching with respect to a given object trajectory, and the experimental evaluation of the proposed model.

1   Introduction

Last years have witnessed a tremendous increase in the number of mobile devices available on the market. Advances in position technology and the widespread use of communication standards, such as GPRS, Bluetooth, Wi-Fi, or WiMAX prompt manufacturers to offer mobile devices supplied with high resolution displays and positioning sensors. Global positioning systems (GPS) are becoming affordable and accurate, thus enabling the deployment of position-aware applications. Examples of mobile devices that profit from location-based services and applications include mobile phones, digital cameras, personal digital assistants, vehicles, and many others.

Ongoing adoption of mobile devices results in an increasing demand for location-based services and applications. Most of location-based services require accurate or approximate position of a mobile client to provide functionality. Examples of such services include management of traffic, navigational service, way-finding, location-based advertising, or movement coordination. In a typical scenario, a moving object periodically informs the positioning framework of its current location. Between position disclosures the location of a mobile object remains unknown. Due to the unreliable nature of portable mobile devices and

A. Levi et al. (Eds.): ISCIS 2006, LNCS 4263, pp. 583–592, 2006.
© Springer-Verlag Berlin Heidelberg 2006

inherent global positioning systems limitations, such as congestions, existence of urban canyons (areas not covered by positioning signals, e.g. subterranean parking garages), or signal losses caused by natural phenomena, the location of a mobile object is often not known for a longer period of time. In such case, an efficient method for predicting possible location of a moving object is required.

Most location-based services demand a fast and reliable location prediction method. The unceasing stream of data generated by positioning sensors, combined with thousands of mobile devices communicating over a wireless channel, make traditional prediction methods obsolete. Sophisticated methods using complex models may yield accurate results, but are computationally unfeasible in mobile environment. For instance, simulation is sometimes used for mimicking the behavior of mobile objects. The quality of simulation depends on numerous parameters governing the movement model. Often, the cost involved in the computation of the model is prohibitively high. In addition, the environment in which mobile objects reside can be dynamic and difficult to capture. For instance, a simple two-dimensional model of a city may not adapt to frequent changes in city topography caused by road construction. Another serious drawback of the currently used location prediction techniques is the fact that most techniques make little or no use of the huge amounts of historical data. Movement data acquired from other moving objects hide valuable knowledge about moving object behavior. In particular, patterns describing popular movement trajectories can be discovered when mining historical data. Alas, data mining techniques are usually (incorrectly) considered too slow and too computationally expensive for real-time location prediction.

Many location-based services may sacrifice prediction accuracy for prediction speed. We follow this paradigm by simplifying our model and resigning from exact modeling of the topography of the movement environment. Instead, we mine historical movement data to discover frequent trajectories traversed by moving objects. These frequent trajectories are further used as an approximate model of the topography. For each object, whose exact location is not known, we perform fast matching of object's trajectory with appropriate frequent trajectories to build a probabilistic model of object location. Our method is fast and efficient, because expensive computations, e.g. mining for frequent trajectories, are performed periodically and offline. Runtime location prediction consists only in trajectory matching, which is a far less arduous task. Another advantage of our approach is the fact that it is independent of a given topography of the movement environment. Our original contribution includes using historical movement data to build an approximate environment model, the design of the *AprioriTraj* algorithm to discover frequent trajectories, the development of four trajectory matching strategies, and the experimental evaluation of the proposal.

The paper is organized as follows. Section 2 presents the related work on the subject. In Section 3 we introduce basic definitions used throughout the paper. The *AprioriTraj* algorithm and trajectory matching strategies are presented in Section 4. The results of conducted experiments are reported in Section 5. We conclude in Section 6 with a brief summary and the future work agenda.

2   Related Work

Significant research effort has been undertaken in both mobile computing and spatial data mining domains. Research on tracking of moving objects resulted in several proposals for predicting future object locations. The method presented in [9] uses recent movement history of an object and combines it with recursive motion functions for objects with unknown motion patterns. An interesting proposal of using time-series analysis enriched with travel speed simulation to predict future trajectory of a moving object is formulated in [12]. A complex model that considers location prediction with accuracy guarantees is presented in [11]. A simulation-based approach to future trajectory prediction based on a non-linear movement model can be found in [10].

Since the advent of spatial data mining [6] many methods and algorithms were developed [4]. However, the problem of mining trajectories of moving objects remained relatively unchallenged until recently. Advances in this field include the proposal to cluster similar trajectories [7] and to use periodic patterns appearing in a single trajectory as the basis for location prediction [8]. A very interesting algorithm for mining patterns from imprecise trajectories of moving objects can be found in [13]. All these works extend the basic framework of periodic sequential patterns [5] and frequent sequential patterns [2]. Our work is strongly influenced by the approach presented in [13]. However, [13] deals primarily with uncertainty in moving object trajectories. The authors propose a new match measure for uncertain trajectories and devise the TrajPattern algorithm for mining sequential patterns that is not based on the Apriori algorithm. On the other hand, the method presented in this paper follows the support-based framework for discovering patterns and uses an Apriori-like algorithm to discover simple movement rules.

3   Basic Definitions

Given a database of moving object locations, where the movement of objects is constrained to a specified area. Let $O = \{o_1, \ldots, o_m\}$ denote the set of objects. Let the location of the j-th object during i-th measurement be denoted as $l_j^i = \left(x_j^i, y_j^i\right)$. The domain of location coordinates is continuous, but the smallest unit of location measurement provides a natural discretization of the input data. However, the level of granularity of this natural discretization is too detailed when compared to the number of moving objects or the number of locations registered for a single object. Therefore, any patterns discovered at the raw data level cannot be generalized. To overcome this obstacle we superimpose a grid on the movement area. The grid consists of square cells of the constant size, denoted as *grid_size*. Each edge can be traversed in two directions, vertical edges can be traversed eastwards and westwards, whereas horizontal edges can be traversed northwards and southwards.

An ordered list of consecutive location measurements for a given object constitutes a trajectory of the object, denoted as $t_j = \langle l_j^0, l_j^1, \ldots, l_j^n \rangle$. Alternatively, the trajectory of an object can be represented as an ordered list of segments, where each segment is defined by two consecutive location measurements of an object, $t_j = \langle s_j^0, s_j^1, \ldots, s_j^{n-1} \rangle$, where $s_j^i = (l_j^i, l_j^{i+1})$. Note that each segment can be replaced with an ordered list of edges traversed by that segment. This replacement transforms the original continuous coordinates domain into a discretized domain of edges. Finally, we represent a moving object trajectory as an ordered list of edges traversed by the trajectory. Let e_{pq} denote an edge. Then, the trajectory of the j-th object is $t_j = \left\langle (e_{p_0 q_0}, d_0)_j, (e_{p_1 q_1}, d_1)_j, \ldots \right\rangle$, where $d_i \in \{ne, sw\}$ denotes the direction in which the edge was traversed (north-east and south-west, respectively).

Let E be the set of all edges. The cardinality of the set E is given by

$$|E| = \left\lceil \frac{a}{grid\_size} \right\rceil * \left(\left\lceil \frac{b}{grid\_size} \right\rceil + 1 \right) + \left(\left\lceil \frac{a}{grid\_size} \right\rceil + 1 \right) * \left\lceil \frac{b}{grid\_size} \right\rceil$$

where $a = \max_{ij}\{x_j^i\} - \min_{ij}\{x_j^i\}$, $b = \max_{ij}\{y_j^i\} - \min_{ij}\{y_j^i\}$.

Let D denote the set of all trajectories, $D = \{t_1, t_2, \ldots, t_n\}$. The support of an edge e_{pq} is the number of trajectories that traverse the edge in a given direction. Note that each edge has two values of support, northeastward and southwestward. An edge e_{pq} is frequent, if its support exceeds the user-defined threshold of *minsup*. Given a trajectory t_j. The length of the trajectory, denoted as *length* (t_j), is the number of edges constituting the trajectory t_j. Given two trajectories t_i and t_j. The trajectory t_i is a sub-trajectory of t_j (the trajectory t_j contains the trajectory t_i, denoted $t_j \supseteq t_i$) if the list of edges constituting t_i is a continuous sublist of the list of edges in t_j and the directions of traversal of edges in t_i are the same as the directions of traversal of corresponding edges in t_j. Trajectories t_i and t_j are adjacent if there exists a trajectory t_k, such that *length* $(t_k) = 2$ and $(e_{p_{max} q_{max}}, d_{max})_i = (e_{p_0 q_0}, d_0)_k \wedge (e_{p_0 q_0}, d_0)_j = (e_{p_1 q_1}, d_1)_k$ (i.e., the last element of the trajectory t_i is the same as the first element of the trajectory t_k and the first element of the trajectory t_j is the same as the second element of the trajectory t_k). The concatenation of trajectories $t_i \| t_j$ is a trajectory

$$t_l = \left\langle (e_{p_0 q_0}, d_0)_i, \ldots, (e_{p_{max} q_{max}}, d_{max})_i, (e_{p_0 q_0}, d_0)_j, \ldots, (e_{p_{max} q_{max}}, d_{max})_j \right\rangle.$$

The support of the trajectory t_j is the number of trajectories in D that contain t_j. A given trajectory t_j is frequent if the support of t_j exceeds the user-defined threshold of *minsup*. The set of all frequent trajectories is denoted as L. Obviously, a frequent trajectory must consist of frequent edges only, furthermore, each sub-trajectory of a frequent trajectory is also frequent.

A movement rule is an expression of the form $t_i \Rightarrow t_j$ where $t_i, t_j \in L$, t_i and t_j are adjacent trajectories and $t_i \| t_j$ is a frequent trajectory. The trajectory t_i is called the antecedent of the rule, the trajectory t_j is called the consequent of the rule. Contrary to the original formulation of association rule mining we do not require the antecedent and the consequent of a rule to be disjunctive.

The *support* of the movement rule $t_i \Rightarrow t_j$ is defined as the support of $t_i \| t_j$,

$$support\,(t_i \Rightarrow t_j) = \frac{|t_k \in D : t_k \supseteq (t_i \| t_j)|}{|D|}$$

The *confidence* of the movement rule $t_i \Rightarrow t_j$ is the conditional probability of t_j given t_i,

$$confidence\,(t_i \Rightarrow t_j) = P\,(t_j | t_i) = \frac{support\,(t_i \| t_j)}{support\,(t_i)}$$

The problem of prediction of location of moving objects based on frequent trajectories can be decomposed into two subproblems:

- generate all movement rules with support and confidence greater than user-defined thresholds of *minsup* and *minconf*, respectively,
- match discovered movement rules with the trajectory of a moving object for which the current location is to be determined.

4   Prediction of Location

To solve the problem of generating movement rules we use a modified version of the well-known *Apriori* algorithm [1]. The outline of our *AprioriTraj* algorithm is depicted in Figure 1. First, we find all frequent trajectories of the length 1 (i.e., all frequent edges). Next, we concatenate adjacent frequent edges to form candidate trajectories of the length 2. We perform a full database scan to determine actual support counts for candidate trajectories and we determine L_2, the set of frequent trajectories of the length 2. Next, we iteratively find sets of frequent trajectories of the length k based on frequent trajectories of the length $(k-1)$ found so far. In each iteration we form a set of k-element candidate trajectories by combining overlapping frequent trajectories. We consider two trajectories t_i and t_j to be overlapping, if the trajectory resulting from removing the first edge from t_i is the same as the trajectory resulting from removing the last edge from t_j (e.g., trajectories $\langle A, B, C, D \rangle$ and $\langle B, C, D, E \rangle$ are overlapping, whereas trajectories $\langle A, C, D, E \rangle$ and $\langle B, C, D, E \rangle$ are not). Two overlapping trajectories t_i and t_j are used to generate a candidate trajectory t_{ij} by concatenating the last edge of t_j to t_i (e.g., the concatenation of $\langle A, B, C, D \rangle$ and $\langle B, C, D, E \rangle$ yields $\langle A, B, C, D, E \rangle$). Contrary to the *Apriori* algorithm, we do not have to verify candidate trajectories for the containment of infrequent sub-trajectories, because the above generation procedure does not produce any superfluous candidate trajectories.

When all frequent trajectories have been found, the task of generating movement rules is straightforward. Each frequent trajectory t_i of the length l can be used to generate movement rules by splitting the trajectory t_i into $(l-1)$ pairs of sub-trajectories (t_i', t_i''), such that for each pair $t_i' \| t_i'' = t_i$ and the splitting point is chosen after i-th $(i = 1, 2, \ldots, l-1)$ element of the trajectory t_i. For each pair $(t_i' \| t_i'')$ we have to verify that $confidence\,(t_i' \Rightarrow t_i'') = support\,(t_i)\,/\,support\,(t_i') \geq minconf$, otherwise we reject the rule $t_i' \Rightarrow t_i''$.

Require: L_1, the set of all frequent trajectories of the length 1
 1: $C_2 = \{t_i \| t_j : t_i \in L_1 \wedge t_j \in L_1 \wedge t_i, t_j \text{ are adjacent}\}$
 2: **for all** trajectories $t \in D$ **do**
 3:    **for all** candidate trajectories $c \in C_2$ **do**
 4:       **if** $t \supseteq c$ **then**
 5:          $c.count ++;$
 6:       **end if**
 7:    **end for**
 8: **end for**
 9: $L_2 = \{t \in C_2 : support\,(t) \geq minsup\}$
10: **for** $k = 3; L_{k-1} \neq \emptyset; k++$ **do**
11:    **for all** trajectories $t_i \in L_{k-1}$ **do**
12:       **for all** trajectories $t_j \in L_{k-1}$ **do**
13:          **if** $\forall n \in \langle 1, k-1 \rangle\, (e_{p_n q_n}, d_n)_i = \left(e_{p_{n-1} q_{n-1}}, d_{n-1}\right)_j$ **then**
14:             $C_k = C_k \cup t_{ij}$, where $t_{ij} = t_i \| \left(e_{p_{max} q_{max}}, d_{max}\right)_j;$
15:          **end if**
16:       **end for**
17:    **end for**
18:    **for all** trajectories $t \in D$ **do**
19:       **for all** candidate trajectories $c \in C_k$ **do**
20:          **if** $t \subseteq c$ **then**
21:             $c.count ++;$
22:          **end if**
23:       **end for**
24:    **end for**
25:    $L_k = \{t \in C_k : support\,(t) \geq minsup\}$
26: **end for**
27: $Answer = \bigcup_{i=1}^{k} L_i$

Fig. 1. *AprioriTraj* algorithm

Let us now focus on the problem of matching discovered movement rules with the trajectory of a moving object. Given a moving object q with a trajectory t_q. We are searching for movement rules $t_i \Rightarrow t_j$ such that:

- $t_i \supseteq t_q$ and the last edge in both t_i and t_q is the same,
- $t_q \supseteq t_i$ and the last edge in both t_i and t_q is the same,
- t_i and t_q are the same.

In all above cases the consequent t_j is used as a prediction of the location of the moving object q in subsequent moments of time. Unfortunately, for a given trajectory t_q too many movement rules can be matched for making an informed decision about possible location of q. A naive approach of ranking matched movement rules based solely on confidence fails, because it does not consider lengths of the rules, thus prefers very short rules that are often useless for predicting the location of a moving object. Furthermore, this approach does not consider the coverage of matched rules with the trajectory t_q. This motivates us to devise new strategies of matched movement rule selection, presented briefly below.

4.1 Simple Strategy

$$\arg\max_{t_i \Rightarrow t_j} \frac{|t_i|}{|t_q|} * confidence\,(t_i \Rightarrow t_j)$$

The drawback of the simple strategy is the fact that it does not consider the length of the consequent of the movement rule. Also, the simple strategy treats the length of the consequent linearly, which may lead to the situation where a long covering movement rule with low confidence is preferred to a shorter but more credible movement rule. Nevertheless, when the trajectory t_q is very short (the history of movement of the object q is almost unknown), then the simple strategy is appropriate.

4.2 Polynomial Strategy

$$\arg\max_{t_i \Rightarrow t_j} \frac{1}{2} \left(\sqrt{\frac{|t_i|}{|c_1|}} + \sqrt{\frac{|t_j|}{|c_2|}} \right) * confidence\,(t_i \Rightarrow t_j)$$

where c_1 and c_2 are the lengths of the longest antecedent and consequent in the rule set, respectively. This strategy is fair and balanced, it represents a reasonable compromise between the simplicity of the simple strategy and the complexity of the logarithmic strategy presented next.

4.3 Logarithmic Strategy

$$\arg\max_{t_i \Rightarrow t_j} \left(w_1 + w_2 * \log_{|c_1|} |t_i| + w_3 * \log_{|c_2|} |t_j| \right) * confidence\,(t_i \Rightarrow t_j)$$

where $w_1 + w_2 + w_3 = 1$. Weights w_1, w_2, w_3 are used to shift emphasis on the confidence factor, the relative length of the antecedent, or the relative length of the consequent of the movement rule. The use of the logarithm smooths the differences between long movement rules and, at the same time, accentuates the differences between short movement rules.

4.4 Aggregate Strategy

Often, discovered movement rules can be grouped into sets of similar rules. In particular, rules sharing the same antecedent can be regarded as a family of rules that predict the movement in a given direction with the confidence of prediction diminishing with the length of the consequent. Let us assume that all movement rules have been grouped according to their antecedent. The aggregate strategy selects the following movement rule

$$\arg\max_{t_i \Rightarrow t_j} \frac{|t_i|}{|t_q|} * \frac{|t_j|}{|c_2|} * \frac{\sum_{t_x \Rightarrow t_y \in G} |t_y| * confidence\,(t_x \Rightarrow t_y)}{\sum_{t_x \Rightarrow t_y \in G} |t_y|}$$

where G denotes the group to which belongs the rule $t_i \Rightarrow t_j$ and c_2 denotes the length of the longest consequent in the rule set. The aggregate strategy considers the coverage factor, the relative length of the antecedent, and the predictive power of the group of related movement rules. The main drawback of this strategy is the computational cost involved in grouping of the movement rules. It is worth emphasizing that the four strategies of movement rule selection presented above are complementary and can be used simultaneously depending on the nature of the trajectory t_q.

5   Experimental Results

The data used in our experiments have been generated by the Network-based Generator of Moving Objects [3]. Maximum velocity has been set to 150 and the number of time units has been set to 100. For each distinct number of moving objects 30 different instances of the database have been generated. All experiments were conducted on a Pentium Centrino 1.8 GHz computer with 1GB RAM running Windows XP.

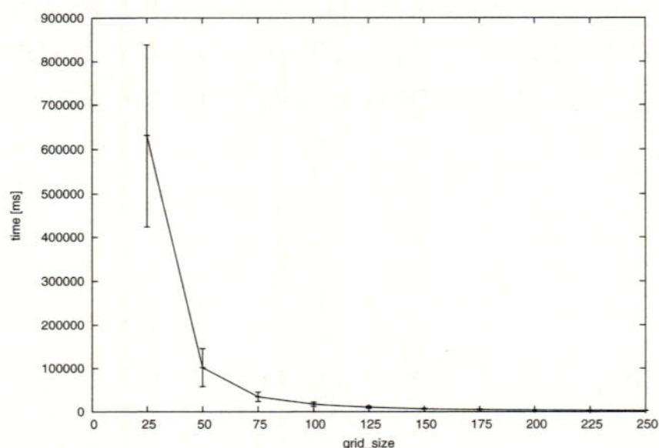

Fig. 2. time vs grid_size

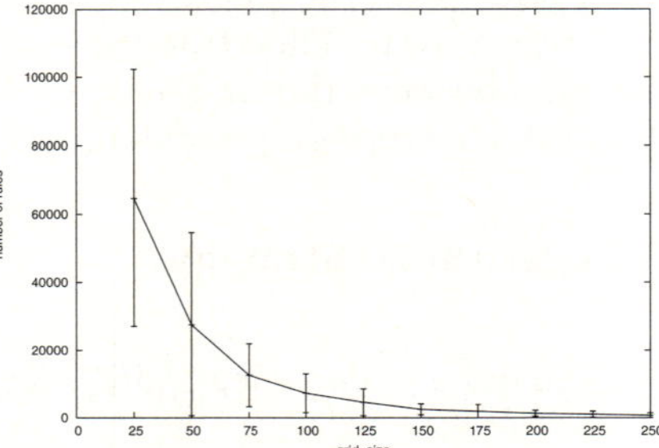

Fig. 3. rules vs. grid_size

Figures 2 and 3 present the execution time and the number of discovered rules when varying the *grid_size* parameter in the range $\langle 25 \div 250 \rangle$ for a fixed number of 300 moving objects and *minsup* = 0.03. As can be easily seen, low values of the *grid_size* parameter produce large numbers of movement rules. We also observe a significant variation in the averaged results over 30 database instances. For small values of *grid_size* discovered rules are too detailed and do not generalize well for prediction of movement of other objects. Interestingly, the execution time and the number of discovered movement rules drop significantly for larger values of *grid_size*.

The impact of the number of moving objects on the execution time and the number of discovered movement rules is depicted in Figures 4 and 5 (*grid_size* = 250, *minsup* = 0.01). A linear dependence of the execution time on the number of moving objects guarantees scalability of the proposed solution. The decrease of

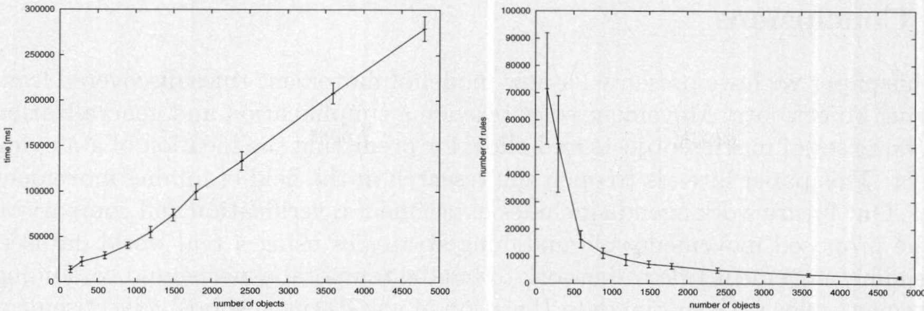

Fig. 4. time vs. number of objects   **Fig. 5.** rules vs. number of objects

the number of discovered movement rules is caused by the increase in the absolute value of *minsup*, because adding new moving objects increases the minimum number of objects that have to traverse an edge to make it frequent. New objects are spread over the movement area uniformly, effectively decreasing support counts of most edges.

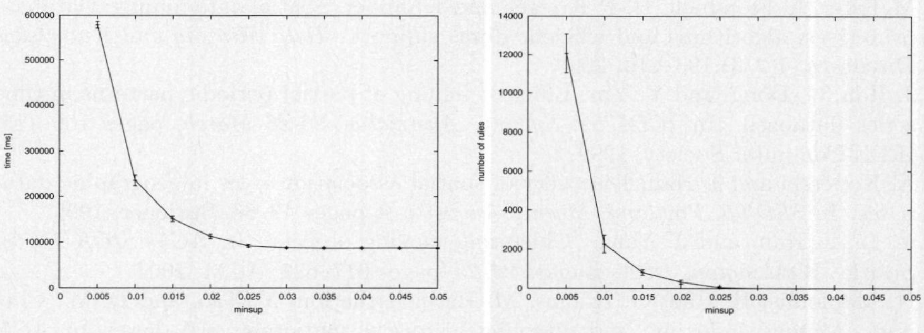

Fig. 6. time vs. *minsup*   **Fig. 7.** rules vs. *minsup*

The influence of the varying *minsup* parameter on the execution time and the number of discovered movement rules is presented in Figures 6 and 7 (*grid_size* = 250, 4800 moving objects). Starting from *minsup* = 0.025 the execution time remains almost constant, because the number of discovered movement rules falls below 50 for larger values of *minsup*.

We have also conducted experiments on predicting the location of an object for different movement rule matching strategies. We refrain from presenting the results of these experiments due to their unreliable nature. The results were skewed by the properties of the synthetic data. The uniform distribution of moving objects across the examined area caused no evident differences between employed matching strategies.

6   Conclusions

In this paper we have presented a new model of movement rules discovered from moving object data. Movement rules provide a simplification and generalization of a large set of moving objects and allow for predicting the location of a moving object. This paper intends to open the research in the field of mining movement rules. Our future work agenda includes experimental verification and comparison of the proposed movement rule matching strategies using a real world dataset, extending movement rule framework to handle temporal aspects, and combining movement rules with spatial data (location of gas stations, shops, advertisement billboards) to make informed decisions based on the intensity of traffic.

References

1. R. Agrawal and R. Srikant. Fast algorithms for mining association rules in large databases. In *VLDB'94, September 12-15, Santiago de Chile, Chile*, pages 487–499. Morgan Kaufmann, 1994.
2. R. Agrawal and R. Srikant. Mining sequential patterns. In *ICDE'95, Taipei, Taiwan, March 6-10*, pages 3–14. IEEE Computer Society, 1995.
3. T. Brinkhoff. A framework for generating network-based moving objects. *GeoInformatica*, 6(2):153–180, 2002.
4. M. Ester, A. Frommelt, H.-P. Kriegel, and J. Sander. Spatial data mining: Database primitives, algorithms and efficient dbms support. *Data Mininig and Knowledge Discovery*, 4(2/3):193–216, 2000.
5. J. Han, G. Dong, and Y. Yin. Efficient mining of partial periodic patterns in time series database. In *ICDE'99, Sydney, Austrialia, 23-26 March*, pages 106–115. IEEE Computer Society, 1999.
6. K. Koperski and J. Han. Discovery of spatial association rules in geographic databases. In *SSD'95, Portland, Maine, August 6-9*, pages 47–66. Springer, 1995.
7. Y. Li, J. Han, and J. Yang. Clustering moving objects. In *ACM SIGKDD'04, Seattle, Washington, USA, August 22-25*, pages 617–622. ACM, 2004.
8. N. Mamoulis, H. Cao, G. Kollios, M. Hadjieleftheriou, Y. Tao, and D. W. Cheung. Mining, indexing, and querying historical spatiotemporal data. In *ACM SIGKDD'04, Seattle, Washington, USA, August 22-25*, pages 236–245. ACM, 2004.
9. Y. Tao, C. Faloutsos, D. Papadias, and B. Liu. Prediction and indexing of moving objects with unknown motion patterns. In *ACM SIGMOD'04, Paris, France, June 13-18*, pages 611–622. ACM, 2004.
10. G. Trajcevski, O. Wolfson, B. Xu, and P. Nelson. Real-time traffic updates in moving objects databases. In *DEXA'02, Aix-en-Provence, France, 2-6 September*, pages 698–704. IEEE Computer Society, 2002.
11. O. Wolfson and H. Yin. Accuracy and resource concumption in tracking and location prediction. In *SSTD'03, Santorini, Greece*, pages 325–343. Springer, 2003.
12. B. Xu and O. Wolfson. Time-series prediction with applications to traffic and moving objects databases. In *MobiDE 2003, September 19, 2003, San Diego, California, USA*, pages 56–60. ACM, 2003.
13. J. Yang and M. Hu. Trajpattern: Mining sequential patterns from imprecise trajectories of mobile objects. In *EDBT'06, Munich, Germany, March 26-31*, pages 664–681. Springer, 2006.

A Framework for Visualizing Association Mining Results

Gürdal Ertek[1] and Ayhan Demiriz[2]

[1] Sabanci University
Faculty of Engineering and Natural Sciences
Orhanli, Tuzla, 34956, Istanbul, Turkey
ertekg@sabanciuniv.edu
[2] Department of Industrial Engineering
Sakarya University
54187, Sakarya, Turkey
ademiriz@gmail.com

Abstract. Association mining is one of the most used data mining techniques due to interpretable and actionable results. In this study we propose a framework to visualize the association mining results, specifically frequent itemsets and association rules, as graphs. We demonstrate the applicability and usefulness of our approach through a Market Basket Analysis (MBA) case study where we visually explore the data mining results for a supermarket data set. In this case study we derive several interesting insights regarding the relationships among the items and suggest how they can be used as basis for decision making in retailing.

1 Introduction

Association mining is an increasingly used data mining and business tool among practitioners and business analysts [7]. Interpretable and actionable results of association mining can be considered as the major reasons for the popularity of this type of data mining tools. Association rules can be classified based on several criteria, as outlined in [11]. In this paper, we focus on single-dimensional, single-level boolean association rules, in the context of market basket analysis.

By utilizing efficient algorithms such as Apriori [2] to analyze very large transactional data -frequently from transactional sales data- will result in a large set of association rules. Commonly, finding the association rules from very large data sets is considered and emphasized as the most challenging step in association mining. Often, results are presented in a text (or table) format with some querying and sorting functionalities. The rules include "if" clauses by default. The structure of such rules is as follows: "If the customer purchases Item A, then with probability $C\%$ he/she will buy Item B."

This probability, $C\%$, is referred to as *confidence level*. More formally, the confidence level can be computed as follows: $C = \frac{frequency(A \cap B)}{frequency(A)}$, where $A \cap B$ refers to the transactions that have both Item A and Item B. Confidence level is also equivalent to the conditional probability of having Item B given Item A.

A. Levi et al. (Eds.): ISCIS 2006, LNCS 4263, pp. 593–602, 2006.

Another important statistic in association mining is the *support level*. Support level is basically equal to the fraction of the transactions that have both Item A and Item B. Thus the support level S is computed as follows: $S = \frac{frequency(A \cap B)}{T}$ where T is equal to the total number of the transactions. Left and right hand sides of the rule are called *antecedent* and *consequent* of the rule respectively.

There exists an extensive literature where a multitude of interestingness measures for association rules are suggested [22] and efficient data mining algorithms are presented for deriving these measures. However, there is considerably less work that focuses on the interpretation of the association mining results.

Information visualization, a growing field of research in computer science [6,8,13], investigates ways of visually representing multi-dimensional data with the purpose of knowledge discovery. The significance and the impact of information visualization is reflected by the development and availability of highly user-friendly and successful software tools such as Miner3D [18], Spotfire [21], Advizor [1], DBMiner [11], and IBM Intelligent Miner Visualization [15].

Our motivation for this study stems from the idea that visualizing the results of association mining can help end-users significantly by enabling them to derive previously unknown insights. We provide a framework that is easy to implement (since it simply merges two existing fields of computer science) and that provides a flexible and human-centered way of discovering insights.

In spite of successful visualization tools mentioned above, the visualization of the association mining results in particular is somewhat a fertile field of study. Some of the studies done in this field are summarized in the next section. We then introduce our proposed framework in Section 3. We explain our implementation in Section 4. We report our findings from the case study in Section 5. We then conclude with future research directions in Section 6.

2   Literature Review

The visualization of association mining results has attracted attention recently, due to the invention of information visualization schemes such as parallel coordinate plots (||-coords). Here we summarize some of the studies that we believe are the most interesting.

Hofmann et al. [14] elegantly visualize association rules through Mosaic plots and Double Decker plots. While Mosaic plots allow display of association rules with two items in the antecedent, Double Decker plots enable visualization of association rules with more items in the antecedent. The interestingness measure of "differences of confidence" can be directly seen in Double Decker plots. Discovering intersection and sequential structures are also discussed.

Kopanakis and Theodoulidis [17] present several visualization schemes for displaying and exploring association rules, including bar charts, grid form models, and ||-coords. In their extensive work they also discuss a similarity based approach for the layout of multiple association rules on the screen.

Two popular approaches for visualizing association rules are summarized in [23]: The first, matrix based approach, maps items and itemsets in the antecedent and consequent to the X and Y axes respectively. Wong et al. [23] bring an alternative to this approach by mapping rules -instead of items- to the X axis. In the second, directed graph approach, the items and rules are mapped to nodes and edges of a directed graph respectively. Our framework departs from the second approach since we map both the items *and* the rules to nodes.

3   Proposed Framework

We propose a graph-based framework to visualize and interpret the results of well-known association mining algorithms as directed graphs. In our visualizations, the items, the itemsets, and the association rules are all represented as nodes. Edges represent the links between the items and the itemsets or associations.

In visualizing frequent itemsets (Figure 1) the nodes that represent the items are shown with no color, whereas the nodes that represent the itemsets are colored reflecting the cardinality of the itemsets. For example, in our case study the lightest shade of blue denotes an itemset with two items and the darkest shade of blue denotes an itemset with four items. The sizes (the areas) of the nodes show the support levels. The directed edges symbolize which items constitute a given frequent itemset.

In visualizing association rules (Figure 4), the items are again represented by nodes without coloring, and the rules are shown by colored nodes. The node sizes (the areas) again show the support levels, but this time the node colors show the confidence levels. In our case study, the confidence levels are shown in a linearly mapped yellow-red color spectrum with the yellow representing the lowest and the red representing the highest confidence levels. The directed edges are color-coded depending on whether they are incoming or outgoing edges. Incoming edges of the rule nodes are shown in grey and outgoing are shown in black. For example, in Figure 4 the association rule A01 is indeed (Item 110 $\Rightarrow$ Item 38).

The main idea in our framework is to exploit already existing graph drawing algorithms [3] and software in the information visualization literature [12] for visualization of association mining results which are generated by already existing algorithms and software in the data mining literature [11].

4   Steps in Implementing the Framework

To demonstrate our framework we have carried out a case study using a real word data set from retail industry which we describe in the next section. In this section, we briefly outline the steps in implementing our framework.

The first step is to run an efficient implementation of the Apriori algorithm: We have selected to use the application developed by C. Borgelt which is available on the internet [4] and is well documented.

To generate both the frequent itemsets and association rules, it is required to run Borgelt's application twice because this particular application is capable of generating either the frequent itemsets or the association rules. One important issue that we paid attention to was using the right options while computing the support levels of the association rules. The default computation of the support level in Borgelt's application is different from the original definition by Agrawal and Srikant [2]. The option "-o" is included in command line to adhere to the original definition which we have defined in the Introduction section.

The second step is to translate the results of the Apriori algorithm into a graph specification. In our case study, we carried out this step by converting the support and confidence levels to corresponding node diameters and colors in a spreadsheet.

We then created the graph objects based on the calculated specifications in the previous step. There are a multitude of tools available on the internet for graph visualization [19]. We have selected the yEd Graph Editor [24] for drawing our initial graph and generating visually interpretable graph layouts. yEd implements several types of graph drawing algorithms including those that create hierarchical, organic, orthogonal, and circular layouts. For interested readers, the detailed information on the algorithms and explanations of the various settings can be found under the program's Help menu.

The final step is to run the available graph layout algorithms and try to visually discover interesting and actionable insights. Our case study revealed that different layout algorithms should be selected depending on whether one is visualizing frequent itemsets or association rules, and on the underlying purpose of the analysis e.g. catalog design, shelf layout, and promotional pricing.

5   Case Study: Market Basket Analysis

The benchmark data set used in this study is provided at [10] and initially analyzed in [5] for assortment planning purposes. The data set is composed of 88,163 transactions and was collected at a Belgian supermarket. There are 16,470 unique items in it. The data set lists only the composition of transactions; different visits by the same customer cannot be identified and the monetary value of the transactions are omitted.

In this section, we present our findings through visual analysis of frequent itemsets and association rules. Frequent itemset graphs generated by yEd provided us with guidelines for catalog design and supermarket shelf design. Association rule graph supplied us with inherent relationships between the items and enabled development of promotional pricing strategies.

5.1   Visualizing Frequent Itemsets

Figure 1 depicts the results of the Apriori algorithm that generated the frequent itemsets at support level of 2% for the data set. This graph was drawn by selecting the Classic Organic Layout in yEd. Items that belong to similar frequent itemsets and have high support levels are placed in close proximity of each other. From Figure 1, one can easily notice the Items 39, 48, 32, 41, and 38 have very high support levels, and form frequent itemsets (with up to four elements) among

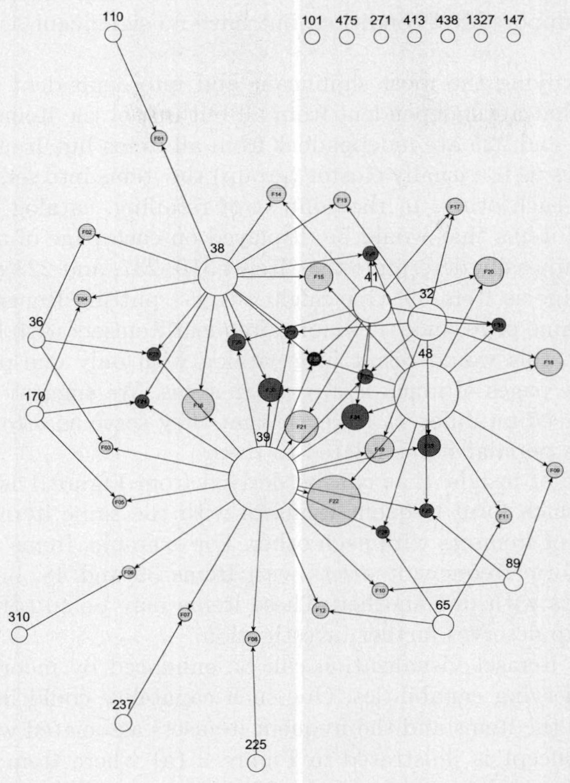

Fig. 1. Visualization of the frequent itemsets through a Classic Organic Layout

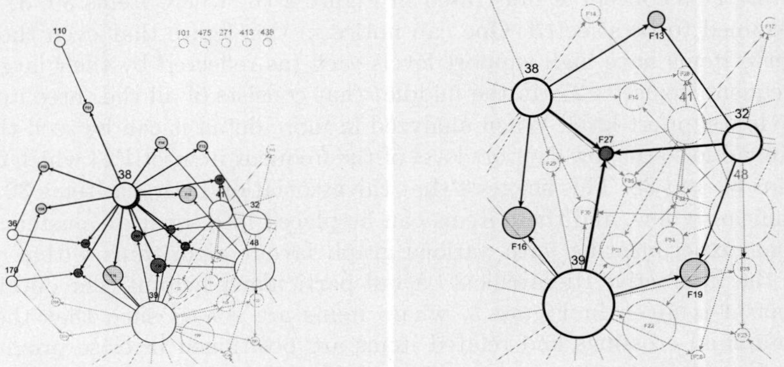

Fig. 2. Querying the visualization of the frequent itemsets (a) Selecting a single item. (b) Selecting three items together.

themselves. On the upper corner of the figure, there is a set of items which meet the minimum support level condition, but have no significant associations with any other item.

Besides identifying the most significant and interdependent items, one can also see items that are independent from all but one of the items. For example, Items 310, 237, and 225 are independent from all items but Item 39. This phenomenon enables us to visually cluster (group) the items into sets that are fairly independent of each other. In the context of retailing, catalog design requires selecting sets of items that would be displayed on each page of a catalog. From Figure 1, one can easily determine that Items 310, 237, and 225 could be on the same catalog page as Item 39. One might suggest putting Items 39, 48, 32, 41, and 38 on the same page since these form frequent itemsets with high confidence levels. However, this would result in a catalog with only one page of popular items and many pages of much less popular items. We suggest that the popular items be placed on different pages so that they serve as *attractors*, drawing attention to less popular items related to them.

Another type of insight that can be derived from Figure 1 is the identification of items which form frequent itemsets with the same item(s) but do not form any frequent itemsets with each other. For example, Items 65 and 89 each independently form frequent itemsets with Items 39 and 48, but do not form frequent itemsets with one another. These items may be substitute items and their relationship deserves further investigation.

The frequent itemset visualization can be enhanced by incorporating interactive visual querying capabilities. One such capability could be that once an item is selected, the items and the frequent itemsets associated with it are highlighted. This concept is illustrated in Figure 2 (a) where Item 38 is assumed to be selected. It can be seen that Item 38 plays a very influential role since it forms frequent itemsets with seven of the 13 items. When two or more items are selected, only the frequent itemsets associated with all of them could be highlighted. Thus selecting more than one item could serve as a query with an AND operator. This concept is illustrated in Figure 2 (b) where Items 39, 32 and 38 are assumed to be selected. One can notice in this figure that even though all the three items have high support levels each (as reflected by their large sizes) the frequent itemset F27 (in the middle) that consists of all the three items has a very low support level. When analyzed in more detail it can be seen that this is mainly due to the low support level of the frequent itemset F13 which consists of Items 32 and 38. This suggests that the association between Items 32 and 38 is significantly low, and these items can be placed into separate clusters.

When experimenting with various graph layout algorithms within yEd we found the Interactive Hierarchical Layout particularly helpful. The obtained visualization is given in Figure 3, where items are sorted such that the edges have minimal crossings and related items are positioned in close proximity to each other. This visualization can be used directly in planning the supermarket shelf layouts. For example assuming that we would place these items into a single aisle in the supermarket and that all the items have same unit volume, we can lay out the items according to their positions in Figure 3, allocating shelf space proportional to their node sizes (support levels).

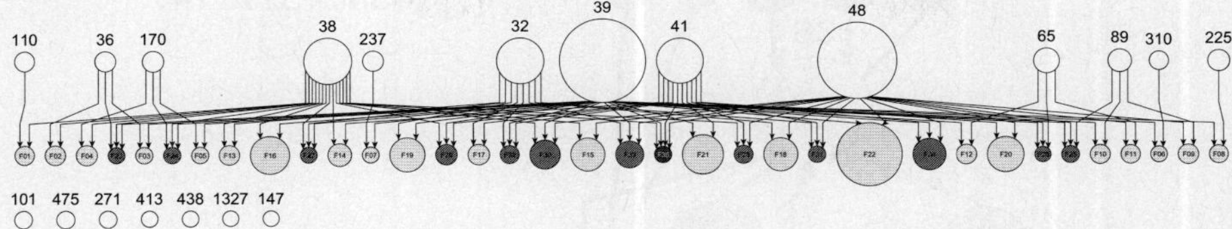

Fig. 3. Visualization of the frequent itemsets through an Interactive Hierarchical Layout

Of course in a real world setting there would be many aisles and the items would not have the same unit volume. For adopting our approach to the former situation we can pursue the following steps: We start with the analysis of a Classic Organic Layout as in Figure 1, and determine from this graph groups of items that will go into aisles together. When forming the groups we try to make sure that the total area of the items in each group is roughly the same. Once the groups are determined we can generate and analyze an Interactive Hierarchical Layout as in Figure 3 for each group and then decide on the shelf layouts at each aisle. Incorporating the situation where the items have significantly varying unit volumes is a more challenging task, since it requires consideration of these volumes in addition to consideration of the support levels.

5.2   Visualizing Association Rules

Figure 4 depicts the results of the Apriori algorithm that generated the association rules at support level of 2% and confidence level of 20% for the data set. This graph was drawn by selecting the Classic Hierarchical Layout in yEd and visualizes 27 association rules. In the graph, only rules with a single item in the antecedent are shown.

The figure shows which items are "sales drivers" that push the sales of other items. For example one can observe at the top of the figure that the rules A01 (Item 110 $\Rightarrow$ Item 38), A02 (Item 36 $\Rightarrow$ Item 38), and A04 (Item 170 $\Rightarrow$ Item 38) all have high confidence levels, as reflected by their red colors. This observation related with high confidence levels can be verified by seeing that the node sizes of the rules A01, A02, and A04 are almost same as the node sizes of Items 110, 36, and 170. For increasing the sales of Item 38 in a retail setting we could use the insights that we gained from Figure 4. Initiating a promotional campaign for any combination of Items 110, 36, or 170 and placing these items next to Item 38 could boost sales for Item 38. This type of a campaign should especially be considered if the unit profits of the driver items (which reside in the antecedent of the association rule) are lower than the unit profit of the item whose sale is to be boosted (which resides in the antecedent of the association rule).

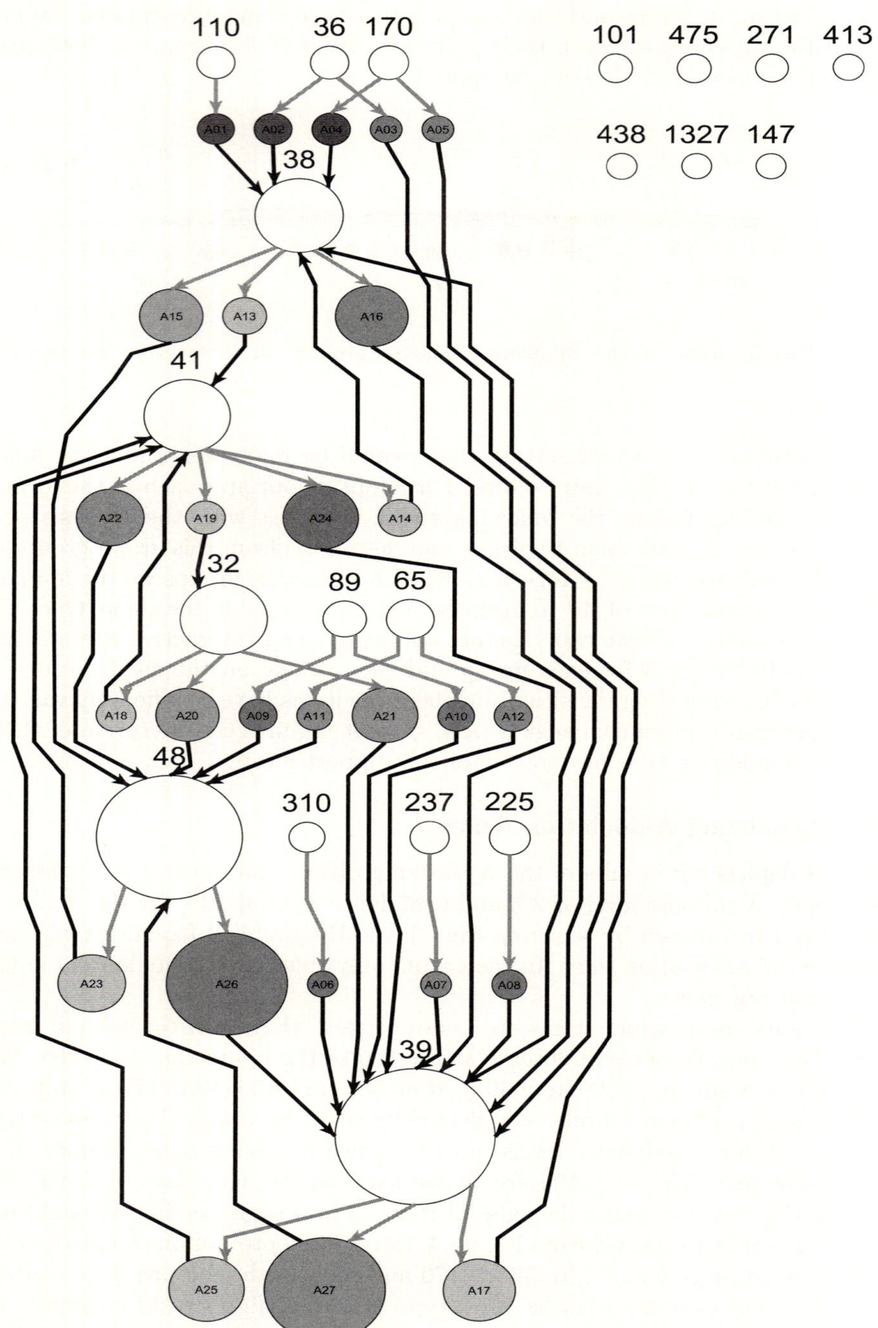

Fig. 4. Visualization of the association rules through an Interactive Hierarchical Layout

We can also identify Items 32, 89, 65, 310, 237, and 225 as sales drivers since they have an indegree of zero (except Item 32) and affect sales of "downstream" items with a high confidence.

6   Conclusions and Future Work

We have introduced a novel framework for knowledge discovery from association mining results. We demonstrated the applicability of our framework through a market basket analysis case study where we visualize the frequent itemsets and binary association rules derived from transactional sales data of a Belgian supermarket.

Ideally, the steps in our framework should be carried out automatically by a single integrated program or at least from within a single modelling and analysis environment that readily communicates with the association mining and graph visualization software. Such a software does not currently exist.

In the retail industry new products emerge and consumer preferences change constantly. Thus one would be interested in laying the foundation of an analysis framework that can fit to the dynamic nature of retailing data. Our framework can be adapted for analysis of frequent itemsets and association rules over time by incorporating latest research on evolving graphs [9].

Another avenue of future research is testing other graph visualization algorithms and software [19] and investigating whether new insights can be discovered by their application. For example, Pajek graph visualization software [20] enables the mapping of attributes to line thickness, which is not possible in yEd. The visualizations that we presented in this paper were all 2D. It is an interesting research question to determine whether exploring association rules in 3D can enable new styles of analysis and new types of insights.

As a final word, we conclude by remarking that visualization of association mining results in particular, and data mining results in general is a promising area of future research. Educational, research, government and business institutions can benefit significantly from the symbiosis of data mining and information visualization disciplines.

References

1. http://www.advizorsolutions.com
2. Agrawal, R., Srikant, R.: Fast algorithms for mining association rules. Proceedings of the 20th VLDB Conference,Santiago, Chile. (1994) 487–499
3. Battista, G. D., Eades, P., Tamassia, R., Tollis, I. G.: Graph Drawing: Algorithms for the Visualization of Graphs. Prentice Hall PTR.(1998)
4. http://fuzzy.cs.uni-magdeburg.de/~borgelt/apriori.html
5. Brijs, T., Swinnen, G., Vanhoof, K., Wets, G.: The use of association rules for product assortment decisions: a case study. Proceedings of the Fifth International Conference on Knowledge Discovery and Data Mining, San Diego (USA), (1999) 254–260.

6. de Oliveira, M. C. F., Levkowitz, H.: From visual data exploration to visual data mining: a survey. IEEE Transactions on Visualization and Computer Graphics **9**, no.3 (2003) 378–394

7. Demiriz, A.: Enhancing product recommender systems on sparse binary data. Journal of Data Mining and Knowledge Discovery. **9**, no.2 (2004) 378–394

8. Eick, S. G.: Visual discovery and analysis. IEEE Transactions on Visualization and Computer Graphics **6**, no.1 (2000) 44–58

9. Erten, D. A., Harding, P. J., Kobourov, S. G., Wampler, K., Yee, G.: GraphAEL: Graph animations with evolving layouts. Lecture Notes in Computer Science. **2913**, (2004) 98–110

10. http://fimi.cs.helsinki.fi/data/

11. Han, J., Kamber, M.: Data Mining Concepts and Techniques. Morgan Kaufman Publishers. (2001)

12. Herman, I., Melançon, G., Marshall, M. S.: Graph visualization and navigation in information visualization: A survey. IEEE Transactions on Visualization and Computer Graphics. **6**, no.1 (2000) 24–43

13. Hoffman, P. E., Grinstein, G. G.: A survey of visualizations for high-dimensional data mining. Chapter 2, Information visualization in data mining and knowledge discovery, Eds: Fayyad, U., Grinstein, G. G., Wierse, A. (2002) 47–82

14. Hofmann, H., Siebes, A. P. J. M., Wilhelm, A. F. X.: Visualizing association rules with interactive mosaic plots. Proceedings of the Sixth International Conference on Knowledge Discovery and Data Mining. (2000) 227–235

15. http://www-306.ibm.com/software/data/iminer/visualization/

16. Keim, D. A.: Information visualization and visual data mining. IEEE Transactions on Visualization and Computer Graphics. **8**, no.1 (2002) 1–8

17. Kopanakis, I., Theodoulidis, B.: Visual data mining modeling techniques for the visualization of mining outcomes. Journal of Visual Languages and Computing. **14** (2003) 543–589

18. http://www.miner3d.com/

19. http://www.netvis.org/resources.php

20. http://vlado.fmf.uni-lj.si/pub/networks/pajek/

21. http://www.spotfire.com/

22. Tan, P., Kumar, V., Srivastava, J.: Selecting the right interestingness measure for association patterns. Proceedings of SIGKDD. (2002) 32–41

23. Wong, P. C., Whitney, P., Thomas, J.: Visualizing association rules for text mining. Proceedings of the 1999 IEEE Symposium on Information Visualization. (1999)

24. http://www.yworks.com/

Credential-Based Policies Management in an Access Control Framework Protecting XML Resources

Konstantina Stoupa, Zisis Simeoforidis, and Athena Vakali

Department of Informatics, Aristotle University of Thessaloniki, Greece
kstoupa@acn.gr, zsimaiof@csd.auth.gr, avakali@csd.auth.gr

Abstract. XML has been widely adopted for Web data representation under various applications (such as DBMSs, Digital Libraries etc). Therefore, access to XML data sources has become a crucial issue. In this paper we introduce a credential-based access control framework for protecting XML resources. Under this framework, we propose the use of access policy files containing policies concerning a specific credentials type. Moreover, we propose the reorganization of the policies in these files based on their frequency of use (the more frequently it is used the higher in the file it is placed). Our main goal is to improve request servicing times. Several experiments have been conducted which are carried out either on single request or on multiple requests base. The proposed framework is proven quite beneficial for protecting XML-based frameworks such as digital libraries or any other data resources whose format is expressed in XML.

1   Introduction

Web large-scale adoption has resulted in massive amount of data exchanged daily, and in this context, large scale access control mechanisms have been considered essential in order to prevent unauthorized access to critical resources. Thus, several research efforts and various access control models have been proposed (a description of the most well-known access control models is given in [6], [8]). In an effort to reduce the increasing number of policies required for protecting resources from the wide and heterogeneous clients accessing modern Internet-based environments, modern access control models such as Credentials-based access control model [9] have been proposed. In such models, each subject is associated with some properties (forming credentials) and thus we express policies of the form: *"clients under 18 years old can gain access to documents belonging into the topic* non-adult staff*"*.

Among the various languages proposed for expressing credentials and generally protected resources over the Web, XML has become the most popular standard for both modeling resources and expressing security policies. XACML is a standardized framework using an XML-based language for expressing policies. In this paper, we adopt XML to define and organize credentials and access control policies over sets of XML-structured documents (typically stored in large-scale repositories).

A. Levi et al. (Eds.): ISCIS 2006, LNCS 4263, pp. 603–612, 2006.

1.1 Related Work

Several credentials-based access control frameworks have been designed to protect XML documents. Adam et. al. in [1] propose a credentials-based access control module appropriate for high volume libraries. This model authorizes subjects with specific properties (e.g. age>18) to gain access to protected resources related to a specific concept. Access control authorizations are stored altogether in a *policy base* (as it is called) which is a unique file containing policies and the servicing of a request demand the scanning of the whole policy base leading to high response times.

Author-X [2] is a CBAC framework able to control access to XML documents. Again subjects are characterized by credentials and authorizations are assigned to credentials and not to subject identities. Author-X specializes its protection mechanisms on XML documents. It is an innovative system that introduces methods for reducing the number of policies that have to be specified for a specific file such as the positive and negative policies. Author-X defines as a *policy base* an XML file that contains the access policies for a single file. Each file under system's protection must have a corresponding policy-base file.

Additionally the MaX mechanism proposed in [3] is a credentials-based system for enforcing access control, specifically tailored to both Digital Libraries (DLs) and Web environments. Key features of MaX are the support for credential and content-based access control to DL and Web documents, and its full integration with standard Internet rating systems. The access policies regard User Groups and the total of the policies is stored inside a policy base which is typically a file. MaX was also the first framework that made use of the credential type hierarchy. This hierarchy is based upon the idea that to make the task of credential specification easier, credentials with similar structures are grouped into *credential-types*, organised into a *credential-type hierarchy*.

1.2 Paper's Contribution

Although several research efforts focus on introducing access control modules (adopting various models) protecting XML resources, few proposals have been made in order to optimize the access request evaluation process. Murata et. al. [5] have introduced the use of static analysis in improving access queries and thus decreasing time delays in request servicing. Ferrari et. al. [4] propose the use of Access Control XML (AC-XML) documents containing for each object (either XML document or DTD) the associated policies.

In this paper we propose an innovative CBAC access control utility protecting XML documents and supporting credential type hierarchy where great concern is given in adopting such policy organization in order to improve the request servicing time. A wide range of Web-based non-CBAC security systems also exists which use either embedded Operating System's techniques, such as the NTFS or databases to control the denial or granting of access to resources. These systems offer very small response times but lack ease of administration as they use single file or directory access control. We try to provide a framework with response times competitive to those of non-CBAC systems, without abolishing the benefits of CBAC models at the fields of administration and policy definition. The effectiveness of our proposal is proved by experimental results. The proposed system can be *used* for the protection of XML-based digital libraries accesses through Internet and generally in order to protect XML-defined resources. For example, web services, image files whose structure is given in XML, etc.

The proposed CBAC framework uses XML to represent resources, credential types (the properties that a subject belonging in this type should have, e.g. student, secretary, etc.), credentials (instances of credential types, e.g. a specific student with specific values in the student properties) and policies but our main focus is to use such policy organization in order to improve response time. The proposed improvements concern the organization of the policy warehouse:

- *Grouping of policies according to credential types they refer to*: our policy warehouse consists of so many XML *access policy files (AP files)* as the number of credentials types are. Each file contains only the policies that refer to the specific type. Therefore, when a request is received, only the associated AP file is scanned. The frameworks discussed in [1] and [3] do not use such an organization and all of the policies are stored into the same file. Thus, the policy file can be extended endlessly and in order to service a request all of this huge policy file should be scanned. On the other hand, Author-X builds one policy file for each protected object. As the protection of files is directed on policies regarding a single file and not a group of physical entities, the majority of the CBAC model benefits is lost. As a result of this architecture, changing the policies by the administrator becomes a very difficult task.

- *Grouping policies according to the topic of the object they refer to*: moreover to the previous grouping, the policies inside an XML access policy file are grouped according to the topic of objects they refer to. Therefore, by receiving a request, the access control module should search only a specific part of the associated policy file and not all of it.

- *Adoption of credential type hierarchy:* Each AP file also contains the policies related to the super credential types. By this the credentials hierarchy parsing does not take place during access request servicing phase (as it is in [3]) but during idle times when the access policy files are built.

- *Reorganization of policies in the AP file according to the frequency of their use*: since some policies are triggered more often than others, in intervals we reorganize policies in each category of AP files according to the frequency of their use. Thus, the policies that are more likely to be triggered again will be at the beginning of the part of the AP file that should be scanned.

The rest of the paper is organized as follows: Section 2 introduces the basic concepts and definitions involved in credential-based access control. Section 3 describes the proposed framework and the functionality of each involved module is discussed. Section 4 has the results of several experiments which have been carried out to prove the effectiveness of our proposal for optimizing request evaluation time. Finally, Section 5 has the conclusions and future work ideas.

2 Credential Based Access Control: Basic Issues

In a typical Credentials Based Access Control System, the system controls which users have access to resources based on their credentials. Access rights are grouped by credential types names, and access to resources is restricted to users who have been authorized to assume the associated role. Here, we formally define the basic components on which our access control module relies. These components are: the protected resources (*objects*), the *subjects* which are characterized by their credentials and the *access modes* supported by the implemented system. Protected resources are valid XML documents following a specific Document Type Definition (DTD).

Objects are the protected resources and they are XML documents and XML Document Type Definitions (DTDs). Therefore, an object can be represented as a 2-tuple (*oid*, *t*) where *oid* is the identity of the object and *t* is the topic where the object belongs. Each object is associated with one topic. Moreover, a finer-grained access control can be achieved if we also denote as objects specific parts of an XML document. In the implemented framework we have not considered such a case but it is in our future plans.

Since the proposed framework is a CBAC one, each subject is associated with a list of properties building his *credentials* assigned during subscription. Each user is associated with a *credentials type* which consists of definition of several properties. Credentials are instances of credential types, i.e. having specific values on the properties. Credentials of a user are stored into XML files whose DTD depicts the credential type they belong to.

In order to service a request, the system should scan an access policy file consisting of several policies. Each policy is a 3-tuple of the form *(subject, object, access_mode)* where *subject* can be a credentials identifier, a credentials type or a credentials expression, *object* can be a whole XML document, or a DTD or part of a document and *access_mode* ϵ {read, write} is the access privilege.

Policies are triggered by requests sent by the client. Requests can be of the form: *(subject, access_mode, object)* where *subject* is a credentials identifier, *access_mode* can be read or write and *object* is an object identifier.

X-Univ - A Case study Scenario : in the following of the paper we will refer to a scenario simulating a university. A university consists of university members which can be students, secretaries or professors. Moreover, the protected resources can be XML files or DTDs which may be grouped into several topics, e.g. courses staff, payroll documents, professors CVs etc. We assume that each object is associated with an identifier known as *object id*. This identifier remains unchanged through life of the document. Often objects belonging into the same *topic* have common protection requirements. Therefore, XML documents are categorized according to their topic. As an example consider the case of having to protect various documents related to the courses, e.g. timetables, exercises, manuals, etc. It is quite sure that subjects sharing similar credentials will have similar authorizations to every object belonging in this topic. Each object is associated with a specific topic but every subject may be interested in various topics. The following is an example of credential type:

```
(student, {(name, string), (type, (postgraduate |
undergraduate)), (semester, (1...8))}).
```

Fig.1 depicts a credential types hierarchy related to our scenario.

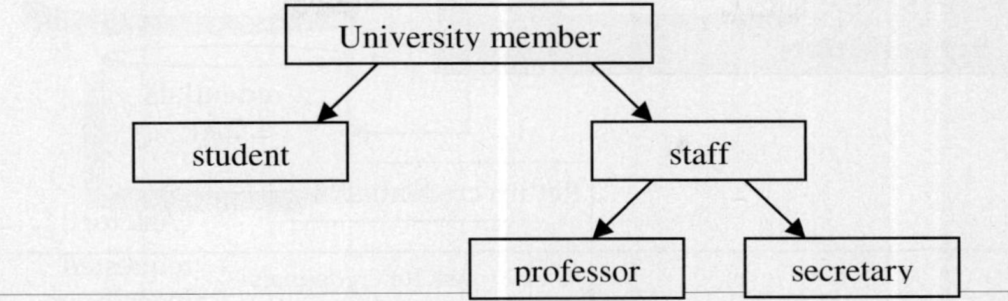

Fig. 1. A credential types hierarchy for the university scenario

According to the scenario described some examples of credentials are:

```
(student, 1, (name: Ntina, dept: computer science,
                semester: 5, type: undergraduate))
(professor, 10, (name: Athena, dept: physics, course:
                Nuclear Physics, type: postgraduate))
```

In our model only positive policies are defined and in case no policy is expressed servicing a specific request, access is denied. Some examples of policies are the following:

```
Policy1=(student/dept[.="Physics"],
                        physics_courses.xml,read)
Policy2=(professor,courses,read)
```

The first policy defines that every student belonging into the physics department is allowed to read `physics_courses.xml`, while the second one defines that all professors are allowed to read documents belonging into the `courses` topic.

3   The Proposed Framework

We propose a credentials-based framework which controls access to XML files and whole groups of files belonging into the same topic, in a quick and secure way, by assigning credentials to system's clients (i.e subjects).

The proposed framework (Fig. 2) consists of several XML-based LDAP directories storing required information about the subject, the objects and the policies. In the credential types LDAP, the XML-based definitions of all credential types are stored (e.g in the X-Univ example, student, secretary, etc.). The credentials of each client following one of those types are stored into credentials LDAP. Since our aim is the improvement of response time, access control policies are organized into XML files according to credentials type they refer to. Each AP file is further organized according to the topic of the object a policy refers to. The reason we have adopted LDAP directories as storage model is due to the fact that in LDAP, data are organized as a tree like XML documents. Therefore, the transformation from the XML data model to the LDAP data model is not a complex task.

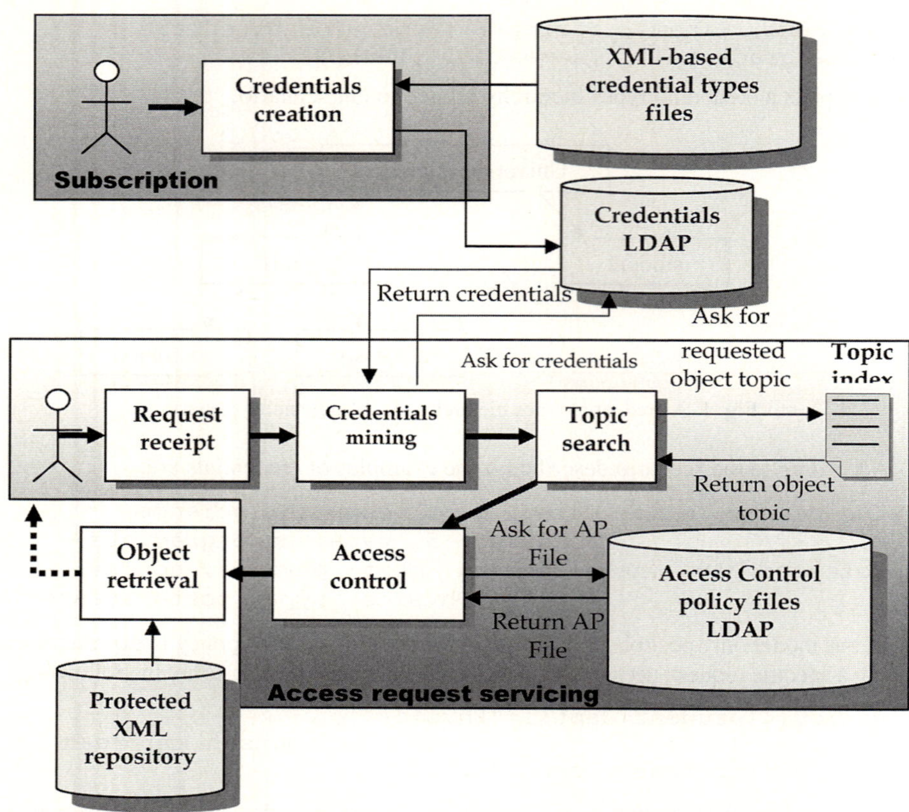

Fig. 2. The architecture of the optimized access control utility

Fig. 3 depicts the AP file related to the credential type "student". The policies in this file are organized according to the topic of object they refer to (in this example one topic is shown: courses) and each category contains both specific and general policies. The object in the specific policies is an object identifier, i.e. a specific XML file, while in the general policies the object is a topic identifier. In order to avoid the parsing of the credential type hierarchy during the access control phase (something that is done in [3]), this file also contains the specific and general policies related to the super credential types (in our example the type "university members"). Thus, upon the receipt of a request originating from a subject belonging into a specific credential type, the associated AP file is opened and the part associated with the requested object topic is scanned.

Each policy has an attribute "frequency" which is increased by one every time a policy is triggered. During idle times, an administrative module scans each policy file and reorganizes policies according to the frequency of their use. Thus, the most frequently used policies will be forwarded at the beginning of the file in order to optimize the response time.

```
<policy_file type="student">
<topic value="courses">
  <policy frequency="23">
      <subject>...</subject> <object>...</object>
      <access_mode>...</access_mode>
  </policy>
  </topic>
</policy_file>
```

Fig. 3. An example of an Access Policy (AP) File

Using the previously defined resources, the function of our framework is divided into two sections: (a) the subscription phase and (b) the access request servicing phase. During the subscription phase the client communicates into the system in order to define its credentials. According to the credential type the client follows, the framework ask him to give values to the properties associated with this type. The subject credentials are then stored into a separate XML file stored into the XML-based credentials warehouse.

The main functionality of the environment is presented during the access request servicing. After the subject has logged into the system, it sends an HTTP access request to Access Control Server. Each HTTP request has to comply with the following schema: *http:// ServerIPAddress : ActivePort / RequestedDocumentName.* From the time a request is received until the time the subject will receive an answer (positive or negative) the following modules are triggered:

- *Credential mining*: according the subject identity, the appropriate file containing its credentials is opened.
- *Topic search*: this module finds the topic that the requested object belongs to.
- *Access control*: this module opens the access policy file associated with the credential type the subject owns and goes to that part of this file containing policies related to the topic the requested object belongs to. Of course the policies are organized according to the frequency of their use and therefore it is very possible to find the appropriate policy at the beginning of the scanned part. If a policy is triggered, a positive answer will be returned to the subject otherwise access will not be allowed. The object retrieval module will be triggered only if a positive answer is returned by the access control module.

4   Experimentation

In order to check the effectiveness of the proposed framework we have implemented it using Java. The parsing of XML files depicting credentials and policies has been done using Xerxes and SAX. The experiments were conducted using both synthetic and real access requests. Synthetic requests were stored into a single file from where they were retrieved while real requests were received through http port. According to the X-Univ scenario we have built three access policy files (AP files) (one for every credential type, student, secretary, professor). Each access policy file contained 100 policies of the form discussed in section 2. The AP files followed the format shown in

Fig. 3. Moreover, we have also built a separate unified policy file containing all of the policies totally unorganized, as they were the policy bases in [3] and [1]. We have conducted experiments using both synthetic workload consisting of 100 requests stored into a file and real workload consisting of requests coming to the server through http messages. In this section we will refer to our proposal as *"AP Files Approach"* and to the generally used method were only one policy file is used as *"Unified Policy File Approach"*.

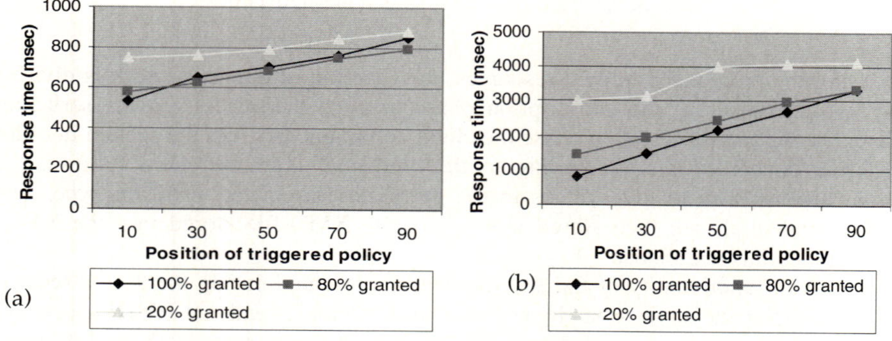

Fig. 4. Response times against the position of the policy that is triggered. In both cases three lines are depicted, when 100% of the requests were granted, 80% were granted and 20% were granted. (a) For AP Files Approach, (b) For Unified Policy File Approach.

Synthetic workload

Since the response time depends on the position in the policy file of the policy that is triggered, the experiments depicted in Fig. 4(a) and (b) show the response times of both approaches when the triggered policy is found at the 10% first policies, at 50%, 70% and 90%. Moreover, we have depicted the response times when all of the requests were granted, when 20% of them were granted or 80%. Comparing Fig. 4(a) and (b) we realize that the AP Files Approach achieves much better response times. (e.g. if all requests are granted and the triggered policies are found at the middle of the total of policies that are to be scanned, the AP Files Approach response time is 701 msec while in the other approach we have 2163 ms.). In all cases our proposal is three times faster.

Fig.5(a) depicts the response times for servicing one request for both approaches. Again the x-axis contains the position of the triggered policy. In case of the AP File approach the response time remains unchanged independently of the policy position and it is at least two times lower than that of the Unified Policy File Approach.

Real workload

We have also tested the behaviour of the two approaches in case or receiving real requests. Fig. 5(b) depicts the behavior of the AP file approach in case it receives one request through http message and the triggered policy is at beginning of the policies that should be scanned, 20% after the beginning, 40%, 60%, 80% and at the end. It is obvious that when using synthetic workload we achieve lower response times.

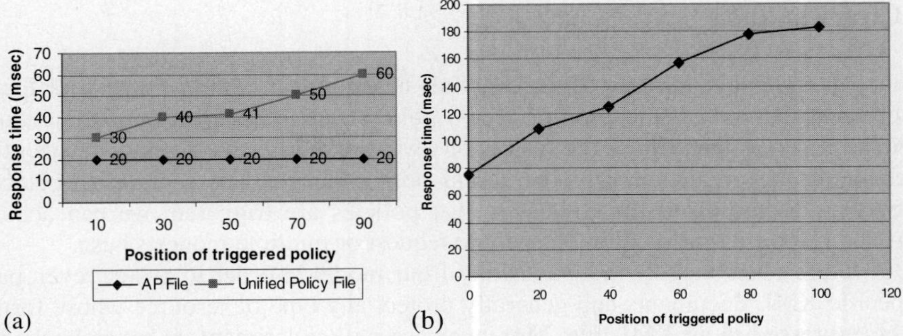

Fig. 5. Response time for servicing one request in both approaches against the position in the file of the triggered policy (a) when request originates from synthetic workload, (b)when the request is received through http.

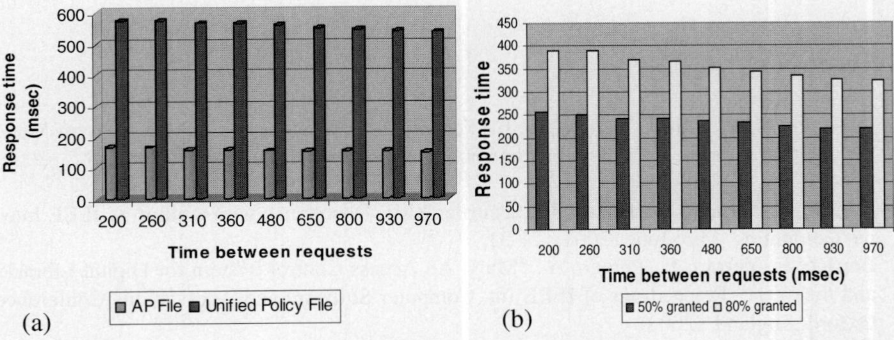

Fig. 6. (a) Response time for both approaches according to the time interval between two requests (real workload), (b) Response time for the AP File approach against the time interval between two incoming requests. Each line refers to a different percentage of granted requests.

Commenting Fig. 6(a) we shall notice that in the AP File approach shows much better response time than the Unified Policy File approach. It is quite obvious that in the AP file approach there is an almost linear increase of the response time as the time interval increases. Nevertheless, that is of minor importance because the increase is of a few milliseconds, which is an amount of time that could be barely noticed by a human user. So we conclude, that this slight time increase is very satisfactory, compared to the large intervals.

Studying the behaviour of the AP File Approach when requests are received through http, Fig. 6(b) depicts the framework's average response time compared with the time interval between two requests, in three different situations. The purple column represents the framework's behavior when 50% of the received requests are serviced by a policy at the end of the scanned area and the white one when 80% are serviced by a policy in this part of the area. Satisfactory times are achieved even in the third situation, where the 80% of the requests trigger policies at the end of a policy file.

5   Conclusions

In this paper we have introduced a credentials-based access control framework focusing on an optimized organization of access policy base in order to improve request servicing time. By presenting the results of several experiments we have proven that by changing the organization of the access policy base and by reorganizing access policy files according to the frequency that policies are triggered, we can achieve improved response times, either on a single request or multiple requests base.

Our future plans include the extension of our model in order to protect even parts of specific XML documents and generally protect any type of resource whose format can be expressed in an XML file. Moreover, we will experiment on several scheduling algorithms to find which is the most appropriate for reorganizing access policy files according to the frequencies of the triggered policies. Finally, we plan to modify this framework to support Internet-accessed environments where users are unknown and their credentials are sent along with their request signed by a trusted authority.

References

1. R. Adam, N. R., Atluri, V., Bertino, E., Ferrari, E.: A Content-based Authorization Model for Digital Libraries. IEEE Transactions on Knowledge and Data Engineering, 14(2) (2002), 296-315
2. Bertino, E., Castano, S., Ferrari, E.: Securing XML Documents with Author-X. IEEE Internet Computing, May-June (2001), 21-31
3. Bertino, E., Ferrari, E., Perego, A.: "MaX: An Access Control System for Digital Libraries and the Web", Proceedings of IEEE Int. Computer Software and Applications Conference, Oxford, England, (2002)
4. Carminati, B., Ferrari, E.: AC-XML Documents: Improving the Performance of a Web Access Control Module. Proceedings of the 10th ACM Symposium of Access Control Models and Technologies, Stockholm, Sweden, (2005)
5. Murata, M., Tozawa, A., Kudo, M., Hada, S.: XML Access Control Using Static Analysis. Proceedings of the 10th ACM Conference on Computer and Communications Security, Washington D.C., U.S.A., (2003)
6. Pallis, G., Stoupa, K., Vakali, A.: Storage and Access Control Issues for XML Documents. In: Taniar, D., Rahayu, J. W. (eds.): Web Information Systems. Idea Group Publishing, (2004), 104-140
7. Sandhu, R. S., Coyne, E. J., Feinstein H. L.: Role-Based Access Control Models. IEEE Computer (1996) 38-47.
8. Stoupa, K., Vakali, A.: Policies for Web Security Services. In Ferrari, E., Thuraisingham, B. (eds.): Web and Information Security, Idea Group Publishing (2006), 52-72
9. Winslett, M., Ching, N., Jones, V., Slepchin, I.: Using Digital Credentials on the World-Wide Web. Journal on Computer Security, 5 (1997), 255-267

Evaluating Proposals in Web Services Negotiation*

Yonglei Yao, Fangchun Yang, and Sen Su

State Key Laboratory of Networking & Switching Technology
Beijing University of Posts & Telecommunications (BUPT), Beijing 100876, China
{yaoyl, fcyang, susen}@bupt.edu.cn

Abstract. Negotiation is a crucial stage of Web Services interaction lifecycle. By exchanging a sequence of proposals in the negotiation stage, a service provider and a consumer try to establish a formal contract, to specify agreed terms on the service, particularly terms on non-functional aspects. In this paper, we propose an approach for proposal evaluation, one of the key decisions in negotiation that determines the acceptability of a proposal. Fuzzy truth propositions are employed to represent the restrictions attached to a service, and a utility function is used to capture the negotiator's preferences over service attributes. The overall acceptability of the proposal can be determined by the restriction obedience and the utility of values for service attributes, collectively. Based on the acceptability of a proposal, a negotiator can decide whether to accept it as a contract, then enact with the party that offers the proposal.

1 Introduction

Semantic Web Services are a set of technologies that will transform the Web from a collection of static information into an infrastructure for distributed computing. Over the past several years, we have seen a growing interest in the research on Semantic Web Services. However, to date, much of the research in this area has concentrated on the problem of service discovery (e.g. [1, 2]) and composition (e.g. [3, 4]). Relatively fewer work addresses the problem of service negotiation, especially little has been done on decision making mechanisms in negotiation, to our knowledge.

Negotiation is a crucial stage of the interaction lifecycle between a service consumer and a service provider [7, 8]. Generally, it is consisted of a sequence of proposal exchanges between the two parties, with the goal of establishing a formal contract, to specify agreed terms on the service, particularly terms on non-functional aspects. Given the ability to negotiate, consumers can continuously customize their needs, and providers can tailor their offers. In particular, multiple service providers can collaborate and coordinate with each other in order to satisfy a request that they can't do alone. In short, negotiation can enable richer and more flexible interactions between Semantic Web Services, and as a result, fully realize their capabilities.

---

* The work presented in this paper was Supported by the National Basic Research and Development Program (973 program) of China (2003CB314806), the Program for New Century Excellent Talents in University (No: NCET-05-0114), and the program for Changjiang Scholars and Innovative Research Team in University (PCSIRT).

A. Levi et al. (Eds.): ISCIS 2006, LNCS 4263, pp. 613–621, 2006.

In the negotiation process, the decisions faced by consumers and providers are often a combination of proposal generation decisions (what initial proposal should be, and what counter proposal to submit if the opponent's offer is unacceptable) and proposal evaluation decisions (how much is the satisfaction degree of a proposal, and if it is acceptable). This paper concentrates predominantly on the latter. In more detail, we employ fuzzy truth propositions to represent restrictions attached to a service, and use truth values of these propositions to denote the restriction obedience. Negotiator's preferences over measurable service attributes are captured by a mathematical function, which calculates the utility of attribute values. The restriction obedience and the utility of a proposal collectively determine the proposal's overall acceptability. As the final step, empirical tests are conducted to evaluate the approach.

The rest of this paper is structured as follows. Section 2 presents the basic concepts related to fuzzy mathematics that will be used in this paper. Section 3 discusses the evaluating algorithm and in section 4 the algorithm is empirically evaluated. Section 5 summarizes related work and finally, section 6 concludes.

2   Preliminaries

In this section, we briefly present the key concepts and notations related to fuzzy logic [5, 6]. These concepts and notations provide the underpinning of the negotiation model and the algorithm for proposal evaluation.

Definition 1. A *fuzzy truth proposition system* is a 5-tuple $(F, T, \wedge, \vee, \neg)$, where

1. $F = \{ f_i \mid i = 1, 2 \dots n \}$ is a set of *primitive propositions*,
2. $T : F \rightarrow [0,1]$ is a *truth function*, which associate each primitive proposition f in F with a *truth* $T(f) \in [0,1]$,
3. $\wedge, \vee$ and $\neg$ are logical operators that can combine primitive propositions into composite ones.

The truth of a composite proposition c, $T(c)$, is calculated recursively as:

$$T(\neg c_0) = 1 - T(c_0),$$
$$T(c_1 \wedge c_2) = \min\{T(c_1), T(c_2)\}, \tag{1}$$
$$T(c_1 \vee c_2) = \max\{T(c_1), T(c_2)\}$$

Where c_0, c_1 and c_2 are primitive or composite propositions.

3   Proposal Evaluation

In the negotiation process, the negotiator (a service consumer or provider) and its opponent continuously exchange proposals according to some protocol, until an agreement is made or the negotiation process is terminated because the time deadline is reached. In a negotiation round, when receiving a proposal form its opponent, the negotiator first need to evaluate the proposal, to determine if a deal can be made or if not, how to react in the next round.

The algorithm we propose evaluates a proposal in a step-by-step fashion. Firstly, the algorithm determines to what extent the negotiator's restrictions will be satisfied by the proposal. Secondly, the algorithm decides whether the negotiator can obey the opponent's restrictions. Finally, the algorithm computes the utility if accepting the values assigned to the service attributes by the opponent, in terms of an additive scoring system. Then all the three collectively determine the overall acceptability of the proposal. As the first step, we will introduce the negotiator model. Then the algorithm for proposal evaluation is presented, followed by an example in a book buying scenario to illustrate the operation of the algorithm.

3.1 The Negotiator Model

The following represents our conceptualization of a service negotiator. The model considers not only service attributes, but also attached restrictions from negotiators.

Definition 2. A negotiator is a 4-tuple knowledge system *(P, R, A, τ)*, where:

1. $P = (F_p, T_p)$ is a fuzzy truth proposition system, representing the negotiator's *profile model*. $F_p = \{f_i \mid i = 1,....,s\}$ is a set of primitive fuzzy propositions, and $T_p : F_p \rightarrow [0,1]$ is a truth function. This is the background information it uses to evaluate to what degree it can satisfy the opponent's restrictions.

2. $R = (F_r, T_r)$ is also a fuzzy truth proposition system that denotes the negotiator's *restriction model*. $F_r = \{f_j \mid j = 1,.....,t\}$ is a set of primitive fuzzy propositions, and $T_r : F_r \rightarrow [0,1]$ is a truth function. This is the set of restrictions that the negotiator requests its opponent to try to satisfy.

3. $A = \{(a_k, w_k, d_k, v_k) \mid k = 1,....,n\}$ is the *requirement model*, which describes its preferences over measurable non-functional attributes of the service. Where:
   (1) a_k denotes an attribute of the service.
   (2) w_k denotes a_k's weight (or importance). These weights are normalized, i.e. $\sum_{1 \leq k \leq n} W_k = 1$.
   (3) $d_k = [min_k,\ max_k]$ denotes the intervals of values for quantitative term a_k acceptable for the negotiator. Values for qualitative issues, on the other hand, are defined over a fully ordered domain, i.e., $d_k = <q_1, q_2, ... q_m>$.
   (4) $v_k: d_k \rightarrow [0,\ 1]$ is a scoring function for issue a_k, which calculates the utility of a value of a_k in the range of its acceptable values.
   With these elements in place, it is possible to compute the utility of a proposal, i.e., the utility that a negotiator can obtain if accepting a vector of values for service attributes, which is in the form of $X = < x_1, x_2, x_3, ... x_n >$ (where x_k denotes a value for service attribute $a_{k,} 1 \leq k \leq n$):

$$U(X) = \sum_{k=1}^{n} w_k v_k(x_k) \tag{2}$$

4. $\tau \in [0,1]$ is the acceptability threshold which the proposal under evaluated must surpass to be acceptable for the negotiator.

In the above model, we consider not only preferences over various service attributes, but also restrictions attached to the service by negotiators. Generally speaking, these restrictions can be classified into two categories. The first class consists of "crisp" restrictions that the opponent must satisfy. If a proposal can't satisfy all the restrictions in this class, it will be ranked as completely unacceptable. This class of restrictions is represented as crisp truth propositions, which can be regarded as a special case of fuzzy truth propositions. The second class includes restrictions that can be partially satisfied, i.e., they have truth values between "completely true" and "completely false". Even though a proposal can't satisfy some restrictions in this class, it may be accepted. These restrictions can be represented as fuzzy truth propositions naturally. For the above reasons, we chose the notion of fuzzy truth propositions to represent the restrictions that attached to the service under negotiated.

3.2   The Evaluating Algorithm

First, we give the formal definition of a proposal that a negotiator receives, which can be viewed as consisting of three components: (1) the restriction that the party offering the proposal requests the negotiator to try to satisfy, (2) restriction that it can satisfy the negotiator, (3) a vector values for the service attributes.

Definition 3. A proposal is a 3-tupple $\text{Proposal} = (c, d, X)$ where:

1. c is a composite fuzzy truth proposition represented as a Boolean expression of $f_1,....,f_s \in F_p$, which denotes the restriction that the party offering the proposal requests the negotiator to try to satisfy.
2. d is the restriction that the party offering the proposal can satisfy the negotiator, which is expressed as a Boolean expression of $f_1^{'},....,f_t^{'} \in F_r$.
3. $X =< x_1, x_2, x_3, ... x_n >$ is a vector of values for measurable service attributes. x_k denotes a value assigned to service attribute $a_k\,(1 \le k \le n)$.

At a negotiation round, the negotiator receives a proposal from its opponent and evaluates it based on the knowledge in hand. With all the knowledge in place (definition 1, 2 and 3), the acceptability of a proposal can be calculated based on three components: (1) the *satisfaction degree* that the restrictions of the negotiator can be satisfied, (2) the *restriction obedience*, which denotes the extent that the negotiator can satisfy the restrictions requested by the proposal, (3) the *utility* that the negotiator can obtain if she accept the values of the service attributes assigned by the proposal. Then all these three components collectively determine the proposal's acceptability.

The *satisfaction degree* of restrictions requested by the negotiator can be expressed as (see definition 2 for T_r and τ, and definition 3 for d):

$$\alpha = \begin{cases} 0, & \text{if } T_r(d)=0 \\ (1\text{-}\tau)T_r(d)+\tau, & \text{otherwise} \end{cases} \tag{3}$$

Where $T_r(d)$ can be computed as:

$$T_r(d) = d^{'}(T_r(f_1^{'}),....,T_r(f_t^{'})) \tag{4}$$

If $T_r(d)$ equal to 0, a conclusion can be drawn that the proposal can't satisfy some of the "crisp" restrictions that must be satisfied. Otherwise, all the restrictions can be satisfied to some degree, and the function $(1-\tau)T_r(d)+\tau$ assures that the satisfaction degree surpasses the *acceptability threshold* of the negotiator.

Similarly, the *restriction obedience*, i.e., the extent to which the negotiator can satisfy the restrictions requested by the proposal, can be calculated as (see definition 2 for T_p and definition 3 for c):

$$\beta = \begin{cases} 0, & if\ T_p(c)=0 \\ (1\text{-}\tau)T_p(c)+\tau, & otherwise \end{cases} \tag{5}$$

Where $T_p(c)$ is computed as:

$$T_p(c) = c'(T_p(f_1),.....,T_p(f_s)) \tag{6}$$

Based on equation (2), the *utility* that the negotiator can obtain if she accepts the values assigned to the service attributes by the opponent offering the proposal is expressed as (see definition 2 for $U(X)$ and definition 3 for X):

$$\mu = U(X) = \sum_{k=1}^{n} w_k v_k(x_k) \tag{7}$$

In terms of equation (3)-(7), as the final step, the acceptability of the proposal is:

$$acceptability = \min\{\alpha, \beta, \mu\} \tag{8}$$

If the *acceptability* is equal to or greater than the *acceptability threshold*, the negotiator will accept the proposal as a formal contract between the two parties, and the negotiation process terminates successfully with a deal. Otherwise, the negotiator will generate a counter proposal if the time deadline is not coming.

3.3 An Example

In this section, we present an example in a book buying scenario where a buyer wants to buy a book from an online book seller, to demonstrate the operation and practicality of the evaluating algorithm.

We start from the buyer model *(P, R, A, τ)* (see definition 2).
- The *profile model P* consists of the following two facts: she is a resident of Beijing, and she likes to pay in check to the degree of 0.8.   Formally, $P = (F_p, T_p)$,

  $F_p = \{f_1 = resideInBeijing, f_2 = payInCheck\}$ and $T_p(f_1)=1$, $T_p(f_2)=0.8$.

- The *restriction model R* includes three constraints: the seller must deliver the book to her office, if failed she likes to be noticed to the degree of 0.7, and a reward of bookmark is valuable for her to the degree of 0.6. Formally, $R = (F_r, T_r)$,

  $F_r = \{f_1' = deliverToOffice, f_2' = failureNotification, f_3' = rewardBookmark\}$, $T_r(f_1')=1$,
  and $T_r(f_2')=0.7, T_r(f_3')=0.6$.

- There are two service attributes she would negotiate with the seller: price and delivery date, with weight of 0.7 and 0.3 respectively. The acceptable interval of values for price is [40, 50], and [1, 7] for delivery date. The scoring functions for the two attributes are in the form of following:

$$u_p(p) = \begin{cases} 1, & \text{if } p{<}40 \\ \dfrac{50-p}{50-40}, & p\in[40,50] \end{cases}, \quad u_d(d) = \frac{7-d}{7-1}, \quad d \in [1,7] \tag{9}$$

- The acceptability, τ, is set to 0.5.

Suppose a proposal offered by the seller consists of the following (see definition 3):
- The restriction that the seller requests the buyer to satisfy is represented as a composite truth proposition $c = resideInBeijing \wedge payInCash$.
- The restriction that the seller can satisfy is also represented as a composite truth proposition $d = deliverToOffice \wedge failureNotificaiton \wedge no\,Re\,ward$.
- The value vector of service attributes is $< price = 42,\ deliveryDate = 3 >$.

With the domain knowledge and the proposal in place, the buyer calculates the acceptability in the following steps:

Step 1. Calculate the *satisfaction degree*:

$$\begin{aligned} T_r(d) &= T_r(f_1' \wedge f_2' \wedge \neg f_3') \\ &= \min\{T_r(f_1'), T_r(f_2'), 1 - T_r(f_3')\} \\ &= 0.4 \end{aligned} \tag{10}$$

$$\alpha = (1-\tau)T_r(d) + \tau = 0.7$$

Step 2. Calculate the *restriction obedience*:

$$\begin{aligned} T_p(c) &= T_p(f_1 \wedge \neg f_2) \\ &= \min\{T_p(f_1), 1 - T_p(f_2)\} \\ &= 0.2 \end{aligned} \tag{11}$$

$$\beta = (1-\tau)T_p(c) + \tau = 0.6$$

Step 3. Calculate the *utility* of the values for services attributes:

$$\begin{aligned} \mu &= w_p \times u_p(42) + w_d \times u_d(3) \\ &= 0.7 \times \frac{50-42}{10} + 0.3 \times \frac{7-3}{6} \\ &= 0.76 \end{aligned} \tag{12}$$

Step 4. Calculate the *acceptability* of the proposal:

$$acceptability = \min\{\alpha, \beta, \mu\} = 0.6 \tag{13}$$

Because the *acceptability* is greater than the *acceptability threshold*, the proposal can be accepted by the buyer, and a deal is made.

4   Empirical Evaluation

Two experimental tests have been undertaken to provide an initial evaluation of the operational performance of our algorithm.

In the first experiment, we ran the algorithm 20 times. Every time, taking a bookselling service as an example, we asked a volunteer (a buyer) the following questions:

- What restrictions can she satisfy the seller (*profile model*)?
- What restrictions does she demand (*restriction model*)?
- What are the acceptable intervals of values for price and delivery time?
- What is the importance (the weight) of price and delivery time, respectively?

Based on the answers to the above questions, we established the negotiator (consumer) model and submitted the model to the algorithm. Then we submitted ten service proposals to the volunteer and the evaluating algorithm, asking them to select the most satisfying one. These proposals were designed by the authors so that they could satisfy the volunteer with different degrees. For 16 times, the volunteer and the algorithm selected the same proposal. For 3 times, the algorithm evaluated the proposal that the volunteer selected with the second highest satisfaction degree, and just for 1 time, with the third highest satisfaction degree.

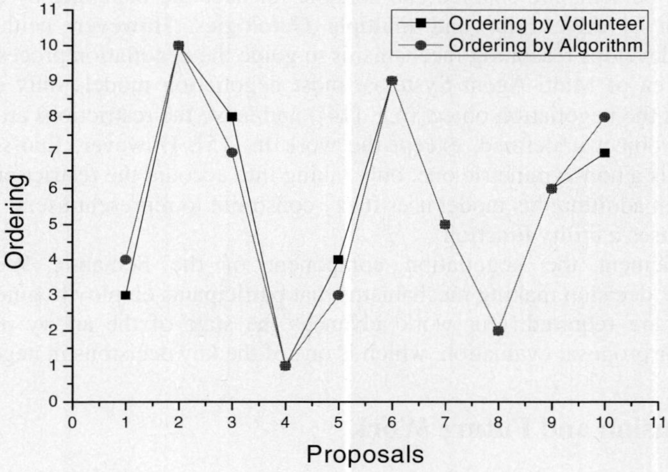

Fig. 1. User and Algorithm Ordering

In the second experiment, we also took the bookselling service as an example, and established the consumer model by interaction with a volunteer. Then we again submitted ten service proposals to the volunteer and the evaluating algorithm, and asked them to order these proposals. The result is presented in figure 1.

From the results of the two experiments, a conclusion can be drawn that our evaluation algorithm can compute the acceptability of a service proposal in the manner that is consistent with the real-word users' preferences.

5   Related Work

The significance of the negotiation stage in the Semantic Web Services interaction lifecycle has been realized for several years [7, 8], and there are increasing interests in research on service negotiation. However, most work focuses on negotiation model and/or negotiation protocol. Little has been done on the decision making mechanisms that participants can employ to guide their actions in negotiation.

Hung et al [10] propose an XML language called WS-Negotiation for Web Services negotiation, which contains three parts: negotiation message, negotiation protocol and negotiation strategies. However, in this basic model for WS-Negotiation, the decision making mechanisms are undefined.

A broker capable of offering negotiation and bargaining support to facilitate the matching of Web Services is presented in [11]. But the protocol and decision-making mechanisms for negotiation are not presented. In [13], the authors discuss their work on adapting some of the research in the multi-agent systems community to facilitate negotiation between web services. However, much of the work has concentrated on the negotiation protocol, not the decision making mechanisms.

WS-Agreement [12] is a recently proposed and emerging protocol for specifying contract proposals and contracts in the context of Web Services negotiation. A formal definition of the WS-Agreement is given in [16] and the schema is extended by adding tags to accommodate states for re-negotiation. In [9], WS-Agreement is extended to be semantic-enabled and suitable for accurate matching by employing a combination of ARL rules and multiple Ontologies. However, neither of these researches develops reasoning mechanisms to guide the negotiation process.

In the area of Multi-Agent Systems, most negotiation models only consider the attributes of the negotiation object (e.g. [14]) and leave the restrictions attached to the negotiation object undefined, except the work in [15]. However, Luo's negotiation model [15] is a non-symmetric one, only taking into account the restrictions requested by buyers. In addition, his model uses fuzzy constraint to represent users' preferences, while ours uses a utility function.

To implement the negotiation component of the Semantic Web Services architecture, decision making mechanisms that participants employ to guide actions in negotiation are required. Our work advances the state of the art by proposing an approach for proposal evaluation, which is one of the key decisions in negotiation.

6   Conclusion and Future Work

Negotiation is an important stage of the interaction lifecycle between a service consumer and a provider, and our work makes complementary contributions to the research on Web Services negotiation. In this paper, we introduce our preliminary work on proposal evaluation, which is one of the key decisions in the negotiation process. We show how to uses fuzzy truth propositions to describe restrictions attached to the service under negotiated, and to represent users' preference with a simple utility function. Then, an algorithm for proposal evaluation is proposed, computing the acceptability of a proposal step-by-step. Given the algorithm we develop, a service consumer or provider can determine whether a proposal offered by the opponent is acceptable, and whether a deal can be made.

Future work includes implementing a protocol for proposal exchange in a dynamic and open environment, developing strategies for generating initial proposal or counter-proposals if the opponent's last offer is not acceptable, and as the last step, investigating the effectiveness of these mechanisms with real world use cases.

References

[1]   K. Sivashanmugam, K. Verma and A. Sheth, Discovery of Web Services in a Federated Registry Environment, in proceedings of 2004 IEEE International Conference on Web Services, pp 270 - 278, 6-9 July 2004

[2]   Z. Shen, J. Su, Web service discovery based on behavior signatures, in proceedings of 2005 IEEE International Conference on Services Computing, Volume 1, pp 279 - 286, 11-15 July 2005

[3]   V. Agarwal, K. Dasgupta, N. Karnik, A. Kumar, A. Kundu, S. Mittal and B. Srivastava, A Service Creation Environment Based on End to End Composition of Web Services, Proceedings of the fourteenth International World Wide Web Conference (WWW 2005), pp 128-137, Chiba, Japan, May 10–14, 2005

[4]   Z. Maamar, S.K. Mostefaoui and H. Yahyaoui, Toward an Agent-Based and Context-Oriented Approach for Web Services Composition, Knowledge and Data Engineering, IEEE Transactions on, Volume 17, Issue 5, May 2005, pp 686 – 697

[5]   L. Zadeh, Fuzzy sets, Inform. and Control, 8 (1965), pp. 338–353.

[6]   L. Zadeh, The calculus of fuzzy restrictions, in: L.A. Zadeh, et al. (Eds.), Fuzzy Sets and Applications to Cognitive and Decision Making Processes, Academic Press, New York, 1975, pp. 1–39.

[7]   C. Preist, A Conceptual Architecture for Semantic Web Services, In proceeding of International Semantic Web Conference, Hiroshima, Japan, 8-11 November 2004

[8]   M. Burstein, C. Bussler, T. Finin, M.N. Huhns, M. Paolucci, A.P. Sheth, S.Williams and M. Zaremba, A semantic Web services architecture, Internet Computing, Volume 9, Issue 5, pp 72-81, Sept.-Oct. 2005

[9]   N. Oldham, K. Verma, A. Sheth, F. Hakimpour, Semantic WS-Agreement Partner Selection, Proceedings of the 15th International World Wide Web Conference (WWW 2006), Edinburgh Scotland, May 23-26, 2006

[10] Patrick C. K. Hung, Haifei Li, Jun-Jang Jeng, WS-Negotiation: an overview of research issues, Proc. HICSS 2004, Jan. 5-8, 2004

[11] Tung Bui and A. Gachet, Web Services for Negotiation and Bargaining in Electronic Markets: Design Requirements and Implementation Framework, Proceedings of the 38th Annual Hawaii International Conference on System Sciences, pp 38 - 38, 03-06 Jan, 2005

[12] A. Andrieux, C. Czajkowski, A. Dan, K. Keahey, H. Ludwig, J. Pruyne, J. Rofrano, S. Tuecke, M. Xu, Web Services Agreement Specification (WS-Agreement), June 29 2005

[13] S. Paurobally, V. Tamma, and M. Wooldridge, Cooperation and Agreement between Semantic Web Services, W3C Workshop on Frameworks for Semantics in Web Services, Innsbruck, Austria, June 2005.

[14] P. Faratin, C. Sierra and N.R. Jennings, Using Similarity Criteria to Make Negotiation Trade-Offs, In Journal of Artificial Intelligence 142 (2) 205-237, 2003

[15] X. Luo, N.R. Jennings, N. Shadbolt, H. Leung, and J.H. Lee, A fuzzy constraint based model for bilateral multi-issue negotiations in semi-competitive environments, Artificial Intelligence Journal 148 (1-2) pp. 53-102,2003

[16] M. Aiello, G. Frankova, and D. Malfatti, What's in an Agreement? An Analysis and an Extension of WS-Agreement, Proc. 3rd ICSOC, 2005

Nested Bitemporal Relational Algebra

Abdullah Uz Tansel[1] and Canan Eren Atay[2]

[1] Baruch College & Graduate Center, CUNY New York, NY 10100 U.S.A
tansel@baruch.cuny.edu
[2] Department of Computer Science, Dokuz Eylul University, Izmir 35160, Turkey
canan@cs.deu.edu.tr

Abstract. We introduce a nested bitemporal relational data model that allows arbitrary levels of nesting. Bitemporal data is attached to attributes. The fundamental construct for representing temporal data is a bitemporal atom that consists of three parts: transaction time, valid time and a value. We have defined algebra for the nested bitemporal relational model. The algebra includes operations to manipulate bitemporal data, to restructure nested bitemporal relations and to rollback database to a designated state in the past. We have also defined the concept of 'context' for using temporal data. Bitemporal context is for auditing purposes and rollback context is for querying past states of a bitemporal database.

1   Introduction

Conventional databases capture only the most current state of the real world, and serve a wide spectrum of applications well. However, it is desirable for a database system to maintain past, present and possible future versions of data. After an update operation when the new values arrive, the past state is discarded and forgotten completely. This results in a loss of valuable information as time progresses. It is hard to identify an application that does not evolve over time. In a wide range of database applications (i.e. employee data, student registration histories, bank account balance, cash flow over time, stock market data, medical records of a hospital, etc.) storing and querying time-varying data are required. For such applications, a temporal database that maintains time-varying data would be an ideal solution.

A temporal database may capture, either the history of objects and their attributes (*valid time*), or the history of database activity (*transaction time*). However, bitemporal database systems support both valid time and transaction time [1]. Valid time is used to model time varying states of an object and its attributes. These states may be in the past, present or even in the future. Transaction time, on the other hand, denotes the times of changes as they are recorded in the database. It may not extend beyond the current time and is system generated. Having only valid time captures the history of an object but does not preserve the history of retroactive and postactive changes. Having only transaction time does not carry historical or future data i.e. validity period of data values. On the other hand, bitemporal databases model our changing knowledge of the changing world, hence associate data values with facts

A. Levi et al. (Eds.): ISCIS 2006, LNCS 4263, pp. 622 – 633, 2006.

and specify when the facts were valid, thereby providing a complete history of data values and their changes.

In this paper, we augment nested relations [19, 20] with both valid time and transaction time dimensions. In Nested Bitemporal Relational Model (NBRM), the valid and transaction timestamps are attached to attributes and arbitrary levels of nesting is allowed to represent histories of entities and their relationships. A nested bitemporal relation scheme is defined inductively on the nesting depth of a scheme [16]. This approach represents a four-dimensional view of temporal data and does not lead to data redundancy. To the best of our knowledge, attribute time stamping and arbitrarily nested relations have not been studied before. Moreover, NBRM can be built on top of commercially available object-relational DBMS that supports nested relations and user-defined datatypes [6] that are also available in SQL99 [7].

We present a Nested Bitemporal Relational Algebra (NBRA) for the Nested Bitemporal Relational Model by extending our earlier work [16, 22]. NBRA has the five basic operators of the relational algebra and restructuring operators of the nested relations for handling bitemporal data. In addition to these, we extend the rollback operator of [3] to rollback a nested bitemporal relation to its state at a given time point, time interval or temporal element [15]. We introduce the concept of *context* to visualize the temporal data. There are four contexts: snapshot, valid time, rollback and bitemporal. *Snapshot context* refers to the current data only. *Valid time context* represent the history of a database as of *now*. *Rollback context* allows viewing the state of a bitemporal database as of a specified time. In the *bitemporal context,* an entire database is available. We use bitemporal and rollback context in defining NBRA operations. Bitemporal context and Rollback context is used to query updates and errors in the evolution of a database for auditing purposes, and to query past states of a bitemporal database, respectively.

The remainder of the article is as follows. The next section presents a brief survey of the bitemporal databases. The basic concepts and the model are introduced in section 3. Section 4 defines NBRA. Section 5 gives examples to illustrate how valid time and transaction time are used in a bitemporal database. Section 6 concludes the paper and points to directions for future research.

2   Related Work

In the past three decades, numerous temporal extensions to the relational data model and relational query languages have been proposed. The first book on the temporal databases by Tansel et al. covers in detail the theory, design and implementation issues of temporal databases [8]. Tansel and Tin identified requirements crucial in representing temporal data and provided a metric for comparing the expressive power of temporal query languages [9].

There are two common approaches in extending the relational data model with respect to how the timestamps are attached; tuple timestamping and attribute timestamping. Tuple timestamping uses the first normal-form (1NF) relations [10, 11, 2, 3, 4] and attribute timestamping requires non-first normal-form (N1NF) relations [12, 13, 14, 15, 5, 21, 16, 9]. In the case of tuple timestamping, a separate relation is required for each time dependent attribute unless they change simultaneously. Non-time-varying attributes are grouped into a different relation. A relation scheme is augmented with two (four) time attributes to designate the time reference of its tuples. Tuple time stamping uses all of the advantages of traditional relational databases. However, each time varying attribute should be in a separate relation, which results in many small relations.

In the case of attribute timestamping, N1NF relations are used, and timestamps are attached to attribute values. Entire data about an object being modeled can be stored in one tuple of the N1NF relation. Entire history of an object is stored in one tuple. Thus, values in a tuple that are not affected by an update do not have to be repeated. All time-varying attributes can be modeled in one relation

Clifford and Croker's algebra is based on lifespans and used an interpolation function for determining the time reference of the attribute values [12]. Tansel incorporated a temporal dimension to nested relations by extending the (N1NF) nested relations for modeling and manipulating temporal data. He attached temporal sets to the attributes [16]. He developed algebra and calculus languages for historical relational databases. The temporal elements and the concept of homogeneity were introduced in [15]. Gadia defined temporal versions of algebra and calculus languages where snapshot semantics was used. Salzberg studied timestamping of the transaction time dimension after commit and analyzed timeslice queries in [18].

There are several earlier studies on bitemporal databases. Ben-Zvi proposed a model for bitemporal databases, a temporal query language, storage architecture, indexing, recovery, synchronization and implementation for valid and transaction times [2]. Tuples are augmented with five implicit attribute values; effective-time-start, effective-time-stop, registration-time-start, registration-time-end and deletion-time. Snodgrass attached four implicit attributes to each time varying relation [3] and designed the temporal query language TQuel which is a derivative of QUEL of INGRES database management system. Gadia and Bhargava attached two dimensional temporal elements as valid and transaction timestamps to attribute values. Their model was designed as a comprehensive formalism for updates and errors [5]. They defined new operators to capture the updated data and to query stored relations by considering their specific semantics and defining various types of users in [21]. Jensen, Soo and Snodgrass proposed Bitemporal Conceptual Data Model, BCDM, that timestamps tuples with bitemporal elements and it is valid-time coalesced [4].

The concept of context is a generalization of user categories introduced by Gadia and Bhargava [21] and database types introduced by Snodgrass [3]. Our nested bitemporal relations are similar to Gadia and Bhargava's model, however, the way we query the bitemporal data is different. Their approach works by cutting snapshots whereas we define our algebra operations at attribute level. In BCDM, bitemporal timestamps are implicitly attached to attribute of a relation that contains only one bitemporal attribute [4]. Therefore, our model is more general and comprehensive than BCDM since it keeps the entire bitemporal history of an object or a relationship in one tuple.

3   Data Model

3.1   Preliminaries

The set U is the universe that consists of atomic values such as integers, reals, characters and the value null. A subset of U represents time, T. T is discrete, linearly ordered set under less than or equal to ($\leq$) relationship and isomorphic to natural numbers. We assume that time values range over integers 0, 1, 2, *now*. The symbol 0 represents the relative origin of time and *now* is a special variable that denotes the current time.

In the context of time, any interval $[t_i, t_{i+n}]$ is a consecutive subset of T that can be enumerated as $\{t_i, t_{i+1}, \ldots t_{i+n}\}$. This interval can be closed or open at its ends. The interval $[t_i, t_{i+n}]$ is closed at both ends; it includes t_i and t_{i+n} and all the time points between them. On the other hand, $[t_i, t_{i+n+1})$ is closed at the beginning and open at the end; it does not include t_{i+n+1}. Set operations (union, intersection, and difference) can be defined on intervals but intervals are not closed under these operations. A *temporal set* is any subset of T. A *temporal element* is a temporal set that is represented by the maximal intervals corresponding to its subsets having consecutive time points, i.e. a finite union of disjoint maximal intervals in T [15]. The smallest interval, hence temporal element may be considered as [t, t] where t is a time instant. The largest interval or temporal element is [0, *now*]. For example, [37, 40) and [50, *now*] are intervals. Time points of these intervals are [37, 38, 39, 40) and (41, *now*]. [37, 39] $\cup$ [40, *now*] is a temporal element.

A relation scheme $R(A_1, A_2, \ldots, A_n)$, is made up of the relation name R and a list of attributes $A_1, A_2, \ldots, A_n$ which we also denote as att(R).

The focus of our paper is on attribute time stamped nested bitemporal relations. For most applications, a few level of nesting would be sufficient to model temporal data. For the sake of generality, we will allow arbitrary levels of nesting. Each attribute's value is recorded as a *temporal atom*: <transaction time, valid time, value> triplet, where transaction time and valid time components can be represented as a time point, a time interval or a temporal element. In a temporal atom, either the transaction time or the valid time may be missing, but not both. A bitemporal atom in the form of <TT, VT, V> means V is valid for the time period VT, and this fact is recorded in the database system for the time period TT. A valid time atom has the form <VT, V>, whereas a transaction time atom is in the form of <TT, V>. TT and VT may not be empty; (TT, VT $\subseteq$ T) and (V $\in$ U). We use the term temporal atom to mean any one of the three types of atoms.

In case the time intervals are used, a temporal atom is $<[TT_l, TT_u), [VT_l, VT_u), V>$, where TT_l is the transaction time lower bound, TT_u is the transaction time upper bound, VT_l is the valid time lower bound, VT_u is the valid time upper bound and V is the data value. The interval that includes *now* as an upper bound such as $[TT_l, now]$ or $[VT_l, now]$ is closed and an expanding interval since the value of *now* changes as time progresses. In the remainder of the paper, we opted to use intervals to represent time for the ease of representation. Temporal elements can also be equivalently used.

3.2 Nested Bitemporal Relations

Atom is the basic undefined term on which the recursive definitions of nested temporal relations are built. An atom takes its values from **U**. A temporal atom has time components and a value component and is defined by atoms.

The basis of the inductive definition of a nested bitemporal relation scheme is a bitemporal tuple scheme, which consists of a sequence of attribute names that are atoms, temporal atoms, or nested relation schemes. A nested temporal relation scheme is defined out of a tuple scheme. Each scheme has an order which is an ordinal value that indicates it's nesting depth. An atom has order zero. A tuple scheme's order is the same as the maximal order of its components. The order of a bitemporal relation scheme is one more than the order of the tuple scheme over which it is defined. Following is the inductive definition of bitemporal tuple and bitemporal nested temporal relation schemes.

Order Zero Scheme:
   t:= tuple: $<t(1), ..., t(n)>$ for n>0. Each t(i) is an atom or a temporal atom.
Order k + 1 Scheme: It could be either a bitemporal tuple scheme or a bitemporal nested relation scheme.

   i. **t:= tuple:** $<t(1), ..., t(n)>$ for n>0. Each t(i) is an atom, a temporal atom or bitemporal nested relation scheme of order k + 1 or less. At least one component of t must be a relation scheme of order k + 1.

   ii. **r:= relation:** $<t>$ where t is the bitemporal tuple scheme $<t(1), ..., t(n)>$. Each t(i) has a scheme of order k or less and at least one t(i) has a scheme of order k. For notational convenience, we will write **r:= relation:** $<t(1), ..., t(n)>$ [16].

Table 1. A Nested Bitemporal Relation, EMP. (Note that DEPARTMENTand SALARY-H are column of EMP and displaced on the next line to save space.)

E#	ENAME	ADDRESS-H	BIRTH-	
		ADDRESS	DATE	
E_1	James	$<[1, now], [1, now], a_1>$	1980	
E_2	Carol	$\{<[12, 27), [15, 27), a_3>,$ $<[28, 40), [28, 40), a_1>,$ $<[41, 45), [41, 45), a_3>,$ $<[53, now], [55, now], a_3>\}$	1990	
E_3	Liz	$\{<[15,56), [18,56), a_4>,$ $<[57, now], [57, now], a_6>\}$	1982	

DEPARTMENT		SALARY-H
DNAME-H	MANAGER-H	SALARY
DNAME	MANAGER	
$<[1, now), [1, now), Marketing>$	$<[1, now], [1, now], James>$	$\{<[1, 8), [1, 10), 25K>,$ $<[9, 20), [11, 22), 30K>,$ $<[21,32), [23, 34), 32K>,$ $<[33, now], [35, now], 40K>\}$
$\{<[14, 45), [15, 45), TechS.>,$ $<[53, now], [55, now], TechS.$ $>\}$	$\{<[14, 45), [15, 45), James>,$ $<[53, now], [53, now], Liz>\}$	$\{<[14, 21), [15, 25), 20K>,$ $<[22, 45), [26, 45), 22K>,$ $<[53, now], [55, now], 25K>\}$
$<[15, now], [18, now], Sales>$	$\{<[15, 25), [15, now], Carol>,$ $<[26, now], [15, now], James>\}$	$\{<[15, 27), [18, 30), 22K>,$ $<[28, 39), [31, 42), 24K>,$ $<[40, now], [43, now], 26K>\}$

EXAMPLE: Following is the definition for a bitemporal nested relation scheme EMP depicted in table 1. Note that EMP has redundant data and is not properly designed. We just use it to illustrate our model and bitemporal nested relational algebra.

EMP: = **relation** <e>
e: = **tuple** : <E#, ENAME, ADDRESS-H, BIRTH-DATE, DEPARTMENT,
            SALARY-H>
ADDRESS-H: = **relation** : <ADDRESS>
DEPARTMENT: = **relation** : <DNAME-H, MANAGER-H>
SALARY-H: = **relation** : <SALARY>
DNAME-H: = **relation** : <DNAME>
MANAGER-H: = **relation** : <MANAGER>
E#, ENAME, BIRTH-DATE: = **tuple** <atom>
ADDRESS, DNAME, MANAGER, SALARY: = tuple <bitemporal atom>

4 Nested Bitemporal Relational Algebra

In querying a bitemporal database, we use a context. There are two commonly used contexts: bitemporal context and rollback context. In bitemporal context, we refer to a bitemporal relation, considering the entire bitemporal history. This context is useful for auditing queries and to investigate the history of corrected errors. In the rollback context, we restrict a bitemporal relation to its state at a given time point (interval or temporal element). The notation $R_{t,X}$ stands for the rollback context and it refers to the state of the bitemporal relation R at time t for the attributes in X. Rollback context is useful for specifying queries involving a state of a bitemporal database. We will first define the bitemporal relational algebra operations for the bitemporal context. Then we will proceed to the definitions of the operations for the rollback context. Let E be a nested bitemporal relation with the scheme **Relation** E: <e(1), ..., e(n)>. EV(E) represents the evaluation of E.

4.1 Bitemporal Context

Set Operations ($\cup$, $\cap$, $-$): In order to apply set operations on two bitemporal nested relations, R and S, they must have the same bitemporal relational schemes. The scheme of the resultant structure is also the same as the schemes R and S.

$$EV(R \cup S) = \{t \mid t \in EV(R) \vee t \in EV(S)\}$$
$$EV(R \cap S) = \{t \mid t \in EV(R) \wedge t \in EV(S)\}$$
$$EV(R - S) = \{t \mid t \in EV(R) - t \in EV(S)\}$$

Projection (π): If $X \subseteq$ att(E) then $EV\left(\pi_x(E)\right) = \{s[x] \mid s \in EV(E)\}$

This operation eliminates the identical (duplicate) tuples.

Selection (σ): $EV\left(\sigma_F(E)\right) = \{s \mid s \in EV(E) \wedge F \text{ is } true\}$

The formula F is made up of the conditions in the form of i **op** j where **op** is one of $\{=, \neq, <, \leq, >, \geq\}$ and i and j are attribute names or integers showing the position of attributes in E. In a condition, components of a bitemporal atom can be used. As we already mentioned, A.TT, A.VT and A.V refer to the transaction time, valid time and value components of attribute A whose values are bitemporal atoms. Moreover, $A.TT_l$, $A.TT_u$, $A.VT_l$ and $A.VT_u$ refer to the lower and upper bounds of the intervals for the transaction and valid times, respectively. The equality (=) and non-equality ($\neq$) tests can be applied on atoms, bitemporal atoms, or sets (relations). On the other hand, comparison operators $\{<, \leq, >, \geq\}$ can only be applied on atoms or atomic components of bitemporal atoms. Connectives $\wedge, \vee, \neg$ are used to build complex formulas. For the convenience of the user, we also provide set membership operator, $\{\in\}$. However, it can be expressed by other operations of bitemporal relational algebra [16]. Using these basic set of formulas, a much larger class of selection formulas can be derived.

Cartesian Product ($\times$): Let R has the scheme <r(1), ..., r(n)>, and S has the scheme <s(1), ..., s(m)>.
E = R x S. Then, E = <e(1), ..., e(n+m)>, where
    e(i)=r(i) for $1 \leq i \leq n$
    e(n+j)=s(j) for $1 \leq j \leq m$
$$E\,(R \times S) = EV\,(R) \times EV\,(S)$$

Unnesting (μ) [17, 19]: Unnesting operation is defined to flatten a nested relation. Unnest is applied on the attribute i of a bitemporal relation R where it is a set of atoms or bitemporal atoms. A new tuple is created for each atom or bitemporal atom in the set and the remaining attribute values are repeated. If unnest is applied on every time-varying set valued attributes in relation R, the result becomes a flat (1NF) relation, made up of atoms or bitemporal atoms.

The columns created by unnesting are appended to the end of E's scheme for notational convenience.

Let R be a bitemporal relation with the scheme <r(1), ..., r(n)> where <u(1), ..., u(m)> is the scheme of r(k), $1 \leq k \leq n$.
$E = \mu_k(R)$, where
    e(i)=r(i) for $1 \leq i \leq k-1$
    e(i)=r(i+1) for $k \leq i \leq n-1$
    e(i)=u(i-n+1) for $n \leq i \leq n+m-1$

$$EV\,(E) = \left\{ s \,\middle|\, \exists r \exists y \left(\begin{array}{l} r \in EV\,(R) \wedge y \in r[k] \wedge s[i] = r[i] \, for \, 1 \leq i \leq k-1 \wedge \\ s[i] = r[i+1] \, for \, k \leq i \leq n-1 \wedge s[i] = r[i-n+1] \, for \, n \leq i \leq n+m-1 \end{array} \right) \right\}$$

Nesting (v) [17, 19]: Let R be a bitemporal relation with the scheme <r(1), ..., r(n)> and $Y = \{i_1, i_2, ..., i_k\}$ is the set of k attributes in R, where $0 < k < \deg(R)$ for some k, and X is the set of remaining attributes in R, i.e. $\{1, ..., n-Y\}$. Let the arity of X be m.
$E = v_{m+1 \leftarrow Y}(R)$ where
    e(j)=r(p) for $1 \leq j \leq n-k$, $p \in X$
    e(n-k+1)=relation:<r(i_1),...,r(i_k)>

$$EV(E) = \left\{ s \,\middle|\, \exists r \,\middle|\, \begin{array}{l} r \in EV(R) \wedge s[j] = r[p] \, for \, 1 \le j \le n-k, p \in X \wedge \\ s[n-k+1] = \left\{ z \,\middle|\, \exists u \,\middle|\, \begin{array}{l} u \in E(R) \wedge u[p] = r[p] \, for \, p \in X \wedge \\ z[j] = u[i_j] \, for \, 1 \le j \le k \end{array} \right\} \end{array} \right\}$$

Relation R is partitioned where the attributes in X have the same values. For each partition, one new tuple is formed in EV(E). Newly generated tuple's X attributes' values are the same and the values of attributes in Y are formed into a set that is added as the last column of the result. This newly formed set may not be empty. Applying repeated nesting operations on a flattened version of a nested bitemporal relation produces the original structure provided that certain conditions are met since nest is not always the inverse operation for unnest.

Slice (§): Let R be a bitemporal relation, k and p are two of its attributes whose values are bitemporal atoms, $1 \le k, p \le n$, $k \ne p$ and θ is one of $\{\cup, \cap, \neg\}$,
$E = \S_{\theta, k, p}(R)$
E has the same scheme as R and E's evaluation is as follows.

$$EV(E) = \left\{ s \,\middle|\, \exists r \,\middle|\, \begin{array}{l} r \in EV(R) \wedge s[i] = r[j] \, for \, 1 \le i \le n, i \ne k, i \ne p \wedge s[k].V = r[k].V \wedge \\ s[k].TT = r[k].TT \; \theta \; r[p].TT \wedge s[k].VT = r[k].VT \; \theta \; r[p].VT \wedge \\ s[k].TT \ne \varnothing \wedge s[k].VT \ne \varnothing \end{array} \right\}$$

This operation changes k^{th} attribute's bitemporal time component according to the time of pth attribute by the specified operator, i.e. union, intersection or set difference. The result may not be empty; i.e. the resulting transaction time or the valid time may not be empty. The intersection operator implements the "when" predicate of natural languages.

Bitemporal atom decomposition (δ): Let R have the bitemporal relation scheme <r(1), ..., r(n)>, k is a bitemporal attribute, $1 \le k \le n$ and $t \le now$.
$E = \delta_k(R)$
This operation splits the kth attribute of R into its components: transaction time, valid time and the value of the attribute. They are placed at the end of relation R as five new attributes. Note that the bounds of valid time interval and the transaction time interval are represented as four separate attributes.
E's scheme is:
    e(i)=r(i) for $1 \le i \le k-1$
    e(i)=r(i+1) for $k \le i \le n-1$
e(n)   := **tuple** <atom>,   e (n+1) := **tuple** <atom>,   e (n+2) := **tuple** <atom>
e (n+3) := **tuple** <atom>,   e (n+4) := **tuple** <atom>

$$EV(E) = \left\{ s \,\middle|\, \exists r \,\middle|\, \begin{array}{l} r \in EV(R_x) \wedge s[i] = r[i] \, for \, 1 \le i < k-1 \wedge s[i] = r[i+1] \, for \, k < i \le n-1 \\ \wedge s[n] = r[k].TT_l \wedge s[n+1] = r[k].TT_u \wedge s[n+2] = r[k].VT_l \\ \wedge s[n+3] = r[k].VT_u \wedge s[n+4] = r[k].V \end{array} \right\}$$

Bitemporal atom formation (r): Let R have the bitemporal relation scheme $<r(1)$, ..., $r(n)>$, and k^{th}, l^{th}, m^{th} and q^{th} attributes are the time attributes, and p^{th} attribute is an atom.

$E = r_{k, l, m, q, p}(R)$

This operation combines the kth, l^{th}, m^{th}, q^{th}, and p^{th} attributes of R into a new column in E. Number of attributes in relation R reduced by four.

E's scheme is:

   $e(i) = r(j)$ for $1 \le i \le n\text{-}2$, $1 \le j \le n$

   $e(n\text{-}1) = $ **tuple** $:= <$bitemporal atom$>$

$r(k) := $ **tuple** $<$atom$>$, $r(l) := $ **tuple** $<$atom$>$, $r(m) := $ **tuple** $<$atom$>$

$r(q) := $ **tuple** $<$atom$>$, $r(p) := $ **tuple** $<$atom$>$

$$EV(E) = \left\{ s \middle| \exists r \middle| \begin{array}{l} r \in EV(R_x) \wedge s[i] = r[j] \, for \, 1 \le i \le n-2, \, 1 \le j \le n, j \ne k, j \ne l, j \ne m, j \ne q, j \ne p \\ \wedge s[n-4].TT_i = r[k] \wedge s[n-4].TT_u = r[l] \\ \wedge s[n-4].VT_i = r[m] \wedge s[n-4].VT_u = r[q] \wedge s[n-4].V = r[p] \\ \wedge s[n-4].TT_i \ne \varnothing \wedge s[n-4].TT_u \ne \varnothing \wedge s[n-4].VT_i \ne \varnothing \wedge s[n-4].VT_u \ne \varnothing \end{array} \right\}$$

4.2   Rollback Context

Rollback context is defined as a bitemporal relation rolled back to a given time. Bitemporal relational algebra operations work on the rolled back bitemporal relations.

Set Operations ($\cup$, $\cap$, $-$): In order to apply set operations on two rolledbacked bitemporal relations, R and S, they must have the same relational schemes and refer to the same database state t where $t < now$. The scheme of the resultant structure is also the same as the schemes of R and S. The notation R_t indicates that the relation R is rolled back to time t. In other words, all the bitemporal attributes of R are rolled back to time t. We also use the notation $R_{t,X}$ where X is a subset of R's bitemporal attributes and t is a time. In this case rollback is applied only to the attributes in X, and not the entire set of attributes in R.

$$EV(R_t \cup S_t) = EV(R_t) \cup EV(R_t)$$
$$EV(R_t \cap S_t) = EV(R_t) \cap EV(R_t)$$
$$EV(R_t - S_t) = EV(R_t) - EV(R_t)$$

Projection (π): If $X \subseteq att(E)$ then $EV\left(\pi_x(E_t)\right) = \left\{ s[x] \middle| s \in EV(E_t) \right\}$

This operation eliminates the identical tuples in the result.

Selection (σ): $EV\left(\sigma_F(E_t)\right) = \left\{ s \middle| s \in EV(E_t) \wedge F \text{ is true} \right\}$

The selection operation applies to the state of database at a designated time, t. That is, first the relation is rolled back to time t, then the selection operation is applied. If time t is omitted it defaults to now. The formula F is the same as in bitemporal context.

Cartesian Product (x): Let R_t has the scheme $<r(1), ..., r(n)>$ and S_t has the scheme $<s(1), ..., s(m)>$.

$E_t = R_t$ x S_t. Then, $E = <e(1), ..., e(n+m)>$ where
$\quad$ e(i)=r(i) for 1≤i≤n
$\quad$ e(n+j)=s(j) for 1≤j≤m
$$E\left(R_t \times S_{t'}\right) = EV\left(R_t\right) \times EV\left(S_{t'}\right)$$

Rollback (ρ): Let R be a bitemporal relation scheme, $<r(1), ..., r(n)>$ where $r(k)$ is a bitemporal attribute. Let t be a time point or an interval such that t < *now*.
$E_t = \rho_{t,\,k}(R)$
The rollback operator is defined as:

$$\rho_{t,k}(R) = \left\{ \begin{array}{l} s \left| (\exists u)\, R(u) \wedge \left(s[i] = u[i]\; for\; i = 1,...,n; i \neq k\right) \wedge \right. \\[2ex] s[k] = \left\{ z \left| (\exists x)(x \in u[k]) \wedge \left(\begin{array}{l} (x.TT_l \leq t < x.TT_u \wedge z = k) \vee \\ \left(\begin{array}{l} z = x \wedge x.TTl < t \wedge \\ \neg \left(\begin{array}{l} (\exists y)\, y \in u[k] \\ \wedge\; y.VT \cap x.VT \neq \varnothing \\ \wedge\; y.TT_l \leq t < x.TT_u \end{array} \right) \end{array} \right) \end{array} \right) \right. \right\} \end{array} \right\}$$

$\quad$ The result contains bitemporal atoms such that its TT includes the time t. If we want to cut the transaction time of these bitemporal atoms so that y only includes time t then we can replace in the above formula z=x by the expression z = < [t, t+1), x.TT, x.V>

$\quad$ To rollback an entire bitemporal relation, we apply the rollback operation on each bitemporal attribute. Let R be a bitemporal relation with the scheme $<r(1), ..., r(n)>$ and i, j, k, ... be its bitemporal attributes.

$$\rho(R) = \rho_i\left(\rho_j ... \left(\rho_k(R)\right)\right)$$

$\quad$ The other operations, nest, unnest, bitemporal atom decomposition and bitemporal formation are similarly defined. To save space, we omitted their definitions.

5   Bitemporal Queries

We now give examples by using the nested bitemporal relation, EMP, depicted in table 1 to illustrate the use of nested bitemporal relational algebra operations. We use position indexes instead of attribute names to avoid the common attributes introduced by the join operation. Note that notation 3.V, 3.TT and 3.VT represent the value, transaction time and valid time bitemporal set components of the attribute number 3, respectively. Consider that *now* is 60 at the time of the queries.

Q1: Who was Liz's manager between time 15 and 30 as of [15, 20]?

$$\pi_9\left(\sigma_{2\,=\,'Liz'\wedge\,(9.VTl\geq15\wedge9.VTu\leq30)}\left(\rho_{[15,20],\,9}\left(\mu_8\left(\mu_5(EMP)\right)\right)\right)\right)$$

Q2: What salary values are stored in the database between times 15 and 30?

$$\pi_{1,\,7.V}\left(\sigma_{(7.TTl\geq15\wedge7.TTu\leq30)}\left(\mu_6(EMP)\right)\right)$$

Q3: What is the employee number of the employees who shared the same addresses at the same time? When was it?

$$\pi_{1,3,8,7}\left(\S_{\cap,\,3.VT,\,7.VT}\left(\sigma_{3.V\,=\,7.V}\left(\mu_3\left(EMP\right)\times\left(\mu_3\left(EMP\right)\right)\right)\right)\right)$$

MANAGER
Carol, [15, 25), [26, 30)
James, [26, 30), [26, 30)

a) Answer to Q1

E#	SALARY
E_1	30K
E_1	32K
E_2	20K
E_2	22K
E_3	22K
E_3	24K

b) Answer to Q2

E#	ADDRESS	E#	ADDRESS
E_1	<[1, *now*], [1, *now*], a$_1$>	E_2	<[28, 40), [28, 40), a$_1$>

c) Answer to Q3

Fig. 1. Answers to queries Q1 through Q3

6 Conclusion

In this paper, we propose using nested relations to manage the temporal data. We call the data model nested bitemporal data model and it includes both valid time and transaction time. Valid time and transaction time are attached to attributes. Each attribute value is either an atomic value or a bitemporal atom which consists of three components; a value, its validity period and the time this data is recorded in the database. We have defined the concept of a context for the bitemporal database. The database can be viewed in valid time, rollback, or bitemporal context. Bitemporal context is for auditing purposes whereas rollback context is for querying past states of a bitemporal database. Retroactive and postactive changes are maintained.

A Nested Bitemporal Relational Algebra is defined for the proposed model and it has operations defined at the attribute level and facilitates query optimization. We define a rollback operator which allows access to a database state at any time point, time interval or temporal element.

In contrast to 1NF relations, nested bitemporal relations are more complex structures. Their storage and query processing may involve complications that may lead to inefficiencies in query processing. However, many of the queries may not require the restructuring operations and can be directly processed by a scan of the stored bitemporal nested relation. We plan to explore query processing and its optimization in our future studies.

We are working on the nested bitemporal relational calculus for the proposed model and plan to add bitemporal support to SQL. We will also implement as a test bed a nested bitemporal database on a commercially available Object Relational Databases System that supports nested relations through user-defined data types. Bitemporal aggregates, bitemporal integrity constraints and query optimization the nested bitemporal relational model are other possible research areas we plan to pursue. We also plan to use the test bed to demonstrate the feasibility of our solutions and to evaluate their performance.

Acknowledgments. First author's research is supported by a grant from the PSC_CUNY Research Award Program.

References

1. Snodgrass, R.T., Ahn, I.: A Taxonomy of Time in Databases, Proc. ACM SIGMOD Conf. (1985) 236-246
2. Ben-Zvi, J.: The Time Relational Model, PhD dissertation, Univ. of California at Los Angeles, (1982)
3. Snodgrass, R.T.: The Temporal Query Language TQuel, ACM Transactions on Database Systems, 12(2), (1987) 247-298
4. Jensen, C. S., Soo, M. D., Snodgrass, R. T.: Unifying Temporal Data Models Via a Conceptual Model, Information Systems, (1994) 19(7):513–547
5. Gadia, S. K., Bhargava, G.: A Formal Treatment of Updates and Errors in a Relational Database, TR97-14, Department of Computer Science, Iowa State University, (1989)
6. Stonebraker, M., Moore, D.: Object-relational DBMSs: Tracking the Next Great Wave, Morgan Kaufmann, (1999)
7. Melton, J., Understanding Object-Relational and Other Advanced Features, Morgan Kaufmann Publishers, San Francisco, (2003)
8. Tansel, A. U., Clifford, J., Gadia, S., Jajodia, S., Segev, A., Snodgrass, R.: Temporal Databases: Theory, Design, and Implementation, Benjamin Cummings, (1993)
9. Tansel, A. U., Tin, E.: Expressive Power of Temporal Relational Query Languages, IEEE Transactions on Knowledge and Data Engineering, Vol. 9, No. 1, Jan. (1997)
10. Lorentzos, N.: The Interval-extented Relational Model and Its Application to Valid-time Databases, Ch 3. In A. Tansel et al., Temporal Databases, Benjamin/Cummings (1993)
11. Sarda, N. L.: Extensions to SQL for Historical Databases, IEEE Trans. Knowledge and Data Eng., vol. 2, no. 2, (1990) 220-230
12. Clifford, J., Croker, A.: The Historical Relational Data Model (HRDM) and Algebra Based on Lifespans, Proc. Third Int'l Conf. Data Eng., Los Angeles, Feb. (1987) 528–537
13. Clifford, J., Tansel, A. U.: On an algebra for Historical Relational Databases: Two views, ACM SIGMOD International Conference on Management of Data, (1985)
14. Tansel, A. U.: Adding Time Dimension to Relational Model and Extending Relational Algebra, Information Systems, 11, No. 4, pp. 343–355, (1986)
15. Gadia, S. K.: A Homogeneous Relational Model and Query Languages for Temporal Databases, ACM Transactions on Database Systems, December (1988)
16. Tansel, A. U.: Temporal Relational Data Model, IEEE Transactions on Knowledge and Data Engineering, Vol. 9, No. 3, June (1997)
17. Schek, H. J., Scholl S.: An Algebra for the Relational Model with Relation-Valued Attributes, Information Systems, 11 (2), (1986)
18. Salzberg, B.: Timestamping After Commit, Parallel and Distributed Inf. Systems, (1994)
19. Ozsoyoglu, M. Z., Ozsoyoglu, G.: An Extension of relational Algebra for Summary Tables, Proceedings of the 2nd Intl Workshop on SDB Management, (1983)
20. Tansel, A. U., Garnett, L.: Nested Historical Relations, Proc. ACM SIGMOD Conf., (1989)
21. Bhargava, G., Gadia, S.: Relational Database Systems with Zero Information Loss, IEEE Transactions on Knowledge and Data engineering Vol.5, No.1, (1993)
22. Garnett, L., Tansel, A. U.: Equivalence of the Relational Algebra and Calculus for Nested Relations, Computers Math. Applications Vol.23, No 10, (1992) 3-25

A Protocol for Reconciling Recovery and High-Availability in Replicated Databases*

J.E. Armendáriz-Iñigo[1], F.D. Muñoz-Escoí[2], H. Decker[2],
J.R. Juárez-Rodríguez[1], and J.R. González de Mendívil[1]

[1] Universidad Pública de Navarra, Campus de Arrosadía, s/n, 31006 Pamplona, Spain
[2] Instituto Tecnológico de Informática, Campus de Vera, 46071 Valencia, Spain
{enrique.armendariz, jr.juarez, mendivil}@unavarra.es,
{fmunyoz, hendrik}@iti.upv.es

Abstract. We describe a recovery protocol which boosts availability, fault tolerance and performance by enabling failed network nodes to resume an active role immediately after they start recovering. The protocol is designed to work in tandem with middleware-based eager update-everywhere strategies and related group communication systems. The latter provide view synchrony, i.e., knowledge about currently reachable nodes and about the status of messages delivered by faulty and alive nodes. That enables a fast replay of missed updates which defines dynamic database recovery partition. Thus, speeding up the recovery of failed nodes which, together with the rest of the network, may seamlessly continue to process transactions even before their recovery has completed. We specify the protocol in terms of the procedures executed with every message and event of interest and outline a correctness proof.

1 Introduction

For distributed systems, high availability, fault tolerance and performance are properties of key importance. They are achieved by data replication, and can be further boosted by speeding up the recovery of failed network nodes. For distributed databases, replication is usually classified by the orthogonal distinctions of eager or lazy update propagation, on one hand, and executing updates in a dedicated "primary copy" node or permitting update execution everywhere in the network, on the other [1,2,3]. For many applications that are distributed over wide areas while requiring strong consistency, e.g., OLTP databases, eager update-everywhere replication is the policy of choice. Solutions which guarantee (possibly relaxed) ACID properties and efficient conflict reconciliation for eager update-everywhere replication have been proposed in [4,5,6,7,8,9,10]. These protocols exploit view synchrony and primitives as provided by a Group Communication System (GCS) [11], as well as some optimization techniques for improving scalability [7]. Replication consistency is achieved either by means of total-order multicast procedures [1], by priorities [9], or by epidemic algorithms [10]. Protocols are implemented either as extensions of the DBMS core [5,7] or modules of a middleware architecture [6,7,8,9].

---

* This work has been supported by the Spanish government research grant TIC2003-09420-C02.

A. Levi et al. (Eds.): ISCIS 2006, LNCS 4263, pp. 634–644, 2006.

A weak point of virtually all solutions published so far is that they do not cope well with network dynamics such as the recovery of failed nodes [4,5,8,9,10]. Recovery protocols bring back temporarily disconnected or crashed nodes to an active state which is consistent with the alive rest of the network. In many replication architectures, recovery is treated only superficially, if at all. Recover is addressed in [6,12] and, to a lesser extent, in [7,13,14].

In this paper, we propose a recovery protocol designed to work in tandem with eager update-everywhere protocols, in the framework of any replication middleware. It distinguishes itself from known protocols of the same type by dispensing with the need of maintaining logs and classifying conflicts. Rather, it enables recovering nodes to fully take part in ongoing transactions as soon as the recovery process has been initiated, without waiting for its completion. It makes use of virtual synchrony and takes advantage of ideas proposed in [15] and previous work [6,12,14].

Roughly, the main idea is as follows. Once a node re-joins the network after failure, an alive "recoverer" node is appointed. It informs the joining node about the updates it has missed during its failure. Thus a dynamic database partition (hereafter DB-partition) of missed data items, grouped by missed views, is established, in recovering and recoverer nodes, merely by some standard SQL statements. The recoverer will hold each DB-partition as long as the data transfer of that DB-partition is going on. Previously alive nodes may continue to access data belonging to the DB-partition. Once the DB-partitions are set in the recovering node, it will start processing transactions, which are, however, blocked when trying to access a DB-partition. Once the partitions are set in the recoverer, it continues processing local and remote transactions as before. It will only block for update operations over the DB-partition.

The remainder is structured as follows: in Section 2, the assumed architecture model is introduced. Section 3 contains a formalization of our recovery protocol. Section 4 outlines a correctness proof. Related work is addressed in section 5. Section 6 concludes the paper.

2   Architecture Model

Throughout, we assume a distribution topology of N database nodes communicating by message exchange via a GCS. We assume full replication, i.e., each node contains a copy of the entire database and each transaction is executed on each replica. Users and applications submit transactions to the system. The middleware forwards them to the respectively nearest (local) node for execution. Each transaction consists of a set of SQL statements. The execution of transactions is assumed to be coordinated by some eager update-everywhere replication protocol ensuring 1CS [4,10,16,17].

Group Communication System. A GCS provides communication and membership services, supporting virtual synchrony [11]. We assume a partially synchronous system and a *partial amnesia crash* [18] failure model. The communication service has a reliable multicast. The membership service provides the notion of *view*, i.e., currently connected and alive nodes. Changes in the composition of a view (addition or deletion) are reported to the recovery protocol. We assume a primary component membership [11], where views installed by all nodes are totally ordered (i.e., there are no concurrent views), and for each pair of consecutive views there is at least one process that remains operational in both. We use *strong* virtual synchrony to ensure that messages are delivered in the same view they were multicast and that two sites transiting to a new view have delivered the same set of messages in the previous view [11,19]. Thus, the set of updated data items in an installed view is determined, and can be stored as meta-data for recovery in the database of alive nodes. Hence, whenever there are failed nodes by the time a transaction commits, the identifier of each updated data item is stored. Thus, it is easy to determine the DB-partitions of missed objects whenever a failed node rejoins the network, as both the view at failure time and the view at recovery time is known.

DBMS. We assume a DBMS ensuring ACID transactions and complying with the serializable transaction isolation level [20]. The DBMS is supposed to interface with the middleware via JDBC. An extra metadata table, named MISSED, is needed to store information for recovering nodes after failure. It contains three fields: VIEW_ID, SITES and OIDS. VIEW_ID contains the view identifier by which crashed or not yet recovered nodes can be selected. SITES contains all nodes that are still crashed or have not recovered yet the given view. OIDS contains the set of data items updated in that view. MISSED is maintained by triggers and stored procedures. The stored procedures *recover_me* and *recover_other* block or abort transactions at recovery startup time: the first is invoked in the recovering node as a dummy UPDATE SQL statement on the data to be recovered, while the second is invoked at the recoverer, for rolling back all previous transactions that have attempted an update, after which it performs a SELECT FOR UPDATE SQL statement over the given DB-partition. This prevents local transactions from modifying rows inside the recovery DB-partition. Afterwards, as mentioned before, transactions trying to update data belonging to the DB-partition are blocked whereas read access is permitted. Each time a node crashes, a new entry is added in MISSED. A stored procedure fills the first two fields of this new row. Hence, whenever a transaction commits, it assigns its write set to the third field. To prevent an indefinite growth of this table, garbage is cleaned off at the end of recovery. Once there is no more node left at the recovered view, the corresponding row is dropped. Superfluous multiple recovery of the same data item in different views is avoided by checking whether the item is included in previous views whose nodes are a subset of the current view. Another stored procedure, invoked by the recoverer, determines and sends the metadata missed by recovering nodes. Correspondingly, recovering nodes invoke, for each meta-data row, information transferred to them by the recoverer.

Transaction Execution and Replication Protocol. We assume that a transaction $t = \langle node, view\_id \rangle$ firstly is executed at its master node (it is a *local transaction* at this node, $t.node = i$) and interacts via the replication protocol with the rest of nodes at commit time according to ROWAA, executing remote transactions at them. The $view\_id$ is left for recovery purposes. This recovery protocol can be thought as the recovery part of a generic eager update-everywhere protocols [4,9,16]. Their transaction execution is based on two messages: *remote*, which propagates updates to execute the remote transaction once it has been processed at its master node; and, *commit*, which globally commits transactions.

3   Recovery Protocol Behaviour

Protocol Outline. The DB-partitions are grouped by the node identifier of the *recovering* node and the missed view identifier; this ensures a unique identifier throughout the whole system. DB-partitions are exclusively created at recoverer and recovering nodes by special transactions called *recovery transactions*, that are started at the delivery of the recovery metainformation by a unique *recoverer* node. These transactions behave as normal transactions except that they have the $t.view\_id$ field equals to the DB-partition. Once a DB-partition has been set up by its associated recovery transaction at the *recoverer* node, it sends the missed updates of that DB-partition to the respective *recovering* node. Currently update transactions executing on the *recoverer* node will be rolled back if they conflict with the DB-partition as it is set up in the *recoverer* node. Afterwards, if a transaction executed at the *recoverer* attempts to modify a data item belonging to the DB-partition then it will get blocked; in other words, read-only access is permitted in these DB-partitions at the *recoverer* node. Respectively, the recovery protocol will block the access to a DB-partition for user transactions issued in its associated *recovering* node. Therefore, user transactions at *recovering* nodes will even commit as long as they do not interfere with their own DB-partitions. Besides, local user transactions on *recovering* nodes may start as soon as they reach the *recovering* state. This state is reached at a *recovering* node when all its associated DB-partitions have been set. When the DB-partitions is set at the *recoverer* node, it sends the state of the data items contained in the DB-partition. Once they are sent, the DB-partition is released at the *recoverer* node even though the *recovering* node has not finished its recovery process. As missed updates are applied in the underlying DBMS, the *recovering* node multicasts a message that notifies the recovery of a given view. The process continues until all missed changes are applied in the *recovering* node. During this recovery process a node may also fail. If it is a *recovering* node, then all its associated DB-partitions will be released on the *recoverer* node. In case of a failure of a *recoverer* node, the new oldest alive node will continue with the recovery process.

Protocol Description. Table 1 summarizes the state variables and functions used. We have to consider different actions each time a view change event is fired by the GCS. The protocol is described in Figure 1, it is described in terms of the procedures executed with every message and event of interest. Since they use shared variables, we assume each one of these procedures is executed in one atomic step.

Site Failure. Initially all nodes are up and *alive*. Afterwards, some node (or several with no loss of generality) may fail firing a view change event. The recovery protocol executes of the $leave_i$ action, see Figure 1. All nodes change the state associated to that node to *crashed*; besides, a new entry in the MISSED table is added for this new view identifier containing (as it was mentioned before): the new view identifier and the failed node. User transactions will continue working as usual. However, the recovery protocol will rollback all remote transactions coming from the *crashed* node. Besides, if the *crashed* node was *recovering*, all its associated recovery transactions in the *recoverer* node would be aborted too. If the failed node was the *recoverer*, then the protocol must choose another *alive* node to be the new *recoverer*. This new *recoverer* node will create the DB-partitions pending to be transferred and then it will perform the object transfer to

Table 1. State variables kept by each node and functions with their description

$status$	An array containing the state of all transactions in the system.
$view_{current}$	Set with the nodes in the current group view and the view identifier.
$view_{previous}$	Set with the nodes in the previous group view and the view identifier.
$states$	An array containing the state of all nodes in the system: $\{crashed,$ $pending\_metadata, joining, recovering, recoverer, alive\}$.
$views$	An array containing the view identifier of all nodes when they finally got recovered.
$oids\_missed$	It represents the `OIDS` field of the `MISSED` indexed by `VIEW_ID`.
$nodes\_missed$	It represents the `SITES` field of the `MISSED` indexed by `VIEW_ID`.
$to\_recover$	An array containing the set of recovery transactions for each node.
$min\_oids\_missed(nodes)$	It returns the set of object identifiers missed by $nodes$.
$min\_nodes\_missed(nodes)$	It returns the nodes not yet recovered during the failure of $nodes$.
$oldest\_alive()$	It checks the $states$ and $views$ variable to determine if this node is the oldest one.
$fulfill\_metainfo(states,$ $views, oids, nodes)$	It fulfills the metadata information in a recovering node.
$gen\_rec\_transactions(j)$	It generates the proper set of recovery transactions by inspection of $missed$ and $views$ variable for node j.
$getObjects(t)$	It gets the set of objects associated to this DB-partition, once it is set up.
$setObjects(t, ops)$	It applies the missed updates associated to this DB-partition, once it is set up.

$recovering$ and $joining$ nodes. If there exists any node whose state is $pending\_metadata$ it will start the recovery process for this node.

Site Recovery. The membership monitor will enable the $join_i$ action to notify that a node has rejoined the system (see Figure 1). These new nodes must firstly update their recovery metadata information. Hence, they are in the $pending\_metadata$ state, and may not start executing local transactions until they reach the $recovering$ state, i.e. all DB-partitions are set. The recovery protocol will choose one node as the $recoverer$ by the function $oldest\_alive$, in our case, the oldest one. Once a node is elected, it multicasts its state variables that corresponds to the oldest $crashed$ node that has joint in this new installed view. One can note that there is no object state transfer at this stage. More actions have to be done while dealing with the join of new nodes. Hence, current local transactions of previously alive nodes in the pre_commit or $committable$ states must multicast the $remote$ message, along with their $commit$ message [12]. Otherwise, as these transactions are waiting for the $remote$ message coming from previously alive nodes, all new alive nodes will receive a $commit$ message from a remote transaction they did not know about its existence.

```
leave_i
  nodes ← view_previous \ view_current;
  ∀ t ∈ T:
    // Abort all update transactions from failed nodes //
    if t.node ∈ nodes then
      DB_i.abort(t); status_i[t] ← aborted
    // Abort all (possible) recovery transactions //
    // from failed nodes //
    else if t ∈ {t': t' ∈ to_recover_i[k],
        k ∈ nodes} then
      DB_i.abort(t); status_i[t] ← aborted;
  ∀ k ∈ nodes, states_i[k] ∈ {joining, recovering,
      alive} :
    states_i[k] ← crashed;
    views_i[k] ← view_previous;
  // A failed node was the recoverer //
  if ∃ r ∈ nodes: states_i[r] = recoverer then
    states_i[r] ← crashed;
    views_i[r] ← view_previous;
    states_i[oldest_alive()] ← recoverer;
    if i = oldest_alive() then
      // Transfer missed objects' states to recovering nodes //
      ∀ j ∈ {n ∈ N: states_i[n] ∈ {joining,
          recovering}} :
        ∀ t ∈ generate_rec_transactions(j):
          to_recover_i[j] ←
              to_recover_i[j] ∪ {t};
          DB_i.begin(t);
          DB_i.recover_other(t, oids_mis-
              sed_i[t.view_id]);
          status_i[t] ← blocked;
      // Send recov. metadata to pending_metadata nodes //
      nodes' ← {p ∈ view_current :
          states_i[p].state = pending_metadata};
      sendRMulticast(⟨recovery_start, i, nodes',
          states_i, views_i, min_oids_missed(nodes'),
          min_nodes_missed(nodes')⟩, nodes').

join_i
  nodes ← view_current \ view_previous;
  if i = oldest_alive() then
    sendRMulticast(⟨recovery_start, i, nodes,
        states_i, views_i, min_oids_missed(nodes),
        min_nodes_missed(nodes)⟩, view_current);
  ∀ j ∈ nodes: states_i[j] ← pending_metadata;.


msg_recovery_start_i(⟨recovery_start, recov_id,
    nodes, m_states, m_views, m_oids_missed,
    m_nodes_missed⟩)
  fulfill_metainfo(m_states, m_views, m_missed);
  states_i[recov_id] ← recoverer;
  ∀ j ∈ nodes:
    states_i[j] ← joining;
    if states_i[i] ∈ {joining, recoverer} then
      ∀ t ∈ generate_rec_transactions(j):
        to_recover_i[j] ← to_recover_i[j] ∪ {t};
        DB_i.begin(t);
        if j ≠ i then
          DB_i.recover_other(t, oids_-
              missed_i[t.view_id])
        else
          DB_i.recover_me(t, oids_-
              missed_i[t.view_id]);
        status_i[t] ← blocked.
// Executed only at the recoverer once the //
// DB-partition associated to t is set //
send_missed_i(t)
  sendRUnicast(⟨missed, t, getObjects(t)⟩, t.node);
  to_recover_i[i] ← to_recover_i[i] \ {t};
  DB_i.commit(t); status_i[t] ← committed.

// Executed only at the recovering once the //
// DB-partition associated to t is set //
msg_missed_i(⟨missed, t, objs⟩)
  setObjects(t, objs);
  DB_i.commit(t); status_i[t] ← committed;
  sendRMulticast(⟨view_recovered,
      t.view_id, i⟩).

msg_view_recovered_i(⟨view_recovered,
    view_id, id⟩)
  states_i[id] ← recovering;
  nodes_missed_i[view_id] ←
      nodes_missed_i[view_id] \ {id};
  if (∀ z ∈ {0, V_i.id} : id ∉ nodes_missed_i[z]) then
    states_i[id] ← alive;
    views_i[id] ← view_current;
    if (∀ j ∈ view_current: states_i[j] ∈
        {alive, recoverer}) then
      ∀ j ∈ view_current: states_i[j] ← alive.
```

Fig. 1. Specific actions to be executed by the recovery protocol

The Beginning of the Recovery Process. It starts with the $msg\_recovery\_start$ message. The $pending\_metadadata$ nodes change their state to $joining$. The $joining$ nodes update their metadata recovery information. As soon as the metadata information is updated the recovery protocol will set up the DB-partitions on $joining$ nodes. Let us focus on its own associated recovery transactions inserted in the respective $to\_recover$ fields. Each recovery transaction will submit two operations to the database at the recovering node. The first time, it will invoke the $recover\_me$ database stored procedure to set up DB-partitions (once all of them are established, the $joining$ node will change its state to $recovering$. Hence, user transactions will be able to start working on the $recovering$ node, even though it has not ended its recovery process. The second operation will be the application of missed updates during the object state transfer, as we will see next. Meanwhile, the $recoverer$ node generates the DB-partitions by the invocation of another specific recovery database procedure called *recover_other*. The recovery transaction performs two operations in the *recoverer* node, it sets up the DB-partition and retrieves the missed updates that the recovery protocol transfers to the *recovering*, or still *joining*, node. At this time, the DB-partition will be released (the recovery transaction committed) at the *recoverer* node. The rest of nodes will continue working as usual. If they execute transactions that update data items belonging to a DB-partition, they will be blocked in the *recoverer* and the *recovering* nodes.

Transferring Missed Updates to the Recovering Site. This step of the recovery process is englobed inside the $send\_missed_i(t)$ and its respective $msg\_missed_i(\langle missed, t, objs\rangle)$ actions, since updates are submitted to the DB_i module. The $objs$ field contains the state of objects missed by i during $t.view$. This process will be repeatedly invoked if there are more than one missed view by the *recovering* node, as each execution of this pair of actions only involves a single view missed data transfer. This action will be enabled once its associated transaction has blocked the DB-partition of the *recovering*, or still *joining*, node. This action will multicast a *view_recovered* message to all alive nodes.

Finalization of the Recovery Process. Once all missed updates are successfully applied, the recovery process finishes. In the following we will describe how the recovery process deals with the end of the recovery process of a given node. As we have said during the data transfer, all missed updates are grouped by views where the *recovering* node was *crashed*. Hence, each time it finishes the update, it will notify the rest of nodes about the completion of the view recovery. The execution of the msg_view_re-$covered_i(t, \langle view\_recovered, view\_id, j\rangle)$, with j as the node identifier being recovered and $view\_id$ as the recovered view identifier, is enabled once the message has been delivered by the GCS. This action updates the variable $nodes\_missed_i$ as it removes the *recovering* node from the entry $view\_id$. It also updates the $states_i$ if it is the last recovery DB-partition of the *recovering* node setting it to *alive*. Besides, if there are no more DB-partitions to be recovered by the *recoverer* node it is also set to *alive*.

4   Correctness

We make a basic assumption about the system's behavior: there is always a primary component and at least one node with all its DB-partitions in the *alive* state transits from one view to the next one.

Lemma 1 (Absence of Lost Updates in Executions without View Changes). *If no failures and view changes occur during the recovery procedure, and the recovery procedure is executed to completion, a node $j \in N$ can resume transaction processing in that DB-partition without missing any update.*

Proof (Outline). Let ν_{id} denote the last installed view identifier at the recovering node i before it crashed and the set of recovery DB-partitions as: $\{\mathcal{P}_{\nu_{id}+1}, \mathcal{P}_{\nu_{id}+2}, \ldots \mathcal{P}_{\mathcal{V}_i.id-1}\}$. Let us denote $\{t_{r_{\nu_{id}+1}}, t_{r_{\nu_{id}+2}}, \ldots, t_{r_{\mathcal{V}_i.id-1}}\}$ as the set of recovery transactions associated to each previous DB-partition that must be applied. In the same way, let us denote $t_1, \ldots, t_f$ be the set of generated transactions during the recovery process, assume they are ordered by the time they were firstly committed. Let us denote by t_{rec}, as the last committed transaction before the chosen recoverer switches from the *alive* to the *recoverer* state. The set of concurrent transactions with the recovery process are: $\{t_{rec+1}, \ldots, t_f\}$. Hence, we have split the sequence of transactions into intervals.

Subsequence $\{t_1, \ldots, t_{rec}\}$. The underlying transactional system guarantees transactional atomicity. Thus, upon restart, a node cannot have lost any of these transactions and the effects of uncommitted transactions do not appear in the system, by means of the *recover_other* database stored procedure. These transactions are the ones that have attempted to update a DB-partition. No transaction has been issued by the recovering node whose $states_i[i] \in \{$pending_metadata, joining$\}$ i.e. $\forall t \in \{t_1 \ldots t_{rec}\}: t.node \neq i$. These committed transactions are applied at all alive nodes in the same order since they are total-order delivered. This implies that some objects may be sent twice, firstly as a user transaction, and afterwards, in a recovery message.

Subsequence $\{t_{rec+1} \ldots t_f\}$. All DB-partitions are set. Transactions committed in this interval comprised data belonging to data not contained in DB-partitions or yet recovered. As these transactions are totally ordered by the GCS, the serialization is consistent at all nodes. Thereby, and since no failures occur, the subsequence $\{t_{rec+1} \ldots t_f\}$ is applied to the underlying system in its entirety at all alive nodes.

Subsequence $\{t_{r_{\nu_{id+1}}}, \ldots, t_{r_{\nu_i.id-1}}\}$. Each one of these transactions encloses a set of user transactions issued in each missed view. These transactions will be committed as soon as they are received (freeing its associated DB-partition). Again, as there are no failures all mised updates will be applied at i and it will switch to the *alive* state.

Subsequence $\{t_{f+1}, \ldots\}$. These transactions correspond to all alive nodes in the *alive* state and will be governed by TORPE, which guarantees the application of updates serially at all alive nodes. Since no transaction can be lost in any subsequence, the theorem is proved. ∎

Lemma 2 (Absence of Lost Updates after a View Change). *A node* $i \in N$ *with* $states_i[i] \in \{pending\_metadata, joining, recovering\}$ *in view* $\mathcal{V}_i$ *that transits to view* $\mathcal{V}_{i+1}$ *resumes the recovery process without missing any update.*

Proof. During the processing of the view change under consideration, if the recoverer has crashed (either in *alive* or *recoverer* state), a new one is elected. Otherwise, the recoverer from the previous view continues as recoverer. In either case, the recoverer in view $\mathcal{V}_{i+1}$ will start the recovery thread, which will multicast the missed updates from the last installed view of the recovering node i, referred as ν_i.

Case $(alive, pending\_metadata)$. In this case, none has received the recovery metadata message, so a new node is elected as the recoverer and sends the *recovery_start* message to the recovering node which restarts the recovery process. By uniform delivery of messages, it ill not be the case that there are a *recoverer* and the recovering node is still in the *pending_metadata* state (see *msg_recovery_start* action in Figure 1).

Cases $(recoverer, joining/recovering)$. The former recoverer has sent the DB-partitions to be set, but it failed during the data transfer of missed updates. At worst, for all DB-partitions to be sent (see *msg_view_recovered* action in Figure 1, that notifies the recovery of a given view). This may imply that some missed views have been transferred by the former *recoverer* node but its application has not finished at the *recovering* node and hence they are multicast twice. However, this second message will be discarded (see *msg_view_recovered* action in Figure 1). Hence, the recovery process will continue by the new recoverer, as soon as its DB-partitions are set, with the data transfer of left missed updates. As it has been seen, recovery is resumed without missing any update thereby proving the Lemma.   ∎

It is important to note that due to the non-total-ordering nature of the recovery transaction generation and the application of missed updates, the *recovering* node will not read 1CS values, during the recovery process. This is the price to pay to maintain a higher degree of concurrency and availability. However, once all updates are applied our recovery protocol guarantees that it is 1CS.

Theorem 1 (1-Copy-Serializable Recovery). *Upon successful completion of the recovery procedure, a recovering node reflects a state compatible with the actual 1CS execution that took place.*

Proof. According to Lemmas 1 and 2, a recovering node that resumes normal processing at transaction t_{f+1}, reflects the state of all committed transactions. The recovering node applies transactions in the delivery order. The recoverer sends committed transactions (they were totally ordered by the 1CS replication protocol) grouped by views. Moreover, this order is the same as they were originally applied at the recoverer in the given view. Moreover, metadata is total order consistent by the total order delivery of installed views. Hence, the serialization order at the recovering node cannot contradict the serialization order at the recoverer node. Since we are assuming the recoverer node is correct, the state resulting after the recovery procedure is completed at the recovering node is necessarily 1CS.   ∎

5   Related Work

There are several alternatives for recovering database replicas. In [14], some on-line reconfiguration solutions are proposed. The first of them accomplishes data transfer within the GCS, during the view change [21]. The drawback is that the GCS is unaware of changes. Thus, it transfers the whole database, during which the current state remains frozen, which impedes high availability. The second solution in [14] therefore proposes an incremental data transfer by the DBMS, using standard techniques. By assigning the recovery tasks to one node, say $\mathcal{R}$, the rest of all alive nodes may remain on-line. During data transfer, $\mathcal{R}$ and the recovering nodes remain off-line, while transactions are queued until recovery terminates. As opposed to that, our recovery proposal permits to start running transactions at *all* nodes as soon as the recovery partition is set.

The three recovery protocols proposed in [12], based on the replication protocols in [4], also use virtual synchrony. The first, *single broadcast recovery*, makes use of *loggers*, i.e., nodes that store logs about view changes, transaction commits and update messages. Upon installment of a new view, update message delivery is delayed until the new node has exchanged messages with a logger and the latter has signalled recovery termination. In the second, called *log update*, loggers must check if there are on-going transactions at non-failed nodes during a view change since the commit message is contained in the new view. Hence, upon recovery, logged data about all missed remote messages must be transferred. This drawback is overcome by the third approach, called *augmented broadcast*. Upon installment of a new view, it shifts additional processing to the transaction master nodes, by including the write set ws of each on-going transaction t that broadcast ws in an earlier view in the commit message of t. As opposed to that, we neither delay update messages as in *single broadcast recovery*, nor do we use logs to maintain the information to be transferred to the recovering node as in *log update*, nor do we need to modify the recovery protocol as in *single broadcast recovery*.

In the recovery protocol of [19], the database is partitioned such that each node is the owner of one or several partitions. A partition owner $\mathcal{O}$ appoints a recoverer node to transfer the log of missed updates to a recovering node $\mathcal{R}$. Transactions are not blocked during recovery. $\mathcal{R}$ start executing transactions as soon as forwarded messages have been applied. In a sense, this is better than in our approach since there is no inactivity phase in any node. However, transactions may only be executed on $\mathcal{O}$. For longer failure periods, this entails large, time-consuming log transfers, while we only need to transfers the most up-to-date version of modified data.

6   Conclusion

We have proposed a new solution for speeding up recovery of failed nodes in distributed databases using eager update everywhere replication. Our solution takes advantage of strong view synchrony and a reliable multicast provided by a GCS. The database schema is modified by adding a table containing, for each view: the crashed nodes and the set of updated data items. The GCS also supports node recovery, by grouping missed updates by the views in which they occurred. This grouping forms the basic data unit for our replication protocol (DB-partition). Once a node recovers from failure, a set of partitions is established at all alive nodes (as many as views missed by the recovering node). Thus, alive nodes that are neither recoverer nor recovering nodes may continue to access data of these partitions as before. The recovering node cannot access these data. It may however start to accept user transactions as soon as the DB-partitions are set up on it. This is the major achievement of our recovery protocol, since it significantly enhances the availability of recovering replicas. In theory, such capabilities have been required from recovery protocol standards since a long time, but up to now, no solution is known which would be comparable to our protocol. Future work will adapt the presented solutions to the incorporation of nodes joining ad-hoc networks.

References

1. Gray, J., Helland, P., O'Neil, P.E., Shasha, D.: The dangers of replication and a solution. In: SIGMOD Conference. (1996) 173–182
2. Wiesmann, M., Pedone, F., Schiper, A., Kemme, B., Alonso, G.: Understanding replication in databases and distributed systems. In: ICDCS. (2000) 464–474
3. Muñoz-Escoí, F.D., Irún-Briz, L., Decker, H.: Database replication protocols. In: Encyclopedia of Database Technologies and Applications. (2005) 153–157
4. Kemme, B., Alonso, G.: A new approach to developing and implementing eager database replication protocols. ACM Trans. Database Syst. **25**(3) (2000) 333–379

5. Kemme, B., Pedone, F., Alonso, G., Schiper, A., Wiesmann, M.: Using optimistic atomic broadcast in transaction processing systems. IEEE TKDE **15**(4) (2003) 1018–1032
6. Patiño-Martínez, M., Jiménez-Peris, R., Kemme, B., Alonso, G.: MIDDLE-R: Consistent database replication at the middleware level. ACM TOCS **23**(4) (2005) 375–423
7. Wu, S., Kemme, B.: Postgres-R(SI): Combining replica control with concurrency control based on snapshot isolation. In: ICDE, IEEE-CS (2005) 422–433
8. Lin, Y., Kemme, B., Patiño-Martínez, M., Jiménez-Peris, R.: Middleware based data replication providing snapshot isolation. In: SIGMOD Conference. (2005)
9. Armendáriz, J.E., Juárez, J.R., Garitagoitia, J.R., González de Mendívil, J.R., Muñoz-Escoí, F.D.: Implementing database replication protocols based on O2PL in a middleware architecture. In: DBA'06. (2006) 176–181
10. Holliday, J., Steinke, R.C., Agrawal, D., Abbadi, A.E.: Epidemic algorithms for replicated databases. IEEE Trans. Knowl. Data Eng. **15**(5) (2003) 1218–1238
11. Chockler, G., Keidar, I., Vitenberg, R.: Group communication specifications: a comprehensive study. ACM Comput. Surv. **33**(4) (2001) 427–469
12. Holliday, J.: Replicated database recovery using multicast communication. In: NCA, IEEE-CS (2001) 104–107
13. Elnikety, S., Pedone, F., Zwaenopoel, W.: Database replication using generalized snapshot isolation. In: SRDS, IEEE-CS (2005)
14. Kemme, B., Bartoli, A., Babaoglu, Ö.: Online reconfiguration in replicated databases based on group communication. In: DSN, IEEE-CS (2001) 117–130
15. Armendáriz-Iñigo, J.E., González de Mendívil, J.R., Muñoz-Escoí, F.D.: A lock based algorithm for concurrency control and recovery in a middleware replication software architecture. In: HICSS, IEEE Computer Society (2005)
16. Armendáriz, J.E., Garitagoitia, J.R., González de Mendívil, J.R., Muñoz-Escoí, F.D.: Design of a MidO2PL database replication protocol in the MADIS middleware architecture. In: AINA - Vol. 2, IEEE-CS (2006) 861–865
17. Bernstein, P.A., Hadzilacos, V., Goodman, N.: Concurrency Control and Recovery in Database Systems. Addison Wesley (1987)
18. Cristian, F.: Understanding fault-tolerant distributed systems. Commun. ACM **34**(2) (1991) 56–78
19. Jiménez-Peris, R., Patiño-Martínez, M., Alonso, G.: Non-intrusive, parallel recovery of replicated data. In: SRDS, IEEE-CS (2002) 150–159
20. Berenson, H., Bernstein, P.A., Gray, J., Melton, J., O'Neil, E.J., O'Neil, P.E.: A critique of ANSI SQL isolation levels. In: SIGMOD Conference, ACM Press (1995) 1–10
21. Birman, K., Cooper, R., Joseph, T., Marzullo, K., Makpangou, M., Kane, K., Schmuck, F., Wood, M.: The ISIS - system manual, Version 2.1. Technical report, Dept. of Computer Science, Cornell University (1993)

Migrating a Hierarchical Legacy Database Application onto an XML-Based Service-Oriented Web Platform

Özgür Yürekten[1,2], Kıvanç Dinçer[2], Berk Akar[2], Müberra Sungur[2],
and Elif Kurtaran Özbudak[2]

[1] Dept. of Computer Engineering, Gazi University, Maltepe, Ankara, Turkey
[2] TUBITAK-UEKAE/G222 Unit, Atatürk Blv. No:211/20, Kavaklıdere, Ankara, Turkey
{ozgur.yurekten, kivanc.dincer, berk.akar,
muberra.sungur, elif.kurtaran}@tubitak.gov.tr

Abstract. We present a case study where a mission-critical legacy hierarchical database, EWIRDB (Electronic Warfare Integrated Reprogramming Database), and its application software are migrated onto a service-oriented web architecture that is based on an XML-based database. EWIRDB stores its data in an extensible tree structure and serves many purposes of supporting EW systems reprogramming, research, development, test, and evaluation; modeling, and simulation, acquisition; and training. We present the historical stages of this migration that helped us to understand the issues and converge to the most appropriate solution eventually. We conclude that recently emerging web service technologies together with native XML database support meet the unique migration requirements of the EWIRDB and its legacy database application. We believe that the proposed solution addresses an almost 20-year old problem in the EW domain problem and forms an appropriate base for porting some other applications with similar requirements in other domains.

1   Introduction

A legacy information system is any information system that significantly resists modification and evaluation to meet new and constantly changing business requirements [14]. Replacement of a legacy information system requires two steps: just the introduction of the new software is not enough; the migration of the data from the old system to the new one is also needed [13]. Legacy database systems are typically mission-critical and rely on large databases that are modeled as networked or hierarchical, or sometimes just as plain flat files [15].

In this paper, we present a case study about migrating a legacy database system onto a modern architecture by exploiting some of the latest web technologies. The EWIRDB (Electronic Warfare Integrated Reprogramming Database) was developed initially by the US Air Force in the 1970's as the primary Department of Defense (DoD) approved source for technical parametric and performance data on non-communications emitters and associated systems. Originally, the EWIRDB was conceived to support software reprogramming of EW combat systems such as radar warning receivers, combat identification systems, electronic jammers, anti-radiation

A. Levi et al. (Eds.): ISCIS 2006, LNCS 4263, pp. 645 – 654, 2006.

missiles and various other target sensing systems that serve to enhance wartime survivability and effectiveness [12]. But today, the EWIRDB not only supports reprogramming, but also serves the additional purposes of supporting EW systems research, development, test, and evaluation; modeling, and simulation, acquisition; and training all over the world.

The EWIRDB is described in terms of a data-implementation model without a legitimate semantic data model. In its original implementation, its tree-structured data was stored in a hierarchical database and organized as text files having thousands of nodes. The hierarchical tree is inherently arbitrary, extensible and reliant in the use of reference codes to link related pieces of data throughout the hierarchy. This data model of the EWIRDB is quite problematic for migration. The hierarchical database has to be migrated without losing the extensibility and flexibility of the tree structure. In addition, several extensions besides the existent capabilities of the original database application software are required. For example, the non-intuitive hierarchical organization and coding scheme prevent the user from gaining meaningful view of an emitter's performance parameters in the original application [9]. Some remedies in the GUI are required in this direction. The named legacy database application did not have the capabilities to support transaction logic, security, and concurrent access. These capabilities are required to be supported by the application after migration.

We here discuss the related issues and present the migration of the legacy database and its standard application software onto an object-oriented, a relational, a native XML database and eventually using web services to support other secondary applications that use the database.

The rest of the paper is organized as follows; In Section 2 we describe the related work, in Section 3 we present the three phases of the migration and finally we summarize our contributions. The paper presented here is based on publicly open literature and resources.

2 Related Work

Some et al.[1] present a hierarchical XML database developed to assist in technology Return On Investment (ROI) analysis and the technology portfolio optimization. They report their findings on the limitations of relational databases in defining hierarchical data. The XML database fixes the depth of the tree structure so it is not sufficiently flexible for adding new nodes into various levels as required in our case.

Sokic et al. [4] propose a native XML database solution for a web content management system. It is pointed out that hierarchical data transformation steps were reduced using an XML database. The proposed solution is constrained on the implemented database schema. It is shown that it is easier and more efficient to maintain the data consistency in an XML database than it is in a file system. The graphical user interface uses the native XML database only for showing the data with eXtensible Stylesheet Language (XSLT).

Syllabus XML database system keeps all the data related to educational content and presents a web service via http that is used for a curriculum analyzing system [2].

In Philippi et al.'s work [3], an XML database is proposed on ontology-based semantic integration of life science databases. Their work points out that the XML database is capable of storing all kinds of complex biological data easily.

There are also some specific studies [9, 10, 11 and 12] in the literature directly on the EWIRDB targeted to migrate and convert the data stored in, into the relational, networked and object-oriented databases. These studies are based on conversion of tree structures to the database models. They show that migrating an extendible tree structure stored in a hierarchical database to relational/object-oriented models is not completely feasible. Lee et al.[10] claimed that only 20% of the EWIRDB tree structure could be modeled using any of these database schemes.

3   Migration Phases

While the hierarchical database models were being used extensively in 1980s when the above mentioned database was developed, surpassing hardware limitations and emerging new technologies have promised to model the database in other representations. Hierarchical data in general can be managed as text files, by existing Database Management Systems (DBMS), such as relational or object-oriented, or by so-called native XML databases [7]. However, based on some previous studies [9 and 10], it seemed problematic to migrate the EWIRDB structure to the first two models. Coyne in his thesis [9] concludes that managing so many created database objects corresponding to data nodes in the hierarchical tree structure, keeping a flexible model and presenting data with a user-friendly GUI were difficult. Based on this information and this experience, we ignored this model in our study.

A tree structure that has thousands of nodes could be also modeled as relational by breaking down the tree structure into many normalized smaller tables related by primary key–foreign key relationships. Normalizing inherently hierarchical data lead to complex database designs that are time-consuming and inefficient to implement and operate [1]. Such a relational model has almost the same problems with the object-oriented database model therefore this alternative was eliminated too.

Below, we present our three migration trials that we see more promising in historical order.

3.1   Phase 1: Migration to Dynamic Relational Database Models

The tree structure that has thousands of nodes could be modeled as relational based on a dynamic table structure. Rather than the classical approach described above, it seemed more appropriate to proceed in this direction.

Two relational tables, called STRUCT (Table 1) and DATA (Table 2) tables, are designed to provide a dynamic and extensible tree structure and store the hierarchical data. Each node of the tree is stored as a record in the STRUCT and a column is used to refer to its parent. Data nodes are stored in the DATA table with a foreign-key that has reference to the corresponding STRUCT table. Data types of the nodes are represented as string values. The conversion of a node's value to its real data type is made using the UNIT column of the STRUCT table.

Table 1. STRUCT Table

Column Name	Description
ENTITY_ID	Unique id for tree node .
ENTITY_NAME	Name of tree node.
UNIT	Unit of data stored in the tree node. Data types of nodes defined automatically and pre-defined units were used in the implementation.
LOGGING_INSTRUCTION	Business rules for entering or updating data.
PARENT	Parent node of this node.
DESCRIPTION	Description for tree node.

Table 2. DATA Table

Column Name	Description
EMITTER_ID	Unique id for each emitter.
ENTITY_ID	Foreign-key to STRUCT table.
VALUE	Value stored in emitter node - stored as a string. Using UNIT column of STRUCT, application level data type conversion is done.

The application that uses the dynamic relational database is based on a two-tier (Client and Server Tiers) architecture and the Java programming language is selected for development. Fig. 1 shows the component model of this software architecture. Oracle 9i relational database is used for the server tier whereas the client tier is developed as a desktop application. A Sample GUI is shown in Fig. 2.

Required data is accessed and updated via the SQL Engine module. Data stored in the relational database is converted to the tree model and vice versa using the Hierarchical/Relational Converter module. While doing this conversion, the Validation module checks the consistency of data and informs the user in case of inconsistencies. The GUI module provides view, update, delete, query, export and import capabilities on both the tree structure and the actual data.

Based on the development of dynamic relational database model, we have conceived the following points and extended the requirements accordingly:

- The implementation of data query mechanisms and the presentation of the values are difficult since all data values are stored as string data types.
- Since the tree structure and the data are stored in different tables, the relations between these tables are obtained by primary-key and foreign-key relationships. As a business rule, a value for the child can be entered only if a parent node has an entered value. Before filling a parent node's values, child fields can be defined in the dynamic relational model. There must be additional controls to handle this situation.

- Data in the dynamic relational model must be converted to tree model before it is used, to understand its structure. The stored data is not readable directly by the users.
- It must provide service to data analysis tools as well as to multiple users. The current type of architecture cannot easily support this desired feature.

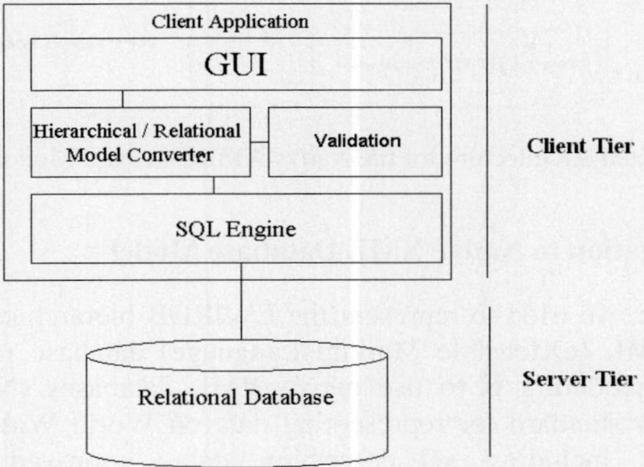

Fig. 1. Selected architecture for Dynamic Relational Database Model (Phase 1)

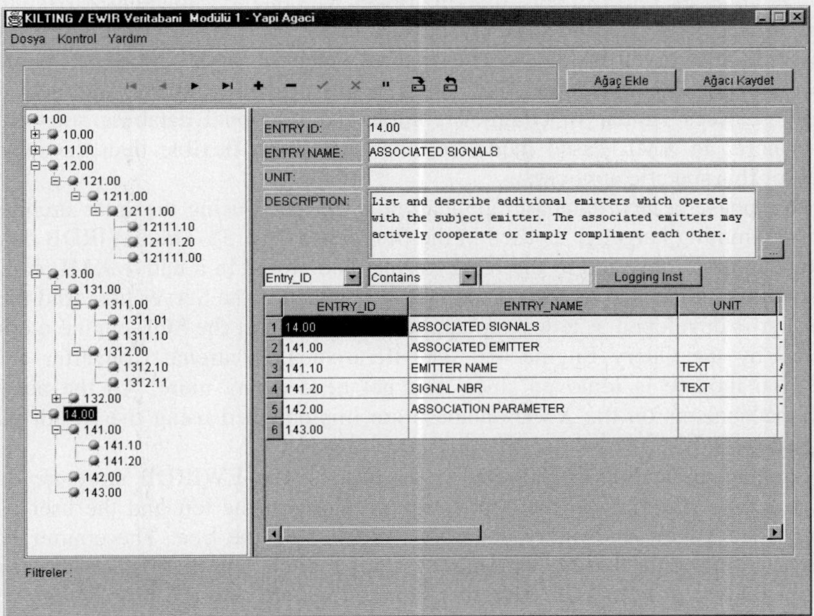

Fig. 2. A Snapshot of the Tree Structure Update GUI

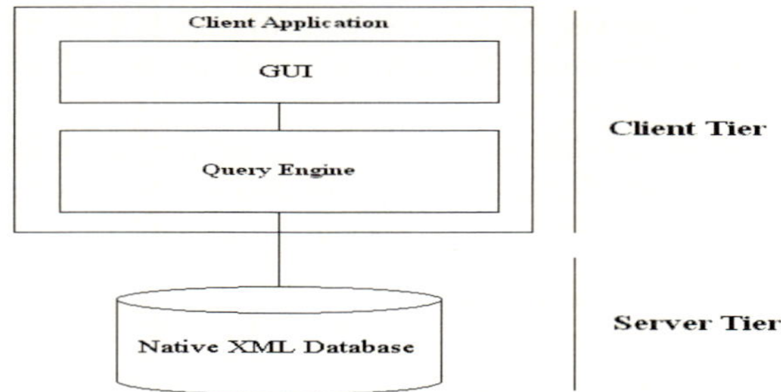

Fig. 3. Selected Architecture for the Native XML Database Model (Phase 2)

3.2   Phase 2: Migration to Native XML Database Model

In the second phase, we tried to represent the EWIRDB hierarchical database model with the native XML (eXtensible Markup Language) database model. The recent trend of database modeling is to use native XML databases (NXD). XML has emerged as a major standard for representing data on World Wide Web. XML has numerous benefits including self-describing data, improved readability and standardization [6]. There is much current interest in publishing and viewing databases as XML documents [8]. Many XML storage models have been proposed to manage XML data [7].

Hierarchical data, like in our problem domain, can be represented as XML data and stored in an XML database. A small portion of XML code that describes this representation is given in Fig. 4. This type of database model allows developers to represent hierarchical data in XML form while providing query, transaction and security services similar to common commercial relational database software [1]. Furthermore, an XML based model is inherently more flexible than the relational model for this specific application.

In this phase, a new database application is designed using the same architecture and programming language as used in the first phase (Fig. 3). The EWIRDB database structure is first converted to the XML format and stored in a native XML database, namely the Xindice Native XML Database [17] which is the Server tier. And the new Client tier is developed as a desktop application. Note that the SQL engine module is replaced by the Query Engine and the Hierarchical/Relational Converter and the Validation module is removed since it is not needed any more. All the necessary query mechanisms on the XML database are implemented using the XPath [18] as proposed by W3C.

A sample application GUI is shown in Fig. 5. The EWIRDB structure data is presented in a tree view in the application window on the left and the user can do update, create, view and query operations directly on the tree. The emitter data is retrieved from the database using Query Engine module and the results are shown in the GUI. Different colors are effectively used for notifying the user of empty data nodes or different data types.

```xml
<?xml version="1.0"?>
<DATA>
    <NAME>
        A0000
    </NAME>
    <PARAMETERS>
        <FOLDER title=" 1 A0000" code="1" >
            <ID>000000000001.00</ID>
            <NAME>A0000</NAME>
            <TYPE></TYPE>
            <MIN></MIN>
            <MAX></MAX>
        <FOLDER title=" 10 GENERAL INFORMATION" code="1" >
            <ID>000000000010.00</ID>
            <NAME>GENERAL INFORMATION</NAME>
            <TYPE></TYPE>
            <MIN></MIN>
            <MAX></MAX>
            <LEAF title=" 10.04 RELATED ELINT NOTATION" code="2"  >
                <ID>000000000010.04</ID>
                <NAME>RELATED ELINT NOTATION</NAME>
                <TYPE>TEXT</TYPE>
                <MIN>A1</MIN>
                <MAX></MAX>
            </LEAF>
```

Fig. 4. XML Representation of a Sample Node (details omitted)

After the development of this application, we have obtained the following results:

- Presentation of the data in a native XML database is much easier than the one in a relational database.
- Desktop applications are not suitable for multi-user applications since the data is retrieved and manipulated by the client directly.
- The developed application is superior to the previously implemented ones since the users can define their own custom hierarchical database structure and update previously defined database structure when required.
- With this alternative, no efficient interface to the database is yet available for analysis tools. We must define an interface that supports loose coupling between the database and the client applications.

3.3 Phase 3: Migration to Native XML Database Model with Web Services

The new major trend for software architecture is the service-oriented one, using web services technology: a collection of XML-based standards that provide a means for passing information between applications using XML documents [16]. The final and most complete implementation for the EWIRDB is designed by combining the web services with an XML-based database used in Phase 2. Not only the users but also different analysis tools require access to the EWIRDB. Therefore, the Query Engine is converted to a web service that allows any client that wants to access the database communicate with this service via internet/intranet using WSDL [21].

The final application is based on a three-tier architecture and implemented using Java (Fig. 6). The server tier contains the eXist [19] native XML database. The presentation tier was developed with JSF [22] and Servlets [23]. Web browser is used as a thin client tier. A very simple snapshot is shown in Fig. 7.

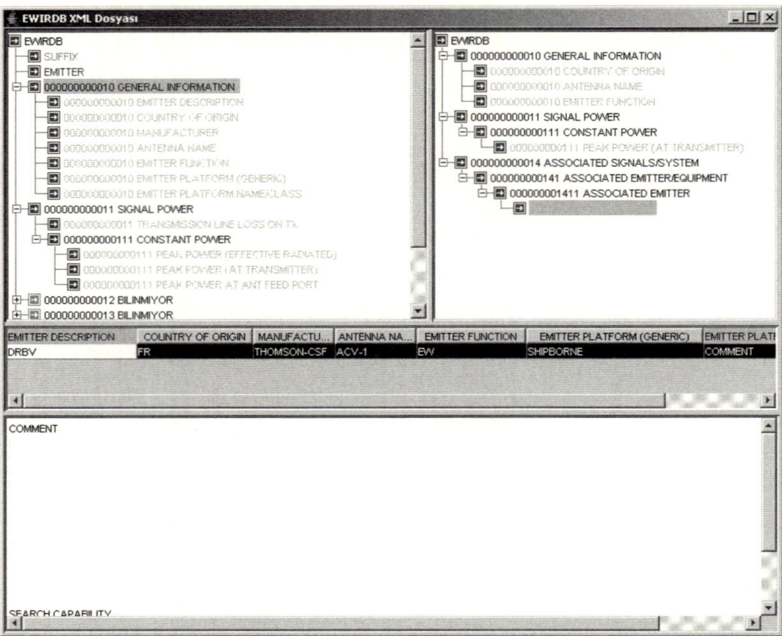

Fig. 5. A Snapshot of the Hierarchical Database Update GUI (Phase 2) (details omitted)

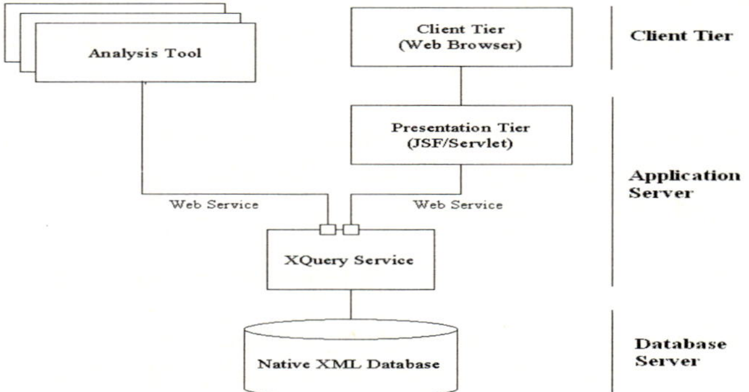

Fig. 6. Selected Architecture for Native XML Database with Web Services (Phase 3)

We have reached the following results after this phase:

- All second phase features are readily supported and also new web service, XQuery [20] and web client features are added in this case.
- A loosely coupled and platform-/language-independent application interface is defined.
- The application has a user-friendly, intuitive and obvious web-based graphical user interface; database can be accessed using a web browser via internet/intranet.

- Architecturally, all web browsers and applications which support web services and placed on the same network become a client of the database. Therefore, analysis tools and other clients can easily access and modify the database.
- Components, which are required for the domain, are developed using JSF, and also supports custom component development.

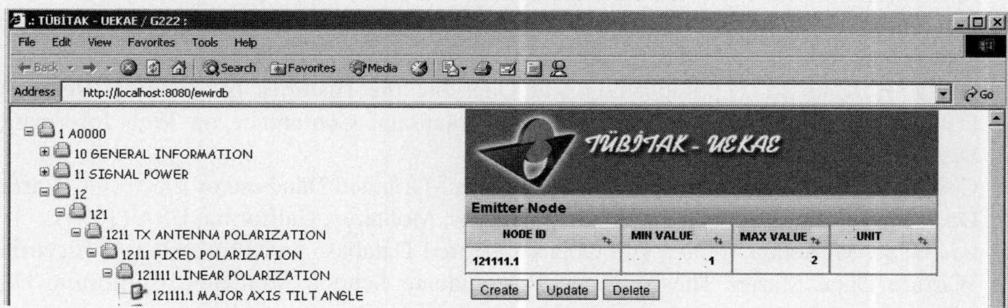

Fig. 7. A Snapshot of the Web-Based GUI (Phase 3)

4 Conclusion

We present the three stages of the EWIRDB migration trials that helped us to understand the important issues and eventually to converge to the most appropriate solution. . Based on the experiences of previous researchers and our own trials summarized here, we conclude that the proposed solution, detailed in phase 3, is more preferable and advantageous than other alternative models on relational, dynamic relational and object-oriented databases. In our solution, we keep the EWIRDB data on a native XML database and provide database query web services for external client applications. This satisfies the unique migration requirements of the EWIRDB, its standard database application, and other client applications that use the database. We believe that this proposes a simple and feasible solution for an almost 20-year old problem in the EW domain.

Acknowledgements. We would like to thank to Asst.Prof. Hasan Şakir Bilge, the thesis advisor of Ö. Yürekten, for his contribution to the performance of Phase 3.

References

1. Some, R.R., A. Czikmantory, A., Neff, J., Marshall, M.: XML Hierarchical Database for Missions and Technologies. IEEE Aerospace Conference Proceedings (2004)
2. Ida, M., Nozawa, T., Yoshikane, F., Miyazaki, K., Kita, H.: Syllabus Database and Web Service on Higher Education. 7th International Conference on Advanced Communication Technology (ICACT 2005), Seoul, Korea (2005)
3. Philippi, S., Köhler, J.: Using XML Technology for the Ontology-Based Semantic Integration of Life Science Databases. IEEE Transactions on Information Technology in Biomedicine, Vol. 8, No. 2 (2004)

4. Sokic, M., Matic, V., Bazent, A.: Web Content Management System Based on XML Database. Internationales Congress Centrum (ICC), Berlin, Germany (2001)
5. Molitoris, J. J.: Use Of COTS XML and Web Technology for Current and Future C2 Systems. XML Conference & Exposition, Philadelphia, USA (2003)
6. Lu, H., Yu, J. X., Wang, G., Zheng, S., Jiang, H., Yu, G., Zhou, A.: What Makes the Differences: Benchmarking XML Database Implementations. Proc.of the 19th International Conference on Data Engineering (ICDE'03). IEEE (2003)
7. Lawrence, R.: The Space Efficiency of XML. Information and Software Technology 46 (2004) 753-759
8. Wang, F., Zaniolo, C.: Publishing and Querying the Histories of Archived Relational Databases in XML. Proc.of the Fourth International Conference on Web Information Systems Engineering (WISE'03). IEEE (2003)
9. Coyne, K. M.: Design and Analysis of an Object-Oriented Database of Electronic Warfare Data. Master Thesis, Naval Postgraduate School, Monterey, California, USA (1996)
10. Lee, J. J., McKenna, T. D.: The Object-Oriented Database and Processing of Electronic Warfare Data. Master Thesis, Naval Postgraduate School, Monterey, California, USA (1996)
11. Scrivener, D. N., Renell, R. D.: Reactivation of Relational Interface in M2DBMS and Implementation of EWIR Database. Master Thesis, Naval Postgraduate School, Monterey, California, USA (1996)
12. Werre, T. J., Diehl, B. A.: The Activation and Testing the Network CODASYL-DML Interface of the M2DBMS Using the EWIR Database. Master Thesis, Naval Postgraduate School, Monterey, California, USA (1996)
13. Keller, A., Turner, P.: Migrating to Object Data Management. OOPSLA Workshop on Legacy Systems and Object Technology, Austin, Texas (1995)
14. Brodie, M. L., Stonebraker, M.: Migrating Legacy Systems: Gateways, Interfaces and the Incremental Approach. Morgan Kaufman Publishers (1995)
15. Van Deursen, A.: Understanding Legacy Architectures. Landelijk Architectuur Congres, Zeist (2001)
16. Apshankar, K., Waterhouse, M., Zhang, L. J., O'Riordan, D., Sadhwani, D., Siddiqui, B., Thelin, J., Hanson, J. J., Mittal, K., Irani, R., Myerson, J. M., Samtani, G., Clark, M., Hankinson, W., Wiggers, C., Samtani, G., O'Riordan, D., Irani, R., Myerson, J. M.: Web Services Business Strategies and Architectures. Expert Press (2002)
17. Apache Xindice. http://xml.apache.org/xindice
18. W3C XML Path Langiage (Xpath). http://www.w3.org/TR/xpath
19. W3C Xquery 1.0: An XML Query Language. http://www.w3.org/TR/xquery
20. eXist Open Source Native XML Database. http://exist.sourceforge.net
21. W3C Web Services Description Language (WSDL) 1.1. http://www.w3.org/TR/wsdl
22. Sun Developer Network, Java Platform Enterprise Edition, Java Server Faces Technology. http://java.sun.com/javaee/javaserverfaces
23. Sun Developer Network, J2EE Java Servlet Technology. http://java.sun.com/products/servlet

Power-Aware Processors for Wireless Sensor Networks

Gürhan Küçük and Can Başaran

Department of Computer Engineering,
Yeditepe University, 34755 Istanbul, Turkey
{gkucuk, cbasaran}@cse.yeditepe.edu.tr

Abstract. Today, wireless sensor networks (WSNs) enable us to run a new range of applications from habitat monitoring, to military and medical applications. A typical WSN node is composed of several sensors, a radio communication interface, a microprocessor, and a limited power supply. In many WSN applications, such as forest fire monitoring or intruder detection, user intervention and battery replenishment is not possible. Since the battery lifetime is directly related to the amount of processing and communication involved in these nodes, optimal resource usage becomes a major issue. A typical WSN application may sense and process very close or constant data values for long durations, when the environmental conditions are stable. This is a common behavior that can be exploited to reduce the power consumption of WSN nodes. This study combines two orthogonal techniques to reduce the energy dissipation of the processor component of the sensor nodes. First, we briefly discuss silent-store filtering *MoteCache*. Second, we utilize Content-Aware Data MAnagement (CADMA) on top of MoteCache architecture to achieve further energy savings and performance improvements. The complexity increase introduced by CADMA is also compensated by further complexity reduction in MoteCache. Our optimal configuration reduces the total node energy, and hence increases the node lifetime, by 19.4% on the average across a wide variety of simulated sensor benchmarks. Our complexity-aware configuration with a minimum MoteCache size achieves not only energy savings up to 16.2% but also performance improvements up to 4.3%, on the average.

1 Introduction

Recent advances in process technologies and the shrinking sizes of radio communication devices and sensors allowed researchers to combine three operations (i.e. sensing, communication and computation) into tiny devices called wireless sensor nodes. Once these devices are scattered through the environment, they can easily construct data-oriented networks known as wireless sensor networks (WSNs). Today, there is a vast number of application scenarios involving WSNs in business, military, medical and science domains.

The lifetime, scalability, response time and effective sampling frequency are among the most critical parameters of WSNs, and they are closely related to one of the most difficult resource constraint to meet: the power consumption. The WSN

A. Levi et al. (Eds.): ISCIS 2006, LNCS 4263, pp. 655–664, 2006.

nodes are designed to be battery-operated, since they may be utilized in any kind of environment including thick forestry, volcanic mountains and oceanbeds. Consequently, everything must be designed to be power-aware in these networks.

The introduction of small-scale operating systems, such as TinyOS [1], ambientRT [2], and computation-/communication-intensive applications significantly increases the energy consumption of the processor component of WSN nodes. In [3], the researchers show that the processor itself dissipates 35% of the total energy budget of the MICA2 platform while running *Surge*, a TinyOS monitoring application. In [4], the authors claim similar energy values when running a TinyDB query reporting light and accelerometer readings once every minute. In [5], the researchers find that the energy consumption of the processor/memory component for raw data compression is higher than the energy consumption of raw data transmission. Similarly, today most of the WSN applications avoid extensive computations and choose to transfer raw data to server machines to increase the lifetime of the sensor nodes. On the contrary, our proposed design encourages the WSN application developers to design less centralized applications by distributing the computation work and reducing the network traffic among the nodes.

After observations of the results from our departmental testbed and various simulations, we found two important characteristics of WSN data:

1) **Temporal and value locality:** Sensor network applications have periodic behavior. Especially, monitoring applications, such as *Surge*, may sense and work on constant data and constant memory locations for long durations. We showed that we considerably reduce the energy dissipation of the WSN processors by caching commonly used data in a small number of latches (*MoteCache*) [6]. Then, we also showed that most of the store instructions in WSN applications are silent (these instructions write values that exactly match the values that are already stored at the memory address that is being written), and proposed to filter them by extending the MoteCache architecture.

2) **Common data values:** Further, we found that there are some common data values flowing through the datapath. In this study, we propose a technique called Content-Aware Data MAnagement (CADMA) that exploits this behavior and boosts our energy savings by reducing the read/write energy not only in SRAM but also in register file. When combined with MoteCache, we show that we can even increase the performance of the processor as much as 14%.

In this study, we mainly focus on MICA2 platform [7] which includes an AVR-RISC processor, ATmega128L, with Harvard architecture (i.e., two main memory spaces, 4Kx8 bytes of SRAM data memory and 64Kx16 bytes of flash program memory space [8]). Nevertheless, our techniques are platform-independent and can be easily applied to other sensor platforms such as TelosB, moteiv and EYES sensor nodes. Moreover, these platforms utilize 16-bit microprocessors (compared to 8-bit microprocessor of the MICA2 platform). Thus, we strongly believe that our techniques will achieve much better energy savings in these new platforms.

We begin by presenting a brief summary of MoteCache design in Section 2 followed by CADMA design in Section 3. The simulation methodology is given in

Section 4, and our results are presented in Section 5. Finally, we discuss the related work in Section 6, and conclude our study in Section 7.

2   MoteCache

We now summarize the design of MoteCache (MC) which is a small SRAM buffer structure that exploits temporal locality of data in WSN applications [6]. In MC, each row consists of data buffers and an associative content-addressable memory (CAM) for holding the tags corresponding to the contents of these buffers. The idea is to cache data values of the N most recently accessed addresses in a N-byte MC [9, 10]. A read access in the MC structure proceeds as follows:

Cycle 1. MoteCache Tag Comparison: As soon as the address is computed, its tag part is compared associatively with the tag numbers associated with the contents of the MC. If there is a match (MC-hit), the scheduled readout of the memory is cancelled, potentially saving energy wasted in reading out the row from the memory.

Cycle 2. Data Steering: In case of a MC-hit, data is read from the corresponding MC entry[1]. When the associative match, using the CAM, fails (MC-miss), the memory access continues in this cycle and the data is read out into a MC entry selected as a victim, based on the least recently used (LRU) replacement policy.

Writing to a MC entry has analogous steps, followed by a step that installs the update into the tag and data part of the corresponding MC entry. We study the writeback policy, since it is more suitable for our power-aware design.

2.1   The MoteCache Configurations

1) Direct-Mapped MoteCache (DMMC): This configuration mimics the behavior of an ordinary direct-mapped cache. Since the SRAM of the MICA2 platform contains a single byte at each line, the direct-mapped cache is organized to contain a single byte at each of its sets. The DMMC configuration has the smallest latency among all, since we can read data in parallel with the tag comparison as soon as the address is available.

2) Set-Associative MoteCache (SAMC): In order to reduce the possible conflict misses of the DMMC configuration; we also decided to try the set-associative cache configuration. This configuration is similar to a standard set-associative cache configuration, and requires the activation of more comparators in a single access.

3) Fully-Associative MoteCache (FAMC): This configuration activates all the tag/address comparators for each memory access. Therefore, it dissipates more power compared to other configurations, and its latency is not better than the DMMC configuration since it has additional multiplexer delay.

As locality of reference guarantees that there is a good chance of producing a MC-hit. Figure 1 shows that MC-hit rate is more than 89%, on the average, for the SAMC configuration with maximum size (8x8). The lowest hit rate is observed in the smallest DMMC configuration (4x1) as 18.4%. Please refer to Table 1 in Section 4 for the details of the simulated WSN benchmarks.

---

[1] To increase processor performance, data can be read from the MC at the end of the first cycle.

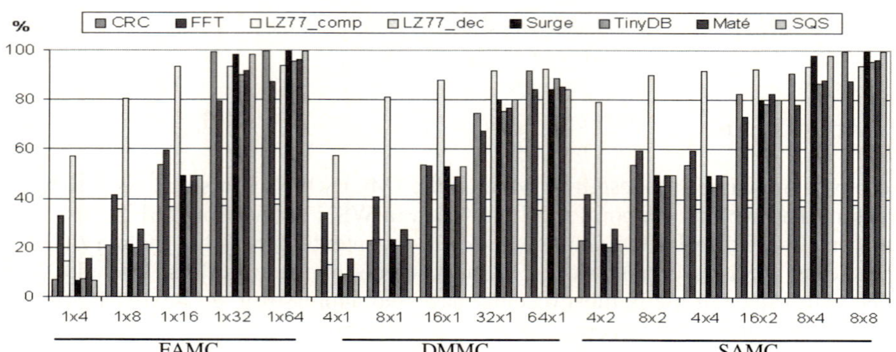

Fig. 1. Hit ratios to various MC configurations (s x a, s: set no, a: associativity)

2.2 Silent-Store Filtering MoteCache

When a store instruction writes a value that actually matches the value already stored at the memory address being written, the operation is called a *silent store* [11]. They have no effect on machine state, and we showed that detection and removal of these instructions may considerably improve the lifetime of WSNs [6]. Figure 2 shows the percentages of silent store instructions in our simulated benchmarks. Across all WSN benchmarks, the average percentage of silent stores is 81.6%.

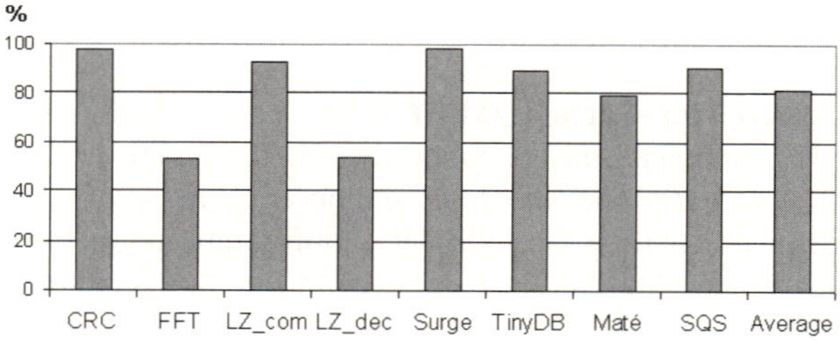

Fig. 2. Percentages of silent stores in WSN benchmarks

We increase the functionality of the *dirty-bit* in our writeback MC for detecting and removing silent stores. Therefore, the *dirty-bit* is renamed to *dirty&noisy-bit* (DN) A data value is written back to SRAM only when it is *dirty* (i.e. it is modified) and also *noisy* (i.e. if the new data value is different than the one stored before.) A write access in the silent-store filtering MC structure proceeds as follows:

1. MC-hit and Silent Store Detection: After a MC-hit, the data value to be written is compared with the data value of the corresponding MC line. If there is no match, the DN-bit of that MC line is set to indicate that the store instruction is *noisy*.

2. MC-miss and Writeback: After a MC-miss, we select a victim line. If the DN-bit of the victim line is set, the standard MC writeback procedure is followed. Otherwise, we just replace the MC line and cancel the rest of the writeback process, since the MC and SRAM data are already in sync.

3   Content-Aware Data Management (CADMA)

In this section, we describe the details of our proposed technique in this study: Content-Aware Data MAnagement (CADMA.) During our simulations, we observed that there are some common data values (specifically, 0, 1, 2 and 3) flowing in the datapath. Figure 3 shows that, across all simulated benchmarks, 48.4% of the SRAM data and 56.7% of the register file data are composed of these common data values.

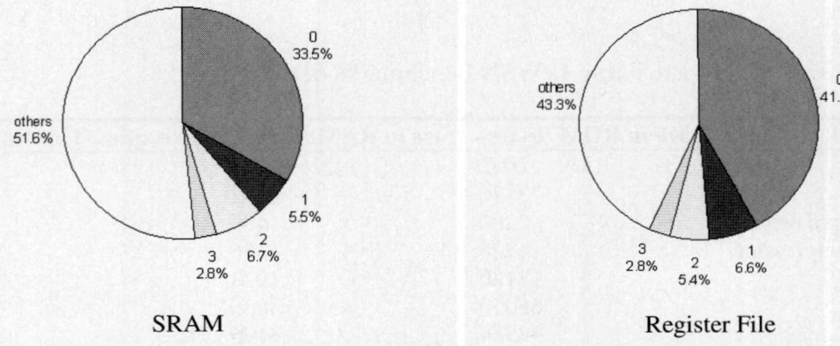

Fig. 3. Average occurrence percentages of data values in SRAM and register file

The idea behind CADMA is to exploit this phenomenon to reduce energy dissipation of SRAM, MC and register file. For this purpose, we introduce an additional bit, common data (CD), to each line of these structures. The CD operations are as follows:

1. Data Write + CD Set: The CD bit is set when there is a register/memory write operation trying to store a common data value[2]. In that case, CADMA only writes 3 bits (one CD bit + the two least significant bits of the common data value) for that byte. Note that, for all of the common data values (0, 1, 2 and 3), there is no need for any encoding/decoding process, since they already fit into the least significant 2 bits.

When the data value is not one of the four common data values, on the other hand, CADMA writes 9 bits (one CD bit + the eight bits of data value) dissipating slightly more power compared to the baseline case.

2. Data Read + CD Probe: A read operation with CADMA starts by probing the CD bit. When it is set, CADMA only activates the read operation for the two least significant bitlines. By canceling the read from the other six bitlines, CADMA achieves significant power savings in all three structures. In this case, the rest of the byte is constructed by setting the six most significant bits to logic-0.

If CD bit is not set, on the other hand, the standard procedure for data read operation is followed. Then again, slightly more power is dissipated (reading 9 bits: one CD bit + the eight bits of data value) compared to the baseline case.

In this study, we integrated CADMA within MC, SRAM, and register file structures. In our experiments, across all simulated benchmarks, we observed that CADMA boosts our processor energy savings as much as 10% and sensor node's total energy savings by 5% compared to the bare MC discussed in [6].

---

[2] A simple hard-wired circuit, which checks if all the six most significant bits of data are zero, may easily detect a common data value.

4 Simulation Methodology

The most important requirement of this study was using a simulator which not only accurately models ATmega128L processor of MICA2 platform in a cycle-accurate way, but also simulates sensor networks in various topologies. We found *Avrora*, the AVR Simulation and Analysis Framework [12], quite suitable to our needs. For all simulated benchmarks, a three-node network topology is used. Table 1 gives the details of the benchmarks used in this study:

Table 1. WSN benchmarks details

Benchmark	Size in ROM (bytes)	Size in RAM (bytes)	Execution Time (mins)
CRC	1072	1492	5
FFT	3120	1332	5
LZ77 Compression	2700	486	5
LZ77 Decompression	1228	356	5
Surge	17120	1928	50
TinyDB	65050	3036	50
Maté	38974	3196	50
SeMA/SQS	22346	2175	50

- CRC implements a CRC32 algorithm continuously running on 448 bytes of data.
- FFT benchmark is a discrete Fast Fourier Transform on 256 bytes of data. This transformation is executed within an infinite loop [13].
- LZ77 compression is again enclosed in an infinite loop and works on 448 bytes of data taken from the header file of an *excel* file.
- LZ77 decompression is the decompression of the compressed data obtained from the LZ77 compression. This data is 330 bytes long[3].
- Surge is a TinyOS core application to demonstrate multihop routing.
- TinyDB application is used to execute the query "select light from sensors".
- Maté (BombillaMica) is used with a script that reads light sensor readings in every 10ms and sends them through RF interface after 10 readings [14].
- SeMA/SQS is used to execute the query "select temperature from sensors each second" [15]. The query results are sent to the base station after each reading.

4.1 Calculation of MC Energy Dissipation

We modified *Avrora* to record transitions at the level of bits for the processor/memory components. We combined the simulator results with energy per transition measurements obtained from the SPICE simulations of the actual component layouts for 0.35μ CMOS technology. We modified the energy model of Avrora to accurately model very fine-grain, instruction-level energy dissipations of the processor. For accurate energy savings estimations, we also considered detailed energy dissipations of the additional CADMA logic.

---

[3] CRC, FFT and LZ77 applications trigger radio communication every 2 seconds to imitate typical WSN applications.

5   Results and Discussions

Figure 4 shows our energy savings for selected silent-store filtering MC configurations. Notice that, even the smallest MC configuration (4x1) saves more than 57% of the memory access energy, on the average. The optimum configuration is found to be the 8x4 configuration, since it gives similar savings compared to the MC configurations twice of its size (80.6% of 8x4 vs. 81.4% of 8x8 – not shown in the Figure.)

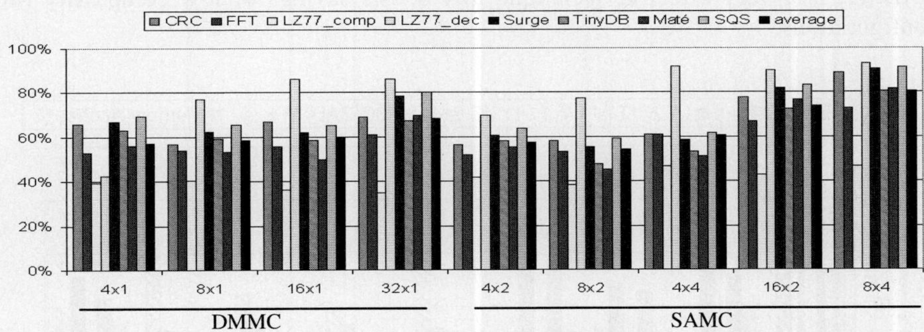

Fig. 4. Average savings on memory access energy dissipation for various MC configurations with the silent-store filter (s x a, s: set no, a: associativity)

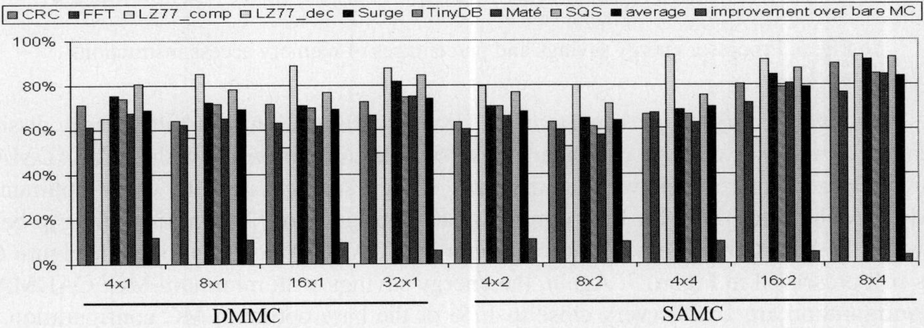

Fig. 5. Average savings on memory access energy dissipation for MC/CADMA

When we apply CADMA on top of these MC results, the energy savings gap between the minimum (DMMC 4x1) and the maximum (SAMC 8x4) configurations almost disappears (70% of 4x1 vs. 84% of 8x4). In Figure 5, we also show the percentage of improvement in the energy savings compared to the bare MC case (the rightmost bar.) Again, notice that the integration of CADMA architecture with the previously proposed MC makes the minimum MC configuration quite feasible.

We then compute the effect of CADMA on total processor energy savings. The rightmost bar in Figure 6 shows that 41% of total instructions are memory read/write instructions, on the average. When we apply these figures to our optimal configuration

(SAMC 8x4), we find that the total processor energy savings are 51.3% (Figure 6). Note that CADMA extracts additional energy savings from register file (with bare MC, total processor energy savings stay at 46.5%, on the average).

When we focus on the minimum MC configuration, energy savings due to CADMA become much more clear. Total processor savings of MC/CADMA combination are 44%, on the average. Notice that, these savings are very close to the savings of bare optimum MC configuration. The energy savings of bare minimum MC configuration are as low as 34%, on the average. These results show that CADMA is a very effective technique that boosts savings of low complexity MC configurations.

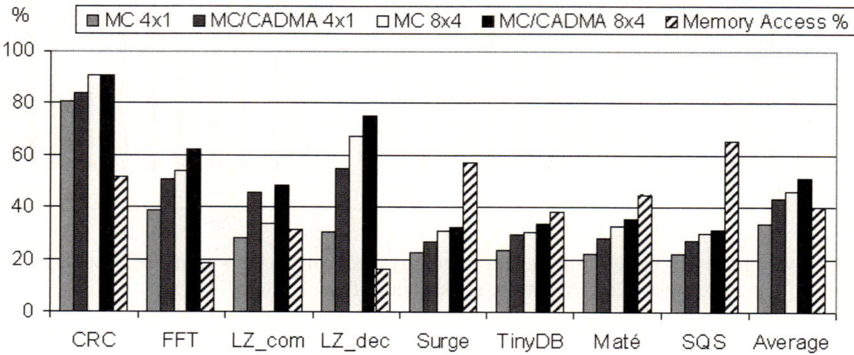

Fig. 6. Processor energy savings and percentages of memory access instructions

Next, we identify the percentage of CPU energy dissipation over total energy dissipation of a sensor node to compute the possible lifetime increase with MC/CADMA architecture. Figure 7 shows that the total energy savings are 19.3% for optimum MC/CADMA and 17% for bare optimum MC configuration. Notice that, the gap between the bare minimum MC and minimum MC/CADMA configurations in Figure 6 is still preserved in Figure 7. Again, the energy savings with minimum MC/ CADMA configuration are 16.2% (very close to 17% of the bare optimum MC configuration.) The energy savings for the bare minimum MC configuration are 11.7%, on the average. These energy savings are directly related to lifetime improvement of the node running that specific application.

Finally, we also studied the possible performance improvements when we assume that we can access to a MC structure in the first cycle of a memory operation. In Figure 8, we give these results for three DMMC configurations: 4x1, 8x1 and 16x1. The minimum configuration improves the performance by 4.3%, on the average, whereas 8x1 and 16x1 improve it by 8% and 14%, respectively. These figures also indicate that when the latency of our MC/CADMA architecture and address computation cannot be squeezed into a single cycle period, we can still increase the cycle time and tolerate slight performance penalties.

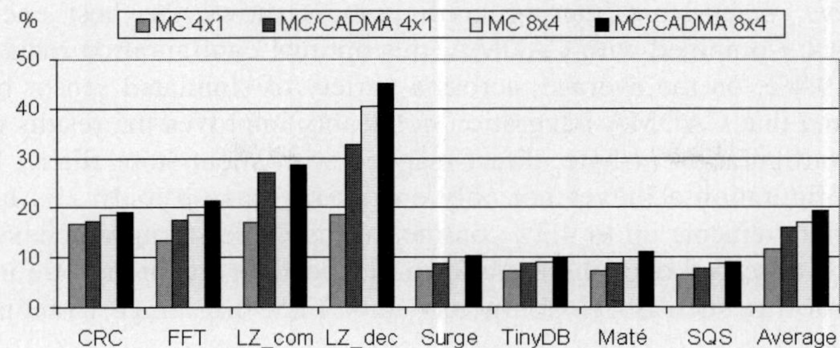

Fig. 7. Node-level energy savings and lifetime improvements

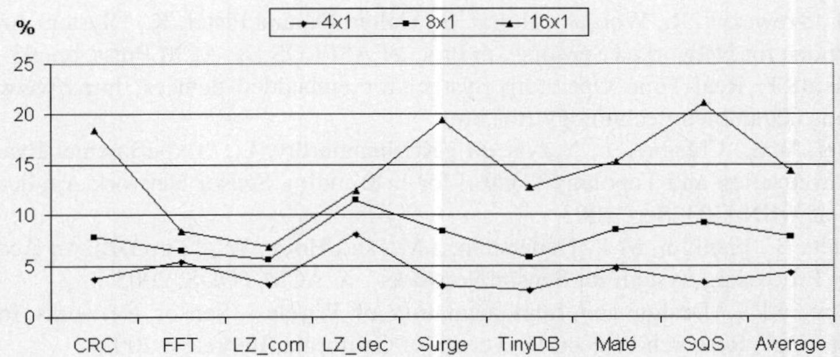

Fig. 8. Possible performance improvements with various DMMC configurations

6   Related Work

In the literature, there are various studies that target energy-efficient microprocessors for wireless sensor nodes [16, 17, 18]. In [16], the authors present SNAP/LE, an event-driven microprocessor for sensor networks. They avoid the TinyOS overhead by their asynchronous, event-driven approach. In [17], the authors seek to fully leverage the event-driven nature of applications. They study the application domain of sensor networks and they seek to replace the basic functionality of a general-purpose microcontroller with a modularized, event-driven system. In [6], we utilize a cache structure (MoteCache) to reduce the energy dissipation of the memory component of the MICA2 platform. In this study, we introduce a platform-independent technique and integrate it with the MoteCache for further reducing the energy dissipation in various processor structures of WSN nodes.

7   Concluding Remarks

In this study, we proposed a platform-independent MC/CADMA architecture for reducing the energy dissipation of the processor/memory component of wireless sensor nodes. We studied various MC configurations and found that 32-byte, 4-way, set-associative, silent-store-filtering configuration shows the best energy/lifetime characteristics. Combined with CADMA, this optimal configuration reduces the node energy by 19.4%, on the average, across a variety of simulated sensor benchmarks. We also found that CADMA integration noticeably improves the results of the minimum MC configuration (4-byte, direct-mapped with silent-store filter.) We showed that this configuration achieves not only energy savings up to 16.2%, but also performance improvements up to 4.3%, on the average. We strongly believe that better results can be observed once these platform-independent techniques are implemented in newer platforms, such as TelosB, moteiv and EYES, that utilize 16-bit processors.

References

1. Hill J., Szewczyk, R., Woo, A., Hollar, S., Culler, D., and Pister, K., "System Architecture Directions for Networked Sensors", in Proc. of ASPLOS IX, ACM Press, pp. 93-104
2. AmbientRT: Real-Time Operating System for embedded devices, http://www.ambient-systems.net/ambient/technology-rtos.htm.
3. Conner, W.S., Chhabra, J., Yarvis, M., Krishnamurthy, L., "Experimental Evaluation of Synchronization and Topology Control for In-Building Sensor Network Applications", in Proc. of WSNA'03, Sep. 2003
4. Madden, S., Franklin, M.J., Hellerstein, J.M., and Hong, W., "TinyDB: An Acquisitional Query Processing System for Sensor Networks", in ACM TODS, 2005
5. Polastre, J.R., "Design and Implementation of Wireless Sensor Networks for Habitat Monitoring", Research Project, University of California, Berkeley, 2003
6. Kucuk, G., Basaran, C., "Reducing Energy Dissipation of Wireless Sensor Processors Using Silent-Store Filtering MoteCache", in Proc. of PATMOS'06, France, 2006
7. Crossbow Technology, Inc., http://www.xbow.com
8. Lynch, C., O'Reilly, F., "Processor Choice for Wireless Sensor Networks", in Proc. of Workshop on Real-World Wireless Sensor Networks (REALWSN'05), 2005
9. Ghose, K. and Kamble, M., "Reducing Power in Superscalar Processor Caches Using Subbanking, Multiple Line Buffers and Bit-Line Segmentation", in ISLPED'99, 1999
10. Kucuk, G. et al., "Energy-Efficient Register Renaming", in Proc. of PATMOS'03, Torino, Italy, September 2003. Published as LNCS 2799, pp.219-228
11. Lepak, K.M., Bell, G.B., and Lipasti, M.H., "Silent Stores and Store Value Locality", in IEEE Transactions on Computers, (50) 11, Nov. 2001
12. Titzer, B. et al., "Avrora: Scalable Sensor Network Simulation with Precise Timing", In 4th International Conference on Information Processing in Sensor Networks, 2005
13. Numerical recipes in C, http://www.library.cornell.edu/nr/cbookcpdf.html
14. Levis, P., Culler, D. "Maté: A Tiny Virtual Machine for Sensor Networks", in Proc. of the ASPLOS X, 2002
15. Baydere, S., Ergin, M.A., "An Architectural Approach to Service Access in Wireless Ad Hoc Networks", in Proc. of Wireless and Optical Communications Conference, 2002
16. Ekanayake, V. et al., "An Ultra Low-Power Processor for Sensor Networks", in Proc. ASPLOS, Oct. 2004
17. Hempstead, M. et al., "An Ultra Low Power System Architecture for Sensor Network Applications", in the Proc. of 32nd ISCA'05, Wisconsin, USA, 2005
18. Warneke, B.A. and Pister, K.S., "An Ultra-Low Energy Microcontroller for Smart Dust Wireless Sensor Networks", in Proc. ISSCC, Jan. 2005

Effects of Asynchronism and Neighborhood Size on Clustering in Self-propelled Particle Systems[*]

Andaç T. Şamiloğlu[1,2], Veysel Gazi[1], and A. Buğra Koku[2]

[1] TOBB University of Economics and Technology, Department of Electrical and Electronics Engineering, Söğütözü Cad., No: 43, Söğütözü, 06560 Ankara, Turkey
[2] Middle East Technical University, Mechanical Engineering Department, İnönü Bulvarı, Çankaya, Ankara, Turkey

Abstract. In this study, we analyze the effects of asynchronism and neighborhood size on the collective motion of multi-agent systems. Many studies performed on the collective motion of self propelled particle systems or basically a class of multi-agent systems are modeled to be synchronous. However, in nature and in robotic applications the autonomous agents mostly act asynchronously. Therefore, a model based on the asynchronous actions of agents is developed. The agents/particles are assumed to move with constant speed and asynchronously update their direction of motion based on a nearest-neighbors rule. Based on these rules simulations are performed and the effects of asynchronism and neighborhood size on the clustering performance are investigated.

1 Introduction

The collective motion of organisms like schools of fish, herds of quadrupeds, flocks of flying birds, and groups of migrating bacteria, molds, ants, or pedestrians is an interesting area studied by many biologists, physicists, and even engineers in recent years. An interesting study on this subject was performed by Vicsek et al. in [1]. In that work, they considered a self-propelled particle system with dynamics based on the simple rule "at each time step a given particle driven with a constant absolute velocity assumes the average direction of motion of the particles in its neighborhood of radius r with some random perturbation added" [1], and investigated clustering, transport, and phase transition in non-equilibrium systems. They showed that their model results in a rich, realistic dynamics despite the simplicity of the model. In [2] and [3] the authors study biologically inspired, inherently non-equilibrium models consisting of self-propelled particles. Similar to [1] the particles move on a plane with constant speed and interact with their neighbors by choosing at each time step a velocity direction equal to the average direction of their neighbors. In [2], they showed that the far-from-equilibrium system of self-propelled particles can be described using the framework of classical critical phenomena and analysis show new features when compared with the analogous equilibrium systems, and in [3] the

---

[*] This work was supported by the Scientific and Technological Research Council of Turkey (TÜBİTAK) under grant 104E170.

A. Levi et al. (Eds.): ISCIS 2006, LNCS 4263, pp. 665–676, 2006.

authors summarize some of the results of large-scale simulations and theoretical approaches about the effects of noise and dimensionality on the scaling behavior of such systems. In [4] Czirók et al. introduce a generic phenomenological model for the collective motion of bacteria on a solid agar surface taking into account nutrient diffusion, reproduction, and sporulation of bacteria, extracellular slime deposition, chemo-regulation, and inhomogeneous population. The model is based on a ferromagnetic-like coupling of the velocities of self-propelled particles and is capable of describing the hydrodynamics on the intermediate level. In [5] the authors demonstrate that a system of self-propelled particles exhibits spontaneous symmetry breaking and self-organization in one dimension. They derived a new continuum theory that can account for the development of the symmetry broken state. The collective motion of organisms in the presence of fluctuations is discussed in [6]. In this study Vicsek utilized the simple rule of motion of particles as in [1]. The author demonstrated that there is a transition from disordered to ordered motion at the finite noise level and particles segregate into lanes or jam into a crystalline structure in a model of pedestrians.

In [7], Savkin gives a qualitative analysis of the dynamics of a system of several mobile robots coordinating their motion using simple local nearest neighbor rules referring to Vicsek's model in [1]. The author states that under some assumptions the headings of all robots will be eventually same. Similar analysis was performed by Jadbabaie et. al. in [8], where they consider both discrete and continuous models as well as leaderless and leader based situation and show that under certain connectivity conditions the heading of all the agents will converge to the same value, thus providing in a sense a theoretical explanation to the results obtained by Vicsek et. al.

A discrete model consisting of self-propelled particles that obey simple interaction rules is studied in [9]. The authors showed that the model can self-organize and exhibit coherent localized solutions in one-dimensional and in two-dimensional space. Furthermore, they develop a continuum version of their discrete model and show the agreement between these models.

In many studies performed on the collective motion of multiagent systems, the behaviors of agents are set to be synchronous. However, in nature and in robotic applications the autonomous agents mostly act asynchronously. Therefore a model based on the asynchronous actions of agents would be more realistic and implementable. For this reason, in this study we will develop an asynchronous version of the model developed by Vicsek [1] and investigate the effects of asynchronism and the neighborhood size in the coordination of agents striving to travel with a common heading.

2   Problem Formulation

We consider a multiagent system consisting of n so called self-propelled or self-driven particles each of which, similar to the model by Vicsek [1], moves based on the dynamics

$$x_i(t+1) = x_i(t) + v\cos(\theta_i(t+1))$$
$$y_i(t+1) = y_i(t) + v\sin(\theta_i(t+1)) \quad i = 1, ..., n$$

where $x_i(t), y_i(t) \in \mathbb{R}$ denote the cartesian position coordinates of agent i and $\theta_i(t) \in \mathbb{R}$ denotes its orientation angle at time t. We assume that v is constant and equal for all agents. In other words, we assume that all the agents move with the same constant speed in possibly different directions (determined by their orientation angles θ_i). Moreover, we assume that the agents have limited sensing capabilities and can "see" or "sense" the other agents which are within a circle of radius δ from it and call these agents its neighbors. Furthermore, it is assumed that the agents update their orientation based on its own current orientation and the orientation of its current neighbors. In particular, we assume that the agent tries to move in the average direction of motion of its current neighbors (including its own current direction).

As a difference from the previous studies we assume that each agent can perform the behaviors at totally different time instants. Moreover, sensing (or measurement) process may include delays. Also since each agent operates on its own local clock without a need for synchronization with the other agents, we introduce a set of time indices T^i, $i = 1, 2, ..., n$, at which the agent i updates its orientation θ_i. It is assumed that at the other instances the agent i does not perform orientation calculation. Therefore, $\theta_i(t)$'s are updated at $t \in T^i$ where T^i of each agent are independent.

Let

$$N_i(t) = \{j : \mid j \neq i, \ (x_i(t) - x_j(t))^2 + (y_i(t) - y_j(t))^2 \leq \delta^2\}$$

denote the set of neighbors of agent i at time t and $|N_i(t)|$ denote the number of agents in the set $N_i(t)$.

Then, the orientation dynamics of the agents are given by the following "nearest neighbor rule"

$$\theta_i(t+1) = \frac{1}{1 + |N_i(t)|}\left(\theta_i(t) + \sum_{j \in N_i(\tau_j(t))} \theta_j(\tau_j^i(t))\right), \quad t \in T^i, \tag{1a}$$

$$\theta_i(t+1) = \theta_i(t), \quad t \notin T^i, \tag{1b}$$

where $\tau_j^i(t)$ satisfies $0 \leq \tau_j^i(t) \leq t$. It represents the delays in sensing the orientation of agent $j \in N_i(\tau_j^i(t))$ by agent i at time t. We assume that at time t agent i knows $\theta_j(\tau_j^i(t))$ instead of the actual $\theta_j(t)$ about the orientation of agent j. In other words, $\theta_j^i(\tau_j(t))$ is the *perceived orientation* of agent j by agent i at time t. Consequently, if agent i has not yet obtained any information about the jth agent's orientation and still has the initial orientation information, then $\tau_j^i(t) = 0$ whereas $\tau_j^i(t) = t$ means that agent i has the current orientation information of the jth agent. The difference between the current time t and the value of the variable $\tau_j^i(t)$ i.e.,$(t - \tau_j^i(t))$ is the delay occurring due to the sensory, computing and/or communication processes or other reasons. We believe that the above model is more realistic (compared to the earlier studies performed with synchronism assumption) since in real world applications (robots coordinating to achieve a common orientation) or animal flocks (schooling behavior of fishes) usually there is an asynchrony between agents and time delays are also possible. In our model we utilize the study on the relation between the synchronism and asynchronism in the parallel computing systems in [10].

The asynchronism between the agents (i.e. robots, fish) may be at different levels due to the characteristics of each agent itself or some environmental disturbance. In some multiagent systems the asynchrony may be negligible (leading to a synchronism assumption) and the behavior of these systems may be computable or predictable. On the other hand, in some systems asynchronism may drastically change the performance of the system. In these kind of systems the behaviors of agents may be difficult to predict. Nevertheless, unbounded or excessively long delays in the information flow or acting of the agents may result in the violation of "agent interaction" concept of multiagent systems. In other words, it might be difficult to view the systems experiencing unbounded or excessively long delays as a single multiagent system. This is because an agent that never performs sensing or never acts cannot be considered as a member of the group. Therefore, the level of asynchronism should be limited in such a way that the agents still can interact and form a single multiagent system. Hence, here we state an assumption which establishes a bound on the maximum possible time delay as well as guarantees uniformity in the updates of the agents.

Assumption 1. *There exists a positive integer B such that*
(a) For every i and every $t \geq 0$, at least one of the elements of the set $\{t, t + 1, \ldots, t + B - 1\}$ belongs to T^i.
(b) There holds $t - B < \tau_j^i(t) \leq t \quad \forall i \quad t \geq 0, t \in T^i$

This assumption basically states that (i) every agent uniformly performs update or change in its orientation (based on 1a) in at most B time steps; (ii) the delay in sensing the orientation of the neighbors of the agent is bounded as well by at most B time steps. This assumption in a sense restricts the level of asynchronism in the system. Systems satisfying Assumption 1 are being referred to as partially asynchronous systems in the parallel and distribution computation literature [10]. In the following section we perform an empirical simulation study of the effect of B on the performance of the system. Moreover, we study also the effect of the neighborhood size δ (the sensing range of the agents) on the performance of the system.

3   Numerical Simulations and Discussions

We simulated the motion of $n = 50$ agents. Initially the agents are localized in a square region of size 100×100 units and the constant speed of all of the agents is set to 1 unit/sec. The simulations are performed for $T = 200$ time steps. The agents perform updates depending on a stochastic function of B. The probability of update of an agent is distributed along the interval $t \in (t - B, t)$ such that it is

$1/(B-\Omega+1)$ where Ω is the number of steps that the agent has performed since the last update. The initial positions and orientations of agents are generated randomly once and for each simulation the same initial conditions are utilized. We also provide some simulation results performed for different initial conditions generated randomly to show that the results presented below are not specific to particular initial positions and conditions.

In order to measure the performance we used the following error criteria based on the distances between agents and orientation differences between agents.

$$e_d(t) = \sum_{i=1}^{n-1} \sum_{j=i+1}^{n} ||z_i(t) - z_j(t)|| \quad and \quad e_\theta(t) = \sum_{i=1}^{n-1} \sum_{j=i+1}^{n} ||\theta_i(t) - \theta_j(t)||$$

where $z_i(t) = [x_i(t), y_i(t)]^T$ is the position vector of agent i. We call $e_d(t)$ as the *total distance between agents* at time t and $e_\theta(t)$ as the *sum of orientation differences between agents* at time t.

We have conducted simulations in order to determine the effects of asynchronism and time delays on the cluster formation. Note that agent i and j belong to the same cluster at time t if $||z_i(t) - z_j(t)|| \leq \delta$. We have conducted simulations both by varying B and δ.

3.1   Effect of B

The simulations are performed for several B values to see the effects of level of asynchrony in the orientation information of nearest neighbors. The radius of the circles for nearest neighbor rule is set to $\delta = 20$ units. Note that in all simulations $B = 0$ corresponds to the synchronous case.

In Figures 1 (a) and (b) we plotted $e_d(t)$ and $e_\theta(t)$ at the end of simulations $(t = T)$ for various B values. It is seen that as the B value increases the values of both $e_d(T)$ and $e_\theta(T)$ increase. The total distance between agents is greater for higher B values. This is an expected result when we consider the delays in actions and orientation sensing of agents during asynchronous coordination. On the other hand the increase in the sum of orientation differences $e_\theta(T)$ means that the number of agents moving with different headings increase and also the difference between the heading of clusters increase since the orientation adjustment becomes less often due to higher delays.

In Figure 1 (c) the number of clusters at the last step of simulations versus B are presented. As the B value gets higher the number of clusters increases. Figure 1 (d) shows the cluster formation at the beginning of the simulations. Here the arrow heads present the location and orientation of agents. The connecting lines between two agents shows that those two agents are neighbors of each other. The headings of agents are different but most of them belong to a single cluster. In the Figures 2 (a) and (b) the cluster formations at the last step of simulations are shown for $B = 0$ (synchronous case) and $B = 60$, respectively. As seen the agents form large clusters for $B = 0$ while they spread away with significantly different headings for the case $B = 60$. For better understanding of the cluster formations we present the trajectories of agents in the Figures 2 (c) and (d) for

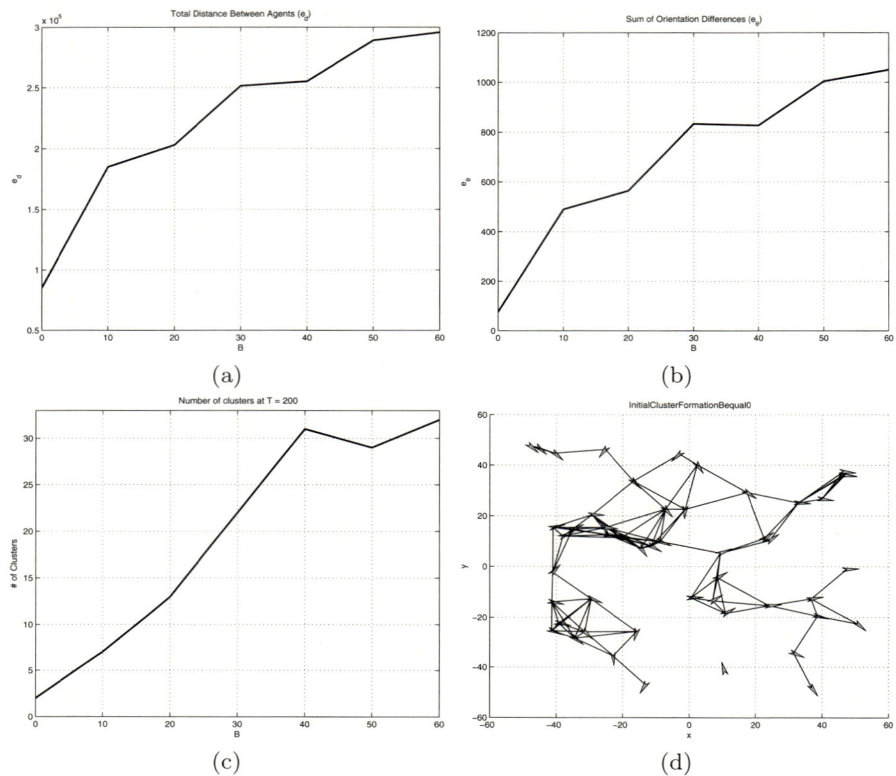

Fig. 1. Change of (a) $e_d(t)$, (b) $e_\theta(t)$, and (c) the number of clusters with respect to B. (d) Cluster formation at the beginning of simulations.

$B = 0$ and $B = 60$, respectively. While the agents mostly keep clustered and orient their motion in common direction in the synchronous ($B = 0$) case, the group tends to disperse and the clusters are dissolved as the value B (the level of asynchronism and the amount of time delay) increases. These are logically expected results

3.2   Effect of δ

In this part we simulated the motion of agents for different radius of circles δ in the nearest neighbor rule or basically for different neighborhood sizes. The simulations are performed for two different cases: (i) $B = 0$ (synchronous case) (ii) $B = 10$ (asynchronous case). The simulation parameters are the same as the previous simulations (Section 3.1) except now the δ values are changing between $\delta = 6$ and $\delta = 30$ with steps of 2.

Figures 3 (a) and (b) show $e_d(T)$ and $e_\theta(T)$, respectively for various δ values. It is seen that as the δ value gets larger the values of $e_d(T)$ and $e_\theta(T)$ decrease.

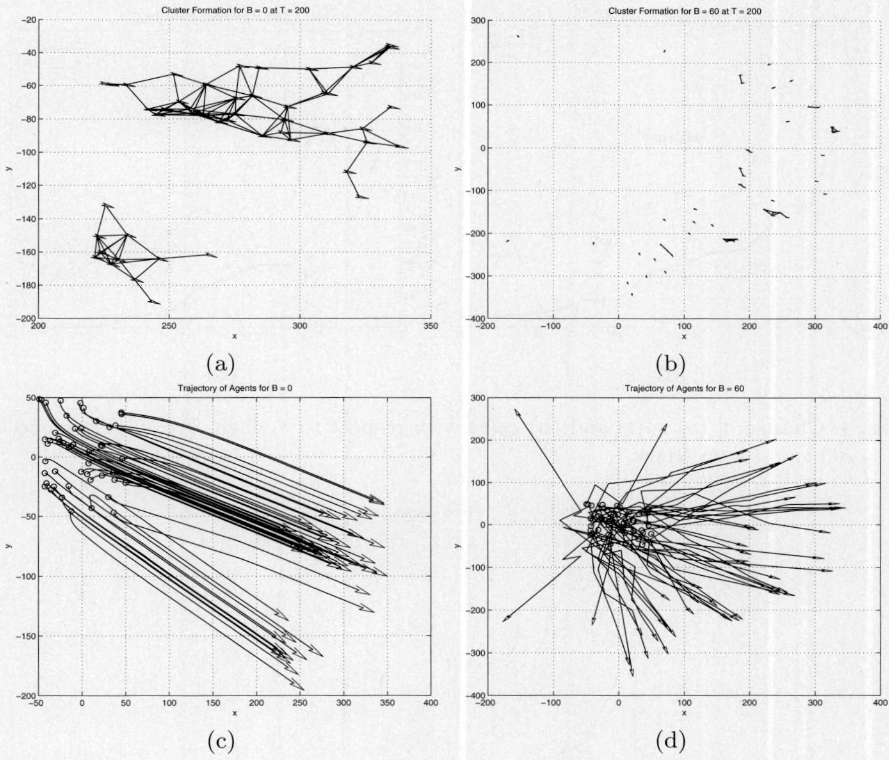

Fig. 2. Clusters formation at the end of simulation for (a) $B = 0$ (synchronous case), (b) $B = 60$ (asynchronous case). Trajectory of agents during the simulation for (c) $B = 0$ (synchronous case), (d) $B = 60$ (asynchronous case).

As the neighborhood size increases the interaction of agents gets denser and hence coordination gets better. Therefore, most of the agents move with the same heading leading to smaller distance and orientation errors. On the other hand the errors for the asynchronous case ($B = 10$) are larger than the ones found for the synchronous case ($B = 0$) as expected.

In Figure 4 we see the change of number of cluster formations at the last step of simulations with respect to δ when $B = 0$ and $B = 10$. It is clear that as the δ values rise the number of clusters formed are decreasing and the heading of each cluster gets closer to each other. As seen, as the δ value increase the cluster formations falls down to single cluster formation for $B = 0$. Again the synchronous case shows better performance than the asynchronous case (the number of clusters is around 5 for $B = 10$).

In Figures 5 (a) and (b) the clusters formed at the beginning of simulations are displayed for $\delta = 6$ and $\delta = 30$, respectively for the case of $B = 0$. As seen for $\delta = 6$ there are many clusters such that each agent forms a different

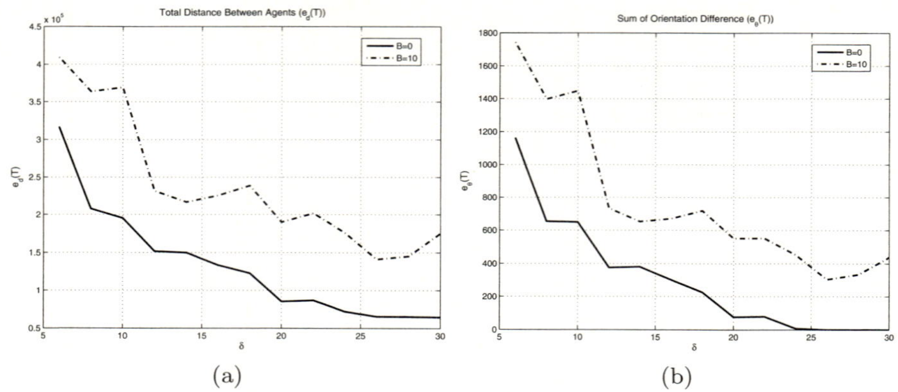

Fig. 3. Change of (a) $e_d(t)$ and (b) $e_\theta(t)$ with respect to δ when $B = 0$, at the end of $T = 200$ simulation steps

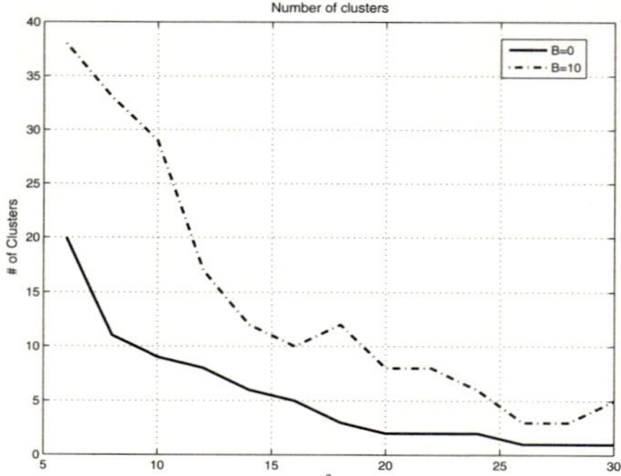

Fig. 4. Change of number of clusters with respect to δ

single cluster whereas for $\delta = 30$ all of the agents belong to a single cluster. When we simulated with different initial conditions we end up with the results in the Figures 6 (a) and (b). As expected the agents spread away when the neighborhood size is small and they form a single cluster with common heading when the neighborhood size is large. For better visualization the trajectory of agents for $\delta = 6$ and $\delta = 30$ are shown in Figures 6 (c) and (d).

In Figures 7 (a) and (b) the clusters formed at the end of simulations are displayed when $B = 10$ for $\delta = 6$ and $\delta = 30$, respectively. As expected the agents spread away when the neighborhood size is small and they form less number of clusters when the neighborhood size is large. Note that for the synchronous case the agents form a single cluster when $\delta = 30$. However, this is not the case for the asynchronous setting since there are three clusters. Again the trajectory of agents are shown in Figures 7 (c) and (d).

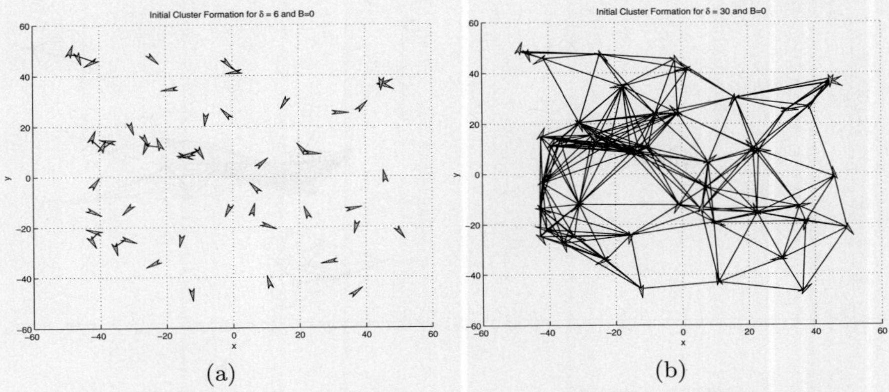

Fig. 5. (a) Initial cluster formation for $\delta = 6$, and (b) $\delta = 30$ when $B = 0$

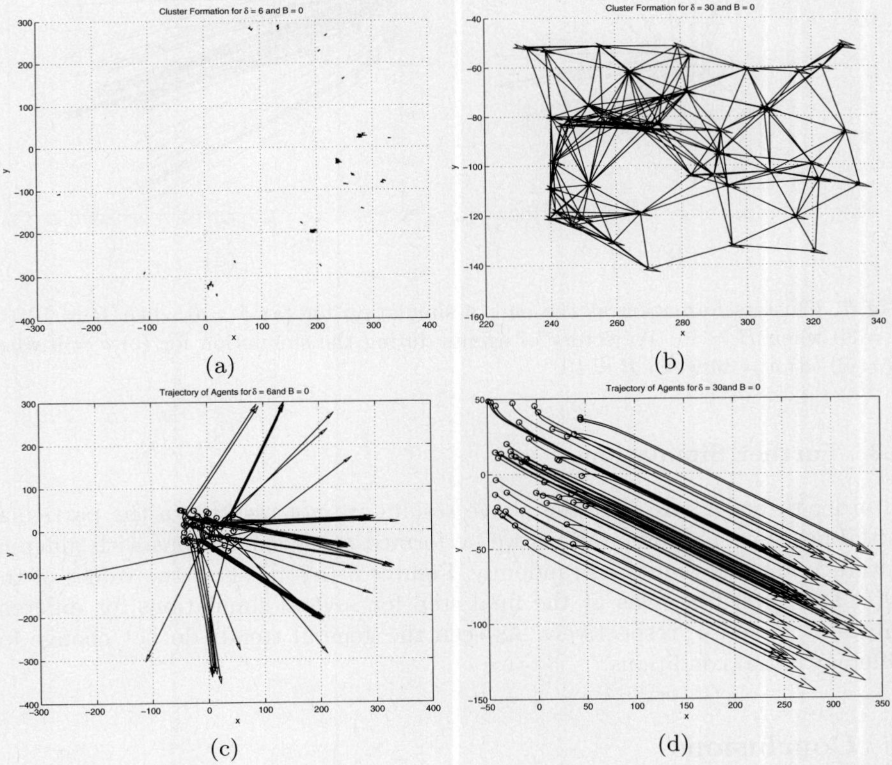

Fig. 6. Clusters formation at the end of simulation for (a) $\delta = 6$, and (b) $\delta = 30$ when $B = 0$. Trajectory of agents during the simulation for (c) $\delta = 6$, and (d) $\delta = 30$ when $B = 0$.

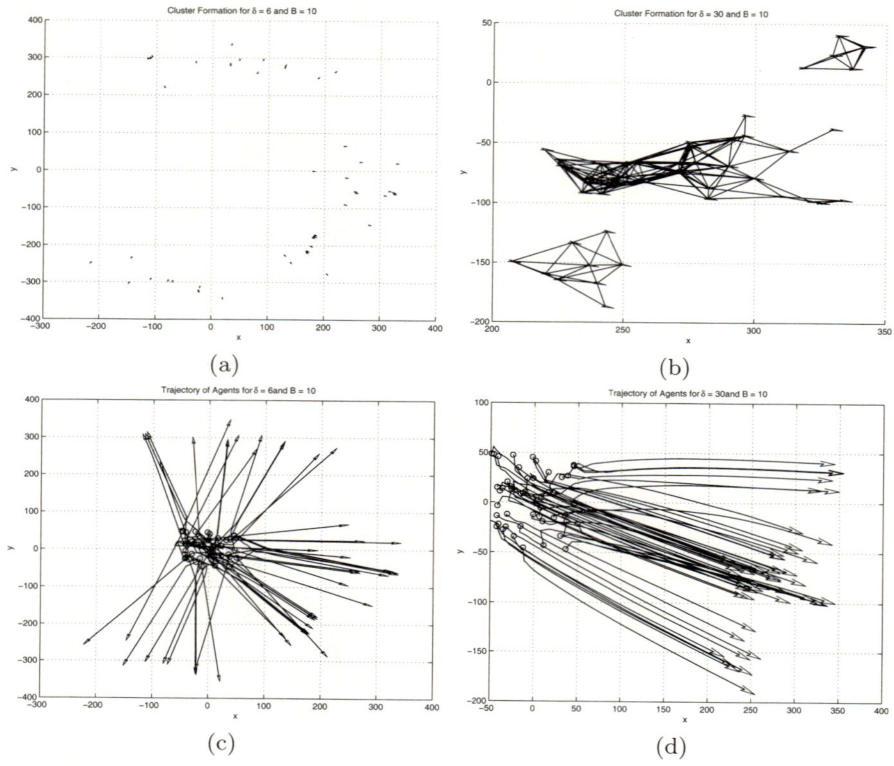

Fig. 7. Clusters formation at the end of simulation for (a) $\delta = 6$ when $B = 10$ (b) $\delta = 30$ when $B = 10$. Trajectory of agents during the simulation for (c) $\delta = 6$ when $B = 10$ (d) $\delta = 30$ when $B = 10$.

3.3   Further Simulations

In order to make sure that the above results are not specific to the particular initial positions and orientations we performed many simulations with different initial conditions generated randomly. Figures 8 (a)-(d) show the values of the $e_d(t)$ and $e_\theta(t)$ functions at the final step for several simulations for different values of B and δ, respectively. As seen the general trends do not change for different initial conditions.

4   Conclusions

In this study, we analyzed the effects of asynchronism and neighborhood size on the collective motion of multi-agent systems with respect to simulation based results. The agents try to orient themselves in the same direction depending on simple interaction rules while at the same time moving with constant speed.

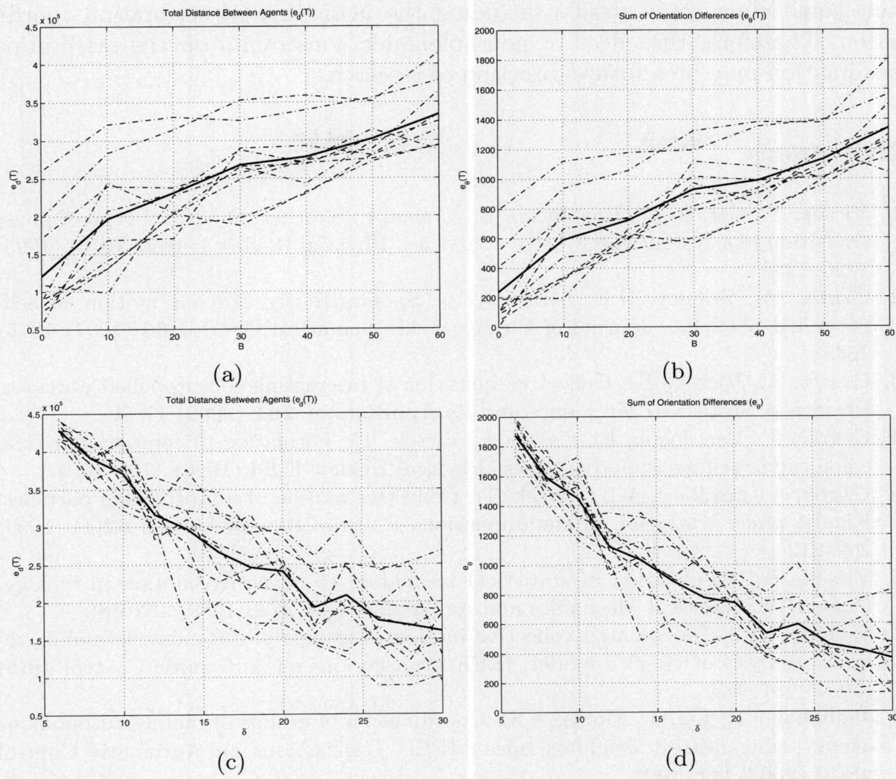

Fig. 8. (a) Total distance between agents $(e_d(T))$ changing with respect to B (b) total orientation difference between agents $(e_\theta(T))$ changing with respect to B (c) total distance between agents $(e_d(T))$ changing with respect to δ $(B = 10)$ (d) total orientation difference between agents $(e_\theta(T))$ changing with respect to δ $(B = 10)$ for several random initial positions and orientations (The average of all simulations is the solid line)

We performed several simulations and discussed the effects of asynchronism and neighborhood size on the cluster formation. The high level of asynchronism results in degraded performance in the collective motion. The neighborhood size which may be thought as the capability of gathering information about other agents and local environment, also has significant effects on the collective motion of agents. As this capability increases the agents coordination performance increases as well.

In conclusion, this study utilized an intensive simulation study leading to the aforementioned results. Even though the simulations suggest these results to be conclusive a rigorous analytical analysis is essential. Another important issue to be pointed out is that the agents used in this study are assumed to be holonomic in the analytic model and simulations. Initial investigation (not shown here) for the case in which the agents have constraints on turning (non-holonomic case) show some unexpected results including the instability of orientation coordination. Therefore, the effect of non-holonomic constraints on the orientation coordination may be a future direction of research.

References

1. Vicsek, T., Czirók, A., Ben-Jacob, E., Cohen, I., Shochet, O.: Novel type of phase transition in a system of self-driven particles. Physical Review Letters **75**(6) (1995) 1226–1229
2. Czirók, A., Stanley, H.E., Vicsek, T.: Spontaneously ordered motion of self-propelled particles. Journal of Physics A Mathematical General **30** (1997) 1375–1385
3. Czirok, A., Vicsek, T.: Collective behavior of interacting self-propelled particles. Physica A Statistical Mechanics and its Applications **281** (2000) 17–29
4. Czirók, A., Ben-Jacob, E., Cohen, I., Vicsek, T.: Formation of complex bacterial colonies via self-generated vortices. Physical Review E **54** (1996) 1791–1801
5. Czirók, A., Barabási, A.L., Vicsek, T.: Collective motion of self-propelled particles: Kinetic phase transition in one dimension. Physical Review Letters **82**(1) (1999) 209–212
6. Vicsek, T.: Application of statistical mechanics to collective motion in biology. Physica A Statistical Mechanics and its Applications **274** (1999) 182–189
7. Savkin, A.V.: Coordinated collective motion of groups of autonomous mobile robots: Analysis of vicsek's model. IEEE Transactions on Automatic Control **49**(6) (2004) 981–983
8. Jadbabaie, A., Lin, J., Morse, A.S.: Coordination of groups of mobile autonomous agents using nearest neighbor rules. IEEE Transactions on Automatic Control **48**(6) (2003) 988–1001
9. Levine, H., Rappel, W.J., Cohen, I.: Self-organization in systems of self-propelled particles. Physical Review E **63**(17101) (2000) 1–4
10. Bertsekas, D.P., Tsitsiklis, J.N.: Parallel and Distributed Computation: Numerical Methods. Athena Scientific, Belmont, MA (1997)

Virtual-ROM: A New Demand Paging Component for RTOS and NAND Flash Memory Based Mobile Devices

Hyojun Kim, Jihyun In, DongHoon Ham,
SongHo Yoon, and Dongkun Shin

Samsung Electronics, Software Laboratories, Mobile Software Platform Team
416 Maetan-3Dong, Yeongtong-Gu, Suwon-City, Kyenggi-Do, Korea 443-742
{zartoven, jh_in, dh.ham, bluesol, dongkun.shin}@samsung.com

Abstract. Similiar to a hard disk, NAND flash memory must be accessed in sector unit, and cannot be used for code storage without copying its contents to RAM. A virtual memory technique is promising as a RAM saving solution. However, it can not be easily used without the operating system supports, and it is not suitable for real time systems because it causes unpredicted execution delays.

Virtual-ROM is a light-weight demand paging solution designed for RTOS based mobile devices. It is OS-independent, easy-to-use, and well optimized for NAND flash memory. Because it occupies only a restricted address space, real time tasks can be free from unpredictable execution delays by being excluded from Virtual-ROM. Our trace driven simulation showed that its performance is similar to 70ns NOR flash memory, and our real taget adaptation for a CDMA mobile phone showed that it saved about 30% RAM usage.

Keywords: Mobile, Virtual Memory, Demand Paging, Shadowing, RTOS, NAND Flash Memory.

1 Introduction

Flash memory is widely used for mobile devices due to its versatile features such as non-volatility, solid-state reliability, and low power consumption. The most common flash types are NOR and NAND flash memories. NOR flash memory is particularly well suited for code storage because it supports execute-in-place (XIP) functionality, while NAND flash memory is commonly used for data storage because of its high density and low price [1]. According to an IDC report in 2005 [2], the price of 512Mbit NAND flash memory is now only 15% of NOR flash memory.

As the applications in mobile consumer devices grow in their code and data size with multimedia functionality, NAND flash memory is rapidly replacing NOR flash memory even for code storage. To use NAND flash memory as code storage, the *shadowing* technique is required. Because NAND flash memory does not support XIP, its contents must be copied to RAM during the boot process, and the process is called *shadowing*. However, it causes two side effects: increased RAM usage and delayed boot time. Especially, RAM usage is critical because it has a deep relationship with production costs and power consumption. Moreover, [3] shows that

A. Levi et al. (Eds.): ISCIS 2006, LNCS 4263, pp. 677 – 686, 2006.

RAM price increases exponentially by its capacity. The predicted price of 512Mbits DRAM is \$3.62 while the price of 1Gbits DRAM is \$22.64 in 2006. Therefore, RAM saving solutions can be critically required for extremely small mobile devices.

Mobile phone systems are facing up to the problem of insufficient memory. Recent featured phones have 64Mbytes RAM, but it is not sufficient because they are increasingly absorbing various functions from other devices such as MP3 players, digital camcorders, and car navigation systems.

We can consider the virtual memory technique of conventional operating systems [4] to reduce RAM usage instead of *shadowing*, and it can expand memory capacity with secondary storage, virtually. However, we cannot use the virtual memory based operating system such as Embedded Linux for mobile phones because the communication protocol stack codes of mobile phone can not be ported to non-RTOS. Therefore, it is necessary to figure out our own demand paging component solution which can be applied to existing RTOS based applications without interference of real-time task execution.

To apply demand paging on mobile devices using real-time operating system (RTOS) and NAND flash memory, unpredicted execution delays of virtual memory systems must be handled in order not to break time dead-lines of real-time tasks. Then, in order to get better performance, the physical characteristics of NAND flash memory must be considered. NAND Flash memory is relatively fast for reading but writing is slow and complicated because of its erasure operation and wear-leveling requirement.

Obviously, it is impossible to use demand paging without execution delays. Therefore, we tried to figure out a graceful architecture where we can selectively use demand paging. That means, the portion of the image related with real time tasks will be excluded from demand paging in our solution. However, the portion is small compared to non-real time tasks in mobile phone systems, and the situation may be similar in other types of mobile consumer devices, fortunately.

We designed a Virtual-ROM for a component based demand paging solution. As its name implies, it influences only the restricted memory space of a processor, and is read-only. For a developer, it is almost the same as a ROM component except that the access to it may be unpredictably delayed by demand paging process.

Fig. 1 shows the difference between the virtual memory of a conventional operating system and a Virtual-ROM. In a virtual memory system (Fig.1. (a)), a user-process can see only a virtual memory space. If a required page is absent in physical memory at a particular moment, the process must wait until the page is loaded by kernel. Fig. 1(b) shows the example of an RTOS-based system's memory space. Normally, an application can see all of the physical memory space. Sometimes, the address mapping can be remapped with a memory management unit statically, but it does not influence the execution of real-time tasks. Fig.1(c) shows an example of the memory space of the system using Virtual-ROM. The Virtual-ROM influences only the restricted memory region. A user can see both physical memory space (outside the Virtual-ROM) and virtual memory space (inside the Virtual-ROM). We can guarantee that Virtual-ROM does not influence real time task execution by excluding the code and data related with real-time tasks from the Virtual-ROM.

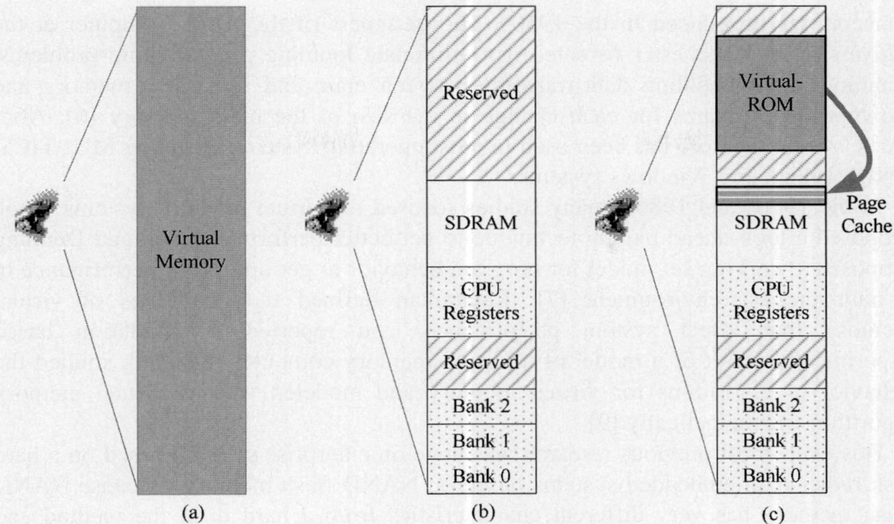

Fig. 1. Examples of the memory spaces of (a) Virtual Memory system, (b) RTOS system, and (c) Virtual-ROM applied RTOS system

Another advantage of Virtual-ROM is its portability. Because Virtual-ROM controls restrict page translation table entries, which are related to its address region, it can be applied to any RTOS that does not change virtual to physical address mapping dynamically for a Virtual-ROM region.

In order to realize our innovative idea on Virtual-ROM, we implemented a Virtual-ROM component for an ARM9 cored processor, and applied it to a commercial CDMA mobile phone. With Virtual-ROM, we were able to successfully save about 30% RAM space. For performance evaluation, the Virtual-ROM was compared with NOR flash memory by trace driven simulation. Extensive simulations with twenty-six traces from SPEC CPU2000 benchmarks [5], show that the overall performance of Virtual-ROM is similar to the performance of NOR flash memory with 70ns access speed.

The rest of the paper is organized as follows: Section 2 outlines the related works in the area of virtual memory and NAND flash memory, and section 3 describes Virtual-ROM design and structure. Section 4 describes the evaluation method and the results briefly, and Section 5 concludes.

2   Related Work

Because of the importance and long history of virtual memory, many researchers have studied it, and many noticeable results have been presented. The virtual memory concept was introduced in the 1950s. The designers of the Atlas Computer at the University of Manchester invented it to eliminate looming programming problems: planning and scheduling data transfers between main and secondary memory and recompiling programs for each change in the size of the main memory [6]. After Atlas, virtual memory has been used in most operating systems including MULTICS, UNIX, Linux, and Windows systems.

In the 1970s and 1980s, many studies focused on virtual memory systems. Leon proposed a look-ahead paging technique to get better performance [6], and Denning proposed a working set model for program behavior to get optimized performance in a multi-process environment [7]. Rajaraman defined the primitives of virtual memory that affect system performance, and reported a simulation based experimental result of a model of a virtual memory computer [8]. Alok studied the behavior of algorithms for virtual memory and modeled various virtual memory algorithms mathematically [9].

However, most previous research was done on enterprise systems based on a hard disk rather than embedded systems based on NAND flash memory. Because NAND flash memory has very different characteristics from a hard disk, the method and effect of the virtual memory change in a NAND flash memory based virtual memory system.

There have been some researches on NAND flash memory based virtual memory techniques for mobile devices. Park et al. proposed a NAND XIP architecture [10] to emulate the functionalities of NOR flash memory with NAND flash memory, SRAM, and additional hardware logic. They tried to replace NOR flash memory physically with their hardware based solution by using demand paging technique for the purpose. In the NAND XIP architecture, the demanded pages are read from NAND flash memory to the internal SRAM by hardware logic. During the demand paging process, the CPU is pended by a CPU wait signal. NAND XIP is very similar to Virtual-ROM because both are for ROM emulation with NAND flash memory to replace NOR flash memory. However, the methods of approaching the problem are different. While Virtual-ROM emulates ROM with a memory management unit and an exception mechanism, NAND XIP uses additional hardware logic and additional SRAM. NAND XIP is more powerful because of its hardware, but Virtual-ROM is cheaper and more flexible because it needs no additional hardware logic.

NAND flash memory based demand paging in Embedded Linux has also been researched [11]. An energy-aware demand paging technique to lower the energy consumption of embedded systems was presented. It considered the characteristics of the interactive embedded applications with large memory footprints. In the research, they showed that a NAND flash memory based demand paging system consumed less energy than systems based on a shadowing technique. They also proposed a flash memory aware page replacement policy, named Clean-First LRU, which can reduce the number of write and erase operations in NAND flash memory. The algorithm gives a higher priority to clean pages than dirty pages in selecting a victim page because the cost of writing is much higher than the cost of reading in NAND flash memory.

For low-end embedded systems without memory management units, Park et al. proposed a compiler-assisted demand paging technique [12]. In this research, they proposed a kind of automatic overlay technique with a compiler post-pass analysis of an ELF executable image and page manager. This research is similar to Virtual-ROM because both methods are for read-only code and data in NAND flash memory. But the baseline was different. Compiler-assisted demand paging is for systems that do not have a memory management unit, but Virtual-ROM is for systems that have a memory management unit. Because Virtual-ROM uses hardware memory manage unit, it is much faster and easier to use than compiler-assisted demand paging. However, Virtual-ROM cannot be applied to systems that do not have a memory management unit.

There have also been trials to change the traditional virtual memory framework. Kieran and David proposed a new method to take over page replacement in the operating system virtual memory implementation [13]. In the method, page-cache management was done by application. However, unlike our approach most parts still remain as a roll of the operating system. Our Virtual-ROM is completely independent of a particular operating system.

3 Virtual-ROM

Virtual-ROM is designed as a standalone component to maximize portability. Fig. 2 shows the internal structure of the Virtual-ROM component. It consists of three modules: the *Interface module*, the *Fault Handling module*, and the *Page Cache Management module*. The *Interface module* initializes the page translation table, and installs the exception handler for the Virtual-ROM component. The *Fault Handling module* handles page faults at run time, and the *Page Cache Management module* manages the page cache with its page replacement algorithm.

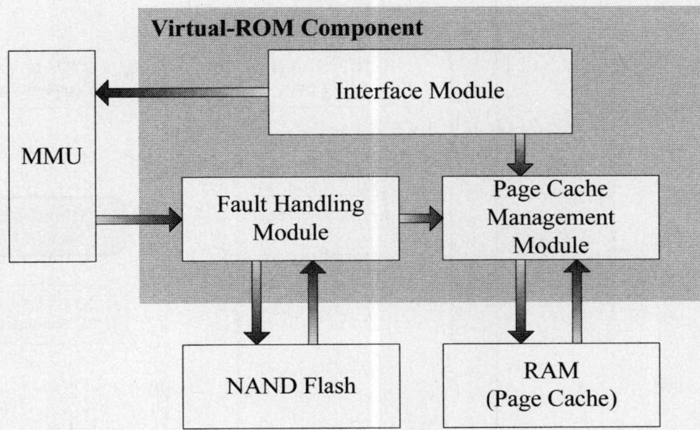

Fig. 2. Virtual-ROM component internal structure: Virtual-ROM consists of three internal modules: the Interface module, Fault Handling module, and Page Cache Management module

3.1 Virtual-ROM Activation Process

Virtual-ROM must be activated after the memory management unit is initialized. Even in RTOS, the memory management unit is commonly used to control cache on/off, to remap memory mapping statically, and sometimes to protect memory. Because the Virtual-ROM also has to use the memory management unit, the Virtual-ROM must be activated after the RTOS board support package (BSP) initializes the memory management unit. Virtual-ROM requires the partial memory space of a processor, and does not influence the outside of the Virtual-ROM region. Because the level 1 page translation table is mandatory to enable the memory management unit, the RTOS BSP builds the page translation table up to the platform's memory configuration during the boot process.

The Virtual-ROM activation API builds a level-2 page translation table to use small mapping units such as 4Kbytes and 1Kbytes pages. To use the two-level page translation, it finds the existing level-1 page translation table's base address and modifies its entries, which are associated with the Virtual-ROM region. **Fig. 3**(a) shows the status when a Virtual-ROM component completes the building of the page translation table.

After building the page translation table for the Virtual-ROM region, it installs its own prefetch and data abort exception handlers. The page fault exception is the core mechanism which is supported by the hardware memory management unit for demand paging. The Virtual-ROM component hooks the existing exception handlers, as shown in **Fig. 3**(b), to catch the CPU control for page fault exceptions. The Virtual-ROM's exception handler checks whether a page fault occurs in the Virtual-ROM region. If the exception occurs outside the Virtual-ROM region, it bypasses the exception to the original handler. The *Fault Handling module* in **Fig. 2** includes the Virtual-ROM's exception handlers. Finally, the Virtual-ROM *Interface module* allocates heap memory for the page cache, and passes it to the *Page Cache Management module* to initialize its data structure by calling the initialization API of the module.

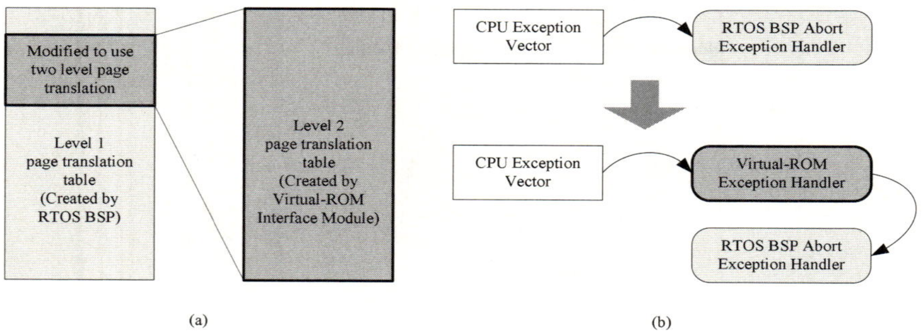

Fig. 3. Virtual-ROM activation process: (a) Modification of the level 1 page translation table, and creation of the level 2 page translation table. (b) The exception handlers of the Virtual-ROM are installed to catch the page translation aborts.

The following code example shows the activation process of the Virtual-ROM in Nucleus OS environment. As shown in the below code example, the Virtual-ROM must be activated after the memory management unit is initialized.

```
/* Nucleus C level initialization. It is called from
   int_pid.s after stack initialization */

void * BoardInit(void *pFreeMem)
{
    __rt_lib_init();
    GPIOInit();
    InitDbgSerial(115200);
    InitHWTimer();

    pFreeMem = MMU_Init(pFreeMem);

    VROM_Init(0x60000000, /* Virtual-ROM Base Address */
              0x01700000, /* Virtual-ROM Size (23MB)  */
              pFreeMem,    /* Page Cache Base Address  */
              0x00500000, /* Page Cache Size   (5MB)   */
              PART_ID_VROM) /* NAND partition ID       */

    pFreeMem += 0x00500000;
    pFreeMem = LCDInit(pFreeMem);
    TimerInit(TICK2SEC);

    return pFreeMem;
}
```

3.2   Page Fault Handling Process in Virtual-ROM

When a page fault occurs, the exception handler of *Fault Handling module* is called. It finds out the exception address, and checks whether the fault occurs inside the Virtual-ROM region. If the fault occurs outside the Virtual-ROM region, it bypasses the fault to the original exception handler of the system. Otherwise, it services the page fault. Then, it requests the *Page Cache Management module* to make a free page frame. Because the Virtual-ROM is read-only, the contents on the victim page can just be flushed without write-back. Then, it reads the required page from the NAND flash memory, and changes the page translation table entry. **Fig. 4** shows the procedure.

Because the ARM processor does not have any hardware support of reference bit for the LRU page replacement algorithm, the Virtual-ROM uses an LRU approximation algorithm: a Clock algorithm with two arms [14]. A pseudo-fault technique is used to sense the page access pattern. The pseudo-fault is not a real fault, so page reading form NAND flash memory is not necessary.

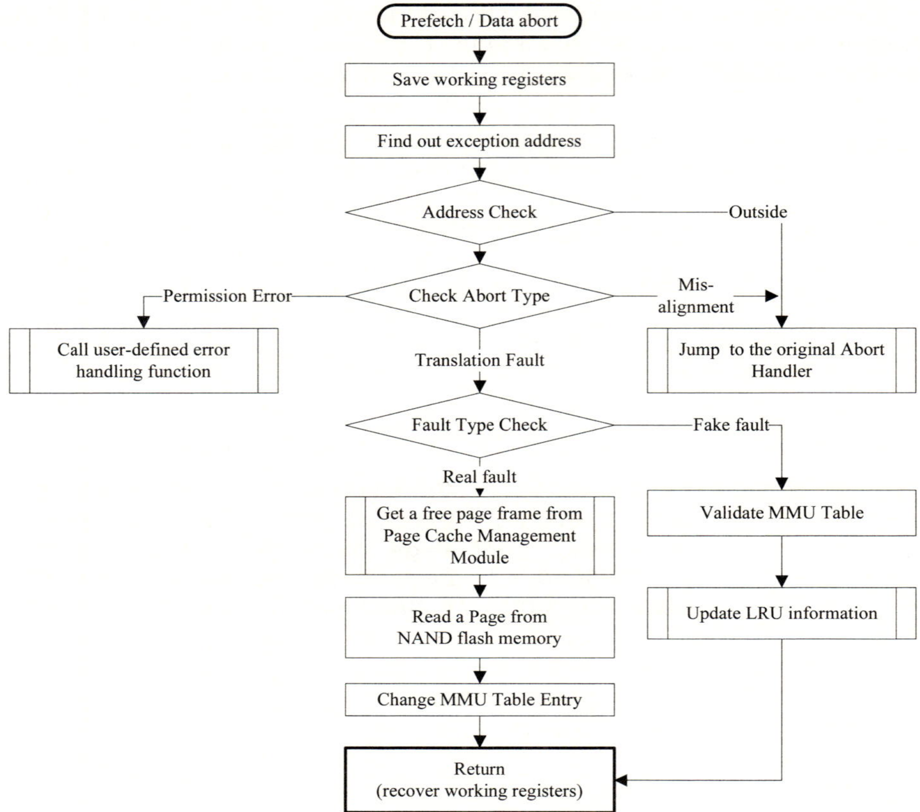

Fig. 4. The page fault handling process in the Virtual-ROM component: The system checks whether the exception occurs inside the Virtual-ROM, and then services the exceptions

4   Evaluation

To evaluate the Virtual-ROM performance, we performed a trace-driven simulation with SPEC 2000 CPU benchmark code access traces. We measured the required parameters from the real implementation of Virtual-ROM on ARM920T core evaluation board for the simulation. The page fault handling time was about 130us, 190us, and 310us for 1Kbyte, 2Kbyte, and 4Kbyte page configurations, respectively.

The traces were obtained from the public Trace Distribution Center [15]. A total of 100 millions traces for each benchmark of the SPEC CPU 2000 (CINT 2000 12 benchmarks, 14 CFP2000 benchmarks) was available. Because the Virtual-ROM is read-only, we extracted only the code traces, and about 65% of the traces were extracted. We simulated the code accesses with the traces, and calculated the time took for all traces. **Fig. 5** shows our simulation results. The results show that the 1K paged Virtual-ROM is comparable with 70ns NOR flash memory.

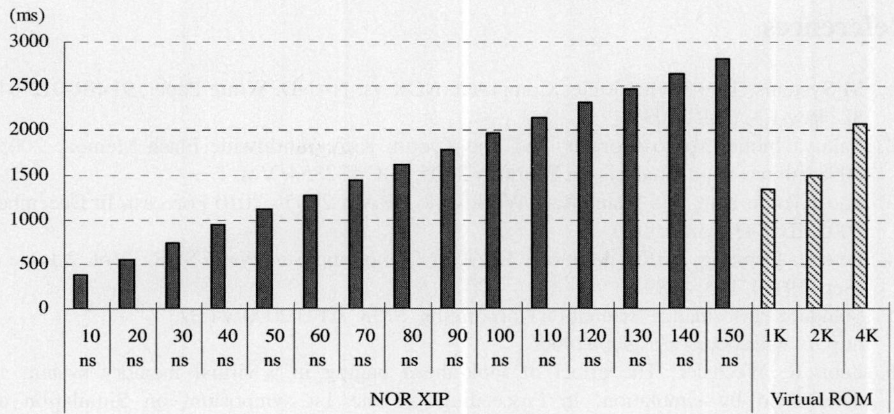

Fig. 5. Trace driven simulation result. The simulator calculates access time for the given address traces. The result above shows the total sum of all simulation results with 26 SPEC CPU 2000 benchmarks.

We applied the Virtual-ROM to a CDMA mobile phone with an ARM926EJ processor, 384Mbytes NAND flash memory, and 64Mbytes SDRAM. Previously, the phone used 29Mbytes RAM for shadowing purposes. We divided 29Mbytes of shadowing image into two partitions: a 6Mbyte shadowing partition that includes real-time tasks and 23Mbytes of Virtual-ROM partition. Because we gave 5Mbytes RAM for the page cache for the Virtual-ROM, we were able to save 18Mbytes of RAM successfully.

5   Conclusion

In this paper, we have proposed an RTOS based demand paging component, a Virtual-ROM to save shadowing RAM in NAND flash memory based mobile devices. Virtual-ROM enables a developer to use virtual and physical memory at the same time. Moreover, its simple but efficient design with a minimized porting cost makes it easier to apply to existing mobile applications.

Our trace driven simulation shows that the performance of the Virtual-ROM is comparable with 70ns NOR flash memory for the traces from SPEC CPU 2000 26 benchmarks. Furthermore, we were able to save about 30% of RAM from CDMA mobile phones with Virtual-ROM resulting in a significant reduction in production costs.

Further research is required to determine which code should be excluded from the Virtual-ROM region for real-time guarantee. For this purpose, we are planning to develop a methodology that includes a run-time profiler and a static image analyzer.

References

1. M-Systems, Two Technologies Compared: NOR vs. NAND. White Paper, 91-SR-012-04-8L, Rev 1.1, (Jul. 2003).
2. Takuya Inoue, Mario Morales, and Soo-Kyoum Kim, Worldwide Flash Memory 2005-2008 Forecast and Analysis. In February 2005, IDC #32854, Vol. 1.
3. Soo-Kyoum Kim, and Shane Rau, Worldwide DRAM 2005 - 2010 Forecast, In December 2005, IDC #34658, Vol.1.
4. Peter J. Denning, Virtual Memory. In ACM Computing Surveys (CSUR), Vol. 2 Issue 3 (Sep. 1970), 153 – 189.
5. Standard Performance Evaluation Corporation, SPEC CPU 2000 V1.3, http://www.spec.org/osg/cpu2000/
6. Leon R. Wechsler, The effect of look-ahead paging in a virtual memory system as determined by simulation. In Proceedings of the 1st symposium on Simulation of computer systems, (1973), 234 – 241.
7. Peter J, Denning, The working set model for program behavior. In Communications of the ACM, Vol.11, Issue 5 (May 1968), 323 – 333.
8. M. K. Rajaraman, Performance of a virtual memory: some experimental results. In ACM SIGMETRICS Performance Evaluation Review, Vol. 8, Issue 4, (1979), 63 – 68.
9. Alok Aggarwal, Virtual memory algorithms. In Proceedings of the twentieth annual ACM symposium on Theory of computing, (1988), 173 – 185.
10. Chanik Park, Jaeyu Seo, Sunhwan Bae, Hyojun Kim, Shinhan Kim, and Bumsoo Kim, A low-cost memory architecture with NAND XIP for mobile embedded systems. In Proceedings of CODES+ISSS'03 (Oct. 2003), 138 – 143.
11. Chanik Park, Jeong-Uk Kang, Seon-Yeong Park, and Jin-Soo Kim, Energy-aware demand paging on NAND flash-based embedded storages. In Proceedings of the 2004 international symposium on Low power electronics and design (Aug. 2004), 338 – 343.
12. Chanik Park, Junghee Lim, Kiwon Kwon, Jaejin Lee, and Sang Lyul Min, Compiler-assisted demand paging for embedded systems with flash memory, In Proceedings of the 4th ACM international conference on Embedded software EMSOFT '04 (Sep. 2004), 114 – 124.
13. Kieran Harty, and David R. Cheirton, Application-controlled physical memory using external page-cache management. In Proceedings of the fifth international conference on Architectural support for programming languages and operating systems (1992), 187 – 197.
14. Babaoglu, O. and Joy, W.N., Converting a swap-based system to do paging in an architecture lacking page-referenced bits. In Proceedings of Eighth ACM Symposium on Operating Systmes Principles (Dec. 1981), 78 – 86.
15. Performance Evaluation Laboratory of Brigham Young University, Trace Distribution Center, http://tds.cs.byu.edu/tds/index.jsp

Model-Driven Development of RTOS-Based Embedded Software[*]

Ji Chan Maeng, Dongjin Na, Yongsoon Lee, and Minsoo Ryu[**]

Computer Engineering Department, College of Information and Communications,
Hanyang University, Korea
`msryu@hanyang.ac.kr`

Abstract. There is a growing interest in the model-driven software development as a viable solution to the increasing complexity of embedded software. An important characteristic of a model-driven approach is that it allows a developer to focus on high-level models rather than low-level details, thereby raising the level of abstraction at which a developer can work. Therefore, the model-driven approach can provide a significant productivity gain and improved maintainability. One of the most noticeable approaches is the OMG's MDA (Model-Driven Architecture), which is a de facto standard. Unfortunately, MDA provides little support for the development of RTOS-based embedded software since it focuses primarily on middleware target platforms such as EJB, Web Services, .NET, and CORBA. In this paper, we present a model-driven approach to RTOS-based embedded software development and an automated tool that can produce RTOS-specific code. Our contributions are two fold. First, we propose generic RTOS APIs (Application Programming Interfaces) that can capture most of typical RTOS services that can be used as a means for describing application's RTOS-related behavior at an early design stage. We then present a transformation tool that can generate fully functional code by transforming generic RTOS APIs into RTOS-specific APIs. Our tool, called TransPI, is able to produce 'C' code for POSIX-compliant RTOSs, and is also configurable to target other RTOSs that do not conform to the POSIX standard.

1   Introduction

Model-driven software development is becoming a viable solution to increasing software complexity. A model-driven approach allows a developer to work at a high level of abstraction without being concerned about specifics of hardware and software [4,12]. A developer just needs to focus on building an abstract model, and automated tools can be used for model-to-code transformation [3,14]. Consequently, the model-driven approach can provide significant advantages in terms of productivity and maintenance.

[*] This work was supported in part by the Korea Research Foundation Grant funded by the Korean Government (MOEHRD) KRF-2005-041-D00625 and by IT Leading R&D Support Project funded the Ministry of Information and Communication.
[**] Corresponding author.

A. Levi et al. (Eds.): ISCIS 2006, LNCS 4263, pp. 687–696, 2006.
© Springer-Verlag Berlin Heidelberg 2006

Model-Driven Architecture (MDA) of the Object Management Group (OMG) is a de facto standard of model-driven software development [1]. An important characteristic of MDA is to separate the specification of abstract system behavior and functionality from the specification of concrete implementation details. To do so, MDA depends on two important types of models, Platform Independent Model (PIM) and Platform Specific Model (PSM). A PIM is a model that does not rely on any implementation technologies. A PSM is a model that contains enough implementation details so that code can be generated from it. With these models, there exist two stages of model mapping in MDA, PIM-to-PSM mapping and PSM-to-code mapping.

However, current MDA provides little support for the development of RTOS-based embedded software as it focuses primarily on middleware target platforms such as EJB, Web Services, .NET, and CORBA [5]. Note that the use of such middleware platforms allows applications to run independent of programming language and underlying operating system, thereby providing better productivity and portability. However, typical embedded systems have distinguishing requirements such as real-time performance and scarce resources. These requirements are often satisfied by adopting a real-time operating system, whereas the use of middleware makes the system encumbered with considerable runtime overheads [2]. As a result, many embedded applications are designed and implemented to run directly on top of RTOS (Real-Time Operating System).

In this paper, we present a model-driven approach for the development of RTOS-based embedded software. The proposed approach is very similar to MDA. The major difference is a special emphasis on RTOS platforms. Our approach can capture application's RTOS-related behavior at an early design stage and produce a concrete RTOS-specific implementation at the final stage. To do so, we defined generic RTOS APIs (Application Programming Interfaces), which represent generic RTOS services and are used as a means for incorporating abstract RTOS-related behavior into an application design model. We then developed a transformation tool that can generate code by transforming generic RTOS APIs into RTOS-specific APIs. Our tool, called TransPI, is able to produce 'C' code aimed at POSIX-compliant RTOSs, and is also configurable to target other RTOSs that do not conform to the POSIX standard [6].

There exist many commercial CASE tools such as Rose, Rhapsody, and Tau [9,10,11] for model-driven software development, which have been widely used in industry long before the release of MDA by OMG. Although these tools allow a developer to create a high-level application model and automatically generates final code from the application model, there is no PSM-like models that could address platform-specific issues. Instead, the above tools commonly use a virtual machine layer to achieve platform independence. For example, Rhapsody produces platform independent code from a model and directly runs it on an OS-dependent adapter. The OS adapter handles interaction with the underlying RTOS as a run-time environment. We believe that our transformation-based approach is superior to the virtual machine approach in two aspects. First, the transformation-based approach do not cause extra run-time overheads that would be incurred by the use of a virtual machine layer. A virtual machine should have wrapper functions that invoke real RTOS calls, and this incurs extra overheads both in time and space for every function call. This may be a serious problem for many performance- and resource-critical embedded systems. Second, the transformation-based approach can provide another important benefit for maintaining legacy software that was not developed through a model-driven approach. For example, it is possible to extend transformation tools to support reverse transformation, i.e., code-to-model transformation. Reverse transformation would allow a developer to derive a model from legacy code and then generate another code for a different target RTOS, or to change the legacy software by modifying the derived model and regenerating code. We will show that our transformation tool is able to generate RIC (RTOS Independent Code) from RSC (RTOS Specific Code), i.e., reverse transformation.

The rest of this paper is organized as follows. Section 2 describes how to develop generic RTOS APIs and how to use them for RTOS behavior modeling. Section 3 describes the design of TransPI. Section 4 presents its implementation and experimental results. Section 5 concludes this paper.

2 RTOS-Centric Model-Driven Software Development

In order to develop a model-driven methodology for RTOS-based embedded software development, it is important to answer two questions; (1) how to specify application's RTOS-related behavior in a platform-independent manner, and (2) how to transform the RTOS-related behavior into functional code on a specific RTOS platform. In this section, we attempt to find an answer to the first question.

2.1 Overall Approach

This work is a result of a collaborative project, called HOPES, between the Seoul National University and Hanyang University. The goal of HOPES was to develop an integrated model-based tool set aimed at embedded software development [7,8]. As shown in Figure 1, our design approach progresses in three stages. Firstly, an Application Behavior Model (ABM) is created through specification of application's functionality with a data flow model [15,18] and generic RTOS APIs. Secondly, an intermediate form of code, called RTOS Independent Code (RIC) is produced by a code synthesizer produces. Lastly, a target RTOS is chosen and the RIC is transformed into RTOS Specific Code (RSC) through TransPI. In the HOPES project, our role was to support the mapping of RIC to RSC, and the work reported here contains our major contributions made for the HOPES project. Specifically, they include generic RTOS APIs to capture application's RTOS-related behavior and an automated tool for RIC-to-RSC transformation.

2.2 Development of Generic RTOS APIs

An important observation about RTOS-based applications is that their RTOS-related behavior can be described by their invocation of RTOS APIs

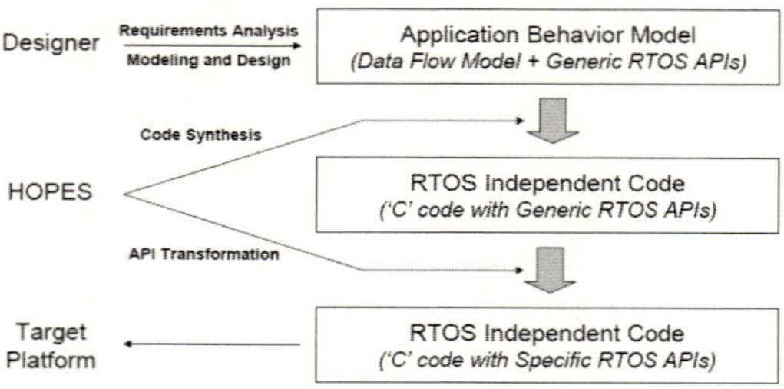

Fig. 1. Development flow within our model-driven approach

(Application Programming Interfaces). A typical RTOS provides various services including task management, memory management, file system management, and I/O management. Examples are networking through socket APIs and inter-process communications through message queue APIs. This observation led us to abstract RTOS APIs for the specification of RTOS-related behavior. Note that a usual RTOS provides more than hundreds of APIs whose semantics and syntax are different across RTOSs. This motivated us to take POSIX 1003.1-2004 standard as a starting point, and we abstracted a reasonable number of generic RTOS APIs from POSIX APIs.

IEEE POSIX is a set of standards that define the application programming interfaces (APIs) for UNIX-based software. The latest version is POSIX Standard 1003.1-2004 which consists of four major components; Base Definitions volume, System Interfaces volume, Shell and Utilities volume, and Rationale (Informative) volume. Among these, the System Interfaces volume defines the actual OS APIs, which amounts to 1023 APIs.

The POSIX System Interfaces can be categorized into eight classes as shown in Table 1. It is important to note that the POSIX standard is not restricted to OS-related services. The POSIX standard has been designed to cover all the aspects of application programming. Examples include mathematical functions such as sin( ) and cos( ) functions. In fact, the POSIX set is a superset of the standard C library functions (ISO/IEC 9899:1999) and the mathematical functions are supported by the standard C library (math.h).

The definition of generic RTOS APIs was rather straightforward. Our approach was to first group related POSIX APIs and organize them into coherent clusters, and then remove redundant or RTOS-irrelevant APIs from them. Note that the POSIX API set contains a number of APIs that have similar functionalities. For example, printf( ), fprintf( ), and sprintf( ) have an identical function of printing formatted data except they print to different display targets.

Our taxonomy of POSIX APIs is different from that of POSIX Standard since the POSIX includes many OS-irrelevant APIs as well. Ours is based on a typical RTOS structure in which there exist five RTOS components; task manager, memory manager, file manager, network manager, and device manager.

We reclassified POSIX APIs into eight categories based on this RTOS structure in mind while separately considering real-time and power management

Table 1. POSIX Standard 1003.1-2004 System Interfaces (1023 APIs in total)

Category	POSIX APIs
Signal	alarm, kill, signal, ... (32 APIs)
Standard I/O Streams	printf, scanf, getc, putc, calloc, ... (137 APIs)
STREAMS	ioctl, getmsg, putmsg, fattach, ... (8 APIs)
XSI Interprocess Communication	msgget, msgctl, semctl, shmctl, ... (11 APIs)
Realtime	pthread_barrier_wait, mq_open, ... (113 APIs)
Threads	pthread_create, pthread_exit, ... (68 APIs)
Sockets	socket, accept, bind, ... (28 APIs)
Tracing	posix_trace_attr_init, posix_trace_start, ... (50 APIs)
Others	sin, cos, tan, asinh, ... (676 APIs)

Table 2. Generic RTOS APIs (85 APIs in total)

Category	Generic RTOS APIs
Task Management	EXEC, EXIT, FORK, THREAD_CREATE, THREAD_DETACH, THREAD_EXIT, THREAD_JOIN, ... (21 APIs)
Real-Time Services	MQ_RECEIVE, MQ_SEND, MQ_SETATTR, SEM_POST, SEM_WAIT, SCHEDGETPARAM, ... (15 APIs)
Power Management	PM_EN_RESOURCE, PM_DIS_RESOURCE, ... (8 APIs)
Memory Management	MEMALLOC, MMAP, MUNMAP, FREE (4 APIs)
File Management	CHDIR, CLOSE, MKDIR, OPEN, READ, ... (17 APIs)
Network Management	SOCK_ACCEPT, SOCK_BIND, ... (9 APIs)
Device Management	IOCTL, POLL, SELECT (3 APIs)
Others	CTIME, GETITIMER, GETTIMEOFDAY, ... (8 APIs)

issues. We then defined a set of generic RTOS APIs for each category. The derived generic RTOS APIs are given in Table 2.

2.3   Specification of RTOS-Related Behavior

Based on generic RTOS APIs, the application's RTOS-related behavior can be easily incorporated into a top-level ABM (application behavior model). This can be best explained through the following example. Figure 2 shows a top-level data flow diagram of H.263 decoder example, which was also used in our experiments. The H.263 decoder consists of five major components: main controller, AVI Reader, Divx decoder, MPEG audio decoder, and frame buffer manager. The main controller is responsible for the execution and coordination of the other four elements by using appropriate RTOS services. Specifically, it creates four threads for pipelined concurrent execution of AVI Reader, Divx decoder, MPEG audio decoder, and frame buffer manager. This requires the main controller to invoke three generic RTOS APIs, THREAD_CREATE, THREAD_JOIN, and THREAD_EXIT. Similarly, the other four components rely on generic RTOS APIs to perform their required functions such as access to multimedia data residing on secondary storage, dynamic allocation of required memory, and destruction of threads.

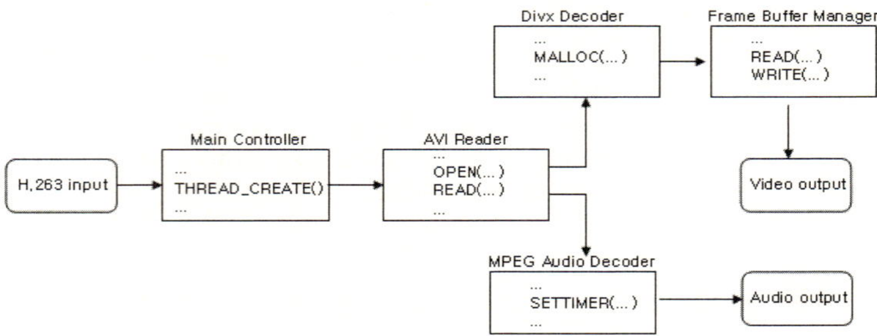

Fig. 2. RTOS-related behavior specification with generic RTOS APIs

Note that the above example has been constructed through the entire HOPES tool set. Our approach to the application's behavioral modeling uses a data flow model for describing overall functionality and an extended finite state machine model [8] for specifying detailed behavior of each component. Each component in Figure 2 has been modeled as a finite state machine, whose precise behavior can be specified by a set of states, events, guard conditions, and actions. Here, we do not delve into how the extended finite state machine can specify detailed behavior. Interested readers are referred to [8].

3   Transformation of Generic RTOS APIs

Once application's RTOS-related behavior has been specified using generic RTOS APIs, the specified behavior can then be transformed into a concrete RTOS-specific implementation through API transformation. This process is automated by our API translator, called TransPI. In this section, we describe how TransPI performs the API transformation.

An important goal of our API translator development is configurability, which is crucial for handling a diversity of target RTOSs ranging from POSIX-compliant RTOSs to those that do not support POSIX APIs. To achieve configurability, we designed a rule-based API translator. TransPI relies on a set of rules that govern transformation of generic RTOS APIs into RTOS-specific APIs. TransPI allows a developer to modify these transformation rules and/or add new rules. Therefore, TransPI can be configured to target any particular RTOS by specifying transformation rules specific to the chosen RTOS.

3.1 API Usage Patterns

Through a preliminary investigation, we found that many generic RTOS APIs have some patterns in their usage. For example, a SEM_WAIT( ) that attempts to acquire a lock must be followed by a SEM_POST( ) that releases the lock. Furthermore, when these APIs are transformed into RSC, some extra routines such as sem_open( ) and sem_close( ) should also be added at proper locations in the code.

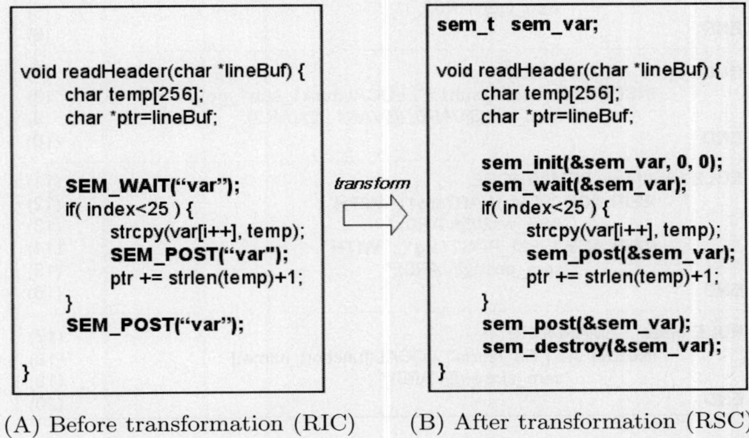

(A) Before transformation (RIC)   (B) After transformation (RSC)

Fig. 3. Transformation of SEMAPHORE pattern into POSIX compliant C code

To handle such patterns in our transformation, we introduced a notion of API pattern into the design of TransPI. We defined an API pattern as a group of one or more APIs that must be used in a synchronous manner to meet their predefined semantics. Figure 3 illustrates an example of RIC and its transformation into POSIX compliant RSC. It shows that SEM_WAIT and SEM_POST constitute a SEMAPHORE pattern and that the transformation replaces SEM_WAIT and SEM_POST with sem_wait( ) and sem_post( ), respectively. The transformation also inserts additional code including: the declaration of a semaphore variable, sem_init( ), and sem_destroy( ).

3.2 Transformation Language and Rules

We defined a dedicated transformation language that can be used to specify transformation rules. The key elements of the transformation language include 7 directives: INCLUDE AT, DECLARE AT, INITIALIZE AT, INSERT AT, REPLACE BY, FINALIZE AT, and DELETE.

- INCLUDE AT: include a required header file at a specified location.
- DECLARE AT: declare variables at a specified location.
- INITIALIZE AT: insert an initialization routine at a specified location.

- INSERT AT: insert a code fragment at a specified location.
- REPLACE WITH: replace a code fragment with at a specified code.
- FINALIZE AT: insert a finalization routine at a specified location.
- DELETE: delete a specified code fragment.

```
RULE initialize_SEMAPHORE                                          (1)
        INCLUDE AT ["task1_sub1.c", HEADER]                        (2)
                "#include <semaphore.h>"                            (3)
        DECLARE AT ["task1_sub1.c", LOCAL(task1_sub1_go)]          (4)
                "sem_t @VAR0;",                                     (5)
END                                                                (6)

RULE open_SEMAPHORE                                                (7)
        INSERT AT ["task1_sub1.c", LOCAL(task1_sub1_go)]           (8)
                "sem_init(@VAR0, @VAR1, @VAR2);",                  (9)
END                                                                (10)

RULE transform_SEMAPHORE                                           (11)
        REPLACE "SEM_WAIT(arg1);" WITH                             (12)
                "sem_wait(@VAR0);"                                 (13)
        REPLACE "SEM_POST(arg1);" WITH                             (14)
                "sem_post(@VAR0);"                                 (15)
END                                                                (16)

RULE close_SEMAPHORE                                               (17)
        INSERT AT ["file_name", LOCAL(function_name)]              (18)
                "sem_close(@VAR0);"                                (19)
END                                                                (20)
```

Fig. 4. Transformation rules for SEMAPHORE pattern

The above directives allow us to specify a family of transformation rules for each API pattern. Generally, each pattern can have at most five transformation rules: initialize, open, transform, close, and finalize rules. Figure 4 illustrates the transformation rules for SEMAPHORE pattern, which is subject to four transformation rules.

3.3   Implementation

TransPI has been implemented in C, and consists of the following three major stages.

- Stage 1 (initialization): It reads in two configuration files, one for a list of API patterns and the other for a set of transformation rules.
- Stage 2 (model analysis): It accepts RIC as input and identifies generic APIs and patterns.
- Stage 3 (code generation): It performs a two-pass transformation based on given transformation. In the first pass, it transforms individual generic RTOS APIs into RTOS-specific APIs. In the second pass, it inserts extra code segment per API pattern.

Note that TransPI allows for reverse transformation, i.e., generation of RIC from RSC. This can be done by providing TransPI with a set of rules for reverse transformation. It is straightforward to derive reverse transformation rules from forward transformation rules. Here, due to space limitation, we do not include how to create a reverse transformation rule with a forward transformation rule.

4   Empirical Study

We performed intensive tests on TransPI using Open POSIX Test Suite [20]. Open POSIX Test Suite is freely available on the Web and provides a lot of C code that had been written with POSIX APIs. To see if our tool can produce operational code for POSIX compliant RTOSs, we manually converted the POSIX APIs in the original Test Suite C code into generic RTOS APIs and then transformed them back into POSIX-compliant C.

We also validated TransPI through a case study on H.263 decoder development. In preliminary work, we had constructed a RIC that consists of five RIC files, MainController.ric, AviReader.ric, DivxDecoder.ric, MpegAudioDecoder.ric, and FrameBufferManager.ric. TransPI was then used to transform each RIC file into POSIX-compliant C code. We compiled the resulting files and successfully executed the resulting H.263 decoder on top of Linux [13].

5   Conclusion

In this paper we presented a model-driven approach and a support tool for the development of RTOSbased embedded software. Our major contributions are: (1) generic RTOS APIs that can be used to specify RTOS-related behavior at modeling level, and (2) an automated tool that can produce RTOSspecific code from RTOS-independent code.

We are currently extending TransPI to support automatic reverse transformation. Note that even with current implementation of TransPI, it is able to reverse-transform 'C' code into a model provided that rules for reverse transformation are given. However, specification of reverse transformation rules is very time-consuming and errorprone. To alleviate this problem, we are working on another tool that can automatically generate reverse transformation rules from forward transformation rules.

References

1. Thomas O. Meservy and Kurt D. Fenstermacher: Transforming Software Development: An MDA Road Map. IEEE Computer, Vol. 38(9) (2005) 52–58
2. Pieter Van Gorp, Dirk Janssens, and Tracy Gardner, Write Once, Deploy N: a Performance Oriented MDA Case Study. Proceedings of the 8th IEEE International Enterprise Distributed Object Computing Conference, (2004) 123–134
3. Jana Koehler, Rainer Hauser, Shubir Kapoor, Fred Y. Wu, and Santhosh Kumaran: A Model-Driven Transformation Method. Proceedings of the 7th IEEE International Enterprise Distributed Object Computing Conference, (2003) 186–197

4. Joao Paulo Almeida, Remco Dijkman, Marten van Sinderen, and Luis Ferreira Pires: On the Notion of Abstract Platform in MDA Development. Proceedings of the 8th IEEE International Enterprise Distributed Object Computing Conference, (2004) 253–263
5. Object Management Group Inc.: MDA Guide v1.0.1. http://www.omg.org, (June 2003)
6. The Open Group: The Open Group Base Specification Issue 6, IEEE Std 1003.1, 2004 Edition. http://www.unix.org, (2004)
7. HOPES. http://peace.snu.ac.kr/hopes, (2005)
8. Soonhoi Ha: Hardware/Software Co-design of Multimedia Embedded Systems: PeaCE Approach. white paper, (2004)
9. International Business Machines Corporation: Rational Rose-RT. http://www.ibm.com
10. I-Logix: Rhapsody. http://www.ilogix.com/
11. Telelogic AB: TAU. http://www.telelogic.com/
12. Stephen J. Mellor, Kendall Scott, Axel Uhl and Dirk Weise: MDA Distilled: Principles of Model- Driven Architecture. Addison Wesley, (2004)
13. Ji Chan Meang, Jong-Hyuk Kim, and Minsoo Ryu, An RTOS API Translator for Model-Driven Embedded Software Development. Proceedings of the IEEE International Conference on Embedded and Real-Time Computing Systems and Applications, (2006)
14. Anneke Kleppe, Jos Warmer and Wim Bast: MDA Explained: The Model Driven Architecture: Practice and Promise. Addison Wesley, (2003)
15. David Harel: Statecharts: A visual formalism for complex systems. Science of Computer Programming, Vol. 8(3) (June 1987) 231-274
16. Grady Booch, James Rumbaugh, and Ivar Jacobson: The Unified Modeling Language User Guide. Addison Wesley, (1999)
17. Object Management Group Inc.: CORBA/IIOP Specification. http://www.omg.org
18. Dohyung Kim and Soonhoi Ha: Static Analysis and Automatic Code Synthesis of flexible FSM Model. ASP-DAC 2005, (January 2005)
19. Stephen J. Mellor and Marc J. Balcer: Executable UML: A Foundation for Model-Driven Architecture. Addison Wesley, (2002)
20. Open POSIX Test Suite from A GPL Open Source Project. http://posixtest.sourceforge.net/

A Target Oriented Agent to Collect Specific Information in a Chat Medium

Cemal Köse and Özcan Özyurt

Department of Computer Engineering,
Faculty of Engineering,
Karadeniz Technical University,
61080 Trabzon, Turkey
{ckose, oozyurt}@ktu.edu.tr

Abstract. Internet and chat mediums provide important and quite useful information about human life in different societies such as their current interests, habits, social behaviors and criminal tendency. In this study, we have presented an intelligent identification system that is designed to identify the sex of a person in a Turkish chat medium. To do this task, a target oriented chat agent is implemented. A simple discrimination function is proposed for sex identification. The system also uses a semantic analysis method to determine the sex of the chatters. Here, the sex identification is taken as an example in the information extraction in chat mediums. This proposed identification system employs the agent and acquires data from a chat medium, and then automatically detects the chatter's sex from the information exchanged between the agent and chatter. The system has achieved accuracy about 90% in the sex identification in a real chat medium.

Keywords: Natural Language Processing, Chat Conversations, Sex Identification, Machine Learning, Intelligent Agent.

1 Introduction

Many research projects on intelligent systems and agents have been launched to collect and extract information from different mediums such as Internet, especially chat, and other communication mediums. These systems possess a common core approach to learn a probabilistic profile of chatters in the mediums, and then they use the profile to find, or classify the information collected from the mediums [1], [2], [3]. A chat medium contains a vast amount of information potentially relevant to a society's current interests, habits, social behaviors, crime rate and tendency [4], [5]. Users may spend a large portion of their time to find out information in chat mediums. Therefore, a sample identification system is implemented to determine chatter's sex identity in chat mediums An intelligent agent, as a chat engine, may also help the users in finding the interested information in the medium [2], [3]. Here, the target oriented agent tries to collect specific information from a targeted chatter in chat mediums. The agent automatically adapts itself to the chatter's behavior and assists users collecting information from the medium [1], [6], [7]. Thus, understanding of a natural language by a machine comprises the process of transforming a sentence into

A. Levi et al. (Eds.): ISCIS 2006, LNCS 4263, pp. 697–706, 2006.

an internal representation [8], [9]. So, the system concludes relationships and decisions according to the resulting representations by employing the process of determining the meaning of sentences in natural language.

In this study, an intelligent identification system is proposed to collect and evaluate information from chat mediums for sex identification. In particular, an intelligent sex identification method is described. Performance of the system is measured in real chat mediums. The rest of this paper is organized as follows. A summary of the grammar of Turkish language is given in Section 2. Methods for semantic and pragmatic analysis of Turkish and the design of the agent are explained in Section 3. A detailed description of the identification system is also presented the same section. The implementation and results are discussed in Section 4. The conclusion and future work are given in Section 5.

2   Turkish Language

Languages may be classified according to their structures and origins. Ural-Altaic languages are one of the most commonly spoken languages in the world. Turkic languages that belong to the group of Ural-Altaic languages form a subfamily of the Altaic languages, and Turkish is an Oghuz oriented member of Turkic language family. Turkish language has several noticeable characteristics. One of them is adding one or more suffixes to a word producing many new words [10], [11]. Suffixes in Turkish may be divided into two groups as inflectional and derivational suffixes. Inflectional suffixes determine state, condition, case, number, person and tense of the words. Adding a derivational suffix to a noun or a verb changes the meaning of the word and generates a new word used for a different concept. Another characteristic of the Turkish language is the vowel and consonant harmony. Turkish languages have two kinds of vowel harmony. The vowels in Turkish language are grouped as front and back vowels. The front vowels are produced at the front of the mouth and back vowels are produced at the back of the mouth. Turkish words can contain only one kind of vowel and all suffixes added to the word must conform to the vowel of the syllable preceding them [11], [12]. Turkish language has also consonant harmony as well. If a morpheme follows a word ending in constants k, p, t or ç, the last constant of the word changes to constants g-ğ, b, d or c respectively.

2.1   Morphological Analysis

Turkish is an agglutinative language with respect to word structures formed by productive affixations of derivational and inflectional suffixes added to root words. Therefore, many different words can be constructed from roots and morphemes to describe objects and concepts. Thus, each input from the conversations is first checked for spelling errors considering abbreviations and words are corrected if possible. Generally, two approaches are used to determine and correct the spelling errors according to the type of words [10]. First approaches are frequency or polygram methods. The second approach may correct any word with spelling errors by searching the closest word with suitable suffixes arranged in order [10], [12]. Our system considers the abbreviations and words used in the chat mediums, and effectively employs the "closest word" method to correct words with spelling error.

A two-level morphological model is used to analyze morphological structures in the identification system [13]. These levels are surface and lexical levels. The surface level is the input as represented in original language. The lexical level is decomposed form of the input into morphemes. The sequence of morphemes, appearing in a word, is determined by morphotactics of a language. Therefore, morphologic analysis in Turkish is realized in several steps; determination of the root word of an input word, morphological tests, and determinations of morphemes of the input word. Firstly, the system tries to locate the root and possible following morphemes by checking possible constructions. Secondly, the system goes to the next state. At this state it searches for the possible morphemes. If it does not match with the morpheme, the system goes to the next morpheme. If there are no matching suffixes, the system applies the spelling checker to correct the input word or generates spelling error output for the word.

2.2 Turkish Language Grammar

Turkish language has some syntactical, morphological and grammatical rules that form words and sentences. Syntactically, the structure of sentences in Turkish languages is generally in Subject-Object-Verb (S-O-V) order. However, mainly grammatical structure of Turkish can be defined as S-O-V, but sometimes adults or children may express a sentence in different grammatical structures. In addition to this, important points are kept next to the verb because the verb is the most important part of a sentence and it takes many suffixes changing the meaning of the sentence [12].

Language understanding is a rule-based part of this system that converts natural language sentences into semantic networks. In this application, first, the morphological analysis module accepts an input string from a dialogue and parses it into morphemes morphologically [8], [9], [10]. Thus, the module checks whether the input is syntactically valid, generates a parse tree, and constructs a semantic structure for the input sentence. Then, semantic analysis module analyses the resulting morphemes expressed in the form of a semantic structure. Then, semantic analysis module establishes the semantic network on the input sentence [14]. Here, the main verb of a sentence is the main element of the semantic structure, so the semantic analysis module searches items that are connected by means of various relationships.

3 The Identification System

In a chat conversation, chatter considers the corresponding chatter's sex, and the course and contents of the conversation may mainly be shaped according to the corresponding persons' sexual identity. Therefore, an example identification agent is implemented to determine chatters' sex identity in the chat mediums. To do this, many conversations are acquired from chat mediums designed on purpose, and then statistical results are obtained by analyzing the conversations.

3.1 A Simple Identification Function

Statistical information related to each chosen word is collected from the purposely designed chat and the other Internet chat mediums. By using this statistical information a weighting coefficient is determined for each word in each group. Each weighting coefficient is normalized into the interval of 0-1, and then each coefficient of words in a group is also normalized by the number of words in the group that exists in the conversation. If a word is female dominant, α varies from 0 to 0.5 but if the word is male dominant, α varies from 0.5 to 1.0. Then, a simple discrimination function or equation (1) is used to identify the sex of a person in a chat medium.

$$g_i = (\alpha_{i1} w_1 + \alpha_{i2} w_2 + ,..., + \alpha_{ik} w_k) / \beta_i. \tag{1}$$

$$\beta_i = (\alpha_{i1} + \alpha_{i2} + ,.. + \alpha_{ik}). \tag{2}$$

Where g_i varies from 0 to 1 and determines the chatters' sexual identity as female or male for ith word group, α_{ij} is the jth weighting coefficient of jth word in ith word group, β_i calculated by equation (2) is normalization divider for the current number of existing words in the ith word group, and w_k is the weighting coefficient of a word in a word group for female or male.

These words are also classified in several groups according to their conceptual relations. Thus, the importance of some word groups can be emphasized collectively. So, several word groups are defined considering words acquired from the conversations in the chat mediums. Then, a weighting coefficient is also assigned for each word group. Equation (3) can be used to determine the sex identity of any chatter in a conversation. This function considers each word in conversations separately and collectively.

$$\gamma = (\lambda_{g1} * g_1 + \lambda_{g2} * g_2 + ,..., + \lambda_{gn} * g_n) / \theta. \tag{3}$$

$$\theta = (\lambda_{g1} + \lambda_{g2} + ,... + \lambda_{gn}). \tag{4}$$

Where γ varies from 0 to 1 and determines the chatters sexual identity as female or male, λ_{gi} is the weighting coefficient for ith female or male word group, θ calculated by equation (4) is normalization divider for the current number of existing groups in a conversation, and λ_{gi} is the weighting coefficient of ith groups. Hence, the weighting coefficients of each group are determined according to dominant sexual identity of the group. Then, the sex of the chatters may be identified as female when γ is determined between 0.0 and 0.5. On the other hand, chatters may be identified as male when γ is determined between 0.5 and 1.0.

3.2 Semantic Analysis of Chat Conversations

Some sentences in conversations such as questions, answers and addressed sentences may expose the sex of the chatter. These typical sentences may be obtained from any chat conversation. Therefore, a semantic analyzer may improve the accuracy of the identification system. Input sentences in a conversation are first morphologically analyzed and then the resulting morphemes are semantically analyzed if a familiar sentence patterns are encountered in a chat conversation. Then, a semantic network is formed to establish the semantic relation between the morphemes of the sentence. These semantic relations may contribute to the final decision and strengthen the accuracy of decision of the identification system. Equation (5) and (6) combines the statistic and semantic identification outputs and produces single identification output. Our identification system is also capable of adding new question, reply and addressed sentences to its database by closely monitoring related sentences in conversations in a chat medium.

$$\lambda = (\lambda_{sta} * \gamma_{sta} + \lambda_{sem} * \gamma_{sem}) / \eta. \tag{5}$$

$$\eta = (\lambda_{sta} + \lambda_{sem}). \tag{6}$$

Where λ is the final result that identifies the sex of the chatter, λ_{sta} and λ_{sem} are the statistic and semantic weigh coefficients respectively, γ_{sta} and γ_{sem} are statistic and semantic identifications respectively, and η is the normalization divider.

In a chat conversation, many question-answer, addressed and implication sentences can be used to strengthen the accuracy of decision. For example "Name? *(ismin?)*→ Alan", "Who are you? *(sen kimsin?)* → David", "U *(U)* → Buket" and etc. An addressed sentence may also be used such as "How are you David (Nasılsın? David)", "What is the news Ahmet *(Nbr Ahmnet?)*", "I am fine Ali *(İyidir Ali)*" and etc. Implication sentences can also be accounted in chat conversations as listed in Table 1. For example "I know that Vigro ladies like this *(benim tanıdığım başak burcu bayanları böyle)*", "I am wearing what I wanted to wear. *(istediğimi giyiyiyorum)*", and etc.

Table 1. A semantic and pragmatic analysis of other implying sentences

	Chatter	Sentence	English
S-1	…	..	..
S-0	merix	Evet	Yes
S+1	merix	sen biliyorsun bayan	You know Lady
S+2	GencPrens	benim tanıdığım başak burcu bayanları böyle	I know that vigro ladies like this
S+3	merix	merakın var herhalde	I suppose You are curious
S-1	…	..	..
S-0	GencPrens	bu arada	Meanwhile
S+1	merix	istediğimi giyiyorum	I am wearing what I wanted to wear
S+2	GencPrens	msn adresin varmı?	Do you have msn address?

3.3 Design of the Target Oriented Agent

In a real chat medium, chatters may mislead and misunderstand each other. Therefore, an intelligent chat agent is implemented to minimize or eliminate the effects of these misleading sentences. The chat agent is also able to chat in the chat medium by asking and answering questions according to the past conversations [15], [16]. So, the chat agent will be able to establish a dialogue with chatters and collect information by asking and replying questions purposely and increases the accuracy of the identification.

A natural language understanding system needs large amount of knowledge to understand even a simple chat conversation. This system uses a knowledge base constructed in terms of situations in conversations to understand chat conversations. In a chat sentence, finding out words, and their roles and meanings are important to make the semantic analysis. Fillmore proposed a verb-oriented approach to define the roles of nouns and noun phrases in the action in a sentence [12]. Case grammar and the relation between concepts can be used to make semantic analysis of the sentences in a conversation. These case relationships include object, agent, instrument, location and time. Thus, a centered verb node with various links to the other participant nodes in the action represents the case frame of an input sentence. In parsing a sentence, the system first finds the verb to retrieve the case frame or grammar. Then, the relationship between nodes in the sentence is to be linked by several questions such as "Who?", "What?", "How?, "When?", and "Where?".

On the other hand, a frame identification method reveals the implicit connections of information from the explicitly organized data structures in a chat dialogue [12]. Here, these implicit connections of information are called frames and these frames structures organize the knowledge of the world. The agent adapts itself to a new situation by calling up information from past experiences as structured objects. The information as structured object contains the frame identification information and default information, descriptor of requirements for a frame, procedural information on usage of the structure described, frame, and new instance information. Here, any information is first introduced to this thematic role model, based module and then these information frames are used to comment about an event.

In a typical chat conversation, the proposed agent starts a conversation with a targeted chatter by using the default information acquired from the specially designed chat system. This default knowledge base may be extended by adding new concepts and sentences encountered in any participated conversation. A new concept or sentence is added to the knowledge base if they are not present in any existing knowledge base. A normal conversation between agent and chatter is carried on by considering the case relationships and frame model. In general, the active element of the conversation is decided as the corresponding chatter. Here, the agent carrying on the conversation in a normal manner waits for the sex related concepts and sentences. When a sex related sentence is encountered, the agent focuses more on the subject in a predetermined manner by considering the previous experiences. In other words, the agent follows the conversation by generating more sex related questions and answer from its knowledge base. If the corresponding chatter is not active enough, following the normal introduction of the conversation, the agent starts to generate sex related sentences from the previous knowledge base.

4   Results

In this paper, an intelligent sex identification system is presented to collect information from chat mediums. For sex identification in chat mediums, this system uses a simple discrimination function and employs an intelligent agent. In addition to this, the effectiveness of the system with a semantic analysis method is also enhanced in real chat mediums. About two hundred and three conversations have been collected from specially designed chat and real mediums. For testing, forty-nine of the conversations between ninety-eight chatters are chosen as the training set including forty-four female and fifty-four male. In the identification process, a scale with four levels is used to determine the sex of a person. The outcome of the system is classified into four categories as strongly male or female, male or female, possibly male or female and undecided. Experimental results indicate that the intelligent system is quite efficient in the sex identification in the chat mediums.

The weighting coefficients of the proposed discrimination function for each word are based on the data collected from the chat medium and the weighting coefficients of the word groups are determined experimentally. Conversations are also grouped as male-male conversation, male-female and female-female conversations, and then the performance of the system measured for each group. The results presented in Table 2 shows the evaluation of the identification function for all conversations on the test data collected from the specially designed chat medium. Here, morphological and semantic analyses of the conversations are exploited to improve the accuracy of the system. The accuracy of decisions of the system with the semantic analyzer has reached to 92.2%.

Table 2. The performance of the identification system with the semantic analysis related to the conversation groups

	Male-Male	Male-Female	Female-Female	General
Number of conversations	12	30	7	49
Number of chatters	24	60	14	98
Number of correct decision	20	54	13	87
Number of wrong decisions	2	5	1	8
Number of undecided results	2	1	0	4
Percentage of correct decisions	83.4%	90.0%	92.9%	88.7%
Percentage of wrong decision	8.3%	8.3%	7.1%	8.2%
Percentage of undecided results	8.3%	1.7%	0.0%	3.1%

More than one hundred conversations are recorded from mIRC (mIRC is a shareware Internet Relay Chat) and thirty of them are chosen randomly. In this experiment, five persons are chosen to determine the sex of the chatters in these conversations. These people read the chosen conversations thoroughly and decided about the sex of the chatters. Their decisions were compared to the decision of the identification system. The decision results of the identification system are listed in Table 3. When these results are examined carefully, it has been seen that the accuracy of identification increases for both female and male chatters. About 18.5% of improvement is achieved in general.

Table 3. The performance of identification system with the semantic analysis in the mIRC medium

	Male Chatters	Female Chatters	General
Number of chatters	19	8	27
Number of correct decisions	17	8	25
Number of wrong decisions	2	-	2
Number of undecided decisions	-	-	-
Percentage of correct decisions	89.5%	100%	92.6%
Percentage of wrong decisions	10.5%	0%	7.4%

Fifteen conversations between the chat engine chatters were recorded in the specially designed chat medium. In all these conversations, the case relationships and frame model were used to carry on the normal conversations and the decisions of the identification system are listed in Table 4. In general, the accuracy of identification is about 86% when the agent is employed. As it can be seen from the table, the system achieves a lower performance than expected. Thus, the intelligent agent is still not mature enough and need to be improved for better dialogues. The knowledge base is also very limited and mostly consists of sex related words. Conversations are mostly directed by the chatters rather than the agent and limited number of chatters may not be suitable for the system to show the complete performance. Also, context of the conversation may not be very interesting for the corresponding chatters because the agent is not active enough.

Table 4. The performance of the intelligent system with the intelligent agent

	Male Chatters	Female Chatters	General
Number of chatters	9	6	15
Number of correct decisions	7	6	13
Number of wrong decisions	1	-	1
Number of undecided decisions	1	-	1
Percentage of correct decisions	77.8%	100.0%	86.7%
Percentage of wrong decisions	11.1%	0.0%	6.7%

5   Conclusion and Future Work

In this study, our goal is to collect valuable information from chat mediums. In order to do this, we addressed syntactic, morphologic and semantic analysis, and understanding sentences in chat conversations. Then, a morphological, syntax and semantic analysis modules were implemented. Our right to left morphological and syntactical analyzers determines the root, suffixes and type of word such as object, subject, verb etc. Semantic analyzer makes the meaning out of these outputs to construct the semantic network. This semantic network is used to produce the frame structure. So, the intelligent system is designed for automatic identification of sex of a person from the content of dialogues in a chat medium. A simple discrimination function is used for sex identification. The identification system with the intelligent agent achieves accuracy over 80% in sex identification in chat mediums.

Although some satisfactory results are obtained, the system is still need to be improved. The results obtained from experiments show that the methods proposed for sex identification may also be applied to the other concepts and subjects. Then, another future task is to extend the system to other subjects. A Neural-Fuzzy method, considering the intersection of the word groups, can be employed to determine more precise weighting coefficients for the discrimination function. This could further improve the accuracy of the identification system. In the literature, several other methods are also employed for sex identification. The proposed simple identification method has quite good performance but a comparison between other methods and this method may not be fair since they are evaluated on different data. So, comparing this proposed method with the others may be considered as another important future work.

References

1. Harksoo, K., Choong-Nyoung, S., Jungyun, S.: A dialogue-based information retrieval assistant using shallow NLP techniques in online domains. IEICE Trans. Inf. & Syst., Vol. 5. (2005) 801 – 808
2. Ackerman, M., Billsus, D., Gaffney, S.: Learning Probabilistic User Profiles: Applications to Finding Interesting Web Sites, Notifying Users of Relevant Changes to Web Pages, and Locating Grant Opportunities. AI magazine, Vol. 18. (1997) 47 – 56
3. Baumgartner R., Eiter T., Gottlob G., Herzog M., Koch C.: Information extraction for the semantic. Lecture Notes in Computer Science – Reasoning Web, Vol. 3564. (2005) 275 – 289
4. Elnahrawy, E.: Log-Based Chat Room Monitoring Using Text Categorization: A Comparative Study. The International Conference on Information and Knowledge Sharing, US Virgin Islands (2002)
5. Khan, F.M., Fisher, T.A., Shuler, L., Wu, T., Pottenger, W.M.: Mining Chatroom Conversations for Social and Semantic Interactions. Lehigh University Technical Report LU-CSE-02-011, (2002)
6. Cozar, R.L., Torre De La, A., Segura, J.C.: Testing dialogue system by means of automatic generation of conversations. ELSEVIER–Interacting with Computer, Vol. 14. (2002) 521–546
7. Gorin, A.L., Ricaddi, G., Wright, J.H.: How may I help you?. ELSEVIER-Speech and Communication. Vol. 23. (1997) 113 – 127
8. Kanagaluru, C.S., Janaki, R.D.: The dynamics of language understanding. Language Engineering Conference, Hyderabad, India (2002) 197 – 199
9. Lee, M.C., Leong, R.V.: NLUS - A Prolog Based Natural Language Understanding System. The 4th International Conference on Computing and Information, Toronto, Canada (1992) 204 – 207
10. Solak, A., Oflazer, K.: Parsing agglutinative word structures and its application to spelling checking for Turkish. The 15th International Conference on Computational Linguistic, Vol.1. Nantes France (1992) 39 – 46
11. Hengirmen, M.: Türkçe Dilbilgisi. Engin Yayınevi, Ankara (2002)
12. Nabiyev, V.V.: Yapay Zeka: Problemler-Yöntemler-Algoritmalar. 2. Baskı, Seçkin Yayınevi Ankara (2005)

13. Oflazer, K.: Two-level Description of Turkish Morphology. Literary and Linguistic Computing, Vol. 9. (1994) 137 – 148
14. Woods, W.A.: Transition network grammars for natural language analysis. Communications of the ACM, Vol. 13. (1970) 591 – 606
15. Mashiro, A., Tasuku, O. Kiyoshi, U., Tasuhisa, N.: An Automatic Dialogue System Generator from the Internet Information Contents. 7th European Conference on Speech Communication and Technology, Aalborg Denmark (2001) 1743 – 1746
16. Pinto, D., Branstain, M., Coleman, R., Croft, W., King, M.: QuASM: A System for Question Answering Using Semi-Structured Data. Joint Conference on Digital Libraries, Portland Oregon USA (2002) 46 – 55

Algorithms for Within-Cluster Searches
Using Inverted Files

Ismail Sengor Altingovde, Fazli Can, and Özgür Ulusoy

Department of Computer Engineering, Bilkent University
06800, Ankara, Turkey
{ismaila, canf, oulusoy}@cs.bilkent.edu.tr

Abstract. Information retrieval over clustered document collections has two successive stages: first identifying the best-clusters and then the best-documents in these clusters that are most similar to the user query. In this paper, we assume that an inverted file over the entire document collection is used for the latter stage. We propose and evaluate algorithms for within-cluster searches, i.e., to integrate the best-clusters with the best-documents to obtain the final output including the highest ranked documents only from the best-clusters. Our experiments on a TREC collection including 210,158 documents with several query sets show that an appropriately selected integration algorithm based on the query length and system resources can significantly improve the query evaluation efficiency.

1 Introduction

Document clustering is one of the earliest approaches proposed for improving effectiveness and efficiency of information retrieval (IR) systems [8, 9]. With the fast growth of the Web, the amount of digital text data has also increased enormously in the last decade. This has given rise to a new interest on document clustering, not only due to the historically known promises of effectiveness and efficiency improvements, but also for several other purposes and application areas such as data visualization or preprocessing for several data mining applications. Moreover, the advent of the Web also fueled creation of some of the largest document hierarchies of the digital age. As an alternative to search engines that index all the terms on the Web pages and provide keyword-based searches, Web directories (such as Yahoo! and DMOZ) exist and attract attention of users. Such Web directories are formed by manually assigning Web pages to the categories of a topic hierarchy by human experts.

A user accessing an IR system with document clusters has three possible methods for satisfying his/her information needs: browsing, keyword-based (ad hoc) querying, or browse-based querying (i.e., the user can first browse through the categories until (s)he reaches to the cluster(s) (s)he is interested in and then pose a keyword-based query to be evaluated under this particular cluster(s)). Notice that, for any given IR system involving document clusters (or categories) -either created automatically or manually, for legacy data or Web documents and in a flat or hierarchical structure- the retrieval process involves two basic steps: finding the relevant clusters that best match to the user query and identifying the most relevant documents within these clusters. The first step, best(-matching) cluster selection, can be achieved either automatically

A. Levi et al. (Eds.): ISCIS 2006, LNCS 4263, pp. 707 – 716, 2006.
© Springer-Verlag Berlin Heidelberg 2006

by matching a user query to cluster representatives (centroids), or manually, as provided by user browsing. The second step, best(-matching) document selection, usually involves an inverted index structure of entire document collection, which is employed during the query-document matching. Thus, the result of best-document selection step is a ranked list of all documents in the collection according to their relevance to the query. The best-clusters obtained in the first step is then used to filter the best-documents in the second step, so that only those documents that have the highest similarity to the query and come from the best-clusters remain in the final output set. This integration step of best-clusters and best-documents can be postponed to the point where both sets are separately identified, or can be somehow embedded to best-document selection process. In this paper, we try to figure out how and when the best-cluster set information should be *integrated* while selecting best-documents with a traditional inverted index based query evaluation strategy. Interestingly, although the history of document clustering spans a few decades, the above question at a detail level of practical implementation has only attracted attention very recently and has been discussed in a few research studies [1, 2, 3, 4, 5].

The main contribution of this paper is proposing and evaluating result integration algorithms to identify a query's best-matching documents that lie within a pre-determined set of best-clusters. It is assumed that best-document selection process involves an inverted index structure (IIS) over all documents, which is the case in most practical systems, and thus such an integration step will be required. The integration algorithm would be of critical value for improving query processing efficiency for both traditional IR systems with automatically clustered document collections and Web directories. Note that, the discussion is independent from the manner in which best-clusters are determined, which might be automatic or manual, and the clustering structure, i.e., partitioning or hierarchical. In the experiments, we use multiple query sets and the *Financial Times* database of TREC containing 210,158 documents of size 564 MB to evaluate the proposed algorithms. Our findings reveal that, selecting an appropriate integration algorithm based on the query size is crucial for reducing the query evaluation time.

The rest of the paper is organized as follows. In Section 2, we review the state of the art approaches for cluster searches (CS) using inverted index structures. In Section 3, we describe several query processing alternatives for result integration in cluster searches. In Section 4, the experimental environment is described and the efficiency figures of proposed strategies are extensively evaluated in Section 5. Finally, we conclude in Section 6.

2   State of the Art Approaches for Cluster Search (CS)

As mentioned before, there are two stages of information retrieval for clustered document collections [4, 5]: determining the best-matching clusters to a given query and then computing the best-matching documents from these clusters. During the best-document selection, a complementary step can also be required: integrating the best-cluster set information to the process of best-document selection to obtain the final query result. In Table 1, we list possible file structures to be used for best-document selection stage. We assume that a set of best clusters within which the search will be conducted is already obtained either automatically [4, 5] or manually, i.e., by browsing.

There are recent proposals that aim to eliminate the result integration step, either totally or partially, by using a modified document inverted index file during the best-document selection stage [1, 2, 3, 5]. In what follows, we first review the potential CS implementations that are based on typical document IIS and require a result integration step. After that, we discuss the implementations with modified inverted files that do not require any integration.

Table 1. Typical file structures for best-document selection stage

Best-document selection	
Initial best-document selection	**Result integration**
Document Vectors (DV)	Cluster-document (CD) IIS
Document IIS (IIS)	Document-cluster (DC) IIS

2.1 Cluster Search Implementations with the Result Integration Step

The best-document selection stage can use two file structures: DV (document vectors) and document IIS (inverted index of documents). In this paper, we assume that the documents are represented by vectors, based on vector space model [9]. The DV file includes the actual document vectors, whereas the IIS file stores an inverted index of all documents. An inverted index has a header part, including list of terms (vocabulary) encountered in the collection, and pointers to the posting lists for each term. A posting list for a term consists of the document ids that include the term and is usually ordered according to the document ids or some importance or relevance function that can optimize query processing. Note that, in all practical systems, a document IIS is used to compute query-document similarity, since the DV option is extremely costly (see [4] for a performance evaluation).

Once the best-clusters and best-documents are obtained separately, there are two ways to eliminate the best-documents that are not a member of the best-clusters [2, 3], i.e., to integrate the results of best-cluster and document selection stages. We call these alternatives *"document-id intersection based integration"* and *"cluster-id intersection based integration,"* and describe in detail next.

- *Document-id intersection based integration*: This alternative uses an inverted index such that for each cluster, the documents that fall into this particular cluster are stored (i.e., cluster-document (CD)-IIS). In this case, by using this latter (inverted) index, first the union of all documents that are within the best-clusters are determined, and then the resulting document set is intersected with the best-documents to obtain the final result. Note that, in an IR environment with clustering, such an inverted index of documents per cluster (i.e., a member document list for each cluster) is required in any case, to allow the browsing functionality.

- *Cluster-id intersection based integration*: The second integration alternative is just the reverse: for each document in the best-document set, the cluster(s) in which this document lies is found by using an (inverted) index that stores the list of clusters for each document (i.e., document-cluster (DC)-IIS). Then, the obtained cluster id(s) are intersected with the best-clusters set and if the result is not empty, the document is added to the final query output set.

The first integration alternative would be efficient when the number of documents per cluster is relatively small, whereas the second approach would be more efficient when the best-document set to be processed is small. Also note that, the inverted index required by the second alternative is redundant, as it is the transpose of the CD-IIS that would be implemented in any case to support the browsing functionality. On the other hand, as the integration process required by the first alternative requires first obtaining a union of several document lists and then an intersection, it would be less efficient in terms of query processing time, whereas storing an additional inverted index (DC-IIS) is not a major concern given the storage capabilities of modern systems [2]. In this paper, we focus on the algorithms for the second alternative, cluster-id intersection based integration, which seems to be more practical for large-scale IR systems.

2.2 Cluster Search Implementations Without the Result Integration Step

To avoid the integration step mentioned above, modified document inverted index files are proposed. In [2, 3], document identifiers are created as signatures, which convey information about the hierarchy of clusters in which a document belongs to. However, since the signatures can produce false drops, i.e. only provide an approximate filtering of best-document set, there is still a need for the cluster-id based integration approach to obtain the final query result. In [1, 5], we propose a skip-based IIS that differs from a typical IIS since in posting lists it stores the documents of each cluster in a group adjacent to each other. Remarkably, this skip-based approach is the only one that is fully evaluated for environments with compression [1] and doesn't require any integration step.

Notice that, our work presented here aims to discuss the efficiency of integration algorithms for systems using typical inverted index files. We believe that such large-scale IR systems exist due to possible data and application-specific limitations and reasons (e.g., a modified IIS may not be available if an off-the-shelf product is used to create the inverted index). Thus, present work would be valuable for those IR systems and Web directories employing typical inverted files.

3 Query Processing Algorithms for Cluster-Id Intersection Based Result Integration in Cluster Search

In this paper, we propose algorithms for the cluster-id based result integration approach for CS. It is assumed that the best-clusters set is already obtained automatically (i.e., by query-cluster centroid matching) or manually (i.e., by browsing). Then, a typical ranking query evaluation algorithm that can be employed during the best-document selection would be as shown in Figure 1.

The typical query evaluation as shown in Figure 1 works as follows. For each query term, corresponding posting list is retrieved, and for each document in the posting list, its accumulator array entry is updated by using a similarity measure (such as the cosine measure [10]). When all query terms are processed, a *min-heap* is used to extract the top scoring documents from the accumulator array. The details of this process can be found in [7, 10].

Input: Keyword-based query q
Output: Top-k best-matching documents
In-memory data structures: Document accumulator $DAcc$

(1) For each query term t
(2)   Retrieve I_t, the posting list of term t from document IIS.
(3)   For each $<doc\text{-}id, tf>$ in I_t
(4)   Update accumulator array entry $DAcc\ [doc\text{-}id]$
(5) Build a min-heap of size k for nonzero accumulator entries
(6) Extract the top-k best-matching documents from the heap

Fig. 1. Typical ranking query evaluation algorithm for keyword-based queries

To achieve within-cluster search, once the best-clusters are selected, the best-document selection phase can be implemented in different ways to integrate the best-cluster information. The alternatives differ in answering the following questions: (i) At what point during best-document selection should the cluster-id(s) of a particular document be intersected with the best-cluster ids, and (ii) What kind of data structure should be used to keep best-cluster ids? During query evaluation shown in Figure 1, the cluster ids can be intersected at three different points, yielding three implementation alternatives: (i) before updating the accumulator array for a document, (ii) before inserting a document to the min-heap, or (iii) after extracting the top scoring documents from the min-heap. Two potential data structures to store best-cluster ids are (i) a sorted array of best-clusters, or (ii) a 0/1 mark array in which entries for best clusters are 1 and all others are 0. We discuss these alternatives and their trade-offs in the following.

Intersect Before Update (IBU). In this approach (Figure 2), only those accumulator entries that belong to documents from best-clusters are updated. To achieve this, after a posting list is retrieved for a query term, the cluster to which each document in the posting list belongs is determined and intersected with the best-cluster set. If the document's cluster is found in the best-cluster set, its accumulator entry is updated.

Note that, this alternative would increase the efficiency of the last two steps of the algorithm (i.e., building and extracting from the heap as shown in lines 7-8), since all

---

Input: Keyword-based query q, best-clusters $BestClus$
In-memory data structures: Document accumulator $DAcc$, Document-category (DC) IIS

(1) For each query term t
(2)   Retrieve I_t, the posting list of term t from document IIS.
(3)   For each $<doc\text{-}id, tf>$ in I_t
(4)   Retrieve $I_{doc\text{-}id}$ from DC-IIS and obtain $Clus(doc\text{-}id)$
(5)   If $Clus(doc\text{-}id) \cap BestClus \neq \emptyset$
(6)   Update accumulator array entry $DAcc\ [doc\text{-}id]$
(7) Build a min-heap of size k for nonzero accumulator entries
(8) Extract the top-k best-matching documents from the heap

Fig. 2. The query processing algorithm for intersect before insert (IBU) approach

the nonzero entries in the accumulator array are for the documents that are from best-clusters. On the other hand, the performance of this approach crucially depends on the cost of determining the clusters to which a document belongs (step 4) and cluster-id intersection operation (step 5). For the former operation, the algorithm should access document-cluster (DC) IIS for each element of the posting lists. However, if document-cluster associations are kept in the main memory or cached efficiently, this cost can be avoidable. This seems reasonable, since DC-IIS can be expected to be relatively small in size and can be shared among several query processing threads. For instance, assuming that documents are not repeated in more than one clusters, the main memory requirement to cache the entire DC-IIS would be only $O(D)$, i.e., in the order of document accumulator array. In this paper, without loss of generality, we assume that each document belongs to at most one cluster and the DC-IIS is stored in the main memory.

The cost of cluster ids' intersection is (assuming each document belongs to only one cluster) $O(\log S)$, if a sorted array of size S is used to store best-cluster ids; and $O(1)$ if a 0/1 mark array is used for this purpose. Note that, the data structure for best-clusters can be a sorted array if the memory reserved per query is scarce and/or total number of clusters is quite large. In this case, the document's cluster id can be searched within best-clusters using binary search. A 0/1 mark array is obviously more efficient but can only be preferred if the memory is not a concern and/or number of clusters is relatively small.

Intersect Before Insert (IBI). In this approach, instead of checking the cluster id intersection for each doc-id in each posting list, we do it once for each non-zero accumulator entry while building the heap (Figure 3). This alternative is preferable if the number of non-zero accumulator entries is expected to be low and/or the cost of cluster id intersection is high.

Input: Keyword-based query q, best-clusters *BestClus*
In-memory data structures: Document accumulator *DAcc*, Document-category (DC) IIS

(1) For each query term t
(2)   Retrieve I_t, the posting list of term t from document IIS.
(3)   Update accumulator array entry *DAcc [doc-id]*
(4)   For each DAcc[doc-id] $\neq 0$
(5)   Retrieve $I_{doc\text{-}id}$ from DC-IIS and obtain *Clus(doc-id)*
(6)   If   *Clus(doc-id)*$\cap$ *BestClus* $\neq \emptyset$
(7)   Insert into a min-heap of size k
(8) Extract the top-k best-matching documents from the heap

Fig. 3. The query processing algorithm for intersect before insert (IBI) approach

Intersect After Extract (IAE). In this third approach (Figure 4) the entire query processing works as in Figure 1 and only at the end of the evaluation, the cluster-ids of top-k documents are intersected with the best-clusters. Of course, if some of those k documents are not from the best-clusters, then the build-heap step and extraction should be repeated. To avoid such a repetition, the initial evaluation can be executed for top-L documents, $L > k$. In this case, the cost of cluster-id intersection is negligible as it is postponed at the end of processing and $L \ll D$. On the other hand, it is important to choose L appropriately, if L is much larger than k (e.g., $L = D$ the extreme case), the gains in the intersection stage would be lost during the build-heap and extraction. If L is too small (i.e., very close to k), we may need more than one iteration to find k documents that are in the best-clusters. Thus, IAE alternative will be useful if it can somehow be guaranteed that in a small number of highest scoring documents, there will be at least k documents from the best clusters. More specifically, this approach would be better than the previous alternative only if cluster intersection is costly; and better than the IBU algorithm if both intersection test is expensive and too many nonzero accumulator entries arise.

Input: Keyword-based query q, best-clusters *BestClus*
Output: Top-k best-matching documents *Result*
In-memory data structures: Document accumulator *DAcc,* Document-category (DC) IIS

(1) For each query term t
(2)   Retrieve I_t, the posting list of term t from document IIS.
(3)   For each *<doc-id, tf>* in I_t
(4)   Update accumulator array entry *DAcc [doc-id]*
(5) Build a min-heap of size L $(L>k)$ for nonzero accumulator entries
(6) Extract the top-L best-matching documents from the heap
(7) While size of *Result* < k
(8)   For each doc-id $\in$ top-L
(9)   Retrieve $I_{doc\text{-}id}$ from DC-IIS and obtain *Clus(doc-id)*
(10)   If *Clus(doc-id)* $\cap$ *BestClus* $\neq \emptyset$
(11)   Insert doc-id to the *Result*
(12) If size of *Result* < k
(13)   Set L to M for some $M > L$, go to step (5)

Fig. 4. The query processing algorithm for intersect after extract (IAE) approach

4 Experimental Environment

Document Database and Clustering Structure. In the experiments, *Financial Times* document collection (referred to as the FT database) of TREC Disk 4 is used. The document database includes *210,158* newspaper articles published between 1991 and 1994. The indexing process with the elimination of English stop-words and numbers yields a lexicon of 229,748 terms.

The database is clustered using C3M algorithm [6] in partitioning mode, which yields 1640 clusters and 128 documents per clusters, on the average. An important parameter is the number of best-matching clusters, and following the common practice in earlier works [5] we use 10% of the total number of clusters (i.e., 164 clusters) as the number of best-clusters in the retrieval experiments. The clustering structure and other parameters are validated for FT database in our previous study [5]. In this paper, we provide results for retrieving top-10 documents, i.e., $k =10$.

Queries, Query Matching & Centroid Weighting. We used the TREC-7 query topics corresponding to the FT database of TREC Disk 4 collection (queries 351-400).

In the experiments we use three different types of query sets: *Qshort*, *Qmedium*, *Qlong* including 2.38, 8.16 and 190 terms on the average, respectively. The first two of the query sets are created from the TREC queries, namely *Qshort* queries include TREC query titles, and *Qmedium* queries include both titles and descriptions. The third one, *Qlong*, is created from the top retrieved document of each *Qmedium* query. The *Qlong* set, with extremely long queries, represents "find similar documents" type queries supported by typical Web search engines.

In this study, the document term weights are assigned using the *term frequency* x *inverse document frequency* (IDF) information and using a well-known term weighting formula. During query processing, term weights are normalized by using the document lengths. The term weights for query terms are calculated using the augmented normalized frequency formula [5]. After obtaining weighted document (d) and query (q) vectors in an n dimensional vector space the query-document matching is performed using the well-known cosine formula [5, 10].

For the cluster centroids, we take a simplistic approach and use all cluster member documents' terms as centroid terms. The weight of a centroid term is also computed by the formula *term frequency* x *IDF*. Please see [5] for further details.

5   Experimental Results

The experiments are conducted on a Pentium 4 2.54 GHz PC with 2GB memory and Mandrake Linux operating system. All implementations use C programming language. Unless otherwise stated, we assume that the posting list per query term is read into main memory, processed and then discarded, i.e., more than one term's posting list is not available in memory simultaneously.

Along with the lines of Section 3, we discuss three query processing implementations (IBU, IBI, IAE) and two versions for each such implementation –the version that uses a sorted array (SA) to keep and look up best-clusters, and the version that uses a 0/1 mark array (MA) for the same purpose. During query evaluation, first the queries in the test sets are matched with the cluster centroids to obtain the best-matching clusters (top 10% of clusters). Next, best-documents within these best-clusters are computed using the three possible algorithms with two different data structures (SA, MA) for best clusters. In Table 2, we report in-memory processing time during best-document selection for each strategy, as well as the average number of accumulator update operations, number of nonzero document accumulator entries, number of cluster-id intersection operations and finally number of heap insertion operations.

From Table 2, the following observations can be drawn. For the short and medium length queries (i.e., as in the cases of *Qshort* and *Qmedium* sets) IAE approach is inferior to other two algorithms due to very high costs of build-heap and extract operations. As shown in Table 2, number of heap insertion operations is at least 10 times larger with respect to other algorithms. Note that, in these experiments, we choose L (i.e., the min-heap size) as the total number of documents in the entire collection, which is the extreme condition, to avoid repeating the heap build and extraction steps as discussed in Section 3. If L is set to k (=10), the efficiency of this

Table 2. Efficiency comparison of the integration algorithms (IBU: Intersect Before Update, IBI: Intersect Before Insert, IAE: Intersect After Extract, SA: Sorted Array, MA: Mark Array)

	Time (sec) and operation counts (all averages)	IBU-SA	IBU-MA	IBI-SA	IBI-MA	IAE (SA & MA)
Qshort	Query evaluation time	0.007	**0.005**	0.007	0.006	0.012
	No. of accumulator updates	908	908	9792	9792	9792
	No. of nonzero accumulators	848	848	9462	9462	9462
	No. of intersections	9792	9792	9462	9462	65
	No. of heap insertion calls	848	848	848	848	9462
Qmedium	Query evaluation time	0.018	**0.008**	0.017	0.010	0.044
	No. of accumulator updates	3786	3786	49416	49416	49416
	No. of nonzero accumulators	2899	2899	39496	39496	39496
	No. of intersections	49416	49416	39496	39496	51
	No. of heap insertion calls	2899	2899	2899	2899	39496
Qlong	Query evaluation time	0.448	0.111	0.133	**0.102**	0.338
	No. of accumulator updates	124115	124115	1.8 mil.	1.8 mil.	1.8 mil.
	No. of nonzero accumulators	11718	11718	189510	189510	189510
	No. of intersections	1.8 mil.	1.8 mil.	189510	189510	27
	No. of heap insertion calls	11718	11718	11718	11718	189510

approach also improves significantly (i.e. 0.006, 0.010 and 0.107 versus 0.012, 0.044 and 0.338 seconds for *Qshort*, *Qmedium* and *Qlong*, respectively); however there is always the possibility that all of these top-k documents are not from best clusters; which would require building and extracting from a larger min-heap. Also note that, since IAE-SA and IAE-MA approaches do not differ significantly in terms of performance, their efficiency figures are shown in the same column in Table 2.

On the other hand, assuming that DC-IIS is kept in the main memory, the performance of IBU-SA and IBI-SA approaches seem to be very similar, the same is true for the IBU-MA and IBI-MA approaches. Clearly, the versions that employ a 0/1 mark array to store best clusters are faster than their sorted array based counterparts. If the memory is large enough to keep DC-IIS in memory, IBU-MA approach performs better than IBI-MA and provides up to 15% and 20% reductions in query processing times for *QShort* and *Qmedium*, respectively. If it is impossible to keep DC-IIS in memory, the IAE method with the minimum number of cluster-id intersection operations would be the method of choice, however we envision that this case may not be highly probable given the modern systems' memory capacities. For instance, in our experimental setup, the size of DC-IIS is only around 1 MB.

For very long queries (as in the case of *Qlong* set), again IBU and IBI approaches with MA seem to be the most reasonable implementation candidates given that DC-IIS in in-memory. For this case, IBU-SA suffers from the excessive cost of cluster-id intersection operations and performs even worse than IAE; so if IBU is the choice of implementation, it should be coupled with MA data structure. Nevertheless, IBI-MA approach outperforms IBU-MA in an 8% margin and seems to be the most efficient approach. As before, IAE (with SA or MA) may only be chosen if DC-IIS can not be stored or cached in the main memory.

Our findings show that, depending on the query set properties and main memory availability to store the DC-IIS and best-clusters, the most appropriate query processing approach for within-cluster search should be determined dynamically by the IR system.

6 Conclusion

In this paper, we propose and evaluate within-cluster search algorithms to efficiently integrate the best-clusters and best-documents for cluster-based IR systems using inverted index structures. Our findings reveal that the efficiency of the integration algorithm depends on the query length, and the appropriate algorithm should be chosen dynamically by the IR system considering query properties and available system resources.

Acknowledgments. This work is partially supported by The Scientific and Technical Research Council of Turkey (TÜBİTAK) under the grant no 105E024.

References

1. Altingovde, I.S., Can, F., Demir, E., Ulusoy, O.: Incremental cluster-based retrieval with embedded centroids using compressed cluster-skipping inverted files. Submitted for publication.
2. Cacheda, F., Baeza-Yates, R.: An optimistic model for searching Web directories. In: Proceedings of the 26th European Conf. on IR Research, Sunderland, UK. (2004) 364–377
3. Cacheda, F., Carneiro, V., Guerrero, C., Viña, Á.: Optimization of restricted searches in Web directories using hybrid data structures. In: Proceedings of the 25th European Conference on IR Research (ECIR), Pisa, Italy. (2003) 436–451
4. Can, F.: On the efficiency of best-match cluster searches. Information Processing and Management **30** (3) (1994) 343–361
5. Can, F., Altingovde, I.S., Demir, E.: Efficiency and effectiveness of query processing in cluster-based retrieval. Information Systems **29** (8) (2004) 697–717
6. Can, F., Ozkarahan E. A.: Concepts and effectiveness of the cover-coefficient-based clustering methodology for text databases. ACM TODS **15** (4) (1990) 483–517
7. Cambazoglu, B.B., Aykanat, C.: Performance of query processing implementations in ranking-based text retrieval systems using inverted indices. Information Processing and Management **42** (4) (2006) 875–898
8. van Rijsbergen, C. J.: Information retrieval. 2nd ed. Butterworths, London (1979)
9. Salton, G.: Automatic text processing: the transformation, analysis, and retrieval of information by computer. Addison Wesley, Reading, MA (1989)
10. Witten, I. H., Moffat, A., Bell, T. C.: Managing gigabytes compressing and indexing documents and images. Van Nostrand Reinhold, New York (1994)

Effect of Inverted Index Partitioning Schemes on Performance of Query Processing in Parallel Text Retrieval Systems*

B. Barla Cambazoglu[1], Aytul Catal[2], and Cevdet Aykanat[1]

[1] Bilkent University, Department of Computer Engineering
06800 Bilkent, Ankara, Turkey
{berkant, aykanat}@cs.bilkent.edu.tr
[2] Scientific and Technological Research Council of Turkey (TÜBİTAK)
06100 Kavaklıdere, Ankara, Turkey
aytul.catal@iltaren.tubitak.gov.tr

Abstract. Shared-nothing, parallel text retrieval systems require an inverted index, representing a document collection, to be partitioned among a number of processors. In general, the index can be partitioned based on either the terms or documents in the collection, and the way the partitioning is done greatly affects the query processing performance of the parallel system. In this work, we investigate the effect of these two index partitioning schemes on query processing. We conduct experiments on a 32-node PC cluster, considering the case where index is completely stored in disk. Performance results are reported for a large (30 GB) document collection using an MPI-based parallel query processing implementation.

1   Introduction

The basic duty of a text retrieval system is to process user queries and present the users a set of documents relevant to their queries [1]. For small document collections, processing of a query can be performed over the original collection via full text search. However, for efficient query processing over large collections, an intermediate representation of the collection (i.e., and indexing mechanism) is required. Until the early 90's signature files and suffix arrays were the choice of most text retrieval system designers [2]. In the last decade, inverted index data structure [3,4] replaced these popular structures and currently appears to be the only choice for indexing large document collections.

An inverted index is composed of a set of inverted lists $\mathcal{L} = \{\mathcal{I}_1, \mathcal{I}_2, \ldots, \mathcal{I}_T\}$, where $T = |\mathcal{T}|$ is the size of the vocabulary $\mathcal{T}$ of the indexed document collection $\mathcal{D}$, and an index pointing to the heads of the inverted lists. The index part is usually small enough to fit into the main memory, but inverted lists are stored on the disk. Each list $\mathcal{I}_i \in \mathcal{L}$ is associated with a term $t_i \in \mathcal{T}$. An inverted list contains entries (called postings) for the documents containing the term it is associated

* This work is partially supported by The Scientific and Technological Research Council of Turkey (TÜBİTAK) under project EEEAG-106E069.

A. Levi et al. (Eds.): ISCIS 2006, LNCS 4263, pp. 717–725, 2006.

$\mathcal{T} = \{t_1, t_2, t_3, t_4, t_5, t_6, t_7, t_8\}$

$\mathcal{D} = \{d_1, d_2, d_3, d_4, d_5, d_6, d_7, d_8\}$

$d_1 = \{t_4, t_5\}$ $d_5 = \{t_2, t_6\}$

$d_2 = \{t_2, t_6, t_7\}$ $d_6 = \{t_4\}$

$d_3 = \{t_1, t_2, t_3, t_6, t_7\}$ $d_7 = \{t_3, t_5\}$

$d_4 = \{t_3, t_4, t_5, t_8\}$ $d_8 = \{t_4, t_5\}$

(a) Toy collection

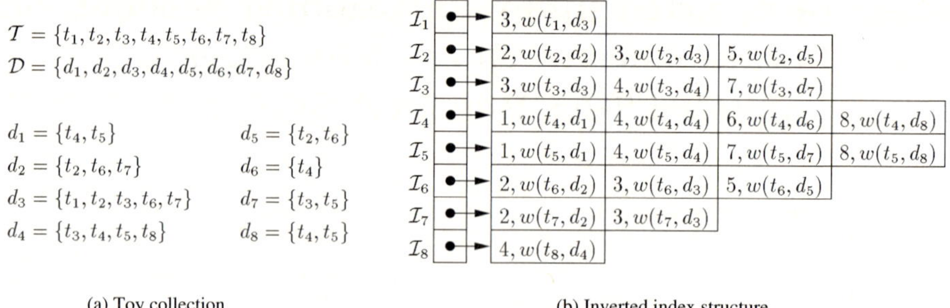

(b) Inverted index structure

Fig. 1. The toy document collection used throughout the paper

with. A posting $p \in \mathcal{I}_i$ consists of a document id field $p.d = j$ and a weight field $p.w = w(t_i, d_j)$ for a document d_j in which term t_i appears. $w(t_i, d_j)$ is a weight which shows the degree of relevance between t_i and d_j using some metric.

Fig. 1-a shows the document collection that we will use throughout the examples in the paper. This toy document collection $\mathcal{D}$ contains $D=8$ documents, and its vocabulary $\mathcal{T}$ has $T=8$ terms. There are $P=21$ posting entries, in the set $\mathcal{P}$ of postings. Fig. 1-b shows the inverted index built for this document collection.

2 Parallel Text Retrieval

In practice, parallel text retrieval architectures can be classified as: inter-query-parallel and intra-query-parallel architectures. In the first type, each processor in the parallel system works as a separate and independent query processor. Incoming user queries are directed to client query processors on a demand-driven basis. Processing of each query is handled solely by a single processor. Intra-query-parallel architectures are typically composed of a single central broker and a number of client processors, each running an index server responsible from a portion of the inverted index. In this architecture, the central broker redirects an incoming query to all client query processors in the system. All processors collaborate in processing of the query and compute partial answer sets of documents. The partial answer sets produced by the client query processors are merged at the central broker into a final answer set, as a final step.

In general, inter-query-parallel architectures obtain better throughput while intra-query-parallel architectures are better at reducing query response times. Further advantages and disadvantages and a brief comparison are provided in [5]. In this work, our focus is on intra-query-parallel text retrieval systems on shared-nothing parallel architectures.

3 Inverted Index Partitioning

In a K-processor, shared-nothing, intra-query-parallel text retrieval system, the inverted index is partitioned among K index servers. The partitioning should be performed taking the storage load of index servers into consideration. If there are $|\mathcal{P}|$ posting entries in the inverted index, each index server S_j in the set $\mathcal{S} = \{S_1, S_2, \ldots, S_K\}$ of index servers should keep an approximately equal amount of posting entries as shown by

$$\mathrm{SLoad}(S_j) \simeq \frac{|\mathcal{P}|}{K}, \qquad \text{for } 1 \le j \le K, \tag{1}$$

where $\mathrm{SLoad}(S_j)$ is the storage load of index server S_j. The storage imbalance should be kept under a satisfactory value.

In general, partitioning of the inverted index can be performed in two different ways: term-based or document-based partitioning. In the term-based partitioning approach, each index server S_j locally keeps a subset $\mathcal{L}_j^{\mathrm{t}}$ of the set $\mathcal{L}$ of all inverted lists, where

$$\mathcal{L}_1^{\mathrm{t}} \cup \mathcal{L}_2^{\mathrm{t}} \cup \ldots \cup \mathcal{L}_K^{\mathrm{t}} = \mathcal{L}, \text{ and} \tag{2}$$

$$\mathcal{L}_i^{\mathrm{t}} \cap \mathcal{L}_j^{\mathrm{t}} = \emptyset, \qquad \text{for } 1 \le i, j \le K, i \ne j. \tag{3}$$

In this technique, all processors are responsible for processing their own set of terms, that is, inverted lists are assigned to index servers as a whole. If an inverted list $\mathcal{I}_i$ is assigned to index server S_j (i.e., $\mathcal{I}_{ji}^{\mathrm{t}} = \mathcal{I}_i$), any index server $\mathcal{S}_k$ other than $\mathcal{S}_j$ has $\mathcal{I}_{ki}^{\mathrm{t}} = \emptyset$.

Alternatively, the partitioning can be based on documents. In the document-based partitioning approach, each processor is responsible for a different set of documents, and an index server stores only the postings that contain the document ids assigned to it. Each index server S_j keeps a set $\mathcal{L}_j^{\mathrm{d}} = \{\mathcal{I}_{j1}, \mathcal{I}_{j2}, \ldots, \mathcal{I}_{jT}\}$ of inverted lists containing subsets $\mathcal{I}_{ji}^{\mathrm{d}}$ of every inverted list $\mathcal{I}_i \in \mathcal{L}$, where

$$\mathcal{I}_{1i}^{\mathrm{d}} \cup \mathcal{I}_{2i}^{\mathrm{d}} \cup \ldots \cup \mathcal{I}_{Ki}^{\mathrm{d}} = \mathcal{I}_i, \qquad \text{for } 1 \le i \le T, \text{ and} \tag{4}$$

$$\mathcal{I}_{ji}^{\mathrm{d}} \cap \mathcal{I}_{ki}^{\mathrm{d}} = \emptyset, \qquad \text{for } 1 \le j, k \le K, j \ne k, 1 \le i \le T, \tag{5}$$

and it is possible to have $\mathcal{I}_{ji}^{\mathrm{d}} = \emptyset$.

In Fig. 2-a and Fig. 2-b, the term- and document-based partitioning strategies are illustrated on our toy document collection for a 3-processor parallel system. The approach followed in this example is to assign the postings to processor in a round-robin fashion according to term and document ids. This technique is used in [6].

4   Previous Work

There are a number of papers on the inverted index partitioning problem in parallel text retrieval systems. We briefly overview three relevant publications.

Tomasic and Garcia-Molina [6] examine four different techniques to partition an inverted index on a shared-nothing distributed system for different hardware configurations. The system and disk organizations described in this paper correspond to the term- and document-based partitioning schemes we previously

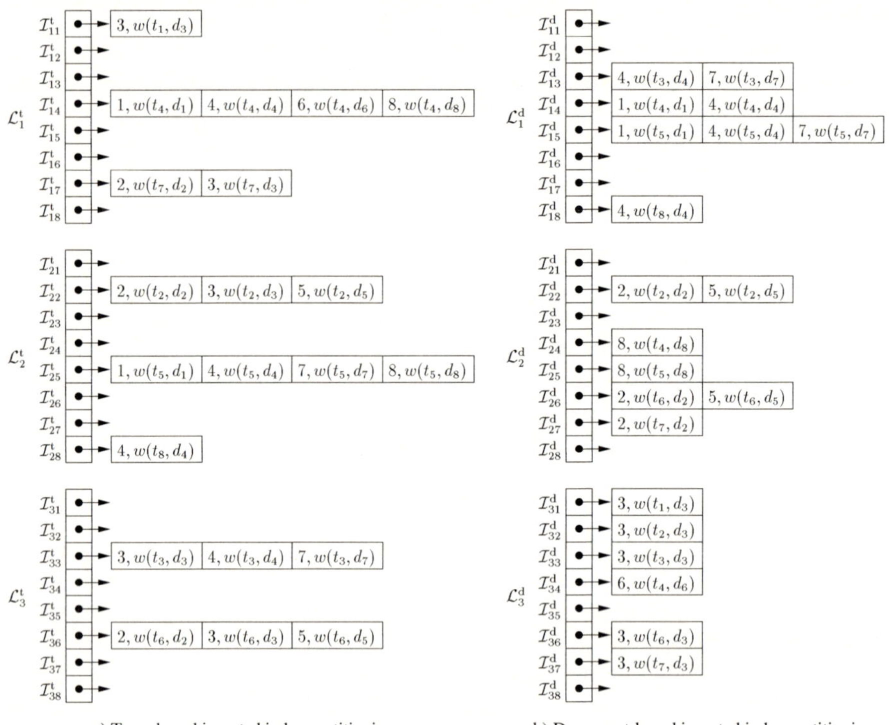

a) Term-based inverted index partitioning   b) Document-based inverted index partitioning

Fig. 2. 3-way term- and document-based partitions for our toy inverted index

described, respectively. The authors verify the performance of the techniques by simulation over a synthetic dataset and use the boolean model for similarity calculations between documents and queries. Their results indicate that document-based partitioning performs well for long documents, whereas term-based partitioning is better on short-document collections.

Jeong and Omiecinski [7] investigate the performance of the two partitioning schemes for a shared-everything multiprocessor system with multiple disks. As in [6], they use the boolean ranking model and work on synthetic datasets. They conduct experiments especially on term skewness. For term-based partitioning, they propose two heuristics for load balancing. In their first heuristic, they partition the posting file with equal posting sizes instead of equal number of terms. In their second heuristic, they consider the term frequencies as well as posting sizes. The results of their simulation show that term-based partitioning is better when term distribution is less skewed in the document collection, and document-based partitioning should be preferred otherwise.

Baeza-Yates and Ribeiro-Neto [8] apply the two partitioning schemes on a shared-nothing parallel system. In their work, they refer to term- and document-based partitioning schemes as global and local index organizations, respectively. For document ranking, they use the vector-space model and conduct their experiments on a real-life document collection. Their results show that term-based

Table 1. A comparison of the previous works on inverted index partitioning

Authors	Tomasic and Garcia-Molina	Jeong and Omiecinski	Riberio-Neto and Baeza-Yates
Year	1993	1995	1999
Target architecture	shared-nothing parallel	multi-disk PC	shared-nothing parallel
Ranking model	boolean	boolean	vector-space
Partitioning model	round-robin	load-balanced	load-balanced
Dataset	synthetic	synthetic	real-life

partitioning performs better than document-based partitioning in the presence of fast communication channels. Table 1 summarizes and compares the above-mentioned works on inverted index partitioning.

All performance results presented so far are based on simulations. In this work, we investigate the effect of the two partitioning schemes using an actual, MPI-based, experimental parallel text retrieval system, Skynet[1], implemented on a 32-node PC cluster.

5   Parallel Query Processing

Processing of a query in a parallel text retrieval system follows several steps. These steps slightly differ depending on whether term-based or document-based inverted index partitioning schemes are employed. In term-based partitioning, since the whole responsibility of a query term is assigned to a single processor, the central broker splits a user query $Q = \{t_{q_1}, t_{q_2}, \ldots, t_{q_Q}\}$ into K subqueries. Each subquery Q_i contains the query terms whose responsibility is assigned to index server S_i, that is, $Q_i = \{q_j : t_{q_j} \in Q \text{ and } \mathcal{I}_{q_j} \in \mathcal{L}_i^t\}$. Then, the central broker sends the subqueries over the network to the index servers. Depending on the query content, it is possible to have $Q_i = \emptyset$, and in that case, no subquery is sent to index server S_i. In document-based partitioning, postings of a term are distributed on many processors. Hence, unless a $K \times T$-bit term-to-processor mapping is stored in the central broker, each index server is sent a copy of the original query, that is, $Q_i = Q$.

Once an index server receives a subquery, it immediately accesses its disk and reads the inverted lists associated with the terms in the subquery. For each query term $t_{q_j} \in Q_i$, inverted list $\mathcal{I}_j$ is fetched from the disk. The weight $p.w$ of each posting $p \in \mathcal{I}_j$ is used to update the corresponding score accumulator for document $p.d$. When all inverted lists are read and accumulator updates are completed, index server S_i transfers the accumulator entries (document ids and scores) to the central broker over the network, forming a partial answer set $\mathcal{A}_i$ for query Q.

During this period, the central broker may be busy with directing other queries to index servers. For the final answer set to the query to be generated, all partial

---

[1] Skynet search engine: available at `http://skynet.cs.bilkent.edu.tr`

answer sets related with the query must be gathered at the central broker. The central broker merges the received K partial answer sets $\mathcal{A}_1, \mathcal{A}_2, \ldots, \mathcal{A}_K$ and returns the most relevant (highly-ranked) document ids as the complete answer set to the user submitted query $\mathcal{Q}$.

In term-based partitioning, accessing a term's inverted list requires a single disk access, but reading the list (i.e., posting I/O) may take a long time since the whole list is stored at a single processor. Similarly, the partial answer sets transmitted by the index servers are long. Hence, the overhead of term-based partitioning is mainly at the network, during the communication of partial answer sets. Especially, in cases where the partial answer sets are long or inverted lists keep additional information such as information on term positions, this communication overhead becomes a bottleneck.

In document-based partitioning, disk accesses are the dominating overhead in total query processing time, especially in the presence of slow disks and a fast network. $O(K)$ disk seeks are required in the worst case to read the inverted list of a term since the complete list is distributed at many processors. However, the inverted lists retrieved from the disk are shorter in length, and hence posting I/O is faster. Moreover, in case the user is interested in only the top s documents, no more than s accumulator entries need to be communicated over the network (no document with a rank of $s+1$ in a partial answer set can take place among the top s documents in the global ranking).

6   Experiments

6.1   Setting

The hardware platform used in the experiments is a 32-node PC cluster interconnected by a Gigabit Ethernet switch. Each node contains an Intel Pentium IV 3.0 GHz processor, 1 GB of RAM, and runs Mandrake Linux, version 10.1. The sequential query processing algorithm is a term-ordered algorithm with static accumulator allocation [9]. The parallel query processing code is implemented in C using the LAM/MPI [10] library.

As the document collection, results of a large crawl performed over the '.edu' domain (i.e., the educational US Web sites) is used. The entire collection is 30 GB and contains 1,883,037 Web pages. After cleansing and stop-word elimination, 3,325,075 distinct index terms remain. The size of the inverted index constructed using this collection is around 2.7 GB. In term-based (document-based) partitioning, terms (documents) are alphabetically sorted and assigned to K index servers in a round-robin fashion using the distribution scheme of [6].

6.2   Results

Table 2 displays the storage imbalance in terms of the number of postings and inverted lists for the two partitioning schemes with varying number of index servers, $K = 2, 8, 32$. This table also shows the total number of disk accesses, the total volume of disk I/O, and the total volume of communication as well

Table 2. Performance comparison of the term- and document-based partitioning

	term-based			document-based		
	K=2	K=8	K=32	K=2	K=8	K=32
imbal. in posting storage (%)	0.7	6.9	17.5	0.1	0.2	0.7
imbal. in inverted list storage (%)	0.0	0.0	0.0	0.8	1.4	3.2
number of disk accesses	272	272	272	543	2161	8619
imbal. in disk accesses (%)	2.9	20.6	64.7	0.2	0.7	0.2
total volume of I/O (MB)	38.6	38.6	38.6	38.6	38.6	38.6
imbal. in I/O (%)	7.4	38.5	123.7	0.0	0.1	0.5
total comm. volume (MB)	36.1	38.0	38.5	33.3	33.3	33.3
imbal. in comm. volume (%)	7.4	38.5	123.7	0.0	0.1	0.5

as the respective imbalances observed in processing a set of 100 queries (having 1 to 5 terms) over the parallel text retrieval system. As expected, the number of disk accesses linearly increases with increasing number of index servers for document-based partitioning and is constant for term-based partitioning. However, the term-based scheme suffers from a considerable load imbalance in disk accesses as the number of index servers increases, i.e., some index servers perform quite more disk accesses than the others. The total volume of communication for transmitting PASs from index servers to the central broker is slightly higher for the case of term-based partitioning. Also, high imbalance rates are observed in posting I/O and hence PAS communication in this type of partitioning.

Fig. 3 shows the query processing performance with increasing number of query terms for different partitioning techniques and numbers of index servers. In this experiment, the central broker submits a single query to the index server and waits for completion of the answer set before submitting the next query. According to the figure, document-based partitioning leads to better response times compared to term-ordered partitioning. This is due to the more balanced distribution of the query processing load on index servers in the case of document-based partitioning. The results show that term-based partitioning is not appropriate for text retrieval systems, where queries arrive to the system infrequently. The poor performance of term-based partitioning is due to the imbalance in the number of disk accesses as well as communication volumes of index servers.

Fig. 4 presents the performance of the system with batch query processing. In these experiments, a batch of 100 queries, each containing between 1 and 5 query terms, was submitted to the system at the same time. The results indicate that term-based partitioning results in better throughput, especially as the number of index servers increases. This is mainly due to the better utilization of index servers and the capability to concurrently process query terms belonging to different queries. For document-based partitioning case, the number of disk accesses becomes a dominating overhead. In our case, after 8 index servers, the throughput starts to decrease.

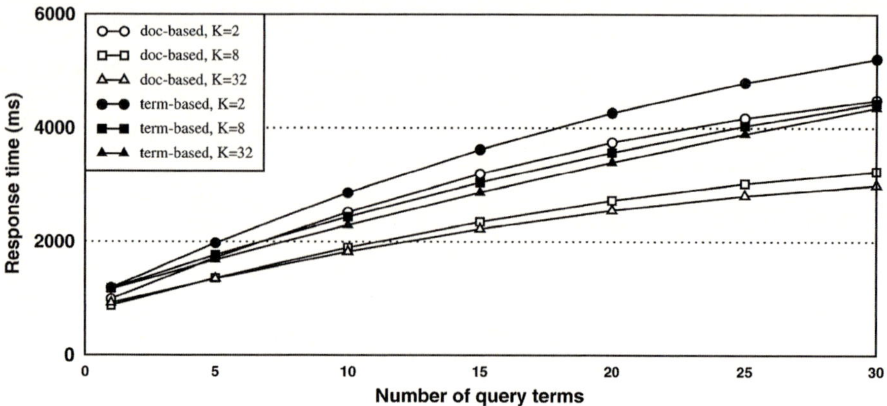

Fig. 3. Response times for varying number of query terms

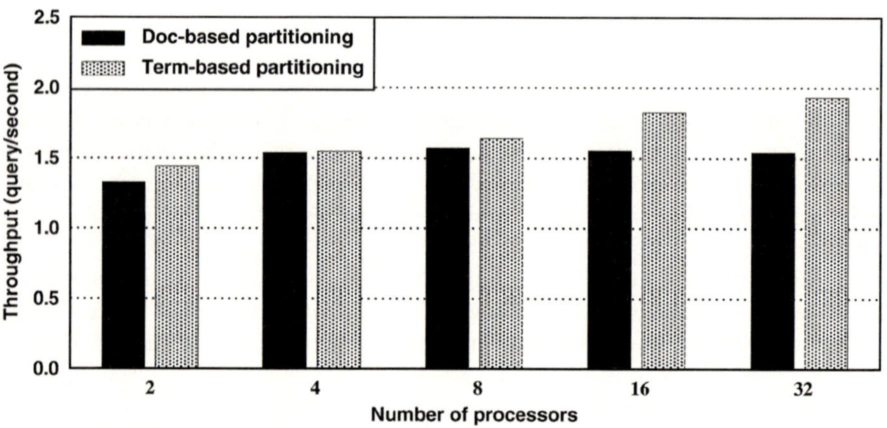

Fig. 4. Throughput with varying number of index servers

7   Conclusion

We have conducted experiments to illustrate the performance of two inverted
index partitioning techniques on a recently-built, 32-node PC cluster system.
We have implemented a parallel text retrieval system capable of working with
both document-based and term-based partitioning schemes. We have conducted
experiments to evaluate the response times and throughput of an MPI-based parallel query processing implementation. The results indicate that, for batch query
processing, term-ordered partitioning produces superior throughput. However,
for the case where queries are infrequently submitted, document-based partitioning should be preferred.

References

1. L. Page, S. Brin, The anatomy of a large-scale hypertextual web search engine. In: Proceedings of the Seventh World-Wide Web Conference. (1998) 107–117
2. Croft, W.B., Savino, P.: Implementing ranking strategies using text signatures. ACM Transactions on Office Information Systems **6**(1) (1988) 42–62
3. Zobel, J., Moffat, A., Sacks-Davis, R.: An efficient indexing technique for full-text database systems. In: Proceedings of the 18th International Conference on Very Large Databases. (1992) 352–362
4. Tomasic, A., Garcia-Molina, H., Shoens, K.: Incremental updates of inverted lists for text document retrieval. In: Proceedings of the 1994 ACM SIGMOD International Conference on Management of Data. (1994) 289–300
5. Baeza-Yates, R., Ribeiro-Neto, B.A.: Modern information retrieval. Addison-Wesley Publishing (1999)
6. Tomasic, A., Garcia-Molina, H.: Performance of inverted indices in shared-nothing distributed text document information retrieval systems. In: Proceedings of the International Conference on Parallel and Distributed Information Systems. (1992) 8–17
7. Jeong, B.S., Omiecinski, E.: Inverted file partitioning schemes in multiple disk systems. IEEE Transactions on Parallel and Distributed Systems **6**(2) (1995) 142–153
8. Ribeiro-Neto, B.A., Barbosa, R.A.: Query performance for tightly coupled distributed digital libraries. In: Proceedings of the Third ACM Conference on Digital Libraries. (1998) 182–190
9. Cambazoglu, B.B., Aykanat, C.: Performance of query processing implementations in ranking-based text retrieval systems using inverted indices. Information Processing and Management **42**(4) (2005) 875–898
10. Burns, G., Daoud, R., Vaigl, J.: LAM: An Open Cluster Environment for MPI. In: Proceedings of the Supercomputing Symposium. (1994) 379–386

Exploiting Social Networks Dynamics for P2P Resource Organisation

Vincenza Carchiolo, Michele Malgeri, Giuseppe Mangioni,
and Vincenzo Nicosia

Dipartimento di Ingegneria Informatica e delle Telecomunicazioni
Facoltà di Ingegneria – Università di Catania
Viale A. Doria 6 – 95100 Catania (Italy)
{car, malgeri, gmangioni, vnicosia}@diit.unict.it

Abstract. In this paper we present a formal description of *PROSA* , a P2P resource management system heavily inspired by social networks. Social networks have been deeply studied in the last two decades in order to understand how communities of people arise and grow. It is a widely known result that networks of social relationships usually evolves to small–worlds, i.e. networks where nodes are strongly connected to neighbours and separated from all other nodes by a small amount of hops. This work shows that algorithms implemented into *PROSA* allow to obtain an efficient small–world P2P network.

1   Introduction

A Peer-to-Peer system consists of computing elements that are connected by a network, addressable in a unique way, and sharing a common communication protocol. All computing elements, equivalently called nodes or peers, have the same functionalities and role. In P2P networks there is no difference between "client" and "server" hosts: a peer acts as a "client" if it requests a resource from the network, while it acts as a "server" if it is requested a resource it is sharing. From this point of view, P2P networks differ a lot from World Wide Web, TCP/IP networks and, in general, from client-server networks.

Studies on P2P networks are focused on two different topics: physical P2P networks (i.e.,P2P networks opposed to hierarchic and centralised TCP/IP networks) and overlay networks (i.e. networks of logical links between hosts over an existing physical network of any type). Our interest is mainly focused on overlay P2P systems: they are probably going to become the most used kind of application–level protocols for resource sharing and organisation.

In this paper we present a novel P2P overlay network, named *PROSA* , heavily inspired by social networks. Social networks are sets of people or groups interconnected by means of acquaintance, interaction, friendship or collaboration links. Many kinds of natural social networks have been deeply studied in the last thirty years [2], and many interesting characteristics of such networks have been discovered. In a real social network relationships among people are of the most importance to guarantee efficient collaboration, resources discovery and

A. Levi et al. (Eds.): ISCIS 2006, LNCS 4263, pp. 726–734, 2006.

fast retrieval of remote people. Nevertheless, not all relationships in a social network are of the same importance: usually links to parents and relatives are stronger than links to friends, which are in turn stronger than links to colleagues and class mets. On the other hand, it is also interesting to note that usually links in a social group evolve in different ways. A large amount of relationships are (and remain) bare "acquaintances"; some of them evolve around time into "friendships", while "relativeness" is typical of very strong links to really trusted people.

This suggests that a P2P network based on a social model should take into account that different kind of links among peers can exist, and that links can evolve from simple acquaintances to friendship.

Results of studies performed by Watts, Strogatz, Newman, Barabasi et al. in the last decades[7] [4] [6] [8] [1] reveal that networks of movie characters, scientific collaborations, food chains, proteins dependence, computers, web pages and many other natural networks usually exhibit emerging properties, such that of being small–worlds. A small–world is a network where distance among nodes grows as a logarithmic function of the network size and similar nodes are strongly connected in clusters.

PROSA tries to build a P2P network based on social relationships, in the hope that such network could naturally evolve to a small–world.

In section 2, we describe **PROSA** and algorithms involved in linking peers and routing queries for resources; in section 3, we report some results about topological properties of **PROSA** network, obtained by simulation; in section 4, we summarise obtained results and plan future work.

2   *PROSA*: A Brief Introduction

As stated above, **PROSA** is a P2P network based on social relationships. More formally, we can model **PROSA** as a directed graph:

$$PROSA = (\mathcal{P}, \mathcal{L}, P_k, Label) \tag{1}$$

$\mathcal{P}$ denotes the set of peers (i.e. vertices), $\mathcal{L}$ is the set of links $l = (s, t)$ (i.e. edges), where t is a neighbour of s. For link $l = (s, t)$, s is the source peer and t is the target peer. All links are directed.

In P2P networks the knowledge of a peer is represented by the resources it shares with other peers. In **PROSA** the mapping $P_k : \mathcal{P} \to \mathcal{C}$, associates peers with resources. For a given peer $s \in \mathcal{P}$, $P_k(s)$ is a compact description of the peer knowledge (PK - *Peer Knowledge*).

Relationships among people are usually based on similarities in interests, culture, hobbies, knowledge and so on. Usually these kind of links evolve from simple "acquaintance–links" to what we called "semantic–links". To implement this behaviour three types of links have been introduced: *Acquaintance–Link* (*AL*), *Temporary Semantic–Link* (*TSL*) and *Full Semantic–Link* (*FSL*). TSLs represent relationships based on a partial knowledge of a peer. They are usually stronger than *AL*s and weaker than *FSL*s.

In $\boldsymbol{PROSA}$, if a given link is a simple AL, it means that the source peer does not know anything about the target peer. If the link is a FSL, the source peer is aware of the kind of knowledge owned by the target peer (i.e. it knows the $P_k(t) <$, where $t \in \mathcal{P}$ is the target peer). Finally, if the link is a TSL, the peer does not know the full $P_k(t)$ of the linked peer; it instead has a *Temporary Peer Knowledge* (TP_k) which is built based on previously received queries from the source peer. Different meanings of links are modelled by means of a labelling function *Label*: for a given link $l = (s,t) \in L$, $Label(l)$ is a vector of two elements $[e, w]$: the former is the link label and the latter is a weight used to model what the source peer knows of the target peer; this is computed as follow:

- if $e = AL \Rightarrow w = \emptyset$
- if $e = TSL \Rightarrow w = TP_k$
- if $e = FSL \Rightarrow w = P_k(t)$

In the next two sections, we give a brief description of how $\boldsymbol{PROSA}$ works. A detailed description of $\boldsymbol{PROSA}$ can be found in [3].

2.1   Peer Joining to $\boldsymbol{PROSA}$

The case of a node that wants to join an existing network is similar to the birth of a child. At the beginning of his life a child "knows" just a couple of people (his parents). A new peer which wants to join, just looks for n peers at random and establishes ALs to them. These links are ALs because a new peer doesn't know anything about its neighbours until he doesn't ask them for resources. This behaviour is quite easy to understand: when a baby comes to life he doesn't know anything about his parents. The $\boldsymbol{PROSA}$ peer joining procedure is represented in algorithm 1..

Algorithm 1. JOIN: Peer s joining to $\boldsymbol{PROSA}$ $(\mathcal{P}, \mathcal{L}, P_k, Label)$

Require: $\boldsymbol{PROSA}$ $(\mathcal{P}, \mathcal{L}, P_k, Label), Peer\ s$
1: $\mathcal{RP} \leftarrow rnd(P, n)$ {Randomly selects n peers of $\boldsymbol{PROSA}$ }
2: $\mathcal{P} \leftarrow \mathcal{P} \cup s$ {Adds s to set of peers}
3: $\mathcal{L} \leftarrow \mathcal{L} \cup \{(s,t), \forall t \in \mathcal{RP}\}$ {Links s with the randomly selected peers}
4: $\forall t \in \mathcal{RP} \Rightarrow Label(p,q) \leftarrow [AL, \emptyset]$ {Sets the previously added links as AL}

2.2 $\boldsymbol{PROSA}$ Dynamics

In order to show how $\boldsymbol{PROSA}$ works, we need to define the structure of a query message. Each query message is a quadruple:

$$Q_M = (qid, q, s, n_r) \qquad (2)$$

where qid is a unique query identifier to ensure that a peer does not respond to a query more then once; q is the query, expressed according to the used knowledge model[1]; $s \in P$ is the source peer and n_r is the number of required results. **PROSA** dynamic behaviour is modelled by Algorithm 2. and is strictly related to queries. When a user (U) of **PROSA** asks for a resource on a peer s, the inquired peer s builds up a query q and specify a certain number of results he wants to obtain n_r. This is equivalent to call $ExecQuery(\textbf{PROSA}, s, \emptyset, n_r)$.

Algorithm 2. ExecQuery: query q originating from peer s executed on peer cur

---

Require: **PROSA** $(\mathcal{P}, \mathcal{L}, P_k, Label)$
Require: $cur, prev \in \mathcal{P}$, $qm \in QueryMessage$
1: $Result \leftarrow \emptyset$
2: **if** $prev \neq \emptyset$ **then**
3:     $UpdateLink(\textbf{PROSA}, cur, prev, q)$
4: **end if**
5: $(Result, numRes) \leftarrow ResourcesRelevance(\textbf{PROSA}, q, cur, n_r)$
6: **if** $numRes = 0$ **then**
7:     $f \rightarrow SelectForwarder(\textbf{PROSA}, cur, q)$
8:     **if** $f \neq \emptyset$ **then**
9:         $ExecQuery(\textbf{PROSA}, f, cur, qm)$
10:     **end if**
11: **else**
12:     $SendMessage(s, cur, Result)$
13:     $\mathcal{L} \leftarrow \mathcal{L} \cup (s, cur)$
14:     $Label(s, cur) \leftarrow [FSL, P_k(cur)]$
15:     **if** $numRes < n_r$ **then**
16:         {– Semantic Flooding –}
17:         **for all** $t \in Neighborhood(cur)$ **do**
18:             $rel \rightarrow PeerRelevance(P_k(t), q)$
19:             **if** $rel > Threshold$ **then**
20:                 $qm \leftarrow (qid, q, s, n_r - numRes)$
21:                 $ExecQuery(\textbf{PROSA}, t, cur, qm)$
22:             **end if**
23:         **end for**
24:     **end if**
25: **end if**

The first time $ExecQuery$ is called, $prev$ is equal to $\emptyset$ and this avoids the execution of instruction number 3. Following calls of $ExecQuery$, i.e. when a peer receives a query forwarded by another peer, use function $UpdateLink$, which updates the link between current peer cur and the forwarding peer $prev$, if necessary. If the requesting peer is an unknown peer, a new TSL link to that peer is added having as weight a Temporary Peer Knowledge(TP_k) based on the received query message. Note that a TP_k can be considered as a "good hint" for the current peer, in order to gain links to other remote peers. It is really

---

[1] If knowledge is modelled by Vector Space Model, for example, q is a state vector of stemmed terms. If knowledge is modelled by onthologies, q is an ontological query, and so on.

probable that the query would be finally answered by some other peer and that the requesting peer will download all resources that matched it. It would be useful to record a link to that peer, just in case that kind of resources would be requested in the future by other peers. If the requesting peer is a TSL for the peer that receives the query, the corresponding TPV (Temporary Peer Vector) in the list is updated. If the requesting peer is a FSL, no updates are performed.

The relevance of a query with respect to the resources hosted by the user's peer is evaluated calling function $ResourcesRelevance$. Two possible cases can hold:

- If none of the hosted resources has a sufficient relevance, the query has to be forwarded to another peer f, called "forwarder". This peer is selected among s neighbours by the function $SelectForwarder$, using the following procedure:
    - Peer s computes the relevance between query q and the weight of each links connecting itself to his neighbourhood.
    - It selects the link with the highest relevance, if any, and forward the query message to it.
    - If the peer has neither $FSLs$ nor $TSLs$, i.e. it has just ALs, the query message is forwarded to one link at random.
  This procedure is described in Algorithm 2., where the subsequent forwards are performed by means of recursive calls to $ExecQuery$.
- If the peer hosts resources with sufficient relevance with respect to q, two sub-cases are possible:
    - The peer has sufficient relevant documents to full-fill the request. In this case a result message is sent to the requesting peer and the query is no more forwarded.
    - The peer has a certain number of relevant documents, but they are not enough to full-fill the request (i.e. they are $< n_r$). In this case a response message is sent to the requester peer, specifying the number of matching documents. The message query is forwarded to all the links in the neighbourhood whose relevance with the query is higher than a given threshold (semantic flooding). The number of matched resources is subtracted from the number of total requested documents before each forward step.

When the requesting peer receives a response message it presents the results to the user. If the user decides to download a certain resource from another peer, the requesting peer contacts the peer owning that resource asking for download. If download is accepted, the resource is sent to the requesting peer.

3   Topological Properties

Algorithms described in section 2 are inspired by the way social relationships among people evolve, in the hope that a network based on those simple rules could naturally become a small–world. That of being a small–world is one of the most desirable properties of a P2P network, since resource retrieval in small–worlds is really efficient. This is mainly due to the fact that small–world networks have a short Average Path Length (APL) and a high Clustering Coefficient (CC). APL is defined as the average number of hops required to reach any other node in the network: if APL is small, all nodes of the network can be easily reached in a few steps starting from whichever other node.

CC can be defined in several ways, depending on the kind of "clustering" you are referring to. We used the definition given in [7], where the clustering coefficient of a node is defined as:

$$CC_n = \frac{E_{n,real}}{E_{n,tot}} \tag{3}$$

where n's neighbours are all the peers to which n as linked to, $E_{n,real}$ is the number of edges between n's neighbours and $E_{n,tot}$ is the maximum number of possible edges between n's neighbours. Note that if k is in the neighbourhood of n, the vice-versa is not guaranteed, due to the fact that links are directed. The clustering coefficient of the whole network is defined as:

$$CC = \frac{1}{|V|} \sum_{n \in V} CC_n \tag{4}$$

i.e. the average clustering coefficient over all nodes.

The CC is an estimate of how strongly nodes are connected to each other and to their neighbourhood. In particular, the definition given in Equation 3 measures the percentage of links among a node neighbours with respect to the total possible number of links among them.

In the following two subsections we show that **PROSA** has both a small APL and a considerable high CC.

3.1   Average Path Length

Since we are focusing on topological properties of a **PROSA** network to show that it is a small–world (i.e. that queries in **PROSA** are answered in a small amount of steps), we estimate the APL as the average length of the path traversed by a query. It is interesting to compare the APL of **PROSA** with the APL of a correspondent random graph, since random graphs usually have a really small average path length.

Given a graph $G(V, E)$ with $|V|$ vertices (nodes) and $|E|$ edges (links) among nodes, the correspondent random graph is a graph G_{rnd} which has the same number of vertices (nodes) and the same number of edges (links) of G, and where each link between two nodes exist with a probability p.

Note that the APL of a random graph can be calculated using equation (5), as reported in [5], where $|V|$ is the number of vertices (nodes) and $|E|$ is the number of edges (links).

$$APL = \frac{\log |V|}{\log (|V|/|E|)} \tag{5}$$

Figure 1 shows the APL for **PROSA** and the correspondent random graph for different number of nodes in the case of 15 performed queries per node. The APL for **PROSA** is about 3.0, for all network sizes, while the APL for the correspondent random graph is between 1.75 and 2.0: the average distance among peers in **PROSA** seems to be independent from the size of the network. This is quite common in real small–world networks.

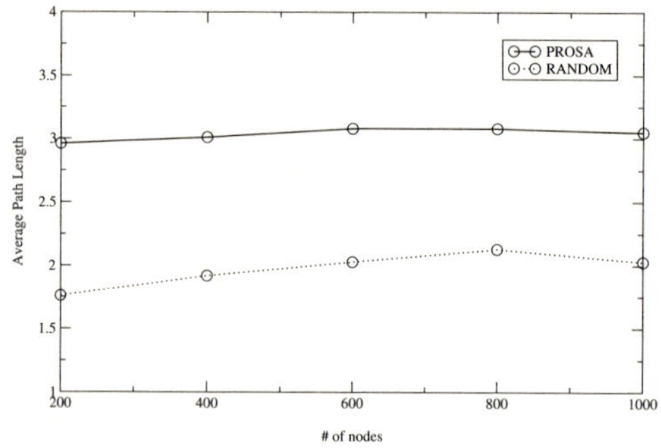

Fig. 1. APL for **PROSA** and random network

It is also interesting to analyse how APL changes when the total number of performed queries increases. Results are reported in Figure 2, where the APL is calculated for windows of 300 queries, with an overlap of 50 queries. Note that the APL for **PROSA** decreases with the number of performed queries. This behaviour heavily depends on the facts that new links among nodes arise whenever a new query is performed (TSLs) or successfully answered (FSLs). The higher the number of performed queries, the higher the probability that a link between two nodes does exist.

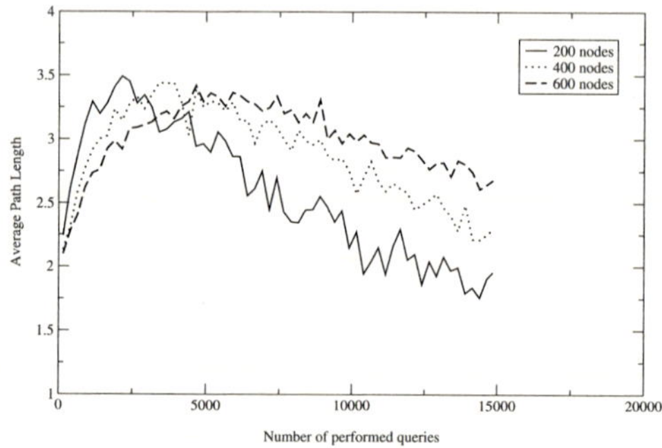

Fig. 2. Running averages of APL for **PROSA** with different network size

3.2   Clustering Coefficient

The clustering (or transitivity) of a network is a measure of how strongly nodes are connected to their neighbourhood. Since links among nodes in **PROSA** are established as a consequence of query forwarding and answering, we suppose that peers with similar knowledge will be eventually linked together. This means that usually peers have a neighbourhood of similar peers, and having strong connections with neighbours could really speed–up resource retrieval.

In Figure 3 the CC of **PROSA** for different number of performed queries is reported, for a network of 200 nodes. Note that the clustering coefficient of the network increases when more queries are performed. This means that nodes in **PROSA** usually forward queries to a small number of other peers so that their aggregation level naturally gets stronger when more queries are issued.

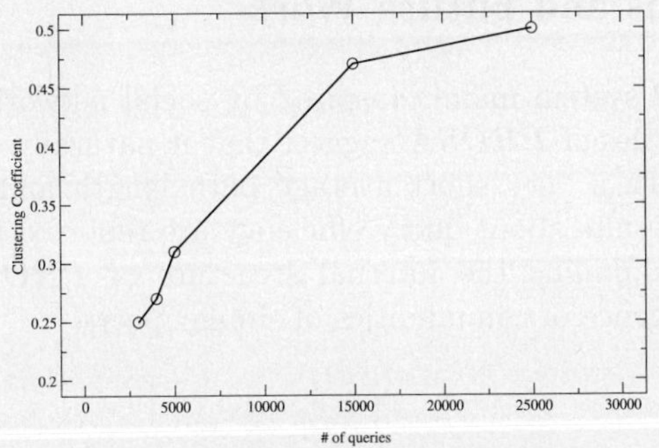

Fig. 3. **PROSA** CC for **PROSA**

It could be interesting to compare **PROSA** clustering coefficient with that of a corresponding random graph. The clustering coefficient of a random graph with $|V|$ vertices (nodes) and $|E|$ edges (links) can be computed using equation 6.

$$CC_{rnd} = \frac{|E|}{|V| \cdot (|V| - 1)} \tag{6}$$

Figure 4 shows the CC for **PROSA** and a correspondent random graph for different network sizes, in the case of 15 performed queries per node. The CC for **PROSA** is from 2.5 to 6 times higher that that of a correspondent random graph, in accordance with CC observed in real small–world networks. This result is quite simple to explain, since nodes in **PROSA** are linked principally to similar peers, i.e. to peers that share the same kind of resources, while being linked to other peers at random. Due to the linking strategy used in **PROSA** , it is really probable that neighbours of a peer are also linked together, and this increases the clustering coefficient.

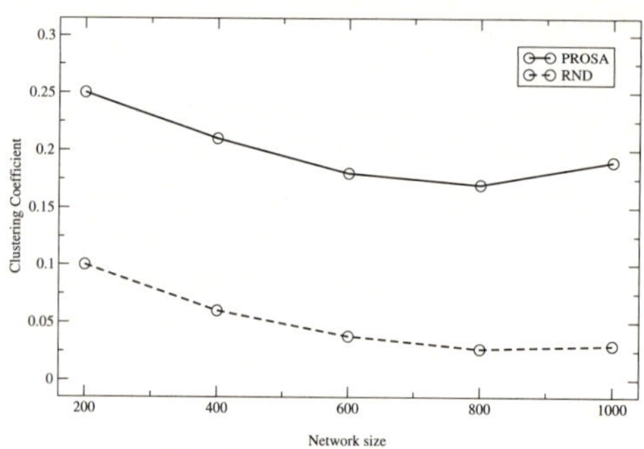

Fig. 4. Clustering coefficient for **PROSA** and the corr. random graph

4   Conclusions and Future Work

PROSA is a P2P system mainly inspired by social networks and behaviours. Topological properties of **PROSA** suggest that it naturally evolves to a small–world network, with a very short average path length and a high clustering coefficient. More results about query efficiency are reported in [3]. Future work includes deeply examining the internal structure of **PROSA** networks and studying the emergence of communities of similar peers.

References

1. Reka Albert and Albert-Laszlo Barabasi. Statistical mechanics of complex networks. *Reviews of Modern Physics*, 74:47, 2002.
2. Mark Buchanan. *Nexus: Small Worlds and the Groundbreaking Theory of Networks.* 2003.
3. V. Carchiolo, M. Malgeri, G. Mangioni, and V. Nicosia. Social behaviours applied to p2p systems: An efficient algorithm for resources organisation. *COPS06 – 2nd International Workshop on Collaborative P2P Information Systems*, June 2006.
4. Scott J. *Social Networks Analysis: A Handbook.* Sage Pubblications, London, 2000.
5. M. E. J. Newman. Scentific collaboration networks. ii. shortest paths, weighted networks, and centrality. *Physical Review E*, 64:016132, 2001.
6. M. E. J. Newman. The structure of scientific collaboration networks. *PROC.NATL.ACAD.SCI.USA*, 98:404, 2001.
7. Duncan J. Watts and Steven H. Strogatz. Collective dynamics of 'small-world' networks. *Nature*, 393:440–442, 1998.
8. R. J. Williams, E. L. Berlow, J. A. Dunne, A.-L. Barabsi, and N. D. Martinez. Two degrees of separation in complex food webs. *Proceedings of the Nat'l Academy of Sciences*, 99:12913–12916, 2002.

Security Considerations in e-Cognocracy

Joan Josep Piles[1], José Luis Salazar[1], José Ruíz[1],
and José María Moreno-Jiménez[2]

[1] Departamento de Ingeniería Electrónica y de Comunicaciones, Universidad de
Zaragoza
[2] Grupo Decisión Multicriterio Zaragoza, Universidad de Zaragoza

Abstract. E-cognocracy [1,2,3] is a cognitive democracy that combines
both representative and participative democracy with two main objectives: (i) to overcome some of the problems associated with the traditional
democratic system (participation, transparency and control) and (ii) to
extract and socially share knowledge related with the scientific resolution
of high complexity problems associated with the governance of society.
E-cognocracy uses the democratic system as a catalyst for the vital or
cognitive process characteristic of living systems, the multicriteria techniques as the methodological aid and the Internet as the communication
and participation support. To capture the decision makers' preferences
and to share the knowledge related with the scientific resolution of the
public decision making problems, the e-voting process of e-cognocracy
has some characteristics that have not been covered by traditional e-
voting systems. In this paper, we present the necessary modifications in
the classical e-voting methods to deal with one of these properties: the
linkage among rounds.

1 Introduction

Historically, the involvement of citizens in their government has been the factor
that has influenced most political changes. All of the parties agree in affirm-
ing that it is desirable to reach the highest participation possible, within the
limitations that involves the efficient operativity of the institutions.

The development of Information and Communication Technologies during the
last years has led the citizens' participation in their own government. The Internet has been the direct cause of that and is a tool that is used widely by
citizens who later will choose their leaders. In that way, the technology evolves
by assimilating the classic exchanges of information, adapting them to its needs.
A clear example has been electronic voting or e-voting. Nevertheless, changes in
the processes of decision making have not been appreciated, even if there have
been proposals on the matter.

We found the reason for that in the shortage of technological means for its
imple-mentation. Herein, we introduce a tool to perform one of those novel ideas:
e-cognocracy.

In Section 2 we present e-cognocracy and its main differences with other e-
voting schemes. Section 3 provides a description of our proposed voting system,

A. Levi et al. (Eds.): ISCIS 2006, LNCS 4263, pp. 735–744, 2006.

as well as a proof that it satisfies the requeriments for its use in e-cognocracy. We offer in Section 4 the details of our implementation and actual deployment of the system. Finally, in Section 5 we provide the final considerations and future job within this project.

2   e-Cognocracy and the e-Voting Process

Recently, a certain democratic fallacy has been discussed because democratic representativeness has not achieved its initial purpose, which is the participation of citizens in their own government. For that reason, many authors have demanded greater participation by the citizens in the governance of the society [4]. One of the solutions proposed is e-cognocracy [1,2,5].

E-cognocracy [1,2,3] is a cognitive democracy that combines both representative and participative democracy with two main objectives: (i) to overcome some of the problems associated with the traditional democratic system (participation, transparency and control) and (ii) to extract and socially share knowledge related with the scientific resolution of high complexity problems associated with the governance of society. It has the final objective of creating a more open, civilized, transparent, and free society that, at the same time, increases the cohesion, the participation, and the connectivity of its citizens, making the society more egalitarian and caring. E-cognocracy uses the democratic system as a catalyst for the vital or cognitive process characteristic of living systems, the multicriteria techniques as the methodological aid and the Internet as the communication and participation support.

It not only provides a framework for greater involvement of the citizenry in its own government, it also solves some of the limitations of traditional democracy, and it provides a process of socialization of the knowledge related to the scientific resolution of problems. The "cognitive" connection between the citizens allows us to establish a network between ideas, cultures and civilizations, helping progress towards the achievement of a new world.

Among all of the tools necessary for the complete development of e-cognocracy, we concentrate on e-voting as the first gathering of information from citizens. E-cognocracy focuses on the extraction of relevant knowledge, including the analysis of the individual and social learning, derived from the scientific resolution of a problem. It uses the e-voting process to incorporate the preferences of the decision makers into the decisional process. To this end, it requires new technological tools [6,7].

From the point of view of the voting process, the key element introduced by e-cognocracy is the linkability of the votes. A classical voting system begins when citizens are asked to participate in the decision making process.

This process starts with a phase of information gathering. In it, each citizen is provided with the greatest amount of information possible from each one of the interested parties (generally, political parties). To give each citizen time to obtain as much information as is possible, usually takes several weeks.

Usually, during that phase, there is no excessive feedback (if any) from the citizens to the interested parties. Polls are performed to get an idea of the existing tendencies, but they affect a very small percentage of the electorate. Furthermore, that leads to a loss of interest, leaving the perception that the only important moment in the entire process is the vote itself.

To get the citizens more involved in this process and to extract the relevant knowledge of the decisional process, we have divided each voting into different rounds. Each voter can vote in as many rounds as he or she wants (but only once in each round). After each round, the results are published and are provided as additional information to the citizens.

For the results of voting in progress, only the last vote of each citizen is entered. Furthermore, all of the history of the different voters can be stored without associating them with specific identities. That way, information is available on the development of the thoughts of the citizenry until they reached a final decision.

To protect the identity of the voter, the individual trails are not publicized. For example, somebody could be paid to vote first A, then B, then C and, finally, D. Depending on the number of rounds, the number of possible combinations becomes sufficiently great that it is relatively safe to say that each person followed a different chain of votes. However, this chain of votes gives us information that will help to determine the reasons for changes in opinion (e.g., not only that people switched from A to B, but that can be a generalized fact after a specific event).

In addition, people are encouraged to put forward their points of view in open forums (anonymously, if that is desired) and the effects of these discussions can be correlated with changes in the opinions of the voters.

2.1 Requirements of e-Voting for the e-Cognocracy

Our system of e-voting started as a tool of e-cognocracy and it requires the following performance properties, most of which are shared with the classical systems of e-voting[8,9]:

Autentication. Only voters in the census shall be able to vote
Democracy. Each voter shall be able to vote only once in each round
Anonymity. A voter shall not be linked to its vote
No coercion. A voter shall not be able to prove its vote
Precision. It shall not be possible to remove a valid vote from the final counting
Reliability. It shall not be possible to include a non-valid vote in the final counting
Veracity. Only each voter can cast its vote
Verifiability. Voters shall be able to verify that their vote has been correctly accounted
Neutrality For each round the vote should be secret until the recount phase
Linkability. Two votes from the same voter in different rounds of the voting shall be linked together, but not to the voter who cast them

3   e-Cognocracy Voting Process

3.1   Previous Work on e-Voting Processes

There are three paradigms for cryptographically secure ballot elections:

Blind signatures[10]. The voters obtain ballots from the authorities, certified and privacy-preserved. This paradigm requires an anonymous channel between the voter and the tallying authorities to hide the user identity at the ballot casting.

Homomorphic encryption[11]. The ballots are encrypted and classified. This enables these schemes a fast tallying process.

Mix-net[12]. A recount authority moves and permutes the ballots, while changing their representation. Moreover, one of the requirements for e-cognocracy is the individual verifiability. A voting scheme has this property if voters can independently verify that their own ballots have been counted correctly. If some inaccuracies have been introduced into the tally, it must be possible to detect them and prove the forgery.

However, the main property of our voting scenario is the linkability. This quality was used in others e-voting schemes to detect double-voting. These schemes use group/ring signatures [13,14]. Nevertheless, almost all existing schemes have signature sizes linear with the signing group, which makes them impractical when used in large-scale voting. The exception is [15], where a short linkable signatures scheme is proposed and it has constant signature size. All of these schemes have a major drawback for our requirements: All the voters have to know all of the eligible voters' public keys. It is more convenient for the voter to be able to vote only with his own credentials, without any more knowledge about the rest of the eligible voters.

For these reasons, we have used the construction of an e-voting scheme from [16] and we have added linkable ability to it.

3.2   Actors in the Voting Process

Voter (V): Each voter must show its preferences in a multi-choice question, and rank them numerically. For each round of the voting the census shall be constant.

Certification Authority (CA): The Certification Authority shall issue the public/private keys and certificates for each actor involved in the process, and will serve as Trusted Third Party with regard to the validation of certificates.

Recount Authority (RA): The Recount Authority is the only entity allowed to decrypt the votes. The Electoral Authority shall provide information enough to link the votes from the same voter, but not to track them to the actual person who cast them.

Electoral Authority server (EA): The Electoral Authority shall keep track of the census, validate the users in the voting process, and sign their votes as a proof of voting. It shall also keep enough data about the votes to know the hash of the last vote from a voter (in order to link them for the Recount Authority) but without actually being able to decrypt them.

In this schema it is assumed that both the Electoral Authority and the Recount Authority do not work together to break the system and are trusted by each other and by the users. However, this is a reasonable assumption for most cases.

3.3   Initialization

The first phase of the voting process is the initialization of the actors involved. In order to keep security, the recount authority as much as the electoral authority will have to obtain a new pair of keys with their respective certificates for each voting process. In addition, the keys of each voter could be initialized, although it is not necessary.

CA Initialization. The CA is initialized only once, before the start of the voting process. It is done by self-signing a certificate issued to itself and distributes it to the parties involved so that they can verify the certificates that this CA issues later.

RA's private key initialization. The Recount Authority must decrypt all the votes with its private key. To avoid possible abuses from a single owner of this key it is possible to split it in different shares, of such form that the data of the ballots are only going to be accessible through the coordination and acceptance of the shareholders.

EA's private key initialization. The Electoral Authority will have a pair of keys and its corresponding certificate to be able to issue blind signatures of each vote, and voting certificates.

Voters registry. The CA will issue a new certificate and a pair of keys to each voter who still does not have them to be able to be registered in the census.

3.4   Voting

1. The questions are presented to the voter, who then makes his choices.
2. Voter identifies himself to EA and sends it a hash of his vote for EA to issue a blind signature of it, and a ticket made from a mix of his identity and a random value that will be signed by EA as well.
3. EA verifies the voter's identity, checking it against the census and that the voter has not already cast its vote in this round.
4. EA issues a blind signature of the vote, and a signature of the ticket, and stores them linked to the voter for future rounds.
5. The voter encrypts his vote and the blinding factor used previously with RA's public key and send them to EA.
6. EA sends to RA:
   - The vote and the blinding factor, encrypted.
   - The blind signature of the vote.
   - The signed ticket.

7. If the voter had previously voted (in other rounds), EA sends to RA a copy of the blind signature of the latest vote, which will be then used by RA to link them.
8. EA sends to V the signature of the ticket to prove that his vote has been stored.

3.5   Recount

- RA makes public the signatures of the tickets, and starts a claims period before the publication of the results.
- RA decrypts the original votes, and uses the secret included with them to get a valid signature from the blind signature.
- RA checks the vote with the signature obtained and verifies that it is correct.
- RA links all the votes from the same voter.
- RA publishes the results of the round/voting.

Let us see whether our voting system is adapted to the requirements imposed on e-cognocracy.

Authentication
- The voters do not send their votes directly to RA; because the EA must insure that the voters are duly included in the census.

Democracy
- To avoid a voter votes more than once in a round, the EA will store which voters have voted in each round.

Anonymity
- All the information provided to RA are encrypted votes and their corresponding blind signatures and signed tickets. With that information, it is impossible to ascertain anything that indicates the identities of the voters.

No coercion
- In exchange for his vote, the voter receives only a signed ticket that is generated randomly and does not bear a relation to the content of the vote.

Precision
- Each voter authenticates itself to the EA, therefore, this one must know the private key, which is impossible to fake, whenever it has a suitable length.

Reliability
- Each voter has a signature of ticket that he or she sent to the EA and a list of these tickets will be published before the recount; therefore, even if RA is compromised, the votes cannot be deleted, since this action will be reported by the affected voters who will present their tickets to support their objection.

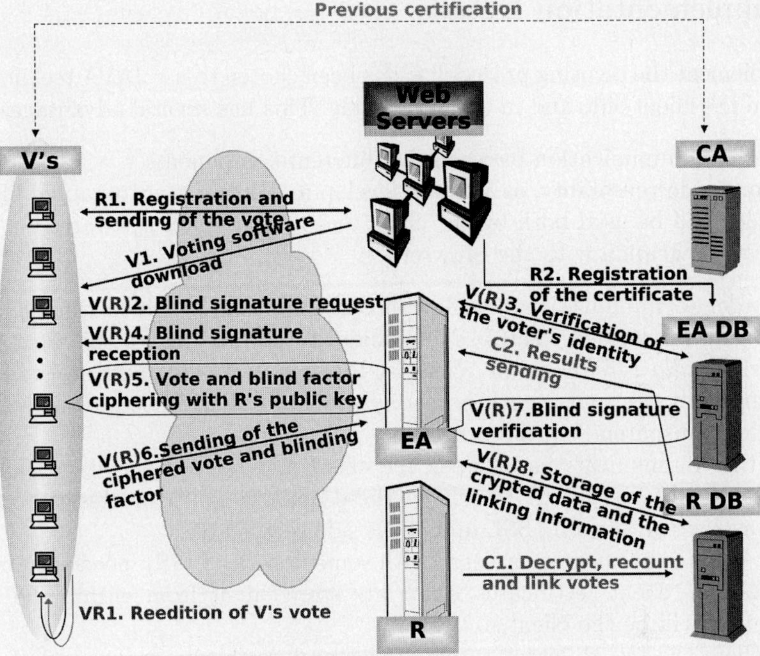

Fig. 1. Our proposed e-voting system

Veracity

- Each vote is stored with a signature from the EA. A vote cannot be introduced for counting (even if RA is compromised), because it would be necessary to obtain a valid signature, and that is not possible without the private key of the EA.

Verifiability

- For each vote received, the EA gives back to the voter a signed ticket. Later, when beginning the recount, R publishes a list of the tickets of the votes cast. If a voter has a vote that is not included in the list, he could report it to the EA so that it undertakes the appropriate action.

Neutrality

- RA decrypts the votes once each round is finished

Linkability

- Along with each vote, the EA sends to RA the blind signature of the last vote cast by the same person. In the recount phase, RA searches among the cast votes, one whose blind signature matches it. In that way, a chain of votes is obtained that stores all of the history of the voter without revealing his identity.

4   Implementation Details

To implement the e-voting protocol, it has been chosen to use JAVA technologies, both in the client side and in the server side. This has several advantages:

- Better communication between the different components.
- More code reusability, as we can develop a series of cryptographic libraries which will be used both by the client and by the server software.
- Easy integration with the browsers.

In order to minimize the number of configurations in which the client side had to run, we decided to choose an standard web browser. In this case, it was selected *Mozilla Firefox* as the reference browser. It has the advantage of being open source, so its source code is readily available, contributing to increase the feeling of transparency in the process.

All the communications between the client and the server will be both authenticated and encrypted. To achieve these goals, it will be necessary to set up an infrastructure allowing SSL and client side certificates.

The browser has been completed with some libraries (*JSS*), needed to be able to access the client certificates which are stored in it from within the JAVA applet that will be the client software.

As there are two different servers (Electoral Authority server and Recount server), there could be two web and application servers, working with two different database servers. None the less, when doing the actual deployment it might happen that it is advisable to put both applications in the same application and/or web server. Likewise, it could be desirable to use two databases in a single database server. This would not be a problem, but it should be taken into account that should the server machine be compromised, the whole voting and recounting system would be broken.

The application server to use will depend on the available infrastructure at the moment of the deployment. In our tests, we used *Tomcat* as application server. It is open source as well, and its capacity for this kind of systems is well proven.

It was chosen to use *MySQL* as a backend to store the data related to the votings (both the actual votes -ciphered and clear-text after the recount- and the information about the votings -question of the voting, number of rounds, period of time for each round...).

4.1   Deployment Details

Our group carried out a deployment of a test voting system. None the less, any future deployments should take into account that the specific details will depend on the available resources. This will be much more important if, as it usually happens, the servers are shared with other applications. The implications for the security of the system must be studied on a case by case basis.

Regarding the choice of software, we used Apache as the webserver and Tomcat 5 as application server, both of them running in LINUX i386 machines. As this was a proof of concept, the system load was expected to be very low. This allowed us to consolidate both services (the Certificate Authority server and the Recount server) within the same Tomcat instance. Likewise, both databases were stored in a single MYSQL server which was executing in the same machine with Apache and Tomcat.

There are several options available to link Apache and Tomcat. The simplest way is running two independent servers listening in different ports (in fact, it would even be possible to have them running in different machines, should the need arise). Notwithstanding this, we chose to use a tighter integration between them using the *JK Connector*. This technology allows to redirect queries that would normally be answered by the Apache server towards the Tomcat application server, in a way that is transparent for the user.

5   Conclusions

We have studied the new challenges that e-cognocracy imposes on traditional methods of voting. We have developed an e-voting system that provides a tool for knowledge extraction and information storage that are needed to achieve a more participative democracy. As we have seen, the key to the linkability of the votes is the separation between the Electoral Authority, who can link the chain of votes to the voter but cannot see the contents of the votes, and the Recount Authority, who can link the votes and decrypt them but without obtaining any type of information about the individual voter. Obviously, a certain degree of trust in the authorities that take part in the process is assumed. The e-voting process proposed for e-cognocracy verifies the ten properties previously established to guaranty the effectiveness of this democratic system. Moreover, it can be applied in a friendly way, without any special kind of technical background. Our future work includes developing other technological tools needed by e-cognocracy. As e-voting provides the raw data, there is still the need for a set of tools which can link the information obtained to the actual social phenomena that helps to form the results obtained in the votation. These tools includes online forum where people can exchange ideas in a controlled way, and the tools needed to extract the relevant or prevalent opinions and match them against the shifts in the voters' opinion.

Acknowledgements

This work has been partially funded under the research projects "Electronic Government. Internet-based Complex Decision Making: e-democracy and e-cognocracy" (Ref. PM2004-052) and "Internet-based Complex Decision Making. Decisional Tools for e-cognocracy" (Ref. TSI2005-02511).

References

1. Moreno-Jiménez, J.M., Polasek, J.M.: e-Democracy and knowledge. a multicriteria framework for the new democratic era. Journal of Multicriteria Decision Analysis **12** (2003) 163–176

2. Moreno-Jiménez, J.M., Polasek, J.M.: e-Cognocracy and the participation of immigrants in e-governance. In: TED Conference on e-government 2005. Electronic democracy: The challenge ahead. Volume 13 of Schriftenreihe Informatik., University Rudolf Trauner-Verlag (2005) 18–26

3. Kersten, G.E.: e-democracy and participatory decision processes: lessons from e-negotiation experiments. Journal of Multi-Criteria Decision Analysis **12**(2-3) (2003) 127–143

4. Roberts, N.: Public Deliberation in an Age of Direct Citizen Participation. The American Review of Public Administration (**34**(4)) 315–353

5. Moreno-Jiménez, J.: Nueva sociedad, nueva democracia. estudios de economía aplicada. (1) (2006) 559–581

6. Lotov, A.: Internet tools for supporting of lay stakeholders in the framework of the democratic paradigm of environmental decision making. Journal of Multi-Criteria Decision Analysis **12**(2-3) (2003) 145–163

7. Insa, R., D., Holgado, J., Moreno, R.: Multicriteria e-negotiation systems for e-democracy. Journal of Multi-Criteria Decision Analysis **12**(2-3) (2003) 213–218

8. Benaloh, J., Tuinstra, D.: Receipt-free secret-ballot elections (extended abstract). In: STOC '94: Proceedings of the twenty-sixth annual ACM symposium on Theory of computing, ACM Press (1994) 544–553

9. Cranor, L.F., Cytron, R.K.: Design and implementation of a practical security-conscious electronic polling system. Technical Report WUCS-96-02, Washington University (1996)

10. Chaum, D.: Blind signatures for untraceable payments. In Chaum, D., Rivest, R.L., , Sherman, A.T., eds.: Advances in Cryptology: Proceedings of Crypto '82. (1982) 199–204

11. Cohen, J.D., Fischer, M.J.: A robust and verifiable cryptographically secure election scheme (extended abstract). In: FOCS. (1985) 372–382

12. Chaum, D.L.: Untraceable electronic mail, return addresses, and digital pseudonyms. Commun. ACM **24**(2) (1981) 84–90

13. Chaum, D., van Heyst, E.: Group signatures. Lecture Notes in Computer Science **547** (1991) 257–265

14. Rivest, R.L., Shamir, A., Tauman, Y.: How to leak a secret. In: ASIACRYPT '01: Proceedings of the 7th International Conference on the Theory and Application of Cryptology and Information Security. Lecture Notes in Computer Science (2001) 552–565

15. Tsang, P.P., Wei, V.K.: Short linkable ring signatures for e-voting, e-cash and attestation. Cryptology ePrint Archive, Report 2004/281 (2004) http://eprint.iacr.org/.

16. Riera, A., Borrell, J.R.J.: Efficient construction of vote-tags to allow open objection to the tally in electronic elections. Inf. Process. Lett. **75**(5) (2000) 211–215

A Dynamic Service Range Management Strategy for Improving Mobile Multicast Protocol Performance[*]

Ping Wang[1], Yunze Cai[2], Jinjie Huang[2], and Xiaoming Xu[2,3]

[1] Dept. of Computer Science & Engineering, Shanghai Jiaotong University,
Dongchuan Road 800, Shanghai 200240, China
Wang_ping@sjtu.edu.cn
[2] Dept. of Automation, Shanghai Jiaotong University,
Dongchuan Road 800, Shanghai 200240, China
{yzcai, huangjinjie, xmxu}@sjtu.edu.cn
[3] University of Shanghai for Science and Technology, Shanghai 200093, China

Abstract. There are many challenges when providing multicast services to mobile hosts (MHs) since host's mobility may cause tree reconstruction, non-optimal routing and the disruption of multicast services. Generally, frequent modifications to multicast tree are avoided as the expense of multicast routing inefficiency and vice versa. Two basic mechanisms, proposed by the IETF in Mobile IP to support multicasting, are two typical cases. This paper introduces a new mobile multicast approach with dynamic service range, which eliminates unnecessary tree reconstruction overhead by utilizing the state of multicast agent, and does not induce significant multicast delivery overhead at the same time. In addition, we present a previous subscription mechanism, which can resume multicast delivery quickly after a MH performs handoff. Simulation results show that the proposed protocol gets an improved performance over the existing protocols in terms of signaling overhead and delay.

1 Introduction

With the rapid improvement in both wireless networks and mobile terminals, great increases have emerged in the fields of services and applications in wireless mobile environment, among which one of the most important and challenging problems is to provide efficient mobility and multicasting support, and to bring the two together in the next generation of IP networks.

The IETF Mobile IP [1, 2] proposes two approaches to support mobile multicast, namely, remote subscription (RS) and bi-directional tunneling (BT). In RS scheme, a MH has to re-subscribe to its desired multicast groups whenever it moves to a new foreign network. This scheme has the advantages of offering an optimal routing path and works well if the MH spends a relatively long time at each foreign network. However, when a MH is highly mobile, it may incur frequent modification of the multicast tree and the tree reconfiguration makes MH experience a lengthy delay.

---

[*] This paper is supported by the National Key Fundamental Research Program (2002cb312200), and the National Natural Science Foundation of China (60575036).

In BT scheme, the home agent (HA) is responsible for managing group membership for its away MHs. Once the HA subscribes to an interesting multicast group, it may forward received multicast packets for its away MHs using the unicast tunneling scheme. The main advantage of this scheme is that the multicast delivery tree will not be updated when host's location changes, which sacrifices routing efficiency because of multicast forwarding across the home network.

There is a tunnel convergence problem in BT scheme. When multiple HAs have MHs on the same foreign network, one copy of every multicast packet is forwarded to the same FA by each HA. To overcome this problem, the MoM [3, 4, 7] protocol chooses one of the HAs as the designated multicast service provider (DMSP). Only the DMSP is allowed to tunnel a copy of multicast packets to the corresponding FA. Therefore, it reduces multicast traffic by decreasing the number of duplicate copies of packets. This scheme, however, introduces DMSP handoff overhead when all MHs of the DMSP for the multicast group move out of the foreign network.

The RBMoM [5] protocol intends to trade off between the shortest delivery path and the frequency of multicast tree reconfiguration by controlling the service range of the multicast home agent (MHA). Each MHA has a specific service range, and a MHA only forwards packets to MHs that are located within the service range. When a MH moves to a new foreign network which is outside the MHA's service range, it must select a new MHA to provide multicast services.

This article distinguishes active and idle multicast agent (MA), and it's unnecessary to reconstruct multicast tree when MA has not forwarded multicast packets for a long time. We just keep track of the location of mobile members if MA is in idle state. Until the MA receives multicast packets, it becomes active and a limited service range of the MA is used to ensure that the routing path is near optimal. In order to reduce the disruption of multicast services due to host's mobility, a previous tunnel is built to trigger the resumption of multicast delivery quickly because of the shortest distance between two neighboring networks. The rest of the paper is organized as follows. Section 2 and 3 present the proposed protocol DRBMoM. Section 4 evaluates the performance of DRBMoM and Section 5 makes a conclusion.

2   DRBMoM Overview

2.1   Design Principle

In general, host's mobility can cause modification of the multicast tree. The purpose of reconstructing multicast tree is to remove triangular routing and offer optimal multicast delivery, but tree reconstruction also lays heavy load on the network since a lot of processing and transmitting overhead is produced. Therefore, most mobile multicast approaches intend to enhance performance by well trading off between the shortest delivery path and the frequency of multicast tree reconfiguration. RS and BT proposed by IETF are at the two ends of the spectrum. RS is the most efficient in multicast delivery, but has the highest rate of multicast tree reconfigurations. In contrast, BT does not require any modification to multicast tree, but it uses possibly long unicast tunnel for multicast packet forwarding. Some improved protocols, such as RBMoM [5] and remote subscription with multicast agent [6], achieve an appropriate balance between routing efficiency and the overhead of tree modifications by changing the size of the service range of multicast agent. Another protocol TBMoM [8] utilizes the characteristic that the mobile multicast has according to the speed of MHs and also achieves good trade off between tree reconstruction overhead and data delivery efficiency.

However, this article achieves a good balance between tree reconstruction overhead and route optimality by dynamically adjusting the service range of multicast agent (MA) according to the state of MA. This idea is not new and it originates from IP paging mechanism in Cellular IP [11], which eliminates unnecessary binding update messages when a MH is idle. Cellular IP just tracks the location of idle hosts in an approximate and efficient manner and MHs do not have to update their location after each handoff, thus minimizing air interface traffic.

Based on above observation, we also distinguish MA's active state from idle state and the service range in MA's active state is limited in order to offer optimal multicast delivery. If a MA has not forwarded multicast packets during a certain period of time, it becomes idle, during which it is unnecessary to reconstruct multicast tree due to host's mobility since no multicast packets are transmitted. The only thing is for MA to track the location of the MH until it changes to be active upon reception of a multicast packet. Therefore, a number of unnecessary tree reconstructions can be avoided.

However, the first arrival multicast packets will be transmitted in MA's idle state before it completes updating the state. If we do not restrict the service range in idle state, a MH may have a long distance to its MA and performance degrades with hops. Therefore, we define a hop limit K_{max} and the service range of MA can't beyond the hop limit.

2.2 Protocol Description

DRBMoM introduces Anchor Multicast Agent (AMA), which is responsible for tunneling multicast data to MHs in its service range. In DRBMoM, an AMA represents an anchor and it can track the location of moving hosts. The service range of AMA is different in active and idle state, which is very interesting for highly MHs that frequently perform handoffs during which the AMA don't forward any multicast data. By restricting the maximum service range of an AMA, the tunnel length between a MH and its multicast agent can be limited.

In DRBMoM, the oldest AMA policy is used to select multicast agent. When a MH enters into a new foreign network which has already subscribed the multicast group, it will receive multicast data directly from the new FA[1] (nFA). Thus, DMSP handoff is avoided and the loss of multicast packets caused by DMSP handoff is minimized. Otherwise, a previous tunnel from the FA in the old foreign network (oFA) the MH just visited to the nFA in the new foreign network is built to forward multicast data. At the same time, the nFA checks if it is out of the service range of MA and it will join the multicast tree if necessary. When multicast packets are forwarded directly to the nFA by a MA, the nFA should request the oFA to delete the previous tunnel if any.

---

[1] In that event, the nFA is an older multicast agent serving for the current network.

3   DRBMoM Protocol Details

3.1   Data Structures

As shown in Fig. 1 (a), each MH maintains a *group information table* about group ID, current multicast agent and its location. According to the group information sent by MH, each FA maintains a *visitor table* to keep track of which MHs are currently at its network, which networks the MHs just visited before they move to current network (i.e., which oFAs), and when these bindings expire. For membership updates, the FA may delete MH's entry from the *visitor table* if its binding expires or it leaves current network. Moreover, there are four lists kept in every FA: *MH list, AMA list, tunnel source list* and *tunnel destination list*. The *AMA list* is the multicast agent which is responsible for forwarding multicast data to current network. The *tunnel source list* is a unicast IP address that indicates from which current FA may receive multicast data and the *tunnel destination list* is a set of unicast IP addresses that indicate to which current FA should send multicast data. When multicast data arrive from AMA directly, current FA requests the FA in the *tunnel source list* to delete the corresponding tunnel. Each AMA maintains a *state table*, which represents current state (i.e., active or idle), the range it can serve and the remaining active timer value. In addition, each AMA keeps *MH list* and *Forwarding list*, which record mobile group members to be served and a set of FAs to which the AMA should forward multicast packets by the unicast tunneling, respectively.

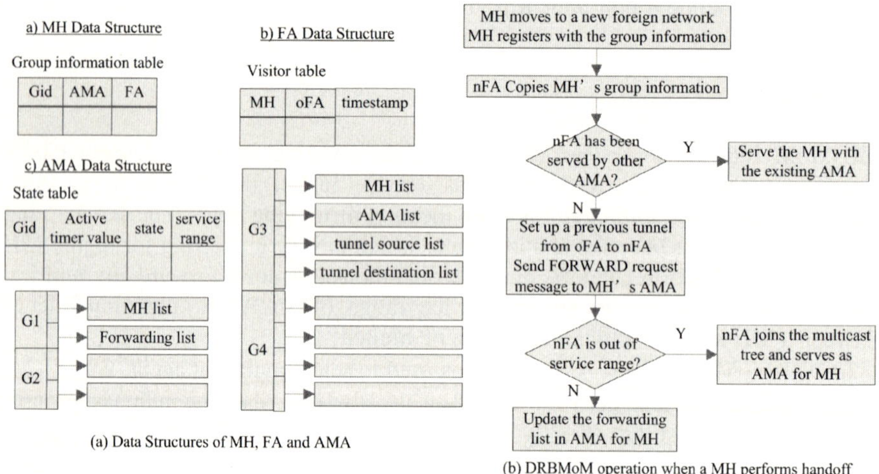

Fig. 1. DRBMoM protocol

3.2   MH's Arrival at a New Foreign Network

When a MH moves into a foreign network and requests a multicast group membership, it registers with the FA of the new network (nFA). The group information may be piggy-backed in the *Registration Request* message. If other MHs in current network have subscribed to the same multicast group, the MH can continue to receive packets for the group since the nFA uses local multicast to deliver the packets to all group members in its network. If the MH is the first member of current network, the nFA checks if it is a multicast tree node. If the nFA finds it has already been in the multicast tree, it will add a new entry for the MH and deliver multicast packets in native multicast over its local link. Otherwise, the nFA requests the FA of the old network the MH just visited (oFA) to build a previous tunnel to transmit multicast data. Meantime, the nFA sends a *FORWARDING request* message to the MH's AMA. The AMA calculates the distance in terms of the path that the message from the nFA travels. If the distance is not beyond the service range, the AMA adds a forwarding entry and sends back a *FORWARDING accepted* message. Otherwise, a *FORWARDING reject* message is sent out as a response. The nFA decides whether to join multicast tree according to the message sent back by the AMA, as shown in Fig. 1 (b). When multicast data forwarded by the AMA arrive, the nFA requests the oFA to delete the previous tunnel.

3.3 Multicast Packet Delivery

When multicast packets arrive, the AMA resets the active timer if it is in active state. Otherwise, the AMA changes the state to be active and sets the active timer with a predetermined value. Accordingly, the service range is set to the range in active state. An *UPDATE request* message with the service range is sent out from the AMA to the FAs in the *Forwarding list* in order to limit the delivery path length. If an AMA has not received multicast packets for a long time during which the active timer expires, the AMA becomes idle and enlarges its service range accordingly.

When multicast packets arrive at a FA, the FA may use link-level multicast to deliver the packets to local members and tunnel the packets to the FAs recorded in the *tunnel destination list* if they exist. If the packets are forwarded by an AMA directly, the FA should send a *DELETE request* message to the FA recorded in the *tunnel source list* if any.

3.4 Group Membership Management

When a MH stays in a foreign network, the MH and the FA will exchange membership message periodically. For a large number of MHs, this might seriously load the FA and its link to the Internet. Indeed, this behavior generates additional traffic that may not be strictly required if each MH sends unsolicited reports at appropriate time intervals, but an initial query message after receiving the first membership report should still be transmitted to notify the MHs about the expected frequency of report transmission and indicate whether or not the AMA mechanism is supported [10].

When a FA detects any change in the group member list through membership reports or expiration of mobile registrations, it communicates the change to the corresponding AMA indicating that it wants to join or leave a multicast group on behalf of the visiting MHs.

3.5 Control Packet Arrival

A control packet arriving at an AMA is either a *FORWARDING request* message or a *FORWARDING stop* message. When a *FORWARDING request* message arrives, the AMA checks whether the FA is in the service range by computing the hop distance the message travels. If so, the AMA adds a forwarding entry about the FA and sends back a *FORWARDING accepted* message. Otherwise, a *FORWARDING reject* message is sent out as a response. If a *FORWARDING stop* message arrives, the AMA deletes the corresponding forwarding entry and sends a *PRUNE request* message to its parent node if it finds that the *MH list* and *Forwarding list* are null.

The control packet arriving at a FA can be classified as *BUILD request* message, *DELETE request* message, *FORWARDING accepted* message, *FORWARDING reject* message and *UPDATE request* message. If a *BUILD request* message arrives, the FA may use the source IP address of this message as the destination endpoint to build a previous tunnel. Provided a *DELETE request* message comes, the FA needs to delete the corresponding tunnel recorded in the *tunnel destination list* and decides whether to request stopping forwarding multicast data from the AMA or the FA in the *tunnel source list* if the *MH list* and *tunnel destination list* become null. A *FORWARDING accepted (reject)* message means the AMA can or cannot forward multicast packets to current network. In the latter case, the FA will join the multicast group. Upon reception of the message with *UPDATE request*, the FA decides whether to join the multicast group by checking whether it is out of the service range. The distance to the AMA is calculated as the hop distance that the message from the AMA travels. The FA joins the multicast tree and serves the visiting MHs directly if it finds out it is out of the service range. A *FORWARDING stop* message will be sent to the previous AMA when the FA joins the multicast group.

4 Performance Evaluations

Performance evaluation of the proposed protocol is performed by discrete-event simulation and the total simulation time is 1000 units. The network topology is assumed to have 8×8 subnets located on *x-y* coordinate system. For simplicity, there is only one multicast group in which only one source is assumed and all group members are mobile. The group member size is varied from 10 to 120. The multicast tree is the source-based shortest path tree and the shortest path length is measured by Dijkstra's algorithm. Initially, MHs are placed randomly among the subnets and random walk mobility model is used as the mobility pattern of the MHs, where a MH moves randomly in one of four directions, with the same probability, 0.25. MHs show diverse mobility rates ranging from 1 (low) to 5 (high). That is, before handoff the time that a MH stays in a subnet is 5, 4, 3, 2 and 1 unit(s), respectively. The interarrival time interval of the multicast packets is a Poisson distribution with mean λ (15units/pkt by default). The active timer is predetermined with 5 units, which means the AMA changes its state from active to idle if it has not received any multicast data in 5 units.

In our proposed scheme, the service range of an AMA in active state (R_{active}) and in idle state (R_{idle}) is set 1 and 3 hop(s) count, respectively. The service range of a MHA in RBMoM (R_{MHA}) is 1 hop count. Three main performance measures are considered, namely, the overhead of tree reconstruction, the delivery overhead of multicast packets and the disruption of multicast services due to host's mobility.

The tree reconstruction overhead is measured by the total number of JOIN and PRUNE operations by MHs during the simulation period, as shown in Fig. 2 (a). In the RS scheme, when a MH moves to a new subnet, the nFA in the new subnet must join the multicast tree for the MH. Meantime, the oFA in the previous subnet the MH just visited must quit from the multicast tree if no subscribers exist. In RBMoM, only when the MH leaves the service range of the MHA, the nFA needs to join the multicast tree. In our scheme, the service range of AMA in idle state is much larger than that in active state, which restricts the reconstruction frequencies when MHs move among subnets without receiving any multicast data. Therefore, RS has the highest reconstruction overhead and RBMoM reduces the reconstructing number greatly. Our scheme lowers signaling overhead again by avoiding unnecessary tree reconstructions. As shown in Fig. 2 (a), there are peak points as the number of MHs increases. This is because after the number of MHs reaches to a certain point, the MHs will populate uniformly in the subnets and the probability that the new subnet a MH moves to has already subscribed the same multicast group becomes large.

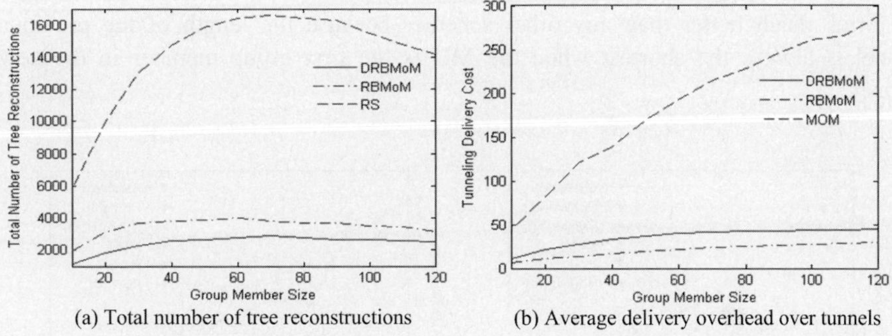

(a) Total number of tree reconstructions   (b) Average delivery overhead over tunnels

Fig. 2. The overhead comparison in tree reconstruction and multicast delivery

Fig. 2 (b) shows the average tunneling length of a multicast packet as a function of the number of MHs. Both RBMoM and DRBMoM have much shorter tunneling length than MoM. This is due to the fact that the tunneling cost in MoM depends on the path length between MHs' FAs and their HAs, while in RBMoM and DRBMoM, the service range of multicast agent restricts the tunneling length. However, when compared with RBMoM, DRBMoM has slightly longer tunneling length. This is because some multicast packets must be forwarded by AMA in its idle state before completing the state update, during which the service range is much larger than that in active state. But compared with the tree reconstruction overhead saved by DRBMoM, this slightly larger cost is trivial.

The disruption of multicast services is calculated as the delay from when the MH gets a care-of address to the time multicast packets can be sent correctly to the new location of the MH, where the path length is used as a metric. In MoM, the disruption is calculated as the length of the path that the registration message travels from the MH to its HA, namely, the wireless link (counted as 1) from the MH to its FA and the path from the FA to the HA. In RS, the disruption means the join delay taken by the tree reconstruction if the MH is the first group member in the new subnet, plus 1 for group membership reports from the MH over the wireless link. In RBMoM, the disruption is 0 if the MH is not the first group member in the new subnet, or is calculated as the length of the path from the nFA to its multicast agent plus 1 for wireless link if the MH is the first group member in the new subnet and it's still within the MHA's service range. Otherwise, the disruption is computed as the join delay taken by the MH plus 1 for wireless link. In our scheme, the delay is 0 if the MH is not the first member in the new subnet, or is 1 if the nFA has already joined the multicast group and there is no other subscriber in the new subnet. Otherwise, the delay is the wireless link from the MH to the nFA and the path from the nFA to the oFA. In general, adding a branch to the multicast tree is more costly than sending a message by unicast along the same path due to the extra processing at each multicast router on the path. We define a *cost factor* (1.5 and 1.3) as the ratio of the cost of adding a branch to the multicast tree to the cost of sending a unicast message along the same path. Fig. 3 (a) and (b) show the average and maximum disruption of multicast service per group member due to handoffs, respectively. Our scheme performs much better than any other schemes because the length of the previous tunnel is always the shortest when the MH is the first group member in the new subnet.

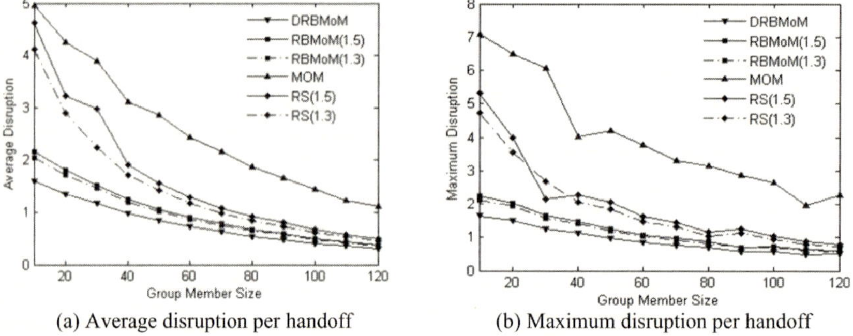

(a) Average disruption per handoff   (b) Maximum disruption per handoff

Fig. 3. The comparison of disruption due to handoff

To study the effect of interarrival time interval of multicast packets and service range on DRBMoM, we evaluate the performance of the proposed scheme under different λ values and service ranges. Because the previous subscription is used in the scheme, the disruption of multicast services hardly changes by using different λ values and service ranges and thus such measure is not given here. Fig. 4 (a) and (b) show the comparison of tree reconstruction cost and tunneling delivery cost under different λ values. As λ value is increased, more tree reconstructions are saved at the expense of longer tunneling delivery path. The reason is that the larger λ value is, the more likely handoff takes place in AMA's idle state and the more difficultly the MHs move out of the service range. Before completing the state update when multicast packets arrive, the more packets will be tunneled to the MHs by AMA in its idle state.

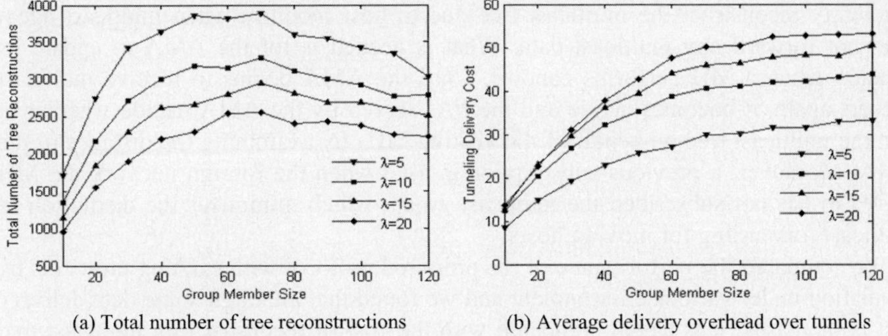

(a) Total number of tree reconstructions   (b) Average delivery overhead over tunnels

Fig. 4. The overhead comparison in tree reconstruction and multicast delivery under different λ values

Fig. 5 (a) and (b) show the comparison of tree reconstruction cost and tunneling delivery cost under different service ranges. Three sets of service ranges are used. For set one, the service range is 1 hop distance in active state (ASR) and 2 hops distance in idle state (ISR); for set 2, ASR is 1 and ISR is 3; for set 3, ASR is 1 and ISR is 4. Because the size of the network used in the simulation is 8×8, we don't consider the situation that the service range in active state is larger than 1 hop distance or the service range in idle state is larger than 4 hops distance. As shown in Fig. 5 (a) and (b), when we increase the service range in idle state (the service range in active state remains unchanged), more tree reconstruction overhead is saved at the cost of more tunneling delivery overhead. The reason is obvious. Tradeoffs may be required to choose the optimum service range in different AMA's states according to λ value.

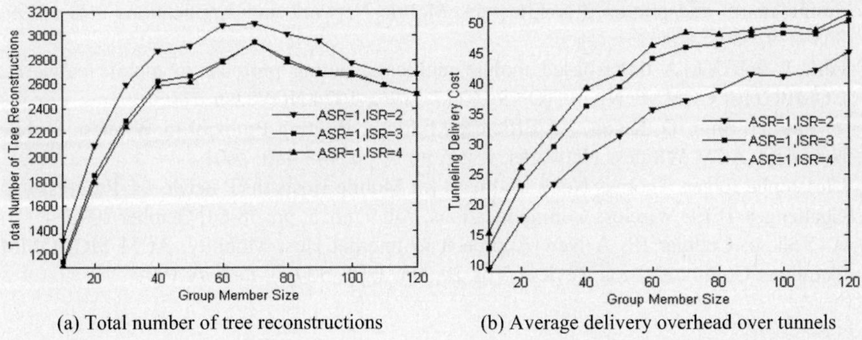

(a) Total number of tree reconstructions   (b) Average delivery overhead over tunnels

Fig. 5. The overhead comparison in tree reconstruction and multicast delivery under different service ranges

5 Conclusion

In this paper, we proposed a dynamic service range based mobile multicast routing protocol, which makes full use of the state of multicast agent. It is unnecessary to frequently reconstruct the multicast tree due to host mobility when multicast agent does not forward any multicast data. What is needed is for the AMA to update its location when a MH performs handoff. Until the AMA begins to receive multicast packets again, it becomes active and the FAs served by the AMA decide whether to join the multicast tree on behalf of the visiting MHs by examining the distance to the AMA. Moreover, a previous subscription is used when the foreign network the MH moves to has not subscribed the multicast group, which minimizes the disruption of multicast forwarding for moving hosts.

We compared the performance of the proposed protocol with existing protocols by simulation under various environment and we found that although some data delivery cost is increased, it is trivial compared with the cost of reconstructing multicast tree saved by DRBMoM. What's more, the disruption of multicast services due to host mobility is reduced greatly.

References

1. C. Perkins, IP mobility support for IPv4, RFC3344, August 2002.
2. D. Johnson, C. Perkins, J. Arkko, Mobility support in IPv6, RFC3775, June 2004.
3. T. Harrison, C. Williamson, W. Mackrell R. Bunt, Mobile multicast (MOM) protocol: multicast support for mobile hosts, in: Proc. of ACM MOBICOM'97 (1997) 151–160.
4. V. Chikarmane, C.L. Williamson, Performance evaluation of the MOM mobile multicast protocol, ACM/Baltzer Mobile Networks and Applications (1998) 189–201.
5. C.R. Lin, K. Cheng, Mobile Multicast Support in IP Network, Proc. IEEE INFOCOM; (2000) 1664–1672.
6. Y. Wang, W. Chen, Supporting IP multicast for mobile hosts, Mobile Networks and Applications 6 (2001) 57-66.
7. V. Chikarmane, C.L. Williamson, Multicast support for mobile host using mobile IP: design issues and proposed architecture, Mobile Network and Applications 3(4) (1999) 365–379.
8. Park J, Suh YJ, A timer-based mobile multicast routing protocol in mobile networks, COMPUTER COMMUNICATIONS 26 (17): 1965-1974 NOV. Jan. 2003.
9. Y. Suh, H. Shin, D. Kwon, An Efficient Multicast Routing Protocol in Wireless Mobile Networks. ACM Wireless Networks, vol. 7, no. 5, pp. 443-453, 2001.
10. Christophe Jelger, Thomas Noel. Multicast for Mobile Hosts in IP networks: Progress and Challenges. IEEE Wireless Communications, vol. 9, no. 5, pp. 58-64, October 2002.
11. A. Valk_o, Cellular IP: A New Approach to Internet Host Mobility, ACM SIGCOMM Computer Communication Review, Vol. 29, No. 1, pp. 50-65., January 1999.

A Survey of Major Challenges and Future Directions for Next Generation Pervasive Computing

Yong-Bin Kang[1] and Yusuf Pisan[2]

[1] Institute for Graphics Interfaces, Republic of Korea
ybkang@igi.re.kr
[2] University of Technology, Sydney, Australia
ypisan@it.uts.edu.au

Abstract. Pervasive computing has emerged as a new computing paradigm with a great deal with appeal in our everyday environment. However, the benefits offered by this new computing paradigm are relatively below our expected standard. This paper discusses the major challenges for the next generation pervasive computing and the difficulties in developing a promising system to meet these challenges. Then, we present a survey that covers relevant existing approaches addressed to overcome the challenges. Finally, we highlight future research directions and present a new intriguing exploration, aiming to broaden the appeal and bridge the gap for the fulfillment of the challenges.

1 Introduction

This paper discusses some of the major challenges for developing a promisingly user-centric computing system, and highlights the future research directions which are yet to be properly addressed to overcome the challenges in a highly embedded interactive computing space.

The development of computing technologies with the advent of a variety of computing devices and applications have been augmenting our everyday environment, seamlessly integrating our activities into the environment. This trend leads to promote a new paradigm of computing, called *pervasive computing* [1]. Thus, pervasive computing environment (PCE) is populated by a collection of users, the computational resources, and the applications, as well as can accommodate the pervasive computing paradigm.

One of the principal goals of pervasive computing is to be user-centric, providing computational support to help and mediate user activities in a natural, non intrusive way [1, 2]. Yet, accomplishing that goal is broad and still largely undeveloped. In order to understand the difficulties to realize that goal, this paper aims at (1) classifying the major three challenges; (2) reviewing some of the major current approaches to meet the challenges; (3) presenting future research directions and a new promising exploration.

This paper is organized as follows. In the next section, we highlight the key challenges that need to be addressed. Section 3 reviews related work. In section 4, our future directions are presented. Finally conclusion remarks close this paper.

A. Levi et al. (Eds.): ISCIS 2006, LNCS 4263, pp. 755–764, 2006.

2   Key Challenges

We highlight the key challenges that need to be addressed to develop a next generation system for pervasive computing based on our observations. These are classified into three major issues and each one is closely related to the others.

2.1   Challenge 1: How to Model Context Information

First and foremost, modeling context information is a significant challenge. Main reasons are considered as follows:

- *Complex Structure*: Most PCEs may form an enormously complex structure consisted of a wide variety of heterogeneous context information [5,6].
- *Dynamic Environment*: The context in a PCE cannot be represented by a fixed prearranged plan, since it is continuously ever-increasing and ever-changing by means of (1) diverse interactions among context; (2) the numerous details that might not be noticed at design time of the PCE [7,8,9].
- *Difficulty in incorporating user preferences*: A true user-centric system needs to encapsulate user preferences into a PCE. However, capturing and understanding the user preferences that may shift over time are a quite difficult problem [10,6].

2.2   Challenge 2: How to Understand Complex Interactions

One of the greatest challenges of pervasive computing is to capture the current status of PCE to support and enhance the user activities in execution task. For this, we believe that diverse interactions happened in PCE must be accurately detected and understood.

There can be occurred several types of interactions in PCE as follows [11, 12, 13]: (1) between users and the environment; (2) among multiple environmental resources; (3) among multiple users; (4) among small social groups(e.g., family, friend); (5) different combination of those types. Understanding those interactions is a quite difficult challenge due to the following reasons:

- *Not explicitly identified*: All the potential interactions cannot be identified by explicit human specification. We do not correctly know what a user like to do, and which services are preferred for user activities at the design time of a PCE [13,14].
- *Dynamic and Complicated Interactions*: Detecting the dynamic interactions among a wide range of different context is also a difficult problem [15,16,17,18, 19,20]. This is still ongoing research issue.
- *Arbitrary Interaction*: It is a common agreement that there can be existed not only the broad patterns of interactions, but also more sophisticated and arbitrary interactions in PCE

2.3   Challenge 3: How to Provide the Most Attractive Services

Lastly, pervasive computing is a user-centric view of computing. This means the best services must be supported to all the users in a PCE. Further, those services should not be contradicted with user preferences. For example, if the dynamic configuration is not consistent with user preferences, the user may be confused or surprised by that change [21]. We embody a minimal set of necessary challenges for this requirement as follows:

- *Eliciting user preferences*: First of all, in order to provide the most attractive services to the users, we must be able to elicit user preferences. Since, however, user preferences are invisible and seamlessly shift over time, it is a significant challenge [6, 10].
- *Providing preference resolution policies*: Within a PCE, every user has different preferences or makes different decisions about the same context. This implies that a particular user might intrude or distract other's preferences intentionally or accidentally. Let us call this situation as *preference confliction*. Since this situation can be commonly happened in the shared environment, harmonizing that confliction is quite important [12, 22].
- *Providing future prediction mechanism*: As Weiser noted [1], the whole purpose of pervasive computing is to provide application that serve humans. For this, we believe that a pervasive computing system should be able to predict future possible actions for use conveniences at a proper place in proper time.
- *Providing collaborative services*: If the interrelated services in the environment are adequately and seamlessly collaborated, we will possibly provide more intelligent services and will improve the quality of the services. We call those services as *collaborative services*.

3   Review of Existing Approaches

There has been a large body of significant research activity for pervasive computing in the last few years both in academia as well as industry. In this section, we briefly review the current status of existing approaches for resolving each challenge discussed above.

3.1   Modeling for Pervasive Computing Environment

It is a fundamental design question how to most appropriately design a model for a PCE being able to capture and encapsulate a large amount of information in the environment. Finding the answer of the question is quite important, because such a model provides computational support for constructing, describing, implementing, and analyzing the patterns of the interaction and coordination among context. We introduce popularly used some of the models heading for this attempt.

Semantic Network is a graph notation for representing the knowledge of the context in patterns of interacted nodes and links [23]. This network is an appropriate model for capturing a vast amount of information entering an Intelligent

Environment, deployed at MIT's AI Laboratory [6]. It can encapsulate many different objects and associations, track, and follow the relationships between them.

CML is designed by Henricken [10] to capture many of the features of context information. CML provides a formal basis for representing and reasoning about some of the properties of context information. CML allows a graphical notation for describing information types, their classification, relevant quality of meta-data, and dependencies among different types of information. A main benefit of CML is sufficiently generic to capture arbitrary types of context information.

Multimodal context [17] was announced to meet the requirement of broader notion in ubiquitous computing system. DAML and DAML+OIL [24], and OWL [25] are ontologies that are a kind of classification for expressing the entities which consist of environment based on W3C's Resource Description Framework(RDF) [26]. Robinson [27] proposes a middleware language that aid in service composition in pervasive computing. It brings together and applying research in the field of Natural Language Processing(NLP), Human Computer Interaction(HCI) and Network Service [28]. Coen [29] introduces a natural language interface to a highly interactive space, known as the Intelligent Room.

Most of these models are required to be formulated by human explicit specification at design time of their PCEs. Thus, those are appropriate for expressing the environment in simply static structure. However, because of the diversity and the dynamics that is expected in a PCE, those modeling methods can be far less suitable to represent a dynamic PCE involving sophisticated interactions. Furthermore, the PCE is ever-changing, even the characteristics of the context are unpredictable (e.g., rapid, unbounded, and time-varying), and thus those are ill-suited to meet the challenges.

3.2   Understanding Interactions in the Environment

In order to capture the diverse interactions in a PCE, several middleware systems have been developed. In PACE Project [30], a middleware was developed for distributed context-aware systems and analyzed the state-of-the-art in middleware for context-aware systems. The PACE consists of four main subsystems such as a context management system, a preference management system, a programming toolkit that facilitates interaction between users and environment, and communication assistance tools.

Dey [17] and Pervasive Computing Group [8] propose middleware systems for detecting the current state, minimizing user distractions. Grimm [31] and Song [32] provide frameworks that can make users simply and easily access services. Mani [13] provides interaction paradigm that utilizes the full potential of the networked, multimedia environment.

Most of these requires the users to pre-arrange the relationships of the interactions between the users and the environment. For example, the one wish to participate in the shared environment must construct and combine their own relationships of interactions. In addition, most interpretation of those interactions are performed in the limited bounds of spaces. Furthermore, those approaches have an inability to dynamically reconfigure the relationships of the interactions. As a result, understanding the interactions in a PCE is still needed to be developed and is a difficult research issue.

3.3 Providing the Best Services to the Users

Very few attempts addressing the issue about improving technique for dynamically eliciting user preferences according to temporal changes has been studied until recently in our observations. Most have been attempted based on *policy-based method* [12,34,33]. The policy-based method allows users to formulate their own preferences by explicit policies if necessary. However, this is only useful at design time, thus it cannot incorporate the dynamic changes of user preferences. Once formulated, these preferences will be gradually staled with the lapse of time, since preferences may shift over time.

We now introduce the representative three models of the policy-based method. Composite Capabilities/Preference Profiles(CC/PP) [35] is a W3C proposed standard [36] for describing device capabilities and preferences with a focus on wireless devices such PDAs and mobile phones. It is suitable for expressing very simple preferences, allowing a system to customize preferences. However, future fledged pervasive systems will require much more sophisticated preferences in order to support seamless adaption to changes in these preferences. Thus, this model is not suitable for future pervasive systems. A more natural preference modeling method based on situation abstraction is developed by Henricksen [22]. In this work, users can express a set of simple and possibly conflicting preferences. In addition, preferences can be grouped into sets and combined by policies. The confliction detection model by Pervasive Computing Group [8] is introduced. This model presents the concept of interest zone which is main basis for conflicting resolution model based on user behavioral patterns.

Regarding the future prediction technique, there has been a large body of research about predicting future situations in static structured spaces. One of the major common features is that these approaches need prior knowledge about their information space. For examples, Chen [37] proposes a prediction model for navigating category on web by inferencing the user access patterns. Letizia [38] and Chi [39] infer user interests from on the web. Yan [40] and Fu [41] cluster the users based on the preference from on the web. Lam [42] proposes a Bayesian approach to track user interest shift.

However, very little research has been performed to predict promising future states of dynamic computing environments. Besides, no attempts to provide intelligent collaborative services for pervasive computing have been addressed until now based on our investigation.

4 Future Directions

This section briefly describes future directions to design a next generation pervasive computing system on the basis of the discussed challenges.

4.1   How to Model Context Information

First, we believe that we need a new model that has a formless schema for a PCE that will not be limited to a particular environment. This model must be able to spontaneously and seamlessly evolve its structure by (1) self-learning from interaction patterns; (2) self-configuring the environment; and (3) self-inferring the future states, according to the environmental changes without human control. Second, we expect that *uniform communication languages and standardized ontologies* will be essential, in order to provide seamless inter-operability and ease of the evolution of a PCE. Third, we believe that a technique for formalizing user preferences into a appropriate model must also be presented.

4.2   How to Understand Complex Interactions

First, we need uniform interfaces to provide single paradigm of data delivery for promoting complex context interactions. Second, based on this interface, we believe that techniques for capturing, organizing, and maintaining the snapshot of the active states of the environment such as user activities or preferences must be developed. Third, we expect that a mechanism for identifying similar groups (community) based on their activities and preferences should be presented, in order not to distract other group members' preferences.

4.3   How to Provide Most Attractive Services

First, in order to elicit user preferences, we believe that a promising criteria for learning the current behavioral patterns of a user need to developed. Because, people usually perform their activities under the influence of their preferences consciously or unconsciously. Second, we believe that a computing technique for the similarity or the dissimilarity measure about the individual preferences must be developed, in order to resolve the preference confliction situations. Third, a new prediction mechanism based on analysis of the prior knowledge about user's previous patterns will be needed. Last, a middleware language and a standard mechanism that aid in incorporating services in pervasive computing must be designed. These services should be fully cooperated all the potential of the computing environment, integrating and manipulating services seamlessly.

4.4   Where Can We Find Promising Possibilities

How can pervasive computing simultaneously broaden its appeal and effectively cope with the future research issues noted above? To answer that question, we present a new intriguing exploration to find a new promising potential by means of investigating the similarities between a biological space and a PCE.

Bioinformatics has arisen from the needs of biologists to utilize and help interpretation the vast amount of data that are constantly being gathered in genomic research [43]. More specifically, we have found that the following common challenges that must be shed light on in human living system are shared in bioinformatics, as well as the biological world has been remarkably successful in solving these problems. [5, 43, 44, 45]:

How to model a genetic network: Human living system forms a huge genetic network composed of non-identical elements (e.g., genes and proteins). Biologists need a new paradigm that is reliable and can deal with the network whose nodes are genes and proteins, and the chemical interactions represented by edges between them. To govern such a constantly expanded large genetic network, a new robust self-organization model is needed. Equally complex situation is occurred in a PCE, where a vertices are diverse entities(e.g., person, devices, and services) and edges are the interactions between them.

Thus, we expect if we more focus on finding the detailed common characteristics from detailed data has been available, and examining generic properties between those two spaces, we will formalize the existence of high-degree of self-organization model far beyond our expectation.

How to enlighten the relationships among genes: Enlightening internal/external relationships among genes in DNA that contains millions of symbols is also a major focus area in biological space. Genes are usually represented by *Strings* to represent DNA, RNA, and sequences of amino acids. Each DNA string contains millions of symbol and metabolic that describes the behavior of cells and their interactions with the network environment.

Some of the most important algorithmic trends in bioinformatics is to study of the relationships among genes such as (1) finding similarities among strings; (2) detecting certain patterns within strings; (3) finding similarities among parts of spatial structures. For these, the remarkable developments of pattern-matching approach has been developed since 1990s. For examples, Basic Local Alignment Search Tool (BLAST) that mimics the behavior of the dynamic programming approach and efficiently yields good results. Another widely used and effective technique is multiple alignment, which helps align several sequences of symbols, so identical symbols are properly lined up.

Therefore, we believe that learning and using those techniques into the computing space of PCEs will be very helpful to detecting, capturing, and analyzing the interactions mechanisms in PCEs.

How to infer new behavior patterns: Inferring new behavior patterns of biological data according to the previous classified clustering data is also one of the major research issues in bioinformatics. Biological data is often characterized by huge size, duplication, unavailability, and sometime unreliability. For this fact, inferring possible sequences from existing data is most essential in biological world. There is much of research about inferring sequences of genes from typical sequences and establishing the likelihood of the patterns for future sequences.

We believe that such inferring techniques will be effectively utilized into the situation requiring dynamic prediction techniques of possible future states(e.g., user activities, preferred services) in PCEs.

The biological world has been remarkably successful in problem solving of the evolution techniques of organisms, the analysis of complex arbitrary interactions, the inference about possible functions, and even cooperative behaviors among the elements in a enormous genetic network. Therefore, we believe that the employment of relevant research topics in bioinformatics will be eventually helpful to find new promising possibilities about the discussed challenges in this paper.

5   Conclusion

In this paper, we briefly discussed some of the important challenges, explored the existing approaches and presented the future research direction issued for developing user-centric pervasive computing.

More specifically, we highlighted the following three challenges that need to be addressed: (1) how to correctly model context information; (2) how to understand the interactions happened in PCEs; (3) how to provide the best services satisfying user preferences. Then, we reviewed some of the relevant existing approaches and their limitations to meet the challenges. Finally, we generated future research directions for realizing the next generation pervasive computing based on our observations. In particular, we suggested the promising possibilities of the involvements of commonly shared topics in bioinformatics, and briefly discussed common features between the biology space and the pervasive computing space.

We hope the issues addressed in this paper will both stimulate further discussion and be more helpful to bridge the gap in a further step towards the next generation pervasive computing technology

References

1. Weiser, M.: The computer of the twenty-first century. Scientific American **3** (1991) 66–75
2. Gupta, S., W.C.Lee, Purakayastha, A., Srimani, P.: An overview of pervasive computing. IEEE Personal Communications **4** (2001) 8–9
3. Dey, A., Abowd, G., Salber, D.: A context-based infrastructure for smart environments. Proceedings of the 1st International Workshop on Managing Interactions in Smart Environments (MANSE '99) (1999) 114–129
4. Sheng, Q.Z., Benatallah, B.: Contextuml - a uml-based modeling language for model-driven development of context-aware web services. Proceedings of the International Conference on Mobile Business (2005) 206–212
5. Barabasi, A., Albert, R.: Emergence of scaling in random netowork. Science **286** (1999) 509–512
6. Peters, S., Shrobe, H.: Using semantic networks for knowledge representation in an intelligent environment. Proceedings of the IEEE International Conference on Pervasive Computing and Communications (2003) 323–329
7. Cetintemel, U., Franklin, M.J., Giles, C.L.: Self-adaptive user profiles for large-scale data delivery. In Proc. of the 16th International Conf. on Data Engineering (2000) 622–633
8. Group, P.C.: Middleware infrastructure for active surroundings. Technical Report TR-CSPG-04-28-001, Information and Communication University (2003)
9. Nelson, G.J.: Context-aware and location systems. A dissertation submitted for the degree of PhD in the University of Cambridge (1998)

10. HENRICKSEN, K., INDULSKA, J., RAKOTONIRAINY, A.: Modeling context information in pervasive computing systems. Proc. of the First International Conference on Pervasive Computing (2002) 15–26
11. Hanssens, N., Kulkarni, A., Tuchida, R., Horton, T.: Building agent-based intelligent workspaces. ABA Conference Proceedings (2002) 675–681
12. Lee, D., Hyun, S.J., Lee, Y.H., Lee, G., Han, S., Kang, S.H., Park, I., Choi, J.: Active surroundings - a group-aware middleware for ubiquitous computing environments. Ubiquitous Computing Workshop 2004 (2004)
13. Mani, A., Sundaram, H., Birchfield, D., Qian, G.: The networked home as a user-centric multimedia system. NRBC '04 - Proceedings of the 2004 ACM workshop on Next-generation residential broadband challenges (2004) 19–30
14. O'Sullivan, D., Lewis, D.: Semantically driven service interoperability for pervasive computing. Proceedings of the 3rd ACM international workshop on Data engineering for wireless and mobile access (2003) 17–24
15. Brumitt, B., Meyers, B., Krumm, J., Kern, A., Shafer, S.A.: Easyliving - technologies for intelligent environments. Proceedings of the 2nd international symposium on Handheld and Ubiquitous Computing (2000) 12–29
16. Coen, M.H.: Design principles for intelligent envrionments. In Proc. of the 1998 National Conference on Artificial Intelligence (AAAI-98) (1998) 37–43
17. Dey, A., Salber, D., Abowd, G.: A conceptual framework and a toolkit for supporting the rapid prototyping of context-aware applications. Human-Computer Interaction **16** (2001) 97–166
18. Garlan, D., Siewiorek, D., Smailagic, A., Steenkiste, P.: Project aura - toward distraction-free pervasive computing. IEEE Pervasive Computing **2** (2002) 22–31
19. Kidd, C., Orr, R., Abowd, G., Atkeson, C., Essa, I., MacIntyre, B., Mynatt, E., Starner, T., Newstetter, W.: The aware home - a living laboratory for ubiquitous computing research. Proceedings of the Second International Workshop on Cooperative Buildings, Integrating Information, Organization, and Architecture (1999) 191–198
20. Kulkarni, A.: Design principles of a reactive behavioral system for the intelligent room. in Bitstream - The MIT Journal of EECS Student Research (2002)
21. Nakajima, T., Fujinami, K., Tokunaga, E., Ishikawa, H.: Middleware design issues for ubiquitous computing. Proceedings of the 3rd international conference on Mobile and ubiquitous multimedia (2004) 55–62
22. HENRICKSEN, K., INDULSKA, J.: A software engineering framework for context-aware pervasive computing. Proc. of the Second IEEE International Conference on Pervasive Computing and Communications (2004) 77–86
23. Sowa, J.F.: Semantic networks. Encyclopedia of Artificial Intelligence (1992)
24. DAML: Darpa markup language. www.daml.org (2003)
25. Dean, M., Connolly, D., van Harmelen, F., Hendler, J., Horrocks, I., McGuinness, D.L., Patel-Schneider, P.F., (editors), L.A.S.: Owl web ontology language 1.0 reference. http://www.w3.org/TR/owl-ref/ (2002)
26. Brickley, D., Guha, R.V.: Resource description framework (rdf) schema specification 1.0 - rdf schema. W3C Working Draft (2003)
27. Robinson, J., Wakeman, I., Owen, T.: Scooby - middleware for service composition in pervasive computing. Proceedings of the 2nd workshop on Middleware for pervasive and ad-hoc computing **77** (2004) 161–166
28. Weeds, J., Keller, B., Weir, D., Wakeman, I., Rimmer, J., Owen, T.: Natural language expression of user policies in pervasive computing environments. Proceedings of OntoLex 2004 (LREC Workshop on Ontologies and Lexical Resources in Distributed Environments (2004)

29. Coen, M., Weisman, L., Thomas, K., Groh, M.: A context sensitive natural language modality for the intelligent room. Proceedings of MANSE'99 (1999)
30. HENRICKSEN, K., INDULSKA, J.: Developing context-aware pervasive computing applications - models and approach. Pervasive and Mobile Computing **2** (2005) 37–64
31. Grimm, R.: System support for pervasive applications. ACM Transactions on Computer Systems **22** (2004) 421–486
32. Song, Z., M., R., Agre, J., Labrou, Y.: Task computing for ubiquitous multimedia services. Proceedings of the 3rd international conference on Mobile and ubiquitous multimedia (2004) 257–262
33. Dunlop, N., Indulska, J., Raymond, K.: Methods for conflict resolution in policy-based management systems. In Proc. of the 7th IEEE International Enterprise Distributed Object Computing Conference (EDOC03) (2003) 98–111
34. Wang, B., Bodily, J., Gupta, S.K.: Supporting persistent social group in ubiquitous computing environments using context-aware ephemeral group service. Proceedings of Pervasive Computing and Commnunications(PERCOM04) (2004) 287–296
35. INDULSKA, J., ROBINSON, R., RAKOTONIRAINY, A., HENRICKSEN, K.: Experiences in using cc/pp in context-aware systems. International Conference on Mobile Data Management (2003) Springer Verlag, LNCS 2574, 247–261
36. F., R., C., W., H., O., G., K.: Composite capability/preference profiles(cc/pp) - structure and vocabularies. W3C Working Draft (2001)
37. M.Chen, LaPaugh, A., Singh, J.: Predicting category accesses for a user in a structured information space. Proceedings of the 25th annual international ACM SIGIR conference on Research and development in information retrieval (2002) 65–72
38. Lieberman, Letizia, H.: An agent that assists web browsing. Proceedings of the 1995 International Joint Conference on Artificial Intelligent (1995) 65–72
39. Chi, E.H., Pirolli, P., Chen, K., Pitkow, J.: Using information scent to model user information needs and actions and the web. Proceedings of the SIGCHI conference on Human factors in computing systems (2001) 490–497
40. Yan, T.W., Jacobsen, M., Garcia-Molina, H., Dayal, U.: From user access patterns to dynamic hypertext linking. Proceedings of the fifth international World Wide Web conference on Computer networks and ISDN systems (1996) 1007–1014
41. Fu, Y., Sandhu, K., , Shih, M.: Fast clustering of web users based on navigation patterns. World Multiconference on Systemics, Cybernetics and Informatics (SCI/ISAS'99) **5** (1999) 560–567
42. Lam, W., Mostafa, J.: Modeling user interest shift using a bayesian approach. Journal of the American Society for Information Science and Technology **5** (2001) 416–429
43. Cohen, J.: Bioinformatics-an introduction for computer scientits. ACM Computing Surveys **36** (2004) 122–158
44. Cohen, J.: Computer science and bioinformatics. COMMUNICATION OF THE ACM **48** (2005) 72–78
45. Hernandez, T., Kambhampati, S.: Integration of biological sources - current systems and challegens ahead. SIGMOD Record **33** (2004) 51–60

Camera-Based Virtual Environment Interaction on Mobile Devices

Tolga Çapın[1], Antonio Haro[2], Vidya Setlur[3], and Stephen Wilkinson[4]

[1] Bilkent University
`tcapin@cs.bilkent.edu.tr`
[2] D4D Technologies
`mail@antonioharo.com`
[3] Nokia
`vidya.setlur@nokia.com`
[4] Texas Instruments
`stephen.wilkinson@ti.com`

Abstract. Mobile virtual environments, with real-time 3D and 2D graphics, are now possible on smart phone and other camera-enabled devices. Using computer vision, the camera sensor can be treated as an input modality in applications by analyzing the incoming live video. We present our tracking algorithm and several mobile virtual environment and gaming prototypes including: a 3D first person shooter, a 2D puzzle game and a simple action game. Camera-based interaction provides a user experience that is not possible through traditional means, and maximizes the use of the limited display size.

Keywords: camera-based interaction, virtual environment, mobile device, computer vision.

1 Introduction

Recent advances in mobile device hardware have made it possible to create mobile virtual and mixed reality environments. It is now possible to align real images spatially with synthetic content in real time [6]. However, to be suitable for real-world applications, key interaction limitations remain, including: a small physical display size, precise registration of virtual content with the real environment, and intuitive user input techniques.

Mobile devices currently support interaction through a joystick or a set of standard keys. Although these modalities are sufficient for simple modes of interaction, more intuitive interaction techniques are needed for mixed reality and virtual environment systems. For a greater degree of immersion, better tracking is essential.

To address these limitations, we present our interaction technique for camera-equipped mobile devices, using the camera sensor as an input device [5]. Our solution is based on analyzing the series of live input images from the camera and estimating the motion of the device. We apply our approach to some of the most interactive application scenarios: navigation and gesture-based interaction in highly interactive 3D virtual environments.

A. Levi et al. (Eds.): ISCIS 2006, LNCS 4263, pp. 765–773, 2006.

While previous work has created 3D and augmented reality game genres that map left/right/up/down camera motions to those exact motions in a game, our work also allows for gesture recognition using the camera's egomotion. For example, a character can be made to jump by shaking the mobile device; our approach recognizes the shaking gesture and maps it to a jump action. In addition, camera motion can be mapped to 3D viewing. This is particularly useful on mobile devices where a limited number of buttons and limited display size make the creation of an immersive gaming experience difficult. By mapping physical motion to 3D viewing transformations in a first-person game, the user has a more immersive experience with no additional hardware or sensors required.

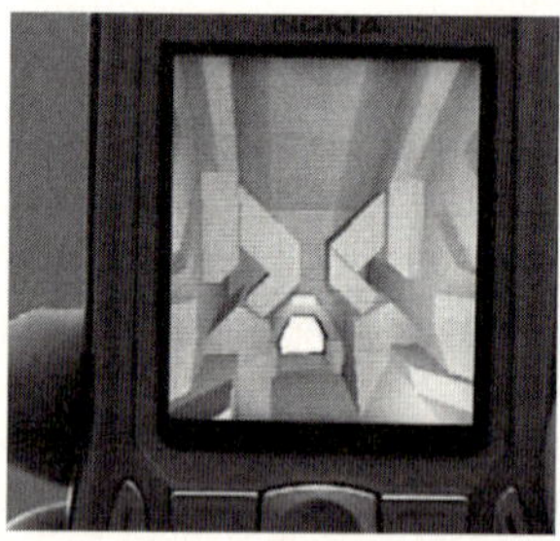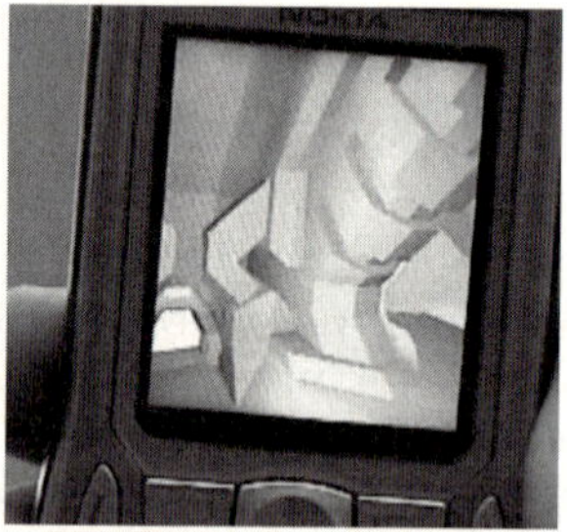

Fig. 1. A 3D virtual environment. The user can move the device up, down, left and right to look around the space. Mapping physical motion to viewing direction in the space creates the illusion of a small window into an environment that surrounds the user.

2   Related Work

Our work is similar to that of Moehring et al. [6], where a 3D model was overlaid on live video captured by a smart phone's on-board camera viewing a set of markers used to capture orientation. Our work does not overlay graphics on video, rather video is analyzed without user-introduced tracking features to determine 2D ego-motion instead of full 3D camera pose. The scroll [8] and peephole [9] displays works are also related as their goals were to estimate 2D device motion towards the creation of more intuitive user interaction. While additional sensors were required in these works, such as mechanical and ultrasonic sensors, we use only the camera as our direction sensor. Doing so allows regular camera-equipped smart phones to have an additional interaction modality without modifying the phone hardware.

Camera-based user interaction has been used in games in several commercial works. The most successful mixed reality platform for gaming presently is Sony's Eyetoy [1], which consists of a 60 fps camera attached to a Sony Playstation 2 game console. Incoming video is analyzed to estimate a player's motion and to segment them from their environment. Our work has similar goals, but is focused on the mobile domain where hardware constraints are more significant. In the mobile domain, a number of mixed reality games are currently available. These range from camera-movement tracking for moving on-screen crosshairs to simple body part region tracking. Mobile games in this category include: Ghostblaster by Futurice Oy, Bitside GmbH's "HyperSpace Invasion" and "Marble Revolution". These are all similar in concept in that the camera can be moved horizontally and vertically to move an on-screen cursor. Camera motions are directly mapped to in-game actions but with no gesture recognition or mapping to 3D interaction as in our work.

Related camera-based tracking work includes the Mozzies game available for the Siemens SX1 mobile phone. While camera motion is indeed estimated in these games to translate sprites accordingly, it should be noted that the detected motion does not need to be exact as the sprites are rendered on top of the video but not attached to any feature. As such, only approximate motion tracking is used. Since our tracked motion needs to match the user's physical motion more precisely, a higher degree of accuracy is required which from our testing is not present in current commercial camera motion tracking-based games. It should also be noted that in these works, only mobile camera motion is used as input; in our work we use the magnitude of the motion and shake detection as well.

Rohs et al. [7] perform tracking based on dividing incoming camera frames into blocks and determine how the blocks move given a set of discrete possible translations and rotations. Our algorithm is instead based on tracking individual corner-like features observed in the entire camera frames. This allows our tracker to recognize sudden camera movements of arbitrary size, as long as some of the features from the previous frame are still visible, at the trade-off of not detecting rotations. Kalman filter based camera motion estimation was demonstrated by Hannuksela et al. [4]. The Kalman tracker has higher motion estimation accuracy, as expected, since Kalman filtering greatly improves the quality of intra-frame matching. However, the computational requirements are significantly greater since several matrix multiplications and inversions are needed per frame. On devices with limited computational resources, our algorithm provides sufficient motion and velocity accuracy for user interaction, freeing computational power for intensive tasks such as collision detection and animation computations, at the trade-off of more limited accuracy, since the temporal filtering in our algorithm cannot match a Kalman filter.

3 Camera-Based Tracking

Our approach is to use the mobile phone's on-board camera as the source of input. The user's physical movement of the device is captured in incoming video, which is analyzed to determine scroll direction and magnitude. The detected direction is sent to the phone's UI event handler exactly as a corresponding mouse event.

3.1 Tracking Algorithm

Our tracking system was implemented on the Symbian OS. We use a feature-based tracking algorithm that determines how corner-like features have moved between the previous frame and the current frame. Finding corner-like features is difficult because traditional corner detectors are too computationally complex for real-time performance in gaming. Edges are easier to detect, however they are not temporally coherent. Instead, edge information in the x and y direction is combined to find corner-like features. The sum of the absolute values of the x and y derivatives, otherwise known as the Sobel operator, provides a practical estimate of corners. All corners cannot be detected using the Sobel operator; however, it provides a useful first-step culling of pixels for additional processing.

Our algorithm is as follows. Frame n is filtered using the Sobel x and y filters. The 50 strongest features per frame are found and the motion of each is estimated using template matching. 15x15 search windows are used to find the features in the next frame since this size is sufficient to capture visually distinct regions and significant intra-frame motion. Once the relative movement direction is determined per feature, the sum of features that have moved in the up, down, left and right directions is totaled to remove temporal inconsistencies. Every 4 frames, the direction with the maximum count is used as the overall camera motion estimate. Since the tracker typically performs at 12 frames per second, the direction estimate is updated several times per second. This is the only temporal filtering needed since the features are robust. The direction estimation fails if at least one feature from the previous frame is not visible in the next frame, which we have not observed in our experiments in various indoor and outdoor environments. In practice, the tracked motion is smooth and amenable for viewpoint selection in virtual environments, especially since the tracker is not computationally expensive.

3.2 Shake Detection

We use motion history images (MHI) [3] to recognize camera shake gestures since MHIs were originally created for action and gesture recognition. MHIs capture motion histories of image sequences in a single grayscale image which can be processed to perform simple, computationally inexpensive gesture recognition.

MHIs are computed by performing background subtraction between the current and previous frames of a video sequence. At locations where the pixel values change, the MHI is updated by decrementing by a pre-defined constant amount. In this manner, the MHI compactly captures the variations of pixel differences at locations in the image across time. By averaging the intensity values of the MHI, the average camera motion magnitude can be estimated. The average camera motion can then be used to detect large, sudden movements or shaking of the device quite reliably and computationally inexpensively.

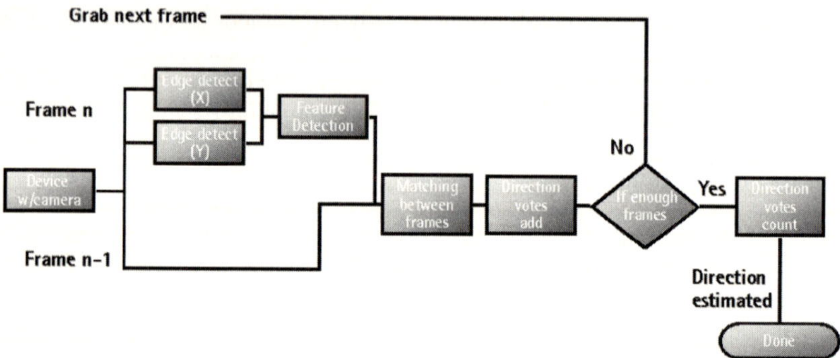

Fig. 2. Our tracker uses the current and previous frame captured by the camera for tracking. Corner like features are detected in the new frame which are matched with the features found in the prior frame so that the prior frame does not have to be reprocessed for features. Direction estimates are accumulated for a number of frames before a movement direction estimate is made.

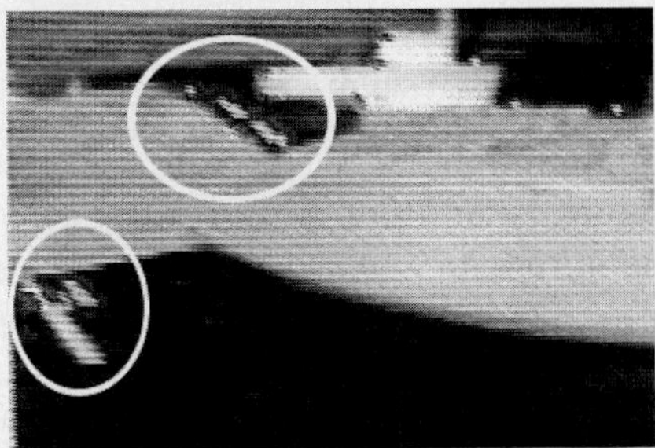

Fig. 3. Feature detection and tracking to estimate 2D camera egomotion. Red pixels are features detected in the current frame, green pixels are features detected in the previous frame (leftward motion shown). The motion of individual features is aggregated to determine global egomotion.

4   Mapping Motion to 3D Interaction

Creating an immersive 3D experience is difficult on mobile devices due to the limited display size. The most immersive experiences are typically created using a combination of large displays reducing peripheral vision as much as possible and/or virtual environment navigation tied to the user's physical motion. In our prototype (Figure 1), we map the user's physical motion to the viewpoint to create the illusion of a window into a 3D world. We have used the tracking and shake recognition algorithms presented to create several mobile 3D game prototypes. In each case, using the camera as the input modality created a user experience not achievable with traditional keypad based input.

Our renderer loads standard Quake III (tm) or Quake III Arena (tm) maps. The rendering is done using the OpenGL ES implementation available on Series 60 based mobile devices. Pre-computed vertex lighting and fixed point calculations are used to improve performance due to the lack of a floating-point unit on our test hardware, a standard Nokia 6630 smart phone. The renderer is able to render realistically lit virtual environments with several thousand polygons per scene at 5-10 frames per second, depending on the environment that is used.

Interaction with the virtual environment is performed with a combination of physical motion and keypad presses. The navigation within the environment is controlled by the directional keys on the keypad. For viewpoint selection, the user looks around in the scene by physically moving the device in the directions that they would like to look. We map the tracked camera motion directions to a trackball as in traditional mouse-based 3D interaction. The game actions are mapped to keypad presses. In this paper, we do not address 3D object interactions such as picking.

5   Mapping Motion to 2D Interaction

Darken et al. [2] have studied 2D and 3D mixed-dimension interaction in virtual environments. They have concluded that a hybrid interface, where 3D and 2D interaction techniques were matched to each individual task, such as object selection, text reading, would be the most preferable solution. We consider that camera-based input can be used for 2D interactions in the virtual environment, as well as those that are 3D. To illustrate real-life applications, we created 2D puzzle and action game prototypes to investigate these ideas using the camera motion and shake detection algorithms presented.

We modified the open source Series 60 port of the "Frozen Bubble" puzzle game, switching the game control from using the keypad to using the camera (Figure 4). In our version, the user moves their mobile device left and right to aim and performs sudden shakes to launch their bubble. This has the effect of significantly changing game play as careful arm motions are now required to aim, instead of a number of button presses. Switching the aiming and launching to be camera-motion based has the result of creating a more physically-accurate aiming experience, which increases the excitement of the game.

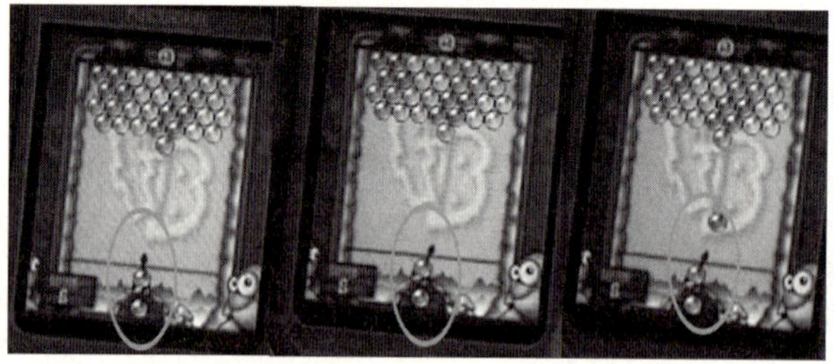

Fig. 4. A 2D puzzle game. Players move the device left and right to aim, and shake the device to launch a bubble. Aiming is more difficult using physical motion than with a keypad, creating a more exciting experience.

We created a camera-based action game prototype as well. Using sprites and artwork from Konami's "Track and Field" game for the Nintendo Entertainment System, a new game (Figure 5) was created. A runner must jump over a never-ending number of approaching hurdles. To jump, the player must time the shaking of their device correctly so that the character does not crash into hurdles. Relying on the

Fig. 5. A 2D action game. The player's character must jump over the hurdles. A jump command is issued by shaking the device at the correct time to avoid tripping on the hurdle.

camera exclusively for input results in a game that is very simple to learn and understand but difficult to master. The timing of a button press is easier than that of a shake since most button press physical motions are very similar, yet most shaking motions are quite different. Consequently, to play well, a player must learn not only the timing needed but also how to perform consistent shaking motions for each hurdle so that the next shake is timed correctly. We believe this additional level of user involvement results in a game that provides richer sensory feedback.

6 Results

We implemented the tracking algorithm and applications in C++ using the Series 60 Second Edition Feature Pack 2 SDK. Our test platform was a Nokia 6630 mobile phone, which features an ARM 9 220mhz processor, 10 megabytes of RAM, 176x208 screen resolution, and a 1.3 megapixel camera capable of capturing frames at 15 fps.

In order to support intuitive and efficient user interaction, it is important to understand what kind of information is provided by the tracking algorithm, and what the limitations are given the output of the tracking algorithm. The most basic but potentially most important input that can be acquired from the tracking algorithm is the two dimensional movement of the mobile device on a plane parallel to the camera in 3D. With this type of data, the camera can be used as an input device to capture the device's movement in up/down, left/right directions, as well as its speed in each direction. Mobile camera-based input has restrictions, primarily due to limitations of mobile device hardware. Forward and backward motion cannot be detected with the current algorithm, so six degree of freedom movement is not supported yet. Forward/backward motion is possible to detect if the algorithm were extended, however this would increase computational demands and reduce the frame rate, impoverishing the user interaction.

Physical movement speed is another challenge for camera-based interaction. The algorithm must perform all of its video analysis in the time between camera frames being captured to support real time interaction.

Thus, there are implicit limits on the computational complexity of the tracking. In addition, there is a fundamental assumption in our algorithm that each frame contains some portion of the prior frame. This assumption is motivated by the observation that users will typically not move their phones erratically when focused on a task. We have also verified our tracking solution in informal experiments and found that it works well in practice. Users usually operate mobile phones with one hand. Mobile phones can also be used anywhere in an office, school, public, home, etc. Considering these environments, there are certain interactions which are not appropriate:

Precise tasks: Precise motion is very difficult holding a mobile device with one hand. Interaction should not require operations like 'move the device 2.5cm up', or 'move the device 34 degrees from the horizontal line.' As a result, camera-based interaction will probably be most useful when navigating large amounts of data, or zoom level dependent data.

Large motion: This restriction is more serious in some environments, such as in crowded public locations. In such situations, it may be advantageous to provide a 'clutch' to turn the tracking on/off. This would emulate the act of lifting a mouse once the edge of a desk is reached in traditional desktop interaction. In our informal testing we did not provide a clutch, however in commercial implementations this is a consideration to keep in mind.

Extended and/or frequent interaction: Using single handed operation, interactions that require extended time and/or frequent movement may fatigue users.

Our approach works best with coarse selections at different speeds and scales of data. It is critical that visual feedback follows physical motion and that the feedback differs according to motion speed, in order to provide an intuitive user experience. The most typical use case is moving the device to scroll UI content such as a list or a document.

7   Conclusions

We introduced a new approach to improve the user experience for interacting with virtual environments on mobile devices. A computer vision-based tracking algorithm was presented to detect both physical motion direction and gestures to permit one-handed physical movement based interaction. A camera was chosen since cameras are now widely available on mobile devices and are very powerful sensors that can be used without introducing new sensors.

We demonstrated our approach in 2D and 3D interaction. In the future, we would like to collect user feedback to determine how to improve user interaction further using mobile cameras. While we applied the camera-based interaction to only viewpoint selections and simple gestures, we would like to investigate its application to navigation, object interactions, and avatar control.

While our tracking algorithm is computationally efficient and works well in practice, there are some situations that cannot be handled. Severe lighting differences will cause the template matching to stop working properly. Motion in front of the camera is ambiguous and can affect tracking results as it is impossible to tell whether the camera is moving or not without either significantly more expensive computations or other sensors. Shadows may confuse the tracking system, but there are known computer vision techniques for robust tracking in the presence of shadows that will be incorporated into the tracking algorithm once additional processing speed is available.

References

1. Campbell D., Computer Vision in Games, Game Developers Conference 2005.
2. Darken R.P., Durost R., Mixed-dimension interaction in virtual environments. VRST2005: pp. 38-45.
3. Davis, J.W. and Bobick, A. The Representation and Recognition of Action Using Temporal Templates, In IEEE International Conference on Computer Vision and Pattern Recognition, August 1997, pp. 928-934.
4. Hannuksela, J., Sangi, P., and Heikkila, J. A Vision-Based Approach for Controlling User Interfaces of Mobile Devices. To appear in IEEE Workshop on Vision for Human-Computer Interaction (V4HCI), 2005.
5. Haro A., Mori K., Capin T., Wilkinson S., Mobile Camera-Based User Interaction. *Proceedings of ICCV-HCI* 2005: 79-89.

6. Moehring, M., Lessig, C., and Bimber, O. Video See-Through AR on Consumer Cell Phones. In *Proceedings of ISMAR 2004*.
7. Rohs, M. Real-world Interaction with Camera-phones, In *2nd International Symposium on Ubiquitous Computing Systems (UCS 2004)*, Tokyo, Japan, November 2004.
8. Siio, I. Scroll Display: Pointing Device for Palm-top Computers, *Asia Pacific Computer Human Interaction 1998* (APCHI 98), Japan, July 15-17, 1998, pp. 243-248.
9. Yee, K-P. Peephole Displays: Pen Interaction on Spatially Aware Handheld Computers, In *Proceedings of CHI'03 Human Factors in Computing Systems*, pp. 1-8.

A Cost Model for an Adaptive Cell-Based Index Structure

Wonik Choi[1], Jinseok Chae[2], Nam-Joong Kim[2], and Mee Young Sung[2]

[1] School of Information and Communication Engineering,
Inha University, Incheon 402-751, Korea
`wichoi@inha.ac.kr`
[2] Department of Computer Science and Engineering,
University of Incheon, Incheon 402-749, Korea
`{jschae, water09z, mysung}@incheon.ac.kr`

Abstract. In this paper, we describe a cost model for an adaptive cell-based index structure which aims at efficient management of immense amounts of spatio-temporal data. We first survey various methods to estimate the performance of R-tree variants. Then, we present our cost model which accurately estimates the number of disk accesses for the adaptive cell-based index structure. To show the accuracy of our model, we perform a detailed analysis using various data sets. The experimental result shows that our model has the average error ratio from 7% to 13%.

1   Introduction

Recent rapid advances in information and communication technologies have been creating new classes of computing environments such as ubiquitous computing or mobile computing. In these new computing environments, the efficient management of immense amounts of spatio-temporal data, e.g. the positions of cars, devices or subscribed users, becomes vital to support various services in ubiquitous computing. Since these spatio-temporal data have geometric and time-varying characteristics, they are continuously evolving and their update volume is typically very large. Therefore, it is highly required to store and retrieve spatio-temporal information efficiently for mobile or ubiquitous computing. Most of the techniques proposed to handle the spatio-temporal data are based on *overlapping* technique and *multiversion* technique. These techniques are two popular techniques for converting an ephemeral structure into an efficient temporal and spatio-temporal index structure. The basic idea is that, to avoid excessive space storage, consecutive logical tress may share common branches so that these branches are stored only once. We use the term overlapping R-trees(OVR-trees) to refer to R-trees using overlapping technique such as HR-tree [NS98]. Also we call R-trees using multiversion technique multiversion R-trees(MVR-trees). BTR-trees [KTF98] and MV3R-tree [TP01] belong to MVR-trees.

The OVR- and MVR-trees, however, are hardly applicable in practice, due mainly to excessive space requirements and high management costs. To address this problem, Choi *et al.* [CML04] proposed a new index structure called *AIM* (*Adaptive cell-based Index for Moving Objects*).

A. Levi et al. (Eds.): ISCIS 2006, LNCS 4263, pp. 774–782, 2006.

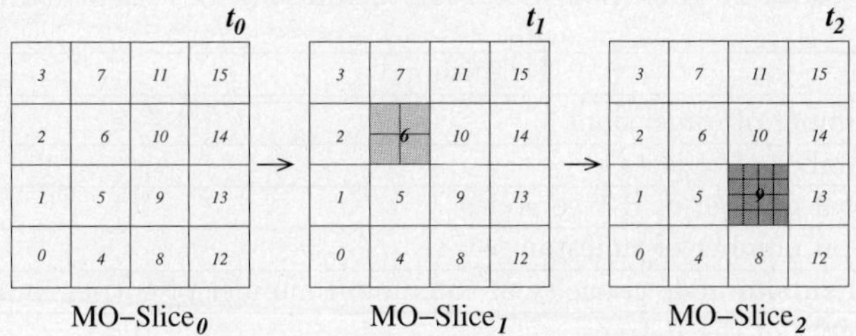

Fig. 1. Adaptive Cell Refinement

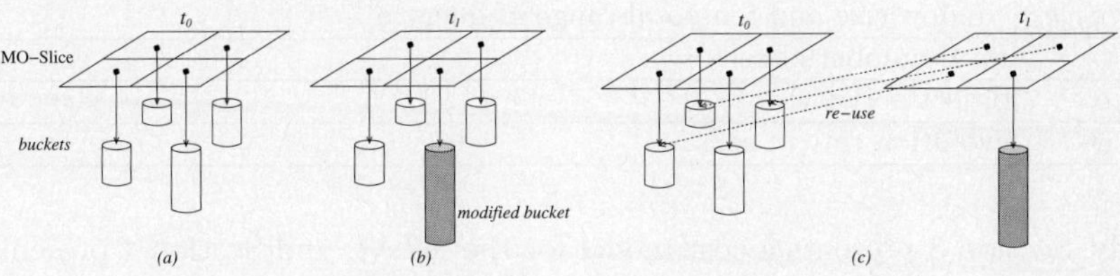

Fig. 2. Overlapping $\mathcal{MO}$-**Slice**s

The $\mathcal{AIM}$ partitions an embedding space-time into a set of fixed-size grid cells to form a cube that keeps growing along the time dimension. Each grid cell stores a bucket of moving objects in its corresponding subspace. The $\mathcal{AIM}$ does not change its basic grid cell structure at each sampled time. Instead, it can refine cells in certain regions to handle data skew by adaptively partitioning cells into smaller sub-cells. Figure 1 shows the adaptive cell refinement technique. Such refined cells can appear and disappear anywhere in the grid, as the mobile objects move around in the space and skewed data regions change over time. The rationale of the $\mathcal{AIM}$ design is to combine the benefits of quadtree (for space decomposition) and hashing method (for bucket storage), without sharing their shortcomings.

As shown in Figure 2, to minimize the storage requirement, the $\mathcal{AIM}$ uses an *overlapping* technique. When a new set of sampled data is added to the $\mathcal{AIM}$, new cells can share data buckets with old cells if the positions of the mobile objects in the old cells remain unchanged. Thus, new data buckets are created only when it needs to accommodate changes made to the data set sampled previously.

Through the extensive performance studies, they observed that The $\mathcal{AIM}$ consumed at most 30% of the space required by OVR- and MVR-trees, and improved query processing time by up to two orders of magnitude compared to OVR- and MVR-trees. Although they presented the extensive performance studies, little work has been carried out on their performance analysis. In this paper, in order to offer clear understanding about the performance of the $\mathcal{AIM}$, we provide a cost model for the $\mathcal{AIM}$. The rest of the paper is organized as follows. Section 2 surveys cost models for overlapping and multiversion structures

Table 1. Table of symbols and definitions for cost model

Symbols	Definitions
d	number of dimensions
n	number of objects
tn	total number of R-tree nodes
T	total number of timestamps
M	maximum node capacity *or* maximum number of entries in a cell
h	height of the R-tree
f	fanout
DA	number of disk accesses for a query window q
$c(c_x, c_y, c_t)$	MBR and temporal range of a node(of R-tree) or cell(of the $\mathcal{AIM}$)
$q(q_x, q_y, q_t)$	window size and temporal range of query q
C	total number of cells
α	object activity
β	evolution rate of cells

briefly. Section 3 presents a cost model for the $\mathcal{AIM}$, and Section 4 presents an experimental evaluation. Finally conclusions are presented in Section 5.

2 Preliminaries : R-Tree Analysis

In this section, we first introduce a variety of techniques proposed in the literature to evaluate the performance of R-trees. Then we survey cost models for OVR- and MVR-trees. Table 1 gives a list of the main symbols that are used frequently in this section.

Faloutsos *et al.* [FSR87] first proposed a model which estimates the performance of R-tree and R^+-tree [SRF87] assuming that the data are uniformly distributed and all the nodes of the tree are full of data. Later, Kamel and Faloutsos [KF93] introduce an analytical formula to evaluate the average number of disk accesses for a query of size $q_x \times q_y$. They define the probability $Prob()$, which means that a node will contribute one disk accesses to a point query, as follows:

$$Prob(point\ query\ retrieves\ node\ p_i) = p_{i,x} * p_{i,y} \tag{1}$$

where p_i is a node which has an MBR of size $p_{i,x} \times p_{i,y}$. $Prob()$ is equivalent to the area of the rectangle $(p_{i,x}, p_{i,y})$ which is the probability that a point fall in the rectangle $(p_{i,x}, p_{i,y})$. Therefore, the expected number of disk accesses $P(q_x, q_y)$ for point queries is:

$$P(0,0) = \sum_{i=1}^{tn} p_{i,x} * p_{i,y} \tag{2}$$

where tn is the total number of tree nodes. For a range query of size $q_x \times q_y$, the expected number of disk accesses $P(q_x, q_y)$ is given by

$$P(q_x, q_y) = \sum_{i=1}^{tn}(p_{i,x} + q_x) * (p_{i,y} + q_y) \tag{3}$$

This is because a range query of size $q_x \times q_y$ is equivalent to a point query, if we expand the nodes by q_x and q_y in the $x-$ and $y-$directions respectively. Then, the node p_i with size $p_{i,x} \times p_{i,y}$ behaves like a node of size $(p_{i,x}+q_x)*(p_{i,y}+q_y)$. Pagel et $al.$ [PSTW93] also independently presented the same approach as the model proposed in [KF93]. The above formula intuitively presents the effects of the node size to the performance of R-trees, but cannot predict the average number of disk accesses. Faloutsos and Kamel [FK94] extended the above formula to really predict the number of disk accesses even for non-uniform data sets. Their model constitutes the first attempt to model R-tree performance for non-uniform distribution superseding the previous work. The estimation of the number of disk accesses DA at level i in their model which is, however, applicable only to point data sets, is given by:

$$DA = \frac{n}{f} \prod_{j=1}^{d}(c_{i,j} + q_j) \tag{4}$$

where $c_{i,j} = \left(\frac{f}{n}\right)^{1/d}$, $\forall\, j = 1, ..., d$, n is the total number of data and d is the number of dimensions.

Theodoridis and Sellis [TS96] proposed an analytical model that supports data sets of any type (point or region data) and distribution (uniform or non-uniform). Specifically, Their model predicts the performance of R-trees using only data properties and, especially, the $amount$ n and the $density$ D of the data set. They defined the density D of a set of n boxes with average size c as the average number of boxes that contain a given point of d-dimensional space. Equivalently, D can be expressed as the ratio of the total sum of the areas of all MBRs over the area of the embedding space. They showed that their model is very accurate, the relative error being usually around $10\% \sim 15\%$. The formula for DA in their model is given by

$$DA = 1 + \sum_{i=1}^{h}\left\{\frac{n}{f^i} \cdot \prod_{j=1}^{d}\left(\left(D_i \cdot \frac{f^i}{n}\right)^{1/d} + q_j\right)\right\} \tag{5}$$

where f is the fanout of the R-tree, $h(= 1 + \lceil \log_f \frac{n}{f} \rceil)$ is the height of the R-tree and D_i refers to the density of node MBRs at level i. The density D_i is expressed as follows:

$$D_i = \left\{1 + \frac{D_{i-1}^{1/d} - 1}{f^{1/d}}\right\}^d, \; i \geq 1 \tag{6}$$

In case of OVR- and MVR-trees, selectivity estimation requires further investigation. To analyze the performance of these structures, the probability that temporal ranges intersect a node must be taken into account. In addition, temporal behavior of objects has a very significant impact on the performance of the *overlapping* and *multiversion* structures. Tao *et al.* [TPZ02] proposed a cost model for the *overlapping* and *multiversion* structures. This is the first work which attempts to predict the node/page accesses and selectivity of *overlapping* and *multiversion* R-trees.

According to their model, the expected number of disk accesses DA for OVR-trees is represented as

$$DA_{OVR} = \sum_{i=0}^{h-1} \left(\frac{n}{f^{i+1}} \left(\sqrt{D_{i+1} \frac{f^{i+1}}{n}} + q_x \right) \left(\sqrt{D_{i+1} \frac{f^{i+1}}{n}} + q_y \right) \right.$$
$$\left. \times \left\{ 1 + \left[1 - \left(1 - \frac{f^{i+1}}{n_\epsilon} \right)^{2\alpha n_\epsilon} \right] (q_t - 1) \right\} \right) \tag{7}$$

On the other hand, the DA of MVR-tree can be written as

$$DA_{MVR} = \sum_{i=0}^{h-1} \left\{ \frac{n}{f^{i+1}} \left(\sqrt{D_{i+1} \frac{f^{i+1}}{n}} + q_x \right) \left(\sqrt{D_{i+1} \frac{f^{i+1}}{n}} + q_y \right) \right.$$
$$\left. \times \left[1 + \frac{\alpha f^{i+1} \cdot (q_t - 1)}{(M - f)^{i+1}} \right] \right\} \tag{8}$$

Through extensive experimentations, they claimed that the above model yield errors below 5% and 15% for uniform and non-uniform data sets, respectively.

3   Cost Model for the $\mathcal{AIM}$

Since the $\mathcal{AIM}$ also adopts *overlapping* technique as mentioned in Section 1, we need to incorporate the model proposed by Tao *et al.* [TPZ02] into our framework in order to analyze the performance of the $\mathcal{AIM}$.

We define a spatio-temporal query as $q(q_x, q_y, q_t)$. Similarly, a cell in the $\mathcal{AIM}$ is defined as $c(c_x, c_y, c_t)$. To answer a spatio-temporal query q, a cell c will be accessed if and only if it intersects q. In other words, the probability, which is denoted as $Prob(c, q)$, that c will be accessed is equivalent to the probability that $c(c_x, c_y, c_t)$ intersects $q(q_x, q_y, q_t)$. Let $Prob_{xy}$ denote the probability that the spatial range(c_x, c_y) intersects (q_x, q_y). Similarly, let $Prob_t$ be the probability that the temporal range(c_t) intersects q_t. Then, since the spatial dimension and the time dimension are independent, $Prob(c, q)$ can be expressed as:

$$Prob(c, q) = Prob_{xy} \cdot Prob_t \tag{9}$$

The $Prob_{xy}$ has been studied in R-tree analysis as shown in Equation (3). By Equation (3), $Prob_{xy}$ should be represented as

$$Prob_{xy} = (c_x + q_x)(c_y + q_y) \tag{10}$$

On the other hand, $Prob_t$ is closely related to temporal behavior of a cell.

$$Prob_t = \frac{C + \beta C(q_t - 1)}{C + \beta C(T - 1)} = \frac{1 + \beta(q_t - 1)}{1 + \beta(T - 1)} \tag{11}$$

where C is the number of all cells, T denotes the number of all the timestamps in history and β means the evolution rate of cells. The denominator of Equation (11) i.e., $C + \beta C(T - 1)$, is computed as follows. Initially there exist C cells in the $\mathcal{AIM}$. Then, at each subsequent timestamp i.e., $(T - 1)$, βC nodes are created.

The evolution rate β is represented as the ratio of the number of cells newly created over the total number of cells. To begin with, we define the *activity* of objects α to present how many objects are updated between two consecutive timestamps. Let n be the total number of objects, and n' the number of objects that change their position at a certain timestamp. Then we define the object activity α as

$$\alpha = \frac{n'}{n} \tag{12}$$

For a data set with α, the total number of changes per timestamp is equal to αn. Then, β corresponds to the probability that a cell is affected by any of these αn changes. Given a change, every cell has the same probability f/n to be affected; thus, the probability for a cell *not* to be affected by a single change is $(1 - f/n)$. Since all the changes are independent, the probability for a cell not to be updated by any of these changes is $(1 - f/n)^{\alpha n}$. Thus we have

$$\beta = 1 - \left(1 - \frac{f}{n}\right)^{\alpha n} \tag{13}$$

Now we can derive $Prob(c, q)$ by combining Equations (10) and (11) as

$$Prob(c, q) = (c_x + q_x)(c_y + q_y) \cdot \frac{1 + \beta(q_t - 1)}{1 + \beta(T - 1)} \tag{14}$$

Since $Prob(c, q)$ means the probability for a node to be accessed in processing query q, the expected number of disk accesses DA is given by Equation (15)

$$\begin{aligned}
DA &= \sum_{every\ cell\ s} Prob(c, q) \\
&= \left[\left(\frac{n}{f} + \beta\frac{n}{f}(T - 1)\right) \cdot Prob(c, q)\right] \\
&= \left[\left(\frac{n}{f} + \beta\frac{n}{f}(T - 1)\right) \cdot (c_x + q_x)(c_y + q_y) \cdot \frac{1 + \beta(q_t - 1)}{1 + \beta(T - 1)}\right]
\end{aligned} \tag{15}$$

Now it remains to estimate c_x and c_y, the average size of cells. Given that there are n/f cells, we have

$$c_x = c_y = \sqrt{\frac{f}{n}} \tag{16}$$

Note that the density D of the $\mathcal{AIM}$ is equal to 1, since the total sum of the areas of all cells is always identical to the area of the embedding space. Finally, combining Equations (9) through (15), the number of disk accesses for the $\mathcal{AIM}$ is presented in Equation (17)

$$DA_{AIM} = \left(\frac{n}{f} \left(\sqrt{\frac{f}{n}} + q_x \right) \left(\sqrt{\frac{f}{n}} + q_y \right) \right.$$

$$\left. \times \left\{ 1 + \left[1 - \left(1 - \frac{f}{n} \right)^{\alpha n} \right] (q_t - 1) \right\} \right) \tag{17}$$

As shown in Equation (7) and Equation (17), the cost model for the $\mathcal{AIM}$ differs from that for *overlapping* R-trees in that the density D for the $\mathcal{AIM}$ is set to 1 and the height h of the $\mathcal{AIM}$ is equal to 1. In addition, in case of *overlapping* R-trees, the total number of changes per timestamp is equal to $2\alpha n$ as shown in Equation (7) since each object update involves one deletion and one insertion. On the other hand, there are only αn insertions in the $\mathcal{AIM}$. Moreover, the fanout f of the $\mathcal{AIM}$ is much lager than that of *overlapping* or *multiversion* R-trees, since a cell of the $\mathcal{AIM}$ stores as little information as possible in each cell, resulting in large fanout.

4   Experimental Evaluation

To show the accuracy of our model, we made several experiments on synthetic data. We used the same data sets that was used in [CML04]. In the experiment shown in Figure 3(a), we compare our cost model to the real performance of the $\mathcal{AIM}$ with a fixed length of time interval($q_t = 10$) and varying query window. As the experimental result shows, the estimates of our model are sufficiently close to the real performance of the $\mathcal{AIM}$. Given the total number of objects n=10,000, activity $\alpha = 5\%$, fanout f for OVR/MVR $= 48$, fanout f for $\mathcal{AIM} = 128$ and a time interval $q_t = 10$, the expected numbers of disk accesses obtained

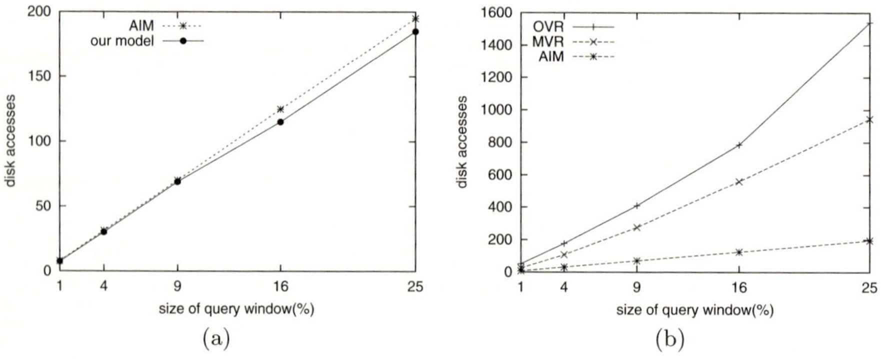

Fig. 3. Expected number of disk accesses for OVR, MVR and the $\mathcal{AIM}$

from Equation (7), (8) and (17) are shown in Figure 3(b). Figure 3(b) shows the disk accesses as a function of size of query window. As expected, the $\mathcal{AIM}$ consistently outperforms both OVR- and MVR-trees. The query cost of OVR-trees grows rapidly with window size and that of MVR-trees increases linearly. The experiment confirmed our cost model up to a relative error of 7-13%. This remaining error is due to cell refinement behavior, which is difficult to include in any formal model.

5   Conclusions

A query optimizer requires performance estimation of a query to choose the most efficient execution plan among all possible plans [SAC+79]. An accurate estimation of the performance is vital to process a query efficiently. Although Choi *et al.* proposed a new index structure called $\mathcal{AIM}$ *(Adaptive cell-based Index for Moving Objects)* to efficiently handle spatio-temporal data, they did not provide the performance analysis of the $\mathcal{AIM}$.

In this paper, in order to offer significant insight into the behavior of the $\mathcal{AIM}$ and provide guidelines about the selection of the most appropriate method in practice, we presented an effective method to estimate the performance of the $\mathcal{AIM}$. To show the accuracy of our model, we performed extensive experiments over various data sets with a reasonable skew distribution. In the experiments, the proposed cost model provided accurate estimation results over various queries with different query windows. The experimental result showed that the proposed model yielded errors below 13%.

Acknowledgments

This work was supported by INHA UNIVERSITY Research Grant.

References

[CML04]   Wonik Choi, Bongki Moon, and Sukho Lee. Adaptive cell-based index for moving objects. *Data & Knowledge Engineering*, 48(1):75–101, 2004.

[FK94]   Christos Faloutsos and Ibrahim Kamel. Beyond Uniformity and Independence: Analysis of R-trees Using the Concept of Fractal Dimension. In *Proceedings of the Thirteenth ACM SIGACT-SIGMOD-SIGART Symposium on Principles of Database Systems*, pages 4–13, Minneapolis, Minnesota, May 1994.

[FSR87]   Christos Faloutsos, Timos K. Sellis, and Nick Roussopoulos. Analysis of Object Oriented Spatial Access Methods. In *Proceedings of the 1987 ACM SIGMOD International Conference on Management of Data*, pages 426–439, San Francisco, California, May 1987.

[KF93]   Ibrahim Kamel and Christos Faloutsos. On Packing R-trees. In Bharat K. Bhargava, Timothy W. Finin, and Yelena Yesha, editors, *Proceedings of the Second International Conference on Information and Knowledge Management*, pages 490–499, Washington, DC, November 1993.

[KTF98]   Anil Kumar, Vassilis J. Tsotras, and Christos Faloutsos. Designing access methods for bitemporal databases. *IEEE Transactions on Knowledge and Data Engineering*, 10(1):1–20, 1998.

[NS98]   Mario A. Nascimento and Jefferson R. O. Silva. Towards historical R-trees. In *Proceedings of the 1998 ACM Symposium on Applied Computing*, pages 235–240, Atlanta, Georgia, February 1998.

[PSTW93]   Bernd-Uwe Pagel, Hans-Werner Six, Heinrich Toben, and Peter Widmayer. Towards an Analysis of Range Query Performance in Spatial Data Structures. In *Proceedings of the Twelfth ACM SIGACT-SIGMOD-SIGART Symposium on Principles of Database Systems*, pages 214–221, Washington, DC, May 1993.

[SAC$^+$79]   Patricia G. Selinger, Morton M. Astrahan, Donald D. Chamberlin, Raymond A. Lorie, and Thomas G. Price. Access Path Selection in a Relational Database Management System. In *Proceedings of the 1979 ACM SIGMOD International Conference on Management of Data*, pages 23–34, Boston, Massachusetts, May 1979.

[SRF87]   Timos K. Sellis, Nick Roussopoulos, and Christos Faloutsos. The R^+-Tree: A Dynamic Index for Multi-Dimensional Objects. In *VLDB'87, Proceedings of 13th International Conference on Very Large Data Bases*, pages 507–518, Brighton, England, September 1987.

[TP01]   Yufei Tao and Dimitris Papadias. MV3R-Tree: A Spatio-Temporal Access Method for Timestamp and Interval queries. In *Proceedings of 27th Int'l. Conf. on Very Large Data Bases*, Roma, Italy, September 2001.

[TPZ02]   Yufei Tao, Dimitris Papadias, and Jun Zhang. Cost models for overlapping and multiversion structures. *ACM Transactions on Database Systems*, 27(3):299–342, 2002.

[TS96]   Yannis Theodoridis and Timos K. Sellis. A Model for the Prediction of R-tree Performance. In *Proceedings of the Fifteenth ACM SIGACT-SIGMOD-SIGART Symposium on Principles of Database Systems*, pages 161–171, Montreal, Canada, June 1996.

Positioning Method for Outdoor Systems in Wireless Sensor Networks

Namkoo Ha and Kijun Han[*]

Department of Computer Engineering,
Kyungpook National University, Daegu, Korea
Phone number: 82-53-950-5557; Fax number: 82-53-957-4846
adama2@netopia.knu.ac.kr, kjhan@knu.ac.kr

Abstract. In recent years, many researchers have actively studied communication protocols for wireless sensor networks. Most works are based on the assumption that each sensor node knows its own geographical position by GPS (Global Positioning System). For this, however, we have to pay an extra cost for implementing GPS modules in sensor nodes, and thus the size of sensor node should become large. In this paper, we propose a method by which all the nodes in the sensing field can recognize their own positions without equipping GPS modules in every node. In our scheme, only some nodes are equipped with the GPS modules when the sensing field is deployed, and the others can find out their positions through communications to GPS nodes. To validate our method, we carried out a computer simulation, and observed that all nodes could successfully recognize their own positions in 3 rounds.

Keywords: Wireless Sensor Networks, Outdoor Systems, Positioning Method, GPS nodes, and No-GPS nodes.

1 Introduction

In recent years, many researches have been actively studied for various applications in wireless sensor networks [1–3]. Specially, lots of communication protocols for MAC (Medium Access Control) and network layers have been proposed: including S-MAC (Sensor MAC) [4][5] in MAC layer and LEACH (Low-Energy Adaptive Clustering Hierarchy) [6], PEGASIS (Power-Efficient Gathering in Sensor Information Systems) [7], and Directed Diffusion [8] in network layer.

All these protocols assume that each sensor node knows its own geographical position or its neighbors' geographical positions, or all nodes' geographical positions [6-10]. To recognize sensor nodes' geographical position, they should be equipped with GPS modules in themselves, which causes an extra cost for implementing sensor nodes as well as a higher energy consumption and a larger size[11][12].

Dragos Niculescu proposed APS (Ad hoc Positioning System) to reduce the cost, price, and size of sensor nodes. APS assumed that three nodes, called the landmark

---

[*] Corresponding author.

A. Levi et al. (Eds.): ISCIS 2006, LNCS 4263, pp. 783–792, 2006.

nodes, know their own positions in the entire field as shown in Fig. 1 [13]. The nodes which do not know their own positions estimate their positions based on the number of hops and relative distance to three landmark nodes, respectively. For this, these landmark nodes flood information on their own positions. Although this method can reduce price and size of the nodes, it takes too long for all nodes to recognize their positions. Also, if there is initially even a small error in the position of landmark node, the error becomes accumulated every flooding time, and can finally exceed an allowable limit.

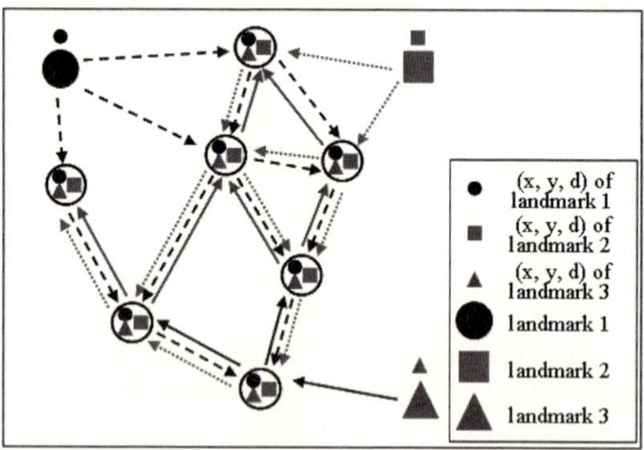

Fig. 1. Procedure of locating method in APS

In this paper, we propose a positioning method, in which some of deploying nodes in sensing field are equipped with the GPS and the other nodes can recognize their own positions through communications to GPS nodes.

The organization of this paper is as follows. Section 2 describes our positioning method, and section 3 presents the validation of our method through computer simulations. Finally, section 4 concludes the paper.

2 Proposed Method

We propose here a method that can recognize positions of no-GPS nodes through communications to the nodes when only some nodes are equipped with the GPS in the sensing field.

2.1 Two Dimensional Case

In a two-dimensional field, any node can find out its own position if there are three or more nodes knowing their positions around it. When N nodes are deployed in the sensing field in a random fashion, the probability that a node exists within the radio range of node n_i is given by

$$p = \frac{A_{n_i}}{A} = \frac{\pi r^2}{M^2} \tag{1}$$

where r is the radius of the radio range, A_{n_i} is n_i's radio range, and A is the size of the whole sensing field with a dimension of $M \times M$.

The probability that a node has k neighbors is represented by

$$f(k) = \binom{N-1}{k} p^k (1-p)^{N-1-k} \tag{2}$$

Therefore, the average number of one-hop neighbors within the sensing coverage of node n_i is

$$\begin{aligned}
\overline{D} &= \sum_{k=1}^{N-1} k \cdot f(k) \\
&= (N-1)p \\
&= (N-1)\frac{\pi r^2}{A}
\end{aligned} \tag{3}$$

The number of nodes with GPS modules required to find out the locations of all nodes in the sensing field, denoted by N_{Ge}, is given by

$$\begin{aligned}
3 &= (N_{Ge}-1)\frac{\pi r^2}{A} \\
\therefore N_{Ge} &= \frac{3A}{\pi r^2} + 1
\end{aligned} \tag{4}$$

The probability that there are 2 or less neighbors around any node is enough small to be ignored. For example, when 400 nodes are deployed in the sensing field with a dimension of 100 x 100 and the radius of the radio range is 10, the probability that there are 0, 1, or 2 neighbors around the node is

$$f_0 + f_1 + f_2 = 2.94301*10^{-6} + 3.80871*10^{-5} + 2.45835*10^{-4} \tag{5}$$

2.2 Three Dimensional Case

Similarly, in a three-dimensional field, any node can find out its own position if there are four or more nodes knowing their positions around it. When there are N nodes deployed in the sensing field with a dimension of $M \times M \times M$ and a volume of V, and a radio range of V_{n_i} at n_i, we can rewrite (1), (3), (4) by (6), (7), (8), respectively.

$$p = \frac{V_{n_i}}{V} = \frac{4\pi r^3}{3V} \tag{6}$$

$$\begin{aligned}
\overline{D} &= \sum_{k=1}^{N-1} k \cdot f(k) \\
&= (N-1)p \\
&= (N-1)\frac{4\pi r^3}{3V}
\end{aligned} \tag{7}$$

$$4 = (N_{Ge} - 1)\frac{4\pi r^3}{3V}$$

$$\therefore N_{Ge} = \frac{3V}{\pi r^3} + 1 \tag{8}$$

In three dimensional case, the probability that there are 3 or less neighbors around any node can be neglected. For example, when 1000 nodes are deployed in the sensing field with a dimension of 50 x 50 x 50 and the radius of the radio range is 10, the probability that there are 3 or less neighbors around the node is

$$f_0 + f_1 + f_2 + f_3 = 1.629*10^{-15} + 5.649*10^{-13} + 9.791*10^{-11} + 1.131*10^{-8} \tag{9}$$

2.3 Positioning Algorithm

In a two dimensional field, any node can find out its position by its position information collected from three or more neighbor nodes that already know their positions. Assume that we are given a node without GPS, denoted by $n_i(x,y)$, whose position is not yet known. If we assume that there are three nodes equipped with GPS module around the node $n_i(x,y)$ as shown in Fig. 2(a), denoted by $G_1(x_1, y_1)$, $G_2(x_2, y_2)$, and $G_3(x_3, y_3)$, then the coordinate of node $n_i(x, y)$ is computed by

$$x = \frac{(y_2 - y_3)(d_1^2 - x_1^2 - y_1^2) + (y_3 - y_1)(d_2^2 - x_2^2 - y_2^2) + (y_1 - y_2)(d_3^2 - x_3^2 - y_3^2)}{2\{(y_2 - y_1)(x_3 - x_1) - (y_3 - y_1)(x_2 - x_1)\}} \tag{10a}$$

$$y = \frac{(x_3 - x_2)(d_1^2 - x_1^2 - y_1^2) + (x_1 - x_3)(d_2^2 - x_2^2 - y_2^2) + (x_2 - x_1)(d_3^2 - x_3^2 - y_3^2)}{2\{(y_2 - y_1)(x_3 - x_1) - (y_3 - y_1)(x_2 - x_1)\}} \tag{10b}$$

where d_1, d_2 and d_3 mean the Euclidean distances from $n_i(x,y)$ to the three nodes, respectively, which are given by

$$d_i^2 = (x - x_i)^2 + (y - y_i)^2 \qquad i = 1,2,3 \tag{11}$$

as shown in Fig. 2(a).

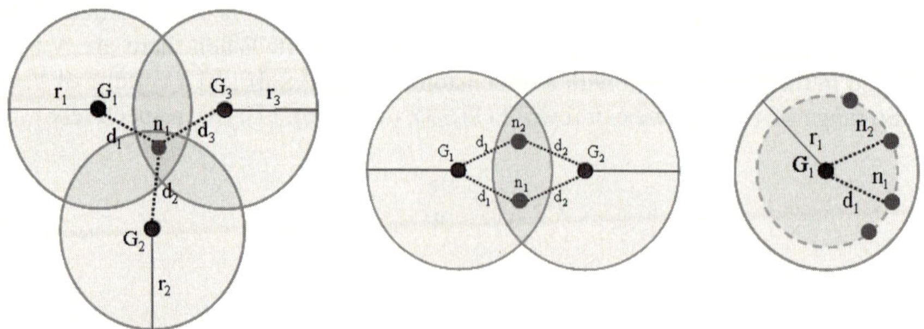

(a) when there are three GPS nodes

(b) when there are two GPS nodes

(c) when there is one GPS node

Fig. 2. Three scenarios for distribution of GPS nodes in two dimensional field

Similarly in a three dimensional field, any node can identify its own position by aid of four or more neighbor nodes that already know their positions. Here, our positioning algorithm is explained for three dimensional field.

Assume that we are given a node without GPS, denoted by $n_i(x,\ y,\ z)$, whose location is not yet identified. When there are three or less nodes equipped with GPS module around $n_i(x,\ y,\ z)$, its location cannot be directly determined as illustrated in Fig. 3(a), (b), and (c). For example, if there is one node equipped with GPS module, $G_1(x_1,\ y_1,\ z_1)$ around the node $n_i(x,\ y,\ z)$ as shown in Fig. 3(a), n_i receives position information from G_1 and it computes d_1 by measuring the signal strength. Therefore, we can determine that n_i is located on surface of a sphere with the radius d_1 which is given by

$$(x - x_1)^2 + (y - y_1)^2 + (z - z_1)^2 = d_1^{\ 2} \tag{12}$$

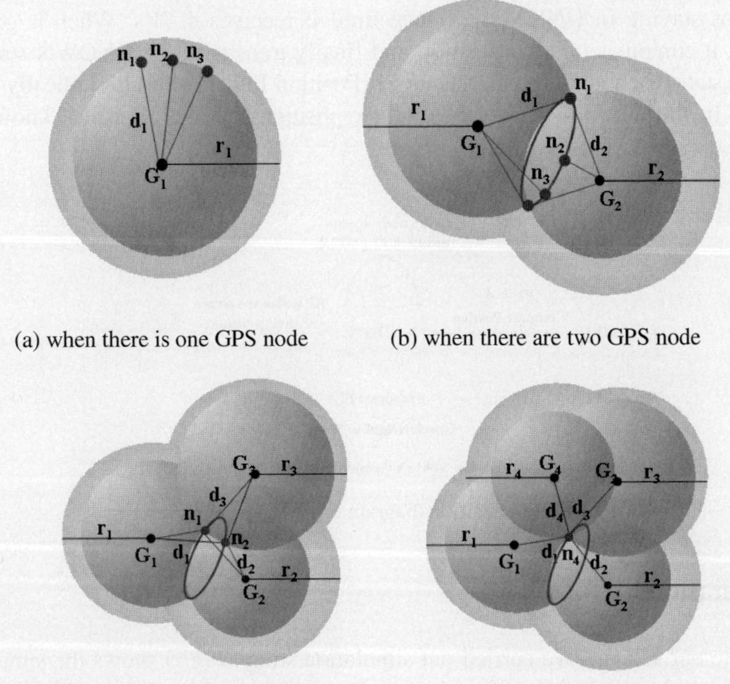

(a) when there is one GPS node   (b) when there are two GPS node

(c) when there are three GPS nodes   (d) when there are four GPS nodes

Fig. 3. Four scenarios for distribution of GPS nodes in three dimensional field

Next, if we assume that there are two nodes equipped with GPS module, $G_1(x_1,\ y_1,\ z_1)$ and $G_2(x_2,\ y_2,\ z_2)$ around the node $n_i(x,\ y,\ z)$ as shown in Fig. 3(b), n_i receives position information from G_1 and G_2 and then it can compute d_1 and d_2 from their signal strengths. So, we can guess that n_i is located anywhere on the circumference which is apart from G_1 and G_2 by d_1 and d_2, respectively.

$$x(x_1 - x_2) + y(y_1 - y_2) + z(z_1 - z_2) = x_1^2 - x_2^2 + y_1^2 - y_2^2 + z_1^2 - z_2^2 + d_2^2 - d_1^2 \qquad (13)$$

If we again assume that there are three nodes equipped with GPS module, $G_1(x_1, y_1, z_1)$, $G_2(x_2, y_2, z_2)$, and $G_3(x_3, y_3, z_3)$ around the node $n_i(x, y, z)$ as shown in Fig. 3(c), then the coordinates of n_i will be one of two points which are apart from G_1, G_2, and G_3, by d_1, d_2, and d_3, respectively.

Now assuming that there are four nodes equipped with GPS module, $G_1(x_1, y_1, z_1)$, $G_2(x_2, y_2, z_2)$, $G_3(x_3, y_3, z_3)$, and $G_4(x_4, y_4, z_4)$ around the node $n_i(x, y, z)$ as shown in Fig. 3(d), then the coordinate of node $n_i(x, y, z)$ can be exactly identified.

To implement our algorithm as a state machine, we define three states: KNOWN, UNKNOWN, FINISH as shown in Fig. 4. Initially, GPS nodes start from KNOWN state while no-GPS nodes begin from UNKNOWN state. Any node in UNKNOWN state keeps staying in UNKNOWN state until it receives 4 PI's. When it gets the fourth PI, it computes its own position and finally transits to the KNOWN state. In KNOWN state, each node broadcasts its PI (Position Information) periodically unless all nodes in the network are aware of their positions. When all nodes know their positions, they go to FINISH state.

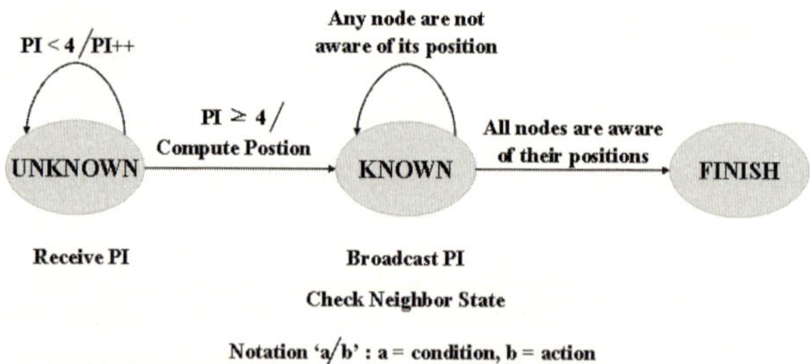

Fig. 4. State transition diagram of node for positioning

3   Simulations

To validate our scheme, we carried out simulation study. Fig. 5 shows the simulation model. We randomly deploy 100 nodes in a square space (50 × 50) or 400 nodes in a square space (100 × 100) in a two dimensional field and 1000 (or 4000 nodes) in a cube space with a dimension of 50 × 50 × 50 (or 100 × 100 × 100). Table 1 shows some parameters and their values used for simulation.

Fig. 6(a) ~ (d) show the average number of neighbor nodes within the radio range of node n_i in eight cases. A sound agreement is observed between the numerical results obtained by Eq. (3) and (7) and the result of computer simulation in two or three dimension field. The number of neighbor nodes is about 12 and 28 in case 1 and

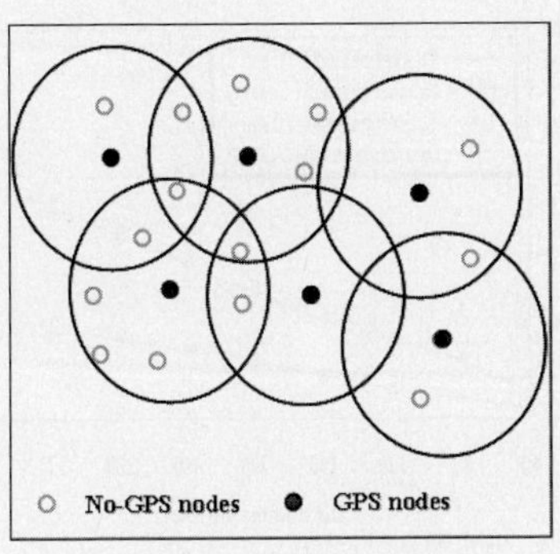

(a) two dimensional field

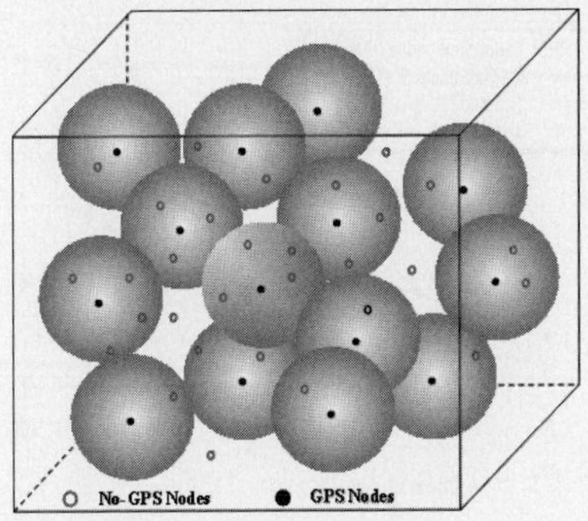

(b) three dimensional field

Fig. 5. Simulation models

Table 1. Simulation parameters and their values in eight scenarios

Two Dimensional Field				
Simulation parameters	Case 1	Case 2	Case 3	Case 4
Map size	50 x 50	100 x 100	50 x 50	100 x 100
Radio range	10	10	15	15
The number of total nodes	100	400	100	400
The number of GPS nodes	24	96	11	43
The number of no-GPS nodes	76	304	89	357
Three Dimensional Field				
Simulation parameters	Case 5	Case 6	Case 7	Case 8
Map size	50 x 50 x 50	100 x 100 x 100	50 x 50 x 50	100 x 100 x 100
Radio range	10	10	15	15
The number of total nodes	1000	4000	1000	4000
The number of GPS nodes	120	955	36	283
The number of no-GPS nodes	880	3045	964	3717

3 in a two dimensional field and 30 and 112 neighbor nodes in case 5 and 7, respectively. This means that if we deploy only three GPS nodes among 12 and 28 nodes, in case 1 and 3 as the situation of two dimensional field, respectively, and if

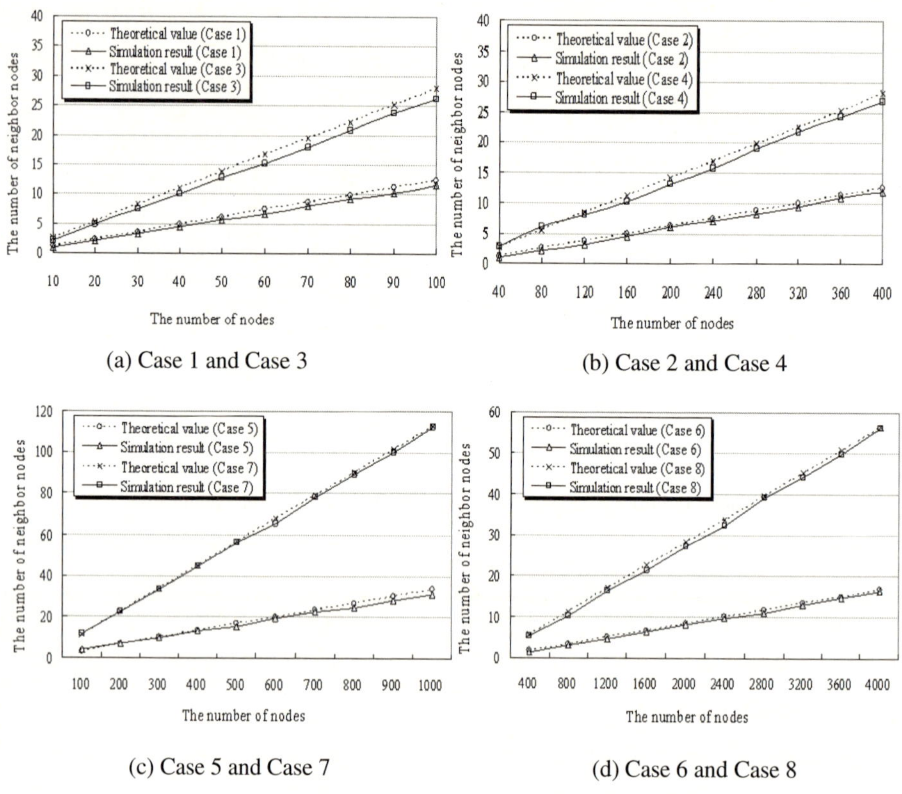

(a) Case 1 and Case 3

(b) Case 2 and Case 4

(c) Case 5 and Case 7

(d) Case 6 and Case 8

Fig. 6. The number of neighbor nodes

we deploy only four GPS nodes in three dimensional field, all nodes can identify their positions in one round, which can greatly save price and make nodes smaller.

Fig. 7 shows how long it will take for all nodes to be aware of their positions. In Fig. 7(a), we see that only 52% and 44% of no-GPS nodes can compute their positions in the first round in case 1 and 3, respectively. In Fig. 7(b), we see that 57% and 66% of no-GPS nodes can compute their positions in the first round in case 5 and 7, respectively. This figure shows that all no-GPS nodes can recognize their positions in the third round for all eight cases.

4   Conclusions

This paper presents a positioning method, in which some of deploying nodes in sensing field are equipped with the GPS and the other nodes can recognize their positions through communications to GPS nodes. The performance of our scheme is evaluated via computer simulations, and the results show that no-GPS nodes can compute their positions in 3 rounds by deploying only some GPS-nodes in the sensing field. Therefore, our scheme saves the price for implementing sensor networks.

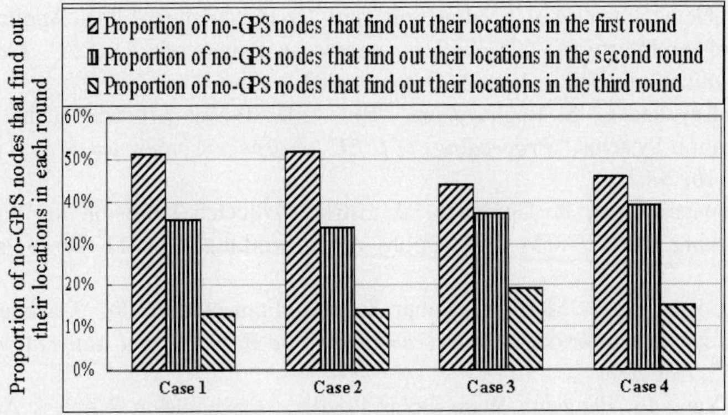

(a) Two dimensional field

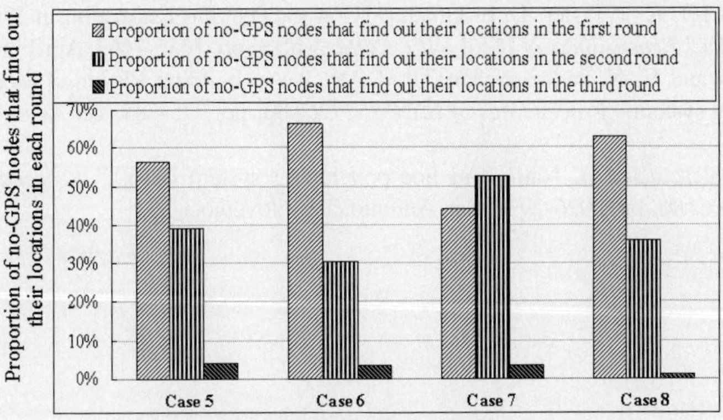

(b) Three dimensional field

Fig. 7. Proportion of no-GPS nodes that find out their locations in each round

References

1. Deepak Ganesan, Alberto Cerpa, Yan Yu, Deborah Estrin, Wei Ye, Jerry Zhao, "Networking Issues in Wireless Sensor Networks," *Journal of Parallel and Distributed Computing*, Vol. 64, Issue 7, pp. 799 – 814, July 2004
2. C.Y. Chong and S.P. Kumar, "Sensor networks: evolution, opportunities and challenges", *Proceedings of the IEEE*, Vol. 91, No. 8, August 2003
3. I. F. Akyildiz, W. Su, Y. Sankarasubramaniam, E. Cayirci, "A survey on sensor networks," *IEEE Communications Magazine*, Vol. 40(8), pp. 102-114, August 2002
4. Wei Ye, John Heidemann, and Deborah Estrin, "An Energy-Efficient MAC Protocol for Wireless Sensor Networks," *In Proceedings of the IEEE Infocom*, pp. 1567–1576, New York, June 2002
5. Wei Ye, John Heidemann, and Deborah Estrin, "Medium access control with coordinated, adaptive sleeping for wireless sensor networks," IEEE/ACM Transactions on Networking. *Technical Report ISI-TR-567*, January 2003

6. W. R. Heinzelman, A. Chandrakasan, and H. Balakrishnan, "An Application-Specific protocol architectures for wireless microsensor networks," *IEEE Transactions on Communications*, Vol. 1, Issue 4, October 2002

7. S. Lindsey and C. S. Raghavendra, "PEGASIS: Power Efficient Gathering in Sensor Information Systems," *Proceedings of IEEE Aerospace Conference*, vol. 3, pp.1125-1130, Mar. 9-16, 2002

8. C. Intanagonwiwat, R. Govindan, D. Estrin, "Directed Diffusion for Wireless Sensor Networking," IEEE/ACM Transactions on Networking, Vol. 11, No. 1, pp. 2-16, Feb. 2003

9. Jorge Cortes, Sonia Martinez, Timur Karatas, Francesco Bullo, "Coverage control for mobile sensing networks," *IEEE Transactions on Robotics and Automation*, vol. 20, pp. 243-255, Apr 2004

10. Xiang-Yang Li, Peng-Jun Wan, Ophir Frieder, "Coverage in Wireless Ad Hoc Sensor Networks," *IEEE TRANSACTIONS ON COMPUTERS*, Vol. 52, No. 6, pp. 753-763, JUNE 2003

11. L. Doherty, K. J. Pister, L. El Ghaoui, "Convex Position Estimation in Wireless Sensor networks," *Proceedings of IEEE INFOCOM*, Vol. 3, pp. 1655-1663, April 2001

12. P. Bahl and V. N. Padmanabhan, "RADAR: An in-building RF based user location and tracking system," *Proceedings of IEEE INFOCOM,* pp. 775-784, Tel Aviv, Israel, March, 2000

13. D. Niculescu and B. Nath, "Ad hoc positioning system (APS)," *Proceedings of IEEE GLOBECOM,* pp. 2926-2931, San Antonio, TX, November 2001

Formal Description of a Runtime Infrastructure for Automatic Distribution of Programs

Omid Bushehrian and Saeed Parsa

Faculty of Computer Engineering, Iran University of Science and Technology
{bushehrian, parsa}@iust.ac.ir

Abstract. Automatic distribution of sequential code is of great concern in applying networks of low cost computers to run computationally intensive code. A major difficulty is to prove that the final distributed code is equivalent with the original sequential code. To achieve this, a formal specification of structure and behavior of the distributed and a formal proof of the equivalence of the operational semantics of the sequential with the final distributed code is presented. To support platform and distributing middleware independence a new architecture is presented.

1 Introduction

With the increasing growth and popularity of the internet and networking techniques, there has been an increasing demand for simple and powerful distributed applications that could be implemented and maintained with a minimum of effort. There have been thorough investigations on automatic distribution of sequential code. Some proposed distribution of Java intermediate code [3][4]. Some others proposed the distribution of multithreaded source code [9]. Apparently, in this approaches the degree of parallelism achieved, depends only on the threads defined by the programmer. Sequential source code distribution has been advocated mostly [8][7][6][5].

We have developed two different frameworks for automatic distribution of sequential Java code [1][2]. A major difficulty with these frameworks has been to prove the equivalence of a distributed code with the original sequential code, independent of any implementation details. To achieve this, a formal specification of the structure and behavior of our frameworks is presented in this paper. An overall description of the building blocks of a general architecture for a distributed code is described in Section 2. Formal specification of the structure of a distributed code is presented in Section 3.1. The behavior of the building blocks of a distributed code is defined in Section 3.2. The equivalence of the states of the memory spaces of the final distributed code and the original sequential code is proved in Section 4.

2 The Architecture

The aim is to provide the possibility of translating a sequential code to a distributed one with minimum effort and independent of the details of the middleware employed

A. Levi et al. (Eds.): ISCIS 2006, LNCS 4263, pp. 793–802, 2006.

to carry out remote method calls. To achieve this, the architecture depicted in Figure 1, is proposed. The advantage of distributing a program code is to speedup its execution by replacing ordinary method calls with remote asynchronous calls. In the first stage of translating a sequential program code into a corresponding distributed code, the class dependency graph of the sequential code is extracted. Then the resulting class dependency graph is clustered. We have developed an environment to investigate genetic clustering algorithms [10]. Each cluster is then, as shown in Figure 1, augmented with three components Port, Distributor and synchronizer.

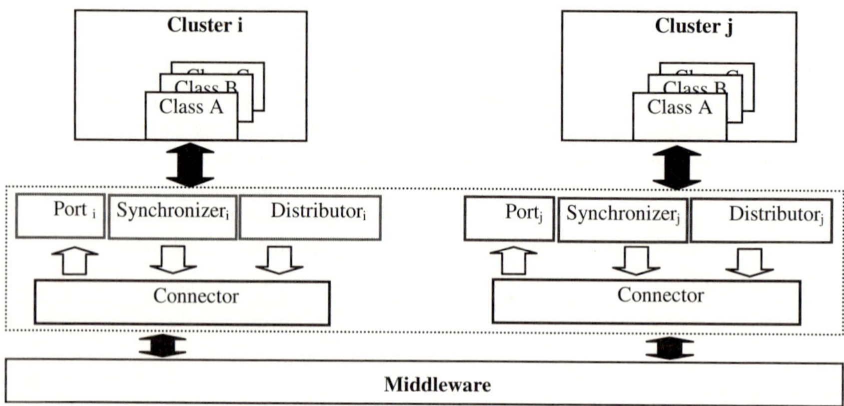

Fig. 1. The Distributed Program Structure

A port component is created for each cluster to facilitate its incoming communications with the other clusters. The Distributor component performs outgoing inter-cluster invocations. The Synchronizer component makes it possible for a caller to receive the value of the reference parameters and the results of remote method calls. Two main approaches, namely *system-wide object references*[11] and *copy/restore*, can be used to transfer parameters in a remote method call. In the *system-wide object references* approach a unique identifier is assigned to each remote object. This identifier addresses the network address of the machine where the object resides plus an indication of the object. All the method calls on this object should be carried out in the machine where the object is initially created. However, if the machine is busy, there will be no speed up compared with the sequential call. Hence, a modified copy/restore approach, has been applied for passing parameters in remote asynchronous invocations. The Synchronizer keeps a record of each remote method call in a table. The record is updated with the values of reference parameters and the return value. A wait statement is inserted at the very first positions where one of the reference parameters or the return value is required. To locate these positions a data dependency analysis approach has been used. The Connector component is the middleware aware part of the suggested architecture. All the inter-cluster communications are carried out through the Connector component. A formal description of the above mentioned components is presented in the following section.

3   Formal Specification

In this Section a formal description of the structure and behavior of the distributed code is presented. Each unit of the distribution is a cluster of the highly related classes. The structure of the cluster and its associated distributing components is presented in section 3.1. The runtime behavior of the distributing mechanism is described in section 3.2.

3.1   Structure

As described above, a distributed program is created by partitioning a given sequential code, and then augmenting a number of components to support asynchronous remote method invocations among partitions. In this Section a formal description of the structure of the distributed program, called *PartitinedCode,* is presented.

> *PartitinedCode* = **set of** cluster,
> $\forall$ Cluster$_i$ $\in$ *PartitinedCode* :   Cluster$_i$ = (CT$_i$, P$_i$, D$_i$, G$_i$,R$_i$)

Where, CT$_i$ addresses a table containing a description of all classes belonging to the Cluster$_i$. The element P$_i$, is the cluster port, providing possibility of asynchronous remote access to the methods of CT$_i$ classes from within the classes of CT$_j$ where   i$\neq$j. The element D$_i$ is the cluster distributor, which provides transparent remote access to the methods of classes in other clusters connected to Cluster$_i$. The element G$_i$ is a map which relates a method in port P$_i$ to a method in one of the classes of CT$_i$. R$_i$ is another map which relates one method in D$_i$ to a method of a remote port P$_k$ where k $\neq$ i. Before specifying these elements formally, some auxiliary definitions are required:

Types	Set of all language types including primitive types and classes
statements	Set of all language statements
identifiers	Set of all valid language identifiers

3.1.1   Classes and Methods in Each Cluster

As described above, the class table of ith cluster, CT$_i$, is defined as a set of classes:

> CT$_i$ = **set of** class
> $\forall$s$_k$ $\in$ CT$_i$: s$_k$= (classname$_k$,T$_k$,F$_k$, M$_k$)
>   where, T$_k$ = **seq of** t , t $\in$ **types**
>   F$_k$ = **seq of** id , id $\in$ **identifiers**, classname$_k$ $\in$ **identifiers** ,
>   len T$_k$ = len F$_k$

In the above definition, **seq of** defines a sequence and the function len returns the length of a sequence. The above definition defines class s$_k$ named classname$_k$, which has fields F$_k$ with types T$_k$ and methods M$_k$. Each method of a class s$_k$ is defined as follows:

> $\forall$ m$_j$ $\in$ M$_k$: m$_j$ = (methodname$_j$,T$_j$,A$_j$, r$_j$, E$_j$) ,
>   where T$_j$ = **seq of** t, t$\in$ **types** , A$_j$ = **seq of** id , id$\in$ **identifiers,**
>   methodname$_j$$\in$ **identifiers**, r$_j$ $\in$ **types**, E$_j$=**seq of** e,e $\in$ **statements,**
>   len T$_j$=len A$_j$

The above definition defines method m_j of a class s_k, named methodname$_j$ which has formal parameters A_j with types T_j and return type r_j and statements E_j.

In a distributed program, there are two sets of call statements, *intra-calls* and *inter-calls*, to define intra-cluster and asynchronous inter-cluster method calls respectively. In cluster Cluster$_r$:

$\forall$ st $\in$ *intra-calls* : st = (s_n , m_i ,V)
> Where: $s_n \in$ CT$_r$, $m_i \in$ M$_n$ and V is a vector of the call statement parameters

$\forall$ st $\in$ *inter-calls* : st=(m_k , V)
> Where: $m_k \in$ D$_r$ (defined bellow)

3.1.2 Port and Distributor

Each cluster Cluster$_i$, is associated with two components, port P_i and distributor D_i, to define methods provided and required by the cluster, respectively. Each cluster, Cluster$_i$, has a single port, P_i, to communicate with the other clusters. The port is defined as a set of methods, which can be accessed from the other clusters by the asynchronous inter-cluster call statements. Each method, m_k, within P_i invokes a method, $G_i(m_k)$, of a class defined within the class table CT$_i$ of the cluster Cluster$_i$.

$P_i =$ **set** of   method,
$\forall$ $m_k \in$ P$_i$: $m_k =$ (methodname$_k$, T$_k$,A$_k$, r$_k$,E$_k$)

Map G_i of Cluster$_i$ is defined as follows:

$G_i =$ **map** P$_i$ **to** M$_i^*$, M$_i^* = \bigcup$M$_n$ where, $s_n \in$ CT$_i$, s_n=(classname$_n$, T$_n$,F$_n$, M$_n$)

G_i maps each method m_k of the port P_i to a method m_t belonging to a class like s_n of Cluster$_i$:

$G_i(m_k) \in$ M$_n$, $G_i(m_k) =$ (methodname$_t$,T$_t$, A$_t$, r$_t$, E$_t$)

The called method, $G_i(m_k)$, has the same name as the method m_k and belongs to one of the classes, s_n, in the cluster Cluster$_i$. The parameter list, A_k, of the method m_k includes the name of the object "objectRef" which references an instance of the class classname$_n$ and the parameters of method m_t :

T$_k =$ [classname$_n$].T$_t$ A$_k =$ ["objectRef"].A$_t$ r$_t =$ r$_k$

In the above definition the concatenation of two sequences are denoted by symbol '.' . Sequence T_t has one more element, classname$_n$, than T_k. Each cluster, Cluster$_i$, has a single distributor D_i as well. D_i delegates the asynchronous inter-cluster calls of Cluster$_i$ to a remote port P_r. In the following definition, R_i maps each method m_k of D_i to a method $R_i(m_k)$ of remote port P_r.

$D_i =$ **set of** method , R$_i$= **map** D$_i$ **to** $\bigcup$P$_r$ for all r $\neq$ i

$\forall$ $m_k \in$ D$_i$: $m_k =$ (methodname$_k$,T$_k$,A$_k$, r$_k$,E$_k$) ,
> $\exists$ P$_r$: R$_i(m_k) \in$ P$_r$, R$_i(m_k) =$ (methodname$_t$,T$_t$,A$_t$, r$_t$,E$_t$) ,
> T$_k =$ T$_t$, A$_k =$ A$_t$, r$_t =$ r$_k$

Finally the following property can be stated for each distributed program *PartitinedCode*:

$$\forall \text{ Cluster}_i \text{ , Cluster}_j \in \textit{PartitinedCode} :$$
$$CT_i \cap CT_j = \phi \text{ , } P_i \cap P_j = \phi$$

3.2 Runtime Elements

In this section, the behavior of the distributing mechanism is described as a set of runtime configurations. In order to perform a remote method call a new configuration is created for the called method, at runtime by the distributor component of the caller. Each configuration represents the behavior of the thread created to perform the remote method. The configuration is removed after the termination of the called method, when the caller receives the return value. A configuration g is defined as tuple $(\sigma_g, S_g, P^i_g, m^j_g, N_g$, State$_g)$ where,

σ_g :   Memory space of the configuration g.

S_g :   Stack of synchronizers of the configuration g.

P^i_g :   the target port of configuration g which belongs to Cluster$_i$

m^j_g: j^{th} method of port P^i which is executed by configuration g

N_g :   Physical network node of configuration g

State$_g$: running state of g, State$_g \in$ {"Suspended","Running","Terminated"}

In the above definitions each element of configuration g is subscripted by the configuration name, g. The configuration port P^i_g is the cluster port which provides access, through one of its methods: m^j_g, to the method which should be executed by g. In the following subsections the elements of the configuration tuple are further described.

3.2.1 Memory Spaces

A new configuration g is created in a workstation N_g whenever an inter-cluster call is delegated asynchronously, through a local distributor D, to a method m^j_g of a remote port, P^i_g. The memory space element of g retains the parameters' value of the method m^j_g, before and after its completion. The memory space element also retains the return value of the method m^j_g.

The memory space σ_g of the configuration g consist of a mapping from variable names to values, written ($x \rightarrow$ v), or from object identifiers to the existing objects, written (obj $\rightarrow$ (classname$_k$, F_k, V_k)) indicating that identifier obj maps to an object of class classname$_k$. F_k and V_k are two sequences of the field names and their values of the class s_k=(classname$_k$,T_k ,F_k , M_k) , $s_k \in CT_i$. For instance consider the following memory space:

$$\sigma = \{(a \rightarrow(A \text{ , } f_1\text{:}b,f_2\text{:}3)),(b \rightarrow(B,f_1\text{:}c)),(c\rightarrow(C))\}$$

This map shows a memory space containing three identifiers pointing to the objects of types A,B and C, respectively. The set $\{a,b,c\}$ is called the domain of this map and is denoted by **dom** σ. Here, the object pointed to by the identifier, *a*, has two attributes f_1 and f_2. f_1 points to *b* which is an object identifier in its turn. The attribute f_2 holds an integer value.

There are two functions called *og* and *serialized* which operate on the memory spaces. The function $og(\sigma,v)$ returns a subset of the memory space, σ, as an object graph containing the object identifier, v, and any object within σ which is accessible via v:

$$og : 2^{\sigma} \times \mathbf{dom}\ \sigma \rightarrow 2^{\sigma},$$

Below, is a recursive definition of the function, *og*:

$$og(\sigma,v) = \begin{cases} \phi\ , & \text{if } v \notin \mathbf{dom}\ \sigma \\ (v \rightarrow \sigma(v)) \cup og(\sigma_i,o_i),\ o_i \in fields(v),\ \sigma_1=\sigma-\{v\},\ \sigma_{i+1}= \sigma_i - \mathbf{dom}\ og(\sigma_i,o_i) \end{cases}$$

The function *og*, traverses the memory space σ and forms a subset of the memory containing the node v and all the nodes accessible via v. The function *fields(v)*, in the above definition of og, returns all the objects, $o_i \in \sigma_i$, immediately accessible via the object $\sigma(v)$.

The *serialized* function returns the value of an object graph w in memory space of configuration g:

$$serialized(g,\ w) = \{(a, \sigma_g(a))\mid a \in \mathbf{dom}\ w\ \}\ w \in 2^{\sigma}$$

3.2.2 Stack of Synchronizers

The synchronizer element, **$\$g$**, of a configuration g keeps a record of the names of all reference parameters, return value and a handle identifying the thread created to execute a remote method, m^j_k, invoked via a method, m, within g, in a table. A new configuration t is created for each remote method invoked within an existing configuration, g. The set D_r and the mapping R_r in the following definition are already defined in section 3.1.2.

$$\$\mathbf{g}\ =\ \text{map}\ (\mathbf{dom}\ \sigma_g)\ \text{to}\ \mathbf{Threads}_g$$

$$\mathbf{Threads}_g = \{t \mid t \text{ is defined as } (\sigma_t, S_t, P^i_t, m^j_t, N_t, State_t)\ \}$$
$$\text{Where g is defined as: } (\sigma_g, S_g, P^r_g, m^s_g, N_g, State_g)$$
$$\forall\ t \in \mathbf{Threads}_g\ \exists\ m \in D_r,\ R_r(m) = m^j_t,\ m^j_t \in P^i_t$$

The synchronizer table is looked up for the names of reference parameters and the return value at the very first positions where one of the reference parameters or the return value is required within g. A *SYNC* statement is inserted at each of these positions. The *SYNC(v)* statement looks up the name v in the synchronizer table to find the handle of the corresponding invoked method. The handle is checked to determine the termination of the invoked method. A synchronizer table is created and pushed into the synchronizer stack, S_g, when entering a new method within g, at runtime.

$$S_g = \text{seq of } \$\mathbf{g}$$

The SYNC method and another method called REG operate on S_g. SYNC(v) is called whenever a variable, v, affected by a remote method call is required within the caller. To get the value of v, the configuration t = $hd(S_g)(v)$ is accessed through the synchronizer stack, S_g. The function $hd(S_g)$ returns the first synchronizer on the top of the stack.

> SYNC(v)
> **pre**: $v \in$ dom $\sigma_g \ \wedge \ t = hd(S_g)(v)$
> **post:**
> $State_t=$"Terminated" $\wedge$
> $\sigma_g= \hat{} \ \sigma_g \ \dagger \ ($ serialized$(t, \cup og(\hat{} \ \sigma_g, v_i))) \cup (\cup og(\sigma_t, v_i)))$,where $\forall \ v_i : hd(S_g) \ (v_i) = t$

In the above definition of SYNC, $\hat{} \ \sigma_g$ indicates the memory space of the caller configuration, g, before the invocation of SYNC; $\dagger$ indicates overriding of $\hat{} \ \sigma$ with the memory space of the called method. After the invocation of SYNC, the caller is suspended until the state, $State_t$ of the target configuration t, becomes *"Terminated"*. The SYNC method uses the memory space of the configuration t, to update the memory space σ_g of the caller configuration, g. The updates are accessed via the *serialized* function, described in section 3.2.1.

The REG(v,t) method records a parameter v passed as a reference parameter in a remote call, together with the called method configuration, t, in the synchronizer table of the caller configuration.

> REG(v, t)
> **pre**: $v \in$ dom σ_g
> $t \in$ Threads$_g$
> **post:**
> $hd(S_g)= hd(^\wedge S_g) \ \dagger \ (v \rightarrow t)$

3.3 Call Statements

As described in section 3.1.1, there are two sets of call statements called *inter-calls* and *Intra-calls*. *Intra-calls* is the set of local invocations in configuration g:

(g is defined as $(\sigma_g, S_g, P^i_g, m^s_g, N_g , State_g)$)
$\forall$ st $\in$ *intra-calls* : st $= (s_n , m_k ,V)$

Where: $s_n \in CT_i$, $m_k \in M_n$ and V is a vector of the call statement parameters
After the completion of a local method, called through a statement in *intra-calls,* the memory space, σ_g, of the caller configuration, g, will be as follows:

(P1): $\sigma_g = \ \hat{} \ \sigma_g \ \dagger \ (\ serialized(g, \cup og(\hat{} \ \sigma_g, v_i)) \cup \cup og(\sigma_g, v_i)), v_i \in V$

Inter-calls, is the set of statements which perform asynchronous remote method calls from within configuration g:

$\forall$ st $\in$ *inter-calls* : st$=(m_k , V)$

Where: $m_k \in D_i$ and g is defined as $(\sigma_g, S_g, P^i_g, m^s_g, N_g , State_g)$
After executing an inter-calls statement, a new configuration t is created and the call parameters are transferred to the memory space of the new configuration t:

(P2): $\sigma_t = \ \cup og(\sigma_g , v_i) \ $, $v_i \in V$

4 Proof of Correctness

To prove that the distributed program code preserves exactly the same semantics as the original sequential code, it is sufficient to prove that the memory space, σ_g, of the caller configuration after completion of the callee will be the same whether the call is performed locally or remotely. To achieve this, the semantics of *inter-calls* and *SYNC* statements, involved in performing inter and intra-cluster calls are specified, firstly, in Section 4.1. These semantics rules are then applied, in section 4.2, to prove the equivalence of the memory spaces.

4.1 Operational Semantics

When a statement *st* in the set *inter-calls* is executed in configuration g, defined as $(\sigma_g, S_g, P^i_g, m^j_g, N_g, State_g)$, a new configuration t is created. All the reference parameters and the return value, v_j, of *st* are recorded in the synchronizer table of the caller configuration, g. Also, t is augmented to the set $Threads_g$:

(R1): $st \in$ *inter-calls* , $m_k \in D_i$, $t \notin Threads_g$:

$st = (m_k , V)$, $v_j \in V \rightarrow Threads_g = Threads_g \cup \{t\}$, $\sigma_t = \bigcup og(\sigma_g , v_j)$,

$state_t =$"*Running*" , $m_t = R_i(m_k)$, $\forall\ v_j \in V: REG(v_j ,t)$

After an inter-cluster invocation the state, $State_t$, of the callee is set to "*Running*". To wait for the value of variable v, affected by the remote method, m_t of configuration t, the state of the caller, $State_g$, is set to "*Suspended*":

(R2): $v \in$ **dom** $hd(S_g)$, $hd(S_g)(v) = t$, $t \in Threads_g$, $State_t \in \{$"*Running*" , "Suspended"$\}$
   : $SYNC(v) \rightarrow State_g =$"*Suspended*"

After the termination of the remote method, m_t, the state of the caller is set to "*Running*".

(R3): $v \in$ **dom** $hd(S_g)$, $hd(S_g)(v) = t$, $t \in Threads_g$, $State_t =$"*Terminated*"
   : $SYNC(v) \rightarrow State_g =$"*Running*"

4.2 The Proof

Suppose that an inter-cluster call statement $st = (m_k, V)$, from within the running configuration g defined as $(\sigma_g, S_g, P^i_g, m^j_g, N_g , State_g)$, calls a method n_s of the remote port P_r in the cluster $Cluster_r$:

$n_s = R_i(m_k)$, $n_s \in P_r$, $Cluster_r = (CT_r , P_r , D_r , G_r , R_r)$

Suppose the method n_s belonging to the destination port P_r calls a method *u* defined in the class, s_n of the class table CT_r:

$G_r(n_s) = u \in M_n$, $s_n = ($ $classname_n$,T_n ,F_n , $M_n)$, $s_n \in CT_r$.

In order to execute st, another configuration t is created. t is defined as $(\sigma_t, S_t, P^i_t, m^j_t, N_t, State_t)$. The value of σ_t after creation of t is initialized with $\bigcup og(\sigma_g, v_i)$, therefore $\sigma_t \subseteq \sigma_g$ before execution of m^j_t. As a result, if the memory space σ_g and network node N_g of configuration g are selected instead of σ_t and N_t respectively in t, the resulting configuration $t'=(\sigma_g, S_t, P^i_t, m^j_t, N_g, State_t)$ changes the memory space of the caller configuration g the same as the configuration $t=(\sigma_t, S_t, P^i_t, m^j_t, N_t, State_t)$ does after corresponding SYNC statement. t' changes the memory space g as follows:

$$\textbf{(L1):} \qquad \sigma_g = \hat{}\,\sigma_g \dagger \; (serialized(g \, , \cup og(\hat{}\,\sigma_g, v_i)) \; \cup \; (\cup og(\sigma_g, v_i) \,) \,)$$

Since (L1) and (P1) are identical, it is obvious that t' changes the memory space of the caller configuration g the same as local call to method u does. Therefore the memory space of the caller configuration g after the SYNC statement will be identical whether the call is performed by t or by a local invocation to u.

Formally:

From $st= (m_k \,, V) \, , \, t \notin Threads_g$

$\qquad Threads_g = Threads_g \cup \{t\} \; , \; \sigma_t = \cup og(\sigma_g \, , \, v_i \,) \; State_t = "Running"$ (R1)

$\qquad$ **From** $\; SYNC(v_i), \, v_i \in V$

$\qquad\qquad State_g = \; "Suspended"$ (R2)

$\qquad\qquad$ **From** $State_t = "Terminated"$

$\qquad\qquad\qquad SYNC(v_i) \rightarrow State_g = "Running"$ (R3)

$\qquad\qquad$ **Infer** post-condition of $SYNC(v_i)$

$\qquad\qquad$ **From** post-condition of $SYNC(v_i)$

$\qquad\qquad\qquad \sigma_g = \hat{}\,\sigma_g \dagger \; (\, serialized(t, \cup og(\hat{}\,\sigma_g, \, v_i)) \cup \cup og(\sigma_t, v_i) \,)$

$\qquad\qquad$ **Infer** $\; \sigma_g = \hat{}\,\sigma_g \dagger \; (serialized(g \, , \cup og(\hat{}\,\sigma_g, v_i)) \; \cup \; (\cup og(\sigma_g, v_i) \,) \,)$ (L1)

$\qquad\qquad$ **Infer** post-condition of $st2=(s_n \, , u \, , V) \in intra\text{-}calls$ (P1)

Infer $st2=(s_n \, , u \, , V)$

5 Conclusions

To prove the equivalence of the operational semantics of a sequential code and its corresponding distributed code, it is sufficient to prove that after completion of a called method the memory space of the caller will be the same whether the call is performed locally or remotely. To achieve this, the state of the memory space of the caller should be defined before and after the completion of the called method. To define the memory space state, the effect of transferring reference parameters and receiving the return value and the value of reference parameters, on the memory spaces of the caller and the called method should be specified. Formal specification of the structure of distributed code makes it possible to define the distributing components and their application. A copy restore approach is preferred for transferring reference parameters in a distributed environment.

References

1. Saeed Parsa, Vahid Khalilpour: Automatic Distribution of Sequential Code Using JavaSymphony Middleware, SOFSEM06 ,LNCS 2006
2. Saeed Parsa, Omid Bushehrian: Automatic Translation of Serial To Distributed Code Using CORBA Event Channels, Lecture Notes in Computer Science, ISCIS 2005

3. Roxana E. Diaconescu, Lei Wang, Michael Franz: Automatic Distribution of Java Byte-Code Based on Dependence Analysis, Technical Report No. 03-18, School of Information and Computer Science, University of California, Irvine, October 2003.

4. Roxana Diaconescu, Lei Wang, Zachary Mouri, Matt Chu: A Compiler and Runtime Infrastructure for Automatic Program Distribution, 19th International Parallel and Distributed Processing Symposium (IPDPS 2005), IEEE ,2005

5. Isabelle Attali, Denis Caromel, Romain Guider: A Step Toward Automatic Distribution of Java Programs, 4th International Conference on Formal Methods for Open Object-Based Distributed Systems (FMOODS 2000), 2000, Stanford, California, USA

6. Mohammad M. Fuad, Michael J. Oudshoorn: AdJava-Automatic Distribution of Java Applications, 25th Australasian Computer Science Conference (ACSC2002), Monash University, Melbourne, 2002

7. PA Felber: Semi-automatic parallelization of java applications, Lecture Notes in Computer Science, Vol. 2888 (January 2003), pp. 1369-1383

8. Michiaki Tatsubori, Toshiyuki Sasaki, Shigeru Chibal, and Kozo Itano: A Bytecode Translator for Distributed Execution of Legacy Java Software, LNCS 2072, pp. 236–255, 2001.

9. Andre Spiegel : Pangaea: An Automatic Distribution Front-End for Java", 4th IEEE Workshop on High-Level Parallel Programming Models and SupportiveEnvironments (HIPS '99), San Juan, Puerto Rico, April 1999.

10. Parsa S, Bushehrian O.: The Design and Implementation of a Tool for Automatic Software Modularization, Journal of Supercomputing, Volume 32, Issue 1, April 2005.

11. Andrew S. TanenBaum, Maarten Van Steen: Distributed Systems Principles and Paradigms, PRENTICE HALL, 2002

Super-Peer Selection Based Framework Using Dynamic Capacity and Similarity

Suhong Min and Dongsub Cho

Department of Computer Science and Engineering,
Ewha Womans University,
Seodaemun-gu, Seoul, 120-750, Korea
`shmin@ewhain.net, dscho@ewha.ac.kr`

Abstract. The peer-to-peer (P2P) systems have grown significantly over the last few years due to their potential for sharing various resources. SP (Super-peer) based P2P systems give the responsibility for query processing to the SPs instead of their OPs (Ordinary-Peer). In these systems, selecting the best SP to join is an important problem, but it has received little attention from the research community. In this study, we propose ISP2P (Intelligent Super-peer based P2P system), which can provide the best SP by analyzing dynamic capacity and similarity between peers. This proposed system can improve scalability and reduce SP's workload by dynamic CPU load, and decrease message traffic by the physical capacity and similarity of content and user behavior.

Keywords: Peer-to-Peer (P2P), Super-Peer, Capacity, Content Similarity, User behavior.

1 Introduction

Peer-to-Peer systems have recently received considerable attention from the networking research community. Initially, only pure P2P systems were considered. That is, all peers were assumed to have the same capabilities. Such systems use a flooding based search in which peers would send a lot of messages in their search to find the desired resource. However, peers with limited capabilities can cause bottlenecks. To improve this situation, a super-peer based hybrid P2P model was proposed. The hybrid P2P model which has been found very effective, is unstructured except for the division of peers into two layers, SP (Super-Peer) and OP (Ordinary-Peer). Each SP is connected to a set of Ops, while OPs are connected to only one SP. The SP deals with all queries instead of OPs [1, 2] so that an OP with low capacity is able to fully participate in the network. It is a feature of the Super-peer based P2P system that the OP should select only one SP for sharing resources and can participate in the network only through the chosen SP. Compared with pure P2P systems, Super-peer based P2P systems have to deal well with a large number of queries from OPs. The selected SP must handle queries efficiently and search for files requested by the OP. Existing systems break peers into OPs and SPs by considering only static capacities, such as the system specifications of peers. These systems pay little attention to a SP's dynamic capacity changes and characteristics of its resources. Often they use simple strategies such as

A. Levi et al. (Eds.): ISCIS 2006, LNCS 4263, pp. 803–812, 2006.

random selection, when an OP chooses a SP. Although this technique is simple, it does not deal well with the heterogeneity of the participating peers both in terms of dynamic capabilities and a content similarity [11]. The best SP selection approach aims to reduce the probability of failure of searching desired files and to improve the entire network performance through the use of only high quality SP's.

In this paper, we have implemented ISP2P (Intelligent Super-peer based P2P system), which can make a decision for the best SP selection with a combination of physical capacity and similarity. We suggest the following three approaches: First, we measure the capacities related to distance cost and the prediction based processing power between peers. Second, we analyze common features indicating the similarity of content of desired files and the similarity of behavior between peers. To do this, we compute the similarity of content between peers with ISM (Intelligent Search Mechanism) algorithm and estimate similar behavior which stands for the duration that both OP and SP are on the P2P network. Finally, in order to give a ranking to SP, we compute max capacity and max similarity.

The main contributions of this paper are: We can reduce the bandwidth cost by selection of best SP. Also we can improve the workload of SP by dynamic prediction based CPU load.

The rest of the paper is organized as follows: Section 2 reviews some related work briefly. Section 3 states the ISP2P system which provides the best super-peer by considering both capacity and similarity; Section 4 shows in detail the procedure of the implementation of our mechanism; we conclude and propose the future work in Section 5.

2 Existing Super-Peer Based P2P System

Recently hybrid P2P model based on Super-peers have supplanted the original pure P2P models. Super-peer based systems classify nodes into SP and OP by considering their capabilities. A super-peer is a node that acts as a centralized server to a subset of clients. These clients (OP) submit queries to their SP and receive results from it. In order to process the query for its OPs, each SP keeps an index of its OP's data. Yang and Garcia-Molina [1] examined the performance tradeoffs in super-peer systems. They and other researchers studied the potential drawbacks of super-peer network and reliability issues [1, 12]. Representative applications based on Super-peer architectures are Gnutella and KaZaA. In case of Gnutella, the original protocol, 0.4 version treats all nodes equal regardless of their bandwidth, CPU power etc. However, it has been observed that the abundance of signaling was a major threat to the scalability of these networks [2]. Gnutella 0.6 version suggested therefore the introduction of a two-level peer hierarchy: ultrapeers and leaf nodes [4]. SP and OP are named ultrapeer and leafnode in Gnutella. A principle goal of the Gnutella 0.6 architecture is to reduce the high message load, which can be observed in a Gnutella 0.4. The Gnutella specification [4] presented some criteria for ultrapeers such as not fire walled, suitable operating system, sufficient bandwidth and sufficient uptime. Peers classified as ultrapeers acts as proxies on behalf of less capable nodes, the so-called leaf nodes. In Gnutella, when leaf nodes connect to one of ultrapeers, they don't consider physical capacities and user behavior between peers. Instead, they simply send Ping message including hop count to connect to ultrapeers in the network [9]. In case of KaZaA, although it is the most popular application based on super-peer architecture, it uses a proprietary protocol with encryption and little is known about the protocols, architectures, and behavior. A recent paper [5] presented the research community with an understanding of how KaZaA operates through some experiments. KaZaA was one of the first P2P systems to exploit this heterogeneity by organizing the peers into two classes, SN (Super Nodes) and ON (Ordinary Nodes) [10]. Like Gnutella, SNs are more powerful in terms of connectivity, bandwidth, CPU power, and non NATed accessibility. When an ON launches the KaZaA application, the ON chooses a parent SN, maintains a semi-permanent TCP connection with its parent SN, and uploads to this SN the meta-data for the files it is sharing.

It has been shown that hybrid systems can reduce network traffic by using SP to handles queries of OP with low capabilities and to locate neighbors and resources. However, current approaches have only a simple strategy for selecting SP. A better way of evaluating potential SPs would further improve the network. We present an efficient SP selection strategy that considers physical capabilities and similarity service in hybrid P2P system.

3 ISP2P System

3.1 System Architecture

We have designed ISP2P (Intelligent Super-peer based P2P system). Proposed system's functions are divided into two kinds; capacity and similarity. First, we calculate the distance cost and dynamic CPU load. The distance cost is measured by values of propagation and transmission delay per hop. The dynamic processing power is calculated by analyzing CPU load changes at different steps and adding more weight to recent CPU load values (or CPU usage). To achieve this, we propose modified EMA (Exponential Moving Average) algorithm which helps us not only to predict the next CPU load value but also to have more accurate CPU load. Second, we explore common features indicating the similarity of content of desired files and the similarity of behavior between peers. We compute the similarity of content between peers with ISM algorithm which applies the Nearest Neighbor classification technique and cosine similarity. And we calculate similar behavior which stands for the duration that both OP and SP are on the P2P network. To do this, we estimate average P2P time slot and used time in it. Each calculated value is used to evaluate SP's score for giving a ranking of SP. The architecture of ISP2P is shown in Fig 1.

3.2 Capacity Measurement

Selecting the best SP, we consider that distance cost between peers and SP's processing power. First, the distance cost should include a transmission delay and a network latency. The distance cost depends on transmission delay and propagation delay between peers. The existing ways still depend on hop count (or TTL) or IP prefix. These methods can not reflect dynamic network changes. Generally, the query transmission delay between an OP and a SP is caused by a variety of environmental factors, that is,

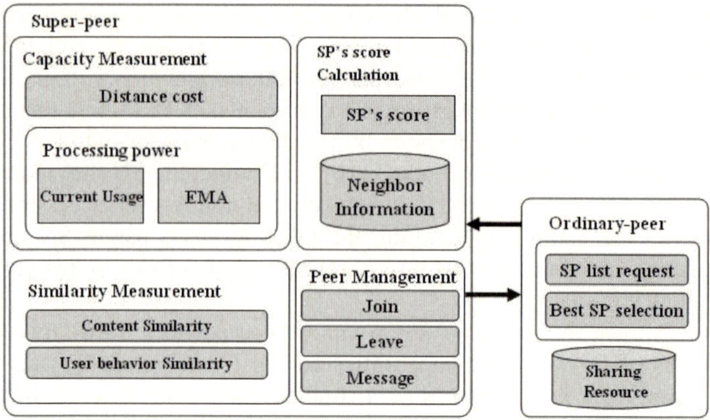

Fig. 1. ISP2P Overviews

distance, link problems and changing router capacity, etc. Therefore, our proposed scheme considers the propagation and transmission delay per hop for distance cost. In this paper, the distance between peers is calculated as follows:

$$T_d = L / R \tag{1}$$

$$P_d = D / S \tag{2}$$

$$D_v = \sum_{i=0}^{\max hop} (T_d + P_d) \tag{3}$$

The formula (1) computes the amount of time required for the peer to push out the packet. L is the packet's length and R is the transmission rate of the link. The formula (2) is the time it takes a bit to propagate from one peer to the next; it is a function of the distance between the two peers. The propagation speed depends on the physical medium of the link (D) and is in the range (D) of 2×10^8 meters/sec to 3×10^8 meters/sec. The propagation delay is the distance between two peers divided by the propagation speed [6]. The distance cost is calculated using (1), (2) and hop count per peer in the formula (3).

Second, we use the CPU load of SP to make a decision the best SP selection and new OP's acceptance. We observe that CPU usage dynamically changes by various conditions such as time, process's status and other traffic. Thus, current CPU usage does not state CPU's status exactly and doesn't predict next CPU load by another new peer's connection. In order to know CPU current status of SP, we modify EMA, one of one-step ahead time series which gives more weight to more recent measurements than to other history data. The original EMA is calculated by the previous EMA value and current CPU usage [7]. EMA value mainly depends on time interval. If time interval increases, it is difficult to reflect recent CPU load, or if time interval is short, we have to calculate EMA frequently. Therefore, we measure the CPU load at 3 steps. Every step has different time intervals. First, we calculate the current CPU usage by short intervals. Second, we estimate MA (Moving Average) value with history dataset returned in 1 step according to middle intervals. Finally, we measure CPU load with modified EMA by long term. If the whole period is 20, current CPU usage, C_t is measured total 20 times at one minute, MA_t is calculated 4 times at 5 minutes intervals, and EMA_t is calculated 2 times at 10 minutes intervals. If OP requires processing power, CPU load of SP is evaluated by means of previous EMA and MA.

The formula for cost of the processing power is

$$C_t = \{c_1, c_2, c_3, \ldots\ldots, c_N\} \tag{4}$$

$$MA_t = \frac{\sum_{i=0}^{n-1} C_{t-i}}{n} \tag{5}$$

$$C_\mu = \alpha \cdot MA_t + (1-\alpha) \cdot EMA_{t-l} \tag{6}$$

$$P_{t+1} = C_\mu + IncrementValue \tag{7}$$

C_t is a set of current CPU values at t time intervals. MA_t is an average value of C_t, and MA_t is a set of MA values, $MA_t = \{ ma_1, ma_2, \ldots, ma_t \}$. C_μ is current EMA, and it means next CPU load as a prediction value. EMA_{t-l} is previous exponential moving average. N means the number of periods for EMA. α is a smoothing constant, $\alpha = 2/(N+1)$. The smoothing constant applies the appropriate weighting to the most recent value relative to the previous EMA. First EMA period's calculation uses MA. After calculating the CPU load of SP with modified EMA, we decide on the acceptance of new OP by expecting the rising traffic. According to take the number of OP, SP have to handle more the number of messages so that it causes CPU load and message response time. To predict increasing traffic by a new peer, we first calculate the threshold of CPU load within the limits of the allowable of OP. And then, we predict the rising traffic by receiving new peer. A SP decides the acceptance or the rejection by the threshold which is computed by Fig. 2. The measured threshold value is that the CPU load is 0.4 (40%). If predicted CPU load is lower than 0.4, a SP takes new OP, or rejects it. Predicted increment CPU load is computed by increasing CPU load by means of the number of average message of new OP. According to [5], the CPU load increase in between 0.05 and 1 whenever new peer joins. As a result, we adopt this value as increment value. The predicted CPU value is as the formula (7). P_{t+1} consist of modified EMA value and $IncrementValue$, which is increasing traffic by taking new peer.

3.3 Similarity Measurement

In this system, we extract common features about content and user behavior between peers. Content based similarity can help OP to be provided with the most relevant content. Also the selected SP is able to offer similar content and similar user behavior, OP can obtain resources through small path length so that we can reduce bandwidth cost. First, we measure the content similarity between OP and SP. To do this, we use ISM algorithm to compute similarity of content. This algorithm uses Nearest Neighbor classification technique and cosine similarity and calculates content's similarity value respectively. In order to search the most relevant answers fast and efficiently, we study ISM which was proposed in [8]. This algorithm is to help the querying peer to find the most relevant answers to its query. To achieve this, a peer estimates for each query, which of its peers are more likely to reply to this query, and propagates the query the message to those peers only. The peer received query calculates content similarity as following:

$$Psimp_k(P_i, q) = \sum Qsim(q_j, q)^\alpha \tag{1}$$

$$Qsim(q_j, q) = \frac{q_j \cdot q}{\left|\vec{q_j}\right| \times \left|\vec{q}\right|} \tag{2}$$

$$= \frac{\sum_{t=1}^{t} w_{i,j} \times w_{i,q}}{\sqrt{\sum_{i=1}^{t} W^2_{i,j}} \times \sqrt{\sum_{t=1}^{t} W^2_{i,q}}}$$

The *Qsim* is the cosine similarity. In order to find the most likely peers to answer a given query we need a function *Qsim*: $Q^2 \rightarrow [0,1]$ (where Q is the query space), to compute the similarity between queries. The cosine similarity metric has been used extensively in information retrieval, and we use this distance function in our setting. Let L be the set of all words that have appeared in queries. We define a |L| - dimensional space where each query is a vector. q_j is one of the K most similar queries to q. The parameter α, which allows us to add some weight for the most similar queries. For example, where α is very large, *Psim* reduces to one-nearest neighbor. If $\alpha =1$, *Psim* adds up the similarity of all queries that have been answered by the peer.

Second, we measure the similarity degree of user behavior. In order to know similarity information about P2P service use behavior in both OP and SP, we calculate similarity behavior between OP and SP in user time slot and used time in this paper. Super-peer based P2P system, OP is affected by SP's network status, that is, which is on or offline. If SP is mainly in other time slot compared to OP or SP's used time is smaller than OP, OP has to frequently replace SP in the middle of P2P utilization. As a result, proposed system considers SP's time slot and the used time in it, when OP selects SP and it makes OP select the most similar SP. The procedure is as follows: First, we check the average time slot and used time in it of peers who record their own log information about user service usage time. In order to do this, we classify time into different slots as below.

Table 1. Time slot

# of time slot	Time (A.M)	# of time slot	Time (P.M)
1	0 ~ 3	5	12 ~ 3
2	3 ~ 6	6	3 ~ 6
3	6 ~ 9	7	6 ~ 9
4	9 ~ 12	8	9 ~ 12

Second, after peers get the average time slot, they array it along the order of the mo st frequent used time slot. And also OP adopts the weight to each sequence of them. T he following formula shows the computation of similar behavior between OP and SP.

$$
Tsim_N = \frac{\sum_{i=0}^{N} \alpha(n-i)(p_i \cap q^{\alpha})}{\sum_{i=0}^{n} (n-i)}
\tag{3}
$$

Assuming N is a set of time zone of OP, p, the individual value belongs to N is compared with the time slot of SP, q. For example, if OP, p, has n time slots, it is compared with SP, q, as many as n and the weight is added with respect to the most frequently used values. The order of SP, α, is taken into consideration simultaneously.

3.4 Ranking of Super-Peer

In order to make a ranked set of SPs, OP gets scores such as, max capacity and max similarity between SP and OP.

Max Capacity: SP calculates the max capacity including physical capacities such as distance cost and processing power between SP and OP. The max capacity is measure d by distance cost, $d \in D$ and processing power $p \in P$. The max capacity is expre ssed as follows: $MC_i : d_i \times p_i \mapsto [0,1]$. If distance cost of SP_i, d_i is 0.8 and processi ng power, p_i is 0.5, the max capacity value between SP_i and OP is 0.4

Max Similarity: SP measures the max similarity which means the similarity of conte nt and user behavior in subsection 3.3. The max similarity is calculated by content si milarity value, $c \in C$ and user behavior value, $u \in U$ between SP and OP. The max similarity is $MS_i : c_i \times u_i \mapsto [0,1]$. If the value is 0, SP and OP are not similar at al l, if the value is 1, they match exactly.

The OP should select best SP of a ranked set of SP. The ranking value is calculated by the max capacity and the max similarity of returned SP. A ranked set of SP is $sp \in SP$ and the ranking value expresses as following: $SP_i : MC_i \times MS_i \mapsto [0,1]$. If the ranking value of SP_1 and SP_2 is relatively 0.5 and 0.8, OP selects SP_2 as best SP.

4 Experiment Evaluations

In this section, we present the simulation model used to evaluate the performance of our SP selection method and determine the weights of the SP factors. We also discuss simulation results. The simulation model is implemented in C++ using CSIM [13]. The network setup and performance metrics are shown in Table 1. It consists of a number of OPs and SPs. OPs join the network and request services or provide them during their lifetimes and then disconnect from the network. All peers repeat these processes during the simulation time.

Table 2. Default parameter settings

Parameters	Default Values
SIMTIME	30000
The number of OP	100 ~ 1000
The number of SP	10
CPU power factor	{1.0,1.5,2.0,2.5,3.0}
The range of distance	10 ~ 100ms
contents	10
The delay per hop	100ms
Max hop	7

In our simulation, we verify that the proposed system can improve scalability and bandwidth cost by considering dynamic capacity and Similarity. First, we do experiment with SP's workload. When SP takes new OP, it calculates the predicted CPU load as section 3.2.2. The acceptance of new OP depends on the threshold of CPU load of SP. Fig. 2 shows that the average message response time increases as the CPU load varies. We can see the response time rate is increased when CPU load is over 40%. Therefore, we indicate the threshold at this point and SP can allow a new OP when CPU load of SP is less than 40%. We do experiment whether SP can stably deal with queries from OP's. In Fig. 3, the performance is compared as the number of peer varies. We compare the dynamic acceptance with the static way which restricts the number of OP's. Fig. 3 shows that dynamic SP have better performance as the number of OP's increases. When SP reflects on current CPU load and expecting increment traffic by another OP, SP can participate in network more scalable, even though peers increases. On the other hand, the conventional way, a static scheme displays the exponential growth of response time as peers increase. Hence, we can improve the performance of SP's workload and scalability by dynamic acceptance of OP. Second, based on the physical capacity and the similarity, we examine the influence of message traffic on various ratios of peers. Fig. 4 shows the message traffic size as peers increase. We

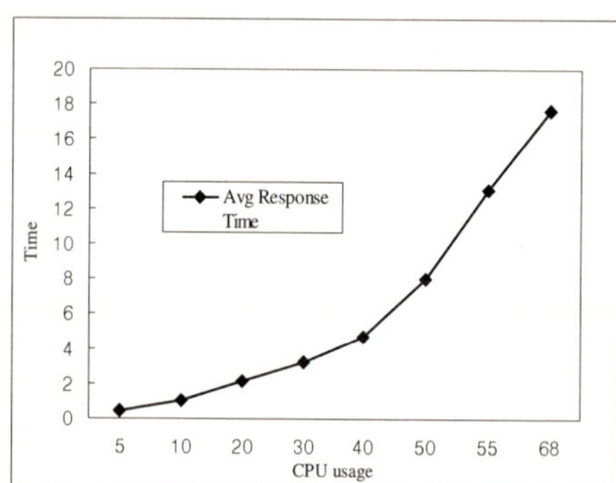

Fig. 2. CPU usage vs. Response time

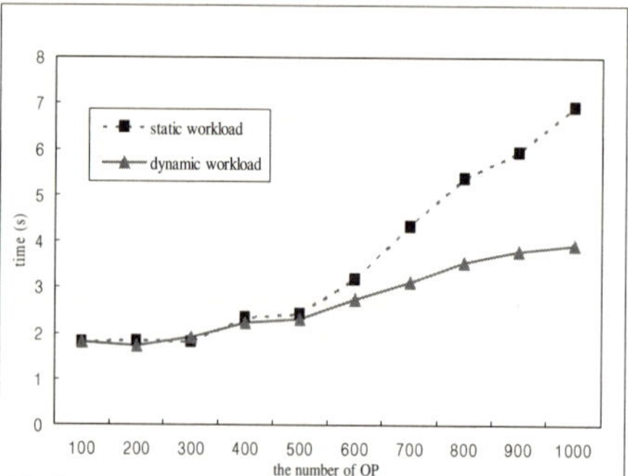

Fig. 3. SP's workload vs. Response time

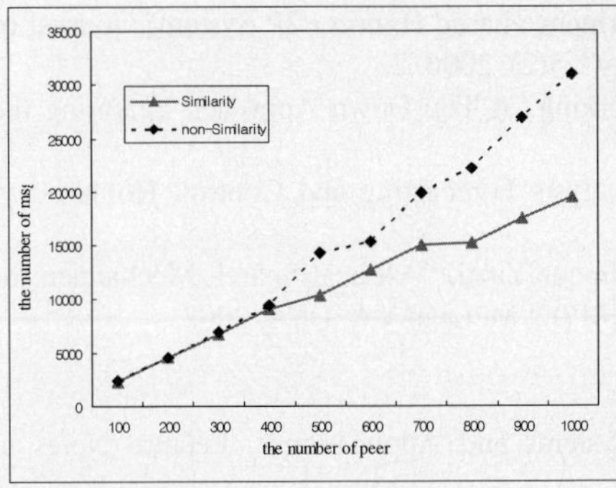

Fig. 4. The number of peer vs. Message traffic

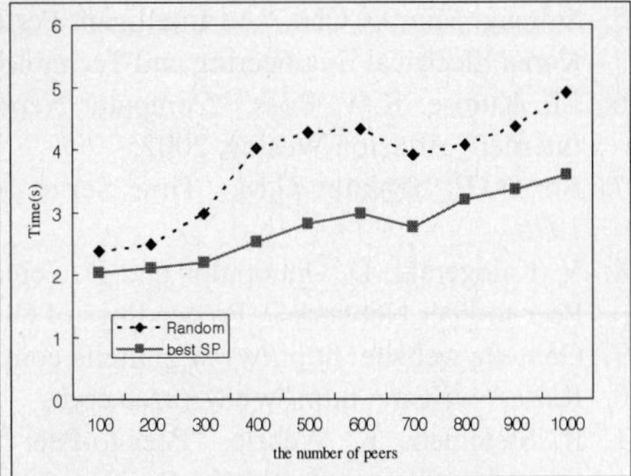

Fig. 5. Random SP vs. Best SP

compare the performance of proposed system with a conventional approach. Fig. 5 shows that the message traffic can be reduced in a network when OP selects the SP with similar contents. Fig. 5 shows the message response time as peers increase. We demonstrate the effectiveness of proposed system which can cause good performance of both OP and SP by dynamic physical capacity and similarity between peers.

5   Conclusion and Future Work

We have presented the ISP2P system for providing the best super-peer. In the Super-Peer based P2P system, SP is supposed to handle all queries received from OP. As a result, selecting SP is important problem, but it has received little attention from the research community and most of the existing systems only select SP at random. In this paper, we have started this exploration by looking at the problem of selecting the best SP. We focus on selecting the best SP by analyzing capacity and similarity between peers. This proposed system can improve scalability and reduce SP's workload by dynamic CPU load, and decrease message traffic by the capacity and similarity of content and user behavior. We plan to implement additional features in the future work such as mechanism that allows monitoring of traffic between peers and strategies for topology self-organization.

References

1. B. Yang, H. Garcia-Molina, "Designing a super-peer network", IEEE International Conference on Data Engineering, Bangalore, India, March 2003.
2. Y. Chawathe , S. Ratnasamy , L. Breslau , N. Lanham and S. Shenker, "Making Gnutella-like P2P systems scalable", Proceedings of the 2003 conference on Applications, technologies, architectures, and protocols for computer communications, Karlsruhe, Germany, August 25-29, 2003.
3. J. Liang, R. Kumar, K Ross, "The KaZaA Overlay: A Measurement Study", Proceedings of the Fifth New York Metro Area Networking Workshop, 2005.
4. Gnutella protocol spec. v.0.6 - http://rfc-gnutella.sourceforge.net/src/rfc-0_6-draft.html

5. Suhong. Min, D. Cho, "An Intelligent Performance based Hybrid P2P System", Journal of Korea Electrical Engineering and Technology", 5(2). 2006. 2.
6. J.F. Kurose, K.W. Ross, "Computer Networking: A Top-Down Approach Featuring the Internet", Addsion Wesley, 2002.
7. Box, G.E., Jenkins, G.M, "Time Series Analysis Forecasting and Control, Holden day, 1976.
8. V. Kalogeraki, D. Gnuopulos and D. Zeinalipour-Yazti, "A Local Search Mechanism for Peer-to-Peer Networks", Proceedings of CIKM'02, McLean VA, USA, 2002.
9. Gnutella website: http://www.gnutella.com.
10. KaZaA website: http://www.kazaa.com.
11. R. Steinmetz, K. Wehrle, "Peer-to-Peer Systems and Applications", Lecture Notes in Computer Science, Vol. 3485 Springer 2005.
12. L. Xiao, Z. Zhuang, Y. Liu, "Dynamic Layer Management in Superpeer Architectures", IEEE Transactions on parallel and distributed systems, 16(11), Nov. 2005.
13. CSIM Development toolkit for simulation and modeling. http://www.mesquite.com.

A General Graph Model for Representing Exact Communication Volume in Parallel Sparse Matrix–Vector Multiplication

Aleksandar Trifunović and William Knottenbelt

Department of Computing, Imperial College London, South Kensington Campus,
London SW7 2AZ, UK
{at701, wjk}@doc.ic.ac.uk

Abstract. In this paper, we present a new graph model of sparse matrix decomposition for parallel sparse matrix–vector multiplication. Our model differs from previous graph-based approaches in two main respects. Firstly, our model is based on edge colouring rather than vertex partitioning. Secondly, our model is able to correctly quantify and minimise the total communication volume of the parallel sparse matrix–vector multiplication while maintaining the computational load balance across the processors. We show that our graph edge colouring model is equivalent to the fine-grained hypergraph partitioning-based sparse matrix decomposition model. We conjecture that the existence of such a graph model should lead to faster serial and parallel sparse matrix decomposition heuristics and associated tools.

1 Introduction

Parallel sparse matrix–vector multiplication is the core operation in iterative solvers for large-scale linear systems and eigensystems. Major application areas include Markov modelling, linear programming and PageRank computation.

Efficient parallel sparse matrix–vector multiplication requires intelligent *a priori* partitioning of the sparse matrix non-zeros across the processors to ensure that interprocessor communication is minimised subject to a load balancing constraint. The problem of sparse matrix decomposition can be reformulated in terms of a graph or hypergraph partitioning problem. These partitioning problems are NP-hard [10], so (sub-optimal) heuristic algorithms are used in practice. The resulting graph or hypergraph partition is then used to direct the distribution of matrix elements across processors.

The limits of the existing graph partitioning approaches are outlined in [11,8,4]. For example, in the case of one-dimensional row-wise or column-wise partitioning of a sparse matrix for parallel sparse matrix–vector multiplication, existing graph models cannot optimise the exact communication volume; instead, they operate indirectly by optimising an upper bound on the communication volume.

On the other hand, hypergraph models that correctly represent the total communication volume have been proposed and are thus preferred to graph models

A. Levi et al. (Eds.): ISCIS 2006, LNCS 4263, pp. 813–824, 2006.
© Springer-Verlag Berlin Heidelberg 2006

in practical applications. Moreover, recently two parallel hypergraph partitioning algorithms have also been developed and implemented [17,16,15,7]. However, graph models do have the advantage that heuristic algorithms operating on graphs are faster and are significantly easier to parallelise than heuristic algorithms that operate on hypergraphs [15,7].

This paper presents a bipartite graph model for parallel sparse matrix–vector multiplication that correctly models the total interprocessor communication volume while maintaining the computational load balance. The graph model is derived from the fine-grained hypergraph model presented by Çatalyürek and Aykanat in [5]. The edges in the graph model the non-zeros in the matrix and thus instead of partitioning the set of vertices, as in existing graph and hypergraph sparse matrix decomposition models, our model requires the colouring of the edges of the graph so that a colouring objective is minimised. Whereas the widely accepted meaning of the phrase "edge colouring" is that the edges of the graph are coloured such that edges incident on the same vertex have different colours, the edge colouring that we seek imposes no such restriction, i.e. we admit colourings where distinct edges incident on the same vertex are of the same colour. The colouring objective correctly models the total interprocessor communication volume, while the computational load balance is maintained by the constraint limiting the number of edges (matrix non-zeros) that can be assigned the same colour.

We anticipate that the advantages of our graph model over existing hypergraph models will be twofold. Firstly, heuristic algorithms for minimising the edge-colouring objective in a graph should be faster than heuristic algorithms for the corresponding hypergraph partitioning problem and secondly, the edge-colouring algorithms should yield more efficient parallel algorithms than their hypergraph partitioning counterparts, as indicated by respective state-of-the-art algorithms for graph and hypergraph partitioning.

The remainder of this paper is organized as follows. Section 2 describes the models used in sparse matrix decomposition for parallel sparse matrix–vector multiplication. Section 3 describes the main contribution of our paper, the graph edge colouring model. Section 4 concludes and considers future directions for this work.

2   Decomposition Models for Parallel Sparse Matrix–Vector Multiplication

2.1   Preliminaries

Consider a sparse $m \times n$ matrix $\mathbf{A}$. We require that the sparse matrix–vector product $\mathbf{A}\mathbf{x} = \mathbf{b}$ is distributed across p processors, where $\mathbf{x}$ and $\mathbf{b}$ are dense n- and m-vectors respectively. In [19], Vastenhouw and Bisseling note that the natural parallel algorithm, with an arbitrary non-overlapping distribution of the matrix and the vectors across the processors, has the following general form:

1. Each processor sends its components x_j to those processors that possess a non-zero a_{ij} in column j.

2. Each processor computes the products $a_{ij}x_j$ for its non-zeros a_{ij} and adds the results for the same row index i. This yields a set of contributions b_{is}, where s is the processor identifier $1 \leq s \leq p$.
3. Each processor sends its non-zero contributions b_{is} to the processor that is assigned vector element b_i.
4. Each processor adds the contributions received for its components b_i, giving $b_i = \sum_{s=1}^{p} b_{is}$.

In common with other authors (e.g. [19,2]), we assume that the processors synchronize globally between the above phases. The computational requirement of step 2 dominates that of step 4 [19]; henceforth we assume that the computational load of the entire parallel sparse matrix–vector multiplication algorithm can be represented by the computational load induced during step 2 only.

It is noted in [2] that the decomposition of the sparse matrix $\mathbf{A}$ to the p processors may be done in one of the following ways:

1. One-dimensional [4]; entire rows (or columns) of the matrix are allocated to individual processors. This has the effect of making the communication step 3 (or 1 in the column case) in the parallel sparse matrix–vector multiplication pipeline redundant.
2. Two-dimensional Cartesian [6]; each processor receives a submatrix defined by a partition of rows and columns of $\mathbf{A}$.
3. Two-dimensional non-Cartesian with the Mondriaan structure [19]; obtained by recursively bipartitioning the matrix in either the row or column direction.
4. Arbitrary (fine-grained) two-dimensional [5]; each non-zero is assigned individually to a processor. This is the most general decomposition.

The above decompositions of the sparse matrix $\mathbf{A}$ to the p processors are usually modelled as a graph or hypergraph partitioning problem.

2.2 Graph and Hypergraph Partitioning

Given a finite set of m vertices, $V = \{v_1, \ldots, v_m\}$, a hypergraph on V is a set system, here denoted $H(V, \mathcal{E})$, such that $\mathcal{E} \subset \mathcal{P}(V)$, where $\mathcal{P}(V)$ is the power set of V. The set $\mathcal{E} = \{e_1, \ldots, e_n\}$ is said to be the set of hyperedges of the hypergraph. When $\mathcal{E} \subset V^{(2)}$, each hyperedge has cardinality two and the resulting set system is known as a *graph*. Henceforth, definitions are given in terms of hypergraphs (although they also hold for graphs) and whenever we specifically need to distinguish between a graph and a hypergraph, the graph shall be denoted by $G(V, \mathcal{E})$.

A hyperedge $e \in \mathcal{E}$ is said to be incident on a vertex $v \in V$ in a hypergraph $H(V, \mathcal{E})$ if, and only if, $v \in e$. The incidence matrix of a hypergraph $H(V, \mathcal{E})$, $V = \{v_1, \ldots, v_m\}$ and $\mathcal{E} = \{e_1, \ldots, e_n\}$, is the $m \times n$ matrix $\mathbf{M} = (m_{ij})$, with entries

$$m_{ij} = \begin{cases} 1 \text{ if } v_i \in e_j \\ 0 \text{ otherwise} \end{cases} \tag{1}$$

In a hyperedge- and vertex-weighted hypergraph, each hyperedge $e \in \mathcal{E}$ and each vertex $v \in V$ are assigned a scalar weight.

A partition Π of a hypergraph $H(V, \mathcal{E})$ is a finite collection of subsets of V (called parts), such that $P \cap P' = \emptyset$ is true for all $P, P' \in \Pi$ and $\bigcup_i P_i = V$. The weight $w(P)$ of a part $P \in \Pi$ is given by the sum of the constituent vertex weights. Given a real-valued balance criterion $0 < \epsilon < 1$, the k-way hypergraph partitioning problem requires a k-way partition Π that satisfies

$$w(P_i) < (1 + \epsilon)W_{avg} \tag{2}$$

for all $1 \leq i \leq k$ (where $W_{avg} = \sum_{i=1}^{k} w(P_i)/k$) and is such that some partitioning objective function f_p is minimised.

For sparse matrix decomposition problems, the partitioning objective of interest is the $k-1$ metric [4]. Here, each hyperedge $e \in \mathcal{E}$ contributes $(\lambda(e) - 1)w(e)$ to the objective function, where $\lambda(e)$ is the number of parts spanned by, and $w(e)$ the weight of, hyperedge e:

$$f_p(\Pi) = \sum_{e \in \mathcal{E}} (\lambda(e) - 1)w(e) \tag{3}$$

Note that for graph partitioning this reduces to the edge-cut metric, since the cardinality of each edge is two.

2.3   Related Work

In [12], Hendrickson and Kolda outline a bipartite graph partitioning-based model for decomposition of a general rectangular non-symmetric sparse matrix. The non-zero structure of a sparse matrix $\mathbf{A}$ corresponds to an undirected bipartite graph $G(V, \mathcal{E})$. We have $V = \mathcal{R} \cup \mathcal{C}$, such that $\mathcal{R} = \{r_1, \ldots, r_m\}$ and $\mathcal{C} = \{c_1, \ldots, c_n\}$ and $(r_i, c_j) \in \mathcal{E}$ if and only if $a_{ij} \neq 0$. In the row decomposition-based model, the weight of the row vertices $\{v \in \mathcal{R}\}$ is given by the number of non-zeros in each row. The column vertices $\{v \in \mathcal{C}\}$ and the edges have unit weights. The partitioning constraint requires that the total weight of vertices from $\mathcal{R}$ allocated to each processor is approximately the same. It is noted that an exact representation of the communication volume may be given by $\sum_i(\lambda(c_i) - 1)$, where $\lambda(c_i)$ is the number of distinct parts that neighbours of $c_i \in \mathcal{C}$ have been allocated to. The authors chose to approximate this metric with the number of edges cut (and thus approximately model the total communication volume) because of the difficulties in minimising the metric that yields the exact communication volume.

Incidentally, in this work we derive a bipartite graph with the same topological structure; however, we use a different weighting on the vertices so as to model the most general sparse matrix decomposition; further, we correctly quantify the total communication volume using a graph edge colouring metric.

Hypergraph partitioning was first applied in sparse matrix decomposition for parallel sparse matrix–vector multiplication by Çatalyürek and Aykanat in [4]. They proposed a one-dimensional decomposition model for a square non-symmetric sparse matrix; without loss of generality, we here describe the row-based decomposition.

The sparsity pattern of the sparse matrix $\mathbf{A}$ is interpreted as the incidence matrix of a hypergraph $H(V, \mathcal{E})$. The rows of $\mathbf{A}$ are interpreted as the vertices and the columns of $\mathbf{A}$ the hyperedges in H. The weight of vertex $v_i \in V$ (modelling row i in $\mathbf{A}$) is given by the number of non-zero elements in row i. The vector elements x_i and b_i are allocated to the processor that is allocated row i of $\mathbf{A}$. Because the authors assumed a symmetric partitioning of the vectors $\mathbf{x}$ and $\mathbf{b}$ (entries x_i and b_i always allocated to the same processor), in order for the $k - 1$ metric to correctly represent the total communication volume of the parallel sparse matrix–vector multiplication, a "dummy" non-zero a_{ii} is added to the model whenever $a_{ii} = 0$. Note that in general the addition of dummy non-zeros is not necessary. For a general $m \times n$ sparse matrix, provided that the vector component x_i is assigned to a processor allocated a non-zero in column i and the vector component b_j is assigned to a processor allocated a non-zero in row j, the $k - 1$ metric will correctly represent the total communication volume of the parallel sparse matrix–vector multiplication under a one-dimensional decomposition.

In [6], Çatalyürek and Aykanat extend the one-dimensional model to a coarse-grained two-dimensional one. The model yields a cartesian partitioning of the matrix; the rows are partitioned into α sets R_π using the one-dimensional row-based hypergraph partitioning model and the columns are partitioned into β sets C_π using the column-based one-dimensional hypergraph partitioning model. The $p = \alpha\beta$ cartesian products $R_\pi \times C_\pi$ are assigned to processors with the (symmetric) vector distribution given by the distribution of the matrix diagonal.

Vastenhouw and Bisseling [19] propose recursive bipartitioning of the general sparse matrix, alternating between the row and column directions. They show that when partitioning a general sparse matrix, its submatrices can be partitioned independently while still correctly modelling the total communication volume.

In [5], Çatalyürek and Aykanat propose a hypergraph model for the most general sparse matrix decomposition. In this fine-grained model, each $a_{ij} \neq 0$ is modelled by a vertex $v \in V$, so that a p-way partition Π of the hypergraph $H(V, \mathcal{E})$ will correspond to an assignment of the matrix non-zeros to p processors. The causes of communication between processors in steps 1 and 3 of the parallel sparse matrix–vector multiplication pipeline define the hyperedges of the hypergraph model. In step 1, the processor with non-zero a_{ij} requires vector element x_j for computation during step 2. This results in a communication of x_j to the processor assigned a_{ij} if x_j had been assigned to a different processor. The dependence between the non-zeros in column j of the matrix $\mathbf{A}$ and vector element x_j can be modelled by a hyperedge, whose constituent vertices are the non-zeros of column j of the matrix $\mathbf{A}$. Such hyperedges are henceforth called column hyperedges. In [5], a "dummy" non-zero a_{ii} is added to the model if $a_{ii} = 0$, because symmetric partitioning of the vectors $\mathbf{x}$ and $\mathbf{b}$ is used. The construction of hyperedges modelling the communication requirements in step 3 is identical, except that now the communication requirement depends on the partitioning of the vector $\mathbf{b}$. These hyperedges are called row hyperedges. The $k - 1$ metric evaluated on partitions of this hypergraph then correctly models the total communication volume.

This fine-grained two-dimensional model is essentially a generalisation of the one dimensional model (in which either only row or only column hyperedges are present). As previously noted in the case of the one-dimensional decomposition, the addition of dummy non-zeros is also not necessary in the two-dimensional model provided the vector component x_j is assigned to a processor allocated a non-zero in column j and the vector component b_i is assigned to a processor allocated a non-zero in row i.

In [18,2], the problem of vector partitioning is considered with the aim of improving the communication balance and reducing the number of messages sent between the processors, while maintaining the overall communication volume. Provided we are prepared to accept an arbitrary partition of vectors $\mathbf{x}$ and $\mathbf{b}$ across the processors, the problem of vector partitioning is orthogonal to the problem of partitioning the sparse matrix; we know that for any given matrix partition produced by one of the hypergraph partitioning-based decomposition models and the total communication volume given by the $k - 1$ metric, there exists a partition of the vectors $\mathbf{x}$ and $\mathbf{b}$ across the processors that yields the claimed total communication volume. Here we will not explicitly consider the problem of vector partitioning when describing our graph-based model, but note instead that incorporating vector partitioning heuristics within a model for the total communication volume is an area of ongoing research [1].

3   The General Graph Model

In this section, we derive our graph colouring-based model for sparse matrix decomposition. We show that our model yields a bipartite graph, which is in fact the same bipartite graph that results from applying the model of Hendrickson and Kolda [12], described in Section 2.3.

3.1   Graph Model Construction

We note that the transpose of the incidence matrix, $\mathbf{M}^T$, defines the *dual* hypergraph $H^*(V^*, \mathcal{E}^*)$ [3]. Duality is commutative, so that $H(V, \mathcal{E})$ is also the dual of $H^*(V^*, \mathcal{E}^*)$.

The hyperedges in H correspond to vertices in H^* and the vertices in H to the hyperedges in H^*. To see this, let $e_i \in \mathcal{E}$ and $e_j \in \mathcal{E}$ denote the ith and j^{th} hyperedges in H. Then, the ith and j^{th} vertices in the dual hypergraph H^* are connected by a hyperedge $e^* \in \mathcal{E}^*$ only if there exists some vertex $v \in V$ such that $v \in e_i$ and $v \in e_j$. The hyperedge e^* in the dual H^* is in direct correspondence with the vertex v. Let $\delta : V \to \mathcal{E}^*$ denote the (invertible) function that maps the vertices in H to hyperedges in H^*.

Let H denote the hypergraph arising from the most general (fine-grained) sparse matrix decomposition model described in Section 2.3 and consider H^*, its dual. Because each vertex v in V (that represents a non-zero in $\mathbf{A}$) is incident on exactly one row and one column hyperedge, the incidence matrix $\mathbf{M}$ has two non-zeros in each row and thus the incidence matrix of the dual $\mathbf{M}^T$ has exactly two non-zeros in each column. Clearly, the dual hypergraph H^* is then a graph. Moreover, this graph is bipartite. To see this, consider vertices $v^*, w^* \in V^*$ that correspond to row hyperedges in the hypergraph arising from the hypergraph model H. Because the row hyperedges share no common vertices in H, v^* and w^* are not connected. A similar argument using column hyperedges shows that (hyper)edges in H^* only connect vertices corresponding to column hyperedges in H with vertices corresponding to row hyperedges in H. Henceforth, when referring to the dual of the hypergraph arising from the two-dimensional fine-grained model, we will denote it $G(V^*, \mathcal{E}^*)$.

To see that a bipartite graph with the same structure as $G(V^*, \mathcal{E}^*)$ also arises from the model of Hendrickson and Kolda [12], described in Section 2.3, note that the sets of vertices $\mathcal{R}$ and $\mathcal{C}$ in Hendrickson and Kolda's model are the sets of vertices in the dual graph corresponding to row and column hyperedges in the fine-grained hypergraph model. Hendrickson and Kolda partition the set $\mathcal{R}$ across the processors, which corresponds to allocating row hyperedges in the fine-grained hypergraph model to processors. Because row hyperedges in the fine-grained model just define the rows of the sparse matrix $\mathbf{A}$, we can (correctly) deduce that the model of Hendrickson and Kolda is in fact a row-wise one-dimensional sparse matrix decomposition.

3.2   The Communication Cost Metric

Having constructed the bipartite graph model $G(V^*, \mathcal{E}^*)$, we define a communication cost metric that correctly models both the total communication volume and the computational load induced on each processor during the parallel sparse matrix–vector multiplication. We know that the hypergraph partitioning problem with the $k-1$ objective achieves this for the hypergraph model $H(V, \mathcal{E})$ with incidence matrix $\mathbf{M}$.

The weight of each vertex $v^* \in V^*$ is set to the weight of the corresponding hyperedge in H and the weight of each (hyper)edge $e^* \in \mathcal{E}^*$ is set to the weight of the corresponding vertex in V. We seek an edge colouring of G (i.e. an assignment of colours to edges in $\mathcal{E}^*$) using p colours and allowing edges incident on the same vertex to be assigned the same colour. Let $c(e^*)$ denote the colour assigned to edge e^* and let C_i, $1 \le i \le p$ be the colours used. The colouring must satisfy the following constraint (for each $1 \le i \le p$):

$$\sum_{\{e^* \in \mathcal{E}^* \mid c(e^*) = C_i\}} w(e^*) < (1 + \epsilon)W_{avg} \tag{4}$$

where ϵ is the prescribed balance criterion and $W_{avg} = \sum_{e^* \in \mathcal{E}^*} w(e^*)/p$. Because the weight of each edge $e^* \in \mathcal{E}^*$ is set to the weight of the corresponding vertex in V, the total edge-weight allocated a distinct colour exactly corresponds to the computational load induced on the processor represented by that colour (as there are p colours and p processors).

The colouring objective is defined in terms of the number of distinct colours that are "induced" onto each vertex by edges connected to it. An edge $e^* \in \mathcal{E}^*$, assigned the colour C_i, $1 \leq i \leq p$, also induces the colour C_i onto a vertex $v^* \in V^*$ if and only if $v^* \in e^*$. The colouring objective is to minimise the function f_c given by

$$f_c(G) = \sum_{v^* \in V^*} w(v^*)(\sigma(v^*) - 1) \tag{5}$$

where $\sigma(v^*)$ represents the number of distinct colours induced onto vertex v^* by edges incident on it.

Proposition 1. *Minimising the colouring objective in Equation 5 subject to the constraint in Equation 2 is equivalent to minimising the total communication volume of parallel sparse matrix–vector multiplication while maintaining an overall computational load balance across the processors.*

Proof. Since the colouring constraint in Equation 4 is equivalent to maintaining the imbalance in computational load within a (prescribed) factor of ϵ, it remains to show that Equation 5 yields the total communication volume of parallel sparse matrix–vector multiplication. To achieve this, it is enough to show that the colouring objective $f_c(G)$ for the graph G is equivalent to the $k - 1$ hypergraph partitioning objective for (its dual) hypergraph H.

Let $\mathbf{M}$ be the incidence matrix of the hypergraph H, so that $\mathbf{M}^T$ is the incidence matrix of its dual graph G.

Now, consider the computation of the $k - 1$ objective ($f_p(\Pi)$ in Equation 3) on a partition Π of H. In order to compute the sum in Equation 3, we need to traverse the matrix $\mathbf{M}$ column-by-column. To compute $\lambda(e_i)$ for column (hyperedge) e_i, we consider each non-zero in the ith column. The allocation of vertices (rows of $\mathbf{M}$) to parts associates a part (processor) with each non-zero in $\mathbf{M}$ so that $\lambda(e_i)$ is given by the number of distinct parts associated with the non-zeros in column i.

To compute $f_c(G)$, we traverse the matrix $\mathbf{M}^T$ row-by-row. The quantity $\sigma(v_i^*)$ is computed by considering each non-zero in the ith row of $\mathbf{M}^T$, so that $\sigma(v_i^*)$ is given by the number of distinct colours associated with the non-zeros in row i. But this is equivalent to traversing the matrix $\mathbf{M}$ column-by-column and computing the number of distinct colours associated with the non-zeros in column i. To obtain the edge colouring of the graph G that is equivalent to the partition Π (in terms of the total communication volume and computational load across the processors), assign colour C_j to edge e^* whenever the vertex $v = \delta^{-1}(e^*)$ is assigned to part P_j, for all edges $e^* \in \mathcal{E}^*$ ($1 \leq j \leq p$). □

3.3   Worked Example

Consider the sparse matrix shown in Figure 1, and consider a decomposition of this matrix over two processors. A one-dimensional row-wise partitioning based

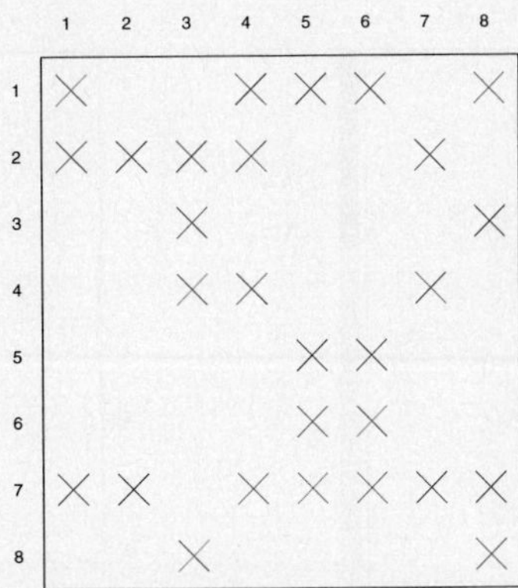

Fig. 1. Sample sparse matrix for decomposition across 2 processors

on a 1D hypergraph model with a 10% balance constraint results in the decomposition shown in Figure 2. Matrix and vector elements assigned to processor 1 are coloured red; those assigned to processor 2 are coloured green. The resulting total communication volume per sparse matrix–vector product is 6, and there is a slight computational load imbalance (15 vs. 13 non-zero matrix elements).

Figure 4 shows our bipartite graph model, with edges coloured so as to minimize the colouring objective of Equation 5 under ideal load balance. The resulting fine-grained sparse matrix decomposition is shown in Figure 3. The resulting total communication volume per sparse matrix–vector product is 3, with no load imbalance. Precisely the same decomposition emerges from a 2D fine-grained hypergraph model based on vertex partitioning.

3.4   A Discussion of the Graph Model

In Section 3.2, we showed that our graph colouring-based model is as expressive as the general fine-grained two-dimensional hypergraph partitioning-based sparse matrix decomposition model. In this section, we briefly discuss possible modifications of existing graph and hypergraph partitioning algorithms to the given graph edge colouring problem and the anticipated advantages over existing hypergraph-based models. Of course, this does not preclude alternative approaches to the edge colouring problem.

The multilevel approach yields algorithms of choice for both graph and hypergraph partitioning [15]. Reduction in complexity of the original problem instance for our graph colouring objective is also possible via the multilevel method.

Consider the coarsening procedure for a graph $G(V^*, \mathcal{E}^*)$. Given vertices $u, v, w \in V^*$ and edges $(u, v), (u, w), (v, w) \in \mathcal{E}^*$, one could match the vertices u and v so that they form a cluster $c = \{u, v\}$ (a vertex in the coarse graph replacing u and v, whose weight is set to the sum of the weights of u and v). Then, the edges (u, w) and (v, w) will be replaced in the coarser graph by the edge (c, w), whose weight is set to be the sum of the weights of the edges (u, w) and (v, w). The edge (u, v) is replaced with the "edge" consisting of only vertex c,

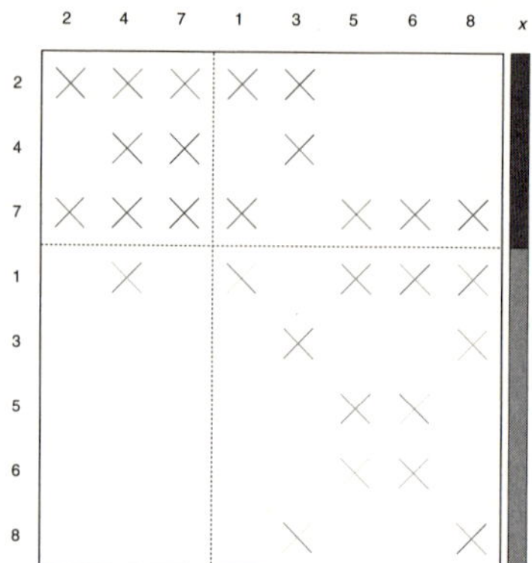

Fig. 2. Row-wise sparse matrix decomposition under 1D hypergraph model

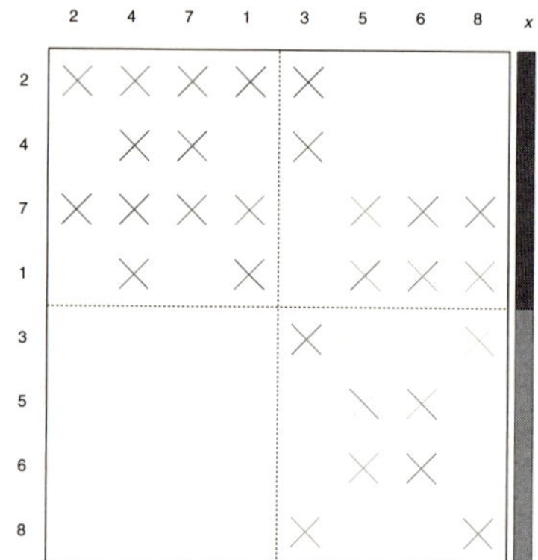

Fig. 3. Fine-grained sparse matrix decomposition under bipartite graph model

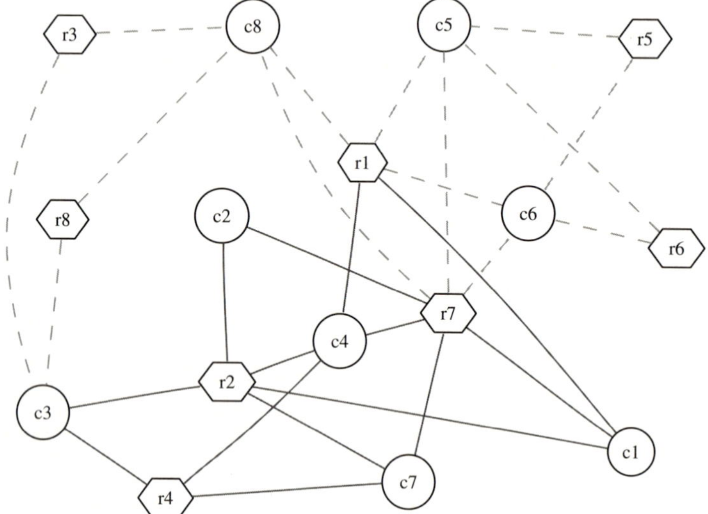

Fig. 4. Bipartite graph model with optimal balanced edge colouring

(c). However, unlike coarsening in the context of partitioning, we cannot discard the edge (c), since the colour assigned to this edge will (potentially) contribute to the colouring objective. We can, though, replace all duplicate edges with a single instance of the edge, setting its weight as the sum of the weights of the duplicate edges. The only difference between the coarse graphs produced by coarsening algorithms in the context of graph partitioning and the graph colouring, respectively, will be the (at most) $|V^*|$ additional singleton edges in the graph colouring case, where V^* is the set of vertices in the coarsest graph. Like uncoarsening in a multilevel partitioning algorithm, a colouring of the coarse graph can be projected onto the finer graph while maintaining the value of the colouring objective. We thus foresee that coarsening algorithms developed for graph partitioning could be applied in the graph colouring context. We also expect that iterative improvement algorithms such as the Fiduccia and Mattheyses algorithm [9] may be applied to our graph colouring problem. Feasible moves are defined as colour changes of edges, such that the overall colouring imbalance satisfies the prescribed constraints (cf. Equation 2).

We foresee two main advantages of the multilevel graph edge colouring algorithms over their multilevel hypergraph partitioning counterparts in the context of sparse matrix decomposition. As graph partitioning algorithms are in general faster than corresponding hypergraph partitioning algorithms, we conjecture than the graph colouring model will yield faster algorithms than the corresponding hypergraph partitioning algorithms. We also anticipate that the graph colouring algorithms will offer significantly more scope for parallelism than the corresponding hypergraph partitioning algorithms. This is attributed to the fact that the cardinalities of hyperedges in a hypergraph may vary from one to an upper bound given by the cardinality of the vertex set, whereas the cardinality of every edge in a graph is two. Indeed, existing parallel multilevel graph partitioning algorithms have demonstrated more natural parallelism than has been hitherto shown for hypergraph partitioning [13,14,20,7,15].

4   Conclusion and Future Work

In this paper we have presented a new graph edge colouring-based model of sparse matrix decomposition for parallel sparse matrix–vector multiplication. Unlike previous graph-based models, our model correctly quantifies the total communication volume of parallel sparse matrix–vector multiplication. Because the edge-colouring algorithms operate on a graph instead of a hypergraph (as the hitherto used partitioning algorithms do), we conjecture that our model will lead to faster sparse matrix decomposition algorithms.

The initial focus of our future work will be an implementation of a multilevel graph edge colouring algorithm in order to empirically evaluate the feasibility of our model and provide a benchmark comparison with respect to existing hypergraph partitioning-based models.

References

1. R.H. Bisseling, January 2006. Personal communication.
2. R.H. Bisseling and W. Meesen. Communication balancing in parallel sparse matrix–vector multiplication. *Electronic Transactions on Numerical Analysis: Special Volume on Combinatorial Scientific Computing*, 21:47–65, 2005.
3. B. Bollobás. *Combinatorics*. Cambridge University Press, 1986.
4. U.V. Çatalyürek and C. Aykanat. Hypergraph Partitioning-based Decomposition for Parallel Sparse–Matrix Vector Multiplication. *IEEE Transactions on Parallel and Distributed Systems*, 10(7):673–693, 1999.

5. U.V. Çatalyürek and C. Aykanat. A fine-grain hypergraph model for 2D decomposition of sparse matrices. In *Proc. 8th International Workshop on Solving Irregularly Structured Problems in Parallel*, San Francisco, USA, April 2001.

6. U.V. Çatalyürek and C. Aykanat. *PaToH: Partitioning Tool for Hypergraphs, Version 3.0*, 2001.

7. K.D. Devine, E.G. Boman, R.T. Heaphy, R.H. Bisseling, and U.V. Çatalyürek. Parallel hypergraph partitioning for scientific computing. In *Proc. 20th IEEE International Parallel and Distributed Processing Symposium*, 2006.

8. K.D. Devine, E.G. Boman, R.T. Heaphy, B.A. Hendrickson, J.D. Teresco, J.Faik, J.E. Flaherty, and L.G. Gervasio. New Challenges in Dynamic Load Balancing. *Applied Numerical Mathematics*, 52(2–3):133–152, 2005.

9. C.M. Fiduccia and R.M. Mattheyses. A Linear Time Heuristic For Improving Network Partitions. In *Proc. 19th IEEE Design Automation Conference*, pages 175–181, 1982.

10. M.R. Garey and D.S. Johnson. *Computers and Intractability: A Guide to the Theory of NP-Completeness*. W.H. Freeman and Co., 1979.

11. B.A. Hendrickson. Graph Partitioning and Parallel Solvers: Has the Emperor No Clothes. In *Proc. Irregular'98*, volume 1457 of *LNCS*, pages 218–225. Springer, 1998.

12. B.A. Hendrickson and T.G. Kolda. Partitioning Rectangular and Structurally Nonsymmetric Sparse Matrices for Parallel Processing. *SIAM Journal of Scientific Computing*, 21(6):248–272, 2000.

13. G. Karypis and V. Kumar. A Fast and High Quality Multilevel Scheme for Partitioning Irregular Graphs. *SIAM Journal on Scientific Computing*, 20(1):359–392, 1999.

14. G. Karypis, K. Schloegel, and V. Kumar. *ParMeTiS: Parallel Graph Partitioning and Sparse Matrix Ordering Library, Version 3.0*. University of Minnesota, 2002.

15. A. Trifunović. *Parallel Algorithms for Hypergraph Partitioning*. PhD thesis, Imperial College London, February 2006.

16. A. Trifunović and W.J. Knottenbelt. A Parallel Algorithm for Multilevel k-way Hypergraph Partitioning. In *Proc. 3rd International Symposium on Parallel and Distributed Computing*, pages 114–121, University College Cork, Ireland, July 2004.

17. A. Trifunović and W.J. Knottenbelt. Towards a Parallel Disk-Based Algorithm for Multilevel k-way Hypergraph Partitioning. In *Proc. 5th Workshop on Parallel and Distributed Scientific and Engineering Computing*, April 2004.

18. B. Uçar and C. Aykanat. Encapsulating Multiple Communication-Cost Metrics in Partitioning Sparse Rectangular Matrices for Parallel Matrix–Vector Multiples. *SIAM Journal on Scientific Computing*, 25(6):1837–1859, 2004.

19. B. Vastenhouw and R.H. Bisseling. A Two-Dimensional Data Distribution Method for Parallel Sparse Matrix–Vector Multiplication. *SIAM Review*, 47(1):67–95, 2005.

20. C. Walshaw, M. Cross, and M. G. Everett. Parallel dynamic graph partitioning for adaptive unstructured meshes. *J. Parallel Distrib. Comput.*, 47(2):102–108, 1997.

Safety of Rollback-Recovery Protocol Maintaining WFR Session Guarantee*

Jerzy Brzeziński, Anna Kobusińska, and Jacek Kobusiński

Institute of Computing Science
Poznań University of Technology, Poland
{Jerzy.Brzezinski, Anna.Kobusinska, Jacek.Kobusinski}@cs.put.poznan.pl

Abstract. This paper addresses a problem of integrating the consistency management of Writes Follow Reads (WFR) session guarantee with recovery mechanisms in distributed mobile systems. To solve such a problem, rollback-recovery protocol rVsWFR, providing WFR consistency model for mobile clients and unreliable servers is proposed. The costs of rollback-recovery in rVsWFR protocol are minimized by exploiting the semantics of clients' operations and the properties of WFR session guarantee. The paper includes the proof of safety property of the presented protocol.

Keywords: fault tolerance, rollback-recovery, large scale system, mobile users, Writes Follow Reads session guarantee.

1 Introduction

Applications in the mobile domain usually tend to be structured as client-server interactions. In many of such applications, clients accessing data are not bound to particular servers but during a session they can switch from one replicated server to another. Due to clients' switching, a new dimension of complexity is added to the problem of replica consistency which should be tackled from the new, clients' perspective. For this reason, *session guarantees* [1], also called *client-centric* consistency models, have been proposed to define required properties of the system observed from clients' point of view. Four session guarantees have been defined: *Read Your Writes* (RYW), *Monotonic Writes* (MW), *Monotonic Reads* (MR) and *Writes Follow Reads* (WFR). RYW expresses the user's expectation not to miss their own modifications performed in the past, MW ensures that the order of writes issued by a single client is preserved, MR ensures that the client's observations of data storage are monotonic, and finally, WFR keeps the track of causal dependencies resulting from the operations issued by a client.

In this paper, we focus our attention on the WFR session guarantee. To illustrate its applications let us consider a distributed system, which consists of two servers that maintain object replicas x and y, and a client that checks the current

---

* This work was supported in part by the State Committee for Scientific Research (KBN), Poland, under grant KBN 3 T11C 073 28.

A. Levi et al. (Eds.): ISCIS 2006, LNCS 4263, pp. 825–833, 2006.

value of replica x and, depending on that value, writes 1 or 0 into replica y. The request of reading the value of the replica x issued by the client is obtained and performed by server S_1. After completing the read operation at server S_1, the client decides to switch to another server S_2 (due to connection problems with S_1 for example). As a result, the final value of replica y at server S_2 may not be consistent with local replica of x, i.e. it can be set to 0 if $x > 0$, because the value of x was checked at another server. The use of WFR will guarantee that, before performing the write on y, the state of x will be updated.

WFR session guarantee is provided by appropriate consistency protocols [1, 2]. These protocols should provide it despite servers' failures in order to meet the increased reliability requirements of distributed mobile systems. Unfortunately, as far as we know, none of the proposed consistency protocols preserving WFR is fault-tolerant [3]. Therefore, this paper addresses a problem of integrating the consistency management of WFR session guarantee in distributed mobile systems, with recovery mechanisms [4, 5, 6, 7].

To solve such a problem, we introduce rVsWFR protocol, integrating logging and checkpointing techniques with coherence operations of previously proposed VsSG consistency protocol [2, 3]. Consequently, the proposed protocol offers a way to overcome servers' failures transparently to the client, at the same time preserving WFR session guarantee . The rVsWFR protocol is optimized in terms of checkpointing overhead, taking into account the specific requirements of WFR session guarantee. Moreover, correctness analysis of the protocol is carried out and its safety property is formally proved.

2   Related Work

Session guarantees have been introduced in the context of Bayou replicated storage system [1] to allow mobile clients to implicitly define sets of writes that must be performed by servers. Since in Bayou, each server's state is maintained in the database, adding a persistent and crash resisting log is enough to provide fault–tolerance in the case of server's failure. CASCADE — a caching service for distributed CORBA objects [8] is another system using consistency conditions based on session guarantees. In CASCADE, it is assumed that processes do not crash during the execution and all communication links are eventually operational. The Globe system [9] follows the approach similar to CASCADE, by providing a flexible framework for associating various replication coherence models with distributed objects. Among the coherence models supported by Globe are also client-based models, although they are combined with object-based consistency models in a single framework. Session guarantees are also provided in OceanStore [10], a global persistent data store, which provides a consistent, highly-available, and durable storage utility atop an infrastructure comprised of untrusted servers. Finally, Pastis — a highly scable, multi-user, peer-to-peer file system [11] implements a consistency model based on RYW session guarantee. In Pastis, it is assumed that at least one replica is not faulty and all users allowed to write to a given file trust one another regarding the update of that file.

3   System Model, Definitions and Notations

Throughout this paper, a large scale replicated distributed storage system is considered. The system consists of a number of unreliable *servers* holding a full copy of *shared objects* and *clients* running applications that access these objects. The storage replicated by servers does not imply any particular data model or organization. Clients are mobile, i.e. they can switch from one server to another during application execution. To access shared object, clients select a single server and send a direct request to this server. Operations are issued by clients synchronously, and are basically divided into *reads* and *writes*, denoted respectively by r and w. The server, which first obtains a write from a client, is responsible for assigning it a globally unique identifier. Clients can concurrently submit conflicting writes at different servers, e.g. writes that modify the overlapping parts of data storage. Operations on shared objects issued by client C_i are ordered by relation $\overset{C_i}{\rightarrow}$ called *client issue order*. Server S_j performs operations in an order represented by relation $\overset{S_j}{\rightarrowtail}$.

In the paper, it is assumed that clients perceive the data from the replicated storage according to *Writes Follow Reads* session guarantee. To meet the requirements of WFR, a server should update its state by performing all writes that have influenced all previous reads of the client, before performing a new write issued by this client . Formal definition of WFR is based on the notion of *relevant writes*, denoted by $RW(r)$, which represents a set of writes that have influenced the current state of objects observed by read r [3]. Formally, Writes Follow Reads session guarantee is defined as follows [3]:

Definition 1. *Writes Follow Reads (WFR) session guarantee is a property meaning that:*

$$\forall C_i \, \forall S_j \left[r \overset{C_i}{\rightarrow} w|_{S_j} \implies \forall w_k \in RW(r) : w_k \overset{S_j}{\rightarrowtail} w \right]$$

Data consistency in rVsWFR protocol is managed by VsSG *consistency protocol* [2] which uses a concept of server-based version vectors, having the following form: $V_{S_j} = \begin{bmatrix} v_1 \, v_2 \, ... \, v_{N_S} \end{bmatrix}$, where N_S is a total number of servers in the system, and single position v_i is the number of writes performed by server S_j. Every write in VsSG protocol is labeled with a *vector timestamp*, set to the current value of vector clock V_{S_j} of server S_j, performing the write for the first time. The vector timestamp of write w is returned by function $T : \mathcal{O} \mapsto V$. All the writes performed by the server in the past are kept in set $\mathcal{O}_{S_j}$. Moreover, identifiers of clients from whom S_j has received read requests are stored in set CR_{S_j}. For each client C_i, the number of writes relevant to reads issued by C_i is kept in $RW_{S_j}[i]$. On the client's side, vector W_{C_i} representing writes issued by this client is maintained. The sequence of past writes is called *history*. A formal definition of history is given below:

Definition 2. *A history H_{S_j} at time moment t, is a linearly ordered set $\left(\mathcal{O}_{S_j}, \overset{S_j}{\rightarrowtail} \right)$, where $\mathcal{O}_{S_j}$ is a set of writes performed by server S_j, till the time t and relation $\overset{S_j}{\rightarrowtail}$ represents an execution order of writes.*

The VsSG protocol eventually propagates all writes to all servers. During the synchronization of servers, their histories are *concatenated*. The concatenation of histories H_{S_j} and H_{S_k}, denoted by $H_{S_j} \oplus H_{S_k}$, consists in adding new operations from H_{S_k} at the end of H_{S_j}, at the same time preserving the appropriate relations [2].

In the paper, we assume the *crash-recovery* model of failures, i.e. servers may crash and recover after crashing a finite number of times [12]. Servers can fail at arbitrary moments and any such a failure is required to be eventually detected. Below, we propose formal definitions of fault-tolerance mechanisms used by rVsWFR protocol:

Definition 3. *Log Log_{S_j} is a set of triples:*

$$\left\{ \langle i_1, o_1, T(o_1) \rangle \ \langle i_2, o_2, T(o_2) \rangle \ ... \ \langle i_n, o_n, T(o_n) \rangle \right\},$$

where i_n represents the identifier of the client issuing a write operation $o_n \in \mathcal{O}_{S_j}$ and $T(o_n)$ is timestamp of o_n.

During a rollback-recovery procedure, operations from the log are executed according to their timestamps, from the earliest to the latest one.

Definition 4. *Checkpoint $Ckpt_{S_j}$ is a couple $\langle V_{S_j}, H_{S_j} \rangle$, of version vector V_{S_j} and history H_{S_j} maintained by server S_j at time t, where t is a moment of taking a checkpoint.*

In this paper, we assume that log and checkpoint are saved by the server in the stable storage, able to survive all failures [4]. Additionally, we assume that the newly taken checkpoint replaces the previous one, so just one checkpoint for each server is kept in the stable storage.

4   The rVsWFR Protocol

The VsSG consistency protocol assumes that servers are reliable, i.e. they do not crash. Such assumption might be consider not plausible and too strong for certain mobile distributed systems. Therefore, the rVsWFR protocol, which equips the VsSG protocol with fault-tolerance mechanisms, has been proposed.

For every client C_i executing write w, results of all the writes relevant to read r issued by C_i and preceding w in client's issue order, cannot be lost, if WFR is to be preserved. On the other hand, results of all the writes that have modified the state of the server observed by read r are not essential for preserving WFR, until read r is not followed by write issued by the same client.

Upon sending a request $\langle o \rangle$
to server S_j **at client** C_i

1: $W \leftarrow \mathbf{0}$
2: **if** iswrite(o) **then**
3:     $W \leftarrow \max(W, R_{C_i})$
4: **end if**
5: send $\langle o, W, i \rangle$ to S_j

Upon receiving a request $\langle o, W, i \rangle$
from client C_i **at server** S_j

6: **while** $\left(V_{S_j} \not\geq W\right)$ **do**
7:    wait()
8: **end while**
9: **if** iswrite(o) **then**
10:     $V_{S_j}[j] \leftarrow V_{S_j}[j] + 1$
11:     timestamp o with V_{S_j}
12:     $Log_{S_j} \leftarrow Log_{S_j} \cup \langle i, o, T(o) \rangle$
13:     perform o and store results in res
14:     $H_{S_j} \leftarrow H_{S_j} \oplus \{o\}$
15:     $nWrites \leftarrow nWrites + 1$
16:     **if** $i \in CR_{S_j}$ **then**
17:         **if** $(RW_{S_j}[i] > 0)$ **then**
18:             $Ckpt_{S_j} \leftarrow \langle V_{S_j}, H_{S_j} \rangle$
19:             $Log_{S_j} \leftarrow \emptyset$
20:             $CR_{S_j} \leftarrow \emptyset$
21:             $nWrites \leftarrow 0$
22:             $RW_{S_j} \leftarrow \mathbf{0}$
23:         **end if**
24:     **end if**
25: **end if**
26: **if not** iswrite(o) **then**
27:     **if** $i \notin CR_{S_j}$ **then**
28:         $CR_{S_j} \leftarrow CR_{S_j} \cup i$
29:     **end if**
30:     $RW_{S_j}[i] \leftarrow nWrites$
31:     perform o and store results in res
32: **end if**
33: send $\langle o, res, V_{S_j} \rangle$ to C_i

Upon receiving a reply $\langle o, res, W \rangle$
from server S_j **at client** C_i

34: **if** iswrite(o) **then**
35:     $W_{C_i} \leftarrow \max(W_{C_i}, W)$
36: **else**
37:     $R_{C_i} \leftarrow \max(R_{C_i}, W)$
38: **end if**
39: deliver $\langle res \rangle$

Every Δt **at server** S_j

40: **foreach** $S_k \neq S_j$ **do**
41:     send $\langle S_j, H_{S_j} \rangle$ to S_k
42: **end for**

Upon receiving an update $\langle S_k, H \rangle$
at server S_j

43: **foreach** $w_i \in H$ **do**
44:     **if** $V_{S_j} \not\geq T(w_i)$ **then**
45:         perform w_i
46:         $V_{S_j} \leftarrow \max(V_{S_j}, T(w_i))$
47:         $H_{S_j} \leftarrow H_{S_j} \oplus \{w_i\}$
48:     **end if**
49: **end for**
50: signal()

On rollback-recovery
51: $\langle V_{S_j}, H_{S_j} \rangle \leftarrow Ckpt_{S_j}$
52: $Log'_{S_j} \leftarrow Log_{S_j}$
53: **foreach** $o'_j \in Log'_{S_j}$ **do**
54:     **choose** $\langle i', o'_i, T(o'_i) \rangle$ **with minimal** $T(o'_j)$ **from** Log'_{S_j} **where** $T(o'_j) > V_{S_j}$
55:     $V_{S_j}[j] \leftarrow V_{S_j}[j] + 1$
56:     perform o'_j
57:     $H_{S_j} \leftarrow H_{S_j} \oplus \{o'_j\}$
58:     $nWrites \leftarrow nWrites + 1$
59: **end for**

Fig. 1. Checkpointing and rollback-recovery rVsWFR protocol

Unfortunately, at the moment of performing the operation, the server does not possess the knowledge, whether in the future a client will issue a write request, or not. Therefore, to preserve WFR, rVsWFR protocol must ensure that results of all writes issued by the client are not lost in the case of server's failure and its recovery. It is performed by logging in the stable storage the operation issued by a client and its timestamp. Additionally, the server state is checkpointed occasionally to bound the length of a message log. Logging and checkpointing operations are integrated with operations of VsSG consistency protocol.

The server, which obtains the write request directly from client C_i, logs the request to stable storage (Fig. 1, l. 12) if it fulfills WFR (l. 6)[2]. It is important that logging of write takes place before performing this request (l. 13). Such an order is crucial, as the operation, which is performed but not logged, may be lost in the case of subsequent failures. The moment of taking a checkpoint is determined by obtaining a write request which follows a read one, issued by the same client and observing the modified server's state. (l. 18). Saving the state of server earlier is excessive, as when read request is not followed by a write one (l. 16) or there are no writes relevant to such a read (l. 17), WFR is not violated. Essential is the fact, that firstly the checkpoint is taken, and only afterwards, the content of log Log_{S_j} is cleared. (l. 19).

After a failure occurrence, a failed server restarts from the latest checkpoint (l. 51) and replays operations from the log (l. 53-59) according to their timestamps, from the earliest to the latest one. Writes received from other servers during update procedure (l. 43-47) are lost in the result of failure occurrence. However, by assumption, such writes are saved in the stable storage (in the log or in the checkpoint) of servers that received them directly from clients. Hence, lost writes will be obtained again in consecutive synchronizations.

5   Safety of rVsWFR Protocol

Lemma 1. *Every write operation w issued by client C_i and performed by server S_j that received w directly from client C_i, is kept in checkpoint $Ckpt_{S_j}$ or in log Log_{S_j}.*

Proof. Let us consider write operation w issued by client C_i and obtained by server S_j. From the algorithm:

1. Server S_j, before performing the request w, adds it to log Log_{S_j} (l. 12). Since logging of w takes place before performing it (l. 13), then, even in the case of failure, operation w remains in the log.
2. Clearing log Log_{S_j} (l. 19) is made after the checkpoint is taken (l. 18). Therefore, the server failure, which occurs after clearing the log, does not affect safety of the algorithm because writes from the log are already stored in the checkpoint.
3. After the checkpoint is taken but before the log is cleared (between lines 18 -19), the writes issued by client C_i and performed by server S_j are stored in both the checkpoint $Ckpt_{S_j}$ and the log Log_{S_j}.

Lemma 2. *The rollback-recovery procedure recovers all write operations issued by clients and performed by server S_j that were logged in log Log_{S_j} at the moment of server S_j failure.*

Proof. Let us assume that server S_j fails. After the failure, operations from the log are recovered (l. 53) and cause the update of vector V_{S_j} (l. 55). Afterwards, they are performed by S_j (l. 56) and added to history H_{S_j}(l. 57). Assume now, that failures occur during the recovery procedure. Due to such failures, the results of operations that have already been recovered are lost again. However, since log Log_{S_j} is cleared (l. 19) only after the checkpoint is taken (l. 18) and it is not modified during the rollback-recovery procedure (l. 52), the log's content is not changed. Hence, the recovery procedure can be started from the beginning without loss of any operation issued by clients and performed by server S_j after the moment of taking checkpoint.

Lemma 3. *Operations required by WFR and obtained during synchronization with other servers, after recovery of S_j, are performed again before new writes from a client are applied.*

Proof. By contradiction, let us assume that server S_j has performed a new write operation w_2, obtained from client C_i, before performing operation w_1 again, received during a former synchronization and lost because of S_j failure. Further, assume that results of w_1 are observed by read operation r, issued by client C_i before w_2. According to VsSG protocol [2], while executing w_2 the condition $V_{S_j} \geq R_{C_i}$ is fulfilled (l. 6) .

Assume further, that w_1 issued by C_i before w_2, is performed by server S_k. Server S_j, in the result of synchronization with S_k, performs w_1 and updates its version vector, modifying V_{S_j} at least in the position k (l. 46). Such a modified vector is sent by S_j to client C_i in reply to read r issued by C_i. At the client's side, the obtained reply modifies vector R_{C_i}, at least in position $k : R_{C_i} \leftarrow \max(R_{C_i}, W)$ (l. 37). However, if the failure of S_j occurs, the state of S_j is recovered accordingly to values stored in $Ckpt_{S_j}$ (l. 51) and in Log_{S_j} (l. 53-59). While recovering operations from the log, the vector V_{S_j} is updated only in position j. Thus, the recovered value of $V_{S_j}[k]$ does not reflect the information on w_1. Hence, until the next update message is obtained, $V_{S_j}[k] < R_{C_i}[k]$, which contradicts the assumption.

Lemma 4. *The server performs new write operation issued by a client only after all writes performed before the failure are recovered.*

Proof. By contradiction, let us assume that there is a write operation w performed by server S_j before its failure, which results have been observed by read operation r issued by client C_i. Further, assume that w has not been recovered yet, and that the server has performed a new write operation obtained from C_i. According to underlying VsSG protocol [2] for server S_j that performs the new write operation, the condition $V_{S_j} \geq R_{C_i}$ is fulfilled (l. 6).

The receipt of write w issued by a client causes the update of a server version vector: $V_{S_j}[j] \leftarrow V_{S_j}[j] + 1$ and results in timestamping w with the unique identifier (l. 11). The reply to read request r that observes the result of w, contains the modified vector V_{S_j} (l. 33). On the client's side, the receipt of reply modifies vector R_{C_i}: $R_{C_i} \leftarrow \max(R_{C_i}, W)$ (l. 37). As the result, R_{C_i} is updated at least in position j: $R_{C_i}[j] \leftarrow j + 1$. If there is write operation w performed by server S_j before the failure that has not been recovered yet, then $V_{S_j}[j] <$

$R_{C_i}[j]$, which follows from the ordering of recovered operations (l. 54). This is a contradiction to $V_{S_j} \geq R_{C_i}$. Hence, the new write operation cannot be performed until all the previous writes relevant to read issued by a client are recovered.

Theorem 1. *WFR session guarantee is preserved by rVsWFR protocol for clients requesting it, even in the presence of server failures.*

Proof. It has been proved in [2] that when none of servers fails, WFR session guarantee holds .

In rVsWFR protocol every write operation performed by server S_j is saved in the checkpoint or in the log (Lemma 1). After the server failure, all operations from the checkpoint and the log are recovered (Lemma 2). All recovered write operations are applied before new writes issued by the client are performed (Lemma 4). The operations obtained by S_j during synchronization procedure, which are lost because of S_j failure, are also performed once again before new writes from C_i (Lemma 3). Hence, for any client C_i and any server S_j, WFR session guarantee is preserved by the rollback–recovery rVsWFR protocol, despite server failures.

6   Conclusions

This paper has dealt with the problem of integrating the consistency management of distributed systems with mobile clients with the recovery mechanisms. To solve such a problem, the rollback-recovery protocol rVsWFR, preserving WFR session guarantee has been proposed and its correctness in terms of safety has been formally proved.

The proposed protocol takes advantage of the known rollback-recovery techniques like logging and checkpointing. However, while applying these techniques, the semantics of operations is taken into account. Consequently, in rVsWFR protocol, only the operations essential to provide WFR are logged, so checkpoints are optimized with respect to WFR session guarantee requirements.

Our future work encompasses the development of rollback-recovery protocols which preserve other session guarantees. Moreover, to evaluate the overhead of rVsWFR protocol quantitatively, appropriate simulation experiments will be carried out.

References

1. Terry, D.B., Demers, A.J., Petersen, K., Spreitzer, M., Theimer, M., Welch, B.W.: Session guarantees for weakly consistent replicated data. In: Proc. of the Third Int. Conf. on Parallel and Distributed Information Systems (PDIS 94), Austin, USA, IEEE Computer Society (1994) 140–149
2. Brzeziński, J., Sobaniec, C., Wawrzyniak, D.: Safety of a server-based version vector protocol implementing session guarantees. In: Proc. of Int. Conf. on Computational Science (ICCS2005), LNCS 3516, Atlanta, USA (2005) 423–430

3. Sobaniec, C.: Consistency Protocols of Session Guarantees in Distributed Mobile Systems. PhD thesis, Institute of Computing Science, Poznan University of Technology (2005)
4. Elmootazbellah, N., Elnozahy, Lorenzo, A., Wang, Y.M., Johnson, D.: A survey of rollback-recovery protocols in message-passing systems. ACM Computing Surveys **34** (2002) 375–408
5. Pradhan, D., P.Krishna, Vaidya, N.: Recovery in mobile environments: Design and trade-off analysis. Proc. of the 26th International Symposium on Fault-Tolerant Computing (1996) 16–25
6. Tanaka, K., Higaki, H., Takizawa, M.: Object-based checkpoints in distributed systems. Journal of computer system science and Engineering **13** (1998) 125–131
7. Brzeziński, J., Szychowiak, M.: An extended coherence protocol for recoverable dsm systems with causal consistency. Proceedings of the International Conference on Computational Science **LNCS 3037** (2004) 475–482
8. Chockler, G., Dolev, D., Friedman, R., Vitenberg, R.: Implementing a caching service for distributed CORBA objects. In: Proc. of Middleware 2000: IFIP/ACM Int. Conf. on Distributed Systems Platforms. (2000) 1–23
9. Kermarrec, A.M., Kuz, I., van Steen, M., Tanenbaum, A.S.: A framework for consistent, replicated Web objects. In: Proc. of the 18th Int. Conf. on Distributed Computing Systems (ICDCS). (1998)
10. Kubiatowicz, J., Bindel, D., Chen, Y., Czerwinski, S., Eaton, P., Geels, D., Gummadi, R., Rhea, S., Weatherspoon, H., Weimer, W., Wells, C., Zhao, B.: Oceanstore: An architecture for global-scale persistent storage. Proceedings of the 9th International Conference on Architectural Support for Programming Languages and Operating Systems (ASPLOS 2000) (2000)
11. Picconi, F., Busca, J.M., Sens, P.: Pastis: a highly-scalable multi-user peer-to-peer file system. EuroPar 2005 (2005) 1173–1182
12. Guerraoui, R., Rodrigues, L.: Introduction to distributed algorithms. Springer-Verlag (2004)

3-D Parallel Implementation of the Wave-Equation PML Algorithm Using Distributed System

Oyku Akaydin and Omar Ramadan

Department of Computer Engineering, Eastern Mediterranean University, Gazimagusa,
Mersin 10, Turkey
{oyku.akaydin, omar.ramadan}@emu.edu.tr

Abstract. This paper describes an implementation of the three-dimensional
(3-D) parallel algorithm for the wave-equation perfectly matched layer (WE-
PML) formulations. The parallel approach is based on domain decomposition
technique, and uses the Message Passing Interface (MPI) system. To simplify
the parallelization strategy, two-dimensional Cartesian topology and derived
data types of MPI are used. The performance of the parallel algorithm has been
studied using distributed computing method, and performed on a network of
PCs interconnected with Ethernet. A speedup factor of 12.9 has been achieved
on the 16 PCs system, as compared to one PC case, for a large size problem.

Keywords: Wave-equation, perfectly matched layer, parallelizing, Message
Passing Interface, interprocess communication, process topology.

1 Introduction

The Finite-Difference Time-Domain (FDTD) [1] is one of the most widely used
numerical method for solving electromagnetic problems [2]. The main advantage of
the FDTD method is that it is a straightforward solution of the six-coupled field
components of the Maxwell's curl equations. This method computes the electric and
the magnetic field components by discretizing the Maxwell's curl equations both in
time and space, and then solving the discretized equations in a time marching
sequence by alternatively calculating the electric and magnetic fields in the
computational domain.

In a linear, homogeneous, isotropic and lossless medium, the normalized
Maxwell's equations can be written in the frequency domain as

$$c\nabla \times \mathbf{E} = -j\omega\mathbf{H} \tag{1}$$

$$c\nabla \times \mathbf{H} = j\omega\mathbf{E} \tag{2}$$

where E and H are, respectively, the electric and the magnetic field vectors and c is
the speed of light. Equations (1) and (2) can be decomposed into a system of six first
order scalar differential equations in terms of E_x, E_y, E_z, H_x, H_y, and H_z fields. For
example, E_z can be written as

A. Levi et al. (Eds.): ISCIS 2006, LNCS 4263, pp. 834–843, 2006.
© Springer-Verlag Berlin Heidelberg 2006

$$\frac{\partial E_z}{\partial t} = c \left(\frac{\partial H_y}{\partial x} - \frac{\partial H_x}{\partial y} \right) \tag{3}$$

Applying central-difference in both space and time to (3), E_z can be computed at the (i, j, k) cell as

$$E_{z_{i,j,k}}^{n+1} = E_{z_{i,j,k}}^{n} + \frac{c\Delta t}{\Delta} \left(H_{y_{i,j,k}}^{n+1/2} - H_{y_{i-1,j,k}}^{n+1/2} - H_{x_{i,j,k}}^{n+1/2} + H_{x_{i,j-1,k}}^{n+1/2} \right) \tag{4}$$

where Δt is the time step size and $\Delta = \Delta x = \Delta y = \Delta z$ is the space cell size in the $x-$, $y-$, and $z-$ directions.

Wave-equation FDTD (WE-FDTD) method is another FDTD algorithm, and it is introduced for solving the scalar Helmholtz wave-equation in source-free domains [3]. Unlike the FDTD, the WE-FDTD allows computing any single field component without the necessity of computing the other field components.

For large problems, the domain size becomes large, and the solution of these problems requires large computational time and memory storage. The key solution to overcome this challenge requires parallel implementations. Different techniques have been introduced for the parallel implementation of the FDTD method [4]-[6].

When the FDTD or the WE-FDTD methods are used for modelling open region problems, suitable Absorbing Boundary Conditions (ABCs) are needed at the outer domain in order to truncate the computational domain. Perfectly matched layer (PML) formulations have been introduced for truncating the FDTD domains [7]. In this approach, all field components and additional auxiliary variables are needed to be computed. Recently, new PML formulations have been introduced for truncating the WE-FDTD domains [8]. This new PML, named as the wave-equation PML (WE-PML), allows computing any single field component without the necessity of computing the other field components. Hence, significant savings in the computational time and memory storage requirements can be achieved.

In this paper, the performance of the parallel WE-PML algorithm has been studied for a three-dimensional (3-D) domain. In this algorithm, the computational domain is divided into subdomains using two-dimensional topology, and each subdomain is assigned to one process. Numerical simulations of this algorithm have been carried out on a network of PCs using the Message Passing Interface (MPI) [9], [10] as the message passing system.

The paper is organized as follows. In section 2, the formulations of the WE-PML algorithm are presented. In section 3, the parallelization technique using the MPI system is described. Section 4 includes the simulation results of the parallel algorithm. Finally, a summary and conclusions are included in section 5.

2 Wave Equation PML Formulations

Using the stretched coordinate PML formulations [11], the frequency domain modified Maxwell's equations in the PML region can be written as

$$c\nabla_s \times \mathbf{E} = -j\omega\mathbf{H} \tag{5}$$

$$c\nabla_s \times \mathbf{H} = j\omega\mathbf{E} \tag{6}$$

where

$$\nabla_s = \sum \hat{a}_\eta \frac{1}{S_\eta} \frac{\partial}{\partial \eta} \tag{7}$$

where S_η, ($\eta = x, y, z$), is the PML stretched coordinate variables defined as [11]

$$S_\eta = 1 + \frac{\sigma_\eta}{j\omega\varepsilon_o} \tag{8}$$

where σ_η is the conductivity profile in the PML region along the η-direction. Assuming a source free PML region, i. e., $\nabla_s.\mathbf{E} = \mathbf{0}$, (5) and (6) can be written in terms of the E_z field component, as an example, as [8]

$$\frac{1}{c^2}(j\omega)^2 E_z = \sum_{\eta=x,y,z} \frac{j\omega}{j\omega+\sigma_\eta/\varepsilon_o} \frac{\partial}{\partial \eta} \frac{j\omega}{j\omega+\sigma_\eta/\varepsilon_o} \frac{\partial}{\partial \eta} E_z \tag{9}$$

Equation (9) represents the modified Helmholtz wave equation in the PML region. It should be pointed out that (9) can be applied in the non-PML region, i. e., in the inner WE-FDTD computational domain, by setting only σ_η, ($\eta = x, y, z$), to zero. Using the relation $j\omega \to \partial/\partial t$, (9) can be written in the time domain as

$$\frac{1}{c^2}\frac{\partial}{\partial t} E_z = \frac{\partial}{\partial t} \sum_{\eta=x,y,z} F_{zx} \tag{10}$$

where the variables $F_{z\eta}$, ($\eta = x, y$ or z), are given by

$$\frac{\partial}{\partial t} F_{z\eta} + \sigma_\eta/\varepsilon_o F_{z\eta} = \frac{\partial}{\partial \eta} P_{z\eta} \tag{11}$$

$$\frac{\partial}{\partial t} P_{z\eta} + \sigma_\eta/\varepsilon_o P_{z\eta} = \frac{\partial}{\partial \eta} E_z \tag{12}$$

Using Yee's FDTD algorithm [2], (10) can be discretized as,

$$E_{z_{i,j,k}}^{n+1} = E_{z_{i,j,k}}^{n} + \sum_{\eta=x,y,z} \left(F_{z\eta_{i,j,k}}^{n+1} - F_{z\eta_{i,j,k}}^{n} \right) \tag{13}$$

where the auxiliary variables $F_{z\eta_{i,j,k}}^{n+1}$, ($\eta = x, y, z$), are obtained by discretizing (11) and (12). As an example, F_{zx} and P_{zx} can be updated [8] as

$$F_{zx_{i,j,k}}^{n+1} = g_{zx1}(i) F_{zx_{i,j,k}}^{n} + g_{zx2}(i) \left(P_{zx_{i,j,k}}^{n+1} - P_{zx_{i-1,j,k}}^{n+1} \right) \tag{14}$$

$$P_{zx_{i,j,k}}^{n+1} = g_{zx1}(i+1/2) P_{zx_{i,j,k}}^{n} + g_{zx2}(i+1/2) \left(E_{z_{i+1,j,k}}^{n+1} - E_{z_{i-1,j,k}}^{n+1} \right) \tag{15}$$

where

$$g_{zx1}(i) = \frac{1-\alpha_x(i)}{1+\alpha_x(i)}, \, g_{zx2}(i) = \frac{c\,\Delta t/\Delta}{1+\alpha_x(i)}, \, \text{ for } \alpha_x(i) = \frac{\Delta t \sigma_x(i)}{2\varepsilon_o} \tag{16}$$

In the same manner, $F_{z\eta_{i,j,k}}^{n+1}$, $(\eta = y, z)$, can be obtained from (11) and (12) [8].

3   Parallelizing the WE-PML Algorithm Using the MPI

To parallelize the WE-PML algorithm, domain decomposition is used to distribute the computations among the processes, and communication between the processes is performed using the MPI system. Having N processes, 3-D computational domain is divided into N subdomains of almost equal size, and each subdomain is assigned to one process.

In MPI, a set of N processes which take part in communication event is represented by a communicator where each process is assigned a rank between 0 and N-1. Processes in the communicator are arranged in topological patterns. A topology describes the preferred communication pattern for the processes in the communicator and provides a mechanism for naming the processes in a way that fits the communication better. Topologies are useful for applications with specific communication patterns that match the topology structure.

3.1   Creation of Cartesian Topology

A Cartesian topology has a grid like structure which is defined by the number of dimensions and the number of processes in each dimension. Each process in the Cartesian topology is connected to its neighbors in the grid, and communication is performed among the processes at neighboring grid points. A Cartesian topology is suitable for an application which requires 4-way nearest neighbor communications for a grid based data.

In this parallel algorithm, the computational domain, defined as a Cartesian grid, is divided into subdomains using two-dimensional topology along the x– and y– directions, as shown in Fig. 1. No division is done along the z– direction. Hence, the algorithm requires 4-way nearest neighbor communications, left-right and up-down communications. In order to facilitate the distribution of the subdomains and the communication between neighboring processes the Cartesian topology facility of MPI is used.

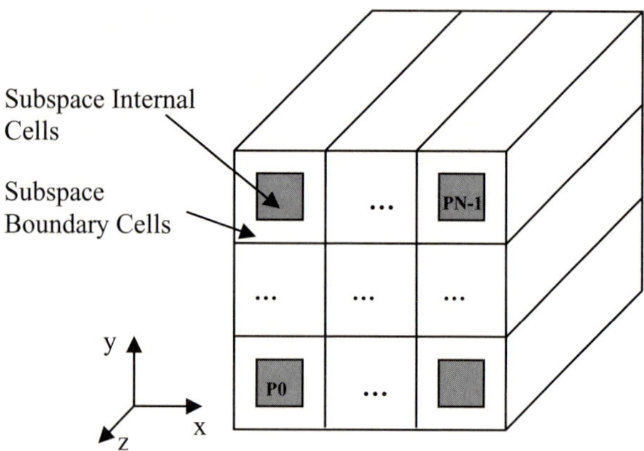

Fig. 1. Computational domain partitioning using two-dimensional topology

The two-dimensional Cartesian topology of processes is created by the following function:

MPI_Cart_create(MPI_COMM_WORLD,ndims,dims,periods,reorder,&comm_cart)

where

MPI_COMM_WORLD	: default communicator
ndims = 2	: # of dimensions of Cartesian topology
dims(0:1)	: number of processes in each dimension
periods(0:1) = 0	: whether the dimension is periodic (1) or not (0)
reorder = 0	: whether the ranking is reordered or not
comm_cart	: new communicator with the Cartesian topology associated

After the topology has been created, to determine the process information in Cartesian topology the following functions are used:

MPI_Comm_rank(comm_cart,&procidcart)
MPI_Cart_coords(comm_cart,procidcart,ndims,proccoord)
MPI_Cart_shift(comm_cart,rightleft,right,&left_n &right_n)
MPI_Cart_shift(comm_cart,updown,up,&down_n,&up_n)

where, within *comm_cart*, processes find about their new rank numbers, their Cartesian coordinates, and their nearest neighbours at left, right, up, and down.

3.2 Communication Using Derived Data Types

To calculate F_{zx}, F_{zy}, P_{zx}, and P_{zy} at the subdomain boundaries, data from the neighboring subdomains are needed. Fig. 2 shows the complete data to be exchanged at the boundaries of a subdomain for two-dimensional topology. It should be pointed out that the left-right communications operate on the y-z surface, and the up-down communications operate on the x-z surface.

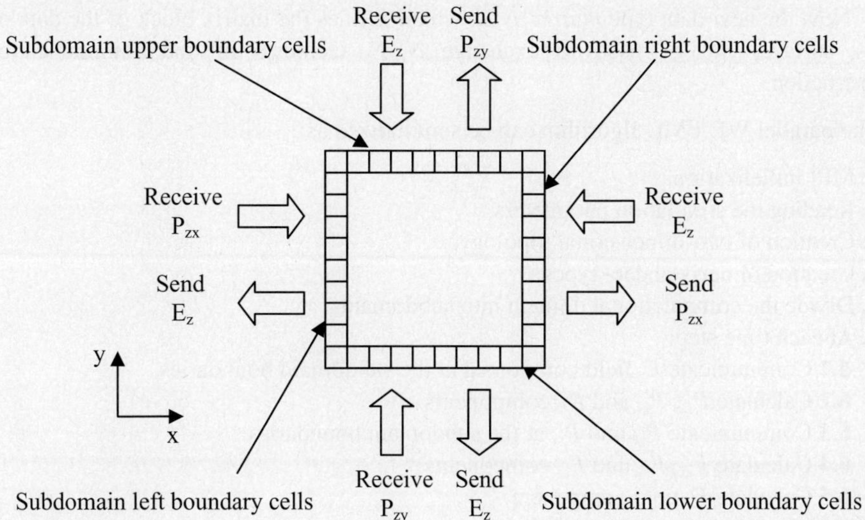

Fig. 2. Communications at the boundaries of a subdomain for the parallel implementation of the WE-PML algorithm

For a subdomain size of $N_x \times N_y \times N_z$ cells, where N_η is the number of cells in the η-direction, it requires $N_y \times N_z$ communication instructions for y-z surface and $N_x \times N_z$ communication instructions for x-z surface. Since communications are considered as an overhead, to minimize the overhead, the number of communication instructions must be minimized and the size of the messages must be maximized. In this algorithm, this is achieved by grouping the data into blocks of data before the transfer. According to the surfaces that will be exchanged, two groups, or blocks, of data are used. One block for x-z surface and one block for y-z surface.

In C, for the 3-D array with x, y, z directions, the data are contiguous along the z axis, and noncontiguous along the axis x and y. Hence, the data on y-z surface are contiguous and can be exchanged as a group of N_y*N_z elements in one communication instruction. However, the data on x-z surface are noncontiguous and must be defined as a group of contiguous elements. To do this, derived data types of MPI, which group the data even having noncontiguous memory addresses, are used.

The matrix block for x-z surface is defined by the following functions:

MPI_Type_contiguous(N_z,MPI_DOUBLE,&column_type)
*MPI_Type_hvector(N_x,1,2*N_y* N_z*sizeof MPI_DOUBLE,column_type,*
    &matrix_type)

The function *MPI_Type_contiguous* is used to define a vector, or column, type which is a block of N_z contiguous elements. Then a matrix type of N_x noncontiguous blocks each having N_z contiguous elements is defined using the function *MPI_Type_hvector*.

Now the new data type *matrix_type*, which defines the matrix block of the data on x-z surface, can be used to exchange N_x*N_z elements in one communication instruction.

The parallel WE-PML algorithm can be summarized as:

1. MPI initialization.
2. Reading the simulation parameters.
3. Creation of two-dimensional topology.
4. Creation of derived data types.
5. Divide the computational domain into subdomains.
6. At each time step:
    6.1 Communicate E_z field component at the subdomain boundaries.
    6.2 Calculate P_{zx}, P_{zy} and P_{zz} components.
    6.3 Communicate P_{zx} and P_{zy} at the subdomain boundaries.
    6.4 Calculate F_{zx}, F_{zy} and F_{zz} components.
    6.5 Calculate E_z field component.
7. MPI finalization.

4 Simulation Study

Performance of the WE-PML algorithm has been studied in 3-D domains. In the tests, a point source excites a 3-D domain at its center. The tests were carried out for different number of processors and for different computational domain sizes, on a network of 2.2 GHz Pentium 4 PCs with 512 MB of memory each. Note that each PC has one processor and each processor runs only one process. The PCs were interconnected with a 100 Mbps Ethernet and they use the MPICH2 implementation of the MPI library.

Table 1 shows the approximate amount of memory required for the serial implementation of the proposed WE-PML algorithm. The amount of memory was calculated as

$$Approximate\ Memory = N_x \times N_y \times N_z \times (7 \times 8) \tag{17}$$

where each cell contains one field value and six auxiliary values, totally seven values, and each value is stored as a double precision floating point number (8 Bytes). The memory required to solve large problems can exceed the physical memory that is available on one PC. Hence, using a distributed memory parallel architecture we can reduce the memory required per PC. A number of PCs connected to an Ethernet network can be considered as a distributed memory parallel architecture. Thus, by increasing the number of PCs we also increase the number of processors so the amount memory available. Beside this, as the number of PCs is increased, after decomposition of the computational domain the local domain size per PC decreases and fits within the physical memory of each individual PC.

Table 1. Memory requirements for different computational domain sizes

Grid Size $(N_x \times N_y \times N_z)$	Approximate Memory (MBytes)
240×240×40	129.02
360×360×40	290.30
480×480×40	516.10
600×600×40	806.40

Table 2 shows the total simulation time for the parallel implementation of the WE-PML algorithm as obtained by using one, four, eight and sixteen PCs for four different domain sizes $(N_x \times N_y \times N_z)$. Due to memory limitations, the largest domain sizes could not be tested on small number of PCs and are represented by N/A, not available. In Table 1 it can be seen that 480×480×40 cells requires approximately 516.10 MB of memory which is less than the memory available on one PC (512 MB).

Table 2. Simulation time for the parallel implementation of the WE-PML algorithm for different domain sizes

Method	WE-PML			
Grid Size	Number of PCs			
$(N_x \times N_y \times N_z)$	1 PC	4 PCs	8 PCs	16 PCs
240×240×40	249.63 s	69.80 s	39.19 s	22.42 s
360×360×40	567.85 s	151.26 s	81.86 s	44.02 s
480×480×40	N/A	269.52 s	144.24 s	98.44 s
600×600×40	N/A	417.73 s	218.96 s	136.29 s

Fig. 3 shows the total simulation time needed to update the field components for the WE-PML parallel algorithm. The results are presented as a function of the number of cells in the domain, i. e., $N_x N_y N_z$.

In Table 2 and Fig. 3, the results for PC=1 are displayed up to 5,184,000 cells (360×360×40), since there is no enough memory for a single PC to compute domain sizes above. The speedup of the WE-PML parallel algorithm was also measured. In this paper, the speedup was calculated as

$$S(N) = T(1)/T(N) \tag{18}$$

where $T(1)$ is the time needed to solve the problem using one PC and $T(N)$ is the time needed to solve the same problem using N PCs. Fig. 4 shows the speedup obtained with four, eight and sixteen PCs for the parallel implementation of the WE-PML algorithm. For the purpose of comparison, the ideal speedup was also shown. The speedup results for larger domain sizes are not displayed since the simulation results of PC=1 for these domain sizes are not available. From Fig. 4 it can be observed that as the computational domain size increases, the efficiency of the parallel algorithm increases.

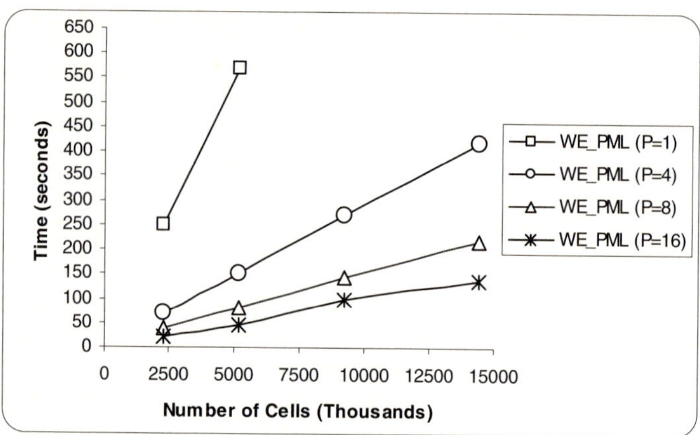

Fig. 3. Total simulation time for the parallel implementation of the WE-PML algorithm as a function of the number of cells in the domain ($N_x N_y N_z$)

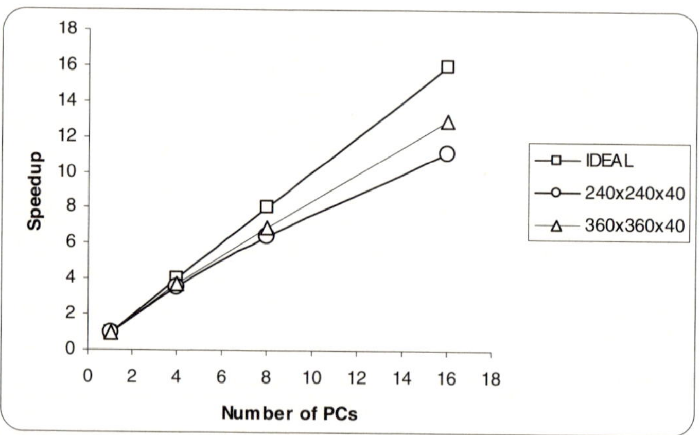

Fig. 4. Speed-up using the parallel implementation of the proposed WE-PML algorithm

5   Conclusions

In this paper, parallel implementation of the WE-PML algorithm has been studied using the MPI system. The performance of the proposed parallel algorithm has been studied by using a point source radiating in 3-D domain. Using distributed memory computing model not only the computational time is decreased but also the amount of memory available to solve the parallel algorithm is increased and hence larger domain sizes could be analyzed. Finally, it has been observed that the parallel implementation of the WE-PML algorithm provides a significant reduction compared with the sequential case. A speedup factor of 12.9 has been achieved on the 16 PCs system, as compared to one PC case, for a large size problem.

References

1. Yee, K. S.: Numerical solution of initial boundary value problems involving Maxwell's equations in isotropic media. IEEE Transaction on Antennas and Propagation. **14** (1996) 302-307
2. Taflove, A.: Computational electrodynamics: The Finite-Difference Time-Domain Method. Artech House, Boston, London, (1995)
3. Aoyagi, P.H., Lee, J.-F., and Mittra, R.: A hybrid Yee algorithm/scalar-wave equation approach. IEEE Transaction Microwave Theory and Techniques. **41** (1993) 1593-1600
4. Varadarajan, V., and Mittra, R.: Finite-difference time domain (FDTD) analysis using distributed computing. IEEE Microwave and Guided Wave Letters. **4** (1994) 144-145
5. Hoteit, H., Sauleau, R., Philippe, B., Coquet, P., and Daniel, J.P.: Vetor and parallel implementations for the FDTD analysis of millimeter wave planar antennas. International Journal of High Speed Computing. **10** (1999) 1-25
6. Guiffaut, C., and Mahdjoubi, K.: A parallel FDTD algorithm using the MPI library. IEEE Antennas and Propagation Magazine. **43** (2001) 94-103
7. Gedney S.D.: An anisotropic perfectly matched layer absorbing medium for the truncation of FDTD lattices. IEEE Transactions on Antennas and Propagation. **44** (1996) 1630-1639
8. Ramadan, O., and Oztoprak, A.Y.: An efficient implementation of the PML for truncating FDTD domains. Microwave and Optical Technology Letters. **36** (2003) 55-60
9. Gropp, W., Lusk, E., and Skjellum, A.: Using MPI: Potable parallel Programming with the Message-Passing Interface. MIT Press, Cambridge, Mass. 1994
10. Pacheco, P.S.: Parallel Programming with MPI, Morgan Kaufmann Publishers, San Francisco. Calif. (1997)
11. Chew, W.C., and Weedon, W.H.: A 3-D perfectly matched medium from modified Maxwell's equations with stretched coordinates. Microwave and Optical Technology Letters. **7** (1994) 599-604

Trustworthy Distributed Algorithm Design to Defend Distance Cheating in Link-Weighted ALM

Dan Li[1], Jianping Wu[1], Yong Cui[1], Jiangchuan Liu[2], and Ke Xu[1]

[1] Department of Computer Science, Tsinghua University, Beijing, P.R. China
`{lidan, cy, xuke}@csnet1.cs.tsinghua.edu.cn,`
`jianping@cernet.edu.cn`
[2] School of Computing Science, Simon Fraser University, British Columbia, Canada
`jcliu@cs.sfu.ca`

Abstract. In link-weighted Application Layer Multicast (ALM), each selfish and strategic end-host receiver may cheat in distance measurement to obtain a better position in the ALM tree. Distance cheating of ALM receivers might lead the ALM tree to be sub-optimal and unstable. We proposed a VCG-based cheat-proof mechanism to defend this kind of cheating behavior in previous work. Based on the theoretical framework, a practical algorithm is designed in this paper, which runs distributedly on ALM receivers. The primary characteristic of the distributed algorithm lies in that it is trustworthy to enforce each selfish receiver to fulfill the algorithm truthfully, which is not considered in other similar studies. Simulations results further suggest that the algorithm is effective in defending distance cheating in link-weighted ALM.

1   Introduction

Application Layer Multicast (ALM) is an efficient supplement to IP Multicast for group communication. However, since ALM tree is composed of selfish and strategic end hosts, there is a potential trouble of trust in ALM. Unlike the obedient routers in IP Multicast, each end host can choose its own strategy to optimize its private utility rather than obeying the demands of the multicast protocol to optimize the global utility.

In link-weighted ALM, receivers usually measure the distances to each other, which constructs the control topology. The ALM tree is built from the control topology and dynamically adjusted to suite the change of network topology. Meanwhile, the utility, which an ALM receiver gets from receiving the multicast data, differs according to its position in the ALM tree. Therefore, when measuring the distances to other receivers, each receiver has both the motivation and the chance to cheat to obtain a better position in the ALM tree. Section 3 will detail the problem.

The distance cheating behavior of ALM receivers has negative impacts on both the efficiency and the stability of the ALM tree [1~2]. We proposed a VCG based theoretical cheat-proof mechanism to defend this kind of distance cheating in previous work [3]. However, how to design a practical algorithm to realize the cheat-proof mechanism is also challenging. In this paper, we try to design a trustworthy distributed algorithm. On one hand, the algorithm is distributed considering the computing feasibility. On the

A. Levi et al. (Eds.): ISCIS 2006, LNCS 4263, pp. 844–853, 2006.

other hand, the algorithm is trustworthy to avoid cheating behaviors when the algorithm is fulfilled by selfish receivers, which is not considered in other similar studies according to our knowledge. Our algorithm does not depend on any specific ALM protocol. It can be regarded as a general algorithm and can be easily integrated into current ALM protocols. Simulations results show that the algorithm is effective in defending distance cheating in link-weighted ALM.

2 Related Work

Currently proposed ALM protocols can be roughly classified into three categories: single-tree based protocols [4~6], multiple-tree based protocols [7~9], and mesh based protocols [10~12]. In all these ALM protocols, tree is the most common structure. Even in mesh based ALM, the ultimate objective is still to use a tree. In link-weighted ALM, an efficient ALM tree is constructed based on the distance information collected between participating nodes. However, since ALM receivers are selfish and strategic end hosts, they might cheat in distance measurement to influence the tree construction. Mathy et al. put forward the distance cheating problem of ALM receivers [1]. They also studied the impact of this kind of cheating behavior on the link stress and stretch of ALM tree. Li et al. made further researches and found that distance cheating also brought ALM tree into instability [2]. We proposed a VCG based cheat-proof mechanism against distance cheating of ALM receivers in previous work [3], which is the first explicit solution to the problem as far as we know. However, it is just a theoretical solution framework. How to design a practical algorithm to realize the cheat-proof mechanism is also challenging, which is covered in this paper.

As for the selfishness problems in ALM, Yuen et al. design VCG based incentive algorithms to defend node throughput cheating, in both single rate session and variable rate sessions [13]. But the payment to each node is computed by the node itself, which may result in further cheating behavior if the payment fulfillment by third-party is considered. Wang et al. design strategy-proof algorithm to calculate the payment to each selfish relay agent [14]. In their model, it is a steiner tree problem to find the optimal tree spanning all receivers, which is well known as NP-Hard. So they do not use the VCG mechanism, which may fail in this case. There also lacks mechanism to enforce selfish agents to implement the payment scheme correctly.

3 Problem Statement and Theoretical Solution Framework

3.1 Distance Cheating Problem in Link-Weighted ALM

We consider a general ALM model, in which all the nodes are autonomous end-hosts. Although all ALM nodes can communicate directly with each other in theory, for scalability reason, each node only maintains a number of other nodes, which is called the neighbors. When a node joins an ALM session, it is assigned with some neighbors, and these neighbors are dynamically adjusted to suite network change. The neighboring relationship between all nodes (including the source) constructs the ALM *control topology*. Each node dynamically asks for the source-to-end distance on neighbors and measures the distances from neighbors to it (note that the distances between two neighbors are asymmetric). Based on the learned information of neighbors, each node selects a parent from them. The parent selection of all nodes results in the *data topology*, also called the ALM tree.

ALM nodes not only get the benefit of receiving data, but also bear the burden of forwarding data to their children. Therefore, each selfish ALM node has the motivation to cheat about its private information to obtain a better position in the ALM tree. Some information exchange integrated in the ALM protocols may be hard to modify, for example, the telling of the source-to-end delay to neighbors, and the forwarding of the available data segments to children. However, the distance measurement between neighbors can be easily modified by strategic nodes. For example, node j wants to measure the distance from neighbor node k to it and sends a measurement probe to node k (maybe a ping command). Node k can hold the measurement probe for a while (maybe just delay the received ping command by several seconds). Then the RTT distance from node k to node j measured by node j will be exaggerated and the probability of node j selecting node k as the parent will be decreased. This behavior at node k can be viewed as cheat because it exaggerates its distance to node j.

For ease of exposition, we list the major notations in this paper in Table 1.

Table 1. List of Notations

q_i	The parent of node i
D_i	The set of all descendant nodes of node i
T_i	The set of nods in the sub-tree rooted from node i ($T_i = D_i \cup \{i\}$)
X_i	The children set of node i
X_j^{-i}	The children set of node j after node i withdraws from the multicast session
A^{-i}	The set of nodes in the ALM tree that have an alternative path to receive multicast data when node i withdraws from the multicast session
$\overline{A^{-i}}$	The set of nodes in the ALM tree that have no other path to receive multicast data when node i withdraws from the multicast session
l_{mn}	The distance from node m to node n
d_i	The source-to-end distance of node i
d_j^{-i}	The source-to-end distance of node j when node i withdraws from the multicast session
c	The cost for each node to forward a unit data to a child
$B(d_j)$	The benefit of node j from receiving multicast data with the source-to-end distance of d_j

3.2 VCG Based Cheat-Proof Mechanism Against Distance Cheating

Distance cheating in link-weighted ALM has negative impact on both the efficiency and the stability of ALM tree. Since all participating nodes are as well receivers, the finding of the optimal tree spanning all receivers is a Polynomial problem. The well-studied VCG mechanism is the natural way to solve this problem. We proposed a VCG based cheat-proof mechanism in previous work [3]. After introducing a well-designed payment policy, each node has to behave honestly in distance measurement to maximize its own welfare, which is the sum of the utility from receiving multicast data and the additional payment to it.

As analyzed by VCG mechanism in [3], the utility of an ALM node i is

$$u_i = B(d_i) - \mid X_i \mid c \tag{1}$$

where $B(.)$ is a non-increasing function of d_i.

The payment to an ALM node i is

$$
\begin{aligned}
p_i &= \sum_{j \in D_i \cap A^{-i}} [B(d_j) - B(d_j^{-i})] + \sum_{j \in D_i \cap \overline{A^{-i}}} B(d_j) \\
&\quad + (\sum_{j \in (D_i \cap A^{-i}) \cup \overline{T_i}} \mid X_j^{-i} \mid - \sum_{j \neq i} \mid X_j \mid)c \\
&= \sum_{j \in D_i \cap A^{-i}} [B(d_j) - B(d_j^{-i})] + \sum_{j \in D_i \cap \overline{A^{-i}}} B(d_j) + (\mid X_i \mid - \mid D_i \cap \overline{A^{-i}} \mid - 1)c
\end{aligned}
\tag{2}
$$

If node i is a leaf node, i.e., $D_i = \Phi$ and $\mid X_i \mid = 0$, the above payment can be simplified as

$$p_i^{leaf} = -c \tag{3}$$

The welfare of an ALM node i is the sum of its utility and the payment to it.

$$
\begin{aligned}
w_i &= u_i + p_i \\
&= B(d_i) - \mid X_i \mid c + \sum_{j \in D_i \cap A^{-i}} [B(d_j) - B(d_j^{-i})] \\
&\quad + \sum_{j \in D_i \cap \overline{A^{-i}}} B(d_j) + (\mid X_i \mid - \mid D_i \cap \overline{A^{-i}} \mid - 1)c \\
&= \sum_{j \in T_i} B(d_j) - \sum_{j \in D_i \cap A^{-i}} B(d_j^{-i}) - (\mid D_i \cap \overline{A^{-i}} \mid + 1)c
\end{aligned}
\tag{4}
$$

4   Trustworthy Distributed Algorithm Design

We design a practical algorithm to realize the cheat-proof mechanism mentioned in the previous section. It is worth noting that, the VCG mechanism is efficient, but not necessarily budget-balanced, i.e., the total payments to all agents can be positive or negative. Hence, a trustable third-party server is necessary to bear the deficit or the surplus of the public system. Fortunately, even without a dedicated server, the source node can act as the trustable third-party as well, because its benefit is associated with the overall outcome of the ALM tree, while not that of individual nodes.

We point out in [3] that we suggest that the payment to node i be computed by its children in X_i. Intuitively, this choice works because the information demanded for computation do not pass node i, so it has no chance to cheat to increase its payment. We now formally prove that any rational node $j \in X_i$ has no motivation to cheat about the payment to node i when it reports the result to the third-party. First, decreasing the payment to node i may cause node i to leave from the multicast session. Since node j has chosen i as its parent, its welfare cannot be further improved by choosing another parent. Hence, a rational node j will not cheat to decrease the payment to node i; Second, the welfare of node j has already been maximized when it reports the actual payment to node i to the third-party. Increasing the payment to node i will not bring any additional benefit to node j. Hence, a rational and selfish node j has not motivation to increase the payment to node j.

In summary, the payment about any node i will be reported truthfully by each of its children after computation. The detailed computation is given by Eq. (5), which extends Eq. (4) to reflect the calculation framework,

$$
\begin{aligned}
p_i &= \sum_{j \in D_i \cap A^{-i}} [B(d_j) - B(d_j^{-i})] + \sum_{j \in D_i \cap \overline{A^{-i}}} B(d_j) + (\mid X_i \mid - \mid D_i \cap \overline{A^{-i}} \mid - 1)c \\
&= \sum_{k \in X_i} \{ \sum_{j \in T_k \cap A^{-i}} [B(d_j) - B(d_j^{-i})] + \sum_{j \in T_k \cap \overline{A^{-i}}} B(d_j) - \mid T_k \cap \overline{A^{-i}} \mid c \} \\
&\quad + (\mid X_i \mid - 1)c
\end{aligned}
\tag{5}
$$

Let
$$
p_{ik1} = \sum_{j \in T_k \cap A^{-i}} [B(d_j) - B(d_j^{-i})] \quad , \quad p_{ik2} = \sum_{j \in T_k \cap \overline{A^{-i}}} B(d_j) \quad , \quad p_{ik3} = \mid T_k \cap \overline{A^{-i}} \mid c \quad ,
$$

$p_i' = (\mid X_i \mid - 1)c$, and $p_{ik} = p_{ik1} + p_{ik2} - p_{ik3}$. Eq. (5) can be simplified to Eq. (6).

$$
p_i = \sum_{k \in X_i} \{ p_{ik1} + p_{ik2} - p_{ik3} \} + p_i' = \sum_{k \in X_i} p_{ik} + p_i'
\tag{6}
$$

As illustrated in Eq. (6), each child k of node i computes p_{ik}, and reports the result to the third-party. The third-party sums all p_{ik}, adds p', and figures out the total payment to node i. A special case is the leaf nodes, which have no children in the ALM. However, according to Eq. (3), the payment to each leaf node is a constant, $-c$. Hence, if a node i has no payment reported, it is regarded as a leaf node by the third-party, and its payment is set to $-c$.

If we use l_{mn} to denote the distance from node m to node n in the ALM tree, each node i sends the following information of every node $j \in T_i$ to q_i: the source-to-end distance of node j with the participation of q_j, i.e., d_j; the source-to-end distance of node j when node q_j withdraws; i.e., $d_j^{-q_j}$; and the distance from q_j to j, i.e., $l_{q_j j}$. The information set $\{ d_j, d_j^{-q_j}, l_{q_j j} \}$ is called a record of node j, and all the records of $j \in T_i$ is called the record set of node i.

There are two types of messages exchanged in our algorithm, the record message and the payment message. The record message is sent from an ALM node i to its parent q_i in the ALM tree, containing the record set of node i. The payment message is sent from an ALM node i to the third-party, containing the payment that node i computes for its parent.

We next give the algorithm details of the computation in Fig. 1 through Fig. 6, among which, Fig. 1 through 4 are executed in each ALM node, and Fig. 5 through 6 are executed in the trustable third-party.

Fig. 1 is a function recordSetCompute(), which is for node i that executes this function to compute its record set. Each node i periodically sends the record message to its parent, as shown in Fig. 2. After receiving a record message from one of its children, node i stores all the corresponding records locally, for future computation of its own record and the payment to its parent. This is illustrated in Fig. 3. Fig. 4 shows how node i computes $p_{q_i i}$ and sends the payment message to the third-party containing $p_{q_i i}$. The record set for computing $p_{q_i i}$ is obtained in Fig. 1. Upon receiving $p_{q_i i}$, the third-party stores all the information locally, and updates parents set Y, as well as children set Z, as shown in Fig. 5. Fig. 6 shows how the third-party computes the payment to each receiver in the ALM. For node $i \in Y$, p_i is calculated by summing all reported p_{ik}, plus p_i'. Any node $j \in Z \cap \overline{Y}$ is assumed as a leaf node, and assigned the payment of $-c$.

<table>
<tr><td>1</td><td>void recordSetCompute()</td></tr>
<tr><td>2</td><td> if $d_i^{-q_i} \neq \infty$ // i has a second best parent</td></tr>
<tr><td>3</td><td>   for each $j \in D_i$</td></tr>
<tr><td>4</td><td> $d_j^{-q_i} \leftarrow d_i^{-q_i} + l_{ij}$ // still select i as parent</td></tr>
<tr><td>5</td><td>   end for</td></tr>
<tr><td>6</td><td> else   // i has no other potential parents</td></tr>
<tr><td>7</td><td>   for each $j \in D_i$</td></tr>
<tr><td>8</td><td> $d_j^{-q_i} \leftarrow d_j^{-i}$ // same as when i withdraws</td></tr>
<tr><td>9</td><td>   end for</td></tr>
<tr><td>10</td><td> end if</td></tr>
<tr><td>11</td><td> for each $j \in D_i$</td></tr>
<tr><td>12</td><td> $l_{qj} \leftarrow l_{qi} + l_{ij}$</td></tr>
<tr><td>13</td><td> end for</td></tr>
</table>

Fig. 1. Record set computation on node i

<table>
<tr><td>1</td><td>void recordMsgSend()</td></tr>
<tr><td>2</td><td> recordSetCompute() // recompute records before sending to parent</td></tr>
<tr><td>3</td><td> $msg.type \leftarrow record$ // record message</td></tr>
<tr><td>4</td><td> $msg.record \leftarrow \Phi$</td></tr>
<tr><td>5</td><td> for each $j \in T_i$</td></tr>
<tr><td>6</td><td> $msg.record \leftarrow msg.record \cup \{d_j, d_j^{-q_i}, l_{qj}\}$</td></tr>
<tr><td>7</td><td> end for</td></tr>
<tr><td>8</td><td> msgSendToParent(msg)</td></tr>
</table>

Fig. 2. Sending record message on node i

```
1    void recordMsgReceive()
2      msg ← msgRcvFromChild()
3      s ← msg.source
4      if s ∈ X_i
5        for each j ∈ T_s  // record message containing records
                           // of all nodes in T_s
6          d_j ← msg.d_j
7          d_j^{-i} ← msg.d_j^{-i}
8          l_ij ← msg.l_ij
9        end for
10     end if
```

Fig. 3. Receiving record message on node i

```
1    void paymentMsgSend()
2      recordSetCompute() // recompute records before computing
                          // payment about parent
3      p_{q_i i1} ← 0  // Eq. (5) and Eq. (6)
4      p_{q_i i2} ← 0  // Eq. (5) and Eq. (6)
5      p_{q_i i3} ← 0  // Eq. (5) and Eq. (6)
6      r ← 0  // to calculate | T_i ∩ \overline{A^{-q_i}} |, Eq. (5) and Eq. (6)
7      for each j ∈ T_i
8        if d_j^{-q_i} ≠ ∞   // nodes in T_i ∩ A^{-q_i}
9          p_{q_i i1} ← p_{q_i i1} + B(d_j) − B(d_j^{-q_i})
10       else        // nodes in T_i ∩ \overline{A^{-q_i}}
11         p_{q_i i2} ← p_{q_i i2} + B(d_j)
12         r ← r+1
13       end if
14     end for
15     p_{q_i i3} ← r*c    // nodes in T_i ∩ \overline{A^{-q_i}}
16     p_{q_i i} ← p_{q_i i1} + p_{q_i i2} − p_{q_i i3}
17     msg.type ← payment   // payment message
18     msg.parent ← i
19     msg.payment ← p_{q_i i}
20     msgSendtoThirdParty( msg )
```

Fig. 4. Sending payment message on node i

```
1    void paymentMsgReceive()
2        msg ← msgRcvFromALMnodes()
3        s ← msg.source
4        q ← msg.parent
5        p_qs ← msg.payment  // s reports the payment about q
6        Y ← Y ∪ q  // parent set
7        Z ← Z ∪ s  // children set
```

Fig. 5. Receiving payment message on the third-party

```
1    void paymentsCompute()
2        for each q ∈ Y  // non-leaf nodes
3            p_q ← 0
4            r ← 0    // to calculate | X_q |, Eq. (5) and Eq. (6)
5            for each s ∈ Z
6                if p_qs ≠ 0  // s ∈ X_q
7                    p_q ← p_q + p_qs  // Eq. (5) and Eq. (6)
8                    r ← r + 1
9                end if
10           end for
11           p_q ← p_q + (r − 1) * c   // Eq. (5) and Eq. (6)
12       end for
13       for each j ∈ Z ∩ Ȳ  // leaf nodes
14           p_j ← −c  // Eq. (3)
15       end for
```

Fig. 6. Payments computation on the third-party

5 Simulations

We conduct extensive simulations to study the effectiveness of our cheat-proof algorithm. Unless otherwise specified, we use the following default settings in our simulation. We use the random model to generate network topology by GT-ITM. The topology is composed of 1000 routers, and the link delays between connected routers are within [10ms, 500ms]. 501 ALM nodes (1 source and 500 receivers) are attached to 501 routers randomly selected from the 1000 routers, each node assigned with some neighbors (reflected by the edge probability of ALM control topology, e). The ALM tree is built using the shortest path tree algorithm upon the ALM control topology. We assume $B(d_i) = 500/d_i$, $c = 0.5$, thus $u_i = 500/d_i - 0.5 * | X_i |$. The quantification of the utility function will not affect the generalization of our discussion.

We study the welfare of each node i under different selfish policies. Assuming that all other receivers are telling the truth, we define the *truth gain* of node i as the difference between its welfares with and without telling the truth. Apparently, any rational node i will tell the truth if and only if its truth gain is non-negative.

When a node cheats its distance to other nodes, we define the *cheating degree* as the multiple times of the exaggerated distance over the actual distance, denoted by h. We show the truth gains of all receivers over cheating degree and the edge probability of ALM control topology in Figs. 7 and 8, respectively. In Fig. 7, we fix the edge probability of ALM control topology to 60%, and change the cheating degree from 50%, 100%, to 200%. In Fig. 8, we fix the cheating degree to 100%, and change the edge probability of ALM control topology from 10%, 40%, to 80%.

All these figures show that the truth gain of an individual receiver is always non-negative, suggesting that an individual receiver achieves its maximum welfare when telling the truth. In other words, each rational node has no motivation to cheat. Furthermore, the figures suggest that the truth gain increases when the cheating degree is higher, or when the edge probability of ALM control topology is lower.

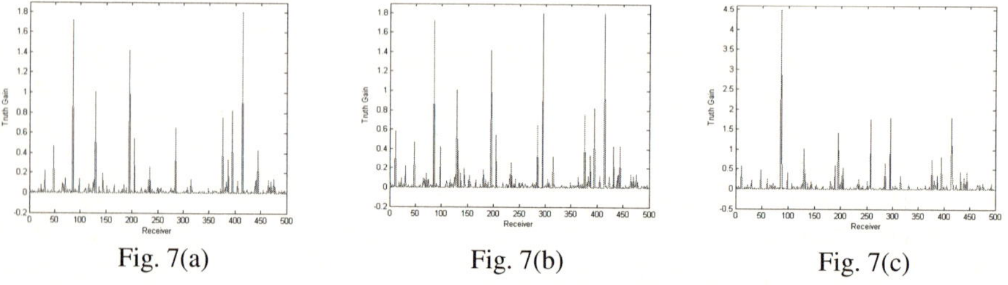

Fig. 7(a)   Fig. 7(b)   Fig. 7(c)

Fig. 7. Truth gain of each receiver (n=500, e=60%). (a) h=50%; (b) h=100%; (c) h=200%.

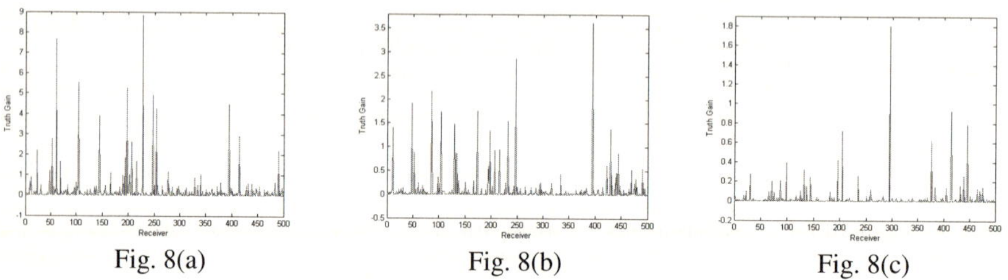

Fig. 8(a)   Fig. 8(b)   Fig. 8(c)

Fig. 8. Truth gain of each receiver (n=500, h=100%). (a) e=10%; (b) e=40%; (c) e=80%.

6 Conclusion and Future Work

We designed a practical algorithm in this paper to thoroughly solve the distance cheating problem in link-weighted ALM, which is based on the VCG motivated theoretical framework we proposed in previous work. The primary characteristic of the algorithm is that it is not only distributed for computing feasibility, but also able to avoid cheating behaviors when it is fulfilled by selfish receivers. Extensive simulation shows that our algorithm is effective in defending receiver cheating.

ALM-based applications are used more and more widely today. How to ensure efficient, reliable and truthful data propagation is always a hot topic, and it will still be the aims of our future work.

References

1. L. Mathy, and N. Blundell, "Impact of Simple Cheating in Application-Level Multicast", in Proceedings of IEEE INFOCOM 2004, Hong Kong, China, Mar 2004
2. D. Li, Y. Cui, K. Xu, and J. Wu, "Impact of Receiver Cheating on the Stability of ALM Tree", in Proceedings of IEEE GLOBECOM 2005, St. Louis, Missouri, USA, Nov/Dec 2005
3. D. Li, J. Wu, Y. Cui, J. Liu, and K. Xu, "A VCG based Cheat-proof Mechanism against Distance Cheating of ALM Receivers", Technical Report, http://netlab.cs.tsinghua.edu.cn
4. Y. H. Chu, S. G. Rao, and H. Zhang, "A Case for End System Multicast", in Proceedings of ACM Sigmetrics 2000, Santa Clara, CA, USA, Jun 2000
5. S. Banerjee, B. Bhattacharjee, and C. Kommareddy, "Scalable Application Layer Multicast", in Proceedings of ACM SIGCOMM 2002, Pittsburgh, PA, USA, Aug 2002
6. D. Pendarakis, S. Shi, D. Verma, and M. Waldvogel, "ALMI: An Application Level Multicast Infrastructure", in Proceedings of USITS 2001, San Francisco, CA, USA, Mar 2001
7. M. Castro, P. Druschel, A. Kermarrec, A. Nandi, A. Rowstron, and A. Singh, "SplitStream: High-bandwidth Content Distribution in Cooperative Environments", in Proceedings of ACM SOSP 2003, New York, USA, 2003
8. D. Kostic, A. Rodriguez, J. Albrecht, and A. Vahdat, "Bullet: High Bandwidth Data Dissemination Using an Overlay Mesh", in Proceedings of ACM SOSP, New York, USA, 2003
9. V. N. Padmanabhan, H. J. Wang, P. A. Chou, and K. Sripanidkulchai, "Distributing Streaming Media Content Using Cooperative Networking", In Proceedings of NOSSDAV 2002, Miami Beach, FL, USA, May 2002
10. R. Rejaie and S. Stafford, "A framework for architecting peer-to-peer receiver-driven overlays," in Proceedings of NOSSDAV 2004, Cork, Ireland, Jun 2004
11. X. Zhang, J. Liu, B. Li, and T. P. Yum, "DONet: A data-driven overlay network for efficient live media streaming," in Proceedings of IEEE INFOCOM 2005, Miami, FL, USA, Mar 2005
12. M. Hefeeda, A. Habib, B. Botev, D. Xu, and B. Bhargava, "PROMISE: Peer-to-peer media streaming using CollectCast", in Proceedings of ACM Multimedia 2003, Berkeley, CA, Nov 2003
13. S. Yuen, and B. Li, "Cheat-proof Mechanisms for Dynamic Multicast Tree Formation in Overlay Networks", in Proceedings of IEEE INFOCOM 2005, Miami, FL, USA, Mar 2005
14. W. Wang, X. Li, Z. Suny, and Y. Wang, "Design Multicast Protocols for Non-Cooperative Networks", in Proceedings of IEEE INFOCOM 2005, Miami, FL, USA, Mar 2005

jEQN a Java-Based Language for the Distributed Simulation of Queueing Networks

Andrea D'Ambrogio, Daniele Gianni, and Giuseppe Iazeolla

Dept. of Computer Science
University of Roma TorVergata
Roma, Italy
{dambro, gianni, iazeolla}@info.uniroma2.it

Abstract. The increasing pervasiveness of large scale networks is bringing distributed simulation (DS) to the reach of academic and business communities besides the traditional military ones. This gives academics and industry the advantage of using larger execution platforms and of reusing locally implemented simulation models as building blocks of much larger models. Developing a distributed simulator however requires learning how to use a given DS standard (such as HLA), that implies a non-negligible amount of effort. This paper addresses the problem of defining a language that can equivalently support the development of local or distributed simulators, making the use of the DS standard transparent. The HLA standard is dealt with, but the method can be extended to any other DS standard. The language (called jEQN) addresses the extended queueing network (EQN) domain, and thus it also includes primitives to facilitate the development of queueing network distributed simulators.

1 Introduction

Distributed simulation (DS) programs are generally harder to develop [1] than local ones since a distribution infrastructure has to be implemented to deal with communication, concurrency and synchronization issues. Many successful languages and tools are available to simulate extended queueing networks [2] (EQN), such as QNAP [3], RESQ [4], etc. Such languages however only support local simulation and their extension to include DS facilities can be very problematic. Existing mechanisms to extend such languages are based on the use of wrapping techniques, which however can lead to unstable code and poor maintainability [5]. On the other hand, existing languages that support DS, such as PDNS [6], Dis-SimJava [7], D-SOL [8] and μSik [9], neither support EQN modeling, nor are easily extensible to support it.

The introduced language, called jEQN, provides appropriate primitives to facilitate the development of EQN distributed simulation models basing on the HLA standard [10].

The system consists of a Java library organized into four software layers, that provide abstractions to isolate the developer from the underlying HLA services and from the discrete event simulation (DES) mechanisms.

A. Levi et al. (Eds.): ISCIS 2006, LNCS 4263, pp. 854–865, 2006.
© Springer-Verlag Berlin Heidelberg 2006

By use of jEQN no extra effort is required to the developer to implement a distributed EQN simulator with respect to a local one and all advantages of the Java language can be exploited.

The paper is organized as follows: Section 2 illustrates the overall jEQN layered architecture, Section 3 describes the details of each layer and Section 4 gives an example of jEQN use. For the sake of conciseness no description is given of the HLA standard [10].

2 jEQN Overall Description

DS standards give support in the development of distributed simulation programs by providing the necessary distribution infrastructure, but a non-negligible amount of effort remains necessary to incorporate the standard into each individual program. By use of jEQN a DS program can be developed without such a specific extra effort. Developers can thus concentrate themselves on the description of the simulation model. This lowers down the developer's effort of average experienced by around 30% and the one of beginners by around 60%. Besides that, a saving takes place of all the effort necessary to implement the code for the interactions and synchronizations between federates and RTI and for the EQN component logic (for about 1.25 MM per federate, according to the SED effort model [11] for an estimated saving of 3.5 K lines of code per federate).

In the present version of jEQN, the simulations programs operate according to the process interaction (PI) paradigm [12]. Other simulation paradigms can however be easily implemented, such as the event sequencing (ES) and the activity scanning (AS) paradigm.

The jEQN architecture consists of four layers that separate the jEQN program from the HLA infrastructure (layer 0). Layer 1 is the bottom layer and layer 4 the uppermost one, as illustrated in Fig. 1, with: *Layer 4* the jEQN program, *Layer 3* the jEQN simulation language (the EQN primitives), *Layer 2* the execution container (the simulation engines), *Layer 1* the DES abstraction (the PI discrete event mechanisms) and finally *Layer 0* the DS infrastructure (HLA in the present implementation).

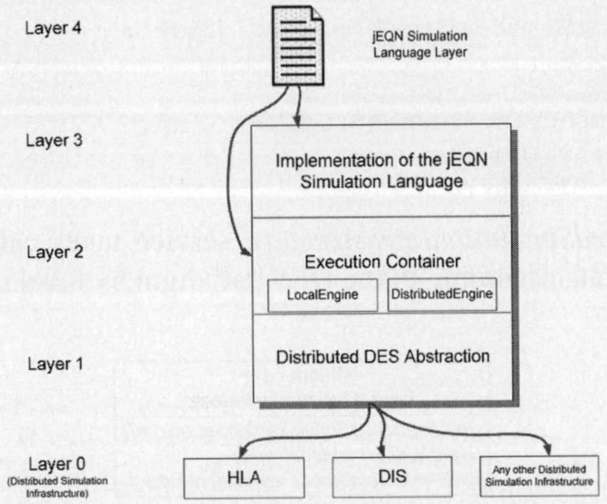

Fig. 1. jEQN layered Architecture

3   jEQN Detailed Description

This section provides a detailed description of the role of the jEQN layers 1 to 4.

3.1   Layer 1

This layer implements the DES services basing on HLA services. This is done by giving the HLA Run Time Infrastructure (RTI) [10] the necessary configuration to support the DES time-advancement and by invoking specific HLA services, as shown next in Section 3.1.1. By the presence of this layer, the layer 2 programs shall only be required to know about DES services.

Layer 1 also incorporates the *Federation Manager* that creates the federation, controls the federation along its life cycle and cares of providing a DES-based execution. This layer includes HLA interface implementations [10] needed to build up the HLA environment and to invoke the HLA services. It is also includes the Java class *HLAEvent* that encapsulates the HLA event data type to help decouple the layer 1's logic from the underlying DS infrastructure.

A specific *LogicalTimeFactoryFromSimpleDataType* interface has been developed to further decouple the layer from the specific HLA implementation.

Layer 1 interface to layer 2. This interface consists of the implementation of three DES services as illustrated in Fig. 2 where each service is based on HLA services as follows:

```
initDistributedSimulationInfrastructure():
        publish(HLAEventClass); subscribe(HLAEventClass);
        enableTimeConstrained(); enableTimeRegulated();
        synchronizationPointAchieved(readyToRun);
        wait(readyToRun);

waitNextDistributedEvent():
        do
                t_future=t_current+t_advancingStep;
                timeAdvanceRequest(t_future);
                wait(timeGrant);
        while not (eventReceived);

waitNextDistributedEventBeforeTime(in t: time):
        do
                t_future=t_current+t_advancingStep;
                timeAdvanceRequest(t_future);
                wait(timeGrant);
        while not eventReceived) or (t_current<t));
```

The *initDistributedSimulationInfrastructure* service takes care of initializing the HLA system to operate according to the DES paradigm by invoking the HLA services

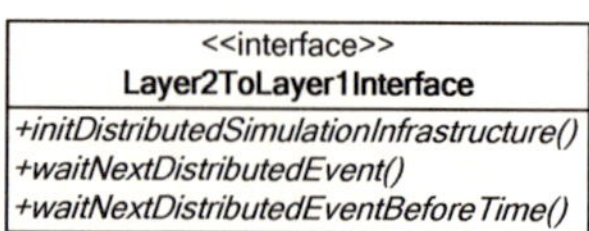

Fig. 2. Layer 2 to 1 interface

publish(HLAEventClass), subscribe(HLAEventClass) etc; the *waitNextDistributedEvent* and *waitNextDistributedEventBeforeTime* services implement the homonym DES paradigm services by invoking the HLA *timeAdvanceRequest* and waiting for the *timeAdvanceGrant.*

The 1-to-0 and 0-to-1 interfaces. The layer 1 to layer 0 interface depends on the specific DS infrastructure used at layer 0. In this paper HLA case, the interface consists of a subset of the FederateAmbassador and RTIambassador services, with the former taking care of the 0-to-1 direction and the latter of the 1-to-0. The detail of such services is shown in Fig. 3a and 3b, of immediate understanding in HLA terms [10].

3.2 Layer 2

This layer is the execution container of the layer 3 programs. Its architecture is based on the concepts of *simulation component* and *simulation engine.*

A *simulation component* represents the basic building block of the simulator. Components can be grouped into *entities, events, ports* and *links,* whose relationship is illustrated in Fig. 4. The meta model of the generic layer 2 component consists of an abstract definition that is specialized into the local version and then further into the distributed version. Since of the hierarchical structure the layer 3 programs need not to know in which (local or distributed) execution context they are run and programs are coded independently of that. Such a context will be known only at simulation instantiation time.

The 1-to-2 interface consists of the *scheduleEvent* service that inserts the generic event *e* into the list of events, as shown in Fig. 5a that also illustrates the interface between layer 2 and 3 (3-to-2) consisting of the components registration and the engine activation command.

Engines. The simulation engine is responsible for the simulation initialization and execution and implements the PI paradigm. Fig. 5b illustrates the engines hierarchy, according to which an abstract engine is refined into a simulation engine for local execution and into a simulation engine for distributed execution.

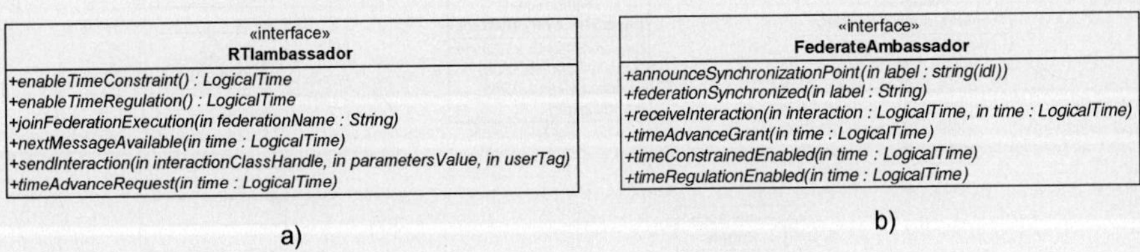

Fig. 3. a) 1-to-0 interface, b) 0-to-1 interface

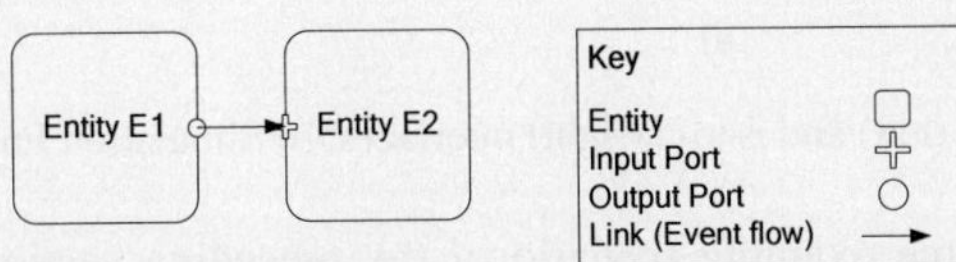

Fig. 4. Relationships between simulation components

Local Simulation Engine. The operation of the local simulation engine basically consists of a cycle for the instantiation of all simulation entities followed by the scheduling of events that determines which entity has to be next activated for execution. Let us refer to the Fig. 4 schema, and consider a very simple simulation, in which the two entities reside on a common host and are thus connected by use of a local link (i.e., a SimpleLink). Entity E1 sends to entity E2 an event every 4 seconds containing the wall clock time. When receiving the event, entity E2 prints out such time. The sequence of steps carried out by the local simulation engine is as follows:

step 1.   the engine starts E1 and E2;
step 2.   E2 asks the engine to be blocked waiting for the next incoming event;
step 3.   the engine stops E2
step 4.   E1 sends an event to its output port;
step 5.   the engine forwards the event to E2 by use of the local link
step 6.   E1 asks the engine to be stopped for 4 seconds;
step 7.   the engine schedules a wake-up event for E1 at time = current time + 4 seconds;
step 8.   the engine wakes up E2 since of the new event;
step 9.   E2 receives the new event;
step 10. E2 prints the data associated to the event
step 11. the engine wakes up E1
step 12. the engine returns to step2.

Distributed simulation engine. The distributed engine has to present to the layer 3 entities the same framework of the local simulation engine. Therefore it has to provide methods for the management of the distributed simulation, the time advancement, the transparent reception of distributed events, the transparent scheduling and sending of distributed events.

Distributed events are scheduled and sent as if they were local events. The only difference being the type of port through which the event is sent. If the port (or the recipient) is local, then the event is managed by the local simulation engine. If the port (or the recipient) is distributed, the distributed simulation engine creates a distributed event and sends it out.

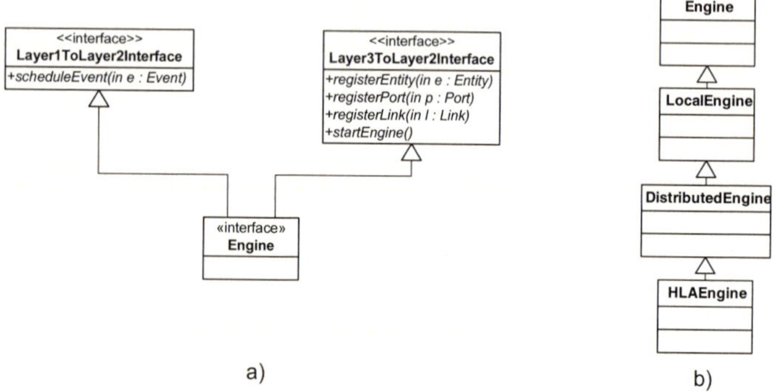

Fig. 5. a) 1-to-2 (left) and 3-to-2 (right) interfaces, b) Simulation Engines hierarchy

Assuming the same example scenario of the preceding section, with E1 and E2 now running on two different hosts (E1 under engine En1 on host H1, and E2 under En2 on host H2), the following sequence of steps can be recognized:

step 1.   En1 starts E1 and En2 starts E2;
step 2.   E2 asks En2 to be blocked waiting for the next incoming event;
step 3.   En2 stops E2;
step 4.   En2 waits for a distributed incoming event;
step 5.   E1 sends an event to its output port;
step 6.   En1 forwards the event to the E2 by use of the distributed link
step 7.   E1 asks En1 to be stopped for 4 seconds;
step 8.   En1 schedules a wake-up event for E1 at time = current time + 4 seconds;
step 9.   En2 receives the distributed event sent by En1 and schedules it as a local event
step 10.   En2 wakes up E2 since of the new event;
step 11.   E2 receives the new event;
step 12.   E2 prints the data associated to the event
step 13.   En1 receives the distributed time grant
step 14.   En1 wakes up E1
step 15.   the engines return to step 2

Entities and Events. An *entity* is a logical process, the fundamental building block in the PI simulation paradigm. The jEQN library provides the *EntityRef* interface, a root class that defines a common abstraction of entity references. Such a class is specialized into *Entity*, for local entities, and *DISEntityRef*, a proxy class, for remote entities. Specific entities (e.g. sources, service centers, etc, in a queueing system) needed for a particular simulation are obtained as specializations of the Entity class. By implementing the *body()* method of the entity the simulator developer determines the entity behaviour, that is how the entity reacts when events are received.

Entities use the services of the simulation engine by an abstract interface that hides the implementation details of the engine. The developer is only required to use the standard *send()* and *wait()* services, which are invoked by entities to send or receive events, respectively.

Events, as already mentioned, include all types of events required by the PI paradigm, such as start events, notify events, sleep events and so forth.

Events are implemented as classes that include attributes such as sender, recipient, time, tag and data, and methods to serialize/deserialize themselves when exchanged by remote entities in a distributed simulation.

Ports. A *port* is used by a simulation entity to exchange events with other entities. The main advantage of using ports is that entities may interact without directly referencing to each other. This increases their degree of reusability.

A port can be of output or input type. Entities send events to output ports and receive events from input ports. Each port is characterized by its owner (the entity to which it belongs) and the link to which it is connected.

Layer 2 provides both local ports (to exchange events between local entities) and distributed ports (to exchange events with remote entities). The only difference being in the fact that local ports have owner entity of `Entity` type and connecting link of `Link` type, while distributed ports have owner entity of `DisEntityRef` type and connecting link of `DisLink` type.

Links. The *links* connect the output ports of sending entities to the input ports of receiving entities. They decouple sending entities from receiving ones, and implement one-to-one, one-to-many, many-to-one and many-to-many associations between sending entities and receiving entities.

In analogy to the other components, links can be either local (`SimpleLink`) or distributed (`DisLink`) links. Local links connect local ports, while distributed links connect local output to remote input ports.

3.3 Layer 3

This layer contains the EQN components, consisting of: 1) user sources, 2) waiting systems, 3) service centers, 4) routers, 5) special nodes and, 6) support components. By support components we mean components (e.g. users, service requests, probabilities, etc.) that do not play an active role in the simulation but are used as objects to exchange information or to parametrize the EQN components.

Each component specializes a corresponding layer 2 Entity class by specifying its own behaviour (reaction to external events) and the input and output ports. To obtain component reusability, flexible parametrization and decoupling functionalities are used:

- parameters that do not affect the component behaviour (such as data structures to store users, service request generators, etc.) are not incorporated in the component and are passed as parameters from the outside;
- parameters that instead affect it (e.g. the source termination condition, etc) are obtained through inheritance from the base component.

In the following, only the source and the waiting system are described, for the sake of brevity.

Source. This component generates each time a user, sends it through its output port and then checks the termination condition, before generating a new user in the next interarrival time. The component parametrization includes the termination condition, the interarrival time and the user type. The first affects the component behaviour, and so it is obtained through inheritance from the source base component, the latter two do not affect it and are thus passed from the outside. Fig. 6 gives the class diagram of the Source.

The termination condition parameter is obtained by use of an abstract method, *terminateCondition()*. The method includes the simple attribute *false* in the case of endless source, or the *usersGenerated = usersToGenerate* condition in case of finite source.

The interarrival time parameter does not affect the component behaviour and thus it is obtained by passing an implementation of the numeric stream interface jRand *NumericStream* [13] that gives the next number in sequence and is implemented by a specific Java class.

In this way, specific types of *UserGenerator* (e.g. *SingleCatUsersGenerator* or *MultiCatUsersGenerator)* can be defined by inheritance, and thus passed as parameters to the source component.

Waiting system. This component consists of a *users queue* and a *service time generator*. In the traditional modeling approach the service time generator is part of the service center definition. In jEQN it is made it part of the waiting system in order to facilitate the implementation of time-dependent service disciplines.

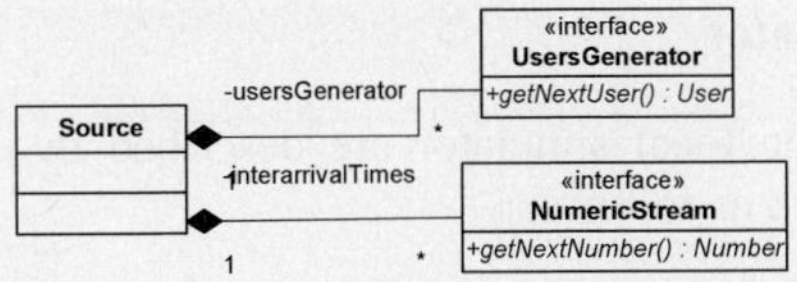

Fig. 6. Source class diagram

The component holds three ports: user *input* port from the preceding entity (generally a router or a service center), user *output* port towards the successor entity (generally a service center) and user *flow control* port needed by the successor entity to request a new user from the waiting system.

Fig. 7 illustrates the *users queue* of the component. It can be seen how specific types of *UsersQueue* (e.g. *SingleUsersQueue* or *MultiUsersQueue)* can be defined by inheritance, and thus passed as parameters to the waiting system. Fig. 7 also illustrates how the *MultiUsersQueue* is composed of a multiplicity of *SingleUsersQueue* and of a *QueueAssigner* that implements the queue dispatching policy.

There are several kinds of waiting systems (WS) in the queueing networks domain, which can be classified into WS with preemptive or non-preemptive service, WS with single or multi queue, WS with given service discipline (FIFO, LIFO, Shortest Time First WS, etc).

Only the preemptive / non-preemptive service affects the WS behaviour and so the relating parameter is obtained in jEQN by inheritance; the remaining service types do not affect the WS behaviour and so the relating parameters are passed in jEQN from the outside.

3.4 Layer 4

This is the layer where the jEQN simulation programs are developed. Such programs mainly consist of jEQN statements that allocate layer 3 components. Such statements are expressed according to standard Java syntax. For example:

```
userGenerator.addUsersGenerator(new SingleCatUsersGenerator(category0));
```

is a primitive that invokes the *addUsersGenerator* method of the userGenerator component in order to allocate a *SingleCatUsersGenerator* of category0 into a multicategory user generator. Besides primitives, the program also includes methods to allocate a layer 2 execution container, e.g. a LocalEngine or a DistributedEngine. Such methods are invoked at beginning of each program. For example: `Engine engine = new LocalEngine().`

4 jEQN Example

In this section a jEQN program developed to simulate an EQN model is illustrated in two versions: a local version (to be run on a single host) and a three host distributed version. The model (Fig. 8) is a closed network consisting of: a finite source that generates 10 users with exponential interarrival times; three service centers, each with gaussian service times and four-queues FIFO waiting system; a router that directs users between centers.

4.1 The Local Simulator

The components of the local simulator are described in jEQN according the Java syntax and are allocated as follows:

```
// Source and related components
#1.    MultiCatUsersGenerator ug =new MultiCatUsersGenerator(new
          UniformStream(0,3));
#2.    Category c<i> = new Category("<i>");
#3.    ug.addUsersGenerator(new SingleCatUsersGenerator(c<i>));
#4.    FiniteSource s = new FiniteSource("source", ug, new
                ExponentialStream(lambda), numberOfUsers);
```

where, statement #1 is a generator that distributes users uniformly among categories 0 to 3; statement #2 (for $<i> = 0$ to 3) defines such categories by assigning them conventional names (0 through 3); statement #3 (for $<i> = 0$ to 3) allocates a *Single-CatUsersGenerator* of the specified category to the *MultiCatUsersGenerator*, and statement #4, defines the exponential interarrival time source and the number of users to be generated.

```
//WaitingSystem and related components
#5.    CategoryBasedQueuesAssigner qa0 =new CategoryBasedQueuesAssigner();
#6.    qa0.addCategoryToQueueMapping(category<i>, <i>, "Queue<i>");
#7.    MultiUsersQueues mq0 = new ScanMultiUsersQueues(qa0);
#8.    mq0.addUsersQueue(new InfiniteFIFOUsersQueueVector());
#9.    ResourceRequestGenerator rg0=new SingleCatResourceRequestGenerator
          (new NormalStream(mu, sigma);
#10.   WaitingSystem ws0 = new WaitingSystem("multiQueue0", mq0, rg0);

//ServiceCenter
#11.   ServiceCenter sc0 = new DoubleNonPreemptiveServiceCenter("sc0")
```

where statements #5 and #6 (for $<i> = 0$ to 3) associate the users categories to the respective queues of center 0; statements #7 and #8 (to be seen repeated for each queue) allocate the waiting system *MultiUsersQueues* and define the service disciplines; statement #9 allocates the service time gaussian generator to service center 0, statement #10 allocates the *WaitingSystem* component, and statement #11 allocates the service center 0 as a non-preemptive center.

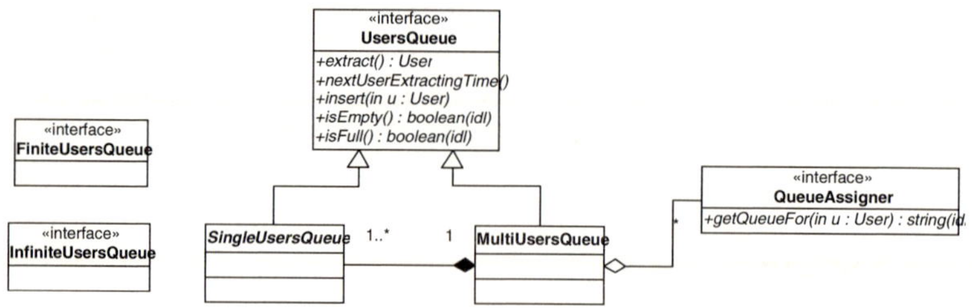

Fig. 7. Class diagram of the WaitingSystem Users Queue

WaitingSystems no.1 and 2 of Fig. 8 and service centers no.1 and 2 are defined in a similar way and are not illustrated here for the sake of brevity.

```
//Router
#12.    double rp[] = {0.7, 0.3};
#13.    Router r = new ProbabilityBasedRouter("router", rp);
```

where statements #12 and #13 define the router and the associated probabilities. The connections between the model entities are defined by allocating link components, each between an output and input port as by statements #14 and #15 (to be seen repeated for <j> = 1 to 3) for the waiting system-service center link, by statements #16 and #17 for the router-waiting system 2 and 3 link; and finally by statements #18 and #19 for the source, service centers 1 and 2-waiting system1 link.

```
// Links
#14.    new SimpleLink(ws<j>.getUsersOutPort(),sc<j>.getUsersInPort());
#15.    newSimpleLink(sc<j>.getUsersSynchPort(),ws<j>.getUsersSynchPort())
#16.    new SimpleLink(r.getUsersOutPort(0),ws2.getUsersInPort());
#17.    new SimpleLink(r.getUsersOutPort(1),ws3.getUsersInPort());
#18.    MultiSenderLink msl = new MultiSenderLink(ws1.getUsersInPort());
#19.    msl.connectWith({s, sc2, sc3}.getUsersOutPort());
```

The duration of the simulation run is defined by statement #20 below:

```
#20.    engine.setSimulationEnd(simulatedTime);
```

and the simulator engine is made ready to start by statement #21 below:

```
#21.    engine.start();
```

The actual run is then launched by use of the conventional Java run command.

The programs to collect the simulation output statistics at each component site are part of the components themselves and are not shown here for the sake of brevity.

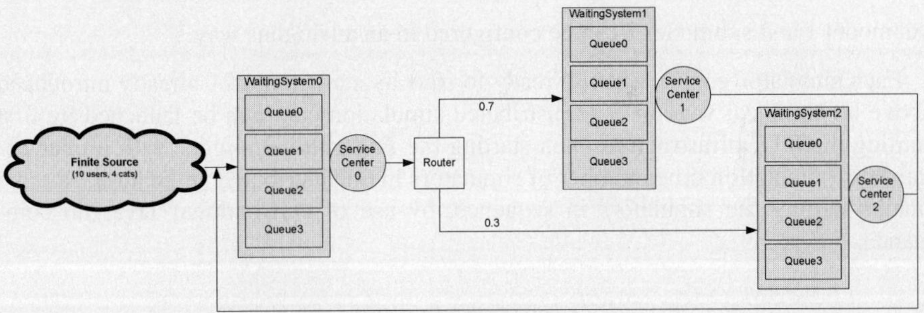

Fig. 8. The simulated example

4.2   The Distributed Simulator

Now assume a distributed simulator of the Fig 8 EQN model has to be developed consisting of three programs simulating the following submodels: submodel 0 = {source, waiting system 0, service center 0, router}; submodel 1 = {waiting system 1, service center 1}; submodel 2 = {waiting system 2, service center 2}. To this purpose, it is sufficient to copy and paste the statements of the local simulator as follows:

1. *submodel 0 (running on host 0):* source and user categories (statements #1 through #4), waitingSystem 0 (statements #5 through #10), serviceCenter 0 (statement #11) and router (statements #12 and #13);

2. *submodel 1 (running on host 1):* user categories (statement #2), waitingSystem 1 (statements #5 through #10 properly updated with system name) and serviceCenter 1 (statement #11 properly updated with center name);

3. *submodel 2 (running on host2):* user categories (statement #2), waitingSystem 2 (statements #5 through #10 properly updated with system name) and serviceCenter 2 (statement #11 properly updated with center name).

Next, statements are introduced to configure submodels 0, 1 and 2.

Submodel 0 configuration:

Statement #22 (for <j> = 1 to 2) below declares local references for submodel 0 to remote entities *ws1* and *ws2* residing on *host1* and *host2* respectively:

```
#22.    EntityRef ws<j>Ref = new EntityRef("host<j>", "waitingSystem<j>");
```

Statement #23 (for <j> = 1 to 2) below declares local references to the input ports of the WaitingSystem 1 and 2:

```
#23.    DisInPort ws<j>InPort = new DisInPort("usersInPort", ws<j>Ref);
```

The links between the submodel 0 router and the remote entities are established by statement #24(for <j> = 1 to 2) below:

```
#24.    new DisSimpleLink(r.getUsersOutPort(<j>), ws<j>.getUsersInPort());
```

Submodel 1 and 2 configuration:

Submodel 1 and submodel 2 can be configured in an analogous way.

Each simulator engine is made ready to start by statement #21 already introduced above for the local version. The distributed simulation can then be launched by first starting the RTI infrastructure, then starting the *FederationManager* with proper parameters (simulation time, number of simulators in the distributed simulation, etc) and finally starting the simulators in sequence, by use of conventional Java run commands.

5 Conclusions

The problem of defining a simulation language that can equivalently support local or distributed simulation by the transparent use of DS standards (in particular the HLA standard) has been addressed. The introduced language, called jEQN, facilitates the development of local or HLA-based distributed simulation programs of extended queueing networks (EQN) and yields a significant savings in effort.

The jEQN primitives and the HLA facilities are implemented as a Java library organized into four software layers that provide abstractions to isolate the developer from the implementation of underlying services, including HLA services. By use of jEQN no extra effort is required to implement a distributed EQN simulator with respect to a local one. An example development of a jEQN simulator has been presented to show how the distributed version is obtained with practically no extra effort with respect to the local one.

References

1. R. Fujimoto, Parallel and Distributed Simulation Systems, Wiley (2000)
2. G. Bolch, S. Greiner, H. de Meer and K. Trivedi, Queueing Networks and Markov Chains, Wiley (1998)
3. M. Veran and D. Portier, "QNAP2: A Portable Environment for Queueing Systems Modelling", Raport de Recherche 314, INRIA, Jun, 1984
4. C. Sauer, E. MacNair and S. Salza, A Language for Extended Queuing Network Models, *IBM Journal of Research and Development*, Vol. 24, n. 6, Nov, 1980
5. A. Verbraeck, "Component-based Distributed Simulation", *Proceedings of the 18th Workshop on Parallel and Distributed Simulation (PADS'04)*, pp. 141-148, Kuftein, Austria, May, 2004
6. G. Riley, M. Ammar, R. Fujimoto, A. Park, K. Perumalla and D. Xu, "A Federated Approach to Distributed Network Simulation", *ACM Transaction on Modeling and Computer Simulation (TOMACS)*, Vol. 14, n. 2, Apr, 2004
7. E. Page, R. Moose and S. Griffin, "Web-based Simulation in SimJava using Remote Method Invocation", *Proceedings of the 1997 Winter Simulation Conference*, pp 468-474, Atlanta, GA, Dec, 1997
8. P. Jacobs, N. Lang and A. Verbraeck, "D-SOL: A Distributed Java Based Discrete Event Simulation Architecture", *Proceedings of the 2002 Winter Simulation Conference*, pp 793-800, San Diego, CA, 8-11 Dec, 2002
9. K. Perumalla, "μsik: A Micro-kernel for Parallel/Distributed Simulation Systems", *Proceedings of the 19th Workshop on Parallel and Distributed Simulation (PADS'05)*, pp 59-68, Monterey, CA, Jun, 2005
10. IEEE, Standard for Modeling and Simulation (M&S) High Level Architecture (HLA) – framework and rules, Technical Report 1516, IEEE (2000)
11. R. Grable, J. Jernigan, C. Pogue and D. Divis, "Metrics for Small Projects: Experiences at the SED", *IEEE Software*, March-April 1999, pp 21-29
12. R. Nance, "The time and state relationships in simulation modeling", *Communications of the ACM*, Vol. 24 n. 4, 173-179, Apr, 1981.
13. D. Gianni, "jRand: a flexible and extendible framework for number sequences for simulation programs", RI.09.03, Dept. of Computer Science, Software Eng. Lab., University of Rome TorVergata, Dec, 2003

Exact Performance Measures for Peer-to-Peer Epidemic Information Diffusion

Öznur Özkasap[1,*], Emine Şule Yazıcı[2], Selda Küçükçifçi[2,**], and Mine Çağlar[2]

[1] Department of Computer Engineering
[2] Department of Mathematics
Koç University, Istanbul, Turkey
{oozkasap, eyazici, skucukcifci, mcaglar}@ku.edu.tr

Abstract. We consider peer-to-peer anti-entropy paradigms for epidemic information diffusion, namely pull, push and hybrid cases, and provide exact performance measures for them. Major benefits of the proposed epidemic algorithms are that they are fully distributed, utilize local information only via pair-wise interactions, and provide eventual consistency, scalability and communication topology-independence. Our contribution is the derivation of exact expressions for infection probabilities through elaborated counting techniques on a digraph. Considering the first passage times of a Markov chain based on these probabilities, we find the expected message delay experienced by each peer and its overall mean as a function of initial number of infectious peers. In terms of these criteria, the hybrid approach outperforms pull and push paradigms, and push is better than the pull case. Such theoretical results would be beneficial when integrating the models in several peer-to-peer distributed application scenarios.

Keywords: peer-to-peer, epidemic, anti-entropy, counting, Markov chain.

1 Introduction

An efficient approach for information diffusion in distributed systems is to utilize epidemic algorithms that involve pair-wise propagation of updates. Epidemic algorithms are fully distributed and randomized approaches such that every peer in an information diffusion session picks a (subset of the other) peer(s) randomly for efficient propagation of updates, that happens through periodic rounds. The underlying epidemics theory for the biological systems study the spreading of infectious diseases through a population [1]. When applied to an information diffusion application, such protocols have beneficial features such as scalability, robustness against failures and provision of eventual consistency. We investigate variations of the epidemic algorithms used in the context of distributed information diffusion and derive exact performance measures for them.

* Research supported by TUBITAK (The Scientific and Technical Research Council of Turkey) under CAREER Award Grant 104E064.
** Research partly supported by TUBA (Turkish Academy of Sciences).

A. Levi et al. (Eds.): ISCIS 2006, LNCS 4263, pp. 866–876, 2006.

One of the first studies that applies epidemic methods to computer systems used the idea for spreading updates in a replicated database [2]. Several succeeding work utilized epidemic (or sometimes so called gossip-style, to reflect rumor propagation in a social network) communication in a variety of contexts such as large-scale direct mail systems [3], group membership tracking [4], support for replicated services [5], message garbage collection [6], failure detection [7], loss recovery in reliable multicast [8], and distributed information management [9]. [10] gives an overview of epidemic information dissemination where the focus is on four design constraints namely, membership, network awareness, buffer management, and message filtering.

There are different classes of epidemic processes one of which is referred to as anti-entropy. In anti-entropy, information diffusion progresses periodically via fixed length time periods, typically larger than the maximum round trip time between peers, and called rounds. In each round, every peer picks another site at random, and shares its state information. We study three approaches for update-exchange; namely, pull, push and hybrid cases as particular models of anti-entropy. When a peer holding information to be shared picks a peer lacking that information and if this triggers dissemination from the holding peer to the lacking peer, we say the dissemination occurs in pull fashion. In contrast, if information dissemination is triggered when a peer lacking a particular information picks a peer holding that information, it has occurred in push fashion. The third approach is a hybrid of the two where information diffusion takes place in both ways. In [11], pull and push anti-entropy approaches are compared through a binomial probability distribution for information flow where push approach is shown to be superior in terms of message latency.

In this study, we develop exact performance measures for the pull, push and hybrid information diffusion models of anti-entropy. The number of peers lacking information to be shared forms a Markov chain advancing in rounds. The transition probabilities on the chain are derived through elaborated counting techniques on a digraph exactly, with no resort to approximate probability distributions that rely on several independence assumptions. Indeed, we show that the binomial model for the pull approach in [11] is only approximate, whereas it is exact for the push approach. We analyze the exact dynamics through the Markov chain with no assumptions on any parameters. In particular, we compute the expected delay of each peer as well as per arbitrary peer with respect to the initial number of members holding information in the population. The hybrid approach outperforms pull and push paradigms, and push is better than the pull case. Such results would be beneficial when integrating the models in several distributed scenarios such as replicated servers, loss recovery, failure detection and group membership management.

Previously, exact as well as asymptotical distributions have been studied for different epidemic models. In [12, 13], the epidemic process is defined on a random graph. In [14], the infection is spread through random contact in a manner less structured than a random graph and simpler than anti-entropy.

The paper is organized as follows. In Sect. 2, our models for the pull, push and hybrid anti-entropy are explained. The exact probability distributions are derived in Sect. 3. In Sect. 4, the Markov chain formulation and delay computations are given. Finally, Sect. 5 includes the conclusions and future work.

2   Model Descriptions

A popular distribution model based on the theory of epidemics is the anti-entropy [1]. According to the terminology of epidemiology, a peer holding information or an update it is willing to share is called *infectious*. A peer is called *susceptible* if it has not yet received an update. In the anti-entropy process, non-faulty peers are always either susceptible or infectious. Data diffusion progresses periodically via rounds of epidemics. In each round, every peer picks another site at random, and exchanges its state information with the selected one. We study the following approaches for update-exchange that execute in a fully distributed manner.

Pull Approach: When an infectious peer (holding data to be shared) picks a susceptible peer (lacking the specific data) randomly, this triggers data dissemination from infectious peer to the susceptible. Steps involved in the dissemination between two such peers is depicted in Fig.1(a) where infectious peer (on the left) has data labelled A. The infectious peer sends a digest (also referred to as gossip) message including its state information. On receiving digest and comparing it with its local data, the susceptible peer finds out it lacks A and sends a request for A back to the infectious. Upon getting request, infectious peer sends a retransmission of data A which causes the other peer to be infectious for A. In fact, each peer in the system performs state exchange periodically and concurrently with the others. Moreover, each peer may have a set of data in its local buffer. Therefore, a digest message generated by a peer would consist of the state information on the current contents of its message buffer. Spreading updates is triggered by susceptible peers when they are picked as gossip destinations by infectious peers.

Push Approach: If a susceptible peer picks an infectious peer randomly, and sends its state information, this triggers information dissemination from infectious peer to the susceptible. Steps involved in the dissemination between two such peers is depicted in Fig.1(b) where infectious peer (on the left) has data labelled A. The infectious peer on receiving digest and comparing it with its local data finds out that the digest owner lacks A and directly retransmits, or pushes data A which causes the other peer to become infectious for A. As illustrated in the figure, in the push approach, no request messages are used. Spreading updates is triggered by infectious peers when they are selected as gossip targets by susceptible peers.

Hybrid Approach: This is a hybrid of two approaches described above. As illustrated in Fig.1(c), when a peer sends its digest to a randomly selected peer in the population, this may trigger data dissemination at both peers. Consider the case where a peer has data A and the other has data B. When the former

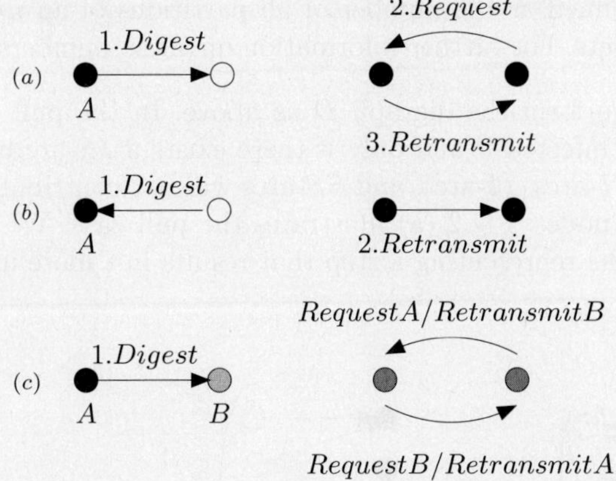

Fig. 1. Model Descriptions

selects the latter as the digest target in a given round, information A and B would be disseminated to the peer that lack it using pull-based or push-based approaches together. This approach is useful for delay sensitive applications since it decreases overall delay during data dissemination at the cost of possible duplicate data transmissions.

3   Exact Diffusion Probabilities

In this section, we will restrict our attention to the processes of distributing a single data message. Therefore, a peer with a copy of the data message is referred to as infectious; otherwise, it would be susceptible. Each step of this diffusion process can be represented by a digraph D where a peer in the population corresponds to a node of the digraph (We will assume there are n peers in the population). If the node u chooses to communicate with the node v then there will be an arc with the tail u and the head v in D. Since each node chooses exactly one node at each step the out degree of each node will be 1 in D. The number of all possible such digraphs with n nodes is $(n-1)^n$. All of these digraphs are equally likely for each step of this process. Therefore, we will count the number of digraphs that infect i more nodes and take the ratio of this number with the number of all possible digraphs to find the probability of infecting i more nodes. Note that if there are k infectious nodes, after one step there will be $k+i$ infectious nodes, where $k+i = 1, 2, \ldots, n$.

Let S be the set of all susceptible nodes and I be the set of all infectious nodes with $|I| = k$ and $|S| = n - k$. For simplicity, we will denote arcs with susceptible heads and infectious tails by IS-arcs, similarly arcs with infectious heads and susceptible tails, infectious heads and infectious tails, and susceptible heads and susceptible tails will be represented by SI-arcs, II-arcs, and SS-arcs, respectively. Note that D is the disjoint union of four subgraphs formed by IS-arcs, SI-arcs, II-arcs, and SS-arcs. Let $S(n, k)$ denote the Stirling number of second kind defined as the number of all partitions of an n-element set into k nonempty subsets. For further information on these numbers see [15].

Pull Case: We form the digraph D as above. In the pull case, a susceptible node s will be infected if and only if there exists a IS-arc in D with the head s. Therefore, SI-arcs, II-arcs, and SS-arcs will not contribute to the number of new infectious nodes. Fig.2 (a) illustrates the pull case. We will determine the number digraphs representing a step that results in i more infectious nodes.

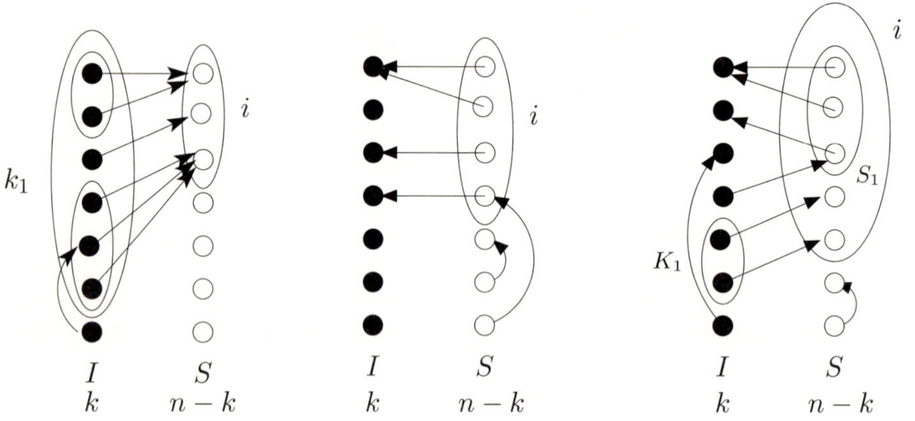

Fig. 2. (a) Pull Case (b) Push Case (c) Hybrid Case

The number of different possible subgraphs formed by SI-arcs and SS-arcs is $(n-1)^{n-k}$, since each of the $n-k$ nodes in S can be adjacent to $n-1$ different nodes.

Now we need to count the number of different possible subgraphs that can be formed by IS-arcs and II-arcs. Let k_1 be the number of IS-arcs. Note that k_1 has to be at least i since each IS-arc infects at most one new node in S also there are $\binom{k}{k_1}$ such k_1-subsets of I. We have $k - k_1$ II-arcs. The number of different possible subgraphs formed by these arcs is $(k-1)^{k-k_1}$. Finally we will count the number of different subgraphs that can be formed by IS-arcs. Among $n-k$ susceptible nodes there are $\binom{n-k}{i}$ different i-subsets of S that may be infected. There are $S(k_1,i)i!$ different ways for k_1 nodes to infect exactly i new nodes. So Therefore, the number of different subgraphs that can be formed by IS-arcs and II-arcs is $\sum_{k_1=i}^{k} \binom{k}{k_1}(k-1)^{k-k_1}\binom{n-k}{i}S(k_1,i)i!$. Hence, the probability of infecting i more nodes in the next step given $|I| = k$ is

$$p(i|k) = \frac{(n-1)^{n-k}\binom{n-k}{i}i! \sum_{k_1=i}^{k} \binom{k}{k_1}(k-1)^{k-k_1}S(k_1,i)}{(n-1)^n}$$

$$= \frac{\binom{n-k}{i} i! \sum_{k_1=i}^{k} \binom{k}{k_1} (k-1)^{k-k_1} S(k_1, i)}{(n-1)^k} .$$

where $k = 2, 3 \ldots, n-1$ and $i = 0, 1, \ldots, n-k$.

For the case $k = 1$, we can easily see that $p(0|1) = 0$ and $p(1|1) = 1$.

In [11], a binomial probability distribution model is assumed for the infection probabilities at each step. It turns out that this is only approximate since the distribution found above is not binomial.

Push Case: In the push case, a susceptible node s will be infected if and only if there exists a SI-arc with the tail s. Therefore, IS-arcs, II-arcs, and SS-arcs will not contribute to the number of new infectious nodes.

Fig.2 (b) illustrates the push case. The number different possible subgraphs formed by IS-arcs and II-arcs is $(n-1)^k$. Since i new nodes will be infected there are i SI-arcs and $\binom{n-k}{i}$ different i-subsets of S. For each SI-arc there are k different choices for the head of the arc, therefore there are $\binom{n-k}{i} k^i$ different possible subgraphs formed by these arcs. Finally, as there are $n-k-i$ SS-arcs, the number different possible subgraphs formed by SS-arcs is $(n-k-1)^{n-k-i}$. Hence, the probability of infecting i more nodes after the step given $|I| = k$ is

$$p(i|k) = \frac{(n-1)^k \binom{n-k}{i} k^i (n-k-1)^{n-k-i}}{(n-1)^n} = \frac{\binom{n-k}{i} k^i (n-k-1)^{n-k-i}}{(n-1)^{n-k}} .$$

where $k = 1, 2, \ldots, n-2$ and $i = 0, 1, \ldots, n-k$.

Clearly, when $k = n-1$, we get $p(0|k) = 0$ and $p(1|k) = 1$. The probability distribution above can be rewritten as

$$\binom{n-k}{i} \left(\frac{k}{n-1}\right)^i \left(\frac{n-k-1}{n-1}\right)^{n-k-i}$$

which can now be recognized as binomial distribution with parameters $n-k$ and success probability $k/(n-1)$. This coincides with the distribution modeled in [11] through probabilistic arguments. The only difference is that the number of possible nodes among which an infectious node chooses to communicate is rounded as n in [11]. In fact, it is $n-1$ as given in the present analysis.

Hybrid Case: In the hybrid case, a susceptible node s will be infected if and only if there exists either a SI-arc with the tail s or an IS-arc with the head s. Therefore, II-arcs and SS-arcs will not contribute to the number of new infectious nodes.

Fig.2 (c) illustrates the hybrid case. There are i new infectious nodes and $\binom{n-k}{i}$ different i-subsets of S. Let S_1 be the set of the tails of SI-arcs where $|S_1| = i_1$. There are $\binom{i}{i_1}$ i_1- subsets of each i-set. The number different possible subgraphs formed by SI-arcs and SS-arcs is $\binom{n-k}{i} \binom{i}{i_1} k^{i_1} (n-k-1)^{n-k-i_1}$.

Let K_1 be the set of nodes that are the tails of the IS-arcs whose heads are in $S \setminus S_1$, where $|K_1| = k_1$. There are $\binom{k}{k_1}$ different ways to choose K_1. These k_1 arcs will infect $i - i_1$ new nodes and there are $S(k_1, i - i_1)(i - i_1)!$ different ways to do this. Finally the remaining $k - k_1$ arcs can be chosen in $(k - 1 + i_1)^{k-k_1}$ different ways. Therefore, the number of different possible subgraphs formed by IS and II-arcs can be calculated as

$$\Theta_{k,i}(k_1, i_1) = \sum_{k_1 = i - i_1}^{k} \binom{k}{k_1} (k - 1 + i_1)^{k-k_1} S(k_1, i - i_1)(i - i_1)!.$$

Hence, the probability of infecting i more nodes in the next step given $|I| = k$ is

$$p(i|k) = \frac{\binom{n-k}{i}}{(n-1)^n} \sum_{i_1 = 0}^{i} \binom{i}{i_1} k^{i_1} (n - k - 1)^{n-k-i_1} \Theta_{k,i}(k_1, i_1)$$

where $k = 2, 3 \ldots, n - 2$ and $i = 0, 1, \ldots, n - k$.

Now, we will consider the end points. If $k = n - 1$, $p(0|k) = 0$ and $p(1|k) = 1$. If $k = 1$, $p(0|1) = 0$ and $p(i|1) = \dfrac{\binom{n-1}{i} i (n - 2)^{n-i-1} (n - 1)}{(n - 1)^n}$ for all $i \geq 1$. There can be $\binom{n-1}{i}$ different i-subsets of S and i different possibilities for the head of the SI-arc, call this node u. There are $n - 1$ possibilities for the arc with the tail u. The arcs coming out of the rest of the $i - 1$ nodes will have heads in I and there is a unique way to do this. Finally the remaining $n - i - 1$ arcs can be chosen in $(n - 2)^{n-i-1}$ different ways.

4   Expected Delay Per Peer

Many stochastic models of epidemic processes are based on the fact that the number of infectious peers, equivalently the number of susceptibles as the population size n is fixed, forms a Markov chain [1]. In existing models, the transition probabilities are modeled according to a probability distribution or left as rates to be estimated from the network due to the complexity of the problem. What is accomplished in Sect. 3 is that we have analyzed the true dynamics taking place at each transition of the Markov chain with no assumptions on any parameters. Using the analytical expressions derived for the transition probabilities, we find the message delay in this section.

The Markov chain under consideration is $\{I_t : t = 0, 1, 2, \ldots\}$ where I_t denotes the number of infectious processes at time t. The transition probabilities $P_{kj} = P\{I_{t+1} = j | I_t = k\}$ can be obtained from $p(i|k)$ given in the previous section by

$$P_{kj} = p(j - k|k) \qquad j = k, k + 1, \ldots, n$$

where $j - k$ is the number of newly infected peers. Clearly, $P_{kj} = 0$ if $j < k$. In [11], the authors show that the delay experienced by each peer can be found by considering the first passage time of I_t to a specific set of states. Let $s_{i\bar{j}}$ denote the first passage time from state i to the set of states $\bar{j} = \{j, j+1, \ldots, n\}$, for $i = 1, 2, \ldots, j-1$. The expected time for the jth infection to occur, or the mean delay that the jth member to receive the message experiences, is given by $s_{k\bar{j}}$ when the initial number of infectious peers I_0 is k. In order to find $s_{k\bar{j}}$ even for a single k value, one needs to solve the set of equations

$$(I - P_{\bar{j}})S_{\bar{j}} = \underline{1} \tag{1}$$

where $P_{\bar{j}}$ is the upper left $j-1 \times j-1$ portion of matrix P, I is the $j-1 \times j-1$ identity matrix, $S_{\bar{j}} = [s_{1\bar{j}}, s_{2\bar{j}}, \ldots, s_{j-1,\bar{j}}]^{\text{T}}$ and $\underline{1}$ is a vector of 1's [11]. Since P is upper triangular, solving system (1) does not pose any numerical difficulties.

The delay experienced by each peer is an important performance measure from user perspective. In Fig.3, the peers in the order they receive the message are plotted against expected number of rounds for different starting number k of infectious peers, for k=1,25,75 and n=100. That is, $s_{k\bar{j}}$ appears in the x-coordinate for $j = k, k+1, \ldots, n$ and $I_0 = k$. Hybrid approach performs significantly better than the others. Although push approach is only slightly better than pull case in terms of mean delay when $k = 1$, its total time to disseminate to the whole population is much lower than the other. The delay is clearly lower for push case when $k > 1$. On the other hand, some peers have lower expected delay in the course of the information diffusion process when $k = 1$ such as the 10th to 15th peers in the order of receiving the message.

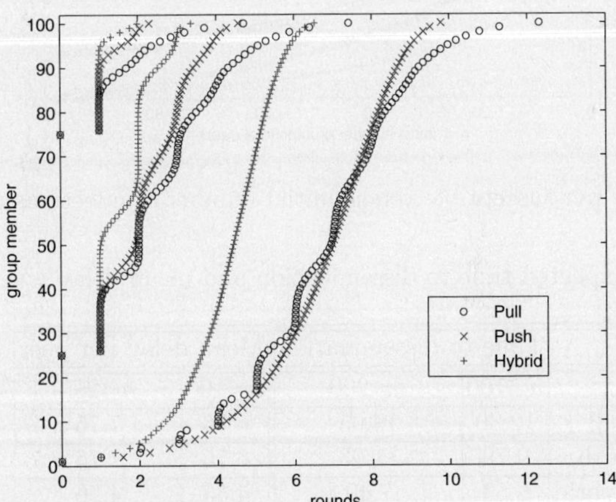

Fig. 3. Peers ordered according to their expected delays given in rounds, for 1, 25 and 75 starting number of infectious peers and n=100

Mean delay experienced per susceptible peer is depicted in Fig.4. In terms of this performance measure, the pull and push approaches behave similarly for small k, and the hybrid approach behaves like push case as k increases to n.

In [11], binomial distribution is used for modeling one step of epidemics for pull and push approaches. This happens to be the exact distribution for only push case as indicated in section 3.2. On the other hand, the model of pull case estimates the true probabilities pessimistically in [11]. The pull approach does not behave as poorly as predicted by the binomial model there.

The advantage of epidemic dissemination, in particular the anti entropy paradigm, is its scalability with respect to population size. That is why the foregoing analysis is repeated for n=200. The results being similar to $n = 100$ are not given here. In order to demonstrate scalability, we have tabulated the expected time of dissemination to the whole population and the mean delay per peer in Tab. 1. These values are consistent with the prediction of asymptotical results for epidemic processes that the delay values increase only logarithmically as n increases.

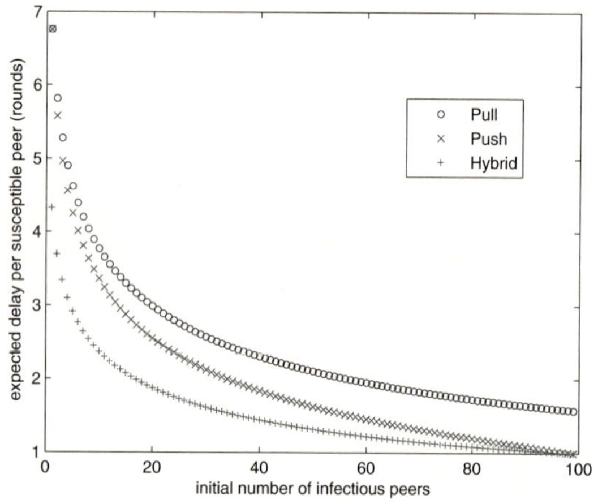

Fig. 4. Mean delay per susceptible versus initial number of infectious peers for n=100

Table 1. Expected time to dissemination and mean delay when $I_0 = 1$

	Time to dissemination		Mean delay per peer	
	n=100	n=200	n=100	n=200
Pull	12.30	14.05	6.76	7.75
Push	9.79	11.03	6.75	7.75
Hybrid	6.53	7.40	4.33	4.96

5   Conclusions and Future Work

We have derived the exact probability distributions for the pull, push and hybrid information diffusion models of anti-entropy. To the best of our knowledge, this study is the first one deriving exact distributions which would be helpful in performance analysis of these epidemic diffusion models. In contrast, previous results rely on simplified models of epidemics usually requiring estimation of several parameters. Our findings show that the binomial model used previously for pull case is not accurate whereas the model for push case is exact. There exists no previous probability model for the hybrid case, the exact distribution of which is derived in this paper.

We have computed the expected delay of each peer as well as per arbitrary peer exactly, depending on the initial number of infectious members in the population. The hybrid approach outperforms pull and push paradigms, and push is better than pull case. Such results would be beneficial when integrating the models in several distributed scenarios such as replicated servers, loss recovery, failure detection and group membership management. Since the probability distributions found in this paper are exact, any possible discrepancies with real measurements of networks or their simulations can lead us to scrutinize other aspects such as overhead associated with each approach. For instance, the duplicate messages associated with the hybrid case due to both pull and push deliveries are worth counting in order to determine any trade off with the superiority of this case.

Dissemination of only one message has been considered. Initialization with a bigger volume of content such as in file sharing applications can be analyzed, the possibility of gossiping to more than one peer and partial knowledge of membership could also be incorporated as future work. Finally, evaluating the probabilities $p(i|k)$ are not computationally intensive, but accuracy is a concern for large group sizes although can be handled with the state of the art computing abilities. On the other hand, asymptotic expressions for large n would be useful.

References

1. N. T. J. Bailey. *The Mathematical Theory of Infectious Diseases and its Applications*. Charles Griffin and Compan, London, 1975.
2. A. Demers, D.Greene, C. Hauser, W. Irish, J. Larson, S. Shenker, H. Sturgis, D. Swinehart, and D. Terry. Epidemic algorithms for replicated database maintenance. In *Proc. of the Sixth ACM Symp. on Principles of Distributed Computing*, 1–12, 1987.
3. A. Birrell, R. Levin, R. Needham, M. Schroeder. Grapevine: Providing availability using lazy replication. *ACM Transactions on Computer Systems*, 10(4):360–391, 1992.
4. R. Golding and K. Taylor. *Group Membership in the Epidemic Style*. Technical Report, UCSC-CRL-92-13, University of California at Santa Cruz, 1992.
5. R. Ladin, B. Lishov, L. Shrira, and S.Ghemawat. An exercise in distributed computing. *Communications of the ACM*, 25(4):260–274, 1982.
6. K. Guo. *Scalable Message Stability Detection Protocols*. Ph.D. dissertation, Cornell University, Dept. of Computer Science, 1998.
7. R. van Renesse, Y. Minsky, and M. Hayden. A gossip-style failure detection service. In *Proceedings of Middleware98*, 55–70, 1998.
8. K. Birman, M. Hayden, O. Ozkasap, Z. Xiao, M. Budiu, and Y. Minsky. Bimodal multicast. *ACM Transactions on Computer Systems*, 17(2):41–88, 1999.
9. R. van Renesse, K. Birman, W. Vogels. Astrolabe: A robust and scalable technology for distributed system monitoring, management, and data mining. *ACM Transactions on Computer Systems*, 21(2):164–206, 2003.

10. P. Eugster, R. Guerraoui, A.-M. Kermarrec, and L. Massoulie. Epidemic information dissemination in distributed systems. *IEEE Computer*, 60–67, May 2004.
11. M. Çağlar, Ö. Özkasap. A chain-binomial model for pull and push-based information diffusion. *Proc. of IEEE ICC*, 2006.
12. I. B. Gertsbakh. Epidemic Process on a Random Graph: Some Preliminary Results. *J. Appl. Prob.*, 14:427–438, 1977.
13. Jerzy Jaworski. Epidemic Processes on Digraphs of Random Mappings. *J. Appl. Prob.*, 36:780–798, 1999.
14. Boris Pittel. On Spreading a Rumor. *SIAM Journal on Applied Mathematics*, 47(1):213–223, 1987.
15. J. H. van Lint and R. M. Wilson. *A Course in Combinatorics*. Cambridge University Press, 1992.

A Leader Election Protocol for Timed Asynchronous Distributed Systems

Amirhasan Amintabar[1], Alexander Kostin[1], and Ljudmila Ilushechkina[2]

[1] Comp. Eng. Dep., Eastern Mediterranean University, Magusa, Turkey
{Amirhasan.Amintabar, Alexander.Kostin}@emu.edu.tr
[2] Software Eng. Dep., Moscow Inst. of Electronic Tech., Russia
ljuda_il@fromru.com

Abstract. A leader election protocol for timed asynchronous distributed systems is presented. The proposed scheme is based on reliable multicast where all participating processes of the group will receive protocol messages. In this protocol, the group members do not need to know each other's addresses to communicate. Also, they do not have to make any reconfiguration if some members crash, join or leave the group. The paper describes the proposed protocol, estimates its performance in simulation and compares this simulation with an analytical model. It is found that the communication complexity of the protocol is of O(N). As simulation formalism, a class of extended Petri nets was used.

Keywords: Timed asynchronous distributed system, leader election.

1 Introduction

Leader election is a fundamental problem that arises in many areas of distributed computing. The goal of a distributed leader election protocol is to select exactly one of the processes to play some particular role as a master. The problem of leader election was investigated for the first time in detail by Garcia Molina in 1982 [1].

With a few exceptions [4], [5], [10], all known leader election algorithms are based on unicast communication between processes [2], [11], [12], [13], [14]. This means that participating processes should know the explicit addressing information about processes in the group. Such a scheme considerably complicates handling of changes in the group membership of processes, since each process must be given the necessary group membership information.

In our recent work [8], a leader election scheme is proposed that is based on multicast group communication. Using multicast mode considerably simplifies problems of addressing of group members and group membership management. An important additional benefit of using a multicast mode is a relatively simple way of maintaining of state information in leaders, when the current leader crashes and a new leader is elected. However, the scheme in [8] implies that the underlying distributed system is synchronous. In particular, such a distributed system requires an upper bound on the time of delivering messages from a source to destinations [9]. This requirement is difficult to achieve in real networks.

A. Levi et al. (Eds.): ISCIS 2006, LNCS 4263, pp. 877–886, 2006.

Our multicast-based leader election scheme [8] is extended for the use in a general environment of timed asynchronous distributed systems. In a timed asynchronous distributed system, communication delays and scheduling delays are unbounded, although most messages arrive at their destinations within a known delay and most actual scheduling delays at processing nodes are shorter than some known period [9].

Due to absence of an upper bound on the time of delivering messages, it is possible that, at some time intervals, there can be more than one leader in the system. However, the protocol is tolerable to such situation; since it is capable to remove redundant leaders once the first request for a service is multicast by any involved process. In the paper, Section 2 describes the system model. Section 3 explains the protocol and the crash model of the leader. Section 4 discusses time-outs and the communication complexity. Section 5 contains the simulation. Finally, Section 6 concludes the paper.

2   The System Model and Assumptions

The underlying distributed system can be viewed logically as a finite population queuing system with N processes, one of which, in addition to its specific application task, holds the leader of the system. All the processes communicate using reliable multicast which guarantees that all the group members receive the messages [3].

A normal process behaves in the following way. Basically it performs some application specific task, which is called the main work of the process in this paper. At the end of a step of the main work, the process generates a request for a service from the leader and multicasts it to the group of processes, one of which is the leader process. After this, it does not send more requests until a reply from the existing leader arrives or specific time-out elapses.

The leader process is responsible to serve the incoming request messages. For example, in the simplest case, this service could be just to generate the next sequence number and send it by multicasting to the requesting process. In particular, the sequence number can be the number of reply messages sent by the leader to the process group up to now. Since the leader sends its reply messages through multicasting, all the other processes in this group will receive each reply message and can learn the latest sequence number.

Each normal process assumes that there is a leader somewhere in the system unless it suspects the absence of it, when no reply arrives during a specific time-out. To minimize the communication traffic of the protocol, it is assumed that only processes that sent a request during some time window, but did not receive a reply message from the leader, participate in the election of a new leader.

It is also assumed that the crash of the leader implies the crash of the entire process that holds the leader. Furthermore, we assume for simplicity that the processes which participate in the election do not crash during the election procedure. This restriction will be dropped in a more elaborate version of the protocol by introducing an additional time-out. Finally, no process is allowed to send requests to get a service from the leader during the election.

3   Description of the Protocol

In this section, an informal description of the proposed protocol is given and its state diagram is explained. As we stated above, the protocol is for timed asynchronous distributed systems. It is based on multicast messaging with the following types:

REQ: It is a request message that a process sends to get some service from the leader.

REP: A reply message sent by the leader. Each process upon receipt of a *REP* message updates its information about the current state of the system, such as the latest sequence number, and uses it if it has been destined to this process.

WBL: This message represents the desire of a process to become a leader ("I want to be a leader"). A process starts an election by multicasting a *WBL* message. Then recipients realizes that an election is going on in the system and does not send request messages any more until the current election finishes and a new leader is established.

IAL: This message means "I am the leader" and is used by the current leader to announce this fact to all other processes. Any other process receiving it realizes that the current election has finished. *WBL* and *IAL* are considered as *election messages*.

In the steady state of the system, there is a leader serving processes. In this state, each process routinely multicasts *REQ* messages to get some service from the leader. The leader, in return, replies to each *REQ* message by multicasting a *REP* message.

If, for some *REQ* message sent by a process P_i, no *REP* message has received during a time-out T_0, then process P_i will think that the leader is crashed or absent. From this moment of time, process P_i starts an election by multicasting a *WBL* message and starting a specific time-out T_1. If, during time-out T_1, another *WBL* is received from some other process P_j, then there is a *conflict* between two processes P_i and P_j that want to become a leader. To resolve the conflict, after elapsing T_1, each process involved in the conflict starts a random delay T_2 and becomes idle. The process, in which T_2 elapses first, resends its *WBL* message and restarts time-out T_1. If this process receives no further *WBL* during T_1 then it is the winner and multicasts an *IAL* message to announce it to all the processes in the group. However, if a conflict happens again, the procedure will continue until one of the processes wins.

Every process running the protocol keeps a set of state variables that represent the system as seen by the process. The most important variables are as follows:

LEDR: A process sets its LEDR variable to zero, on receipt of a *WBL* message, meaning an election started and no leader is available yet. Correspondingly, on receipt of an *IAL* message the process sets LEDR to 1, means the election has ended.

CNFL: It is used in conflict detection. A process, before sending a *WBL* message, sets its CNFL variable to zero. Arrival of a *WBL* from other processes makes CNFL to 1.

SEQN: The latest sequence number is provided by the current leader and is multicast to all the processes in *REP* messages. All the processes, upon receipt of a *REP* message, update their own variable SEQN to the new value received from the leader.

The most recent sequence number generated by the previous leader is the only value that a new leader must know. As the result of multicasting of reply messages by the leader, this number becomes known to each process in the group. Therefore, when a process becomes the new leader, it can continue to provide sequence numbers without any interruption in the service. A new process joining the group sets its variable SEQN to -1 and upon receipt of the first *REP* message from the current leader, sets SEQN to the correct value.

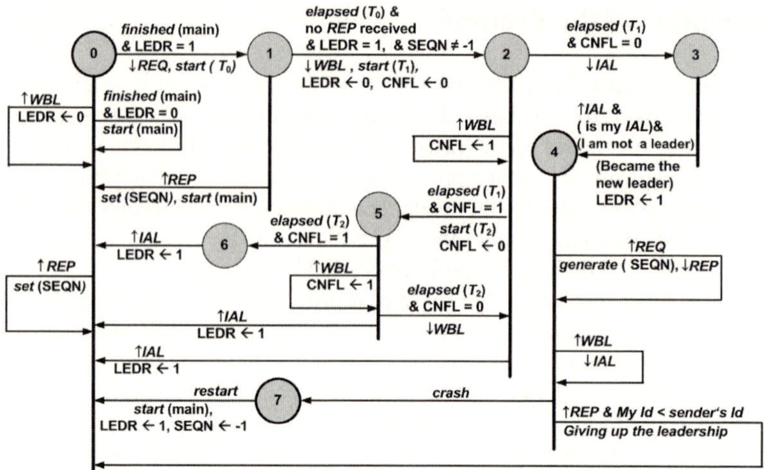

Fig. 1. A process state diagram. 0, 4 and 7 are main work, leadership and crash states.

A formalized specification of the protocol is presented here in the form of a simplified state diagram in Fig. 1. States of the diagram have the following meanings: 0 – the process is performing a step of its main work (or thinking); 1 – the process has sent a *REQ* message and is running time-out T_0; 2 – the process has initiated an election by sending a *WBL* message and is running time-out T_1; 3 – the process has sent an *IAL* message and is expecting to become the new leader; 4 – the process has received its own *IAL* message and has become the new leader; 5 – the process is running back-off delay T_2; 6 – the process is waiting for the election to finish; 7 – the process has crashed or left the system.

In the diagram, expressions over transition arcs are predicates in terms of events, logical statements, and functions. Expressions under transition arcs represent actions performed by the protocol if the corresponding logical expression over this transition arc is true. The events, predicates and functions have the following meanings: ↑X – a message of type X is received from some process; ↓X – the process multicasts a message of type X to other processes; *start* (T_i) – the process starts time-out T_i; *elapsed* (T_i) – delay or time-out T_i elapsed; *start* (main) – the process starts a step of its main work; *finished* (main) – the process completed a step of its main work; *set* (SEQN) – the process extracts the current sequence number from the arrived *REP* message and assigns it to SEQN; *generate* (SEQN) – the leader generates the next sequence number to be multicast in *REP* messages; *crash*() – the process crashed or left; *restart*() – the process restarted or joined the group.

As was mentioned in Sect. 1, the protocol tolerates existence of more than one leader during some time intervals. With more than one leader, a response to the *REQ* message will be a few multicast *REP* messages, from each leader. Therefore, each leader will receive *REP* message sent by the other leaders, and hence will realize their existence. In such a case, each leader behaves in the following way. If it receives a

REP message from a leader process which has a higher identifier, it gives up the leadership. Since there is only one of these leaders which has the highest identifier, there will be left only one leader in the system.

4 Time Outs, Delays and Communication Complexity

As was explained in Sect. 3, the protocol uses a few time-out and delays. Let us consider guidelines to estimate their values or ranges. Let τ_d be the interval during which, with high probability, a multicast message is delivered in the underlying network from a source process to all processes in the group. Then the value of the time-out T_0 is taken to wait for a reply after multicasting a *REQ* message by a process, must satisfy the inequality

$$T_0 > 2\tau_d + T_S, \tag{1}$$

where $2\tau_d$ is the amount of time for a message to be delivered from a source process to the most remote process in the group and back, and T_S is the maximal time of serving a request by the leader. Similarly, time-out T_1 must satisfy the inequality

$$T_1 > 2\tau_d, \tag{2}$$

which means that a process sending a *WBL* message must wait for a possible conflicting message during some window. Using a large value of time-out T_1 has no benefit for the traffic complexity of the protocol, as the conflict detection of the participating processes happens during the first $2\tau_d$ time of T_1. However, too large T_1 will increase the duration of the election procedure.

As explained in Sect. 3, random back-off delay T_2 is used for conflict resolution among processes. It is sufficient to use, for T_2, the uniform probability distribution in range $((T_2)_{min}, (T_2)_{max})$. This delay should not be too small. The expressions

$$(T_2)_{min} > 2\tau_d, \ (T_2)_{max} - (T_2)_{min} > 2\tau_d, \tag{3}$$

guarantee with high probability, that most sent *WBL* messages reach the processes during the window time $((T_2)_{min}, (T_2)_{max})$.

The duration of a step of the main work of a process in the group is assumed to be a random exponentially distributed variable with parameter $1/T_{main}$. Accordingly, mean values of the duration of the leader interval, and crash interval are random exponentially distributed with parameters $1/T_{lead}$ and $1/T_{crash}$. As assumed in Sect. 2, both leader interval and crash interval are large comparing to the mean time of the main work of a process, service time of a leader, and values of T_0, T_1, and T_2;

$$T_{lead}, T_{crash} \gg T_{main,}, T_S, T_0, T_1, \text{ and } T_2. \tag{4}$$

Thus, in our estimation, we neglect the possibility of a crashed leader rejoin the election procedure. When the leader process crashes, N-1 processes remain in the system. Let's λ_w denote the Poisson rate at which a process initiates a *WBL* message. It can be shown that

$$\lambda_w = 1/(T_{main} + T_0). \tag{5}$$

This is because in a group with no leader, a process which finished its main work will initiate a *WBL* message after elapsing time out T_0.

Indeed, a process may generate a *WBL* message only after it finishes a step of its main work during T_{main}, sends a *REQ* message and waits for time-out T_0 to elapse.

After the leader crashes, sooner or later one of the remaining *N-1* processes detects the absence of the leader and sends the first *WBL* message to start the election. Let's call this process *initiator process*. If another process also detects the leader's crash at the same time, the election will go to *competition phase*, see State 5 in Fig. 1. Any other process from remaining *N-2* processes can participate in the election only if it detects the leader's crash and sends a *WBL* message during the window time τ_d of the initiator process. This is the period starting from the moment when the first *WBL* message was sent to the network, to the moment when this message reaches all other *N-2* processes. This is because a process does not participate in the election if it already received a *WBL* message from some other processes.

The *communication complexity* of the proposed protocol is defined as the expected number of messages sent by all participating processes per election. There are two types of messaging traffics: messages related to ordinary interaction of the processes with the leader and messages relevant to the election procedure. Only the latter types of messages need to be taken into account to estimate the communication complexity of the protocol. It can be expressed as the sum that includes of the first *WBL* message sent by the *initiator process*, the number of *WBL* messages sent by *N-2* processes during the competition phase, and finally, one *IAL* message at the end of the election:

$$CC = 1 + CC_c + 1 = 2 + CC_c, \tag{6}$$

where CC_c denotes the number of *WBL* messages during the competition phase. The expected number of messages during interval τ_d of the first *WBL* message sent to the network by the *initiator process* is:

$$C_1 = (N - 2)\, \lambda_w\, \tau_d. \tag{7}$$

From now, an average of C_1 processes will start their random back-off time T_2. According to the protocol, if an involved process receives a *WBL* message during this time, it gives up the election and leaves the competition (State 6 of Fig. 1), otherwise after elapsing T_2 it sends another *WBL* and waits (in State 5) to see whether any conflicting *WBL* arrives. At this stage, the expected number of *WBL* messages can be approximated as follows:

$$C_2 = C_1\, \tau_d\, /\, R(T_2), \tag{8}$$

where $R(T_2)=((T_2)_{max} - (T_2)_{min})$ is the range of random time-out T_2 . After that, C_2 number of processes will continue the election procedure, which will result in the following number of the *WBL* messages:

$$C_3 = C_2\, \tau_d\, /\, R(T_2). \tag{9}$$

The procedure will continue until no conflict happens during T_2. Hence for the k_{th} competition stage, the expected number of *WBL* messages is:

$$C_k = C_{k-1}\, \tau_d\, /\, R(T_2) = C_1\, (\tau_d\, /\, R(T_2))^{k-1}, \; k = 2, 3, \tag{10}$$

Recall that at the end of each competition phase (if happens), there is one final *WBL* message which closes the competition and is sent by the winning process. Hence, the expected number of this message equals to the expected number of times an election goes to competition phase. That is when during the τ_d of the *initiator process* at least one more other process multicasts a *WBL* message. Let's denote the average number of this *WBL* message by C_f, then

$$C_f = (1 - \frac{e^{\tau_d \lambda_w (N-2)} \times \tau_d \lambda_w (N-2)^0}{0!}) \times 1 = 1 - e^{\tau_d \lambda_w (N-2)}. \tag{11}$$

So, the expected number of messages during a competition phase of an election is:

$$CC_c = C_f + C_1 + C_2 + C_3 + \ldots C_k = C_f + C_1 \sum_{k=0}^{\infty} (\frac{\tau_d}{R(T_2)})^k. \tag{12}$$

Finally, from (6), (11) and (12), the total average number of *WBL* massages during the complete election procedure can be approximated by the expression:

$$CC = 2 + \frac{(N-2)\tau_d}{(T_0 + T_{main})(1 - \tau_d /((T_2)_{max} - (T_2)_{min}))} + 1 - e^{\tau_d \lambda_w (N-2)}, \tag{13}$$

that is the expected number of messages of types *WBL* and *IAL* during an election procedure. As one can see from this expression, the communication complexity is of $O(N)$, so that the protocol can be considered as scalable with respect to the number of participating processes.

5   Simulation Performance Study of the Protocol

To investigate the proposed protocol of distributed leader election in more depth, its detailed formalized model was developed and an extensive simulation study was carried out. As a modeling formalism, a class of extended Petri nets, belonging to timed colored Petri nets, was used [6]. The simulation was carried out in the simulation system Winsim based on these Petri nets and implemented in Windows operating system [6]. The simulation model, in terms of extended Petri nets, was organized as a set of segments, each of which representing activity of one process. The number of segments representing processes could be varied to simulate the protocol with different number of processes in the group. The segments were linked to a model of a network.

The number of processes in the model was varied from 3 to 24. For each of the three loads of the leader, low (0.10) medium (0.50), and high (0.90), and given number of processes, the communication complexity of the protocol M was estimated in simulation by using the following expression:

$$M = \frac{1}{k} \sum_{i=1}^{k} (W_i + I_i), \tag{14}$$

where W_i and I_i are the numbers of *WBL* and *IAL* messages during election i, and k is the number of elections in a simulation run. Since, from a simulation point of view,

the protocol can be considered as a non-terminating system, its steady-state performance measures are of interest. To decrease the effect of the transient state, each run
was long enough to ensure that about 2000 elections happened in the system.

The correct setting of values of time-outs T_0 and T_1 is crucial for the proper protocol behavior. Based on the specified delivery time of messages in the model of the
underlying network and taking into account the protocol's assumptions, the following
values of time-outs were fixed in simulation experiments: $T_0 = T_1 = 500$ ms and T_2 is
random uniformly distributed in the range (40 - 100) ms. It is also assumed in the experiments that the distribution of the leader's life, the leader's crash and service time
of requests by the leader are exponentially distributed with the following mean times:
$T_{lead} = 30000$ ms, mean time of a leader's life in the system; $T_{crash} = 10000$ ms, mean
time of a leader's crash and $T_{serv} = 25$ ms, mean service time of a request. Finally, it is
also assumed that the duration of a step of the main work of a process is distributed
exponentially with the mean time T_{main} that was varied.

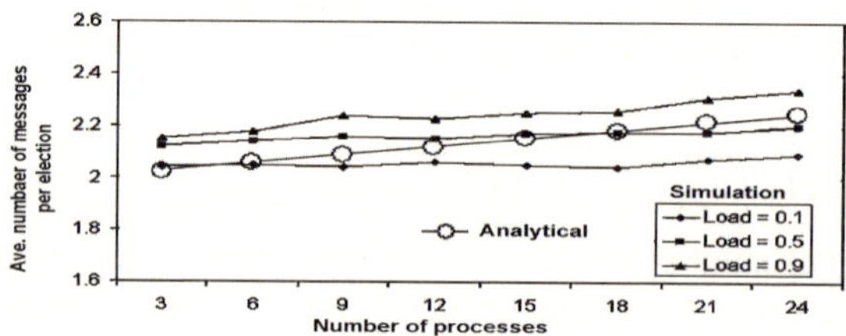

Fig. 2. Comparison of the simulation results to the analytical results

By changing the value of T_{main}, the performance of the protocol was investigated under different loads of the leader for different number of processes. The comparison of
the simulation results with analytical estimations for the average number of messages
per election is illustrated in Fig. 2.

These results show that the communication complexity increases slowly with the
number of processes. In fact, most often only one process detects the failure of the
leader, so that only two *election messages*, *WBL* and *IAL*, are multicast during an election. However, the number of election messages increases when the load of the leader
becomes high. In this case two factors contribute to affect the number of messages per
election. First, since the leader becomes busier, the timeout T_0 in a process that sent a
request can elapse and the process would erroneously start an election. Second, in a
large group, two or more processes can more often start an election at about the same
time, which will increase the number of conflicting *WBL* messages. However, as
shown in Fig. 2, even in a loaded system with 24 processes, communication complexity does not grow considerably. This complexity for such a system is around 2.4. Thus,
when the number of processes increases from 3 to 24, the communication complexity
rises less than 10%.

It is highly desirable that small changes of values of time-outs and delays do not
yield significantly different performance results of the protocol. This is especially
important for time-out T_0, since it serves to detect the crash of the leader. A short

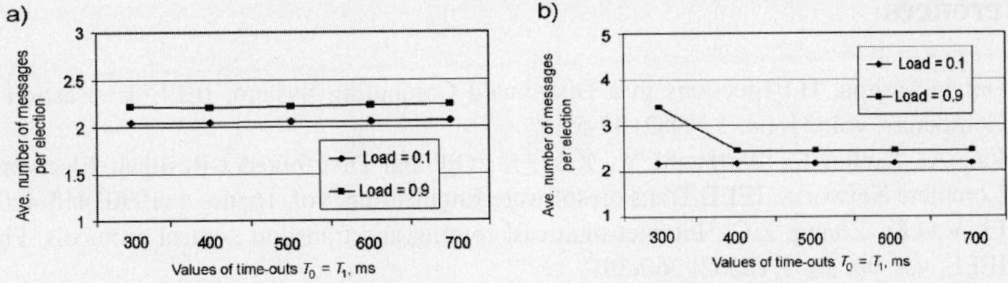

Fig. 3. Robustness to changes of time-outs T_0, T_1: a) 6 processes, b) 24 processes

time-out T_0 makes the processes erroneously think that there is no leader in the system when it elapse before any reply arrives from the leader. The time-out T_1 is also important since it serves to detect a conflict between the election participants. The time-out T_2 just spreads starting time of resending their *WBL* messages. To test the robustness of the protocol with respect to changes of time-outs T_0 and T_1, a sensitivity analysis has been carried out by simulation. The sensitivity analysis was done with low (0.10) and high (0.90) loads of the leader for 6 and 24 processes. The results are presented in Fig. 3.a and Fig. 3.b, respectively.

The graphs in both Figures do not exhibit any clear dependence of the communication complexity on time-outs T_0 and T_1 in a low loaded system. However, in a loaded system with relatively large number of processes, insufficient time-outs will increase the communication complexity. In particular, for a system with 24 processes and load = 0.90, short time outs $T_0 = T_1 = 300$ ms mislead the processes to initiate fake elections. However, reasonable values of time-outs do not degrade the performance of the protocol. As can be seen from Fig. 3.b, time-outs T_0 and T_1 can be chosen from the range between 400 to 700 ms with no effect on the performance.

6 Conclusion

A novel distributed leader election protocol is described for timed asynchronous systems. In timed synchronous systems there is no strict upper bound on communication delays. This may cause existence of more than one leader in the system for a short time. However, it was shown that all the redundant leaders except one will soon give up their leadership.

The behavior of the protocol was studied by extensive simulation in terms of extended Petri nets. The results of simulation and estimation showed that the protocol is scalable with respect to the number of processes. The estimation results also confirm the fact that communication complexity of the protocol is of O(N).

It is essential that the algorithm does not need any system reconfiguration when a new process joins the system or a process leaves the system. The system also quickly recovers when the current leader crashes, since all the processes possess enough information about the latest state of the system. If any of the processes becomes a new leader, it already has the necessary state information.

References

1. Garcia-Molina, H.: Elections in a Distributed Computing System, IEEE Transaction on Computers, vol. 31, no. 1 (1982) 47-59
2. Itai, A., Kutten S., Wolfstahl Y., Zaks, S.: Optimal Distributed t-Resilient Election in Complete Networks. IEEE Trans on software Engineering, vol. 16, no. 4 (1990) 415-420
3. Li, V.O.K., Zhang, Z.C.: Internet multicast routing and transport control protocols. Proc. IEEE, vol. 90, no. 3, (2002) 360-391
4. Donahoo, M.J., Ainapure, S.R.: Scalable multicast representative member selection. Proc. IEEE Infocom, March (2001) 259-268
5. Cidon, I., Mokryn, O.: Propagation and Leader Election in a Multihop Broadcast Environment. DISC98, Distributed Computing, 12th Inter. Symp., Greece (1998) 104-118
6. Kostin, A. and Ilushechkina, L.: Winsim: A Tool for Performance Evaluation of Parallel and Distributed Systems. LNCS, vol. 3261, (2004) 312-321
7. Banks, J., Carson, J.S., B.L., Nelson, Nicol, D.M.: Discrete- Event System Simulation. 3rd ed., Prentice-Hall (2001)
8. Amintabar, A., Kostin, A., Ilushechkina, L.: Simulation of a Novel Leader Election Protocol with the Use of Petri Nets. 9th IEEE International Symposium on Distributed Simulation and Real-time Applications, (DS-RT) Canada (2005) 283-289
9. Cristian, F., Fetzer C.: The timed asynchronous distributed system model, IEEE Transactions on Parallel and Distributed Systems, vol. 10, Iss 6, June (1999) 642 – 657
10. Raz, D., Shavitt, Y., Lixia Zhang.: Distributed council election. IEEE/ACM Transactions on Networking, Volume 12, Issue 3, June (2004) 483 – 492
11. Vasudevan, S., DeCleene, B., Immerman, N., Kurose, J., Towsley, D.: Leader Election Algorithms for Wireless Ad Hoc Networks. Proceedings of the DARPA Information Survivability Conference and Exposition (DISCEX'03) IEEE, vol. 1 (2003) 261-273
12. Singh, G.: Leader Election in the Presence of Link Failures. IEEE Transactions on Parallel and Distributed Systems, vol. 7, no. 3 (1996) 231-236
13. Nakano, K., Olariu, S.: A Survey on Leader Election Protocols for Radio Networks. International Symposium on Parallel Architectures, Algorithms and Networks (ISPAN '02), May (2002) 71-76
14. Yamashita, M., Kameda, T.: Leader Election Problem on Networks in which Processor Identity Numbers Are Not Distinct. IEEE Transactions on Parallel and Distributed Systems, vol. 10, no. 9, (1999) 878-887

Computing the Steady-State Distribution of G-networks with Synchronized Partial Flushing[*]

J.M. Fourneau and F. Quessette

PRiSM, Université de Versailles St-Quentin en Yvelines,
45 av. des Etats Unis, 78 035 Versailles Cedex, France

Abstract. We have shown in [5, 4, 3] that G-networks with synchronized partial flushing still have a product form steady-state distribution. These networks may have very complex dynamics where an arbitrary number of customers leave an arbitrary number of queues at the same time. The network flow equation are non linear and the usual approaches to solve them fail. We present here a new numerical algorithm which is based on a transform of the G-network to a classical G-network with triggers. We show that the flow equation are transformed by a classical elimination procedure. This new result puts more emphasis on the importance of flow equations following the approach recently proposed by Gelenbe in [2].

1   Introduction

The concept of Generalized networks (G-networks for short) has been introduced by Gelenbe in [7]. These networks contain customers and signals. In the first papers on this topic, signals were also denoted as negative customers. Signals are not queued in the network. They are sent to a queue, and disappear instantaneously. But before they disappear they may act upon some customers present in the queue. As customers may at the completion of their service become signals and be routed into another queue, G-networks exhibit some synchronized transitions which are not modeled by Jackson networks.

Various effects of signal have been investigated to prove a product form solution. They always imply that the customer in service leaves the queue immediately. So the synchronizations described by G-networks contain the simultaneous departures of several customers from several queues. These networks have a steady-state product form solution under usual Markovian assumptions: Poisson arrivals of external customers and signals, i.i.d. exponential service times, probabilistic routing. We also assume that the queues have an infinite capacity. The usual proof consists of the algebraic resolution of the global balance equations, assuming that a flow equation associated with the system has a unique solution. However the flow equations are non linear and we have to prove that they have a solution and derive to new algorithms to find it.

[*] This research is partially supported by project SMS, programme ANR non thématique 2005.

A. Levi et al. (Eds.): ISCIS 2006, LNCS 4263, pp. 887–896, 2006.

The existence problem was generally addressed in all the papers which describe a new product form solution. But the numerical computation of the solution is ignored. Usually it is reported that a fixed point operation is sufficient to find the flow solution. In [1] we have proved an algorithm to compute the solution of the flow equations for networks with positive and negative customers. This sandwich algorithm provides at each step an upper bound and a lower bound of the solution. However neither this algorithm nor the naive fixed point iteration can provide a solution for some recent G-networks based on more complex interaction of customers and signals.

Here we study the flow equations associated with a class of G-networks with a periodic list of deletions. Such networks of queues, denoted as synchronized partial flushing G-networks, are proved to have a product form distribution [5]. In such networks, a signal deletes a customer in each queue in an ordered list and it iterates on these deletions until the smallest queue becomes empty. We state that the fixed point iteration does not provide the numerical solution for the flow. Then we develop a network transform to obtain a simpler G-network. This network still has product form solution. Its flow equation is not the same. As the network is simpler we can generalize the sandwich algorithm in a straight forward manner. We prove that the solutions of the complex network can be found from the solution of the simple network by a simple elimination algorithm. This new statement puts more emphasis on the flow equations and strengthen the idea recently developed by Gelenbe in [2] on the importance of these equations.

The following of the paper is organized as follows. In Section 2 we present an example of a G-network with a complex dynamic with product form and we show that the naive fixed point iteration does not lead to a solution. We show that this transform preserves the numerical values of the solution even if the flow equation is not the same. For the sake of readability, we prefer showing an example. Then in Section 3 we detail the network transform to obtain a G-network with triggers and the algorithm to compute its steady-state distribution. It is important to remark that this network transform may have other applications: for instance the analysis of the stability region. It may also help to understand more deeply this new type of product form network whose dynamics are quite complex.

2   Three Queues with Synchronized Partial Flushing

Consider the following G-network with three queues. The services are exponential with rate μ_i for station i. The customers move between stations according to an arbitrary routing matrix R. The external customers arrive according to Poisson processes with rate λ_i^+ for station i. There are no external signals. At the completion of its service in station 1, a customer may enter station 2 as a signal with probability $P^-[1,2] = p$. The signal acts upon queue 2 and queue 3 even if it is sent to queue 2. First the signal deletes a customer in queue 2 if there is any. Then it applies the same action to queue 3 and it iterates deleting a customer in queue 2 and queue 3. If at any time the queue visited is empty the signal stops and disappears. More formally, let $n_2(t)$ and $n_3(t)$ be the number of customers in queue 2 and 3 respectively, just before the arrival of a signal at queue 2. The signal acts as follows:

$$\begin{cases} \text{If } n_2(t) \leq n_3(t) \text{ then } n_2(t+\epsilon) = 0 \text{ and } n_3(t+\epsilon) = n_3(t) - n_2(t) \\ \text{If } n_2(t) > n_3(t) \text{ then } n_2(t+\epsilon) = n_2(t) - n_3(t) - 1 \text{ and } n_3(t+\epsilon) = 0 \end{cases} \quad (1)$$

This network is a simple example of G-networks with synchronized partial flushing which has been defined and studied by Verchère et al [5, 4].

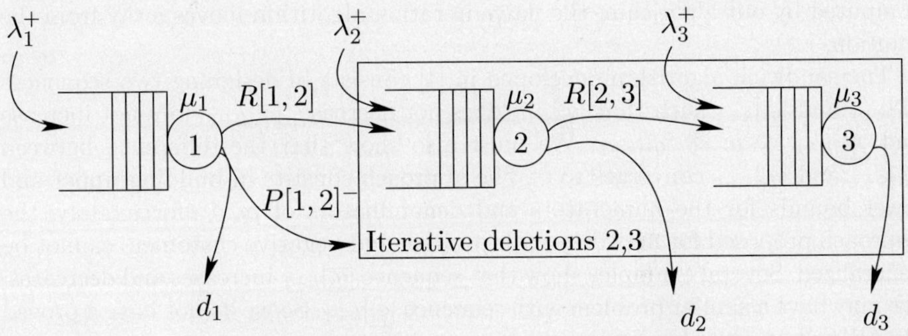

Fig. 1. Network with synchronized partial flushing

It has been proved in [5, 4] that G-networks with synchronized partial flushing have a product form solution. The proof is, as usual with G-network, based on the global balance equation. We summarize the result in the following property to put more emphasis on the second and third parts of the flow equation which makes the problem difficult to solve numerically:

Property 1. *If there exists a solution* $(\rho)_{i=1..3}$ *to the following non linear flow equation,*

$$\begin{cases} \rho_1 = \dfrac{\lambda_1^+ + \sum_{j=1}^3 \rho_j \mu_j R[j,1]}{\mu_1} \\[3ex] \rho_2 = \dfrac{\lambda_2^+ + \sum_{j=1}^3 \rho_j \mu_j R[j,2]}{\mu_2 + \dfrac{\mu_1 \rho_1 P^-[1,2]}{1 - \rho_2 \rho_3}} \\[3ex] \rho_3 = \dfrac{\lambda_3^+ + \sum_{j=1}^3 \rho_j \mu_j R[j,3]}{\mu_3 + \dfrac{\mu_1 \rho_1 P^-[1,2] \rho_2}{1 - \rho_2 \rho_3}} \end{cases} \quad (2)$$

such that $\rho_i < 1$ *for all* $i = 1, 2, 3$, *then the network has a steady-state distribution with product form solution:* $p(n) = \prod_{i=1}^3 (1 - \rho_i) \rho_i^{n_i}$.

Of course, the general results are more complex than this simple example. The network may contain classes of customers and several scheduling disciplines. Note also that when the list of deletions is a singleton, a queue which receives a signal is emptied. This model of queues with catastrophes (i.e. deletion of all the customers) was extensively studied following Gelenbe's pioneering work [9].

2.1   Iteration Fails

Let us consider the usual fixed point algorithm $x^{n+1} = F(x^n)$. We just give here several experimental results. First the naive iteration $x^{n+1} = F(x^n)$ may converge or fail depending of the numerical parameters of the problem (service and arrival rates, routing matrices). This is typically the case when we consider a network where some deletion lists are singletons. Even worse, the naive iteration is not stable in some cases. If we initialize the sequences with the exact solution computed by our algorithm, the naive iteration algorithm moves away from the solution.

The sandwich algorithm developed in [1] consists in designing two sequences $[\overline{q_i}]_{k+1}$ and $[\underline{q_i}]_{k+1}$ such that $[\underline{q_i}]_{k+1}$ does not decrease, $[\overline{q_i}]_{k+1}$ does not increase and $[\underline{q_i}]_{k+1} \leq \rho_i \leq [\overline{q_i}]_{k+1}$. We must also show that the difference between $[\overline{q_i}]_{k+1}$ and $[\underline{q_i}]_{k+1}$ converges to 0. The approach consists in building upper and lower bounds for the numerators and denominators of ρ_i. Unfortunately, the approach proposed for networks with positive and negative customers cannot be generalized. Several examples show that sequence $[\overline{q_i}]_{k+1}$ increases and decreases. We may have a similar problem with sequence $[\underline{q_i}]_{k+1}$. So we do not have a proved algorithm but some heuristics which may converge or not.

3   Network Transform

The aim of this Section is to show how we can transform a G-network with synchronized partial flushing into a G-network with triggers such that the solution of the former can be deduced from the solution of the latter. We begin by an example based on the network presented in the last Section. First we recall some definitions and results on G-networks with triggers.

3.1   G-networks with Triggers

In [8], Gelenbe generalized the first definition of signals (denoted as negative customers). These signals trigger customer movements between queues. So synchronizations between three queues are considered and the transitions with two departures and one arrival appear in the Markov chain. The routing is described by three matrices P^+ (the routing of customers), P^- (the routing of signals) and Q (the routing of customers triggered by the signals). The network is open and there are N queues. A customer which leaves queue i at its service completion goes to queue j either as a customer with probability $P^+[i, j]$, or as a signal with probability $P^-[i, j]$. It may also leave the network with probability d_i and we have for all i: $\sum_{j=1}^{N} P^+[i, j] + \sum_{j=1}^{N} P^-[i, j] + d_i = 1$. In a G-network with triggers, when a signal arrives at a non-empty queue (say queue j), it triggers a customer from queue j to queue k with probability $Q[j, k]$. If queue j is empty, then the signal has no effect. Q is a transition probability matrix: for all j, $\sum_{k=1}^{N} Q[j, k] = 1$. Service times are i.i.d exponential with rate μ_i and external arrivals of customers and signals follow Poisson processes with rate λ_i^+ and λ_i^- respectively. The fundamental result about these networks is the proof of a product form solution which is established in [8].

Theorem 1. *(Gelenbe) Consider an open G-network, if the non linear flow equation*

$$\rho_i = \frac{\lambda_i^+ + \sum_j \mu_j \rho_j P^+[j, i] + \sum_j \sum_k \mu_j \rho_j P^-[j, k] \rho_k Q[k, i]}{\mu_i + \sum_j \mu_j \rho_j P^-[j, i]} \tag{3}$$

has a solution such that $\rho_i < 1$, $\forall i \in [1..N]$, then the steady-state distribution exists and has a product form: $p(\boldsymbol{n}) = \prod_{i=1}^{N}(1 - \rho_i)\rho_i^{n_i}$.

For the example we describe now, we only need a single class network. However in general we use a generalization of the previous theorem with several classes of signals and triggers to represent the routes.

3.2   An Example of Network Transform

Consider now the G-network with triggers depicted in figure 2. Stations 1 to 3 are the same as in the former example. We assume that queue 1 may send a signal to queue 2 (with probability $P^-[1, 2] = p$). When a signal arrives at queue 2 it moves a customer from queue 2 to queue 4. After a service in queue 4 the customer is sent to queue 3 as a signal with probability 1. In that queue, the signal triggers a customer to queue 5. In queue 5, the customer receives service and is routed as a signal to queue 2 where it can again triggers a customer. The routing of customers and signals is completely specified by the three routing matrices associated with a G-network with triggers:

$$P^+ = \begin{pmatrix} & 0\,0 \\ R & 0\,0 \\ & 0\,0 \\ 0\,0\,0\,0\,0 \\ 0\,0\,0\,0\,0 \end{pmatrix} \quad P^- = \begin{pmatrix} 0\,p\,0\,0\,0 \\ 0\,0\,0\,0\,0 \\ 0\,0\,0\,0\,0 \\ 0\,0\,1\,0\,0 \\ 0\,1\,0\,0\,0 \end{pmatrix} \quad Q = \begin{pmatrix} 0\,0\,0\,0\,0 \\ 0\,0\,0\,1\,0 \\ 0\,0\,0\,0\,1 \\ 0\,0\,0\,0\,0 \\ 0\,0\,0\,0\,0 \end{pmatrix} \tag{4}$$

R denotes the routing matrix of the network considered in Section 2. We assume that the external arrivals only take place in queue 1, 2 and 3 with the same rate λ_i^+ as in the previous model.

Let μ be the service rate in stations 4 and 5. Remember that the service times have an exponential distribution and the steady-state distribution has a product form for all values of μ_i such that $\rho_i < 1$. Let us consider the assumptions made on the arrival rates in queues 4 and 5 and on the routing, and compute the value of ρ_4 and ρ_5 from equations 3.

$$\rho_4 = \frac{\mu_1 \rho_1 P^-[1, 2]\rho_2 + \mu_5 \rho_5 \rho_2}{\mu_4} \quad and \quad \rho_5 = \frac{\mu_4 \rho_4 \rho_3}{\mu_5} \tag{5}$$

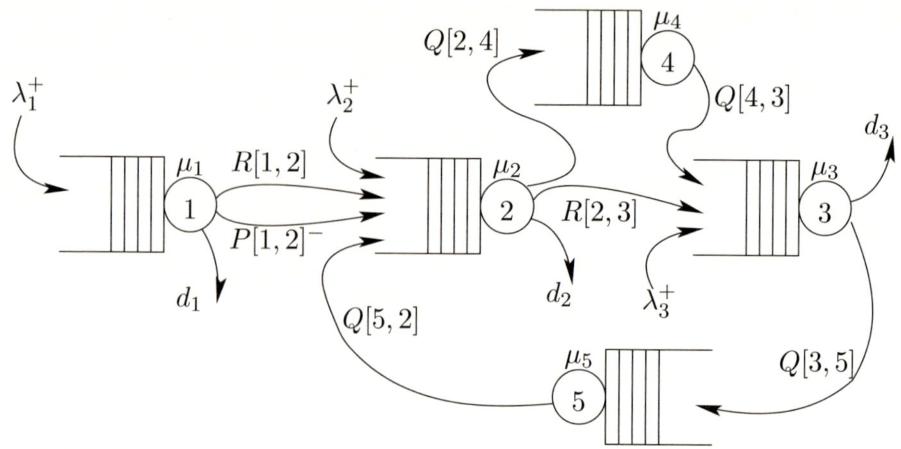

Fig. 2. Associated G-network with trigger

We can perform an algebraic elimination to obtain the values of $\mu_4\rho_4$ and $\mu_5\rho_5$ as functions of the parameters of the three other queues. Clearly:

$$\mu_4\rho_4 = \frac{\mu_1\rho_1\rho_2 P^-[1,2]}{1-\rho_2\rho_3} \quad and \quad \mu_5\rho_5 = \frac{\mu_1\rho_1\rho_2\rho_3 P^-[1,2]}{1-\rho_2\rho_3} \tag{6}$$

Now we can substitute all the values of $\mu_4\rho_4$ and $\mu_5\rho_5$ used in the definitions of ρ_2 and ρ_3.

$$\rho_2 = \frac{\lambda_2^+ + \sum_{j=1}^3 \mu_j\rho_j R[j,2]}{\mu_2 + \mu_1\rho_1 P^-[1,2] + \mu_5\rho_5} = \frac{\lambda_2^+ + \sum_{j=1}^3 \mu_j\rho_j R[j,2]}{\mu_2 + \frac{\mu_1\rho_1 P^-[1,2]}{1-\rho_2\rho_3}} \tag{7}$$

Similarly,

$$\rho_3 = \frac{\lambda_3^+ + \sum_{j=1}^3 \mu_j\rho_j R[j,3]}{\mu_3 + \mu_4\rho_4} = \frac{\lambda_3^+ + \sum_{j=1}^3 \mu_j\rho_j R[j,3]}{\mu_3 + \frac{\mu_1\rho_1\rho_2 P^-[1,2]}{1-\rho_2\rho_3}} \tag{8}$$

Finally we notice that the definition of ρ_1 does not take into account ρ_4 and ρ_5. We now have a complete definition of ρ_i by a fixed point system and this system is exactly the one considered in Section 2 which describes a G-network with synchronized partial flushing. Clearly these two systems have the same solution. We just have to check that the transform does not add constraints which cannot be satisfied. Indeed we must have $\rho_1 < 1$ for all queue index i and the set is larger for the G-network with triggers. Clearly it is sufficient to consider large values for μ_4 and μ_5. Thus we do not check the stability constraint (i.e. $\rho < 1$) for the queues we add. The algorithm consists in designing a new network with triggers from the network with partial flushing and use a sandwich algorithm to solve the G-network with triggers flow equation.

3.3   Algorithm

The algorithm consists of into two steps: the network transformation and the numerical resolution of the G-network with triggers. The initial network with synchronized flushing has M queues while the G-network with triggers has N queues and C classes of signals. Like in Kelly's networks, the classes are associated with the routes. However we do not need customer class, we only consider classes of triggers. The network transformation associates a route and some queues with a signal. If the routes do not intersect, it is not necessary to use classes but, for the sake of generality, we present here the multiple class model which is sufficient for our network transform. These networks are a simple generalization of the single class model shown in theorem 1. The classes of signals are used to represent routing: for instance, $P^-[c, j, i]$ denotes the probability for a customer to move from queue j to queue i as a class c signal at a service completion. The customer in service is moved by a signal of any class but it moves according to the routing matrix of the signal. The flow equation for this multiple class G-network with synchronized flushing is a simple generalization of the one stated in Theorem 1:

$$\rho_i = \frac{\lambda_i^+ + \sum_j \mu_j \rho_j P^+[j, i] + \sum_j \sum_k \sum_c \mu_j \rho_j P^-[c, j, k] \rho_k Q[c, k, i]}{\mu_i + \sum_j \mu_j \rho_j \sum_c P^-[c, j, i]} \tag{9}$$

Let us now briefly discuss the network transformation.

Network Transformation: A signal description in the G-network with synchronized flushing model is an ordered list of queues. A list can not contain more than one occurrence of a queue index. We associate a signal class in the G-network with triggers to each list in the G-network with synchronized flushing.

Consider a signal of class c arriving at queue l_1 from queue j and whose list is $(l_1, l_2, \ldots, l_L)$. We add L queues numbered between $K + 1$ and $K + L$ where K is an arbitrary integer chosen to avoid index confusion between the queues. The transition rate in these new queues is μ and it is sufficiently large to avoid stability problem for these queues. We extend the size of the customer routing matrix but we do not add customer transitions neither between these new queues nor between new queues and old queues. We add two new routing matrices: one describing the transition from a customer to a class c signal and one describing the movement of the customer triggered by a class c signal.

- When queue l_i receives a class c signal it triggers a customer movement to queue $K + i + 1$.
- A class c signal is sent with probability 1 at the end of its service in queue $K + i$. The signal is sent to queue with index l_i.

Numerical Resolution: We consider, for any queue index i, six sequences of real numbers $[\overline{q_i}]_k$, $[\underline{q_i}]_k$, $[\overline{\lambda_i^+}]_k$, $[\underline{\lambda_i^+}]_k$, $[\overline{\lambda_i^-}]_k$, $[\underline{\lambda_i^-}]_k$ defined by induction on k as follows :

$$
\begin{cases}
[\overline{\lambda_i^+}]_k = \lambda_i^+ + \sum_j P^+[j,i]\mu_j[\overline{q_j}]_k + \sum_m \sum_j \sum_c P^-[c,j,m]\mu_j[\overline{q_j}]_k Q[c,m,i][\overline{q_m}]_k \\[2ex]
[\underline{\lambda_i^+}]_k = \lambda_i^+ + \sum_j P^+[j,i]\mu_j[\underline{q_j}]_k + \sum_m \sum_j \sum_c P^-[c,j,m]\mu_j[\underline{q_j}]_k Q[c,m,i][\underline{q_m}]_k \\[2ex]
[\overline{\lambda_i^-}]_k = \sum_{j=1}^{N}\sum_{c=1}^{C} P^-[c,j,i]\mu_j[\overline{q_j}]_k \\[2ex]
[\underline{\lambda_i^-}]_k = \sum_{j=1}^{N}\sum_{c=1}^{C} P^-[c,j,i]\mu_j[\underline{q_j}]_k \\[2ex]
[\overline{q_i}]_{k+1} = \min\left(1, [\overline{\lambda_i^+}]_k \, / \, (\mu_i + [\underline{\lambda_i^-}]_k)\right) \\[2ex]
[\underline{q_i}]_{k+1} = \min\left(1, [\underline{\lambda_i^+}]_k \, / \, (\mu_i + [\overline{\lambda_i^-}]_k)\right)
\end{cases}
\tag{10}
$$

with $[\underline{q_i}]_0 = 0$ and $[\overline{q_i}]_0 = 1$ for the initialization. We iterate the computations of the sequences until the algorithm stops when a lower bound $[\underline{q_i}]_{k+1}$ reaches 1 or when $\sum_i([\overline{q_i}]_{k+1} - [\underline{q_i}]_{k+1})$ becomes smaller than a threshold ϵ. Numerical experiments showed that the algorithm converges quite quickly to the solution. Note that the stationary condition is now included into the fixed point system since $[\overline{q_i}]_{k+1}$ and $[\underline{q_i}]_{k+1}$ are positive and smaller than or equal to 1.

Property 2. *Due to the initialization and the definition of the sequences, we have:*

- $[\underline{q_i}]_{k+1} \le \rho_i \le [\overline{q_i}]_{k+1}$,
- *the sequences $[\underline{q_i}]_{k+1}$ do not decrease with k*
- *and the sequences $[\overline{q_i}]_{k+1}$ do not increase with k.*

The proof is based on an induction on k and it is omitted.

This is not sufficient to obtain a solution. We must also prove that the difference between $[\underline{q_i}]_{k+1}$ and $[\overline{q_i}]_{k+1}$ convergess to 0. The following property gives a sufficient condition for the algorithm to converge.

Property 3. *If $P^+ + P^- + P^-Q$ is sub-stochastic, then the algorithm converges to a solution.*

The proof is a straightforward generalization of the method stated in [1] that we cannot derive here due to the size of the paper. Note that for networks with positive and negative customers, matrix Q has all its entries equal to 0. Therefore for that simple case the condition is that matrix $P^+ + P^-$ is sub-stochastic. That can be trivially verified for open G-networks with positive and negative customers.

However for G-networks with trigger that condition is not necessarily satisfied due to the definition of the routing matrices. Of course, as usual in an open G-network, matrix $P^+ + P^-$ is sub-stochastic but adding $P^- Q$ may lead to a matrix whose rows sum up to more than 1.0. We are still working to improve the algorithm and its proof.

We have implemented the sandwich algorithm on the network of Section 2 before and after the transformation. It depends on the values of the parameters, but the algorithm always converges with the network of five queues and most of the time, the algorithm fails on the network with three queues. The number of iterations needed for a 10^{-20} accuracy for `double` type variable in C language is less than 100. The time for these iterations is negligible due to the small size of the example.

4   Concluding Remarks: Time Renormalization, Infinite Service Rate and Product Form

Following Gelenbe [2] we must stress again the importance of flow equation. G-networks with resets are completely different from Jackson's networks. They have the same state space but do not have the same transitions. However, even if their global balance equations are different they share the same flow equation.

Here we have considered two models with product form. They do not have exactly the same state space (the smallest is included into the largest one). Again the transitions are quite different. But we can transform the flow equations using an elimination procedure to obtain the simpler flow equations.

We have used this elimination to solve numerically the flow equation but other applications of this transform are currently under study: for instance, the stability region analysis. Assume that the network has n free parameters (arrival rates, services rates, routing matrices). Let us denote by the stability region the subset of R^n such that the flow equations have solutions ρ_i strictly smaller than 1.0. Thus the product form solution exists. Clearly our transform provides a one to one mapping between the stability region of a G-network with partial flushing and the stability region of a G-network with triggers.

We think that it is important to explain why some networks share the same flow equations and what is the stochastic operator associated with this algebraic elimination of ρ_i inside a flow equation. Intuitively, this is related to the service rate being infinite in that queue. Consider the G-network with triggers. If the service rate in queues 4 and 5 is infinite, then the service times and the sojourn times are zero; the services in these stations are instantaneous. Of course we cannot say that we still have a product form solution (at least it is still an open problem that a product form solution is kept when service rates become infinite). At least we can describe the behavior of the queueing network. Consider now the effect of a signal which enters queue 2 arriving from queue 1. Assume that there are some customers in queues 2 and 3 at this time. The signal triggers a customer to queue 4 where it is instantaneously transformed into a signal which joins queue 3. The second part of the cycle is also performed immediately: the signal moves a customer from queue 3 to queue 5 where it is transformed into a signal to enter queue 2. Clearly, the signal will continue to delete customers from queues 2 and 3 until it vanishes because it enters an empty queue. So the signal of trigger acts exactly as a signal of partial flushing when we make some service rates infinite. The equivalence between these two models suggests that the product form is always preserved when some services are instantaneous. We hope that we will be able to prove that conjecture in the near future.

It may be worthy to remark how complex can be the behavior of a network of queues which combines triggers and instantaneous services. The dynamics always imply multiple departures as the superposition of transitions $(-1, -1, +1)$ where the arrival $(+1)$ vanishes immediately to create a new part of the synchronizations. Clearly, the dynamics never allow the synchronized arrival of customers; it is already known that such a behavior does not preserve product form solution.

Similarly the resets studied in [2] can be associated with distributions which are reached after an infinite time or an infinite number of transitions and a correct renormalization. We are still working on this property and we expect that such an approach can provide new results and knowledge on the product form of networks of queues.

References

1. J.M. Fourneau, "Computing the steady-state distribution of networks with positive and negative customers", $13^t h$ IMACS World Congress on Computation and Applied Mathematics, Dublin, 1991.
2. J.M. Fourneau and E. Gelenbe, "Flow Equivalence and Stochastic Equivalence in G-Networks", Computational Management Science, V1, N2, pp 179–192, 2004.
3. J.M. Fourneau, L. Kloul and F. Quessette, "Multiple Class Generalized Networks with iterated deletions", Performance Evaluation, Elsevier, V42, pp 1-20, 2000
4. J.M. Fourneau, L. Kloul and D. Verchère, "Multiple Class G-Networks with list oriented deletions", European Journal on Operation Research, V 126, pp 250-272, 2000
5. J.M. Fourneau, N. Pekergin and D. Verchère, "Reseaux généralisées avec synchronisations cycliques", RAIRO-RO, V32, N3, 1998, pp 353-372.
6. E. Gelenbe, "Random neural networks with negative and positive signals and product form solution", Neural Computation, V1(N4), pp 502–510, 1990.
7. E. Gelenbe, "Product form queueing networks with negative and positive customers", Journal of Applied Probability, V28, pp 656–663, 1991.
8. E. Gelenbe, "G-networks with triggered customer movement", Journal of Applied Probability, V 30, pp 742–748, 1993.
9. E. Gelenbe, "G-networks with signals and batch removals", Probability in the Engineering and Informational Sciences, V 7, pp 335–342, 1993.

Worst-Case Analysis of Router Networks with Rival Queueing Models

Nalan Gülpınar[1], Pete Harrison[2], and Berç Rustem[2]

[1] Warwick Business School
University of Warwick, Coventry CV4 7AL, UK
Nalan.Gulpinar@wbs.ac.uk
[2] Department of Computing
Imperial College London, London SW7 2AZ, UK
{pgh, br}@doc.ic.ac.uk

Abstract. A robust, worst-case design framework is developed for a tandem router network based on rival queueing models. Worst-case design is concerned with determining the best design or strategy in the most hostile operating environment, i.e. simultaneously with worst-case model parameters. In the router network, end-to-end performance is computed as the mean transmission delay subject to an upper limit on the rate of losses and finite capacity queueing and recovery buffers. The worst-case optimal ratio of arrival-buffer size to recovery-buffer size is determined, which is a critical quantity that affects both loss rate and transmission time. The impact of the retransmission probability is also investigated.

Keywords: Worst-case analysis, queueing theory, router design.

1   Introduction

We consider worst-case analysis – so-called minimax – for the design of a router network using discrete state Markov queueing models. In view of the diverse design options, such models have many adjustable parameters and choosing the best set for a particular performance objective is a delicate and time-consuming task. An optimisation approach based on queueing theory is introduced to automate this task. Each rival model optimizes the end-to-end performance of the network. Specifically, the mean end-to-end delay is minimized subject to an upper limit on the rate of losses, which may be due to either full buffers or corrupted data. Losses at a full buffer are inferred by a time-out whereas corrupted data is detected immediately on receipt of a packet at a router, causing a N-ACK to be sent upstream. Recovery buffers are used to hold successfully transmitted packets so that an expensive resend from source can be avoided. The performance of such networks is measured in terms of the optimal ratio of arrival buffer size to recovery buffer size, which is a critical quantity that affects both loss rate and transmission time. For more information on these control systems and their rival models, the reader is referred to [3] and [6].

There are various well established theories that have been applied to model systems such as router networks. These have, in turn, led to the development of

A. Levi et al. (Eds.): ISCIS 2006, LNCS 4263, pp. 897–907, 2006.

different rival models purporting to represent their performance. In such circumstances, there is uncertainty about which model to use in the detailed design of a network.

A model-based router design entails a reasonable specification of the underlying model and an appropriate characterization of uncertainty. The latter can be an exogenous effect, a parameter's approximation or uncertainty regarding the structure of the model, which must be flexible enough to admit alternate structures. In this paper, we introduce a robust worst-case router design taking into account three rival queueing models developed for a tandem network with certain feedback mechanisms. This is achieved by a pooling of the models. The pooling that yields the optimal buffer sizes which is robust to model choice is formulated as a constrained minimax problem. The minimization is over the decision variables and the maximization is over the choice of rival models.

The general minimax optimization problem can be defined as:

$$\min_{x \in X} \max_{v \in V} \; F(x, v), \tag{1}$$

where $X \subset R^n$, $V \subset R^m$ and $F : R^{n+m} \to R$. The aim of the worst-case approach is to minimize the objective function with respect to the worst possible outcome of the uncertain variables v. Therefore, x is chosen to minimize the objective function, whereas nature or an artificial environment chooses v to maximize it. If V is a finite set, such as $V = \{v_1, v_2, \cdots, v_k\}$, then (1) becomes the discrete minimax problem. Introducing $f^j(x) = F(x, v_j)$ for $j = 1, 2, ..., k$, the discrete minimax problem can be formulated as

$$\min_{x \in X} \quad \max_{j=1,2,...,k} \; f^j(x) \tag{2}$$

It can be shown that minimax problem (2) is equivalent to the following mathematical programming problem:

$$\min_{x,z} \; z,$$

$$s.t. \; f^j(x) \le z, \quad \forall j = 1, 2, ..., k, \tag{3}$$

The performance of the actual decision has a *non-inferiority property* and the robustness of minimax arises from its optimality condition. Let x^*, v^* be an optimal solution of the general minimax problem (1). Then, the following inequality is valid for all feasible v_j

$$F(x^*, v^*) \ge F(x^*, v_j)$$

This inequality simply states the optimality of v^* and also signifies the robustness of minimax: the expected performance is *guaranteed* to be at the level given by the worst-case and will *improve* if any scenario other than the worst-case v^* is realized.

The rest of the paper is organised as follows. In section 2, the tandem router network model is described in terms of its parameters and constraints. In section 3, we define the worst-case performance optimization problem for this network and in section 4 present our computational experiments with numerical results. The paper concludes in section 5.

2 Tandem Router Network

Consider a two-node, tandem network of internal routers with a sender (source) node and receiver (destination) node at the ends. At each node there are arrival (for queueing) and recovery buffers. The model is depicted in Figure 1. We assume that batches arrive (from the sender) at the first router node as a Poisson process with constant arrival rate λ_0 batches per unit time and batch size with specified probability distribution, mean b. The arrivals wait if the node is busy and there is space in the buffer. Notice that in an M/M/1 queueing model λ_0 denotes the number of arrival packets per unit time with $b = 1$. The departure process from this queue is also approximated as Poisson with unit batches. The

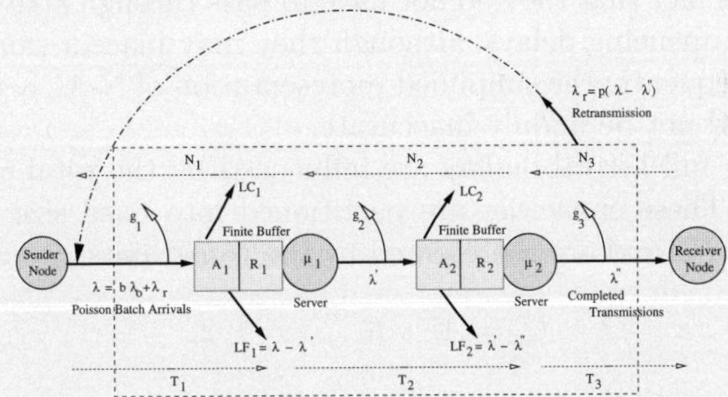

Fig. 1. A two-node router network with batch arrivals

packets are served when they reach the front of the arrival queue. A service time includes the time to look up router tables, manage header information and dispatch the packet so that the next can be processed. It is assumed to be either an exponential random variable, for an M/M/1 queue, or generally distributed, for an M/G/1 queue. Customers' service times are independent of each other and of the arrival process. The service rates at nodes 1 and 2 are denoted by μ_1 and μ_2, respectively.

Any arrival packet is either transferred successfully or else is lost. Losses arise due to either a *full buffer* whereupon there is no acknowledgement (ACK) or *corrupted data on arrival at a buffer*. We assume that garbage is not buffered but that a negative acknowledgement (N-ACK) is sent upstream instead. A loss due to a full buffer will cause an additional transmission delay by a timeout of duration much greater than the per-link transmission time – specified here by a multiple of the estimated end-to-end delay. Losses might also occur due to incorrect routing, a wrong entry or a late update in the routing table at a node. The effect on the sender (and receiver) is the same as a full-buffer loss, however, and we make no distinction in our model.

Packets are stored in the recovery buffer when any arrival (not overflow or garbage) to node 1 or node 2 has been successfully processed and sent on. If full, the oldest packet is deleted from the recovery buffer, which therefore operates in a round-robin, cyclic fashion.

Let λ_r be the net rate at which packets are resent to the sender node due to losses of all types. The total rate of arrivals, including retransmissions, is therefore $\lambda = b\lambda_0 + \lambda_r$ where λ_0 is the total rate of external arrivals from various user input streams.

The probabilities that a packet is lost because of corruption that leads to garbage data arriving at node 1, node 2 and the receiver are g_1, g_2 and g_3, respectively. Such garbage is detected on arrival at a node, before joining the queue, and causes a N-ACK to be sent upstream to the sender. We assume that acknowledgements are processed fast, at high priority and do not incur queueing delays. More precisely, N-ACKs (and ACKs) are generated fast by a process running on a node's arrival buffer and an ACK packet is sent back to the previous node's *output* buffer. Because of the high priority of ACKs and N-ACKs and the fact that they do not have to pass through arrival buffers, they suffer negligible queueing delays, although they may place a small overhead on the nodes. Consequently the simplified representation of N-ACK transmission in our model should not be unduly inaccurate.

Losses due to full arrival buffers are influenced by the total capacities C_i of nodes $i = 1, 2$. These capacities are partitioned into fixed size arrival A_i and recovery buffers R_i, and are represented by the constraints

$$C_i = A_i + R_i, \quad i = 1, 2$$

Referring to Figure 1, N_1, N_2 and N_3 are the N-ACK delays from node 1 to the sender, from node 2 to the node 1, and from the receiver to node 2, respectively. Let T_1, T_2 and T_3 be the transmission delays for packets passing over the links between the sender and node 1, node 1 and node 2, and node 2 and the receiver node, respectively. Hence the transmission delay for successful packets, excluding the time spent in the nodes, is $T = T_1 + T_2 + T_3$. Let τ_1 and τ_2 denote the throughputs of servers 1 and 2 respectively. The net equilibrium arrival rate to nodes 1 and 2 are $\lambda_1' = \lambda(1 - g_1)$ and $\lambda_2' = \tau_1(1 - g_2 + g_2 q_1)$, respectively. The respective server utilizations ρ_1, ρ_2 are therefore

$$\rho_1 = \frac{\lambda_1'}{\mu_1} \quad \text{and} \quad \rho_2 = \frac{\lambda_2'}{\mu_2}$$

The net rate at which packets are resent by the sender node due to losses of all types is defined as the *retransmission rate*, λ_r, and computed as

$$\lambda_r = p(\lambda - \lambda_3')$$

where $\lambda_3' = \tau_2(1 - g_3 + g_3[q_2 + q_1'(1 - q_2)])$ is the rate at which non-garbage packets arrive at the receiver, designated node 3 (i.e. the 'goodput' of the network). During transmission, total losses should not exceed a specified maximum *loss rate* β, measured conventionally as a fraction β of the external packet arrival rate. This implies

$$(1 - p)(\lambda - \lambda_3') \le \beta b \lambda_0$$

The (assumed) Poisson arrivals comprise external and retransmitted packets with rate λ_1' packets per unit time at node 1 and λ_2' packets per unit time at node 2. The throughput of successful transmissions from node i is then obtained approximately by direct analysis of the corresponding finite capacity $M/M/1/A_i$ queue $(i = 1, 2)$ as

$$\tau_1 = \frac{\rho_1 \left(1 - \rho_1^{A_1}\right) \mu_1}{1 - \rho_1^{A_1+1}} \quad \tau_2 = \frac{\rho_2 \left(1 - \rho_2^{A_2}\right) \mu_2}{1 - \rho_2^{A_2+1}}$$

Let f_i define the probability that a packet is rejected at node i due to a full buffer. The probabilities of successful packets being transmitted from node 1 and node 2 are respectively represented by:

$$\frac{\tau_1}{\lambda} = (1 - g_1)(1 - f_1), \quad \frac{\tau_2}{\lambda_2'} = (1 - f_2)$$

The probability that a packet is successfully transmitted from the network arrives correctly at the receiver is the ratio λ_3'/τ_2.

The user also defines the probability p of retransmission, $0 \le p \le 1$, which is incorporated in the optimization model. When $p = 0$, no retransmissions are allowed so losses are higher but congestion is lower. When $p = 1$, there is always a retransmission attempt and so there are no losses due to full buffers since the number of retransmissions is unlimited. This causes extra load on the network which might result in heavy congestion and hence significantly longer delays.

2.1   Rival Model Specifications

We develop a worst-case design of router networks with three discrete state queueing models. The first rival model $(j = 1)$ has $M/M/1$ queueing at both nodes. The second model $(j = 2)$ uses the $M/G/1$ waiting time result, with batch arrivals, at node 1 and the $M/M/1$ waiting time formula at node 2. The third model $(j = 3)$ has two $M/G/1$ queues, with batch arrivals at node 1 and with unit arrivals at node 2. Each queueing network model determines the mean end-to-end transmission time (also called response time) in terms of its (pre-specified) input parameters.

Response Time in a M/G/1 Queue with Batches

Let $G_X(z)$ denote the probability generating function of a discrete random variable X and let $T^*(\theta) = E[e^{-\theta T}]$ denote the Laplace-Stieltjes transform of the probability distribution of a (continuous) random variable T, where $E[.]$ denotes expectation. Let the service time random variable for a single customer at a queue be S, with mean $1/\mu$, and let the *batch* (Poisson) arrival rate be λ and the batch size random variable be N with mean $\overline{N} = b$. Let S_B be the service time random variable for *batches* with size distributed as N. The sojourn time, or waiting time, W, of a customer (in a batch) is the sum of the time it spends waiting to start service and its service time. We consider the *last customer in a batch*. The last customer enters the queue with its batch and the batch completes its service when the last customer is served. Hence, the service completion of the last customer in a batch represents the completion of the batch, i.e. successful transmission of the message, and the waiting time of the last customer is also the waiting time of the batch.

The Laplace-Stieltjes transform of the response time distribution in such an $M/GI/1/\infty$ queue with unit arrivals is:

$$W_U^* = \frac{(1-\rho)\theta S^*(\theta)}{\theta - \lambda(1 - S^*(\theta))}$$

For an $M/GI/1/\infty$ queue with batch arrivals of random size N, the Laplace-Stieltjes transform of batch-service time distribution, denoted by S_B^*, can be obtained as

$$S_B^*(\theta) = E[e^{-\theta S_B}] = E[E[e^{-\theta(S_1+S_2+\cdots+S_N)}|N]]$$
$$= E[(E[e^{-\theta S}])^N] = G_N(S^*(\theta))$$

Then the Laplace-Stieltjes transform of the *batch* response time distribution in such an $M/GI/1/\infty$ queue with batch arrivals becomes

$$W_B^* = \frac{(1-\rho)\theta G_N(S^*(\theta))}{\theta - \lambda(1 - G_N(S^*(\theta)))}$$

Moments of Network Response Times

Let $B^{(k)}$ and $T_s^{(k)}$ respectively denote the kth factorial moment of batch size and the Laplace-Stieltjes transform of the service time distribution in the above $M/GI/1/\infty$ queue. That is, $B^{(k)} = G_N^{(k)}(1) = E[N(N-1)...(N-k+1)]$ and $T_s^{(k)} = S_B^{*(k)}(0) = (-1)^k E[S^k]$. The mean waiting time at node 1 is approximated as the M/G/1 response time with batch arrivals, i.e. $\overline{W}_1 = -W_B^{*\,'}(\theta)|_{\theta=0}$ where

$$W_B^{*\,'}(0) = \frac{-2\mu_1(1-\rho_1)b - \lambda_1'[B^{(2)} - b + b\mu_1^2 T_s^{(2)}]}{2\mu_1(\mu_1 - \lambda_1' b)}$$

The expected response time at node 2, $\overline{W}_2$, is approximated as the M/G/1 response time with unit arrivals, i.e. $\overline{W}_2 = -W_U^{*\,'}(\theta)|_{\theta=0}$ where

$$W_U^{*\,'}(0) = \frac{-\lambda_2'\mu_2 T_s^{(2)} - 2(1-\rho_2)}{2(\mu_2 - \lambda_2')}$$

For each queueing model, the mean response times at nodes 1 and 2 are summarised in Table 1. The total expected response time $\overline{W}_j$ for models $j = 1, 2, 3$ is

Table 1. Mean response times at nodes 1 and 2

Rival Models	Mean Response Time at Node 1	Mean Response Time at Node 2
Model 1 MM1: $j = 1$	M/M/1 queue $\overline{W}_1^1 = \dfrac{(1-(A_1+1)\rho_1^{A_1}+A_1\rho_1^{A_1+1})}{\mu_1(1-\rho_1)(1-\rho_1^{A_1})}$	M/M/1 queue $\overline{W}_2^1 = \dfrac{(1-(A_2+1)\rho_2^{A_2}+A_2\rho_2^{A_2+1})}{\mu_2(1-\rho_2)(1-\rho_2^{A_2})}$
Model 2 MG1-D: $j = 2$	M/G/1 queue with batch arrivals $\overline{W}_1^2 = \dfrac{\lambda B^{(2)}-3\lambda b+\lambda b\mu_1^2 T_s^{(2)}+2\mu_1 b}{2\mu_1(\mu_1-\lambda b)}$	M/M/1 queue $\overline{W}_2^2 = \dfrac{1-(A_2+1)\rho_2^{A_2}+A_2\rho_2^{A_2+1}}{\mu_2(1-\rho_2)(1-\rho_2^{A_2})}$
Model 3 MG1-2: $j = 3$	M/G/1 queue with batch arrivals $\overline{W}_1^3 = \dfrac{2\mu_1(1-\rho_1)b+\lambda_1'[B^{(2)}-b+b\mu_1^2 T_s^{(2)}]}{2\mu_1(\mu_1-\lambda_1' b)}$	M/G/1 queue with unit arrivals $\overline{W}_2^3 = \dfrac{\lambda_2'\mu_2 T_s^{(2)}+2(1-\rho_2)}{2(\mu_2-\lambda_2')}$

defined as the combined time spent in the two nodes on a successful transmission attempt. This is computed as the sum of the expected response times at each node, $\overline{W}_j = \overline{W}_1^j + \overline{W}_2^j$.

Failed packets, due to either corrupted data or loss at a full arrival buffer, retry a number of times given by the retry-probability p. Because each retry is made independently of previous attempts, this number of attempts is a geometric random variable with parameter p (for a persistently failing transmission). The overhead at any attempt, L, incurred by a failed transmission, i.e. the elapsed time between the start of that attempt and the start of the next attempt, consists of:

- the time-out delay set to $k(\overline{W}_j + T)$ (k mean successful transmission times) for packets lost due to a full buffer;
- the time elapsed between the instant that the failure is detected—i.e. by detection of garbage on arrival at a node—and the instant the re-sent packet is received.

Therefore, for each rival model specification $j = 1, 2, 3$, the mean overhead, $\overline{L}_j$, takes into account each of the possible failures above and their probabilities of occurrence. In addition to retransmissions, which incur a time-penalty in our model, there is a possibility that a transmission will be abandoned, i.e. 'lost forever', in the event that a retransmission is not tried, with probability $1-p$. Such a loss is assigned a more severe time penalty of $k'(W_j + T)$ where $k' > k$ and acquisition time penalty of $k'' > 0$. Let F_m be the probability of a loss forever at the mth attempt. This is computed as

$$F_m^j = \left(1 - \frac{\lambda_3'}{\lambda}\right)(1 - p)\left(1 - \frac{\lambda_3'}{\lambda}\right)^{m-1} p^{m-1}$$

Let CF_m^j be the cost random variable for transmissions that end after m attempts: i.e. are either successful, with cost equal to response time, or lost forever, with cost being the above loss penalty. CF_m^j is given in the following table, together with its associated probability. The mean of the cost function is obtained in terms of mean response time delays and time penalties as

Table 2. Cost random variable and corresponding probabilities

Function	CF_m^j	Probability
Response Time	$W_j + T + (m-1)L_j$	$\frac{\lambda_3'}{\lambda}\left[p\left(1 - \frac{\lambda_3'}{\lambda}\right)\right]^{m-1}$
Loss Penalty	$k'(W_j + T) + k'' + (m-1)L_j$	F_m^j

$$\overline{CF}_j = \frac{\lambda_3'(\overline{W}_j + T) + p\overline{L}_j(\lambda - \lambda_3')\left[p\lambda_3' + \lambda(1-p)\right]}{\lambda(1-p) + p\lambda_3'} + \frac{(1-p)(\lambda - \lambda_3')\left[k'(\overline{W}_j + T) + k''\right]}{\lambda(1-p) + p\lambda_3'}$$

3 Worst-Case Robust Router Design

Performance optimization models (denoted by $j = 1, 2, 3$) minimize the mean of the end-to-end delay subject to an upper limit on the rate of losses. The worst-case approach is now to minimize the objective function with respect to the worst possible outcome of the uncertain variables. Wise decision making would therefore entail the incorporation of all scenarios to provide an integrated and consistent framework. In this paper we propose worst-case robust optimal design for router networks. In risk management terms, such robust strategy would ensure that performance is optimal in the worst-case and this will further improve if the worst-case scenarios do not materialize.

The minimax approach considers all rival models simultaneously and is formulated as

$$\min_{A_i, R_i, f_i, \lambda, \lambda_r, \lambda', \lambda'', \lambda'''} \max_j \left\{\overline{CF}_j\right\}$$

An equivalent nonlinear programming formulation of this minimax problem [5] is as follows;

$$\min \nu$$
$$\text{s.t} \quad \overline{CF}_j \leq \nu \qquad\qquad j = 1, 2, 3$$
$$(1-p)(\lambda - \lambda''') \leq \beta b \lambda_0$$
$$A_i + R_i = C_i \qquad\qquad i = 1, 2$$
$$\lambda_r, \lambda', \lambda'', \lambda''', A_i, R_i, f_i \geq 0 \qquad\qquad i = 1, 2$$

We note that there may well be more than one scenario corresponding to the worst-case. This noninferiority is the guaranteed performance character of minimax. Min-max optimization is more robust as regards the realization of worst-case scenarios than considering a single scenario or an arbitrary pooling of scenarios. It is suitable for situations which need protection against the risks of adopting a wrong model specification scenario since the minimax model constructs an optimal design simultaneously with the most pessimistic model specification.

4   Numerical Results

The optimization model described in the previous section was implemented and integrated with a software package called *mqueue*, which has been written in C++ and uses the nonlinear solver E04UCF, Nag Library [4], to optimize the transmission time. In our computational experiments, the parameters, which were input to the optimization model, are as follows: the service rates at nodes 1 and 2 are $\mu_1 = \mu_2 = 1.0E+06$, the probabilities of garbage data at the nodes are $g_1 = g_2 = 0.0002$ and $g_3 = 0.001$, the acknowledgement delays are $N_1 = N_2 = N_3 = \frac{1.0}{10.0 \times \mu_1}$, and the link transmission delays are $T_1 = T_2 = T_3 = \frac{1.0}{10.0 \times \mu_1}$. All computational experiments are carried out on a 3 GHz Pentium 4, running Linux with 256Meg of RAM. Partly in order to motivate the optimization model, we first considered the mean transmission time over the range of retransmission probabilities, $0 \le p \le 1$ in Figure 2. The arrival buffer size at node 2 is fixed at 10 and the arrival rate is chosen to be 90% of the service rate of each node. The graph on the right in Figure 2 is a plot of $\overline{W}$ (the Z-axis) versus retransmission probability p (the Y-axis) and arrival buffer size at node 1, A_1 (the X-axis).

Although not realistic, this network being overloaded with excessively high accepted loss rate, these parameters were chosen to reveal interesting performance characteristics, in particular optimum operating points, to illustrate our approach. In the left graph, the optimum buffer size at node 1 is around 20.

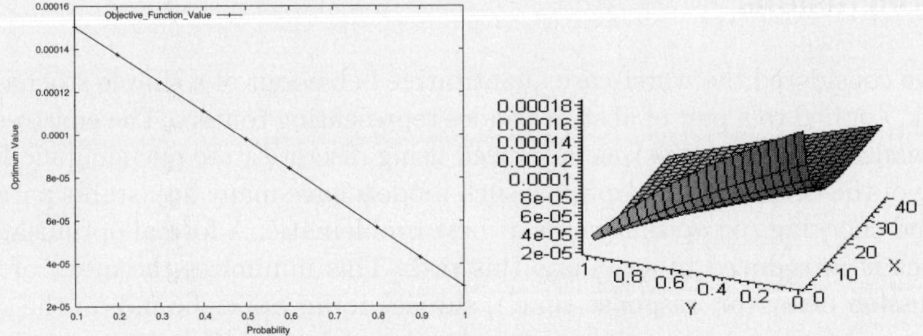

Fig. 2. Mean cost function versus retry probabilities with and without optimization

This clearly verifies that the minimum mean transmission time is obtained at the optimum arrival and recovery buffer size.

In order to show the impact of batch size distribution on the arrival and recovery buffer sizes, we ran the optimization model based on an M/G/1 queue with constant (deterministic) and geometric batch size distributions. In the numerical experiments, the mean batch size was 3. The results suggest that the distributions do not have a big impact on the model; i.e. both constant and geometric distributions behave in a similar way in terms of the optimal buffer sizes. For illustrative purposes, we only present the results obtained with constant batch size distribution.

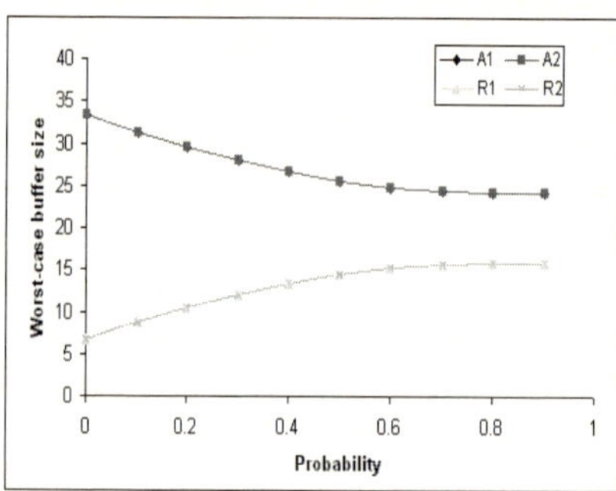
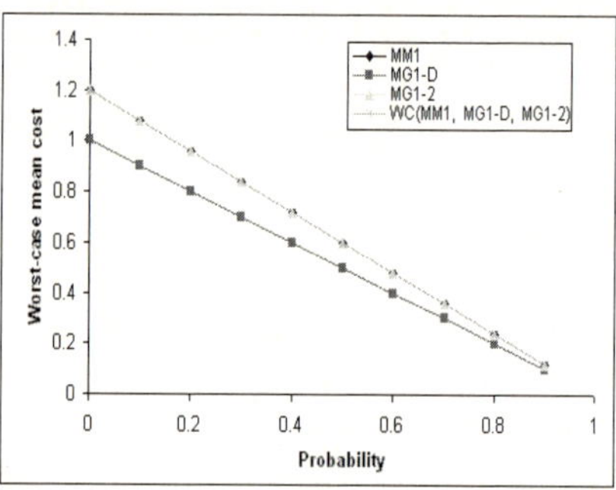

Fig. 3. Worst-case arrival and recovery buffer sizes and worst-case expected cost versus retry probabilities

We next carried out experiments to illustrate the utility of the minimax optimization model, varying the value of the user-defined retransmission probabilities $0 \leq p \leq 1$. Figure 3 shows the effect of worst-case strategy on buffer size and mean response time (left) and worst-case mean cost (right). The results show that the robust worst-case model specification coincides with model 1 and model 3. In addition minimax approach yields a cautious strategy to avoid excessive performance.

5   Conclusions

We have considered the worst-case quantitative behaviour of a simple stochastic network, applied to a pair of abstract nodes representing routers. The end-to-end performance of the network was optimized using discrete state queueing models. In view of the diverse design options, such models have many adjustable parameters and choosing the optimal set is at best problematic. A formal optimisation approach is introduced to automate this task. This minimizes the mean of the transmission delay (or 'response time'), subject to an upper bound on the rate of losses and finite capacity queueing and recovery buffers. It can also optimize a combination of mean and variance by a relatively straightforward model extension; see [6]. A two-node network was chosen for its simplicity in illustrating our approach, but it is clear that arbitrary sized networks could equally well be accommodated at greater computational effort.

The robust, worst-case design strategy that we introduced optimizes an objective function simultaneously with the worst-case model specifications. The guaranteed performance is optimal in the worst-case and will improve further if the worst-case scenarios do not materialize. The worst-case optimal ratio of arrival-buffer size to recovery-buffer size was determined, which is a critical quantity that affects both loss rate and transmission time. The impact of the retransmission probability was also investigated.

Forthcoming research will address, in particular, stochastic fluid models, with continuous state. These represent a number of packets in a buffer by a volume of fluid in a reservoir. Together with external fluid-flows, representing users' traffic streams, these fluid levels affect the rates of fluid flow into and out of the reservoirs. The present minimax models will be applied in the context of both discrete queueing models and stochastic fluid models, giving a more diverse and meaningful risk-based design strategy.

References

1. J. Borje, H.A. Lund, A. Wirkestrand, "Real-time Routers for Wireless Networks", *Ericsson Review Journal*, Vol 76, 4, 1999, pp. 190–197.
2. P.G, Harrison, N.M. Patel, *Performance Modeling of Communication Networks and Computer Architectures*, Addison-Wesley Publishing, 1992.
3. N. Gulpinar, P.G, Harrison, B. Rustem, L-F Pau, "An Optimization Model for a Two-Node Router Network", *MASCOTS 2004*, pp. 147–156.
4. NAG Library, `http://www.nag.co.uk`, The Numerical Algorithms Group, Oxford.
5. B. Rustem and M. Howe, *Algorithms for Worst-Case Design and Applications to Risk Management*, Princeton University Press, London and New Jersey, (2002).
6. N. Gulpinar, P. Harrison, B. Rustem, L.F. Pau, "Performance Optimization of a Router Network with Batch Arrivals", Submitted to *Journal of Cluster Computing*.
7. K.C. So, K.E. Chin, "Performance Bounds on Multiserver Exponential Tandem Queues with Finite Buffers", *European Journal of Operations Research*, Vol 63, 3, 1992, pp. 463–477.

An Anomaly Intrusion Detection Approach Using Cellular Neural Networks

Zhongxue Yang[1] and Adem Karahoca[2]

[1] Department of Computer Science, Nanjing Xiaozhuang University, Nanjing, China
alpha5336@yahoo.com
[2] Department of Computer Engineering, Faculty of Engineering, Bahcesehir University, Istanbul, Turkey
akarahoca@bahcesehir.edu.tr

Abstract. This paper presents an anomaly detection approach for the network intrusion detection based on Cellular Neural Networks (CNN) model. CNN has features with multi-dimensional array of neurons and local interconnections among cells. Recurrent Perceptron Learning Algorithm (RPLA) is used to learn the templates and bias in CNN classifier. Experiments with KDD Cup 1999 network traffic connections which have been preprocessed with methods of features selection and normalization have shown that CNN model is effective for intrusion detection. In contrast to back propagation neural network, CNN model exhibits an excellent performance owing to the higher attack detection rate with lower false positive rate.

Keywords: Intrusion detection system, Cellular Neural Networks, Data Mining.

1 Introduction

Security gaps of the Internet, threaten computer network systems. It has been a research area concerned with developing a secure and robust network and computer systems. Many security techniques and policies have been used to protect important data and computer system from being destroyed only as the first line defense, such as firewall, and encryption. A firewall acts as a defense of network or computer system, but it merely reduces exposure rather than monitors or eliminates vulnerabilities in computer systems [1].

An Intrusion Detection System (IDS) is a system for monitoring and detecting data traffic or user behavior to identify intruders [2]. Actually, most intrusion detection techniques are based on the assumption that intrusive activities can be detected by observing a deviation from the normal or expected behavior of the system or the users. The model of normal or valid behavior is extracted from reference information collected by various means. The IDS later compares this model with the current activity. When a deviation is observed, an alarm is generated. Recently, many approaches have been used to detect intrusions such as artificial intelligence [3], statistical analysis [4], neural networks [5], and data mining with decision tree algorithm [6].

A. Levi et al. (Eds.): ISCIS 2006, LNCS 4263, pp. 908–917, 2006.

In this paper, CNN model is proposed for intrusion detection process and also compared with a back propagation algorithm. CNN has features with multi-dimensional array of neurons and local interconnections among cells. The CNN model can detect both well-known and novel intrusions in real time automatically and efficiently, which works in a way of online detecting novel intrusions, classifying them into different classes according to a given criterion, real-time training new CNN classifier into the existing IDS.

The rest of the paper is organized as follows. In section 2, intrusion detection is reviewed. Section 3 includes preprocessing operation of the raw data. In section 4, CNN model is introduced. Simulation experiments on anomaly detection are given in section 5, and the performance of the CNN model is evaluated also. Finally, this paper is concluded in section 6.

2   Overview of Intrusion Detection

An intrusion is an unauthorized access or the use of computer or network system resources. By an IDS is software with the functions of detecting, identifying and responding to unauthorized or abnormal activities on a target system [7]. The major functions performed by IDS are: (1) to monitor and analyze user and system activities, (2) to maintain the integrity of critical system and data files, (3) to recognize activity patterns reflecting known attacks, (4) to respond automatically to detect activities, and (5) to report the outcome of detection process [8].

Generally, the methodology of intrusion detection is categorized into misuse detection and anomaly detection. The misuse detection model utilizes the well-known weakness of a target domain to identify intrusions. Thus, misuse detection is mostly used to detect well-known intrusions. The novel intrusions, however, will be detected unsuccessfully in this method. Anomaly detection suffers from the accuracy problem, as building an accurate model, avoiding false negative rate, may not reflect the complex dynamic nature of computer systems, leading to false positive rate. Misuse detection, by virtue of the simpler scope of the objects being modeled, can attain high levels of accuracy [8].

3   Data Preparation

3.1   The Raw Data

The data set used in the experiment is "KDD Cup 1999 Data"[9]. The raw data includes a wide variety of intrusions simulated in the network of US Air Force. Four major attack categories were chosen to group attack components with regard to the actions and goal of attacker. Denials of Service (DoS) attacks have the goal of limiting or denying service provided by to a user, a computer, or network. A common example is SYN-Flood attack, where the attacker floods the victim host with more

TCP connection requests than it can handle, causing the host to be unable to respond to valid requests for service; probe attacks have the goal of gaining knowledge of existence or configuration of a computer system or network. A common example is the IPsweep attack where the attacker sweeps one or more IP addresses in a given range to determine which addresses correspond to live hosts; Remote-to-local (R2L) attacks have the goal of gaining local access to a computer or network to which the attacker previously only had remote access. Examples are attempting to guess a password to illegally login to a computer system and the "IMAP" buffer-overflow, where a specifically crafted binary string sent during an "IMAP" mail connection yields access to the Linux system, for a particular version of IMAPD; User-to-root (U2R) attacks have the goal of gaining root or super-user access on a particular computer or system on which the attacker previously had user-level access. Common examples of U2R's are buffer-overflow attacks on various operating system programs. Fig.1. shows labeled network traffic data in the training data set.

0,tcp,private,RSTR,0,0,0,0,0,0,0,0,0,0,0,0,0,0,0,0,0,0,0,0,1,1,0.00,0.00,1.00,1.00,1.00,0.00,0.00,255,1,0.00,1.0
0,1.00,0.00,0.00,0.00,1.00,1.00,probe
175,tcp,http,SF,198,174,0,0,0,0,0,1,0,0,0,0,0,0,0,0,0,0,0,0,16,25,0.00,0.00,0.00,0.00,1.00,0.00,0.16,16,255,1.00
,0.00,0.06,0.02,0.00,0.00,0.00,0.01,normal
0,icmp,ecr_i,SF,1032,0,0,0,0,0,0,0,0,0,0,0,0,0,0,0,0,0,0,0,511,511,0.00,0.00,0.00,0.00,1.00,0.00,0.00,255,255,1
.00,0.00,1.00,0.00,0.00,0.00,0.00,0.00,dos
0,tcp,ftp_data,SF,334,0,0,0,0,0,0,1,0,0,0,0,0,0,0,0,0,0,0,1,1,0.00,0.00,0.00,0.00,1.00,0.00,0.00,1,5,1.00,0.00,1
.00,0.40,0.00,0.00,0.00,0.00,r2l
0,tcp,ftp_data,SF,0,5828,0,0,0,0,0,1,0,0,0,0,0,0,0,0,0,0,0,0,2,2,0.00,0.00,0.00,0.00,1.00,0.00,0.00,2,2,1.00,0.00,
1.00,0.00,0.00,0.00,0.00,0.00,u2r

Fig. 1. Network traffic data in the training data set

In the training data, 24 attack types are provided and 14 types are included in the testing data set. In test data set, a number of new attacks are added that are not presented in the training data. This makes the intrusion detecting practicability. Each of these data record has 41 unique features, including 34 numeric and 7 discrete features that its value can be converted to numeric value.

3.2 Feature Selection

Some of the 41 features in each of network traffic recorders may be redundant or contribute little to the detection process since the information they attach is contained in other features. Extraneous features can even make it harder to detect suspicious behavior patterns. In [10], it has been demonstrated that a large number of features are unimportant and may be eliminated, without significantly lowering the performance of the IDS. As shown in Table 1, 18 features are selected from the available set because they are typically present in network data packets. In these selected features, 12 of them are continuous features and the others are discrete which can be converted to a numeric value.

Table 1. Selected features (type: **c**ontinuous, **d**iscrete)

Features	Description	Type
duration	Length (number of seconds) of the connection	C
protocol_type	TCP=0, UDP=1, ICMP=2, Unknown=3	D
service	network service on the destination; HTTP=0, SMTP=1, FTP=2, Telnet=3, …	D
src_bytes	number of data bytes from source to destination	C
dst_bytes	number of data bytes from destination to source	C
land	1 if connection is from/to the same host/port; 0 otherwise	D
wrong_frag	number of "wrong" fragments	C
num_fail_log	number of failed login attempt	C
logged_in	1 if successfully logged in; 0 otherwise	D
root_shell	1 if root shell is obtained; 0 otherwise	D
No_file_creat	number of file creation operations	C
is_guest_login	1 if the login is a "guest" login; 0 otherwise	D
count	number of connections to the same host	C
srv_count	number of connections to the same service	C
serror_rate	% of connections that have "SYN" errors to the same host in the past 2 seconds	C
src_serror_rate	% of connections that have "SYN" errors to the same service	C
diff_srv_rate	% of connections to the different services in the past 2 seconds	C
diff_host_count	number of connections to different hosts	C

3.3 Data Normalization

An attribute is normalized by scaling its values so that they fall within a small specific range, such as 0 to 1. Normalization is particularly useful for classification algorithms involving neural networks, or distance measurements such as nearest-neighbor classification and clustering. Normalizing the input values for the training samples will help speed up the learning phase. There are so many methods for data normalization as min-max normalization, z-score normalization, and normalization by decimal scaling [11]. The data is normalized by a linear (min-max) normalization method as seen in Eq.(1). Also, it has good performance and simplicity.

$$\overline{x}_i(j) = \frac{x_i(j) - x_{\min}(j)}{x_{\max}(j) - x_{\min}(j)} \tag{1}$$

$$x_{\max}(j) = Max(x_i(j)), \ i = 1,2,\ldots,n \ , \ x_{\min}(j) = Min(x_i(j)), \ i = 1,2,\ldots,n$$

4 Cellular Neural Networks Methodology

4.1 Overview of the CNN Model

Cellular neural networks (CNN) were introduced in [12] and investigated as a fine-grained parallel model of computation both for simulation spatial dynamics of non-linear phenomenon. CNN can be viewed as a hybrid of cellular automaton (CA) and artificial neural network (ANN) [13]. Like CA it consists of a huge number of simple processing elements (cells), usually placed in the nodes of an orthogonal or hexagonal grid, each cell being connected to a set of nearest neighbors. Like in the ANN the connections are weighted, and each cell computes its output as a non-linear function of its internal state, which is updated depending on the sum of weighted outputs of its neighbors. A CNN is a nonlinear analog circuit which processes signals in real time and this new architecture is able to perform time-consuming tasks, such as signal processing, image processing and solving partial differential equations. CNN is also particularly applied to perform feature extraction and some complicated data classification. A 3-D scheme of CNN is explained in [14], which can be extended to dimensions CNN model (actually, this model can be defined in arbitrary dimensions, such as 1-D, 2-D, and so forth.).

In the cell circuit, E_{ij} is independent nonlinear current source. C is a linear capacitor and R_x, R_y are linear resistors. I is independent voltage source namely bias. $I_{xu}(i,j,w;k,l,z)$ and $I_{xy}(i,j,w;k,l,z)$ are linear voltage controlled current sources with $I_{xy}(i,j,w;k,l,z)=A(i,j,w;k,l,z)y_{klz}$ characteristics and $I_{xu}(i,j,w;k,l,z)=B(i,j,w;k,l,z)u_{klz}$. The constant coefficient $A(i,j,w;k,l,z)$ and $B(i,j,w;k,l,z)$ are known as cloning templates and arranged in A-template or feedback template and B-template or control template also, respectively. The CNN is therefore described by the state equations as shown in equations (2) and (3) of all cells by applying Kirchoff's Current Law (KCL) and Kirchoff's Voltage Law (KVL).

$$C\frac{dx_{ijw}(t)}{dt} = -\frac{1}{R_x}x_{ijw}(t) + \sum_{C(k,l,z)\in N_r(i,j,w)} A(i,j,w;k,l,z)y_{klz} + \sum_{C(k,l,z)\in N_r(i,j,w)} B(i,j,w;k,l,z)u_{klz} + I \qquad (2)$$

where

$$N_r(i,j,w) = \{C(k,l,z) \mid \max(|k-i|,|l-j|,|z-w|) \leq r\} \qquad (3)$$

with $1 \leq k \leq M$, $1 \leq l \leq N$, $1 \leq z \leq P$ is the r-neighborhood and

$$x_{ijw}(0) = x_{ijw_0}; \ |x_{ijw_0}| \leq 1; \ C>0; \ R_x>0; \ A(i,j,w;k,l,z)= A(k,l,z;i,j,w).$$

A dimensions r-neighborhood contains $(2r+1)^n$ cells where r represents the neighbor radius and n denotes the dimensions of CNN model.

4.2 Algorithm of CNN for Intrusion Detection

In our study, we use 2-D CNN architecture to train a classifier for intrusion detection, so equations (2) and (3) can be rewritten as equations (4) and (5):

$$y_{ij}(n) = f(x_{ij}(n)) = \frac{1}{2}(|x_{ij}(n)+1| - |x_{ij}(n)-1|) \qquad (4)$$

$$x_{ij}(n+1) = -x_{ij}(n) + \sum_{(k,l)\in N_r(i,j)} A_{i,j;k,l}(n)y_{kl} + \sum_{(k,l)\in N_r(i,j)} B_{i,j;k,l}(n)u_{kl} + I \qquad (5)$$

Assuming that each cell is connected to its 1-neighborhood neighbors only, A, B and I are identically repeated in the neighborhood of every neuron as:

$$A = \begin{bmatrix} A_{1,1} & A_{1,2} & A_{1,3} \\ A_{2,1} & A_{2,2} & A_{2,3} \\ A_{3,1} & A_{3,2} & A_{3,3} \end{bmatrix} \quad B = \begin{bmatrix} B_{1,1} & B_{1,2} & B_{1,3} \\ B_{2,1} & B_{2,2} & B_{2,3} \\ B_{3,1} & B_{3,2} & B_{3,3} \end{bmatrix} \quad I = I_{1\times1}$$

From the definition and equations, it can be derived that the network behavior of a CNN depends upon a set of template parameters. Initial state of cells and the weights values of the A and B matrices. In most common case this template set contains $2\times(2r+1)^n+1$ parameters and in our case 19 parameters are to be taken into account. All of these parameters can be found using a training algorithm, or by defining local rules for a given global task. If template parameters' values for the local rules are found, simulations are very helpful to test the dynamic global behavior of the entire clone of cells. In order to find the set of template parameters, learning is the most efficient and general method to solve this problem. Learning algorithm(LA) is used to realize the matching of input and output by adjusting the value of template parameters. Recurrent Perceptron Learning Algorithm (RPLA) is used to learn and train CNN model to find the template parameters [15]. Basically, updated weight parameters in RPLA are defined as equation (6).

$$w(n+1) = w(n) + 2\eta\varepsilon(n)V(n) \tag{6}$$

where $w(n)$ is the weight vector at iterations n, η is the learning rate, $V(n)$ is input vector, $\varepsilon(n)$ is error function defined as equation (7).

$$\varepsilon(n) = \frac{1}{2}\sum(y(n)-d)^2 \tag{7}$$

where $y(n)$ is the steady state of output of the actual output and d is the desired output. We can define input vector $V(n)$ using input data $u=(u_0,u_1,.....,u_{N-1})$ and output data $y=(y_0,y_1,.....,y_{N-1})$ as form of equation (8).

$$V(n) = (y(n)u_1) \tag{8}$$

where the output y changes by the state variable x while input data u is fixed as the initial condition. At the same time, for stability, the templates A, B should be symmetrically defined as follows

$$A = \begin{bmatrix} a_1 & a_2 & a_3 \\ a_2 & a_4 & a_5 \\ a_3 & a_5 & a_1 \end{bmatrix} \quad B = \begin{bmatrix} b_1 & b_2 & b_3 \\ b_2 & b_4 & b_5 \\ b_3 & b_5 & b_1 \end{bmatrix}.$$

So, the weight vector can be described as below form which has only 11 parameters instead of 19. $w=(a_1,a_2,a_3,a_4,a_5,b_1,b_2,b_3,b_4,b_5,I)$, here, equation (6) can be rewritten as equation (9) by using equation (7) and (8) to replace.

$$w(n+1) = w(n) + \eta\frac{1}{2}\sum(y(n)-d)^2(y(n)u_1) \tag{9}$$

LA ran for minimizing the error function $\varepsilon(n)$ (ideally, $\varepsilon(n)$ is zero) and the problem of learning can be formulated as an optimization problem. While training is finalized, by using eq.(9) the updated weight vector is converted to template A, B and bias I.

5   Simulation Experiment on Intrusion Detection

5.1   Performance Parameters

Several performance measures have been defined to evaluate the effectiveness of IDS. Most evaluated metrics are attack detection rate (false negative rate) and false positive rate. Attack detection rate defines the percentage of the number of detected attacks in relation to the number of overall attacks, which is in inverse proportion to the false negative rate. However, false positive rate is defined as the percentage of the number of misclassified processes in relation to the number of normal processes (Eq.(10)).

$$attack\ detection\ rate = \frac{number\ of\ detected\ attacks}{number\ of\ attacks} \times 100\%$$

$$false\ negative\ rate = \frac{number\ of\ false\ detected\ attacks}{number\ of\ attacks} \times 100\% \tag{10}$$

$$false\ positive\ rate = \frac{number\ of\ misclassified\ processes}{number\ of\ normal\ processes} \times 100\%$$

The IDS with higher attack detection rate and lower false negative rate is regarded as good performance system.

5.2   Learning Templates

RPLA is used as learning templates for CNN model as follows:
S1. Choose the proper templates for CNN and initialize the templates;
S2. Preset the learning rate, the value of total error and the number of iterations;
S3. Run the test for each individual template;
S4. Select a set of training data randomly and put them into the networks;
S5. Adjust (increase/decrease) the value of each template parameter by using the equation (9); Increase the iteration parameter. Compare with maximum iteration value. If the iteration value is greater than the iteration limit, then go S7.
S6. Compare the actual output with desire output and compute the total error value by using Eq.(7). If the total error can reach the preset value go to next step, else go S3.
S7. Finish the training session.

   In the training process, 1000 iterations have been made and the value of total error reached to about 10-5 where learning rate is 0.1. Thus, the templates and bias are estimated as follows:

$$A = \begin{bmatrix} 0 & 0 & 0 \\ 0 & 2.8 & 0 \\ 0 & 0 & 0 \end{bmatrix} \quad B = \begin{bmatrix} -1 & -1 & -1 \\ -1 & 5 & -1 \\ -1 & -1 & -1 \end{bmatrix} \quad I = -2$$

Consequently, these parameters can be applied to classify the network traffic data by using the created CNN model.

5.3 Simulation Results

In intrusion detection, the Receiver Operating Characteristic (ROC) curve is typically used to measure the performance of method. The ROC curve indicates how the detection rate changes as the thresholds are varied to generate more or fewer false alarms. The ROC curve is a plot of intrusion detection accuracy against the false positive probability that tradeoffs detection accuracy against the analyst workload [16]. It can be obtained by varying the detection threshold. We created a test data set to evaluate the performance of the CNN classifier algorithm. 20000 instances which cover all of categories are selected randomly from training data set including 320 attack instances. For comparison, the same test data set is applied to back propagation neural network (BPNN) which is trained by the same data set as that of CNN model. The results of experiment on anomaly detection with methods of CNN and BPNN are shown in Table 2, Table 3 and fig. 2.

Table 2. The results of CNN model (threshold: 0.23-0.38, real=19680)

Threshold	Attacks		Normal processes	Attack detection rate (%)	False positive rate (%)
	discovered	real	misclassified		
0.23	320	320	3726	100.00	18.93
0.24	318	320	1272	99.38	6.40
0.26	318	320	913	99.38	4.64
0.27	316	320	905	98.75	4.60
0.29	316	320	405	98.75	2.06
0.32	153	320	392	47.81	1.99
0.37	152	320	78	47.50	0.40
0.38	103	320	5	32.19	0.03

Table 3. The results of Back Propagation NN model (threshold: 0.15-0.29, real=19680)

Threshold	Attacks		Normal processes	Attack detection rate (%)	False positive rate (%)
	discovered	real	misclassified		
0.15	320	320	5872	100.00	29.84
0.16	315	320	3907	98.44	19.85
0.17	315	320	2465	98.44	12.53
0.18	310	320	693	96.88	3.52
0.19	106	320	532	33.13	2.70
0.22	102	320	130	31.88	0.66
0.25	97	320	19	30.31	0.10
0.29	89	320	10	27.81	0.05

The anomaly detection ROC curves for CNN and BP neural network are shown together in fig. 2 and each curve depicts the relationships between attack detection rate and false positive rate based on different threshold which varied from 0.23 to 0.38 of CNN and 0.15 to 0.29 of BP neural network. As depicted in Fig. 2., CNN model can exhibit superior performance than BP neural network in that CNN model provides the lowest false positive rate of 18.93% rather than 29.84% of BP neural network model when the attack detection rate reaches 100%. Moreover, the convergence of CNN model is faster than that of BP neural network model. The curve jumps sharply from 47.81% to 98.75% of attack detection rate as the threshold decreases in CNN model, and this occurrence appears in the BPNN model as well.

This might be the result of insufficient training datasets, which made the models incomplete, which causes model outputs to be close, and consequently could not be classified with any threshold [16]. The threshold of 0.29 in the detecting process with the CNN model, however, may be an optimum selection while taking the balance between attack detection rate and false positive rate into account in real-life intrusion detection.

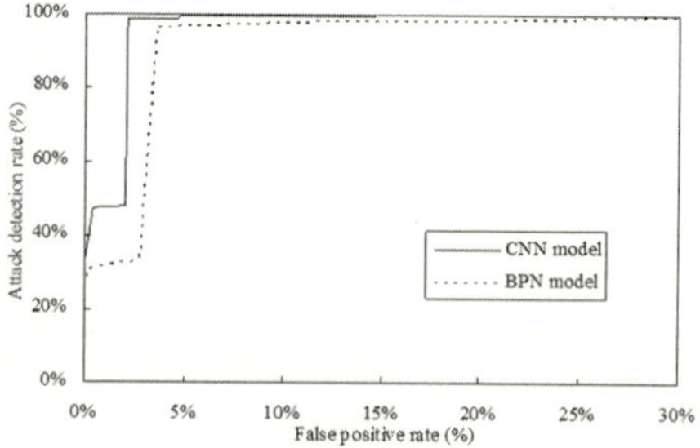

Fig. 2. Anomaly detection ROC curves for CNN and BPN models

6 Conclusion and Future Directions

In this paper, we have proposed an approach to intrusion detection using CNN. CNN has emerged as a powerful and practically realizable paradigm of multidimensional, locally connected, nonlinear processor arrays and it has been used in many research fields including data mining. RPLA has been employed to train the CNN model as a classifier. Experiments with KDD Cup 1999 connection traffic data which has been preprocessed such as features selection and normalization have shown that this model is able to effectively detect intrusive behaviors. We have also demonstrated performance comparisons to BPNN using the same data set and the results have shown that the CNN model exhibits superior performance with higher attack detection rate and lower false positive rate. Comparisons of various algorithms can provide more selections to improve the performance of CNN model.

References

1. Ghosh, A., Wanken, J., Charron, F.: Detecting anomalous and unknown intrusions against programs. In: Proc. 1998 Annual Computer Security Applications Conf., ACSAC_98, Los Alamitos, CA, USA, December 1998. IEEE Computer Soc. (1998) 259–267.
2. Anderson, J.,P.: Computer security threat monitoring and surveillance, Technical Report, James P. Anderson Company, Fort Washington, PA, April (1980).

3. Frank, J.: Artificial Intelligence and Intrusion Detection: Current and future directions. In Proceedings of the 17th National Computer Security Conference, (1994).

4. Helman,P., Bhangoo,J. A.: Statistically base system for prioritizing information exploration under uncertainty . IEEE Transactions on Systems, Man and Cybernetics, Part A: Systems and Humans, Vol. 27. (1997) 449-466.

5. Ghosh, A., Schwartzbard, A.: A study in using neural networks for anomaly and misuse detection. Proceedings of the Eighth USENIX Security Symposium, (1999) 141-152.

6. Depren, O., Topallar, M., Anarim, E., Ciliz, M.K., An intelligent intrusion detection system (IDS) for anomaly and misuse detection in computer networks, Expert Systems with Applications, Vol. 29(4) (2005) 713-722

7. Denning, D.E. An intrusion detection model.: IEEE Trans. S.E., SE-13 (2),(1987) 222-232.

8. Veroerd T, Hunt R.: Intrusion detection techniques and approaches. Computer Communications Vol. 25. (2002) 1356-1365.

9. KDD Cup 1999 Data. http://kdd.ics.uci.edu/databases/kddcup.html.1999

10. Sung AH, Mukkamala S.: Identifying important features for intrusion detection using support vector machines and neural networks. Proceedings of international symposium on applications and the internet (SAINT 2003), (2003) 209-217

11. Han,J., and Kamber,M.: Data Mining: Concepts and Techniques, Morgan Kaufmann Pubilisher, (2000)

12. Chua L. O., Yang, L.: Cellular Neural Networks: theory and application, IEEE Trans. Circuits and Systems, Vol. 35. (1998) 1257-1290.

13. Pudov, S.: Learning of cellular neural networks. Future Generation Computer Systems Vol.17. (2001) 689-697.

14. Fortuna, L. Arena, P. Balya, D. Zarandy, A.: Cellular neural networks: a paradigm for nonlinear spatio-temporal processing, Circuits and Systems Magazine, Vol.1(4) (2001) 6-21

15. Guzelis C., Karamahmut., S.: Recurrent Perceptron Learning Algorithm for Completely Stable Cellular Neural Networks. Proc. Third IEEE Int. Workshop on Cellular Neural Network and Applications, Rome, Italy, (1994) 177-182.

16. Wun-Hwa, C., Sheng-Hsun, H., Hwang-Pin, S.: Application of SVM and ANN for intrusion detection. Computers & Operations Research Vol. 32. (2005) 2617-2634.

A Lookup Table Model for Time-Memory Trade-Off Attacks on Binary Additive Stream Ciphers

Imran Erguler[1,2] and Emin Anarim[2]

[1] UEKAE-TUBITAK P.K.: 74, 41470, Gebze, Kocaeli, Turkey
`ierguler@uekae.tubitak.gov.tr`
[2] Electrical-Electronics Engineering Department, Bogazici University,
34342 Bebek, Istanbul, Turkey
`anarim@boun.edu.tr`

Abstract. In this study, we present a novel technique which can speed up the internal state reversion part of time-memory trade-off attacks on binary additive stream ciphers at the expense of requiring more pre-computational time. The technique also solves the difficulties that an attacker may face through running some stream generators backwards.

1 Introduction

A binary additive stream cipher is a synchronous stream cipher in which the key stream, plaintext, and ciphertext digits are binary digits, and the output function is the XOR function [1]. These stream ciphers have many applications in secure communications, since they offer required security for high data rate applications and have algorithms that are popular in fast implementations.

It is well known that the most of the attacks on stream ciphers are known plaintext attacks. For these types of attacks, attacker assumes knowledge of a piece of plaintext and its corresponding ciphertext so a piece of key stream sequence [2]. The goal of the attacker can be to find the unknown part of the plaintext, or most of the time to obtain secret encryption key K.

For binary additive stream ciphers, key stream sequences are independent from plaintext and a common lookup table could be used in analysis of different ciphertext blocks. Therefore cryptanalytic time-memory trade-off is an efficient known plaintext attack type for stream ciphers. Babbage and Golic independently described a time-memory trade-off technique known as BG attack for stream ciphers in [3] and [4] respectively. In [5], A. Biryukov et. al. presented an improved time-memory trade-off attack against stream ciphers by using the Hellman's time-memory tradeoff principle for block ciphers [6]. According to these models, by using known key stream sequence and a lookup table, possible internal state of the stream generator is determined. Afterwards, if the attacker wants to obtain rest of the plaintext it runs the generator forwards or if he wants to find the secret encryption key K, he needs to run generator backwards. However for some stream generators such as A5/1 GSM stream cipher, state of the generator changes in an irregular manner [4]. In those cases, there may be more than one solution for the previous state of any internal state. Although

A. Levi et al. (Eds.): ISCIS 2006, LNCS 4263, pp. 918–923, 2006.

possible number of solutions for initial state yielding the same internal state is a very small integer, it grows up as branches of a tree through reversing to initial state. This problem can be also valid for other some clock controlled stream generators or generators that are based on high order nonlinear feedback shift registers. This paper proposes that, by using a modified lookup table model for time-memory trade-off attacks, internal state reversion to find secret key K becomes practical and simpler, if number of different initial states yielding the same internal state at some time in future and the same output sequence is very likely to be a very small integer.

The outline of the paper is as follows: In Section 2, we describe the proposed model and construction of the tables. In Section 3, the advantage of the attack compared to BG attack model is investigated. Section 4 gives the required complexities of the proposed model. Finally, in Section 5 conclusions of the study are given.

2   The Proposed Model

The attack based on our proposed model consists of two parts; constructing the lookup tables and the lookup stage. In the first part, two lookup tables whose size determines the required memory are built up. The first table is used to reach the initial state of the stream generator from an internal state and the second table is used to find the corresponding internal state from the known key stream sequence. Let N represent total solution space of the generator internal state. Before preparation of the first table, attacker should decide at most how many possible windows of $\log(N)$ consecutive bits provided from the known key stream he will use in cryptanalysis. Let the attacker chose this number as D. Then the first table can be formed as follows: Firstly a random sample of M different $\log(N)$- bit blocks which are candidates for the internal state are chosen from the solution space N as Y_1, Y_2, Y_3................ Y_M. Then each Y_i, representing the internal state, is run forwards for D-1 times according to the state transition function of the stream generator. So if $Y_i(0)$ is the beginning state of Y_i, $Y_i(D-1)$ will be state of the Y_i after D -1 state transitions. Finally, each $Y_i(0)$-$Y_i(D-1)$ pair is stored as shown in Fig.1. Notice that the internal states of Y_i are not stored to use memory efficiently, since they can be reached by running $Y_i(0)$ forward directions.

$$Y_1(0) ----- > Y_1(D-1)$$
$$Y_2(0) ----- > Y_2(D-1)$$
$$Y_3(0) ----- > Y_3(D-1)$$
$$\vdots \qquad\qquad \vdots$$
$$Y_M(0) ----- > Y_M(D-1)$$

Fig. 1. The lookup table; the arrow represents the state transition function

The second table begins at where the first one ends. It is constructed as follows: Firstly each $Y_i(D\text{-}1)$, stored in second column of the first table, is taken as an internal state of the stream generator and from this state $\log(N)$ bits output stream is generated. Then generated output bit string and corresponding $Y_i(D\text{-}1)$ are stored as $Y_i(D\text{-}1)\text{-}z^i$ pairs in the second lookup table which is depicted in Fig. 2.

In the lookup stage, it is assumed that the attacker gets n consecutive key stream sequence bits; this known sequence provides $n\text{-}\log(N)+1$ overlapping $\log(N)$ bit blocks. The bits at bit positions between 1 and $\log(N)$ make up the first successive $\log(N)$ bit sequence so called s_1 and the bits at bit positions between $n\text{-}\log(N)+1$ and n make up the last block so called s_D. Then for each sequence, a search is made to find whether a match occurs between the sequence and the output column of the second lookup table as in case of the BG attack. If s_t matches with z^k (t is the matched sequence number), the corresponding $Y_k(D\text{-}1)$ which produced z^k is found in the second table. Since $Y_k(D\text{-}1)$ in fact produced s_t, if $Y_k(D\text{-}t)$ is obtained, the initial state of stream generator is determined with a high probability. To obtain $Y_k(D\text{-}t)$; firstly the $Y_k(0)$, corresponding to $Y_k(D\text{-}1)$ is found from the first lookup table, then $Y_k(0)$ is run forwards for $D\text{-}t$ times and $Y_k(D\text{-}t)$ which is the initial state is obtained. In the following part, whole realization part is summarized:

- Search all successive $\log(N)$ bit sequences (s_1, s_2,.... s_D) of the known key stream sequence in output column of the second lookup table.
- If a match occurs between s_t and z^k, then corresponding $Y_k(D\text{-}1)$ is found in the second table.
- Next, $Y_k(0)$ corresponding to $Y_k(D\text{-}1)$ in the first table, is run forwards for ($D\text{-}t$) times, where t is matched sequence number.
- Running $Y_k(0)$ forwards ($D\text{-}t$) times, the desired initial state of stream generator is obtained with high probability.
- Then by running forwards the candidate initial state of the stream generator, key stream sequence is produced and this is checked with the known key stream sequence to ensure that the obtained initial state is true.

$$Y_1(D-1) \Rightarrow z^1$$
$$Y_2(D-1) \Rightarrow z^2$$
$$Y_3(D-1) \Rightarrow z^3$$
$$\vdots \qquad\qquad \vdots$$
$$\vdots \qquad\qquad \vdots$$
$$Y_M(D-1) \Rightarrow z^M$$

Fig. 2. Second lookup table; $Y_i(D\text{-}1)$ represents the internal state of the stream generator and z^i denotes the generated $\log(N)$ bits of output from this state

Actually, when we look at the tables in Fig.1 and Fig.2, it can be seen that output of first table is input of the second table so they can be combined as one table as shown in Fig.3. So $Y_i(D\text{-}1)$ column is discarded to use memory efficiently .

Some binary additive stream ciphers go through an initial phase in which the cipher is clocked but no key stream is produced. Thus in such cases, information about the first state for the key stream does not lead to the initial state of the cipher. If attacker knows r times the cipher is clocked from initial state to the state that the first bit is generated (for A5/1, r is 100), he can also use the proposed model with a modified version. Instead of running each $Y_i(0)$ D-1 times in construction of the table, each $Y_i(0)$ is run $D+r$-1 times now. Also in the lookup stage, if s_t matches with z^k, $Y_k(0)$ is run D-t+r times, to obtain the desired initial state of stream generator with high probability.

$$Y_1(0) \Rightarrow z^1$$
$$Y_2(0) \Rightarrow z^2$$
$$Y_3(0) \Rightarrow z^3$$
$$\vdots \qquad \vdots$$
$$\vdots \qquad \vdots$$
$$Y_M(0) \Rightarrow z^M$$

Fig. 3. Combination of the first and second lookup tables; $Y_i(D$-1$)$ terms are discarded and only $Y_i(0)$ and z^i pairs are stored

3   Advantage of the Attack

In the classical BG time-memory trade-off attack, obtaining the internal state of the generator is the same as in the proposed model. However internal state reversion may be much complex and impractical according to stream cipher design. For example, according to GSM A5/1 stream cipher design, 4 states can converge to a common state in one clock cycle, so number of predecessors of an internal state may be 4. The branching process presented in [4] seems practical for A5/1, but for some stream cipher designs distance from internal states to initial state can be long enough opposed to A5/1 design and the attacker's internal state reversion attempt can be impractical or result in high time complexity. Also if the expected number of predecessors of any internal state is greater than 1, the expected number of vertices in the first t levels of tree grows exponentially in t, so getting initial state may become infeasible. It is a crucial difficulty that the attacker may face in BG type attack. On the other hand by using the proposed model the attacker obtain the possible initial state of the generator in only D-t state transitions.

4   The Complexities

The success of the attack can be expressed from the birthday paradox; two random subsets of a space with N points are likely to intersect if the product of their sizes exceeds N [5]. When D possible windows are used in the lookup stage, the trade-off curve of the attack becomes $DM=N$. Note that the attacker should reduce number of search attempts by using less log(N)-bit windows, though amount of available known key stream sequence can be more than required. Therefore the attack time T can be changed from D towards 1 for any $1 \leq T \leq D$, with satisfying the general trade-off equation as follows:

$$TM=N. \tag{1}$$

The total memory required to store the lookup table is $2M$log(N) bits, since there are M rows with two columns in the proposed table and each element in the table is log(N) bits length. Both memory requirement and time requirement of our model in getting the internal state is same as that of the BG model. Because in case of BG model, required internal state reversion time has also to be added to T, BG model requires more time in real time phase, compared to the proposed model. Let P denote the time required by pre-processing phase of the attack. According to the BG attack, if we ignore the logarithmic factors, pre-computational time becomes $P=M$. On the other hand, in the formation of the proposed table, the pre-computational time of our attack is $M(D$-1) state transition time much more than that of BG attack, because each sample is run forwards D-1 times more. However this extra time amount belongs to pre-processing phase of the attack and can be accepted by considering the fact that this table is generated once but can be used several times. If the number of possible solutions for the initial state of the stream generator yielding the same internal state is with high probability one or a very small positive integer, by using our model retrieving the initial state from any found internal state is simpler than branching process mentioned in [4]. Therefore computational time of the attack can be reduced.

5 Conclusion

In this study, we have presented a new model in construction of the lookup table described in BG time-memory trade-off attack. The aim of the attacker can be to find the secret encryption key K, rather than getting rest of the plaintext by running the generator forwards. In those cases, if the target stream cipher has a high resistance in internal state reversion, our proposed model can become very useful to obtain initial state of the generator from any internal state.

The memory requirement of the attack is $2M$log(N) which is same as that of BG model. Although our model results in extra amount of time ($M(D$-1) state transition time) in pre-processing phase of the attack, it can reduce computational time of the attack in appropriate situations and can improve the time taken to reach possible initial states. Also for some stream cipher designs, this model makes the impractical internal state reversions possible.

References

1. Menezes, A., van Oorschot, P. C., Vanstone, S. A.: Handbook of Applied Cryptography. CRC Press Inc., (1997)
2. Schneier, B.: Applied Cryptography. 2nd edn. John Wiley and Sons, New York (1996)

3. Babbage, S.: A Space/Time Trade-Off in Exhaustive Search Attacks on Stream Ciphers. In: European Convention on Security and Detection IEE Conference Publication. 408 (1995)
4. Golic, J.: Cryptanalysis of Alleged A5 Stream Cipher. In: Fumy, W. (eds.): EUROCRYPT 1997. Lecture Notes in Computer Science, Vol. 1233. Springer-Verlag, Berlin Heidelberg New York (1997) 239–255
5. Biryukov, A., Shamir, A.: Cryptanalytic Time/Memory/Data Trade-Offs for Stream Ciphers. In: Okamoto, T. (eds.): ASIACRYPT 2000. Lecture Notes in Computer Science, Vol. 1976. Springer-Verlag, Berlin Heidelberg New York (2000) 1–13
6. Hellman, M. E.: A Cryptanalytic Time-Memory Trade-Off. IEEE Trans. Inform. Theory 26 (1980) 525-530

Improved Merkle Cryptosystem (IMC)

Attila Altay Yavuz[1], Emin Anarim[2], and Fatih Alagoz[1]

[1] Bogazici University, Department of Computer Engineering,
Bebek, Istanbul 34342, Turkey
[2] Bogazici University, Department of Electrical and Electronic Engineering,
Bebek, Istanbul 80815, Turkey
{attila.yavuz, fatih.alagoz}@boun.edu.tr
anarim@boun.edu.tr

Abstract. Merkle Cryptosystem (MC) is the first cryptosystem which introduces general concept of the public key cryptography. In this paper, we propose Improved Merkle Cryptosystem (IMC), which has significant security advantages over both MC and a variant of MC (VMC). In IMC, cryptographic hash functions and a new puzzle structure are used together in order to increase the security of MC and VMC. The key agreement value, which is send as clear text in VMC, is hidden using cryptographic hash function in IMC. Also, in order to increase security of the key agreement value, auxiliary keys are used. Notice that, in IMC, computational advantages of VMC remain unchanged while its security is increased. Utilizing computational advantages of VMC, IMC has also security and storage advantages over original MC. It is shown that, with these improvements, IMC can provide as high security as some well-known public key cryptosystems while MC and VMC can not provide same security due to performance problems.

Keywords: Cryptography, Merkle Cryptosystem, Key Establishment, Encryption.

1   Introduction

Public key cryptography made significant impact on secure and authenticated communication systems [1]. Many different public key cryptography algorithms have been developed based on different mathematical approaches [2]. RSA, which is based on factorization of large numbers into prime factors and El-Gamal cryptosystem, which is based on hardness of Discrete Logarithm Problem (DLP), are well-known and fundamental public key cryptosystems [3]. Also, Elliptic Curve Cryptography (ECC) [4] which is based on DLP over EC is one the most widely used cryptosystem utilizing DLP. Apart from these, new public key cryptosystems such as NTRU (N-th degree TRUncated polynomial ring) [5], which is based on lattice problem, have also been proposed.

However, the first cryptosystem, which provides a solution to the secure communication problem over insecure channels without pre-established secrets, is Merkle Cryptosystem (MC) [6]. In MC, communicating parties use 'puzzles',

A. Levi et al. (Eds.): ISCIS 2006, LNCS 4263, pp. 924–934, 2006.

which are feasible for them to solve but infeasible for an attacker to solve. A Variant of MC (VMC) [7] utilizes MC with block ciphers and uses a different puzzle generation technique from MC. VMC method has some advantages over original MC.

In this paper, we propose Improved Merkle Cryptosystem (IMC) that increases the security of the both MC and VMC. In VMC, the index, which is used for key agreement, is sent in clear text. This approach causes significant security degradation. In IMC, we use a different puzzle structure and cryptographic hash functions to increase security of VMC. IMC utilizes puzzle generation method of VMC but uses auxiliary key to increase security of messages transmitted over network. Also, in order to hide key agreement value, we use cryptographic hash functions. Thus, adversary can not understand which puzzle communicating parties agree on (auxiliary keys increases security of the hashed key agreement value). In addition to this, computational advantages of the VMC remain unchanged while its security is significantly increased. Shifting computational advantages of communicating parties to the overall system security, IMC can also provide higher security than original MC. Moreover, puzzle structure of IMC provides storage advantages over original MC method. We also show that, with these improvements, IMC can provide as high security as some well-known public key cryptosystems while MC and VMC can not provide same security due to performance issues.

The rest of the paper is organized as follows: In Section 2, we discussed MC and VMC algorithms together with their security analysis. In Section 3, we present our IMC algorithm and its properties. In Section 4, we give detailed analysis of IMC algorithm and compare IMC to MC and VMC. Also, comparison of IMC for various criteria to some well-known public key cryptosystems and MC-VMC is given. In Section 5, we present conclusion and future works.

2   MC and VMC

2.1   Merkle Cryptosystem (MC)

Merkle Cryptosystem (MC), also known as Merkle Puzzle, is the first cryptosystem having public key cryptography properties [6]. Suppose that, Alice and Bob want to secretly communicate over an insecure channel without pre-established secrets. Alice creates a set of puzzles that are feasible to solve for Bob. These puzzles are derived from secret values using secret keys that are short enough such that Bob can realize brute force attack on them. Each puzzle contains a session key that will be used for future communication and a pseudo-index which makes possible secret key establishment. In addition, each puzzle is added the required redundancy that allows Bob to perform the brute force attack. Bob selects one of the puzzles and performs a brute force attack on it. Bob stops brute force attack when he detects recognizable redundancy value. Bob recovers pseudo-index and session key from solved puzzle and sends pseudo-index to Alice. Alice searches this pseudo-index in her pseudo-index list and find corresponding real index which Bob has chosen. Consequently, Bob and Alice agree on a secret session key which corresponds to the selected real index. Adversary (Oscar) only obverses pseudo-index, which does not reveal any information about which key Bob has chosen. Thus, adversary has to make brute force attack to all puzzles. Here, Bob makes brute force attack only one puzzle while adversary makes brute force attack to all puzzles.

Apart from being the first cryptosystem which introduces general concept of the public key cryptography, principles of MC are used in many security applications. For instance, puzzle principle of MC is used in time-lock puzzles [8]. In time-lock puzzles, the idea is that a secret is transformed in such a way that any machines, running continuously, take at least a certain amount of time to solve the puzzles in order to recover the secret. This minimum amount of time is the relative release time with respect to the start of solving the puzzle and could be different for different machines [9]. In addition to this, puzzle concept of MC is used to combat against junk mails and is used to prevent DoS (Denial of Service) attacks utilizing client puzzles [10].

Notations, which are used in MC, are given below:

P : Public key vector (puzzles), K : Secret key vector that is used to generate P, K_s : Session key vector. $P_i \in P$, $K_i \in K$ and $K_{s_i} \in K_s$ for $1 \leq i \leq N$ where $N = 2^m$. m: The parameter which, determines number of elements in the P, K and K_s vectors. $|Var|$ denotes the bit length of the variable Var and $||$ denotes concatenation operation. In MC, bit length of the secret key is represented by $n' = |K_i|$ and bit length of the single puzzle is represented by $t = |P_i|$. $(E-D)_K$: Symmetric encryption and decryption functions using secret key K. r : Index number used for key agreement. S : The recognizable redundancy value.

Original version of MC is described below:

1. Alice generates puzzles $P_i = E_{K_i}(S||r_i||K_{s_i})$ for $1 \leq i \leq N$ where $N = 2^m$. Alice sends vector P to Bob.

2. Bob selects one of the puzzle say j'th puzzle and realizes a brute force attack to P_j. When brute force attack is completed, Bob decrypts the puzzle $(S||r_j||K_{s_j}) = D_{K_j}(P_j)$. Bob verifies S and recover r_j and K_{s_j}.

3. Bob sends index r_j to Alice in clear text. Notice that this index r_j is a pseudo-index and only Alice knows which real index corresponds to pseudo-index r_j. Suppose that pseudo-index r_j corresponds i'th puzzle. Then, Alice knows that Bob has chosen i'th puzzle P_i from P.

4. Alice and Bob agree on the secret session key K_{s_i} and use this key for future communication.

In this system, symmetric encryption function can be an appropriate block cipher such as DES or AES [11]. Notice that, n' i.e., that is the bit length of the K_i should be selected carefully. It should allow Bob to realize a brute force attack on P_i but should not be so small such that it weakens the whole cryptosystem. In the first version of the MC, n' is selected as 20 bits. Also, some versions select $n' = m$ so that number of puzzles and bit length of the single puzzle are equal to each other. In MC, Oscar can listen the communication channel and observe index r_j . However, since index r_j does not reveal which puzzle Bob chooses, Oscar has to realize brute force attack to whole puzzles in order to understand which puzzle Bob has chosen. In original MC, bit length of single puzzle P_i is $|t| = (S||r_i||K_{s_i})$ where $t > n'$. This property increases storage requirements of the original MC. Notice that, reasonable bit length of $n' \leq 50$. Complexity of the MC is summarized at Table 1.

Table 1. Computational and Storage Complexity of MC

	Computational Complexity	Storage Complexity
Alice	$O(\ 2^m\ )$	
Bob	$O(\ 2^{n'}\ )$	$O(2^m) * t$
Oscar	$O(\ 2^{m+n'}\ )$	

2.2 Variant of Merkle Cryptosystem (VMC)

Many variations of MC have been reported in literature. One of the variant (VMC), which is given in [7], uses larger key bit length for each puzzle. Also, puzzle generation method of VMC is different from MC. For this reason, it is not feasible for Bob to attack each puzzle similar to the original MC. This method uses another public key X to generate public key vector such that length of the public key vector can be used to reduce search space of the participant of the communication. However, this method sends real index in clear text that significantly reduces brute force attack effort of Oscar. Parameters, which are used in VMC, are given below:

X : The public key value, which is used to generate public key vector P. Bit length of the single puzzle is equal to bit length of the secret key, $|P_i| = |K_i| = n$. Notice that, reasonable bit length of the $n \approx 64$ bits.

VMC algorithm is described below:

1. Alice generates puzzles $P_i = E_{K_i}(X)$ for $1 \leq i \leq N$ where $N = 2^m$. Alice sends vector P and public key X to Bob.

2. Bob generates random keys $l_1, l_2, ...$ and encrypts X with them. Bob compares results with elements in vector P such that there is a collision between encrypted value and one of the elements of vector P. Suppose that collision occurs for l_j. Consequently, $E_{l_j}(X) = P_{K_i}(X)$ and $l_j = K_i$. Bob finds the i'th puzzle in vector P via this collision search.

3. Bob sends index i in clear text together with encrypted message $M' = E_{K_i}(M)$. Bob sends (M', i) to Alice. Optionally, Bob might generate a session key K_s, $K_s' = E_{K_i}(K_s)$ and sends (K_s', i) to Alice.

4. Alice obtains index i and understands that Bob uses i'th key for secret communication. Alice decrypts message or session key $M = D_{K_i}(M')$ or $K_s = D_{K_i}(K_s')$.

Complexity of the VMC is summarized at Table 2.

Note that, VMC uses block ciphers to generate puzzles. The bit length of a single puzzle (n) is smaller than the key bit length of the block cipher such as AES having 128,192 or 256 bit key size in order to make collision search

Table 2. Computational and Storage Complexity of VMC

	Computational Complexity	Storage Complexity
Alice	$O(2^m)$	
Bob	$O(2^{n-m})$	$O(2^m) * n$
Oscar	$O(2^n)$	

possible for Bob. In this situation, first n bit of the block cipher key is used as variable part while remainder part is used as constant to obtain n bit security. In remainder of the paper, n is used in this context.

2.3   Advantages and Disadvantages of VMC to MC

Most important contribution of VMC is that the computational effort of Bob to find a secret key, is reduced from $O(2^{n})$ to $O(2^{n-m})$. The reason is that, Bob realizes a collision search using advantages of large number of puzzles. In collision search, as explained in VMC step 2, Bob generates random keys and discovers corresponding private key with the probability of $Pr(Collision) = 2^m/2^n$. However, in original MC, number of puzzles does not give any contribution for reducing computational effort of Bob. The reason is that, Bob directly chooses one of the puzzles and realizes a brute force attack to the puzzle with $O(2^n)$ computational complexity.

VMC uses computational advantages of Bob to generate puzzles that have larger key bit length. Instead of giving Bob shorter time to determine a key, it is possible to keep collision search to constant but increase the bit length of single puzzle n. This approach increases computational effort of Oscar to break a single puzzle.

In VMC, Bob sends key agreement index i in clear text together with encrypted message as described in VMC step 3. Sending index in clear text causes significant security problem and drastically reduces the computational effort that Oscar has to perform, compared to the original MC. Notice that, in MC, Bob sends his selected index in clear text but the index sent by Bob does not correspond to the real index for the puzzle that Bob has found. Alice generates a puzzle in the MC step 1 such that it contains a pseudo-index which is known only by Alice. In MC Step 3, this pseudo-index is sent in clear text and does not reveal any information about the real index that Bob has found. Thus, brute force attack effort of Oscar is in the order of $O(2^{n+m})$. However, in VMC, sending real index i in clear text (Step 3) reduces the effort required to attack by Oscar from $O(2^{n+m})$ to $O(2^n)$. Note that the high number of puzzles, which is $N = 2^m$, become useless to prevent attack of Oscar, since Oscar can observe real index and realizes brute force attack directly to the selected puzzle. Sending index in clear text may give small advantages compared to the original MC such that Alice does not make a search for pseudo-index. However, this search effort is completely insignificant since Alice stores pseudo-indices sorted and finds a corresponding real index easily. However, sending real index in clear text causes a significant security degradation that can not be compared with neglible search time advantage.

3   Improved Merkle Cryptosystem (IMC)

In this section, we present details of our Improved Merkle Cryptosystem (IMC). We make improvements over MC and VMC for three major points. Firstly, we increase security of the VMC by eliminating security problem which stems from sending real index in clear text. Notice that, computational advantages of Bob in VMC remain unchanged while security of the cryptosystem is increased. Secondly, we use auxiliary secret keys, which increase security of the hashed secret value transmitted over network for key agreement. This approach provides security advantages over VMC for transmitted packets over network. Thirdly, we show that IMC reduces storage requirements and bandwidth consumption of Bob and Alice.

Following additional notations are used:

H : Cryptographic hash function. This hash function should be a secure hash function such as SHA family [12] or a cryptographic hash function having variable length output property (this may provide advantage for different bandwidth requirements of communication). y_i : Auxiliary secret key which is used to increase bit length security of the hashed message transmitted over network, P_i^* : Public key which is generated using y_i auxiliary keys. K_{s_a} and K_{s_b} denote session keys, which are generated by Alice and Bob, respectively. h : Secret hashed vector where $h_i \in h$, for all i, $1 \leq i \leq N$ where $N = 2^m$. $PRNG$: Pseudo Random Number Generator.

IMC algorithm is described below:

1.Alice generates auxiliary secret keys y_i and puzzle pairs $P_i = E_{K_i}(X)$, $P_i^* = E_{K_i}(y_i)$ for $1 \leq i \leq N$ where $N = 2^m$. Alice sends (P_i, P_i^*, X) for all i to Bob and stores (K_i, y_i) pairs as secret key pairs.

2. Alice generates hashed secret key vector h, $h_i = H(K_i||y_i)$ for $1 \leq i \leq N$ where $N = 2^m$. Alice stores h as secret key vector. She can store vector h in two different ways. Details for storage of vector h are given in Section 4.2.

3. Bob obtains (P_i, P_i^*, X) for $1 \leq i \leq N$ where $N = 2^m$. Then he generates random keys l_j similar to VMC step 2 such that $while(v, search\ on\ P_i)\{l_j = PRNG(), v = E_{l_j}(X), move\ indices\}$. If $(P_i == E_{l_j}(X))$ then $K_i = l_j$ and Bob finds one of the secret keys K_i. Using K_i, Bob decrypts P_i^* and obtains secret auxiliary key $y_i = D_{K_i}(P_i^*)$.

4. Bob calculates $h' = H(K_i||y_i)$ and sends h' value to Alice. Notice that, only Alice knows K_i and y_i and using these secret key pairs, only Alice can calculate and verify h' value. Since one-way properties of H, Oscar can not find K_i and y_i from h'.

5. Session key agreement can be done with three different ways:

- *Alice decides session key:* Bob sends h' to Alice. Alice searches h' over vector h. If she finds then Alice and Bob agree on key $(K_i||y_i)$. Alice generates session key K_{s_s} and calculates $K_{s_s}' = E_{K_i||y_i}(K_{s_s})$ and sends K_{s_s}' to Bob. Bob decrypts K_{s_s}' and obtains $K_{s_s} = D_{K_i||y_i}(K_{s_s}')$. Alice and Bob agree on session key K_{s_s}.
- *Bob decides session key:* Bob generates K_{s_b} and calculates $K_{s_b}' = E_{K_i||y_i}(K_{s_b})$. Bob sends (h', K_{s_b}') pair to Alice. Alice searches h' over vector h. If she finds then Alice and Bob agree on key $(K_i||y_i)$. Alice decrypts K_{s_b}' and obtains $K_{s_b} = D_{K_i||y_i}(K_{s_b}')$. Alice and Bob agree on session key K_{s_b}.
- *Alice and Bob jointly decide session key:* Alice and Bob agree on $(K_i||y_i)$ similar to steps above and they exchange K_{s_s} and K_{s_b} session keys. They calculate their joint session key $K_s' = K_{s_s} \oplus K_{s_b}$.

4 Analysis and Comparison of IMC

In this section, we analyze properties of IMC and compare it to the MC and VMC. Also, we compare the security of IMC to the some well-known public key cryptosystems. Firstly, we analyze security properties and advantages of IMC over MC and VMC showing that IMC provides higher security than MC and VMC. Secondly, we present storage advantages of IMC over MC and mention some additional techniques to reduce storage requirements of IMC.

4.1 Security Analysis and Advantages of IMC

In IMC, in order to hide key agreement value, which is secret key $(K_i||y_i)$, we calculate hash of $(K_i||y_i)$, $h' = H((K_i||y_i))$ and transmit h' over network. Due to one-way property of cryptographic hash functions, Oscar can not find $(K_i||y_i)$ from h'. With our improvement, in order to obtain $(K_i||y_i)$, Oscar has to realize brute force attack to all puzzles ($N = 2^m$ puzzles). Since brute force attack to a single puzzle requires $O(2^n)$ computational effort, total computational effort of Oscar becomes $O(2^{n+m})$. In VMC, since real index is sent in clear text, Oscar knows which index Bob has chosen. Thus, computational effort of Oscar in VMC is only $O(2^n)$. In table 3, we can see security advantages of the IMC over VMC ($O(2^{n+m}) > O(2^n)$).

IMC can use larger key bit length for a single puzzle by shifting computational advantages of Bob to the overall system security (properties of VMC). Shifting computational advantages of Bob to the key bit length of a single puzzle (parameter for overall system security), we can select n such that $n > n'$. Thus, $O(2^{n+m}) > O(2^{n'+m})$ and IMC can provide higher security than MC using this approach. In table 3, advantages of IMC over MC can be seen. In addition to this, in table 3, security/performance advantage of IMC over MC and VMC is shown. It is calculated by dividing computational effort of Oscar to the computational effort of Bob. This gives us a criterion about the efficiency of the cryptosystem. We can see that both MC and VMC have $O(2^m)$ security/performance value while IMC has $O(2^{n+m})/O(2^{n-m}) = O(2^{2m})$ which is more efficient than MC and VMC.

Another improvement of IMC is that it uses auxiliary key y_i to increase bit length security of the hashed key agreement value h'. Suppose that Oscar obtain h' value by eavesdropping. In order to find $(K_i\|y_i)$ from h', Oscar should try all possible $O(2^{2n})$ key space for detecting a one-to-one mapping among generated random keys and h' value. One-way properties of cryptographic hash function does not allow Oscar to recover $(K_i\|y_i)$ from h' without brute force attack under the assumption of random behavior of hash functions [13]. Notice that, $|(K_i\|y_i)| = 2n$ and for $n \simeq 70$ bits, $|(K_i\|y_i)| = 140$ bits. This provides the security in the order of $O(2^{140})$. If only $h' = H(K_i)$ was used instead of $h' = H(K_i\|y_i)$ then brute force effort of Oscar would have been $O(2^n)$. Under this condition, security of the transmitted message over network $(O(2^n))$ would have been lower than security of overall system cryptosystem ($O(2^{n+m})$) and Oscar would have broken system easily by attacking h' value instead of P_i puzzles. The main idea behind of the using auxiliary keys is preventing IMC from this attack. In VMC, messages transmitted over network are encrypted using only n bit K_i keys. Thus, IMC provides higher security for messages transmitted over network (including key agreement value) than that of the VMC. In MC, session keys are embedded into puzzle P_i. When Bob solves the puzzle, he uses session key to encrypt message, which is transmitted over network. Thus, message security of MC depends on key bit length of the session key and overall security of the cryptosystem. Results are summarized at Table 3.

4.2 Storage Analysis and Advantages of IMC

IMC has storage advantages over MC. In MC, a single puzzle P_i contains three components, which are S, r_i, and K_{s_i}, respectively (total t bits). These additional components increase bit length of a single puzzle and cause significant storage and transmission load. However, in IMC, there are puzzle pairs (P_i, P_i^*) each of them having $2n$ bit length. Thus, for $N = 2^m$ puzzles, IMC provides $O(2^m t - 2^{m+1}n) = O(2^m(t - 2n))$ storage advantages over MC. For example, bit length of a single puzzle in MC with 40 bit redundancy, 40 bit pseudo-index and 128 bit session key are approximately $t \approx 208$ bit. In IMC, the bit length of a key can be selected up to 70 bits (due to storage and computational limits). Thus, bit length of a single puzzle pair is $2n \approx 140$ *bits*. Consequently, for $m \approx 30$, IMC provides storage advantages up to $(2^{30} * 68) \simeq 1\ GB$ for these settings when compared to MC. Important point is that, same amount of gain is also obtained for network bandwidth consumption. Notice that, VMC has a small storage advantages when compared to IMC (IMC : $O(2 * 2^m n)$, VMC: $O(2^m n)$). However, for corresponding small storage load, IMC has significant security advantages over VMC. These results can also be observed in table 3.

Apart from these, in IMC step 2, we have discussed that secret key vector h can be stored in two different ways. This is a tradeoff approach among storage and computational resources of Alice. If Alice has sufficient storage resources, she stores vector h permanently. Then, whenever a key agreement occurs, Alice directly searches h' over vector h for key agreement. This approach provides computational resource advantage. However, if Alice does not have sufficient storage capability, for each key agreement, she dynamically generates h_i elements using (K_i, y_i) secret key pairs and compares h_i with h' to find a match. Thus, Alice does not have to store vector h permanently. Since cryptographic hash functions are fast, with feasible amount of puzzle ($N = 2^m, m \approx 30$), search operation becomes feasible. This approach provides storage advantage.

Table 3. Comparion of IMC to MV and VMC

		MC	VMC	IMC
	Alice	2^m	2^m	2^m
Computational Complexity	Bob	$2^{n'}$	2^{n-m}	2^{n-m}
	Oscar	2^{n+m}	2^n	2^{n+m}
	Alice	$2^m t$	$2^m n$	$2^{m+1} n$
Storage Complexity	Bob	$2^m t \to 1$	$2^m n \to 1$	$2^{m+1} n \to 1$
	Oscar	$2^m t$	$2^m n$	$2^{m+1} n$
Security Comparison		2^{n+m}	2^n	2^{n+m}
Security/Computational		2^m	2^m	2^{2m}
Message Security		$|K_s|$	2^n	2^{2n}

4.3 Comparison of IMC with MC, VMC and Some Well-Known Public Key Cryptosystems

Table 4 demonstrates comparison of the IMC with MC, VMC and some well-known public key cryptosystems. Symmetric Cryptosystem Bit Length (SCBL) security gives total bit length strength of the MC, VMC and IMC to resist attack of Oscar. For example, 100 bits mean that computational effort of Oscar to break cryptosystem is equivalent to break 100 bits block cipher. Note that, it does not mean that bit length of the key that will be used for block cipher is 100 bits, but total effort (using all puzzles in the system) corresponds to 100 bits security. To reach this security level, parameters $m \simeq 30$ bits, $n' = 40$ bits and $n = 70$ bits are selected for today's and near future feasible memory and computational possibilities. Brute force attack capability of Bob is selected as 2^{40} that allows feasible search time for key agreement. Storage capability of Alice and Bob is selected as approximately $2^{30} \cdot 140$ bits so that it is feasible for current hardware possibilities. Using these parameters, maximum security available for the MC is 2^{70}. In IMC, using aforementioned improvements, security level can be reached up to 2^{100} bits ($O(2^{n+m})$) that extends approximate lifespan of the cryptosystem to 30 years (Table 4) [14]. For these parameters, providing more than 70 bit security becomes infeasible both for MC and VMC. Remainder parts of the table 4 shows equivalent bit length security level for various public key cryptosystems and their related lifespan and economical cost values. Corresponding values for symmetric key bit length security are obtained from [14]. For these comparisons, [15] can also be used. With these interpretations, we see that IMC can provide as high security as some well-known public key cryptosystems. In table 4, following abbreviations are used: $PKCL$: Public Key Cryptography bit Length. CAS: Classical Asymmetric Cryptography like RSA. $SDLF$: Sub Group Discrete Logarithm problem Field. EC: Elliptic Curve. LB: Lower Bound.

Table 4. Comparison of IMC with VMC-MC and some well-known public key cryptosystems for various criteria

SCBL	MC	70	Infeasible for Participants				
	VMC	70	Infeasible for Participants				
	IMC	70	76	82	88	94	100
PKCL	CAS	952	1279	1613	2054	2560	3137
	SDLF	704	960	1248	1632	2080	2592
	SDL Key Size	125	135	145	156	167	178
	EC Size	132	155	173	197	218	240
Infeasible Number of MIPS Years		$8 \cdot 10^9$	$5 \cdot 10^{11}$	$2 \cdot 10^{13}$	$2 \cdot 10^{15}$	$1 \cdot 10^{17}$	$8 \cdot 10^{18}$
LB for HW attack cost for 1 day breaking		$1 \cdot 10^8$	$3 \cdot 10^8$	$4 \cdot 10^8$	$7 \cdot 10^8$	$1 \cdot 10^9$	$2 \cdot 10^9$
Corresponding Lifespan		2000	2008	2015	2023	2031	2039

5 Conclusion and Future Works

In this study, we propose Improved Merkle Cryptosystem (IMC), which can be considered as an alternative method for key agreement schemes, based on only symmetric cryptosystem and cryptographic hash functions without requiring a Trusted Third Part (TTP). As a novelty, IMC uses cryptographic hash functions and auxiliary keys to increase security of MC and VMC. Unlike VMC, IMC hides key agreement value using cryptographic hash functions and enhances the security of key agreement value utilizing auxiliary keys. These approaches provide significant security advantages over VMC. Since IMC utilizes some advantages of VMC over MC, IMC also provides higher security than MC. Different puzzle structure of IMC reduces storage requirement of the cryptosystem when compared to MC. Our improvements provide a solution to use MC for long term security, which is compatible with some well-known public key cryptosystems, within today's feasible hardware possibilities.

MC does not provide security against active attacks such as message replay and injection attacks. As a future work, we consider using IMC to develop a key agreement scheme, which can provide major cryptographic goals such as confidentiality, integrity, authentication and unforgeability together. In order to this, we consider using some principles of signcryption [16]. We will integrate IMC with a signcryption based key exchange schemes [17], which uses nonce and time-stamps to prevent cryptosystem from active attacks. We believe that, this integrated cryptosystem, Signcryption Type Authentic Key Establishment scheme (STAKE), will solve active attack problems of IMC and will provide additional cryptographic goals.

Acknowledgements

This work is supported by the State Planning Organization of Turkey under "Next Generation Satellite Networks Project", and Bogaziçi University Research Affairs.

References

1. W. Diffie and M. E. Hellman. New Directions in Cryptography, IEEE Trans. Information Theory, vol. IT-22, Nov. 1976, pp: 644 654.
2. Ueli Maurer. Cryptography 2000 -10 Years Back, 10 Years Ahead, Lecture Notes in Computer Science, Springer-Verlag, vol. 2000, pp.63-85, 2001.
3. Standard specifications for public key cryptography. IEEE P1363/D13, November 1999.
4. D. Johnson, A. Menezes. The Elliptic curve digital signature algorithm (ECDSA)", February 24, 2000.
5. J. Hoffstein, J. Pipher, and J.H. Silverman, NTRU: A Ring-Based Public Key Cryptosystem, Proceedings of ANTS III, Portland, June 1998.
6. R. C. Merkle. Secure Communications over Insecure Channels, Communications of the ACM 21(4), pp294–299 (April 1978).
7. Chris Mitchell. Public key encryption using block ciphers, technical report RHUL-MA-2003-6, 9 September (Department of Mathematics, Royal Holloway, University of London), 2001.
8. R. L. Rivest, A. Shamir, and D. A. Wagner. Time-lock puzzles and timed-release crypto, MIT LCS Tech. Report MIT/LCS/TR-684, 1996.
9. Aldar C.-F. Chan, Ian F. Blake. Scalable, Server-Passive, User-Anonymous Timed Release Cryptography, icdcs, pp. 504-513, 25th IEEE International Conference on Distributed Computing Systems (ICDCS'05), 2005.
10. D. Dean and A. Stubblefield. Using client puzzles to protect TLS, Proceedings of the USENIX Security Symposium, August 2001.
11. NIST. Specifications for the Advanced Encryption Standard(AES). Federal Information Processing Standards Publications (FIPS PUB) 197, November 2001. U.S. Department of Commerce, N.I.S.T.
12. NIST. Secure Hash Standard. Federal Information Processing Standards Publications(FIPS PUB) 180-2, August 26, 2002. U.S. Department of Commerce, N.I.S.T.
13. D. Stinson. Cryptography Theory and Practice. CRC Press, Inc., Third Edition, 2005.
14. Arjen K. Lenstra and Eric R. Verheul. Selecting cryptographic key sizes, Journal of Cryptology, 14(4):255–293, 2001.
15. A.K. Lenstra. Unbelievable security, Proceedings Asiacrypt 2001, LNCS 2248, Springer-Verlag 2001, 67-86.
16. Y. Zheng. Digital signcryption or how to achieve Cost(Signature Encryption) $\ll$ Cost(Signature) + Cost(Encryption). Advances in Cryptology – Crypto'97, Lecture Notes in Computer Science, Vol. 1294, pp. 165-179, Springer-Verlag, 1997.
17. Y. Zheng. Shortened digital signature, signcryption, and compact and unforgeable key agreement schemes (A contribution to IEEE P1363 Standard for Public Key Cryptography), July 1998.

Threshold Cryptography Based on Asmuth-Bloom Secret Sharing[*]

Kamer Kaya[**], Ali Aydın Selçuk, and Zahir Tezcan

Department of Computer Engineering
Bilkent University
Ankara, 06800, Turkey
{kamer, selcuk, zahir}@cs.bilkent.edu.tr

Abstract. In this paper, we investigate how threshold cryptography can be conducted with the Asmuth-Bloom secret sharing scheme and present two novel function sharing schemes, one for the RSA signature and the other for the ElGamal decryption functions, based on the Asmuth-Bloom scheme. To the best of our knowledge, these are the first threshold cryptosystems realized using the Asmuth-Bloom secret sharing. The proposed schemes compare favorably to the earlier function sharing schemes in performance as well as in certain theoretical aspects.

1 Introduction

Threshold cryptography deals with the problem of sharing a highly sensitive secret among a group of n users so that only when a sufficient number t of them come together can the secret be reconstructed. Well-known secret sharing schemes (SSS) in the literature include Shamir [8] based on polynomial interpolation, Blakley [2] based on hyperplane geometry, and Asmuth-Bloom [1] based on the Chinese Remainder Theorem.

A further requirement of a threshold cryptosystem can be that the subject function (e.g., a digitial signature) should be computable without the involved parties disclosing their secret shares. This is known as the *function sharing problem.* A function sharing scheme (FSS) requires distributing the function's computation according to the underlying SSS such that each part of the computation can be carried out by a different user and then the partial results can be combined to yield the function's value without disclosing the individual secrets. Several protocols for secret sharing [1, 2, 8] and function sharing [4, 3, 5, 7, 9] have been proposed in the literature. Nearly all existing solutions for function sharing have been based on the Shamir SSS [8].

In this paper, we show how sharing of cryptographic functions can be achieved using the Asmuth-Bloom secret sharing scheme. We give two novel FSSs, one

---

[*] This work is supported in part by the Turkish Scientific and Technological Research Agency (TÜBİTAK), under grant number EEEAG-105E065.

[**] Supported by the Turkish Scientific and Technological Research Agency (TÜBİTAK) Ph.D. scholarship.

A. Levi et al. (Eds.): ISCIS 2006, LNCS 4263, pp. 935–942, 2006.

for the RSA signature and the other for the ElGamal decryption functions, both based on the Asmuth-Bloom SSS. The proposed schemes, to the best of our knowledge, are the first realization of function sharing based on the Asmuth-Bloom SSS.

The organization of the paper is as follows: In Section 2, we give an overview of threshold cryptography and review the existing secret and function sharing schemes in the literature. In Section 3, we discuss the Asmuth-Bloom SSS in detail. After describing the proposed FSSs in Section 4, the paper is concluded with an assessment of the proposed schemes in Section 5.

2   Background

In this section, we give an overview of the field of threshold cryptography and discuss briefly some of the main secret and function sharing schemes in the literature.

2.1   Secret Sharing Schemes

The problem of secret sharing and the first solutions to it were introduced independently by Shamir [8] and Blakley [2] in 1979. A (t, n)-secret sharing scheme is used to distribute a secret d among n people such that any coalition of size t or more can construct d but smaller coalitions cannot. Furthermore, a SSS is said to be *perfect* if coalitions smaller than t cannot obtain *any* information on d; i.e., the candidate space for d cannot be reduced even by one candidate by using $t - 1$ or fewer shares.

The first scheme for sharing a secret was proposed by Shamir [8] based on polynomial interpolation. To obtain a (t, n) secret sharing, a random polynomial $f(x) = a_{t-1}x^{t-1} + a_{t-2}x^{t-2} + \ldots + a_0$ is generated over $\mathbb{Z}_p[x]$ where p is a prime number and $a_0 = d$ is the secret. The share of the ith party is $y_i = f(i)$, $1 \leq i \leq n$. If t or more parties come together, they can construct the polynomial by Lagrangian interpolation and obtain the secret, but any smaller coalitions cannot.

Another interesting SSS is the scheme proposed by Blakley [2]. In a t dimensional space, a system of t non-parallel, non-degenerate hyperplanes intersect at a single point. In Blakley's scheme, a point in the t dimensional space (or, its first coordinate) is taken as the secret and each party is given a hyperplane passing through that point. When t users come together, they can uniquely identify the secret point, but any smaller coalition cannot.

A fundamentally different SSS is the scheme of Asmuth and Bloom [1], which shares a secret among the parties using modular arithmetic and reconstructs it by the Chinese Remainder Theorem. We describe this scheme in detail in Section 3.

2.2   Function Sharing Schemes

Function sharing schemes were first introduced by Desmedt et al. [4] in 1989. key-dependent function is distributed among n people such that any coalition of size t or more can evaluate the function but smaller coalitions cannot. When a coalition $\mathcal{S}$ is to evaluate the function, the ith user in $\mathcal{S}$ computes his own partial result by using his share y_i and sends it to a platform which combines these partial results. Unlike in a secret sharing scheme, the platform here need not be trusted since the user shares are not disclosed to the platform.

FSSs are typically used to distribute the private key operations in a public key cryptosystem (i.e., the decryption and signature operations) among several parties. Sharing a private key operation in a threshold fashion requires first choosing a suitable SSS to share the private key. Then the subject function must be arranged according to this SSS such that combining the partial results from any t parties will yield the operation's result correctly. This is usually a challanging task and requires some ingenious techniques.

Several solutions for sharing the RSA and ElGamal private key operations have been proposed in the literature [4, 3, 5, 6, 7, 9]. Almost all of these schemes are based on the Shamir SSS, with the only exception of one scheme in [4] based on Blakley. Lagrangian interpolation used in the secret reconstruction phase of Shamir's scheme makes it a suitable choice for function sharing, but it also provides several challenges. One of the most significant challenges is the computation of inverses in $\mathbb{Z}_{\phi(N)}$ for sharing the RSA function where $\phi(N)$ should not be known by the users. The first solution to this problem, albeit a relatively less efficient one, was proposed by Desmedt and Frankel [3], which solved the problem by making the dealer compute all potentially needed inverses at the setup time and distribute them to users mixed with the shares. A more elegant solution was found a few years later by De Santis et al. [7]. They carried the arithmetic into a cyclotomic extension of $\mathbb{Z}$, which enabled computing the inverses without knowing $\phi(N)$. Finally, a very practical and ingenious solution was given by Shoup [9] where he removed the need of taking inverses in Lagrangian interpolation altogether by a slight modification in the RSA signature function.

To the best of our knowledge, so far no function sharing schemes based on the Asmuth-Bloom SSS have been proposed in the literature. We show in this paper that the Asmuth-Bloom scheme in fact can be a more suitable choice for function sharing than its alternatives, and the fundamental challanges of function sharing with other SSSs do not exist for the Asmuth-Bloom scheme.

3   Asmuth-Bloom Secret Sharing Scheme

In the Asmuth-Bloom SSS, sharing and reconstruction of the secret are done as follows:

- *Sharing Phase:* To share a secret d among a group of n users, the dealer does the following:
   1. A set of pairwise relatively prime integers $m_0 < m_1 < m_2 < \ldots < m_n$, where $m_0 > d$ is a prime, are chosen such that

$$\prod_{i=1}^{t} m_i > m_0 \prod_{i=1}^{t-1} m_{n-i+1}.$$

(1)

2. Let M denote $\prod_{i=1}^{t} m_i$. The dealer computes

$$y = d + a m_0$$

where a is a positive integer generated randomly subject to the condition that $0 \leq y < M$.

3. The share of the ith user, $1 \leq i \leq n$, is

$$y_i = y \bmod m_i.$$

− *Construction Phase:*

Assume $\mathcal{S}$ is a coalition of t users to construct the secret. Let $M_{\mathcal{S}}$ denote $\prod_{i \in \mathcal{S}} m_i$.

1. Given the system

$$y \equiv y_i \quad (\bmod\ m_i)$$

for $i \in \mathcal{S}$, solve y in $\mathbb{Z}_{M_{\mathcal{S}}}$ using the Chinese Remainder Theorem.

2. Compute the secret as

$$d = y \bmod m_0.$$

According to the Chinese Remainder Theorem, y can be determined uniquely in $\mathbb{Z}_{M_{\mathcal{S}}}$. Since $y < M \leq M_{\mathcal{S}}$ the solution is also unique in $\mathbb{Z}_M$.

The Asmuth-Bloom SSS is a perfect sharing scheme: Assume a coalition $\mathcal{S}'$ of size $t-1$ has gathered and let y' be the unique solution for y in $\mathbb{Z}_{M_{\mathcal{S}'}}$. According to (1), $M/M_{\mathcal{S}'} > m_0$, hence $y' + j M_{\mathcal{S}'}$ is smaller than M for $j < m_0$. Since $\gcd(m_0, M_{\mathcal{S}'}) = 1$, all $(y' + j M_{\mathcal{S}'}) \bmod m_0$ are distinct for $0 \leq j < m_0$, and there are m_0 of them. That is, d can be any integer from $\mathbb{Z}_{m_0}$, and the coalition $\mathcal{S}'$ obtains no information on d.

4   Function Sharing Based on the Asmuth-Bloom Scheme

In this section, we present two novel FSSs based on the Asmuth-Bloom SSS for sharing the RSA signature and ElGamal decryption functions.

In the original Asmuth-Bloom SSS, the authors proposed a recursive process to solve the system $y \equiv y_i \pmod{m_i}$. Here, we give a direct solution which is more suitable for function sharing. Suppose $\mathcal{S}$ is a coalition of t users gathered to construct the secret d.

1. Let $M_{\mathcal{S}\setminus\{i\}}$ denote $\prod_{j \in S, j \neq i} m_j$ and $M'_{\mathcal{S},i}$ be the multiplicative inverse of $M_{\mathcal{S}\setminus\{i\}}$ in $\mathbb{Z}_{m_i}$, i.e.,

$$M_{\mathcal{S}\setminus\{i\}} M'_{\mathcal{S},i} \equiv 1 \quad (\bmod\ m_i).$$

First, the ith user computes

$$u_i = y_i M'_{\mathcal{S},i} M_{\mathcal{S}\setminus\{i\}} \bmod M_{\mathcal{S}}.$$

2. y is computed as

$$y = \sum_{i \in \mathcal{S}} u_i \bmod M_{\mathcal{S}}. \tag{2}$$

3. The secret d is computed as

$$d = y \bmod m_0.$$

As a separate point, note that m_0 in the Asmuth-Bloom SSS need not be a prime, and the scheme works correctly for a composite m_0 as long as m_0 is relatively prime to m_i, $1 \le i \le n$.

Also note that m_0 need not be known during the secret construction process until the 3rd step above. In the FSSs described below, m_i, $1 \le i \le n$, are known by all users, but m_0 is kept secret by the dealer unless otherwise is stated.

4.1 Sharing of the RSA Signature Function

The following is a FSS based on the Asmuth-Bloom SSS for the RSA signature function:

1. In the RSA setup, choose the RSA primes $p = 2p' + 1$ and $q = 2q' + 1$ where p' and q' are also large random primes. $N = pq$ is computed and the public key e and private key d are chosen from $\mathbb{Z}^*_{\phi(N)}$ where $ed \equiv 1 \pmod{\phi(N)}$. Use Asmuth-Bloom SSS for sharing d with $m_0 = \phi(N) = 4p'q'$.
2. Let w be the message to be signed and assume a coalition $\mathcal{S}$ of size t wants to obtain the signature $s = w^d \bmod N$. The ith person in the coalition knows m_j for all $j \in \mathcal{S}$ and $y_i = y \bmod m_i$ as its secret share.
3. Each user $i \in \mathcal{S}$ computes

$$u_i = y_i M'_{\mathcal{S},i} M_{\mathcal{S}\setminus\{i\}} \bmod M_{\mathcal{S}}, \tag{3}$$

$$s_i = w^{u_i} \bmod N. \tag{4}$$

4. The *incomplete signature* $\bar{s}$ is obtained by combining the s_i values

$$\bar{s} = \prod_{i \in \mathcal{S}} s_i \bmod N. \tag{5}$$

5. Let $\lambda = w^{-M_{\mathcal{S}}} \bmod N$ be the *corrector*. The partial signature can be corrected by trying

$$(\bar{s}\lambda^j)^e = \bar{s}^e (\lambda^e)^j \stackrel{?}{\equiv} w \pmod{N} \tag{6}$$

for $0 \le j < t$. Then the signature s is computed by

$$s = \bar{s}\lambda^\delta \bmod N$$

where δ denotes the value of j that satisfies (6).

We call the signature $\bar{s}$ generated in (5) *incomplete* since we need to obtain $y = \sum_{i \in \mathcal{S}} u_i \bmod M_{\mathcal{S}}$ as the exponent of w. Once this is achieved, we have $w^y \equiv w^d \pmod{N}$ as $y = d + am_0$ for some a and we chose $m_0 = \phi(N)$.

Note that the equality in (6) must hold for some $j \le t - 1$ since the u_i values were already reduced modulo $M_{\mathcal{S}}$. So, combining t of them in (5) will give $d + am_0 + \delta M_{\mathcal{S}}$ in the exponent for some $\delta \le t - 1$. Thus in (5), we obtained

$$\bar{s} = w^{d + \delta M_{\mathcal{S}}} \bmod N \equiv sw^{\delta M_{\mathcal{S}}} \bmod N \equiv s\lambda^{-\delta} \bmod N$$

and for $j = \delta$, equation (6) will hold. Also note that the mappings $w^e \bmod N$ and $w^d \bmod N$ are bijections in $\mathbb{Z}_N$, hence there will be a unique value of $s = \bar{s}\lambda^j$ which satisfies (6).

4.2   Sharing of the ElGamal Decryption Function

The following is a FSS based on the Asmuth-Bloom SSS for the ElGamal decryption function:

1. In ElGamal setup, choose $p = 2q + 1$ where q is a large random prime and let g be a generator of $\mathbb{Z}_p^*$. Let $\alpha \in \{1, \ldots, p - 1\}$ and $\beta = g^\alpha \bmod p$ be the private and the public key, respectively. Use Asmuth-Bloom SSS for sharing the private key α with $m_0 = 2q$.
2. Let (c_1, c_2) be the ciphertext to be decrypted where $c_1 = g^k \bmod p$ for some $k \in \{1, \ldots, p - 1\}$ and $c_2 = \beta^k w$ where w is the plaintext message. The coalition $\mathcal{S}$ of t users wants to obtain the plaintext $w = sc_2 \bmod p$ for $s = (c_1^\alpha)^{-1} \bmod p$. The ith person in the coalition knows m_j for all $j \in \mathcal{S}$ and $y_i = y \bmod m_i$ as its secret share.
3. Each user $i \in \mathcal{S}$ computes

$$u_i = y_i M_{\mathcal{S},i}' M_{\mathcal{S} \setminus \{i\}} \bmod M_{\mathcal{S}}, \tag{7}$$

$$s_i = c_1^{-u_i} \bmod p, \tag{8}$$

$$\beta_i = g^{u_i} \bmod p. \tag{9}$$

4. The *incomplete decryptor* $\bar{s}$ is obtained by combining the s_i values

$$\bar{s} = \prod_{i \in \mathcal{S}} s_i \bmod p. \tag{10}$$

5. The β_i values will be used to find the exponent which will be used to correct the incomplete decryptor. Compute the incomplete public key $\bar{\beta}$ as

$$\bar{\beta} = \prod_{i \in \mathcal{S}} \beta_i \bmod p. \tag{11}$$

Let $\lambda_s = c_1^{M_{\mathcal{S}}} \bmod p$ and $\lambda_\beta = g^{-M_{\mathcal{S}}} \bmod p$ be the *correctors* for s and β, respectively. The corrector exponent δ can be obtained by trying

$$\bar{\beta}\lambda_\beta^j \overset{?}{\equiv} \beta \pmod{p} \tag{12}$$

for $0 \le j < t$.

6. Compute the plaintext message w as

$$s = \bar{s}\lambda_s{}^\delta \bmod p, \tag{13}$$

$$w = sc_2 \bmod p. \tag{14}$$

where δ denotes the value for j that satisfies (12).

As in the case of RSA, the decryptor $\bar{s}$ is *incomplete* since we need to obtain $y = \sum_{i \in \mathcal{S}} u_i \bmod M_\mathcal{S}$ as the exponent of c_1^{-1}. Once this is achieved, $(c_1^{-1})^y \equiv (c_1^{-1})^\alpha \pmod{N}$ since $y = \alpha + a\phi(p)$ for some a.

When the equality in (12) holds we know that $\beta = g^\alpha \bmod p$ is the correct public key. This equality must hold for one j value, denoted by δ, in the given interval because since the u_i values in (7) and (9) are first reduced in modulo $M_\mathcal{S}$. So, combining t of them will give $\alpha + am_0 + \delta M_\mathcal{S}$ in the exponent in (11) for some $\delta \leq t - 1$. Thus in (11), we obtained

$$\bar{\beta} = g^{\alpha + am_0 + \delta M_\mathcal{S}} \bmod p \equiv g^{\alpha + \delta M_\mathcal{S}} \equiv \beta g^{\delta M_\mathcal{S}} \equiv \beta \lambda_\beta^{-\delta} \pmod{p}$$

and for $j = \delta$ equality must hold. Actually, in (11) and (12), our purpose is not computing the public key since it is already known. We want to find the corrector exponent δ to obtain s, which is also equal to one we use to obtain β. The equality can be verified as seen below:

$$s \equiv c_1{}^{-\alpha} \equiv \beta^{-r} \pmod{p}$$

$$\equiv \left(g^{-(\alpha + (\delta - \delta)M_\mathcal{S})}\right)^r \pmod{p}$$

$$\equiv c_1{}^{-(\alpha + am_0 + \delta M_\mathcal{S})}\left(c_1{}^{M_\mathcal{S}}\right)^\delta \equiv \bar{s}\lambda_s{}^\delta \pmod{p}$$

5   Discussion of the Proposed Schemes

In this paper, sharing of the RSA signature and ElGamal decryption functions with the Asmuth-Bloom SSS is investigated. Previous solutions for sharing these functions were typically based on the Shamir SSS [4, 3, 7, 9] and in one occasion, the Blakley SSS was used for ElGamal decryption [4]. To the best of our knowledge, the schemes described in this paper are the first that use the Asmuth-Bloom SSS for function sharing.

Computational complexity of the proposed schemes also compare quite favorably to the earlier proposals. In a straightforward implementation, each user needs to do $t+1$ multiplications, one inversion, and one exponentiation for computing a partial result, which is comparable to the earlier schemes and in fact better than most of them [4, 3, 7, 9]. Combining the partial results takes $t - 1$ multiplications, plus possibly a correction phase which takes an exponentiation and $t - 1$ multiplications.

Acknowledgments

We would like to thank İsmail Güloğlu for some very informative discussions and his comments on this paper.

References

[1] C. Asmuth and J. Bloom. A modular approach to key safeguarding. *IEEE Trans. Information Theory*, 29(2):208–210, 1983.

[2] G. Blakley. Safeguarding cryptographic keys. In *Proc. of AFIPS National Computer Conference*, 1979.

[3] Y. Desmedt. Some recent research aspects of threshold cryptography. In *Information Security, First International Workshop ISW '97*, number 1196 in Lecture Notes in Computer Science, pages 158–173. Springer-Verlag, 1997.

[4] Y. Desmedt and Y. Frankel. Threshold cryptosystems. In *Proc. of Crypto'89*, number 435 in Lecture Notes in Computer Science, pages 307–315. Springer-Verlag, 1990.

[5] Y. Desmedt and Y. Frankel. Homomorphic zero-knowledge threshold schemes over any finite abelian group. *SIAM Journal on Discrete Mathematics*, 7(4):667–679, 1994.

[6] R. Gennaro, S.Jarecki, H. Krawczyk, and T. Rabin. Robust threshold dss signatures. *Inf. Comput.*, 164(1):54–84, 2001.

[7] A. De Santis, Y. Desmedt, Y. Frankel, and M. Yung. How to share a function securely? In *Proc. of STOC94*, pages 522–533, 1994.

[8] A. Shamir. How to share a secret. *Comm. ACM*, 22(11):612–613, 1979.

[9] V. Shoup. Practical threshold signatures. In *Proc. of EUROCRYPT 2000, Lecture Notes in Computer Science, LNCS 1807*, pages 207–220, 2000.

Capture Resilient ElGamal Signature Protocols[*]

Hüseyin Acan[1], Kamer Kaya[2,**], and Ali Aydın Selçuk[2]

[1] Bilkent University, Department of Mathematics
`acan@fen.bilkent.edu.tr`
[2] Bilkent University, Department of Computer Engineering
`{kamer, selcuk}@cs.bilkent.edu.tr`

Abstract. One of the fundamental problems of public key cryptography is protecting the private key. Private keys are too long to be remembered by the user, and storing them in the device which performs the private key operation is insecure as long as the device is subject to capture. In this paper, we propose server-assisted protocols for the ElGamal signature scheme which make the system capture resilient in the sense that the security of the system is not compromised even if the signature device is captured. The protocols also have a key disabling feature which allows a user to disable the device's private key in case both the device and the password of the user are compromised simultaneously.

1 Introduction

In public key cryptosystems, protecting the private key is a crucial problem. The keys are too long to be remembered by the users, and the devices which perform the private key operations may be subject to capture. This problem is even more significant if the device is a mobile authentication token such as a smart card or a hand-held device. An intuitive solution to this problem would be keeping the private key encrypted with the user's password in the device. However, in that case an offline dictionary attack on the password may be sufficient to obtain the private key if the device is captured, since the password by its very nature is a weak secret.

To make the devices resilient to capture, the private key can be stored in a server and the device can download it whenever a private-key operation is to be performed. To ensure that only the legitimate user can transfer the private key, an authentication to the server with the user's password is also required. However, the server itself has to be trusted and it must also be not subject to compromise in this solution.

MacKenzie and Reiter [4] avoided the requirement of a trusted server with a neat solution and gave a generic protocol framework to achieve capture resilience with different public key crpytosystems. They extended their technique

---

[*] This work is supported in part by the Turkish Scientific and Technological Research Agency (TÜBİTAK), grant number EEEAG-105E065.

[**] Supported by the Turkish Scientific and Technological Research Agency (TÜBİTAK) Ph.D. scholarship.

A. Levi et al. (Eds.): ISCIS 2006, LNCS 4263, pp. 943–951, 2006.

to develop RSA based signature [7] and ElGamal based decryption [2] protocols. The protocols also supported a key disabling feature if the device and the user's password are both compromised simultaneously.

What has been remarkably missing in the literature has been a capture resilient solution for ElGamal based signature systems [2]. ElGamal is the most commonly used signature algorithm after RSA, and it is especially significant for being the underlying algorithm of NIST's Digital Signature Standard [5]. Its elliptic curve versions are particularly popular in smart card authentication applications. In this paper, we extend the work of MacKenzie and Reiter to the ElGamal signature protocols and show how capture resilience can be achieved in the systems which use this algorithm for authentication. We consider two different versions of the ElGamal signature algorithm and present a capture resilient protocol for each of them.

The rest of this paper is organized as follows: In Section 2, we summarize the related background. After explaining the notation and the framework in Section 3, we present the capture resilient ElGamal signature protocols in Section 4. Section 5 concludes the paper with ideas for future research.

2   Background

The problem of using public key authentication techniques where the users are able to remember only weak passwords has been studied in the literature for several years. Capture resilience is an important feature of such techniques since the devices are subject to being captured. Obviously, if the private key of a device is stored in the device, the system would not be capture resilient. In 1999, Perlman and Kaufman [6] designed a strong password protocol where the private key is not stored in the device and downloaded from the server when needed. This idea requires an additional authentication mechanism which uses only a weak password to ensure that the private key is downloaded only by the legitimate user.

The idea of storing the private key in the server can also be used for obtaining capture resilience. However, storing the private key of the device in the server is secure only if the server is trusted and not subject to compromise. It is obvious that by capturing the server, an adversary can mount an offline dictionary attack even if the private key is encrypted with the weak password. MacKenzie and Reiter [4] solved this problem by storing a ticket in the device which includes the private key information. This ticket is encrypted with the public key of the server and contains the private key information encrypted with the password. Based on this idea, they proposed a generic private key retrieval protocol which does not require the server to be trusted.

MacKenzie and Reiter extended their ideas in the generic private key retrieval protocol and proposed RSA-based signature and ElGamal-based decryption protocols which supported capture resilience and also key disabling. Key disabling preserves the security of the system in case that the device is captured and the user password is compromised. In that case, the legitimate user can disable his private key by sending a request to the server and, if this request is valid, the server will ignore future signature/decryption requests with tickets associated with the old private key. To achieve capture resilience, MacKenzie and Reiter proposed to divide the private key information into two. The first one, the server's share, is encrypted with the public key of the server and stored in the device whereas the second one is produced from the password and a random number stored in the device. The protocols proposed in [4] are secure if one of the device or the server is compromised alone; however, if both are compromised simultaneously, the password can be broken by a dictionary attack and the private key can be obtained.

3   Framework

In our framework, the device and the server are connected through a public network where the attackers are able to eavesdrop and inject messages. Both the device and the server has a public-private key pair, (PK_{dvc}, SK_{dvc}), and (PK_{svr}, SK_{svr}), respectively. We use E and D to denote the public key encryption and decryption operations with these keys. The legitimate user of the device creates a valid ElGamal signature for a message m by cooperation with the server. The cooperation is needed since the device cannot use SK_{dev} without the help from the server. The security of the signing operation is provided by a user password denoted by π.

We follow the attack and adversary models of MacKenzie and Reiter [4] where there are various adversary types. Each adversary type is assumed to be able to control the network, so an adversary can read all the messages going through the network and control the inputs to the device and the server. In addition, an adversary can capture a subset of $\{\pi, dvc, svr\}$ and learn all of the static contents of the captured resources. The type of an adversary is specified with respect to a capture set $S \subset \{\pi, dvc, svr\}$ where $ADV(S)$ denotes an adversary who captured the components in S.

Here we give the definition and notation for the ElGamal signature schemes used in the proposed protocol:

3.1   ElGamal Signatures

Let g be a generator of $\mathbb{Z}_p^*$ where p is a large prime. The private key is $SK_{dvc} = x$ where $\gcd(x, p-1) = 1$. The public key is $PK_{dvc} = (y, g, p)$ where $y = g^x \bmod p$. To sign a message m, the signer chooses a random ephemeral key k such that $\gcd(k, p-1) = 1$ and computes $r = g^k \bmod p$. Then he computes the signature s by using a cryptographic hash function $h : \{0,1\}^* \to \mathbb{Z}_p$ and sends $\sigma = (r, s)$ as the signature. The receiver can verify the signature by checking an equation in modulo p. A detailed discussion of the ElGamal signature scheme can be found in [2].

There are several variants of the ElGamal signature algorithm where s is defined differently [3]. Two important variants used in our protocols are as follows:

1. In the first variant, the signature is computed as

$$s = xr + kh(m) \bmod (p - 1)$$

   and the verification equation is

$$g^s \stackrel{?}{=} y^r r^{h(m)} \bmod p.$$

2. In the second one, the signature is computed as

$$s = xh(m) + kr \bmod (p - 1)$$

   and the verification equation is

$$g^s \stackrel{?}{=} y^{h(m)} r^r \bmod p.$$

4   Capture Resilient ElGamal Signature Protocols

In this section, we propose two capture resilient signature protocols for the El-Gamal signature algorithm. The protocols proposed here are based on the ideas in [4] but differ significantly in the details since the distribution techniques of MacKenzie and Reiter do not apply due to the significantly different nature of the ElGamal signature algorithm. In our protocol, the private key of the user is shared between the server and the device. When a user wants to sign a message m, the device, which was previously initialized with π by the legitimate user, signs m by cooperation with the server. At the first step of our protocol, the device is authenticated to the server with π and sends the server's share of the private key x with m. One part of the signature is computed by the server with its share of x. Upon receiving the partial signature from the server, the device computes the other part with its share which is produced from π.

As mentioned above, proposed protocols also support a key disabling operation when both π and dvc are compromised. Disabling a key means sending a message to the server to ignore the future requests with the corresponding private key. Hence, the adversary cannot forge signatures by cooperation with the server after key disabling.

We present the details of the protocol in two phases. The first phase is the device initialization phase where the required data for the protocols are generated in the device. Some of these data are stored in the device and some are deleted immediately. The second phase is the signature protocol where the device signs a message with the help of the server. After introducing the signature protocols, we describe the key disabling operation and then we conclude this section with the security analysis.

4.1   Device Initialization

The static data required for the protocols is produced in the device initialization phase. The notation $A \leftarrow_R B$ denotes that A is randomly chosen from the elements of B with a uniform distribution. In the proposed protocols, random numbers are chosen from κ-bit numbers where κ can be considered as a security parameter for the protocols:

$$t \leftarrow_R \{0,1\}^\kappa$$
$$u \leftarrow_R h_{dsbl}(t)$$
$$v \leftarrow_R \{0,1\}^\kappa$$
$$a \leftarrow_R \{0,1\}^\kappa$$
$$b \leftarrow h(\pi)$$
$$x_1 \leftarrow f(v,\pi)$$
$$x_2 \leftarrow x - x_1 \bmod (p-1)$$
$$\tau \leftarrow E_{PK_{svr}}(a,b,u,x_2,g,p)$$

The values t and u are computed to be used in the key disabling phase. The random number a is chosen to be used in generating the message authentication codes(MAC). The function f takes two arguments and computes $x_1 \in \mathbb{Z}_p$, the device's share of x. The ticket τ, which contains x_2, the server's share of x, is encrypted with PK_{svr} to guarantee that an adversary cannot see the share. The values v, a, t and τ are stored on the device and, u, b, x, x_1, x_2 and π are deleted from the device immediately after the device initialization.

4.2   Signature Protocol

The device starts this phase with the values stored in the device initialization phase, the password π and the message m to be signed by using the private key x of the device. The two variants of our protocols are illustrated in Fig.1 and Fig.2. These protocols differ only in the signature equation, hence the notation used in both is same. To start the protocol the device first chooses two κ-bit random numbers ρ and k_1 and then computes β, the hash of π. Then $r_1 = g^{k_1} \bmod p$ is computed to generate r used in the ElGamal signature scheme described in the previous section. The protocol message γ is obtained by encrypting m, β, ρ and r_1 with PK_{svr} and sent to the server with the ticket τ and a MAC $\delta = mac_a(\gamma, \tau)$.

Upon receiving γ, δ and τ, server first checks if the messages and the password π used by the device are authentic. Then it chooses a random number k_2 and computes $r_2 = g^{k_2} \bmod p$. Note that k_1 and k_2 are random numbers whose sum, k, is the ephemeral key used in the ElGamal signature scheme. After computing r, the server computes the partial signature s_2 and sends them to the device by masking them with ρ.

When the device gets r and $\eta = s_2 \oplus \rho$, it computes his partial signature and combines it with the one sent by the server. Then it checks the validity of s and outputs the signature if it is valid.

<table>
<tr><td>DEVICE</td><td>SERVER</td></tr>
</table>

$\beta \leftarrow h(\pi)$
$\rho \leftarrow_R \{0,1\}^\kappa$
$k_1 \leftarrow_R \{0,1\}^\kappa$
$r_1 \leftarrow g^{k_1} \bmod p$
$\gamma \leftarrow E_{PK_{svr}}(m, \beta, \rho, r_1)$
$\delta \leftarrow mac_a(\gamma, \tau)$

$$\xrightarrow{\gamma, \delta, \tau}$$

$(a, b, u, x_2, g, p) \leftarrow D_{SK_{svr}}(\tau)$
abort if $mac_a(\gamma, \tau) \neq \delta$
$(m, \beta, \rho, r_1) \leftarrow D_{SK_{svr}}(\gamma)$
abort if $\beta \neq b$
$k_2 \leftarrow_R \{0,1\}^\kappa$
$r_2 \leftarrow g^{k_2} \bmod p$
$r \leftarrow r_1 r_2 \bmod p$
$s_2 \leftarrow (x_2 r + k_2 h(m)) \bmod (p-1)$
$\eta \leftarrow \rho \oplus s_2$

$$\xleftarrow{\eta, r}$$

$s_2 \leftarrow \rho \oplus \eta$
$x_1 \leftarrow f(v, \pi)$
$s_1 \leftarrow (x_1 r + k_1 h(m)) \bmod (p-1)$
$s \leftarrow (s_1 + s_2) \bmod (p-1)$
abort if $g^s \neq y^r r^{h(m)}$
return (r, s)

Fig. 1. Capture resilient ElGamal signature protocol, the 1st variant: $s = xr + kh(m)$

4.3   Key Disabling

It is obvious that an adversary $ADV\{dvc, \pi\}$ can forge signatures by impersonating the user of the device. In the proposed protocols, the legitimate user has a key disabling option to disable his private key in these cases. To start the key disabling mechanism, the legitimate user sends τ and t to the server, hence these values must be kept offline. Upon receiving a disabling request, the server decrypts the ticket and checks if $u \stackrel{?}{=} h_{dsbl}(t)$ where h_{dsbl} is a hash function. If the equality holds, server puts τ to the disabled list and refuses to respond to requests with this ticket.

4.4   Security Analysis

As stated earlier, the device is connected to a server through a public network and adversaries are able to see and control the messages to the device and the

$$\text{DEVICE} \hspace{5cm} \text{SERVER}$$

$$\beta \leftarrow h(\pi)$$
$$\rho \leftarrow_R \{0,1\}^\kappa$$
$$k_1 \leftarrow_R \{0,1\}^\kappa$$
$$r_1 \leftarrow g^{k_1} \bmod p$$
$$\gamma \leftarrow E_{PK_{svr}}(m,\beta,\rho,r_1)$$
$$\delta \leftarrow mac_a(\gamma,\tau)$$

$$\xrightarrow{\gamma,\delta,\tau}$$

$$(a,b,u,x_2,g,p) \leftarrow D_{SK_{svr}}(\tau)$$
$$\text{abort if } mac_a(\gamma,\tau) \neq \delta$$
$$(m,\beta,\rho,r_1) \leftarrow D_{SK_{svr}}(\gamma)$$
$$\text{abort if } \beta \neq b$$
$$k_2 \leftarrow_R \{0,1\}^\kappa$$
$$r_2 \leftarrow g^{k_2} \bmod p$$
$$r \leftarrow r_1 r_2 \bmod p$$
$$s_2 \leftarrow (x_2 h(m) + k_2 r) \bmod (p-1)$$
$$\eta \leftarrow \rho \oplus s_2$$

$$\xleftarrow{\eta,r}$$

$$s_2 \leftarrow \rho \oplus \eta$$
$$x_1 \leftarrow f(v,\pi)$$
$$s_1 \leftarrow (x_1 h(m) + k_1 r) \bmod (p-1)$$
$$s \leftarrow (s_1 + s_2) \bmod (p-1)$$
$$\text{abort if } g^s \neq y^{h(m)} r^r$$
$$\text{return } (r,s)$$

Fig. 2. Capture resilient ElGamal signature protocol, the 2nd variant: $s = xh(m) + kr$

server. Here we discuss the security of the proposed protocols against four types of adversaries:

1. $ADV\{dvc\}$: This adversary captured the device, but cannot initiate the protocol since he does not know π. However, he can perform an online guessing attack to find π by observing the responses of the server to his invocations. The success probability of this attack is simply $q/|D|$ where D is the password space and q is the number of invocations. Given that only a negligible fraction of the password space can be tried in an online guessing attack, the system is secure against this type of attack.

   The only information the adversary can obtain by eavesdropping is the signature of a message m since all the messages are encrypted. He can obtain neither the partial signatures nor any other information related to them.

2. $ADV\{\pi, svr\}$: This adversary type has all the static data stored in the server and has also obtained the password. He knows the public values PK_{dvc}, g,

p and PK_{svr}. Furthermore, he knows SK_{svr}; so he can decrypt the ticket τ and find the values a, b, u and x_2. He can also obtain r_1, ρ, and m by decrypting γ.

For this type of adversary, obtaining the private key x is equivalent to obtaining x_1. Having π is not sufficient for an offline dictionary attack since v is also required, which is unknown to the adversary. By eavesdropping or impersonating the server, he can obtain valid s_2 values for a valid signature s. The partial signature of the device, s_1, can be computed by subtracting s_2 from s. However, s_1 is not sufficient to obtain x_1 since k_1 is also required but it is an unknown for the adversary. Note that k_1 cannot be obtained from r_1 because this is equivalent to the discrete log problem.

3. $ADV\{dvc, svr\}$: If all components of the system are broken but the password π, the attacker can always try to find π by an offline dictionary attack. In this case, the dictionary attack will be done by comparing the hash of the password guess to b, which can be obtained by decrypting the ticket. If the password is broken, the attacker can forge signatures.

   If the password is not broken, obtaining the private key x will be equivalent to obtaining x_1 for this type of adversary. By eavesdropping or impersonating the server, he can obtain a valid partial signature of the server, s_2, for a valid signature s so he can also obtain s_1. However, these values are not sufficient to obtain x_1 because similar to the $ADV\{\pi, svr\}$ this adversary type suffers from the lack of k_1 which is an unknown to the adversary.

4. $ADV\{\pi, dvc\}$: If the device and the password are compromised simultaneously, the attacker will be virtually indistinguishable from the legitimate user and can forge signatures by cooperation with the server until the legitimate user of the device disables his private key. For this type of adversary, obtaining the private key is equivalent to obtaining x_2. With a procedure similar to the ones above, this adversary can obtain s_1 and s_2 for a valid signature s however he still suffers from the lack of k_2 to obtain x_2.

5 Conclusions and Future Work

In this paper, we proposed two ElGamal based signature protocols for capture resilient devices. It is obvious that storing the private keys in the device make the devices vulnerable to capture. Encrypting the private key with a weak password is also insufficient since an offline dictionary attack can always be performed once the device is captured. In this paper, we extended the approach of MacKenzie and Reiter [4] to the ElGamal signature scheme which is the fundamental of many important systems. The proposed protocols provide a server assisted solution for ElGamal-based authentication which makes the systems resilient to capture of the devices.

Future work on this problem may include a formal security analysis of the proposed protocols possibly using the random oracle model [1]. Techniques used by MacKenzie and Reiter [4] to prove the security of their protocols for RSA signature and ElGamal decryption protocols do not directly apply to the ElGamal signature scheme due to the more involved structure of the latter. A formal proof of a similar nature may be possible but would require more creative approaches with the random oracle model.

References

[1] M. Bellare and P. Rogaway. Random oracles are practical: A paradigm for designing efficient protocols. In *ACM Conference on Computer and Communications Security*, pages 62–73, 1993.

[2] T. ElGamal. A public-key cryptosystem and a signature scheme based on discrete logarithms. *IEEE Trans. Information Theory*, 31(4):469–472, 1985.

[3] P. Horster, H. Petersen, and M. Michels. Meta-elgamal signature schemes. In *CCS '94: Proceedings of the 2nd ACM Conference on Computer and communications security*, pages 96–107, New York, NY, USA, 1994. ACM Press.

[4] P. MacKenzie and M. K. Reiter. Networked cryptographic devices resilient to capture. *International Journal of Information Security*, 2(1):1–20, 2003.

[5] NIST. The digital signature standard. *Commun. ACM*, 35(7):36–40, 1992.

[6] R. Perlman and C. Kaufman. Secure password-based protocol for downloading a private key. In *Proc. of Network and Distributed System Security*, 1999.

[7] R. L. Rivest, A. Shamir, and L. M. Adelman. A method for obtaining digital signatures and public-key cryptosystems. *Comm. of the ACM*, 21(2):120–126, 1978.

A New Efficient Protocol for Authentication and Certificate Status Management in Personal Area Networks*

Chul Sur[1], Jong-Phil Yang[1], and Kyung Hyune Rhee[2]

[1] Department of Computer Science, Pukyong National University,
599-1, Daeyeon3-Dong, Nam-Gu, Busan 608-737, Republic of Korea
{kahlil, bogus}@pknu.ac.kr
[2] Division of Electronic, Computer and Telecommunication Engineering,
Pukyong National University
khrhee@pknu.ac.kr

Abstract. In this paper we propose a new efficient authentication protocol that reduces a burden of computation for digital signature generation/verification on mobile devices in the personal area network. In particular, we focus on eliminating the traditional public key operations on mobile devices without any assistance of a signature server. Moreover, the proposed protocol provides a simplified procedure for certificate status management to alleviate communication and computational costs on mobile devices in the personal area network.

Keywords: Personal Area Network, Efficient Authentication, Simplified Certificate Status Management, One-Time Signature.

1   Introduction

The next generation of mobile communications are expected to be different from current ones in relation to both the type of accesses to the networks and the terminals used to access the networks. Especially, distributed multi-function mobile terminals may consist of several different configurable components which are connected through local wireless communication within physical proximity to each other and to the user or users. A Personal Area Network (PAN) is the interconnection of fixed, portable, or moving components within a range of an individual operating space, typically within a range of 10 meters. In PAN the communication between components should be secure and authenticated since private information and personal data will be transmitted over radio links. Secure and authenticated communication can be achieved by means of proper security protocols and appropriate security associations among PAN components.

For the sake of supporting key management in a PAN, a personal CA, which is responsible for generating public key certificates for all mobile devices within

* This work was supported by grant No. R01-2006-000-10260-0 from the Basic Research Program of the Korea Science & Engineering Foundation.

A. Levi et al. (Eds.): ISCIS 2006, LNCS 4263, pp. 952–962, 2006.

the PAN, was introduced in [3]. The personal CA is used by an ordinary user at home or small office deployment distinguished from large scale or global CA functions. The initialization phase of [3] extends the concept of imprinting [11] to bootstrap all mobile devices with public key certificates. After all the mobile devices have been imprinted with their public key certificates, mobile devices may launch routine operations of the PAN by means of the traditional public key signature schemes.

The personal PKI concept seems to be properly applied to PAN environment. However, the personal PKI concept leaves at least two important challenging problems unaddressed: (1) The traditional public key signature schemes put resource-constrained mobile devices to formidable workloads since a digital signature is a computationally complex operation. (2) To manage certificate status information, no optimization was devised and the conventional certificate status management schemes were considered. Consequently, to design efficient authentication protocol and certificate status management that addresses the aforementioned problems is a promising challenge for PAN environment.

Our Contribution. In this paper, we propose a new efficient authentication protocol that reduces computational overheads for generating and verifying signatures on mobile devices. Especially, we focus on eliminating the traditional public key operations on mobile devices by means of one-time signature scheme, and differentiating it from previously proposed server-assisted signatures relied on assistances of a signature server. As a result, the proposed protocol gets rid of inherent drawbacks of server-assisted signatures such as problematic disputes, and high computational and storage requirements on the server side. Moreover, our protocol provides simplified procedure for certificate status management based on hash chain to alleviate communication and computational costs for checking certificate status information.

The rest of the paper is organized as follows. The next section describes preliminaries to induce the motivation of the paper. We outline our system model in Section 3. The proposed protocol that provides efficient authentication and certificate status management on mobile devices in PAN is presented in Section 4. In Section 5, we give the security and performance evaluations of the proposed protocol. Finally, we conclude the paper in Section 5.

2   Preliminaries

2.1   One-Time Signature and Fractal Merkle Tree Traveral

One-time signature (OTS for short) schemes are digital signature mechanisms which can be used to sign, at most, one message[6]. One-time signature schemes have the advantages that signature generation and verification are very efficient, and further, more secure since these schemes are only based on one-way functions, as opposed to trapdoor functions that are used in traditional public key signature schemes.

Despite of aforementioned advantages, one-time signature schemes have been considered to be impractical due to two main reasons: (1) the signature size is relatively long in comparison with traditional public key signatures. (2) their "one-timed-ness", i.e., key generation is required for each usage, thus implying that the public key must be distributed in a authentic fashion which is done most typically using a public key signature. As a result, the benefit of usefulness of quick and efficient one-way function is apparently lost.

In order to decrease the length of one-time signatures, a message digest should be calculated using hash function, just like traditional public key signature schemes, and then one-time signature scheme should be applied to the message digest. In this case, if a message digest would be the SHA-1 function which has a 160 bits output, we need 168 secrets to sign the message digest[6].

Merkle introduced the idea of using a hash tree to authenticate a large number of one-time signatures[7]. An important notion in Merkle's proposal is that of an *authentication path*: the values of all the nodes that are siblings of nodes on the path between a given leaf and the root. In [5], Jakobsson *et al.* presented *a fractal Merkle trees for the sequential traversal* of such a Merkle hash tree, which provides the authentication path for each leaf when the leaves are used one after the other. In this scheme, the total space required is bounded by $1.5log^2 N/loglogN$ hash values, and the worst-case computational effort is $2logN/loglogN$ hash function evaluations per output. Recently, Naor *et al.* showed that the combined scheme of Merkle's one-time signature scheme with Jakobsson *et al.*'s algorithm provides fast signature times with low signature sizes and storage requirements through experimental results[8].

2.2 Modified Efficient Public Key Framework

In [12], Zhou *et al.* proposed a new public-key framework, in which the maximum lifetime of a certificate is divided into short periods and the certificate could expire at the end of any period under the control of the certificate owner. They intended to establish a new public key framework that exempts the CA from testifying the validity of a certificate, once the certificate has been issued by the CA. However, Zhou's framework has considerable problems for practical implementation. That is, it is an unreasonable framework to authenticate an unidentified user based on some information submitted by the unidentified user in exempting CA. In particular, a malicious user can always generate valid signatures without any restriction. To overcome this drawback, [12] introduced a new trust party called security server. However, the security server is not only a redundant entity, but also requires an additional cost to be maintained securely.

Alternatively, we introduce *control window* mechanism to make Zhou's public-key framework above more suitable for realistic implementation.

Definition 1 (Control Window). Control Window *describes a time period that the verifier can trust the status of the sender's certificate only based on the sender's hash chain.*

Upon control window mechanism, CA sets the size of the control window of the user at the certificate issuance. The user can control the status of his/her certificate by using hash chain, and the verifier only trusts the user's hash chain during the control window. At the end point of the control window, the verifier queries certificate status information to CA.

3   System Model

3.1   Design Principles

In this section, we firstly clarify our design principles in order to efficiently provide authentication and certificate status management among mobile devices in PAN environment. The concerns of our design are summarized as follows:

- *Eliminating Public Key Operations on Mobile Devices.* Since traditional public key signature schemes generally require computationally complex operations in terms of signature generation and even verification, they may not even be appropriate for resource-constrained mobile devices in PAN, which may have 8-bit or 16-bit microcontrollers running at very low CPU speeds. Therefore, designing an authentication protocol which does not perform any public key operations is a promising challenge in PAN environment.

- *No Assistance of a Signature Server.* To avoid cumbersome public key signature generations, some cryptographic protocols which depend upon a signature server were presented[1][2]. However, these approaches put a heavy burden on the server side or, both the server and the mobile device side in terms of high storage requirement for resolving problematic disputes. Furthermore, these approaches do not eliminate public key operation on verifier side and suffer from round-trip delay since all signing procedures are carried out through the signature server. Consequently, it is desirable to design an authentication protocol without assistance of the signature server.

- *Small Computational and Communication Overheads for Validating Certificate Status.* Although online certificate status checking mechanism such as OCSP[10] seems a good choice since mobile devices can retrieve timely certificate status information with moderate resources usages in comparison with CRLs[4], the personal CA suffers from heavy communication workloads as well as computational overheads as it requires computing lots of signatures. Therefore, to mitigate the personal CA's workloads, it is necessary to reduce the number of the personal CA's signature generations and total communication passes.

3.2   Architecture

To define architectural model more clearly, we assume the followings:

- A PAN consists of portable or moving components that communicate with each other via wireless interfaces.
- At the constituting the PAN, all the security associations required for making PAN routine operations secure are set up. That is, every mobile device equipped with the PAN is bootstrapped with these security quantities and certificates during the initial phase.

A PAN is composed of a personal CA and mobile devices in our system model. The descriptions of system components are as follows:

- **Personal CA:** Personal CA is a unique trusted third party in the PAN, and it has a display and a simple input device to give its commands. Also, it is permanently available online to provide all other PAN components with certificates and certificate status information.
- **Mobile Devices:** Components equipped with the PAN, which have networking capability and likely low computing power.

In our system model, every mobile device is bootstrapped with a pair of public/secret key and its own certificate during the initial phase, described in the subsequent section. After all mobile devices have been imprinted with their security quantities, mobile devices which wish to sign and verify a message carry out the proposed authentication protocol.

3.3   Notations

We use the following notations to describe the protocols:

- PCA, M : the identities of personal CA and mobile device, respectively.
- $h()$: a cryptographic secure one-way hash function.
- SK_X : a randomly chosen secret key of the mobile device X.
- $sk_X^{i,j}$: the secrets of each one-time signature of the mobile device X, where

$$sk_X^{i,j} = h(SK_X|i|j)$$

  i is the signature number, j is the index of the secret, and $|$ is the concatenation of messages.
- $pk_X^{i,j} := h(sk_X^{i,j})$: the commitment for each $sk_X^{i,j}$.
- $PLC_X^i := h(pk_X^{i,1}|\cdots|pk_X^{i,t})$: the i-th public leaf commitment, which is the hash of all the commitments of a single one-time signature.
- PK_X : a public key of the mobile device X, which is the tree root of a fractal Merkle hash tree.
- $AuthPath_X^i$: the authentication path of the i-th public leaf commitment of the mobile device X.
- VK_X^{n-i} : the i-th validation key of the mobile device X. Based on a randomly chosen secret quantity VK_X from the range of $h()$, the mobile device X computes the hash chain $VK_X^0, VK_X^1, \cdots, VK_X^n$, where

$$VK_X^0 = VK_X, VK_X^i = h_X^i(VK_X) = h_X(VK_X^{i-1})$$

VK_X^n constitutes X's *root validation key*, VK_X^{n-i} is X's *current validation key*.

- Sig_X^i : the i-th one-time signature of the mobile device X.
- $Cert_X$: a certificate of the mobile device X.

4   System Operations

4.1   Initialization Protocol

The initialization protocol is the modified version of manual authentication protocol[3] that inherently settles key distribution problem in one-time signature scheme. The detailed steps of the protocol are as follows:

Step 1. The personal CA sends its identifier PCA and public key PK_{PCA} to a mobile device.

Step 2. The mobile device randomly generates two secret quantities SK_M and VK_M. Starting with these values, the mobile device performs the followings:

- Generates the one-time secrets/commitments pairs and the corresponding public leaf commitments according to the total number of signatures n (Taking into account the PAN environment, we assume that the total number of signature is less than 2^{16}).
- Initializes a fractal Merkle hash tree of height $logn$, and computes a public key PK_M, with the public leaf commitments values PLC_M^i as its leaves, where $i = 1, \cdots, n$.
- Generates $VK_M^n = h^n(VK_M)$ as the root validation key.
- Sets the signature number $i = 0$.

Then, the mobile device submits M, PK_M, n, VK_M^n to the personal CA.

Step 3. Both the personal CA and the mobile device carry out the following manual authentication:

- The personal CA generates a random key k and computes a MAC as a function of $PCA, PK_{PCA}, M, PK_M, n, VK_M^n$ by using the random key k. The MAC and the key k are then displayed by the personal CA.
- The user now types MAC and k into the mobile device, which uses k to recompute MAC value (using its stored versions of the public keys and associated data as input).

If two values agree then the mobile device gives a success signal to the user. Otherwise it gives a failure signal.

Step 4. If the mobile device emits a success indication, the user instructs the personal CA to generate a certificate. In order to generate the certificate, the personal CA sets up a control window CW according to the system security policy and issues the certificate signed by one-time signature for the mobile device together with the authentication path $AuthPath_{PCA}^i$ of the certificate.

$$Cert_M = \{Ser\#, M, PK_M, n, VK_M^n, CW, Sig_{PCA}^i\},$$

where $Ser\#$ is a serial number.

Step 5. The mobile device checks the followings to verify the correctness of the issued certificate.

- Verifies the one-time signature of the personal CA on the certificate by the use of PK_{PCA} and $AuthPath_{PCA}^i$.
- Checks whether the data fields within the certificate are valid as expected.

If all the checks are successful, the protocol is now completed.

4.2   Efficient Authentication and Certificate Status Management Protocol

In this section, we present a new efficient authentication protocol that provides fast signature generation and verification without any assistance of a signature server, and offers simplified certificate status checking by means of control window mechanism. The detailed descriptions of the protocol are as follows:

Signature Generation. A mobile device M_s which wishes to sign a message m performs the followings:

- Proceeds Merkle's one-time signature scheme[6] as follows:
  - Increments the signature number i
  - Calculates a message digest $md = h(m)$ and sets C = number of '0'-bits in md, and then sets $msg = md||C$.
  - Generates $\{sk_{M_s}^{i,j}\}_{j=1}^t$ and the corresponding $\{pk_{M_s}^{i,j}\}_{j=1}^t$, where $t=|msg|$.
  - Calculates $Sig_{M_s}^i = \{sk_{M_s}^{i,j} \, \forall j \in \{j|msg_j = 1\}, \, pk_{M_s}^{i,j} \, \forall j \in \{j|msg_j = 0\}\}$.
- Computes $AuthPath_{M_s}^i$ and updates authentication path using fractal Merkle tree algorithm[5].
- Calculates the current validation key $VK_{M_s}^{n-i}$.

Then, sends $m, Sig_{M_s}^i, AuthPath_{M_s}^i$ together with the signature counter i and the current validation key $VK_{M_s}^{n-i}$ to an intended mobile device M_v.

Signature Verification. The mobile device M_v proceeds the followings to check the status of the mobile device M_s:

- Obtains $Cert_{M_s}$ and queries whether the status of $Cert_{M_s}$ is valid or not.
- Verifies the current validation key based on the root validation key in the obtained certificate, i.e., $h^i(VK_{M_s}^{n-i}) \stackrel{?}{=} VK_{M_s}^n$.
- If all the checks are successful, the mobile device M_v caches $Cert_{M_s}$ and sets the current local time as starting trust time and the ending trust time based on the control window in $Cert_{M_s}$.

To verify the received signature, the mobile device M_v performs as follows:

- Calculates a message digest $md' = h(m)$ and sets $C' =$ number of '0'-bits in md', and then sets $msg' = md'||C'$.
- Sets $Sig'_{M_s} = Sig_{M_s}$ by denoting $Sig'_{M_s} = \{sig'_j\}_{j=1}^t$, where $t = |msg'|$ and updates $sig'_j \longleftarrow h(sig'_j), \forall j \in \{j|msg'_j = 1\}$, and then calculates $PLC^i_{M_s} = \{sig'_1|\cdots|sig'_t\}$.
- Iteratively hashes $PLC^i_{M_s}$ with $AuthPath^i_{M_s}$ and compares the result to PK_{M_s} in the certificate $Cert_{M_s}$.

In comparison with previously proposed server-assisted signatures[1][2] to reduce computational overheads on resource-constrained mobile devices, the proposed protocol does not need to perform any public key operations and employ any signature server at all.

Also, the verifier needs not to query the signer's certificate status information to the personal CA during the period of control window since the verifier trusts the signer's certificate based on the hash chain in the certificate up to the ending trust point. As a result, our protocol provides moderate communication and computational overheads for validating certificate status compared with OCSP[10] and CRLs[4].

5   Evaluations

In this section, we give evaluations of the proposed protocol in terms of the security and performance points of view.

5.1   Security Evaluations

To provide secure operations, it is necessary to prove the security of both one-time signature scheme and control window mechanism used in the proposed protocols. Clearly, we require that message digest hash function $h()$ is collision-resistant. Then, it is sufficient that: if the one-way hash function $h()$ used for committing secrets and hash operations in the Merkle's one-time signature scheme is a collision-resistant function which implies preimage-resistant, no signature for a message $m' \neq m$ can be forged.

Regarding the security of control window mechanism, it is obvious that: to forge the mobile device's current validation key corresponding to the i-th one-time signature, an adversary should compute on his own the $(n - i)$-th $h()$-inverse of the root validation key VK^n in the mobile device's certificate, which is computationally infeasible work.

5.2   Performance Evaluations

Table 1. shows the comparisons between the most efficient server-assisted signature[1] and the proposed protocol in terms of computational and storage requirements on system components. Note that computational requirement of our protocol for signer is comparable with [1] without putting a heavy burden on the server. Furthermore, signature verification of our protocol is more efficient than

Table 1. Comparisons of Computational and Storage Requirements

	Component	[1]	Proposed protocol
Computational Requirement (for signature)	Signer	$(m+1)H$	$(m+1)H + 1T_c$
	Server	$(p+2)H + 1S$	-
	Verifier	$1H + 1V$	$(p+2)H + 1T_v$
Storage Requirement	Signer	mH	$2K + 1C + 1A$
	Server	$(m+p+1)H$	-
	Verifier	$1Cert$	$1Cert$

H: hash computation, S: traditional signature generation, V: traditional signature verification, p: number of hash computation to verify OTS, m: number of public commitments in OTS, K: size of security quantity, C: size of signature counter, A: size of hash tree for authentication path, T_c: computation of authentication path, T_v: verification of authentication path.

[1] since verifier does not perform traditional signature verification, but only needs to perform one-way hash computations. In particular, we solve the main problem in [1] that are the high storage requirement on the server by removing the signature server. Recall server-assisted signatures must store all signatures for resolving problematic disputes. In addition, considering storage requirement on the signer, our protocol only requires 1.9 KB approximately. (two 20 bytes security quantities and 1920 bytes hash tree along with 4 bytes signature counter) while [1] requires about 3.3 KB ($168 * 20$ bytes $= 3.3$ KB approximately.)

Upon taking into consideration of the efficiency of control window mechanism, clearly our protocol reduces the number of signature generations and communication passes of the personal CA since the verifier does not query certificate status information to the personal CA during the period of control window. To have concrete and general measurements in terms of communication costs, we consider the following parameters[9] to compare communication costs with CRLs and OCSP:

- n : Estimated total number of certificates ($n = 300,000$).
- p : Estimated fraction of certificate that will be revoked prior to their expiration ($p = 0.1$).

Table 2. Comparisons of Daily Communication Costs

Scheme	Communication Cost (bits)
CRLs	1.803×10^{11}
OCSP	3.132×10^{8}
Our Proposal	2.046×10^{8}

CRLs daily cost: $T \cdot (p \cdot n \cdot l_{sn} + l_{sig}) + q \cdot (p \cdot n \cdot l_{sn} + l_{sig})$
OCSP daily cost: $q \cdot l_{sn} + q \cdot l_{sig}$
Our protocol daily cost: $\frac{q \cdot l_{sn}}{C} + \frac{q \cdot l_{sig}}{C} + q \cdot l_{hash}$

- q : Estimated number of certificate status queries issued per day ($q = 300,000$).
- T : Number of updates per day ($T = 2$, the periodic update occurs per 12 hours).
- C : Size of control window in our protocol ($C = 2$, the length of control window is two days).
- l_{sn} : Number of bits needed to hold a certificate serial number ($l_{sn} = 20$).
- l_{sig}, l_{hash} : Length of signature and hash value ($l_{sig} = 1,024, l_{hash} = 160$).

Table 2. gives the estimated daily communication costs according to three certificate status management schemes. If we make use of control window mechanism instead of OCSP, then communication cost for certificate status management can be diminished by 65%.

6   Conclusion

In this paper, we have proposed a new protocol to reduce a burden of computation for digital signature generation and verification on the PAN components, and simplify the procedure of certificate status management in the PAN. Compared with sever-assisted signatures, the proposed protocol does not require performing any public key operations at all without assistance of a signature server. Based on hash chain technique, and further, the proposed protocol alleviates communication and computational costs for checking certificate status information. Consequently, our protocol is quite attractive to PAN components which are resource-constrained devices.

References

1. K. Bicakci and N. Baykal, "Server assisted signature revisited," *Topics in Cryptology - CT-RSA 2003*, pp.143-156 March 2003.
2. X. Ding, D. Mazzocchi and G. Tsudik, "Experimenting with Server-Aided Signatures," *2002 Network and Distributed Systems Security Symposium (NDSS'02)*, February 2002.
3. C. Gehrmann, K. Nyberg and C. Mitchell, "The personal CA - PKI for a Personal Area Network," *Proceedings - IST Mobile & Wireless Communications Summit 2002*, June 2002.
4. R. Housley, W. Ford, W. Polk and D. Solo, "Internet X.509 public key infrastructure certificate and CRL profile," *RFC 2459*, January 1999.
5. M. Jakobsson, F. Leighton, S. Micali and M. Szydlo, "Fractal Merkel tree representation and traversal," *Topics in Cryptology - CT-RSA 2003*, pp.314-326, 2003.
6. R. C. Merkle, "A digital signatures based on a conventional encryption function," *Advances in Cryptology - CRYPTO'87*, pp.369-378, 1987.
7. R. C. Merkle, "A certified digital signature," *Advances in Cryptology - CRYPTO'89*, pp.218-238, 1989
8. D. Naor, A. Shenhav and A. Wool, "One-Time Signature Revisited: Have They Become Practical?," Cryptology ePrint Archive, Report 2005/442, 2005.

9. M. Naor and K. Nissim, "Certificate revocation and certificate update," *The 7th USENIX Security Symposium*, January 1998.
10. M. Myers, R. Ankney, A. Malpani, S. Galperin and C. Adams, "X.509 Internet public key infrastructure on-line certificate status protocol (OCSP)," *RFC 2560*, June 1999.
11. F. Stajano and R. Anderson, "The resurrecting duckling: security issues for ad-hoc wireless networks," *The 7th International Workshop on Security Protocols*, pp.172-194, 1999.
12. J. Zhou, F. Fao and R. Deng, "An Efficient Public-Key Framework," *The 5th International Conference on Information and Communications Security*, pp.88-99, October 2003.

A New Image Encryption Algorithm Based on One-Dimensional Polynomial Chaotic Maps

Amir Akhavan[1], Hadi Mahmodi[2], and Afshin Akhshani[2]

[1] Department of Engineering, IAU, Urmia, Iran
[2] Department of Physics, IAU, Urmia, Iran
afshin_akhshani@yahoo.com

Abstract. In recent years, a growing number of cryptosystems based on chaos have been proposed, however, most of them encounter with some problems such as: low level of security and small key space. Chaotic maps have good properties such as ergodicity, sensitivity to initial conditions and control parameters, etc. Due to these features, they are good candidate for information encryption. In this paper, encryption based on the Polynomial Chaotic Maps ($PCMs$) is proposed. The theoretic and simulation results state that the proposed algorithm has many properties such as high speed and large key space and high security. Therefore it is suitable for practical use in the secure communications.

1   Introduction

Over the past decade, there has been a tremendous interest in studying the behaviour of chaotic systems. They are characterized by sensitive dependence on initial conditions, similarity to random behaviour and system parameters. The close relationship between chaos and cryptography makes chaotic encryption a natural candidate for secure communication and cryptography [1,2].There exist two main approaches to chaotic cryptosystems: analog and digital mode. This paper chiefly focuses on the chaotic digital encryption techniques. In recent years, a growing number of cryptosystems based on chaos have been proposed [3,4,5,6], many of them fundamentally flawed by a lack of robustness and security [7]. To overcome the drawbacks, we present algorithm based on Polynomial Chaotic Maps ($PCMs$) for improving security [8]. Since digital images are usually represented as two-dimensional arrays, so we applied these kind of maps in two direction of image. Meanwhile, to confuse the relationship between cipher-image and plain-image, a diffusion process among pixels is performed. It is found that the mentioned map is particularly suitable for image encryption and transmission applications. Taking advantage of the exceptionally good properties of maps e.g. measurability, ergodicity, having long intervals compared to other map's intervals.

The rest of the paper is organized as follows. A new chaotic algorithm based on $PCMs$ is introduced briefly in section 2. In section 3 the experimental analysis are given. In section 4, security of the chaotic encryption algorithm is discussed. Finally, section 5 concludes the paper.

A. Levi et al. (Eds.): ISCIS 2006, LNCS 4263, pp. 963–971, 2006.

2   A New Algorithm Based on *PCMs*

2.1   One-Parameter Families of Chaotic Maps

One of the exactly solvable, one dimensional maps or the map with invariant measure is the well known Ulam-Von Neumann map [9] $f(x) = x(1-x)$ (Logistic map for $\mu = 1$). Here we generalize these maps to a Hierarchy of one-parameter families of maps with invariant measure, where the map of reference [10] is topologically conjugate to the first map (generalized Ulam-Von Neumann) of this hierarchy.

These one-parameter families of chaotic maps of the interval $[0, 1]$ with an invariant measure can be defined as the ratio of polynomials of degree N [8]:

$$\Phi_N^{(1)}(x, \alpha) = \frac{\alpha^2 (T_N(\sqrt{x}))^2}{1 + (\alpha^2 - 1)(T_N(\sqrt{x})^2)}, \qquad Type\,I \tag{1}$$

$$\Phi_N^{(2)}(x, \alpha) = \frac{\alpha^2 (U_N(\sqrt{(1-x)}))^2}{1 + (\alpha^2 - 1)(U_N(\sqrt{(1-x)})^2)}, \quad Type\,II \tag{2}$$

Also $T_N(U_n(x))$ are Chebyshev polynomials of type I (type II), respectively. where N is an integer greater than one.

These maps have interesting property, that is, for even values of N the $\Phi^{(1)}(\alpha, x)(\Phi^{(2)}(\alpha, x))$ maps have only a fixed point attractor $x = 1(x = 0)$ provided that their parameter belongs to interval $(N, \infty)((0, \frac{1}{N}))$ while, at $\alpha \geq N$ $(\alpha \geq \frac{1}{N})$ they bifurcate to chaotic regime without having any period doubling or period-n-tupling scenario and remain chaotic for all $\alpha \in (0, N)$ $(\alpha \in (\frac{1}{N}, \infty))$ but for odd values of N, these maps have only fixed point attractor $x = 0$ for $\alpha \in (\frac{1}{N}, N)$, again they bifurcate to chaotic regime at $\alpha \geq \frac{1}{N}$, and remain chaotic for $\alpha \in (0, \frac{1}{N})$, finally they bifurcate at $\alpha = N$ to have $x = 1$ as fixed point attractor for all $\alpha \in (\frac{1}{N}, \infty)$(see [8] for details and mathematical proof). From now, depending on the situation we will consider one of these maps $(Type\,I, II)$. Perhaps this interesting property is due to existence of invariant measure for a range of values of parameter of these maps. For example, we give below some of these maps:

$$\phi_2^{(1)} = \frac{\alpha^2 (2x - 1)^2}{4x(1 - x) + \alpha^2 (2x - 1)^2}, \tag{3}$$

$$\phi_2^{(2)} = \frac{4\alpha^2 x(1 - x)}{1 + 4(\alpha^2 - 1)x(1 - x)}, \tag{4}$$

$$\phi_3^{(1)} = \phi_3^{(2)} = \frac{\alpha^2 x(4x - 3)^2}{\alpha^2 x(4x - 3)^2 + (1 - x)(4x - 1)^2}, \cdot \tag{5}$$

2.2   New Proposed Algorithm

In this section, we discuss the properties of the proposed cryptosystem as well as step by step procedure of encryption processes. Here in this paper we proposedto use a hierarchy of One-dimensional families of maps of the interval [0,1] for encryption/decryption process. In chaos theory, Kolmogorov entropy is defined to measure the decreasing rate of the information. In ergodic systems, since the one-dimensional chaotic maps, Kolmogorov entropy is equal to Lyapunov exponent [11], and also a possible way to describe the key space might be in terms of positive Lyapunov exponents so we choose a chaotic region (see Fig.1). The following equations are yielded using equations Type I, II. We used a block diagram shown in Fig. 2.

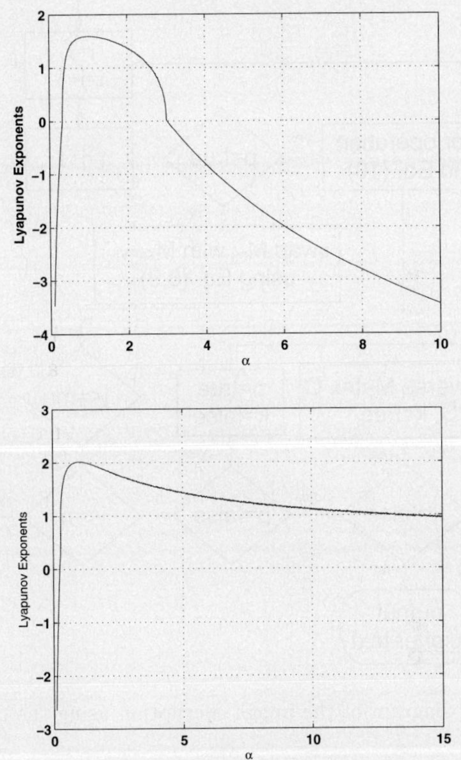

Fig. 1. Lyapunov Exponents plot of PCMs: (a)Type I, (b)Type II

$$\phi_5^{(1)} = \phi_5^{(2)} = \tag{6}$$

$$\frac{\alpha^2 x(16x^2 - 20x + 5)^2}{\alpha^2 x(16x^2 - 20x + 5)^2 + (1 - x)(16x^2 - (2x - 1))}$$

$$\phi_4^{(2)} = \frac{16\alpha^2 x(1 - x)(1 - 2x)^2}{(1 - 8x + 8x^2)^2 + 16\alpha^2 x(1 - x)(1 - 2x)^2} \tag{7}$$

$$x_p = \lfloor \phi_4 \times 10^{14} \rfloor \ mod \ 256 \tag{8}$$

$$y_p = \lfloor \phi_5 \times 10^{14} \rfloor \ mod \ 256 \tag{9}$$

$$C_{ij} = C_p \oplus M_{ij} \oplus \{\lfloor \phi_5 \times 10^{14} \rfloor \ mod \ 256\} \tag{10}$$

C_p is the previous encrypted pixels values.

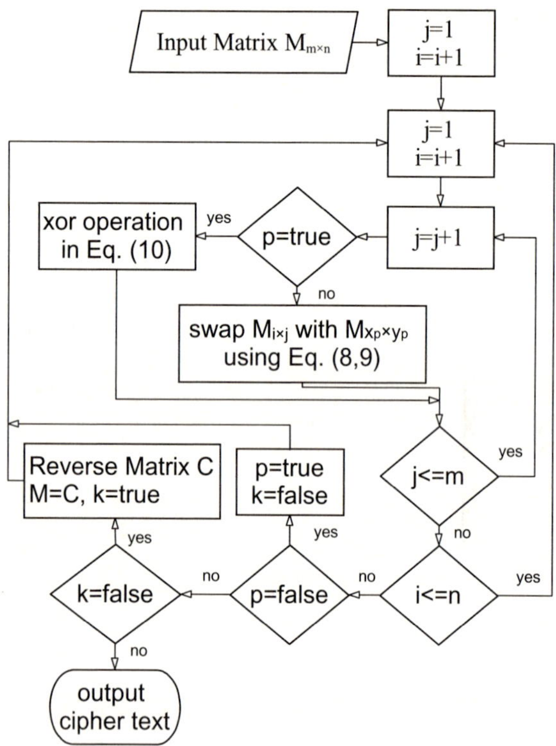

Fig. 2. Block diagram of the image encryption using the chaotic map

Step 1. Set encryption key for the plain-image, including structural parameters.

Step 2. Permute image data using Eq. (6),(7),(8) and (9) and proposed new method of swapping pixels in both directions.

Step 3. Xor permuted data Eq. (7) and (10).

Step 4. Pass encrypted image to an image object.

The decryption algorithm is similar to the encryption algorithm but receiving encryption key and operating with the encrypted image. Therefore, the dynamical properties of the $PCMs$ yield more security than other maps. This feature is very useful in secure communications.

3   Experimental Analysis

In this section, simulation results have shown the effectiveness of the above algorithm which is based on the proposed cryptosystem. Experimental analysis of the new algorithm presented in this paper has been done with "Pepper" image $I_{m \times n}$. Fig. (3) shows the experimental results with Pepper image. Fig. 3(a) is the 256 grey-scale Pepper plain-image of size 256×256. Fig. 3(b) is its encrypted image with the encryption keys that shown in Table 1. As shown in Fig. 3(b), the encrypted image is rough-and-tumble and unknowable. It can be seen that the decrypted image is clear and correct without any distortion. But if we use a wrong key, we will get an unexpected image. Undoubtedly, the multiple secret keys are secure enough even if a chosen plaintext/ciphertext attack is adopted. By the use of long chaotic map interval, the sensitivity to initial conditions which is the main characteristics of chaos guarantees the security of

(a)   (b)

Fig. 3. Image encryption and decryption result:(a) Plain-image,(b) Cipher-image image

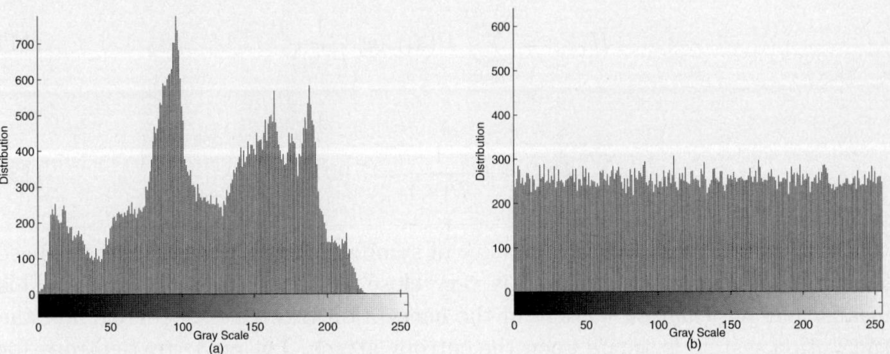

Fig. 4. Histogram of the images:(a) Histogram of plain-image,(b) Histogram of cipher-image

Table 1. Parameters of PCMs used for encryption

XOR		Permutation			
α	6	x_1	0.632432	y_1	0.732532
x	0.2	α_x	1.101554	α_y	3.5874

this scheme. The proposed algorithm is implemented using Visual C++ running on a personal computer with 2.4 GHz Pentium IV,Intel celeron 256 Mb RAM and 80 Gb hard-disk capacities. The average time used in encryption/decryption on 256 grey-scale images of size 256×256 is less than ≈ 0.2s. Statistical analysis has been performed on the proposed image encryption algorithm, demonstrating its superior confusion and diffusion properties which strongly resist statistical attacks. From the Fig. 4(b), one can see that the histogram of the ciphered image is fairly uniform and is significantly different from that of the original image Fig. 4(a).

4   Security Analysis

Some security analysis has been performed on the proposed image encryption scheme, including the most important ones like key space analysis, information entropy and statistical analysis, which has demonstrated the satisfactory security of the new scheme, as demonstrated in the following. Key space size is the total number of different keys that can be used in the encryption. Cryptosystem is completely sensitive to all secret keys. If the precision is 10^{-14}, the key space size for initial conditions is 2^{312}.

4.1   Information Entropy

It is well known that the entropy H of a symbol source S can be calculated as:

$$H(S) = \sum_{i=0}^{2N-1} P(s_i) \log \frac{1}{P(s_i)}, \tag{11}$$

$$= \sum_{i=0}^{255} P(s_i) \log \frac{1}{P(s_i)} = 7.9975 \approx 8 \tag{12}$$

where $P(s_i)$ represents the probability of symbol s_i and log represents the base 2 logarithm. The value obtained is very close to the theoretical value 8. This means that information leakage in the encryption process is negligible and the encryption system is secure upon the entropy attack. The ciphertext entropy for a value of s=256 is calculated using Eq.(11) and is listed in Table 2. Apparently, the proposed algorithm compared with the existing algorithms such as [3,12,13] is better.

Table 2. Entropy value for the ciphertext of different sources m

m	256
Ideal	8
Baptista's	7.926
Wong's	7.969
Xiang	7.995
Proposed	7.997

4.2   Correlation of Two Adjacent Pixels

To test the correlation between two adjacent pixels in plain-image and ciphered image, the following procedure was carried out. Randomly select 1000 pairs of two adjacent (in vertical, horizontal, and diagonal direction) pixels from plain-images and ciphered image, and calculate the correlation coefficients [13], respectively by using the following two formulas:

$$cov(x, y) = \frac{1}{N} \sum_{i=1}^{N} (x_i - E(x))(y_i - E(y)), \tag{13}$$

$$r_{xy} = \frac{cov(x, y)}{\sqrt{D(x)}\sqrt{D(y)}} \tag{14}$$

$$E(x) = \frac{1}{N} \sum_{i=1}^{N} x_i, \tag{15}$$

$$D(x) = \frac{1}{N} \sum_{i=1}^{N} (x_i - E(x))^2, \tag{16}$$

Where, $E(x)$ is the estimation of mathematical expectations of x, $D(x)$ is the estimation of variance of x, and $cov(x, y)$ is the estimation of covariance between x and y. where x and y are grey-scale values of two adjacent pixels in the image (see Table 3).

Table 3. Correlation coefficients of two adjacent pixels in two images

	Plain image	Ciphered image
Horizontal	0.9686	0.00094
Vertical	0.9616	0.00026
Diagonal	0.9331	0.0019

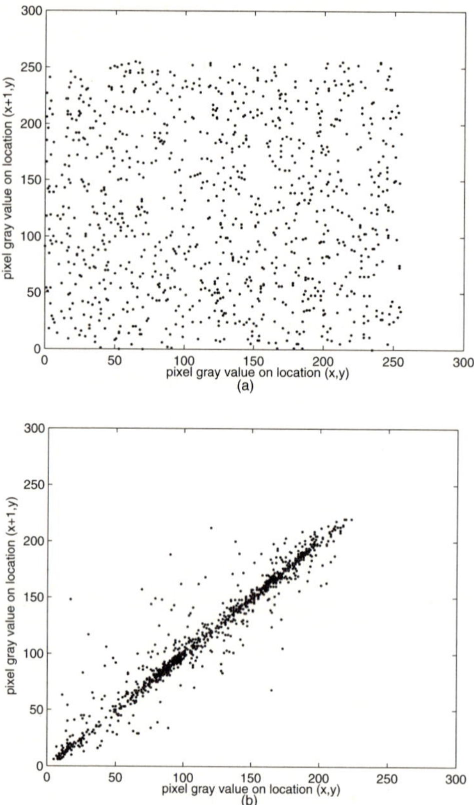

Fig. 5. Correlations of two horizontally adjacent pixels in the plain-image and in the cipher-image: (a) Correlation analysis of cipher-image, (b) Correlation analysis of plain-image

5   Conclusion

In this paper, an algorithm for image encryption based on one dimensional polynomial chaotic maps of interval [0, 1] is investigated [8]. These maps which are defined as ratios of polynomials of degree N have interesting property such as invariant measure, Ergodicity, variable control parameters in the two interval $[\frac{1}{N}, N]$ for odd N and $[\frac{1}{N}, \infty)$ for even N, Capability of calculation KS-entropy and ability to construct composition form of maps [15]. This new scheme employs the chaotic map (PCMs I, II) to shuffle the positions of image pixels and uses another chaotic map (PCMs II) to confuse the relationship between cipher-image and plain-image, thereby significantly increasing its resistance to various attacks such as the statistical and differential attacks. Our experiments show that even a simple algorithm can achieve a rather good estimation. Moreover, the encryption time is acceptable while the length of ciphertext is the same as that of the plaintext. The analysis indicates that the algorithm can satisfy all the performance requirements of high level of security and enough large key space. It is practicable and reliable, with high potential to be adopted for Internet image encryption, transmission applications and other information security fields.

References

1. R. Brown, L.O. Chua, Clarifying chaos: Examples and counterexamples, Int.J.Bifur. Chaos **6(2)** (1996) pp.219-242.
2. J. Fridrich, Symmetric ciphirs based on two-dimensional chaotic maps, Int. J. Bifurcation and Chaos **8(6)** (1998) 1259-1284.
3. M. S. Baptista , Cryptography with chaos, Physics Letters A, **240** (1998) 50-54.
4. W.-K. Wong, L.-P. Lee, K.-W. Wong, A modified chaotic cryptographic method, Comput. Phys. Commun. **138** (2001)234.
5. K.-W. Wong, A fast chaotic cryptographic scheme with dynamic look-up table, Phys. Lett. A **298** (2002) 238.
6. Z.-H. Guan, F. Huang, W. Guan, Chaos-based image encryption algorithm ,Phys. Lett. A **346** (2005), pp.153-157.
7. VI. Ponomarenko, MD. Prokhorov. Extracting information masked by the chaotic signal of a time-delay system, Phys. Rev. E. **66** (2002), pp.026215-21.
8. M.A. Jafarizadeh, S. Behnia, S. Khorram, and H.Nagshara, Hierarchy of Chaotic Maps with an Invariant Measure J. Stat. Phys. (2001) 104(516), 1013.
9. K. Umeno, Method of constructing exactly solvable chaos, Phys. Rev. E 55, 5280-5284(1997).
10. T. Gilbert, C.D.Ferguson and J.R.Dorfman. Field driven thermostated systems: A nonlinear multibaker map, Phys. Rev. E **59** (1999) 364-371.
11. G. Keller, Equilibrium States in a Ergodic Theory. Cambrige University Press, (1998) 23-30.
12. K.-W. Wong, S.-W. Ho, C.-K. Yung, A chaotic cryptography scheme for generating short ciphertext, Phys. Lett. A **310** (2003) 67.
13. T. Xiang, X. Liao, G. Tang, Y. Chen, K.-W. Wong,A novel block cryptosystem based on iterating a chaotic map, Physics Letters A **349**(2006)109115.
14. G. Chen, Y. Mao,C. Chui, A symmetric image encryption scheme based on 3d chaotic cat maps, Chaos Solitons Fractals, **21** (2004) 749-61.
15. M.A. Jafarizadeh, S. Behnia., Hierarchy of Chaotic Maps with an Invariant Measure and their Compositions, J. Nonlinear Math.Phys. 9(1),(2002), pp.1-16.

A Non-committing Encryption Scheme Based on Quadratic Residue*

Feiyu Lei, Wen Chen, and Kefei Chen

Department of Computer Science and Engineering,
Shanghai Jiao Tong University,
1954 Hua Shan Road, Shanghai, 200030
aflylei@gmail.com

Abstract. This paper presents a non-committing encryption scheme based on quadratic residue. It is a solution to adaptive security of multiparty computation with non-erasing parties in the cryptographic model. The scheme is more efficient than all previous non-committing encryption schemes. Furthermore, we give security proofs.

Keywords: information security, multiparty computation, adaptive security, non-committing encryption, quadratic residue.

1 Introduction

1.1 Multiparty Computation

In 1982, Yao [17] proposed the *multiparty computation* (MPC) for the first time from the famous millionaires problem. Afterwards many research about multiparty computation have sprung up rapidly, i.e. [5] [8] [9] [10]. In general, secure multiparty computation is defined that allows a set of parties without Trusted Third Party to compute an arbitrary agreed function of their private inputs in a secure way, even if an adversary may corrupt some of the parties and use this to learn information he should not know. Electronic Auction, Electronic Voting and Threshold Signature are familiar examples of MPC.

1.2 Security of MPC

The security of an MPC protocol π [12] [1] [4] should be satisfied with the following: the adversary $\mathcal{A}$'s view about the protocol π in **the real-life model** can be simulated by a dummy adversary θ that runs in **the ideal model**.

In **the real-life model**, the parties executing the protocol π (no Trusted Third Party). The adversary $\mathcal{A}$ is able to see internal data and protocol messages of π .

In **the ideal model**, we still have the $\mathcal{A}$, but π is replaced by an ideal functionality $\mathcal{F}$ that plays a role of Trusted Third Party. The parties only offer

* This work was partially supported under NFSC 60273049,60303026,90104005.

A. Levi et al. (Eds.): ISCIS 2006, LNCS 4263, pp. 972–980, 2006.

the inputs $(x_1, ..., x_n)$ to $\mathcal{F}$, then $\mathcal{F}$ outputs $(y_1, ..., y_n)$. Obviously, the ideal model is unconditionally secure.

The real protocol π doesn't exist in the ideal model. $\mathcal{A}$ can't see any internal data and protocol messages of π due to the inexistence of π. Then the dummy adversary θ is constructed in order to supply fake internal data and protocol messages in the ideal model to $\mathcal{A}$. We always call the dummy adversary θ simulator. If the simulator θ's view is indistinguishable from the real adversary $\mathcal{A}$'s view, we may refer that the protocol π is secure.

1.3 Non-committing Encryption and Related Works

The security of multiparty computation with an adaptive adversary is called *adaptive security*. **The adaptive security meets obstacles with non-erasing parties in cryptographic model**. (Note: Channels in cryptographic model are insecure and the adversary is restricted to probabilistic polynomial time. The secure channel in the cryptographic model can be achieved through encryption on the communication.)

Non-erasing parties are not trusted to erase his sensitive information so that the dummy simulated ciphertexts generated by the simulator θ may not be consistent with the plaintexts that is obtained from the later corrupted sender's memory. The simulation is failed for the scenario. For example, we assume a multiparty protocol π has n non-erasing parties and an adaptive adversary $\mathcal{A}$. After one party *Alice* sends another party *Bob* the ciphertext c of plaintext m through RSA encryption on the channel, *Alice* and *Bob* don't erase the plaintext m, and m will be in their memory or disk. Firstly, Nobody is corrupted by $\mathcal{A}$. When *Alice* sends *Bob* the ciphertext c, the simulator provides $\mathcal{A}$ with dummy cipertext c'. But after $\mathcal{A}$ corrupts *Alice*, $\mathcal{A}$ obtains m and *Alice*'s encipher RSA key from *Alice* memory or disk. Then $\mathcal{A}$ finds out m cannot match c'. So the simulator fails on the RSA encryption, and the protocol π is not secure.

As non-erasing parties became the obstacles of adaptive security, Beaver and Haber [3] firstly suggested that each party should erase his all historical information immediately. This is a direct and efficient way that the simulator θ doesn't need care about the relationship between the dummy ciphertexts and the actual plaintexts. But, in real life we cannot prevent some parties from recording information, i.e. automatic backups.

In order to solve the problem, Canetti et al. [6] introduced an ingenious primitive called **non-committing encryption**. It substitutes for the traditional public key encryption, which is used to obtain secure channels in the cryptographic model mentioned. Non-committing encryption is roughly characterized as follows. In traditional encryption schemes, the ciphertexts may be regarded as a commitment [15] of the sender to the plaintexts. Anyone can request the sender later to show the process how the plaintexts was encrypted and decrypted. It is obviously that a ciphertext cannot be decrypted as two plaintexts '0' or '1'. In a non-committing encryption scheme a simulator is able to generate dummy ciphertexts that look like actual ones, and can be later "opened" as encryptions of either '0' or '1' so that the ciphertext is not a commitment to the plaintext.

Canetti's scheme [6] has great expansion factor $\Omega(k^2)$ where k is security parameter, i.e. it sends k^2 bits for per plaintext bit communicated. The communication overhead is too high.

Subsequently, Beaver [2] presented another non-committing encryption based on the Diffie-Hellman problem with small expansion factor $\mathcal{O}(k)$. *Up to now, Beaver's scheme is the most efficient scheme in the literature.* Beaver's scheme is described as follows.

- Public: prime p, subgroup generator g, Let $\mathcal{R}(S)$ denote the uniformly random distribution over finite set S.
- Alice: $c \leftarrow \mathcal{R}(\{0,1\})$, $a \leftarrow \mathcal{R}(Z_{p-1})$, $x_c \leftarrow g^a modp$, $x_{1-c} \leftarrow \mathcal{R}(\langle g \rangle)$
- Alice→Bob: (x_0, x_1)
- Bob: $d \leftarrow \mathcal{R}(\{0,1\})$, $b \leftarrow \mathcal{R}(Z_{p-1})$, $y_d \leftarrow g^b modp$, $y_{1-d} \leftarrow \mathcal{R}(\langle g \rangle)$, $z_d \leftarrow x_d^b modp$, $z_{1-d} \leftarrow \mathcal{R}(\langle g \rangle)$
- Bob→Alice: (y_0, y_1, z_0, z_1)
- Alice: if $y_c^a = z_d$ then $s \leftarrow 0$ else $s \leftarrow 1$, if $s = 0$ then $f \leftarrow m \oplus c$ else $f \leftarrow 0$
- Alice→Bob: (s, f)
- Bob: if $s = 0$, then $m \leftarrow f \oplus d$, conclude succeed else conclude fail.

Recently, Damgard and Nielsen [7] proposed a scheme based on a general complexity assumption. The scheme is regarded as a generalization of Beaver's scheme, and it needs simulatable public-key systems.

In 2001, Nielsen [16] pointed out that non-committing encryption is too easy in the random oracle model, and proved that the scheme is not non-committing if the oracle is instantiated. The random oracle is too ideal to exist in real life.

Although the improvements of Beaver, Damgard and Nielsen [2] [7] just decreased Canetti's expansion factor [6] from $\Omega(k^2)$ to $\mathcal{O}(k)$, they all neglected that the computational cost is another important element to determine the efficiency of a scheme. We pointed out that all schemes mentioned above [6] [2] [7] are not efficient for they need too much expensive computational costs. For instance, if Alice sends a n bits message to Bob, Beaver scheme [2] needs at least $4n$ modular exponetiantions, and Damgard and Nielsen scheme [7] needs at least $2n$ public encryption and decryption operations.

1.4   Our Contributions

The motivation of this paper is **to reduce the computational costs** of non-committing encryption, and inherit the small expansion factor from Beaver scheme [2].

Our contributions are as follows.

- In this paper we present an efficient non-committing encryption based on quadratic residue. The main idea is to evaluate a one-time pad bit by Legendre symbol computation with the running time $\mathcal{O}(k^2)$ bit operations where k is the security parameter. It is a modification of technique in [11].

- We adopt a quadratic residue property of Blum integers to simulate a real protocol perfectly. Although $\mathcal{A}$ can corrupt sender later and obtain the secret key of sender, $\mathcal{A}$ believe that the dummy ciphertext is consistent with the real plaintext.
- Furthermore, the scheme has also expansion factor only $\mathcal{O}(k)$ as Beaver scheme.
- The scheme doesn't need simulatable public-key systems [7] and random oracles [16].

Note that: As all the previous schemes above assumed [6] [2] [7], we also consider a network in our scheme that provides authenticated, service undeniable, point-to-point connections.

The rest of the paper is organized as follows. At first, we introduce quadratic residue in section 2. In section 3, we propose a new non-committing encryption scheme based on quadratic residue. Then we give a proof of security of the presented scheme in section 4. Section 5 is the conclusion.

2 Quadratic Residue

Quadratic Residue [13]: Let n be an integer (Note: In this paper, we assume that it is infeasible to factorize n.), $a \in Z_n^*$ is said to be a quadratic residue modulo n, if there exists an $x \in Z_n^*$ such that $x^2 \equiv a \, mod \, n$. If no such x exists, then a is called a quadratic non-residue modulo n. The set of all quadratic residues modulo n is denoted by Q_n and the set of all quadratic non-residues modulo n is denoted by $\widetilde{Q_n}$. Let p be an odd prime and a an integer. The Legendre symbol $\left(\frac{a}{p}\right)$ is defined to be:

Case0:$\left(\frac{a}{p}\right) = 0$ if $p|a$,
Case1:$\left(\frac{a}{p}\right) = 1$ if $a \in Q_p$,
Case2:$\left(\frac{a}{p}\right) = -1$ if $a \in \widetilde{Q_p}$.

Fact1: Let n be a product of two distinct odd primes p and q. Then $a \in Z_n^*$ is a quadratic residue modulo n if and only if $a \in Q_p$ and $a \in Q_q$.
Fact2: n is a Blum integer if $n = pq$ and (p, q) are distinct odd primes such as $p \equiv q \equiv 3 \, mod \, 4$. Then $\left(\frac{-1}{p}\right) = \left(\frac{-1}{q}\right) = -1$.

3 The Proposed Non-committing Encryption Scheme

We present the protocol for a single attempt which Alice transmits a one-bit message m in Figure 1. Let $\mathcal{R}(S)$ denote the uniformly random distribution over set S. Alice's public key is a Blum integer $N_a = p_a q_a$, and her secret key is p_a and q_a.

Firstly, It is easy to see that the most expensive computation in our scheme is to compute Legendre symbol. Let k denote a security parameter, where $k = |p| = |q| \geq 512 bits$. So the scheme has a running time of $\mathcal{O}(k^2)$ bit operations.

Our proposed scheme

- Alice: $c \leftarrow \mathcal{R}(\{0,1\})$, $r_c \leftarrow \mathcal{R}(Z_{N_a}^*)$ such that $\left(\frac{r_c}{p_a}\right) = \left(\frac{r_c}{q_a}\right) = 1$, $r_{1-c} = -r_c \bmod N_a$.
- Alice→Bob: (r_0, r_1).
- Bob: $d \leftarrow \mathcal{R}(\{0,1\})$, $k_0, k_1 \leftarrow \mathcal{R}(Z_{N_a}^*)$, $l_0 \equiv k_0^2 \bmod N_a$, $l_1 \equiv k_1^2 \bmod N_a$, $x_d \equiv l_d r_d \bmod N_a$, $x_{1-d} \equiv l_{1-d} r_{1-d} \bmod N_a$
- Bob→Alice: (x_0, x_1)
- Alice: if $\left(\frac{x_c}{p_a}\right) = \left(\frac{x_c}{q_a}\right) = 1$ then $s \leftarrow 0$ else $s \leftarrow 1$, if $s = 0$ then $f \leftarrow m \oplus c$ else $f \leftarrow 0$
- Alice→Bob: (s, f)
- Bob: if $s = 0$, then $m \leftarrow f \oplus d$, conclude succeed else conclude fail.

Fig. 1. Our proposed scheme

The most expensive computation in Beaver's scheme is modular exponentiation, and running time is $\mathcal{O}(k^3)$ bit operations. Secondly, the communication costs of a single attempt to transfer one-bit message is $4k + 4k + 2$ bits. So the scheme has also expansion factor only $\mathcal{O}(k)$ as Beaver scheme. The Table 1 shows our scheme is more efficient than all schemes proposed before, and we needn't the random oracle model(ROM).

Table 1. Comparison with previous schemes

	Canetti [6]	Beaver [2]	Damgard [7]	Nielsen [16]	Our Scheme
Running Time	$\mathcal{O}(k^3)$	$\mathcal{O}(k^3)$	$\mathcal{O}(k^3)$	$\mathcal{O}(k^3)$	$\mathcal{O}(k^2)$
Expansion Factor	$\Omega(k^2)$	$\mathcal{O}(k)$	$\mathcal{O}(k)$	$\mathcal{O}(k)$	$\mathcal{O}(k)$
In the ROM	No	No	No	yes	No

4   Security Proofs

We affirm that our scheme is a secure non-committing encryption if the confidentiality and non-committing property are both satisfied. We illustrate a successful simulation to prove ***Theorem1*** which shows the main expected non-committing property in the scheme. Then we use ***Theorem2*** to prove the scheme is a secure encryption to provide confidentiality.

Firstly, we give two lemmas to support ***Theorem1*** and ***Theorem2***.

Lemma 1. It is difficult to compute the square roots modulo N when N is a large composite integer for which the prime factors are unknown.

Lemma 2. It is difficult to estimate whether an integer is a quadratic residue modulo N when N is a large composite integer whose prime factors are unknown.

We believe that ***Lemma1*** and ***Lemma2*** [13] are folklores so that the proofs are ignored.

Theorem 1. *There doesn't exist a probabilistic polynomial time algorithm with $P_r > 1/2$ to distinguish a real conversation from a simulated one that simulated by the simulator θ.*

Proof. Now we illustrate a simulation conducted by the simulator θ. If the simulator θ's view is indistinguishable from the real adversary $\mathcal{A}$'s view, we may refer that the encryption provides non-committing property.

We begin with the simulation without corruption requests. Alice and Bob in the simulation are denoted by *Alice* and *Bob* respectively that they are dummy simulated parties.

- $Alice{:}c \leftarrow \mathcal{R}(\{0,1\}), e \leftarrow \mathcal{R}(Z^*_{N_a}), r_c \equiv e^2 \bmod N_a, r_{1-c} \equiv -r_c \bmod N_a$
- $Alice \rightarrow Bob{:} (r_0, r_1)$
- $Bob{:}s \leftarrow \mathcal{R}(\{0,1\}),$
  if $s = 0$, then
  $k_0, k_1 \leftarrow \mathcal{R}(Z^*_{N_a}), l_0 \equiv k_0^2 \bmod N_a, l_1 \equiv k_1^2 \bmod N_a,$
  $x_0 \equiv l_0 r_0 \bmod N_a, x_1 \equiv l_1 r_1 \bmod N_a,$
  else
  $c \leftarrow \mathcal{R}(\{0,1\}), d \leftarrow 1 - c$
  $k_0, k_1 \leftarrow \mathcal{R}(Z^*_{N_a}), l_0 \equiv k_0^2 \bmod N_a, l_1 \equiv k_1^2 \bmod N_a,$
  $x_d \equiv l_d r_d \bmod N_a, x_{1-d} \equiv l_{1-d} r_{1-d} \bmod N_a$
- $Bob \rightarrow Alice{:} (x_0, x_1)$
- $Alice{:}$ if $s = 0$, then $f \leftarrow \mathcal{R}(\{0,1\})$ else $f \leftarrow 0$
- $Alice \rightarrow Bob{:} (s, f)$

Namely in all, the simulator θ generates three simulated protocol messages: $(r_0, r_1), (x_0, x_1), (s, f)$.

Next, we analyze the corruption requests in the simulation. According to the time point of coming corruption requests, there are the same four cases that are clearly written in [2].

Case 0: Before any protocol messages are sent, the real adversary $\mathcal{A}$ makes its first corruption request.
Case 1: After Alice sends her first message, but before Bob sends his message, the real adversary $\mathcal{A}$ makes its first corruption request.
Case 2: After Alice and Bob have sent their first message, the real adversary $\mathcal{A}$ makes its first corruption request.
Case 3: After Alice and Bob have sent all messages, the real adversary $\mathcal{A}$ makes its first corruption request.

When corruption requests coming, the simulator θ corrupts the same dummy simulated parties as $\mathcal{A}$ does in the real protocol. We subdivide the four cases into 0A, 0B, 1A, 1B, 2A, 2B, 3A, 3B, that indicates whether $\mathcal{A}$ selects Alice or Bob to corrupt first.

Case 0.A: θ obtains *Alice*'s input m and Alice's secret key (p_a, q_a) from corrupting *Alice* and reports (m, p_a, q_a) as *Alice*'s view.
Case 0.B: Reports nothing as Bob's view.
Case 1.A: θ obtains Alice's input m and Alice's secret key (p_a, q_a) from corrupting *Alice*. θ performs

$c \leftarrow \mathcal{R}(\{0,1\}), e \leftarrow \mathcal{R}(Z^*_{N_a}), r_c \equiv e^2 \bmod N_a, r_{1-c} \equiv -r_c \bmod N_a, \theta$ reports $(m, p_a, q_a, c, r_0, r_1)$ as *Alice*'s view. patches *Bob*'s view with (r_0, r_1).

Case 1.B: θ performs $c \leftarrow \mathcal{R}(\{0,1\}), e \leftarrow \mathcal{R}(Z^*_{N_a}), r_c \equiv e^2 \bmod N_a, r_{1-c} \equiv -r_c \bmod N_a$ and patches *Bob* 'view with (r_0, r_1).

Case 2.A: θ obtains *Alice*'s input m and Alice's secret key (p_a, q_a) from corrupting *Alice*. performs

$c \leftarrow \mathcal{R}(\{0,1\}), e \leftarrow \mathcal{R}(Z^*_{N_a}), r_c \equiv e^2 \bmod N_a, r_{1-c} \equiv -r_c \bmod N_a, \theta$ reports $(m, p_a, q_a, c, r_0, r_1)$

$d \leftarrow \mathcal{R}(\{0,1\}), k_0, k_1 \leftarrow \mathcal{R}(Z^*_{N_a}), l_0 \equiv k_0^2 \bmod N_a, l_1 \equiv k_1^2 \bmod N_a$

$x_d \equiv l_d r_d \bmod N_a, x_{1-d} \equiv l_{1-d} r_{1-d} \bmod N_a$.

θ reports $(m, p_a, q_a, c, r_0, r_1, x_0, x_1)$ as *Alice*'s view. θ patches *Bob*' view with $(r_0, r_1, d, k_0, k_1, l_0, l_1, x_0, x_1)$

Case 2.B: θ performs

$c \leftarrow \mathcal{R}(\{0,1\}), e \leftarrow \mathcal{R}(Z^*_{N_a}), r_c \equiv e^2 \bmod N_a, r_{1-c} \equiv -r_c \bmod N_a, \theta$ reports $(m, p_a, q_a, c, r_0, r_1)$

$d \leftarrow \mathcal{R}(\{0,1\}), k_0, k_1 \leftarrow \mathcal{R}(Z^*_{N_a}), l_0 \equiv k_0^2 \bmod N_a, l_1 \equiv k_1^2 \bmod N_a$

$x_d \equiv l_d r_d \bmod N_a, x_{1-d} \equiv l_{1-d} r_{1-d} \bmod N_a$.

θ reports (c, r_0, r_1, x_0, x_1) as *Alice*'s view. θ patches *Bob*' view with $(r_0, r_1, d, k_0, k_1, l_0, l_1, x_0, x_1)$

Case 3.A: θ obtains *Alice*'s (m, p_a, q_a) from corrupting *Alice*. At this point, θ does as follows:

If $s = 0$, θ performs $c \leftarrow m \oplus f, d \leftarrow c, e \leftarrow \mathcal{R}(Z^*_{N_a}), r_c \equiv e^2 \bmod N_a, r_{1-c} \equiv -r_c \bmod N_a$,

$k_0, k_1 \leftarrow \mathcal{R}(Z^*_{N_a}), l_0 \equiv k_0^2 \bmod N_a, l_1 \equiv k_1^2 \bmod N_a$

$x_d \equiv l_d r_d \bmod N_a, x_{1-d} \equiv l_{1-d} r_{1-d} \bmod N_a$. θ reports $(m, p_a, q_a, c, r_0, r_1, x_0, x_1, s, f)$ as *Alice*'s view. θ patches *Bob*' view with $(r_0, r_1, d, k_0, k_1, l_0, l_1, x_0, x_1, s, f)$

If $s = 1$, θ has already chosen values for $(m, p_a, q_a, r_0, r_1, c, d, k_0, k_1, l_0, l_1, x_0, x_1)$ in the simulation without corruption requests.

θ reports $(m, c, r_0, r_1, x_0, x_1, s, f)$ as *Alice*'s view. θ patches *Bob*' view with $(m, d, r_0, r_1, k_0, k_1, l_0, l_1, x_0, x_1, s, f)$.

Case 3.B: θ obtains bit m from corrupting *Bob*. At this point, θ does as in *Case 3.A*. Then θ reports $(m, c, r_0, r_1, x_0, x_1, s, f)$ as *Alice*'s view. θ patches *Bob*' view with

$(m, d, r_0, r_1, k_0, k_1, l_0, l_1, x_0, x_1, s, f)$.

Thus, the simulation is completed. Next, we consider the difference between a real conversation and a simulated one. In a real conversation, Alice performs $\left(\frac{r_c}{p_a}\right) = \left(\frac{r_c}{q_a}\right) = 1, r_{1-c} = -r_c \bmod N_a$. In a simulated conversation, *Alice* performs $e \leftarrow \mathcal{R}(Z^*_{N_a}), r_c \equiv e^2 \bmod N_a, r_{1-c} \equiv -r_c \bmod N_a$. According to **Lemma2**, no one even who has prime factors of N_a can distinguish them with $P_r > 1/2$. Then we also similarly conclude that no one can distinguish the x_0, x_1 in a real conversation and x_0, x_1 in a simulated conversation with $P_r > 1/2$. Namely, there doesn't exist a probabilistic polynomial time algorithm with $P_r > 1/2$ to distinguish a real conversation and a simulated one. $\qquad\qquad\square$

According to **Theorem1**, the simulator completes the successful simulation, in which the simulator can efficiently generate dummy ciphertexts that can be opened as plaintexts '0' or '1'. The dummy ciphertexts in the simulation are indistinguishable from the actual ciphertexts in the real protocol. This is just the non-committing property.

Theorem 2. *Given (r_0, r_1, x_0, x_1) in a real or simulated conversation that described above, there doesn't exist a probabilistic polynomial time algorithm with $P_r > 1/2$ to evaluate the bit c or d in a simulated or real conversation that described above.*

Proof. As we assume that the special network setting mentioned as Section 1.4, we do not consider the IND-CPA, IND-CCA2 .et al games [14], even they are the popular formal security proofs about encryption schemes. Namely, the scheme satisfied confidentiality if the ciphertexts are secure against eavesdroppers although they are able to corrupt parties. We begin with consider a real conversation. According to **Lemma1** and **Lemma2**, r_0, r_1 and x_0, x_1 leak no knowledge about (c, d) for the useful knowledge only lies in the index $\{0, 1\}$ which is random chosen by Alice and Bob. So no one can evaluate the bit c or d with $P_r > 1/2$ in a real conversation that described above.

The proof in a simulated conversation is similar to that in a real conversation mentioned as above. $\square$

According to **Theorem2**, the shared enciper key as one-time pad bit is secure against eavesdroppers. Therefore, the encryption operation is secure as theoretically unbreakable one-time pad [16].

In summary, according to **Theorem1** and **Theorem2**, our scheme is a secure efficient non-committing encryption.

5   Conclusion

In this paper, we present an efficient non-committing encryption scheme based on quadratic residue that is a solution for adaptive security of multiparty computation with non-erasing parties. Our scheme is more efficient than all schemes proposed before.

References

1. D.Beaver, Foundations of secure interactive computing. In Joan Feigenbaum, editor, Advances in Cryptology - Crypto'91, pages 377-391, Berlin, 1991. Springer-Verlag. Lecture Notes in Computer Science Volume 576.
2. D.Beaver, Plug and play encryption. In Burt kaliski, editor, Advances in Cryptology - Crypto'97, pages 75-89, Berlin, 1997. Springer-Verlag. Lecture Notes in Computer Science Volume 1294
3. D.Beaver, S.Haber, Cryptographic protocols provably secure against dynamic adversaries. Advances in Cryptology - Eurocrypt '92 proceedins, pages 307-323, Berlin, 1993. Springer-Verlag. Lecture Notes in Computer Science Volume 658.

4. Ran Canetti, Security and composition of multi-party cryptographic protocols. Obtainable from the Theory of Cryptography Library, august 1999.
5. Ronald Cramer and Ivan Damgard. Multiparty computation, an introduction Http://www.daimi.au.dk/ ivan/mpc.ps, 2003
6. Ran Canetti, Uri Feige, Oded Goldreich, and Moni Naor. Adaptively secure multiparty computation. In Proceedings of the Twenty-Eighth Annual ACM Symposium on the Theory of Computing, pages 639-648, Philadelphia, Pennsylvania, 22-24 May 1996.
7. Ivan Damgard and Jesoer B.Nielsen, Improved non-committing encryption schemes based on a general complexity assumption. In Mihir Bellare, editor, Advances in Cryptology - Crypto'2000, pages 432-450, Berlin, 2000. Springer-Verlag. Lecture Notes in Computer Science Volume 1880.
8. S.Goldwasser. S. Goldwasser. Multi-party computations: past and present. In ACM Symposium on Principles of Distributed Computing, 1997
9. O. Goldreich, S. Micali, and A. Wigderson. How to play any mental game. In Proceedings of the 19th Annual ACM Symposium on Theory of Computing, pages 218-229, 1987.
10. S. Goldwasser and L. Levin, Fair Computation of General Functions in Presence of Immoral Majority , CRYPTO, 1990.
11. S. Goldwasser and S.Micali, Probabilistic encryption and how to play mental poker keeping secret all partial information, Proceeding of 14th ACM Symposium, on the Theory of Computing, pages 365-377, 1982.
12. S.Micali and P.Rogaway, Secure computaion. In Joan Feigenbaum, editor, Advances in Cryptology - Crypto'91, pages 392-404, Berlin, 1991. Springer-Verlag. Lecture Notes in Computer Science Volume 576.
13. Menezes, A.J., Van Oorschot,P., and Vanstone,S.A., Handbook of applied cryptography, (CRC Press, Boca Raton,1997)
14. Wenbo Mao, Modern Cryptography: Theory and Practice, (Prentice-Hall, PTR, 2004)
15. M.Naor, Bit commitment using pseudo-randomness. Advances in Cryptology - Crypto'89, pages 128-136, Berlin, 1990. Springer-Verlag.
16. Jesoer B.Nielsen. Non-committing encryption is too easy in the Random Oracle Model. Basic Research in Computer Science Report, December 2001.20pp
17. Andrew C.Yao, Protocols for secure computations (extended abstract). In 23rd Annual Symposium on Foundations of Computer Science [16], pages 160-164.

Biometric Cryptosystem Using Online Signatures

Alisher Kholmatov and Berrin Yanikoglu

Faculty of Engineering and Natural Sciences
Sabanci University
Istanbul 34956 Turkey
alisher@su.sabanciuniv.edu, berrin@sabanciuniv.edu

Abstract. Biometric cryptosystems combine cryptography and biometrics to benefit from the strengths of both fields. In such systems, while cryptography provides high and adjustable security levels, biometrics brings in non-repudiation and eliminates the need to remember passwords or to carry tokens etc. In this work, we present a biometric cryptosystem which uses online signatures, based on the fuzzy vault scheme of Jules et al. The fuzzy vault scheme releases a previously stored key when the biometric data presented for verification matches the previously stored template hidden in a vault. The online signature of a person is a behavioral biometric which is widely accepted as the formal way of approving documents, bank transactions, etc. As such, biometric-based key release using online signatures may have many application areas.

We extract minutiae points (trajectory crossings, endings and points of high curvature) from online signatures and use those during the locking & unlocking phases of the vault. We present our preliminary results and demonstrate that high security level (128 bit encryption key length) can be achieved using online signatures.

1 Introduction

Biometric authentication is the task of verifying the identity of individuals based on their physiological (e.g. fingerprint, face) or behavioral traits (e.g. signature). During authentication, biometric traits of a person are matched against the stored biometric profile of the claimed identity and access is granted if there is sufficient match. Biometric systems are gaining popularity as more trustable alternatives to password-based security systems, since there are no passwords to remember and biometrics cannot be stolen and are difficult to copy. Biometrics also provide non-repudiation (an authenticated user cannot deny having done so) to some degree because of the difficulty in copying or stealing someone's biometrics.

On the other hand, biometric traits are known to be variable and noisy. The same biometric may change between consecutive acquisitions (due to injury, ageing, even mood etc.) and noise can be introduced to a biometric signal by an acquisition device or the environment. While it would be very convenient to

A. Levi et al. (Eds.): ISCIS 2006, LNCS 4263, pp. 981–990, 2006.

use biometric traits for encryption, for instance someone using his fingerprint or handwritten signature to encrypt a document and securely send it over public network, this seems very difficult due to the aforementioned variability of the biometric signals and the fact that encryption and decryption operations cannot tolerate the perturbation of even a single bit. In its most basic sense, generating a cryptographic key directly from a biometric trait, for instance fingerprints, has not been very successful, as it involves obtaining an *exact* key from a highly variable data. For instance Feng and Wah has only been able to generate a 40-bit private key from online signatures with an 8% equal error rate (the key extracted from a genuine signature is not correct or a forgery successfully extracts the key) [1].

Recent research has focused on combining cryptography and biometrics to take advantage of the benefits of both fields [2][3][4][5][6]. While biometrics provide non-repudiation and convenience, traditional cryptography provides adjustable levels of security and can be used not just for authentication, but also for encryption. Uludag et al. makes the distinction between two general approaches within what they call *crypto-biometric systems*, according to the coupling level of cryptography and biometrics [7]: *Biometrics-based key release* refers to the use of biometric authentication to release a previously stored cryptographic key. Biometric authentication is used as a wrapper, adding convenience to traditional cryptography where the user would have been in charge of remembering his/her key; however the two techniques are only loosely coupled. *Biometrics-based key generation* refers to extracting/generating a cryptographic key from a biometric template or construct. In this case, biometrics and cryptography are tightly coupled: the secret key is bound to the biometric information and the biometric template is not stored in plain form.

According to the above definition, recent work of Juels et al. [2] and Tuyls et al. [3] are classified as biometrics-based key generation, as they require a tight coupling of cryptography and biometrics. In particular, the *fuzzy vault* construct of Juels et al. forms the basis of this paper. Jules and Wattenberg proposed the *fuzzy commitment* scheme [8]; later Juels and Sudan extended it to the *fuzzy vault* scheme [2] and described how it can be used to construct/release an encryption key using one's biometrics: a secret (cryptographic key) is "locked" using a biometric data of a person such that someone who possesses a substantial amount of the locking elements (e.g. another reading of the same biometric) would be able to decrypt the secret. Note that the fuzzy vault scheme is classified as a key-generation scheme in Uludag et al., because of its tight coupling of cryptography and biometrics [7]. However, in the sense that the biometric data releases a previously stored key, it can also be seen as a releasing mechanism.

Yang and Verbauwhede and Uludag et al. [9, 10] implemented the fuzzy vault using fingerprints, making simplifying assumptions about the biometric data. In this paper we present an implementation of the fuzzy vault construct using online signatures.

2   Previous Work

2.1   Fuzzy Vault

Jules and Sudan proposed a scheme called *fuzzy vault*, which they call an error tolerant encryption operation [2]. Fuzzy vault scheme provides a framework to encrypt ("lock") some secret value (eg. cryptographic key) using an unordered set of locking elements as a key, such that someone who possesses a substantial amount of the locking elements will be able to decrypt the secret. It is based on the difficulty of the polynomial reconstruction problem. The encoding and decoding are done as follows:

Assume that Alice wants to secure her cryptographic key S (a random bit stream) using an arbitrary set of elements A. She selects a polynomial $P(x)$ of degree D and encodes S into the polynomial's coefficients. Encoding can be achieved by slicing S into non-overlapping bit chunks and then mapping these onto the coefficients. The mapping must be invertible meaning that the coefficients can be unambiguously mapped back to the corresponding bit chunks, which when concatenated will reconstruct the S. Then, Alice evaluates the polynomial at each element of her set A and stores these evaluation pairs into the set G, where $G = \{(a_1, P(a_1)), (a_2, P(a_2)), ..., (a_N, P(a_N))\}$, $a_i \in A$ and $|A| = N$. Finally, she generates a random set R of pairs such that none of the pairs in that set lie on the polynomial; and she merges the sets G and R into a final set, to obtain the vault, which she then makes public. Note that within the vault, it is not known which points belong to G and which ones belong to R. All the steps required to lock a secret in the Fuzzy Vault are graphically represented in Figure 1.

Now suppose that Bob has his own set of elements B and he wants to find out ("unlock") Alice's secret locked in the vault. He will be able to do so only if his set B largely overlaps with Alice's A, so as to identify a substantial number of the pairs that lie on the polynomial, from the vault. Given at least $D + 1$ pairs that lie on the polynomial, he applies one of the known polynomial reconstruction techniques (eg. Lagrange interpolating polynomial) to reconstruct the polynomial and thus extracts her secret S. Notice that if Bob does not know which of the points of the vault lie on the polynomial, it should be computationally infeasible for him to unlock the vault.

Whereas perturbation of a single bit in a key of a classical cryptosystem (eg. AES, RSA) hinders decryption completely, the fuzzy vault allows for some minor differences between the encryption & decryption keys; here the unordered sets used to lock & unlock the vault. This fuzziness is necessary for use with biometrics since different measurements of the same biometric often result in (slightly) different signals. Furthermore, for most of the known biometric signals, it is hard to establish a consistent ordering within the measured features. For instance two impressions of the same fingerprint can have substantial distortion and the number of features may vary between the two impressions.

Since the fuzzy vault scheme can tolerate some difference between the locking & unlocking sets and does not requiring ordering amongst the set elements,

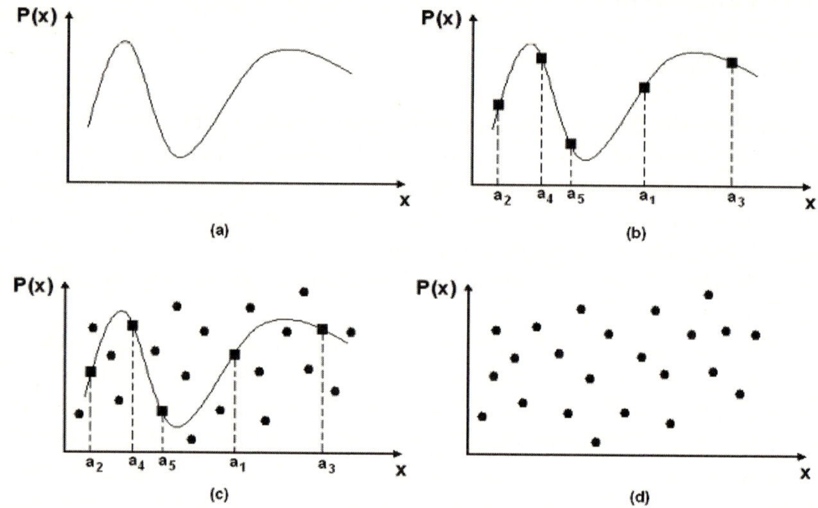

Fig. 1. Vault *Locking* phase: (a) Create a polynomial by encoding the *Secret* as its co-efficients. (b) Project genuine features onto the polynomial: a_i represents the subject's i'th feature. (c) Randomly create chaff points (represented by small black circles) and add to the Vault. (d) Final appearance of the Vault, as stored to the system database.

it has a potential to be used in biometric cryptosystems. However it is not straightforward how to implement a fuzzy vault using a particular biometric data, due to the difficulty of matching the template and query biometric signals (i.e. locking and unlocking sets, respectively) within the presence of random data (the chaff points).

2.2 Fuzzy Vault with Fingerprints

Uludag et al. [10] demonstrated a preliminary implementation of the fuzzy vault scheme using fingerprints. Yang and Verbauwhede [9] also implemented the fuzzy vault with fingerprints, but they made the assumption that rotation & transla-tion invariant features can be reliably extracted from minutiae -which is difficult in practice. Furthermore, they store reference minutia point along with the vault, which may leak some information.

We will review the system by Uludag et al. as it relates the most to our proposed scheme. Minutia points of template & query fingerprints were used as locking & unlocking sets, respectively, to lock a 128-bit long data (S) which forms the cryptographic key. More precisely, the values obtained by concatenation of the corresponding x & y coordinates of minutiae points were used as set elements. To make sure that the desired S was unlocked from the vault through an error-prone process, cyclic redundancy check bits (16 bits) were concatenated to S. Then, S, together with its check bits, was divided into non-overlapping chunks (16 bits each), giving the coefficients of an 8th degree polynomial. To lock the secret, template minutiae set was projected onto this polynomial and random chaff points not lying on the polynomial are added, to form the vault. Based on their empirical estimations, they used only 18 minutia points and 200 chaff points.

To unlock the secret, i.e. reconstruct S, they first match the query minutia set with the abscissa part of the vault and identify candidate points lying on the polynomial. Since $D + 1$ points are required to reconstruct a polynomial of degree D, all possible 9 point combinations of the candidate set are tried, to find the one with the correct check bits. S is successfully unlocked when the check bits verify. Authors report a 79% of correct reconstruction rate with 0% false accept rate.

To bypass the problem of matching the minutiae points and finding an upper bound for the performance of the scheme, authors have used a fingerprint database where minutia points and the correspondence between template & query fingerprints were established by an expert. During their experiments, the minutiae sets of mating fingerprints were pre-aligned (i.e. rotated & translated) according to the established correspondence, and used as such.

3   Proposed Method

In this section we demonstrate an implementation of the fuzzy vault scheme using online signatures. Online (dynamic) signatures are captured by pressure-sensitive tablets that extract dynamic properties of a signature in addition to its shape, which is the only available information in offline (static) signatures found on bank checks and documents. Dynamic features include the number and order of the strokes, the overall speed of the signature, the pen pressure at each point, etc. and make the signature more unique and more difficult to forge. Throughout the rest of the paper, we use the term signature to mean an online signature, unless otherwise specified.

For a given biometric, finding a representation which is suitable for the fuzzy vault scheme can be a challenging problem. In this work, we use the event points of a signature, namely crossings, endings and points of high curvature on the signature's trajectory, as features to lock and unlock the vault. Hereafter, these points will be called minutiae points, due to their similarity to the minutiae points defining branch and end points in fingerprints. Figure 2 demonstrates an example signature with marked minutiae points points.

Currently, the minutiae points are marked manually by experts in order to measure the maximum performance attainable in a system using the suggested features. This way, we guarantee that there are no error introduced by an automatic minutiae extraction algorithm; though minutiae extraction using dynamical information is not a complex problem.

Note that these minutiae points do not capture the timing of a signature, nor the ordering of the strokes; in fact they only use the shape of the signature. Despite this fact, the results are very promising in comparison to the results obtained with previous implementations of fuzzy vault. Since the features only depend on the shape of the signature, the proposed method could also be used with offline signatures, though using offline signatures in a cryptosystem is not very meaningful.

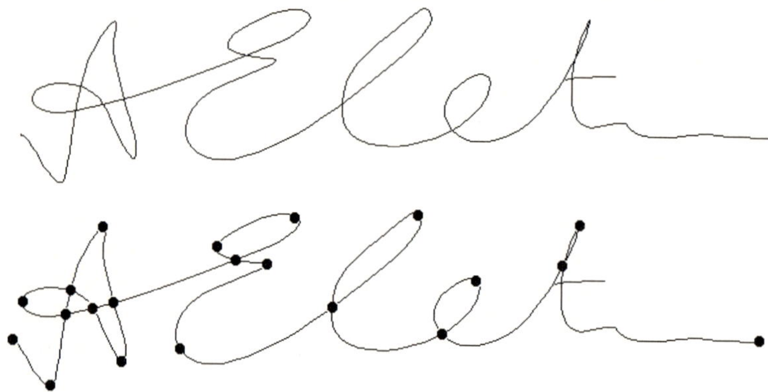

Fig. 2. The Figure demonstrates a genuine signature (on top) and minutiae points marked for that signature (at the bottom)

During the locking phase, we concatenate the x & y coordinates of minutiae points and project these on to the secret polynomial as described in Section 2.1. Minutiae coordinates and their corresponding projections, along with random chaff points constitute the locking set of the vault. Although chaff points are created randomly, special attention must be paid to their number and placements, so as not to leak information. If chaff points are generated too close to minutiae points, the unlocking performance will be reduced since chaff points located in close proximity to genuine points may be mistakenly matched during the unlocking phase. If chaff points are generated too close to other chaff points, they may be easy to detect if the attacker knows the closest possible distance between two genuine points (i.e. distance between minutiae). If there are too few chaff points, decoding the secret becomes easier as there are fewer combinations of points to choose from to reconstruct the secret polynomial. Finally, chaff points must be homogeneously distributed in the vault space; otherwise, they may leak information, enabling an attacker to reduce his search space and decrease the vault's strength. Figure 3 shows a sample vault which is generated within this system.

During the unlocking phase, the correspondence between points of unlocking minutiae set and those of the vault must be determined. Although there are numerous point matching algorithms, we used exhaustive matching to reduce the error which may be introduced by the matching algorithm. Exhaustive matching is performed by applying all possible rotations & translations (in the vault space) to the unlocking set, to find the alignment with the most number of matching points. Figure 4 shows the result of matching genuine (left) and forgery (right) minutiae sets with the vault (matched vault points are circled). As can be seen, while the genuine set substantially overlaps with the vault's genuine points, the forgery set does not.

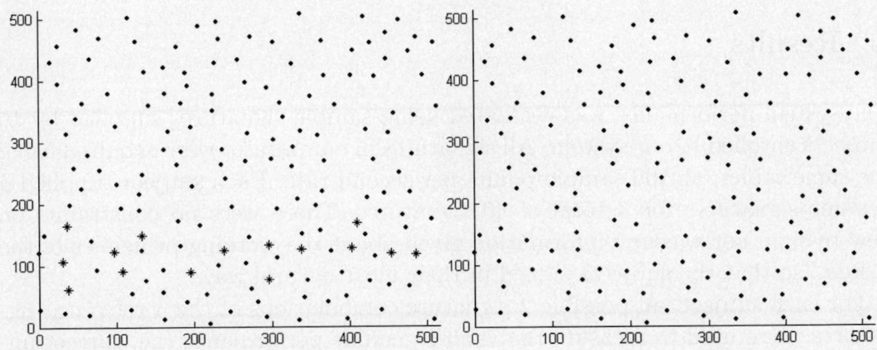

Fig. 3. Fuzzy Vault Locking: genuine points (stars) and chaff (dots) points are represented separately on the left for the sake of clarity. The actual vault shown on the right, only contains the points without any information about their source (genuine or chaff).

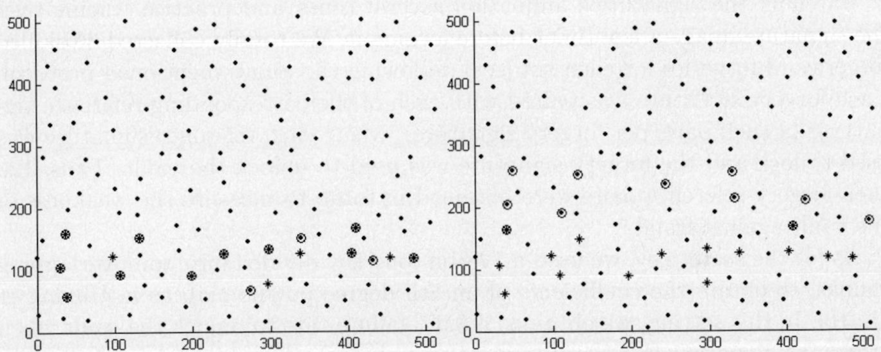

Fig. 4. Fuzzy Vault Matching: matching of genuine (left) and forgery (right) minutiae sets with the vault from Fig. 3. matched vault points are shown circled and minutiae (stars) and chaff (dots) points of the vault are represented differently for the sake of clarity

As the result of matching, we obtain a candidate set of points which are used for decoding the secret key: During each iteration of the decoding phase, we select $D + 1$ points from the candidate set where D is the degree of the secret polynomial and use them to decode the secret as described in Section 2.1.

During the locking phase, a cryptographic hash of the secret is stored in the system database along with the vault. During unlocking, we calculate the hash of the decoded secret and compare it with the one stored in the system's database. Decoding phase terminates when both hash values match (secret is decoded) or when the maximum number of iterations is performed (secret not revealed). These steps are based on the fuzzy vault implementation of Uludag et al. [10].

4   Results

The system performance was evaluated using sample signatures supplied by 10 subjects enrolled to our system. All signatures in our dataset were acquired using the same tablet, at 100 sample points per second rate. Each subject supplied 4 genuine signatures for a total of 40 signatures. There were no constraints on how to sign, nor was any information given about the working principles of the system, so that the subjects signed in their most natural way.

For each subject, all possible 2-signature combinations of the 4 reference signatures, were used to measure the vault's genuine performance (i.e. correct unlocking rate of the vault). Thus, 6 such signature pairs were obtained for each user and 60 such pairs were tested in total.

To collect skilled forgeries, we added a signing simulation module to our system. Simulation module animates the signing process of a given signature so that the forger could see not only the signature trajectory's points sequence but also the signing dynamics (speed and acceleration). Forgers had a chance of watching the signature's animation several times and practice tracing over the signature image a few times before forging it. We totally collected 30 skilled forgeries (3 forgeries for each subject), following the above mentioned protocol. Each forgery signature was paired with each of the corresponding reference signatures (4 such pairs per forgery signature), where each reference signature was used to lock and the forgery signature was used to unlock the vault. Thus, 120 such forgery-reference pairs were obtained in total, to measure the weakness of the vault against fraud.

As for the secret key, we used a 128-bit long key divided into non-overlapping chunks, to obtain the coefficients of an 8th degree polynomial, as in Uludag et al. [10]. In this setting, we obtained a 8.3% failure rate to unlock the vault when a genuine signature was presented (i.e. can be considered as false reject rate) and 2.5% false unlocking rate when the vault was attempted to be opened using forgery signatures. These results are quite promising compared to previous work in this area. Most of the failures in unlocking the vault with genuine signatures were due to the high variability within reference signatures (genuine points did not successfully match the genuine template points stored in the vault). On the other hand, false unlocking errors were due to the fact that the geometric minutiae points do not incorporate dynamic features of the user, losing discriminative information about the signatures. The false accept rate can be reduced by increasing the polynomial degree, of course at the expense of a slight increase in FRR. Conversely, FRR can be lowered by more efficient chaff point generation, which could assure that the number of genuine points matching chaff points doesn't exceed a certain threshold.

On average, it took approximately 30 seconds to unlock a vault with it's corresponding genuine signature. Troughout the test a notebook computer with Intel Celeron (M) 1.5GHz and 512 megabyte of RAM hardware configuration was used. All algorithms were implemented using Matlab.

5   Summary and Conclusion

Biometric cryptosystems combine cryptography and biometrics to take advantage of the benefits of both fields: while biometrics provide non-repudiation and convenience, traditional cryptography provides adjustable levels of security and can be used not just for authentication, but also for encryption. Fuzzy Vault scheme [2] is a promising framework for such systems, as it doesn't require an ordered representation of the biometric and it can tolerate variations within the biometric to some extent.

We demonstrated an implementation of the Fuzzy Vault scheme using online signatures, running in real time. Even though our method is a relatively straightforward extension of the fuzzy vault scheme implementation by Uludag et al. [10], the issues encountered in implementing the fuzzy vault with online signatures are non-trivial. Besides, this is the first realisation of the scheme using online signatures, demonstrating very promising performance results.

Acknowledgments

We would like to thank TUBİTAK (The Scientific and Technical Research Council of Turkey) for the Ph.D. fellowship support granted to Alisher Kholmatov throughout this research.

References

1. Feng, H., Wah, C.: Private key generation from on-line handwritten signatures. Information Management & Computer Security, **10/4** (2002) 159–164
2. Juels, A., Sudan, M.: A fuzzy vault scheme. IEEE International Symposium on Information Theory (2002) 408
3. Tuyls, P., Verbitskiy, E., Ignatenko, T., Denteneer, D., Akkermans, T.: Privacy protected biometric templates: Acoustic ear identification. Proceedings of SPIE: Biometric Technology for Human Identification **Vol. 5404** (2004) 176–182
4. Davida, G., Frankel, Y., Matt, B.: On enabling secure applications through on-line biometric identification. In IEEE Symposium on Privacy and Security (1998) 408
5. Soutar, C., Roberge, D., Stojanov, S., Gilroy, R., Kumar, B.V.: Biometric encryption using image processing. In Proc. SPIE, Optical Security and Counterfeit Deterrence Techniques II **Vol. 3314** (1998) 178–188
6. Linnartz, J., Tuyls, P.: New shielding functions to enhance privacy and prevent misuse of biometric templates. Proceeding of AVBPA (LNCS 2688) (2003) 393–402
7. Uludag, U., Pankanti, S., Prabhakar, S., Jain, A.: Biometric cryptosystems: Issues and challenges. In: Proceedings of the IEEE. Volume 92(6). (2004)

8. Juels, A., Wattenberg, M.: A fuzzy commitment scheme. Conference on Computer and Communications Security, ACM Press. (1999) 28–36
9. Yang, S., Verbauwhede, I.: Secure fuzzy vault based fingerprint verification system. Signals, Systems and Computers, 2004. Conference Record of the Thirty-Eighth Asilomar Conference on (2004) 577–581
10. Uludag, U., Pankanti, S., Jain., A.: Fuzzy vault for fingerprints. Proceeding of International Conference on Audio- and Video-Based Biometric Person Authentication (2005) 310–319

Finite Field Polynomial Multiplication in the Frequency Domain with Application to Elliptic Curve Cryptography

Selçuk Baktır and Berk Sunar

Worcester Polytechnic Institute
100 Institute Road, Worcester, MA 01609, USA
{selcuk, sunar}@wpi.edu

Abstract. We introduce an efficient method for computing Montgomery products of polynomials in the *frequency domain*. The discrete Fourier transform (DFT) based method originally proposed for integer multiplication provides an extremely efficient method with the best asymptotic complexity, i.e. $O(m \log m \log \log m)$, for multiplication of m-bit integers or $(m-1)^{st}$ degree polynomials. However, the original DFT method bears significant overhead due to the conversions between the time and the frequency domains which makes it impractical for short operands as used in many applications. In this work, we introduce *DFT modular multiplication* which performs the entire modular multiplication (including the reduction step) in the frequency domain, and thus eliminates costly back and forth conversions. We show that, especially in computationally constrained platforms, multiplication of finite field elements may be achieved more efficiently in the frequency domain than in the time domain for operand sizes relevant to elliptic curve cryptography (ECC). To the best of our knowledge, this is the first work that proposes the use of frequency domain arithmetic for ECC and shows that it can be efficient.

Keywords: Finite field multiplication, DFT, elliptic curve cryptography.

1 Introduction

Finite fields have many applications in coding theory [2,1], cryptography [11,4,13], and digital signal processing [3]. Hence efficient implementation of finite field arithmetic operations is crucial. Multiplication of finite field elements is commonly implemented in terms of modular multiplication of polynomials realized in two steps: ordinary polynomial multiplication and modular reduction of the result by the field generating polynomial. Unlike modular reduction which has only linear complexity, i.e. $O(m)$, for polynomials of degree $m - 1$ when a fixed special modulus is chosen, polynomial multiplication with the classical *schoolbook method* has quadratic complexity, i.e. $O(m^2)$, given in terms of the number of coefficient multiplications and additions. This complexity may be improved to $O(m^{\log_2 3})$ using the Karatsuba algorithm [8]. However, despite the significant improvement

A. Levi et al. (Eds.): ISCIS 2006, LNCS 4263, pp. 991–1001, 2006.

gained by the Karatsuba algorithm, the complexity is still not optimal. Furthermore, the implementation of the Karatsuba algorithm is more burdensome due to its recursive nature. The known fastest multiplication algorithm, introduced by Schönhage and Strassen [16], performs multiplication in the frequency domain using the fast Fourier transform (FFT) [6] with complexity $O(m \log m \log \log m)$ for multiplication of m-bit integers or m-coefficient polynomials [7]. Unfortunately, the FFT based algorithm becomes efficient and useful in practice only for very large operands, e.g. larger than 1000 bits in size, due to the overhead associated with the forward and inverse Fourier transform operations.

When the transformation computations between the time and frequency domains are not considered, frequency domain polynomial multiplication (without modular reduction) has surprisingly low *linear*, i.e. $O(m)$, complexity. Sadly, no efficient method for performing modular reduction is known to exist in the frequency domain, and therefore one needs to convert the result of a polynomial multiplication operation back to the time domain to perform modular reduction bearing significant overhead. In this paper we propose an algorithm for achieving modular reduction in the frequency domain. Thus, the entire finite field multiplication, including modular reduction, can be carried out in the frequency domain. In many finite field applications a chain of arithmetic operations is performed rather than a solitary one. Using our method, after an initial conversion step all intermediary operations may be computed in the frequency domain. Therefore, there will be no need for conversion before and after every single finite field multiplication except before the very first and after the very last ones.

2   Background

Number Theoretic Transform (NTT)

Number theoretic transform over a ring, also known as *the discrete Fourier transform over a finite field*, was introduced by Pollard [14]. For a finite field $GF(q)$ and a generic sequence (a) of length d whose entries are from $GF(q)$, the forward NTT of (a) over $GF(q)$, denoted by (A), can be computed as

$$A_j = \sum_{i=0}^{d-1} a_i r^{ij} \ , \ 0 \le j \le d-1 \ . \tag{1}$$

Likewise, the inverse NTT of (A) over $GF(q)$ can be computed as

$$a_i = \frac{1}{d} \cdot \sum_{j=0}^{d-1} A_j r^{-ij} \ , \ 0 \le i \le d-1 \ . \tag{2}$$

Here we refer to the elements of (a) and (A) by a_i and A_i, respectively, for $0 \le i \le d-1$. Also, we will refer to (a) and (A) as the *time and frequency domain* sequences, respectively. The above NTT computations over $GF(q)$ are defined by utilizing a d-th primitive root of unity, denoted by r, from $GF(q)$ or a finite extension of it. Note that unlike the complex number $r = e^{j2\pi/d}$ generally used as the d-th primitive root of unity in the discrete Fourier transform (DFT) computations, a finite field element r can be utilized for the same purpose in an NTT. A number theoretic transform of special interest is *Mersenne transform*, which is an NTT with arithmetic modulo a Mersenne number $M_n = 2^n - 1$ [15]. Hence, if q is a Mersenne prime, then the NTT over $GF(q)$ is a Mersenne transform.

Mersenne transform allows for very efficient forward and inverse DFT operations for $r = \pm 2^k$, where k is an integer. Multiplication of an n-bit number with integer powers of 2^k modulo M_n can be achieved with a simple bitwise left rotation of the n-bit number, e.g. multiplication of an n-bit number with $(2^k)^i$ modulo M_n can be achieved with a simple bitwise left rotation by $ki \bmod n$ bits. Similarly, multiplication of an n-bit number with integer powers of -2^k modulo M_n can be achieved with a simple bitwise left rotation of the number, in addition to a negation if the power of -2^k is odd. Hence, when $r = \pm 2^k$ all of the multiplications by powers of r in the forward and inverse DFT computations in a Mersenne transform can be achieved with simple bitwise rotations. In this case, for a transform length of d, the forward DFT computation can be achieved with only $(d-1)^2$ simple rotations and $d(d-1)$ additions/subtractions avoiding any multiplications. For the inverse DFT computation additional d constant multiplications with $1/d$ are performed. For a more detailed complexity analysis of Mersenne transform, we refer the interested reader to [15].

Note that the sequence length d and the dth primitive root of unity r are dependent on each other and can not be chosen independently. In a Mersenne transform over $GF(q)$, where $q = M_n = 2^n - 1$ is a Mersenne prime, $r = \pm 2^k$ can take the values $2, -2$ and 2^2. Hence, the following equalities hold determining the relationship between d and r:

$$d = \begin{cases} n, & r = 2 . \\ 2n, & r = -2 . \\ n, & r = 2^2 . \end{cases}$$

An extremely efficient method for computing the DFT is the fast Fourier transform (FFT) [6]. The FFT algorithm works by exploiting the symmetry of the DFT computation and the periodicity of the dth primitive root of unity r when the sequence length d is a composite number. For instance, if a sequence is of even length, i.e. if its length d is divisible by two, then by applying the FFT the DFT computation of this d-element sequence is basically reduced to DFT computations of two $(d/2)$-element sequences, namely the sequence comprising only the even indexed elements of the original sequence and the sequence comprising only the odd indexed elements of the original sequence. When d is a power of two, the same approach can easily be applied recursively surprisingly reducing the $O(d^2)$ complexity of the DFT computation to $O(d \log_2 d)$. However, we would like to note that for the case of Mersenne transform modulo a Mersenne prime $M_n = 2^n - 1$, and when $r = \pm 2^k$, the allowable sequence length d is either the prime number n (for $r = 2$ or $r = 2^2$) or $2n$ (for $r = -2$). Hence, either $d = n$ is prime and the FFT algorithm can not be applied at all or $d = 2n$

and only a single level of recursion is allowed in the FFT computation which would have limited computational advantage.

Multiplication in $GF(q^m)$ Using NTT

Cyclic convolution of any two d-element sequences (a) and (b) in the time domain results in another d-element sequence (c) and can be computed as follows:

$$c_i = \sum_{j=0}^{d-1} a_j b_{i-j \bmod d} , \quad 0 \leq i \leq d-1 . \tag{3}$$

The above convolution operation in the time domain is equivalent to the following computation in the frequency domain:

$$C_i = A_i \cdot B_i , \quad 0 \leq i \leq d-1 . \tag{4}$$

Thus, convolution of two d-element sequences in the time domain, with complexity $O(d^2)$, has a surprisingly low $O(d)$ complexity in the frequency domain.

Multiplication of two polynomials is basically the same as the *acyclic (linear) convolution* of the polynomial coefficients. We have seen that cyclic convolution can be performed very efficiently in the frequency domain by pairwise coefficient multiplications, hence it will be wise to represent an element of $GF(q^m)$, in polynomial representation an $(m-1)^{st}$ degree polynomial with coefficients in $GF(q)$, with at least a $d = (2m-1)$ element sequence by appending zeros at the end, so that the cyclic convolution of two such sequences will be equivalent to their acyclic convolution and give us their polynomial multiplication. We can form sequences by taking the ordered coefficients of polynomials. For instance, $a(x) = a_0 + a_1 x + a_2 x^2 + \ldots + a_{m-1} x^{m-1}$, an element of $GF(q^m)$ in polynomial representation, can be interpreted as the sequence $(a) = (a_0, a_1, a_2, \ldots, a_{m-1}, 0, 0, \ldots, 0)$ after appending $d - m$ zeros to the right. For $a(x), b(x) \in GF(q^m)$ the cyclic convolution of (a) and (b) yields a sequence (c) whose first $2m-1$ entries can be interpreted as the coefficients of $c(x) = a(x) \cdot b(x)$. The following straightforward algorithm (Algorithm 1) realizes the polynomial multiplication $c(x) = a(x) \cdot b(x)$.

Algorithm 1. Polynomial Multiplication by Direct Application of DFT

Input: $a(x), b(x) \in GF(q^m)$
Output: $c(x) = a(x) \cdot b(x)$
 1: Interpret $a(x)$ and $b(x)$ as the sequences (a) and (b) with length $d \geq 2m - 1$

 2: Convert (a) and (b) into (A) and (B) using the NTT as in (1)
 3: Multiply (A) with (B) to compute (C) as in (4)
 4: Convert (C) to (c) using the inverse NTT as in (2)
 5: Interpret the first $2m - 1$ coefficients of (c) as the coefficients of $c(x) = a(x) \cdot b(x)$
 6: Return $c(x)$

Note that with Algorithm 1 the polynomial product $c(x) = a(x) \cdot b(x)$ is computed in the frequency domain but the final reduction by the field generating polynomial remains to be computed. One needs to convert (C) back to the time domain to do the modular reduction, so that further multiplications can be performed on it using the same method. In the next section, we introduce *DFT modular multiplication* which performs both polynomial multiplication and modular reduction in the frequency domain and thus avoids conversions between the time and frequency domains.

3   Modular Multiplication in the Frequency Domain

In many finite field applications, a chain of arithmetic operations needs to be performed. For example, in elliptic curve cryptography a scalar point product is computed by applying a chain of finite field additions, subtractions, multiplications, squarings and inversions on the input point coordinates [5]. The Montgomery residue representation has proven to be useful in this computation [12], [10], [9]. In using this method, first the operands are converted to their respective Montgomery residue representations, then utilizing Montgomery arithmetic the desired computation is implemented, and finally the result is converted back to the normal integer or polynomial representation. If there is a large number of operations performed in the Montgomery domain, due to the efficiency of the intervening computations, the forward and backward conversion operations become affordable. We introduce the same notion for the frequency domain. We find an arithmetic operation in the frequency domain that is equivalent to Montgomery multiplication in the time domain. In the remainder of this section, we introduce the *DFT modular multiplication* algorithm which allows for both polynomial multiplication and modular reduction operations in the frequency domain.

3.1   The DFT Modular Multiplication Algorithm

We use (f) and (x) to represent the d-element sequences for the irreducible field generating polynomial $f(x)$ and the constant polynomial $x \in GF(q^m)$, respectively, in the time domain. We denote the NTTs of (f) and (x) with (F) and (X), respectively, and let F_i and X_i, for $0 \leq i \leq d - 1$, denote their elements. For instance, the constant polynomial x is represented in the time domain with the d-element sequence $(x) = (0, 1, 0, 0, \cdots, 0)$ and its frequency domain representation is $(X) = (1, r, r^2, r^3, r^4, r^5, \ldots, r^{d-1})$.

DFT modular multiplication presented with Algorithm 2 consists of two parts: multiplication (steps $1 - 3$) and Montgomery reduction (steps $4 - 13$). Multiplication is performed by simple pairwise multiplication of the coefficients of the frequency domain sequence representations of the input operands. Reduction is more complex and performed by Montgomery reduction in the frequency domain. In the reduction process the normalized field generating polynomial $f'(x) = f(x)/f_0 \bmod q$ is used. Hence, $f'(x)$ is equivalent to $f(x)$ but normalized to have $f'(0) = 1$. We let (f') and (F') denote the d-element time and frequency domain sequence representations for $f'(x)$, where $f'_i = f_i/f_0 \bmod q$ and $F'_i = F_i/f_0 \bmod q$, respectively, for $0 \le i \le d-1$.

Algorithm 2. DFT Modular Multiplication

Input: (A), (B) which represent $a(x), b(x) \in GF(q^m)$ in the frequency domain
Output: (C) which represents $c(x) = a(x) \cdot b(x) \cdot x^{-(m-1)} \bmod f(x)$ in the frequency domain

1: **for** $i = 0$ to $d-1$ **do**
2:     $C_i \leftarrow A_i \cdot B_i$
3: **end for**
4: **for** $j = 0$ to $m-2$ **do**
5:     $S \leftarrow 0$
6:     **for** $i = 0$ to $d-1$ **do**
7:         $S \leftarrow S + C_i$
8:     **end for**
9:     $S \leftarrow -S/d$
10:     **for** $i = 0$ to $d-1$ **do**
11:         $C_i \leftarrow (C_i + F'_i \cdot S) \cdot X_i^{-1}$
12:     **end for**
13: **end for**
14: Return (C)

Proof of Correctness

DFT modular multiplication is a direct adaptation of Montgomery multiplication for the frequency domain. Polynomial multiplication part of the algorithm (steps $1-3$) is performed via simple pairwise multiplications. As a result, the polynomial $c(x) = a(x) \cdot b(x)$ is obtained. In the modular reduction part (steps $4-13$), S is computed such that $(c(x) + S \cdot f'(x))$ is a multiple of x. This is accomplished by computing $-c_0$, the negative of the first coefficient in the time domain sequence (c) and then by making c_0 zero by adding $S \cdot (F')$ to (C) in the frequency domain. Then again in the frequency domain, $(c(x) + S \cdot f'(x))$ is divided by x and the result, which is congruent to $c(x) \cdot x^{-1}$ modulo $f(x)$ in the time domain, is obtained. This division of $(c(x) + S \cdot f'(x))$ by x is accomplished in the frequency domain by dividing $(C) + (F') \cdot S$ by (X) (Step 11). By repeating steps $5-12$ of the algorithm $m-1$ times the final result (C), which represents $a(x) \cdot b(x) \cdot x^{-(m-1)} \bmod f(x)$ in the frequency domain, is obtained.

$\square$

For $d \approx 2m$, modular multiplication in $GF(q^m)$ with the DFT modular multiplication algorithm requires $4m^2 - m - 1$ multiplications and $4m^2 - 4m$ additions in the ground field $GF(q)$, while the schoolbook method requires only m^2 multiplications and $(m-1)^2$ additions ignoring the cost of modular reduction. Nevertheless, this complexity may be improved dramatically by using special values for q, r, d and the irreducible field generating polynomial $f(x)$ as we will see in the next section.

3.2   Utilizing Efficient Parameters for DFT Modular Multiplication

Using the smallest possible sequence length d, satisfying $d \geq 2m - 1$, will lead to the smallest number of arithmetic operations in the computation of DFT modular multiplication. Optimally, $d = 2m - 1$ will lead to the least number of arithmetic operations.

As mentioned in section 2, using a Mersenne prime as the modulus and selection of $r = \pm 2^k$, where k is an integer, will allow for extremely efficient modular multiplication with $r^i = (\pm 2^k)^i$. This modular multiplication can be achieved with a simple bitwise rotation (in addition to a negation when $r = -2^k$ and i is odd) which is inexpensive. In the DFT modular multiplication algorithm, this property may be exploited if q is chosen as a Mersenne prime and r is chosen as $r = \pm 2^k$. In that case, in step 11 of the algorithm multiplications with $X_i^{-1} = r^{-i} = (\pm 2^k)^{-i} = (\pm 1)^i \cdot 2^{-ki \bmod d}$ become simple $(-ki \bmod d)$-bit left-rotations (in addition to a negation when $r = -2^k$ and i is odd), which have negligible cost compared to a regular multiplication. Also, note that when q is a Mersenne prime, negation of an element of $GF(q)$ can be achieved by simply flipping its bits. Multiplications with F_i' in step 11 can also be avoided in a similar fashion for special $f(x)$. For instance, for the binomial $f(x) = x^m \pm r^{s_0}$ with s_0 an integer, $F_i' = \pm r^{mi - s_0 \bmod d} + 1$ and hence for $r = \pm 2^k$ multiplications with F_i' can be achieved with only one bitwise rotation and one addition/subtraction. Likewise, for the trinomial $f(x) = x^m \pm r^{s_{m'}} x^{m'} \pm r^{s_0}$ or $f(x) = x^m \mp r^{s_{m'}} x^{m'} \pm r^{s_0}$, where s_m' and s_0 are integers, $F_i' = \pm r^{mi - s_0} + r^{m'i + s_{m'} - s_0} + 1$ or $F_i' = \pm r^{mi - s_0} - r^{m'i + s_{m'} - s_0} + 1$, respectively, and hence multiplications with F_i' can be achieved with only two bitwise rotations and two additions/subtractions. Finally, we would like to caution the reader that all these parameters q, d, r and $f(x)$ are dependent on each other and can not be chosen independently.

3.3   Existence of Efficient Parameters

In Table 1 we give a list of parameters that would yield efficient multiplication in $GF(q^m)$ using the DFT modular multiplication algorithm for operand sizes relevant to elliptic curve cryptography. For every case listed in Table 1, one can verify that there exist many special irreducible binomials of the form $x^m \pm 2^s$, or trinomials of the form $x^m \pm r^{s_1} x_1 \pm r^{s_0}$ or $x^m \pm r^{s_1} x_1 \mp r^{s_0}$, as field generating polynomials that would allow for efficient DFT modular multiplication.

4   Complexity of DFT Modular Multiplication

In this section, we present the complexity of DFT modular multiplication for a practical set of parameters relevant to ECC and compare it with two other efficient methods, namely the direct application of DFT multiplication with time domain modular reduction (Algorithm 1) and the Karatsuba algorithm [8]. In our complexity analysis we assume the use of Mersenne prime finite field characteristics as q, irreducible field generating binomials of the form $f(x) = x^m \pm 2^{s_0}$,

Table 1. List of some $q = M_n$, m, d and $r = \pm 2^k$ values for efficient DFT modular multiplication in $GF(q^m)$ for ECC over finite fields of size 143 to 403 bits

$q = M_n = 2^n - 1$	m	d	r	equivalent binary field size
$2^{13} - 1$	11	26	-2	$\sim 2^{143}$
$2^{13} - 1$	12	26	-2	$\sim 2^{156}$
$2^{13} - 1$	13	26	-2	$\sim 2^{169}$
$2^{17} - 1$	9	17	2^2 or 2	$\sim 2^{153}$
$2^{17} - 1$	11	34	-2	$\sim 2^{187}$
$2^{17} - 1$	12	34	-2	$\sim 2^{204}$
$2^{17} - 1$	13	34	-2	$\sim 2^{221}$
$2^{17} - 1$	14	34	-2	$\sim 2^{238}$
$2^{17} - 1$	15	34	-2	$\sim 2^{255}$
$2^{17} - 1$	16	34	-2	$\sim 2^{272}$
$2^{17} - 1$	17	34	-2	$\sim 2^{289}$
$2^{19} - 1$	10	19	2^2 or 2	$\sim 2^{190}$
$2^{19} - 1$	11	38	-2	$\sim 2^{209}$
$2^{19} - 1$	12	38	-2	$\sim 2^{228}$
$2^{19} - 1$	13	38	-2	$\sim 2^{247}$
$2^{19} - 1$	14	38	-2	$\sim 2^{266}$
$2^{19} - 1$	15	38	-2	$\sim 2^{285}$
$2^{19} - 1$	16	38	-2	$\sim 2^{304}$
$2^{19} - 1$	17	38	-2	$\sim 2^{323}$
$2^{19} - 1$	18	38	-2	$\sim 2^{342}$
$2^{19} - 1$	19	38	-2	$\sim 2^{361}$
$2^{31} - 1$	11	31	2^2 or 2	$\sim 2^{341}$
$2^{31} - 1$	12	31	2^2 or 2	$\sim 2^{372}$
$2^{31} - 1$	13	31	2^2 or 2	$\sim 2^{403}$

d-th primitive root of unity $r = \pm 2^k$ and sequence length $d \approx 2m$. The field parameters we use, such as low Hamming weight field generating polynomial and Mersenne prime field characteristics, lead to efficient implementation of multiplication for all three methods. Therefore, for the selected parameters, we can safely assume that our comparisons are fair. In Table 2, we present the complexities of multiplication in $GF(q^m)$ in terms of $GF(q)$ operations for all three approaches when such ideal parameters are used. Note that the astonishingly low $O(m)$ complexity of Algorithms 1 and 2 in terms of the number of $GF(q)$ multiplications is achieved under the ideal conditions with these efficient field parameters together with the choice of $r = \pm 2^k$. The complexity presented for the Karatsuba algorithm is only an approximate one for the case when m is a power of two. For the best complexities of the Karatsuba algorithm for different extension degrees, the reader is referred to [17].

Clearly, the complexity of DFT modular multiplication (Algorithm 2) is an improvement upon the direct DFT approach (Algorithm 1). Moreover, since DFT modular multiplication requires significantly less number of complex operations such as multiplication and constant multiplication, its overall performance appears to be better than the Karatsuba algorithm, for computationally constrained platforms where multiplication is significantly more expensive compared to simpler operations such as addition, subtraction or bitwise rotation.

Table 2. Complexity of multiplication in $GF(q^m)$ in terms of the number of $GF(q)$ operations when $f(x) = x^m + 2^{s_0}$, q is a Mersenne prime and $d \approx 2m$

	Algorithm 1	Karatsuba	Algorithm 2
#Multiplication	$\approx 2m$	$\approx m^{\log_2 3}$	$\approx 2m$
#Const. Mult.	$\approx 2m$	$-$	$m - 1$
#Add./Subtr.	$\approx 8m^2 - 4m$	$\approx 6m^{\log_2 3} - 7m + 1$	$\approx 6m^2 - 6m$
#Rotation	$\approx 8m^2 - 8m + 2$	$m - 1$	$\approx 4m^2 - 4m$

Multiplication operation is inherently more complex than addition, subtraction or bitwise rotation. Therefore a multiplier circuit either runs much slower or it is designed significantly larger in area to run as fast. A straightforward low power/small area implementation of an n-bit multiplication can be achieved via n additions and n shift operations. Therefore, in serialized hardware implementation the complexity of an n-bit multiplication may be assumed to be roughly equal to the complexity of n additions and n shift operations. Using the same approach, we may assume that multiplication by a constant n-bit number can be achieved with $n/2$ shifts and $n/2$ additions on average. Under these assumptions, Table 3 gives the complexities of modular multiplication in $GF(q^{13})$ for all three methods when $q = 2^{13} - 1$ and $GF(q^{13})$ is constructed using the irreducible binomial $f(x) = x^{13} - 2$. The table also includes the total number of clock cycles that a single multiplication with these methods takes, assuming addition/subtraction and rotation operations all take a single clock cycle. Note that this finite field has size $\sim 2^{169}$ and is chosen to be representative for elliptic curve cryptography. We would like to note that all values in Table 3 are

Table 3. Complexity of multiplication in $GF(q^{13})$ where $f(x) = x^{13} - 2$, $q = 2^{13} - 1$, $d = 26$ and $r = -2$

	Algorithm 1	Karatsuba	Algorithm 2
#Multiplication	26	91	26
#Const. Mult.	26	$-$	12
#Add./Subtr.	1300	390	936
#Rotation	1250	12	624
#Total Clock Cycles	3564	2768	2392

obtained directly from Table 2, except for the exact complexity of Karatsuba multiplication for $GF(q^{13})$ which we draw from [17] .

Finally, we would like to note that for composite values of d, the FFT algorithm would apply to both Algorithm 1 and Algorithm 2 similarly for efficient computations. However, since in our case d does not take highly composite values (see Table 1), the speed up gained by possible application of FFT would be limited. Hence, for the generality and simplicity of our analysis, we did not consider the effect of using FFT in our complexity derivations.

5   Future Work

The DFT modular multiplication algorithm presented in this paper may efficiently apply to binary fields, i.e. $GF(2^m)$, or prime fields, i.e. $GF(p)$, as well by using similar efficient parameters and methods. We identify investigation of such efficient parameters and methods, as well as architectures for their efficient implementations, as future research directions.

6   Conclusion

We introduced the DFT modular multiplication algorithm which performs modular multiplication in the frequency domain using Montgomery reduction. The DFT based multiplication technique, which performs multiplication in the frequency domain, is known to be very efficient. Nevertheless, due to the lack of a frequency domain reduction algorithm, for performing modular reductions conversion to the time domain is needed, which adds a significant overhead and makes the DFT based multiplication algorithms impractical for small operands, e.g. less than 1000 bits in length. In this work, by allowing for modular reductions in the frequency domain the overhead of back and forth conversions between the frequency and the time domains is avoided, and thus efficient finite field multiplication is made possible for cryptographic operand sizes. We have shown that with our method, especially in computationally constrained platforms, finite field multiplication can be achieved more efficiently in the frequency domain than in the time domain for even small finite field sizes, e.g. ~ 160 bits, relevant to elliptic curve cryptography.

Acknowledgements

This work was supported by NSF CAREER award ANI-0133297.

References

1. E. R. Berlekamp. *Algebraic Coding Theory*. McGraw-Hill, New York, New York, USA, 1968.
2. R. E. Blahut. *Theory and Practice of Error Control Codes*. Addison-Wesley, Reading, Massachusetts, USA, 1983.
3. R. E. Blahut. *Fast Algorithms for Digital Signal Processing*. Addison-Wesley, Reading, Massachusetts, USA, 1985.
4. I.F. Blake, X.H. Gao, R.C. Mullin, S.A. Vanstone, and T. Yaghgoobin. *Applications of Finite Fields*. Kluwer Academic, 1999.
5. I.F. Blake, G. Seroussi, and N. Smart. *Elliptic Curves in Cryptography*. Cambridge University Press, London Mathematical Society Lecture Notes Series 265, 1999.

6. J. Cooley and J. Tukey. An Algorithm for the Machine Calculation of Complex Fourier Series. *Mathematics of Computation*, 19:297–301, 1965.

7. R. Crandall and C. Pomerance. *Prime Numbers*. Springer-Verlag, New York, NY, USA, 2001.

8. A. Karatsuba and Y. Ofman. Multiplication of Multidigit Numbers on Automata. *Sov. Phys. Dokl. (English translation)*, 7(7):595–596, 1963.

9. Ç. K Koç and T. Acar. Montgomery Multplication in $GF(2^k)$. *Design, Codes, and Cryptography*, 14(1):57–69, 1998.

10. Ç. K Koç, T. Acar, and B. Kaliski. Analyzing and Comparing Montgomery Multiplication Algorithms. *IEEE Micro*, pages 26–33, June 1996.

11. R. J. McEliece. *Finite Fields for Computer Scientists and Engineers*. Kluwer Academic Publishers, 2nd edition, 1989.

12. P. L. Montgomery. Modular Multiplication without Trial Division. *Mathematics of Computation*, 44(170):519–521, April 1985.

13. C. Paar. *Efficient VLSI Architectures for Bit-Parallel Computation in Galois Fields*. PhD thesis, (Engl. transl.), Institute for Experimental Mathematics, University of Essen, Essen, Germany, June 1994. ISBN 3–18–332810–0.

14. J. M. Pollard. The Fast Fourier Transform in a Finite Field. *Mathematics of Computation*, 25:365–374, 1971.

15. C. M. Rader. Discrete Convolutions via Mersenne Transforms. *IEEE Transactions on Computers*, C-21(12):1269–1273, December 1972.

16. A. Schönhage and V. Strassen. Schnelle Multiplikation großer Zahlen. *Computing*, 7:281–292, 1971.

17. A. Weimerskirch and C. Paar. Generalizations of the Karatsuba Algorithm for Efficient Implementations. Technical report, Department of Electrical Engineering and Information Sciences, Ruhr-Universität Bochum, Germany.

A Threshold Proxy Signature Scheme with Nonrepudiation and Anonymity

Yuan Yumin

Department of Mathematics and Physics, Xiamen University of Technology,
Xiamen 361005, P.R. China
yuanymp@163.com

Abstract. In 2004, Shao pointed out that both Sun et al.'s and Hsu et al.'s threshold proxy signature schemes are vulnerable to coalition attack. For enhancing the security, Shao proposed an improved scheme with anonymity to outsiders. This signature scheme is meaningless to any outsider because there is no way for him to prove each individual proxy signing public key validity. We further propose a practical threshold proxy signature scheme to remedy this drawback. The new scheme has the following advantages: (1) Any verifier can check whether the authors of the proxy signature belong to the designated proxy group by the original signer, while outsiders cannot find the actual signers; (2) The original signer can identify the actual proxy signers; (3) The verification of the proxy signing public keys of the proxy signers and the threshold proxy signature can be accomplished within a signature verification procedure simultaneously.

Keywords: Digital signature, proxy signature, threshold proxy signature, anonymity, nonrepudiation.

1 Introduction

1996, Mambo, Usuda, and Okamoto first proposed the concept of proxy signature [1,2]. In the proxy signature scheme, an original signer is allowed to delegate his signing power to a designated person, called the proxy signer, and the proxy signer is able to sign the message on behalf of the original signer.

In some cases, the original signer may delegate his signing power to the specified proxy group for sharing signing responsibility. To achieve such purpose, by integrating the concepts of proxy signature and threshold signature, the concept of a (t, n) threshold proxy signature scheme was proposed. In such a (t, n) threshold proxy signature scheme, the original signer delegates his signing capability to a designated proxy group of n members, and only t or more proxy signers of the group can represent the proxy group to cooperatively generate a proxy signature on behalf of the original signer, while $t-1$ or less proxy signers cannot. So far, there have been many threshold proxy signature schemes proposed. Sun et al. proposed a new (t, n) threshold proxy signature scheme [3] based on Zhang's threshold proxy signature scheme [4]. Recently, Hsu et al. [5] pointed out that Sun et al.'s scheme suffered from a drawback that it is possible for the proxy signers to alter the threshold value and

A. Levi et al. (Eds.): ISCIS 2006, LNCS 4263, pp. 1002–1010, 2006.

proposed an improvement. In 2004, Shao [6] showed that both Sun et al.'s scheme [3] and Hsu et al.'s improvement [5] are not secure against coalition attack, that is, any t or more malicious proxy signers can conspire together against the original signer. This coalition attack is inherent in many threshold signature schemes [7-10] using secret sharing techniques. To resist this attack, Shao [6] proposed an improved scheme with anonymity to outsiders by using secondary public keys to hide the identities of the proxy signers. However, the secondary public keys suffer from the authentication problem, in fact, Shao's scheme doesn't provide authentication of the secondary public keys by outsiders. In practice, such scheme is obviously impractical and insecure. Devising a secure threshold proxy signature scheme providing both against the collusion attack and anonymity were until now an open problem. To solve this problem, we further propose a practical threshold proxy signature scheme. The improved threshold proxy scheme will still maintain the advantage of Shao's scheme that the original signer can identify the actual signers, while any outsider cannot trace the actual signers. Furthermore, the novel scheme provides that any verifier can check whether the authors of the proxy signature belong to the proxy group designated by the original signer. Furthermore, the authenticity of the individual proxy signing public key of each user can be checked without any extra certificates and can be carried out simultaneously with the corresponding signature verification.

The rest of the paper is organized as follows: Shao's signature scheme is briefly reviewed in Section 2. Then, our cryptanalysis of Shao's scheme is given in Section 3. In Section 4, we propose a new threshold proxy signature scheme. The security analysis of our scheme is given in section 5. Finally, our conclusion will be in Section 6.

2   Brief Review of Shao's Improvement Scheme

Let p be a large prime, q be a prime factor q of $p-1$, g be an element of order q over $GF(p)$, and $h(\cdot)$ a secure one-way hash function. The parameters (p, q, g) and the function $h(\cdot)$ are made public. The private key and the public key for each user P_i are $x_i \in \mathbb{Z}_q$ and $y_i = g^{x_i} \bmod p$, respectively. Suppose that an original signer P_0 with a key pair (x_0, y_0) wants to delegate his signing power to a proxy group $G = \{P_1, P_2, \ldots, P_n\}$ of n proxy signers in such a way that a proxy signature can be created by any subset of t or more proxy signers from G. Shao's scheme can be divided into the following two stages: proxy share generation stage and proxy signature generation stage.

2.1   Proxy Share Generation

Secondary private/public key generation:

1. Each proxy signer P_i chooses a secondary private key v_i and computes the corresponding secondary public key $z_i = g^{v_i} \bmod p$.

2. The proxy signer chooses a random integer w in $\mathbb{Z}_q$ and computes $r' = g^w \bmod p$, $s' = w + (x_i y_i + v_i z_i) h(r', z_i, C) \bmod q$, where C commits as a proxy

signer. Then the proxy signer P_i sends $(r', y_0^w s', y_0^w z_i, y_0^w C \bmod p)$ to the original signer P_0.

3. Upon receiving $(r', y_0^w s', y_0^w z_i, y_0^w C \bmod p)$, the original signer P_0 computes $y_0^w = (r')^{x_0} \bmod p$ and recovers (r', s', z_i, C) . Then he verifies the secondary public key z_i and the commit C by checking the following equation: $g^{s'} = (y_i^{y_i} z_i^{z_i})^{h(r', z_i, C)} r' \bmod p$.

For delegating the signing power to G ,

1. The original signer P_0 chooses a random integer k in $\mathbb{Z}_q$ and computes $r = g^k \bmod p$, $s = (x_0 h(r, \mathrm{PGID}) + k)t^{-1} \bmod q$, where PGID records the proxy status, containing the identity and the public key y_0 of the original signer, the secondary public keys $(z_1, z_2, \dots, z_n)$ of the proxy signers, the threshold value t and the expiration time of the delegation. Then the original signer P_0 broadcasts (r, s, PGID) to each proxy signer P_i .

2. Each proxy signer can verify (r, s, PGID) by checking the equation

$$g^{ts} = y_0^{h(r, \mathrm{PGID})} r \bmod p$$

2.2 Proxy Signature Generation

Let m be the message to be signed. Without loss of generality, let $P_1, P_2, \dots, P_t$ be t proxy signers with the secondary public keys $z_1, z_2, \dots, z_t$, respectively, who want to cooperatively generate the proxy signature for m. Each participant proxy signer P_i chooses a random integer k_i in $\mathbb{Z}_q$, and computes and broadcasts $Y_i = g^{k_i} \bmod p$. Then each participant computes $Y = \prod_{i=1}^{t} Y_i \bmod p$, $T_i = (s + v_i h(r, \mathrm{PGID}))h(m) + k_i Y \bmod q$ and broadcasts (i, T_i) . Consequently, the proxy signature of m is $(r, \mathrm{PGID}, Y, T, (1, 2, \dots, t))$, where $T = \sum_{i=1}^{t} T_i \bmod q$. The verification equation of the proxy

$$g^T = \left(\left(y_0 \prod_{i=1}^{t} z_i \right)^{h(r, \mathrm{PGID})} r \right)^{h(m)} Y^Y \bmod p$$

where $(1, 2, \dots, t)$ can be denoted by an integer, the i th bit of which is equal to 1 if and only if the secondary public key z_i is involved in the verification equation.

3   Cryptanalysis of Shao's Scheme

Shao claims that in his scheme [6], it's impossible that z_i is a false secondary public key. The reason is that other proxy signers in the proxy group can detect such proxy signatures since they know the actual signers and defend themselves by asking the original signer to reveal (r_i', s_i', z_i, C_i) committed by each proxy signer involved in the forged proxy signatures. This implies only the proxy signers can find whether there is any false secondary public key using in a proxy signature. It may be impractical and unreasonable for some applications since once the original signer uses false secondary public keys to forge threshold proxy signatures, any outsider cannot detect such wrong proxy signatures. The reason for this is that the outsider is unable to distinguish whether $(z_1, z_2, \ldots, z_n)$ is created by the legal proxy signers, unless he asks the original signer to reveal (r_i', s_i', z_i, C_i) (but this violates the anonymous property to outsider).

4 The Proposed Scheme

In this section, we will propose a new scheme to remedy the weakness as described in Section 3. Similar to Shao's scheme, by using the proxy signing public keys, the identities of the proxy signers are hided in our scheme. In addition, our scheme provides the verification of the authenticity of proxy signing public keys of proxy signers within the signature verification procedure to guard against the original signer's forge attack.

The proposed scheme is divided into three stages: proxy share generation, proxy signature generation, and proxy signature verification. Besides, the notations $\{p, q, g, P_i, x_i, y_i, h(\cdot)\}$ are the same as those in the Shao's scheme. Our scheme is composed of the following procedure.

4.1 Proxy Share Generation

Suppose that the original signer P_0 wants to delegate the signing power to the proxy group G. Each proxy signer $P_i \in G$ first chooses his proxy signing private key and sends the corresponding public key to the original signer to make the proxy group identity PGID. Then, each proxy signer signs the proxy group identity PGID, to achieve the correctness of his proxy signing private key containing in PGID. After that, the original signers P_0 signs PGID to generate the proxy share. In the following, the details are given.

1. Each proxy signer $P_i \in G$ selects a random integer $k_i \in \mathbb{Z}_q^*$, computes $K_i = g^{k_i} \bmod p$, and broadcasts K_i to the other $n-1$ proxy signers in the proxy group.

2. Each proxy signer P_i chooses a proxy signing private key v_i and computes the corresponding public key $z_i = g^{v_i} \bmod p$. Then, P_i computes $k_i' = y_0^{k_i} \bmod p$, $z_i^* = h(k_i')z_i$, and sends (K_i, z_i^*) to the original signer.

3. Upon receiving all (K_i, z_i^*), the original signer P_0 first computes $k_i' = y_0^{k_i} = K_i^{x_0} \bmod p$, $h(k_i')$, and recovers z_i by using $h(k_i')$. Then, P_0 chooses a random integer $k_0 \in \mathbb{Z}_q^*$ and computes $K_0 = g^{k_0} \bmod p$. After that, P_0 broadcasts $(K_0,$ PGID) to each proxy signer P_i in G, where PGID records the proxy status,

containing the identity of the original signer, the identities of the proxy signers in G, the proxy signing public keys $(z_1, z_2, \dots, z_n)$ of the proxy signers, the threshold value t and the expiration time of the delegation.

4. After receiving PGID, each $P_i \in G$ checks the correctness of his proxy signing public key containing in PGID. If so, P_i computes $K = \prod_{j=0}^{n} K_j \mod p$ and uses his private key x_i and proxy signing private key v_i to compute $s_i = x_i y_i h(K, \text{PGID}) + v_i + k_i \mod q$. At last, he sends $k_i' s_i$ to P_0.

5. After receiving all $k_i' s_i$ (for $i = 1, 2, \dots, n$), the original signer P_0 recovers s_i by using k_i'. Then, he checks the validity of (s_i, z_i, K_i) by the following equation:

$$g^{s_i} = \left(y_i^{y_i}\right)^{h(K,\text{PGID})} z_i K_i \mod p \qquad (1)$$

If it does not, P_0 requests the corresponding proxy signer to deliver a new one. If all s_i's are valid, P_0 computes $s_0 = x_0 y_0 h(K, \text{PGID}) + k_0 \mod q$ and broadcasts s to $P_i \in G$, where $s = s_0 + \sum_{i=1}^{n} s_i \mod q$.

6. After receiving s, each $P_i \in G$ can validate it using the following equation

$$g^{s} = \left(y_0^{y_0} \prod_{i=1}^{n} y_i^{y_i}\right)^{h(K,\text{PGID})} \prod_{i=1}^{n} z_i K \mod p \qquad (2)$$

If it holds, P_i accepts s as a valid proxy share.

4.2 Proxy Signature Generation

Without loss of generality, let $\{P_i \mid i \in A\}$ be t' proxy signers in the proxy group G, where $t \le t' \le n$, $A \subset \{1, 2, \dots, n\}$ and $|A| = t'$, who want to cooperatively generate a proxy signature for the message m on behalf of the original signer. Let $\text{ASPK} = (z_i \mid i \in A)$ be the actual signers' proxy signing public keys, to generate the proxy signature for m, each participant proxy signer P_i ($i \in A$) executes the following steps:

1. P_i ($i \in A$) chooses a random number $r_i \in \mathbb{Z}_q^*$, computes $R_i = g^{r_i} \mod p$, and broadcasts (R_i, i).

2. Each participant proxy signer computes $R = \prod_{i \in A} R_i \mod p$, $T_i = (t'^{-1} \cdot s - v_i) h(R, \text{ASPK}, \text{PGID}, m) + r_i \mod q$ as the individual signature of m, and broadcasts (T_i, i).

3. Upon receipt of T_i ($i \in A$), each participant validates the individual signature (R_i, T_i) of m by checking the following equation:

$$g^{T_i} = \left(\left(\left(y_0^{y_0} \prod_{j=1}^{n} y_j^{y_j}\right)^{h(K,\text{PGID})} \prod_{j=1}^{n} z_j K\right)^{t'^{-1}} z_i^{-1}\right)^{h(R,\text{ASPK},\text{PGID},m)} R_i \mod p \qquad (3)$$

If all T_i's are verified, he computes $T = \sum_{i \in A} T_i \bmod q$. Consequently, the proxy signature of m is $(PGID, K, R, T, ASPK)$.

4.3 Proxy Signature Verification

When a verifier receives a signature $(PGID, K, R, T, ASPK, m)$, he should run the following steps to verify its validity.

1. Check the validity of $PGID$.
2. Verify the following equation:

$$g^T = \left(\left(y_0^{y_0} \prod_{i=1}^{n} y_i^{y_i} \right)^{h(K, PGID)} \left(\prod_{i \notin A} z_i \right) K \right)^{h(R, ASPK, PGID, m)} R \bmod p \tag{4}$$

If it holds, the proxy signature $(PGID, K, R, T, ASPK, m)$ is accepted, otherwise, it will be rejected.

5 Analysis of the New Scheme

Now we will analyze the security of our scheme. The security of the proposed scheme is based on the difficulty of computing discrete logarithm and the difficulty of solving one-way function inverse. Several possible attacks will be considered, but none of them can successfully break the scheme.

5.1 Anonymity

Assume that an attacker wants to know the identities of the actual signers from a proxy signature. If he has intercepted K_i, z_i^* and $k_i' s_i$ sent to the original signer by the proxy signer P_i, and obtains the corresponding proxy signature $(PGID, K, R, T, ASPK, m)$ afterward, he attempts to disclose the identity of the proxy signer who sent K_i, z_i^* and $k_i' s_i$. Though he can compute $h(k_i')$ by $h(k_i') = z_i^* / z_i$, here z_i is obtained by $PGID$, he cannot know k_i' because of the difficulty of solving one-way function inverse. Consequently, he cannot obtain s_i from $k_i' s_i$. Since s_i that is a signature on $PGID$ signed by proxy signer P_i is unknown, the attacker cannot find any information on the relationship between the proxy signing public key z_i and the public key y_i of the proxy signer P_i from the public information. Identifying the actual signers is computationally hard for any outsider in our threshold proxy signature.

5.2 Security Against Chosen Message Attack

Theorem 1. *If an attacker can forge an individual signature* $(PGID, ASPK, K, R, R_i, T_i)$ *for message m satisfying Eq.(3), in probabilistic polynomial time (PPT) with* *non-negligible probability, then he can also compute discrete logs in PPT with non-negligible probability.*

Proof. The exact probabilistic analysis is based on the forking lemma of [11,12], and is quite similar to the one for the standard Schnorr signature scheme. If a chosen message attack produces with non-negligible probability a valid signature $(\text{PGID}, \text{ASPK}, K, R, R_i, T_i, m)$ on the message m, then a replay of this attack produces with non-negligible probability another valid signature $(\text{PGID}, \text{ASPK}, K, R, R_i, T_i', m')$ with $h_2 \neq h_2'$, where $h_2 = h(R, \text{ASPK}, \text{PGID}, m)$ and $h_2' = h(R, \text{ASPK}, \text{PGID}, m')$. Using the verification equation (3), we obtain

$$g^{T_i} = \left(\left(g^s \right)^{t^{-1}} z_i^{-1} \right)^{h_2} R_i \bmod p \ \text{ and } \ g^{T_i'} = \left(\left(g^s \right)^{t^{-1}} z_i^{-1} \right)^{h_2'} R_i \bmod p$$

So $g^{s \cdot t^{-1} - v_i} = \left(g^s \right)^{t^{-1}} z_i^{-1} = g^{(T_i - T_i')/(h_2 - h_2')} \bmod p$. He can compute $\sigma_i = t'^{-1} \cdot s - v_i$, the discrete log of $\left(g^s \right)^{t^{-1}} z_i^{-1}$, by $\sigma_i = (T_i - T_i')(h_2 - h_2')^{-1} \bmod q$. Therefore, he can obtain the proxy signer P_i's the proxy signing private key $v_i = t'^{-1} \cdot s - (T_i - T_i')(h_2 - h_2')^{-1} \bmod q$ as long as he knows proxy share s. $\square$

For the same reason, we have **Theorem 2.**

Theorem 2. *If an attacker can forge an proxy signature $(\text{PGID}, \text{ASPK}, K, R, T)$ for message m satisfying Eq.(3), in PPT with non-negligible probability, then he can also compute discrete logs in PPT with non-negligible probability.*

5.3 Security Against Chosen Proxy Signing Key Attack

Lemma (the forking lemma). *If an attacker can forge a valid proxy signature $(\text{PGID}, K, R, T, \text{ASPK}, m)$ with the proxy signing public keys $(z_i \mid i \notin A)$, in PPT with non-negligible probability, then he can forge the valid proxy signature $(\text{PGID}', K', R, T', \text{ASPK}', m)$ with the proxy signing public keys $(z_i' \mid i \notin A)$, in PPT with non-negligible probability, such that $\left(\prod_{i \notin A} z_i \right) K = \left(\prod_{i \notin A} z_i' \right) K'$, while $(z_i \mid i \notin A) \neq (z_i' \mid i \notin A)$.*

Proof. (proof Sketch) Similar to the proof of the Forking Lemma [11,12], by replays of with the same random tapes $\left(\prod_{i \notin A} z_i \right) K$ and R but different choices of oracles h_1 and h_2, as done in the Forking Lemma [11,12], we can obtain two valid proxy signatures $(\text{PGID}, K, R, T, \text{ASPK}, m)$ and $(\text{PGID}', K', R, T', \text{ASPK}, m)$, in PPT with non-negligible probability, such that $h_1 \neq h_1'$ and $h_2 \neq h_2'$, where $h_1 = h(K, \text{PGID})$, $h_1' = h(K', \text{PGID}')$, $h_2 = h(R, \text{ASPK}, \text{PGID}, m)$ and $h_2' = h(R, \text{ASPK}', \text{PGID}', m)$. $\square$

Theorem 3. *If an attacker can forge a valid proxy signature* $(\text{PGID}, K, R, T, \text{ASPK}, m)$ *with false proxy signing public keys* $(z_i \mid i \notin A)$, *in PPT with non-negligible probability, then he can also compute discrete logs in PPT with non-negligible probability.*

Proof. If the attacker can forge valid proxy signature by choosing false proxy signing public keys, *in PPT with non-negligible probability*, by using the forking lemma twice, he can obtains three valid proxy signatures $(\text{PGID}^{(j)}, K^{(j)}, R, T^{(j)}, \text{ASPK}^{(j)}, m)$ (for $j = 1, 2, 3$), with non-negligible probability, such that $\left(\prod_{i \notin A} z_i^{(1)} \right) K^{(1)} = \left(\prod_{i \notin A} z_i^{(2)} \right) \cdot K^{(2)} = \left(\prod_{i \notin A} z_i^{(3)} \right) K^{(3)}$, while the determinant $D = \begin{vmatrix} h_1^{(1)} h_2^{(1)} - h_1^{(2)} h_2^{(2)} & h_2^{(1)} - h_2^{(2)} \\ h_1^{(1)} h_2^{(1)} - h_1^{(3)} h_2^{(3)} & h_2^{(1)} - h_2^{(3)} \end{vmatrix} \neq 0$, where $h_1^{(j)} = h(K^{(j)}, \text{PGID}^{(j)})$ and $h_2^{(j)} = h(R, \text{ASPK}^{(j)}, \text{PGID}^{(j)}, m)$ (for $j = 1, 2, 3$). Using the verification equation (4), we obtain

$$g^{T^{(j)}} = \left(\left(y_0^{y_0} \prod_{i=1}^{n} y_i^{y_i} \right)^{h_1^{(j)}} \left(\prod_{i \notin A} z_i^{(j)} \right) K^{(j)} \right)^{h_2^{(j)}} R \bmod p$$

Let $g^{\sigma} = \left(\prod_{i \notin A} z_i^{(j)} \right) K^{(j)} \bmod p$. For $j, l = 1, 2, 3$ and $j \neq l$,

$$g^{T^{(j)} - T^{(l)}} = g^{\sum_{i=0}^{n} x_i y_i (h_1^{(j)} h_2^{(j)} - h_1^{(l)} h_2^{(l)}) + \sigma(h_2^{(j)} - h_2^{(l)})} \bmod p$$

Thus

$$\begin{cases} \sum_{i=0}^{n} x_i y_i (h_1^{(1)} h_2^{(1)} - h_1^{(2)} h_2^{(2)}) + \sigma(h_2^{(1)} - h_2^{(2)}) = T^{(1)} - T^{(2)} \\ \sum_{i=0}^{n} x_i y_i (h_1^{(1)} h_2^{(1)} - h_1^{(3)} h_2^{(3)}) + \sigma(h_2^{(1)} - h_2^{(3)}) = T^{(1)} - T^{(3)} \end{cases} \tag{5}$$

Note that the two equations in Eq. (5) contain only two unknown symbols, and the determinant of coefficient $D \neq 0$. Therefore, by Cramer's rule, two simultaneous equations in Eq. (5) has unique solution, that is, the secrets $\sum_{i=0}^{n} x_i y_i$, σ can be obtained, while $\sum_{i=0}^{n} x_i y_i$ is the discrete log of $\prod_{i=0}^{n} y_i^{y_i}$. □

From **Theorem [1,2,3]**, we know that in the random oracle model, our proposed threshold proxy signature is secure against chosen message attack, chosen proxy signing key attack and chosen proxy group identity PGID attack. Therefore, it provides unforgeability and nonrepudiation.

6 Conclusion

In this paper, we show that Shao's scheme doesn't provide authentication of the proxy signing public keys by outsiders. To overcome this flaw, we propose further a scheme with nonrepudiation and anonymity. As compared with Shao's scheme, the new scheme not only inherits the advantage of Shao's scheme that any outsider is incapable of identifying the actual signers, but also takes the advantage of that any one can verify the validity of the proxy signing public keys. Moreover the verification of the proxy signing public keys of the proxy signers and threshold proxy signature can be accomplished within a signature verification procedure simultaneously while the relation between the proxy signer and his proxy signing public key is still kept in secret.

Acknowledgements. The author of this paper would like to thank the anonymous reviewers for their suggestions and comments.

References

1. Mambo, M., Usuda, K., Okamoto, E.: Proxy signatures: Delegation of the power to sign message. IEICE Transaction of Fundamentals E79-A (9) (1996) 1338–1354.
2. Mambo, M., Usuda, K. Okamoto, E.: Proxy signatures for delegation signing operation. Proceedings of 3rd ACM Conference on Computer and Communication Security (1996) 48–57.
3. Sun, H.M., Lee, N.Y., Hwang, T.: Threshold proxy signature scheme. IEE Proc., Comput. Digit. Tech, 146 (5) (1999) 259– 263.
4. Zhang, K.: Threshold Proxy Signature Schemes. Proc. Information Security Workshop (ISW'97), LNCS 1396, Springer-Verlag, (1997) 282-290.
5. Hsu, C.L., Wu, T.S., Wu, T.C.: Improvement of threshold proxy signature scheme. Applied Mathematics and Computation, Volume 136, Issues 2-3, 15 March 2003, 315-321.
6. Shao, Z.: Improvement of threshold proxy signature scheme. Computer Standards & Interfaces, Volume 27, Issue 1, November (2004) 53-59.
7. Wu, T.S., Hsu, C.L.: Threshold signature scheme using self-certified public keys. The Journal of Systems and Software, vol. 67, (2003) 89-97.
8. Wang, M., Liu, Z.J.: An identity-based proxy ring signature scheme from bilinear pairings. Computer and Information Technology (CIT'05) (2005) 695 – 699.
9. Cheng, X.G., Liu, J.M., Wang, X.M.: An Identity-Based Signature and Its Threshold Version. Advanced Information Networking and Applications (AINA'05) Volume 1 (2005) 973-977.
10. Yu, Y.L., Chen, T.S.: An efficient threshold group signature scheme. Applied Mathematics and Computation 167 (2005) 362–371.
11. Pointcheval, D., Stern, J.: Security proofs for signatures, In: Eurocrypt'96, LNCS, vol. 1070, Springer-Verlag, Berlin Heidelberg New York (1996) 387–398.
12. Pointcheval, D., Stern, J.: Security arguments for digital signatures and blind signatures, J. Cryptol. 13 (3). Springer-Verlag, Berlin Heidelberg New York (2000) 361– 396.

Deterministic Analysis of Balancedness in Symmetric Cryptography*

Candelaria Hernández-Goya[1] and Amparo Fúster-Sabater[2]

[1] Dept. of Statistics, Operations Research and Computation
University of La Laguna
38271 La Laguna, Tenerife, Spain
mchgoya@ull.es
[2] Instituto de Física Aplicada, C.S.I.C.
Serrano 144, 28006 Madrid, Spain
amparo@iec.csic.es

Abstract. An efficient algorithm to compute the degree of balancedness in LFSR-based sequence generators has been developed. The computation is realized by means of logic operations on bit-strings. Emphasis is on the computational features of this algorithm. The procedure checks deviation of balancedness from standard values for this type of generators with application in symmetric cryptography.

Keywords: Confidentiality, bit-string algorithm, balancedness, cryptography.

1   Introduction

Computer users have become aware of the importance of security mechanisms when dealing with transactions of information. Nowadays, security services as confidentiality are required in all kind of scenarios, from leisure to industrial applications (pay-per-view tv, videoconferences, wireless communication: UMTS, Bluetooth, e-commerce, etc.)

Confidentiality makes use of an encryption function currently called *cipher* that converts the *plaintext* into the *ciphertext*. Ciphers are usually divided into two large classes: stream ciphers and block-ciphers. Stream ciphers are very fast (in fact, the fastest among the encryption procedures) so they are implemented in many technological applications e.g. the stream cipher RC4 [9] used in Microsoft Word and Excel, algorithms A5 in GSM communications [5] or the encryption system E0 used in the Bluetooth specifications. Stream ciphers try to imitate the ultimate one-time pad cipher and are supposed to be good pseudorandom generators capable of stretching a short secret seed (the secret key) into a long sequence of seemingly random bits. This key-stream is then XORed with the plaintext in order to obtain the ciphertext. Most generators producing key-stream sequence are based on Linear Feedback Shift Registers (LFSRs) [4]. The

---

* Research supported by Ministerio de Educación y Ciencia (Spain) under grants SEG2004-04352-C04-03 and SEG2004-02418.

A. Levi et al. (Eds.): ISCIS 2006, LNCS 4263, pp. 1011–1020, 2006.

pseudorandom output sequence is a periodic sequence generated as the image of a nonlinear Boolean function in the LFSR stages.

Balancedness in the output sequence is a necessary although never sufficient condition that every cryptographic generator must satisfy. Roughly speaking, a binary sequence is balanced if it has approximately the same number of $1's$ as $0's$. Due to the long period of the generated sequence ($T \simeq 10^{38}$ bits in current cryptographic applications), it is unfeasible to produce an entire cycle of such a sequence and then count the number of $1's$ and $0's$. Therefore, in practical design of binary generators, portions of the output sequence are chosen randomly and statistical tests (frequency test or monobit test [8]) are applied to all these subsequences. Nevertheless, passing the previous tests merely provides *probabilistic evidence* that the generator produces a balanced sequence (see [10]).

In the present work, balancedness of LFSR-based generators has been treated in a *deterministic way*. In fact, an efficient bit-string algorithm allows one to compute the exact number of $1's$ (number of $0's$) in the output sequence without producing the whole sequence. The general expression of the number of $1's$ is obtained as a function of the generator parameters. The number of $0's$ is just the sequence period minus the number of $1's$. In this way, the degree of balancedness of the sequence can be perfectly checked: the obtained number of $1's$ ($0's$) is compared with the value required for this sequence to be balanced (half the period $\pm$ a tolerance interval). In case of non-accordance, the LFSR-based generator must be rejected. Thus, the procedure here developed can be considered as a first selective criterium for acceptance/rejection of this type of generators.

The computational method is based exclusively on the handling of binary strings by means of logic operations. Indeed, the general expression of the number of digits is just an interpretation of such binary strings. Numerical results of the computation are presented as well as the complexity of the algorithm has been analyzed. In brief, the algorithm can be executed on a simple PC computer with adequate time and memory requirements. Thus, the procedure can be applied to cryptographic generators proposed and published in the open literature.

2   Fundamentals and Basic Concepts

Several basic concepts and definitions to be used throughout the paper are presented in this section.

A minterm of L binary variables (a_0, a_1, ..., a_{L-1}) is the logic product of the L variables, where each variable can be in its true or complementary form. For L variables, there exist 2^L different minterms. If a minterm includes the variables a_i ... a_j in their true form while the rest are in complementary form, then such a minterm is denoted by $A_{i...j}$. Since a binary sequence generator is characterized by a Boolean function, two different representations of such functions are considered:

(i) *Algebraic Normal Form (A.N.F.)* ([7], [11]) expresses the function as the exclusive-OR sum of logic products in the L variables, for instance

$$F_1(a_0, a_1, ..., a_{L-1}) = a_0\, a_1\, a_{L-1} \oplus a_1\, a_{L-2} \oplus a_{L-1},$$

(ii) *Minterm representation* ([7], [11]) expresses the function as a linear combination of its minterms, for instance

$$F_2(a_0, a_1, ..., a_{L-1}) = A_{012} \oplus A_{0L-2} \oplus A_{2\,L-2\,L-1}.$$

A binary LFSR is an electronic device with L memory elements (stages), cyclic shifting and linear feedback [4]. An LFSR-based generator is a nonlinear Boolean function F in A.N.F. whose input variables are the binary contents of the LFSR stages. At each new clock pulse, the new binary contents of the stages will be the new input variables of the function F. In this way, the generator produces the successive bits of the output sequence.

Next, let us introduce the dual function of F.

Definition 1. *The dual function of F, notated Φ_F, is a nonlinear Boolean function that substitutes each term $a_i\, a_j \dots a_k$ of F for its corresponding minterm $A_{ij\dots k}$. The function Φ_F is an involution.*

$$F(a_i) = a_0\, a_1 \oplus a_2 \quad \Rightarrow \quad \Phi_F(a_i) = A_{01} \oplus A_2.$$

A minterm function is a minterm of L variables expressed in A.N.F. Every minterm function can be easily obtained by expanding out the corresponding minterm. Let $A_{i\dots j}$ be a minterm with d indexes $(1 \le d \le L)$. According to [3], its corresponding minterm function is perfectly characterized. In fact, the total number of terms is:

$$\text{No. of terms} = 2^{L-d}. \tag{1}$$

In addition, the number of terms of each order as well as the particular form of these terms are perfectly characterized too.

On the other hand, every minterm function considered as an generator applied to the L stages of an LFSR generates a canonical sequence with a unique 1 and period $T = 2^L - 1$ (see [10]). In brief, every LFSR-based generator can be expressed as a linear combination of its minterms and each minterm provides the output sequence with a unique 1. Thus, the basic idea of this work can be summarized as follows:

The number of minterms in the expression of F equals the number of $1's$ in the output sequence. Therefore, the aim is double: (i) to express the Boolean function in terms of its minterms, (ii) to count the number of such minterms.

As every cryptographic generator is designed in Algebraic Normal Form, the Boolean function F has first to be converted from its A.N.F. into its minterm expansion. The conversion procedure is carried out as follows [7]:

Input: A nonlinear function F given in A.N.F.

For instance, $F(a_0, a_1, a_2) = a_0\, a_2 \oplus a_1\, a_2 \oplus a_1.$

 − *Step 1:* Compute Φ_F

$$\Phi_F(a_0,\, a_1,\, a_2) = A_{02} \oplus A_{12} \oplus A_1.$$

 − *Step 2:* Substitute every minterm by its corresponding function in A.N.F. and cancel common terms

$$\Phi_F(a_0,\, a_1,\, a_2) = a_0\,\overline{a}_1\,a_2 \oplus \overline{a}_0\,a_1\,a_2 \oplus \overline{a}_0\,a_1\,\overline{a}_2 =$$

$$a_0\,a_1\,a_2 \oplus a_0\,a_1 \oplus a_0\,a_2 \oplus a_1.$$

 − *Step 3:* Compute $F(a_i) = \Phi_F \circ \Phi_F$

$$F(a_0,\, a_1,\, a_2) = \Phi_F(\Phi_F(a_0,\, a_1,\, a_2)) = A_{012} \oplus A_{01} \oplus A_{02} \oplus A_1.$$

Output: F expressed in terms of its minterms.
The number of minterms in step 3 (or equivalently the number of terms in step 2) coincides with the number of 1's in the generated sequence.

3   An Efficient Algorithm to Compute the Degree of Balancedness in Binary Generators

An algorithm that automates the comparison among the different terms in Φ_F, checks the cancelled terms and computes the number of final terms is presented. Such an algorithm is based on an L-bit string representation.

3.1   Specific Terminology for the Implementation

First of all some simplifications in the notation are introduced. A Greek letter (for example α) will represent the set of indexes $ij\ldots k$ above described to label the minterms, i.e. $A_{ij\ldots k} = A_\alpha$. A similar notation will be used for the product of LFSR stages, $a_i\,a_j\ldots a_k = a_{ij\ldots k} = a_\alpha$. According to this notation, the nonlinear function F and its dual function Φ_F can be rewritten as $F = \sum_{\oplus} a_{\alpha_i}$ and $\Phi_F = \sum_{\oplus} A_{\alpha_i}$, respectively. In the previous section, it was told that the minterm function A_α had in total $2^{L-d(\alpha)}$ terms, $d(\alpha)$ being the number of indexes in α. In order to implement this algorithm, every minterm function A_α is represented by a L-bit string numbered $0, 1, \ldots, L-1$ from right to left. If the n-th index is in the set α $(n \in \alpha)$, then the n-th bit of such a string takes the value 1; otherwise, the value will be 0. Thus, $d(\alpha)$ equals the number of 1's in the L-bit string that represents A_α.

Definition 2. *We call maximum common development (m.c.d.) of two minterm functions A_α and A_β, notated $MD(A_\alpha, A_\beta)$, to the minterm A_χ such that $\chi = \alpha \cup \beta$.*

Under the L-bit string representation of the minterms, the m.c.d. can be realized by means of a bitwise OR operation between the binary strings of both functions. The m.c.d. represents all the terms that A_α and A_β have in common. If two minterms A_α and A_β are added, $A_\alpha \oplus A_\beta$, then the terms corresponding to their m.c.d. are cancelled. Thus, the total number of terms in $A_\alpha \oplus A_\beta$ is the number of terms in A_α plus the number of terms in A_β minus twice the number of terms in the m.c.d., that is $2^{L-d(\alpha)} + 2^{L-d(\beta)} - 2 \cdot 2^{L-d(\alpha \cup \beta)}$.

Definition 3. *The auxiliary function H is defined as $H = \sum_i s_i A_{\alpha_i}$, s_i being an integer with sign that specifies how many times the function A_{a_i} is contained in H.*

In a symbolic way, H indicates whether the minterms A_{α_i} are added (sign $+$) or cancelled (sign $-$) as well as how many times such terms have been added or cancelled. Remark that the m.c.d. can be applied to the functions H too. Keeping in mind all these definitions, we can now describe the algorithm.

3.2   The Algorithm

Let $F = \sum_\oplus a_{\alpha_i}$ $(i = 1, ..., N)$ be a nonlinear Boolean function of N terms applied to the stages of an LFSR. In order to compute the number of $1's$ (notated $\mathcal{U}_F$) in the generated sequence, the following algorithm is introduced:

- *Step 1:* Define the function Φ_F from the N terms a_{α_i} of F. Initialize the function H with a null value, $H_0 = \oslash$.
- *Step 2:* Run this loop from $i = 1$ to $i = N$: update $H_i = H_{i-1} + A_{\alpha_i} - 2 \cdot MD(A_{\alpha_i}, H_{i-1})$.
- *Step 3:* From the final form of $H_N = \sum_j s_j A_{\beta_j}$, compute the number of $1's$ in the generated sequence by means of the expression $\mathcal{U}_F = \sum_j s_j \cdot 2^{L-d(\beta_j)}$.

Next subsections consider different features that can be derived from this algorithm.

3.3   Generators with Guaranteed Balancedness

From the previous algorithm, it can be noticed that if a minterm in Φ_F, for instance A_{α_N}, includes a unique non-repeated index, then at the N-th loop, the final updating of H is:

$$H_N = H_{N-1} + A_{\alpha_N} - 2 \cdot MD(A_{\alpha_N}, H_{N-1}).$$

Nevertheless, the terms $2 \cdot MD(A_{\alpha_N}, H_{N-1})$ and H_{N-1} in the second member contains exactly the same binary strings except for the new index. Thus, regarding the number of $1's$, we have for every pair of quasi-equal strings:

$$2^{L-k} - 2 \cdot 2^{L-k-1} = 2^{L-k} - 2^{L-k} = 0$$

for any k. Therefore, the final number of $1's$ in the sequence generated is due exclusively to the contribution of the term A_{α_N}. Thus, $\mathcal{U}_F = 2^{L-1}$.

Consequently, the output sequence of such generators will be balanced. That is the case of the TOYOCRYPT-HR1 keystream generator for the stream cipher TOYOCRYPT-HS1 [2]. In fact, this pseudorandom binary generator employs a LFSR of length $L = 128$ where the last stage, notated a_{127}, appears as a unique term with non-repeated index in the generating function F. In this practical example and according to the previous algorithm balancedness in the output sequence is always guaranteed.

This algorithm may be useful not only in the the analysis of non-linear filters, but also when the generators belong to the categories of combination generators or mutual clock controlled ones.

The shrinking generator fits in this second group. It is a binary sequence generator [1] composed of two LFSRs: a control register, LFSR A, that decimates the sequence produced by the other register, LFSR B. We denote by L_A, L_B their corresponding lengths where $(L_A, L_B) = 1$ and $L_A < L_B$.

The sequence produced by the LFSR A, that is $\{a_i\}$, controls the bits of the sequence produced by the LFSR B, that is $\{b_i\}$, which are included in the output sequence $\{c_j\}$ (the shrunken sequence). The decimation rule P is described as follows: If $a_i = 1$, then $c_j = b_i$. Otherwise b_i is discarded.

The period of the shrunken sequence [1] is $T = (2^{L_B} - 1)2^{(L_A-1)}$. The generating function in terms of a Boolean function has an only term: $F = a_0 b_0$, as the decimation affects the period of the output sequence but never the number of $1's$. In order to fix the L-bit strings, very low values are assigned to the lengths of the LFSRs: $L_A = 2, L_B = 3$ with $((L_A, L_B) = 1)$, thus $L = 5$. According to the previous section, we proceed:

Step 1.- $\Phi_F = A_0 B_0$ and its string format is: $M_{\alpha_1} = A_0 B_0 = 001\ 01$. H is initialized $H_0 = \oslash$.

Step 2.- The loop consists of just one iteration $i = 1$: $H_1 = \oslash + 001\ 01 - \oslash = 001\ 01$.

Step 3.- Finally: $\mathcal{U}_F = 2^{L_A-1} 2^{L_B-1}$.

For lengths of the LFSRs in a cryptographic range $L_i \approx 64$ the number of $1's$ in the output sequence is $\simeq T/2$. Consequently, the generated sequence is quasi balanced.

3.4   Remarks on the Algorithm Implementation

This section gathers some key factors taken into account in the implementation of the algorithm in order to enhance its efficiency.

This implementation has been carried out using the ANSI C programming language, since the operations to develop are mainly boolean operations involving the bit strings A_{α_i}. Hence, it has been an advantage that ANSI C provides so powerful bitwise operators.

The function Φ_F has been simulated through a linked list where each element contains an unsigned integer representing the corresponding minterm (field value) and a second signed integer (field coefficient) that will be used later in the construction of the MD list. This second field corresponds to the times the current minterm has been added or cancelled along the algorithm execution and until the current stage.

It should be noticed that storing the binary strings as unsigned integers allows to reduce the operations involved in this procedure to bitwise OR operations among the strings A_{α_i}. Once the list Φ_F has been built, the iterations described in 3.2 commence. During each iteration the construction of a new list corresponding to $MD(A_{\alpha_i}, H_{i-1})$ is required. The remaining calculations consists of linking the list obtained in the previous iterations (H_{i-1}) with the MD list and the minterm analyzed in the present stage. This action does not suppose neither memory consumption nor computation since the elements in MD have a field value greater or equal than the one associated to the terms included in H_i so far. Summing up, the computational effort required at each step is scarce. When deciding a criteria for inserting the minterms in the list representing the function Φ_F, the increasing order defined over the field value was chosen. However, at the time of analyzing the results, the conclusion that the order in which the minterms were analyzed affects the number of comparisons was reached. This brought in the necessity of evaluating the algorithm considering different sort criteria. This result was confirmed through statistical analysis. Finally, after the trials developed (Table 1) it can be stated that when building the list MD and highly frequent indexes appear, a great deal of repeated binary strings are obtained, whereas the minterms with bizarre indexes generate many more elements to be inserted in the list. If the rare strings are inserted at the beginning of the process, then the auxiliary list H_i would grow quickly and such strings should be "dragged" along all the calculations. In spite of this dependency, the size of the final list H_N is the same whatever it may be the order in which the functions A_{α_i} are compared.

The list H_N is used in step 3 to calculate the number of ones in the binary sequence. The operations needed in order to do so are not significantly expensive, since the more complex operation in this step is just determining the hamming weight of the minterms contained in the list.

The worst-case complexity of the algorithm was analyzed finding out that the order was $O(N2^N)$ (it is determined by the length of the list MD). However, this analysis is no realistic when applying to LFSR based generators since it would imply that all the indexes in the minterms functions are different. In terms of the LFSR-based generator, this means that the sequence generated does not even fulfill the short terms statistics properties. The experiments carried out suggests that in order to optimize the implementation a codification where the most common index will have assigned to the least significant bit in the minterm representations, the second most common index will correspond to the following bit and so forth should be used.

3.5   Practical Result of the Computation

This subsection deals with the description of the results obtained through the experiments. The trials were developed using a machine (tarja) located at the

Computing Research Support Service at the ULL whose architecture is the following. It has 64 Intel Itanium 2 processors at 1.5GHz. and 256 Gb. RAM. Table 1 shows the time (expressed in seconds) and memory (expressed in bytes) required by checking balancedness for different non linear functions.

In order to obtain nonlinear filters suitable for using in stream ciphers, the hints given in [4] were used at the time of defining the anlysed functions. Concretely, the LFSRs used where maximal ones and their lengths were defined as prime numbers. Another characteristic of the functions examined was defining the number of minterms as L/2 ($N = L/2$). Twenty of these functions were randomly generated for each length. The numbers contained in that table corresponds to the average time calculated for each method and each length. In order to appreciate the difference among the time consumed by each method the standard deviation is also provided. Time consumption dependency on the order

Table 1. Time and memory consumption in different insertion methods

L	Insertion Methods				Standard Deviation	Memory
	Decreasing	Increasing	Beginning	End		
5	0.0000755	0.0000308	0.0000721	0.0000283	0.000029	21.47
7	0.0000564	0.000148	0.0000794	0.0000413	0.000047	62.74
11	0.0000570	0.0000433	0.0000946	0.0000991	0.000026	228.21
13	0.0000732	0.0000583	0.0001069	0.0001148	0.000025	346.80
17	0.0002202	0.0003853	0.0002365	0.0002386	0.0000910	1078.40
19	0.0003468	0.0002441	0.0003342	0.0003167	0.0000560	1364.00
23	0.0011043	0.0006879	0.0009427	0.0007270	0.0002099	2301.33
29	0.0338849	0.0245308	0.0274779	0.0242933	0.0047825	21952.40
31	0.0327866	0.0161485	0.0221186	0.0243141	0.0084289	17282.80
37	0.5035322	0.2087113	0.2676401	0.2894309	0.1560113	63697.20
41	3.3322934	1.7652361	2.0834449	3.6767633	0.8283063	183164.00
43	7.4994210	2.9651031	4.5740873	3.6412809	2.2987840	223734.40
53	269.7338189	97.4952237	142.5837833	185.7441535	89.3180118	1280148.50
61	1715.9855528	515.3584146	809.9829705	566.8828017	625.7195635	2597063.20

in which the terms are analyzed is also shown in the previous table (Table 1).

A memory consumption analysis is included in Table 2 and Figure 1. The function used here has a minterm $A_{\alpha_{33}}$ which appears for the first time. The table compares the memory requirements when this minterm is analyzed at the beginning of the execution, when it is included in the last iteration and when increasing and decreasing order is used. There, it is possible to appreciate a substantial increase in the size of the lists when such a minterm is included at the beginning of the analysis. This is due to the memory increment experienced ($\Delta(M_i) = M_i - M_{i-1}$) during the construction of the list H_i at each iteration. The value $\Delta(M_i)$ represents the partial memory spent in the $i - th$ minterm evaluation. These data are shown in afore mentioned table. Unlike it could be

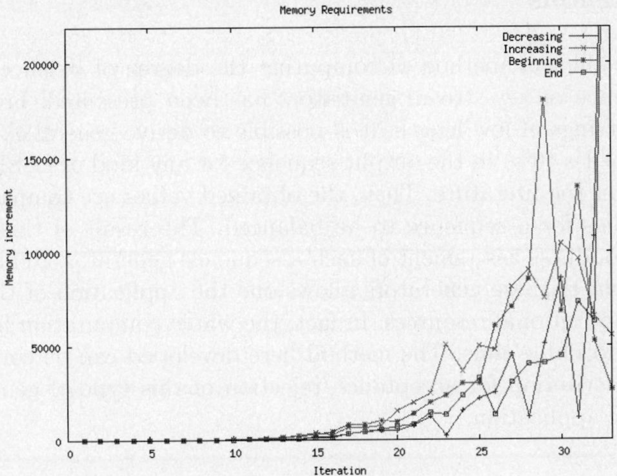

Fig. 1. Memory consumption in the different methods

expected, the function $\Delta(M_i)$ is not monotonically increasing since when a new minterm A_{α_i} is examined, the length of the list H_i may not change, or it even may decrease, depending on the indexes of the minterm analyzed at the current iteration. The sections with maximum slopes in the graphic correspond to those minterms with indexes no present in the elements analyzed so far, while the plateaus section are associated to the complementary set.

Table 2. Memory consumption

	Memory increment (Bytes)			
Step	Decreasing order	Increasing order	Inserting at the beginning	Inserting at the end
1	1	1	1	1
5	16	8	16	12
10	182	272	446	186
15	1346	3684	2652	1105
20	5021	15512	9650	7144
25	22248	50124	29986	32813
30	86040	103998	67942	44660
33	422229	55156	26896	422229

As conclusion of this section, it is worth pointing out that the algorithm has been tested for cases of practical interest in Cryptography obtaining reasonable time measures.

The application developed is still susceptible of improvements. In fact, we are now changing the data structures in order to build a parallel version that allows us to obtain results for filters based on longer LFSRs.

4   Conclusions

An easy and efficient method of computing the degree of balancedness in the output sequence of key-stream generators has been presented. From the handling of bit-strings of low length, it is possible to derive general expressions for the number of $1's$ $(0's)$ in the output sequence for any kind of LFSR-based generator found in the literature. Then, the obtained values are compared with the expected values for a sequence to be balanced. The result of this comparison implies the goodness assessment of such a sequence generator. Remark that the particular form of these generators allows one the application of the algorithm with low computational resources. In fact, the whole computation has been carried out in affordable time. The method here developed can be considered as a first selective criterion for acceptance/rejection of this type of generators with cryptographic application.

References

1. D. Coppersmith, H. Krawczyk, Y. Mansour, "The Shrinking Generator", CRYPTO'93, LNCS Springer Verlag, Vol. 773, 1994, pp. 22-39.
2. CRYPTREC project- cryptographic evaluation for Japanese Electronic Government, www.ipa.go.jp/security/enc/CRYPTREC/index-e.html
3. A. Fúster-Sabater and P. García-Mochales, Aspects of pseudorandomness in non-linear generators of binary sequences, Information Processing Letters, 85 (2003), 111-116.
4. S.W. Golomb, Shift Register-Sequences, Aegean Park Press, Laguna Hill, 1982.
5. GSM, *Global Systems for Mobile Communications*, available at http://cryptome.org/gsm-a512.htm
6. R. Lidl and H. Niederreiter, Introduction to Finite Fields and Their Applications, Cambridge: Cambridge University Press, 1986.
7. D. Mange, Analysis and Synthesis of Logic Systems, Artech House, INC., Norwood 1986.
8. A.J. Menezes *et al.*, Handbook of Applied Cryptography, New York:CRC Press, 1997.
9. R.L. Rivest, "The RC4 Encryption Algorithm". RSA Data Security, Inc., March 12, 1992.
10. R.A. Rueppel, Analysis and Design of Stream Ciphers, New York:Springer-Verlag, 1986.
11. L. Wang, A.E. Almani, Fast conversion algorithm for very large Boolean functions, Electron. Lett. 36 (2000) 1370-1371.

Test Suite Reduction Based on Dependence Analysis

Guy-Vincent Jourdan, Panitee Ritthiruangdech, and Hasan Ural

School of Information Technology and Engineering (SITE)
University of Ottawa
800 King Edward Avenue
Ottawa, Ontario, Canada, K1N 6N5
{gvj, pritthir, ural}@site.uottawa.ca

Abstract. A test suite, constructed either manually or automatically using a coverage criterion, can be reduced without significantly reducing its fault-detection capability by eliminating all but one of the equivalent test cases from each class of equivalent test cases of the test suite. In this paper, we use the analysis of control and data dependencies in an EFSM model of the system requirements to identify patterns of interaction among the elements of the EFSM that affect a requirement under test. These patterns are used to identify equivalent test cases w.r.t. the requirement under test; only one test case per equivalence class is kept, and equivalence classes that are not covered by any test cases are flagged. A software tool - Test Suite Reduction (TSR) based on above concept- is introduced. This tool is implemented in C++ and Java languages and runs on Sun workstations under Solaris Sparc 5.8. Additionally, the results of the application of TSR to several examples are also presented.

1 Introduction

Requirement-based test generation is a model-based technique for generating suites of test cases related to individual requirements [1] which are described in the Extended Finite State Machine (EFSM) model [2]. Depending on the selected test strategy, the EFSM may then be used to automatically generate test cases related to individual requirements. Adaptations of commonly used test generation strategies in software testing, such as branch coverage, all-uses coverage and constrained path coverage to the EFSM model are reported in the literature[3, 4, 5, 2]. Generally, these test generation strategies are used to test the entire system functionality, referred to as complete testing, i.e., to test all features and requirements. Such complete testing is very labor-intensive and expensive due to a considerably large number of test cases that are generated. Therefore, requirement-based selective test generation has been proposed to support partial system testing with respect to a set of selected requirements [1]. Test suites generated by requirement-based selective testing are considerably smaller than those generated by complete system testing; however, the number of test cases may still be very large. Since the cost of executing large number of test cases is very high, the problem of test suite reduction arises.

A. Levi et al. (Eds.): ISCIS 2006, LNCS 4263, pp. 1021–1030, 2006.

In [3], an approach for the reduction of requirement-based test suites using EFSM dependence analysis has been proposed. Two types of dependencies, namely control dependence and data dependence are identified in an EFSM model representing the system requirements. Those dependencies are analyzed to yield patterns of interaction among the elements of the EFSM model. Subsequently, equivalent tests are identified: two tests are equivalent if both exhibit the same pattern of interaction w.r.t. the requirement under test. Therefore, one of them can be removed from the test suite.

In this paper, the approach in [3] has been placed in a formal setting and expanded to cover larger subsets of EFSM based representations of requirements. Test suite reduction algorithms based on those two methods have been developed. Then, the approach in [3] has been extended to identify patterns of interactions that are not covered by any test case in the test suite (lack of coverage of such patterns may affect the fault detection capability of the test suite). Finally, a test suite reduction tool has been implemented and case studies have been performed to confirm the expected reduction in the size of test suites. The remainder of this paper is organized as follows: Section 2 reviews formal definition of EFSM and introduces the concepts related to dependence analysis in the EFSM model. Section 3 presents the overview of the functionality and the structure of TSR. Section 4 contains the results of applications of TSR to several examples. Finally, in Section 5, the conclusions and future work are presented.

2   Preliminaries

EFSM: EFSM is an extension of the classical Finite State Machine (FSM), which adds parameters to inputs and outputs of an FSM and variables, enabling predicate, and actions into transitions of an FSM. An EFSM can be formally represented as a nine-tuple $(S, s_{en}, s_{ex}, I, O, P_I, P_O, V, T)$, where S is a finite set of states, s_{en} is the entry, s_{ex} is the exit state, I is a finite set of input interactions, O is a finite set of output interactions, P_I is a finite set of input interaction parameters, P_O is a finite set of output interaction parameters, V is a finite set of variables and T is a finite set of transitions.

Each element of T is a 5-tuple $t = (s_s, s_d, i, g, a)$ where s_s and s_d are states in S representing the *starting state* and the *terminating state* of t, respectively. i is an input interaction in I that triggers t. g is the *enabling condition* which is a Boolean expression over elements of P_I and V that must be evaluated to be *true* for t to be executable. a is a sequence of actions that take place when t is executed such as assigning or modifying the values of variables, initiating output interactions, starting and stopping timers and performing procedure calls.

An EFSM can be graphically represented by a digraph $G = (V, E)$ where V is a set of nodes, each representing a state in S and E is a set of edges, each representing a transition in T. For instance, Figure 1 shows an EFSM describing the requirements for a simplified Automatic Teller Machine (ATM) System. In this paper, we assume that requirements can be represented as a single EFSM and each requirement can be adequately represented by a single transition in this EFSM.

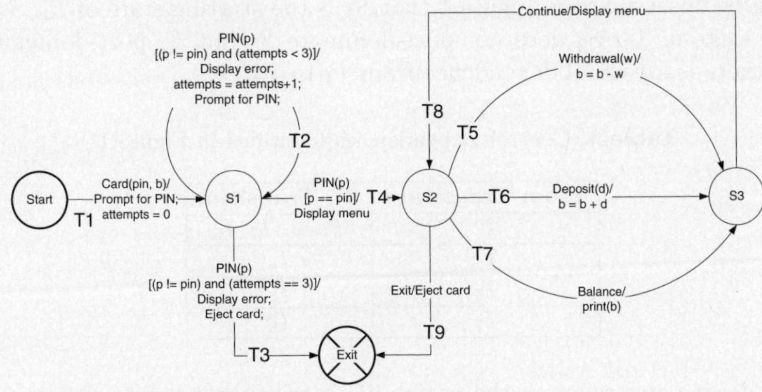

Fig. 1. The EFSM Model of the simplified ATM system [3]

Classification of Variable Occurrence: In an EFSM, each variable $\in P_I \cup P_O \cup V$ at a transition is classified as being a definition, a computational use, or a predicate use which are referred to as a def, c-use, or p-use, respectively. A *definition* (def) of a variable v at transition t (denoted by d_t^v) is an occurrence of v by which a value is assigned to v (e.g., an occurrence of v on the left hand side of assignment statement, for instance, the definition of "attempts" at transition T_1 in Figure 1). A use of a variable v is an occurrence of v by which the value of v is referred. Each use occurrence is also further classified as a computational use (c-use) or a predicate use (p-use) [6, 7]. A c-use of a variable v at transition t (denoted by c_t^v) is a use of v that occurs in the right hand side of an assignment statement, as an argument in a procedure call or an output statement, for instance, the use of variable "b" at transition T_5 in Figure 1. A p-use of a variable v at transition t (denoted by p_t^v) is a use that occurs in a Boolean expression corresponding to the enabling condition of t, for instance, the use of variable "pin" at transition T_4 in Figure 1.

Dependence Analysis: In an EFSM, there are two types of dependencies between transitions, namely data dependence and control dependence [3].

The concept of *control dependence* in an EFSM is extended from the notion of control dependence defined for a program control graph [8]. In an EFSM, a control dependence captures the notion that one transition may potentially affect traversal of another transition and is based on the concept of post-dominance. Let us give the concept of post-dominance [3] first.

Let S_1 and S_2 be states (nodes) and t be an outgoing transition of S_1 in an EFSM. State S_2 *post-dominates* state S_1 if S_2 is on every path from S_1 to the exit state. State S_2 *post-dominates* transition t if S_2 is on every path from S_1 to the exit state through t. Let t_i and t_k be outgoing transitions from S_1 and S_2 respectively. There is a control dependence from transition t_i to transition t_k if S_2 does not post-dominate S_1 and S_2 post-dominates transition t_i.

It can be observed from Figure 1 that S_1 is the starting state of T_4, S_2 is the starting state of T_6, S_2 does not post-dominate S_1 but S_2 post-dominates T_4. Hence, there is a control dependence from T_4 to T_6.

Table 1. Control Dependencies Identified in Figure 1

From Transition	To Transition
T_4	T_5, T_6, T_7, T_9
T_5	T_8
T_6	T_8
T_7	T_8

Data dependence relies on the notion of associations between definitions and uses of variables where one transition defines a value of a variable and the same or another transition uses this value. Formally, there exists a data dependence from transition t_i to transition t_k w.r.t. a variable v if

1. $d_{t_i}^v$ is the last definition of v in t_i
2. $u_{t_k}^v$ is a c-use or p-use of v in t_k before v is redefined (if at all) in t_k
3. there exists a def-clear path $(t_i, t_{i+1}, \cdots, t_{k-1}, t_k)$ w.r.t. v from t_i to t_k, i.e., a path where there are no definitions of v at transitions t_{i+1} to t_{k-1}.

For example, in Figure 1, there is a data dependence from T_1 to T_6 w.r.t. b due to the fact that b is defined in T_1, b is used in T_6 and there is a def-clear path w.r.t. b from T_1 to T_6 (namely $T_1T_4T_6$). All data dependencies identified for the EFSM in Figure 1 are shown in Table 2.

Static Dependence Graph (SDG): Control and data dependencies in an EFSM can be graphically represented as a directed graph where each node represents a transition and each edge represents either control dependence or data dependence. For example, Figure 2 shows the static dependence graph of the EFSM given in Figure 1 constructed by using the control and data dependencies between transitions given in Table 1 and Table 2.

Static Interaction Pattern (SIP): The static interaction pattern (SIP) of a test case (also called a *test sequence*, a complete sequence of transitions that starts at the entry node and ends at the exit node of the EFSM) w.r.t. a transition under test (TUT), is a sub-graph of the SDG, such that data and control dependence edges in SIP "influence" the TUT. The SIP of a test case w.r.t a TUT is unique. To construct the SIP of a test case, control and data dependencies that are encountered during the traversal of the test sequence are identified and represented as a sub-graph of the SDG called sub-SDG. The control and data dependencies that influence the TUT are of particular interest. Such dependencies can be identified by traversing the sub-SDG *backward* from the TUT and marking all traversed nodes and edges. All unmarked nodes and edges are removed from the sub-SDG. As a consequence, the resulting sub-SDG consists only of control and data dependencies that influence the TUT. For example the SIP of Test_1 $= T_1T_4T_5T_8T_5T_8T_9$ w.r.t. TUT T_5 is presented in Figure 3.

Table 2. Data Dependencies Identified in Figure 1

From Transition	To Transition	w.r.t. variable	def-clear path
T_1	T_2	attempts or pin	T_1T_2
T_1	T_3	pin	$T_1T_2T_2T_2T_3$
T_1	T_4	pin	T_1T_4
T_1	T_5	b	$T_1T_4T_5$
T_1	T_6	b	$T_1T_4T_6$
T_1	T_7	b	$T_1T_4T_7$
T_2	T_2	attempts or pin	T_2T_2
T_2	T_3	attempts	T_2T_3
T_5	T_5	b	$T_5T_8T_5$
T_5	T_6	b	$T_5T_8T_6$
T_5	T_7	b	$T_5T_8T_7$
T_6	T_5	b	$T_6T_8T_5$
T_6	T_6	b	$T_6T_8T_6$
T_6	T_7	b	$T_6T_8T_7$

Dynamic Interaction Pattern (DIP): The dynamic interaction pattern (DIP) of a test sequence w.r.t. a TUT, is derived from the SDG, such that data and control dependence edges in DIP "influence" the TUT. To construct a DIP, in principle, is similar to construct a SIP from a test case except that repetitions of the same dependence during the traversal of a test sequence are taken into account. To do so, for a given test case, each traversed transition is represented as a separate node in the dependence graph called Dynamic Dependence Graph (DDG), even if the same transition has already been traversed before. Each identified control and data dependence during the traversal is represented as an edge between two nodes (transitions) in DDG. Then, dependencies that influence the TUT are identified by traversing backwards from the TUT and marking all traversed nodes and edges. Then all unmarked nodes and edges are removed

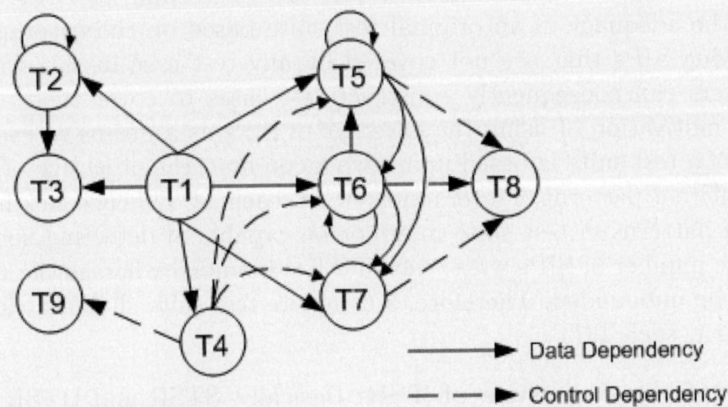

Fig. 2. The SDG of the ATM EFSM

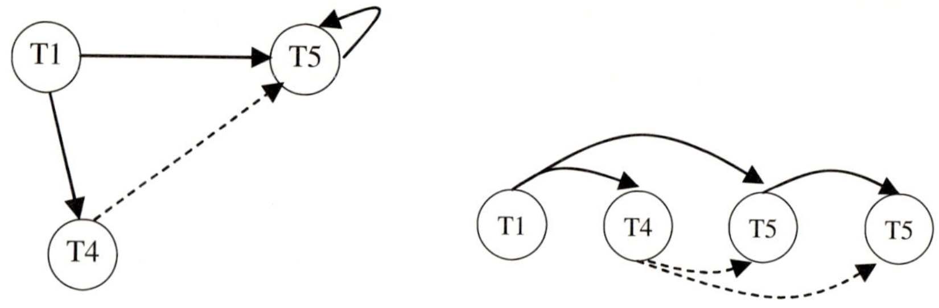

Fig. 3. SIP of Test_1 w.r.t. T_5 **Fig. 4.** DIP of Test_1 w.r.t. T_5

from the DDG. The resulting graph is the DIP. For example, Figure 4 shows the DIP of Test_1 $= T_1 T_4 T_5 T_8 T_5 T_8 T_9$ with TUT$= T_5$.

We can form equivalence classes on the SIPs and on the DIPs, so that test cases in the same class have the same SIP (resp. DIP). Test cases belonging to the same equivalence class provide equivalent testing of the static (resp. dynamic) interaction patterns. Consequently, only one test case per equivalence class is needed and the other test cases can be discarded.

3 TSR

Based on the concept of test suite reduction using either static or dynamic interaction pattern [3], the *Test Suite Reduction* (TSR) [9] program has been developed and implemented in C++ and Java languages and runs on Sun workstations under Solaris Sparc 5.8. TSR is built to reduce the number of test cases in a given test suite by eliminating equivalent test cases, according to the definition of either SIP or DIP.

Overview of the Functionality of TSR: TSR is made up of two programs, STSR and DTSR. STSR reduces the number of test cases according to SIPs whereas DTSR reduces the number of test cases according to DIPs. TSR also evaluates the adequacy of an original test suite based on the coverage of SIPs by identifying SIPs that are not covered by any test case in the original test suite. Testers can consequently construct test cases to cover these uncovered SIPs. The motivation of using the coverage of SIPs as a means to evaluate the adequacy of a test suite is based upon two facts: first, the objective of testing is to cover different patterns of interactions w.r.t. each TUT; hence lacking of some interaction patterns, a test suite may not be capable of detecting some faults. Second, the number of SIPs w.r.t. each TUT is bounded whereas the number of DIPs may be unbounded. Therefore, a complete test suite should at least cover all SIPs w.r.t. each TUT.

Overview of the Structure of TSR: Basically, STSR and DTSR have the same architecture and perform the following tasks: the construction of SDG (phase 1), the identification of equivalent test cases (and uncovered SIPs by STSR) (phase 2) and the construction of the reduced test suite (phase 3).

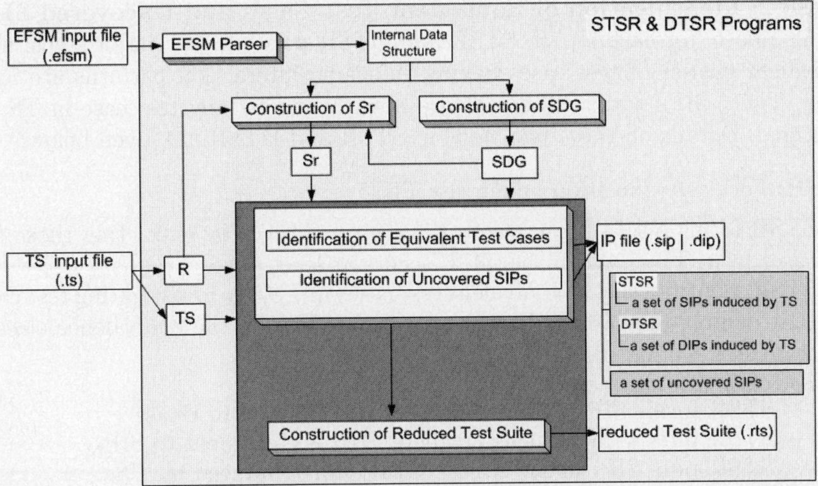

Fig. 5. Structure of STSR and DTSR Programs

As shown in Figure 5, STSR and DTSR require two input files: one for the EFSM (".efsm") and the other for the original test suite (".ts"). A ".ts" file consists of a set of requirements where each requirement is represented by a TUT and a collection of test cases. STSR and DTSR each generate two output files: a reduced test suite file (".rts"), where redundant test cases have been eliminated, and an interaction pattern (IP) file. An IP file represents, for each TUT, two sets of interaction patterns. The first set consists of unique interaction patterns induced by test cases in a ".ts" file, which are either SIPs or DIPs w.r.t. the TUT. Each interaction pattern comes with a group of equivalent test cases that exhibit it. The second set consists of SIPs w.r.t. the TUT that are not covered by any test case in the ".ts" file. The extension of the IP file is ".sip" for STSR and ".dip" for DTSR.

Phase 1: Construction of SDG and S_r: This phase is identical for both STSR and DTSR. The programs first verify that the two input files specify a test suite that belong to the EFSM system (e.g., by checking if efsm ids in ".efsm" and ".ts" files are identical). Then, the ".efsm" file is analyzed and parsed using Unix's Lex and Yacc, to get the EFSM, classify the variables and their occurrences in each transition, and form the EFSM internal data structure. Based on this internal data structure, control and data dependencies are identified and captured to build the SDG of the EFSM. Finally, a set S_r of all possible SIPs w.r.t. each TUT r is constructed. A set of TUTs, R, and a collection of test cases, TS, are extracted from the ".ts" file. TSR implements the algorithm proposed in [10] to generate S_r. The complexity of SDG generation is quadratic in the size of the set of states in the EFSM [10].

Phase 2: Identification of Equivalent Test Cases and Uncovered SIPs:
In this phase, for each $r \in R$, STSR and DTSR perform two major steps: first,
equivalent classes of test cases having the same interaction patterns are identified, Then, SIPs w.r.t. TUT that are not covered by any test case in TS are
identified. Details on these two steps in STSR and DTSR are given below:

STSR: For each transition under test TUT:
1. STSR forms a set of test cases (TS_r) w.r.t. TUT r by extracting those test
   cases from TS in which the TUT occurs at least once.
2. STSR identifies sets of equivalent test cases in TS_r by investigating test cases
   that exhibit the same SIP. Thus, let $TS_r(\text{SIP}_i)$ be the equivalence class of
   test cases having the same SIP_i.
   For each test case $tc \in TS_r$,
   - STSR forms SIP_{tc} from tc using SDG obtained in Phase 1
   - STSR puts tc in $TS_r(\text{SIP}_i)$ where SIP_i is equivalent to SIP_{tc}.
   - STSR puts SIP_i in the set S_r' of SIPs for r induced by TS_r.
3. STSR exports all $\text{SIP}_r \in S_r'$ as well as a group of test cases from $TS_r(\text{SIP}_i)$
   into ".sip" file.
4. STSR inputs a set of all possible SIPs w.r.t. the TUT r, S_r.
5. STSR identifies which $\text{SIP}_r \in S_r$ (if any) is not covered by any $tc \in TS_r$
   using S_r and S_r' (obtained in Step 1). STSR reports $S_r - S_r'$ by appending
   such information to ".sip" file.

DTSR: DTSR performs this phase like STSR, but using DIPs instead of SIPs.
For item 2., DTSR must first form the DDG_{tc} from each test case $tc \in TS_r$
and then generate DIP_{tc} from DDG_{tc}. At item 5., in order to identify uncovered
SIPs, DTSR maps DIP_{tc} into a SIP_{tc} by collapsing group of nodes representing
the same transition into a single node.

Phase 3: Construction of Reduced Test Suite: In the previous phase,
equivalent test cases that exhibit the same interaction pattern (SIP or DIP) w.r.t.
the TUT have been identified. Therefore, reduced test suite can be constructed
by simply selecting randomly one test case from each equivalence class of test
cases having the same interaction pattern w.r.t. the TUT.
More formally,

STSR	DTSR
1: let RTS = $\{tc\|tc$ is a test case$\}$;	1: let RTS = $\{tc\|tc$ is a test case$\}$;
2: RTS $\leftarrow \emptyset$	2: RTS $\leftarrow \emptyset$
3: **for** each $r \in R$ in the TS file **do**	3: **for** each $r \in R$ in the TS file **do**
4: RTS$_r \leftarrow \emptyset$	4: RTS$_r \leftarrow \emptyset$
5: **for** $i = 1$ to $\|S_r\|$ **do**	5: **for** $i = 1$ to $\|D_r\|$ **do**
6: select randomly one tc from $TS_r(\text{SIP}_i)$	6: select randomly one tc from $TS_r(\text{DIP}_i)$
7: RTS$_r \leftarrow$ RTS$_r \cup \{tc\}$	7: RTS$_r \leftarrow$ RTS$_r \cup \{tc\}$
8: **end for**	8: **end for**
9: RTS $\leftarrow$ RTS $\cup$ RTS$_r$	9: RTS $\leftarrow$ RTS $\cup$ RTS$_r$
10: **end for**	10: **end for**

At this point, STSR and DTSR have formed the reduced test suite and exported it to an ".rts" file (including efsm id and sets of TUTs) where the repetitive test cases have been eliminated.

4   Applications of TSR to Several Examples

TSR has been applied to three systems: ATM, Cruise Control System (CCS) and Vending Machine System(VMS). For each system, the following process has been carried out:

1. Formal representation of the requirements in an EFSM model;
2. Manual generation of test suites according to branch coverage, all-uses coverage [7] and IPO_2-df-Chains coverage criteria [5].
3. Reduction of the test suites constructed in step 2 using STSR and DTSR.

Space limitation prevents us to provide the details of our findings (see [11]). The results of the case studies show that STSR and DTSR do not considerably reduce the size of the test suites derived from branch coverage. This is caused by the very small size of such test suites. For example, in ATM system, there is only one test case for each TUT; therefore, the percentage of reduction w.r.t. each TUT is equal to 0%. However, when the size of the test suites becomes larger as obtained by another test suite generation strategy (especially IPO_2-df-Chains coverage), TSR is successful in its aim of reducing the test suites. For example, for CCS, significant reduction (73 to 99%) is achieved.

TSR also validates the coverage of the reduced test suite by evaluating the adequacy of the reduced test suite based on the coverage of SIPs. To do so, TSR identifies a set of SIPs that are not covered by any test case in the original test suite and reports such uncovered SIPs. For example, in VMS, TSR identifies between 44 and 74 missing SIPs for various TUTs. Testers can consequently construct test cases to cover such uncovered SIPs; therefore, as a consequence, TSR may enhance the capability of the reduced test suite in its interaction coverage.

5   Conclusion and Future Work

A large test suite can be reduced by eliminating all but one of the equivalent test cases from each class of equivalent test cases of the test suite. The analysis of EFSM dependence (control and data dependence) is shown to identify classes of equivalent test cases. In particular, such analysis yields two types of interaction patterns that affect a requirement under test: Static Interaction Pattern (SIP) and Dynamic Interaction Pattern (DIP), which are in turn used to identify equivalent test cases w.r.t. the requirement under test. Two tests are considered being equivalent w.r.t. the requirement under test if both exhibit the same interaction pattern; hence, one of them can be discarded from the test suite. TSR has been developed as a tool for supporting the concept of test suite reduction using

EFSM dependence analysis. It has been shown from the application of TSR to several examples that TSR can significantly reduce the number of test cases.

In the future research, we are planning to develop a strategy to select a representative test case for each equivalence class. This would require a fault model which considers the effects of the input parameter values on revealing faults. In addition, we plan to implement another feature in TSR such that it can automatically generate test cases with respect to a set of missing SIPs. As such, TSR can enhance the capability of the reduced test suite in fault-detection.

References

1. Tahat, L., Vaysburg, B., Korel, B., Bader, A.: Requirement-based automated black-box test generation. In: IEEE COMPSAC. (2001) 489–495
2. Bourhfir, C., Dssouli, R., Aboulhamid, E.M.: Automatic test generation for EFSM-based systems. Tech. Rep. IRO 1043, University of Montreal (1996)
3. Vaysburg, B., Tahat, L., Korel, B.: Dependence analysis in reduction of requirement based test suites. In: International Symposium on Software Testing and Analysis (ISSTA'02), Roma, Italy, ACM Press (2002) 107–111 ISBN: 1-58113-562-9.
4. Saleh, K., Ural, H., Williams, A.: Test generation based on control and data dependencies within system specifications in sdl. Computer Communications **23** (2000) 609–627
5. Ural, H., Yang, B.: A test sequence selection method for protocol testing. IEEE Transactions on Communications **39** (1991) 514–523
6. Rapps, S., Weyuker, E.J.: Selecting software test data using data flow information. IEEE Trans. Software Eng. **11** (1985) 367–375
7. Frankl, P.G., Weyuker, E.J.: An applicable family of data flow testing criteria. IEEE Trans. Software Eng. **14** (1988) 1483–1498
8. Ferrante, K., Ottenstein, K., Warren, J.: The program dependence graph and its use in optimization. ACM Trans. Progr. Lang. & Systems **9** (1987) 319–349
9. Ural, H. *et al.*: TSR. http://www.site.uottawa.ca/~ural/TSR (2006)
10. Chemli, O.: Reduced test suite generation. University of Ottawa, Master Thesis in Computer Science (2006)
11. Ritthiruangdech, P.: Test suite reduction using sdl and efsm dependency analysis. University of Ottawa, Master Thesis in Computer Science (2004)

Realism in Project-Based
Software Engineering Courses:
Rewards, Risks, and Recommendations

Pierre Flener[*]

Computing Science Division, Department of Information Technology
Uppsala University, Box 337, 751 05 Uppsala, Sweden
Pierre.Flener@it.uu.se

Abstract. A software engineering course is often the capstone of a general undergraduate curriculum in computer science. It is usually at least partly a project-based course, with the intention that student groups can deploy their already acquired skills on programming, verification, databases, and human-computer interaction, while applying the new material about requirements, architecture, and project management on a project. I have taught a software engineering course six times, using a combination of ideas that I have never seen elsewhere, with a strong emphasis on realism. I here reflect on the rewards and risks of this approach, and make some recommendations for future offerings.

1   Introduction

The discipline of *software engineering* proposes a set of principles, techniques, and tools for the multi-person development of correct and efficient software within an allocated time and budget, in response to a perceived software need. The required coordination efforts set it apart from *programming*, which is typically a one-person activity and starts (normally) from a precise specification. Such programming-in-the-small is just one of the many activities within a software engineering project, also known as programming-in-the-large. The other activities include requirements elicitation and specification, architecture specification, validation and verification, and project management.

A software engineering course is often the capstone of a general undergraduate curriculum in computer science. It is often the last course taught in the final year,[1] and builds on top of courses on programming, verification, databases, human-computer interaction, and so on. The concepts of requirements, architecture, and project management are often covered for the first time in a software engineering course. It is usually at least partly a project-based course, with the intention that student groups can deploy their already acquired skills while

---

[*] Currently a Visiting Faculty Member at Sabancı University in İstanbul, Turkey.
[1] The 'big picture' is of course taught in some introductory first-year course.

A. Levi et al. (Eds.): ISCIS 2006, LNCS 4263, pp. 1031–1039, 2006.

applying the new material on a project. In that case, the pedagogical approach taken fits the modern drive for *problem-based learning* [6]. There is a flourishing literature on how to teach software engineering, witness the *ACM/IEEE Curriculum Guidelines for Undergraduate Degree Programs in Software Engineering* (`http://sites.computer.org/ccse/`),[2] the *Conference on Software Engineering Education and Training* (CSEE&T) annual series [1], and numerous articles in software engineering journals, as well as in the general computer science education or research conferences and journals.

2   My Software Engineering Course

I have taught a software engineering course six times, namely from 1995 to 1997 at the Computer Engineering and Information Science department of Bilkent University in Ankara, Turkey, and from 1999 to 2001 at the Information Science department of Uppsala University, Sweden.[3] Both courses were taught to fourth-year students in a project-based way. The first time I gave the course, I had thought long and hard about it. I come up with a combination of ideas that I have never seen elsewhere, namely:

- The instructor is the *coach* for all the teams.
- The instructor is the (*external*) *client*, with a software need well outside the area of expertise of probably all the students.
- The client is *insecure* about the actual software need, is largely *ignorant* about programming and computer issues, and even has *mind changes* about some objectives after receiving the first two deliverables.
- The first two deliverables are *revised at least once*, so as to accommodate feedback from the coach and the mind changes of the client.
- The software is *neither implemented nor validated and verified*, mainly for time reasons.

In the following, I will describe the course in more detail. See `http://user.it.uu.se/~pierref/courses/SE/` for its most recent incarnation, developed from the feedback on the previous five offerings.

2.1   Goals and Overview

My main objective is to make the students familiar with the fundamental principles and techniques of software engineering. This will allow the students to acquire further knowledge later, be it through advanced courses or through self-study and practice. This also means that my lectures have a slightly theoretical flavour, as they discuss *no* particular tools. Once the fundamental principles

---

[2] These guidelines did not exist yet when I last taught the course.

[3] The software engineering course at my current department was in able hands when I moved there in late 2001.

and techniques are understood, the usage of tools is eased, whereas the study of any particular tools would not prepare the students for the usage of other tools nor of the better ones that are bound to emerge. Furthermore, the usage of tools without understanding their underlying principles and techniques is outright dangerous. The focus is on understanding why a particular principle or technique should be applied, or why it should not be applied, rather than only on how to apply it.

Some practice of software engineering is acquired by the students through the specification and design (but *not* the implementation, validation, and verification) of a software application, as a project for teams of about five students. For comparison purposes, the *same* project is assigned to all teams. The topic is at my discretion, but is chosen so as to be most likely *outside* the expertise of *all* the students.[4] Such a project for an *external client* has the advantage of learning what it means not to decide in-house what the requirements actually are, so that the client *must* be consulted on *every* single issue.

For pedagogical purposes, the first two deliverables are *revised* at least once, so as to learn that no such document is ever perfect, because of evolution of the requirements and because of errors in content and style. It is this essential feature of my course that makes it impossible to have the teams go on to the implementation, validation, and verification of their software, as the usually allocated time span of the course is too short. In any case, it is debatable whether a course should allow students to spend so much time applying something they have already learned in other courses, despite the joys of seeing one's product in action (if it ever runs): I have seen software engineering project-based courses degenerate into programming fests once the teams were stuck in the morass of their poor early decisions, with the hope that an actually running software product would sway the instructor.

Major methodological decisions are taken by the instructor, but the actual choice of techniques, notations, and tools is left to the teams, under the instructor's *coaching*. As a textbook, I used (the first version of) the excellent *Fundamentals of Software Engineering* [2] at Bilkent University, but switched to *Software Engineering: Theory and Practice* [4] at Uppsala University, while awaiting the now available second edition of the former. For the project management, we followed the introductory version of the *Team Software Process* (TSPi) [3] at Uppsala University. The students used or adapted its on-line supplements, such as the forms and the support tool. For the requirements process, we followed the *Volere* methodology [5] at Uppsala University. The students used or adapted its on-line Volere Requirements Specification Template.

---

[4] Five times, I decided on software support for the various chairs of scientific conferences. Having been a programme (co-)chair of three conferences and several workshops, with no or very little software support, made me a very convincing client. One of my Bilkent students actually went on and developed a commercial product from my requirements. In the meantime, there is a flurry of such products, enabling inspiration for the project over the internet, though the topic retains its mystery to most students.

2.2   The Project

Upon filled-out TSPi forms from each student, indicating their strengths, weaknesses, role preferences, and teammate preferences, the instructor divides the class into teams (ideally of size 5, otherwise of size 6), and assigns a TSPi management role[5] to each team member. Of course, in addition to their TSPi role, every team member is a software engineer and is expected to contribute to the entire project. The instructor is the coach for all the teams, as well as their client. The *same* project is then launched by all the teams. It is designed to be not feasible properly by less than 4 students, to avoid free-loading students.

Through appointments with the client, each team elaborates a **requirements specification** for a software helping to solve the problem. The client may be accidentally inconsistent or incomplete about the software need across the various requirements elicitation sessions. However, I also deliberately sneak in some inconsistency and incompleteness, in order to see whether the team eventually detects that or not. Upon constructive feedback from the client and coach, each team eventually has to produce two more versions of their requirements specification, because of errors and inadequacies in earlier versions or because the client has mind changes on some objectives. I do the latter deliberately after the second version. The teams are explicitly warned to plan for change.

Each team also has to come up with an **architecture specification** corresponding to their requirements specification, starting from its second version. Upon constructive feedback from the coach,[6] each team eventually has to produce a second version of their architecture specification, corresponding to the third version of the requirements specification, because of errors and inadequacies in the first version or because of the mind changes in the requirements.

Finally, *without* actually writing the software (according to the third requirements specification and the second architecture specification), each team has to produce a **test plan** according to which they would validate and verify the software, such that it would give them a reasonable degree of confidence.

2.3   Additional Realism

Just like in real life, it is not unusual for team members to quit (by dropping the course) or be temporarily unable to perform. Also, teams can break apart because of internal tensions. The teams are asked to have contingency plans for all this, and in any case the team leaders have weekly meetings with the coach to report on leadership issues.

I have toyed with the idea of letting the teams freely swap members, if not to operate myself such swaps. However, project re-staffing is considered bad practice because the effort of integrating a new engineer usually does not pay off, especially in struggling projects. Also, as all teams would be affected by and learn from such realism, this may be considered unfair by the designated students,

---

[5] Team leader, development manager, planning manager, quality and process manager, or support manager.

[6] Clients usually do not look at the architecture specification.

unless they volunteer. Hence I have never carried out such an experiment, except when a team shrank below critical mass and I distributed its members over willing teams. It was a decision I regretted later on, as the team was very good and its ex-members lost much of their motivation while trying to integrate into their new teams.

Another way of conveying how hard it is to be integrated into an ongoing project is to rotate the documents among the teams at some checkpoint. If warned about this, the teams would take extra care to leave nothing undocumented. However, I decided this would be too drastic an experiment.

2.4   Student Evaluation

Within the exam, each team has a two-hour oral project postmortem with me, only over the final versions of their documents for the project, and, if need be, over some of the course material:

- 30% of the grade depend on the requirements specification;
- 20% of the grade depend on the architecture specification;
- 10% of the grade depend on the test plan;
- 20% of the grade depend on participation in the classroom and in meetings with the client, coach, or instructor, including the exam;
- 20% of the grade depend on participation in internal team meetings, according to an anonymous TSPi peer-evaluation conducted at the exam.

The re-exam is a written exam over the course material. It is reserved for those who failed the first exam and thus actually participated in a project team, as the project is a mandatory part of the course and can only be taken while the course takes place.

3   Course/Teacher Evaluation: Rewards and Risks

In general, my students overall loved this course, witness the following excerpts from the course and teacher evaluations, identifying the **rewards** of this course:

"Course workload, project, content, lessons, organisation, etc were excellent. I really think I can take advantage of what I learned in this course."

"The lectures have been *very* interesting and the course is the *best* in preparing us, the students, for real-life work at companies. [...] The attitude against students feels professional. The instructor really wants us to learn much of the course and prepare us for industry."

"The teacher kept a good balance between academic and industry-related issues, so we can feel this course to be very useful when we start working."

I have also received various emails from former students after they spent a few years in industry as software engineers. Examples are:

> "I want to thank you so sincerely for all the knowledge you shared with us in the classes. I just wish I paid a little more attention. [...] The software engineering course you taught me is still my main reference (I still have the Software Engineering book we used as reference in the class and the class notes that some of which I took and many others were copied)." — A Bilkent'96 graduate, in May 1999

> "I had found myself at particular ease compared to many others and was nominated internal quality auditor and a vice-manager of quality assurance. I have to recognize that your course has been my guiding line through more than a year of work. And I'm indebted to you for your excellent tutorship and owe you this modest regard." — A Bilkent'97 graduate, in August 1998

However, is is impossible to have all the students on one's side, and many students who appreciated the course also came up with constructive criticism, which I always addressed in the next offering. There are indeed also **risks** in teaching the course this way, as shown in the following.

The most common complaints were about the inordinate workload, though this was usually confessed to be self-induced, witness an open letter to future classes:

> "We did not start working on the first version of the requirements specification document on the time that Dr Flener has suggested. [...] The problems cascaded to the other documents as well [...] extremely difficult to cope with. [...] Just start working on time, the rest must be enjoyable." — The Bilkent software engineering class of 1997

As hinted in this letter, I did earnestly warn the students that getting started early and well will enormously pay off. I did so every year, and no team ever heeded this advice, only to bitterly regret it later on.

Several students used the phrase 'shock therapy' for my realism-based approach, referring to the impact of the client's mind changes after the first architecture specification has been handed in. Despite my clear admonitions to expect the unexpected and to plan for change, and despite the mildness of the mind changes, if not my hoodwinking about what they might be, that impact was usually traumatic. Some students found the idea quite good, but others commented as follows:

> "I experienced more shock than learning during this course."

> "If your aim was to make our projects fail, then you have succeeded."

Learning from one's mistakes is certainly a powerful learning method, but it should not become the only or major one (unconsciously) deployed in a course. Unfortunately, a software engineering project staffed entirely by undergraduate students seems predestined to run into trouble, unless significant amounts of coaching and predecessor courses are available.

Among the most serious objections was also the following:

> "The student life/work environment is completely different from the real world and there is no way and no need for trying hard to impose any similarity."

As the more positive comments above indicate, this may be an opinion that only some students form. The only way to remedy this seems to teach the course without any project work, which is generally not done. Maybe such students, especially those who think they will not become actual software engineers, can be offered to take a theoretical exam instead of doing the project team work.

4   Instructor's Viewpoint: Rewards and Risks

It is very **rewarding** to see one's students get the best out of team work and eventually hand in quite good final versions of their deliverables. The improvement compared to their initial versions is usually amazing, which confirms the merit of abolishing write-once documents in courses. Seeing the students rebound from poor initial choices and from the client's mind changes is also a gratifying sign that the material taught eventually pays off.

However, the amount of time (and manpower) necessary to properly conduct the course the way described is usually not allocated by study directors. This leads to severe **risks** for the instructor, as argued next.

A recurring advice in the software engineering education literature [1] is that a single instructor cannot effectively coach projects involving more than 25 to 30 students. I never needed to enforce this quota, but was once forced (for department finance reasons) to teach 35 students. It was a gruelling time, as I did not want to compromise too much on my team-wise coaching. I enforced strict, but generous, time limits for reading each submitted document. The students that year correctly complained that my annotations often just pointed to problems but did not address how to fix them. Since every team also had a strict, but generous, time budget to interview or consult me, it was hard for them to get access to all my feedback on their progress.

Even with fewer than 25 to 30 students, it is very hard to adequately conduct the course this way. Even if the instructor spends (a lot) more time than allocated to the course, drawing on spare time to do so, some students may be unsympathetic to such dedication. They may fail to weigh it in when writing course and teacher evaluations, or they may consider it unnecessary for lack of their own motivation, if not unwarranted. Despite the (much) higher weight of the positive evaluations, this kind of comments hurts.

Finally, recent industry trends such as extreme programming, the anarchic community-based development of (excellent) software such as the Linux operating system, and the so-called web-speed development of software before the burst of the IT bubble in 2001 go a long way in undermining student belief in the relevance of a classical academic software engineering course, where there is much focus on project management and non-software deliverables. As long as there are projects successfully conducted with, and because of, that more organised and slower approach, the instructor must be able to motivate the latter to the students, lest they think learning something irrelevant in practice.

5   Recommendations

If I were to teach the course again, I would still teach it the way I did so far and described here, but I would try and comply with the following recommendations. They stem from my own observations and most of them were repeatedly asked for by the students. Their implementation is often beyond the power of the instructor, but rather a policy change by the department.

The student experience is likely to be more meaningful and less painful if there were *predecessor courses on requirements specification and software architecture.* After just a few lectures on these topics, which have entire textbooks dedicated to them, within a software engineering course, the students are not ready to properly deploy and extrapolate that knowledge on even small projects within just a handful of weeks.

Similarly, a *predecessor course on technical writing (and typesetting)* is absolutely essential. A software engineering course is the wrong place to start actually teaching these important skills, and comes too late for that in the curriculum anyway. Even students not destined for graduate studies will benefit from such a course, namely when writing course reports such as on their internship, as well as in their professional careers. Even a *predecessor course on rhetoric* would be beneficial, as many students find it hard to phrase good questions when interviewing the client. Good communication skills are essential to software engineers, despite the popular perception that they must be so-called geeks.

The instructor must enforce a limit of 25 to 30 students, especially if alone. Finding competent teaching assistants and making their contribution consistent with the one of the instructor is very hard, so ways need to be found to involve other instructors. For instance, the coaching of software engineering course projects should involve more people than its instructor. Most computer science departments have requirements, architecture, database, human-computer interaction, or validation and verification experts, who ought to coach all the teams on their topic and thereby reinforce what they already taught them in previous courses. Even in this scenario, the actual instructor can probably not handle more than 30 students.

A full-speed ten-week-period[7] is way too short to conduct the course as outlined here. Beyond the (debatable) loss of the implementation, validation, and verification of the software product, the price to pay is that not enough necessary material can be taught and exercised on small problems on time before having to be deployed on an actual project. In any case, software-project cost estimation methods, such as COCOMO, reveal five-person-teams as incompatible with ten-week-projects. The predecessor courses mentioned above would help in that direction. Otherwise, a *half-speed full-semester course* should be scheduled.

---

[7] As used in Sweden.

The *TSPi roles* and their detailed descriptions are much appreciated by the students to give structure and guidance to their teams and activities. If the project does not involve actual programming, validation, and verification, then the development manager and quality and process manager roles need to be given more work than prescribed in [3]. However, the students invariably perceived the TSPi management paperwork to be suffocating, so it ought to be carefully tuned down.

Learning from peers can also be added. For instance, each team can review the documents of another team, in addition to the reviews done by the client and coach.

Acknowledgements

I am deeply indebted to my former software engineering students, for making this course so enjoyable.

References

1. *Conference on Software Engineering Education and Training* (CSEE&T) annual series. Early proceedings in Lecture Notes in Computer Science at Springer-Verlag, later ones at IEEE Computer Society Press. 1987–present.
2. Ghezzi, Carlo and Jazayeri, Mehdi and Mandrioli, Dino. *Fundamentals of Software Engineering*, second edition. Prentice-Hall, 2003.
3. Humphrey, Watts S. *TSPi – Introduction to the Team Software Process*. Addison-Wesley, 2000.
4. Pfleeger, Shari Lawrence. *Software Engineering: Theory and Practice*, second edition. Prentice-Hall, 2001.
5. Robertson, Suzanne and Robertson, James. *Mastering the Requirements Process*. Addison-Wesley, 1999.
6. Woods, Donald R. *Problem-Based Learning: How to Gain the Most from PBL, Helping Your Students Gain the Most from PBL*, and *Resources to Gain the Most from PBL*. Department of Chemical Engineering, McMaster University, Canada.

Problems of Adiabatic Quantum Program Design

Evgeniya Khusnitdinova[1] and A.C. Cem Say[2]

Computer Engineering Department, Boğaziçi University, Istanbul, Turkey
[1] jenya1981@gmail.com, [2] say@boun.edu.tr

Abstract. Although several quantum programming languages have already been proposed, none of these are based on the newly discovered adiabatic evolution approach. We examine some flow control constructs like loops and branching from the adiabatic quantum perspective to illustrate the main design problems as a first step towards the development of an adiabatic quantum programming infrastructure.

1   Introduction

In 1982, the physicist Richard Feynman pointed out that quantum computers may perform certain tasks more efficiently than classical computers [6]. Since then, the young field of quantum computation has enjoyed a rapid growth and excited a lot of interest. Many quantum algorithms have been discovered, the most notable being Shor's famous algorithm [11] for polynomial-time factorization. However, there does not yet seem to be a unifying set of principles by which quantum algorithms are developed; this makes it hard to discover new quantum algorithms.

In 2000, a new paradigm for designing quantum algorithms, namely, the model of quantum computation by adiabatic evolution, was discovered by Farhi et al. [5]. Adiabatic quantum computation is done by tracking the evolution of a Hamiltonian from the known ground state to a ground state which encodes the desired result by a quantum computer. It was established that this model is polynomially equivalent to the standard model of quantum circuits [1], nevertheless, it provides a completely different way of constructing quantum algorithms and reasoning about them.

In parallel to the work on quantum algorithms, efforts were started to develop quantum programming languages. Several imperative quantum programming languages were introduced, such as the earliest proposal by Knill [7] in 1996, followed by QCL [8], qGCL [13], and a quantum extension of C++ by Bettelli [3]. Some studies were done in the direction of functional quantum programming languages, such as QFC [2], QML [9], and linear lambda calculus for quantum computation [12].

Till the present moment, none of the research on quantum programming languages was done within the framework of adiabatic quantum computation. We acknowledge the main problem in adiabatic quantum computation to be the lack of insight that common programmers have about the design of Hamiltonians. In this paper, we examine some flow control constructs like loops and branching from an adiabatic quantum perspective to illustrate the main design issues, as a first step towards the

A. Levi et al. (Eds.): ISCIS 2006, LNCS 4263, pp. 1040–1049, 2006.

development of an adiabatic quantum programming infrastructure. It is hoped that looking at the topic from this "programming" perspective could also provide a better understanding of adiabatic quantum computation.

2 Basics of Adiabatic Quantum Computation

2.1 Schrödinger's Equation and the Adiabatic Theorem

The state of a quantum system is described by a unit vector $|\psi\rangle$ in a Hilbert space. The evolution of the system in time is defined by the Second Postulate of Quantum Mechanics, and is described by the Schrödinger Equation:

$$i\hbar \frac{d|\psi(t)\rangle}{dt} = H(t)|\psi(t)\rangle, \tag{1}$$

where $\hbar$ is a constant (Planck's constant), and H is a hermitian operator.

The adiabatic theorem tells how to follow the evolution of the quantum system described by the Schrödinger equation under certain conditions.

Let Hamiltonian $H(s)$ be a smooth operator in a Hilbert space of dimension N. Take $H(s) = H(t/T)$, where t is a real time variable ($0 \le t \le T$), and s is a re-scaled time variable ($0 \le s \le 1$), so that T controls the rate at which $H(s)$ varies. Define the instantaneous eigenvectors $|\varphi_i\rangle$ and eigenvalues E_i of $H(s)$ by:

$$H(s)|\varphi_i(H(s))\rangle = E_i(s)|\varphi_i(H(s))\rangle, \tag{2}$$

with $E_0(s) \le E_1(s) \le ... \le E_{N-1}(s)$. Define

$$g_{min} = \min_{0 \le s \le 1}(E_1(s) - E_0(s)). \tag{3}$$

This is called the spectral gap of $H(s)$.

The Adiabatic Theorem. Let $H(s)$ be a function from [0, 1] to the vector space of Hamiltonians on n qubits. Assume $H(s)$ is continuous, has a unique ground state, for every $s \in [0,1]$, and is differentiable in all but possibly finitely many points. Let $\varepsilon > 0$ and assume that the following adiabatic condition holds for all points $s \in (0,1)$ where the derivative is defined:

$$T\varepsilon \ge (g_{min})^{-2} \cdot \left\| \frac{d}{ds} H(s) \right\| \tag{4}$$

Then, a quantum system that is initialized at time 0 with the ground state of $H(0)$ $|\psi(0)\rangle = |\varphi_g(H(0))\rangle$, and evolves according to the dynamics of the Hamiltonian

$H(s)$, ends up at re-scaled time 1 at a state $|\psi(1)\rangle$ that is within ε^c distance from $|\varphi_g(H(1))\rangle$ for some constant $c > 0$.

Informally, the adiabatic theorem affirms that for large T the final state of the system is very close to the ground state of $H(1)$. Just how large T should be for this to happen is determined by the spectral gap of the Hamiltonians $H(s)$.

2.2 Adiabatic Quantum Computation

Suppose we have a quantum system of n qubits with a time-dependent Hamiltonian $H(t)$. The rules of Quantum Mechanics say that the state of a quantum system $|\psi(t)\rangle$ changes according to (1). A specification of $H(t)$ and an initial state of the quantum system $|\psi(0)\rangle$, both chosen so that at a time T a state $|\psi(T)\rangle$ gives the answer to our problem, can be viewed as a quantum computer program.

In designing our quantum computer program we can take advantage of the Adiabatic Theorem above which claims that a quantum system will stay near its instantaneous ground state if the Hamiltonian that governs its evolution varies slowly enough.

To follow this, we have to construct a time-dependent Hamiltonian $H(s)$ and initialize our quantum system so that the initial state of the system is the ground state of $H(0)$. Also, for each specific problem that we want to solve by an adiabatic quantum computation (AQC) algorithm, the answer to that problem has to be encoded in the ground state of $H(1)$. Although we may be able to construct such $H(s)$ easily for a specific problem, it may be computationally difficult to find its final ground state.

As was mentioned above, the parameter s can be chosen as $s = t/T$, where t is real time and T is a constant which also determines the duration of the algorithm, so that $H(s) = H(t/T) = \tilde{H}(t)$ (from now on, $H(t)$ will be used with the meaning of $\tilde{H}(t)$). Therefore, if our quantum system starts at $t = 0$ in the ground state of $H(0)$, that is $|\psi_g(0)\rangle$, and if $H(t)$ varies slowly, then the evolving state vector $|\psi(t)\rangle$ will remain close to the instantaneous ground state $|\psi_g(t)\rangle$ of $H(t)$, and in particular, at time $t = T$, $|\psi(T)\rangle$ will be close to a solution of our problem.

So, the general AQC algorithm is designed and used as follows:

1. A time-dependent Hamiltonian $H(t)$ is constructed so that the initial state of the system is the given ground state of $H(0)$ and a ground state of $H(T)$ encodes the solution of the particular problem;
2. T is selected big enough;
3. The system undergoes Schrödinger evolution for time T; at the end of which the final state of the system $|\psi(T)\rangle$ will be very close to the solution;
4. The qubits of state $|\psi(T)\rangle$ are measured.

2.3 Comparison of Standard and Adiabatic Quantum Computation

Standard quantum computation in terms of quantum gates and AQC in terms of Hamiltonians are equivalent. The method of construction of a quantum circuit corresponding to a given Hamiltonian was shown in [5]. In the reverse direction, the Hamiltonian corresponding to a given quantum circuit can be constructed as described in [1], thus proving the equivalence of these two models.

Nevertheless, there are certain qualitative differences between two models. The major is that standard quantum computation in terms of gates constitutes a sequential process of applying one gate after the other. Time is measured as the number of operations performed during the computation. On the contrary, AQC is a single application of a Hamiltonian, which is continuous in real time. Evolution time plays a very important role, since the result of the AQ program depends on the duration of the program.

3 Adiabatic Quantum Programming

While reading this section, it may be interesting to keep in mind that this is probably how the introduction of a future textbook on AQ programming will look like. This naturally suggests that some changes will be needed to be made in computer science curricula, to keep up with this fundamentally new approach to computation.

3.1 Low-Level Specification of Adiabatic Quantum Programming

A unit of quantum information in AQ programming is the quantum bit – qubit. Qubits can be manipulated via two fundamental operations – application of a Hamiltonian and measurement.

Application of a Hamiltonian is an operation over a system of qubits for a specified duration T, which changes the states of the qubits in a continuous way. In adiabatic quantum computing we are interested in quantum states which constitute a ground state of a Hamiltonian.

Measurement is the operation of observing the state of a system of qubits. Measurement causes the state of observed qubits to collapse to either 0 or 1, thus converting them to classical bits.

In an adiabatic quantum program (AQP) there are three distinctive stages: initialization, application of a Hamiltonian and final measurement. During initialization, the state of a system of qubits is set to be the ground state of a Hamiltonian. For that reason, we construct the Hamiltonian so that its ground state at the beginning is an easy-to-prepare state. The application of this Hamiltonian is the main computational action in an AQP. Finally, we perform a measurement to read the result of the computation.

A complete specification of a particular AQP means specification of the initial state which is also the ground state of the Hamiltonian in the beginning, specification of the Hamiltonian which performs a particular computational task, as well as specification of the running time of the program. Note that the number of qubits necessary to perform a particular computational task can be derived from the dimension of the Hamiltonian by taking its logarithm. Therefore, we can talk about an AQP as a mapping of three variables which maps the quantum state of qubits to a classical state of bits:

$$\text{AQP}\left(\left|\psi_{init}\right\rangle, H, T\right) : \left|\psi_{init}\right\rangle \rightarrow \{0,1\}^n \tag{5}$$

3.2 Designing a Hamiltonian

The "Hamiltonian," which is the main object of AQ programming, is a smooth time-dependent hermitian operator. There is no standard way or ready procedure of designing a Hamiltonian. Having in mind that the aim is to specify a state without knowing it by assigning it a property of being a ground state of a Hamiltonian at the end of the computation, the main approach adopted in the design of the AQPs in the literature has been to formulate them as interpolations between two time-independent Hamiltonians – initial H_{init} and final H_{final}, e.g.:

$$H(s) = sH_{init} + (1-s)H_{final}, \tag{6}$$

where $s = t/T$ is the rescaled time parameter. As was already mentioned above, the initial Hamiltonian is chosen so that its ground state is an easy-to-prepare state and the final Hamiltonian is so that its ground state encodes the result of the AQP. Note that the "speed" of such a Hamiltonian $H(t)$ is $\left\|\frac{dH(t)}{dt}\right\| = \left\|\frac{H_{final} - H_{init}}{T}\right\|$ and therefore is in inverse dependence of T: if T is bigger then $H(t)$ varies slower. The correctness of an AQC algorithm strongly depends on the choice of T: the slower the Hamiltonian varies, the more correctly the algorithm works.

For certain problems like 3-SAT and similar problems of finding a satisfying assignment for a Boolean formula, the final Hamiltonian can be specified by means of a so-called energy function [5]. In those cases, an energy function for a particular clause in the Boolean formula is a function of bit values corresponding to Boolean variables of a certain clause: the function gives 0 if the bit values correspond to a satisfying assignment of a clause, and it gives 1 otherwise. The total energy function for the Boolean formula is the sum of energy functions for each clause contained in the formula. Clearly, the minimum of the total energy function corresponds to the assignment for Boolean variables which violates minimum number (i.e. possibly zero) of clauses. The final Hamiltonian is a quantum operator in a Hilbert space, whose eigenvectors are standard basis vectors of the Hilbert space with eigenvalues equal to values of energy function for the corresponding assignments of Boolean variables encoded in basis vectors (a system of n qubits constitutes 2^n basis vectors of a Hilbert space). The smallest eigenvalue possible is 0, and the corresponding eigenvector is a ground state of H_{final} which describes the satisfying assignment of the given Boolean formula (or, in the case of existence of multiple satisfying assignments, the uniform superposition of satisfying assignments). In this context, solving a 3-SAT problem is equivalent to finding a ground state of a final Hamiltonian.

Another known way of designing a Hamiltonian is through a procedure of converting a quantum circuit to an AQP as suggested in [1]. The procedure takes advantage of the so-called 'history state' of the computation and constructs initial and final

Hamiltonians out of the given sequence of quantum gates – unitary transformations. The final state of the AQC is that 'history state' which has a non-negligible projection to a final state of the quantum circuit.

The main components of this conversion procedure which will be used in the next section are given below. For more details, see [1].

$$H_{init} = H_{clockinit} + H_{input} + H_{clock},\tag{7}$$

$$H_{final} = \frac{1}{2}\sum_{l=1}^{L}H_l + H_{input} + H_{clock},\tag{8}$$

$$H_{clockinit} = |1\rangle\langle 1|_1^c,\ H_{input} = \sum_{i=1}^{n}|1\rangle\langle 1|_i \otimes |0\rangle\langle 0|_1^c,\ H_{clock} = \sum_{l=1}^{L}|01\rangle\langle 01|_{l,l+1}^c,\tag{9}$$

$$H_l = I \otimes |100\rangle\langle 100|_{l-1,l,l+1}^c - U_l \otimes |110\rangle\langle 100|_{l-1,l,l+1}^c -$$

$$-U_l^+ \otimes |100\rangle\langle 110|_{l-1,l,l+1}^c + I \otimes |110\rangle\langle 110|_{l-1,l,l+1}^c,\tag{10}$$

where n is the number of qubits involved in the computation, L is the number of gates in the given quantum circuit, U_l is the unitary matrix corresponding to the lth gate, and subscript c denotes so called "clock" qubits. All qubits are initialized to 0.

3.3 Determining the Running Time of an Adiabatic Quantum Program

The correctness of an AQP depends on how slowly the time-dependent Hamiltonian $H(t)$ varies. The Hamiltonian varies slower as T gets larger. When T goes to infinity, the AQC adiabatic quantum algorithm becomes 100% correct, i.e. finds a solution to our problem with 100% probability.

Since we cannot afford infinite time algorithms, we have to accept a probability of finding the solution that is less than 100%, thus running the algorithm for a finite time T. The question is how large we should choose T so that the probability of finding a solution is acceptable.

By various numerical simulations of algorithms for instances of a particular problem, we can calculate the average time needed to reach a desired probability p<1. For example, in [4] the probability 1/8 was chosen as a sensible one. By various numerical simulations of the instances of the problem under consideration, the median time to achieve the probability 1/8 to find the solution was estimated.

This, of course, is not meaningful in the general case: Having to run expensive classical simulations is exactly the rthing that we want to avoid by having a quantum computer. Ideally, we wish to use equation (4) to calculate an appropriate value of T. This, however is not possible in the general case using the current analytical methods [5], and constitutes a major unsolved problem of adiabatic quantum computation: We have interesting algorithms which solve NP-complete problems in a totally new way, but we cannot analyze their time complexities with our present mathematical abilities. This also means that, except in lucky cases where the spectral gap can be computed analytically, the required evolution time, which we specified as part of the input, of an adiabatic program is supposed to be found with guesswork.

3.4 Flow Control Manifestations in Adiabatic Quantum Programs

In this section, we discuss two familiar programming structures – loops and conditional branching – from the perspective of AQ programming, to illustrate the fundamentally different "feel" of the framework. As will be elaborated in the discussion, this is basically an introduction about what *not* to do during adiabatic program design.

3.4.1 Loops

Let us consider how loop structures look in the framework of AQP. The simplest loop format is:

```
DO n times {loop_body}
```

In a standard quantum program, this kind of loop would be implemented as a quantum circuit containing the sub-circuit which corresponds to {loop_body} *n* consecutive times. In an AQP, this will just correspond to a Hamiltonian. In the examples below, Hamiltonians of the body and its loop are constructed and compared.

Example 1. Consider the circuit shown in Fig. 1, and convert it to an AQP. The matrix representation of the $\pi/2$-rotation around the y-axis is:

$$R_y(\pi/2) = \cos(\pi/4) - i\sigma_y \sin(\pi/4) = \frac{1}{\sqrt{2}}\begin{pmatrix} 1 & -1 \\ 1 & 1 \end{pmatrix} \tag{11}$$

According to (7)-(10), $H_{clockinit} = |1\rangle\langle 1|^c$, $H_{input} = |1\rangle\langle 1| \otimes |0\rangle\langle 0|^c$, H_{clock} may be ignored and $H_1 = I \otimes |0\rangle\langle 0|^c - R_y(\pi/2) \otimes |1\rangle\langle 0|^c - R_y^+(\pi/2) \otimes |0\rangle\langle 1|^c + I \otimes |1\rangle\langle 1|^c$.

Therefore, $H_{init} = \begin{pmatrix} 0 & 0 & 0 & 0 \\ 0 & 1 & 0 & 0 \\ 0 & 0 & 1 & 0 \\ 0 & 0 & 0 & 1 \end{pmatrix}$, $H_{final} = \frac{1}{2\sqrt{2}}\begin{pmatrix} \sqrt{2} & -1 & 0 & -1 \\ -1 & \sqrt{2} & 1 & 0 \\ 0 & 1 & 3\sqrt{2} & -1 \\ -1 & 0 & -1 & \sqrt{2} \end{pmatrix}$ and

$$H(s) = (1-s)H_{init} + sH_{final} = \frac{1}{4}\begin{pmatrix} 2s & -\sqrt{2}s & 0 & -\sqrt{2}s \\ -\sqrt{2}s & 4-2s & \sqrt{2}s & 0 \\ 0 & \sqrt{2}s & 4+2s & -\sqrt{2}s \\ -\sqrt{2}s & 0 & -\sqrt{2}s & 4-2s \end{pmatrix} \tag{12}$$

$$|0\rangle \quad \boxed{R_y(\pi/2)} \quad \frac{1}{\sqrt{2}}(|0\rangle + |1\rangle)$$

Fig. 1. Simple quantum circuit involving one qubit and one quantum gate corresponding to the $\pi/2$-rotation around the y-axis

Example 2. Consider the "loop" in Fig. 2, and convert it to an AQP. Again, $H_{clockinit} = |1\rangle\langle 1|_1^c$, $H_{input} = |1\rangle\langle 1| \otimes |0\rangle\langle 0|_1^c$, $H_{clock} = |01\rangle\langle 01|^c$, $H_1 = I \otimes |00\rangle\langle 00|^c -$

$- R_y(\pi/2) \otimes |10\rangle\langle 00|^c - R_y^+(\pi/2) \otimes |00\rangle\langle 10|^c + I \otimes |10\rangle\langle 10|^c$ and $H_2 = I \otimes |10\rangle\langle 10|^c -$

$- R_y(\pi/2) \otimes |11\rangle\langle 10|^c - R_y^+(\pi/2) \otimes |10\rangle\langle 11|^c + I \otimes |11\rangle\langle 11|^c$. Therefore,

$$H_{init} = \begin{pmatrix} 0 & \cdots & & & & & & 0 \\ & 1 & 0 & \cdots & & & & 0 \\ \vdots & 0 & 1 & 0 & \cdots & & & 0 \\ \vdots & & 0 & 1 & 0 & \cdots & & 0 \\ & \vdots & & 0 & 1 & 0 & \cdots & 0 \\ & & \vdots & & 0 & 2 & 0 & 0 \\ & & & \vdots & & 0 & 1 & 0 \\ 0 & 0 & 0 & 0 & 0 & 0 & 0 & 1 \end{pmatrix}, \quad H_{final} = \frac{1}{2\sqrt{2}} \begin{pmatrix} \sqrt{2} & 0 & -1 & 0 & 0 & 0 & -1 & 0 \\ 0 & 2\sqrt{2} & 0 & 0 & 0 & 0 & 0 & 0 \\ -1 & 0 & 2\sqrt{2} & -1 & 1 & 0 & 0 & -1 \\ 0 & 0 & -1 & \sqrt{2} & 0 & 0 & 1 & 0 \\ 0 & 0 & 1 & 0 & 3\sqrt{2} & 0 & -1 & 0 \\ 0 & 0 & 0 & 0 & 0 & 4\sqrt{2} & 0 & 0 \\ -1 & 0 & 0 & 1 & -1 & 0 & 2\sqrt{2} & -1 \\ 0 & 0 & -1 & 0 & 0 & 0 & -1 & \sqrt{2} \end{pmatrix} \text{ and}$$

$$H_{loop}(s) = \frac{1}{4} \begin{pmatrix} 2s & 0 & -\sqrt{2}s & 0 & 0 & 0 & -\sqrt{2}s & 0 \\ 0 & 4 & 0 & 0 & 0 & 0 & 0 & 0 \\ -\sqrt{2}s & 0 & 4 & -\sqrt{2}s & \sqrt{2}s & 0 & 0 & -\sqrt{2}s \\ 0 & 0 & -\sqrt{2}s & 4-2s & 0 & 0 & \sqrt{2}s & 0 \\ 0 & 0 & \sqrt{2}s & 0 & 4+2s & 0 & -\sqrt{2}s & 0 \\ 0 & 0 & 0 & 0 & 0 & 4+4s & 0 & 0 \\ -\sqrt{2}s & 0 & 0 & \sqrt{2}s & -\sqrt{2}s & 0 & 4 & -\sqrt{2}s \\ 0 & 0 & -\sqrt{2}s & 0 & 0 & 0 & -\sqrt{2}s & 4-2s \end{pmatrix}. \tag{13}$$

AQPs in examples 1 and 2, according to [1], all qubits are initialized to 0 and the running time is sensible since the corresponding spectral gaps are not zero.

Compared to (12), (13) has a larger dimension, since more gates are involved in the computation. But what these examples really show is that one really should not be tempted to automatically build one's AQPs by conversion from the circuit model. The obvious equality of a single $R_y(\pi/4)$ (i.e. "not") gate to Fig. 2 makes this point clear: Like in all other kinds of programming, we should develop an insight about the "natural" way to write good programs in this new language. As mentioned above, this will probably require future programming students to learn linear algebra and related mathematical topics as thoroughly as today's physics students as a prerequisite.

Consider the following "hybrid" classical/quantum loop:

```
DO n times {loop_body; measure; check}
```

This loop describes the act of running of an AQP n times consecutively, checking the output for correctness after each run. (This can clearly be deemed efficient only for problems in NP). In practice, due to the probabilistic nature of AQPs, they have to be run several times in this fashion to amplify the probability of success. This causes an n-fold increase in the running time of the originally designed AQP. However, assuming that there are resources available to increase the number of qubits participating in the computation n times, the n copies of the AQP can be run simultaneously, keeping the original running time. The above-mentioned loop can be realized, therefore, by

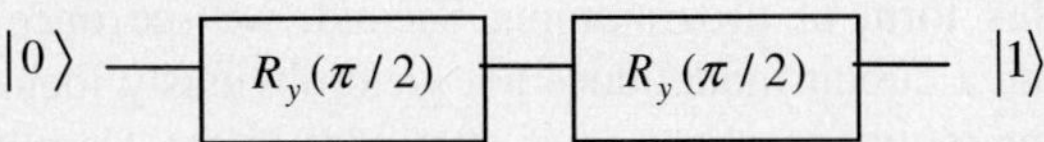

Fig. 2. Simple quantum "loop" circuit involving one qubit and two consecutive quantum gates each corresponding to the $\pi/2$-rotation around the y-axis

an AQP with the new Hamiltonian obtained by taking the tensor product of the original Hamiltonian by itself n times:

$$\text{AQPPll}\left(\left|\psi_{init}\right\rangle^{\otimes poly(n)}, H^{\otimes poly(n)}, T\right) : \left|\psi_{init}\right\rangle^{\otimes poly(n)} \rightarrow \{0,1\}^{n \cdot poly(n)} \qquad (14)$$

3.4.2 Conditional Branching

Classical programs allow the conditional execution of code in dependence on the content of a Boolean variable, i.e. conditional branching:

```
IF condition THEN branch1 ELSE branch2
```

In standard quantum computation, pure quantum conditional branching can be realized using controlled gates. For instance, consider the conditional $\pi/2$-rotation shown in Fig. 3. The unitary matrix of that quantum circuit is:

$$U = \begin{pmatrix} I & 0 \\ 0 & R_y(\frac{\pi}{2}) \end{pmatrix} = \frac{1}{\sqrt{2}} \begin{pmatrix} \sqrt{2} & 0 & 0 & 0 \\ 0 & \sqrt{2} & 0 & 0 \\ 0 & 0 & 1 & -1 \\ 0 & 0 & 1 & 1 \end{pmatrix}.$$

Following Aharonov *et al.*'s converting procedure [1], for this particular circuit,

$$\left|\psi_{init}\right\rangle = \left|100\right\rangle, \quad H_{input} = \left(\left|00\right\rangle\left\langle00\right| + \left|01\right\rangle\left\langle01\right| + \left|11\right\rangle\left\langle11\right|\right) \otimes \left|0\right\rangle\left\langle0\right|^c, \quad H_{clockinit} = \left|1\right\rangle\left\langle1\right|^c,$$

$$H_1 = I \otimes \left|0\right\rangle\left\langle0\right|^c - U \otimes \left|1\right\rangle\left\langle0\right|^c - U^+ \otimes \left|0\right\rangle\left\langle1\right|^c + I \otimes \left|1\right\rangle\left\langle1\right|^c \quad \text{and we ignore} \quad H_{clock}.$$

Explicitly,

$$H_{init} = \begin{pmatrix} 1 & 0 & 0 & 0 & 0 & 0 & 0 & 0 \\ 0 & 1 & 0 & 0 & 0 & 0 & 0 & 0 \\ 0 & 0 & 1 & 0 & 0 & 0 & 0 & 0 \\ 0 & 0 & 0 & 1 & 0 & 0 & 0 & 0 \\ 0 & 0 & 0 & 0 & 0 & 0 & 0 & 0 \\ 0 & 0 & 0 & 0 & 0 & 1 & 0 & 0 \\ 0 & 0 & 0 & 0 & 0 & 0 & 1 & 0 \\ 0 & 0 & 0 & 0 & 0 & 0 & 0 & 1 \end{pmatrix}, \quad H_{final} = \frac{1}{4}\begin{pmatrix} 6 & -2 & 0 & 0 & 0 & 0 & 0 & 0 \\ -2 & 2 & 0 & 0 & 0 & 0 & 0 & 0 \\ 0 & 0 & 6 & -2 & 0 & 0 & 0 & 0 \\ 0 & 0 & -2 & 2 & 0 & 0 & 0 & 0 \\ 0 & 0 & 0 & 0 & 2 & -\sqrt{2} & 0 & -\sqrt{2} \\ 0 & 0 & 0 & 0 & -\sqrt{2} & 2 & \sqrt{2} & 0 \\ 0 & 0 & 0 & 0 & 0 & \sqrt{2} & 6 & -\sqrt{2} \\ 0 & 0 & 0 & 0 & -\sqrt{2} & 0 & -\sqrt{2} & 2 \end{pmatrix} \quad \text{and}$$

$$H_{cond}(s) = \frac{1}{4}\begin{pmatrix} 4+2s & -2s & 0 & 0 & 0 & 0 & 0 & 0 \\ -2s & 4-2s & 0 & 0 & 0 & 0 & 0 & 0 \\ 0 & 0 & 4+2s & -2s & 0 & 0 & 0 & 0 \\ 0 & 0 & -2s & 4-2s & 0 & 0 & 0 & 0 \\ 0 & 0 & 0 & 0 & 2s & -\sqrt{2}s & 0 & -\sqrt{2}s \\ 0 & 0 & 0 & 0 & -\sqrt{2}s & 4-2s & \sqrt{2}s & 0 \\ 0 & 0 & 0 & 0 & 0 & \sqrt{2}s & 4+2s & -\sqrt{2}s \\ 0 & 0 & 0 & 0 & -\sqrt{2}s & 0 & -\sqrt{2}s & 4-2s \end{pmatrix}. \qquad (15)$$

Since $H_{cond}(s)$ has the non-zero gap, the running time for this AQP is sensible.

Two remarks are in order: First, note that, although we give the Hamiltonians explicitly for pedagogical purposes, this is clearly not possible (nor required) when a sizable number of bits constitute our system. The program is supposed to be describeable implicitly, and doing this without knowing the final ground state is what requires ingenuity in this form of programming Second, we see once again that automatic conversion from a circuit model does not yield obviously identifiable patterns corresponding to our intuitions about an if statement in the Hamiltonian. Once again, a "native" design approach is called for.

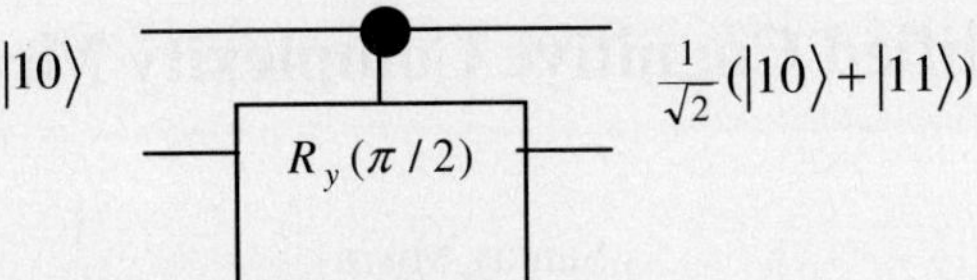

Fig. 3. Simple quantum conditional circuit involving one control and one target qubit and one controlled gate corresponding to the controlled $\pi/2$-rotation around the y-axis

4 Conclusion

Since adiabatic quantum computation was recently shown to have universal computational power, it is only natural to ask how a programming language suitable for this paradigm would look like. We have started to examine this issue by "adiabaticizing" some well-known flow control structures using the technique presented in [1]. As expected, such a direct conversion from programs written in a different paradigm neither yields efficient adiabatic programs, nor seems to be helpful about developing an insight about how to design them. The correct approach would indeed probably rely on the mathematical vocabulary and tools that have already been developed for dealing with these kinds of matrices, [1] and the educational requirements that this imposes on prospective adiabatic programmers are likely to have important consequences for the design of future computer science curricula.

References

1. Aharonov, D., *et al.*: Adiabatic Quantum Computation is Equivalent to Standard Quantum Computation. arXiv:quant-ph/0405098 (2004)
2. Altenkirch, T., *et al.*: A Functional Quantum Programming Language. arXiv:quant-ph/0409065 (2005)
3. Bettelli, S.: Toward an architecture for quantum programming. PhD Thesis, Universita di Trento (2002)
4. Farhi, E., *et al.*: A Quantum Adiabatic Evolution Algorithm Applied to Random Instances of an NP-Complete Problem. arXiv:quant-ph/0104129 (2001)
5. Farhi, E., *et al.*: Quantum Computation by Adiabatic Evolution. arXive:quant-ph/0001106 (2000)
6. Feynman, R.: Simulating Physics with Computers. International Journal of Theoretical Physics 21: 467–488 (1982)
7. Knill, E.: Conventions for Quantum Pseudocode. LANL report LAUR-96-2724 (1996)
8. Ömer, B.: A Procedural Formalism for Quantum Computing, Master thesis, Technical University of Vienna (1998)
9. Selinger, P.: Towards a Quantum Programming Language. Mathematical Structures in Computer Science 14(4): 527-586 (2004)
10. Selinger, P.: A Brief Survey of Quantum Programming Languages. Proceed. of the 7th Int'l Sympos. on Funct. and Logic Progr., Nara, Japan. Springer LNCS 2998, pp. 1-6 (2004)
11. Shor, P.: Algorithms for Quantum Computation: Discrete Logarithms and Factoring. arXiv:quant-ph/9508027 (1994)
12. Van Tonder, A.: A Lambda Calculus for Quantum Computation, arXiv:quant-ph/0307150 (2004)
13. Zuliani. P.: Quantum Programming. PhD Thesis, University of Oxford (2001)

Modified Cognitive Complexity Measure

Sanjay Misra

Department of Computer Engineering
Atilim University, Ankara, Turkey
smisra@atilim.edu.tr

Abstract. In cognitive functional size measure, the functional size is proportional to weighted cognitive complexity of all internal BCS`s and number of input and output. This paper proposes the modification in cognitive functional size complexity measure. The proposed complexity measure is proportional to total occurrence of operators and operands and all internal BCS´s. The operators and operands are equally important in design consideration. Thus, the contribution of the operators, operands and cognitive aspects complete the definition of a complexity measure in terms of cognitive. Accordingly, a new formula is developed for calculating the modified cognitive complexity measure. An attempt has also been made to evaluate modified cognitive complexity measure in terms of nine Weyuker's properties, through examples. It has been found that seven of nine Weyuker's properties have been satisfied by the modified cognitive complexity measure and hence establishes as a well-structured one.

Keywords: Software metrics, cognitive weights, basic control structures, cognitive complexity measure.

1   Introduction

Many efforts have been done to propose such complexity measure, which satisfied most of the parameters of software. Numbers of complexity measures are proposed for this purpose. Some of them are McCabe's cyclomatic number [8], Halstead programming effort [4], Oviedo's data flow complexity measures [10], Basili's measure [2], [3], Wang's cognitive functional size measure [16], Knot complexity [12] and others [1], [5], [6], [7]. All the reported complexity measures are supposed to cover the effectiveness and clarity of software and to provide good estimate of these parameters. Out of the numerous proposed measures, selecting a particular complexity measure is again a problem, as every measure has its own advantages and disadvantages. There is an ongoing effort to find such a comprehensive complexity measure, which addresses most of the parameters of software.

The cognitive complexity measures are in developing phase. Cognitive complexity measures are based on cognitive informatics, which in turn helps in comprehending the software. In cognitive functional size measure, the functional size depends upon internal architecture of the software and input and output. In this proposed metric the occurrence of operators and operands are taken into account in place of number of

A. Levi et al. (Eds.): ISCIS 2006, LNCS 4263, pp. 1050–1059, 2006.

input and output. Cognitive complexity takes into account both the internal architecture of software and I/Os it process. Wang claims that basic control structures are used for building logical software architecture, but operators and operands are equally important and part of design information. Therefore, the contributions of operators and operands have been taken. Once operators and operands have been considered, the number of input and output are automatically included. The occurrence of operators and operands directly affect the internal architecture and as well as to the cognitive complexity of software, which has not taken into consideration in the cognitive functional size approach.

In section two, we discussed the basic definitions of cognitive informatics. In section 3, the proposal of new complexity measure is given. We have evaluated the proposed measure in section 4. Robustness analysis of the proposed measure is given in section 5 with a number of comparative case studies. The conclusion of the paper is given in section 6.

2   Cognitive Weights and Information Contents of Software

In cognitive informatics, the functional complexity of software in design and comprehension is dependent on internal architecture of the software, input and output. Basic control structures (BCS), sequence, branch and iteration [13], [15] are the basic logic building blocks of any software. The cognitive weight of software [16] is the extent of difficulty or relative time and effort for comprehending given software modeled by a number of BCS's. There are two different architectures for calculating W_{bcs}: either all the BCS's are in a linear layout or some BCS's are embedded in others. For the former case, sum of the weights of all n BCS's; are added and for the latter, cognitive weights of inner BCS's are multiplied with the weights of external BCS's. The total cognitive weight of a software component W_c is defined as the sum of cognitive weight of its q linear blocks composed in individuals BCS'S. Since each block may consists of m layers of nesting BCS's, and each layer with n linear BCS's, the total cognitive weight, W_c can be calculated by:

$$W_c = \sum_{j=1}^{q} \left[\prod_{k=1}^{m} \sum_{i=1}^{n} W_c(j,k,i) \right] \tag{1}$$

Wang has also established relations between the software and the cognitive science. According to his theory, [17] software obeys the laws of Informatics and the cognitive science based on the following assertions:

- Software represents computational information.
- Software is a mathematical entity.
- Software is the coded solution to a given program.
- Software is a set of behavioral instructions to computer.

Wang [18] further defines software, as "Software in cognitive informatics is perceived as formally described design information and implemented instructions of computing application". In other words, Wang claims that complexity of any software is in the form of difficulty in understanding the information contained.

Based on the theory of Wang, the cognitive complexity should not only depend on the cognitive weights of basic control structures but also on the operators and operands, which are equally important for design considerations. Therefore, we have modified the previous cognitive functional size approach.

3   Modified Cognitive Complexity Measure

By considering the above theories, the author is in favor of that although cognitive functional size is a good measure but it does not provide the contribution of operators and operands. In this paper, an attempt has been made to establish a very simple relation between operators, operands and the cognitive weights of software. In proposed modified cognitive complexity measure (MCCM), it depends upon:

1. The total number of occurrence of operators and operands. Therefore, the complexity measure due to operators and operands can be calculated as,

$$S_{OO} = N_{i1} + N_{i2} \qquad (2)$$

   Where, N_{i1}: The total number of occurrences of operators.

   N_{i2}: The total number of occurrences of operands.

   S_{OO}: Total number of operators and operands.

2. The cognitive weights of basic control structures. In fact, cognitive weights correspond to the number of executed instructions. For example, if in a simple program without any loop, the weights assigned to such code is one. Cognitive weights of basic control structures are basic building blocks of software and the standard weights for different control structures are given in [16].

Using the above considerations, we suggest a formula for modified cognitive complexity measure:

$$\textbf{Modified Cognitive complexity Measure} = S_{oo} * W_c. \qquad (3)$$

Where, W_c and S_{OO} are given by equation 1 and 2.

In Equation-3, the S_{oo} values are multiplied by W_c values because of the possible higher structure value. For a simple program having only basic control structure the "sequence", W_i will not have any additional contribution to complexity. Therefore, for those programs the complexities are only due to S_{oo}.

The unit of modified cognitive complexity measure is defined as the cognitive weight of the simplest software component with only single number of operator and operand and a linear structured BCS i.e.

MCCM = f (S_{oo}, W_{bcs}) = $(S_{oo} * W_{bcs})$ = 1 Cognitive Complexity Unit (CCU).

The above measure has been illustrated with the help of an example given below.

Example 1. An algorithm to calculate the average of a set of numbers, to illustrate the application of MCCM to measure the complexity.

```
# define N 10
  main ()
  { int count;
    float sum, average, number;
    sum=0;
    count=0;
    while(count<N)
      {
        scanf("%f",&number);
        sum = sum +number;
        count = count +1;
      }
    average= sum/N;
    printf("N=%dsum = %f", N,sum);
    printf("average = %f",average);
  }
```

We illustrate the MCCM to calculate the complexity of the above program as under:

Total number of operands =20.
Total number of operators = 10.
S_{oo}= 20+10= 30.
BCS (sequence) W_1 = 1.
BCS (iteration) W_2 = 3.
$W_c = W_1+W_2=1+3 = 4$.
$\qquad$ MCCM $= S_{oo}* W_c = 30 * 4 = 120$.

Then, the cognitive complexity measure value of the algorithm is 120 CCU.

4   Evaluation of Modified Cognitive Complexity Measure

Weyuker [11] proposed the nine properties to evaluate and compare any software complexity measure. These properties also evaluate the weaknesses of a measure and in turn lead to the definition of good notions of software complexity. With the help of these properties, one can determine the most suitable measure among the different available complexity measures. In the following paragraphs, the modified cognitive complexity measure has been evaluated against nine Weyuker properties for establishing it as a good and comprehensive measure. For this purpose, nine examples given in [7] are considered.

Property 1: $(\exists P)\,(\exists Q)(|\,P\,|\neq|\,Q\,|)$.Where P and Q are program body.
This property states that a measure should not rank all programs as equally complex. The first of the two examples considered in [7] have two internal structures: a sequence and iteration. Total cognitive weight of this algorithm is:
$\quad W =W_1+W_2 = 4$.
Total number of operator and operands are:
$\quad S_{oo}=21$.
Hence, MCCM $= S_{oo}* W_c = 21 * 4 = 84$ CCU.

For the next example in figure 2, here is only one internal structure: a sequential. The total cognitive weight of the BCS's is:

W=1.

Total number of operator and operands are:

S_{oo}=15.

Hence, MCCM = S_{oo}* W_c = 15 * 1   = 15 CCU.

Clearly, from the above two examples where modified cognitive complexity measure is different, this property is satisfied by the proposed measure.

Property 2: Let c be a non-negative number, and then there are only finitely many programs of complexity c.

All programming language consist only finite number of operators, operands and BCS's. For modified cognitive complexity measure, it depends on the number of operators, operands, and cognitive weights, which are all finite in number for any finite length program and there is only finite number of program bodies for a given complexity value. Hence, MCCM holds for this property.

Property 3: There are distinct programs P and Q such that $|\,P\,|=|\,Q\,|$.

Example 3 considered in [7] has two internal structures: a sequential and an iteration .Total cognitive weight of this algorithm is :

$W = W_1 + W_2 = 4.$

Total number of operator and operands are:

S_{oo}= 30.

Hence, MCCM = S_{oo}* W_c = 30 * 4   = 120 CCU.

For the next example in figure 8, there are two internal structures: a sequential and iteration. Total cognitive weight of this algorithm is:

$W = W_1+W_2 = 4.$

Total number of operator and operands are:

S_{oo}=30.

Hence, MCCM = S_{oo}* W_c = 30 * 4   = 120 CCU.

Considering two programs of examples 3 and 8 [7] it is clear that for two distinct programs the modified cognitive complexity measure is same i.e. 120. Therefore, this property is satisfied by the modified cognitive complexity measure.

Property 4: $(\exists P)\,(\exists Q)(P \equiv Q\,\&\,|\,P\,|\neq|\,Q\,|).$

This property states that even though two programs compute the same function, the program complexity is determined by the implementation details. If in example figure 1[7], for loop is replaced by the formula s= (b+1) b/2 (in figure 2.) the output is not affected. For this changed program MCCM is 16 CCU, which is different for MCCM value for example figure 1(MCCM=88 CCU). For measuring the sum of first n integer by two different algorithms, it is observed that the modified cognitive complexity measure for the two algorithms of same object is different. Therefore, this property is also satisfied by the given measure.

Property 5: $(\forall P)\,(\forall Q)\,(|\,P\,| \leq |\,P;Q\,|\,\&\,|\,Q\,| \leq |\,P;Q\,|).$

Modified Cognitive complexity measure is an integer and the set of integers with operator holds the following property:

$(\forall P)\,(\forall Q)\,(P \le P + Q)$ and $(Q \le P + Q)$.

Since this equation and Weyuker's property 5, are analogous and such property 5 is satisfied by modified cognitive complexity measure.

An alternative proof of this property also exists by taking an example of the two-program bodies. For program given in Fig. 4 [7], there is one main program with two-program body. The BCS of the main program and two-program body are given separately.

The program body for finding out the factorial of the number, there are one sequential, and one branch BCS's. Total cognitive weight is given by,

$W=1+2=3$.

For, the program body for finding out the prime number, there are one sequential, one iteration and two branch BCS's. Total cognitive weight is given by,

$W=1+3*2*3=19$.

For the main program body for finding out the prime and factorial of the number, there are one sequential, two call, one branch BCS's. The total cognitive weight of the program is given by,

$W=1+5+21+2=29$.

Total number of operator and operands are:

$S_{oo}=58$.

Hence, MCCM $= S_{oo}*W_c = 58*29 = 1682$ CCU.

For program given in Fig. 5, there is one sequential, one iteration and two branch BCS's. The total cognitive weight is given by,

$W= 1+2*3*2+2=15$ [CCU].

Total number of operator and operands are:

$S_{oo}=25$.

Hence, MCCM $= S_{oo}*W_c = 25*15 = 375$ CCU.

For program given in Fig. 6, there is one sequential, one iteration and one branch BCS's. The total cognitive weight is given by,

$W= 1+2*3=7$.

Total number of operator and operands are:

$S_{oo}=20$.

Hence, MCCM $= S_{oo}*W_c = 20*7 = 140$ CCU.

It is clear from the above example that if we take the two program body, one for calculating the factorial and another for checking for prime whose cognitive weight complexity are 140 and 375 which is less than P+Q i.e. 1682. So property five also holds for this complexity measure.

Property 6a: $(\exists P)\,(\exists Q)\,(\exists R)\,(\,|\,P\,|=|\,Q\,|)\,.\,\&\,\,|\,P;\,R\,|\neq|\,Q;\,R\,|)$.
6b: $(\exists P)\,(\exists Q)\,(\exists R)\,(\,|\,P\,|=|\,Q\,|)\,.\,\&\,\,|\,R;\,P\,|\neq|\,R;\,Q\,|)$.

This property asserts that we can find two program bodies of equal complexity which when separately concatenated to a same third program yields the programs of different complexity. Our measure depends upon the number of operator, operands, and cognitive weights that are the fixed for all programs and joining program R with P and Q adds the same amount of complexity. Hence, this property is not satisfied.

Property 7: There are program bodies P and Q such that Q is formed by permuting the order of the statements of P, and ($| P |\neq| Q |$).
Since MCCS depend on the number of operators and operands and cognitive weights of basic control structures, which are fixed for any program, hence permuting the order of statement in any program will not change the value of MCCM. Hence, the MCCM will not change for the two programs. Thus, MCCM does not hold for this property.

Property 8: If P is renaming of Q, then $| P |=| Q |$.
Modified Cognitive complexity measure gives an integer so renaming of a program cannot change cognitive complexity and as such this property is clearly satisfied by the given complexity measure.

Property 9: ($\exists$P) ($\exists$Q) ($| P |+| Q |$).$<$ ($| P; Q |$).
This property allows for the possibility that as program grows from its component program bodies, additional complexity is introduced. If we take the examples 4, 5 and 6 [7], where modified cognitive complexity measure for two-program bodies are 375 and 140 and for single (combination of both) is 1682. This example proves that this complexity measure satisfies property 9.

In this section, it is proved that MCCM satisfied seven of nine Weyuker's property. The failure to satisfy property 6 and 7 is a weakness of this complexity measure. Since MCCM measures the cognitive weights, operators, and operands, which are fixed for all programs and joining, program R with P and Q adds the same amount of complexity. Therefore, this complexity measure is not satisfied by the property 6. Further, the complexity value for MCCM does not change by changing the position/order of operators, operands and BCS's. Therefore, property seven is not satisfied by proposed measure.

5 Case and Comparative Studies of MCCM

We have taken different 'C' programs from [9] for analysis of the result. We calculated the MCCM for different programs. Then, we compared MCCM with cognitive functional size and components of the proposed measure. The value of modified cognitive complexity measure, cognitive functional size and its components are given in the table [1].

The MCCM for all the programs gives higher complexity values when we compare it with cognitive functional size approach. It can be easily seen that MCCM already includes the considerations of cognitive aspects of CFS. On the other hand, the missing prospective in cognitive functional size measure is the contribution of operators and operands, which is added in the present work.

Kuswaha and Misra [7] have proposed Cognitive Information Complexity Measure (CICM), in which they established the relation between the information contents of the software and cognitive weights. They claim that the amount of information contained in the software is a function of identifiers that hold the information and the operators that perform the operations on the information. It is related to run time, which cannot be interpreted as the design information of software. Further, we have compared MCCM with CICM by taking 10 different examples from [7] as illustrated in table [2].

Table 1. Complexity values for components of MCCM and CFS

No.	Cognitive Weights (CW)	Sum of Operator & Operands (SOO)	Cognitive Functional Size(CFS)	Modified Cognitive Complexity measure (MCCM)	Ref of source code
1	6	10	21	60	Fig 7
2	4	20	8	80	Fig 1
3	3	20	14	60	Fig 6
4	6	17	30	102	Fig 8
5	9	25	30	225	Fig 5
6	3	35	9	105	Fig 2
7	10	52	9	520	Fig 3
8	16	58	46	928	Fig 4

Table 2. Complexity values for MCCM and CICM

ProgramNo.	1	2	3	4	5	6	7	8	9	10
MCCM	88	16	120	1682	375	140	352	120	42	120
CICM	19	3	19	97	19	30	83	22	10	14

A plot for MCCM and CICM is shown in figure 1. The plot shows the trends of modified cognitive complexity measure with cognitive information complexity measure. It is seen that the value of MCCM is very high at two places; it is due to high value of operators and operands. It is worth mentioned that CICM approach is comparatively difficult, more complex and time consuming. In his formulation, one has to calculate the weighted information count of each line of code. Further, in case of MCCM, it is very easy to calculate the complexity value. Therefore, this measure is comparatively and computationally simple. It will help to the developers and practitioners in evaluating the complexity of software, which serves both as analyzer and as a predicator in quantitative software engineering.

MCCM is language independent complexity measure except declarative and functional languages because of non-existence of BCS's for these languages. The language independency of modified cognitive complexity measure can be easily proved by applying it on different implementations for same algorithm in different languages. Since, MCCM measures the cognitive weights, operator, and operands, which are same for all implementations for the same algorithms. This obliviously gives the same complexity values. However, cognitive information complexity measure is not language independent complexity measure.

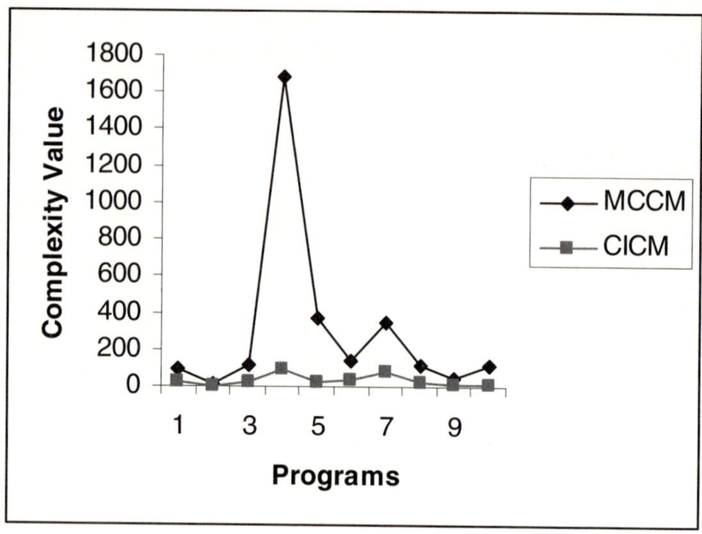

Fig. 1. Comparative graphs for MCCM and CICM

6 Conclusion

A relation between operator, operands and the cognitive weights of software has been proposed. The basic aspect realizing such relation is to be established a simple formula to calculate cognitive complexity measure. In addition, it has been established that besides from basic control structures, the operators and operands are also an important dimension in calculating software complexity. This has been formulated as Modified Cognitive Complexity Measure based on the number of operators, operands and cognitive weights of different BCS's.

Software complexity measures serves both as an analyzer and as a predicator in quantitative software engineering. Software quality is defined as the completeness, correctness, consistency, no misinterpretation, and no ambiguity, feasible and verifiable in both specification and implementation. For a good complexity measure, it is very necessary that the particular complexity measure not only satisfy the above-mentioned property of software quality but also satisfy the nine Weyuker's properties. The software complexity in terms of modified cognitive complexity measure based on operators and operands and cognitive weight, thus as a well-structured complexity measure.

Acknowledgments. I am highly thankful to my colleague Dr. Hurevren Kilic for his valuable comments and suggestions. I am also thankful to Prof. Abraham Akman, chair of the department for his encouragement and support during the work.

References

1. Baker, A.L., Zweben, S. H.: A comparison of Measures of control flow complexity. IEEE Transaction on Software Engineering, 6 (1980) 506-511.
2. Basili, V.R.: Qualitative software complexity models: A summary in tutorial on models and methods for software management and engineering, IEEE Computer Society Press, Los Alamitos, CA, (1980).
3. Basili, V.R., Selby, R.W., Phillips, T.Y.: Metric analysis and data validation across fortran projection. IEEE Transactions on Software Engineering, 9 (1983) 652-663.
4. Halstead, M.H.: Elements of software science. Elsevier North-Holland, New York. 1997.
5. Harrison W.: An entropy-based measure of software complexity. IEEE Transactions on Software Engineering, 18(11)(1992) 1025-1029.
6. Kemola, T., Rilling, J.: A Cognitive Complexity Metric Based on Category Learning. Proceeding of the 2nd IEEE International Conference on Cognitive Informatics, IEEE CS Press, (2003) 1044-1050.
7. Kushwaha, D.S., Misra, A.K.: Robustness Analysis of Cognitive Information Complexity Measure using Weyuker's Properties. ACM SIGSOFT Software Engineering Notes, 31, 1 (2006) 1-6,
8. McCabe, T. H.: A complexity measure. IEEE Transactions Software Engineering, SE-2, 6, (1976) 308-320.
9. Misra, S., Misra, A.K.: Evaluating cognitive complexity measure with Weyuker's properties. Proceedings of third IEEE International Conference on Cognitive Informatics, IEEE CS Press, (2004) 103-108.
10. Oviedo, E.I.: Control flow, data and program complexity. Proc. IEEE COMPSAC, Chicago, IL, (1980) 146-152.
11. Weyuker, E.J.: Evaluating software complexity measure. IEEE Transaction on Software Complexity Measure, 14,9 (1988) 1357-1365.
12. Woodward, M.R., Hennel, M. A., David.: A measure of control flow complexity in program text. IEEE Transaction on Software Engineering, SE-5, 1,(1979) 45-50.
13. Wang, Y.: Component Based Software Measurement in F. Barbier ed. Business Component - Based Software Engineering. 247-262, 2002.
14. Wang, Y.: The real-time process algebra (RTPA). Annuals of Software Engineering An International Journal, 14,(2002)235-274.
15. Wang, Y., Shao, J.: On cognitive informatics, Keynote Lecture. Proceeding of the 1st IEEE International Conference on Cognitive Informatics, (2002) 34-42.
16. Wang, Y., Shao, J.: A new measure of software complexity based on cognitive weight. Can. J. Elect. Comput. Engg. (2003), 69-74.
17. Wang, Y: On cognitive informatics: Foundation of Software Engineering. Proceeding of the 3rd IEEE International Conference on Cognitive Informatics (ICCI'04), IEEE CS Press,(2004) 22-31.
18. Wang, Y.:On the Informatics Laws of Software. Proceeding of the 1st IEEE International Conference on Cognitive Informatics (ICCI'04), IEEE CS Press, (2004)132-141.

Coverage-Based, Prioritized Testing Using Neural Network Clustering

Nida Gökçe[1], Mubariz Eminov[2], and Fevzi Belli[3]

[1] Faculty of Arts and Sciences, Department of Statistics, Mugla University, Turkey
[3] Department of Computer Science, Electrical Engineering and Mathematics,
University of Paderborn, Germany
[1] nidagokce@yahoo.com, [2] emubariz@hotmail.com, [3] belli@upb.de

Abstract. Graph-based algorithms are commonly used to automatically generate test cases for coverage-oriented testing of software systems. Because of time and cost constraints, the entire set of test cases generated by those algorithms cannot be run. It is then essential to prioritize the test cases in sense of a ranking, i.e., to order them according to their significance which usually is given by several attributes of relevant events entailed. This paper suggests unsupervised neural network clustering of test cases for forming preference groups, where adaptive competitive learning algorithm is applied for training the neural network used. A case study demonstrates and validates the approach.

Keywords: Event sequence, pair-wise coverage, clustering, competitive learning, importance degree, test ranking.

1   Introduction

Testing is the traditional validation method in the software industry. There is no justification, however, for any assessment of the correctness of the system under test (SUT) based on the success (or failure) of a single test, because there can potentially be an infinite number of test cases. To overcome this shortcoming of testing concerning completeness, formal methods have been proposed, which introduce models that represent the relevant, desirable features of the SUT. The modeled features are either functional behavior or structural issues of the SUT, leading to *specification-oriented* testing or *implementation-oriented* testing, respectively. Once the model is established, it "guides" the test process to generate and select test cases, which form sets of test cases (also called *test suites*). The selection is ruled by an *adequacy criterion*, which provides a measure of how effective a given set of test cases is in terms of its potential to reveal faults [1]. Most of the existing adequacy criteria are coverage-oriented. Thus, the ratio of the portion of the specification or code that is covered by the given test set in relation to the uncovered portion can then be used as a decisive factor in determining the point in time at which to stop testing (*test termination*).

   This paper is on model-based, specification-oriented testing; i.e., the underlying model represents the system behavior interacting with the user's actions. The system's behavior and user's actions will be viewed here as events, more precisely, as

A. Levi et al. (Eds.): ISCIS 2006, LNCS 4263, pp. 1060–1071, 2006.

desirable events if they are in accordance with the user expectations. Moreover, the approach includes modeling of the faults as *undesirable events*. This represents, mathematically spoken, a complementary view of the behavioral model. The original view and the complementary view make up then the *holistic* view.

A well-known family of algorithms [1-3] utilize combinatorial design all pair-wise interactions that are tested independently and incorporated into a test suite. These algorithms are extension of the greedy algorithms [4] that generate only one test at a time, therefore they are ineffective in terms of both execution time and cost. We prefer here a group of graph-based algorithms introduced in [5-7] and generate test suites through a finite sequence of discrete events. The underlying optimization problem is a generalization of the Chinese Postman Problem (CPP) [8] and algorithms given in [5-7] differ from the well-known ones in that they satisfy not only the constraint that a minimum total length of test sequences is required, but also fulfill the coverage criterion with respect to converging of all event pairs represented graphically. Bad news is that exercising the complete test suite constructed may run out the test budget given by project resources. To overcome this problem in sense of "divide and conquer" principle, a *prioritized* version of the mentioned test generation algorithms is needed. The required prioritization has to schedule the test process, to meet the needs and preferences of test management how to spend the test budget. However, SUT and software objects, i.e., components, architecture, etc., usually have a great variety of features. Therefore, test prioritization entails the determination of order relation(s) for these features. Generally speaking, we have m objects, whereby each object has a number of features that we call *dimension*. Test prioritization problem then reduces to comparison of the test objects of different dimensions. Being of enormous practical relevance, this is a tough problem to solve in general.

Existing approaches to solving this problem usually suggest constructing a density covering array in which all pair-wise interactions are covered [2, 3]. Every t-tuple is then qualified by a number of values to each of which a degree of importance is assigned. In order to capture important interactions among pairs of choices the importance of pairs is defined as the benefit of the tests. Every pair covered by the test contributes to the total benefit of a test suite by its benefit. Therefore, the tests given by a test suite are to be ordered according to the importance of corresponding pairs. However, such interaction-based, prioritized algorithms are computationally complex and thus mostly less effective.

In this paper we suggest a prioritized testing approach that attempts to improve the testing capacity of the algorithm described in [7] as it is of less complexity than the ones known from literature and provides the ordering of the implementation of the tests to be run. For this aim, to each of the tests generated a degree of its importance is assigned. This degree is indirectly determined through estimation of the events qualified by several attributes. These attributes depend on the features of the project and their values are justified by their significance to the user. We give some examples how to define such attributes and assign values to them, based on a graphical representation of corresponding events. Those events compose an unstructured multidimensional data set that is divided into preferable groups the number of which should be determined in advance, because they define "the rules of the game". To obtain those groups we use a clustering scheme based on unsupervised neural network (NN) training of which is performed by an adaptive competitive learning (CL) algorithm. The effectiveness of the proposed testing approach is validated by a case study.

This paper is organized as follows. Section 2 presents the definition of NN-based clustering. Section 3 describes the proposed prioritized graph-based testing approach. Section 4 includes the case study and Section 5 give hints to further research and concludes the paper.

2 Background

2.1 Event Sequence Graphs

[5, 6] introduced a graphical representation of both the behavioral model and the fault model of the SUT which enables a scalable generation and selection of test cases. That work uses *event sequence graphs (ESG)* for representing the user and the system behavior as well as user-system interaction. Basically, an *event* is an externally observable phenomenon, such as an environmental or a user stimulus, or a system response, punctuating different stages of the system activity. A simple example of an ESG is given in Fig 1. Mathematically, an ESG is a labeled graph and may be thought of as an ordered pair *ESG=(α, E)*, where α is a finite set of nodes (vertices) uniquely labeled by some input symbols of the alphabet Σ, denoting events, and *E*: $\alpha \rightarrow \alpha$, a precedence relation, possibly empty, on α. The elements of *E* represent directed arcs (edges) between the nodes in α. Given two nodes *a* and *b* in α, a directed arc *ab* from *a* to *b* signifies that event *b* can follow event *a*, defining an *event pair (EP)* ab. The remaining pairs given by the alphabet Σ form the set of *faulty event pairs (FEP)*, e.g., *ba*. As a convention, a dedicated, start vertex is the *entry* of the ESG whereas a *final* vertex represents the exit, denoted by an incoming and outgoing edge, respectively.

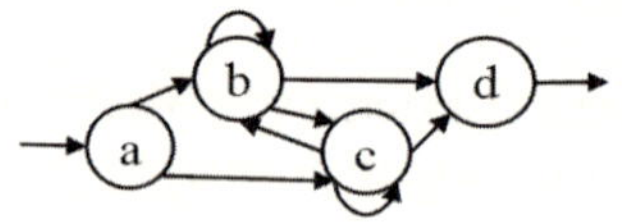

Fig. 1. An event sequence graph

Following some definitions are informally introduced that are sufficient to describe the test generation algorithm.

A sequence of *n+1* consecutive (legal) events that represents the sequence of n arcs is called a *event sequence (ES) of the length n+1*, e.g., an EP (event pair) is an ES of length 2. An ES is *complete* if it starts at the initial state of the ESG and ends at the final event; in this case it is called a *complete ES (CES)*.

A *faulty event sequence (FES) of the length n* consists of n-1 subsequent events that form a (legal) ES of length n-2 plus a concluding, subsequent FEP. An FES is *complete* if it starts at the initial state of the ESG; in this case it is called *faulty complete ES*, abbreviated as *FCES*.

2.2 Neural Network-Based Clustering

Clustering is a technique to generate an optimal partition of a given, supposedly unstructured data set into a predefined number of clusters (or groups). Homogeneity within the groups and heterogeneity between them can be settled by means of unsupervised neural network-based clustering algorithms [12, 14]. Such algorithms (being in NN framework) are known as *learning algorithms* that provide training of NN. We deal with the family of competitive learning (CL) algorithms that are a type of self-organizing networking models. According to these algorithms "winning" weight vector (weights of connections between input and output nodes) or *cluster center* can be adjusted by applying "winner-takes-all" strategy in training phase of the NN under consideration. Clustering requires a data set $X = \{x_1,...,x_n\} \in R^p$ be partitioned into c numbers of clusters each of which contains a data subset S_i. Each cluster is represented by a cluster center (*prototype*) that corresponds to a weight vector $w = (w_1,...,w_p) \in R^p$ and after finding a trained value of all weight vectors $W = \{w_1,...,w_c\}$ a data set $w \in R^p$ is divided into i^{th} cluster by the condition:

$$S_i = \left\{ X \in R^p \, \big\| x - w_i \big\| \leq \big\| x - w_j \big\| \quad \forall i \neq j \right\} \tag{1}$$

Training of the weight vectors according to CL algorithm is executed as follows: Firstly, for a data point $x_k \in R^p$ selected from X the winner weight vector w_w is determined by:

$$w_w = \arg \min_i \left\{ \big\| x_k - w_i \big\| \right\} \qquad k = 1,...,n \qquad i = 1,...,c \tag{2}$$

where $\|.\|$ is *Euclidean distance measure*. Then this vector is adjusted at step t by

$$\Delta w_w(t) = \eta(t)(x_k - w_w) \tag{3}$$

where $\eta(t)$ is a *learning rate*. Secondly, the adjusted winner vector is calculated by

$$w_w(t) = w_w(t-1) + \Delta w_w(t) \tag{4}$$

Training process is iteratively preceded until the convergence condition for the all weight vectors is satisfied. Clearly, the CL algorithm actually seeks for a local minimum (with respect to the predetermined number of clusters) for squared error criterion by applying gradient descent optimization.

If the probability distribution function of a data set is given in advance, then the simple standard CL algorithm described above may get good quality of a clustering minimizing *mean squared error* (*MSE*) defined as [9-14]

$$E = \sum_{i=1}^{c} D_i \tag{5}$$

where D_i be *intra-cluster error* for i^{th} cluster S_i that is determined by

$$D_i = \frac{1}{p}\left(\sum_{x \in S_i} \|x - w_i\|^2\right) \tag{6}$$

However, in general, the distribution is not given in advance; hence the initial values of the weight vectors are randomly allotted. It negatively influences the clustering performance of considered CL algorithm. In order to get a better clustering performance, in this paper we use the adaptive CL algorithm with deleting of weight vectors [9,10,12] the main properties of which are:

a) Both data points $\tilde{x}_k$ and weight vectors $\tilde{w}_i$ are normalized to a unit length, i.e., they are presented as the unit vector.

b) The winner vector is determined by a dot product of data point $\tilde{x}_k$ and weight vector $\tilde{w}_i$ instead of (2)

$$\tilde{w}_w = \arg\max_i \left\{\sum_{j=1}^{p} \tilde{x}_{kj} \tilde{w}_{ij}\right\} \quad k = 1,\ldots,n \qquad i = 1,\ldots,c \tag{7}$$

or through the angle between these vectors as

$$\tilde{w}_w^{\,\theta} = \arg\min_i \{\theta_i\} \qquad i = 1,\ldots,c \tag{8}$$

c) The updating rule of a winner weight vector instead of (3) is based on the adjusting equation [11] expressed as follows

$$\Delta\tilde{w}_w(t) = \eta(t)\left(\frac{\tilde{x}_k}{p} - \tilde{w}_w\right) \tag{9}$$

d) There is a deletion mechanism that (starting with a greater number than the prepared, required number of weight vectors) sequentially eliminates one vector, w_s that has a minimum intra-cluster partition error, i.e., $D_s \geq D_i$, for all i, determined as

$$D_i = \frac{1}{p}\left(\sum_{\overline{x} \in S_i} \tilde{x}\tilde{w}_w\right) \qquad i = 1,\ldots,c \tag{10}$$

and it proceeds until the number of weight vectors is equal to the predetermined one.

Now, the adaptive CL algorithm can be presented as follows:

Step 1. *Initialization*:

Given are initial weight vectors $\left\{ w_1(0), w_2(0), ..., w_c(0) \right\}$, initial number of output neurons l_0, final (predetermined) number of neurons l maximum iteration T_{max}, initial iteration of deletion $t_0 = T_{max} / 3$ and partial iteration $u = T_{max} / 3(l_0 - l + 1)$

Set $t \leftarrow 0$ and $m \leftarrow l_0$

Step 2. *Standard Competitive Learning*:

2.1. Choose an input vector $\tilde{x}_k$ at random among $\left\{ x_1, x_2, ..., x_n \right\}$

2.2. Select a winner $\tilde{w}_i$ according to (10)

2.3. Update the winner $\tilde{w}_w$ vector according to (8)

2.4. Set $t \leftarrow t + 1$

2.5. If $m > l$ and $t = t_0 + u \times q$ than go to Step 3, otherwise go to 2.1.

Step 3. *Deletion Mechanism*:

3.1. Delete $\tilde{w}_s$ calculating D_i according to (10) and checking $D_s \geq D_i$

3.2. Set $m \leftarrow m - 1$

Step 4. *Termination Condition*:

If $t = T_{max}$ then terminate, otherwise go to Step 2.

Thus, after finding a value of weight vectors $\left\{ w_1, ..., w_c \right\}$ that correspond to cluster centers $(v_1, ..., v_c)$, respectively a data set is divided into c groups as follows:

$$S_i = \left\{ X \in R^p \ \middle| \ \sum_{j=1}^{p} \tilde{x}_{kj} \tilde{w}_{ij} \geq \sum_{j=1}^{p} \tilde{x}_{kj} \tilde{w}_{mj} \quad \forall i \neq m \right\} \tag{11}$$

To order the defined groups with respect to their preference degree we compare the length of their mean vectors, a task that is justifiable: the more the value of attributes the better the group. Classification performance of the considered clustering algorithm was estimated by the MSE calculated using expressions (5) and (6). Effectiveness of this algorithm was verified for different types of data sets that have showed less value of MSE [12].

3   Prioritized ESG-Based Testing

We consider the testing process based on the generation of a test suite from ESG that is a discrete model of a SUT. To generate tests, firstly a set of ESGs are derived which are input to the generation algorithm to be applied. We deal with the test generation algorithms [5,7] that generates tests for a given ESG and satisfies the following coverage criteria.

a) Cover all event pairs in the ESG.
b) Cover all faulty event pairs derived by the ESG.

Note that a test suite that satisfies the first criterion consists of CESs while a test suite that satisfies the second consists of FCESs. These algorithms are able to provide the following constraint:

a) The sum of the lengths of the generated CESs should be minimal.
b) The sum of the lengths of the generated FCESs should be minimal.

The constraint on total lengths of the tests generated enable a considerable reduction in the cost of the test execution and thus the algorithms mentioned above can be referred to as the relatively effective ones. However, as stated in Introduction, an entire test suite generated may not be executed due to limited project budget. Such circumstances entail ordering all tests to be checked and exercised as far as they do not exceed the test budget. To solve the test prioritizing problem, several algorithms have been introduced [1,2]. Usually, during the test process for each *n-tuple* (in particular pair-wise) interaction a degree of importance is computationally determined and assigned to the corresponding test case. However, this kind of prioritized testing is computationally complex and hence restricted to deal with short test cases only.

Our prioritized testing approach is based on the use of the ESG-based testing algorithms mentioned above. Note that our test suite consists of CESs which start at the entry of the ESG and end of its exit, representing *walks* (*paths*) through the ESG under consideration. This assumption increases the testing capacity of the algorithms and yields ordering the generated tests, i.e., CESs. The ordering of the CESs is in accordance with their importance degree which is defined indirectly i.e., by estimation of events which are the nodes of ESG and represent objects (modules, components) of SUT. For this aim, firstly events are presented as a *multidimensional data point* $x_k = (x_1,...,x_p)$ where p is the *number of attributes*. Then, a data set $x = \{x_1,...,x_n\} \in R^p$ is constructed where n is the number of events, which being an unstructured one is divided into c groups The number of groups are determined in advance by using the *validity algorithm*, as described in [12-14]. Derivation of groups is provided by using NN clustering as explained in previous section. Afterwards, the constructed groups are ordered on the preference degree according to their length of corresponding mean vector. Finally, the CESs are manually ordered, scaling their preference degrees based on the events which incorporate the preferred group(s). We assume that the behavior of an SUT is correctly specified, i.e., only CESs constructed are analyzed. Additionally, we deal with minimal length of the ES to be covered, i.e., pair-wise coverage is the termination criterion.

Example for Qualifying and Quantifying the Attributes

To qualify an event corresponding to a node in ESG, we propose to use of p=8 attributes that are the dimension of a data point represented in a data set. The name of attributes and definition to them are given below:

x_1 : The *number of occurrence layers* determines the number occurrences of an event within the hierarchically ordered layers, beginning from the top of the ESG (the more the number of layer the more the test cost).

x_2 : The *number of related edges* takes all related edges into account and invokes usage density of a node (an event).

x_3 : The *relationship degree* defines the total number of nodes(events) to be directly and indirectly connected to them

x_4 : The *number of sub-nodes* determines whether a node in the ESG (menu) has subnodes (sub-menus) to be invoked further

x_5 : The *number of belongings* determines the number of occurrences of an event (a node) within one or more CESs (paths) at the same time.

x_6 : The *distance* specifies the position of an event in ESG and determines its distance from the entry and thus the cost for testing.

x_7 : The *balancing degree* determines balancing a node as the sum of all incoming edges (as plus (+)) and outgoing edges (as minus (-)) for a given node.

x_8 : *Average frequency of usage* determines the averaged frequencies each of which indicates how many an event (a node) occurs within the CES.

4   A Case Study

We now present a case study to verify the validity of testing process utilizing the testing approach mentioned in the previous section. The study was conducted using the RealJukebox (RJB) that is a personal music management system to build, manage and play individual digital music library on a personal computer. A complete set of ESGs for the RJB was constructed. Each ESG from this set represents all required sequences of user-system interactions to realize the likely operations. Consequently, the nodes of an ESG are interpreted as operations where an event can be a user input or a system response leading interactively to a succession of user inputs system outputs. Each of the ESGs defines a system sub-function and total of 12 sub-functions are presented in above mentioned study [7].

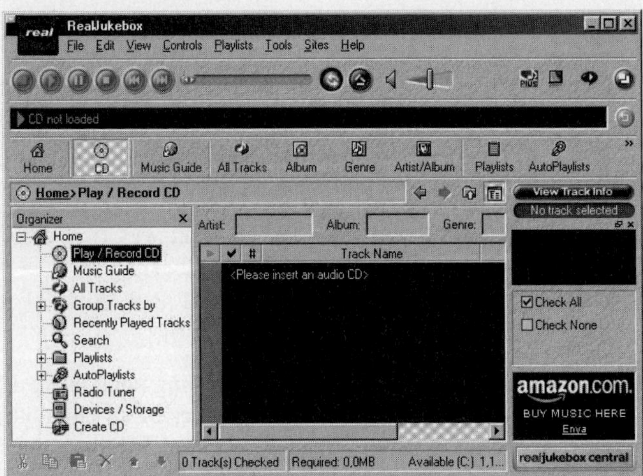

Fig. 2. GUI of RJB

Figure 2 represents the main menu of the SUT, i.e., RJB. At this top level, the GUI has a pull-down menu with the options *File, Edit*, etc., that invoke other components. These sub-options have further sub-options, etc. There are still more window components which can be used to traverse through the entries of the menu and sub-menus, creating many combinations and accordingly, many applications.

Our case study focuses on the testing of ESG that defines the sub-function 3: Edit Playlists and / or Auto Playlists that is shown below. The objective of this study is to verify empirically the correctness of the importance degrees to be assigned to CESs. For this goal, first of all the set of CESs is to be constructed, satisfying both the coverage criterion and the minimal lengths constrain as described as in previous section.

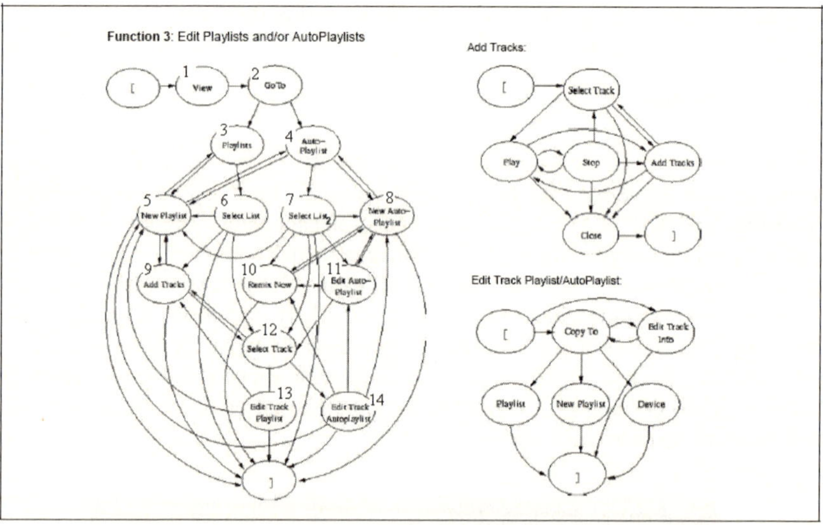

Fig. 3. ESG for Edit Playlist and / or AutoPlaylists Function

According to the test generation algorithm described in Section 3, the CESs generated are listed below:

[1 2 3 5 4 7 8 10 11 12 13 5 9 12 14 11 10 8 4 5 3 6 12 9 5],
[1 2 4 8 11 8 4 7 12 14 8 4 7 5 4 7 11 10],
[1 2 3 6 9 12 13 9 12 14 5 3 6 5 9 12 14], [1 2 4 7 10 11 12 14 10 8]
[1 2 3 6 12 13], [1 2 3 5 9], [1 2 4 7], [1 2 3 6],

As a follow-on step, each event, i.e., the corresponding node in the ESG, is represented as a multidimensional data point using the values of all eight attributes as defined in the previous section. Estimating by means of the ESG, the values of attributes for all events are determined and the data set $X = \{x_1, ..., x_{14}\} \in R^8$ is constructed as follows:

Table 1. Data set of events

Event no	X_1	X_2	X_3	X_4	X_5	X_6	X_7	X_8
1	1	1	13	0	8	1	0	0,1401
2	1	3	12	0	8	2	1	0,1401
3	2	4	9	0	7	21	0	0,1541
4	2	6	12	0	8	19	0	0,1631
5	3	11	11	0	8	25	3	0,1186
6	3	5	11	0	5	22	-3	0,1327
7	3	7	11	0	6	16	-5	0,0129
8	3	9	11	5	6	8	1	0,1156
9	4	7	11	0	6	24	1	0,1522
10	4	7	11	0	5	17	1	0,1119
11	4	7	11	0	5	16	1	0,0634
12	5	8	11	0	9	23	1	0,1237
13	6	5	11	5	3	11	-1	0,0885
14	6	6	11	0	5	17	-4	0,0674

In order to divide the given data set into groups, we apply the adaptive CL algorithm to the NN to train it; this provides a good clustering (see Section 2). To determine the number of groups the V_{sv} *validity index-based algorithm* [14] has been used, resulting in 7 groups. Therefore, the groups S_i, $i = 1,...,7$ are obtained which contain the events given below as follows:

Table 2. Obtained groups of events

Groups	S_1	S_2	S_3	S_4	S_5	S_6	S_7
Length of mean vectors	1,88	1,34	1,66	2,20	1,61	1,77	2,14
Importance degree	3	7	5	1	6	4	2

As mentioned in previous section, the preference degree of the CESs is determined indirectly, depending on the groups of corresponding events to be ordered. Consequently, the comparison of the length of mean vectors for all groups leads to groups that are ordered according to their importance degree (Table 3).

Table 3. Ranking

Order of importance degree	1	2	3	4	5	6	7
Belonging events	9	5,12	4,7,14	3,6	8	1,2	10,11,13

Finally, choosing the events from the ordered groups, we determine a ranking of CESs (paths) according to their descending importance degrees. The assignment of importance degree is based on the rule that is given as follows:

a) The CES the highest degree if that contains the events which belong to the top group with utmost preference degree and more adjacent ones ordered to bottom.

b) The CES (path) has the lowest degree if it contains the events which belong to the group(s) that take place within the lowest part of ordering.
Generated CESs (paths) rank is represented in Table 4.

Table 4. Ranking of CESs (paths)

Preference Degree	CESs (Paths)
1	[1 2 3 5 4 7 8 10 11 12 13 5 9 12 14 11 10 8 4 5 3 6 12 9 5]
2	[1 2 3 6 9 12 13 9 12 14 5 3 6 5 9 12 14]
3	[1 2 4 8 11 8 4 7 12 14 8 4 7 5 4 7 11 10]
4	[1 2 3 5 9]
5	[1 2 4 7]
6	[1 2 3 6]
7	[1 2 3 6 12 13]
8	[1 2 4 7 10 11 12 14 10 8]

The achieved ranking of CESs fully complies with the point of the tester's view. Thus, we determined an ordering of the complete set of CESs (paths) that represent the test suite generated by the test process. Now we have a ranking of test cases to make the decision which test cases are to be primarily tested.

5   Conclusions and Future Work

ESG-based testing algorithms generate software test suites fulfilling the criteria concerning minimal total length of the test sequences required for a complete coverage and their cost of execution. In this paper, test capacity of these algorithms is improved by prioritizing the test process. The approach provides ordering the test cases according to their degrees of importance which are indirectly determined by assessment of the events specified by several attributes. These attributes are defined by means of the graphical representation (ESG) and their classification using unsupervised neural network clustering. The approach is useful when an ordering the tests due to restricted budget and time is required.

Further work is planned to extend the approach to cases where 3 and 4-tuple events coverage is required instead of the pair-wise one as studied in this paper. Additionally, the fuzzy-neural network clustering is to be considered for an alternative - classification and to compare the preciseness of both methods.

References

1. R.V. Binder: *Testing Object-Oriented Systems*. Addison-Wesley, 2000.
2. Bryce, R.C., and Colbourn C.J.: Test Prioritization for Pairwise Interaction Coverage, ACM SIGSOFT Software Engineering Notes, Volume 30, Issue 4 (July 2005)
3. Elbaum, S., Malishevsky, A., and Rothermel, G.: Test Case Prioritization: A Family of Empirical Studies. *IEEE Transactions on Software Engineering*, 182-191, 2002.

4. Cohen, D.M., Dalal, S.R., Freedman, M.L., and Patton, G.C.: The AETG System: An Approach to Testing Based on Combinatorial Design. *IEEE Trans. Software Engineering*, 1997.

5. Belli, F.: Finite-State Testing and analysis of Graphical User Interfaces, *Proc. 12th Int'l. Symp. Softw. Reliability Eng. (ISSRE'01)*,. 43-43, 2001.

6. F. Belli, Ch. J. Budnik, L. White: "Event-Based Modeling, Analysis and Testing of User Interactions – Approach and Case Study". *J. Software Testing, Verification & Reliability*, John Wiley & Sons, 2006, 3-32.

7. F. Belli, Ch. J. Budnik: Test Minimization for Human-Computer Interaction. to appear in *J. of Applied Intelligence*.

8. Edmonds, J., Johnson, E.L.: Matching: Euler Tours and the Chinese Postman, *Math. Programming*, .88-124, 1973.

9. Maeda, M., Miyajima, H., Marashima, S.: An adaptive Learning and Self-deleting Neural Network for Vector Quantization. *IEICE Trans. Fundamentals*, 1996, 1886-1893

10. Maeda, M., Miyajim, H.: Competitive Learning Algorithm Founded on Adaptivity and Sensitivity Deletion Method. *IEICE Trans. Fundamentals*, 2000, 2770-2774

11. Rummelhart, D.E.: Zipser, D.: Competitive Learning. *J. Cognitive Science*, 1985, 75-112.

12. Eminov, M., Gokce, N.: Neural Network Clustering Using Competitive Learning Algorithm, *Proc. TAINN 2005*, 161-168, 2005.

13. Eminov, M.E.: Fuzzy c-Means Based Adaptive Neural Network Clustering. *Proc. TAINN-2003, Int. J. Computational Intelligence*. 2003), 338-343.

14. Kim, D.J., Park, Y.W. and Park, D.J.: A Novel Validity Index for Clusters, *IEICE Trans. Inf & System.*, 2001, 282-285.

Component Oriented Design Based on Axiomatic Design Theory and COSEML

Cengiz Togay and Ali H. Dogru

Middle East Technical University, Computer Engineering Dept.,
06531 Ankara, Turkey
{ctogay, dogru}@ceng.metu.edu.tr

Abstract. A Component Oriented software development method is proposed that uses collaboration diagrams for the definitions of dependencies among the Functional Requirements and Design Parameters according to Axiomatic Design Theory. COSEML is a component oriented graphical modeling language utilizing a single hierarchy diagram to construct systems. Axiomatic design theory provides a systematic approach to application design where developers can see all the determined dependencies among functional requirements and solutions (design parameters) in a matrix. However, axiomatic design has a shortcoming. There is no defined way to create relationships among functional requirements and design parameters. Axiomatic design theory provides basically two axioms that keep the design manageable and cost effective. Axiomatic design has been applied to component oriented software engineering in our previous studies. This research produces a foundation for a framework that combines COSEML and Axiomatic Design Theory, through added capabilities in defining dependencies.

Keywords: Axiomatic Design Theory, COSEML, Collaboration Diagrams.

1 Introduction

A common approach to solving complex problem is the "divide and conquer" approach, that suggests to divide the problem into simpler parts, solve them, and integrate into a viable solution [1, 2]. Component Oriented Software Engineering (COSE) approaches represent a development method for assembling systems from reusable components. Using component technologies is a cost effective way of constructing systems [3]. On the other hand, Axiomatic Design Theory (ADT) [4] is a separate approach that also incorporates a decomposition strategy: Highest-level requirements are mapped to design parameters and a feedback is acquired for decomposing the requirement. A "Zig-Zag" operation between the Functional Requirements (FRs) and Design Parameters (DPs) hence continues towards lower-level requirements and corresponding DPs. As a result, a set of relations among the FRs and DPs is represented in a design matrix.

Both approaches, however, lack a method to aid the decomposition through stating the dependencies among the identified FRs and DPs. Collaboration diagrams defined for COSEML [5, 6] are incorporated to our framework with the purpose to study such

A. Levi et al. (Eds.): ISCIS 2006, LNCS 4263, pp. 1072–1079, 2006.

dependencies. This approach also guides the ADT based process through a scenario centered view; a system function can be traced through a collaboration model and a by-product of this trace is a set of relations among the DPs. A collaboration model specifies dependencies among the services that are related to DPs. The following sections provide more information about the ADT and COSEML.

1.1 Axiomatic Design Theory

Axiomatic Design Theory (ADT) [4] is introduced by Suh at MIT to solve complex engineering problems through a hierarchical scheme. Axiomatic design starts with the more general Functional Requirements (FRs) and Design Parameters (DPs) of the problem and continues systematically toward more detailed FRs and DPs. In the leaf level of hierarchy, DPs define method or attribute names and related FRs defines the purpose of using DPs in software engineering [3, 7]. In the design matrix depicted in Fig. 1.a, "X" represents the relation and "O" represents non-relation. Each FR must be related with at least one DP. For instance, "FR1.1.5" is related with "DP1.1.5" and "DP1.1.1". Relationship among FRs and DPs also creates a relationship among DPs. For implementing "FR1.1.5", "DP1.1.1" must be executed before "DP1.1.5". In other words, "DP1.1.5" can be dependant on "DP1.1.1". Dependency among DPs can be described using Design Structure Matrix (DSM) [8]. Two fundamental axioms of ADT namely independence and information axioms provide cost effective designs. At the end of the design, a design matrix is created. Design matrix contains the FRs and DPs and dependency relationships among them. ADT has been applied to various development approaches such as object oriented [7], component oriented [3], and requirement management media [9].

1.2 COSEML

COSE Modeling Language (COSEML) [10] is a graphical modeling language utilizing a single hierarchy diagram. COSEML supports the Component Oriented Software Engineering (COSE) philosophy. COSE separates the parts of the system (components) from its abstract specification. COSEML hierarchy consists of two parts: Abstractions and Components as shown in Fig. 2. To construct the hierarchy, it starts with the most abstract notations and continues towards component representations. It is assumed that all components are available in domains to form any type of software system. To be effective, available components should be considered while decomposing the system. In component representation, a component can have more than one interface for depicting different aspects of the component. Each interface consists of properties, methods in, methods out, events in, and events out elements. "methods in" and "events in" present published services of component and "methods out" and "events out" present the subscribed services of other components. COSEML also incorporates of "Logical" and "Run- time" collaboration diagrams [5, 6].

Abstract level decomposition forms the static view of the system structure. There is a need for a dynamic model to verify compatibility of static structure with requirements. Therefore, logical collaboration diagrams are used. If a given set of abstractions are not enough to provide the required functionality then decomposition

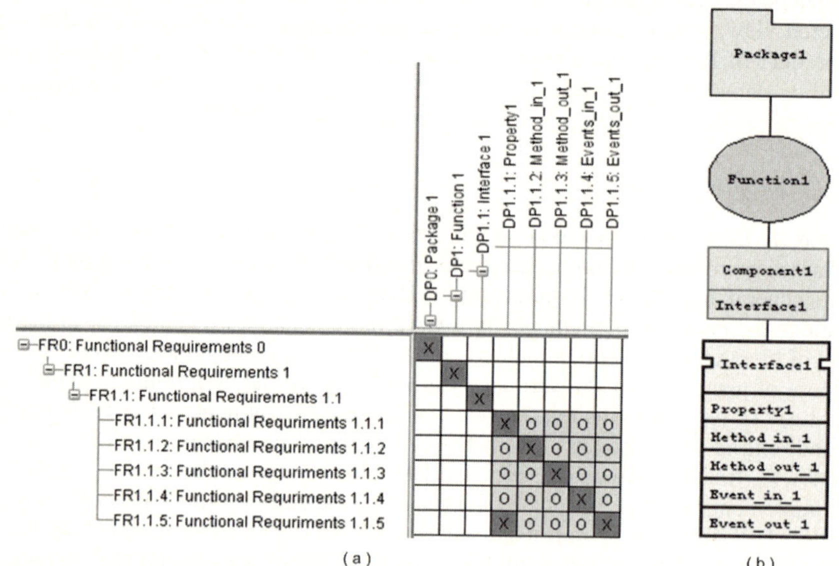

Fig. 1. a) Axiomatic design representation, b) COSEML representation

must be reconsidered. This diagram is also used to find components through using the design matrix. After specifying components, they are verified depending on specific scenarios. Scenarios are prepared using real-time collaboration diagrams.

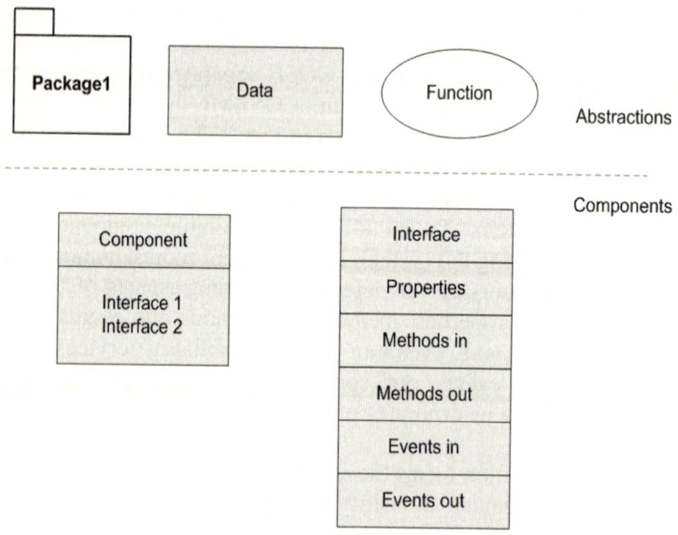

Fig. 2. COSEML symbols used in this study

2 Proposed Approach

Component oriented approaches have not incorporated the relationships among Functional Requirements (FRs) and solutions (Design Parameters (DPs)). Normally, component interfaces consist of property, method and event names. Although interface concepts are important, interfaces do not include enough information to describe components. It is assumed that component names and interface elements carry enough information about themselves. Therefore, we presented a framework [3] that composes the axiomatic design and COSE concepts. This framework provides an environment to design and develop components and applications in a mature domain. A mature domain is formed from components that are designed using this framework. This framework contains the ADT that is used to keep relationships between FRs and DPs. COSEML and design matrix depict the different views of systems. Although they have similarities in representation, they vary especially in low levels. While COSEML presents the system view with components and their integration, design matrix presents the relationships among FRs and DPs (property, method, and event names of components) in low levels as shown in Fig. 1. Creation of design matrices suffers from missing of a method to specify the dependency relationships among FRs and DPs. There is no defined way to form a design matrix. It is completely left to the developer. In this study, collaboration diagrams are used to find these relationships.

The method for developing COSE systems is presented in this section, followed by its application to a hotel reservation system example. The method includes the construction of the COSEML model and the design matrix of ADT corresponding to the system. Collaboration diagrams are utilized for the logical and run-time views of

Table 1. Development Process

Step	Description
1	Construct the COSEML decomposition and compatible design matrix for abstract levels.
2	Prepare the logical collaboration diagrams for abstract functions of COSEML diagram.
3	Specify the available and missing components
4	Add FRs and DPs of components from their design matrices to the system design matrix. If there is no candidate component then define components with interfaces and specify corresponding FRs and DPs in the design matrix.
5	Prepare the real-time collaboration diagrams for each specific scenario.
6	Verify the components' functionality with real-time collaboration diagrams
7	Develop missing components depending on real-time collaboration diagrams and design matrices.
8	Integrate components.

the COSEML, to nominate possible components and to verify their matching with the DPs. Table 1 lists the steps to perform the suggested development method.

The activities can be described on an example. The next section explains these steps while applying them for the design of a hotel reservation system.

2.1 An Example Design

The suggested component oriented development starts with decomposing the system: Hotel, Reservation, and Customer packages are specified. While these packages are depicted in COSEML as shown in Fig. 4, also a design matrix is prepared ("DPs 0-2") as depicted in Fig. 3. Development continues with further decomposition depending on requirements. Therefore, Function and Data abstractions "New Reservation" and "Reservation Table" respectively are added to the diagram as shown in Fig. 4. At the same time, design matrix is expanded with "DPs 1.1-1.4 and 2.1, 2.2". In the second step, logical collaboration diagrams are prepared for each abstract function in the COSEML diagram. Fig. 5 presents a logical collaboration diagram conducted on the "Check In" abstract function. This step is repeated for each abstract function. In step three, candidate components and missing components can be found by investigating existing systems' collaboration diagrams and design matrices in the mature domain. If specified components capability covers more than required functionality then component can be divided to smaller ones for optimization or cost reasons. A functional requirement can be provided with more than one component. In step four, located physical components' interfaces are added to the COSEML diagram as shown in Fig. 4. Therefore, abstractions and physical representations are shown in the same model. Existing components are also added to the design matrix as shown in Fig. 3. Available component's design matrix can help the developer to add its related FRs and DPs to the systems design matrix. If there is no existing component then the developer defines the probable component interface and sets the FRs and DPs in the design matrix. These defined or built component interfaces must be satisfying the scenario requirements. It must be noted that message names in logical collaboration diagrams can be different from method names in component interfaces, especially during early stages of the process. In step five, Run time collaboration diagrams are prepared to depict the details of system behavior satisfying usage scenarios. In step six, each collaboration diagram is used to verify components. At the same time, these diagrams depict dependencies among FRs and DPs in the design matrix. For instance, it can be inferred from Fig. 6 that "DP 1.2.3 Assign_room" method requires the "DP 1.4: Room Information Table" property and "DP 2.1.1: Create" method. These relationships are depicted in the design matrix as shown in Fig. 3. Last two steps are repeated for each specific scenario. In step seven, missing components are developed depending on the prepared interface, and corresponding FRs and DPs in the design matrix. Lastly, components are integrated to the system for an executable application.

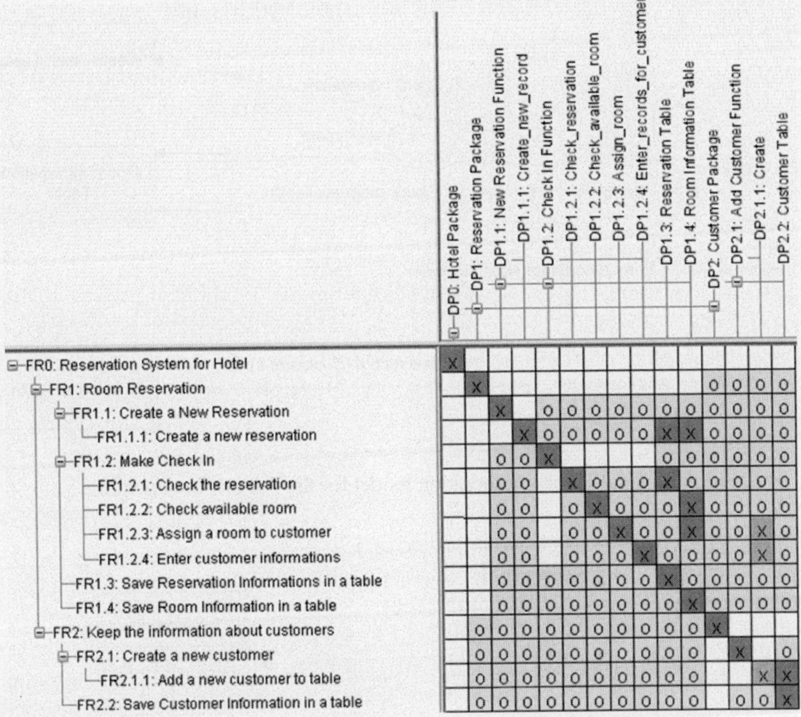

Fig. 3. Design matrix representation of example

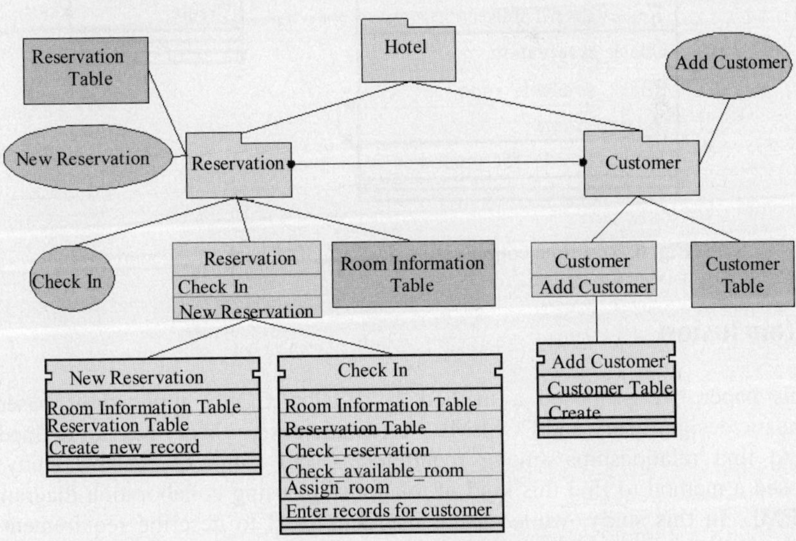

Fig. 4. COSEML representation of example

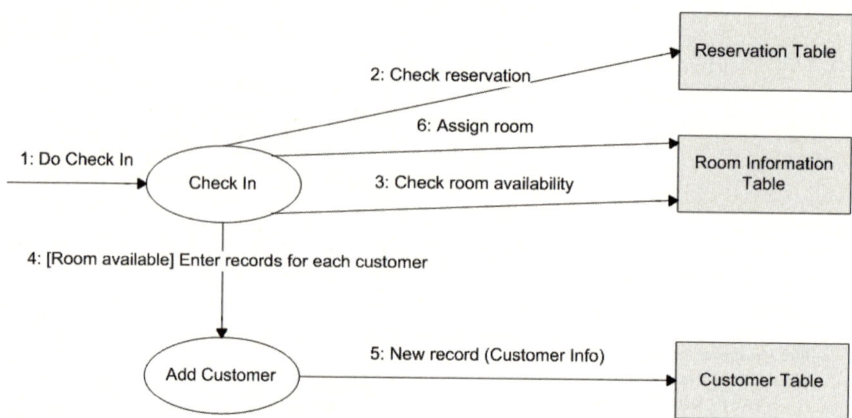

Fig. 5. Logical-level collaboration model for the "Check In" operation

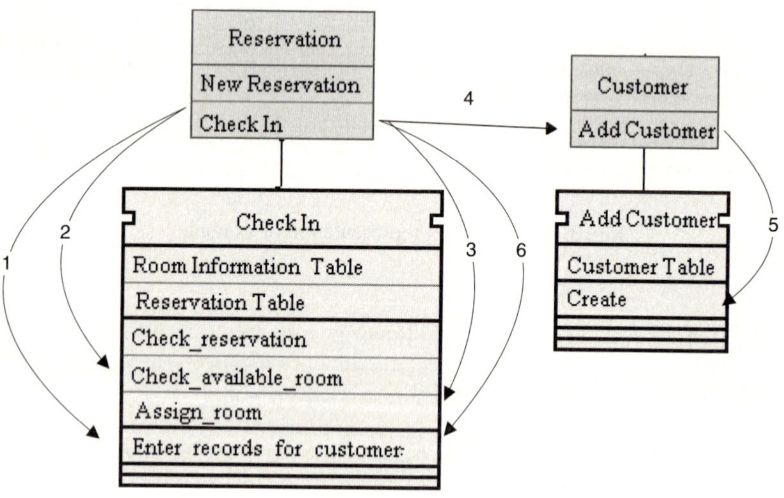

Fig. 6. Run-time collaboration diagram of "Check In" scenario

3 Conclusion

In this paper, we proposed a method to develop COSE applications based on Axiomatic design theory and COSEML. Axiomatic design theory has not defined any way to find relationships among requirements and solutions. In this study, we proposed a method to find this kind of relationships using collaboration diagrams of COSEML. In this study, while design matrix is used to describe requirement and solution relationship, COSEML and its concepts (hierarchy and two levels of collaboration diagrams) provide overall system description. We have conducted several designs based on previous case studies. The missing guidance in the completeness analysis for definition of DPs and their relations has been provided by the collaboration diagrams. It can be observed that component oriented development utilizing a design mechanism is supported to a noticeable extent from the practitioners point of view. Earlier work for including interaction models to COSEML were intended to achieve further automation in composing component based systems: the sequence of messages was the new information. Now it can be observed that besides the sequence information that provides a dependency view, collaboration diagrams support the verification of a component oriented design with respect to usage scenarios. As future work, the proposed method will be used to design High Level Architecture (HLA) based simulations.

References

1. Simon, H.A.: The Science of the Artificial. The MIT Press (1969)
2. Tanik, M.M., Chan, E.S.: Fundamentals of Computing for Software Engineers. Van Nostrand Reinhold New York (1991)
3. Togay, C., Dogru, A.H: A Framework for Component Integration Using Axiomatic Design and Object Model Template for Simulation Applications," Department of Electrical and Computer Engineering University of Alabama, Birmingham, Alabama, Technical Report 2005-11-ECE-001, (2005)
4. Suh, N.P.: Axiomatic Design: Advances and Applications. Oxford University Press New York (2001)
5. Dogru, A.H., Component-Oriented Software Engineering: The Academy of Learning and Advances Studies (The ATLAS) (2006)
6. Tuncel, M.B.: Using Collaboration Diagrams in Component Oriented Modeling. Master Thesis, Middle East Technical University, Computer Engineering Dept. Ankara, Turkey (2006)
7. Do, S.H., Suh, N.P: Systematic OO Programming with Axiomatic Design. IEEE Computer, Vol. 32. (1999), 121-124
8. Steward, D.: System Analysis and Management: Structure, Strategy and Design. Petrocelli Books (1981)
9. Gumus, B., Ertas, A.: Requirement Management and Axiomatic Design. Integrated Design and Process Technology Symposium Kusadasi Turkey (2004)
10. Dogru, A.H., Tanik, M.M: A Process Model for Component-Oriented Software Engineering. IEEE Software, Vol. 20. No. 2. (2003) 34-41

Author Index

Printing: Mercedes-Druck, Berlin
Binding: Stein + Lehmann, Berlin

Lecture Notes in Computer Science

For information about Vols. 1–4179

please contact your bookseller or Springer

Vol. 4222: L. Jiao, L. Wang, X. Gao, J. Liu, F. Wu (Eds.), Advances in Natural Computation, Part II. XLII, 998 pages. 2006.

Vol. 4221: L. Jiao, L. Wang, X. Gao, J. Liu, F. Wu (Eds.), Advances in Natural Computation, Part I. XLI, 992 pages. 2006.

Vol. 4219: D. Zamboni, C. Kruegel (Eds.), Recent Advances in Intrusion Detection. XII, 331 pages. 2006.

Vol. 4218: S. Graf, W. Zhang (Eds.), Automated Technology for Verification and Analysis. XIV, 540 pages. 2006.

Vol. 4217: P. Cuenca, L. Orozco-Barbosa (Eds.), Personal Wireless Communications. XV, 532 pages. 2006.

Vol. 4216: M.R. Berthold, R. Glen, I. Fischer (Eds.), Computational Life Sciences II. XIII, 269 pages. 2006. (Sublibrary LNBI).

Vol. 4215: D.W. Embley, A. Olivé, S. Ram (Eds.), Conceptual Modeling - ER 2006. XVI, 590 pages. 2006.

Vol. 4213: J. Fürnkranz, T. Scheffer, M. Spiliopoulou (Eds.), Knowledge Discovery in Databases: PKDD 2006. XXII, 660 pages. 2006. (Sublibrary LNAI).

Vol. 4212: J. Fürnkranz, T. Scheffer, M. Spiliopoulou (Eds.), Machine Learning: ECML 2006. XXIII, 851 pages. 2006. (Sublibrary LNAI).

Vol. 4211: P. Vogt, Y. Sugita, E. Tuci, C. Nehaniv (Eds.), Symbol Grounding and Beyond. VIII, 237 pages. 2006. (Sublibrary LNAI).

Vol. 4210: C. Priami (Ed.), Computational Methods in Systems Biology. X, 323 pages. 2006. (Sublibrary LNBI).

Vol. 4209: F. Crestani, P. Ferragina, M. Sanderson (Eds.), String Processing and Information Retrieval. XIV, 367 pages. 2006.

Vol. 4208: M. Gerndt, D. Kranzlmüller (Eds.), High Performance Computing and Communications. XXII, 938 pages. 2006.

Vol. 4207: Z. Ésik (Ed.), Computer Science Logic. XII, 627 pages. 2006.

Vol. 4206: P. Dourish, A. Friday (Eds.), UbiComp 2006: Ubiquitous Computing. XIX, 526 pages. 2006.

Vol. 4205: G. Bourque, N. El-Mabrouk (Eds.), Comparative Genomics. X, 231 pages. 2006. (Sublibrary LNBI).

Vol. 4204: F. Benhamou (Ed.), Principles and Practice of Constraint Programming - CP 2006. XVIII, 774 pages. 2006.

Vol. 4203: F. Esposito, Z.W. Raś, D. Malerba, G. Semeraro (Eds.), Foundations of Intelligent Systems. XVIII, 767 pages. 2006. (Sublibrary LNAI).

Vol. 4202: E. Asarin, P. Bouyer (Eds.), Formal Modeling and Analysis of Timed Systems. XI, 369 pages. 2006.

Vol. 4201: Y. Sakakibara, S. Kobayashi, K. Sato, T. Nishino, E. Tomita (Eds.), Grammatical Inference: Algorithms and Applications. XII, 359 pages. 2006. (Sublibrary LNAI).

Vol. 4200: I.F. C. Smith (Ed.), Intelligent Computing in Engineering and Architecture. XIII, 692 pages. 2006. (Sublibrary LNAI).

Vol. 4199: O. Nierstrasz, J. Whittle, D. Harel, G. Reggio (Eds.), Model Driven Engineering Languages and Systems. XVI, 798 pages. 2006.

Vol. 4198: O. Nasraoui, O. Zaiane, M. Spiliopoulou, B. Mobasher, B. Masand, P. Yu (Eds.), Advances in Web Minding and Web Usage Analysis. IX, 177 pages. 2006. (Sublibrary LNAI).

Vol. 4197: M. Raubal, H.J. Miller, A.U. Frank, M.F. Goodchild (Eds.), Geographic, Information Science. XIII, 419 pages. 2006.

Vol. 4196: K. Fischer, I.J. Timm, E. André, N. Zhong (Eds.), Multiagent System Technologies. X, 185 pages. 2006. (Sublibrary LNAI).

Vol. 4195: D. Gaiti, G. Pujolle, E. Al-Shaer, K. Calvert, S. Dobson, G. Leduc, O. Martikainen (Eds.), Autonomic Networking. IX, 316 pages. 2006.

Vol. 4194: V.G. Ganzha, E.W. Mayr, E.V. Vorozhtsov (Eds.), Computer Algebra in Scientific Computing. XI, 313 pages. 2006.

Vol. 4193: T.P. Runarsson, H.-G. Beyer, E. Burke, J.J. Merelo-Guervós, L. D. Whitley, X. Yao (Eds.), Parallel Problem Solving from Nature - PPSN IX. XIX, 1061 pages. 2006.

Vol. 4192: B. Mohr, J.L. Träff, J. Worringen, J. Dongarra (Eds.), Recent Advances in Parallel Virtual Machine and Message Passing Interface. XVI, 414 pages. 2006.

Vol. 4191: R. Larsen, M. Nielsen, J. Sporring (Eds.), Medical Image Computing and Computer-Assisted Intervention – MICCAI 2006, Part II. XXXVIII, 981 pages. 2006.

Vol. 4190: R. Larsen, M. Nielsen, J. Sporring (Eds.), Medical Image Computing and Computer-Assisted Intervention – MICCAI 2006, Part I. XXXVVIII, 949 pages. 2006.

Vol. 4189: D. Gollmann, J. Meier, A. Sabelfeld (Eds.), Computer Security – ESORICS 2006. XI, 548 pages. 2006.

Vol. 4188: P. Sojka, I. Kopeček, K. Pala (Eds.), Text, Speech and Dialogue. XV, 721 pages. 2006. (Sublibrary LNAI).

Vol. 4187: J.J. Alferes, J. Bailey, W. May, U. Schwertel (Eds.), Principles and Practice of Semantic Web Reasoning. XI, 277 pages. 2006.

Vol. 4186: C. Jesshope, C. Egan (Eds.), Advances in Computer Systems Architecture. XIV, 605 pages. 2006.

Vol. 4185: R. Mizoguchi, Z. Shi, F. Giunchiglia (Eds.), The Semantic Web – ASWC 2006. XX, 778 pages. 2006.

Vol. 4184: M. Bravetti, M. Núñez, G. Zavattaro (Eds.), Web Services and Formal Methods. X, 289 pages. 2006.

Vol. 4183: J. Euzenat, J. Domingue (Eds.), Artificial Intelligence: Methodology, Systems, and Applications. XIII, 291 pages. 2006. (Sublibrary LNAI).

Vol. 4182: H.T. Ng, M.-K. Leong, M.-Y. Kan, D. Ji (Eds.), Information Retrieval Technology. XVI, 684 pages. 2006.

Vol. 4180: M. Kohlhase, OMDoc – An Open Markup Format for Mathematical Documents [version 1.2]. XIX, 428 pages. 2006. (Sublibrary LNAI).